Using Computers
A Gateway to Information
AND
Programming in QBasic

Using Computers
A Gateway to Information
AND
Programming in QBasic

Gary B. Shelly
Thomas J. Cashman
Gloria A. Waggoner
William C. Waggoner

Contributing Authors
James S. Quasney
Misty E. Vermaat
Tim J. Walker

boyd & fraser publishing company

An International Thomson Publishing Company

Danvers • Albany • Bonn • Boston • Cincinnati • Detroit • London • Madrid • Melbourne
Mexico City • New York • Paris • San Francisco • Singapore • Tokyo • Toronto • Washington

SHELLY
CASHMAN
SERIES®

Special thanks go to the following reviewers of *Using Computers: A Gateway to Information*.

Paula Bell, Lock Haven University; **Catherine J. Brotherton**, Riverside Community College; **Deborah Fansler**, Purdue University Calumet; **Kenneth Frizane**, Oakton Community College; **E. Colin Ikei**, Long Beach City College; **Gary L. Margot**, Ashland University; **Harry J. Rosenblatt**, College of the Albemarle; **Althea Stevens**, Mid-Plains Community College, McDonald/Belton Campus; and **Mike Waggoner**, Educational Consultant.

© 1995 boyd & fraser publishing company
One Corporate Place • Ferncroft Village
Danvers, Massachusetts 01923

International Thomson Publishing
boyd & fraser publishing company is an ITP company.
The ITP trademark is used under license.

Printed in the United States of America

For more information, contact boyd & fraser publishing company:

boyd & fraser publishing company
One Corporate Place • Ferncroft Village
Danvers, Massachusetts 01923 USA

International Thomson Publishing Europe
Berkshire House 168-173
High Holborn
London, WC1V 7AA, England

Thomas Nelson Australia
102 Dodds Street
South Melbourne 3205
Victoria, Australia

Nelson Canada
1120 Birchmont Road
Scarborough, Ontario
Canada M1K 5G4

International Thomson Editores
Campose Eliseos 385, Piso 7
Col. Polanco
11560 Mexico D.F. Mexico

International Thomson Publishing GmbH
Konigswinterer Strasse 418
53227 Bonn, Germany

International Thomson Publishing Asia
221 Henderson Road
#05-10 Henderson Building
Singapore 0315

International Thomson Publishing Japan
Hirakawacho Kyowa Building, 3F
2-2-1 Hirakawacho
Chiyoda-ku, Tokyo 102, Japan

ISBN 0-7895-0309-3

All rights reserved. No part of this work may be reproduced or used in any form or by any means — graphic, electronic, or mechanical, including photocopying, recording, taping, or information and retrieval systems — without prior written permission from the publisher.

> **SHELLY CASHMAN SERIES®** and **Custom Edition®** are trademarks of International Thomson Publishing, Inc. Names of all other products mentioned herein are used for identification purposes only and may be trademarks and/or registered trademarks of their respective owners. International Thomson Publishing, Inc. and boyd & fraser publishing company disclaim any affiliation, association, or connection with, or sponsorship or endorsement by, such owners.

2 3 4 5 6 7 8 9 10   BC   9 8 7 6 5

Contents in Brief
Using Computers: A Gateway to Information
AND
Programming in QBasic

USING COMPUTERS: A GATEWAY TO INFORMATION

PREFACE		x
CHAPTER 1	An Overview of Computer Concepts	1.1
SPECIAL FEATURE	The Evolution of the Computer Industry	1.32
CHAPTER 2	Computer Software Applications: User Tools	2.1
CHAPTER 3	Input to the Computer	3.1
CHAPTER 4	The System Unit	4.1
SPECIAL FEATURE	Making a Computer Chip	4.35
CHAPTER 5	Output from the Computer	5.1
CHAPTER 6	Secondary Storage	6.1
CHAPTER 7	Communications and Networks	7.1
SPECIAL FEATURE	The Internet	7.43
CHAPTER 8	Operating Systems and System Software	8.1
SPECIAL FEATURE	How to Purchase, Install, and Maintain a Personal Computer	8.29
CHAPTER 9	Information Management: Files and Databases	9.1
CHAPTER 10	Information Systems	10.1
CHAPTER 11	Information Systems Development	11.1
CHAPTER 12	Program Development and Programming Languages	12.1
SPECIAL FEATURE	Multimedia	12.37
CHAPTER 13	Security, Ethics, and Privacy	13.1
CHAPTER 14	Your Future in the Information Age	14.1
SPECIAL FEATURE	Virtual Reality	14.35
	Index for Using Computers: A Gateway to Information	I.1
	Photo Credits for Using Computers: A Gateway to Information	

Contents in Brief *(continued)*

PROGRAMMING IN QBASIC

PROJECT 1	*An Introduction to Programming in QBasic*	*QB1*
PROJECT 2	*Basic Arithmetic Operations and Accumulating Totals*	*QB25*
PROJECT 3	*Decisions*	*QB42*
PROJECT 4	*Interactive Programming, For Loops, and an Introduction to the Top-Down Approach*	*QB62*
PROJECT 5	*Sequential File Processing*	*QB83*
PROJECT 6	*Arrays and Functions*	*QB99*
	Appendix QBasic Debugging Techniques	*QB115*
	Index	*QB118*
	Reference Card	*R.1*

Contents

Using Computers: A Gateway to Information
AND
Programming in QBasic

Preface	x

CHAPTER ONE

An Overview of Computer Concepts

Objectives	1.1
Computer and Information Literacy	1.2
What Is a Computer?	1.4
What Does a Computer Do?	1.4
Why Is a Computer so Powerful?	1.5
Speed	1.5
Reliability	1.6
Storage	1.6
How Does a Computer Know What to Do?	1.6
The Information Processing Cycle	1.7
What Are the Components of a Computer?	1.7
Input Devices	1.7
System Unit	1.8
Output Devices	1.8
Secondary Storage Devices	1.9
Categories of Computers	1.9
Personal Computers	1.10
Servers	1.12
Minicomputers	1.12
Mainframe Computers	1.13
Supercomputers	1.13
Computer Software	1.14
System Software and	
Application Software	1.14
Application Software Packages	1.15
Personal Computer Application	
Software Packages	1.15
What Are the Elements of an	
Information System?	1.16
Connectivity	1.17
An Example of How One Company	
Uses Computers	1.17
Receptionist	1.17
Sales	1.18
Marketing	1.18
Shipping and Receiving	1.19
Manufacturing	1.19
Engineering	1.20
Accounting	1.20
Human Resources	1.20
Information Systems	1.20
Executive	1.21
Summary of How One Company	
Uses Computers	1.21
Computers at Work: Carnegie Mellon:	
Information at Your Dorm Room	1.22
In the Future: Information Appliances	1.23
What You Should Know	1.24
Terms to Remember	1.26
Test Your Knowledge	1.27
Points to Ponder	1.28
Out and About	1.29
In the Lab	1.30

SPECIAL FEATURE

The Evolution of the Computer Industry   1.32

CHAPTER TWO

Computer Software Applications: User Tools

Objectives	2.1
Productivity Software	2.2
User Interface	2.2
Word Processing Software	2.4
Creating	2.5
Editing	2.6
Formatting	2.7
Printing	2.9
Desktop Publishing Software	2.10
Spreadsheet Software	2.12
Database Software	2.18
Presentation Graphics Software	2.20
Data Communications Software	2.22
Electronic Mail Software	2.23
Personal Information Management	2.24
Project Management	2.25
Integrated Software	2.25

Learning Aids and Support Tools for Application Users	2.27
Computer at Work: Productivity Software Use High in Business	2.28
In the Future: Will There Eventually Be Only One Software Superapplication?	2.29
What You Should Know	2.30
Terms to Remember	2.32
Test Your Knowledge	2.33
Points to Ponder	2.34
Out and About	2.35
In the Lab	2.36

CHAPTER THREE

3 Input to the Computer

Objectives	3.1
Overview of the Information Processing Cycle	3.2
What Is Input?	3.2
The Keyboard	3.3
Pointing Devices	3.5
Mouse	3.5
Trackball	3.6
Joystick	3.6
Pen Input Devices	3.7
Touch Screen	3.8
Light Pen	3.9
Digitizer	3.9
Graphics Tablet	3.9
Source Data Automation	3.10
Image Scanner	3.10
Optical Recognition	3.11
Magnetic Ink Character Recognition	3.13
Data Collection Devices	3.14
Terminals	3.15
Multimedia Input Devices	3.16
Sound Input	3.16
Voice Input	3.16
Digital Camera	3.19
Video Input	3.20
Data Accuracy	3.20
Computers at Work: Helping People with Special Needs	3.22
In the Future: "Computer, tell me the status of..."	3.23
What Your Should Know	3.24
Terms to Remember	3.26
Test Your Knowledge	3.27
Points to Ponder	3.28
Out and About	3.29
In the Lab	3.30

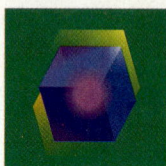

CHAPTER FOUR

4 The System Unit

Objectives	4.1
What Is the System Unit?	4.2
How Data Is Represented Electronically	4.2
ASCII and EBCDIC	4.3
Parity	4.4
The Components of the System Unit	4.5
Motherboard	4.6
Microprocessor and the CPU	4.6
Control Unit	4.6
System Clock	4.7
Arithmetic/Logic Unit	4.7
Registers	4.7
Word Size	4.7
Microprocessor Comparison	4.8
Upgrade Sockets	4.8
Memory	4.9
Random Access Memory	4.9
Read Only Memory	4.11
Memory Speed	4.11
Coprocessors	4.12
Buses	4.12
Expansion Slots	4.13
Ports and Connectors	4.14
Parallel Ports	4.15
Serial Ports	4.15
Bays	4.16
Power Supply	4.16
Sound Components	4.17
Summary of the Components of the System Unit	4.17
Machine Language Instructions	4.18
Types of Processing	4.19
Pipelining	4.19
Parallel Processing	4.20
Neural Network Computers	4.20
Number Systems	4.21
Decimal Number System	4.21
Binary Number System	4.22
Hexadecimal Number System	4.22
Computers at Work: Unparalleled Performance from Parallel Processors	4.24
In the Future: 2,000 MIPS by the Year 2000	4.25
What Your Should Know	4.26
Terms to Remember	4.29
Test Your Knowledge	4.30
Points to Ponder	4.31
Out and About	4.32
In the Lab	4.33

SPECIAL FEATURE
Making a Computer Chip   4.35

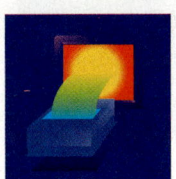

CHAPTER FIVE

Output from the Computer

Objectives	**5.1**
What Is Output?	**5.2**
Reports	5.2
Graphics	5.4
Audio Output	5.4
Video Output	5.5
Multimedia	5.5
Virtual Reality	5.7
Printers	**5.9**
Impact Printers	**5.9**
Dot Matrix Printers	5.10
Band and Chain Printers	5.12
Nonimpact Printers	**5.13**
Ink-Jet Printers	5.13
Page Printers	5.14
Thermal Printers	5.15
Other Types of Printers	**5.16**
Considerations in Choosing a Printer	**5.17**
Display Devices	**5.18**
Resolution	5.18
Color Monitors	5.20
Monochrome Monitors	5.20
Flat Panel Displays	5.20
How Images Are Displayed on a Monitor	5.22
How Color Is Produced	5.23
Other Output Devices	**5.23**
Data Projectors	5.23
Plotters	5.24
Computer Output Microfilm	5.24
Voice Output	5.25
Computers at Work: Notestation – The Key to Getting the Right Music	**5.27**
In the Future: Virtual Reality – Beyond Entertainment	**5.28**
What You Should Know	**5.29**
Terms to Remember	**5.32**
Test Your Knowledge	**5.33**
Points to Ponder	**5.34**
Out and About	**5.35**
In the Lab	**5.36**

CHAPTER SIX

Secondary Storage

Objectives	**6.1**
What Is Secondary Storage?	**6.2**
Magnetic Disk Storage	**6.3**
Diskettes	6.3
Hard Disks	6.8
Data Compression	6.11
RAID	6.13
Other Types of Hard Disks	6.14
Maintaining Data Stored on a Disk	**6.15**
Backup	6.15
Defragmentation	6.15
Magnetic Tape	**6.16**
Cartridge Tape Devices	6.16
Reel-to-Reel Tape Devices	6.17
Storing Data on Magnetic Tape	6.17
Other Forms of Secondary Storage	**6.19**
PC Cards	6.19
Optical Disks	6.19
Solid-State Storage Devices	6.21
Mass Storage Devices	6.21
Special-Purpose Storage Devices	6.22
Computers at Work: American Express Opts for Optical Storage	**6.24**
In the Future: Memory Cubes	**6.25**
What You Should Know	**6.26**
Terms to Remember	**6.29**
Test Your Knowledge	**6.30**
Points to Ponder	**6.31**
Out and About	**6.32**
In the Lab	**6.33**

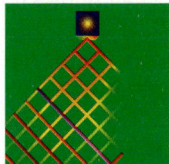

CHAPTER SEVEN

Communications and Networks

Objectives	**7.1**
Examples of How Communications Is Used	**7.2**
Electronic Mail	7.2
Voice Mail	7.3
Teleconferencing	7.3
FAX	7.4
Groupware	7.4

CONTENTS

Telecommuting	7.5
Electronic Data Interchange (EDI)	7.5
Global Positioning Systems (GPS)	7.6
Bulletin Board Systems (BBS)	7.7
Online Services	7.7
What Is Communications?	**7.8**
A Communications System Model	**7.8**
Transmission Media	**7.9**
Twisted Pair Wire	7.9
Coaxial Cable	7.9
Fiber Optics	7.10
Microwave Transmission	7.11
Satellite Transmission	7.11
Wireless Transmission	7.12
An Example of a Communications Channel	7.13
Line Configurations	**7.14**
Point-to-Point Lines	7.14
Multidrop Lines	7.15
Characteristics of Communications Channels	**7.16**
Types of Signals: Digital and Analog	7.16
Transmission Modes: Asynchronous and Synchronous	7.16
Direction of Transmission: Simplex, Half-Duplex, and Full-Duplex	7.17
Transmission Rate	7.17
Communications Equipment	**7.18**
Modems	7.18
Multiplexors	7.19
Front-End Processors	7.19
Network Interface Cards	7.19
Communications Software	**7.20**
Communications Protocols	**7.21**
Communications Networks	**7.21**
Local Area Networks (LANs)	7.21
Wide Area Networks (WANs)	7.24
The Internet	7.24
Network Configurations	**7.25**
Star Network	7.25
Bus Network	7.26
Ring Network	7.26
Connecting Networks	**7.27**
An Example of a Communications Network	**7.28**
Computers at Work: Satellites Help Track Moving Vans	**7.30**
In the Future: The Information Superhighway	**7.31**
What You Should Know	**7.32**
Terms to Remember	**7.36**
Test Your Knowledge	**7.37**
Points to Ponder	**7.38**
Out and About	**7.39**
In the Lab	**7.41**

SPECIAL FEATURE

The Internet — 7.43

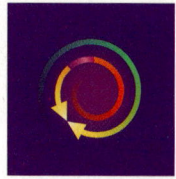

CHAPTER EIGHT

8 *Operating Systems and System Software*

Objectives	**8.1**
What Is System Software?	**8.2**
What Is an Operating System?	**8.2**
Loading an Operating System	**8.3**
Types of Operating Systems	**8.4**
Single Program	8.4
Multitasking	8.4
Multiprocessing	8.5
Virtual Machine	8.5
Functions of Operating Systems	**8.6**
Allocating System Resources	8.6
Monitoring System Activities	8.9
Disk and File Management	8.10
Popular Operating Systems	**8.11**
DOS	8.11
Windows	8.12
Windows NT	8.12
Macintosh	8.13
OS/2	8.13
UNIX	8.13
NextStep	8.15
Other Operating Systems	8.15
Utilities	**8.15**
Language Translators	**8.16**
Computers at Work: NextStep: Objects May Be Closer Than They Appear	**8.17**
In the Future: Is There a Future for Utility Software?	**8.18**
What You Should Know	**8.19**
Terms to Remember	**8.22**
Test Your Knowledge	**8.23**
Points to Ponder	**8.24**
Out and About	**8.25**
In the Lab	**8.27**

SPECIAL FEATURE

How to Purchase, Install, and Maintain a Personal Computer — 8.29

9 CHAPTER NINE

Information Management: Files and Databases

Objectives	9.1
Data Management	9.2
Data Accuracy	9.2
Data Security	9.3
Data Maintenance	9.3
Summary of Data Management	9.3
What Is a File?	9.4
Types of File Organization	9.4
Sequential File Organization	9.4
Indexed File Organization	9.5
Direct File Organization	9.6
Summary of File Organization Concepts	9.8
How Is Data in Files Maintained?	9.9
Adding Records	9.9
Changing Records	9.9
Deleting Records	9.10
Databases: A Better Way to Manage and Organize Data	9.12
What Is a Database?	9.12
Why Use a Database?	9.13
Types of Database Organization	9.14
Hierarchical Database	9.14
Network Database	9.15
Relational Database	9.15
Object-Oriented Database	9.16
Database Management Systems	9.17
Query Languages: Access to the Database	9.18
A Query Example	9.18
Structured Query Language	9.19
Database Administration	9.20
The Database Administrator	9.20
The Responsibility of the User in a Database Management System	9.21
Personal Computer Database Systems	9.21
Computers at Work: Finding Information Among the Data	9.22
In the Future: Nontext Databases	9.23
What You Should Know	9.24
Terms to Remember	9.26
Test Your Knowledge	9.27
Points to Ponder	9.28
Out and About	9.29
In the Lab	9.31

10 CHAPTER TEN

Information Systems

Objectives	10.1
Why Is Information Important to an Organization?	10.2
How Do Managers Use Information?	10.3
Management Levels in an Organization	10.5
Senior Management	10.5
Middle Management	10.6
Operational Management	10.6
Nonmanagement Employees	10.6
Other Approaches to Management Organization	10.6
Qualities of Information	10.8
Types of Information Systems	10.9
Transaction Processing Systems	10.9
Management Information Systems	10.9
Decision Support Systems	10.11
Expert Systems	10.12
Integrated Information Systems	10.13
The Role of Personal Computers in Information Systems	10.14
Computers at Work: Expert Systems Capture and Apply Knowledge	10.15
In the Future: The Virtual Corporation	10.16
What You Should Know	10.17
Terms to Remember	10.19
Test Your Knowledge	10.20
Points to Ponder	10.21
Out and About	10.22
In the Lab	10.23

11 CHAPTER ELEVEN

Information Systems Development

Objectives	11.1
What Is the System Development Life Cycle?	11.2
The Phases of the System Development Lift Cycle	11.2
Project Management	11.2
Documentation	11.3

Who Participates in the System Development Life Cycle?	11.3
Analysis Phase	**11.4**
The Preliminary Investigation	11.4
Detailed System Analysis	11.4
Making the Decision on How to Proceed	11.8
Analysis at Sutherland	**11.9**
Acquisition Phase	**11.10**
What Is Commercial Applications Software?	11.10
Summarizing the Application Requirements	11.11
Identifying Potential Software Vendors	11.11
Evaluating Software Alternatives	11.13
Making the Purchase	11.14
Acquisition at Sutherland	**11.14**
Commercial Applications Versus Custom Software	**11.15**
Customizing Phase	**11.16**
Customizing at Sutherland	**11.16**
Design Phase	**11.17**
Structured Design Methods	11.17
Design Activities	
Testing Design	11.19
Design Review	11.20
Prototyping	11.20
Computer-Aided Software Engineering (CASE)	11.20
Design at Sutherland	**11.21**
Development Phase	**11.22**
Program Development	11.22
Equipment Acquisition	11.22
Development at Sutherland	**11.22**
Implementation Phase	**11.23**
Training and Education	11.23
Conversion	11.23
Post-Implementation Evaluation	11.24
Implementation at Sutherland	**11.24**
Maintenance Phase	**11.25**
Performance Monitoring	11.25
Change Management	11.25
Error Correction	11.25
Maintenance at Sutherland	**11.26**
Computers at Work: The Case for CASE	**11.27**
In the Future: A RADical New Way to Develop Applications	**11.28**
What You Should Know	**11.29**
Terms to Remember	**11.32**
Test Your Knowledge	**11.33**
Points to Ponder	**11.34**
Out and About	**11.35**
In the Lab	**11.36**

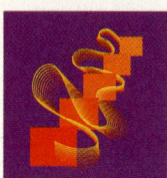

CHAPTER TWELVE

12 Program Development and Programming Languages

Objectives	**12.1**
What Is a Computer Program?	**12.2**
What Is Program Development?	**12.2**
Step 1 – Reviewing the Program Specifications	**12.3**
Step 2 – Designing the Program	**12.4**
Structured Program Design	12.4
Program Design Tools	12.7
Structured Walkthrough	12.8
Step 3 – Coding the Program	**12.9**
Step 4 – Testing the Program	**12.10**
Step 5 – Finalizing Program Documentation	**12.11**
Program Maintenance	**12.11**
What Is a Programming Language?	**12.12**
Categories of Programming Languages	**12.12**
Machine Language	12.12
Assembly Language	12.13
High-Level Languages	12.14
Fourth-Generation Languages	12.15
Application Generators	**12.16**
Object-oriented Programming	**12.17**
Programming Languages Used Today	**12.19**
How to Choose a Programming Language	**12.24**
Computers at Work: COBOL: The Language That Keeps Marching On	**12.25**
In the Future: Computing Naturally	**12.26**
What You Should Know	**12.27**
Terms to Remember	**12.30**
Test Your Knowledge	**12.31**
Points to Ponder	**12.32**
Out and About	**12.33**
In the Lab	**12.34**

SPECIAL FEATURE

Multimedia   12.37

CONTENTS

13 CHAPTER THIRTEEN
Security, Ethics, and Privacy

Objectives	13.1
Computer Security: Risks and Safeguards	13.2
Computer Viruses	13.2
Virus Detection and Removal	13.3
Unauthorized Access and Use	13.4
Hardware Theft	13.8
Software Theft	13.9
Information Theft	13.10
System Failure	13.11
Backup Procedures	13.13
Disaster Recovery Plan	13.14
Developing a Computer Security Plan	13.16
Ethics and the Information Age	13.17
Information Accuracy	13.17
Codes of Conduct	13.18
Information Privacy	13.18
Unauthorized Collection and Use of Information	13.18
Employee Monitoring	13.20
Computers at Work: Active Badges Help Locate Users	13.22
In the Future: Who Will Set the Standards and Methods of Information Privacy?	13.23
What You Should Know	13.24
Terms to Remember	13.27
Test Your Knowledge	13.28
Points to Ponder	13.29
Out and About	13.30
In the Lab	13.31

14 CHAPTER FOURTEEN
Your Future in the Information Age

Objectives	14.1
The Information Processing Industry	14.2
The Computer Equipment Industry	14.2
The Computer Software Industry	14.3
Information Processing Professionals	14.3
What Are the Career Opportunities in Information Processing?	14.4
Working in an Information Systems Department	14.4
Sales	14.5
Service and Repair	14.5
Education and Training	14.6
Consulting	14.6
Compensation and Growth Trends for Information Processing Careers	14.6
Preparing for a Career in Information Processing	14.8
What Are the Fields in the Information Processing Industry?	14.8
Obtaining Education for Information Processing Careers	14.8
Career Development in the Information Processing Industry	14.8
Professional Organizations	14.8
Certification	14.9
Professional Growth and Continuing Education	14.9
Computer Publications	14.10
Trends in Computers and Information Processing	14.11
Digital Convergence	14.11
Artificial Intelligence	14.13
Robotics	14.13
Vision Systems	14.13
Fuzzy Logic	14.13
Agent Software	14.14
Information Systems in Business	14.15
How Will Existing Information Systems Change?	14.15
The Automated Office	14.16
The Digital Factory	14.17
The Computer-Integrated Enterprise	14.19
Bringing the Information Age Home	14.19
The Use of Personal Computers in the Home	14.19
Computers at Work: Rapid Prototyping Using Stereolithography	14.23
In the Future: Human Computer Integration	14.24
What You Should Know	14.25
Terms to Remember	14.28
Test Your Knowledge	14.29
Points to Ponder	14.30
Out and About	14.31
In the Lab	14.33

SPECIAL FEATURE
Virtual Reality — 14.35

Index	I.1
Photo Credits	

Programming in QBasic — QB1

Project One
An Introduction to Programming in QBasic — QB1

The Programming Process — QB1
Sample Program 1 — Patient Listing — QB2
- Program Flowchart — QB2
- The QBasic Program — QB4

The DATA Statement — QB5
The CLS, PRINT, and END Statements — QB6
- The CLS Statement — QB6
- The PRINT Statement — QB6
- The END Statement — QB7

Variables — QB7
The READ Statement — QB7
The DO WHILE and LOOP Statements — QB8
- Testing for the End-of-File — QB9
- Conditions — QB9

Try It Yourself Exercises — QB11
The QB Operating Environment — QB12
- Starting a Session — QB12
- The QB Screen — QB13
  - View Window — QB13
  - Menu Bar — QB14
  - Immediate Window — QB14
  - Status Line — QB14
- Dialog Boxes — QB15
- Cursor Movement Keys — QB15
- Function Keys — QB15
- Terminating a QBasic Session — QB16
- Editing QBasic Programs — QB16
  - Deleting Previously Typed Characters — QB16
  - Changing or Replacing Previously Typed Lines — QB16
  - Adding New Lines — QB16
  - Deleting a Series of Lines — QB16
  - Moving Text — QB17
  - Copying Lines — QB17

Executing Programs and Hard-Copy Output — QB17
- Executing the Current Program — QB17
- Listing Program Lines to the Printer — QB18
- Listing a Portion of the Program to the Printer — QB19
- Printing the Results on the Output Screen — QB20

Saving, Loading, and Erasing Programs — QB20
- File Specifications — QB20
- Saving the Current Program to Disk — QB20
- Loading a Program from Disk — QB21
- Starting a New Program — QB22

The QB Advisor On-Line Help System — QB22
Try It Yourself Exercises — QB23
Student Assignments — QB23

Project Two
Basic Arithmetic Operations and Accumulating Totals — QB25

The LET Statement — QB25
- Expressions — QB25
- Order of Operations — QB26
- The Use of Parentheses in an Expression — QB27

Sample Program 2 — Auto Expense Report — QB27
- Accumulators — QB28
- Program Flowchart — QB29
- The QBasic Program — QB30
  - The DATA Statements — QB30
  - Initialization Module — QB30
  - The Process File Module — QB31
  - End-of-File Processing — QB32
  - The Complete QBasic Program — QB32

Report Editing — QB33
Printing a Report on the Printer — QB38
Try It Yourself Exercises — QB39
Student Assignments — QB40

Project Three
Decisions — QB42

The IF Statement — QB42
Coding If-Then-Else Structures — QB44
- Simple If-Then-Else Structures — QB44
- Nested If-Then-Else Structures — QB46

Sample Program 3 — Video Rental Report — QB47
- Program Flowchart — QB48
- The QBasic Program — QB49
- Discussion of Sample Program 3 — QB50

Logical Operators — QB51
- The NOT Logical Operator — QB51
- The AND Logical Operator — QB52
- The OR Logical Operator — QB53
- Combining Logical Operators — QB53
- The Use of Parentheses in Compound Conditions — QB54

The SELECT CASE Statement — QB54
- Valid Match-Expressions — QB56

Try It Yourself Exercises — QB56
Student Assignments — QB59

▶ PROJECT FOUR
Interactive Programming, For Loops, and an Introductions to the Top-Down Approach — QB62

- **THE INPUT STATEMENT** — QB62
- **THE BEEP AND LOCATE STATEMENTS** — QB64
  - The BEEP Statement — QB64
  - The LOCATE Statement — QB64
- **EDITING DATA ENTERED THROUGH THE KEYBOARD** — QB65
- **SAMPLE PROGRAM 4 — ITEM COST REPORT** — QB66
  - Program Flowchart — QB66
- **THE FOR AND NEXT STATEMENTS** — QB68
  - The QBasic Program — QB69
  - Discussion of Sample Program 4 — QB71
- **AN INTRODUCTION TO THE TOP-DOWN APPROACH** — QB72
  - Implementing the Top-Down Approach — QB73
- **THE GOSUB AND RETURN STATEMENTS** — QB73
  - Discussion of Sample Program 4 Modified — QB77
- **TRY IT YOURSELF EXERCISES** —
- **STUDENT ASSIGNMENTS** — QB80

▶ PROJECT FIVE
Sequential File Processing — QB83

- **FILE ORGANIZATION** — QB83
- **CREATING A SEQUENTIAL DATA FILE** — QB83
  - Opening Sequential Files — QB83
  - Closing Sequential Files — QB84
  - Writing Data to a Sequential File — QB84
- **SAMPLE PROGRAM 5A — CREATING A SEQUENTIAL DATA FILE** — QB85
  - Top-Down Chart and Program Flowcharts — QB86
  - The QBasic Program — QB88
  - Discussion of the Program Solution — QB89
- **READING DATA FROM A SEQUENTIAL DATA FILE** — QB91
  - The INPUT #n Statement — QB91
  - The EOF Function — QB91
- **SAMPLE PROGRAM 5B — PROCESSING A SEQUENTIAL DATA FILE** — QB92
  - Top-Down Chart and Program Flowcharts — QB92
  - The QBasic Program — QB94
  - Discussion of the Program Solution — QB96
- **TRY IT YOURSELF EXERCISES** — QB96
- **STUDENT ASSIGNMENTS** — QB97

▶ PROJECT SIX
Arrays and Functions — QB99

- **ARRAYS** — QB99
- **THE DIM STATEMENT** — QB100
- **SAMPLE PROGRAM 6 — CUSTOMER ACCOUNT TABLE LOOKUP** — QB101
  - Top-Down Chart and Program Flowcharts — QB102
  - The QBasic Program — QB103
    - Initialization Module — QB104
    - Process A Request Module — QB104
- **FUNCTIONS** — QB108
  - Numeric Functions — QB108
    - INT Function — QB108
    - SQR Function — QB108
    - RND Function — QB109
  - String Functions — QB110
    - The DATE$ and TIME$ Functions — QB110
  - Use of the LEFT$, LEN$, MID$, and RIGHT$ Functions — QB110
- **TRY IT YOURSELF EXERCISES** — QB112
- **STUDENT ASSIGNMENTS** — QB113

▶ APPENDIX
Debugging Techniques — QB115

- **EXAMINING VALUES THROUGH THE IMMEDIATE WINDOW** — QB115
- **EXECUTING ONE STATEMENT AT A TIME** — QB115
- **BREAKPOINTS** — QB116
- **TRACING** — QB116
- **SET NEXT STATEMENT** — QB116
- **RECORDING** — QB117
- **WATCH VARIABLES AND WATCHPOINTS** — QB117

▶ QBASIC INDEX — QB118

▶ QBASIC REFERENCE CARD — R.1

Preface

This Shelly Cashman Series textbook provides an up-to-date coverage of computers, their uses, and programming in QBasic than any book ever published. When preparing this book, our single guiding thought was: The book must be relevant to the world of computers today.

Toward that end, with our previous bestsellers as a base, we reviewed each and every aspect of the computer industry to ferret out the essential knowledge a student requires for a well-rounded understanding of using a computer as a tool to produce useful information, whether it be in the home, small business, or large business environments. This includes not only hardware and software, but also the processes and procedures required to successfully program a computer.

As a result, this book was developed with five goals in mind: The material must

- represent the latest in computer technology, particularly with respect to personal computer hardware and software.
- recognize that personal computers have become the backbone of the computer industry and emphasize their use as both stand-alone devices and networked devices.
- focus on using the computer as a productivity tool.
- present the material in an interesting, exciting manner with a format that invites the student to learn. This includes new, color photographs and unique, state-of-the-art drawings that augment the text material.
- provide exercises and lab assignments that allow the student to interact with a computer and actually learn by using the computer.
- present introductory programming concepts using QBasic.

Therefore, not only do we discuss the latest in computer equipment, computer software, and personal computer applications, but we also explain the process required to successfully use these tools to produce useful information. The result is a complete treatment of computers, the computer industry, and programming.

Merely explaining computer concepts without allowing a student to interact with a computer, however, would deprive the student of an essential experience. Therefore, at the end of each of the first fourteen chapters, we have included a series of *In the Lab* exercises that direct the student to use a computer to learn Microsoft Windows and DOS. In addition, a series of special Shelly Cashman Series Interactive Labs allow students to learn computer skills and gain computer knowledge in an online, interactive setting.

Each of the sections of the book, together with the extraordinary instructor's materials, are explained in the following paragraphs.

Objective of the Textbook

Using Computers: A Gateway to Information and Programming in QBasic is intended for use in a one-quarter or one-semester introductory course whose purpose is to provide students with a firm foundation in computer technology, computer nomenclature, the use of computers as productivity tools, and introduce programming using QBasic.

When a student has completed a course using this book, he or she will have an understanding of computers, computer technology, programming, computer hardware and software, and how computers can be used to produce meaningful information. With the experience gained via the *In the Lab* section of the book, the student should be proficient in using computers running under both DOS and Windows.

Chapter Organization of *Using Computers: A Gateway to Information*

Each of the first fourteen chapters is organized to present the optimum amount of material in the most effective manner possible. The text is presented in concise, clearly identified sections and subsections so the student is easily guided through the chapter. Figures (pictures and drawings) are visually separated from the text so the student can read without being encumbered by confusing text, graphics, arrows, and drawings.

Each chapter is organized into the following sections:
- **Objectives**   The objectives for the chapter are clearly stated on the first page of the chapter so the student has an overview of the subject matter.
- **Chapter Introduction**   Each chapter has an introduction that briefs the student on the material within the chapter and the reason the material in the chapter is important.
- **Chapter Text, Pictures, and Drawings**   The major learning material in the chapter is presented as text, pictures, and drawings. The pictures have been chosen for their pedagogical value and provide a valuable addition that allows students to see the actual hardware, software, and other subjects described in the text. The drawings, created with the latest state-of-the-art drawing capabilities of computers, specifically illustrate concepts that are understood more easily through the

use of drawings. The combination of drawings and pictures used in this book sets a new standard for computer textbooks.

- **Computers at Work** At the end of each chapter, an example of computers being used for interesting applications is presented. These examples illustrate points made within the chapter.
- **In the Future** This feature, which appears at the end of each chapter, points out an application or applications that will occur in the future using technology discussed in the chapter.
- **What You Should Know** This clear, step-by-step summary of the material in the chapter will help students review the chapter and prepare for examinations.
- **Terms to Remember** This listing of the key terms found in the chapter together with the page on which the terms are defined will aid students in mastering the chapter material. A complete summary of all key terms in the book, together with their definitions, appear in the Index at the end of the book.
- **Test Your Knowledge** Fill-in and short answer questions, together with a figure from the chapter that must be labeled, help focus the student when reviewing the material within the chapter.
- **Points to Ponder** The computer industry is not without its controversial issues. At the end of each chapter, six scenarios are presented that challenge the student to critically examine the computer industry and rethink his or her perspective of technology in society.
- **Out and About** Computers are found everywhere. This section, appearing at the end of each chapter, provides multiple projects that send the student out of the classroom and into the world where interesting discoveries about computers will take place.
- **In the Lab** Students must interact with and use a computer to complete their introduction to computers. At the end of each chapter, a series of lab exercises are presented for student use. These Labs are:
  - **Windows Labs** Beginning with the simplest exercises within Microsoft Windows, students are led through a series of activities that, by the end of the book, will enable them to be proficient in using Windows.
  - **DOS Labs** As with Windows, students are given a set of exercises that will lead to proficiency in using DOS commands by the end of the course.
  - **Online Labs** Online Labs introduce students to the many online services available when using a personal computer and a modem. This series of exercises at the end of each chapter directs students to use and interact with one or more online services.
- **Shelly Cashman Series Interactive Labs** These unique exercises, developed specifically for this book, are hands-on exercises that use the computer to teach about the computer. The Labs are described in detail on page xxiii.

This chapter organization and the material presented provide an in-depth treatment of introductory computer subjects. Students will finish the course with a complete understanding of computers and how to use computers.

Contents of *Using Computers: A Gateway to Information*

A brief explanation of each of the chapters in this book follows:

Chapter 1 – An Overview of Computer Concepts Introduces the student to the fundamentals of a computer, including the information processing cycle. When the student completes the chapter, he or she will have a firm understanding of the basics of computer processing and will be ready for the more in-depth treatment of subjects in subsequent chapters.

Chapter 2 – Computer Software Applications: User Tools Provides a complete explanation of application software available on computers, with an emphasis on personal computer software that students are likely to use. Numerous examples of the use of software such as word processing, spreadsheets, database, presentation graphics, data communications, electronic mail, and others are included.

Chapter 3 – Input to the Computer Presents the manner in which data is entered into the computer for processing, with primary attention to personal computers. In addition to the keyboard and mouse, pointing devices, scanners, voice input, and other means of entering data into personal computers is closely examined.

Chapter 4 – The System Unit Offers a detailed look inside the system unit. Topics include the motherboard, processors, memory, ports, and other elements that make a personal computer run.

Chapter 5 – Output from the Computer Explores the many means for obtaining useful information from a computer, including printers, display devices, voice output, and plotters. Included is an explanation of the types of output from personal computers, such as reports, graphics, audio output, video output, multimedia, and virtual reality.

Chapter 6 – Secondary Storage   Discusses the manner in which data is stored on a computer. Included are diskettes, hard disk, and cartridge tape systems, among others, together with an explanation of such storage issues as defragmentation and compression.

Chapter 7 – Communications and Networks   Covers communications and networks from a user's perspective. All important subjects are explained, with a special emphasis on local area networks and personal computers.

Chapter 8 – Operating Systems and System Software   Teaches students about operating systems such as DOS, OS/2, and Windows. A clear explanation of difficult subjects such as multitasking and multiprocessing contributes to a student's overall understanding.

Chapter 9 – Information Management: Files and Databases   Emphasizes the care and treatment of data, with particular attention on databases and the capability of accessing data to create meaningful information.

Chapter 10 – Information Systems   Explains that when the computer is used as a tool within an organization, be it small or large, the information from the computer must be organized and presented in its most useful form; details the information needs of various people within an organization.

Chapter 11 – Information Systems Development   Identifies the processes necessary to analyze, design, and implement an information system because effective use of computers and application systems does not happen by accident.

Chapter 12 – Program Development and Programming Languages   Presents all the steps required to produce a robust, functioning program. In addition, the student is exposed to the multitude of available programming languages.

Chapter 13 – Security, Ethics, and Privacy   Explores the effects of computers within society. It also looks at security issues with computers, and in particular how to ensure that data and programs on a computer are not rendered useless by viruses.

Chapter 14 – Your Future in the Information Age   Examines career opportunities in the computer field and discusses the future of the computers in our society

Special Features   Within the book, the special features sections provide an in-depth look at certain aspects of computers. The four special features are:
- The Evolution of the Computer Industry
- Making a Computer Chip
- The Internet
- How to Purchase, Install, and Maintain a Personal Computer
- Multimedia
- Virtual Reality

These contents, together with *In the Lab* and other projects within this book, present a thorough course on computers and computer usage.

Contents of *Programming in QBasic*

Programming in QBasic is designed for a first course on Microsoft QBasic programming. It introduces fundamentals programming concepts, presents the essentials of the Microsoft QBasic language that comes free with versions of DOS 5 and DOS 6, and acquaints students with structured and top-down programming techniques. This portion of the book assumes neither previous experience with computers nor mathematics beyond the high school freshman level. *Programming in QBasic* is organized into six projects. In each project, a problem is presented and then, step by step, it is thoroughly solved with a QBasic program.

- **Project 1 – An Introduction to Programming in QBasic**   The first project introduces students to the program development cycle, the basic characteristics of a QBasic program, and the QBasic operating environment.

- **Project 2 – Basic Arithmetic Operations and Accumulating Totals**   Project 2 presents computations, summary totals, report editing, and printing a report.

- **Project 3 – Decisions**   In this project, students learn about decision making. Topics include the IF statement, implementing If-Then-Else structures, logical operators, and the SELECT CASE statement.

- **Project 4 – Interactive Programming, For Loops, and an Introduction to the Top-Down Approach**   Unlike the first three projects, which use the READ and DATA statements to integrate data into a program, Project 4 shows students how to use the INPUT statement to accomplish this task. Also included is coverage of how to use For loops to implement counter-controlled loops, and how to design top-down programs.

- **Project 5 – Sequential File Processing**   This project introduces students to creating and processing a sequential data file.

- **Project 6 – Arrays and Functions**   In this final project, students learn how to write programs that can look up information in tables; they are then acquainted with the most often used QBasic *built-in* functions.

- **Appendix – QBasic Debugging Techniques**   This appendix introduces students to the debugging features that are built into Microsoft QBasic, specifically the immediate window, stepping one statement at a time, breakpoints, tracing, recording, and watchpoints.

- **Reference Card**   Included at the back of this portion of the book is a reference card that lists all of the statements, functions, and features of Microsoft QBasic.

Programming in QBasic Exercises and Assignments

Each project includes one or more sets of Try It Yourself Exercises and Student Programming Assignments.

- **Try It Yourself Exercises**   Try It Yourself Exercises are paper-and-pencil exercises to help students master the concepts presented. More than 75 such exercises are included; some are complete programs. Also, instructors can use these exercises as a diagnostic tool.

- **Student Programming Assignments**   Student Programming Assignments are field-tested assignments included at the end of each project. Each assignment includes instructions, sample input data, and sample output results.

Instructor's Support Package

The most comprehensive instructor's support package ever developed accompanies *Using Computers: A Gateway to Information* and *Programming in QBasic*. The elements of this package are as follows:

- **Annotated Instructor's Edition (AIE)**   The AIE for *Using Computers: A Gateway to Information* is designed to assist you with your lectures by suggesting transparencies to use, summarizing key points, proposing pertinent questions, offering important tips, and incorporating the answers to the student activities. The several hundred annotations in the AIE fall into three major categories:
    - **Teacher Notes**   Suggest ways to convey an idea effectively; point beyond what is covered in the book; describe the latest uses of computers; explain misconceptions; include quotes, show and tell suggestions, and interesting sidelights
    - **Discussion Topics**   Include questions to ask students that result in classroom discussion
    - **Transparency References**   Recommend transparencies to use at key points in the lecture presentation
- **Multimedia Lecture Presentation System**   The multimedia lecture presentation system was prepared specifically for use with *Using Computers: A Gateway to Information*. The system was developed using Microsoft PowerPoint 4 for Windows. The multimedia lecture presentation system is available on CD-ROM or diskette. The CD-ROM version includes chapter highlights, pictures, and more than one hour of video clips. The pictures and video clips can be viewed during lecture at the discretion of the instructor. The diskette version includes chapter highlights and fewer pictures. The Microsoft PowerPoint presentation viewer is included with both versions so an instructor does not need PowerPoint on his or her computer. The source files of the presentation are supplied, however, so instructors who have Microsoft PowerPoint 4 for Windows on their computers can customize the presentation to meet their students' needs.
- **Instructor's Materials for *Using Computers: A Gateway to Information* include the following:**
    - Detailed lesson plans, including objectives, overviews, and lecture outlines with transparency references for each illustration in each chapter of the book
    - A test bank of True/False, Multiple Choice, and Fill-in questions
    - A lesson plans and test bank diskette, called ElecMan, that includes the detailed lesson plans and test bank for customizing to each instructor's needs
    - Answers to all student activities
    - Black and white transparency masters for every figure in the first eight chapters and actual color transparencies of selected drawings for use in lectures
    - Illustrations for every screen in the *Microsoft Office* portion of this book on CD-ROM – for selection and display in a lecture or to print and make transparencies
    - A lab solutions diskette that contains all the answers to the *In the Lab* exercises in the book
- **Computer-Based LCD Lecture Success System** The Shelly Cashman Series proudly presents the finest LCD learning material available in textbook publishing. The Lecture Success System diskette, together with a personal computer and LCD technology, are used in lieu of transparencies. The system enables you to explain and illustrate the step-by-step, screen-by-screen

development of a project in the textbook without entering large amounts of data, thereby improving your students' grasp of the material. The Lecture Success System leads to a smooth, easy, error-free lecture.

The Lecture Success System diskette comes with files that correspond to key figures in the book. You load the files that pertain to a project and display them as needed. If the students want to see a series of steps a second time, simply reopen the file you want to start with and redo the steps. This presentation system is available to adopters without charge.

- **Video Tapes to Augment Lectures** Complimentary selections from three series, *Computer Applications*, *The Machine That Changed the World*, and *The Computer Revolution*, are available to qualified adopters of *Using Computers: A Gateway to Information*.
- **MicroExam IV** MicroExam IV, a computerized test-generating system, is available free to adopters of any Shelly Cashman Series textbook. It includes all the questions from the test bank previously described. MicroExam IV is an easy-to-use, menu-driven software package that provides instructors with testing flexibility and allows customizing of testing documents.
- **NetTest IV** NetTest IV, available at no cost, allows instructors to take a MicroExam IV file made up of True/False and Multiple Choice questions and proctor a paperless examination in a network environment. The same questions display in a different order on each personal computer in the network. Students have the option of instantaneous feedback. Tests are electronically graded, and an item analysis is produced.
- **Instructor's Materials for *Programming in QBasic*** include the following:
  - Lesson plans with lecture outlines and notes
  - Answers/Solutions to all Try It Yourself Exercises and Student Assignments
  - Test Questions with answer key
  - Transparency Masters for every figure
  - Instructor's Diskette

Student Study Guide

This highly popular supplement contains completely new activities to help solidify the concepts and techniques presented in the text. The Study Guide compliments the end-of-chapter material with short answer, fill-in, and matching questions and other challenging exercises.

Acknowledgments

The Shelly Cashman Series would not be the success it is without the contributions of outstanding publishing professionals. First, and foremost, among them is Becky Herrington, director of production and designer. She is the heart and soul of the Shelly Cashman Series, and it is only through her leadership, dedication, and untiring efforts that superior products are produced.

Under Becky's direction, the following individuals made significant contributions to these books: Ginny Harvey, series administrator and manuscript editor; Peter Schiller, production manager; Ken Russo, senior illustrator and cover art; Mike Bodnar, Greg Herrington and Dave Bonnewitz, illustrators; Jeanne Black, Betty Hopkins, and Michele Todd, typographers; Tracy Murphy, series coordinator; Sue Sebok and Melissa Dowling LaRoe, copy editors; Marilyn Martin and Nancy Lamm, proofreaders; Sarah Evertson and Sarah Bendersky, photo researchers; Marilyn Martin, photo credits; Christina Haley, indexer; Henry Blackham, cover and opener photography; and Dennis Woelky, glass etchings.

Our sincere thanks go to Dennis Tani, who together with Becky Herrington, designed *Using Computers: A Gateway to Information*. In addition, Dennis performed all the layout and typography, executed the magnificent drawings contained in this book, designed the cover, and survived an impossible schedule with goodwill and amazing patience. We salute Dennis's work.

The efforts of our contributing authors helped make this book extraordinary. As always, special recognition for a job well-done must go to Jim Quasney, who quarter-backed this book from its beginning to its final form. Thanks to Tom Walker, president and CEO of boyd & fraser publishing company, for his vision and support of this product.

We hope you find using this book an enriching and rewarding experience.

Gary B. Shelly
Thomas J. Cashman
Gloria A. Waggoner
William C. Waggoner

Shelly Cashman Series – Traditionally Bound Textbooks

The Shelly Cashman Series presents both Windows- and DOS-based personal computer applications in a variety of traditionally bound textbooks, as shown in the table below. For more information, see your ITP representative or call 1-800-423-0563.

	COMPUTERS
Computers	Using Computers: A Gateway to Information
	Using Computers: A Gateway to Information, Brief Edition
Computers and Windows Applications	Using Computers: A Gateway to Information, Brief Edition and Microsoft Office: Introductory Concepts and Techniques (also available in spiral bound)
	Using Computers: A Gateway to Information, Brief Edition and Works 3.0 (also available in spiral bound)
	Complete Computer Concepts and Microsoft Works 2.0 (also available in spiral bound)
Computers and DOS Applications	Complete Computer Concepts and WordPerfect 5.1, Lotus 1-2-3 Release 2.2, and dBASE IV Version 1.1 (also available in spiral bound)
	Complete Computer Concepts and WordPerfect 5.1, Lotus 1-2-3 Release 2.2, and dBASE III PLUS (also available in spiral bound)
Computers and Programming	Using Computers: A Gateway to Information and Programming in QBasic
	Using Computers: A Gateway to Information and Programming in Microsoft BASIC
	WINDOWS APPLICATIONS
Integrated Packages	Microsoft Office: Introductory Concepts and Techniques (also available in spiral bound)
	Microsoft Office: Advanced Concepts and Techniques (also available in spiral bound)
	Microsoft Works 3.0 (also available in spiral bound)
	Microsoft Works 2.0 (also available in spiral bound)
Windows	Microsoft Windows 3.1 Introductory Concepts and Techniques
	Microsoft Windows 3.1 Complete Concepts and Techniques
Windows Applications	Microsoft Word 2.0, Microsoft Excel 4, and Paradox 1.0 (also available in spiral bound)
Word Processing	Microsoft Word 6* • Microsoft Word 2.0
	WordPerfect 6.1* • WordPerfect 6* • WordPerfect 5.2
Spreadsheets	Microsoft Excel 5* • Microsoft Excel 4
	Lotus 1-2-3 Release 5* • Lotus 1-2-3 Release 4*
	Quattro Pro 6 • Quattro Pro 5
Database Management	Paradox 5 • Paradox 4.5 • Paradox 1.0
	Microsoft Access 2*
Presentation Graphics	Microsoft PowerPoint 4*
	DOS APPLICATIONS
Operating Systems	DOS 6 Introductory Concepts and Techniques
	DOS 6 and Microsoft Windows 3.1 Introductory Concepts and Techniques
Integrated Package	Microsoft Works 3.0 (also available in spiral bound)
DOS Applications	WordPerfect 5.1, Lotus 1-2-3 Release 2.2, and dBASE IV Version 1.1 (also available in spiral bound)
	WordPerfect 5.1, Lotus 1-2-3 Release 2.2, and dBASE III PLUS (also available in spiral bound)
Word Processing	WordPerfect 6.0
	WordPerfect 5.1 Step-by-Step Function Key Edition
	WordPerfect 5.1
	WordPerfect 5.1 Function Key Edition
	WordPerfect 4.2 (with Educational Software)
	WordStar 6.0 (with Educational Software)
Spreadsheets	Lotus 1-2-3 Release 4 • Lotus 1-2-3 Release 2.4 • Lotus 1-2-3 Release 2.3
	Lotus 1-2-3 Release 2.2 • Lotus 1-2-3 Release 2.01
	Quattro Pro 3.0
	Quattro with 1-2-3 Menus (with Educational Software)
Database Management	dBASE 5
	dBASE IV Version 1.1
	dBASE III PLUS (with Educational Software)
	Paradox 4.5
	Paradox 3.5 (with Educational Software)
	PROGRAMMING AND NETWORKING
Programming	Microsoft Visual Basic 3.0 for Windows*
	Microsoft BASIC
	QBasic
Networking	Novell Netware for Users
Internet	The Internet: Introductory Concepts and Techniques (UNIX Version)
	The Internet: Introductory Concepts and Techniques (Mosaic Version)

*Also available as a Double Diamond Edition, which is a shortened version of the complete book

Shelly Cashman Series – **Custom Edition** Program

If you do not find a Shelly Cashman Series traditionally bound textbook to fit your needs, boyd & fraser's unique **Custom Edition** program allows you to choose from a number of options and create a textbook perfectly suited to your course. The customized materials are available in a variety of binding styles, including boyd & fraser's patented **Custom Edition** kit, spiral bound, and notebook bound. Features of the **Custom Edition** program are:

- Textbooks that match the content of your course
- Windows- and DOS-based materials for the latest versions of personal computer applications software
- Shelly Cashman Series quality, with the same full-color materials and Shelly Cashman Series pedagogy found in the traditionally bound books
- Affordable pricing so your students receive the **Custom Edition** at a cost similar to that of traditionally bound books

The table on the right summarizes the available materials. For more information, see your ITP representative or call 1-800-423-0563.

COMPUTERS	
Computers	Using Computers: A Gateway to Information
	Using Computers: A Gateway to Information, Brief Edition
	Introduction to Computers (32-page)
OPERATING SYSTEMS	
Windows	Microsoft Windows 3.1 Introductory Concepts and Techniques
	Microsoft Windows 3.1 Complete Concepts and Techniques
DOS	Introduction to DOS 6 (using DOS prompt)
	Introduction to DOS 5.0 (using DOS shell)
	Introduction to DOS 5.0 or earlier (using DOS prompt)
WINDOWS APPLICATIONS	
Integrated Packages	Microsoft Works 3.0
	Microsoft Works 2.0
Microsoft Office	Using Microsoft Office (16-page)
	Object Linking and Embedding (OLE) (32-page)
Word Processing	Microsoft Word 6*
	Microsoft Word 2.0
	WordPerfect 6.1*
	WordPerfect 6*
	WordPerfect 5.2
Spreadsheets	Microsoft Excel 5*
	Microsoft Excel 4
	Lotus 1-2-3 Release 5*
	Lotus 1-2-3 Release 4*
	Quattro Pro 6
	Quattro Pro 5
Database Management	Paradox 5
	Paradox 4.5
	Paradox 1.0
	Microsoft Access 2*
Presentation Graphics	Microsoft PowerPoint 4*
DOS APPLICATIONS	
Integrated Package	Microsoft Works 3.0
Word Processing	WordPerfect 6.0
	WordPerfect 5.1 Step-by-Step Function Key Edition
	WordPerfect 5.1
	WordPerfect 5.1 Function Key Edition
	Microsoft Word 5.0
	WordPerfect 4.2
	WordStar 6.0
Spreadsheets	Lotus 1-2-3 Release 4
	Lotus 1-2-3 Release 2.4
	Lotus 1-2-3 Release 2.3
	Lotus 1-2-3 Release 2.2
	Lotus 1-2-3 Release 2.01
	Quattro Pro 3.0
	Quattro with 1-2-3 Menus
Database Management	dBASE 5
	dBASE IV Version 1.1
	dBASE III PLUS
	Paradox 4.5
	Paradox 3.5
PROGRAMMING AND NETWORKING	
Programming	Microsoft Visual Basic 3.0 for Windows*
	Microsoft BASIC
	QBasic
Networking	Novell Netware for Users
Internet	The Internet: Introductory Concepts and Techniques (UNIX Version)
	The Internet: Introductory Concepts and Techniques (Mosaic Version)

* Also available as a mini-module

In the Lab Exercises
with Shelly Cashman Series Interactive Labs

Each of the chapters in this book concludes with a hands-on exercise section titled *In the Lab*, which consists of Windows, DOS, and Shelly Cashman Series Interactive Labs. The purpose of these Labs is to allow students to use computers so they learn firsthand how computers work. The Labs solidify and reinforce the computer concepts presented in each chapter in a way unparalleled in previous computer textbooks. Students completing these labs will have a firm understanding of how to use computers with both DOS and Windows.

Of particular interest are the Shelly Cashman Series Interactive Labs (below), which help students gain a better understanding of a specific subject covered in a chapter.

Shelly Cashman Series Interactive Labs

Lab	Function	Page
Using the Mouse	Master how to use a mouse. The Lab includes pointing, clicking, double-clicking, and dragging.	1.30
Using the Keyboard	Learn how to use the keyboard. The Lab discusses different categories of keys, including the edit keys, function keys, ESC, CTRL, and ALT keys, and how to press keys simultaneously.	1.30
Scanning Documents	Understand how document scanners work.	3.30
Understanding the Motherboard	Step through the components of the motherboard and build one by adding components. The Lab shows how different motherboard configurations affect the overall speed of a computer.	4.33
Setting Up to Print	See how information flows from the system unit to the printer and how drivers, fonts, and physical connections play a role in generating a printout.	5.36
Configuring Your Display	Recognize the different monitor configurations available, including screen size, display cards, and number of colors.	5.36
Maintaining Your Hard Drive	Understand how files are stored on disk, what causes fragmentation, and how to maintain an efficient hard drive.	6.33
Connecting to the Internet	Learn how a computer is connected to the Internet. The Lab presents using the Internet to access information.	7.41
Evaluating Operating Systems	Evaluate the advantages and disadvantages of different categories of operating systems.	8.27
Working at Your Computer	Learn the basic ergonomic principles that prevent back and neck pain, eye strain, and other computer-related ailments.	8.27
Designing a Database	Create a database structure and optimize a database to support searching.	9.31
Choosing a Programming Language	Differentiate between traditional languages and newer object-oriented languages.	12.34
Keeping Your Computer Virus Free	Learn what a virus is and about the different kinds of viruses. The Lab teaches how to prevent your computer from being infected with a virus.	13.31
Exploring the Computers of the Future	Learn about computers of the future and how they will work.	14.33

CHAPTER ONE

An Overview of Computer Concepts

1

Objectives

After completing this chapter, you will be able to:

- Define computer and information literacy

- Explain the four operations of the information processing cycle: input, process, output, and storage

- Explain how speed, reliability and storage make computers powerful tools

- Identify the major components of a computer

- Identify the categories of computers

- Explain the difference between system software and application software

- Describe how the six elements of an information system work together

Computers play a key role in how individuals work and how they live. Today, even the smallest organizations have computers to help them operate more efficiently. Computers also affect people's lives in many unseen ways. Buying groceries at the supermarket, using an automated teller machine, or making a long-distance phone call all require using computers.

As they have for a number of years, personal computers continue to make an increasing impact on our lives. At home, at work, and in the field, these small systems help us do our work faster, more accurately, and in some cases, in ways that previously would not have been possible.

1.2 Computer and Information Literacy

Today, most people believe that knowing how to use a computer, especially a personal computer, is a basic skill necessary to succeed in business or to function effectively in society. Given the increasing use and availability of computer systems, such knowledge will continue to be an essential skill. Is just knowing how to use a computer, sometimes called **computer literacy**, enough? Many people now believe that a person should be *information literate* as well as *computer literate*. **Information literacy** is defined as knowing how to find, analyze, and use information. It is the ability to gather information from multiple sources, select the relevant material, and organize it into a form that will allow you to make a decision or take a specific action. For example, in shopping for a new car, one approach would be to visit several car dealers and talk to the salespeople about features of the model car in which you are interested. You can take written notes but your information will be limited to what you are told. An information literate person, however, will obtain relevant information about specific vehicles from a variety of sources before making any purchase decision. Such information might include vehicle list price, dealer cost, available options, repair history, and whether or not there have been any recalls. This type of information is available in several consumer-oriented publications and automobile magazines. With these facts, the car buyer is able to make a more informed decision on what car to buy (or not buy). How then do computers relate to information literacy?

COMPUTER AND INFORMATION LITERACY

They relate because increasingly, information on cars and other products, as well as information on finances, upcoming events, travel, and weather, is available from information sources that can be accessed using computers. With communications equipment and software, computers can connect with information sources around the world. Using a computer allows you to obtain up-to-date information in a fast, efficient, and cost-effective manner. Computers have become the tools people use to access and manage information.

The purpose of this book is to give you the knowledge you need to understand how computers work and how computers are used by people and organizations to gather and analyze information to make better decisions.

Chapter 1 gives you an overview of computer concepts. You will begin to learn what a computer is, how it processes data into information, and what elements are necessary for a successful information system. You will also begin to develop a basic vocabulary of computer terminology. While you are reading, remember that this chapter is an overview and that many of the terms and concepts that are introduced will be discussed in more detail in later chapters. *Figure 1-1* shows a variety of computers including personal computers and their applications. As you can see, the use of computer technology is widespread in our world. New uses for computers and improvements to existing technology are continually being developed. Computers affect your life every day and will continue to do so in the future. Learning about computers and their applications will help you to function more effectively in the world.

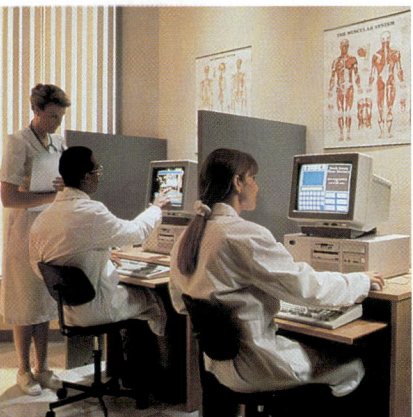

Figure 1-1
Computers being used in a wide variety of applications and professions; new applications are being developed every day.

What Is a Computer?

The most obvious question related to understanding computers and their impact on our lives is, "What is a computer?" A **computer** is an electronic device, operating under the control of instructions stored in its own memory unit, that can accept data (input), process data arithmetically and logically, produce output from the processing, and store the results for future use. While broader definitions of a computer exist, this definition includes a wide range of devices with various capabilities. For example, the tiny microprocessor shown in *Figure 1-2* can be called a computer. Generally, the term is used to describe a collection of devices that function together to process data. An example of the devices that make up a computer is shown in *Figure 1-3*.

What Does a Computer Do?

Whether small or large, computers can perform four general operations. These operations comprise the **information processing cycle** and are: input, process, output, and storage. Collectively, these operations describe the procedures that a computer performs to process data into information and store it for future use.

All computer processing requires data. **Data** refers to the raw facts, including numbers, words, images, and sounds, given to a computer during the input operation. In the processing phase, the computer manipulates the data to create information. **Information** refers to data that has been processed into a meaningul and useful form. The production of information by processing data on a computer is called **information processing,** or sometimes **data processing** (DP). During the output operation, the information created is put

Figure 1-2
Small enough to fool a bumblebee, this microprocessor contains the electronic circuits that perform the operations of a computer.

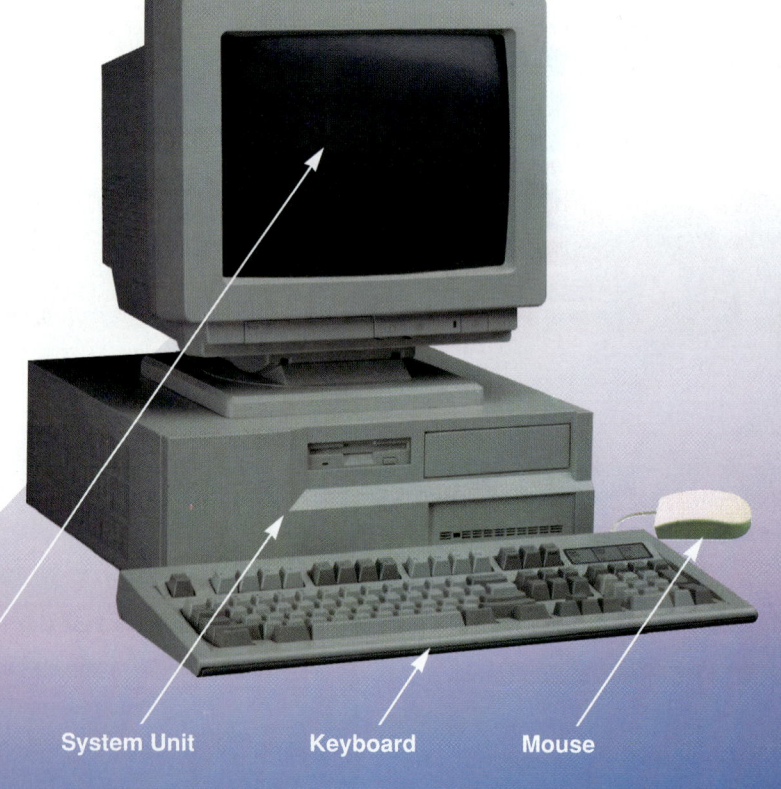

Figure 1-3
Devices that comprise a personal computer system.

Why Is a Computer so Powerful?

The input, process, output, and storage operations that a computer performs may seem very basic and simple. However, the computer's power derives from its capability to perform these operations with speed and reliability and to store large amounts of data and information.

Speed

In a computer, operations occur through the use of electronic circuits contained on small chips as shown in

into some form, such as a printed report, that people can use. The information can also be stored electronically for future use.

The people who either use the computer directly or use the information it provides are called **computer users**, **end users**, or **users**. *Figure 1-4* shows a computer user and demonstrates how the four operations of the information processing cycle can occur on a personal computer. (1) The computer user inputs data by pressing the keys on the keyboard. (2) The data is then processed by the device called the system unit. (3) The output, or results, from the processing are displayed on the screen of the monitor or printed on the printer, providing information to the user. (4) Finally, the output is stored on a disk for future reference.

Figure 1-4 ▶
The use of this personal computer illustrates the four operations of the information processing cycle: input, process, output, and storage.

Storage Input Process Output

Printer

CHAPTER 1 – AN OVERVIEW OF COMPUTER CONCEPTS

How Does a Computer Know What to Do?

For a computer to perform the operations in the information processing cycle, it must be given a detailed set of instructions that tell it exactly what to do. These instructions are called a **computer program**, **program instructions**, or **software**.

Before the information processing cycle for a specific job begins, the computer program corresponding to that job is loaded into the computer's memory. Once the program is loaded, the computer can begin to process data by executing the program's first instruction. The computer executes one program instruction after another until the job is complete.

Figure 1-5 When data flows along these circuits it travels at close to the speed of light. This allows processing to be accomplished in billionths of a second.

Reliability

The electronic components in modern computers are very reliable and seldom fail. In fact, most reports about computer errors are usually traced to other causes, often human mistakes. The high reliability of the components enables the computer to produce accurate results on a consistent basis.

Storage

Computers can store enormous amounts of data and keep that data readily available for processing. Using modern storage methods, the data can be quickly retrieved and processed and then re-stored for future use.

The speed, reliability, and storage capabilities of the computer make it a powerful tool for information processing.

Figure 1-5 Inside a computer are chips and other electronic components that process data in billionths of a second.

The Information Processing Cycle

Your understanding of the information processing cycle introduced in this chapter is fundamental to understanding computers and how they process data into information. To review, the information processing cycle consists of four operations. They are: input, process, output, and storage.

The first three of these operations, **input**, **process**, and **output**, describe the procedures that a computer performs to process data into information. The fourth operation, **storage**, describes a computer's electronic storage capability. As you learn more about computers, you will see that these four operations apply to both the computer equipment and the computer software. The equipment, or devices, of a computer are classified according to the operations they perform. Computer software is made up of instructions that describe how the operations are to be performed.

What Are the Components of a Computer?

Data is processed by specific equipment that is often called computer **hardware**. This equipment consists of: input devices, a system unit, output devices, and secondary storage devices (*Figure 1-6*).

Input Devices

Input devices are used to enter data into a computer. Two common input devices shown in *Figure 1-7* on the next page are the keyboard and the mouse. As the data is entered on the **keyboard**, it is temporarily stored in the computer's memory and displayed on the screen of the monitor. A **mouse** is a type of pointing device used to select processing options or information displayed on the screen. The mouse is used to move a small symbol that appears on the screen. This symbol, called a **mouse pointer** or **pointer**, can be many shapes but is often in the shape of an arrow.

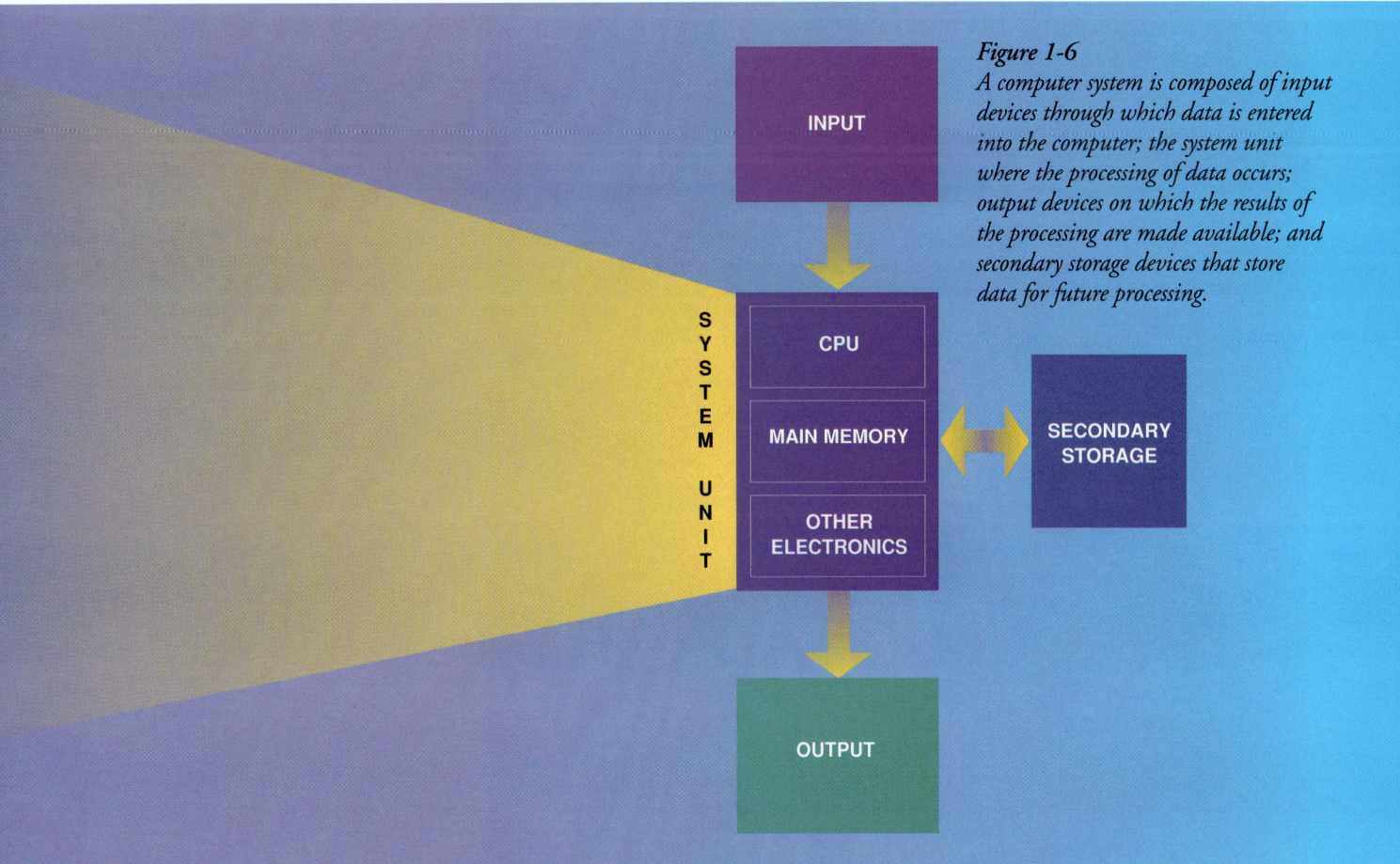

Figure 1-6
A computer system is composed of input devices through which data is entered into the computer; the system unit where the processing of data occurs; output devices on which the results of the processing are made available; and secondary storage devices that store data for future processing.

System Unit

Figure 1-6 on the previous page and *Figure 1-7* show the **system unit** of a computer, which contains the electronic circuits that actually cause the processing of data to occur. The system unit includes the central processing unit, main memory, and other electronic components. The **central processing unit** (CPU) contains a **control unit** that executes the program instructions and an **arithmetic/logic unit** (ALU) that performs math and logic operations. **Arithmetic operations** include numeric calculations such as addition, subtraction, multiplication, and division. Comparisons of data to see if one value is greater than, equal to, or less than another are called **logical operations.**

Main memory, also called **RAM** (**Random Access Memory**) or **primary storage**, temporarily stores data and program instructions when they are being processed.

Other electronics include components that work with the input, output, and storage devices and optional components that enable the computer to communicate with other computers.

Output Devices

Output from a computer can be presented in many forms. The two most commonly used **output devices** are the **printer** and the **monitor** shown in *Figure 1-7*. Other frequently used names for the monitor are the **screen**, or the **CRT**, which stands for **cathode ray tube**.

Figure 1-7
The components of a personal computer system perform the four operations of the information processing cycle.

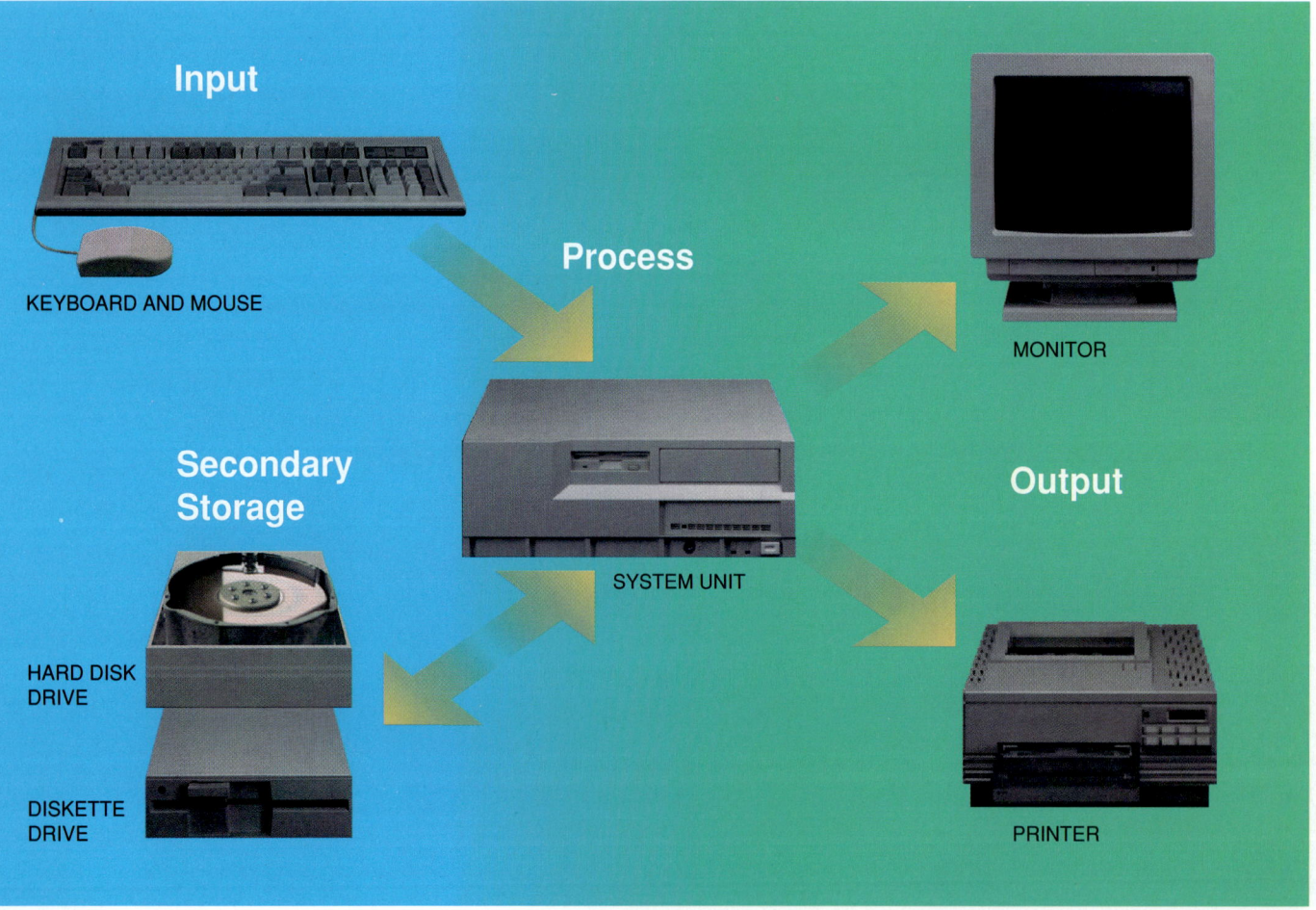

Secondary Storage Devices

Secondary storage devices, sometimes called **auxiliary storage devices,** shown in *Figure 1-7,* store instructions and data when they are not being used by the system unit. A common secondary storage device on personal computers is a diskette drive, which stores data as magnetic areas on a small plastic disk called a **diskette.** Another secondary storage device is called a hard disk drive. **Hard disk** drives contain nonremovable disks and provide larger storage capacities than diskettes.

As you can see, each component shown in *Figure 1-7* plays an important role in information processing. Collectively, this equipment is called a **computer system,** or simply a computer. The term computer is also used to refer to the system unit where the actual processing of data occurs. The input devices, output devices, and secondary storage devices that surround the system unit are sometimes referred to as **peripheral devices.**

Categories of Computers

Figure 1-8 shows the following five major categories of computers: personal computers, servers, minicomputers, mainframe computers, and supercomputers.

Computers are generally classified according to their size, speed, processing capabilities, and price. However, rapid changes in technology make firm definitions of these categories difficult. This year's speed, performance, and price classification of a mainframe might fit next year's classification of a minicomputer. Even though they are not firmly defined, the categories are frequently used and should be generally understood.

CATEGORY	PHYSICAL SIZE	SPEED*	NUMBER OF ONLINE USERS	GENERAL PRICE RANGE
Personal Computer	Hand-held to desktop or tower	1 to 100 MIPS	Usually a single user	Hundreds to several thousand $
Server	Tower or small cabinet	25 to 200 MIPS	2 to 1,000 users	$5,000 to $150,000
Minicomputer	Small cabinet to several large cabinets	Hundreds of MIPS	2 to 4,000 users	$15,000 to several hundred thousand $
Mainframe	Partial to full room of equipment	Hundreds of MIPS	Hundreds to thousands of users	$300,000 to several million $
Supercomputer	Full room of equipment	Thousands of MIPS	Hundreds of users	Several million $ and up

*speed rated in MIPS; each MIP equals one million instructions per second.

Figure 1-8
This table summarizes some of the differences between the categories of computers. Because of rapid changes in technology, these should be considered general guidelines only.

Personal Computers

Personal computers (PCs), shown in *Figure 1-9*, also called **microcomputers** or **micros**, are the small systems that have become so widely used. Classifications within this category include hand-held, palmtop, notebook, subnotebook, laptop, pen, desktop, tower, and workstation. Hand-held, palmtop, notebook, subnotebook, laptop, and pen computers are considered portable computers. Depending on their size and features, personal computer prices range from several hundred to several thousand dollars. The most expensive personal computers are generally under $10,000.

Hand-held computers *(Figure 1-9a)* are usually designed for a specific purpose such as meter reading or inventory counting and are used by workers who are on their feet instead of sitting at a desk.

Palmtop computers *(Figure 1-9b)* often have several built-in or interchangeable personal information management functions such as a calendar to keep track of meetings and events, an address and phone file, and a task list of things to do. Some palmtop computers also have limited capabilities to write correspondence and perform financial analysis. Palmtop computers do not have disk storage devices and usually have a nonstandard keyboard, meaning that the keys are not arranged like a typewriter.

Notebook computers *(Figure 1-9c)* are small enough to be carried in a briefcase but are often transported in their own carrying case. Notebooks are general-purpose computers in that they can run most application software packages. They have standard keyboards and usually have at least one disk drive for storage. Notebooks usually weigh between four and eight pounds.

Subnotebook computers *(Figure 1-9d)* are smaller versions of notebook computers and generally weigh less than four pounds. To save weight and space, some subnotebooks do not have disk drives and use special-purpose memory cards for storage.

Figure 1-9
Personal computers come in many shapes and sizes. Shown in these photos are
(a) hand-held,
(b) palmtop,
(c) notebook,
(d) subnotebook,
(e) laptop,
(f) pen,
(g) personal digital assistant (PDA),
(h) desktop,
(i) tower, and
(j) workstation.

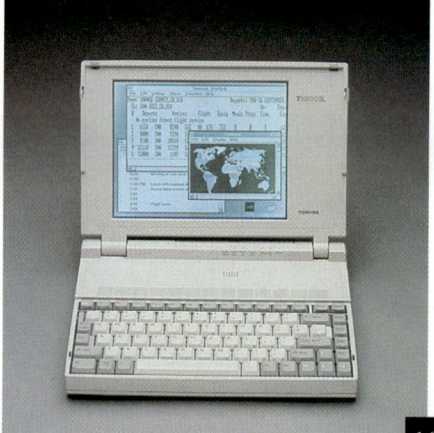

CATEGORIES OF COMPUTERS

Laptop computers *(Figure 1-9e)* are larger versions of notebook computers that weigh between eight and fifteen pounds. The extra weight comes primarily from large-capacity disk storage devices and larger display screens.

Pen computers *(Figure 1-9f)* are specialized portable computers that use a pen-like device to enter data. Sometimes the pen is used to write information on a special input screen and sometimes it is used as a pointing device to select a processing choice presented on the screen. Pen systems have successfully replaced many applications that previously required the user to fill out a form or checklist. The unique feature about pen systems is the special software that allows the system to recognize handwritten input. One type of small pen input system is called a **personal digital assistant** (**PDA**) or **personal communicator**. These hand-held devices are designed for workers on the go and often have built-in communications capabilities that allow the PDA to use voice, fax, or data communications. Apple's Newton PDA *(Figure 1-9g)* has built-in intelligence that assists the user in making entries.

Desktop computers *(Figure 1-9h)* are the most common type of personal computer and are designed to fit conveniently on the surface of a desk or workspace. Desktop computers have separate display screens.

Tower computers *(Figure 1-9i)* are personal computers in an upright case. A full-size tower case provides more room for expanding the system and adding optional equipment. The most powerful personal computers are sometimes only available in tower cases. A mini-tower case, approximately half the size of a full tower case, usually has less expansion room than a desktop computer but takes up less room.

Workstations *(Figure 1-9j)* are expensive high-end personal computers that have powerful calculating and graphics capabilities. Workstations are frequently used by engineers to aid in product design and testing. The term workstation is sometimes used to refer to a personal computer or terminal connected to a network.

1-9e

1-9g

1-9i

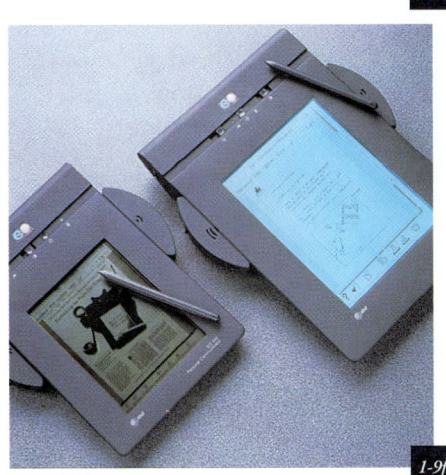
1-9f

1-9h

1-9j

Servers

Server computers, shown in *Figure 1-10*, are designed to support a computer network that allows users to share files, applications software, and hardware such as printers. The term server really describes how a computer is used. Technically, the term could be applied to any of the other categories of computers if they were used to support a network of other computers. However, in recent years manufacturers have built computers specifically designed for network use and the term server is becoming widely used to describe this type of computer. Server computers usually have the following characteristics:

- designed to be connected to one or more networks
- most powerful CPUs available
- capability to add more than one CPU to divide the processing tasks (one manufacturer's server can use up to 32 CPUs)
- large memory capacity
- large disk storage capacity, usually comprised of numerous small disks instead of several large disks
- high-speed internal and external communications

Small servers look like high-end personal computers and are priced in the $5,000 to $20,000 range. The most powerful servers look and function more like minicomputers and are priced as high as $150,000.

Minicomputers

Minicomputers, shown in *Figure 1-11*, are more powerful than personal computers and can support a number of users performing different tasks. Originally developed to perform specific tasks such as engineering calculations, their use grew rapidly as their performance and capabilities increased. Today, many businesses and other organizations use minicomputers for their information processing requirements. These systems can cost from approximately $15,000 up to several hundred thousand dollars. The most powerful minicomputers are called superminicomputers.

Figure 1-11
Minicomputers can perform many of the functions of a mainframe computer but on a smaller scale.

Figure 1-10
Server computers are designed to support a network of other computers. Servers allow the other computers to share data, applications software, and hardware resources such as printers. Small servers are simply powerful personal computers dedicated to a server function. The most powerful servers, however, are more like minicomputers. High-end servers contain multiple CPUs, numerous large-capacity disk drives, and large amounts of memory.

Figure 1-12
Mainframe computers are large, powerful machines that can handle many users concurrently and process large volumes of data.

Mainframe Computers

Mainframe computers, shown in *Figure 1-12*, are large systems that can handle hundreds of users, store large amounts of data, and process transactions at a very high rate. Mainframes usually require a specialized environment including separate air conditioning, cooling, and electrical power. Raised flooring is often built to accommodate the many cables connecting the system components underneath. The price range for mainframes is from several hundred thousand dollars to several million dollars.

Supercomputers

Supercomputers, shown in *Figure 1-13*, are the most powerful category of computers and, accordingly, the most expensive. The capability of these systems to process hundreds of millions of instructions per second is used for such applications as weather forecasting, engineering design and testing, space exploration, and other jobs requiring long, complex calculations *(Figure 1-14)*. These machines cost several million dollars.

Computers of all categories, especially personal computers, are sometimes connected to form **networks** that allow users to share data and computing resources such as software, printers, and storage devices.

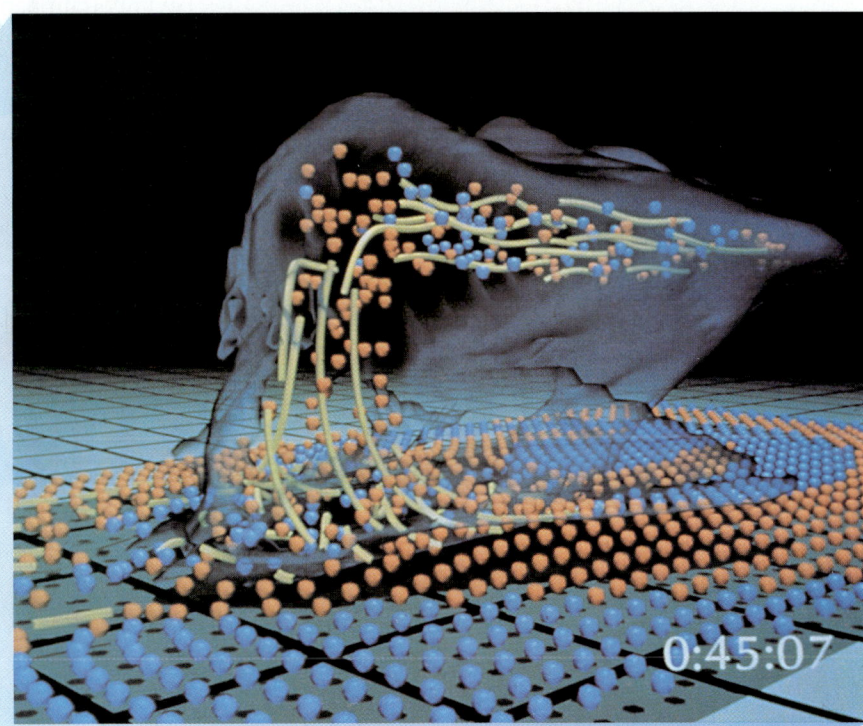

Figure 1-14
This simulated weather pattern was calculated on a supercomputer.

Figure 1-13
Supercomputers are the most powerful and expensive computers.

Computer Software

As mentioned previously, a computer is directed by a series of instructions called a computer program *(Figure 1-15)* that specifies the sequence of operations the computer will perform. To do this, the program must be loaded into the main memory of the computer. Computer programs are commonly referred to as computer software. Many instructions can be used to direct a computer to perform a specific task. For example, some instructions allow data to be entered from a keyboard and stored in main memory; some instructions allow data in main memory to be used in calculations such as adding a series of numbers to obtain a total; some instructions compare two values stored in main memory and direct the computer to perform alternative operations based on the results of the comparison; and some instructions direct the computer to print a report, display information on the screen, draw a color graph on a screen, or store data on a disk.

Most computer programs are written by people with specialized training. These people, called **computer programmers**, write the instructions necessary to direct the computer to process data into information. The instructions must be placed in the correct sequence so the desired results will occur.

Complex programs may require hundreds or even thousands of program instructions. Programmers often follow a plan developed by a **systems analyst** who works with both the user and the programmer to determine and design the desired output of the program.

Computer software is the key to productive use of computers. With the correct software, a computer can become a valuable tool. Software can be categorized into two types: system software and application software.

System Software and Application Software

System software consists of programs that are related to controlling the actual operations of the computer equipment. An important part of the system software is a set of programs called the operating system. The instructions in the **operating system** tell the computer how to perform functions such as how to load, store, and execute an application program and how to transfer data between the input/output devices and main memory. For a computer to operate, an operating system must be stored in the main memory of the computer. Each time a computer is turned on, or restarted, the operating

Figure 1-15
A computer program contains instructions that specify the sequence of operations to be performed. This program is written in a language called QuickBASIC. The program prompts the user for data and then calculates and prints a sales commission amount.

Program:
```
REM Program 1-15
REM Determining a Salesperson's Commission
REM Dave Brame, CIS 204, Div. 01
REM September 30, 1996
REM ************************************
REM Clear Screen
CLS
REM Request Data from Operator
INPUT "Commission rate =====> ", Rate
INPUT "Week 1 sales ========> ", Week1
INPUT "Week 2 sales ========> ", Week2
INPUT "Return sales ========> ", Returns
REM Calculate the Earned Commission
Commission = Rate * (Week1 + Week2 - Returns)
REM Display the Earned Commission
PRINT
PRINT "Earned commission ===>"; Commission
END

[run]
```

Results:
```
Commission rate =====> 0.15
Week 1 sales ========> 1200
Week 2 sales ========> 1500
Return sales ========> 75

Earned commission ===> 393.75
```

system is loaded into the computer and stored in the computer's main memory. Many different operating systems are available for computers. Today, many computers use what is called an **operating environment** that works with the operating system to make the computer system easier to use. Operating environments have a **graphical user interface** (GUI) that provides visual clues such as symbols, called icons, to help the user. Each **icon** represents an application software package, such as word processing, or a file or document where data is stored. Microsoft Windows *(Figure 1-16)* is a graphical user interface that works with the DOS operating system. DOS, which stands for disk operating system, is the most commonly used operating system on personal computers. Apple Macintosh computers also have a graphical user interface built into the Macintosh operating system.

Application software consists of programs that tell a computer how to produce information. When you think of the different ways that people use computers in their careers or in their personal lives, you are thinking of examples of application software. Business, scientific, and educational programs are all examples of application software.

Application Software Packages

Most end users do not write their own programs. In some corporations, the information processing department develops custom software programs for unique company applications. Programs required for common business and personal applications can be purchased from software vendors or stores that sell computer products *(Figure 1-17)*. Purchased programs are often referred to as **application software packages**, or simply **software packages**.

Personal Computer Application Software Packages

Personal computer users often use application software packages. Some of the most widely used packages are word processing, desktop publishing, electronic spreadsheet, presentation graphics, database, communications, and electronic mail.

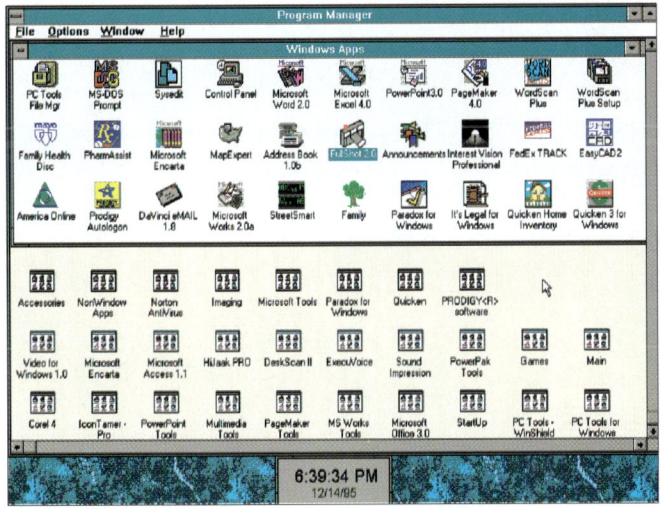

Figure 1-16
A graphical user interface, such as Microsoft Windows, makes the computer easier to use. The small pictures, or symbols, on the main part of the screen are called icons. The icons represent different processing options, such as word processing or electronic spreadsheet applications, the user can choose.

Figure 1-17
Many programs commonly required for business and personal applications can be purchased from computer stores.

What Are the Elements of an Information System?

Obtaining useful and timely information from computer processing requires more than just the equipment and software described so far. Other elements required for successful information processing include accurate data, trained information systems personnel, knowledgeable users, and documented procedures. Together these elements are referred to as an **information system** *(Figure 1-18)*.

For an information system to provide accurate, timely, and useful information, each element in the system must be strong and all of the elements must work together. The equipment must be reliable and capable of handling the expected work load. The software must have been carefully developed and tested, and the data entered to be processed must be accurate. If the data is incorrect, the resulting information produced from it will be incorrect. Properly trained information systems personnel are required to run most medium and large computer systems. Even small networks of personal computers usually have a system administrator to manage the system. Users are sometimes overlooked as an important element of an information system, but with expanding computer use, users are taking increasing responsibility for the successful operation of information systems. This includes responsibility for the accuracy of both the input and output. In addition, users are taking a more active role in the development of computer applications. They work closely with information systems department personnel in the development of computer applications that relate to their areas of work. Finally, all information processing applications should have documented procedures covering not only the computer operations but any other related procedures as well.

Figure 1-18
An information system requires computer equipment; software that runs on the equipment; data the computer processes; people including both computer personnel who manage the equipment and users who use the information the equipment produces; and finally procedures, that help the entire system run efficiently.

Connectivity

Connectivity refers to the capability to connect a computer to other computers. The connection may be temporary, such as when a computer is connected to an online information service provider, or permanent such as when a computer is connected to a network of other computers. Connectivity has had a significant impact on the way people use computers *(Figure 1-19)*. For many years, computers were used as stand-alone devices, limited to the hardware and software resources contained in that computer. However, stand-alone computers are becoming the exception. One study found that most business computers are connected to other computers as part of a network. Even home computers are increasingly used to access other computers to transfer data or to obtain information on practically any subject. You may have heard about the *Information Highway*, the United States government's plan to bring information access into the home of every citizen. This ambitious plan will create a high-speed network that will allow people, with a computer, to access government information and other information and entertainment services. Many people believe that the computer will eventually be used for all forms of communication; written, visual, and sound.

An Example of How One Company Uses Computers

To show you how a typical mid-sized company might use computers, this section will take you on a visual and narrative tour of Hayden Corporation, an automobile parts manufacturer. All of the computers at Hayden are joined together in a network that allows the computer users to communicate with one another and share information.

Receptionist

One of the things you notice when you enter the main lobby of Hayden is the computer sitting on the receptionist's desk *(Figure 1-20)*. Outside calls are answered by the receptionist who transfers them to the appropriate employee. If an employee doesn't answer his or her phone, the receptionist can use the computer to determine the location of the employee. When employees leave their work area for a meeting, lunch, or to travel away from the office, they record their destination or reason for being away using their computer terminal. An employee can also record any special instructions to the receptionist, such as when he or she will return or to hold calls. If a caller wants to leave a voice message, the company phone system, which also uses a computer, can record the message and play it back for the employee when he or she returns or calls in for messages.

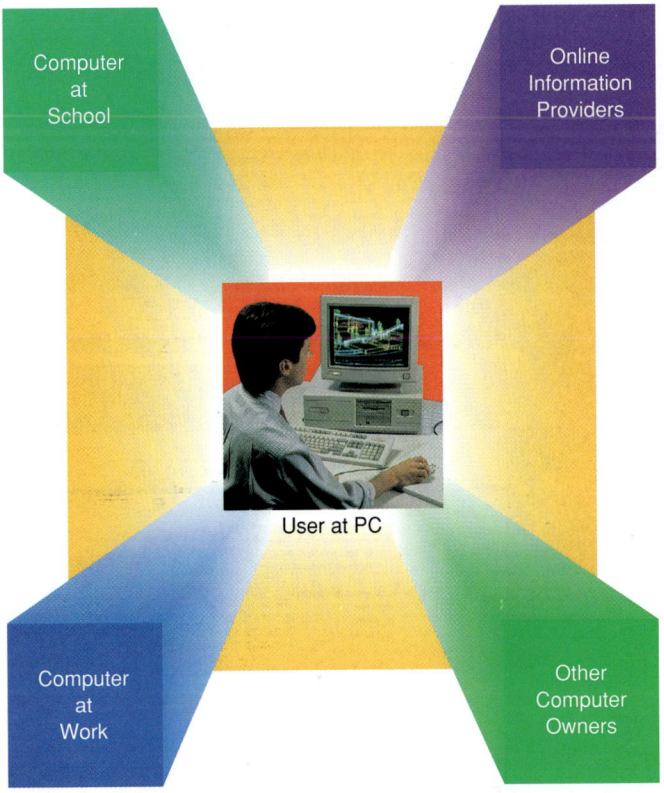

Figure 1-19
Increasingly, computers are connected to other computers to share data and information.

Figure 1-20 *The receptionist uses the computer system to locate employees away from their desks, to record messages, and to help with general correspondence.*

Sales

The Hayden sales department consists of two groups; in-house sales representatives that handle phone-in and mail-in sales orders and the field sales force that makes sales calls at customer locations. The in-house sales staff use headset phones *(Figure 1-21)* so their hands are free to use their computer keyboards. Using the computer while they are on the phone with a customer allows them to check product availability and the customer's credit status. A computer program also recommends products that compliment the products ordered by the customer and displays information on special product promotions. Field sales force representatives use notebook computers and special communications equipment and software to communicate with the Hayden main office. As with the in-house sales staff, they also can check product availability and customer credit status. If they receive a customer order, they can enter it into the Hayden computer system while they are still at the customer site. In addition, the field sales representatives can use the electronic mail capability to check for or send messages.

Marketing

The marketing department uses the computer system for a number of purposes. Desktop publishing, drawing, and graphics software is used to develop all marketing literature *(Figure 1-22)*. Product brochures, print advertising, and product packaging are all produced in-house, saving considerable time and money. The customer service representatives all have computer terminals that allow them to record a variety of customer inquiries. Recording the nature of each customer service inquiry provides for better follow-up (less chance of forgetting an unresolved inquiry) and enables the company to summarize and review why customers are calling. This helps the company identify and resolve potential problems at an early stage. The marketing department also uses a calendar program to schedule product promotions and attendance at trade shows *(Figure 1-23)*.

Figure 1-21
Order entry personnel use the computer to check if the products requested by the customer are in stock. The system automatically displays additional products the customer might need and information on special product promotions.

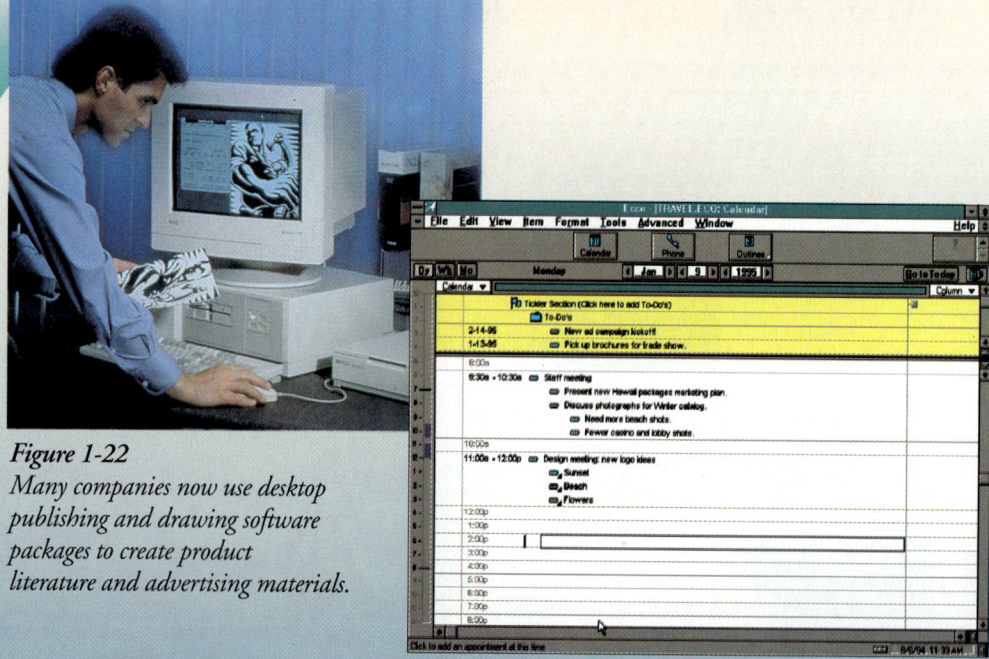

Figure 1-22
Many companies now use desktop publishing and drawing software packages to create product literature and advertising materials.

Figure 1-23
Calendar programs help users plan their schedules.

Shipping and Receiving

The shipping and receiving department uses the computer system to enter transactions that keep Hayden's inventory records accurate *(Figure 1-24)*. Inventory receipts are first checked against computer records to make sure that Hayden receives only what was ordered. If the received goods match what was ordered, only a single entry has to be made to update the on-hand inventory and purchasing records. Shipping transactions are also efficient. If all requested items were in stock, only a single entry is required to decrease the inventory and create the information that will be used to prepare the billing invoice. Shipping information such as the method and time of shipment can be added to the transaction record so the computer system can be used to provide up-to-the-minute status of the customer's order.

Manufacturing

The manufacturing department uses the computer to schedule production and to record the costs of the items produced. Special manufacturing software matches the availability of production resources such as people, machines, and material against the desired product output. This information allows Hayden to efficiently schedule production and tells them when and how much to buy of the raw materials they need to produce their products *(Figure 1-25)*. Actual labor, material, and machine usage is recorded on the manufacturing floor using special terminals designed to be used in industrial environments *(Figure 1-26)*. This information is automatically entered into the computer system to update inventory, production, payroll, and cost accounting records.

Figure 1-25
Special software helps the company manufacture products.

Figure 1-24
Computers help companies keep accurate inventory records.

Figure 1-26
Some computer terminals have been specially designed to withstand the heat, dust, and other conditions of a factory floor.

Engineering

The engineering department uses computer-aided design (CAD) software to design new products *(Figure 1-27)*. CAD software allows the engineers to design and review three-dimensional models of new products on the computer before expensive molds are required. If a design is approved, the CAD software can automatically produce a list of the required parts.

Accounting

The accounting department is one of the largest computer system users. Many of the accounting records are the result of transactions entered in the user departments, such as shipping and receiving and manufacturing. These records are used to pay vendor invoices, bill customers for product sales, and to process the Hayden employee payroll *(Figure 1-28)*. The accounting transactions are automatically summarized to produce Hayden's financial statements that are used internally to monitor financial performance and given to outside organizations such as banks.

Human Resources

The human resources department uses the computer system to keep track of information on existing, past, and potential employees *(Figure 1-29)*. Besides the standard information required for payroll and employee benefits, the system keeps track of employees job skills and training. This information enables the human resource department to review the records of existing employees first when a new job becomes available.

Information Systems

A primary responsibility of the information systems department is to keep the existing system running and to

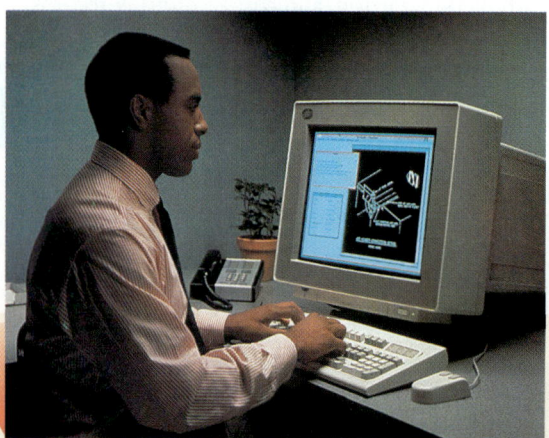

Figure 1-27
Computer-aided design (CAD) software is used to design new products. As with word processing software, CAD programs make the design process easier by allowing the user to make many changes until they are satisfied.

Figure 1-28
Accounting departments were one of the first users of computer systems and still rely heavily on computers to summarize the numerous financial transactions.

Figure 1-29
Human resource departments use computers to keep track of past, present, and potential employees.

determine when and if new equipment or software is required. To help answer these questions, the information systems personnel use diagnostic and performance measurement software that tells them how much the system is being used and if system problems are being encountered *(Figure 1-30)*. A systems analyst works with users to design custom software for user applications for which application software packages do not exist. A computer programmer uses the design to write the program instructions necessary to produce the desired processing results and output.

Executive

The senior management staff of Hayden Corporation (the president and three vice presidents) use the computer for an executive information system (EIS). The EIS summarizes information such as actual sales, order backlog, number of employees, cash on hand, and other performance measures into both a numeric and graphic display *(Figure 1-31)*. The EIS is specifically designed for executives who do not regularly work with computers and who only want to see summarized information.

Summary of How One Company Uses Computers

The computer applications just discussed are only some of the many potential uses of a computer within Hayden Corporation. In addition, employees in each of the departments would use the computer for preparing correspondence, project and task management, budgeting, and sending messages via electronic mail.

As you can see in the Hayden Corporation example, computers are used throughout an organization. Employees use computers to perform a variety of tasks related to their job area. Because of the widespread use of computers, most organizations prefer to hire employees with computer experience and knowledge.

Summary of an Overview of Computer Concepts

This chapter presented a broad introduction to concepts and terminology related to computers. You now have a basic understanding of what a computer is, how it processes data into information, and what elements are necessary for a successful information system. You also have seen some examples of different types of computers and how they are used. Reading the overview of computer concepts in Chapter 1 will help you to more easily understand topics as they are presented in more detail in following chapters.

Figure 1-30
Information system personnel check on how much the computer system is being used with performance measurement software.

Figure 1-31
Executive information system (EIS) software usually includes graphics to convey information to users who do not frequently use the computer and who want summarized information.

COMPUTERS AT WORK

Carnegie Mellon University: Information at Your Dorm Room

Students at Carnegie Mellon University (CMU) can access the latest in research reference materials from the comfort of their dorm rooms. CMU has long been recognized as a leader in computer science education and their Library Information System (LIS) is one of the first decentralized electronic library applications. Using nearly any type of personal computer, CMU's 5,000 students can log into a network that provides information from numerous journals on computer science, artificial intelligence, and other subjects. Eventually, CMU plans on having more than 600 journals available for review online. Some publishers, however, have been reluctant to permit their material to be added to the system. These publishers are concerned about improper use of their materials and loss of subscription revenue. But with the strong overall trend towards electronic publishing, CMU officials are confident that these issues will eventually be resolved. Students without their own personal computers can use systems in the library and at several other locations around the campus. The LIS runs on a campus-wide network supported by seven server computers. Future plans for the LIS include additional server computers, a natural language interface that will make the system easier to use, and expansion of the network to include outside resources such as commercial online services and the Internet.

Figure 1-32

IN THE FUTURE

Information Appliances

Many believe that today's personal computer will evolve into an information appliance. This device will serve as a master control for all your home systems as well as allow you to access and process information from around the world.

Numerous changes will have to take place before any one device can control so many aspects of daily life, but the trend in that direction seems to be firmly established. For one thing, computers can handle different types of information more easily than ever before. Originally limited to text and numbers, computers can now handle sound, sophisticated color graphics, and still images. Movie-length, full-motion video will be available in the near future. Entertainment, hardware, software, and communications companies are forming partnerships to provide video entertainment to individuals on demand. This merging of industries and products is sometimes referred to as digital convergence, the conversion of all types of data into digital input that can be processed and stored by a computer. All forms of voice communications are now heavily computerized, including wireless communication from almost any location on earth.

Even everyday household appliances such as washers, driers, and refrigerators are becoming smarter. These and many other products now use embedded computer chips to help them work more efficiently. Eventually, these embedded computers will be capable of communicating with and be controlled by computers. This will enable you to start dinner and turn on the home air-conditioning before you leave the office; if you work in an office, that is. Another change computers have enabled is working away from the office. With existing communications capabilities, many people work at home and commute to the office electronically.

Can you imagine having to use a remote control to visually search through the 500 or more TV channels that will be available or to look through the directories of five online databases to find information on a single topic? New ways of presenting information will be developed so users can quickly make informed selections from expanded information choices. Smart software will be developed that will perform the necessary research to meet our information requests. Computers will undoubtedly be used to help users sort through all of the information, entertainment, and communications options.

Figure 1-33

What You Should Know

1. **Computer literacy** is knowing how to use a computer and **information literacy** is knowing how to find, analyze, and use information.

2. A **computer** is an electronic device, operating under the control of instructions stored in its own memory unit, that can accept data (input), process data arithmetically and logically, produce output from the processing, and store the results for future use.

3. The **information processing cycle** is composed of four general operations: input, process, output, and storage.

4. All computer processing requires **data**–raw facts, including numbers, words, images, and sounds, given to a computer during the input operation. In the processing phase, the computer manipulates data to create **information**–data that has been processed into a form that has meaning and is useful.

5. **Information processing**, sometimes called **data processing** (DP), is the production of information by processing data on a computer.

6. People who either use the computer directly or use the information it provides are called **computer users**, **end users**, or **users**.

7. A computer's power derives from its capability to perform input, process, output, and storage operations with speed and reliability and to store large amounts of information.

8. A **computer program**, also called **program instructions** or **software**, is a detailed set of instructions that tell a computer exactly what to do.

9. The first three operations of the information processing cycle, **input**, **process**, and **output**, describe the procedures that a computer performs to process data into information. The fourth operation, **storage**, describes a computer's electronic storage capability.

10. Data is processed by specific equipment that is often called computer **hardware**.

11. **Input devices** are used to enter data into a computer. Two common input devices are the **keyboard** and the **mouse**. The mouse is used to move a small symbol, called a **mouse pointer** or **pointer**, that appears on the computer screen.

12. A computer's **system unit** contains the electronic circuits that actually cause the processing of data to occur. The system unit includes the central processing unit, main memory, and other electronic components.

13. The **central processing unit** (CPU) contains a **control unit** that executes the program instructions and an **arithmetic/logic unit** (ALU) that performs math and logic operations. **Arithmetic operations** include numeric calculations such as addition, subtraction, multiplication, and division. **Logical operations** are comparisons of data to see if one value is greater than, less than, or equal to another.

14. **Main memory**, also called **RAM** (**Random Access Memory**) or **primary storage**, temporarily stores data and program instructions when they are being processed.

15. **Output devices** present the output from a computer. The two most commonly used output devices are the **printer** and the **monitor**, also called the **screen** or the **CRT** (which stands for **cathode ray tube**).

16. **Secondary storage devices**, or **auxiliary storage devices**, store instructions and data when they are not being used by the system unit. Common secondary storage devices on personal computers store data as magnetic areas on a **diskette** or **hard disk**.

17. Collectively, the equipment that performs the four operations of the information processing cycle is called a **computer system**. The input devices, output devices, and secondary storage devices that surround the system unit are sometimes referred to as **peripheral devices**.

18. The five major categories of computers are: personal computers, servers, minicomputers, mainframe computers, and supercomputers. Computers are generally classified according to their size, speed, processing capabilities, and price.

What You Should Know

19. **Personal computers**, also called **microcomputers** or **micros**, are the small systems that have become so widely used in recent years. Depending on their size and features, personal computer prices range from several hundred to several thousand dollars. Classifications within this category include **hand-held computers**, **palmtop computers**, **notebook computers**, **subnotebook computers**, **laptop computers**, **pen computers**, (such as a **personal digital assistant** (PDA) or **personal communicator**), **desktop computers**, **tower computers**, and **workstations**.

20. **Server** computers are designed to support a computer network that allows users to share files, applications software, and hardware. Small servers look like high-end personal computers and are priced in the $5,000 to $20,000 range, while the most powerful servers look and function more like minicomputers and are priced as high as $150,000.

21. **Minicomputers** are more powerful than personal computers and can support a number of users performing different tasks. These systems cost from approximately $15,000 to several hundred thousand dollars.

22. **Mainframe** computers are large systems that can handle hundreds of users, store large amounts of data, and process transactions at a very high rate. The price range for mainframes is from several hundred thousand dollars to several million dollars.

23. **Supercomputers**, the most powerful category of computers and, accordingly, the most expensive, are capable of processing hundreds of millions of instructions per second. These machines cost several million dollars.

24. Computers of all categories, especially personal computers, are sometimes connected to form **networks** that allow users to share data and computer resources.

25. Computer programs, commonly referred to as computer software, specify the sequence of operations the computer will perform. **Computer programmers** write the instructions (computer programs) necessary to direct the computer to process data into information. Programmers often follow a plan developed by a **systems analyst**, who works with both the user and the programmer to determine and design the desired output of the program.

26. **System software** consists of programs that are related to controlling the actual operations of the computer equipment. The instructions in the **operating system**, a component of system software, tell the computer how to perform functions such as how to load, store, and execute an application program and how to transfer data between the input/output devices and main memory.

27. Today, many computers use an **operating environment** that works with the operating system to make the computer easier to use. Operating environments have a **graphical user interface** (GUI) that provides visual clues, such as symbols called icons, to help the user. Each **icon** represents an application software package or a file or document where data is stored.

28. **Application software** consists of programs that tell a computer how to produce information. Programs required for common business and personal applications can be purchased from software vendors or stores that sell computer products. Purchased programs are often referred to as **application software packages** or simply **software packages**. Some of the more widely used packages for personal computer users are: word processing, desktop publishing, electronic spreadsheet, presentation graphics, database, communications, and electronic mail software.

29. In addition to a computer system and software, other elements required for successful information processing include accurate data, trained information systems personnel, knowledgeable users, and documented procedures. Together these elements are referred to as an **information system**.

30. **Connectivity** refers to the capability to connect a computer to other computers. The connection may be temporary or permanent.

31. A typical mid-sized company might use computers in a variety of areas, including: the receptionist, sales department, marketing department, shipping and receiving department, manufacturing department, engineering department, accounting department, human resources department, information systems department, and executive level.

32. Because of the widespread use of computers, most organizations prefer to hire employees with computer experience and knowledge.

Terms to Remember

arithmetic/logic unit (ALU) (1.8)
application software (1.15)
application software package (1.15)
arithmetic/logic unit (ALU) (1.8)
arithmetic operation (1.8)
auxiliary storage device (1.9)

cathode ray tube (CRT) (1.8)
central processing unit (CPU) (1.8)
computer (1.4)
computer literacy (1.2)
computer program (1.6)
computer programmer (1.14)
computer system (1.9)
computer users (1.5)
connectivity (1.17)
control unit (1.8)
CPU (central processing unit) (1.8)
CRT (cathode ray tube) (1.8)

data (1.4)
data processing (DP) (1.5)
desktop computer (1.11)
diskette (1.9)
DP (data processing) (1.5)

end users (1.5)

graphical user interface (GUI) (1.15)
GUI (graphical user interface) (1.15)

hand-held computers (1.10)
hard disk (1.9)
hardware (1.7)

icon (1.15)
information (1.4)
information literacy (1.2)
information processing (1.5)
information processing cycle (1.4)
information system (1.16)
input (1.7)
input device (1.7)

keyboard (1.7)

laptop computer (1.11)
logical operation (1.8)

main memory (1.8)
mainframe (1.13)
micro (1.10)
microcomputer (1.10)
minicomputer (1.12)
monitor (1.8)
mouse (1.7)
mouse pointer (1.7)

network (1.13)
notebook computer (1.10)

operating environment (1.15)
operating system (1.14)
output (1.7)
output device (1.8)

palmtop computer (1.10)
PC (personal computer) (1.10)
PDA (personal digital assistant) (1.11)
pen computer (1.11)
peripheral device (1.9)
personal communicator (1.11)
personal computer (PC) (1.10)
personal digital assistant (PDA) (1.11)
pointer (1.7)
primary storage (1.8)
printer (1.8)
process (1.7)
program instructions (1.6)

RAM (Random Access Memory) (1.8)
Random Access Memory (RAM) (1.8)

screen (1.8)
secondary storage device (1.9)
server (1.12)
software (1.6)
software package (1.15)
storage (1.7)
subnotebook computer (1.10)
supercomputer (1.13)
system software (1.14)
system unit (1.8)
systems analyst (1.14)

tower computer (1.11)

users (1.5)

workstation (1.11)

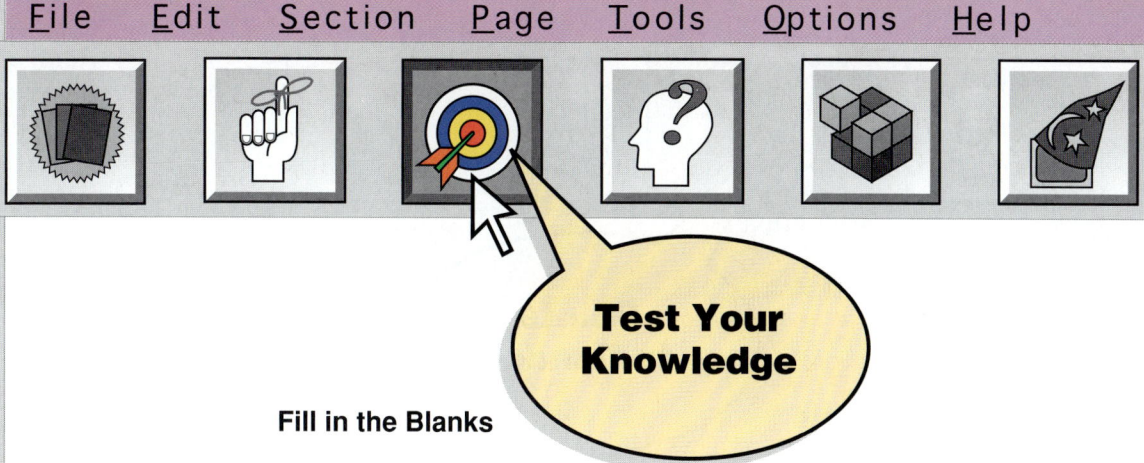

Test Your Knowledge

Fill in the Blanks

1. A(n) _____ is an electronic device, operating under the control of instructions stored in its memory unit, that can accept input, process the input arithmetically and logically, produce output from the processing, and store the results for future use.

2. The four operations of the information processing cycle are: _____, _____, _____, and _____.

3. During information processing, the computer manipulates _____–raw facts given to a computer during the input operation–to create _____–input that has been converted into a form that has meaning and is useful.

4. The central processing unit (CPU) contains a(n) _____ that executes program instructions and a(n) _____ that performs math and logic operations.

5. Collectively, the equipment that performs the four operations of the information processing cycle is called a(n) _____, and the input devices, output devices, and secondary storage devices that surround the system unit are referred to as _____.

4. What is computer software? How is system software different from application software?

5. What is an information system? How do the six elements of an information system work together?

Label the Figure

Instructions: The figure below represents a computer system. In the spaces provided, label the components of the system.

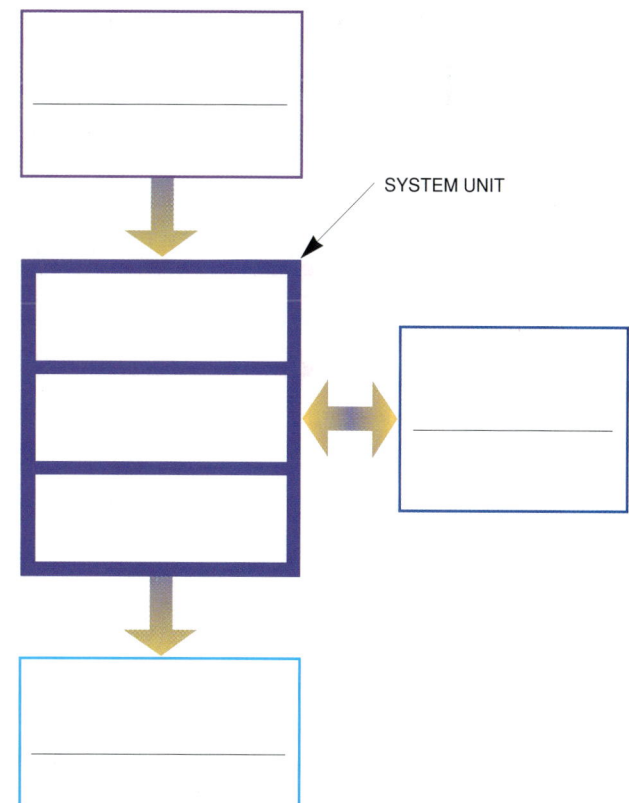

Short Answer

1. What is the difference between computer literacy and information literacy? How do computers relate to information literacy?

2. What three characteristics make the computer such a powerful tool? Describe each.

3. How are computers generally classified? What are the five major categories of computers? Briefly describe each. Why is it difficult to make firm definitions of these categories?

Points to Ponder

1 Cynics once said that it's not *what* you know, it's *who* you know that is important. With the increasing emphasis on information literacy, however, it might be argued that now it's not *what* you know, it's *how you can find out* that is most significant. What do you think? What changes, if any, should schools make to better address information literacy? How should computers be used in schools to enhance information literacy?

2 Some technological innovations, such as the telephone and the automobile, have had a significant impact on society at large, in both positive ways and negative ways. Together with a classmate, present a debate on the ways computers have affected society. One of you should argue that the impact of computers has been primarily positive and the other that the impact has been primarily negative. When the debate is over, and your classmates have had their say, see if you can reach a consensus on whether, overall, society is better off, or worse off, with the proliferation of computers.

3 Despite the reliability of computers, everyone has heard of "computer errors." Describe a situation you are familiar with (either through reading or personal experience) in which a "computer error" occurred. Who, or what, do you feel was responsible for the error? What steps do you think could be taken to ensure that the error does not happen again?

4 Your school has been given a grant to purchase a supercomputer, a mainframe computer, several minicomputers, and a number of personal computers. How do you think each category of computer would be best used in your school? Who should have access to each computer? If the money for personal computers had to be spent on three different types of personal computers, what kind do you think should be purchased and how should they be used?

5 This chapter describes how computers are used in the Hayden Corporation, an automobile manufacturer. You have been hired as a consultant to the Hayden Corporation and asked to provide a worst-case and a best-case scenario. If, due to financial difficulties, the computers in one part of the organization have to be moved to another department, which part of the organization do you feel could best withstand the loss? Why? If, as a result of increased profits, the Hayden Corporation is able to purchase additional computer equipment, where should the equipment go to most benefit the corporation as a whole? Why?

6 From the timeline presented following this chapter, you can see that many of the most notable developments in the computer industry took place over the past thirty years. Draw a hypothetical timeline that chronicles the computer industry over the next twenty years. On your timeline, place and describe at least six developments you think will have a significant impact on the computer industry during the next two decades.

Out and About

1. Visit a library or book store and examine at least three different current magazines aimed at computer users. Write down the name of all three magazines and make a list of the titles of articles in each. Look at the advertisements. What is the most expensive computer equipment advertised? What is the least expensive? What, in your opinion, is the most unusual computer equipment advertised? Do you think each magazine is intended for a particular type of computer user? Why or why not?

2. Interview a person who uses a computer every day at work, and prepare a report on that person's feelings about computers. Some of the questions you might ask are: How is the computer used? Did the person feel any anxiety when first confronted with the computer? What type of computer training did the individual receive? How does the computer make this person's job easier? How does the computer make this person's job more difficult? What kind of computer education would this individual recommend to students interested in going into the same field?

3. Visit a computer vendor and interview the manager or a salesperson. Based on your interview, prepare a report on the demographics of the typical computer buyer at that store. Find the answers to such questions as: What gender are most computer purchasers? In what age range are the buyers? What is their average age? What seems to be the characteristic educational level of a computer buyer? Approximately what is their average income? Why do most purchasers buy a computer?

4. Rent a videotape in which a computer plays a major part–some examples are *2001: A Space Odyssey*, *War Games*, and *Short Circuit*. Watch the videotape, then prepare a report on how the movie makers view computers. What part did the computer play in the movie? In general, was the computer a hero, a villain, or simply the tool of a human character? Why? What was the theme of the movie? What role, if any, did the computer play in promoting the theme?

5. Prepare a detailed report on one of the individuals or events depicted on the timeline following this chapter. Describe the impact the individual or event has had on the computer industry. How do you think the computer industry would be different if the individual had never existed or if the event had never taken place?

6. Visit a store that sells computer software and examine the application software packages. Make a list of at least five application packages you would like to have on your personal computer. Most application software is written for a specific operating system (system software). Write down the name of the operating system with which each of the application packages you selected is designed to work. If one (or more) of your applications does not work with the same operating system as the others, try to locate a similar application package. Your goal is to find five application packages that all work with the same operating system. Make a list of your final five application packages, and note the operating system that they all use. What features, if any, did you have to give up to find five applications that use the same operating system?

In the Lab

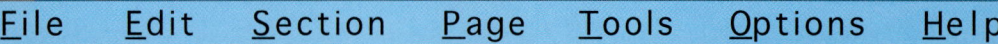

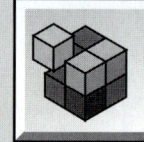

Windows Labs

1 Learning to Use the Mouse With Program Manager on the screen, select the Help menu by pressing the ALT key on the keyboard to activate the menu at the top of the screen and typing the letter H for Help. From the Help menu, choose the Windows Tutorial command by pressing the DOWN ARROW key to highlight it and then press the ENTER key. Windows welcomes you to the tutorial and then displays instructions *(Figure 1-34)*. Type M to begin the mouse lesson. As you move through the mouse lesson, do the following on a sheet of paper: (1) define the terms point, click, double-click, and drag; (2) explain how you would move the mouse pointer to the right if the mouse is on the edge of the right side of your desk. Exit the tutorial by pressing the ESC key and typing the letter Y.

2 Shelly Cashman Series Mouse Lab With Program Manager on the screen, look for the Shelly Cashman Series Labs group window *(Figure 1-36)*. If you do not see it, hold down the CTRL key and press function key F6 until the Shelly Cashman Series Labs group icon is highlighted *(Figure 1-35)*. Release both keys and press the ENTER key. Use the arrow keys to highlight the Shelly Cashman Series program-item icon *(Figure 1-36)*. Press the ENTER key. When the Shelly Cashman Series Labs screen displays *(Figure 1-37)*, use the UP ARROW and DOWN ARROW keys to highlight Using the Mouse. Press the ENTER key. When the introductory screen appears, carefully read the objectives. With your printer turned on, press the P key on the keyboard to print the questions for the Mouse Lab. Fill out the top of the Questions sheet and answer the questions as you step through the Mouse Lab.

3 Shelly Cashman Series Keyboard Lab Follow the instructions in Windows Lab 2 to display the Shelly Cashman Series Labs screen *(Figure 1-37)*. Select Using the Keyboard by pointing to it and clicking the left mouse button. When the initial Keyboard Lab screen displays, carefully read the objectives. With your printer turned on, point to the Print Questions button and click the left mouse button. Fill out the top of the Questions sheet and answer the questions as you step through the Keyboard Lab.

4 Learning the Basics of Microsoft Windows With Program Manager on the screen, point to Help on the menu bar and click the left mouse button. Point to the Windows Tutorial command on the Help menu and click the left mouse button. Windows welcomes you to the tutorial and then displays instructions *(Figure 1-34)*. Type W to begin the Windows Basics lesson. Click the Instructions button and read the instructions. Click the Return to the Tutorial button. Click the Continue button to begin the Windows Basics lesson. As you move through the Windows Basics lesson, use paper and pencil to do the following: (1) describe how to open a group window; (2) name the icons in the Accessories group window; (3) describe how to start an application; (4) describe how to enlarge a window so it fills the computer screen; (5) describe how to resize a window; (6) list the

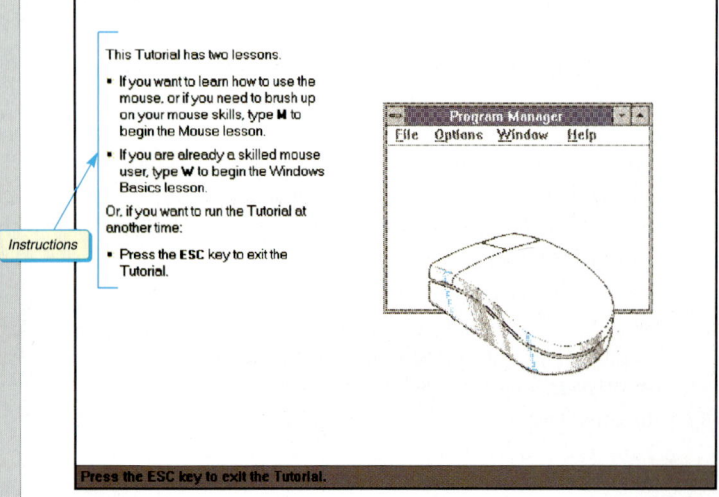

Figure 1-34

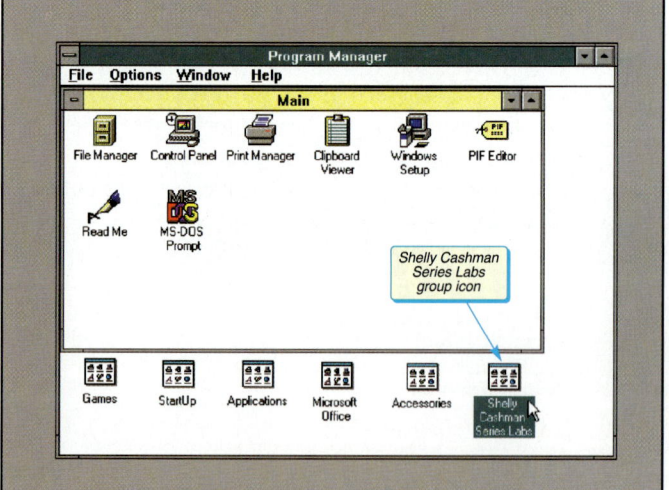

Figure 1-35

commands on the File menu; (7) list the ingredients in the recipe you displayed; (8) name the number of calories in a Strawberry Yogurt Sundae with 2 scoops and nuts; (9) describe how to close an application window. Exit the tutorial.

5 Improving Your Mouse Skills With Program Manager on the screen, double-click the Games group icon to open the Games group window. In the Games group window, double-click the Solitaire program-item icon. When the Solitaire application displays, click its Maximize button. Select the Help menu in the Solitaire window and choose the Contents command. One by one, click the green Help topics to learn how to play Solitaire; then print each Help topic by choosing the Print Topic command from the File menu. To return to the Contents window and select another Help topic, choose the Back button. To close the Solitaire Help window, double-click its Control-menu box. Play the game of Solitaire. To quit Solitaire, double-click the Solitaire window's Control-menu box. Close the Games group window by double-clicking its Control-menu box.

DOS Labs

1 Booting and Rebooting a Personal Computer With your computer turned off, **cold boot** it by turning the power switch on. Once the computer is operational, perform a **warm boot** by holding down the CTRL and ALT keys, pressing the DELETE key, and then releasing all three keys. If your computer has a reset button on the system unit, press and then release it to perform a warm boot. Answer the following questions: (1) Which boot process takes longer? (2) Why isn't there just one key on the keyboard to reboot your computer? (3) Why would you warm boot a computer?

2 Executing a Program Obtain information from your instructor on how to change to the directory on your computer containing the TALRCALC.EXE program. At the DOS prompt, type talrcalc and press the ENTER key. Type John and press the ENTER key. Type 36 and press the ENTER key. Type 196 and press the ENTER key. Ready your printer. Press the PRINT SCREEN key to print the results. Answer the following: (1) What was the input for this program and what hardware was used to accomplish the input? (2) What was the output for this program and what hardware was used for the output? (3) Between the input and the output, what took place to produce the output? Run the program again using these values: Sandy, 28, 140. Print the results.

Online Lab

1 Information About Online Services Following is a list of online services and telephone numbers: Prodigy Service, (800) 776-3449; Genie Online Services, (800) 638-9636; Delphi, (800) 695-4005; CompuServe, (800) 848-8199; and America Online, (800) 827-6364. Call each service to compare monthly rates and hours of free connect time per month. Request a membership kit from any two services.

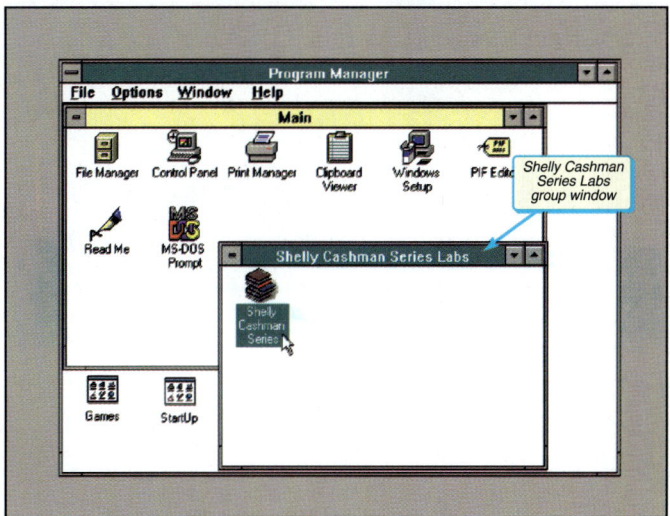

Figure 1-36

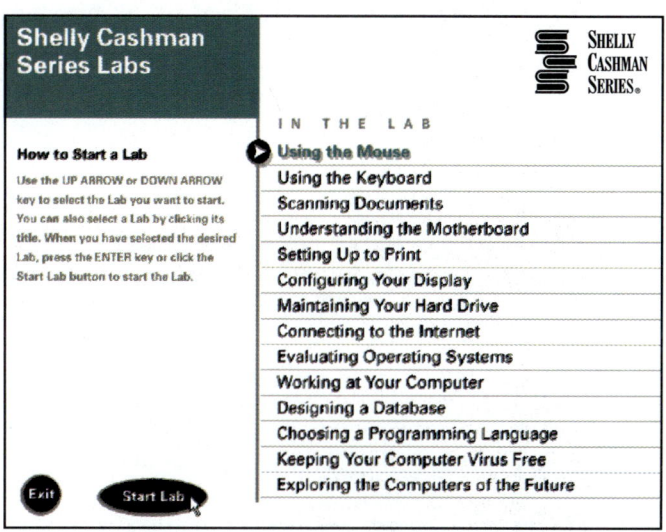

Figure 1-37

1.32 The Evolution of the Computer Industry

The electronic computer industry began more than fifty years ago.

1937

Dr. John V. Atanasoff and his assistant Clifford Berry designed and began to build the first electronic digital computer during the winter of 1937-38. Their machine, the Atanasoff-Berry-Computer, or ABC, provided the foundation for the next advances in electronic digital computers.

1943

During the years 1943 to 1946, Dr. John W. Mauchly and J. Presper Eckert, Jr. completed the ENIAC (Electronic Numerical Integrator and Computer), the first large-scale electronic digital computer. The ENIAC weighed thirty tons, contained 18,000 vacuum tubes, and occupied a thirty-by-fifty-foot space.

1952

In 1952, Dr. Grace Hopper, a mathematician and commodore in the U.S. Navy, wrote a paper describing how to program a computer with symbolic notation instead of the detailed machine language that had been used.

Dr. Hopper was instrumental in developing high-level languages such as COBOL, a business application language introduced in 1960. COBOL uses English-like phrases and runs on most computers, making it one of the more widely used languages in the world.

1953

The IBM model 650 was one of the first widely used computer systems. Originally, IBM planned to produce only 50 machines, but the system was so successful that eventually it manufactured more than 1,000.

Core memory, developed in the early 1950s, provided much larger storage capacities and greater reliability than vacuum tube memory.

This timeline summarizes the major events in the evolution of the computer industry.

1945

Dr. John von Neumann is credited with writing a brilliant report in 1945 describing several new hardware concepts and the use of stored programs. His breakthrough laid the foundation for the digital computers that have since been built.

1951

J. Presper Eckert, Jr., standing left, explains the operations of the UNIVAC I to newsman Walter Cronkite, right. This machine was the first commercially available electronic digital computer.

Public awareness of computers increased when, in 1951, the UNIVAC I, after analyzing only 5% of the tallied vote, correctly predicted that Dwight D. Eisenhower would win the presidential election.

1952

In 1951-52, after much discussion, IBM decided to add computers to its line of business equipment products. This led IBM to become a dominant force in the computer industry.

1957

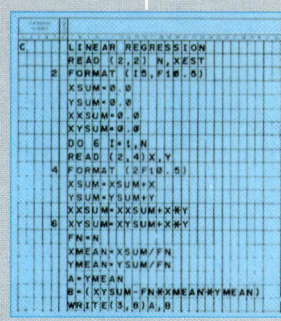

FORTRAN (FORmula TRANslator) was introduced in 1957, proving that efficient, easy-to-use programming languages could be developed. FORTRAN is still in use.

1958

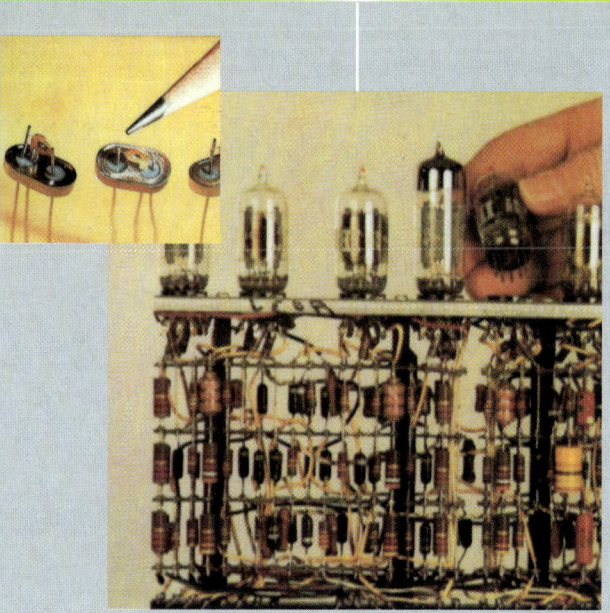

In 1958, computers built with transistors marked the beginning of the second generation of computer hardware. Previous computers built with vacuum tubes were first-generation machines.

1959

By 1959, more than 200 programming languages had been created.

THE EVOLUTION OF THE COMPUTER INDUSTRY

1960

1964

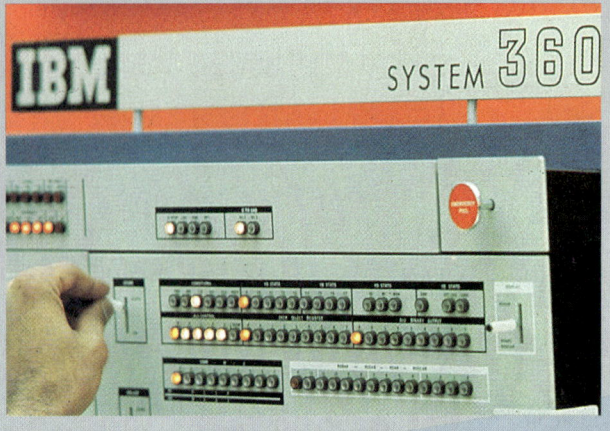

Third-generation computers, with their controlling circuitry stored on chips, were introduced in 1964. The IBM System/360 computers were the first third-generation machines.

From 1958 to 1964, the number of computers in the U.S. grew from 2,500 to 18,000.

1965

In 1965, Dr. John Kemeny of Dartmouth led the development of the BASIC programming language. BASIC is still widely used on personal computers.

1969

In 1969, under pressure from the industry, IBM announced that some of its software would be priced separately from the computer hardware. This "unbundling" allowed software firms to emerge in the industry.

1970

The fourth-generation computers built with chips that used LSI (large-scale integration) arrived in 1970. The chips used in 1965 contained as many as 1,000 circuits. By 1970, the LSI chip contained as many as 15,000.

1975

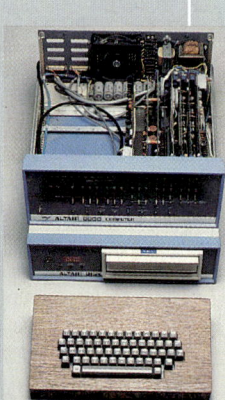

The MITS, Inc. Altair computer, sold in kits for less than $400, was the first commercially successful microcomputer.

ETHERNET, developed at Xerox PARC (Palo Alto Research Center) by Robert Metcalfe, was the first local area network (LAN). Originally designed to link minicomputers, ETHERNET was later extended to personal computers. The LAN allows computers to communicate and share software, data, and peripherals such as printers.

THE EVOLUTION OF THE COMPUTER INDUSTRY

1967   1968   1969

Digital Equipment Corporation (DEC) introduced the first minicomputer in 1965.

The software industry emerged in the 1960s. In 1968, Computer Science Corporation became the first software company to be listed on the New York Stock Exchange.

PASCAL, a structured programming language, was developed by Swiss computer scientist Niklaus Wirth between 1967 and 1971.

In 1969, Dr. Ted Hoff of Intel Corporation developed a microprocessor, or microprogrammmable computer chip, the Intel 4004.

1976   1979

In 1976, Steve Wozniak and Steve Jobs built the first Apple computer.

The first public online information services, CompuServe and the Source, were founded.

The VisiCalc spreadsheet program written by Bob Frankston and Dan Bricklin was introduced in 1979. This product was originally written to run on Apple II computers. Together, VisiCalc and Apple II computers rapidly became successful. Most people consider VisiCalc to be the singlemost important reason why personal computers gained acceptance in the business world.

THE EVOLUTION OF THE COMPUTER INDUSTRY

1980

In 1980, IBM offered Microsoft Corporation's founder, Bill Gates, the opportunity to develop the operating system for the soon-to-be announced IBM personal computer. With the development of MS-DOS, Microsoft achieved tremendous growth and success.

1981

The IBM PC was introduced in 1981, signaling IBM's entrance into the personal computer marketplace. The IBM PC quickly garnered the largest share of the personal computer market and became the personal computer of choice in business.

1982

More than 300,000 personal computers were sold in 1981. In 1982, the number jumped to 3,275,000

1984

Apple introduced the Macintosh computer, which incorporated a unique graphical interface, making it easy to learn.

1987

Several personal computers utilizing the powerful Intel 80386 microprocessor were introduced in 1987. These machines handled processing that previously only large systems could handle.

THE EVOLUTION OF THE COMPUTER INDUSTRY

1983

1984

Instead of choosing a person for its annual award, TIME magazine named the computer "Machine of the Year" for 1982. This event acknowledged the impact of the computer on society.

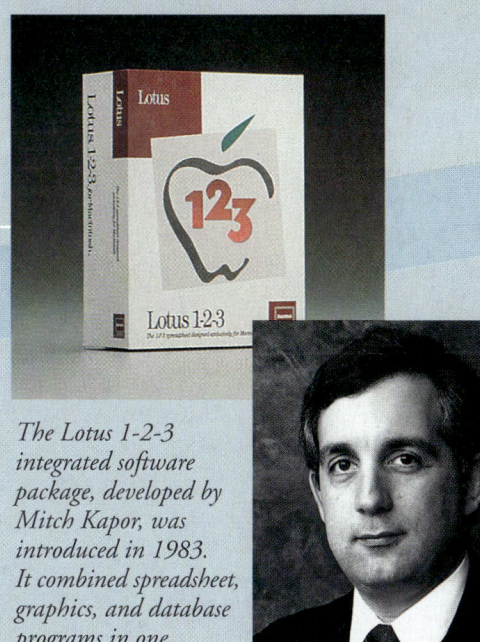

The Lotus 1-2-3 integrated software package, developed by Mitch Kapor, was introduced in 1983. It combined spreadsheet, graphics, and database programs in one package.

IBM introduced a personal computer, called the PC AT, that used the Intel 80286 microprocessor.

1989

1990

The Intel 486 became the world's first 1,000,000 transistor microprocessor. It crammed 1.2 million transistors on a sliver of silicon that measured .4" x .6" and executed instructions at 15 MIPS (million instructions per second) — four times as fast as its predecessor, the 80386 chip. The 80 designation used with previous Intel chips, such as the 80386 and 80286, was dropped with the 486.

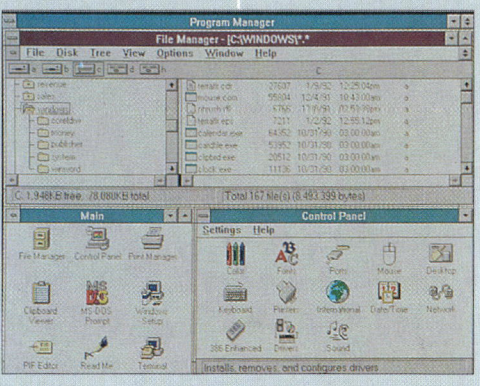

Microsoft released Windows 3.0, a substantially enhanced version of its Windows graphical user interface first introduced in 1985. The software allowed users to run multiple applications on a personal computer and more easily move data from one application to another. The package became an instant success, selling hundreds of thousands of copies.

By 1990, more than 54 million computers were in use in the United States.

THE EVOLUTION OF THE COMPUTER INDUSTRY

1991

The High Performance Computing and Communications (HPCC) initiative, sponsored by U.S. Senator Al Gore, proposed the building of a high-speed network, or digital highway, to connect government research laboratories.

1992

Apple introduced a personal digital assistant (PDA) called the Newton MessagePad. This 7 1/4 -by-4 1/2 -inch personal computer incorporates a pen interface and wireless communications.

1993

Several companies introduced computer systems using the Pentium microprocessor from Intel. The Pentium chip is the successor to the Intel 486 microprocessor. It contains 3.1 million transistors and is able to perform 112 million instructions per second (MIPS).

1993

The Energy Star program, endorsed by the Environmental Protection Agency (EPA), encouraged manufacturers to build computer equipment that meets strict power consumption guidelines. Manufacturers meeting the guidelines can then display the Energy Star logo on their products.

The scope of the network proposed in the 1991 HPCC initiative was significantly expanded to the National Information Infrastructure (NII). The NII is envisioned as a broadband digital network allowing universal access and providing information services, such as government data, training, and medical services, to everyone.

1994

"**We** are crossing a technology threshold that will forever change the way we learn, work, socialize and shop. It will affect all of us, and businesses of every type, in ways far more pervasive than most people realize."

Bill Gates
COMDEX '94

Estimates indicated that more than 16 million personal computers were sold worldwide in 1994 alone.

Approximately 13 million Americans gained access to online information services. More than 8 million had access to the Internet.

CHAPTER TWO

Computer Software Applications: User Tools

2

Objectives

After completing this chapter, you will be able to:

- Identify the most widely used personal computer software applications

- Describe productivity software

- Define and describe a user interface and a graphical user interface

- Explain the key features of each of the major applications

- Explain the advantages of integrated software

- List and describe learning aids and support tools that help users to use personal computer software applications

Today, understanding the applications commonly used on personal computers is considered a part of being computer literate. In fact, a working knowledge of at least some of these applications is now considered by many employers to be a required skill. Because of this, personal computer software applications are discussed early in this book. Learning about each of the most widely used applications will help you understand how people use personal computers in our modern world. Before discussing the applications, the user interface is explained. The user interface controls how the user works with the software and applies to all the applications. After learning about individual applications, you will learn about integrated software; the combination of several applications into a single software package. Finally, some of the aids and tools that are available to help you learn and use software applications are discussed.

Productivity Software

This chapter will introduce you to nine widely used personal computer software applications:
- Word processing
- Desktop publishing
- Spreadsheet
- Database
- Presentation graphics
- Communications
- Electronic mail
- Personal information management
- Project management

These software applications are used by a wide range of organizations and individuals. Because these applications help people perform their work more efficiently, they are sometimes referred to as **productivity software**.

Although these applications are discussed as they are used on personal computers, they are actually available on computers of all sizes. The concepts you will learn about each application package on personal computers will also apply if you are working on a larger system.

User Interface

To more easily learn about productivity software, you need to understand some of the features of a user interface. A **user interface** is the way the user tells the software what to do and the way the computer displays information and processing options to the user. One of the most common user interfaces is the graphical user interface (GUI). The **graphical user interface**, or GUI (pronounced gooey), combines text and graphics to make the software easier to use. Graphical user interfaces include several common features such as windows, icons, menus, and buttons.

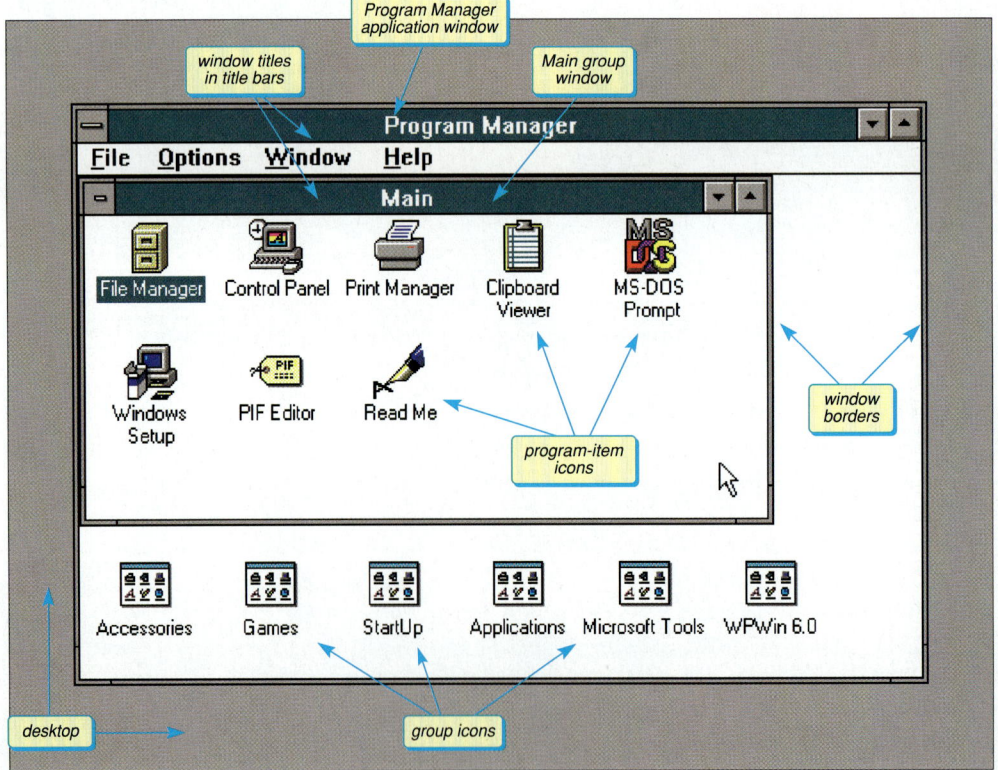

Figure 2-1
Two key features of a graphical user interface (GUI) are windows and icons. Windows are rectangular areas that present information. Icons are symbols that represent processing options or documents. In this screen, there are two windows open; the larger Program Manager window and the smaller Main window contained within the Program Manager window. Several windows can be open at the same time and moved from back to front so all information on a window can be seen. Each of the group icons at the bottom of the screen can be opened into a window such as the Main window.

A **window** is a rectangular area of the screen that is used to present information *(Figure 2-1)*. They are called windows because of their capability to see into another part of a program. Many people consider windows to be like multiple sheets of paper on top of a desk. In the same way that each piece of paper on the desk contains different information, each window on the screen contains different information. Just as papers can be moved from the bottom of a pile to the top of the desk when they are needed, windows can be created on a screen and moved around to show information when it is needed. The term Windows, with a capital W, refers to **Microsoft Windows**, the most popular graphical user interface for personal computers.

Icons are pictures or symbols that are used to represent processing options, such as an application or a program, or documents, such as a letter or spreadsheet *(Figure 2-1)*.

A **menu** is a list of options from which the user can choose. In a graphical user interface, menus often contain a list of related commands. **Commands** are instructions that cause the computer software to perform a specific action. For example, the menu shown in *Figure 2-2* lists commands related to files. Using this menu, the user can work with files by choosing the Open, Move, Copy, or Delete command.

A **button** is an icon (usually a rectangular or circular shape) that causes a specific action to take place. Buttons are selected using a pointing device such as a mouse but can also be activated by using the keyboard. In *Figure 2-3*, the buttons shown are used to control printing a document.

The features of a user interface make it easier for the user to communicate with the computer. You will see examples of these features and how they are used as you learn about the various personal computer applications.

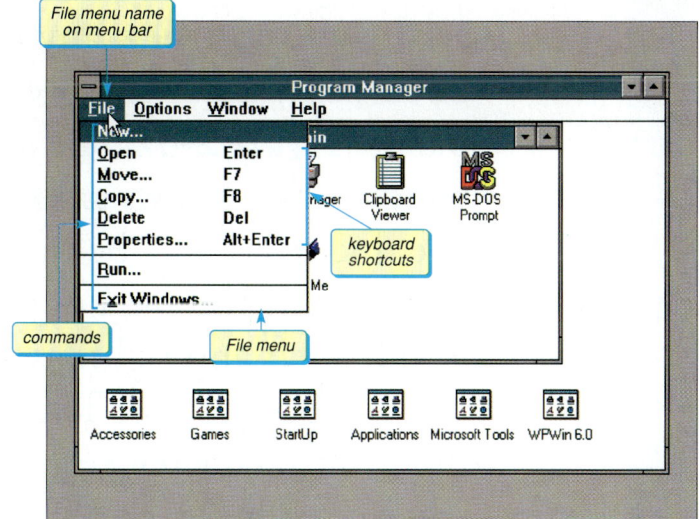

Figure 2-2
A menu is a list of options from which the user can choose. The menu shown on this screen lists commands for file operations. The commands can be chosen with a pointing device or by pressing the keys listed to the right of the commands.

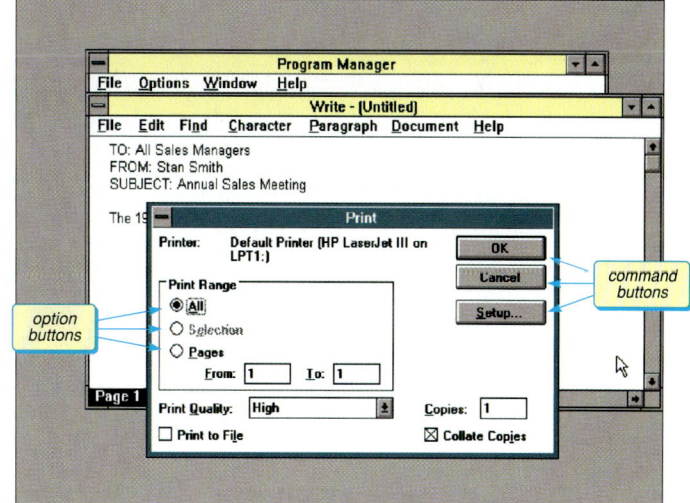

Figure 2-3
A button is an icon that causes a specific action to take place. This screen contains two types of buttons. Option buttons modify the action that will take place. In this example, the option buttons determine what pages are printed. Command buttons start a specific action.

Word Processing Software

The most widely used computer application is word processing. **Word processing software** enables a computer to produce or modify documents that consist primarily of text. Millions of people use word processing software every day to create letters, memos, reports, and other documents. A major advantage of using word processing to produce a document is the capability to easily change what has been done. Because the document is stored electronically, you can add, delete, or rearrange words, sentences, or entire sections. The document can be printed as many times as you like with each copy looking as good as the first. With older methods such as using a typewriter, making changes and reprinting a document take much more time. Using word processing software is also an efficient way of storing documents because many documents can be stored on a disk or diskette. If computers are connected in a network, stored documents can be shared among users.

Today, most people perform word processing using personal computers or larger computer systems such as minicomputers or mainframes. These computers are also used for other applications. **Dedicated word processing systems**, used only for word processing, also exist.

Producing a document using word processing usually consists of four steps: creating, editing, formatting, and printing. A fifth step, saving the document, should be performed frequently throughout the process so work will not be lost.

Creating

Creating a word processi[ng document involves entering] text, usually by using the keybo[ard. Some of the] features used during the creati[ng step include word wrap,] scrolling, and moving the curso[r.]

- Word Wrap. **Word wrap** pr[ovides automatic line breaks] when the text reaches a certa[in point on the screen,] such as the right-hand margi[n. This means the] user can continue typing and [does not have to press the] return or line feed key.

- Scrolling. **Scrolling** is the pr[ocess of moving the text] so the user can view any port[ion of the document. Think of] documents as having been cr[eated on a long roll of] paper *(Figure 2-4)*. The scree[n acts as a] window that allows a portio[n of the document to be viewed.] The document can be moved [up or down behind] the screen window. For wide[r documents, the text can be] scrolled left and right, as wel[l.]

- Moving the Cursor. The **curs[or**, which is an] underline character, rectangle[, or other symbol, indicates] where on the screen the next [character will be entered. Using]

cursor control keys, on the ke[yboard, the cursor can be moved a] character or line at a time. If [the key is held down, the] movement is repeated until th[e key is released. More] efficient ways to move the cu[rsor around the screen include] using the Page Up and Page [Down keys]

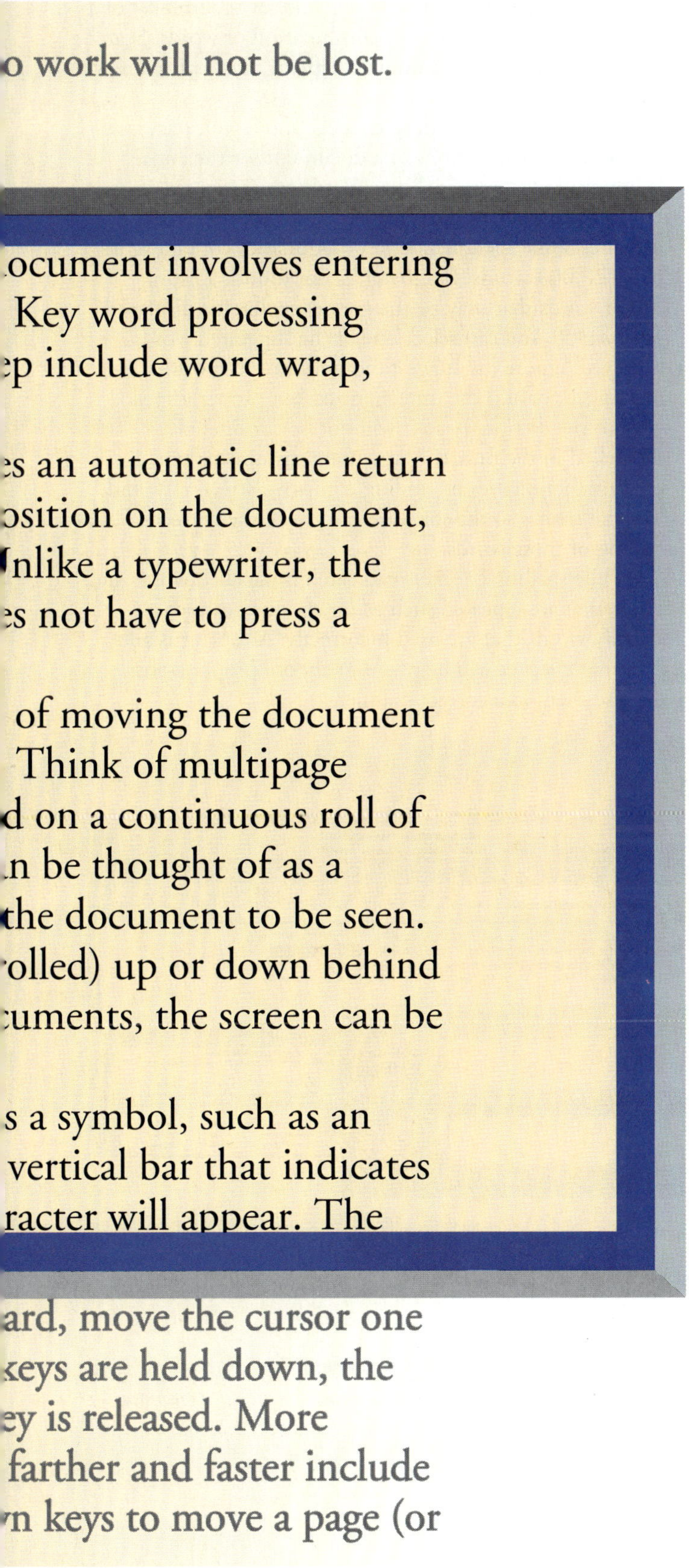

Creating

Creating a word processing document involves entering text, usually by using the keyboard. Key word processing features used during the creating step include word wrap, scrolling, and moving the cursor.

- Word Wrap. **Word wrap** provides an automatic line return when the text reaches a certain position on the document, such as the right-hand margin. Unlike a typewriter, the user can continue typing and does not have to press a return or line feed key.
- Scrolling. **Scrolling** is the process of moving the document so the user can view any portion. Think of multipage documents as having been created on a continuous roll of paper *(Figure 2-4)*. The screen can be thought of as a window that allows a portion of the document to be seen. The document can be moved (scrolled) up or down behind the screen window. For wide documents, the screen can be scrolled left and right, as well.
- Moving the Cursor. The **cursor** is a symbol, such as an underline character, rectangle, or vertical bar that indicates where on the screen the next character will appear. The cursor is moved by using the mouse or keyboard. The cursor control keys, on the keyboard, move the cursor one character or line at a time. If the keys are held down, the movement is repeated until the key is released. More efficient ways to move the cursor farther and faster include using the Page Up and Page Down keys to move a page (or screen) at a time and the Home and End keys to move to the beginning or end of a line. Other key combinations can be used to move to the beginning of words, paragraphs, or the start or end of the document.

Figure 2-4
Scrolling is the process of moving the document so the portion you want to see is displayed on the screen. It's as if the document had been created on a continuous roll of paper. The limited size of the screen only allows you to see a portion of the document. The document can be moved (scrolled) up or down and right or left so any portion of the document that will fit on one screen can be seen.

Editing

Editing is the process of making changes in the content of a document. Word processing editing features include cutting, copying, and pasting, inserting and deleting, and searching and replacing. Advanced editing features include spell checking, using a thesaurus, and grammar checking.

- Cut, Copy, and Paste. To **cut** involves removing a portion of the document and electronically storing it in a temporary location called the **Clipboard**. Whatever is on the Clipboard can be placed somewhere else in the document by giving a **paste** command. When you **copy**, a portion of the document is duplicated.
- Insert and Delete. When you **insert**, you add text to a document. When you **delete**, you remove text. Most word processors are normally in the *insert mode*, meaning that as you type, any existing text is pushed down the page to make room for the new text. However, word processors can be placed in a *typeover mode* (also called *overtype mode*), where new text replaces any existing text.
- Search. The **search** feature lets you find all occurrences of a particular character, word, or combination of words. Search can be used in combination with **replace** to substitute new letters or words for the old.
- Spelling Checker. A **spelling checker** allows you to review individual words, sections of a document, or the entire document for correct spelling. Words are compared to an electronic dictionary included in the word processing software. Some spelling checker dictionaries contain more than 120,000 words. If a match is not found, a list of similar words that may be the correct spelling is displayed *(Figure 2-5)*. You can select one of the suggested words displayed, ignore the suggestions and leave the word unchanged, or add the unrecognized but properly spelled word to the dictionary so it will not be considered misspelled in the future. Many users customize their software dictionaries by adding company, street, city, and personal names so the software can check the correct spelling of those words.

While spelling checkers can catch misspelled words and words that are repeated such as *the the,* they cannot identify words that are used incorrectly. A thesaurus and grammar checker will help you to choose proper words and use them in a correct manner.

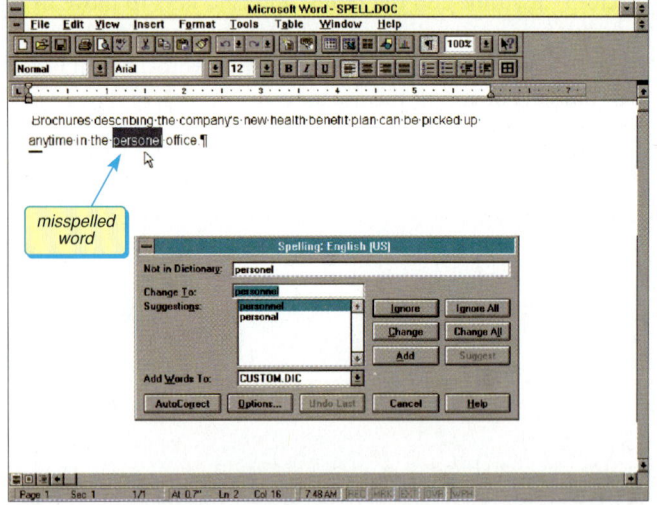

Figure 2-5
A spelling checker identifies words that do not match entries in the spelling checker dictionary. Alternative words are suggested and can be substituted for the unidentified word.

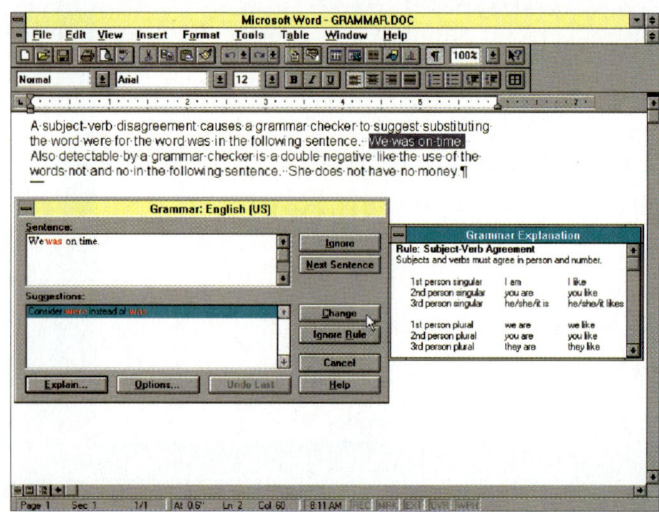

Figure 2-6
Grammar checking software identifies grammar, writing style, and sentence structure errors. As shown on this screen, most grammar checkers offer a possible solution when they detect a problem.

- Thesaurus. A **thesaurus** allows you to look up synonyms for words in a document while you are using your word processor. Using a thesaurus is similar to using a spelling checker. When you want to look up a synonym for a word, you place the cursor on the word to check, and activate the thesaurus with either a keyboard command or by using a pointing device. The thesaurus software displays a list of possible synonyms. If you find a word you would rather use, you select the desired word from the list and the software automatically incorporates it in the document by replacing the previous word.
- Grammar Checker. A **grammar checker** is used to check for grammar, writing style, and sentence structure errors *(Figure 2-6)*. This software can check documents for excessive use of a word or phrase, identify sentences that are too long, and find words that are used out of context such as *four* example.

Formatting

To **format** means to change the appearance of a document. Formatting is important because the overall look of a document can significantly affect its capability to communicate. For documents being sent to clients, it is not unusual to spend more time formatting the document than in entering the text. Word processing features that can be used to format a document include the following *(see Figure 2-7)*:

- Typeface, Font, and Style. A **typeface** is a specific set of characters that are designed the same. Helvetica and Times New Roman are examples of typefaces. The size of a typeface is measured in points. Each **point** is approximately 1/72 of an inch. The text you are reading in this book is ten point type. A specific combination of typeface and point size is called a **font**, though it is common to hear and read of typefaces being called fonts. A particular **style**, such as **bold**, *italics,* or underlining, can be applied to a font to make it stand out.

Figure 2-7
Examples of word processing formatting features.

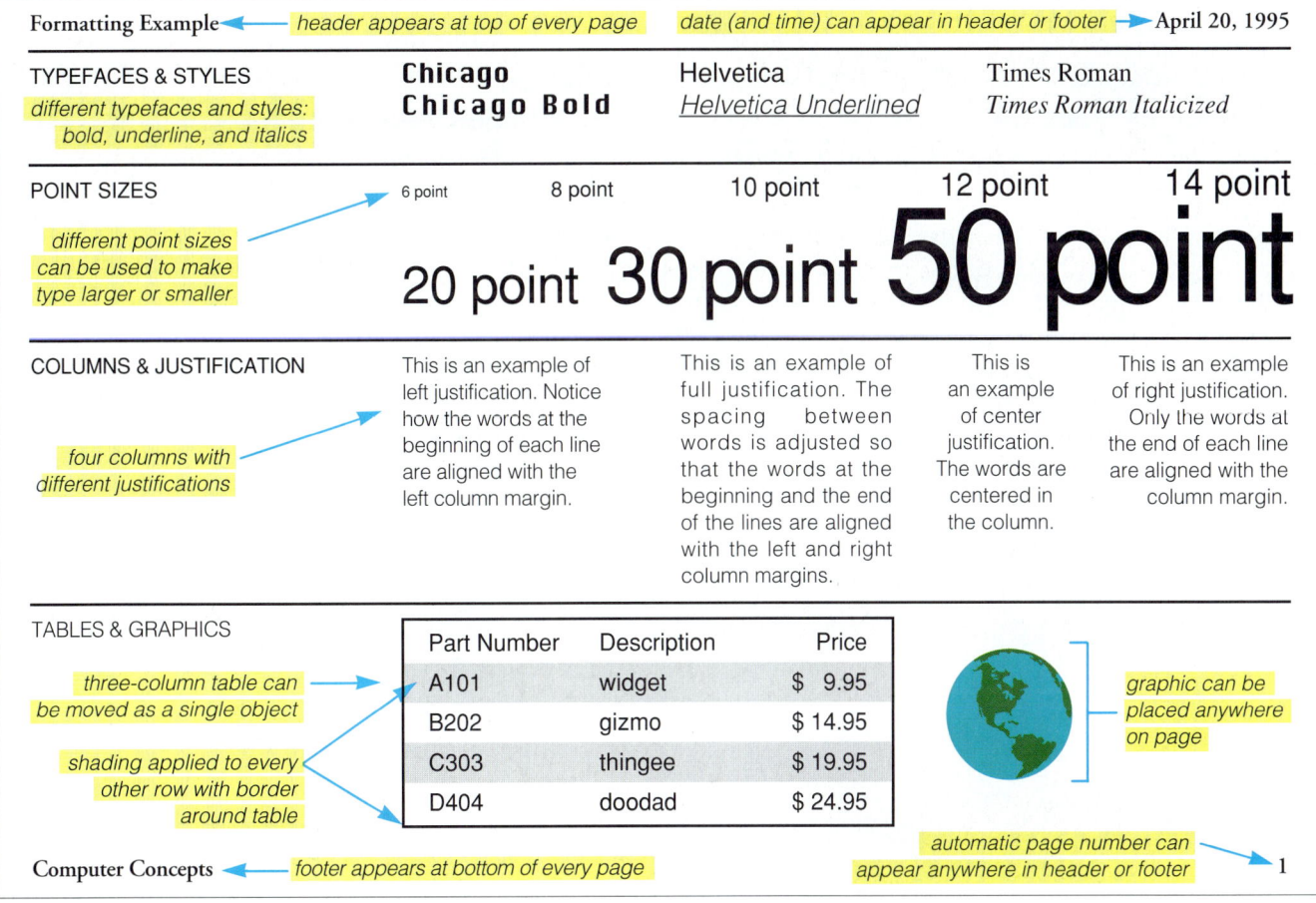

- Margins and Justification. **Margins** specify the space in the border of a page and include the left, right, bottom, and top margin. **Justification**, also called **alignment**, deals with how text is positioned in relation to a fixed reference point, usually a right or left margin. **Full justification** aligns text with both the left and right margins. Left justification and right justification align with the left and right margins only. Centered justification divides the text equally on either side of a reference point, usually the center of the page.
- Spacing. **Spacing** deals with how far apart individual letters (horizontal spacing) and lines of text (vertical spacing) are placed. With **monospacing**, each character takes up the same amount of space. With **proportional spacing**, wide characters, such as a W or M, are given more space than narrow characters, such as an I. **Line spacing** increases the distance from the bottom of one line to the bottom of the next line. Single and double line spacing are the most common, but exact distances can also be specified in some word processing software.
- Columns, Tables, and Graphics. Most word processors can arrange text in two or more columns, like a newspaper or magazine. The text from the bottom of one column automatically flows to the top of the next column. Tables are a way of organizing information in rows and columns. Word processors that support tables enable the user to easily add and change table information and move the entire table as a single item, instead of as individual lines of text. Although word processors are primarily designed to work with text, most can now incorporate graphics such as drawings and pictures. Some graphics are included in word processing packages, however, graphic items are usually created in separate applications and imported (brought into) the word processing document.
- Borders and Shading. Borders and shading can be used to emphasize or highlight sections of a word processing document. A **border** is a decorative line or box that is used with text, graphics, or tables. **Shading** darkens the background area of a section of a document or table. Colors can be used for borders and shading but will print as black or gray unless you have a color printer.

Portrait Orientation

MEMORANDUM

TO: All Village Creek Employees
FROM: Christine Reddings, Training Supervi
DATE: December 1, 1995
SUBJECT: **Computer Training Seminars**

On Monday, January 2, 1996, we will begin using new versions cessing and electronic spreadsheet software. To prepare you fo we are offering the following training seminars.

Word Processing (December 8, 1995, 1:00 p.m. - 4:30 p.m.)

This seminar focuses on the new word processor features. Thro and hands-on exercises, you will create, edit, format, save and p Bring a blank formatted disk to the seminar.

Electronic Spreadsheets (December 12, 1995, 8:00 a.m. - 11.

This seminar addresses the new features of the electronic sprea ware. During the session, you will build worksheets with calculat graphs. Bring a blank formatted disk to the seminar.

Integrating Your Software (December 15, 1995, 2:00 p.m. - 4.

This seminar illustrates how to merge worksheet data and graph processing documents. Bring a disk containing one word proces one electronic spreadsheet file.

These training seminars will be held in Room C-312. Once you h selections(s), please check with your supervisor and then call m 290 to make a reservation.

Landscape Orientation

Village Creek Industries
Personnel Database

Last Name	First Name	Hire Date	Age	Gender	Education	Department	Title	Salary
Hoika	Janice	11/12/71	60	F	BS	R&D	Engineer	52,500
Webb	Marci	2/4/95	34	F	AAS	Computer	Programmer	36,500
Ling	Jodi	2/26/92	25	F	MS	Computer	Analyst	47,400
Webster	Jeffrey	5/22/84	47	M	AAS	R&D	Technician	36,250
Sabol	Lisa	7/15/94	52	F	BS	Marketing	Manager	47,500
Chin	Ben	1/5/89	22	M	HS	Administration	Clerk	18,500
Brown	Jeremiah	9/4/87	29	M	PhD	R&D	Engineer	48,900
Sobalski	Joseph	9/2376	44	M	BS	Marketing	Telemarketer	29,700
Raih	Niki	5/18/79	36	F	AAS	Administration	Receptionist	24,300
Nyguen	Sue	1/17/82	32	F	BS	Computer	Programmer	43,200
Stephens	James	6/22/84	31	M	HS	Mail Room	Clerk	17,400
Rae	Amy	11/26/92	57	F	MS	Production	Manager	52,200
McCarthy	Kevin	1/11/80	62	M	MA	Personnel	Director	57,600
Dolar	Laura	11/2/85	46	F	AA	Production	Supervisor	46,000

Figure 2-8
Most correspondence is printed in portrait orientation; printing across the narrower portion of a sheet of paper. In landscape orientation, the printing goes across the wider portion of the paper.

- Page Numbers, Headers, and Footers. Most word processors can automatically apply page numbers to any location on the page. Page numbers can be started at a particular number and can appear in a font different from the main body of text. **Headers** and **footers** allow you to place the same information at the top or bottom of each page. A company name, report title, date, or page number are examples of items that may appear in a header or footer.
- Style Sheets. A **style sheet** lets you save font and format information so it can be applied to new documents. A style sheet can save you considerable time if you use different formatting techniques on frequently created documents. Company letterhead, a memorandum, or a report that is prepared each month are examples of items that could use style sheets.

Printing

Most word processors give the user many options other than printing a single copy of the entire document.
- Number of Copies and Pages. The capability to print individual pages and a range of pages (for example, pages 2 through 7) is usually available. In addition, the user can specify how many copies are to be printed.
- Portrait and Landscape. **Portrait** printing means that the paper is taller than it is wide. Most letters are printed in portrait orientation. **Landscape** printing means that the paper is wider than it is tall. Tables with a large number of columns are often printed in landscape orientation. See *Figure 2-8* for examples.
- Print Preview. **Print preview** *(Figure 2-9)* allows the user to see on the screen how the document will look when it is printed. In print preview you can see one or more pages. Even though the text may be too small to read, you can review the overall appearance and decide if the page needs additional formatting.

With the features available in word processing packages, users can easily and efficiently create professional looking documents. Packages such as WordPerfect and Microsoft Word may contain enough features to satisfy the desktop publishing needs of many users. However, the document design capabilities of desktop publishing packages still exceed the capabilities of word processing software.

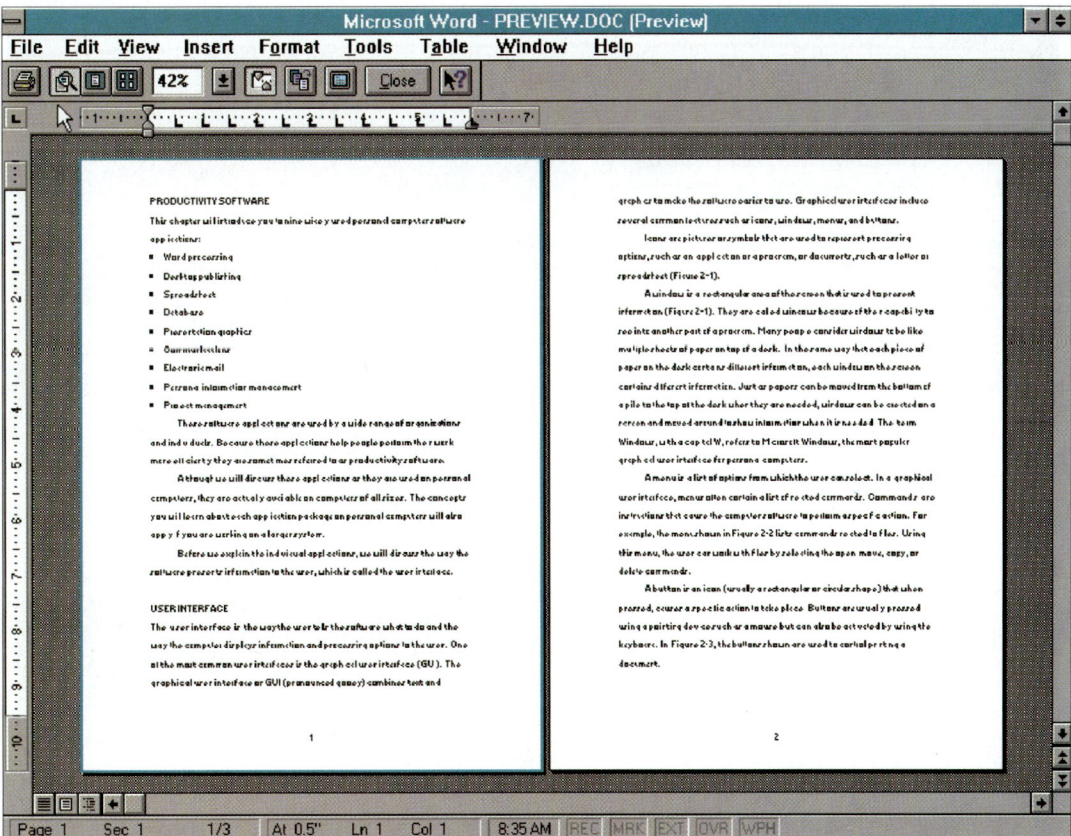

Figure 2-9
Print preview allows you to see on the screen how the document will look when it is printed. This feature helps you decide if the overall appearance of the document is acceptable or if the document needs more formatting.

Desktop Publishing Software

Desktop publishing (DTP) software allows users to design and produce professional looking documents that contain both text and graphics *(Figure 2-10)*. Examples of such documents include newsletters, marketing literature, technical manuals, and annual reports. Documents of this type were previously created by slower, more expensive traditional publishing methods such as typesetting.

Whereas word processing software is designed to manipulate text, DTP software focuses on page composition and layout. **Page composition and layout**, sometimes called **page makeup**, is the process of arranging text and graphics on a document page. The text and graphics used by a DTP program are frequently imported from other software packages. For example, because text manipulation capabilities of word processing packages exceed those offered in DTP packages, text is usually created with a word processor and then transferred into the desktop publishing package. Graphics objects, such as illustrations, and photographs, are also imported from other software packages. Illustration software that is designed for use by artists, such as Corel Draw and Aldus Freehand, is often used to create graphics for DTP documents.

Figure 2-11
Clip art consists of previously created illustrations that can be added to documents. Clip art usually comes in collections of individual images that are grouped by type. These clip art examples are from a business collection.

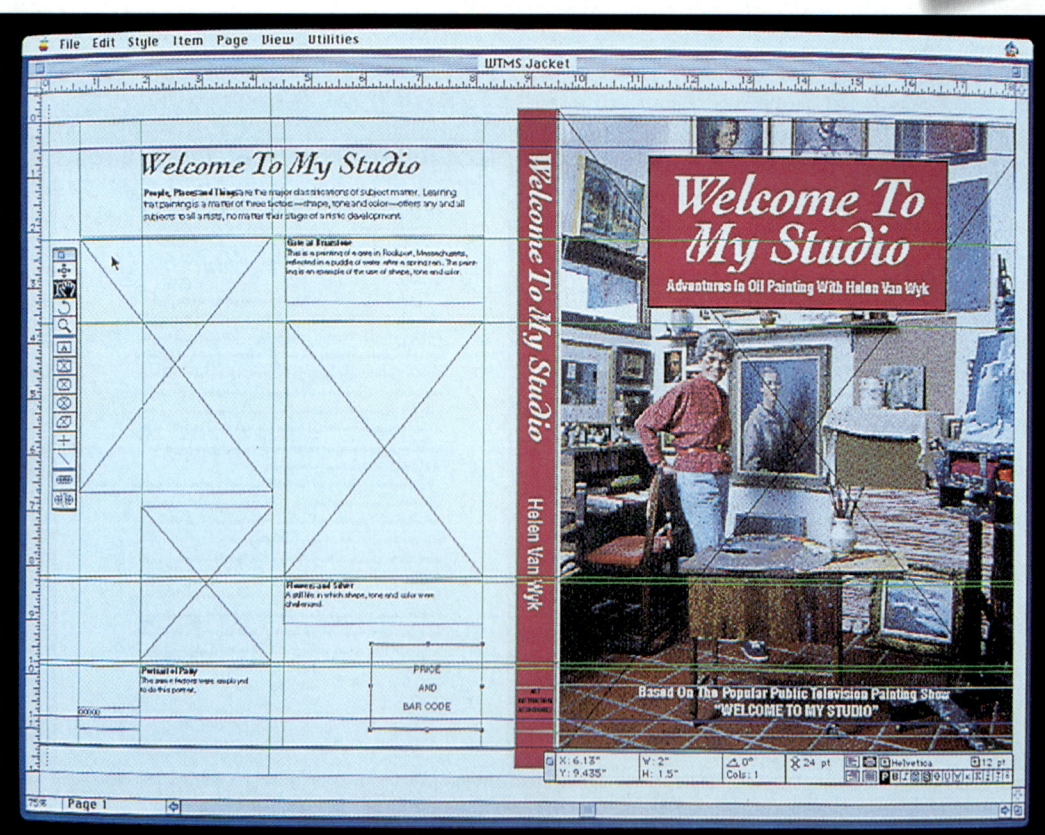

Figure 2-10
Desktop publishing software is used to create professional looking documents that combine text, graphics, illustrations, and photographs.

In addition, DTP documents often make use of previously created art, called **clip art**, that is sold in collections. Collections of clip art contain several hundred to several thousand images grouped by type, such as holidays, vehicles, or people. *Figure 2-11* shows examples of different clip art. Input devices, called scanners, can also be used to import photographs and art into DTP documents.

To aid the user in the process of page layout and design, all DTP programs display information on the screen exactly as it will look when printed. This capability is called WYSIWYG (pronounced whiz-e-wig). **WYSIWYG** is an acronym for What You See Is What You Get. Although many application programs now offer the WYSIWYG feature, DTP software packages were among the first.

Some of the other page composition and layout features that distinguish DTP software include the following (some of these features are illustrated in *Figure 2-12*):
- Capability to increase or decrease the size of graphic objects
- Capability to rotate text and graphics objects
- Backgrounds of different shades, colors, and textures
- Large page sizes (up to 18" by 24")
- Capability to flow text around irregularly shaped objects
- Capability to easily add or delete entire columns or pages
- Rulers and guides for aligning text and graphics
- Precise horizontal and vertical spacing control
- Color control

The capability to print DTP documents relies on a page definition language. A **page definition language**, such as **PostScript**, describes the document to be printed in language the printer can understand. The printer, which includes a page definition language translator, interprets the instructions and prints the document. Using a page definition language enables a DTP document created on one computer system to be printed on another computer with a different printer, as long as the second printer has a compatible page definition language.

With desktop publishing, users can now create professional looking documents on their own computers and produce work that previously could only be done by graphic artists. By using desktop publishing, both the cost and time of producing quality documents is significantly decreased. Popular desktop publishing packages include PageMaker, QuarkXpress, and Corel Ventura.

Figure 2-12
Some of the features available in the PageMaker desktop publishing software package are shown in this screen.

Spreadsheet Software

Spreadsheet software allows you to organize numeric data in a worksheet or table format called an **electronic spreadsheet** or **spreadsheet**. Manual methods, those done by hand, have long been used to organize numeric data in this manner *(Figure 2-13)*. You will see that the data in an electronic spreadsheet is organized in the same manner as it is in a manual spreadsheet. Within a spreadsheet, data is organized vertically in **columns** and horizontally in **rows**. Columns are usually identified by a letter and rows by a number. The intersection where a column and row meet is called a **cell** *(Figure 2-14)*. Cells are named by their location in the spreadsheet. In *Figure 2-14*, the cursor is on cell C2, the intersection of column C and row 2.

Cells may contain three types of data: labels (text), values (numbers), and formulas. The text, or **labels**, as they are called, identify the data and help document the worksheet.

Good spreadsheets contain descriptive labels. The rest of the cells in a spreadsheet may appear to contain numbers, or **values**. However, some of the cells actually contain formulas. The **formulas** perform calculations on the data in the spreadsheet and display the resulting value in the cell containing the formula. Formulas can be created by the user or can use functions that come with the spreadsheet software. **Functions** are stored formulas that perform common calculations, such as adding a range of cells, or generating a value such as the time or date. *Figure 2-15* is a list of functions found in most spreadsheet packages.

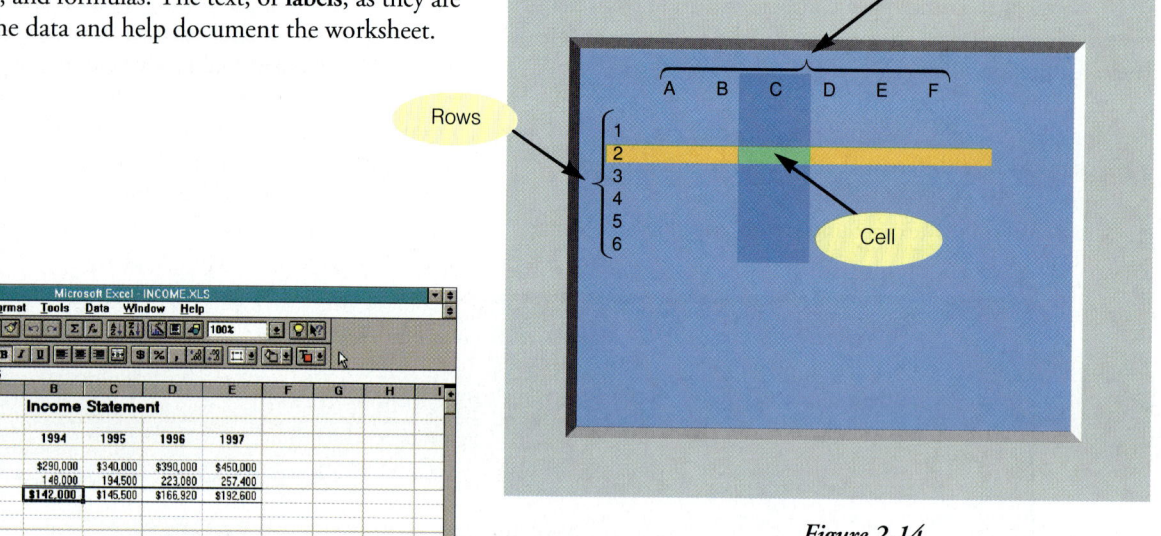

Figure 2-14
In a spreadsheet, columns refer to the vertical lines of data and rows refer to the horizontal lines of data. Columns are identified by letters and rows are identified by numbers. The intersection of a column and row is called a cell.

Figure 2-13
The electronic spreadsheet above still uses the column and row format of the manual spreadsheet on the right.

By developing a simple spreadsheet to calculate the profit and profit % from three months of revenues and costs, you will see how a spreadsheet works. As shown in *Figure 2-16,* the first step in creating the spreadsheet is to enter the labels, or titles. These should be short but descriptive, to help you organize the layout of the data in your spreadsheet.

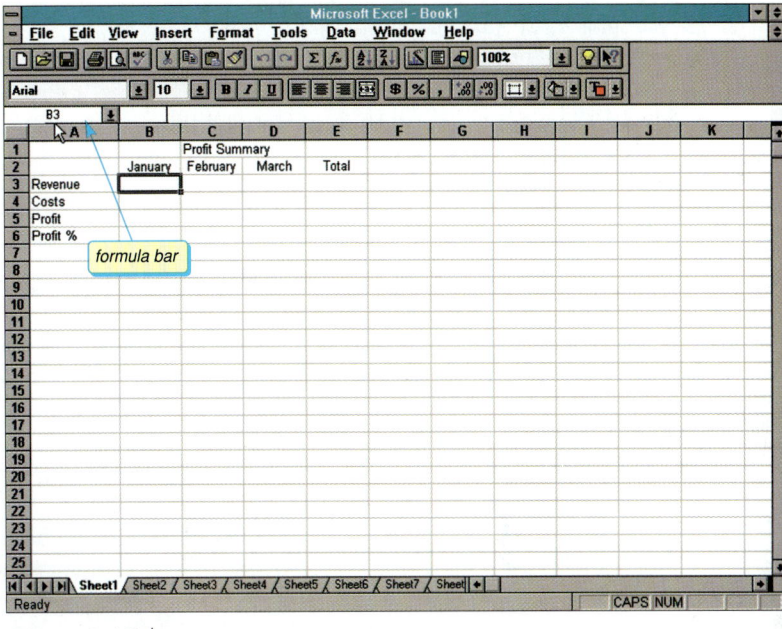

Figure 2-15 ▼
Spreadsheet functions are predefined formulas that perform calculations or return information based on given data. This is just a partial list of some of the more common functions. Probably the most often used function is SUM, which is used to add a range of numbers.

Figure 2-16 ▲
Labels such as January, February, Revenue, and Costs are entered in the spreadsheet to identify columns and rows of data. The formula bar shows the address and contents of the active cell. Here, the active cell is B3 (column B, row 3). Nothing has been entered for this cell, so the formula bar shows only the cell address.

SPREADSHEET FUNCTIONS	
FINANCIAL	
FV (rate, number of periods, payment)	Calculates the future value of an investment.
NPV (rate, range)	Calculates the net present value of an investment.
PMT (rate, number of periods, present value)	Calculates the periodic payment for an annuity.
PV (rate, number of periods, payment)	Calculates the present value of an investment.
RATE (number of periods, payment, present value)	Calculates the periodic interest rate of an annuity.
DAY & TIME	
DATE	Returns the current date.
NOW	Returns the current date and time.
TIME	Returns the current time.
MATHEMATICAL	
ABS (number)	Returns the absolute value of a number.
INT (number)	Rounds a number down to the nearest integer.
LN (number)	Calculates the natural logarithm of a number.
LOG (number, base)	Calculates the logarithm of a number to a specified base.
ROUND (number, number of digits)	Rounds a number to a specified number of digits.
SQRT (number)	Calculates the square root of a number.
SUM (range)	Calculates the total of a range of numbers.
STATISTICAL	
AVERAGE (range)	Calculates the average value of a range of numbers.
COUNT (range)	Counts how many cells in the range have entries.
MAX (range)	Returns the maximum value in a range.
MIN (range)	Returns the minimum value in a range.
STDEV (range)	Calculates the standard deviation of a range of numbers.
LOGICAL	
IF (logical test, value if true, value if false).	Performs a test and returns one value if test is true and another value if test is false.

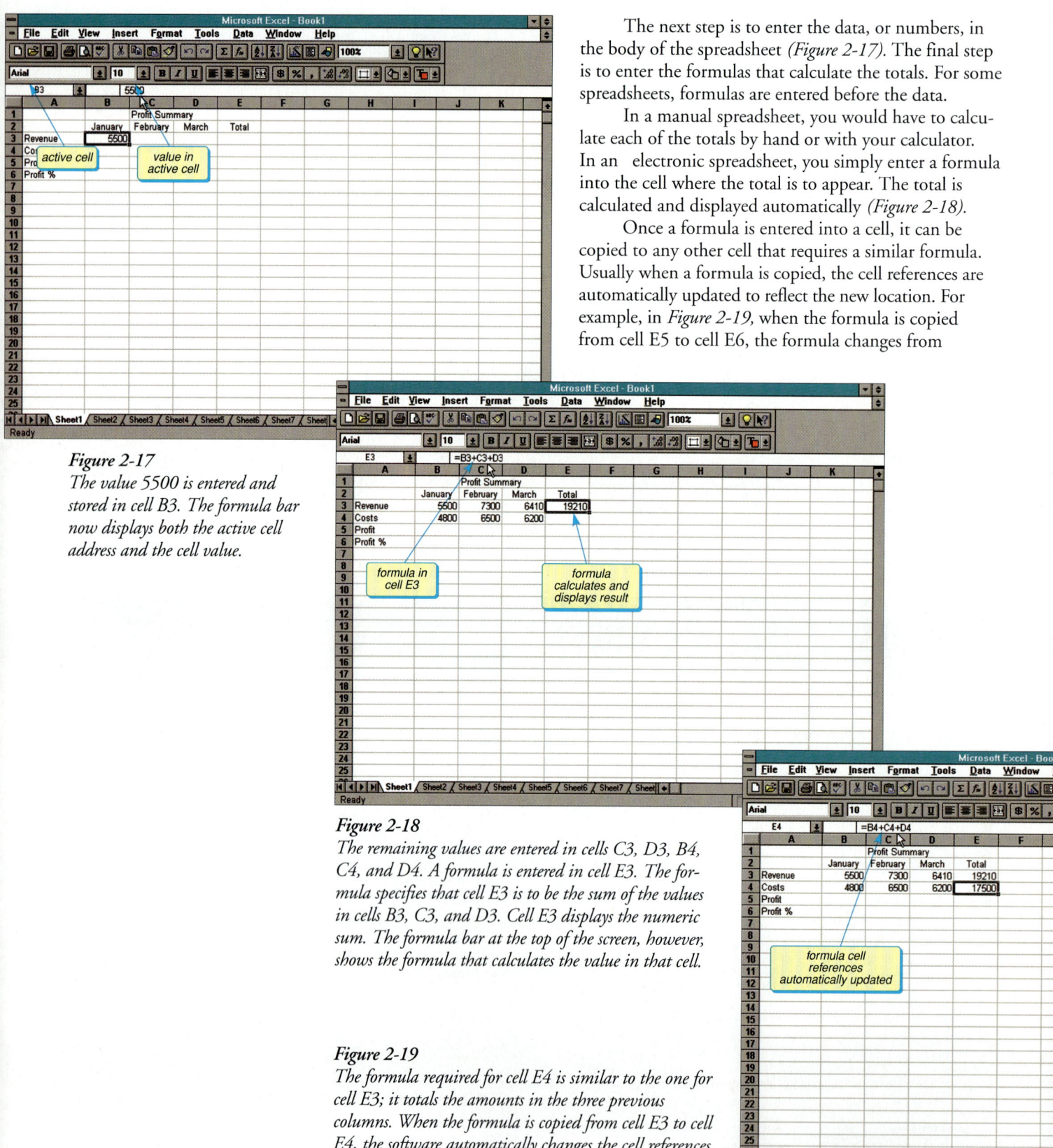

The next step is to enter the data, or numbers, in the body of the spreadsheet *(Figure 2-17)*. The final step is to enter the formulas that calculate the totals. For some spreadsheets, formulas are entered before the data.

In a manual spreadsheet, you would have to calculate each of the totals by hand or with your calculator. In an electronic spreadsheet, you simply enter a formula into the cell where the total is to appear. The total is calculated and displayed automatically *(Figure 2-18)*.

Once a formula is entered into a cell, it can be copied to any other cell that requires a similar formula. Usually when a formula is copied, the cell references are automatically updated to reflect the new location. For example, in *Figure 2-19*, when the formula is copied from cell E5 to cell E6, the formula changes from

Figure 2-17
The value 5500 is entered and stored in cell B3. The formula bar now displays both the active cell address and the cell value.

Figure 2-18
The remaining values are entered in cells C3, D3, B4, C4, and D4. A formula is entered in cell E3. The formula specifies that cell E3 is to be the sum of the values in cells B3, C3, and D3. Cell E3 displays the numeric sum. The formula bar at the top of the screen, however, shows the formula that calculates the value in that cell.

Figure 2-19
The formula required for cell E4 is similar to the one for cell E3; it totals the amounts in the three previous columns. When the formula is copied from cell E3 to cell E4, the software automatically changes the cell references from B3, C3, and D3 to B4, C4, and D4.

B5+C5+D5 to B6+C6+D6. This automatic updating of the formula is called **relative referencing**.

If you are going to copy a formula but always want the formula to refer to the same cell location, you would use **absolute referencing**. For example, if you had a single tax rate that was going to be used to calculate taxes on the amounts in more than one cell, you would make an absolute reference to the cell containing the tax rate. To make a cell an absolute reference, you place a dollar sign in front of the column and row. E5 in a formula would be an absolute reference to cell E5. As the formula is copied, the formula calculations are performed automatically. After entering the remaining formulas, the spreadsheet is complete *(Figure 2-20)*.

One of the more powerful features of the electronic spreadsheet occurs when the data in a spreadsheet changes. To appreciate the capabilities of spreadsheet software, consider how a change is handled in a manual system. When a value in a manual spreadsheet changes, you must erase it and write a new value into the cell. You must also erase all cells that contain calculations referring to the value that changed and then you must recalculate these cells and enter the new result. For example, the row totals and column totals would be updated to reflect changes to any values within their areas. In a large manual spreadsheet, accurately posting changes and updating the values affected would be time consuming and new errors could be introduced. But posting changes on an electronic spreadsheet is easy. You change data in a cell by simply entering in the new value. All other values that are affected are updated automatically. *Figure 2-21* shows that if you change the value in cell C3 from 7300 to 8000, five other cell values will automatically change. On a computer, the updating happens almost instantly.

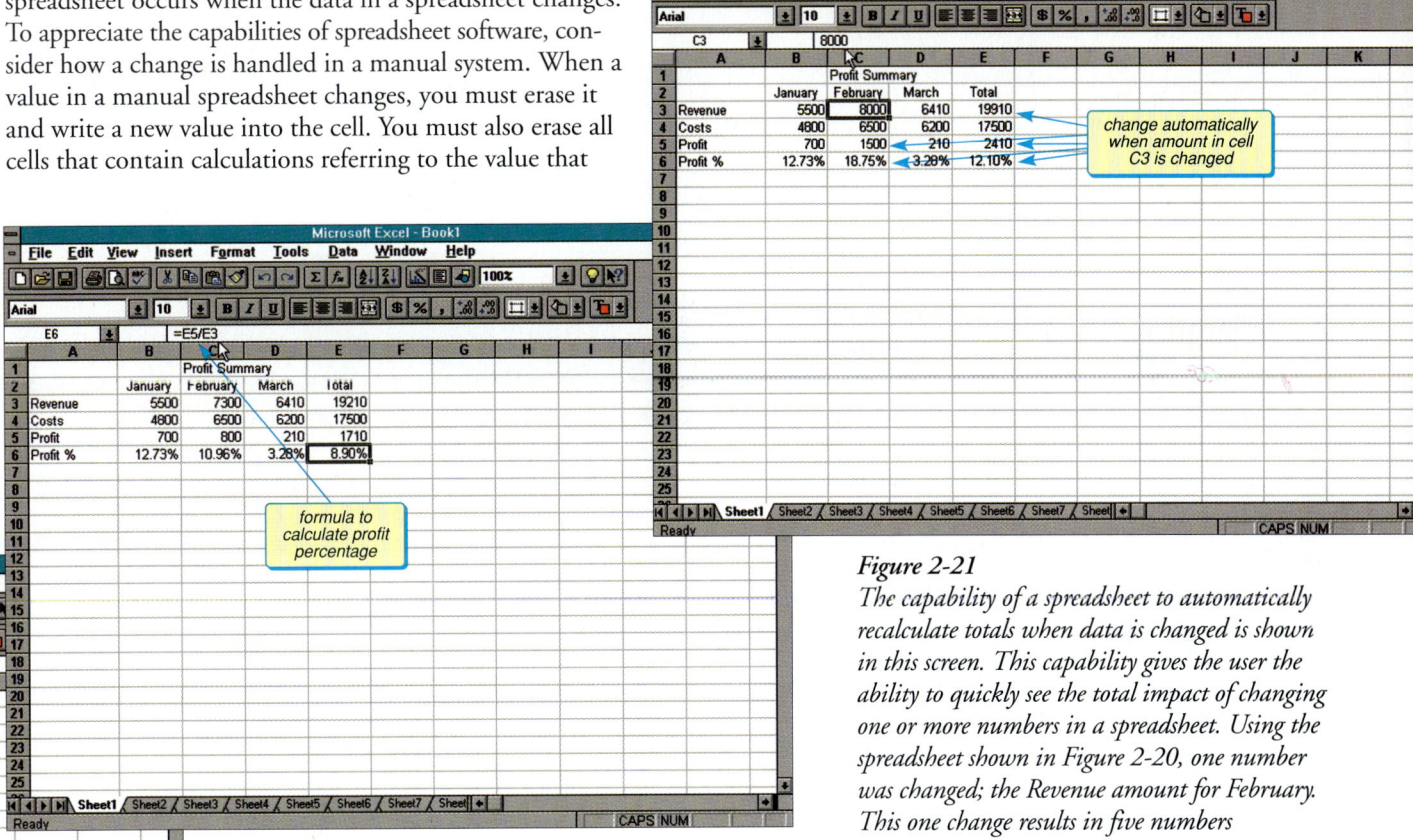

Figure 2-21
The capability of a spreadsheet to automatically recalculate totals when data is changed is shown in this screen. This capability gives the user the ability to quickly see the total impact of changing one or more numbers in a spreadsheet. Using the spreadsheet shown in Figure 2-20, one number was changed; the Revenue amount for February. This one change results in five numbers automatically recalculating in the spreadsheet.

Figure 2-20
In the completed spreadsheet, the value in cell E6 is derived from the formula in the formula bar, which specifies that the value in cell E5 is to be divided by the value in cell E3 (the slash character indicates division).

A spreadsheet's capability to recalculate when data is changed makes it a valuable tool for decision making. This capability is sometimes called **what-if analysis** because the results of different assumptions ("what-if we changed this ...") can be quickly seen.

A standard feature of spreadsheet packages is the capability to create **charts** that graphically present the relationship of numerical data. Visual representation of data in charts often makes it easier to analyze and interpret information. The types of charts provided by spreadsheet packages are sometimes called **analytical graphics** or **business graphics** because they are primarily used for the analysis of numerical data by businesses. *Figure 2-22* shows the chart types offered in one spreadsheet package.

Most of these charts are variations on three basic chart types; line charts, bar charts and pie charts. **Line charts** are effective for showing a trend as indicated by a rising or falling line. If the area below or above a line is filled in with a color or pattern, it is called an area chart. **Bar charts** display bars of various lengths to show the relationship of data *(Figure 2-23)*. The bars can be horizontal, vertical (sometimes called columns), or stacked one on top of the other. **Pie charts**, so called because they look like a pie cut into pieces, are effective for showing the relationship of parts to a whole. Pie charts are often used for budget presentations to show how much each part of the budget is a percentage of the total. To improve their appearance, most charts can be displayed or printed in a three-dimensional (3-D) format.

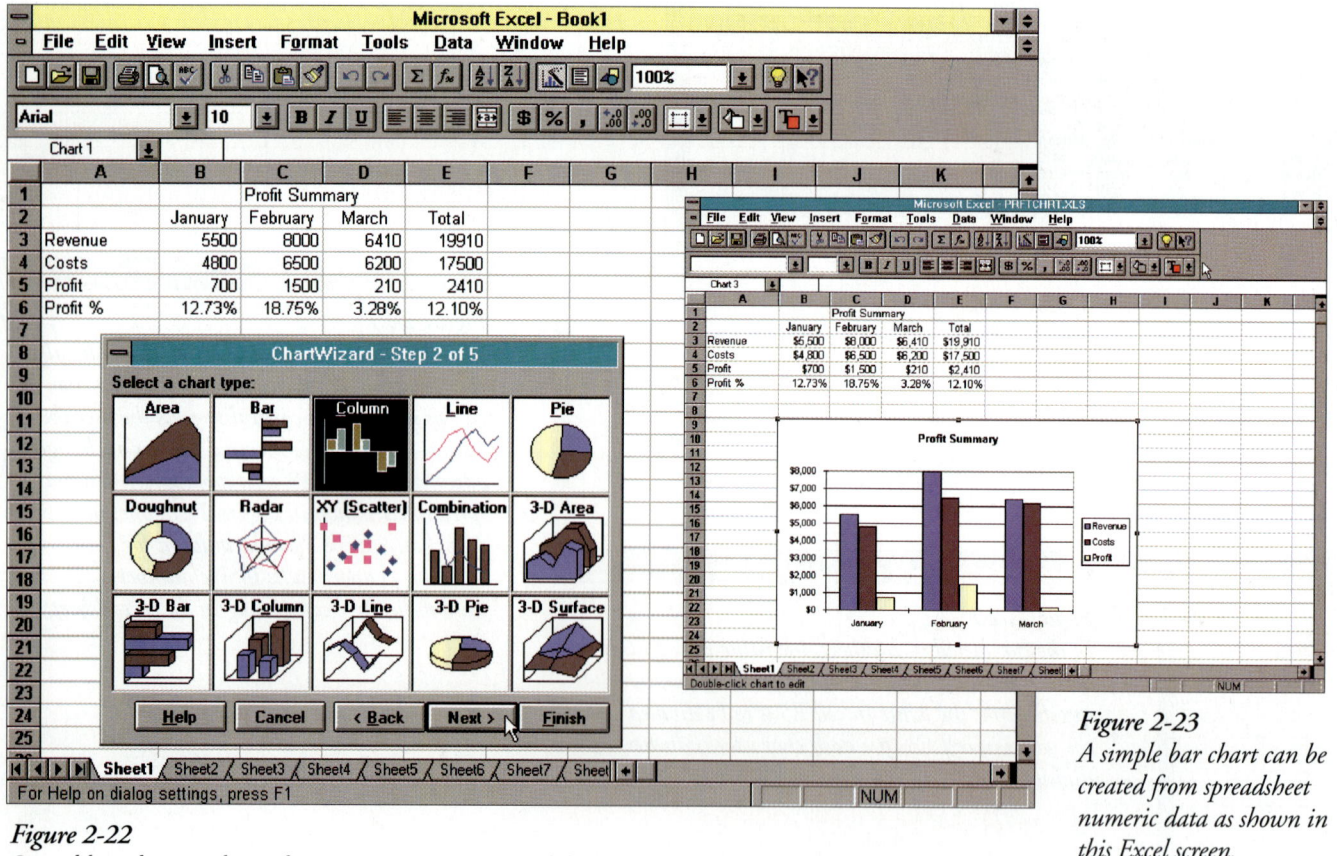

Figure 2-22
Spreadsheet data can be used to create numerous types of charts. This screen shows 15 types of charts that are available with the Microsoft Excel spreadsheet package.

Figure 2-23
A simple bar chart can be created from spreadsheet numeric data as shown in this Excel screen.

Besides the capability to manipulate numbers, spreadsheet packages have many formatting features that can improve the overall appearance of the data. These include typefaces, sizes, and styles, borders and lines, and shading and colors to highlight data. *Figure 2-24* shows the spreadsheet with some of these features added.

Spreadsheets are one of the most popular software packages and have been adapted to a wide range of business and nonbusiness applications. Some of the popular packages used today are Lotus 1-2-3, Microsoft Excel, and Quattro Pro.

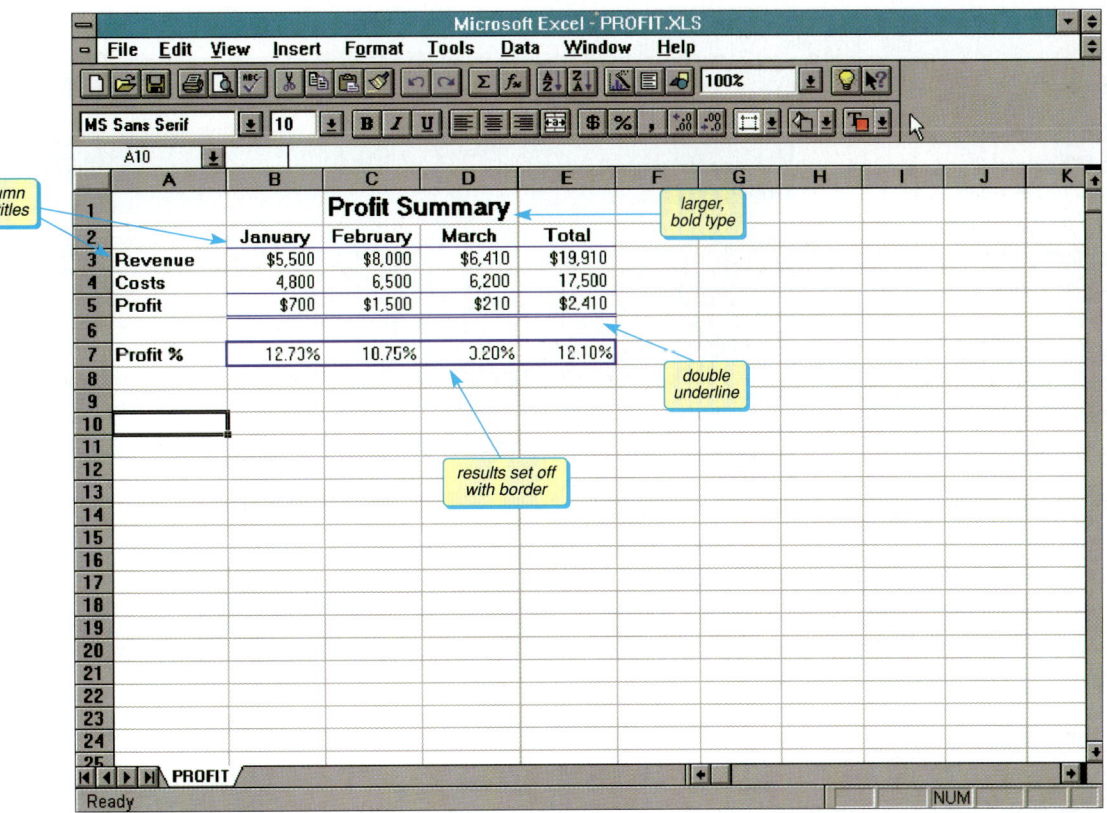

Figure 2-24
This formatted spreadsheet shows how the formatting features improve the appearance of a document.

Database Software

A **database** refers to a collection of data that is stored in files. **Database software** allows you to create a database and to retrieve, manipulate, and update the data that you store in it. In a manual system *(Figure 2-25)*, data is recorded on paper and stored in a filing cabinet. In a database on the computer, the data will be stored in an electronic format on a secondary storage device such as a disk.

When you use a database, you need to be familiar with the terms file, record, and field. Just as in a manual system, the word **file** is a collection of related data that is organized in records. Each **record** contains a collection of related facts called **fields**. For example, an address file might consist of records containing name and address information. All the data that relates to one name would be considered a record. Each fact, such as the street address or phone number, is called a field.

The screens in *Figures 2-26* through *2-29* present the development of a database containing information about the members of a school band booster club. The booster club members donate money to help fund band activities. Besides keeping track of each member's name, address, and phone number, the band director wants to record the amount of money donated and the date the money was received.

A good way to begin creating a database is to make a list of the information you want to record. Each item that you want to keep track of will become a field in the database. Each field should be given a unique name that is short but descriptive. For example, the field name for a member's last name could be LNAME. The field name for a member's first

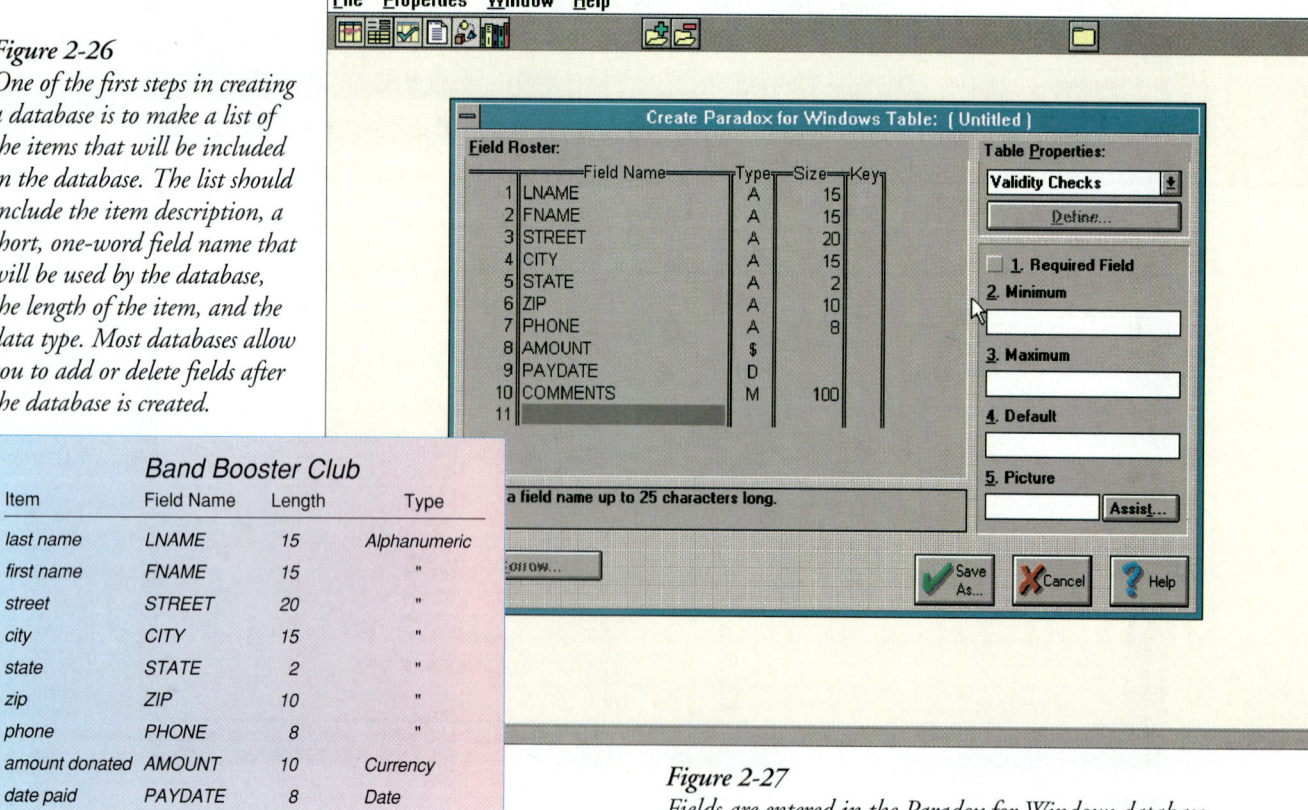

Figure 2-25
A database is similar to a manual system; related data items are stored in files.

Figure 2-26
One of the first steps in creating a database is to make a list of the items that will be included in the database. The list should include the item description, a short, one-word field name that will be used by the database, the length of the item, and the data type. Most databases allow you to add or delete fields after the database is created.

Band Booster Club

Item	Field Name	Length	Type
last name	LNAME	15	Alphanumeric
first name	FNAME	15	"
street	STREET	20	"
city	CITY	15	"
state	STATE	2	"
zip	ZIP	10	"
phone	PHONE	8	"
amount donated	AMOUNT	10	Currency
date paid	PAYDATE	8	Date
comments	COMMENTS	–	Memo

Figure 2-27
Fields are entered in the Paradox for Windows database.

name could be FNAME. Additional information that needs to be decided is the length of each field and the type of information that each field will contain. The type of information could be any of the following:
- **Alphanumeric** – letters, numbers, or special characters
- **Numeric** – numbers only
- **Currency** – dollar and cents amounts
- **Date** – month, day, and year information
- **Memo** – free form text of any type or length

A list of the information necessary for the band booster club is shown in *Figure 2-26*.

Each database program differs slightly in how it requires the user to enter the file and field information. A field entry screen from the Paradox for Windows database software package is shown in *Figure 2-27*.

After the database structure is created by defining the fields, individual database records can be entered. Usually, they are entered one at a time by using the keyboard. However, most database programs also have the capability to import data from other files. The information specified for each field helps the user in entering the data. For example, designating the DATE PAID field as a date field prevents the user from entering anything other than a valid date. Comparing data entered against a predefined format or value is called **validation** and is an important feature of database programs. *Figure 2-28* shows the entry screen for the band booster club data.

After the records are entered, the database can be used to produce information. All or some of the records can be selected and arranged in the order specified by the user. This is one of the most powerful features of a database; the capability to retrieve database information based on criteria specified by the user. For example, suppose the band director wanted to personally call and thank all the booster club members who donated more than $100. A report, called a **query** could be produced that listed the members names, phone numbers, and the amounts and dates donated. An example of such a report is shown in *Figure 2-29*.

As shown in the band boosters club example, database software assists users in creating files and storing, manipulating, and retrieving data. Popular software packages that perform these functions include dBASE, FoxPro, Microsoft Access, and Paradox.

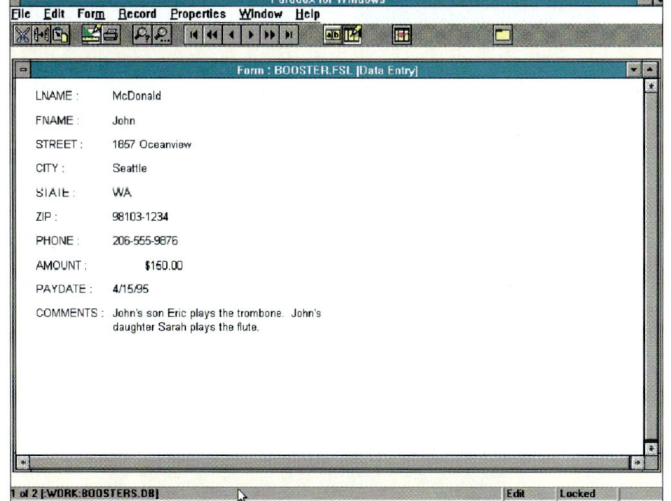

Figure 2-28
Once the database fields are defined, data can be entered. Most database programs automatically create a data entry form based on information that was entered for the fields. This Paradox for Windows data entry form lists each of the database fields in the order they were entered. Advanced database features can be used to design more complex data entry forms.

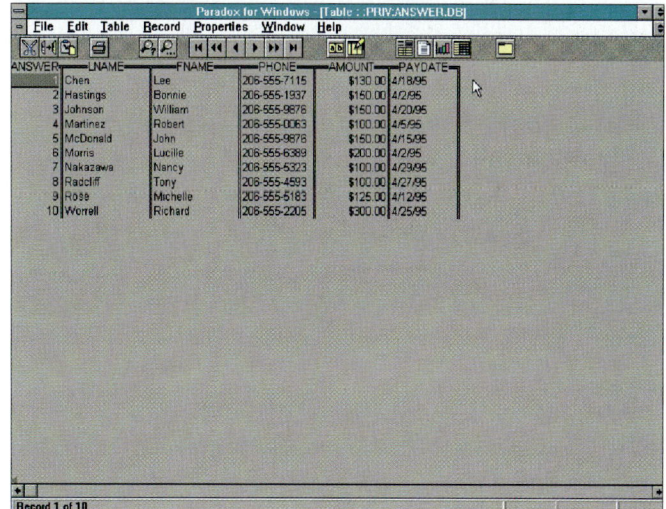

Figure 2-29
Database software packages can produce reports based on criteria specified by the user. For example, this screen shows the result of a request, called a query, that specified the name and phone number of each booster club member that contributed $100 or more. The amount and date of the contribution were also requested. The results of the query can be displayed on the screen or printed.

Presentation Graphics Software

Presentation graphics software allows the user to create documents, called **slides**, that are used in making presentations before a group *(Figure 2-30)*. The slides can be displayed on a large monitor or projected on a screen. Presentation graphics goes beyond analytical graphics by offering the user a wider choice of presentation features. Some of the features included with most presentation graphics packages include:

- Numerous chart types
- Three-dimensional effects for charts, text, and graphics
- Special effects such as shading, shadows, and textures
- Color control that includes preestablished groups of complementary colors for backgrounds, lines and text, shadows, fills, and accents
- Image libraries that include clip art graphics that can be incorporated into the slides; the image libraries are usually business oriented and include illustrations of factories, people, money, and other business-related art

Besides the slides, presentation graphics packages create several other documents that can be used in a presentation *(Figure 2-31)*. *Outlines* include only the text from each slide, usually the slide title and the key points. A *notes page* is used

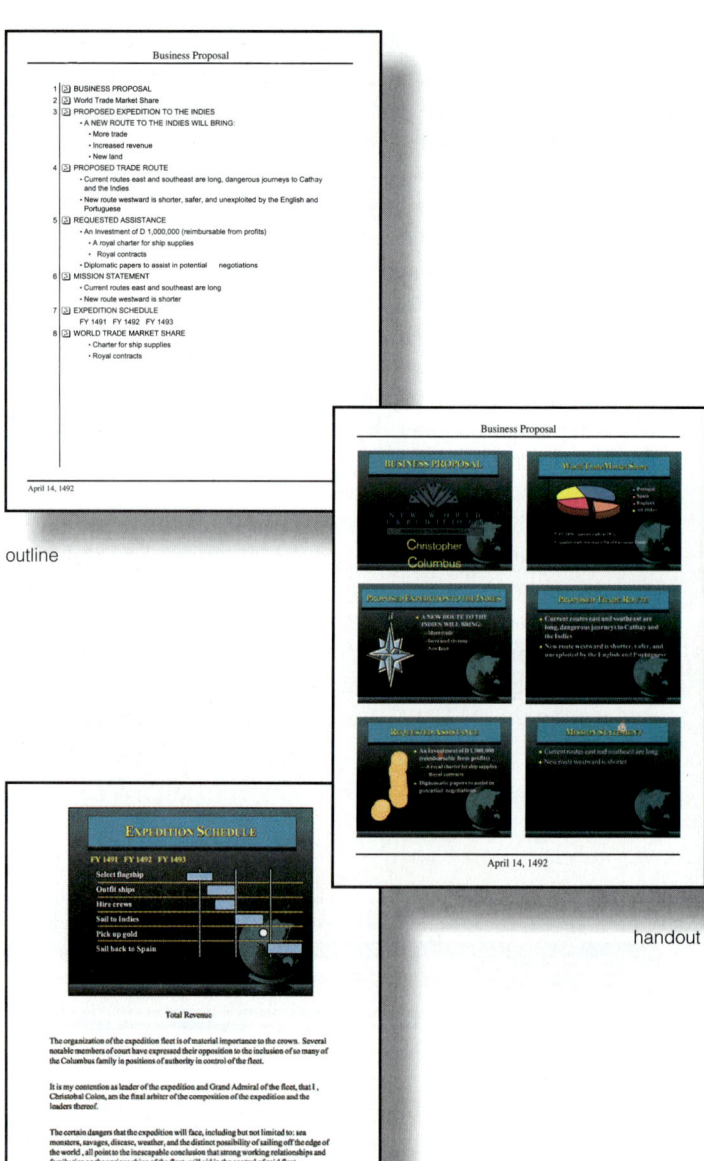

outline

handout

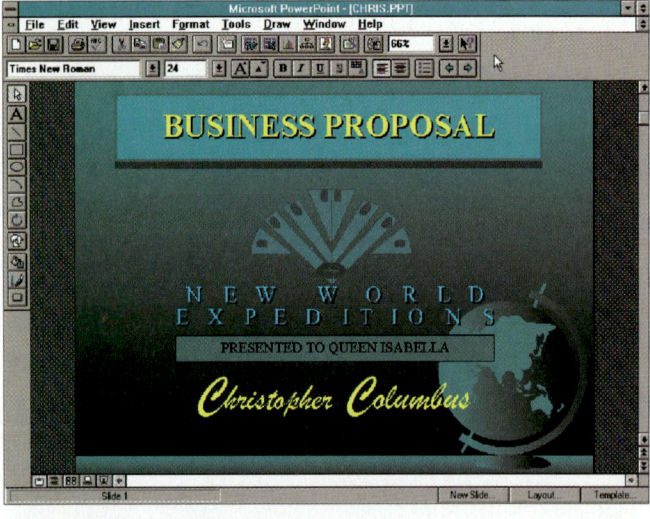

Figure 2-30
Presentation graphics software is used to prepare slides used in making presentations. The slides can be displayed on a computer, projected on a screen, or printed and handed out. The presentation graphics software includes many features to control graphics objects and color to make the slides more visually interesting.

notes page

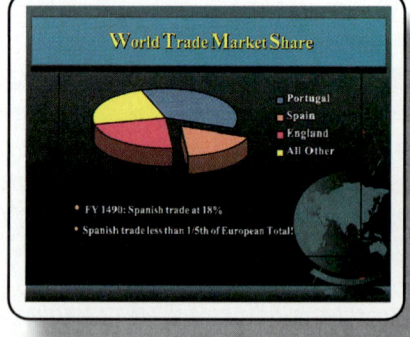

Figure 2-31
Documents that can be created with presentation software packages.

transparency

by the speaker making the presentation and includes a picture of the slide and any notes the speaker wants to see when he or she is discussing the slide. Audience *handouts* include images of two or more slides on a page that can be given to people who attended the presentation.

To help organize and present the slides, presentation graphics packages include slide sorters. A slide sorter presents a screen view similar to how 35mm slides would look on a photographer's light table *(Figure 2-32)*. By using a mouse or other pointing device, the user can arrange the slides in any order. When the slides are arranged in the proper order, they can be displayed one at a time by clicking the mouse or using the keyboard. The presenter can also set up the slides to be automatically displayed with a predetermined time delay between each slide. Special effects can also be applied to the transition between each slide. For example, one slide might slowly dissolve as the other slide comes into view.

Using presentation graphics software allows you to efficiently create professional quality presentations that help communicate information more effectively. Studies have shown that people are more likely to remember information they have seen as well as heard and that they recall 25% more information when it is presented in color. Popular presentation graphics packages include Microsoft PowerPoint, Aldus Persuasion, Lotus Freelance Graphics, and SPC Harvard Graphics.

Figure 2-32
This slide sorter screen shows a miniature version of each slide. Using a pointing device or the keyboard, the slides can be rearranged to change their order of presentation.

Data Communications Software

Data communications software is used to transmit data from one computer to another. For two computers to communicate, they each must have data communications software, data communications equipment, and be connected by some type of link such as a telephone line. Features that most data communications software packages include are:

- A dialing directory of phone numbers that can be used to automatically connect with other computer systems *(Figure 2-33)*
- Automatic redial that lets the user set the number of times the computer will keep trying to connect with another computer if the line is busy; a time delay between call attempts can also be set
- Automatic answer if another user tries to call your computer
- The capability to send or receive one or more data files

Communications software is frequently used by employees that are away from the office. Using communications software (and sometimes other packages such as E-mail), remote employees can check their messages, send messages to other employees, check the quantity of inventory on hand, and enter orders that they have just received from customers.

Communications software is also used to access online services for news, weather, financial, and travel information. Online service companies such as Prodigy and America Online provide a wide range of information for a small monthly fee *(Figure 2-34)*. Other service companies provide detailed information in subject areas such as medicine, finance, or specific industries. Shopping is also available from several services. Online shoppers can read a description and, in some cases, see a picture of a product on their screen. Using a credit card, the product can be ordered. More banks are now offering online banking. The user can review recent financial transactions, transfer money from one account to another, and even pay bills using his or her computer. All of these activities are made possible through the use of data communications software. Popular communications software packages are Crosstalk and Procomm Plus.

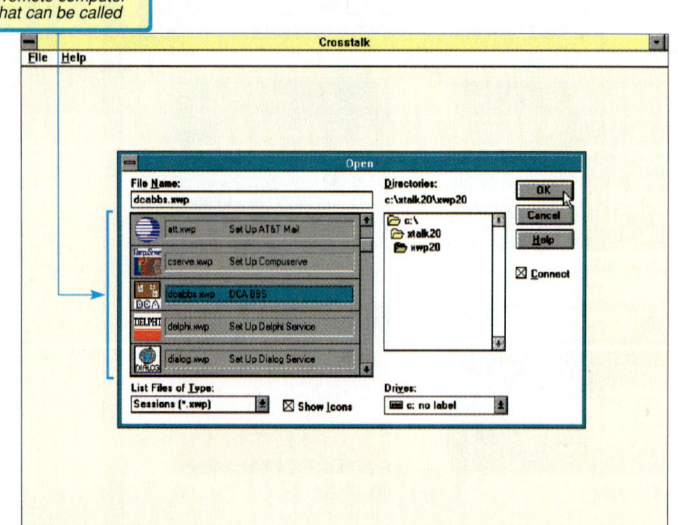

Figure 2-33
Communications programs include dialing directories that make it easier to connect with other computers. In this screen from Crosstalk for Windows, each icon represents a computer that can be called. To make the connection, the user selects the icon with a pointing device or the keyboard. The communications software then dials the other computer using a prestored phone number and establishes the connection.

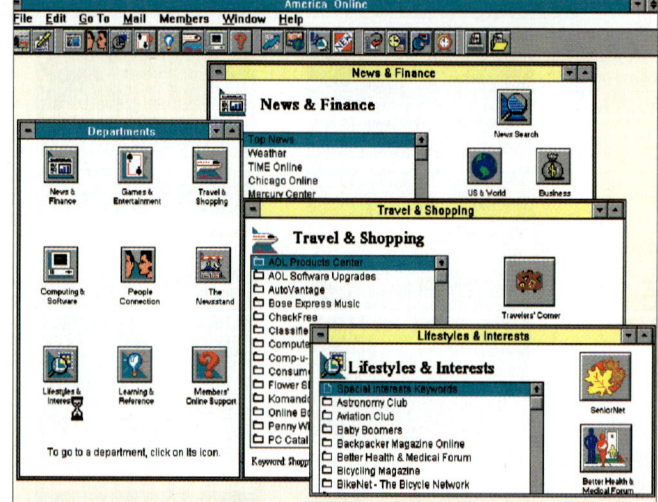

Figure 2-34
Online information services such as America Online offer a wide variety of information to their subscribers. The user needs to have a computer and a modem, a piece of communications equipment that enables the computer to use a phone line to connect to the online service. Communications software is usually provided by the information service.

Electronic Mail Software

Electronic mail software, also called **E-mail,** allows users to send messages to and receive messages from other computer users *(Figure 2-35).* The other users may be on the same computer network or on a separate computer system reached through the use of communications equipment and software. Each E-mail user has a mailbox and an address to which the mail can be sent. To make the sending of messages efficient, E-mail software allows the user to send a single message to a distribution list consisting of two or more individuals. The E-mail software takes care of copying the message and routing it to each person on the distribution list. For example, a message sent to the Department Supervisors distribution list would be routed to each of the department supervisors. E-mail systems usually have a mail waiting alert that notifies a user through a message or sound that a message is waiting to be read even if the user is working in another application.

Although E-mail is primarily used within private organizations, several communications companies (such as MCI) and online services providers (such as Prodigy and America Online) have established public E-mail facilities. For a small monthly fee, users can receive mail from and send mail to other users of the service. E-mail can be especially useful to people whose job keeps them away from the office. Remote workers can dial into their E-mail and send and receive messages at any time of the day. Because of its widespread use, informal rules, called E-mail etiquette, have been developed. These mostly common-sense rules include:

- Keep messages short and to the point.
- Avoid using E-mail for trivia, gossip, or other nonessential communications.
- Keep the distribution list to a minimum.
- Avoid using all capital letters – it is considered the same as yelling.
- It's okay (OK) for you (u) to (2) abbreviate as long as the abbreviation can be easily understood.
- Make the subject as meaningful as possible. Many E-mail systems list a summary of the mail and only show the subject, date, and sender.
- Read your mail regularly and clear messages that are no longer needed.

Popular E-mail packages are Microsoft Mail, Lotus CC:Mail, and Da Vinci eMAIL.

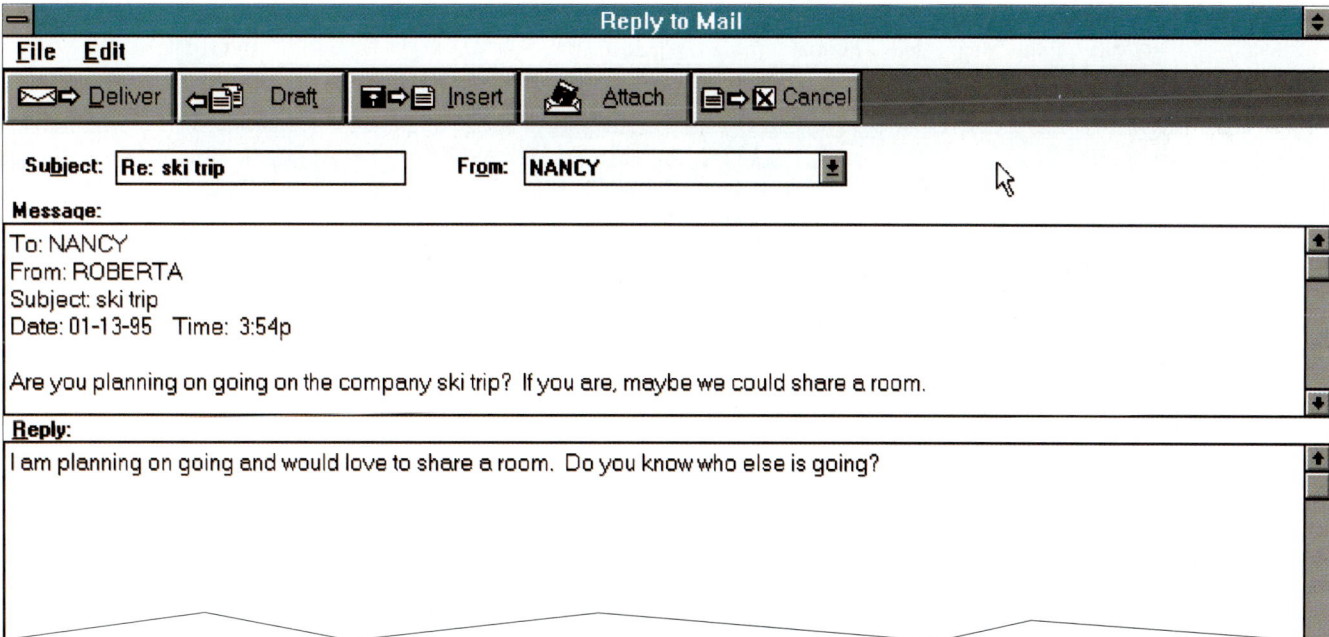

Figure 2-35
Electronic mail allows users to send and receive messages with other computer users. Each user has an electronic mail box to which messages are sent. This screen shows how a user can add a reply to a received message and then send the reply back to the person who sent the original message.

Personal Information Management

Personal information management (PIM) software helps users keep track of the miscellaneous bits of personal information that each of us deals with every day. This information can take many forms: notes to ourselves or from others, phone messages, notes about a current or future project, appointments, and so on. Programs that keep track of this type of information, such as electronic calendars, have been in existence for some time. In recent years, however, such programs have been combined so one package can keep track of all of a user's personal information.

Because of the many types of information that these programs can manage, it is difficult to precisely define personal information software. However, the category can be applied to programs that offer any of the following capabilities: appointment calendars, outliners, electronic notepads, data managers, and text retrieval. Some personal information software packages also include communications software capabilities such as phone dialers and electronic mail.

Appointment calendars allow you to schedule activities for a particular day and time *(Figure 2-36)*. Most of them will warn you if two activities are scheduled for the same time. Outliners allow you to *rough out* an idea by constructing and reorganizing an outline of important points and subpoints. Electronic notepads allow the user to record comments and assign them to one or more categories that can be used to retrieve the comments. Data managers are simple file management systems that allow the input, update, and retrieval of related records such as name and address lists or phone numbers. Text retrieval provides the capability to search files for specific words or phrases such as *Sales Meeting*. Two popular personal information management packages are Ecco and Commence.

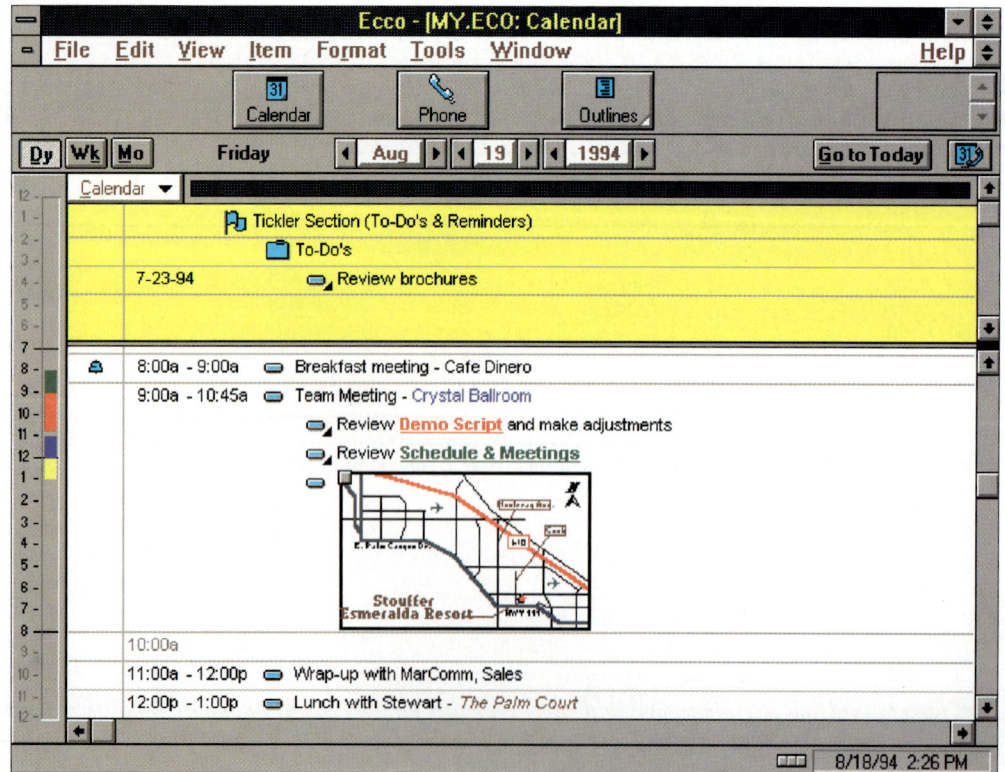

Figure 2-36
Personal information management (PIM) software helps organize and keep track of the many different types of information that people encounter each day. This screen shows the ECCO PIM software. In addition to text, graphics objects, such as the map, can be inserted in the calendar portion of the software.

Project Management

Project management software allows users to plan, schedule, track, and analyze the events, resources, and costs of a project *(Figure 2-37)*. For example, a construction company might use this type of software to manage the building of an apartment complex or a campaign manager might use it to coordinate the many activities of a politician running for office. The value of project management software is that it provides a method for managers to control and manage the variables of a project to help ensure that the project will be completed on time and within budget. Popular project management packages include Timeline and Microsoft Project.

Integrated Software

Software packages such as databases and electronic spreadsheets are generally used independently of each other; but what if you wanted to place information from a database into a spreadsheet? The data in the database would have to be reentered in the spreadsheet. This would be time consuming and errors could be introduced as you reentered the data. The inability of separate programs to easily communicate with one another and use a common set of data has been overcome through the use of integrated software.

Integrated software refers to packages that combine applications such as word processing, spreadsheet, and database into a single, easy-to-use set of programs. Many integrated packages also include communications capabilities. The applications that are included in integrated packages are designed to have a consistent command and menu structure. For example, the command to print a document looks and works the same in each of the integrated applications. Besides a consistent look and feel, a key feature of integrated packages is their capability to pass data quickly and easily from one application to another. For example, revenue and cost information from a database on daily sales could be

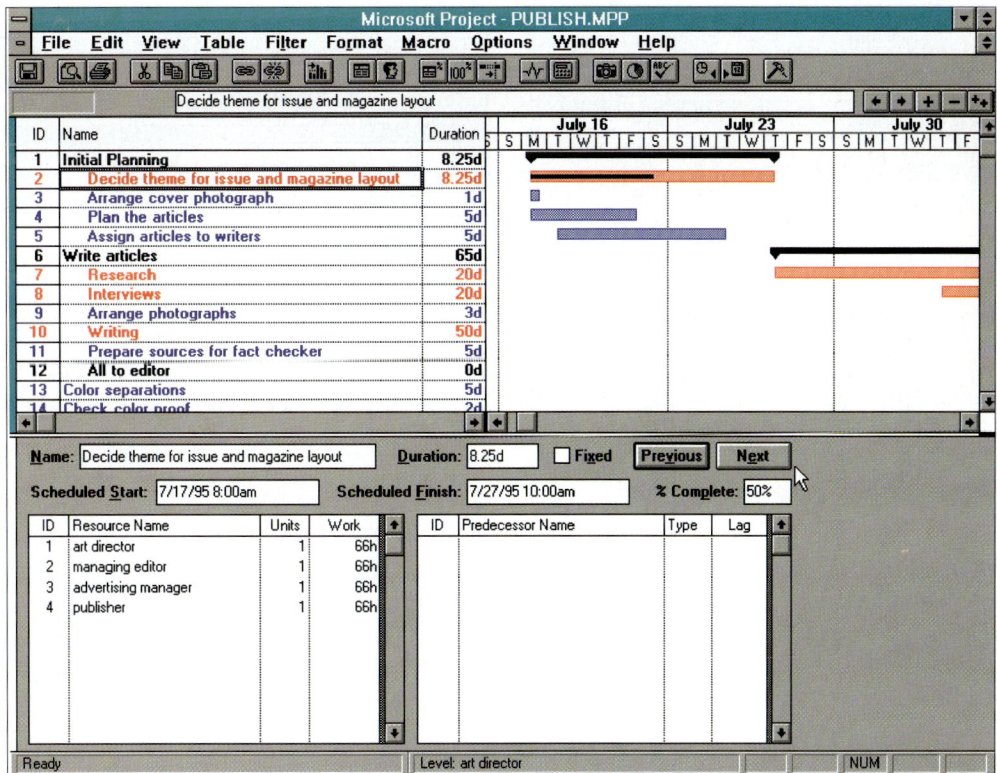

Figure 2-37
Project management software helps you plan and keep track of the tasks and resources necessary to complete a project. This screen shows part of a project plan for publishing a magazine. The most important tasks are listed in red. The bars in the upper right corner, called a Gantt chart, graphically indicate the duration of each task. The bottom portion of the screen identifies the resources required for the highlighted task; in this case, the hours needed from specific individuals.

quickly loaded into a spreadsheet. The spreadsheet could be used to calculate gross profits. Once the calculations are completed, all or a portion of the spreadsheet data can be passed to the word processing application to create a narrative report.

In their early days, integrated packages were criticized as being a collection of good but not great applications. To some extent this is still true. Users who need the most powerful word processor or spreadsheet will probably not be satisfied with the capabilities of an integrated application. For many users, however, the capabilities of today's integrated applications more than meet their needs. Besides the advantages of working well together, integrated applications are less expensive than buying comparable applications separately. Two popular integrated software packages are Microsoft Works and ClarisWorks.

Similar to integrated software are software **suites**; individual applications packaged in the same box and sold for a price that is significantly less than buying the applications individually. Although the use of suites was originally just a pricing strategy, it is becoming more and more like integrated software. First the individual packages were just bundled together for a good price; now they are being modified to work better together and offer the same command and menu structures. For the developer, the advantages of products that look and work the same include shorter development and training time, and easier customer support. Another advantage is that customers who have learned one application package are more likely to buy a second package if they know it works in a similar manner. Popular software suites include Microsoft Office, Lotus SmartSuite, and Novell PerfectOffice.

Figure 2-38
Four ways to learn application software packages.

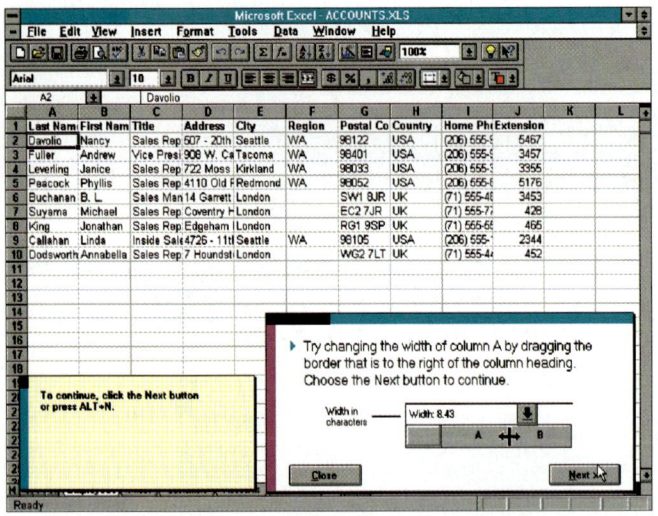

Figure 2-38a
Software tutorials help you learn an application while using the actual software on your computer. This screen shows how the Microsoft Excel tutorial teaches how to change the width of a column in a spreadsheet.

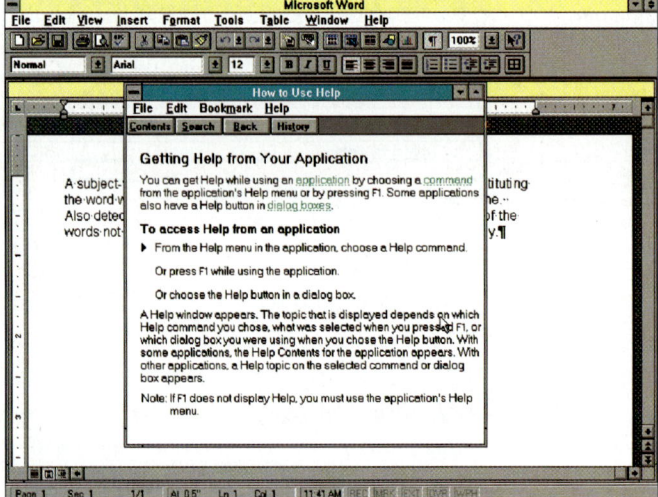

Figure 2-38b
Online help provides assistance without having to leave your application.

Learning Aids and Support Tools for Application Users

Learning to use an application software package involves time and practice. In addition to taking a class to learn how to use a software application, several learning aids and support tools are available to help you including: tutorials, online help, trade books, and keyboard templates *(Figure 2-38)*.

Tutorials are step-by-step instructions using real examples that show you how to use an application. Some tutorials are written manuals, but more tutorials are software based, allowing you to use your computer to learn about a package.

Online help refers to additional instructions that are available within the application. In most packages, a function key is reserved for the help feature. When you are using an application and have a question, pressing the designated *help* key will temporarily overlay your work on the screen with information on how to use the package. When you are finished using the help feature, pressing another key allows you to return to your work.

The documentation that accompanies software packages is frequently organized as reference material. This makes it very useful once you know how to use a package, but difficult to use when you are first learning it. For this reason, many **trade books** are available to help users learn to use the features of personal computer application packages. These books can be found where software is sold and are usually carried in regular bookstores.

Keyboard templates are plastic sheets that fit around a portion of your keyboard. The keyboard commands to select the various features of the application programs are printed on the template. Having a guide to the commands readily available is helpful for both beginners and experienced users. Many application software packages include keyboard templates.

Summary of Personal Computer Software Applications

In this chapter, you have learned about user interfaces and several widely used personal computer applications. The chapter covered the learning aids and support tools available for applications software. Knowledge about these topics increases your computer literacy and helps you to understand how personal computers are being used.

Figure 2-38c
Trade books are available for all popular software applications.

Figure 2-38d
Keyboard templates give you quick reference to software commands.

COMPUTERS AT WORK

Productivity Software Use High in Business

According to a recent report, more than $2 billion of productivity software applications are sold each year. By far, the largest user of this software is business, although home use is increasing. In a survey of 1,000 large businesses, nearly 100% of the companies said they used word processing and spreadsheet software. Close behind at approximately 95% are four applications; database, presentation graphics, communications, and electronic mail. Rounding out the applications were desktop publishing at 84%, project management at 72%, and personal information management at 48%. A survey of smaller businesses ranked the applications in the same order with slightly lower percentages. These results make it clear that productivity software is an essential part of business. Companies and individuals are turning to these software applications to work efficiently and become more productive. Project management is one of the fastest growing applications. Nowadays, practically every manager is a project manager. Likewise, many individuals are now using personal information management (PIM) software to manage their day-to-day activities.

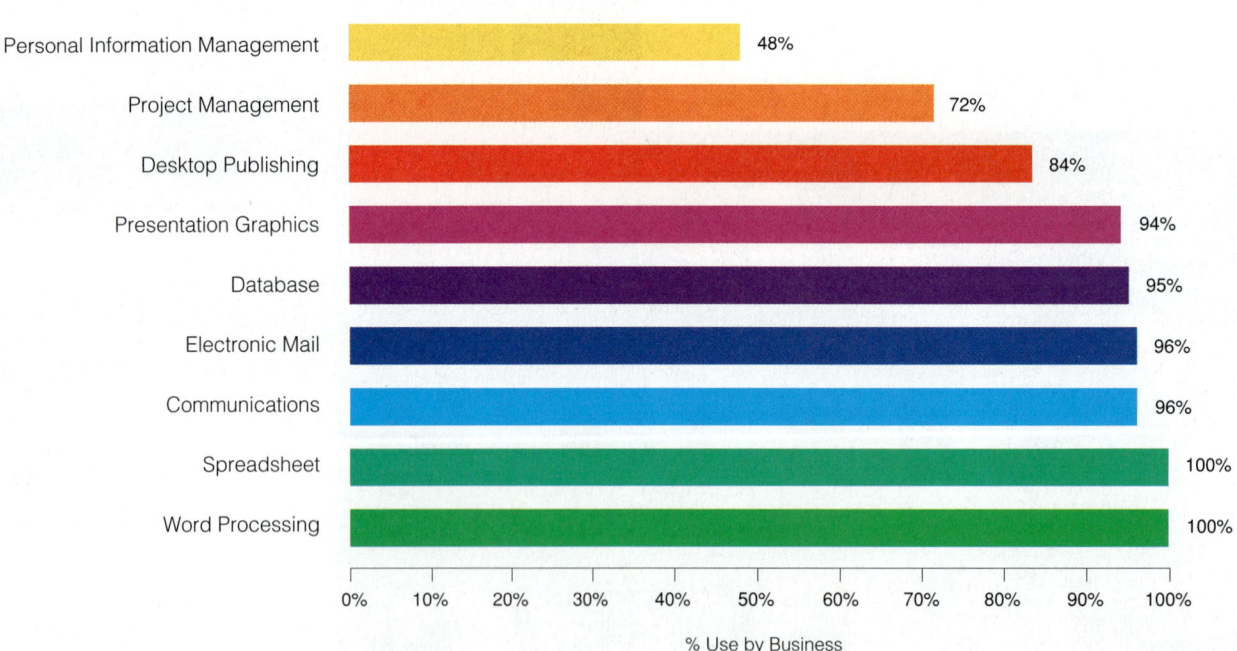

Figure 2-39

IN THE FUTURE

Will There Eventually Be Only One Software Superapplication?

Some people believe that individual software applications such as word processing and spreadsheets will eventually be replaced by a single *super*application that has the combined features of today's separate packages. They believe that the current software applications technology will become more standardized and thus easier to use for different document tasks. Some describe this evolution as a switch from application-oriented computing to document-oriented computing. The idea is that you shouldn't have to worry about what your document might contain before you start working on it. Even though the document may contain text, graphics, a spreadsheet, a chart, sound, or video, the necessary tools should be available as you need them.

Many worry that the trend toward superapplications will lead to less competition in the productivity software industry. Individual application developers will have a hard time competing against suites of applications that offer the user a common interface and one-call support. However, others see a continuing market for applications and individual tools that can be integrated with the superapplication. The same standardization that will enable the individual applications to be combined will enable independent developers to create tools that can replace or be added to the tools of the superapplication. For example, an artist may want a more powerful illustration tool than the one that comes with the superapplication. A salesperson who calls on five customers per day may want a more powerful personal information manager than a salesperson who makes one sales call per week. Other tools, such as a dictionary or a thesaurus, may be customized for specific professions such as law or medicine.

The trend toward the so-called superapplication was started with integrated software. Software suites with common toolbars and menus are the second step. How long will it be before we see ads for DocumentPerfect 1.0?

Figure 2-40

What You Should Know

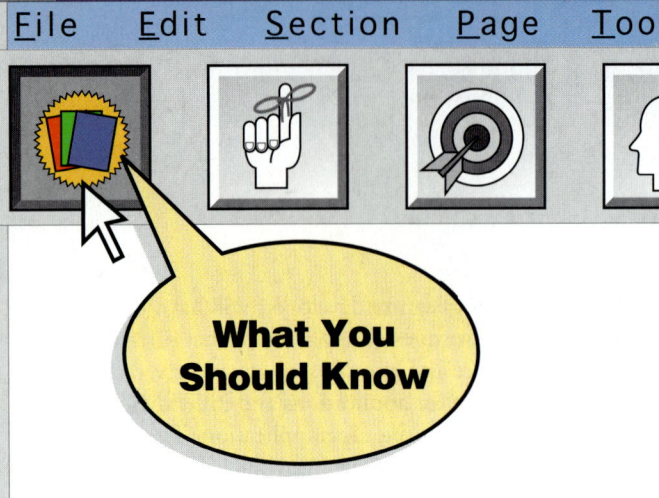

1. Applications that help people perform their work more efficiently are sometimes referred to as **productivity software**.

2. A **user interface** is the way the user tells the software what to do and the way the computer displays information and processing options to the user. A **graphical user interface** (GUI) combines text and graphics to make software easier to use. Graphical user interfaces include several common features such as icons, windows, menus, and buttons.

3. **Icons** are pictures, or symbols, used to represent processing options. A **window** is a rectangular area of the screen that is used to present information. The term Windows refers to **Microsoft Windows**, the most popular graphical user interface for personal computers. A **menu** is a list of options from which the user can choose. In a graphical user interface, menus often contain a list of related **commands**, or instructions, that cause the computer software to perform a specific action. A **button** is an icon that, when selected, causes a specific action to take place.

4. **Word processing** involves the use of a computer to produce or modify documents that consist primarily of text. Although most people perform word processing using personal computers or larger computer systems that can also be used for other applications, **dedicated word processing systems**, that can only be used for word processing, also exist.

5. Producing a document using word processing usually involves the following steps: creating, editing, formatting, printing, and saving.

6. Creating a word processing document entails entering text, usually by using the keyboard. Key word processing features used during this step include **word wrap**, **scrolling**, and moving the **cursor**.

7. **Editing** is the process of making changes in the content of a document. Word processing editing features include **cut** (which electronically places text in a temporary storage location called the **Clipboard**), **paste**, **copy**, **insert**, **delete**, **search**, and **replace**. Other editing features include using a **spelling checker**, **thesaurus**, and **grammar checker**.

8. To **format** means to change the appearance of a document. Word processing features that can be used to format a document include **fonts**, a specific combination of **typeface** and **point** size, and **styles**, such as **bold**, *italic,* or **underline**. Formatting can also involve setting **margins**, changing **justification** or **alignment**, using **full justification**, altering the **spacing** between characters (using **monospacing** or **proportional spacing**), and adjusting **line spacing**. Most word processors can arrange text in columns, organize information in tables, and incorporate graphics. Word processors can also use a **border** or **shading**, and create **headers** and **footers**. A **style sheet** lets you save font and format information so it can be applied to new documents.

9. Most word processors give the user many printing options including number and copies of pages, **portrait** or **landscape orientation**, and **print preview**.

10. **Desktop publishing** (DTP) software allows users to design and produce professional looking documents that contain both text and graphics.

11. DTP software focuses on **page composition** and **layout**, sometimes called **page makeup**, which is the process of arranging text and graphics on a document page. The text and graphics used by a DTP program are frequently imported from other software packages. DTP documents often make use of previously created art, called **clip art**.

12. All DTP programs display information on the screen exactly as it will look when printed, a capability called **WYSIWYG** (an acronym from What You See Is What You Get).

13. The capability to print DTP documents relies on a **page definition language**, such as **PostScript**, which describes the document to be printed in language the printer can understand.

14. **Spreadsheet software** allows you to organize numeric data in a worksheet or table format called an **electronic spreadsheet** or spreadsheet.

15. Within a spreadsheet, data is organized vertically in **columns** and horizontally in **rows**. The intersection where a column and row meet is called a **cell**.

16. Cells may contain three types of data: **labels** (text), **values** (numbers), and **formulas** that perform calculations on the data in the spreadsheet and display the resulting value. **Functions** are stored formulas that perform common calculations. When formulas are copied to another cell, the formula can be automatically updated to the new location (**relative referencing**) or continue to refer to the same cell locations (**absolute referencing**).

17. A spreadsheet's capability to recalculate when data is changed, sometimes called **what-if analysis**, makes it a valuable tool for decision making.

18. A standard feature of spreadsheet packages is the capability to turn numeric data into a **chart** that graphically shows the relationship of numerical data. The types of charts provided by spreadsheet packages are sometimes called **analytical graphics** or **business graphics**, and most are variations on three basic chart types: **line charts**, **bar charts**, and **pie charts**.

19. A **database** refers to a collection of data that is stored in files. **Database software** allows you to create a database and to retrieve, manipulate, and update the data that you store in it.

20. A **file** is a collection of related data that is organized in records. Each **record** contains a collection of related facts called **fields**. A field can contain any of the following types of information: **alphanumeric**, **numeric**, **currency**, **date**, or **memo**.

21. Comparing data entered against a predefined format is called **validation** and is an important feature of database programs.

22. The capability to retrieve database information in a report, called a **query**, based on criteria specified by the user is one of the more powerful features of a database.

23. **Presentation graphics software** allows the user to create documents called **slides** that are used in making presentations before a group to help communicate information more effectively.

24. Some of the features included with most presentation graphics packages include: numerous chart types, three-dimensional effects, special effects, color control, and image libraries. In addition to slides, presentation graphics packages create outlines, notes pages, and audience handouts. Presentation graphics packages also include slide sorters to help organize and present the slides.

25. **Data communications software** is used to transmit data from one computer to another. Features that most data communications software packages include are: a dialing directory of phone numbers, automatic redial, automatic answer, and the capability to send or receive one or more data files.

26. Communications software is frequently used by employees who are away from the office. It is also used to access online services for news, weather, financial, and travel information.

27. **Electronic mail software**, also called **E-mail**, allows users to send messages to and receive messages from other computer users. Although E-mail is primarily used within private organizations, several communications companies and online services have established public E-mail capabilities.

28. **Personal information management** (**PIM**) **software** helps users keep track of the miscellaneous bits of personal information that each of us deals with every day. The category can be applied to programs that offer any of the following capabilities: appointment calendars, outliners, electronic notepads, data managers, and text retrieval.

29. **Project management software** allows users to plan, schedule, track, and analyze the events, resources, and costs of a project.

30. **Integrated software** refers to packages that combine applications such as word processing, spreadsheet, and database into a single, easy-to-use set of programs. The applications have a consistent look and feel and the capability to pass data quickly from one application to another. Similar to integrated software are software **suites**; individual applications packaged in the same box and sold for a price that is significantly less than buying the applications individually.

31. Several learning aids and support tools are available to help you learn to use an application package including: **tutorials**, **online help**, **trade books**, and **keyboard templates**.

Terms to Remember

absolute referencing (2.15)
alignment (2.8)
analytical graphics (2.16)

bar chart (2.16)
bold (2.7)
border (2.8)
business graphics (2.16)
button (2.3)

cell (2.12)
chart (2.16)
clip art (2.11)
Clipboard (2.6)
column (2.12)
command (2.3)
copy (2.6)
currency (2.19)
cursor (2.5)
cut (2.6)

data communications software (2.22)
database (2.18)
database software (2.18)
date (2.19)
dedicated word processing system (2.4)
delete (2.6)
desktop publishing (DTP) software (2.10)

E-mail (2.23)
editing (2.6)
electronic mail software (2.23)
electronic spreadsheet (2.12)

field (2.18)
file (2.18)
font (2.7)
footer (2.9)
format (2.7)
formula (2.12)

full justification (2.8)
functions (2.12)

grammar checker (2.7)
graphical user interface (GUI) (2.2)

header (2.9)

icon (2.3)
insert (2.6)
integrated software (2.25)

justification (2.8)

keyboard template (2.27)

label (2.12)
landscape (2.9)
line chart (2.16)
line spacing (2.8)

margins (2.8)
memo (2.19)
menu (2.3)
Microsoft Windows (2.3)
monospacing (2.8)

numeric (2.19)

online help (2.27)

page composition and layout (2.10)
page definition language (2.11)
page makeup (2.10)
paste (2.6)
personal information management (PIM) software (2.24)
pie chart (2.16)
point (2.7)
portrait (2.9)
PostScript (2.11)
presentation graphics software (2.20)

print preview (2.9)
productivity software (2.2)
project management software (2.25)
proportional spacing (2.8)

query (2.19)

record (2.18)
relative referencing (2.15)
replace (2.6)
row (2.12)

scrolling (2.5)
search (2.6)
shade (2.8)
slides (2.20)
spacing (2.8)
spelling checker (2.6)
spreadsheet (2.12)
spreadsheet software (2.12)
style (2.7)
style sheet (2.9)
suites (2.26)

thesaurus (2.7)
trade books (2.27)
tutorials (2.27)
typeface (2.7)

user interface (2.2)

validation (2.19)
values (2.12)

what-if analysis (2.16)
window (2.3)
word processing software (2.4)
word wrap (2.4)
WYSIWYG (2.11)

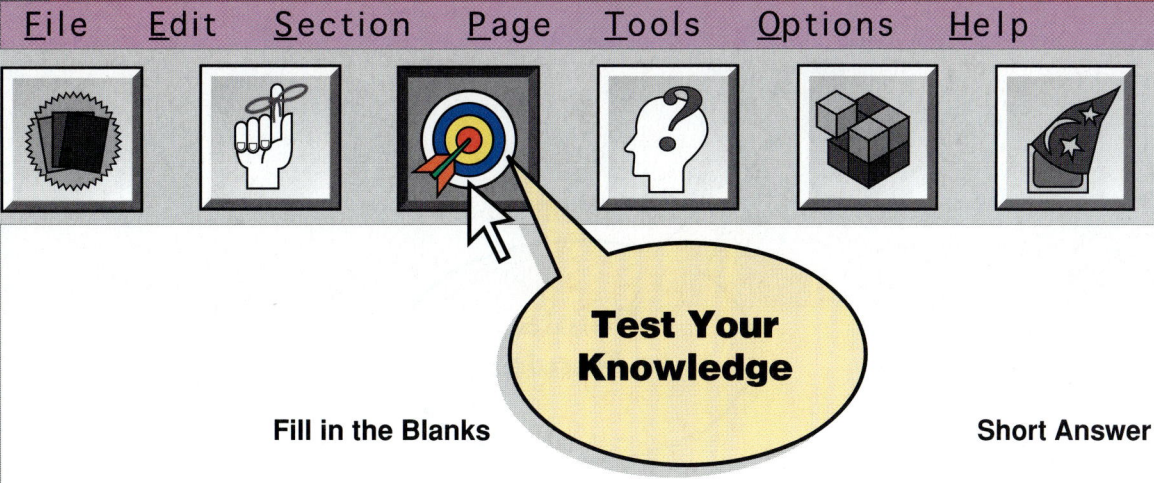

Fill in the Blanks

1. The nine most widely used personal computer software packages are: _____, _____, _____, _____, _____, _____, _____, _____, and _____.

2. Applications that help people perform their work more efficiently are sometimes referred to as _____.

3. A(n) _____ is the way the user tells the software what to do and the way the computer displays information and processing options to the user.

4. _____ refers to packages that combine applications such as word processing, spreadsheet, and database into a single, easy-to-use set of programs.

5. Four learning aids and support tools available for application users are: _____, _____, _____, and _____.

Short Answer

1. What is productivity software? Briefly explain why each of the nine widely used personal computer software applications described in this chapter can be considered productivity software.

2. What is a graphical user interface (GUI)? Describe the several common features included in most graphical user interfaces.

3. How is word processing software different from desktop publishing software (DTP)? Describe some of the major features of each type of software. In what way are word processing software and desktop publishing software used together?

4. What is the purpose of spreadsheet software? Briefly describe an electronic spreadsheet. How can a spreadsheet be a valuable tool for business decision making?

5. How is presentation graphics similar to analytical graphics? How are they different? Briefly describe the materials that can be created with presentation graphics packages. In what way do presentation graphics packages help communicate information more effectively?

Label the Figure

Instructions: The figure on the right shows Productivity Software Use. In the spaces provided label the bars.

Productivity Software Use

- 48%
- 72%
- 84%
- 94%
- 95%
- 96%
- 96%
- 100%
- 100%

% Use by Business

1

Many people believe that word processing software greatly improves the quality of written material by making it easier to create, edit, and print documents. Some word processing software even provides templates–patterns or blueprints for a document–that can be used to produce reports, memos, cover letters, resumes, legal pleadings, even letters to mom! Yet, other people argue that word processing software has become a crutch, making it unnecessary for students to learn the rudiments and nuances of language. These people feel that much of the work produced with word processors is indeed "processed," lacking the beauty, artistry, and individuality of great literature. What effect do you think word processing software has on written communication? Does it result in better work or simply more correct mediocre work? What word processing features, if any, do you feel are particularly valuable to an author?

2

Johann Guttenberg's invention of printing from moveable type had a profound impact on Western thought, making books that were previously available only to a privileged elite accessible to a much wider audience, thereby facilitating the distribution of knowledge. Will desktop publishing (DTP) software have a similar impact? Will previously unpublished writers use desktop publishing software to produce professional looking works that are widely circulated? What effect, if any, do you think desktop publishing will have on the ability of people to produce and gain access to material that reflects unconventional, or not generally accepted, ideas?

3

Your Aunt Agatha has offered to buy you some computer software for your birthday. Because she places a great deal of importance on organization (her socks are stored in alphabetical order by color), she will purchase only database software or personal information management software. How could you use both types of software now? How could you use both types of software in the future? If Aunt Agatha asks you which type of software you would rather have, what would you answer? Why?

4

An increasing number of employees are working at home, using data communications software to transmit data from their personal computer to a computer in the central office. What do you think are the advantages of working at home? What are the disadvantages? Do you feel a worker is likely to be more productive at home or in the office? If you could attend school at home, communicating with your teachers through your personal computer, would you? Why or why not?

5

A woman was once fired when she used her office electronic mail system to complain about her boss. Although she felt her E-mail conversations were private and would not be monitored, she learned, to her chagrin, that she was wrong. Do you think employers have the right to "listen in" to electronic mail conversations? Why or why not? If you "overheard" a fellow employee criticizing your boss on her E-mail system, would you tell your boss? What if you heard the same employee planning a theft of company products? Where do you draw the line?

6

One of the catch phrases in education today is "learning styles," the belief that different people learn things best in different ways. How do you learn things most effectively? Of the four learning aids described in this chapter (tutorials, online help, trade books, and keyboard templates), which fit your learning style best? Why?

Out and About

1. Unlike a graphical user interface, which combines text and graphics, a text interface uses only text, or commands, to communicate with the computer. Many software packages have one version written for use with a graphical user interface (such as Microsoft Windows) and another written for use with a text interface (such as DOS). Visit a computer store and find a software package that has a version written for both types of interfaces (such as WordPerfect for Windows and WordPerfect for DOS). Try out each version. How are they similar? How are they different? Which version is easier to learn? Why? If you were going to buy this software package, would you buy the version used with the graphical user interface or the version used with the text interface? Why?

2. Interview someone who regularly uses one of the productivity tools discussed in this chapter in the course of his or her work to find out his or her feelings about the software. For what purpose is the software used? Why does this person use the particular software package? What does he or she like about the software? What does the individual dislike? How did the person learn to use the software? If free to choose another software package to perform the same task, would this person choose one? Why or why not?

3. Many bookstores and software vendors carry trade books that can help users learn the features of personal computer application packages. Pick a productivity tool, such as spreadsheet software, and visit a bookstore or software vendor to survey the trade books on that tool. For what particular spreadsheet package (e.g., Lotus 1-2-3, Excel, or Quattro Pro) are the most titles available? How difficult do you think it would be to learn each software package using the available trade books? Which trade book do you think is the best? Why? If you were going to purchase a software package solely on the basis of the available trade books, which package would you buy? Why?

4. Make a list of the features listed in this chapter that are provided by word processing or spreadsheet software. Visit a computer vendor and compare two word processing or spreadsheet packages in terms of the features you have listed. Which package is easier to learn? Why? Once you have learned it, which package allows you to do more? If you were to purchase one of the two packages, which would you buy? Why?

5. Do some research on presentations. Make a list of the characteristics of effective presentations, in order from most important to least important. Which of these characteristics can be enhanced through the use of presentation graphics software? How much of a difference in the overall quality of a presentation do you think presentation graphics software can make? Do you think presentation graphics are more helpful in certain presentations than in others? If you had to give a presentation on your favorite subject, would you like to use presentation graphics software? Why or why not?

6. Uncle Ulysses has agreed to buy you an integrated software package of your choice. Visit a software vendor and compare integrated software packages. Which would you ask Uncle Ulysses to buy? Why? If Uncle Ullysses is willing to buy any applications, or a software suite, that are the same price or less than the integrated software package, which would you prefer? Why?

In the Lab

 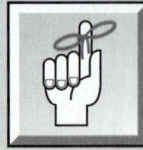    

Windows Labs

1 Creating a Word Processing Document With Program Manager on the screen, double-click the Accessories group icon. Double-click the Write program-item icon to start the Write application. Click the Maximize button in the upper right corner of the Write window to maximize it. Type the first three paragraphs on page 2.4 under the heading Word Processing Software as shown in *Figure 2-41*. To indent the first line of each paragraph, press the TAB key. Only press the ENTER key to begin a new paragraph. Do not bold any words in the paragraphs. At the end of the third paragraph, press the ENTER key twice and type your name.

To make corrections in your document, use the mouse to move the I-beam to the location of the error; then click the mouse to move the insertion point to the error. To erase to the left of the insertion point, press the BACKSPACE key; to erase to the right of the insertion point, press the DELETE key. To insert character(s), move the insertion point immediately to the left of the point of insertion and begin typing.

When your document is correct, save it by inserting a formatted diskette in drive A, choosing the Save command from the File menu, typing a:win2-1 and choosing the OK button. With your printer turned on, print the document by choosing the Print command from the File menu. Close Write by double-clicking its Control-menu box.

2 Formatting a Word Processing Document Start Write as described in Windows Lab 1 and insert your formatted diskette in drive A. Open the document you created in Windows Lab 1 by choosing the Open command from the File menu, typing a:win2-1 in the File Name box, and choosing the OK button. Maximize the Write window.

With the insertion point in the upper left corner of the document, press the ENTER key twice. Position the insertion point back in the upper left corner of the window. Select the Character menu and choose the Enlarge Font command. Choose the Enlarge Font command from the Character menu a second time. Type WORD PROCESSING SOFTWARE. With the insertion point in the title, select the Paragraph menu. Choose the Centered command to center it.

Drag the mouse over the first three words (Word processing software) in the second sentence. Select the Character menu and choose the Bold command. Drag the mouse from the first character in the first paragraph through the last character in the last paragraph to highlight the three paragraphs of text. Select the Paragraph menu and choose the Double Space command to double-space the document *(Figure 2-42)*. Click anywhere in the document to remove the highlight. Practice using the scroll bar to scroll through the document.

Save the document by choosing the Save As command from the File menu. When the Save As dialog box displays, type a:win2-2 in the File Name box and choose the OK button. Print the document. Close Write by double-clicking its Control-menu box.

3 Creating a Drawing With Program Manager on the screen, double-click the Accessories group icon. Double-click the Paintbrush program-item icon. Maximize

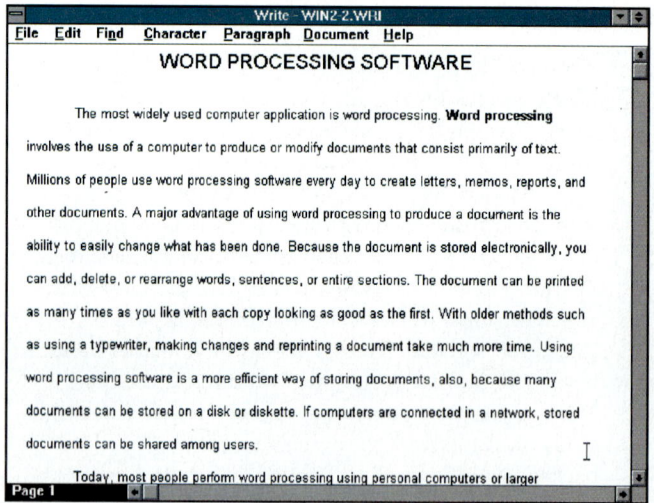

Figure 2-41

Figure 2-42

the Paintbrush window.

Change the background color to royal blue by pointing to the color royal blue in the palette at the bottom of the Paintbrush window and clicking the *right* mouse button. Change the foreground color to yellow by pointing to the color yellow in the palette and clicking the *left* mouse button. Select the File menu and choose the New command. The screen is now royal blue; the drawing you make will be in yellow.

Click the Brush tool. Move the mouse pointer into the blue window. Use the mouse pointer to write your name in cursive so it is similar to *Figure 2-43*. Drag the mouse through your entire name, or release the mouse in between each character. If you make a mistake, choose the Undo command from the Edit menu to erase your last draw.

Save the drawing to your diskette in drive A by choosing the Save command from the File menu. Type a:win2-3 in the File Name box. What extension does Paintbrush attach to its files? Print the drawing by choosing the Print command from the File menu. Close Paintbrush by double-clicking its Control-menu box.

4 Using Help   With Program Manager on the screen, select the Help menu and choose the How to Use Help command. Read the contents of the window *(Figure 2-44)*. Print the contents of the window by choosing the Print Topic command from the File menu. Point to the word *topic,* which has a green dotted underline beneath it and click. What is the definition of the word *topic*? Click the Help Basics topic. Read and print the contents of the Help Basics window. Click the Back button. Close the Help window by double-clicking its Control-menu box.

DOS Labs

1 Creating a Text Document   At the DOS prompt, type edit and press the ENTER key. Press the ESC key when the Welcome message appears. Type the title and first three paragraphs on page 2.4. Press the ENTER key at the end of each line on page 2.4. Press the ENTER key twice between paragraphs. At the end of the third paragraph, press the ENTER key twice and type your name. To make corrections, use the arrow keys to move the cursor to the error. To erase to the left of the cursor, press the BACKSPACE key; to erase to the right of the cursor, press the DELETE key. When your document is correct, insert a formatted diskette in drive A. Press the ALT key to activate the menu. Type F for File menu and S for Save. In the Save As dialog box, type a:dos2-1 as the filename. Press the ENTER key. Print the document by choosing the Print command on the File menu. Choose the Exit command on the File menu.

2 Using FastHelp   At the DOS prompt, type fasthelp and press the ENTER key to display a list of DOS commands and their descriptions. Press the ENTER key to continue through the list. Answer these questions: (1) What is the description of FASTHELP? FORMAT? MORE? (2) Using FastHelp, how do you obtain more information on a specific command?

Online Lab

1 Viewing an Art Gallery   Using one of the two online services you selected in Chapter 1, connect to the service and perform the following tasks: (1) Search the online service for an Art or Graphics Gallery. (2) As you view the artwork, make a list of the titles of the artwork and the artists.

Figure 2-43

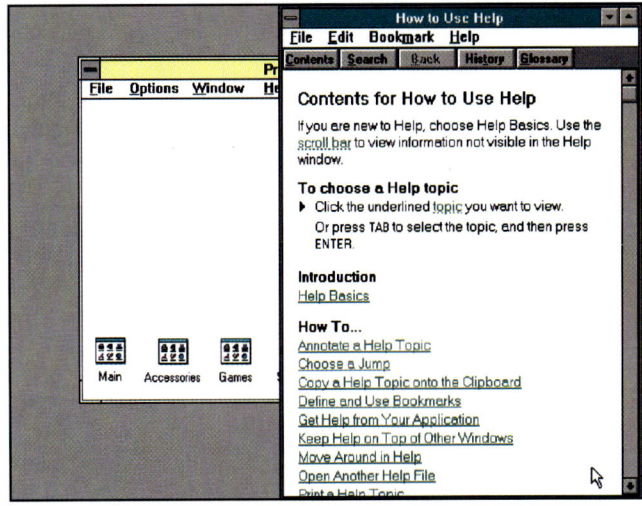

Figure 2-44

CHAPTER THREE

Input to the Computer

3

Objectives

After completing this chapter, you will be able to:

- Review the four operations of the information processing cycle: input, process, output, and storage

- Define the four types of input and how the computer uses each type

- Describe the standard features of keyboards, and explain how to use the cursor control and function keys

- Explain how a mouse works and how it is used

- Describe several input devices other than the keyboard and mouse

- Explain the three types of terminals and how they are used

- Explain multimedia input devices

- Describe procedures used to ensure data accuracy

The information processing cycle is basic to all computers, large or small. It is important that you understand this cycle, for much of your success in understanding computers and what they do depends on having an understanding or feeling for the movement of data as it flows through the information processing cycle and becomes information. This chapter discusses the information processing cycle and describes some of the devices used for input. Certain devices that can be used for both input and storage, such as disk and tape drives, are covered in the chapter on secondary storage.

Overview of the Information Processing Cycle

As you saw in Chapter 1, the information processing cycle consists of four operations: input, processing, output, and storage *(Figure 3-1)*. Regardless of the size and type of computer, these operations process data into a meaningful form called information.

The operations in the information processing cycle are carried out through the combined use of computer equipment, also called computer hardware, and computer software. The computer software, or programs, contain instructions that direct the computer equipment to perform the tasks necessary to process data into information. In the information processing cycle, the input operation must take place before any data can be processed and any information produced and stored.

Figure 3-1
A computer consists of input devices, the system unit, output devices, and secondary storage devices. This equipment, or hardware, is used to perform the operations of the information processing cycle.

What Is Input?

Input refers to the process of entering data, programs, commands, and user responses into main memory. Input also refers to the media (e.g., disks, tapes, documents) that contain these input types. These four types of input are used by a computer in the following ways:

- **Data** refers to the raw facts, including numbers, letters, words, images, and sounds that a computer receives during the input operation and processes to produce information. Although technically speaking, a single item of data should be called a *datum,* it is common and accepted usage to use the word data to represent both singular and plural. Data must be entered and stored in main memory for processing to occur. Data is the most common type of input.
- **Programs** are instructions that direct the computer to perform the necessary operations to process data into information. The program that is loaded and stored in main memory determines the processing that the computer will perform. When a program is first created it is usually input by using a keyboard. Once the program has been entered and stored on secondary storage, it can be transferred to main memory by a command.

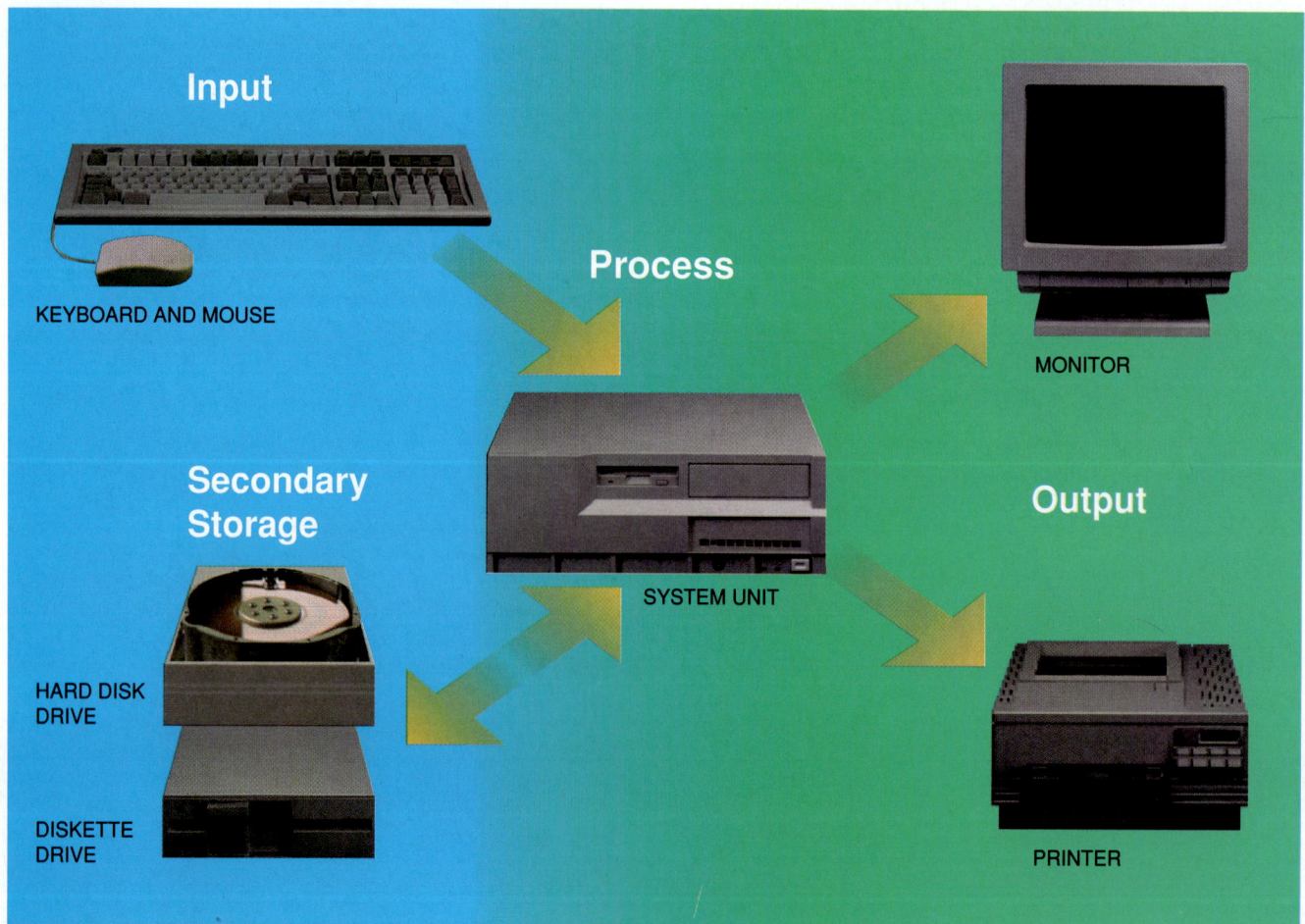

THE KEYBOARD

- **Commands** are key words and phrases that the user inputs to direct the computer to perform certain activities. Commands are usually either entered from the keyboard or selected from a list.
- **User responses** refer to the data that a user inputs to respond to a question or message from the software. One of the most common responses is to answer "Yes" or "No" to a question. Based on the answer, the computer program will perform specific actions. For example, typing the letter Y in response to the message, Do you want to save this file?, will result in the file being saved (written) to the secondary storage device.

The Keyboard

The **keyboard** is the most commonly used input device. Users input data to a computer by pressing the keys on the keyboard. Keyboards are connected to other devices that have screens such as a personal computer or a terminal. As the user enters data through the keyboard, the data displays on the screen.

Keyboards are usually similar to the one shown in *Figure 3-2*. The alphabetic keys are arranged like those on a typewriter. A **numeric keypad** is located on the right-hand side of most keyboards. The numeric keys are arranged in an adding machine or calculator format to allow you to enter numeric data rapidly.

Figure 3-2
A typical keyboard used on personal computers.

Keyboards also contain keys that can be used to position the cursor on the screen. A **cursor** is a symbol, such as an underline character, rectangle, or vertical bar, that indicates where on the screen the next character entered will appear. The keys that move the cursor are called **arrow keys or cursor control keys**. Cursor control keys have an UP ARROW (↑), a DOWN ARROW (↓), a LEFT ARROW (←), and a RIGHT ARROW (→). When you press any of these keys, the cursor moves one space in the same direction as the arrow. In addition, many keyboards contain other cursor control keys, such as the HOME key, which when you press it can send the cursor to a beginning location such as the upper left position of the screen or document. The numeric keypad can also be used to move the cursor. With most keys, if you hold them down they will automatically start to repeat.

Some computer keyboards also contain keys that can alter or edit the text displayed on the screen. For example, the INSERT and DELETE keys allow characters to be inserted into or deleted from data displayed on the screen.

Function keys are keys that can be programmed to accomplish certain tasks that will assist the user. For example, a function key may be programmed for use as a help key when using software such as a word processor. Whenever the function key is pressed, messages will appear that give helpful information about how to use the word processing software. Function keys can also save keystrokes. Sometimes several keystrokes are required to accomplish a certain task, for example, printing a document. Some application software packages are written so the user can either enter the individual keystrokes or press a function key and obtain the same result.

Status lights in the upper right corner of the keyboard indicate if the numeric keypad, capital letters, and scroll locks are turned on.

The ESCAPE (ESC) key is often used by computer software to cancel an instruction or exit from a situation. The use of the ESC key varies among software packages.

The disadvantage of using a keyboard as an input device is that training is required to use it efficiently. Users who lack typing ability are at a disadvantage because of the time they spend looking for the appropriate keys. While other input devices are appropriate in some situations, users should be encouraged to develop their keyboard skills.

Pointing Devices

Pointing devices allow the user to control an on-screen symbol called the **mouse pointer**, or **pointer**, that is usually represented by an arrow-shaped marker (↖). The pointing device is used to move the cursor to a particular location on the screen or to select available software options.

Mouse

The mouse is a unique device used with personal computers and some computer terminals to select processing options or information displayed on the screen. A **mouse** is a small, lightweight input device that easily fits in the palm of your hand *(Figure 3-3)*. You move the device across a flat surface such as a desktop to control the movement of the pointer on a screen.

The mouse is usually attached to the computer by a cable but wireless mouse devices also exist. On the bottom of the mouse is a device, usually a small ball, that senses the movement of the mouse. Electronic circuits in the mouse translate the movement of the mouse into signals that are sent to the computer. The computer uses the mouse signals to move the pointer on the screen in the same direction as the mouse *(Figure 3-4)*. When you move the mouse left on the surface of the table or desk, the pointer moves left on the screen. When you move the mouse right, the pointer moves right, and so on.

On top of the mouse are one or more buttons. By using the mouse to move the pointer on the screen and pressing the buttons on the mouse, you can perform actions such as making menu selections, editing a word processing document, and moving data from one location on the screen to another.

The primary advantage of a mouse is that it is easy to use. With a little practice, a person can use a mouse to point to locations on the screen just as easily as using a finger.

There are two disadvantages of the mouse. The first is that it requires empty desk space where it can be moved about. The second disadvantage is that the user must remove a hand from the keyboard and place it on the mouse whenever the pointer is to be moved or a command is to be given.

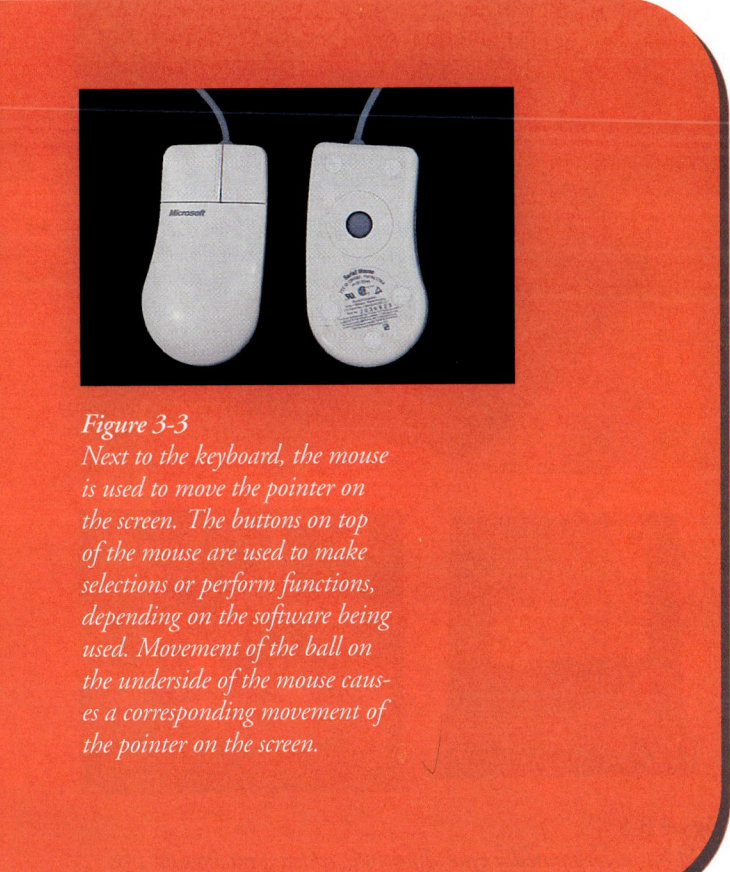

Figure 3-3
Next to the keyboard, the mouse is used to move the pointer on the screen. The buttons on top of the mouse are used to make selections or perform functions, depending on the software being used. Movement of the ball on the underside of the mouse causes a corresponding movement of the pointer on the screen.

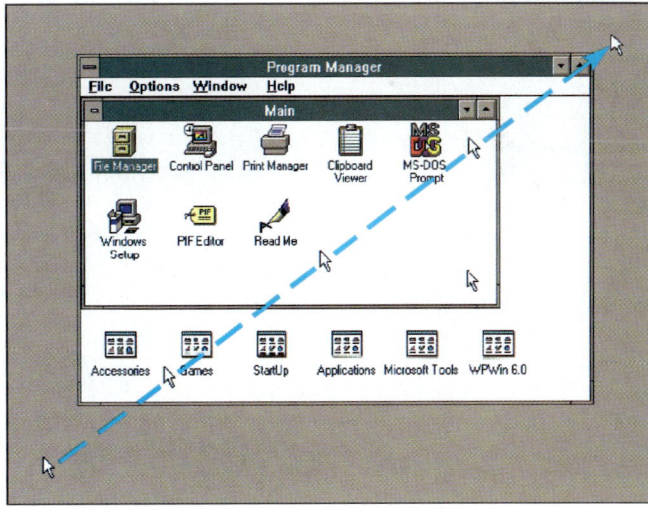

Figure 3-4
As the mouse is moved diagonally across a flat surface, the mouse pointer on the screen moves in a similar direction.

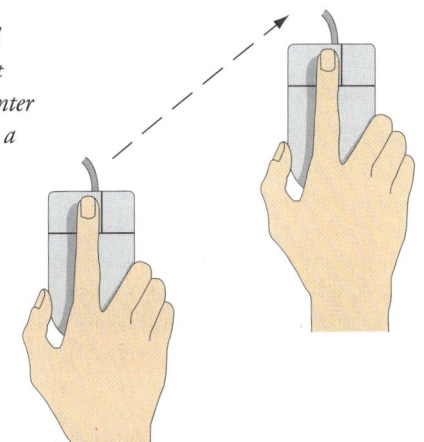

Trackball

A **trackball** is a pointing device like a mouse only with the ball on the top of the device instead of the bottom *(Figure 3-5)*. To move the pointer with a trackball, all you have to do is rotate the ball in the desired direction. With a mouse, you have to move the entire device. To accommodate movement with both the fingers and palms of a hand, the ball on top of a trackball is usually larger than the ball on the bottom of a mouse. The main advantage of a trackball over a mouse is that it doesn't require clear desk space. Smaller trackball units have been designed for use on portable computers *(Figure 3-6)*.

Joystick

A **joystick** uses the movement of a vertical stem to direct the pointer. A full-size joystick, often used with computer games, is usually large enough for the user's hand to wrap around it *(Figure 3-7)*. Full-size joysticks usually have buttons you press to activate certain events, depending on the software. Much smaller joysticks, without buttons, have been incorporated into some portable computers *(Figure 3-8)*. The small joysticks look like a long pencil eraser stuck between the keys. Pressure on the joystick from the user's finger causes the pointer to move.

Figure 3-7
Joysticks are often used with computer games to control the actions of a vehicle or player.

Figure 3-5
The trackball is like a mouse turned upside down. The user rotates the ball to move the cursor and then presses one of the keys shown at the top of the trackball.

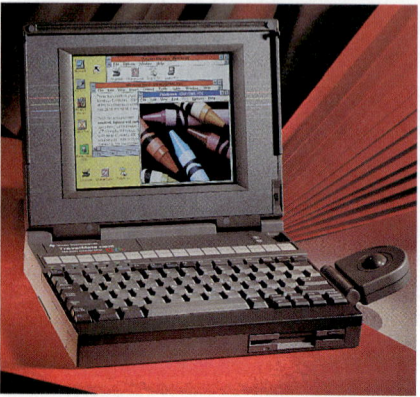

Figure 3-6
Smaller trackball units are often used on portable computers. They are attached to the side of the computer as shown on this Texas Instruments Notebook computer. Sometimes they are built into the computer case.

Figure 3-8
IBM has incorporated a type of joystick, called a trackpoint, into their line of portable computers.

Pen Input Devices

Pen input devices have become increasingly popular in recent years and may eventually be part of most, if not all, computers. Almost all of the personal digital assistant (PDA) class of personal computers use a pen. One advantage is that people who have never used a computer adapt naturally to using a pen as an input device *(Figure 3-9)*.

Pen input devices allow the user to use the pen in three ways; to input data using hand-written characters and shapes the computer can recognize, as a pointing device like a mouse to select items on the screen, and to gesture, which is a way of issuing commands.

Pen computers use special hardware and software to interpret the movement of the pen. When the pen touches the screen, it causes two layers of electrically conductive material to make contact. The computer determines the coordinates for the contact point and darkens that location on the screen. The darkened area on the screen is referred to as **ink**. Handwritten characters are converted into computer text by software that matches the shape of the hand-written character to a database of known shapes. If the software cannot recognize a particular letter, it asks the user to identify it. Most **handwriting recognition software** can be taught to recognize an individual's unique style of writing. In addition to working with character input, graphic recognition software used on pen input devices improves drawings by cleaning up uneven lines. Wavy lines can be straightened and circles can be made perfectly round. Perhaps the most natural use of the pen is as a pointing device. When used this way, the pen functions as a mouse. Pressing the pen against the screen once or twice is the same as using the buttons on a mouse.

Gestures are special symbols made with the pen that issue a command such as delete text. As shown in *Figure 3-10*, many gestures are identical to those used for manual text editing. Gestures can be more efficient than using a mouse or keyboard because they not only identify where you want to make a change but also the type of change to be made.

Pen input devices have already been adapted to many applications that were previously not computerized. Any application where a form has to be filled out is a candidate for a pen input device. One of the largest markets for pen input devices is mobile workers, who spend most of their time away from their desks or offices.

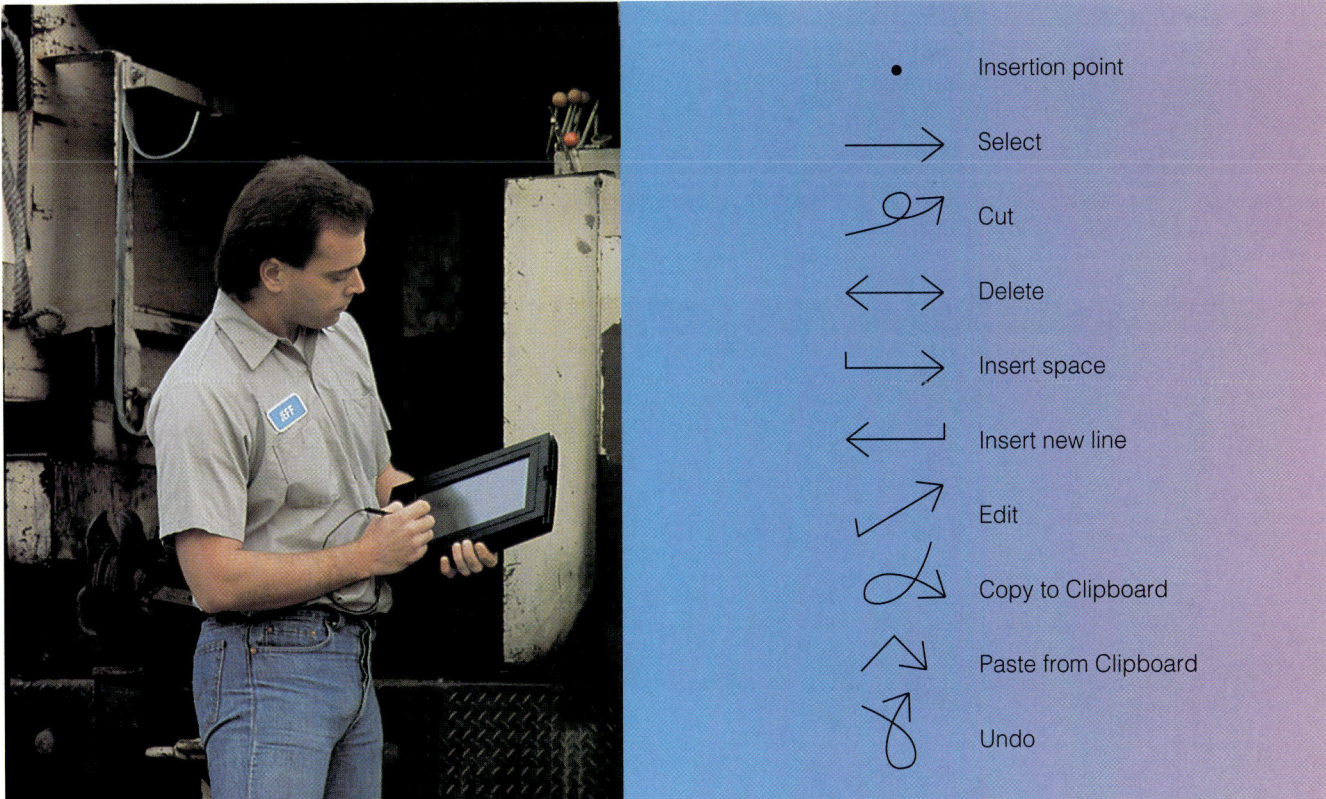

Figure 3-9
Pen input systems allow the user to use a pen to enter data or select processing options without using a keyboard. This method is easy to learn by individuals who have worked with a pencil and paper.

Figure 3-10
Gestures are a way of issuing commands with a pen. Gestures not only tell what you want done but also where you want to make a change. The arrows indicate the direction of the pen movement.

Touch Screen

A **touch screen** allows users to touch areas of the screen to enter data. They let the user interact with a computer by the touch of a finger rather than typing on a keyboard or moving a mouse. The user enters data by touching words or numbers or locations identified on the screen.

Several electronic techniques change a touch on the screen into electronic signals that are interpreted by the computer software. One technique uses beams of infrared light projected across the surface of the screen. A finger or other object touching the screen interrupts the beams, generating an electronic signal. This signal identifies the location on the screen where the touch occurred. The software interprets the signal and performs the required function.

Touch screens are not used to enter large amounts of data. They are used, however, for applications where the user must issue a command to the software to perform a particular task or must choose from a list of options. Touch screens have been successfully installed in kiosks used to provide information in hotels, airports, and other public locations *(Figure 3-11)*.

There are both advantages and disadvantages to touch screens. A significant advantage is that they are very natural to use; that is, people are used to pointing to things. With touch screens, users can point to indicate the processing they want performed by the computer. In addition, touch screens are usually easy for the user to learn. As quickly as pointing a finger, the user's request is processed. There are some disadvantages to touch screens. First, the resolution of the touching area is not precise. Thus, while a user can point to a box or a fairly large area on the screen and the electronics can determine the location of the touch, it is difficult to point to a single character in a word processing application, for example, and indicate that the character should be deleted. In cases such as these, a keyboard or mouse is easier to use. A second disadvantage is that after a period of reaching for the screen, the user's arm could become tired.

Figure 3-11
Touch screens are frequently used for information kiosks. Users touch the screen and receive information about the chosen topic.

Light Pen

A **light pen** is used by touching it on the display screen to create or modify graphics *(Figure 3-12)*. A light cell in the tip of the pen senses light from the screen to determine the pen's location. The light pen can be used to select processing options or to draw on the screen.

Digitizer

A **digitizer** converts points, lines, and curves from a sketch, drawing, or photograph to digital signals and transmits them to a computer *(Figure 3-13)*. The user indicates the data to be input by pressing one or more buttons on the hand-held digitizer device.

Graphics Tablet

A **graphics tablet** works in a manner similar to a digitizer, but it also contains unique characters and commands that can be automatically generated by the person using the tablet *(Figure 3-14)*.

Figure 3-12
The light pen can be used to make selections or to draw directly on the screen. A light cell in the tip of the pen can detect where on the screen the pen is touching. Light pens are often used in engineering applications.

Figure 3-13
Digitizers are used to create original drawings or to trace and reproduce existing drawings. When buttons on the hand-held device are pushed, the location on the drawing is input to the computer. Special software can link the points together to create a drawing that can be modified.

Figure 3-14
The color template on the graphics tablet allows the user to select processing options by placing a hand-held device over the appropriate location on the tablet and pressing a button.

Source Data Automation

Source data automation refers to procedures and equipment designed to make the input process more efficient by eliminating the manual entry of data. Instead of a person entering data using a keyboard, source data automation equipment captures data directly from its original form such as an invoice or an inventory tag. The original form is called a **source document**. In addition to making the input process more efficient, source data automation usually results in a higher input accuracy rate. The following section describes some of the equipment used for source data automation, which is sometimes called **source data collection**.

Image Scanner

An **image scanner**, sometimes called a **page scanner**, is an input device that electronically captures an entire page of text or images such as photographs or art work *(Figure 3-15)*. The scanner converts the text or image on the original document into digital information that can be stored on a disk and processed by the computer. The digitized information can be printed or displayed separately or merged into another document such as a newsletter. Hand-held devices that scan a portion of a page are also available *(Figure 3-16)* as well as color scanners.

Image processing systems use scanners to capture and electronically file documents such as legal documents or documents with signatures or drawings. These systems are like electronic filing cabinets that allow users to rapidly access and review exact reproductions of the original documents *(Figure 3-17)*.

Figure 3-15
The scanner inputs text, graphics, or photographs for use in word processing or desktop publishing applications.

Figure 3-16
A hand-held scanner enters text or graphics less than a page wide. Software allows you to join separately scanned items to make up a complete page.

Figure 3-17
Image processing systems record and store an exact copy of a document. These systems are often used by insurance companies that may need to refer to any of hundreds of thousands of documents.

Optical Recognition

Optical recognition devices use a light source to read codes, marks, and characters and convert them into digital data that can be processed by a computer.

OPTICAL CODES

Optical codes use a pattern or symbols to represent data. The most common optical code is the bar code. A **bar code** consists of a set of vertical lines and spaces of different widths. The bar code is usually either printed on the product package or attached to the product with a label or tag. The bar code reader uses the light pattern from the bar code lines to identify the item. Of the several different types of bar codes, the most familiar is the **universal product code** (UPC). The UPC bar code, used for grocery and retail items, can be translated into a ten-digit number that identifies the product manufacturer and product number *(Figure 3-18)*.

Optical code scanning equipment includes light guns that are aimed at the code and wands that are passed over the code. Grocery stores often use stationary units set in a counter. *Figure 3-19* shows several different types of bar code readers.

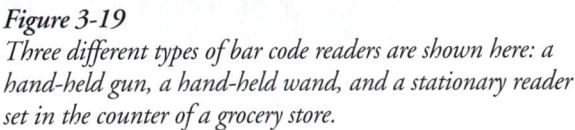

Figure 3-18
Bar codes are a type of optical code found on most grocery and retail items. The universal product code (UPC) bar code is the most common. The numbers printed at the bottom identify the manufacturer and the product and can be used to input the item if the bar code reader fails.

Figure 3-19
Three different types of bar code readers are shown here: a hand-held gun, a hand-held wand, and a stationary reader set in the counter of a grocery store.

OPTICAL MARK RECOGNITION

Optical mark recognition (OMR) devices are often used to process questionnaires or test answer sheets *(Figure 3-20)*. Carefully placed marks on the form indicate responses to questions that are read and interpreted by a computer program.

OPTICAL CHARACTER RECOGNITION

Optical character recognition (OCR) devices are scanners that read typewritten, computer-printed, and in some cases hand-printed characters from ordinary documents. OCR devices range from large machines that automatically read thousands of documents per minute to hand-held wands.

An OCR device scans the shape of a character, compares it with a predefined shape stored in memory, and converts the character into the corresponding computer code. The standard OCR typeface, called OCR-A is illustrated in *Figure 3-21*. The characters are read easily by both people and machines. OCR-B is a set of standard characters widely used in Europe and Japan.

OCR is frequently used for **turn-around documents**, documents designed to be returned *(turned around)* to the organization that created them. Examples of such documents are billing statements from credit card companies and department stores. The portion of the statement that you send back with your payment has your account number, total balance, and payment information printed in optical characters.

Figure 3-20
Optical mark recognition devices are often used for processing questionnaires and test answer sheets. For test scores, the reader marks the incorrect answers and reports the number of correct answers and the average score of all tests.

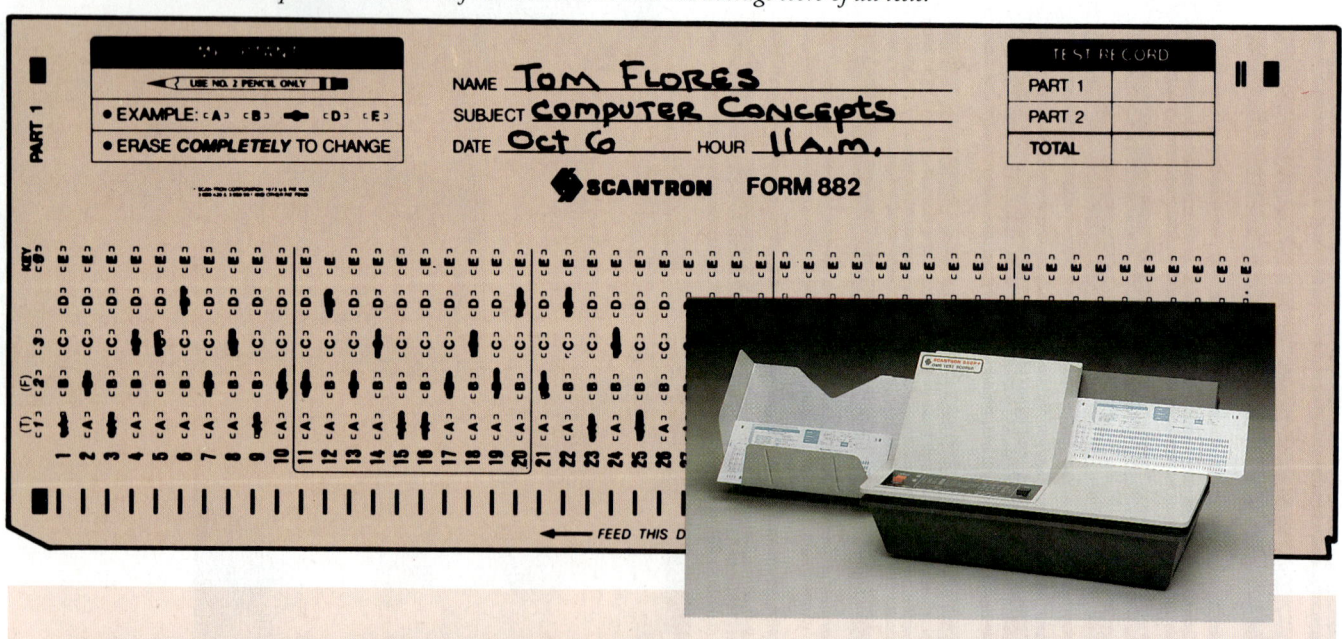

Figure 3-21
In this portion of the OCR-A character set, notice how the characters B and 8 and S and 5 and the number 0 and the letter O are designed differently. Thus, the reading device can easily distinguish between them.

OCR SOFTWARE

OCR software is used with image scanners to convert text images into data that can be processed by word processing software. OCR software works as follows: First the entire page of text is scanned. At this point, the page is considered a single graphic image, just like a picture, and individual words are not identified. Next, the software tries to identify individual letters and words. *Figure 3-22* shows how one OCR software package displays the status during this process. Modern OCR software has a very high success rate and can usually identify more than 98% of the scanned material. Finally, the OCR software displays the text that it could not identify. When the user makes the final corrections, the document may be saved in the word processing format of the user's choice.

Magnetic Ink Character Recognition (MICR)

Magnetic ink character recognition (MICR) characters use a special ink that is magnetized during processing. MICR is used almost exclusively by the banking industry for processing checks. Blank (unused) checks already have the bank code, account number, and check number printed in MICR characters across the bottom. When the check is processed by the bank, the amount of the check is also printed in the lower right corner *(Figure 3-23)*. Together, this information is read by MICR reader-sorter machines *(Figure 3-24 on the next page)* as part of the check-clearing process.

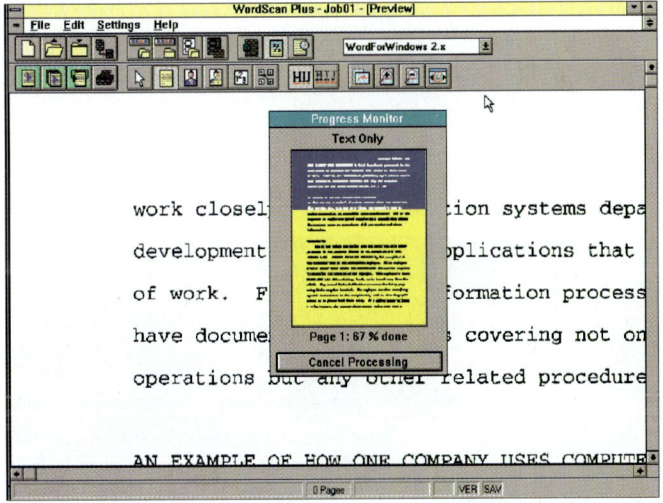

Figure 3-22 ◄
OCR software in the process of converting a page of scanned text into data that can be input to word processing software is shown in this screen. The entire page of text was converted in less than one minute; much faster than the text could be entered using the keyboard.

Figure 3-23 ▼
The MICR characters printed along the bottom edge indicate the bank, account number, and amount of the check. The amount in the lower right corner is added after the check is cashed. The other MICR numbers are preprinted on the check.

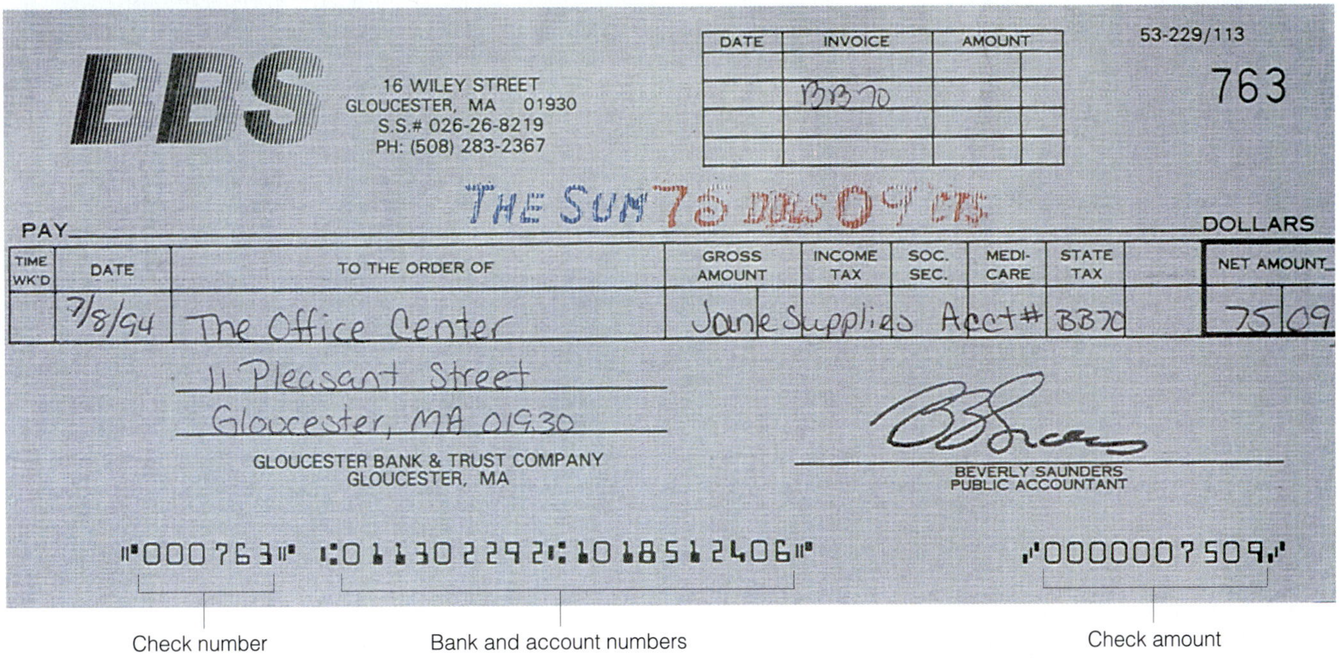

Check number   Bank and account numbers   Check amount

Data Collection Devices

Data collection devices are designed and used for obtaining data at the site where the transaction or event being reported takes place. Oftentimes, data collection equipment is used in factories, warehouses, or other locations where heat, humidity, and cleanliness are difficult to control *(Figure 3-25)*. Data collection equipment must be rugged and easy to use because it is often operated by persons whose primary task is not entering data.

Figure 3-24
This MICR reader-sorter can process more than a thousand documents per minute. After the documents are read, they are sorted into the vertical bins on the right side of the machine. The reader-sorter is connected to a computer so the data is input as the documents are read.

Figure 3-25
Data collection devices are often used in factories and warehouses where heat, humidity, and cleanliness are difficult to control.

Terminals

Terminals, sometimes called **display terminals,** or **video display terminals** (VDTs), consist of a keyboard and a screen. Terminals differ from monitors that only have a viewing screen and no keyboard.

A **dumb terminal** consists of a keyboard and a display screen that are used to enter and transmit data to or receive and display data from a computer to which it is connected. A dumb terminal has no independent processing capability or secondary storage and cannot function as a stand-alone device *(Figure 3-26)*. Dumb terminals are often connected to minicomputers, mainframes, or supercomputers.

Intelligent terminals have built-in processing capabilities and often contain not only the keyboard and screen but also secondary storage devices such as disk drives. Because of their built-in capabilities, these terminals can perform limited processing tasks when they are not communicating directly with the central computer. Intelligent terminals are also known as **programmable terminals** or **smart terminals** because they can be programmed by the user to perform many basic tasks, including arithmetic and logic operations. Personal computers are frequently used as intelligent terminals when they are connected to larger computers.

Special-purpose terminals perform specific jobs and contain features uniquely designed for use in a particular industry. The special-purpose terminal shown in *Figure 3-27* is called a point-of-sale terminal. **Point-of-sale (POS) terminals** allow data to be entered at the time and place where the transaction with a customer occurs, such as in fast-food restaurants or hotels, for example. Point-of-sale terminals serve as input to computers located at the place of business or elsewhere. The data entered is used to maintain sales records, update inventory, make automatic calculations such as sales tax, verify credit, and perform other activities associated with the sales transactions and critical to running the business. Point-of-sale terminals are designed to be easy to operate, requiring little technical knowledge. As shown in *Figure 3-27*, the keys are labeled to assist the user.

Figure 3-26
Dumb terminals have no independent processing capability and cannot function as a stand-alone device. They are usually connected to larger computer systems.

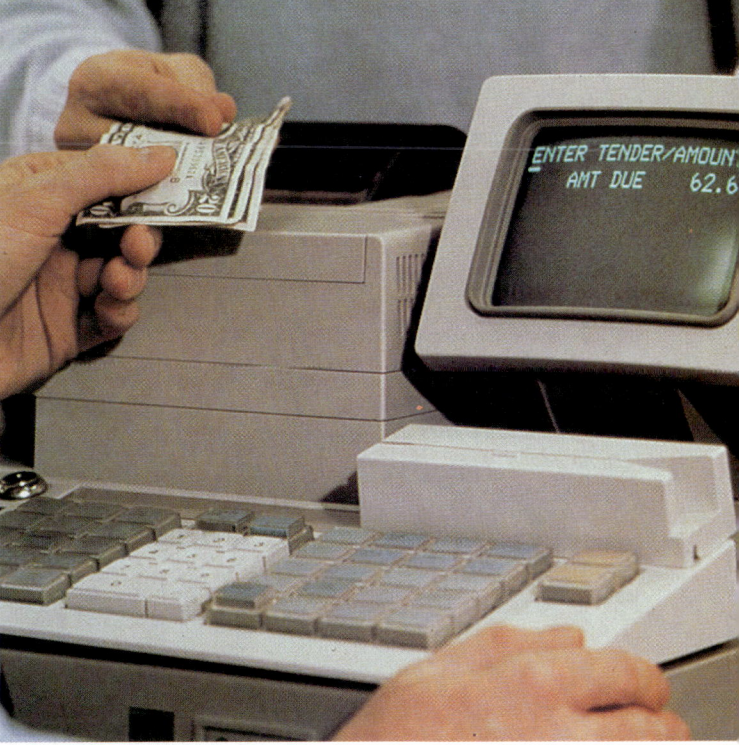

Figure 3-27
Point-of-sale terminals are usually designed for a specific type of business such as a restaurant, hotel, or retail store. Keys are labeled to assist the user in recording transactions.

Multimedia Input Devices

Multimedia is the combination of sound and images with text and graphics. To capture sound and image data, special input devices are required. For personal computers, these input devices consist primarily of electronics contained on a separate card, such as a **sound card** or **video card**, that is installed in the computer.

Sound Input

Sounds are usually recorded with a microphone connected to the sound card or by directly connecting a sound device such as an electronic music keyboard to the sound card. Sound editing software *(Figure 3-28)* allows the user to change the sound after it is recorded.

Voice Input

Voice input, sometimes referred to as speech or voice recognition, allows the user to enter data and issue commands to the computer with spoken words. Some experts think that voice input may eventually be the most common way to operate a computer. Their belief is based on the fact that people can speak much faster than they can type (approximately 200 words per minute speaking and only 40 words per minute for the average typist). In addition, speaking is a more natural means of communicating than using a keyboard, which takes some time to learn.

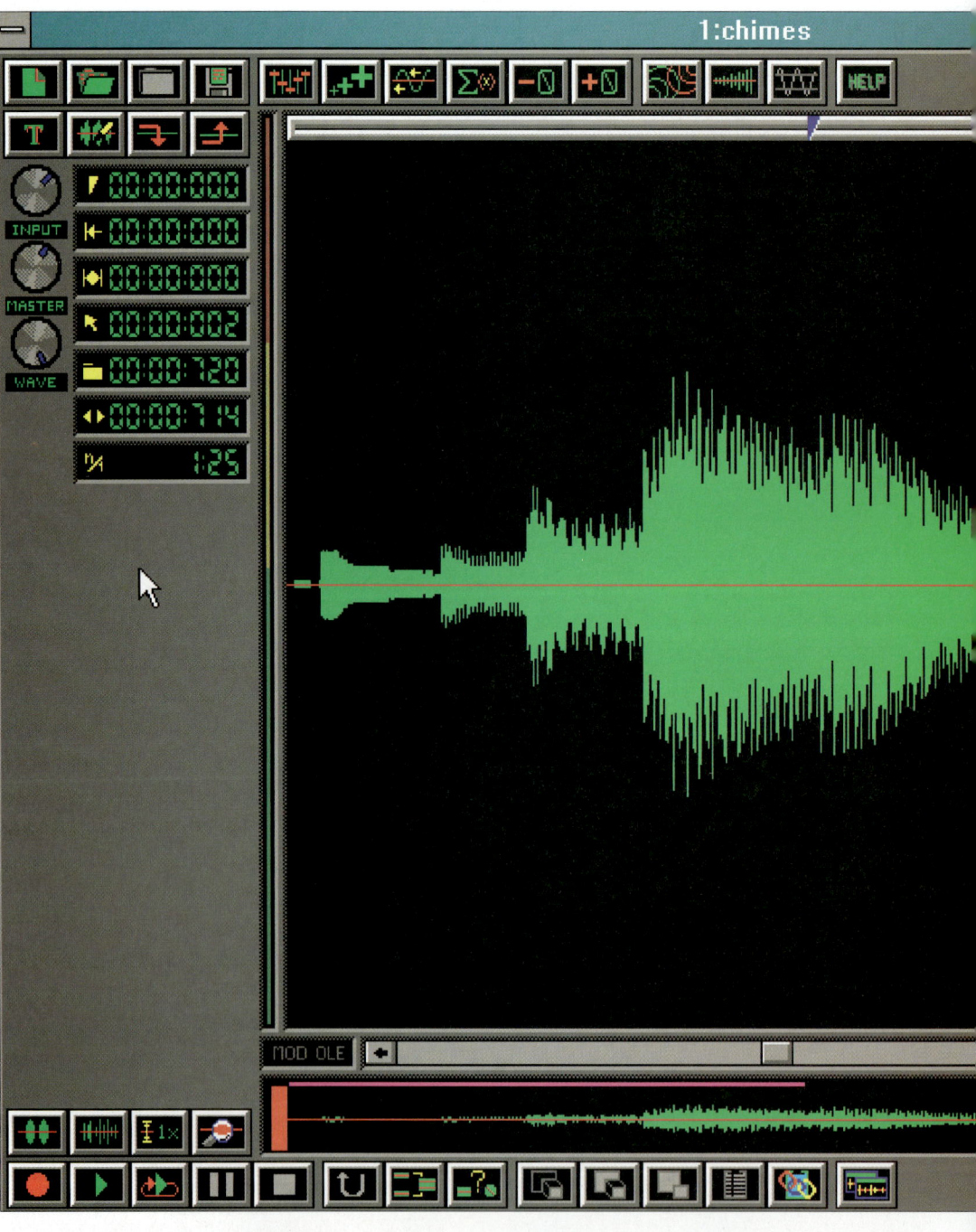

Figure 3-28
Sound editing software allows the user to change sounds that have been digitally recorded. Sounds can be duplicated, speeded up, slowed down, or have special effects such as echo or fade added. This screen represents the sound of chimes.

MULTIMEDIA INPUT DEVICES

Four areas where voice input is used are data entry, command and control, speaker recognition, and speech to text.

In many voice data entry applications, it is as if the user is verbally filling out a form. Standard questions are verbally completed, usually with a limited number of acceptable responses. For example, voice data entry systems are used for product inspections in manufacturing companies. Instead of manually recording data or using a keyboard, the inspector dictates the completed product information into a microphone. This is especially efficient when the inspector's hands and eyes must stay focused on the item being inspected.

Command and control applications use a limited vocabulary of words that cause the computer to perform a specific action such as *save* or *print* a document. Command and control applications are also used to operate certain types of industrial machinery.

Speaker recognition applications are usually security oriented such as restricting physical access to a particular area. Unless a person's voice matches a previously recorded pattern, he or she is denied entry. This type of application has been used in banks, government installations, and other high security locations.

Speech-to-text applications offer the most possibility for the widespread use of voice input. With speech-to-text applications, spoken words are immediately translated into computer text and usually displayed on the screen. One area where speech-to-text applications have been implemented is in medical reporting. Many health professionals now use speech-to-text systems to input the numerous reports that must be maintained on patients *(Figure 3-29)*.

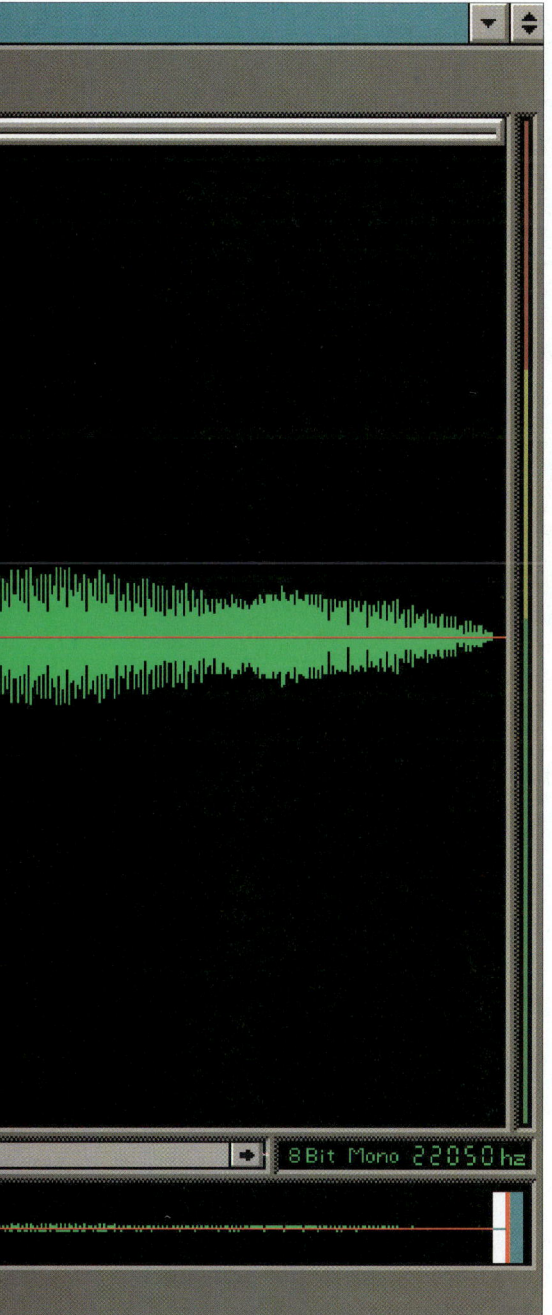

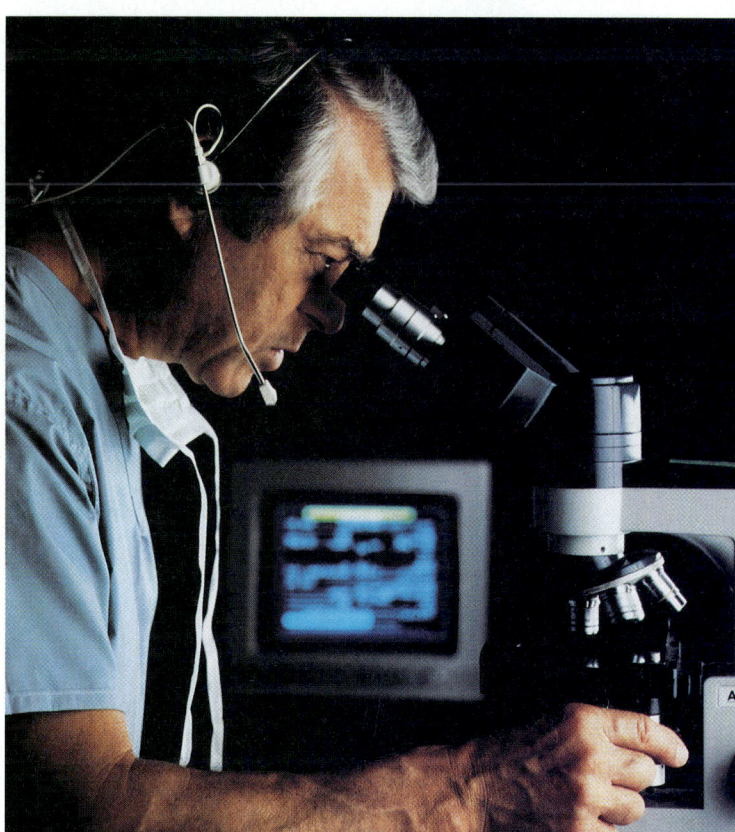

Figure 3-29
Many health care professionals use speech-to-text systems to record information while they are working.

Most voice input systems use a combination of hardware and software to convert spoken words into data the computer can process. The conversion process used by one voice input system developer, shown in *Figure 3-30,* is as follows:
1. The user's voice, consisting of sound waves, is converted into digital form by **digital signal processing** (DSP) circuits that are usually on a separate board added to the computer.
2. The digitized voice input is compared against patterns stored in the voice system's database.
3. Grammar rules are used to resolve possible word conflicts. Based on how a word was used, the computer can usually identify the correct word in cases of words that sound alike such as to, too, and two.
4. Unrecognized words are presented to the user to identify.

With many voice input systems, especially the lower cost systems with limited vocabularies, the user has to train the system to recognize his or her voice. For each of the words in the vocabulary, the user speaks the word. After each word has been spoken several times, the system develops a digital pattern for the word that can be stored on secondary storage. When the user later speaks a word to the system to request a particular action, the system compares the word to the words that were previously entered. When it finds a match, the software performs the activity associated with the word. Such systems are referred to as **speaker dependent** because each person who wants to use the system has to train it to his or her voice. With larger vocabulary systems containing up to 50,000 words, training on individual words is not practical. Instead, developers include multiple patterns, called **voice templates** for each word. These templates include male and female voices as well as regional accents. These systems are called **speaker independent** because most users will not have to train the system to their speech pattern.

Figure 3-30
This diagram shows how one speech recognition company, Kurzweil AI, Inc., converts spoken words to computer input.

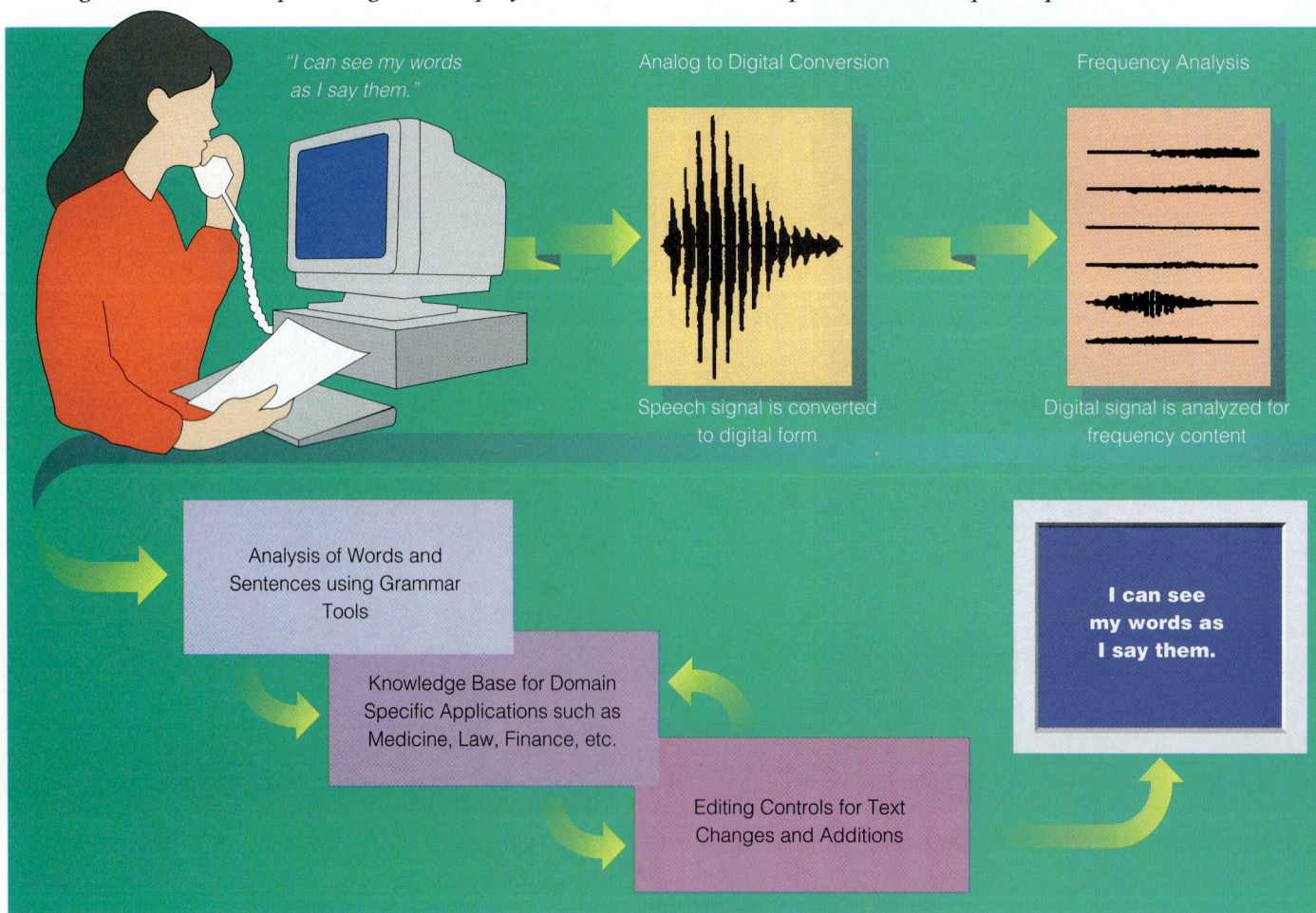

Most speech-to-text systems in use today use **discrete speech recognition** that requires the user to pause slightly between each word. **Continuous speech recognition** systems that allow the user to speak in a flowing conversational tone are not yet widely used because they require more complex software and hardware to separate and make sense of the words. Low cost continuous speech recognition systems are expected to be available for personal computers by the year 2000.

Beyond continuous voice recognition is what is called natural language voice interface. A **natural language voice interface** allows the user to ask a question and have the computer not only convert the question to understandable words but interpret the question and give an appropriate response. For example, think how powerful and easy it would be to use a system if you could simply ask, "How soon can we ship 200 red stainless steel widgets to Boston?" Think about how many different pieces of information the computer might have to pull together to generate a correct response. Such natural language voice recognition systems are not commercially available now but are being developed using powerful computers and sophisticated software.

Digital Camera

Digital cameras record photographs in the form of digital data that can be stored on a computer. No chemical based film is used. Some digital cameras are portable and look similar to traditional film cameras. Other digital cameras are stationary and are connected directly to a computer *(Figure 3-31)*.

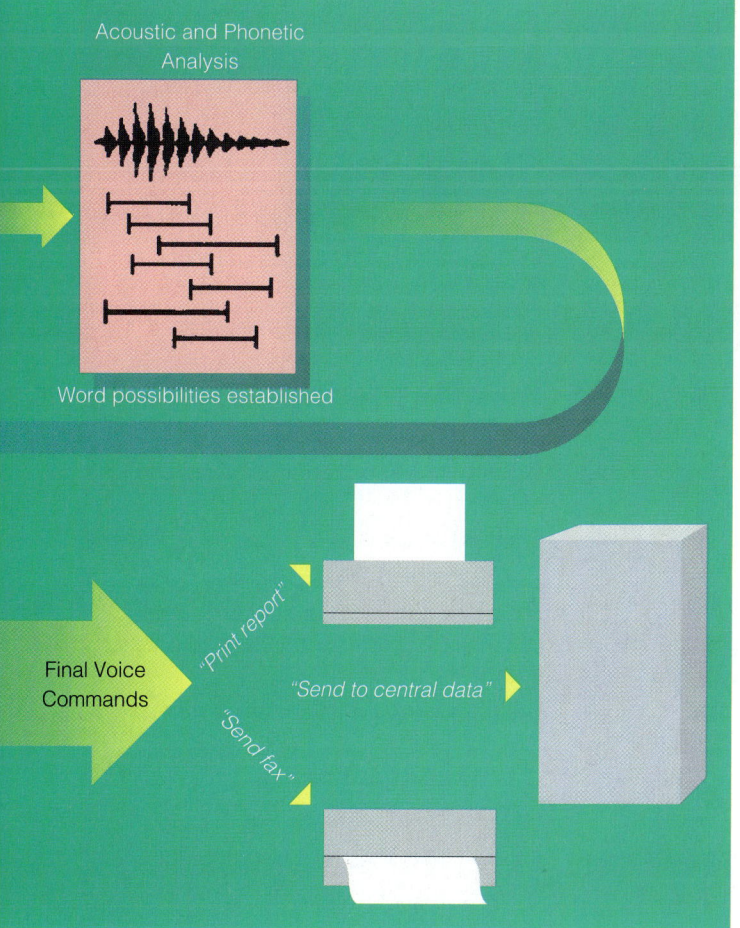

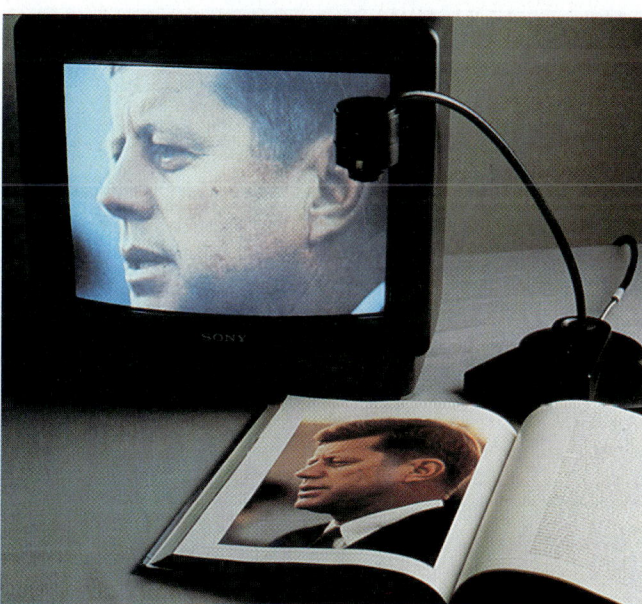

Figure 3-31
The digital camera is used to record digital photographs of documents, products, or people. The camera is connected to a video board installed in the computer.

Many companies use digital cameras to record images of their products for computer based catalogs or to record photos of their employees for personnel records *(Figure 3-32)*.

Video Input

Video material is input to the computer using a video camera or a video recorder using previously recorded material. Video data requires tremendous amounts of storage space, which is why video segments in personal computer applications are often limited to only a few seconds. Improvements in video electronics and software and larger capacity storage devices will enable movie length video data to eventually become available. Video applications currently under development include video repair manuals. Rather that just looking at a photo or diagram, the user could view narrated video segments on how to disassemble and repair a piece of equipment.

The input devices discussed in this chapter are summarized in *Figure 3-33*. When any of these devices are used to input data, it is important that the data is entered accurately. Various procedures are used to help ensure data accuracy.

Figure 3-32
Digital cameras are often used to record photographs of employees that are added to their computer-based personnel records.

Data Accuracy

The procedures developed for controlling input are important because accurate data must be entered into a computer to ensure data integrity. Inaccurate information caused by inaccurate data is often worse than no information at all. The computer jargon term **GIGO** states this point very well; it stands for *Garbage In, Garbage Out*.

Because users are often interacting directly with the computer during the input process, procedures and documentation must be quite clear. Computer programs and procedures must be designed to check for accurate data and should specify the steps to take if the data is not valid. Although different applications will have specific criteria for validating input data, several tests can be performed before the data is processed by the computer. Some of these tests are:

- Tests for data type and format – If data should be of a particular type, such as alphabetic or numeric, then it should be tested for that. Often, a data type test is combined with a data format test. For example, in the United States, the ZIP postal code should either be five digits alone or five digits followed by a dash followed by four digits. Unless the data fits one of those two formats, it should be rejected.

DEVICE	DESCRIPTION
Keyboard	Most commonly used input device; special keys may include numeric keypad, cursor control keys, and function keys
Mouse or Trackball	Used to move pointer and select options
Joystick	Stem device often used as input device for games
Pen Input	Uses pen to input and edit data and select processing options
Touch Screen	User interacts with computer by touching screen with finger
Light Pen	Used to select options or draw on screen
Digitizer	Used to enter or edit drawings
Graphic Tablet	Digitizer with special processing options built into tablet
Image Scanner	Converts text, graphics, or photos into digital input
Optical Recognition	Uses light source to read codes, marks, and characters
MICR	Used in banking to read magnetic ink characters on checks
Data Collection	Used in factories and warehouses to input data at source
Sound Input	Converts sound into digital data
Voice Input	Converts speech into digital data
Digital Camera	Captures digital image of subject or object
Video Input	Converts video into digital data

Figure 3-33
A summary of some of the more common input devices.

- Tests for data reasonableness – A reasonableness check ensures that the data entered is within normal or accepted boundaries. For example, suppose no employee within a company is authorized to work more than 80 hours per week. If the value entered in the hours worked field is greater than 80, the value in the field would be indicated as a probable error.
- Tests for data consistency – In some cases, data entered cannot, by itself, be found to be invalid. If, however, the data is examined in relation to other data entered for the same transaction, discrepancies might be found. For example, in a hotel reservation system, both the check-in and check-out dates are entered. Each date should be checked to make sure it is valid. In addition, the check-out date should be later than the check-in date. If the check-out date is earlier than the check-in date, an error has been made when entering one of the dates *(Figure 3-34)*.
- Tests for transcription and transposition errors – The possibility always exists that an operator will make an error when entering data. A **transcription error** occurs when an error is made in copying the values from a source document. For example, if the operator keys the customer number 7165 when the proper number is 7765, the operator has made a transcription error. A **transposition error** happens when the operator switches two numbers. Such an error has occurred when the number 7765 is entered as 7756. Transcription and transposition errors are often difficult to detect. Usually, some other piece of information must be checked to verify that the data entered is correct. For example, when entering a customer number, the user should verify that the corresponding customer name is correct before proceeding.

Summary of Input to the Computer

Chapter 3 presented an overview of the information processing cycle and discussed how data is organized. Also discussed were the four types of input and a variety of input devices. Procedures used to ensure data accuracy were presented and explained. After reading this chapter, you should have a better overall understanding of computer input.

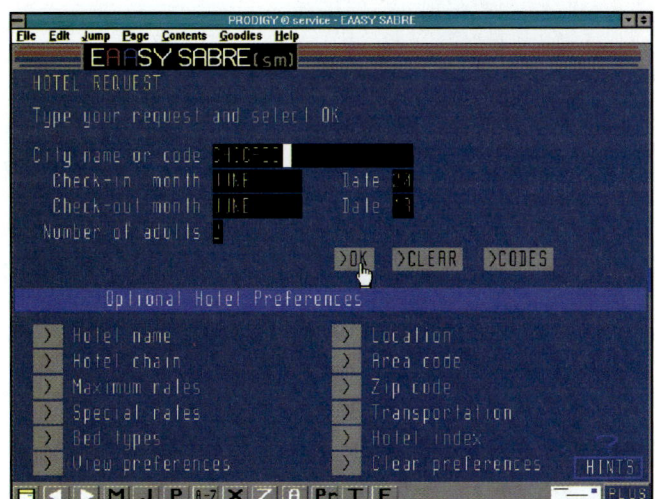
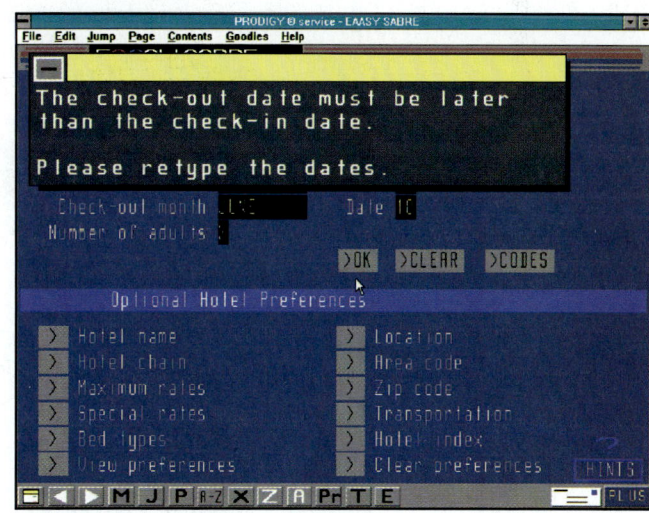

Figure 3-34
One way to check for data accuracy is to compare one piece of data with another and look for logical errors. In this example of a hotel reservation system, the system compared the check-out date with the check-in date. Because the check-out date was earlier than the check-in date, an error message was displayed and the user was asked to reenter the dates.

COMPUTERS AT WORK

Helping People with Special Needs

For physically challenged and disabled individuals, working with standard computers may be either difficult or impossible. Fortunately, special software and hardware, called adaptive, or assistive, technology enables many of these individuals to use computers productively and independently.

Adaptive technology covers a wide range of hardware and software products that help the user make the computer meet his or her special needs. For people with motor disabilities who cannot use a standard keyboard, there are a number of alternative input devices. Most of these devices involve the use of a switch that is controlled by any reliable muscle. One type of switch is even activated by breathing into a tube. The switches are used with special software to select commands or input characters. For those who cannot use their muscles to activate switches, a system exists that is controlled by eye movement. Called Eyegaze, the system uses a camera mounted on the computer and directed at one of the user's eyes. Using the movement of the user's eye, software determines where on the screen the user is looking to within $1/4$ inch accuracy. To activate a choice on the screen, the user has to stare at it for approximately $1/4$ second.

For blind individuals, voice recognition programs allow for verbal input. Software is also available that converts text to Braille and sends it to Braille printers. Both blind and nonverbal individuals use speech synthesis equipment to convert text documents into spoken words. For people with limited vision, several programs are available that magnify information on the screen.

The use of adaptive technology received further encouragement when the Americans with Disabilities Act (ADA) was enacted. Since 1994, the ADA requires that all companies with 15 or more employees make reasonable attempts to accommodate the needs of workers with physical challenges. Many employers are complying with the legislation through the use of personal computers and adaptive technology software and equipment.

Figure 3-35

IN THE FUTURE

"Computer, tell me the status of . . ."

In many science fiction stories, humans have conversations with computers. The human speaks in a natural, conversational tone and the computer responds in a similar manner, sometimes asking questions to clarify the human's statement or request. Many experts believe that this type of natural language interface will one day become the way humans interact with a computer. To provide this capability, however, much more powerful and faster computers will have to be developed. In addition, voice recognition software will have to be significantly improved.

To understand human speech, a computer has to go through four steps: sound analysis, word recognition, sentence or thought construction, and statement context. Sound analysis is the easiest part. Sound waves are converted into the smallest units of speech, called phonemes. During word recognition, the phonemes are joined together to form words. This can be a difficult task because conversational speech often runs one word into another. The problem becomes more difficult during sentence and thought construction. During this process, the identified words are joined together to make a logical statement. As your high school English teacher may have told you, people do not always speak or write in a logical manner using correct grammar. Statement context involves using past statements to provide information about a current statement. For example, say an airline reservation agent told you there were no flights available on the day you wanted to leave, June 20. If you said, "How about the next day?", the computer should know that you now want to check the flights on June 21.

Some experts think that significant breakthroughs in natural speech recognition are just a few years away. Others think that easy to use systems will not be available until after the year 2000. The optimists, however, are already talking about the next human interface challenge; how to read lips!

Do you remember *HAL*, the computer in the movie *2001: A Space Odyssey*?

Figure 3-36

What You Should Know

1. The input operation must take place before any data can be processed and any information produced and stored. **Input** refers to the process of entering data, programs, commands, and user responses into main memory.

2. **Data** refers to the raw facts, including numbers, letters, words, images, and sounds a computer receives during the input operation and processes to produce information. **Programs** are instructions that direct the computer to perform the necessary operations to process data into information. **Commands** are key words and phrases the user inputs to direct the computer to perform certain activities. **User responses** refer to the data a user inputs to respond to a question or message from the software.

3. The **keyboard** is the most commonly used input device. The alphabetic keys are arranged like those on a typewriter, and a **numeric keypad** is located on the right-hand side of most keyboards. A **cursor** is a symbol that indicates where the next character typed will appear on the screen. Other keyboard keys include the **arrow keys** or **cursor control keys**, and **function keys**.

4. Pointing devices allow the user to control an on-screen symbol called the **mouse pointer** or **pointer** that is usually represented by an arrow-shaped marker.

5. A **mouse** is a small, lightweight input device that easily fits in the palm of your hand. Moving the mouse across a flat surface controls the movement of the pointer on the screen, and the buttons on top of the mouse can be used to select options displayed on the screen.

6. A **trackball** is a pointing device like a mouse only with the ball on top of the device instead of on the bottom.

7. A **joystick** uses the movement of a vertical stem to direct the pointer.

8. **Pen input devices** allow the user to use the pen in three ways; to input data using hand-written characters and shapes the computer can recognize, as a pointing device like a mouse to select items on the screen, and to gesture, which is a way of issuing commands. When the pen touches the screen, the computer darkens that location. The darkened area is referred to as **ink**.

9. Most **handwriting recognition software** can be taught to recognize an individual's unique style of writing. **Gestures** are special symbols made with the pen that issue a command.

10. A **touch screen** allows users to touch areas of the screen to enter data. A **light pen** is used by touching it on the display screen to create or modify graphics. A **digitizer** converts points, lines, and curves from a sketch, drawing, or photograph to digital impulses and transmits them to a computer. A **graphics tablet** works in a manner similar to a digitizer, but it also contains unique characters and commands that can be automatically generated by the person using the tablet.

11. **Source data automation**, sometimes called **source data collection**, refers to procedures and equipment designed to make the input process more efficient by eliminating the manual entry of data. Data is captured directly from its original form, called a **source document**.

12. An **image scanner**, sometimes called a **page scanner**, is an input device that electronically captures an entire page of text or images, such as photographs or art work. **Image processing systems** use scanners to capture and electronically file documents.

13. **Optical recognition** devices use a light source to read codes, marks, and characters and convert them into digital data that can be processed by a computer.

14. **Optical codes** use a pattern or symbols to represent data. A **bar code**, the most common optical code, consists of a set of vertical lines and spaces of different widths. There are several different types of bar codes, but the most familiar is the **universal product code** (UPC) used for grocery and retail items.

What You Should Know

15. **Optical mark recognition** (OMR) devices can read carefully placed marks on specially designed documents such as questionnaires or test answer sheets.

16. **Optical character recognition** (OCR) devices are scanners that read typewritten, computer-printed, and in some cases hand-printed characters from ordinary documents. OCR is frequently used for **turn-around documents** that are designed to be returned to the organization that created them.

17. **OCR software** is used with image scanners to convert text images into data that can be processed by word processing software.

18. **Magnetic ink character recognition** (MICR) characters use a special ink that can be magnetized during processing. MICR is used almost exclusively by the banking industry for processing checks.

19. **Data collection devices** are designed and used for obtaining data at the site where the transaction or event being reported takes place. They are often used in rugged locations, such as factories or warehouses, and operated by persons whose primary task is not entering data.

20. Terminals, sometimes called **display terminals** or **video display terminals** (VDTs), consist of a keyboard and a screen. A **dumb terminal** can be used to enter and transmit data to or receive data from a computer to which it is connected. It has no independent processing capability or secondary storage and cannot function as a stand-alone device. **Intelligent terminals**, also known as **programmable terminals** or **smart terminals**, have built-in processing capabilities, can be programmed by the user to perform many basic tasks, and often contain secondary storage devices. **Point-of-sale** (POS) terminals are special-purpose terminals that allow data to be entered at the time and place where the transaction with a customer occurs.

21. **Multimedia** is the combination of sound and images with text and graphics. Personal computers use special input devices consisting primarily of electronics contained on a separate card, such as a **sound card** or **video card**, that are installed in the computer to capture sound and image data.

22. Sounds are usually recorded by connecting a microphone or electronic music keyboard to the sound card. **Voice input** allows the user to enter data and issue commands to the computer with spoken words. The user's voice, consisting of sound waves, is converted into digital form by **digital signal processing** (DSP) circuits. Four areas where voice input is used are data entry, command and control, speaker recognition, and speech-to-text.

23. Voice input systems that must be trained to the voice of each person who wants to use the system are referred to as **speaker dependent**. Voice input systems that contain **voice templates** for each word are called **speaker independent**, because most users will not have to train the system to their speech pattern.

24. Most speech-to-text systems in use today use **discrete speech recognition** that requires the user to pause slightly between each word. **Continuous speech recognition** systems allow the user to speak in a flowing conversational tone but are not yet widely used. A **natural language voice interface** allows the user to ask a question and have the computer not only convert the question to understandable words but to interpret the question and give an appropriate response.

25. **Digital cameras** record photographs in the form of digital data that can be stored on a computer.

26. Video material is input to the computer with a video camera or a video recorder using previously recorded material. Video data requires tremendous amounts of storage space.

27. Inaccurate information caused by inaccurate data is often worse than no information at all. The computer jargon GIGO states this very well; it stands for *Garbage In, Garbage Out.*

28. Several tests can be performed to validate data before it is processed by the computer. Some of these tests are: tests for data type and format, tests for data reasonableness, tests for data consistency, and tests for **transcription errors** (errors made in copying values from a source document) and **transposition errors** (errors made by switching two numbers).

Terms to Remember

arrow keys (3.4)

bar code (3.11)

commands (3.2)
continuous speed recognition (3.19)
cursor (3.4)
cursor control keys (3.4)

data (3.3)
data collection devices (3.14)
digital camera (3.19)
digital signal processing (DSP) (3.18)
digitizer (3.9)
discrete speech recognition (3.19)
display terminals (3.15)
dumb terminals (3.15)

function keys (3.4)

gestures (3.7)
GIGO (Garbage In, Garbage Out) (3.20)
graphics tablet (3.9)

handwriting recognition software (3.7)

image processing systems (3.10)
image scanner (3.10)
ink (3.7)
input (3.2)
intelligent terminals (3.15)

joystick (3.6)

keyboard (3.3)

light pen (3.9)

magnetic ink character recognition (MICR) (3.13)
mouse (3.5)
mouse pointer (3.5)
multimedia (3.16)

natural language voice interface (3.19)
numeric keypad (3.3)

OCR software (3.13)
optical character recognition (OCR) (3.12)
optical codes (3.11)
optical mark recognition (OMR) (3.12)
optical recognition (3.11)

page scanner (3.10)
pen input devices (3.7)
point-of-sale (POS) terminals (3.15)
pointer (3.5)
programmable terminals (3.15)
programs (3.2)

smart terminals (3.15)
sound card (3.16)
source data automation (3.10)
source data collection (3.10)
source document (3.10)
speaker dependent (3.18)
speaker independent (3.18)

touch screen (3.8)
trackball (3.6)
transcription error (3.21)
transposition error (3.21)
turn-around documents (3.12)

universal product code (UPC) (3.11)
user responses (3.3)

video card (3.16)
video display terminals (VDT) (3.15)
voice input (3.16)
voice templates (3.18)

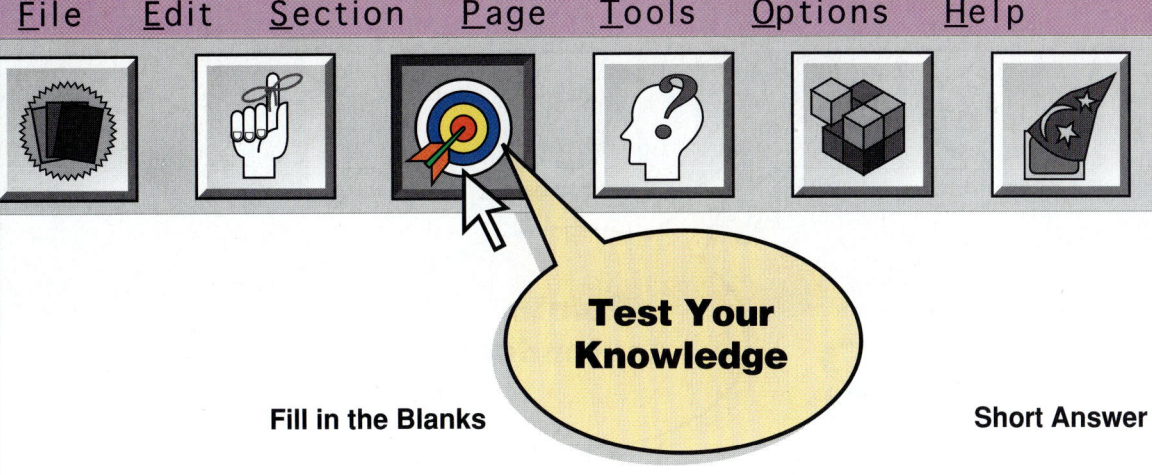

Test Your Knowledge

Fill in the Blanks

1. The information processing cycle consists of four operations: _____, _____, _____, and _____.
2. In the information processing cycle, the _____ operation must take place before any data can be processed and any information produced and stored.
3. A(n) _____ is a pointing device that, by moving it across a flat surface and pressing buttons, can be used to move the pointer and select options on the screen.
4. Three types of terminals are: _____, which can be used to enter, transmit, receive, or display data but have no independent processing capability; _____, which have built-in processing capabilities and often contain disk drives and printers; and _____, which allow data to be entered at the time and place where the transaction with a customer occurs.
5. _____ is the combination of sound and images with text and graphics.

Short Answer

1. What is input? List the four types of input and briefly describe how the computer uses each type.
2. Although a computer keyboard is similar to a typewriter keyboard, a computer keyboard also has keys that are not found on the keyboard of a traditional typewriter. What are some of these keys? For what purpose are these keys used?
3. How are a mouse, trackball, and joystick similar? How are they different? What is the primary advantage of a mouse? What are the disadvantages? What advantage does a trackball have over a mouse?
4. What is a terminal? How is a dumb terminal different from an intelligent terminal? How is a point-of-sale terminal used?
5. Why is data accuracy important? What does the computer jargon term GIGO mean? Briefly describe three tests for data accuracy that can be performed before the data is processed by the computer.

Label the Figure

Instructions: The examples below show gestures; special symbols made with pen input devices. In the spaces provided, list the command issued for each gesture.

Gesture	Command	Gesture	Command
•	_____	←	_____
→	_____	↗	_____
↗ (loop)	_____	↻	_____
↔	_____	⌒	_____
→	_____	↑ (loop)	_____

Points to Ponder

1

The traditional arrangement of letters on a keyboard is sometimes called the QWERTY layout. The name QWERTY comes from the first six keys in the top row of letters. This layout was initially adopted by early typewriters to place the most commonly used letters in locations that were not easily reached, to slow typists down and prevent keys from jamming. Although keys jamming is no longer a problem, most keyboards still use the same design today. A different key arrangement, called the Dvorak layout, places the most commonly used letters on the home row, the row on which your fingers rest. What are the advantages of the Dvorak layout? What are the disadvantages? If a typist was trained to use both keyboard layouts, which do you think would result in faster data input? Why? Will the Dvorak layout ever be widely accepted? Why or why not?

2

At one time, the keyboard was the only means of inputting data into a computer. Although the keyboard remains the most commonly used input device, the mouse has also become almost essential; many makers of computer software require the use of a mouse with their application packages. What does the future of input devices hold? Thirty years from now, will a different pointing device be more popular than the mouse? Will the keyboard be replaced by another input device? Why? Will any input device become an historical oddity, seen only in museums? Why?

3

Pen input devices have been adapted to many applications and are currently being used by sales representatives, delivery services, nurses and doctors, and inventory takers. In what way do you think pen input devices are particularly useful in each of these fields? List some other areas that you feel could use pen input devices and briefly describe how they could be used in each. Do you think a pen input device would be valuable to a student? Why or why not?

4

A recent controversy in one county in New York state involved the use of optical code scanners in grocery stores. Scanners were being used at the check-out counters to determine the price of each purchase and, although prices were indicated on the grocery shelves, they were not marked on individual grocery items. Consumer groups argued that the shelf price tags were hard to read and not having price stickers on each item made it difficult to compare prices. In addition, they claimed that the databases from which the scanners obtained prices were not always accurate and frequently were not updated to reflect sale prices. The grocery stores maintained that the labor involved in individual item pricing would add to the item's cost, and that most of the time their scanned prices were accurate. What do you think? Should grocery stores be required to put a price on each individual item? Why or why not? Can you think of any other way to answer consumer concerns?

5

Although computers have become widespread, many people are still intimidated when forced to input data into a computer. Of the input devices discussed in this chapter, which do you feel would be the easiest to use for someone who is uncomfortable with computers? Why? Which input device do you think requires the most training? If a school decided every student must learn to use one input device, which device do you think should be taught? Why?

6

All input devices require some form of human interaction. A keyboard requires a great deal of human interaction because someone inputting data must not only read the data accurately but also locate and press the correct keys. In contrast, an optical code scanner requires a minimum of human interaction because the user need only pass the optical code in front of the scanner. Keeping in mind the tests described in this chapter, what impact do you think the degree of human interaction has on data accuracy? Why? List at least five input devices in order, from those that require the most human interaction to those that require the least human interaction. Which input devices do you think result in the most accurate input of data? Why?

Out and About

1. Although all computer keyboards may seem alike, the placement of special keys, the space between keys, the feel of the keys, and the noise produced when a key is pressed may vary. Visit a computer vendor and try at least three different types of computer keyboards. Evaluate each keyboard in terms of the suggested characteristics. Which keyboard do you like best? Why? Which keyboard do you like least? Why?

2. Visit a firm or organization that uses computers. Talk with a person involved with computer operations to find out what types of input devices are used. For what purpose is each device used? Has the firm or organization ever experienced problems as a result of inaccurate data being entered into the computer? If so, what kinds of problems? What measures were taken to insure that the problems did not happen again?

3. The wide range of input devices available for computers has helped many physically challenged individuals. Use a library to research the types of input devices that have helped people facing physical challenges. What types of input devices have been used? What input devices have been particularly helpful for people with specific physical disabilities?

4. Optical code scanners are used by retail stores, supermarkets, and libraries. Visit an organization that uses optical code scanners to find out how the scanners are used. What types of information are they able to record? How is the information used? In what way does the information obtained through the use of scanners benefit the organization or the organization's clientele? Were they able to keep track of the same information before they used scanners? Why or why not?

5. Visit a local bank and ask an employee about ATM (automatic teller machine) terminals. How are they used? What kind of information do they obtain? What security measures are provided? What precautions does the bank suggest to ATM users? Has the bank ever had any trouble with their ATMs? If so, what? After interviewing the bank employee, decide whether you think an ATM is a dumb terminal or an intelligent terminal. Why?

6. Visit a computer vendor and select a personal computer system displayed in the store. Make a list of the input devices that can be used with that personal computer, and provide a price for each input device. If you were to purchase that personal computer, which input device or devices would you want to purchase right away? Why? Which input devices do you think you might purchase at a later date? Why? Are there any available input devices that you think you would never buy? Why?

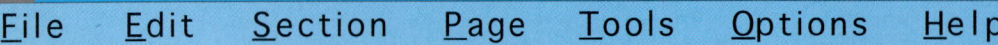

 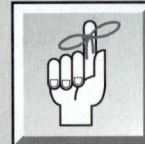   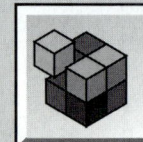 

Windows Labs

1 Displaying Your System Configuration With Program Manager on the screen, double-click the Main group icon. In the Main group window, double-click the Windows Setup program-item icon. Write down the type of display, keyboard, and mouse your computer has. Close Windows Setup by double-clicking its Control-menu box.

2 Customizing the Mouse With Program Manager on the screen, double-click the Main group icon. In the Main group window, double-click the Control Panel program-item icon. In the Control Panel window, double-click the Mouse icon. In your Mouse dialog box, which may be similar to *Figure 3-37*, click the Help button. Read and print all of the Help topics about the Mouse dialog box. To return to the original Help window, click the Back button. Close the Help window.

Test each of the options in the Mouse dialog box. For example, on the Double Click Speed scroll bar, drag the scroll box to Slow. Double-click the Test box to test the speed. A successful double-click reverses the color in the Test box. Test other speeds. Answer the following questions: (1) Why would you want to switch the left and right (primary and secondary) mouse buttons? (2) What are mouse trails? (3) How do you adjust the speed of the mouse? Choose the OK button in the Mouse dialog box. Close Control Panel.

3 Shelly Cashman Series Input Lab Follow the instructions in Windows Lab 2 on page 1.30 to display the Shelly Cashman Series Labs screen. Select Scanning Documents and choose the Start Lab button. When the initial screen displays, carefully read the objectives. With your printer turned on, point to the Print Questions button and click the left mouse button. Fill out the top of the Questions sheet and answer the questions as you step through the Input Lab.

4 Scanning a Photograph Bring a 3 $1/2$" x 5" (or larger) picture of yourself or family members to class. Ask your instructor for assistance in scanning the photograph to create a digital version on your diskette using the first four characters of your last name as the filename. With Program Manager on the screen, double-click the Accessories group icon. Double-click the Paintbrush program-item icon. Use the Open command on the File menu to open the file containing your picture. Your Paintbrush window should be similar to the one shown in *Figure 3-38*. Print the picture using the Print command on the File menu. For extra credit, autograph your picture in Paintbrush and print it. Do not save the autographed picture to your diskette. Close Paintbrush.

5 Using the Mouse and Keyboard to Interact with an Online Program Obtain information from your instructor on the location (path) of the file LOANCALC.EXE. With Program Manager on the screen, select the File menu and choose the Run command. In the Command Line text box, type the path and filename loancalc. For example, type c:\sclabs\loancalc as shown in *Figure 3-39*. Press the ENTER key. The Loan Payment Calculator window displays on the

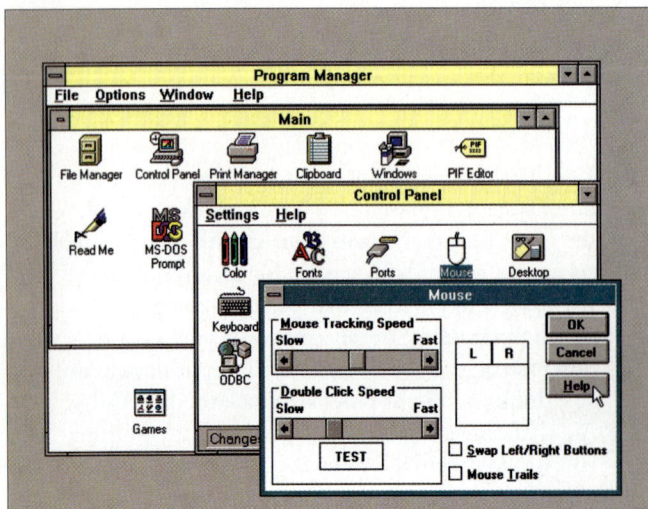

Figure 3-37

Figure 3-38

screen. Type 100000 in the LOAN AMOUNT box. Click the YEARS right scroll arrow or drag the scroll box until the YEARS equals 15. Click the APR right scroll arrow or drag the scroll box until the APR equals 9.75. Click the Calculate button. Note the monthly payment and sum of all payments made *(Figure 3-40)*. Click the Clear button. What is the monthly payment and sum of payments for each of these loan amounts, years, and APRs? (1) 15000, 5, 6.25; (2) 55000, 30, 10.25; (3) 162500, 30, 8; (4) 75550, 15, 9.25; and (5) 9750, 3, 7.5. Click the About button. Who wrote this program? Choose the OK button. Close the Loan Payment Calculator.

6 **More About Using Help** With Program Manager on the screen, select the Help menu and choose the How to Use Help command. One at a time, click the last five topics listed in green at the bottom of the window. Read and print each one. Click the Back button to return to the How to Use Help window. Close the How to Use Help window.

DOS Labs

1 **Using Doskey** At the DOS prompt, type doskey and press the ENTER key. Type dir and press the ENTER key. When the DOS prompt appears again, press the UP ARROW key to recall the dir command and press the ENTER key. Type ver and press the ENTER key. Press the UP ARROW key three times to display one at a time the sequence of commands executed. What is the purpose of the DOSKEY command?

2 **Using the Numeric Keypad to Enter Data** Obtain information from your instructor on how to change to the directory on your computer containing the LOANPAY.EXE program. At the DOS prompt, type loanpay and press the ENTER key. Press the NUM LOCK key on the numeric keypad to turn on Num Lock. When you are prompted, enter 10500 for the loan amount, 11.5 for the rate, and 4.5 for the years using the numeric keypad. What input device did you use to enter the data? List the input prompts, corresponding data items, and output results for the loan program.

3 **Using Help** At the DOS prompt, type help and press the ENTER key. Press F1 to display the How to Use MS-DOS Help window. Read the contents of the window. Print the contents of the window by pressing the ALT key to activate the menu bar, typing F to display the File menu, and typing P to choose the Print command. Finally, press the ENTER key when the Print dialog box displays. With the cursor on the first Help topic, press the ENTER key. Read and print the information. Press ALT+B to return to the prior Help window. One by one, select and print each remaining topic to learn how to use Help. Exit the Help window by selecting the File menu and choosing the Exit command.

Online Lab

1 **Weather Information** Using one of the two online services you selected in Chapter 1, connect to the service and perform the following tasks: (1) Search the online service for Weather Information. (2) Display the United States weather map. Write down the weather information for your part of the country. (3) Display and write down the weather information for Anchorage, AK; Chicago, IL; Los Angeles, CA; Maui, HI; New York, NY; and the city you live in, or one nearby.

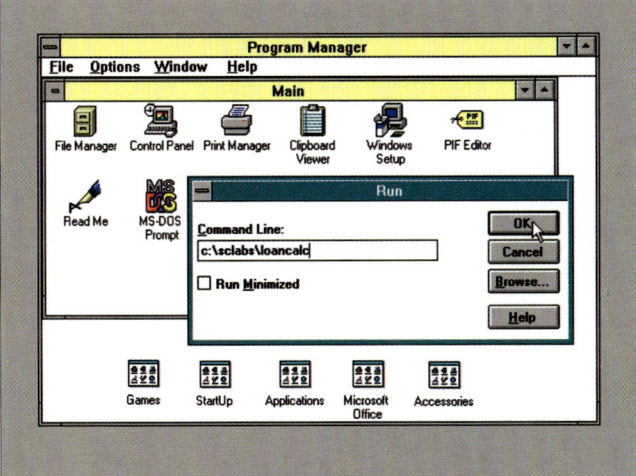

Figure 3-39

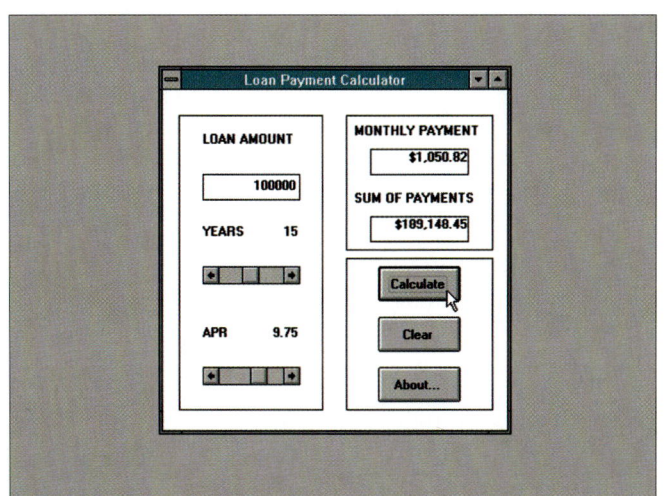

Figure 3-40

CHAPTER FOUR

The System Unit

Objectives

After completing this chapter, you will be able to:

- Define a bit and describe how a series of bits in a byte is used to represent data

- Discuss how the ASCII and EBCDIC codes represent characters

- Identify the components of the system unit and describe their use

- Describe how the CPU uses the four steps of the machine cycle to process data

- Describe the primary use and characteristics of RAM and ROM memory

- Explain the difference between parallel and serial ports

- Describe a machine language instruction and the instruction set of a computer

- Describe various types of processing including pipe-lining, parallel processing, and neural networks

- Convert numbers between the decimal, binary, and hexadecimal number systems

The information processing cycle consists of input, processing, output, and storage operations. When an input operation is completed and both a program and data are stored in main memory, processing operations can begin. During these operations, the system unit executes, or performs, the program instructions and processes the data into information.

Chapter 4 examines the components of the system unit, describes how main memory stores programs and data, and discusses the sequence of operations that occurs when instructions are executed on a computer. These topics are followed by a discussion of types of processing and number systems.

What Is the System Unit?

The term computer is usually used to describe the collection of devices that perform the information processing cycle. This term is also used more specifically to describe the system unit, because this is where the *computing* actually occurs *(Figure 4-1)*. It is in the **system unit** that the computer program instructions are executed and the data is manipulated. The system unit contains the central processing unit, or CPU, main memory, and other electronics *(Figure 4-2)*. To better understand how the system unit processes data, an explanation of how data is represented electronically follows.

How Data Is Represented Electronically

Most computers are **digital computers**, meaning that the data they process, whether it be text, sound, graphics, or video, is first converted into a digital (numeric) value. Converting data into a digital form is called **digitizing**. Other types of computers, called **analog computers**, are designed to process continuously variable data, such as electrical voltage.

You may be thinking that the digital values used by a computer are the numbers 0 through 9. In fact, only the numbers 0 and 1 are used. A 0 is used to represent the electronic state of *off* and a 1 is used to represent the electronic state of *on*. Each off or on digital value is called a **bit**, the smallest unit of data handled by a computer. Bit is short for *bi*nary dig*it*. The binary number system represents quantities by using only two numbers, 0 and 1 *(Figure 4-3)*.

By itself, a bit cannot represent much data. In a group of eight bits, called a **byte**, 256 different possibilities can be represented by using all the combinations of 0s and 1s. This provides enough combinations so a unique code can be assigned to each of the characters that are commonly used, such as the numbers 0 through 9, the uppercase and lowercase

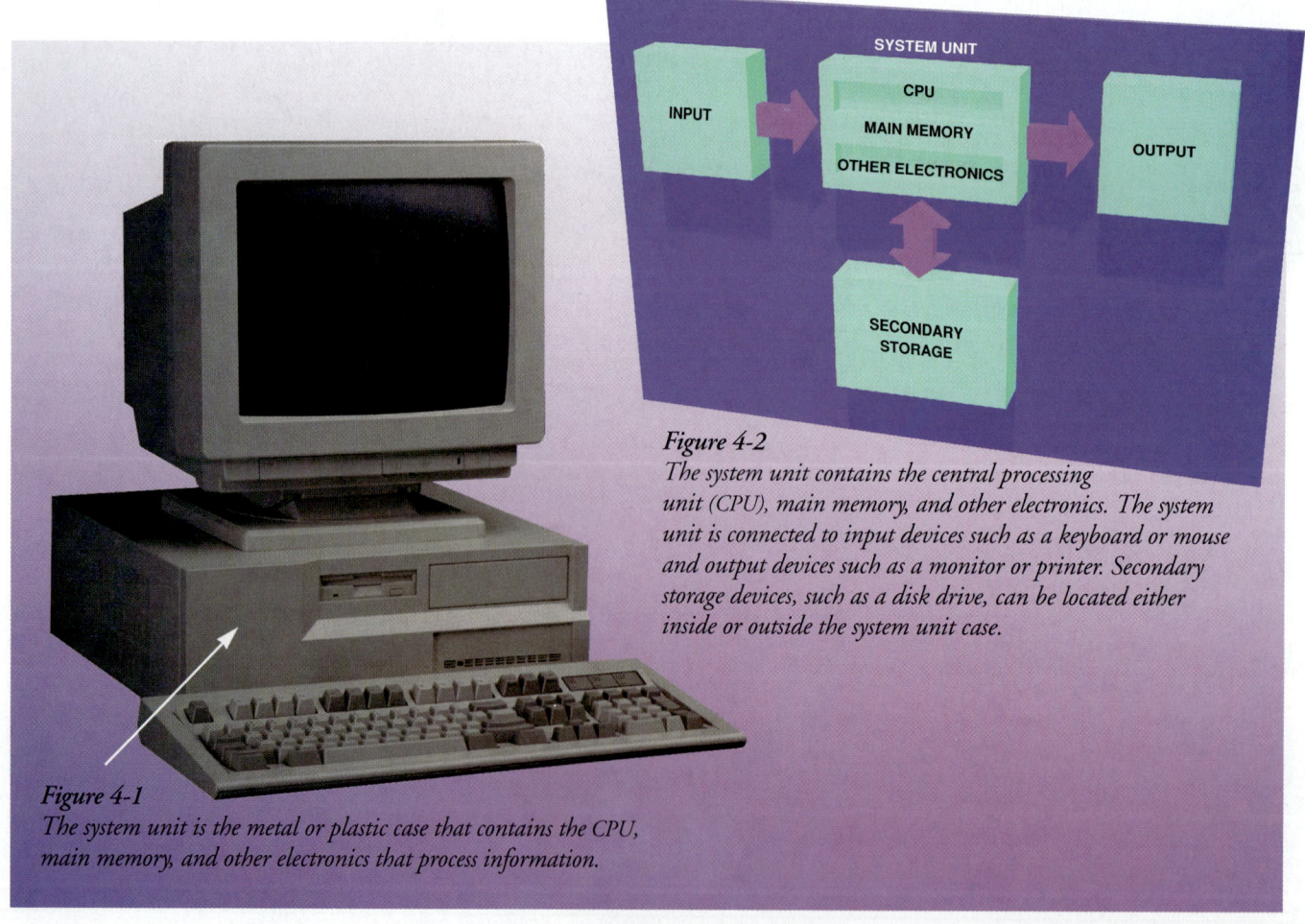

Figure 4-1
The system unit is the metal or plastic case that contains the CPU, main memory, and other electronics that process information.

Figure 4-2
The system unit contains the central processing unit (CPU), main memory, and other electronics. The system unit is connected to input devices such as a keyboard or mouse and output devices such as a monitor or printer. Secondary storage devices, such as a disk drive, can be located either inside or outside the system unit case.

alphabet, foreign characters that require special accent marks such as umlauts (¨) and tildes (~), and special characters such as punctuation marks *(Figure 4-4)*. Several different coding schemes are used on computers.

ASCII and EBCDIC

Two popular codes that represent characters in memory and on secondary storage are the ASCII and EBCDIC codes. The **American Standard Code for Information Interchange**, called **ASCII** (pronounced ask-ee), is the most widely used coding system to represent data. Originally a seven-bit code, ASCII has been expanded to an eight-bit code. ASCII is used on personal computers and minicomputers. The **Extended Binary Coded Decimal Interchange Code**, or EBCDIC (pronounced eb-see-dick) is used primarily on mainframe computers. *Figure 4-5* summarizes these codes. Notice how the combination of bits, represented in binary, is unique for each character.

SYMBOL	ASCII	EBCDIC
0	01100000	11110000
1	01100001	11110001
2	01100010	11110010
3	01100011	11110011
4	01100100	11110100
5	01100101	11110101
6	01100110	11110110
7	01100111	11110111
8	01101000	11111000
9	01101001	11111001
A	01000001	11000001
B	01000010	11000010
C	01000011	11000011
D	01000100	11000100
E	01000101	11000101
F	01000110	11000110
G	01000111	11000111
H	01001000	11001000
I	01001001	11001001
J	01001010	11010001
K	01001011	11010010
L	01001100	11010011
M	01001101	11010100
N	01001110	11010101
O	01001111	11010110
P	01010000	11010111
Q	01010001	11011000
R	01010010	11011001
S	01010011	11100010
T	01010100	11100011
U	01010101	11100100
V	01010110	11100101
W	01010111	11100110
X	01011000	11100111
Y	01011001	11101000
Z	01011010	11101001
!	00100001	01011010
"	00100010	01111111
#	00100011	01111011
$	00100100	01011011
%	00100101	01101100
&	00100110	01010000
(	00101000	01001101
)	00101001	01011101
*	00101010	01011100
+	00101011	01001110

BINARY NUMBER	0	1
BIT	○	●
STATUS	OFF	ON

Figure 4-3
A bit, the smallest unit of data handled by a computer, can either be off or on. The binary numbers 0 and 1 are used to represent off and on, respectively.

0 1 0 0 0 0 0 1
○ ● ○ ○ ○ ○ ○ ●
8–BIT BYTE

Figure 4-4
A graphic representation of an eight-bit byte with two bits on and six bits off. The off bits (open circles) are represented by the binary number 0 and the on bits (solid circles) are represented by the binary number 1. This combination of bits represents the letter A using the ASCII code.

Figure 4-5
Numeric, uppercase alphabetic, and several special characters as they are represented in ASCII and EBCDIC. Each character is represented in binary using a unique ordering of zeros and ones.

When the ASCII or EBCDIC code is used, each character that is represented is stored in one byte of memory. There are also other binary formats, sometimes used by the computer to represent numeric data. For example, a computer may store, or *pack*, two numeric characters in one byte of memory. These binary formats are used by the computer to increase storage and processing efficiency.

Parity

Regardless of whether ASCII, EBCDIC, or other binary methods are used to represent characters in main memory, it is important that the characters be stored accurately. For each byte of memory, most computers have at least one extra bit, called a **parity bit**, that is used by the computer for error checking. A parity bit can detect if one of the bits in a byte has been accidentally changed. While such errors are rare, they can occur because of voltage fluctuations, static electricity, or a memory failure.

Computers are either odd or even parity machines. In computers with **odd parity**, the total number of *on* bits in the byte (including the parity bit) must be an odd number (Figure 4-6). In computers with **even parity**, the total number of *on* bits must be an even number. Parity is checked by the computer each time a memory location is used. When data is moved from one location to another in main memory, the parity bits of both the sending and receiving locations are compared to see if they are the same. If the system detects a difference or if the wrong number of bits is on (e.g., an even number in a system with odd parity), an error message displays. Some computers use multiple parity bits that enable them to detect and correct a single-bit error and detect multiple-bit errors.

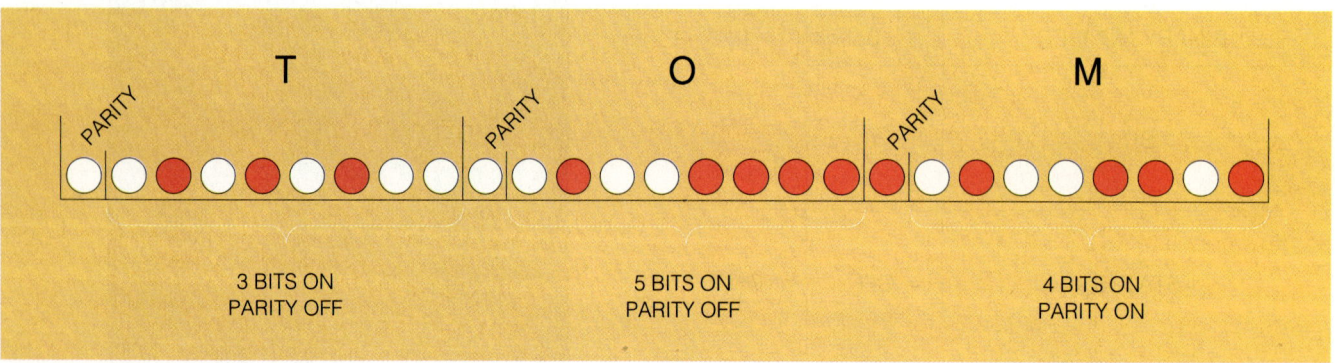

Figure 4-6
In a computer with odd parity, the parity bit is turned on or off to make the total number of on bits (including the parity bit) an odd number. Here, the letters T and O have an odd number of bits so the parity bits are left off. The number of bits for the letter M is even, so in order to achieve parity, the parity bit is turned on.

The Components of the System Unit

The components of the system unit are usually contained in a metal or plastic case. For personal computers, all system unit components are usually in a single box. For larger and more powerful computers, the components may be housed in several cabinets. The components considered part of the system unit and discussed in the following sections include: the motherboard, the microprocessor and CPU, upgrade sockets, memory, coprocessors, buses, expansion slots, ports and connectors, bays, the power supply, and sound components *(Figure 4-7)*.

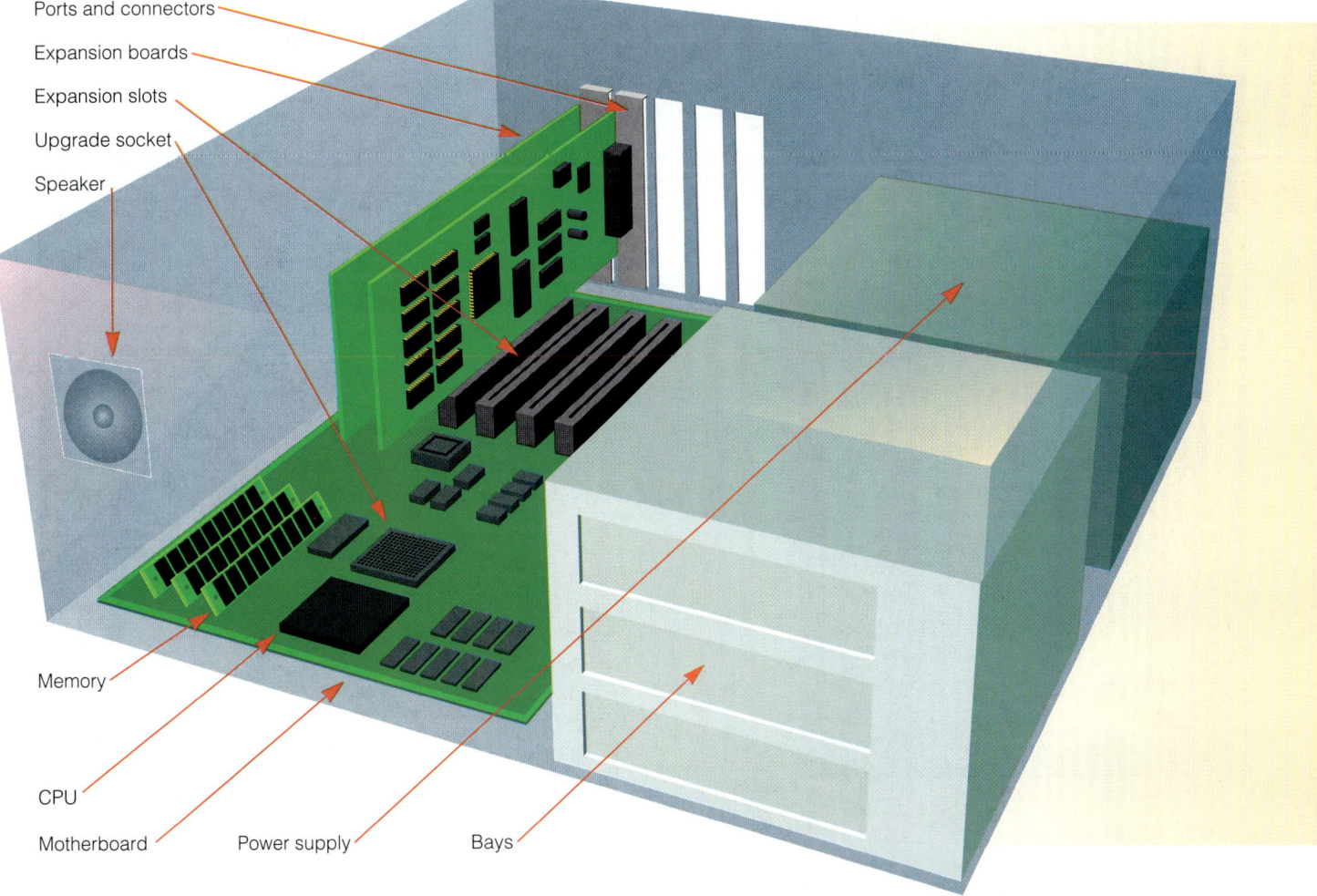

Figure 4-7
The components of the system unit are usually inside a plastic or metal case. This illustration shows how some of the components might be arranged on a typical PC.

Motherboard

The **motherboard**, sometimes called the **main board** or **system board**, is a circuit board that contains most of the electronic components of the system unit. *Figure 4-8* shows a photograph of a personal computer motherboard. One of the main components on the motherboard is the microprocessor.

Microprocessor and the CPU

On a personal computer, the CPU or central processing unit, is contained on a single integrated circuit called a **microprocessor** *(Figure 4-9)* that is located on the motherboard. An **integrated circuit**, also called a **chip** or an **IC**, is a complete electronic circuit that has been etched on a small slice of nonconducting material such as silicon. For mainframe and supercomputers, the CPU consists of one or more circuit boards *(Figure 4-10)*.

The **central processing unit** (CPU) contains the control unit and the arithmetic/logic unit. These two components work together using the program and data stored in main memory to perform the processing operations.

Control Unit

The control unit can be thought of as the *brain* of the computer. Just as the human brain controls the body, the control unit *controls* the computer. The **control unit** operates by repeating the following four operations, called the **machine cycle** *(Figure 4-11):* fetching, decoding, executing, and storing. **Fetching** means obtaining the next program

Figure 4-8
The main circuit board (motherboard) of a personal computer.

◀ *Figure 4-9*
A Pentium microprocessor from Intel Corporation. The microprocessor circuits are located in the center. Small gold wires lead from the circuits to the pins that fit in the microprocessor socket on the motherboard. The pins provide an electronic connection to different parts of the computer.

Figure 4-10 ▶
With PCs, the CPU is contained in a single microprocessor chip. With larger computers, the CPU operations are split among several chips and sometimes more than one circuit board.

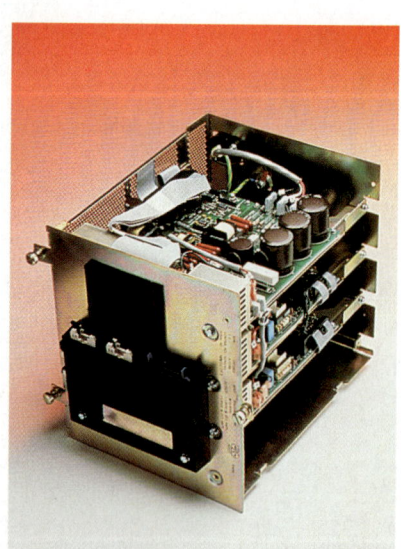

instruction from main memory. **Decoding** is translating the program instruction into the commands the computer can process. **Executing** refers to the actual processing of the computer commands, and **storing** takes place when the result of the instruction is written to main memory.

System Clock

The control unit utilizes the **system clock** to synchronize, or control the timing of, all computer operations. The system clock generates electronic pulses at a fixed rate, measured in **megahertz** (abbreviated **MHz**). One megahertz equals one million pulses per second. The speed of the system clock varies among computers. Some personal computers can operate at speeds in excess of 100 megahertz.

Arithmetic/Logic Unit

The second part of the CPU is the **arithmetic/logic unit** (**ALU**). This unit contains the electronic circuitry necessary to perform arithmetic and logical operations on data. **Arithmetic operations** include addition, subtraction, multiplication, and division. **Logical operations** consist of comparing one data item to another to determine if the first data item is *greater than, equal to,* or *less than* the other. Based on the result of the comparison, different processing may occur. For example, two part numbers in different records can be compared. If they are equal, the part quantity in one record can be added to the quantity in the other record. If they are not equal, the quantities would not be added.

Registers

Both the control unit and the ALU contain **registers**, temporary storage locations for specific types of data. Separate registers exist for the current program instruction, the address of the next instruction, and the values of data being processed.

Word Size

One aspect of the CPU that affects the speed of a computer is the word size. The **word size** is the number of bits the CPU processes at one time. The word size of a machine is measured in bits. CPUs can have 8-bit, 16-bit, 32-bit, or 64-bit word sizes. A CPU with a 16-bit word size can manipulate

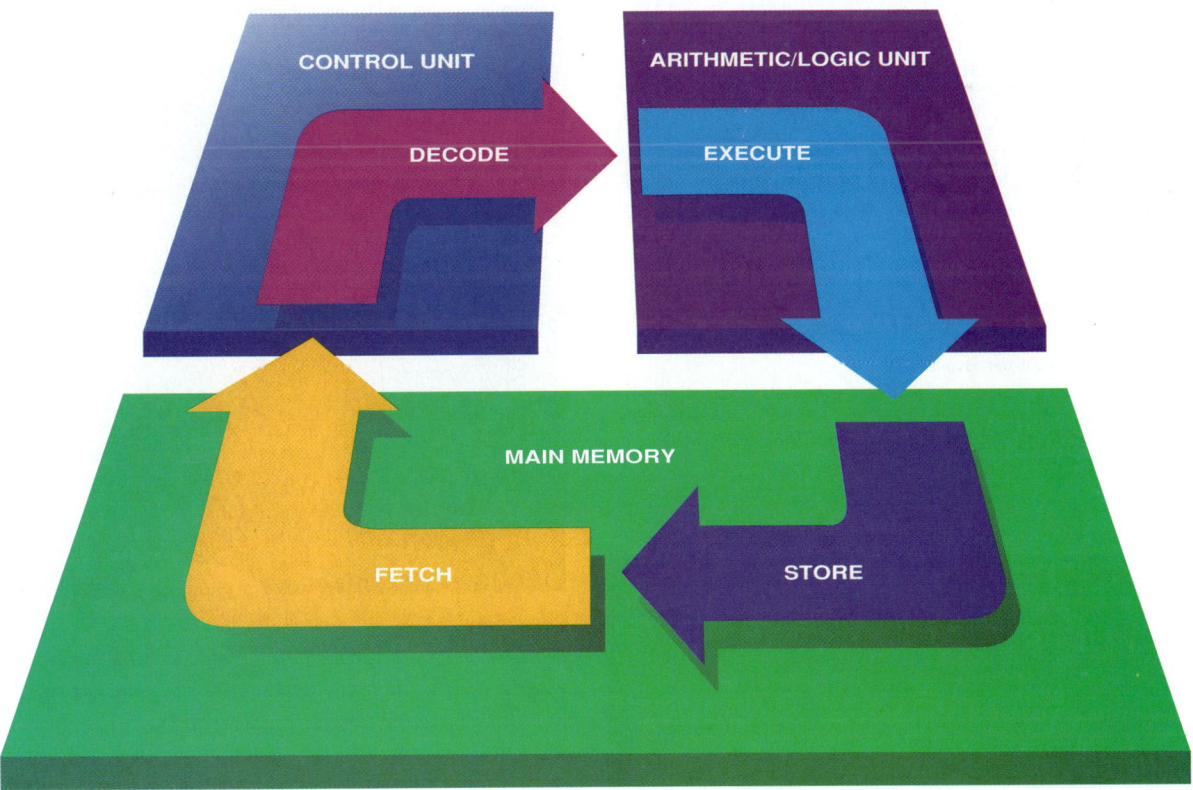

Figure 4-11
The machine cycle consists of four steps; fetching the next instruction, decoding the instruction, executing the instruction, and storing the result. Fetching and decoding are called the instruction cycle. Executing and storing are called the execution cycle.

16 bits at a time. Sometimes, the word size of a computer is given in bytes instead of bits. For example, a word size of 16 bits may be expressed as a word size of two bytes because there are eight bits in a byte. The larger the word size of the CPU, the faster the capability of the computer to process data.

Microprocessor Comparison

Personal computer microprocessors are most often identified by their model number or model name. *Figure 4-12a* summarizes some of the microprocessors currently in use. Microprocessors made by Intel come in several versions designated by letters after the processor name. *Figure 4-12b* explains the differences. Also, when discussing the three Intel processors prior to the Pentium, the "80" in the name/model number is usually not referred to. For example, the 80486 processor is usually referred to as a 486 processor.

Upgrade Sockets

Some motherboards contain empty sockets, called **upgrade sockets** *(Figure 4-13)*, that can be used to install more powerful CPUs or additional memory.

The CPU upgrade sockets enable a user to install a more powerful microprocessor and obtain increased performance without having to buy an entirely new system. With a CPU upgrade socket, the old microprocessor does not have to be removed. When the new microprocessor is installed, the old microprocessor is automatically disabled. Many, but not all, systems can install a more powerful microprocessor even if they do not have a separate CPU upgrade socket. For these systems, the old microprocessor is removed and replaced with the new microprocessor.

Name	Date	Manufacturer	Word Size	Bus Width	Clock Speed (Mhz)	MIPS*
Pentium	1993	Intel	64	64	60-100	112
80486DX	1989	Intel	32	32	25-66	20-54
80386DX	1985	Intel	32	32	16-33	5.5-11.4
80286	1982	Intel	16	16	8-12	1.2-1.7
PowerPC	1994	Motorola	64	64	66-80	>100
68040	1989	Motorola	32	32	25-40	15-35
68030	1987	Motorola	32	32	16-50	12
68020	1984	Motorola	32	32	16-33	5.5
Alpha AXP	1993	Digital	64	64	150	275

*MIPS: millions of instructions per second

Figure 4-12a
A comparison of some of the more widely used microprocessors.

ZIF socket

Figure 4-13
This motherboard includes an upgrade socket that can accept a more powerful Intel microprocessor. This particular type of socket is called a zero insertion force (ZIF) socket. The ZIF socket uses a lever to clamp down on the microprocessor pins and makes the installation of the chip easier. Other types of upgrade sockets require the microprocessor pins to be forced into the socket.

486DX4	Internal speed of chip is three times faster than the speed at which the chip communicates with the rest of the system.
486DX2	Internal speed of chip is two times faster than the speed at which the chip communicates with the rest of the system.
486SX	Does not have internal math coprocessor like 486DX models. Slower and less expensive than DX models.
386SX	32-bit word length but only 16-bit data bus. Slower and less expensive than 386DX.
SL	Low voltage version of 386 and 486 chip. Used primarily in portable computers to extend battery life.

Figure 4-12b
Different versions of Intel microprocessors.

Memory

Memory refers to integrated circuits that store program instructions and data that can be retrieved. Memory chips are installed in the system unit and also on circuit boards that control other computer devices such as printers. The two most common types of memory chips are Random Access Memory (RAM) and Read Only Memory (ROM).

Random Access Memory

Random access memory, or **RAM**, is the name given to the integrated circuits, or chips, that are used for main memory. **Main memory**, or **primary storage**, stores three items: the operating system and other system software that direct and coordinate the computer equipment; the application program instructions that direct the work to be done; and the data currently being processed by the application programs. Data and programs are transferred into and out of RAM, and data stored in RAM is manipulated by computer program instructions.

The basic unit of memory is a byte, which you recall consists of eight bits. Just as a house on a street has a unique address that indicates its location on the street, each byte in the main memory of a computer has an address that indicates its location in memory *(Figure 4-14)*. The number that indicates the location of a byte in memory is called a **memory address**. Whenever the computer references a byte, it does so by using the memory address, or location, of that byte.

The size of main memory is measured in either kilobytes or megabytes. A **kilobyte** (abbreviated as K or KB) is equal to 1,024 bytes, but for discussion purposes, is usually rounded to 1,000 bytes. A **megabyte** (abbreviated as MB) is approximately one million bytes. These terms are also used when discussing the storage capacity of other devices such as disk drives.

RAM memory is said to be **volatile** because the programs and data stored in RAM are erased when the power to the computer is turned off. As long as the power remains on,

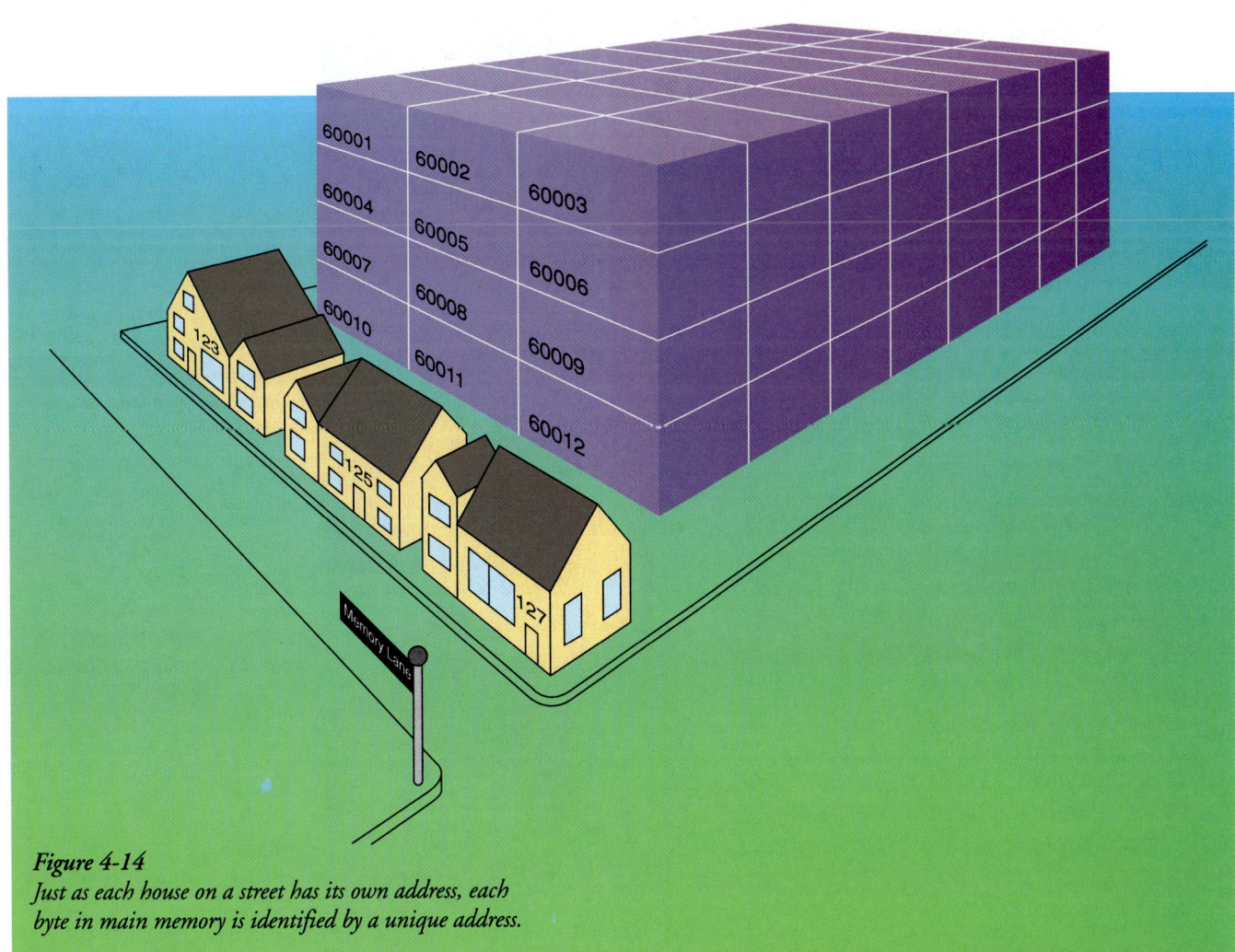

Figure 4-14
Just as each house on a street has its own address, each byte in main memory is identified by a unique address.

the programs and data stored in RAM will remain intact until they are replaced by other programs and data. Programs and data that are needed for future use must be transferred from RAM to secondary storage before the power is turned off. A relatively new type of memory called **flash RAM** or **flash memory** can retain data even when the power is turned off. Flash memory is sometimes used instead of a disk drive in small portable computers.

Today, most RAM memory is installed by using a **SIMM** (single in-line memory module). As shown in *Figure 4-15*, a SIMM is a small circuit board that holds multiple RAM chips. Common SIMM sizes are 1, 2, 4, 8, and 16 megabytes of memory. A SIMM is installed directly on the motherboard.

Some computers improve their processing efficiency by using a limited amount of high-speed RAM memory between the CPU and main memory *(Figure 4-16)*. High-speed memory used in this manner is called **cache memory** (pronounced cash). Cache memory is used to store the most frequently used instructions and data. When the processor needs the next program instruction or data, it first checks the cache memory. If the required instruction or data is present in cache (called a *cache hit*), the processor will execute faster than if the instruction or data has to be retrieved from the slower main memory.

As shown in *Figure 4-17*, memory on personal computers can be divided into four areas. **Conventional memory** is located in the first 640K of RAM and is used for the operating system, programs, and data. **Upper memory** is located between 640K and 1MB of RAM and is used for programs that control input and output devices and other computer hardware. **Extended memory** consists of all memory above 1MB and is used for programs and data. Not all programs are written to use extended memory. Older programs, including many games, must run in conventional memory space or use expanded memory. **Expanded memory** consists of up to 32MB of memory on a memory expansion board. A separate program called an *expanded memory manager* is used to access this memory 16K at a time and transfer the data into upper memory. Newer computers use extended memory and do not have expanded memory.

Figure 4-15
Most RAM memory is installed using a SIMM (single in-line memory module). SIMMs usually contain nine chips mounted on a small circuit board. Each chip represents one of the eight bit positions in a byte plus the parity bit. Common SIMM sizes are 1, 2, 4, 8, and 16 megabytes.

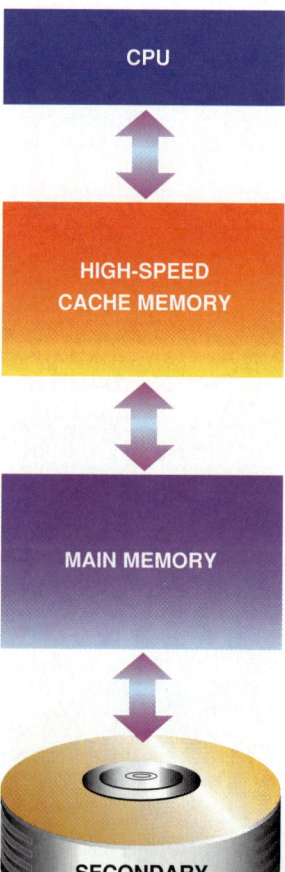

Figure 4-16
Some computers use high-speed cache memory to store frequently used instructions or data. If the required data or instructions are in cache, the processing will execute faster than if the instruction or data has to be retrieved from slower main memory or from secondary storage. Cache memory can consist of separate chips mounted on the motherboard or can be included in the actual CPU.

Read Only Memory

Read only memory (ROM) is the name given to chips that store information or instructions that do not change. For example, ROM is used to store the start up instructions and data used when a computer is first turned on. With ROM, data is permanently recorded in the memory when it is manufactured. ROM memory is described as **nonvolatile** because it retains its contents even when the power is turned off. The data or programs that are stored in ROM can be read and used, but cannot be altered, hence the name *read only*. Many of the special-purpose computers used in automobiles, appliances, and so on use small amounts of ROM to store instructions that will be executed repeatedly. Instructions that are stored in ROM memory are called **firmware** or **microcode**.

Memory Speed

Because of different manufacturing techniques and materials, some types of memory are faster than others. The speed of memory is measured in **nanoseconds**, one billionth of a second. Main memory is comprised of **dynamic** RAM **(DRAM)** chips that have access speeds of 50 to 100 nanoseconds. RAM cache memory is faster and is comprised of **static** RAM **(SRAM)** chips with access times of 10 to 50 nanoseconds. Static RAM chips are not used for main memory because they are larger than dynamic RAM chips and because they cost significantly more to manufacture. Registers designed into the CPU chip are the fastest type of memory with access times of 1 to 10 nanoseconds. ROM memory has access times between 50 and 250 nanoseconds. For comparison purposes, accessing data on a fast hard disk takes between 10 and 20 milliseconds. One **millisecond** is a thousandth of a second. Thus, accessing information in memory with a 70 nanosecond access time is 2,500 times faster than accessing data on a hard disk with a 15 millisecond access time.

Figure 4-17
Memory allocation on a personal computer.

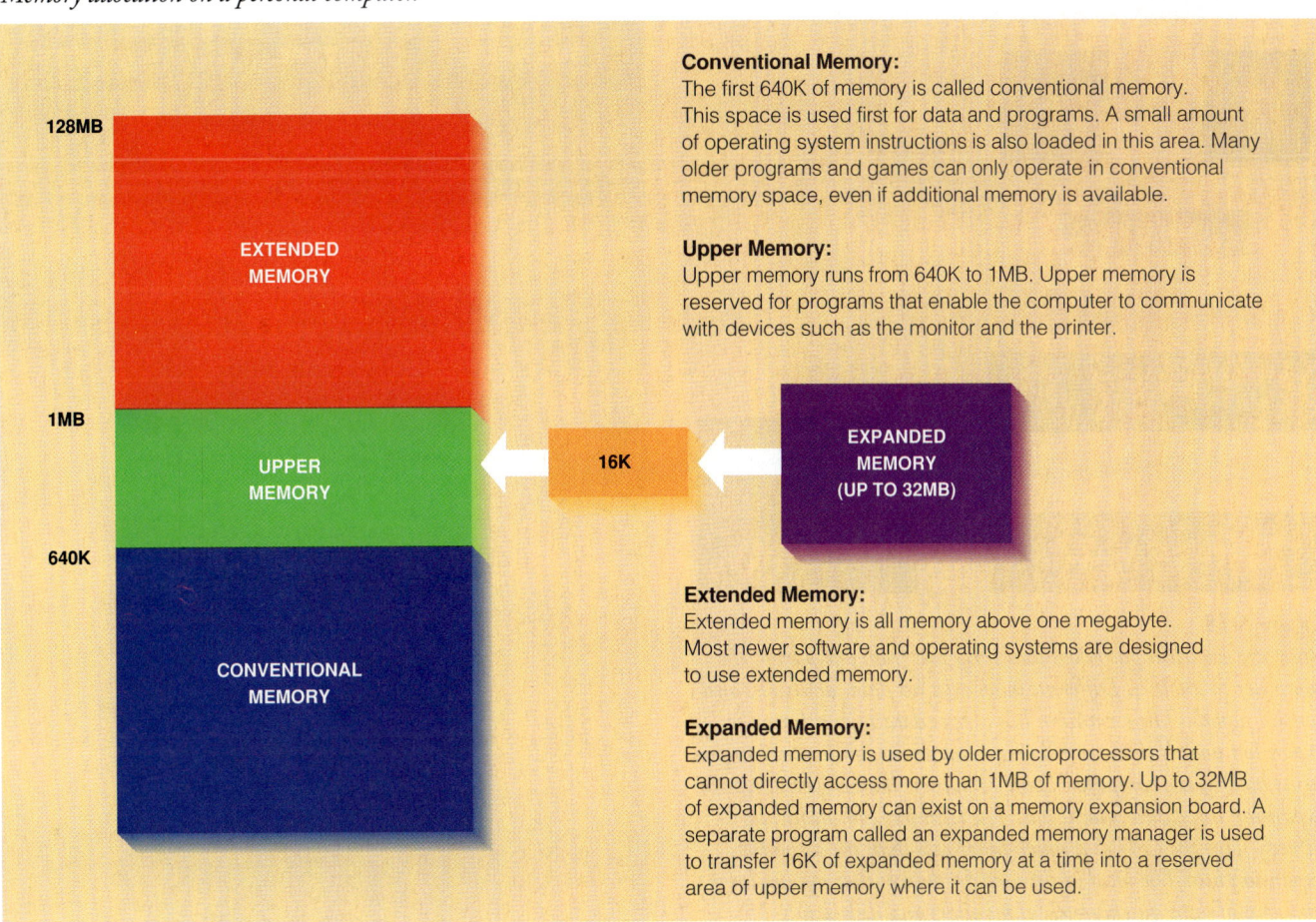

Coprocessors

One way computers increase their productivity is the use of a **coprocessor**, a special microprocessor chip or circuit board designed to perform a specific task. For example, math coprocessors can be added to computers to greatly speed up the processing of numeric calculations. Other types of coprocessors are used to speed up the display of graphics and for communications. Some computers have coprocessors designed into the CPU.

Buses

As previously explained, computers store and process data as a series of electronic bits. These bits are transferred internally within the circuitry of the computer along paths capable of transmitting electrical impulses. Sometimes these paths are actual wires and sometimes they are etched lines on the circuit board or within the CPU chip itself. Any path along which bits are transmitted is called a **bus**. Buses are used to transfer bits from input devices to memory, from memory to the CPU, from the CPU to memory, and from memory to output devices. Separate buses are used for memory addresses, control signals, and data. One type of bus is called an expansion bus.

An **expansion bus** carries the data to and from the expansion slots *(Figure 4-18)*. Personal computers can have different types of expansion buses. Some computers have more than one type present. It is important to know the type of expansion buses on your computer because some devices

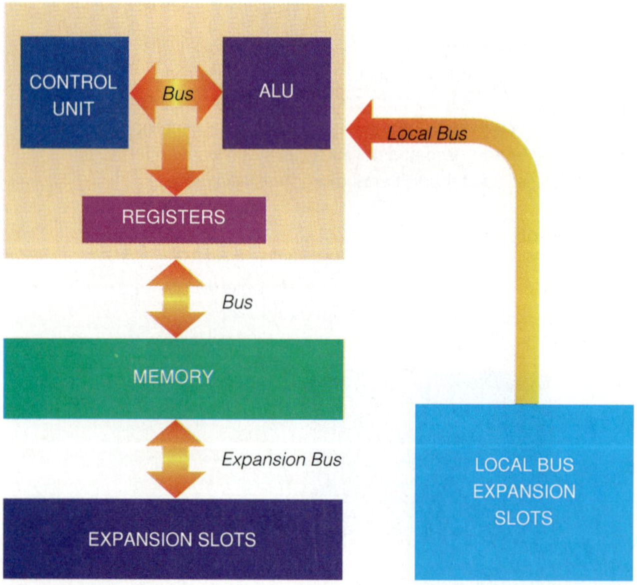

Figure 4-18
Buses are electrical pathways that carry bits from one part of the computer to another. Different buses exist for data, addresses, and control signals. The expansion bus carries data to and from the expansion boards that control peripheral devices and other components used by the computer. Some computers have a special type of expansion bus called a local bus. The local bus communicates directly with the CPU at a much faster rate than the standard expansion bus. The local bus is used for devices that require large amounts of data quickly such as monitors and disk drives.

Figure 4-19
Types of expansion buses found on personal computers.

BUS NAME	TYPE	BITS
XT	standard	8
ISA	standard	16
EISA	standard	32
MCA	standard	16 or 32
VESA or VL	local	32
PCI	local	32 or 64
NuBus	standard	32

Expansion Slots

are designed to work with only one bus type. Most expansion buses connect directly to RAM. To obtain faster performance, some expansion buses bypass RAM and connect directly to the CPU. An expansion bus that connects directly to the CPU is called a **local bus**. *Figure 4-19* lists the most common expansion bus types on personal computers.

Buses can transfer multiples of eight bits at a time. A 16-bit bus has 16 lines and can transmit 16 bits at a time. On a 32-bit bus, bits can be moved from place to place 32 bits at a time, and on a 64-bit bus, bits are moved 64 bits at a time. The larger the number of bits that are handled by a bus, the faster the computer can transfer data. For example, assume a number in memory occupies four eight-bit bytes. With a 16-bit bus, two steps would be required to transfer the data from memory to the CPU because on the 16-bit bus, the data in two eight-bit bytes would be transferred in an individual step. On a 32-bit bus, the entire four bytes could be transferred at one time. The fewer number of transfer steps required, the faster the transfer of data.

An **expansion slot** is a socket designed to hold the circuit board for a device, such as a tape drive or sound card, that adds capability to the computer system. The circuit board for the add-on device is called an **expansion board**. Expansion boards are sometimes called **expansion cards**, **controller cards**, **adapter cards**, or **interface cards**. The expansion card is usually connected to the device it controls by a cable. The socket that holds the card is connected to the expansion bus that transmits data to memory or the CPU. *Figure 4-20* shows an expansion board being placed in an expansion slot on a personal computer motherboard.

A special type of expansion slot is the PCMCIA slot. PCMCIA stands for Personal Computer Memory Card International Association. This group has defined standards for a thin credit card-sized device that can be inserted into a personal computer *(Figure 4-21)*. **PCMCIA cards** are used for additional memory, storage, and communications.

Figure 4-20
An expansion board being inserted into an expansion slot on the motherboard of a personal computer.

Figure 4-21
PCMCIA cards are not much bigger than a credit card and fit in a small slot, usually on the side of a computer. PCMCIA cards are used for additional memory, storage, and communications. Because of their small size, PCMCIA cards are often used on portable computers. The card shown in this photo is a fax/data modem that can be connected to a phone line.

DESCRIPTION
Developed for original IBM PC
Industry Standard Architecture, sometimes called AT bus
Extended Industry Standard Architecture developed by IBM clone manufacturers; backward compatible with ISA bus (ISA cards can run in EISA bus)
Micro Channel Architecture developed by IBM for high-end PS/2 systems
Local bus standard developed by Video Electronics Standards Association
Peripheral Component Interconnect local bus standard developed by Intel
High performance expansion bus used in Apple Macintosh computers

Ports and Connectors

A **port** is a socket used to connect the system unit to a peripheral device such as a printer or a modem. Most of the time, ports are on the back of the system unit *(Figure 4-22)* but they can also be on the front. Ports have different types of couplers, called **connectors**, that are used to attach cables to the peripheral devices. A matching connector is on the end of the cable that attaches to the port. Most connectors are available in two genders – male or female. Male connectors have one or more exposed pins, like the end of an electrical cord you plug into the wall. Female connectors have matching receptacles to accept the pins, like an electrical wall outlet. *Figure 4-23* shows the different type of connectors you may find on a system unit. Ports can either be parallel or serial.

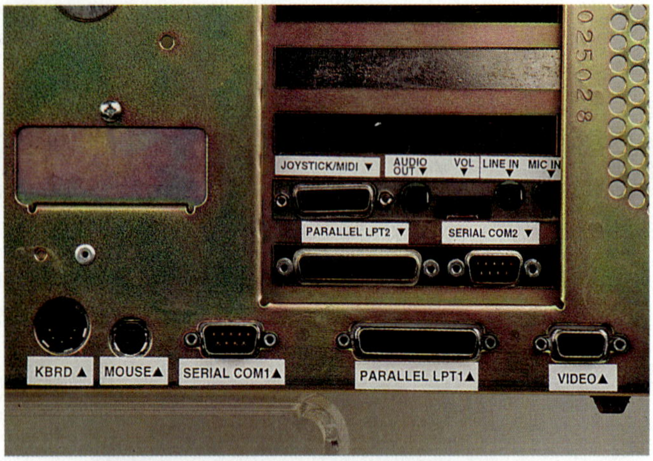
JOYSTICK/MIDI
AUDIO OUT
VOL
LINE IN
MIC IN
PARALLEL LPT2
SERIAL COM2
KBRD
MOUSE
SERIAL COM1
PARALLEL LPT1
VIDEO

Figure 4-22
Ports are sockets used for cables that connect the system unit with devices such as a mouse, keyboard, and printer. Usually, ports are on the back of the system unit.

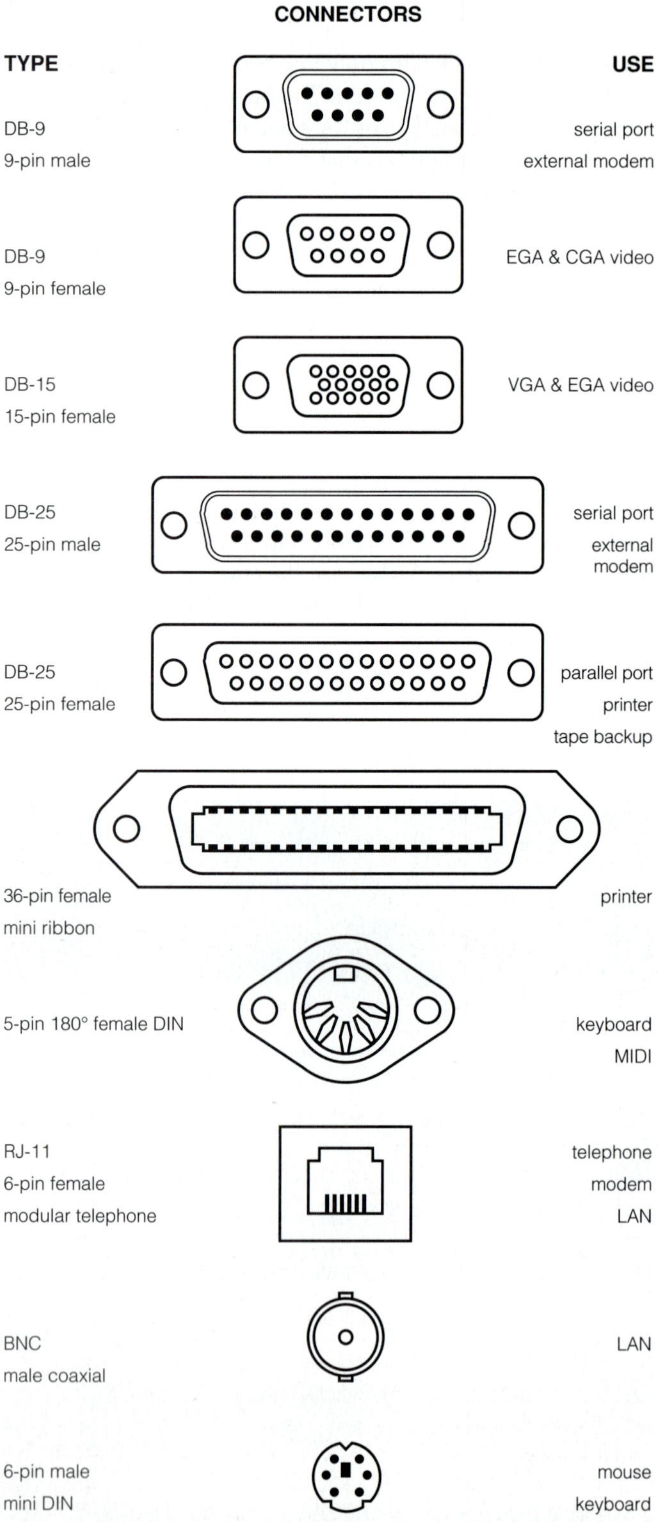
CONNECTORS
TYPE
USE
DB-9
9-pin male
serial port
external modem
DB-9
9-pin female
EGA & CGA video
DB-15
15-pin female
VGA & EGA video
DB-25
25-pin male
serial port
external modem
DB-25
25-pin female
parallel port
printer
tape backup
36-pin female
mini ribbon
printer
5-pin 180° female DIN
keyboard
MIDI
RJ-11
6-pin female
modular telephone
telephone
modem
LAN
BNC
male coaxial
LAN
6-pin male
mini DIN
mouse
keyboard

Figure 4-23
Examples of different types of connectors used to connect devices to the system unit. Adapters are available to join one type of connector with another.

Parallel Ports

Parallel ports are most often used to connect devices that send or receive large amounts of data such as printers or disk and tape drives. **Parallel ports** transfer eight bits (one byte) at a time using a cable that has eight data lines *(Figure 4-24)*. The electrical signals in a parallel cable tend to interfere with one another over a long distance and therefore, parallel cables are usually limited to 50 feet. Personal computer parallel cables are usually six to ten feet long. A special type of parallel port is the SCSI (pronounced scuzzy) port. SCSI stands for small computer system interface. A **SCSI port** can be used to attach up to seven different devices to a single port. The devices must be designed to connect to the SCSI port.

Serial Ports

A **serial port** transmits data one bit at a time *(Figure 4-25)* and is considerably slower than a parallel port. Cables connecting serial ports are smaller than parallel cables and do not generate as much electrical interference. Because of this, serial port cables can be up to 1,000 feet long. Serial ports are used for the mouse, the keyboard, and communication devices such as a modem. A special type of serial port is a MIDI (pronounced *midd-dee*) port. MIDI stands for musical instrument digital interface. A **MIDI port** is a serial port designed to be connected to a musical device such as an electronic keyboard or a music synthesizer.

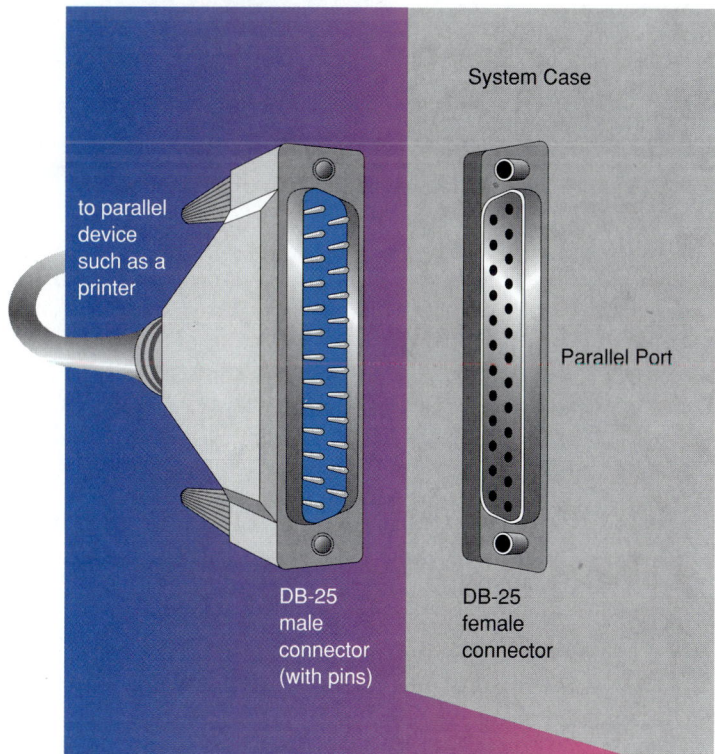

Figure 4-24
Parallel ports transfer eight bits at a time using a cable with eight data lines.

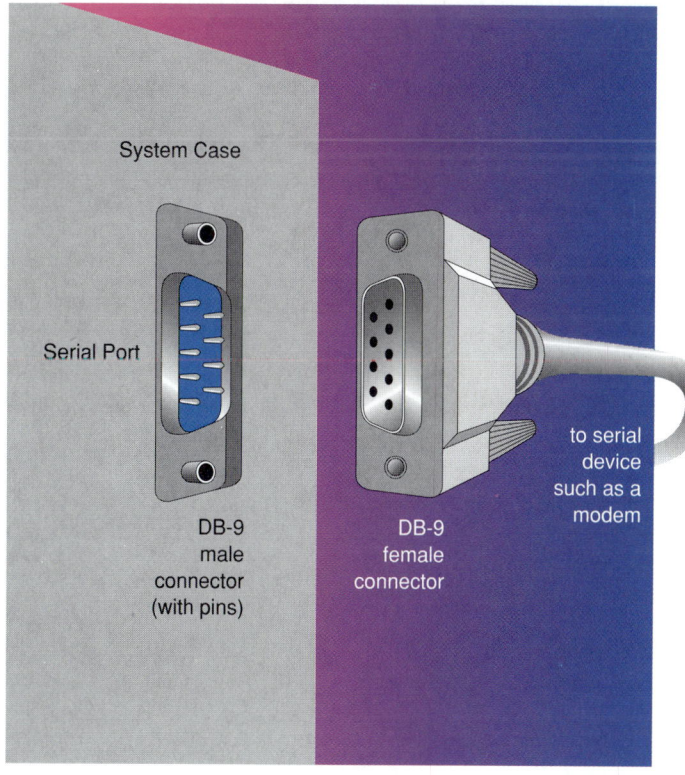

Figure 4-25
Serial ports transfer only one bit at a time and are slower than parallel ports. Separate data lines are used to transmit and receive data. Pin 2 is used to receive data and pin 3 is used to send data.

Bays

A **bay** is an open area inside the system unit used to install additional equipment. Because they are often used for disk and tape drives, these spaces are also called **drive bays**. Mounting brackets called **rails** are sometimes required to install a device in a bay. Two or more bays side by side or on top of one another are called a **cage**. *Figure 4-26* shows a personal computer with a three-bay cage. *External bays* have one end adjacent to an opening in the case. External bays are used for devices that require loading and unloading of storage media such as diskettes, tapes, and CD-ROMs. *Internal bays* are not accessible from outside the case and are used for hard disk drives.

Power Supply

The **power supply** converts the wall outlet electricity (115-120 volts AC) to the lower voltages (5 to 12 volts DC) used by the computer. The power supply also has a fan that provides airflow inside the system unit to help cool the components. The humming noise you hear when you turn on a computer is usually the power supply fan. Personal computer power supplies are rated by wattage and range from 100 to 250 watts. Higher wattage power supplies can support more electronic equipment.

Figure 4-26
Bays, also called drive bays, are usually located beside or on top of one another. Each bay is approximately 1 3/4 inches high by 6 inches wide by 8 inches deep. Two or more bays together are called a cage.

Sound Components

Most personal computers have the capability to generate sounds through a small speaker housed within the system unit. Software allows users to generate a variety of sounds including music and voice. Some computers also have built-in microphones that allow users to record voice messages and other sounds. As you will see in the chapter on output devices, many users enhance the sound-generating capabilities of their systems by installing expansion boards, called sound boards, and by attaching higher quality speakers to their systems.

Summary of the Components of the System Unit

The previous sections have presented information about the various components of the system unit. You should now be able to identify these components and have a more complete understanding about how they operate. The next section will explain how the system unit processes data by executing machine language instructions.

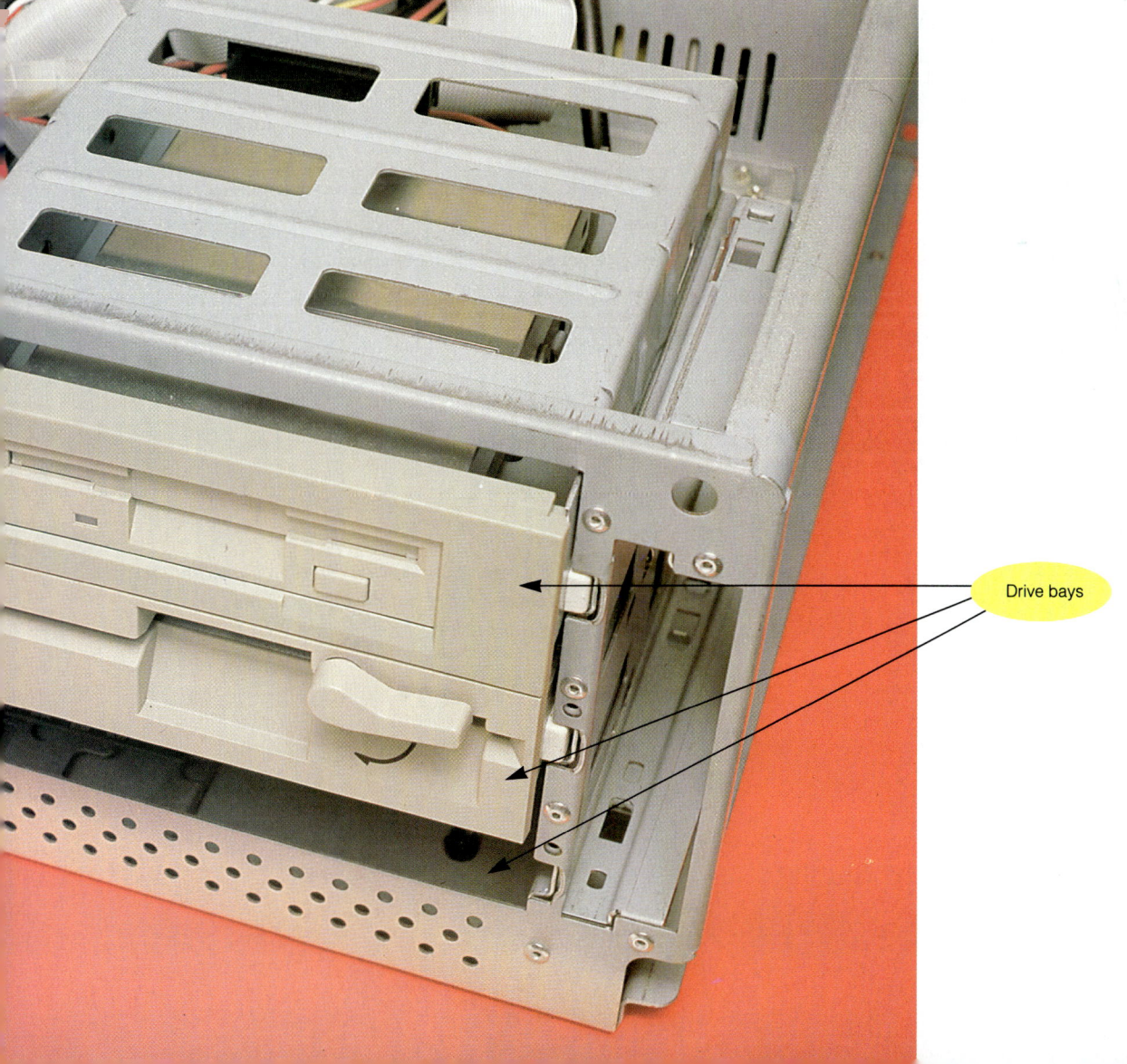

Machine Language Instructions

The system unit gets its directions from programs permanently stored in ROM or temporarily stored in RAM. To execute, program instructions must be in a form, called machine language instructions, the CPU can understand. A **machine language instruction** is binary data that the electronic circuits in the CPU can interpret and convert into one or more of the commands in the computer's instruction set. The **instruction set** contains commands, such as ADD or MOVE, that the computer's circuits can directly perform. Most computers have hundreds of commands in their instruction sets and are referred to as **CISC** computers, standing for *complex instruction set computing* (or *computers*). Studies have shown, however, that as much as 80% of the processing is performed by a small number of frequently used instructions. Based on these findings, some manufacturers have designed CPUs based on RISC technology. **RISC**, which stands for *reduced instruction set computing* (or *computers),* involves reducing the instructions to only those that are most frequently used. Because a RISC computer is designed to execute the frequently used instructions, overall processing capability, or throughput, is increased.

A machine language instruction is composed of two parts. The first part is called an operation code or opcode for short. An **operation code** tells the computer what to do and matches one of the commands in the instruction set. The second part of the machine language instruction is an operand. An **operand** specifies the data or the location of the data that will be used by the instruction. A machine language instruction may have zero to three operands. *Figure 4-27* shows an example of a machine language instruction that adds the number 32 to a register in the CPU.

In the early days, computers actually had to be programmed in machine language instructions using mechanical switches to represent each binary bit. Today, program instructions are written in a readable form using a variety of programming languages. The program instructions are then converted by the computer into machine language instructions. Programming languages and conversion methods are discussed in the chapter on programming languages.

MACHINE LANGUAGE INSTRUCTION		
opcode	operand 1	operand 2
00000101	00100000	00000000
Addition command	the value 32	data register in CPU

Figure 4-27
A PC machine language instruction consists of an operation code (opcode) and up to three operands. This machine language instruction adds the value 32 to a register.

The number of machine language instructions a computer processes in one second is one way of rating the speed of computers. One **MIPS** equals one million instructions per second. Powerful personal computers today are rated at more than 100 MIPS. Another way of rating computer speed is the number of floating-point operations. Floating-point operations are a type of mathematical calculation. The term **megaflop** (**MFLOPS**) is used for millions of floating-point operations per second. **Gigaflop** (**GFLOPS**) is used for billions of floating-point operations per second. Giga is a prefix indicating billion.

Types of Processing

In the discussions thus far, the emphasis has focused on computers with single CPUs processing one instruction at a time. The following section presents variations from this approach.

Pipelining

In most CPUs, the system waits until an instruction completes all four stages of the machine cycle (fetch, decode, execute, and store) before beginning to work on the next instruction. With **pipelining**, a new instruction is started as soon as the preceding instruction moves to the next stage. The result is faster throughput, because by the time the first instruction is in the fourth and final stage of the machine cycle, three other instructions have started to be processed *(Figure 4-28)*. Some CPUs, such as the Intel Pentium, have two or more pipelines that can simultaneously process instructions.

MACHINE CYCLE (without pipelining):

Machine Cycle Stages			
Fetch	Decode	Execute	Store
INSTRUCTION 1	INSTRUCTION 1	INSTRUCTION 1	INSTRUCTION 1 (Results)

MACHINE CYCLE (with pipelining):

Machine Cycle Stages			
Fetch	Decode	Execute	Store
INSTRUCTION 1 INSTRUCTION 2 INSTRUCTION 3 **INSTRUCTION 4**	INSTRUCTION 1 INSTRUCTION 2 **INSTRUCTION 3**	INSTRUCTION 1 **INSTRUCTION 2**	INSTRUCTION 1 (Results)

Figure 4-28
Without pipelining, an instruction moves through the complete machine cycle before the next instruction is started. With pipelining, the CPU starts working on another instruction each time the preceding instruction moves to the next stage of the machine cycle. As shown in the illustration for pipelining, by the time the first instruction has reached the fourth stage of the machine cycle, the next three instructions have started the cycle. Some CPUs have more than one pipeline.

Parallel Processing

Most computers contain one central processing unit (CPU) that processes a single instruction at a time. When one instruction is finished, the CPU begins execution of the next instruction, and so on until the program is completed. This method is known as **serial processing**. **Parallel processing** involves the use of multiple CPUs, each with its own memory. Parallel processors divide up a problem so multiple CPUs can work on their assigned portion of the problem simultaneously *(Figure 4-29)*. As you might expect, parallel processors require special software that can recognize how to divide up problems and bring the results back together again. Parallel processors are often used in supercomputers. **Massively parallel processors** (MPP) use hundreds or thousands of microprocessor CPUs to perform calculations.

Neural Network Computers

Neural network computers use specially designed circuits to simulate the way the human brain processes information, learns, and remembers. Neural network chips form a interconnected system of processors that learn to associate the relative strength or weakness of inputs with specific results (output). Neural network computers are used in applications such as pattern recognition to correctly guess the identity of an object when only hazy or partial information is available. Other applications that use neural network computers are speech recognition and speech synthesis.

Figure 4-29
Parallel processors have multiple CPUs that can divide up parts of the same job or work on different jobs at the same time. Special software is required to divide up the tasks and bring the results together.

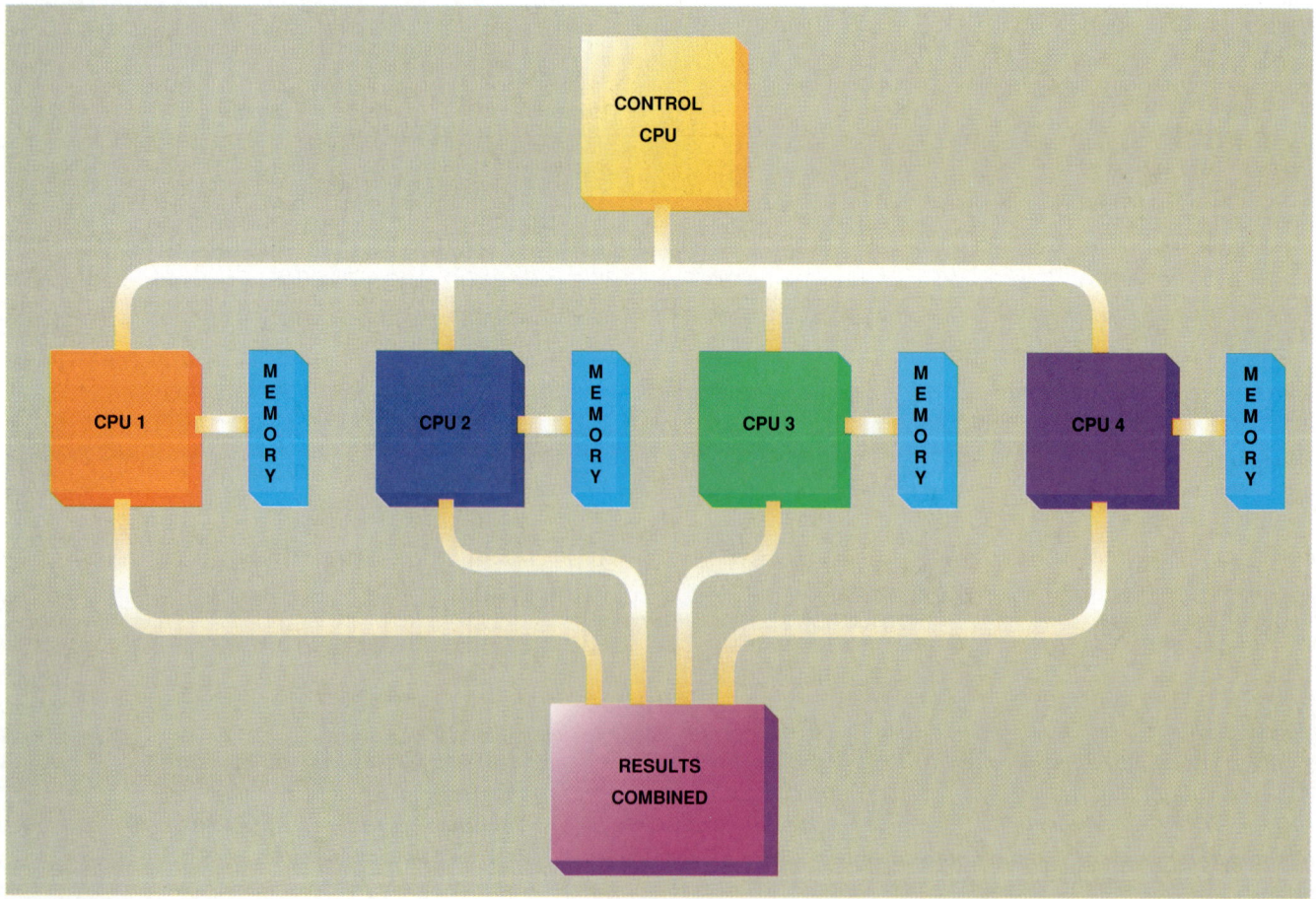

Number Systems

This section describes the number systems that are used with computers. Whereas thorough knowledge of this subject is required for technical computer personnel, a general understanding of number systems and how they relate to computers is all most users need.

As you have seen, the binary (base 2) number system is used to represent the electronic status of the bits in main memory. It is also used for other purposes such as addressing the memory locations. Another number system that is commonly used with computers is **hexadecimal** (base 16). *Figure 4-30* shows how the decimal values 0 through 15 are represented in binary and hexadecimal.

The mathematical principles that apply to the binary and hexadecimal number systems are the same as those that apply to the decimal number system. To help you better understand these principles, this section starts with the familiar decimal system, then progresses to the binary and hexadecimal number systems.

Decimal Number System

The decimal number system is a base 10 number system (*deci* means ten). The *base* of a number system indicates how many symbols are used in it. Decimal uses 10 symbols, 0 through 9. Each of the symbols in the number system has a value associated with it. For example, you know that 3 represents a quantity of three and 5 represents a quantity of five. The decimal number system is also a *positional* number system. This means that in a number such as 143, each position in the number has a value associated with it. When you look at the decimal number 143, you know that the 3 is in the ones, or units, position and represents three ones or (3 x 1); the 4 is in the tens position and represents four tens or (4 x 10); and the 1 is in the hundreds position and represents one hundred or (1 x 100). The number 143 is the sum of the values in each position of the number (100 + 40 + 3 = 143). The chart in *Figure 4-31* shows how the positional values (hundreds, tens, and units) for a number system can be calculated. Starting on the right and working to the left, the base of the number system, in this case 10, is raised to consecutive powers. The value 10^0, or 1, is the positional value for the units position. The value 10^1, or 10, is the positional value for the tens position. The value 10^2, or 100, is the positional value for the hundreds position. These calculations are a mathematical way of determining the place values in a number system.

DECIMAL	BINARY	HEXADECIMAL
0	0000	0
1	0001	1
2	0010	2
3	0011	3
4	0100	4
5	0101	5
6	0110	6
7	0111	7
8	1000	8
9	1001	9
10	1010	A
11	1011	B
12	1100	C
13	1101	D
14	1110	E
15	1111	F

Figure 4-30
The binary and hexadecimal representation of decimal numbers 0 through 15 are shown in this chart. Notice how letters represent the numbers 10 through 15 in the hexadecimal representation.

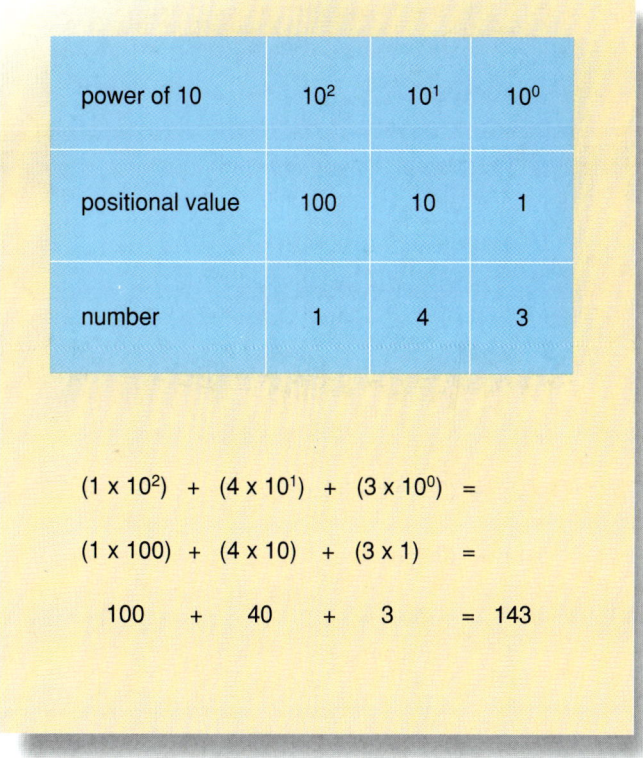

Figure 4-31
The positional values in the decimal number 143 are shown in this chart.

When you use number systems other than decimal, the same principles apply. The base of the number system indicates the number of symbols that are used, and each position in a number system has a value associated with it. The positional value can be calculated by raising the base of the number system to consecutive powers beginning with zero.

Binary Number System

As previously discussed, binary is a base 2 number system (*bi* means two), and the symbols that are used are 0 and 1. Just as each position in a decimal number has a place value associated with it, so does each position in a binary number. To determine the place values for binary, the base of the number system, in this case 2, is raised to consecutive powers *(Figure 4-32)*. To construct a binary number, you place ones in the positions where the corresponding values add up to the quantity you want to represent; you place zeros in the other positions. For example, the binary place values are 8, 4, 2, and 1, and the binary number 1001 has ones in the positions for the values 8 and 1 and zeros in the positions for 4 and 2. Therefore, the quantity represented by binary 1001 is 9 $(8 + 0 + 0 + 1)$.

Hexadecimal Number System

Many computers use a base 16 number system called hexadecimal. The hexadecimal number system uses 16 symbols to represent values. These include the symbols 0 through 9 and A through F *(Figure 4-30* on the previous page*)*. The mathematical principles previously discussed also apply to hexadecimal *(Figure 4-33)*.

The primary reason why the hexadecimal number system is used with computers is because it can represent binary values in a more compact form and because the conversion between the binary and the hexadecimal number systems is very efficient. An eight-digit binary number can be represented by a two-digit hexadecimal number. For example, in the ASCII code, the character M is represented as 01001101. This value can be represented in hexadecimal as 4D. One way to convert this binary number to a hexadecimal number is to divide the binary number (from right to left) into groups of four digits; calculate the value of each group; and then change any two-digit values (10 through 15) into the symbols A through F that are used in hexadecimal *(Figure 4-34)*.

power of 2	2^3	2^2	2^1	2^0
positional value	8	4	2	1
binary	1	0	0	1

$(1 \times 2^3) + (0 \times 2^2) + (0 \times 2^1) + (1 \times 2^0) =$

$(1 \times 8) + (0 \times 4) + (0 \times 2) + (1 \times 1) =$

$8 + 0 + 0 + 1 = 9$

power of 16	16^1	16^0
positional value	16	1
hexadecimal	A	5

$(10 \times 16^1) + (5 \times 16^0) =$

$(10 \times 16) + (5 \times 1) =$

$160 + 5 = 165$

Figure 4-32
Each positional value in a binary number represents a consecutive power of two. Using the positional values, the binary number 1001 can be converted to the decimal number 9.

Figure 4-33
Conversion of the hexadecimal number A5 to the decimal number 165. Notice that the value 10 is substituted for the A during calculations.

Summary of Number Systems

As mentioned at the beginning of the section on number systems, binary and hexadecimal are used primarily by technical computer personnel. A general user does not need a complete understanding of numbering systems. The concepts that you should remember about number systems are that binary is used to represent the electronic status of the bits in main memory and auxiliary storage. Hexadecimal is used to represent binary in a more compact form.

Summary of the System Unit

This chapter examined various aspects of the system unit including its components, how programs and data are stored, and how the processor executes program instructions to process data into information. You have also studied various methods of processing and learned about the various number systems used with computers. Knowing this material will increase your overall understanding of how processing occurs on a computer.

positional value	8421	8421
binary	0100	1101
decimal	4	13
hexadecimal	4	D

Figure 4-34
Conversion of the ASCII code 01001101 for the letter M to the hexadecimal value 4D. Each group of four binary digits is converted to a hexadecimal symbol.

COMPUTERS AT WORK

Unparalleled Performance from Parallel Processors

One way of obtaining improved computer performance is by using more than one CPU. The theory is simple; if one CPU can do a job in one hour, then two CPUs could do the job in 30 minutes, four CPUs in 15 minutes, 60 CPUs in 1 minute, and so on. Although the results aren't as direct as the example (twice the CPUs does not reduce the time in half), significant improvements in performance can be obtained if the work to be done is divided into separate parts that can be worked on simultaneously. Some applications using this approach have been implemented on parallel processors for some time. These applications include automobile crash simulation and weather forecasting. With automobile crash simulation, parallel processors measure the impact and damage at multiple points on the automobile at the same time *(Figure 4-35)*. With weather forecasting, the effect of simultaneous temperature and pressure changes is calculated. Parallel processors are also being applied to commercial applications in several ways. Large-scale parallel processors are being applied to database searches. Kmart, WalMart, and Mervyn's are three retailers that use large parallel processors to sort through millions of transactions in hours to spot sales patterns and trends. For this type of application, the database can be divided among the number of processors available. On a mainframe, the same sales analysis application could take days. On a smaller scale, multiple processors are being implemented at the PC level. The most powerful server computers usually have four or more CPUs to handle the network requirements of up to several thousand users. Microprocessor designers are also incorporating parallel processor designs into the CPU itself. For example, Intel has plans to have four separate but linked CPUs in the chip it plans to build sometime around the year 2000 (see **IN THE FUTURE** on the next page). Existing microprocessor chips, such as the Intel Pentium, have some parts, but not all, of the CPU duplicated. Eventually, all computers will have multiple CPUs working in parallel to produce faster results than any single CPU system.

Figure 4-35

IN THE FUTURE

2,000 MIPS by the Year 2000

By the year 2000, Intel, the world's largest manufacturer of microprocessors, predicts it will have a CPU chip that can perform 2,000 MIPS; 2 billion instructions per second. This is almost ten times faster than microprocessor CPUs currently available. To reach this performance level, Intel will have to continue to pack more transistors onto the slice of silicon that becomes the heart of the microprocessor. Intel's Pentium processor has 3.3 million transistors. Their next generation processor, dubbed the P6, is predicted to have between 6 and 8 million transistors. The 2,000 MIPS processor will have between 50 and 100 million transistors spread among four integrated CPUs. To reach this level of transistor density, the size of the transistors will have to shrink below one-tenth of a micron. A micron is one-millionth of a meter. Current microprocessors have transistor sizes approximately six- to eight-tenths of a micron. For comparison purposes, an average human hair is 75 microns, or approximately 100 times the size of current microprocessor transistors. The clock speed of the microprocessor will also have to improve, probably to about 250 megahertz (each megahertz is one million cycles per second). Current microprocessors run at about 100 to 150 megahertz.

To reach these levels of transistor density and clock speed, microprocessor chip advances will have to continue to meet the prediction of Intel founder Gordon Moore. In 1965, Moore predicted that transistor density, and thus relative computing power, would double every 18 to 24 months. Called Moore's Law, this prediction has so far been amazingly accurate (see *Figure 4-36*). To reach Intel's goal of the 2,000 MIPS chip by the year 2000, the law will have to hold true for a few more years.

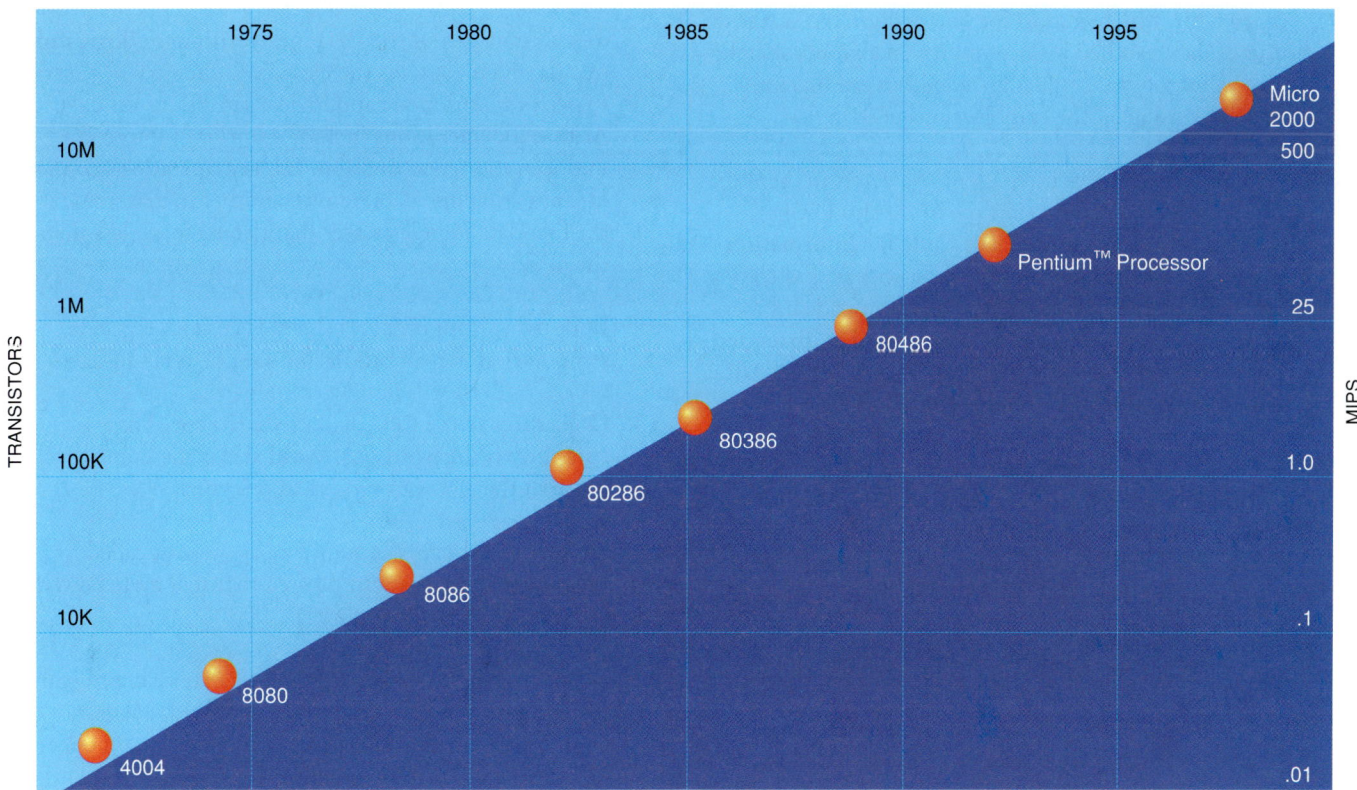

Figure 4-36

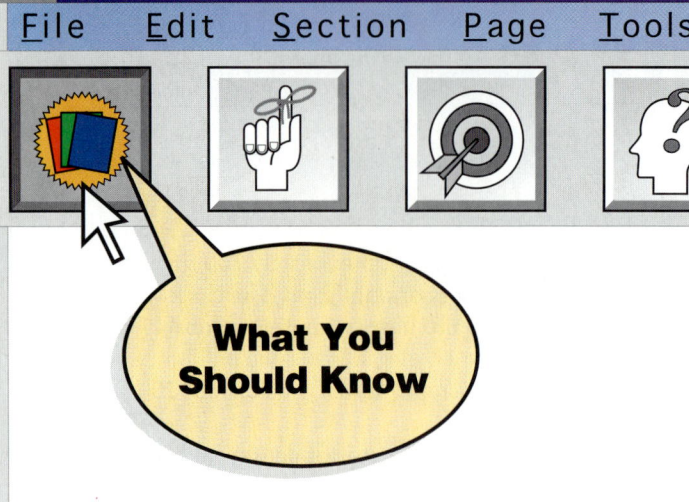

What You Should Know

1. It is in the **system unit** that the computer program instructions are executed and the data is manipulated. The system unit contains the central processing unit, or CPU, main memory, and other electronics.

2. Most computers are **digital computers**, meaning that the data they process is first converted into a digital (numeric) value. Converting data into digital form is called **digitizing**. Other types of computers, called **analog computers**, are designed to process variable data.

3. The digital values used by a computer are 0 (to represent the electronic state of *off*) and 1 (to represent the electronic state of *on*). Each off or on digital value is called a **bit**, which is short for *bi*nary dig*it*, the smallest unit of data handled by a computer. In a group of eight bits, called a **byte**, 256 data possibilities can be represented by using all the combinations of 0s and 1s.

4. Two popular codes that represent characters in memory and on secondary storage are the ASCII and EBCDIC codes. The **American Standard Code for Information Interchange**, called ASCII, is the most widely used coding system to represent data. It is an eight-bit code used on personal computers and minicomputers. The **Extended Binary Coded Decimal Interchange Code**, or EBCDIC, is used primarily on mainframe computers.

5. For each byte of memory, most computers have at least one extra bit, called a **parity bit**, that is used by the computer for error checking. In computers with **odd parity**, the total number of on bits must be an odd number. In computers with **even parity**, the total number of on bits must be an even number.

6. The components considered part of the system unit include: the motherboard, the microprocessor and CPU, upgrade sockets, memory, coprocessors, buses, expansion slots, ports and connectors, bays, the power supply, and sound components.

7. The **motherboard**, sometimes called the **main board** or **system board**, is a circuit board that contains most of the electronic components of the system unit.

8. On a personal computer, the CPU, or central processing unit, is contained on a single integrated circuit, called a **microprocessor**, that is located on the motherboard. An **integrated circuit**, also called a **chip** or an IC, is a complete electronic circuit that has been etched on a small slice of semiconducting material. The **central processing unit** (CPU) contains the control unit and the arithmetic/logic unit.

9. The **control unit** operates by repeating four operations, called the **machine cycle: fetching, decoding, executing,** and **storing**.

10. The control unit utilizes the **system clock** to synchronize all computer operations. The system clock generates electronic pulses at a fixed rate, measured in **megahertz (MHz)**.

11. The second part of the CPU is the **arithmetic/logic unit (ALU)**, which contains the electronic circuitry necessary to perform arithmetic and logical operations on data. **Arithmetic operations** include addition, subtraction, multiplication, and division. **Logical operations** consist of comparing one data item to another to determine if the first data item is greater than, equal to, or less than the other.

12. Both the control unit and the ALU contain **registers**, temporary storage locations for specific types of data.

13. One aspect of the CPU that affects the speed of a computer is the word size. **Word size** is the number of bits that the CPU can process at one time.

14. Some motherboards contain empty sockets, called **upgrade sockets**, that can be used to install more powerful CPUs or additional memory.

15. Memory refers to integrated circuits that store program instructions and data that can be retrieved. Memory chips are installed in the system unit and also on circuit boards that control other computer devices.

What You Should Know

16. **Random access memory**, or **RAM**, is the name given to the integrated circuits, or chips, that are used for main memory. **Main memory**, or **primary storage**, stores three items: the operating system and other system software, the application program instructions, and the data currently being processed. The number that indicates the location of a byte in memory is called a **memory address**. The size of main memory is measured in **kilobytes** (**K** or **KB**) or **megabytes** (**MB**).

17. RAM memory is said to be **volatile** because the programs and data stored in RAM are erased when the power to the computer is turned off. A relatively new type of memory called **flash RAM**, or **flash memory**, retains data even when the power is turned off.

18. Today, most RAM memory is installed by using a **SIMM** (single in-line memory module). Some computers improve their processing efficiency by using a limited amount of high-speed RAM memory, called **cache memory**, between the CPU and main memory to store the most frequently used program instructions or data. Memory on personal computers can be divided into four areas: **conventional memory**, **upper memory**, **extended memory**, and **expanded memory**.

19. **Read only memory** (**ROM**) is the name given to chips that store information or instructions that do not change. ROM memory is described as **nonvolatile** because it retains its contents even when the power is turned off. Instructions that are stored in ROM memory are called **firmware** or **microcode**.

20. The speed of memory is measured in **nanoseconds**, one billionth of a second. Main memory is comprised of **dynamic RAM** (**DRAM**) chips that have access speeds of 50 to 100 nanoseconds. RAM cache memory is faster and is comprised of **static RAM** (**SRAM**) chips with access times of 10 to 50 nanoseconds. Registers designed into the CPU chip are the fastest type of memory with access times of 1 to 10 nanoseconds. ROM memory has access times between 50 and 250 nanoseconds. Accessing data on a fast hard disk drive takes between 10 and 20 **milliseconds** (a thousandth of a second).

21. One way computers can increase their productivity is through the use of a **coprocessor**, a special microprocessor chip or circuit board designed to perform a specific task.

22. Bits are transferred internally within the circuitry of the computer along paths capable of transmitting electrical impulses. Any path along which bits are transmitted is called a **bus**. An **expansion bus** carries data to and from the expansion slots. An expansion bus that connects directly to the CPU is called a **local bus**. Buses can transfer multiples of eight bits at a time.

23. An **expansion slot** is a socket designed to hold the circuit board for a device that adds capability to the computer system. The circuit board for the add-on device is called an **expansion board**. Expansion boards are also sometimes called **expansion cards**, **controller cards**, **adapter cards**, or **interface cards**. **PCMCIA cards** are used for additional memory, storage, and communications.

24. A **port** is a socket used to connect the system unit to a peripheral device such as a printer or a modem. Ports have different types of couplers, called **connectors**, that are used to attach cables to the peripheral devices. **Parallel ports** transfer eight bits (one byte) at a time using a cable that has eight data lines. These ports are most often used to connect devices that send or receive large amounts of data, such as printers or disk and tape drives. A **SCSI port** is a special type of parallel port that attaches up to seven devices to a single port. **Serial ports** transmit data one bit at a time and are considerably slower than parallel ports. These ports are used for the mouse, the keyboard, and communication devices such as a modem. A **MIDI port** is a special type of serial port designed to be connected to a musical device such as an electronic keyboard or music synthesizer.

25. A **bay** is an open area inside the system unit used to install additional equipment. Because they are often used for disk and tape drives, these spaces are also called **drive bays**. Mounting brackets, called **rails**, are sometimes required to install a device in a bay. Two or more bays side by side or on top of one another are called a **cage**.

26. The **power supply** converts the wall outlet electricity (115-120 volts AC) to the lower voltages (5 to 12 volts DC) used by the computer. The power supply also has a fan to help cool the system unit components. Personal computer power supplies range from 100 to 250 watts.

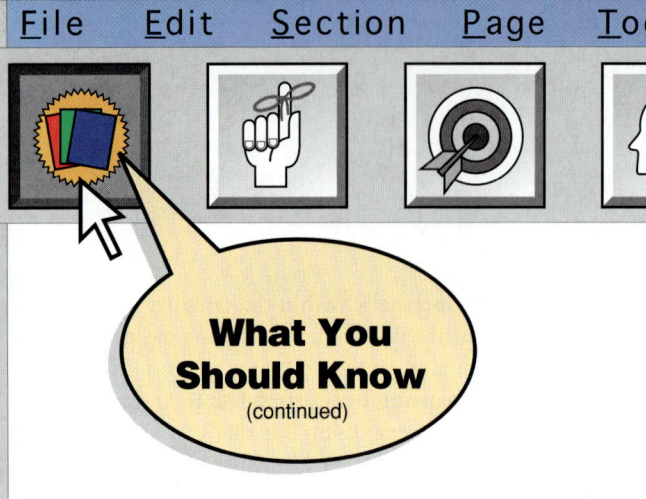

What You Should Know (continued)

27. Most personal computers can generate sounds through a small speaker housed within the system unit. Some computers also have built-in microphones that allow users to record voice messages and other sounds.

28. A **machine language instruction** is binary data that the electronic circuits in the CPU can interpret and convert into one or more commands in the computer's instruction set. The **instruction set** contains commands that the computer's circuits can directly perform. Most computers have hundreds of commands in their instruction set and are referred to as **CISC** computers, standing for *complex instruction set computing* (or *computers*). Some manufacturers have designed CPUs based on **RISC** technology, *or reduced instruction set computing* (or *computers*), which involves reducing the instructions to only those that are most frequently used, thus increasing overall processing capability.

29. The first part of a machine language instruction, called an **operation code**, tells the computer what to do and matches one of the commands in the instruction set. The second part of a machine language instruction, called an **operand**, specifies the data that will be used by the instruction. Although in the early days computers actually had to be programmed in machine language instructions, today program instructions are written in a readable form using a variety of programming languages.

30. The number of machine language instructions that a computer can process in one second is one way of rating the speed of computers. Powerful personal computers today are rated at more than 100 **MIPS** (million instructions per second). Another way of rating computer speed is the number of floating-point operations (a type of mathematical calculation). The term **megaflop** (**MFLOPS**) is used for millions of floating-point operations per second, and **gigaflop** (**GFLOPS**) is used for billions of floating-point operations per second.

31. In most CPUs, the system waits until an instruction completes all four stages of the machine cycle. With **pipelining**, a new instruction is started as soon as the preceding instruction moves to the next stage.

32. Most computers use a method known as **serial processing** in which one central CPU processes a single instruction at a time until the instruction is finished, then begins execution of the next instruction, and so on until the program is completed. **Parallel processing** involves the use of multiple CPUs, each with its own memory. Parallel processors, often used in supercomputers, divide up a problem so multiple CPUs can work on their assigned portion of the problem simultaneously. **Massively parallel processors** (**MPP**) use hundreds or thousands of microprocessor CPUs to perform calculations.

33. **Neural network computers** use specifically designed circuits to simulate the way the human brain processes information.

34. The binary (base 2) number system is used to represent the electronic status of the bits in main memory and secondary storage. The **hexadecimal** (base 16) number system, another number system commonly used with computers, represents binary in a more compact form. The mathematical principles that apply to the binary and hexadecimal number systems are the same as those that apply to the decimal system. The *base* of the number system indicates how many symbols are used in it. Each system is also a *positional* number system, meaning that every position in the number has a value associated with it.

Terms to Remember

adapter cards (4.13)
American Standard Code for Information Interchange (ASCII) (4.3)
Analog computers (4.2)
arithmetic operations (4.7)
arithmetic/logic unit (ALU) (4.7)
ASCII (4.3)

bay (4.6)
bit (4.2)
bus (4.12)
byte (4.2)

cache memory (4.10)
cage (4.16)
central processing unit (CPU) (4.6)
chip (4.6)
CISC (4.18)
connectors (4.14)
control unit (4.6)
controller cards (4.13)
conventional memory (4.10)
coprocessor (4.12)

decoding (4.7)
digital computers (4.2)
digitizing (4.2)
drive bays (4.16)
dynamic RAM (DRAM) (4.11)

EBCDIC (4.3)
even parity (4.4)
executing (4.7)
expanded memory (4.10)
expansion board (4.13)
expansion bus (4.12)
expansion cards (4.13)
expansion slot (4.13)
Extendend Binary Coded Decimal Interchange Code (EBCDIC) (4.3)
extended memory (4.10)

fetching (4.6)
firmware (4.11)
flash memory (4.10)
flash RAM (4.10)

gigaflop (GFLOPS) (4.19)

hexadecimal (4.21)

IC (4.6)
instruction set (4.18)
integrated circuit (4.6)
interface cards (4.13)

kilobyte (K or KB) (4.9)

local bus (4.13)
logical operations (4.7)

machine cycle (4.6)
machine language instruction (4.18)
main board (4.6)
main memory (4.9)
massively parallel processors (MPP) (4.20)
megabyte (MB) (4.9)
megaflop (MFLOPS) (4.19)
megahertz (MHz) (4.7)
memory address (4.9)
microcode (4.11)
microprocessor (4.6)
MIDI port (4.15)
millisecond (4.11)
MIPS (4.19)
motherboard (4.6)

nanoseconds (4.11)
neural network computers (4.20)
nonvolatile (4.11)

odd parity (4.4)
operand (4.18)
operation code (4.18)

parallel ports (4.15)
parallel processing (4.20)
parity bit (4.4)
PCMCIA cards (4.13)
pipelining (4.19)
port (4.14)
power supply (4.16)
primary storage (4.9)

rails (4.16)
RAM (4.9)
random access memory (RAM) (4.9)
read only memory (ROM) (4.11)
registers (4.7)
RISC (4.18)

SCSI port (4.15)
serial port (4.15)
serial processing (4.20)
SIMM (4.10)
static RAM (SRAM) (4.11)
storing (4.7)
system board (4.6)
system clock (4.7)
system unit (4.2)

upgrade sockets (4.8)
upper memory (4.10)

volatile (4.9)

word size (4.7)

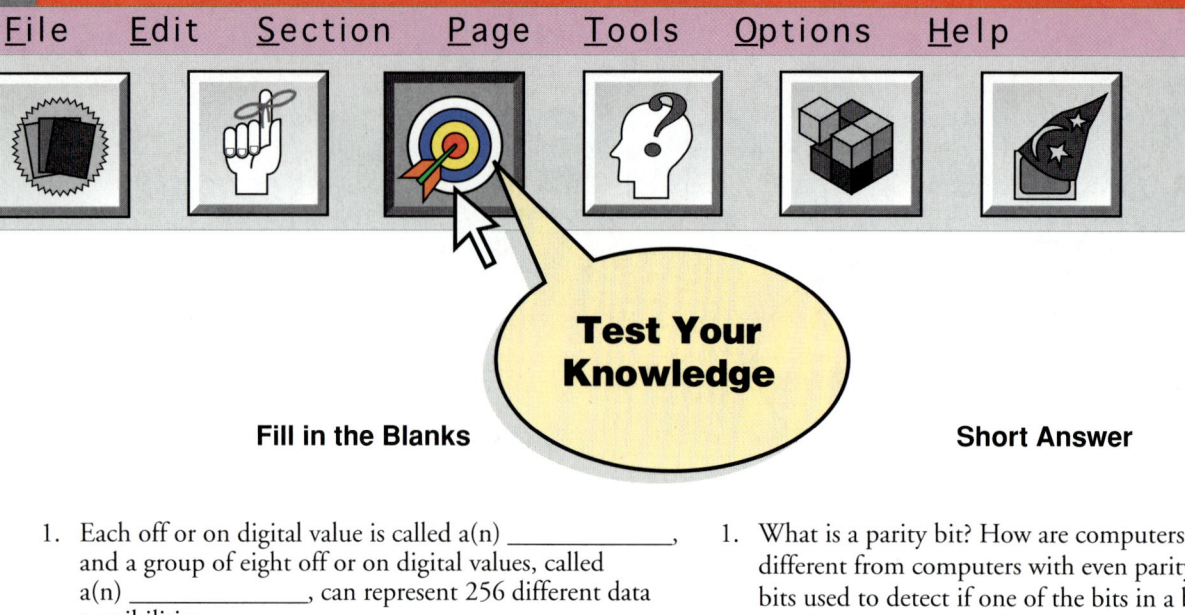

Test Your Knowledge

Fill in the Blanks

1. Each off or on digital value is called a(n) _____, and a group of eight off or on digital values, called a(n) _____, can represent 256 different data possibilities.
2. _____, the most widely used coding system to represent data, is used primarily on personal computers and minicomputers, while _____ is a coding system used primarily on mainframe computers.
3. The four steps of the machine cycle are: _____, _____, _____, and _____.
4. The two parts of a machine language instruction are a(n) _____ that tells the computer what to do and matches one of the commands in the instruction set and a(n) _____ that specifies the data or location of the data that will be used by the instruction.
5. The decimal number _____ can be written as 1101 in the binary number system and as _____ in the hexadecimal number system.

Short Answer

1. What is a parity bit? How are computers with odd parity different from computers with even parity? How are parity bits used to detect if one of the bits in a byte has been accidentally changed when data is moved from one location to another in main memory?
2. How is RAM memory different from ROM memory? For what purpose is each primarily used? What is flash RAM, or flash memory? What is cache memory?
3. How are parallel ports different from serial ports? For what devices are each type of port used? What is a SCSI port? What is a MIDI port?
4. What is an instruction set? How are CISC computers different from computers using RISC technology? Why does RISC technology increase overall processing capability?
5. What is pipelining? How is serial processing different from parallel processing? In what type of computer are parallel processors often used? What is a neural network computer?

Label the Figure

Instructions: Label the parts of the system unit in the spaces provided in the figure below.

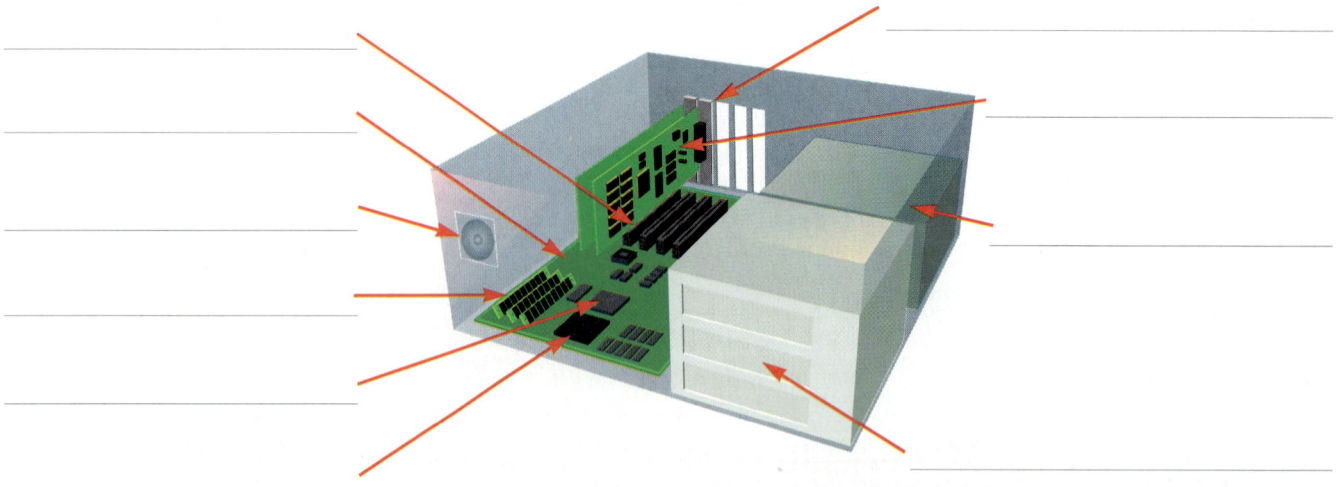

1

Although the four operations in the machine cycle may seem new to you, in a sense you carry out these same operations each time you complete certain ordinary tasks. Think of a simple task in which you perform operations analogous to those in the machine cycle. Explain what parts of accomplishing the task would be considered fetching, decoding, executing, and storing.

2

Some of the terms in this chapter have another meaning in a different context. For example, a bus, any path along which bits are transmitted, can also be defined as a large, motor-driven passenger vehicle. In this case the meanings are similar because one involves the transfer of bits and the other the transfer of people. List some other terms in this chapter that have more than one meaning. Give both meanings. If the meanings are similar, explain how.

3

ENIAC, the first computer, filled an entire room, yet it was less powerful than today's laptop computers. As the processing power and memory of personal computers increases (during the 1980s, the power of PCs expanded tenfold, and over the past twenty years, the capacity of RAM has more than doubled every two years), it is becoming increasingly difficult to define "personal computer," and to separate it from its larger cousins. How do you define personal computer? Do you think your definition will still be valid twenty years from now? Why or why not?

4

Consider the differences between RAM and ROM. In terms of your own memory, what kind of information do you have in your "RAM" memory? What kind of information do you have in your "ROM" memory? What information, if any, do you have stored in your "cache" memory?

5

As a general marketing rule, higher quality results in higher prices. Computers appear to challenge this rule, however, as they become more powerful, smaller, faster, and *less* expensive. An Atari 800 purchased at a computer store in the early 1980s for more than $1,000 could, by the mid-1980s, be replaced by one bought at a toy store for about $70. What do you think will be the impact of the decline in the price of computers? Who will be using computers in the future? What effect will the greater affordability of computers have on education?

6

Because the instruction sets, or microcode, used with IBM computers are completely different from those used with Apple computers, unless special enhancements are made, software that is written for an IBM personal computer cannot be used on an Apple Macintosh computer. Recently, however, under an agreement with IBM and Apple, Motorola has created a new processor, called the PowerPC. This chip will enable IBM and Apple to produce software that takes advantage of each other's applications. IBM systems will be able to run Macintosh applications, and Macintosh systems will be able to run IBM software. Who will benefit from this new chip? Why? Will anyone be harmed by this new development? Why or why not?

Out and About

1. If you own a personal computer or have access to a personal computer, take the cover off the system unit. Make a sketch of the system unit and try to identify as many components of the system unit as you can. Be careful not to touch any of the components. By referring to the computer's *User Guide,* list the computer's specification for some of the components described in this chapter (for example, CPU, CPU speed, bus speed, cache, RAM type, RAM capacity, expansion slots, and power supply).

2. Make a copy of an advertisement in a newspaper or magazine for a personal computer. Highlight any terms in the advertisement that were discussed in this chapter. List the terms, and explain the meaning of each.

3. Visit a computer vendor and compare one of its less expensive personal computer systems to one of its more expensive computer systems. Make a table that shows the differences between their system units (type of microprocessor, RAM capacity, and so on). Do you think the differences justify the discrepancy in price? Why or why not? Are there any other factors (such as included software) that might also affect the price disparity?

4. Two of the earliest computers were the ENIAC (an acronym for Electronic Numerical Integrator and Computer) and UNIVAC I. Both of these computers were enormous – ENIAC filled an entire room and UNIVAC I weighed 16,000 pounds! Visit a library to research these early computers. What were their components? In what ways were they different from today's personal computers? What technological developments have led to laptop computers that have greater capabilities than either the ENIAC or the UNIVAC I?

5. It is sometimes said that, "Software drives hardware." Although this statement has several interpretations, when purchasing a personal computer, it means that the system unit and peripheral devices (hardware) you buy must be capable of running the application programs (software) in which you are interested. Visit a store that sells computer software and make a list of the application programs you would like now and those you may want in the future. Examine the software packages and note the system requirements. On the basis of your findings, what are the minimum system requirements you would demand in a personal computer?

6. The semiconductor industry continues to develop and introduce new microprocessor and memory chips. Using current computer magazines, explore the most recent advances in microchip technology. What are the latest advances? Where are they being made? How do you think these advances will affect the development of personal computers over the next decade? What impact, if any, will these advances have on the way computers are used?

Computer Labs   4.33

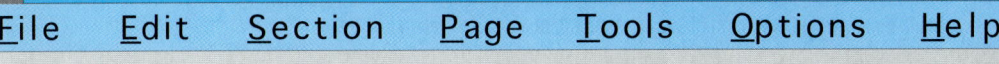

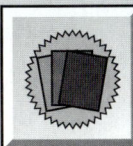    

In the Lab

Windows Labs

1 Setting the Date and Time With Program Manager on the screen, double-click the Main group icon. In the Main group window, double-click the Control Panel program-item icon. In the Control Panel window, double-click the Date/Time icon. In the Date & Time dialog box *(Figure 4-37),* click the Help button. Read and print the Date/Time information. Close the Help window.

Practice changing the system date and time. Answer the following questions: (1) How do you change the system date? (2) How do you change the system time? (3) What applications use the system date and time? Choose the Cancel button in the Date & Time dialog box. Close the Control Panel window by double-clicking its Control-menu box.

2 Using Clock With Program Manager on the screen, double-click the Accessories group icon. Double-click the Clock program-item icon to start the Clock application. Perform the following tasks: (1) Use the mouse to resize the Clock window to the size shown in *Figure 4-38.* (2) Select the Settings menu and choose the Analog command. Select the Settings menu and choose the Digital command. (3) Select the Settings menu and choose the Seconds command. (4) Select the Settings menu and choose the Date command. Select the Settings menu and choose the No Title command. (5) Double-click inside the Clock window to redisplay the title bar. Select the Settings menu and choose the Set Font command. (6) In the Font dialog box, click a variety of fonts in the Font list box; notice the selected font displays in the Sample area. Select a font and choose the OK button. (7) Click the Minimize button in the Clock window. Double-click the Clock icon to display it in normal size.

(8) Describe the function of all the commands in the Settings menu. (9) In *Figure 4-36,* which Clock settings are selected? Close Clock.

3 Shelly Cashman Series Motherboard Lab Follow the instructions in Windows Lab 2 in Chapter 1 on page 1.30 to display the Shelly Cashman Series Labs screen Select Understanding the Motherboard and choose the Start Lab button. When the initial screen displays, carefully read the objectives. With your printer turned on, point to the Print Questions button and click the left mouse button. Fill out the top of the Questions sheet and answer the questions as you step through the Motherboard Lab.

4 Using Calculator to Perform Number System Conversion With Program Manager on the screen, double-click the Accessories group icon. Double-click the Calculator program-item icon to start the Calculator application. Perform the following tasks: (1) Select the View menu and choose the Scientific command to display the scientific calculator *(Figure 4-39* on the next page). (2) Click the Dec option button to select base 10. Enter 16384 by clicking the numeric buttons. Click the Hex option button. What number displays? Click the Bin option button. What number displays? (3) Convert the following base 10 (decimal) numbers to hexadecimal and binary: 7, 16, 32, 64, 4096, and

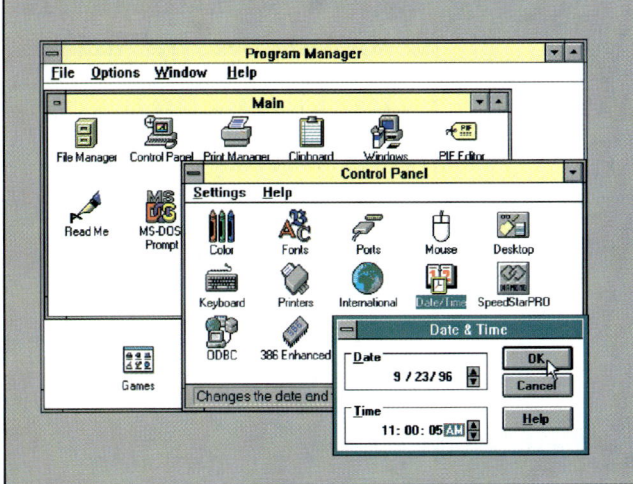

Figure 4-37

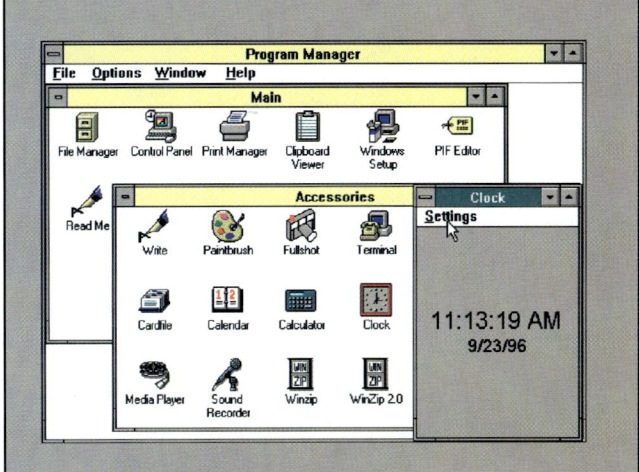

Figure 4-38

In the Lab (continued)

8192. (4) Convert the following base 2 (binary) numbers to decimal and hexadecimal: 100, 11111111, 1010, and 100000111000111. (5) Convert the following base 16 (hexadecimal) numbers to decimal and binary: 64, 3AB, BBB, 49C2, FFFF, ACDB12, and 32AC. Close Calculator.

5 Using Help With Program Manager on the screen, select the Help menu and choose the About Program Manager command. To whom is Windows 3.1 licensed? How much memory is free on your system? What percentage of system resources is free? Choose the OK button.

Select the Help menu and choose the Contents command. When the Program Manager Help window displays (Figure 4-40), print the contents of the window by choosing the Print Topic command from the File menu.

DOS Labs

1 Setting the Date and Time At the DOS prompt, type cls and press the ENTER key to clear the screen. Type date and press the ENTER key. At the Enter new date (mm-dd-yy) prompt, type 11-5-98 and press the ENTER key. Type date and press the ENTER key. What date displays as the current date? At the Enter new date (mm-dd-yy) prompt, enter today's date and press the ENTER key. Press the PRINT SCREEN key.

At the DOS prompt, type cls and press the ENTER key. Type time and press the ENTER key. At the Enter new time prompt, type 14:40 and press the ENTER key. Type time and press the ENTER key. What time displays as the current time? At the Enter new time prompt, enter the current time and press the ENTER key. Press the PRINT SCREEN key.

2 Checking Memory Type cls and press the ENTER key. Type mem and press the ENTER key to display memory information. Press the PRINT SCREEN key. How much of each of these types of memory is on your system: conventional, upper, reserved (adapter), extended, and total? How much expanded memory is on your system? If there is none designated, indicate none. What is the largest executable program size?

3 Using Help At the DOS prompt, type help mem and press the ENTER key to display help about the MEM command. Read and print the information. Read and print the information for the Notes jump topic and the Examples jump topic. Exit the Help window.

Online Lab

1 Electronic Job Hunting Using one of the two online services you selected in Chapter 1, connect to the service and perform the following tasks: (1) Search the online service for job listings. (2) Search the list for Programming positions and write down three openings in your area of the country. (3) Search the list for job openings for your major, and write down three openings in your area of the country. (4) **Extra Credit:** Use electronic mail to enter your resume on the online service. Be advised, you may be contacted.

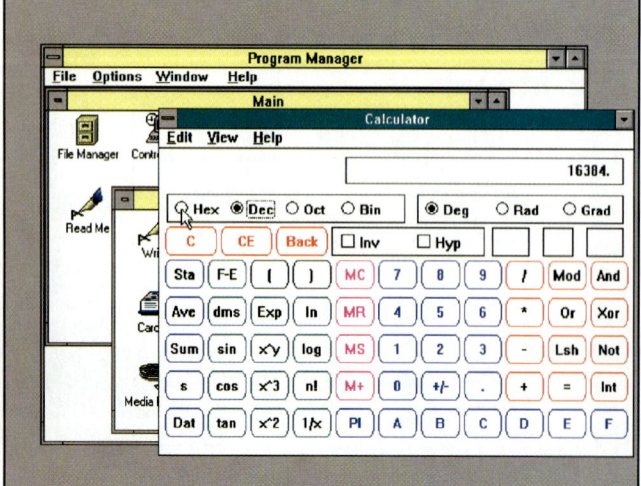

Figure 4-39

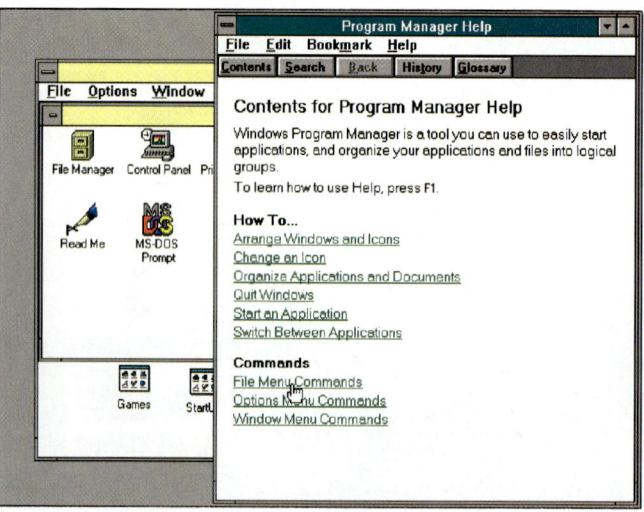

Figure 4-40

Making a Computer Chip

A computer chip is made by building layers of electronic pathways and connections using conducting and non-conducting materials on a surface of silicon. The combination of these materials into specific patterns forms microscopic electronic components such as transistors, diodes, resistors, and capacitors; the basic building blocks of electronic circuits. Connected together on a chip, these components are referred to as an integrated circuit. The application of the conducting and non-conducting materials to the silicon base is done through a series of technically sophisticated chemical and photographic processes. Some of the manufacturing steps are shown in the following photographs.

A computer chip begins with a design developed by engineers using a computer aided circuit design program (1). In order to better review the design, greatly enlarged printouts are prepared. Some chips only take a month or two to design while others may take a year or more. A separate design is required for each layer of the chip. Most chips have at least four to six layers but some have up to fifteen.

Although other materials can be used, the most common raw material used to make chips is silicon crystals (2) that have been refined from quartz rocks. The silicon crystals are melted and formed into a cylinder five to ten inches in diameter and several feet long (3). After being smoothed, the silicon ingot is sliced into wafers four to eight inches in diameter and 4/1000 of an inch thick.

Much of the chip manufacturing process is performed in special laboratories called clean rooms. Because even the smallest particle of dust can ruin a chip, the clean rooms are kept 1000 times cleaner than a hospital operating room. People who work in these facilities must wear special protective clothing called bunny suits (4). Before entering the manufacturing area, the workers remove any dust on their suits in an air shower (5).

After the wafer has been polished and sterilized, it is cleaned in a chemical bath. Because the chemicals used in the cleaning process are dangerous, this step is usually performed

MAKING A COMPUTER CHIP

by a robot (6). After cleaning, the wafers are placed in a diffusion oven where the first layer of material is added to the wafer surface (7). Other materials, called dopants, are added to the surface of the wafer in a process called ion implantation (8). The dopants create areas that will conduct electricity. Channels in these layers of materials are removed in a process called etching. Before etching, a soft gelatin-like emulsion called photoresist is added to the wafer. During photolithography (9), an image of the chip design, called a mask, is used as a negative. The photoresist is exposed to the mask using ultraviolet light. Ultraviolet light is used because its short wavelength can reproduce very small details on the wafer. Up to 100 images of the chip design are exposed on a single wafer. The photoresist exposed to the ultraviolet light becomes hard and the photoresist covered by the chip design on the mask remains soft. The soft photoresist and some of the surface materials are etched away with hot gases leaving what will become the circuit pathways (10). The process of adding material and photoresist to the wafer, exposing it to ultraviolet light, and etching away the unexposed surface, is repeated using a different mask for each layer of the circuit.

4.38 MAKING A COMPUTER CHIP

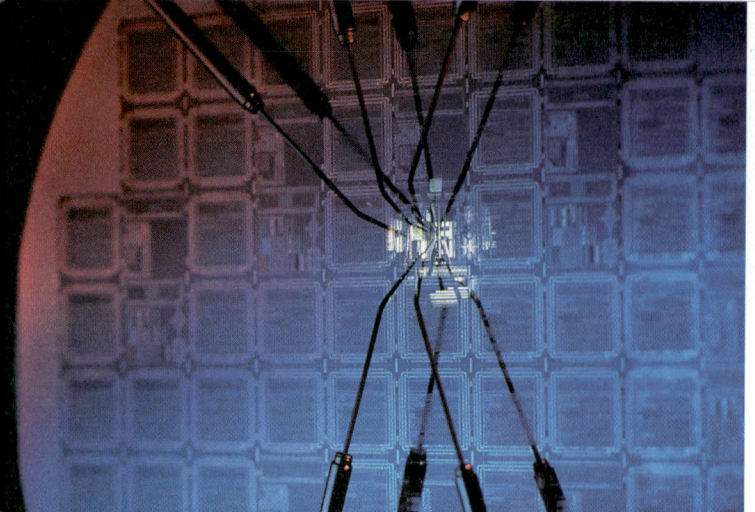

After all circuit layers have been added, individual chips on the wafer are tested by a machine that uses probes to apply electrical current to the chip circuits (11). In a process called dicing, the wafers are cut with a diamond saw (12) into individual chips called die (13). Die that have passed all tests are placed in a ceramic or plastic case called a package (14). Circuits on the chip are connected to pins on the package using gold wires (15). Gold is used because it conducts electricity well and does not corrode. The pins connect the chip to a socket on a circuit board (16).

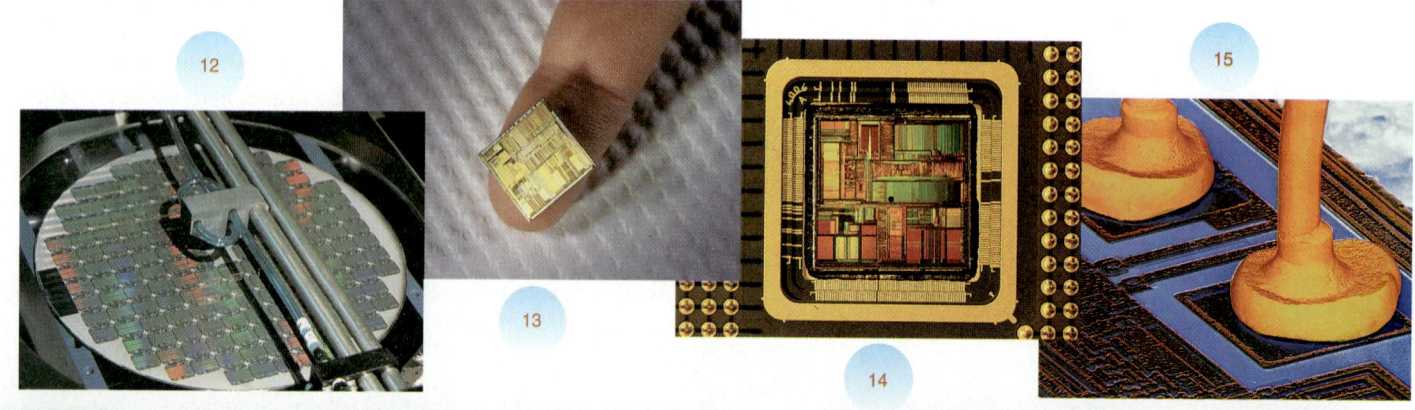

CHAPTER FIVE

Output from the Computer

5

Objectives

After completing this chapter, you will be able to:

- Define the term output

- Describe different types of printed output

- Describe multimedia and virtual reality output

- Explain the difference between impact and nonimpact printers

- Identify different types of display devices

- Explain how images are displayed on a screen

- List and describe other types of output devices used with computers

Output is the way the computer communicates with the user. Most people are familiar with computer printouts and information displayed on a screen, but computer output can take many other forms, as well. This chapter discusses different types of output and the devices computers use to produce output.

What Is Output?

Output is data that has been processed into a useful form called information that can be used by a person or a machine. Output used by a machine, such as a disk or tape file, is usually an intermediate result that eventually will be processed into output that can be used by people.

The type of output generated from the computer depends on the needs of the user and the hardware and software that are used. Two common types of output are reports and graphics. These types of output can be printed on a printer or displayed on a screen. Output that is printed is called **hard copy** and output that is displayed on a screen is called **soft copy**. Other types of output include audio (sound), video (visual images), multimedia, and virtual reality. Multimedia is an exciting method of communicating information that combines several types of output. Virtual reality also combines different types of output to create a simulated, three-dimensional environment that the user can experience using special equipment. Each of these types of output is discussed in the following sections.

Reports

A **report** is information presented in an organized form. Most people think of reports as items printed on paper or displayed on a screen. For example, word processing documents can be considered reports. Information printed on forms such as invoices or payroll checks can also be considered types of reports. One way to classify reports is by who uses them. An **internal report** is used by individuals in the performance of their jobs. For example, a daily sales report that is distributed to sales personnel is an internal report because it is used only by personnel within the organization. An **external report** is used outside the organization. Sales invoices that are printed and mailed to customers are external reports.

Reports can also be classified by the way they present information. The four types of common reports are: narrative reports, detail reports, summary reports, and exception reports.

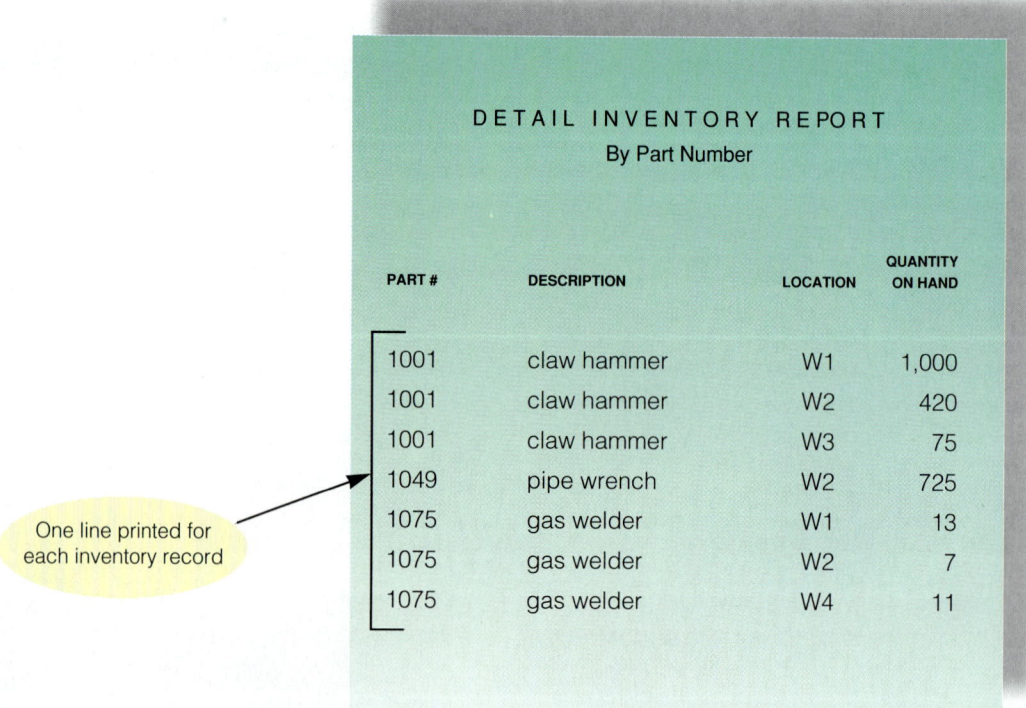

Figure 5-1
The data for this detail report was obtained from each inventory record.

Narrative reports may contain some graphic or numeric information but are primarily text-based reports. These reports, usually prepared with word processing software, include the various types of correspondence commonly used in business such as memos, letters, and sales proposals.

Detail, summary, and exception reports are primarily used to organize and present numeric-based information.

In a **detail report,** each line on the report usually corresponds to one record that has been processed. Detail reports contain a great deal of information and can be quite lengthy. They are usually required by individuals who need access to the day-to-day information that reflects the operating status of the organization. For example, people in the warehouse of a hardware distributor should have access to the location and number of units on hand for each product. The Detail Inventory Report in *Figure 5-1* contains a line for each warehouse location for each part number. Separate inventory records exist for each line on the report.

As the name implies, a **summary report** summarizes data. It contains totals for certain values found in the input records. The report shown in *Figure 5-2* contains a summary of the total quantity on hand for each part. The information on the summary report consists of totals for each part from the information contained in the detail report in *Figure 5-1*. Detail reports frequently contain more information than most managers have time to review. With a summary report, however, a manager can quickly review information in summarized form.

An **exception report** contains information that is outside of *normal* user-specified values or conditions, called the *exception criteria*. Records meeting this criteria are an *exception* to the majority of the data. For example, if an organization wants to know when to reorder inventory items to avoid running out of stock, it would design an exception report. The report would tell which inventory items fell below the reorder points and therefore need to be ordered. An example of such a report is shown in *Figure 5-3*.

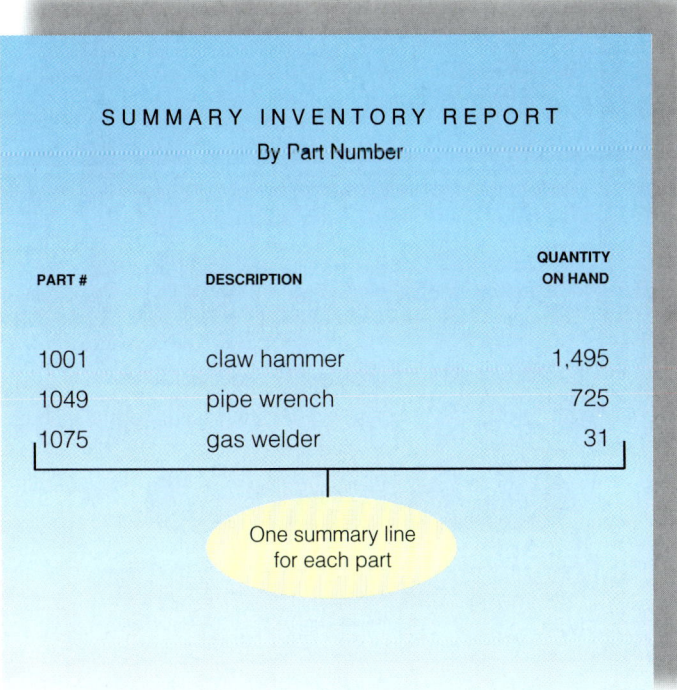

Figure 5-2
The summary report contains the total on-hand quantity for each part. The report can be prepared using the same records that were used to prepare the report in Figure 5-1.

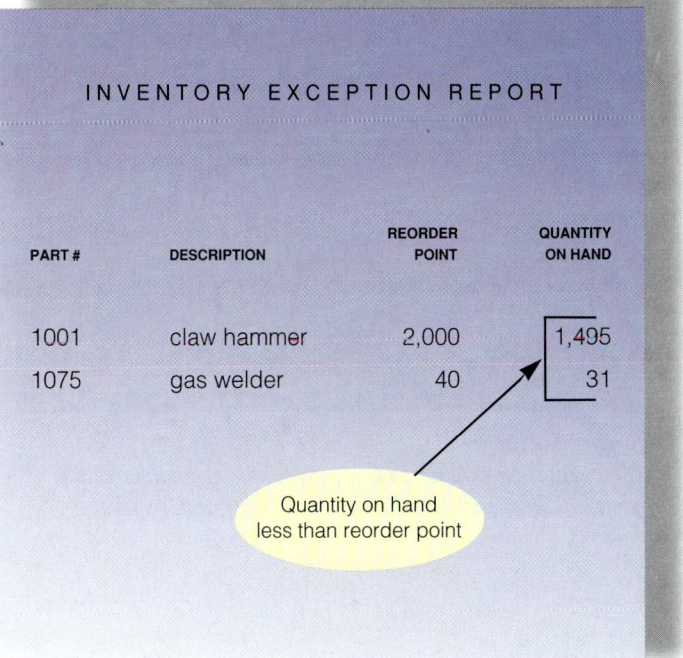

Figure 5-3
The exception report lists inventory items with an on-hand quantity below their reorder points. These parts could have been selected from thousands of inventory records. Only these items met the user's exception criteria.

Exception reports help users focus on situations that may require immediate decisions or specific actions. The advantage of exception reports is that they save time and money. In a large department store, for example, there may be more than 100,000 inventory items. A detail report containing all inventory items could be longer than 2,000 pages. To search through the report to determine the items whose on-hand quantity was less than the reorder point would be a difficult and time-consuming task. The exception report, however, could select these items, which might number 100 to 200, and place them on a two- to four-page report that could be reviewed in just a few minutes.

Reports are also sometimes classified by how often they are produced. **Periodic reports**, also called **scheduled reports**, are produced on a regular basis such as daily, weekly, monthly, or yearly. **On-demand reports** are created whenever they are needed for information that is not required on a scheduled basis.

Graphics

Computer graphics are any nontext pictorial information. One of the early uses of computer graphics was for charts to help analyze numeric information. Charts are now widely used in spreadsheet and presentation graphics software packages *(Figure 5-4)*. In recent years, computer graphics have gone far beyond charting capabilities. **Computer drawing programs** and **computer paint programs** allow an artistic user to create stunning looking works of art. These programs are frequently used for developing advertising and other marketing materials *(Figure 5-5)*. Clip art and photographs are also considered types of computer graphics.

Audio Output

Audio output, sometimes called **audio response**, consists of sounds, including words and music, produced by the computer. An audio output device on a computer is

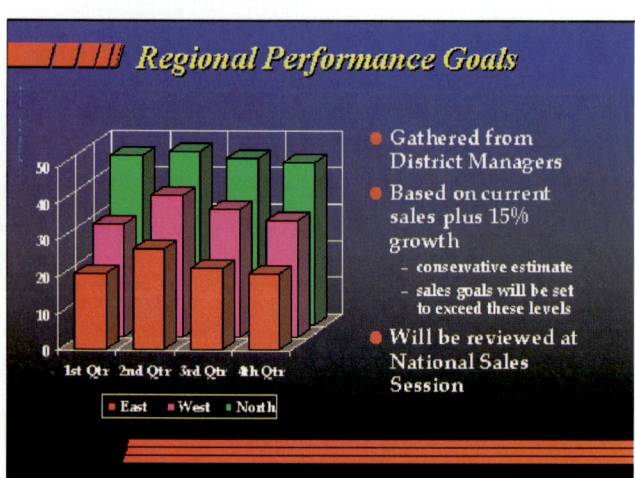

Figure 5-4
A presentation graphics slide is an example of graphics output that combines text, charts based on numeric data, and art.

Figure 5-5
Computer drawing and paint programs are often used by professional artists to create advertising and marketing materials.

a speaker. Most personal computers come with a small speaker (approximately two inches) that is usually located behind an opening on the front or side of the system unit case. Increasingly, personal computer users are adding higher quality stereo speakers to their systems *(Figure 5-6)*. The stereo speakers connect to a port on a sound card that works with sound, voice, and music software.

Video Output

Video output consists of visual images that have been captured with a video input device, such as a VCR or camera, digitized, and directed to an output device such as a computer monitor *(Figure 5-7)*. As was mentioned in Chapter 3, some video input devices can digitize the image as it is captured. Video output can also be directed to a television monitor. Because standard televisions are not designed to handle a computer's digital signals, the video output has to be converted to an analog signal that can be displayed by the television. **High definition television** (**HDTV**) sets are designed for digital signals and may eventually replace computer monitors.

Multimedia

Multimedia is the combination of text, graphics, video, and sound. Some people have described it as a combination of traditional text-based computers and television. Multimedia is really more than just a combination of these previously separate information elements. Multimedia is different because it usually gives the user options on the amount of material to review and the sequence in which the material will be reviewed. For example, a typical multimedia presentation will display text material along with one or more photos or graphic images. Some sound or voice narration may also be provided. In addition, the screen will usually show icons that represent additional material, such as pictures, sounds, animation, or maps, that the user can also choose to review. Most multimedia presentations use a technique, called **hypermedia**, that allows the user to quickly move to related subject areas. An example of these features can be seen in *Figures 5-8* and *5-9* on the next page; screens from Microsoft's multimedia encyclopedia, Encarta. *Figure 5-8* shows text information about the famous jazz musician, Duke Ellington. The small icons at the top of the text material indicate there is an image item (represented by

Figure 5-6
To fully experience computer audio output, many users are adding or purchasing systems with stereo speakers.

Figure 5-7
Use of video output is like a video telephone system; it allows company employees to see the coworker with whom they are talking.

the camera-shaped icon) and a sound item (represented by the speaker-shaped icon) that can also be reviewed. To see or hear these items, the user selects the icon with the mouse. To see related topics, the user can choose the See Also button at the bottom of the screen. When this is done, a list of the topics is presented *(Figure 5-9)*. The user can move directly to any of these topics by selecting one with the mouse.

The Microsoft Encarta multimedia encyclopedia, like most multimedia products available today, is stored on a CD-ROM disk. This type of storage device is required because of the large amounts of data that most multimedia applications require. For example, the Encarta encyclopedia takes more than 550MB of storage space. Full-motion video, which is used sparingly in most multimedia presentations today, can require more than 2 gigabytes of storage for each minute of video. These storage requirements can be reduced through the use of data compression techniques.

Currently, multimedia applications are primarily used in four areas; education, training, entertainment, and information. Information applications include multimedia kiosks that can be found in museums, airports, and hotels *(Figure 5-10)*. Eventually, multimedia techniques will be incorporated into most all software applications.

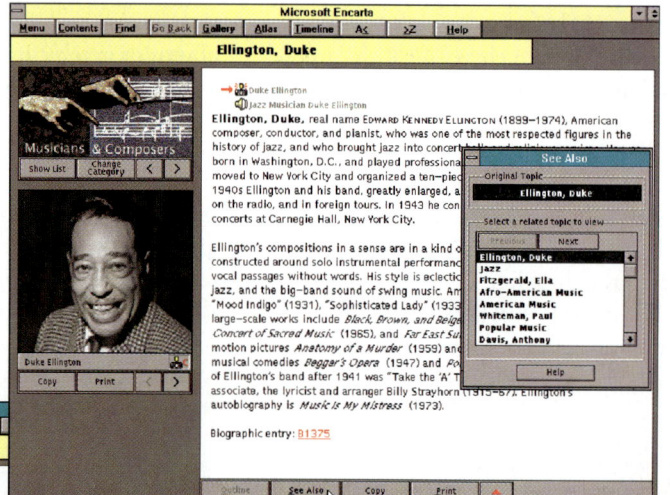

Figure 5-9
When the user chooses the See Also button at the bottom of the screen, a list of related topics is displayed. The user can move directly to any of these topics by selecting one of them with a pointing device.

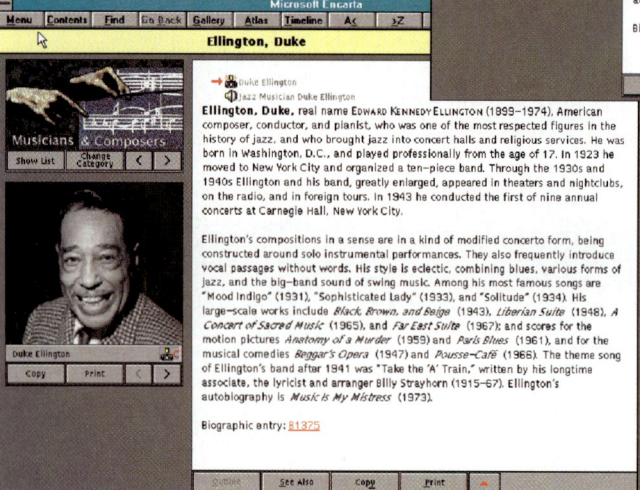

Figure 5-8
The Microsoft Encarta multimedia encyclopedia offers text, graphics, sound, and animation. Clicking the camera-shaped icon at the top of the text displays a photograph of jazz musician Duke Ellington. Clicking the speaker-shaped icon below the camera plays a portion of one of Ellington's compositions.

Figure 5-10
Coca-Cola uses multimedia kiosks to present information on their products and history at their Atlanta visitors center. Multimedia information kiosks are becoming a frequent site in hotels, museums, airports, and other locations where infrequent visitors need to obtain information.

Virtual Reality

Virtual reality (VR) refers to the use of a computer to create an artificial environment that can be experienced by the computer user. In its simplest form, VR software displays what appears to be a three-dimensional view of a place, such as a landscape or a building, that can be explored by the user. Architects are using such software to show clients what proposed construction or remodeling changes will look like *(Figure 5-11)*. In more advanced forms, VR software requires the user to wear specialized headgear, gloves, and body suits to enhance the experience of the artificial environment *(Figure 5-12)*. The headgear includes displays in front of both eyes that project the artificial environment being experienced by the wearer. The glove and body suit sense the motion and direction of the user. Gloves allow the user to pick up and hold items displayed in the virtual environment. Eventually, experts predict, the body suits will provide tactile feedback so the wearer can experience the touch and feel of the virtual world.

Figure 5-11
One of the first practical applications of virtual reality software was in the architectural profession. Architects use VR software to create a model of the project on which they are working. Clients can then walk through the virtual project and specify design changes before the project is built.

Figure 5-12
The virtual reality body suit, called a "Datasuit" by developer VPL research, allows more than 50 different movements of the wearer to be interpreted by the VR software. The software then manipulates the image in the virtual environment, which is displayed in the headset.

Most experts agree that VR is still in its early stages and that practical applications are just now becoming available. The potential applications of VR, however, have many people excited and have kept millions of dollars flowing into VR research.

The general public's first encounter with VR will likely be through a three-dimensional electronic game. One such game is called Dactyl Nightmare *(Figure 5-13)*. Special visors allow the player to *see* the computer-generated environment. Sensors in the surrounding game machine record movement and direction as the player *walks* around the game's electronic landscape. The object of the game is to use a simulated laser gun to shoot other players before they shoot you. Players also have to avoid being snatched by giant green pterodactyls (prehistoric birds) that can carry them high into the sky before letting them crash to the ground. Because of their high cost (more than $50,000) and the special equipment required, VR games are not spreading across the land as fast as pin ball machines once did. Most major metropolitan U.S. cities, however, now have VR arcades installed or planned for the near future.

Commercial applications of VR include a virtual showroom and a virtual office. The showroom lets customers wander among available products and inspect those they find interesting. In the virtual office, created for an office furniture company, clients can see what their selected furniture will look like and can experiment with different furniture arrangements.

As computing power increases, VR applications will be able to be run on lower cost computers. This in turn will increase the number of commercial VR applications and make VR technology available for a wider number of users.

A variety of devices produce the output created in the information processing cycle. The following sections describe the devices most commonly used.

Figure 5-13
Dactyl Nightmare is one of the first virtual reality games available to the public. Players try to shoot each other and avoid being carried away by computer-generated pterodactyls. The screen on the right shows the view seen by one of the players.

Printers

Printing requirements vary greatly among computer users. For example, home computer users may only print a hundred pages or fewer a week. Small business computer users may print several hundred pages a day. Users of mainframe computers, such as large utility companies that send printed bills to hundreds of thousands of customers each month, need printers that are capable of printing thousands of pages per hour. These different needs have resulted in the development of printers with varying speeds, capabilities, and printing methods. Generally, printers can be classified into two groups, impact or nonimpact, based on how they transfer characters to the paper.

Impact Printers

Impact printers transfer the image onto paper by some type of printing mechanism striking the paper, ribbon, and character together. One technique is front striking in which the printing mechanism that forms the character strikes a ribbon against the paper from the front to form an image. This is similar to the method used on typewriters. The second technique utilizes a hammer striking device. The ribbon and paper are struck against the character from the back by a hammer to form the image on the paper *(Figure 5-14)*.

Most impact printers use continuous-form paper. The pages of **continuous-form paper** are connected together for a continuous flow through the printer *(Figure 5-15)*. The advantage of continuous-form paper is that it need not be changed frequently; thousands of pages come connected together. Some impact printers use single-sheet paper. The advantage of using single-sheet paper is that different types of paper, such as letterhead, can be quickly changed.

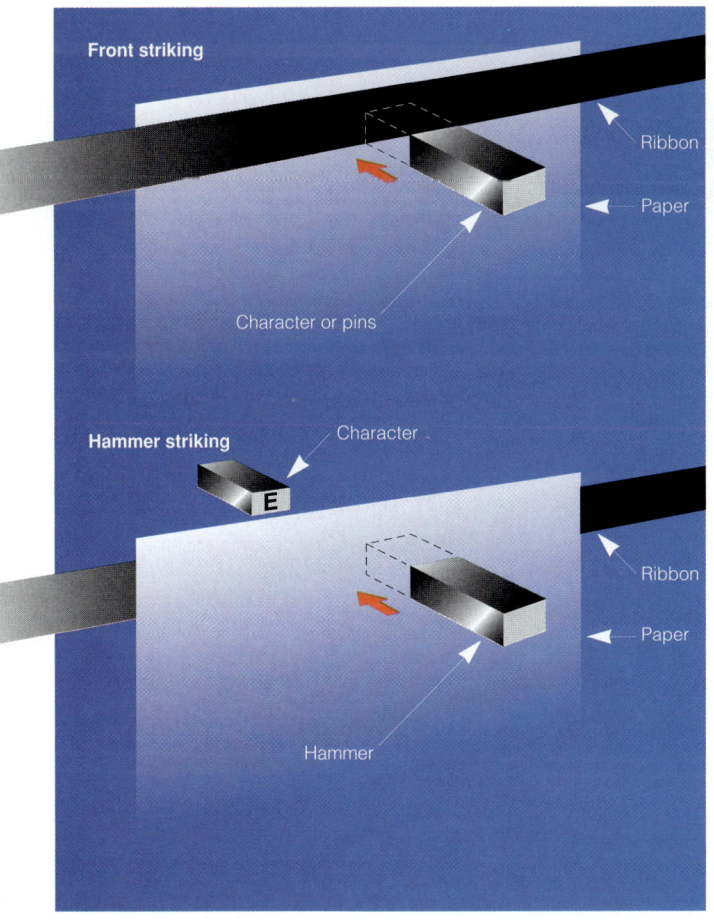

Figure 5-14
Impact printers operate in one of two ways; front striking or hammer striking.

Figure 5-15
Sheets of continuous-form paper are connected together. Small holes on the sides of the paper allow sprockets to pull the paper through the printer. Perforations between each sheet allow the pages to be easily separated.

Dot Matrix Printers

A **dot matrix printer** produces printed images by striking wire pins against an inked ribbon. Its print head consists of a series of small tubes containing wire pins that, when pressed against a ribbon and paper, print small dots. The pins are activated by electromagnets that are arranged in a circular pattern. The combination of small dots printed closely together forms the character *(Figure 5-16)*. Dot matrix printers are used extensively because they are versatile and relatively inexpensive. The printer shown in *Figure 5-17* is a dot matrix printer used with personal computers. *Figure 5-18* shows a dot matrix printer frequently used with larger systems.

To print a character using a dot matrix printer, the character stored in main memory is sent to the printer's electronic circuitry. The printer circuitry activates the pins in the print head that correspond to the pattern of the character to be printed. The selected pins strike the ribbon and paper and print the character. Most dot matrix printers used with personal computers have a single print head that moves across the page. Dot matrix printers used with larger computers usually have fixed print mechanisms at each print position and can print an entire line at one time. Because the individual pins of a dot matrix printer can be activated, a dot matrix printer can be used to print expanded (larger than normal) and condensed (smaller than normal) characters and graphics.

Dot matrix printers can contain a varying number of pins, depending on the manufacturer and the printer model. Print heads consisting of 9 and 24 pins (two vertical rows of 12) are most common. *Figure 5-19* illustrates the formation of the letter E using a nine-pin dot matrix printer.

The speed of impact printers with movable print heads is rated in **characters per second** (**cps**). Depending on the printer model, this speed varies between 50 and 300 cps. The speed of impact printers that print one line at a time is rated in **lines per minute** (**lpm**). High-speed dot matrix printers can print up to 1,200 lpm. The speeds quoted by dot matrix printer manufacturers are usually for what is called draft-quality printing. **Draft-quality** printing uses the minimum

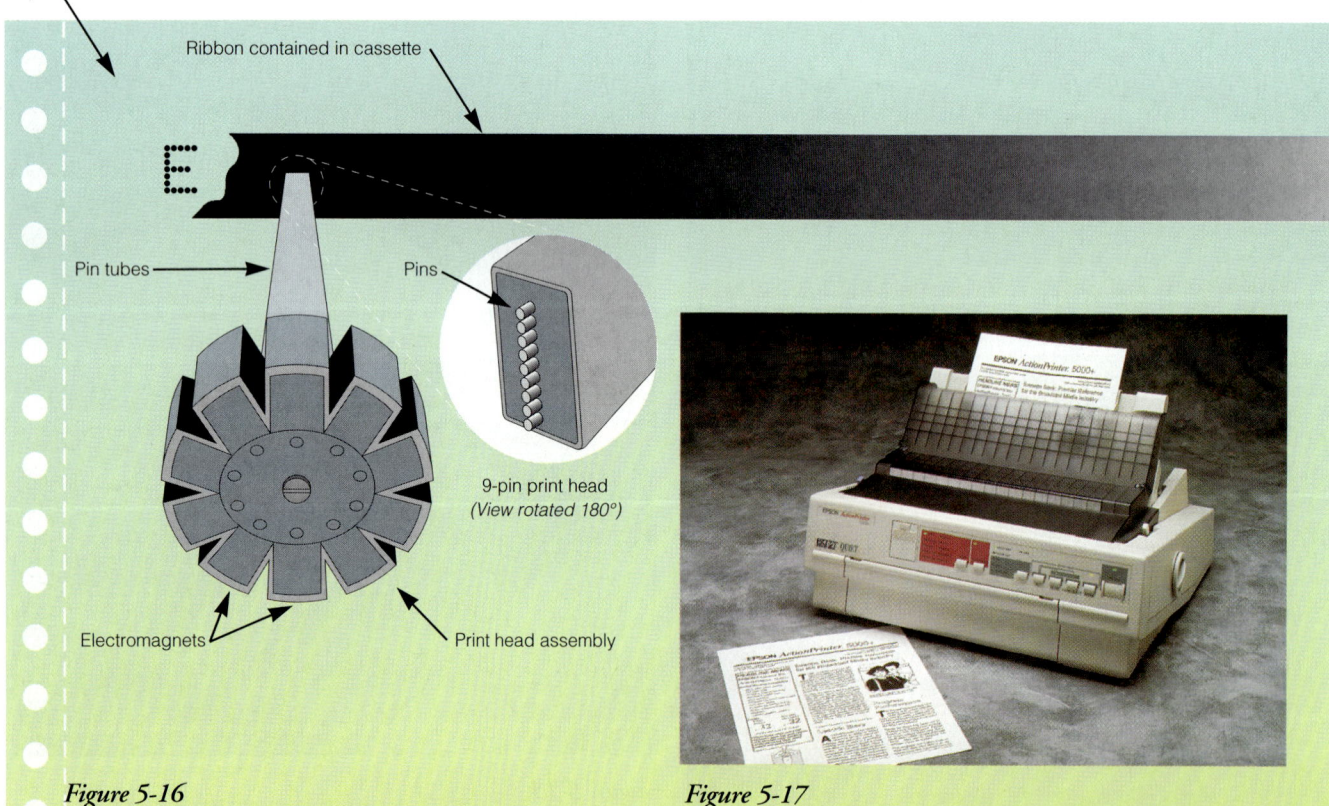

Figure 5-16
The print head assembly for a dot matrix printer consists of a series of pins that are fired at the paper by electromagnets. When activated, the pins push the ribbon into the paper forming an image made up of small dots.

Figure 5-17
Many different types of small dot matrix printers are available for use with personal computers.

number of dots to form a character and achieve the fastest printing speed. Draft quality is fine for internal reports but is not adequate for sending printed material to customers or other outsiders. To achieve a sharper, higher quality look, called **letter quality** (**LQ**) or **near letter quality** (**NLQ**), the printer overlaps the printed dots. Nine-pin print heads accomplish the overlapping by printing the line twice. The character is slightly offset during the second printing. This results in the appearance of solid characters *(Figure 5-20)*. Twenty-four-pin printers can accomplish the overlapping on a single pass because their multiple rows of pins are slightly offset *(Figure 5-21)*.

Dot matrix printers with movable print heads are designed to print in a **bidirectional** manner. That is, the print head, the device that contains the mechanism for transferring the character to the paper, can print as it moves from left to right and from right to left. The printer does this by storing the next line to be printed in its memory and then

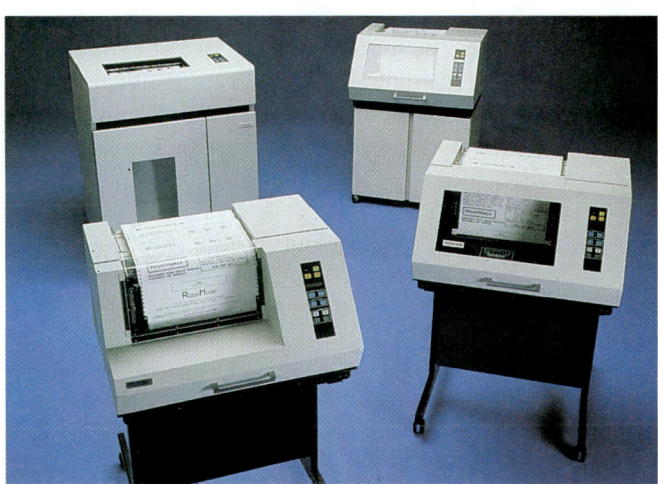

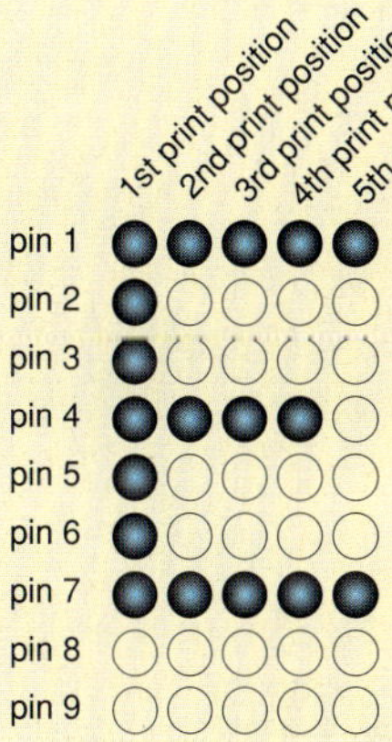

Figure 5-18
Dot matrix printers used with larger systems often have print heads at each print position that allow them to print an entire line at a time.

Figure 5-19
The letter E is formed by a combination of dots. As the nine-pin print head moves from left to right, it fires one or more pins into the ribbon, which makes a dot on the paper. At print position 1, it fires pins 1 through 7. At print positions 2 through 4, it fires pins 1, 4, and 7. At print position 5, it fires pins 1 and 7. Pins 8 and 9 are used for lowercase characters such as g, j, p, q, and y that extend below the line.

Figure 5-20
Overlapping the printed dots gives the appearance of a more solid-looking character that is easier to read.

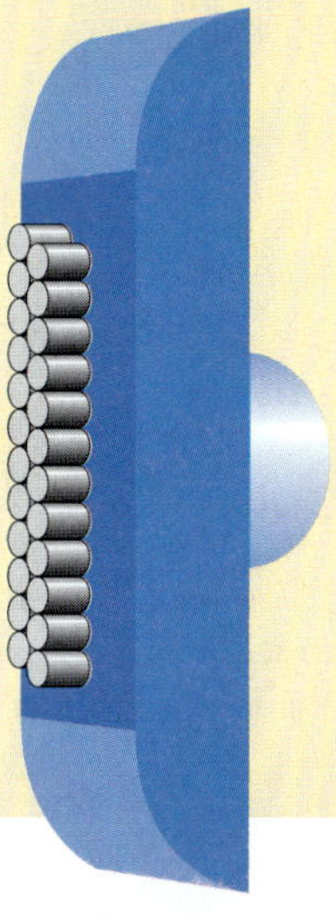

Figure 5-21
The two rows of pins on this 24-pin dot matrix print head are slightly offset (one is higher than the other) so they will overlap and produce a more solid-looking character or a smoother line.

printing the line forward or backward as needed. Bidirectional printing greatly increases the speed of the printer.

The feed mechanism determines how the paper moves through the printer. Two types of feed mechanisms found on dot matrix printers are tractor feed and friction feed. **Tractor feed mechanisms** transport continuous-form paper through the printer by using sprockets, which are small protruding prongs of plastic or metal that fit into holes on each side of the paper. Where it is necessary to feed single sheets of paper into the printer, **friction feed mechanisms** are used. As the name implies, paper is moved through friction feed printers by pressure on the paper and the carriage, as it is on a typewriter. As the carriage rotates, the paper moves through the printer.

Dot matrix printers are built with a standard, medium, or wide carriage. A standard carriage printer can accommodate paper up to 8 1/2 inches wide. A medium carriage can accommodate paper up to 11 inches wide, and a wide carriage printer can accommodate paper up to 14 inches wide.

Some dot matrix printers can print in multiple colors using ribbons that contain the colors red, yellow, and blue in addition to the standard black. Color output is obtained by repeated printing and repositioning of the paper, print head, and ribbon. Such printers can be useful in printing graphs and charts, but other types of color printers offer a higher quality of color output.

Dot matrix printers range in cost from less than $200 for small desktop units to more than $10,000 for heavy-use business models. Most dot matrix printers are available for less than $1,000.

Band and Chain Printers

Band and chain printers are used for high-volume output on large computer systems. **Band printers** use a horizontal, rotating band containing numbers, letters of the alphabet, and selected special characters. The characters are struck by hammers located at each print position behind the paper and ribbon to create a line of print on the paper *(Figure 5-22)*.

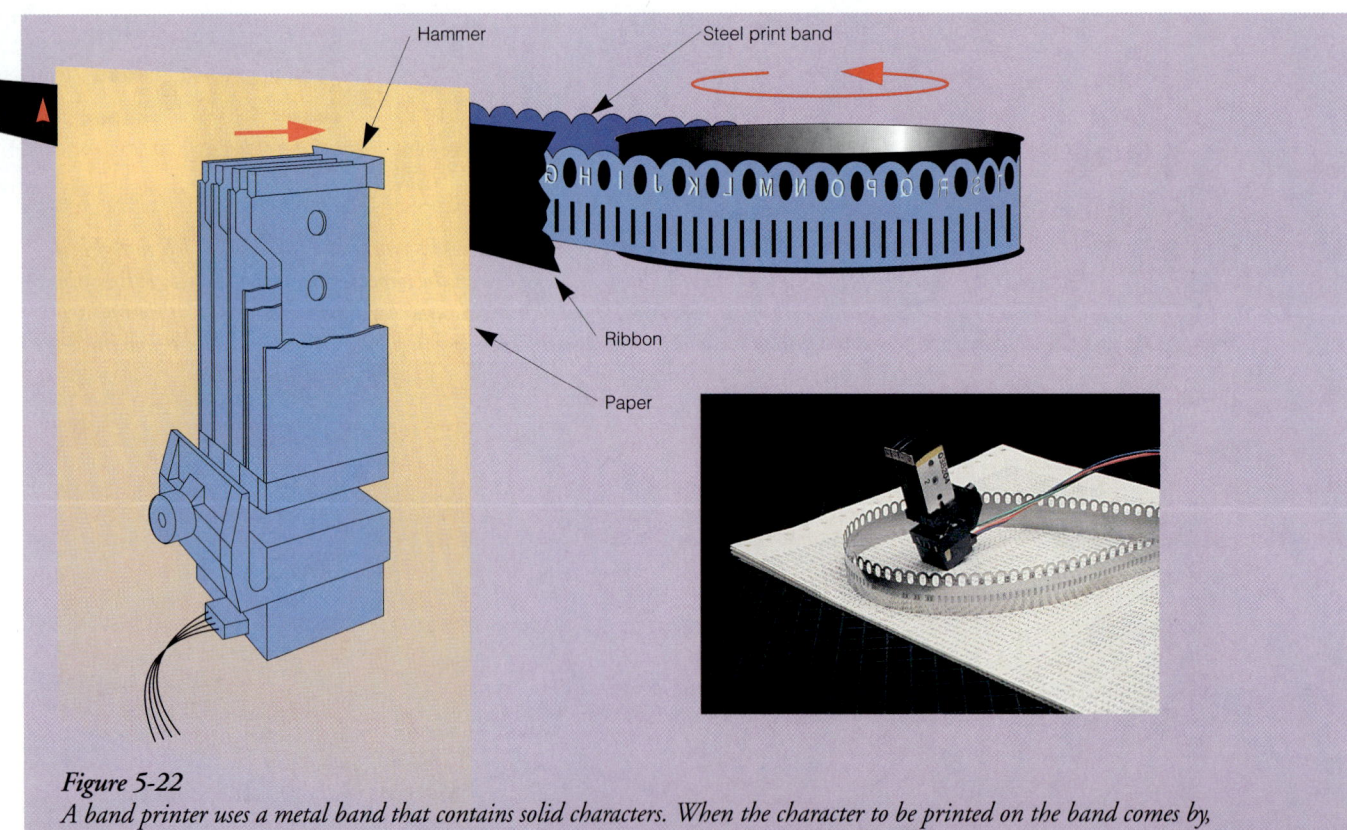

Figure 5-22
A band printer uses a metal band that contains solid characters. When the character to be printed on the band comes by, print hammers strike the paper and the ribbon forcing them into the band to print the character.

Nonimpact Printers

Interchangeable type bands with different fonts can be used on band printers. A band printer can produce up to six carbon copies, has good print quality, high reliability, and depending on the manufacturer and model of the printer, can print in the range of 600 to 2,000 lines per minute.

The **chain printer** is similar to a band printer and contains characters on a rotating chain *(Figure 5-23)*. The chain consists of a series of type slugs that contains the character set. The character set on the type slugs is repeated two or more times on the chain mechanism. The chain rotates at a very high speed. Each possible print position has a hammer that can strike against the back of the paper, forcing the paper and ribbon against the character on the chain. As the chain rotates, the hammer strikes when the character to be printed is in the proper position.

The chain printer produces good print quality up to 3,000 lines per minute.

Nonimpact printing means that printing occurs without having a mechanism striking against a sheet of paper. For example, ink is sprayed against the paper or heat and pressure is used to fuse a fine black powder into the shape of a character.

Just as there are a variety of impact printers, there are also a variety of nonimpact printers. Ink-jet, small page printers, and thermal printers are frequently used on personal computers and small minicomputers. Medium- and high-speed page printers are used on minicomputers, mainframes, and supercomputers. The following sections discuss the various types of nonimpact printers.

Ink-Jet Printers

An **ink-jet printer** sprays tiny drops of ink onto the paper. The print head of an ink-jet printer contains a nozzle with anywhere from 50 to more than 100 small holes *(Figure 5-24)*. Although there are many more of them, the ink holes in the nozzle are similar to the individual pins on a dot matrix

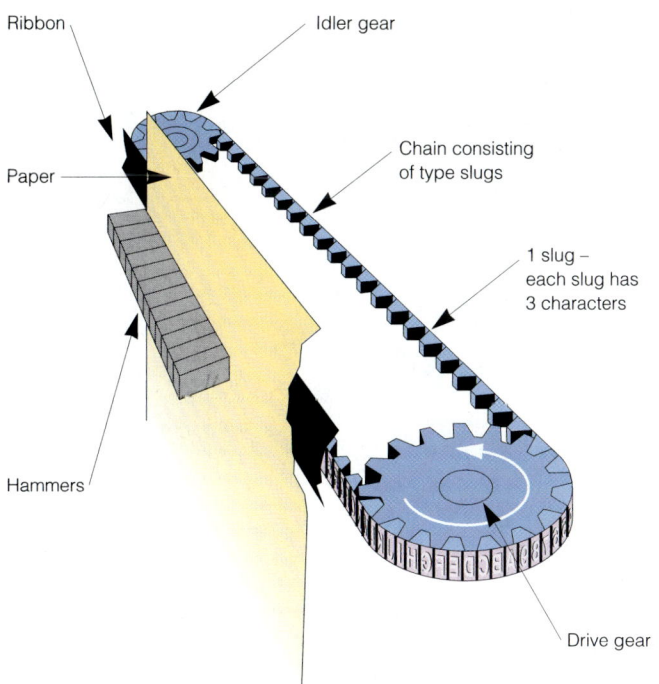

Figure 5-23
The chain printer contains a complete set of characters on several sections of a chain that rotates at a high constant speed. Print hammers are located at each horizontal print position. The paper and ribbon are located between the hammers and the chain. As the chain rotates, the hammers fire when the proper characters are in front of their print positions.

Figure 5-24
The print head of an ink-jet printer contains many tiny holes that act as nozzles to spray drops of ink onto the paper.

printer. Just as any combination of dot matrix pins can be activated, ink can be propelled by heat or pressure through any combination of the nozzle holes to form a character or image on the paper. Ink-jet printers produce high-quality print and graphics and are quiet because the paper is not struck as it is by dot matrix printers. Good quality, single-sheet paper is usually used with ink-jet printers. Lower quality paper can be too soft and cause the ink to bleed. Transparency sheets can also be used. Ink-jet printers print at rates from 30 to 150 cps. Color ink-jet printers are also available *(Figure 5-25)*.

Page Printers

The **page printer** is a nonimpact printer that operates similar to a copying machine. The page printer converts data from the computer into light that is directed to a positively charged revolving drum. Each position on the drum touched by the light becomes negatively charged and attracts the toner (powdered ink). The toner is transferred onto the paper and then fused to the paper by heat and pressure. Several methods are used to direct light to the photosensitive drum and create the text or image that will be transferred to the paper. **Laser printers** use a laser beam aimed at the drum by a spinning mirror *(Figure 5-26)*.

Other page printers use light emitting diode (LED) arrays or liquid crystal shutters (LCS). With these methods, the light can expose thousands of individual points on the drum. Although the light exposure methods of LED and LCS printers are different from laser printers, they are often referred to and classified with laser printers. All page printers produce high-quality text and graphics suitable for business correspondence *(Figure 5-27)*. Color laser printers are available but are very expensive and not yet widely used.

An advantage of page printers is that they usually come with a large number of built-in fonts. As you recall from Chapter 2, a font is a specific combination of *typeface,* such as Courier, and *point size,* the height of the type. Although different fonts can be produced using software, documents using a printer's built-in fonts print faster.

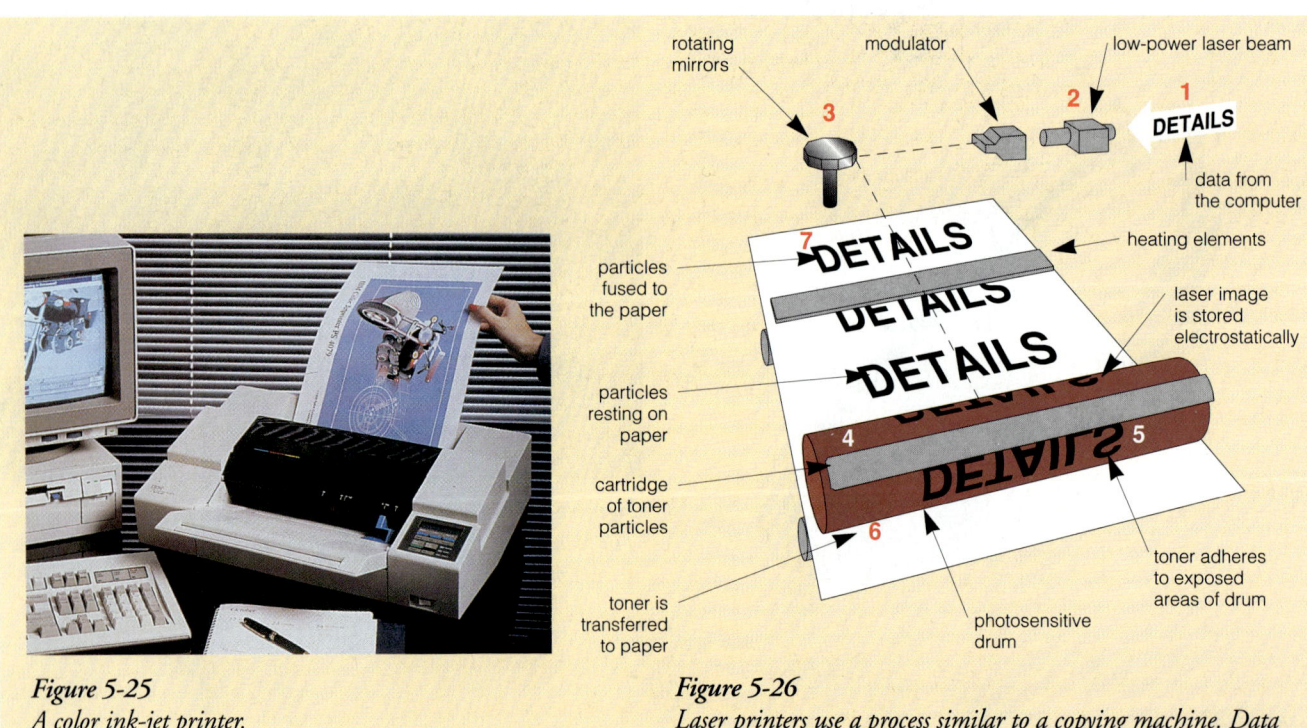

Figure 5-25
A color ink-jet printer.

Figure 5-26
Laser printers use a process similar to a copying machine. Data from the computer, such as the word DETAILS (1), is converted into a laser beam (2) that is directed by a mirror (3) to a photosensitive drum (4). The areas on the drum touched by the laser attract toner particles (5) that are transferred to the paper (6). The toner is fused to the paper with heat and pressure (7).

Page printers are rated by their speed and resolution. Speed is measured in **pages per minute** (**ppm**). Page printers used with individual personal computers range from 4 to 12 ppm and start at less than $500. Page printers supporting multiple users on a network or larger computer range from 16 to 50 ppm and cost from $10,000 to $100,000. High-speed page printers costing as much as several hundred thousand dollars can produce output at the rate of several hundred pages per minute *(Figure 5-28)*. Page printer resolution is measured by the number of **dots per inch** (**dpi**) that can be printed. The more dots, the sharper the image. The resolution of page printers ranges from 240 to 1200 dpi with most printers currently offering 300 or 600 dpi. Page printers usually use individual sheets of paper stored in a removable tray that slides into the printer case. Some page printers have trays that can accommodate different-sized paper while others require separate trays for letter and legal paper. Most page printers have a manual feed slot where individual sheets can be inserted. Transparencies and envelopes can also be printed on page printers.

Thermal Printers

Thermal printers, sometimes called **thermal-transfer printers**, use heat to transfer colored inks from ink sheets onto the printing surface (*Figure 5-29* on the next page). Thermal printers can work with plain paper but produce the best results when higher quality, smooth paper or plastic transparencies are used. A special type of thermal printer using a method called **dye diffusion** uses chemically treated paper to obtain color print quality equal to glossy magazines. Dye diffusion actually varies the color intensity of each dot placed on the page. Most color printers merely alter the pattern of red, blue, yellow, and black dots to create the illusion of different colors. Thermal printers produce output at the rate of one to two pages per minute.

Figure 5-27
Page printers such as the laser printer can produce high-quality text or graphics output.

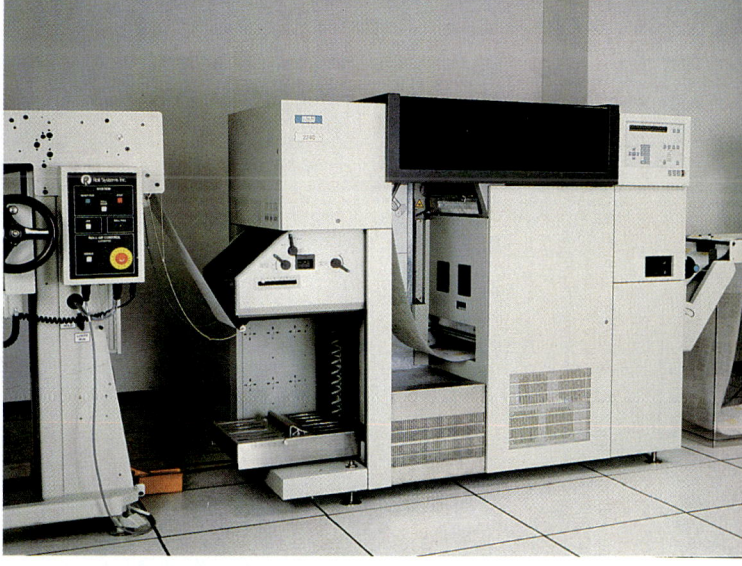

Figure 5-28
High speed laser printers can operate at speeds greater than 200 pages per minute. These printing systems can cost more than $200,000.

Other Types of Printers

In addition to the printers just discussed, there are a number of printers developed for special purposes. These include single label printers, bar code label printers, and portable printers. *Figure 5-30* shows examples of these printers.

Figure 5-29
Thermal-transfer printers are used to produce high-quality color output.

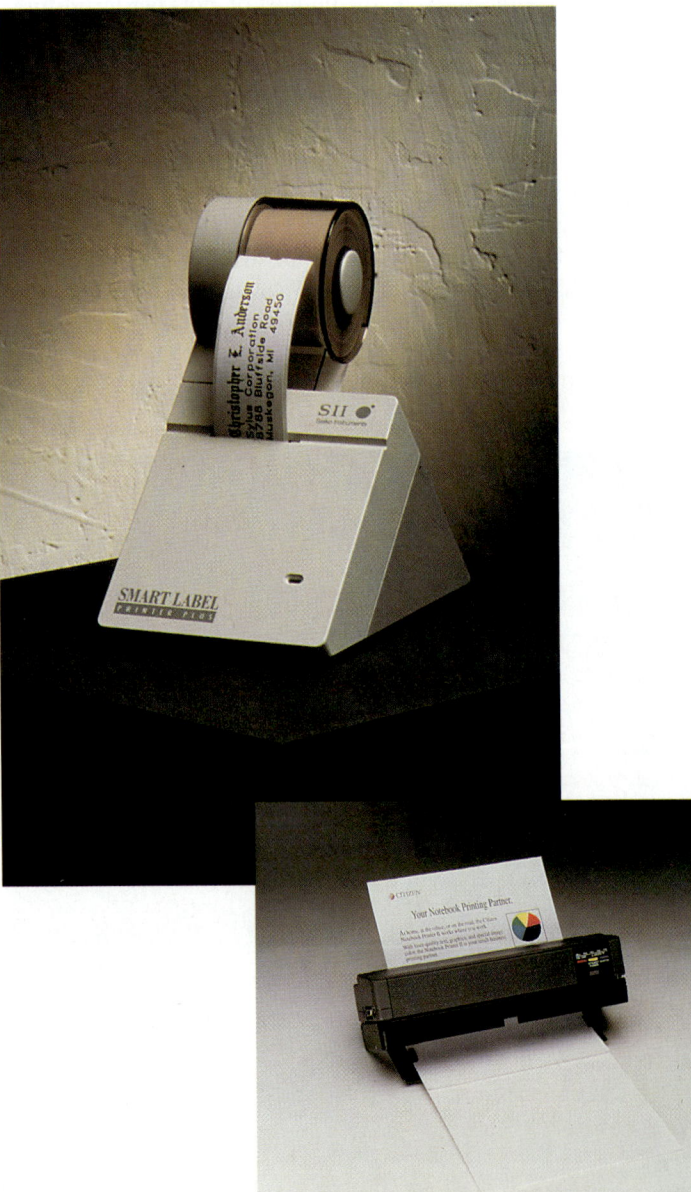

Figure 5-30
Other types of printers, from left to right, include a bar code label printer, a single label printer, and a portable printer designed for use with portable computers.

Summary of Impact and Nonimpact Printers

Impact and nonimpact methods of printing each have advantages and disadvantages. Impact printing can be noisy because the paper is struck when printing occurs. Because the paper is struck, specially treated multipart paper can be used to create multiple copies of a report at one time, such as an invoice, that is routed to different people. Nonimpact printers are quiet, produce high-quality output, and have become the standard for business correspondence. They do not strike the paper, however, and can therefore create only one printed copy at a time. If additional copies are needed, they must each be printed separately. Color output is more attractive, but is slower and more expensive than black and white output for all printer types.

Considerations in Choosing a Printer

In addition to understanding the features and capabilities of the various types of printers that are available, you must consider several other factors before choosing a printer. These include factors such as how much output will be produced and who will use the output. Considering these and the other factors stated in *Figure 5-31* will help you to choose a printer to meet your needs.

Figure 5-31
Questions to consider when choosing a printer.

QUESTION	EXPLANATION
How much output will be produced?	Desktop printers are not designed for continous use. More than several hundred pages a day requires a commercial (business) grade printer. Check a printer's **duty cycle,** the recommended maximum number of copies per month and **mean time between failures (MTBF)**, the estimated time the before a component needs service.
What type of output will be produced?	Make a list of the types of output that will be produced (e.g., reports, transparencies, labels, charts, graphics) and match this list with printer capabilities.
Who will use the output?	Internal-only reports can be prepared on fast, draft-quality printers. External correspondence requires the letter-quality output of a nonimpact printer.
Where will the output be produced?	If the output will be produced at the user's desk or in an open office environment, a sound enclosure may be required to reduce printer noise.
Are multiple copies required?	Only impact printers can produce multiple copies on a single pass.
Is color required?	Color can enhance a document, but color printers are slower and cost more.
Are different fonts needed?	Most, but not all, printers have some built-in fonts. Page printers usually offer the most choices. Software-based fonts are also available.
Where will the printer be located?	Printers close (within 25 feet) to a computer use a faster parallel interface. Printers farther away will use a slower interface or use network cabling.

Display Devices

A **display device** is the visual output device of a computer. The most common type of display device is a monitor. A **monitor** looks like a television and consists of a display surface, called a screen, and a plastic or metal case to house the electrical components. A monitor often has a swivel base that allows the angle of the screen surface to be adjusted. The term **screen** is used to refer to both the surface of any display device and to any type of display device. A **video display terminal** (VDT) is a type of display device that also includes a keyboard. VDTs, also called dumb terminals, are usually connected to larger systems such as minicomputers or mainframes. An older term sometimes used to refer to monitor or VDT display devices is CRT. A **CRT**, which stands for **cathode ray tube**, is actually the large tube inside a monitor or VDT. The front part of the tube is the display surface or screen.

The most widely used monitors are equivalent in size to a 14- to 17-inch television screen. Monitors designed for use with desktop publishing, graphics, or engineering applications come in even larger sizes that can display full-size images of one or sometimes two 8 1/2 by 11-inch pages of data. One company even makes a monitor that can be tilted 90 degrees to display either long or wide pages or two pages side by side *(Figure 5-32)*.

Resolution

The **resolution**, or clarity, of the image on the monitor depends on the number of individual dots displayed on the monitor and the distance between each dot. Each dot that can be illuminated is called a **picture element**, or **pixel**. The pixels are illuminated to form an image on the screen *(Figure 5-33)*. The distance between each pixel is called the **dot pitch**. The greater the number of pixels and the closer they are, the better the monitor resolution. The resolution of a monitor is important, especially when the monitor will be used to display graphics or other nontext information.

Figure 5-32
Portrait Display Labs manufactures a monitor that can be tilted 90 degrees to display long or wide pages or two pages side by side.

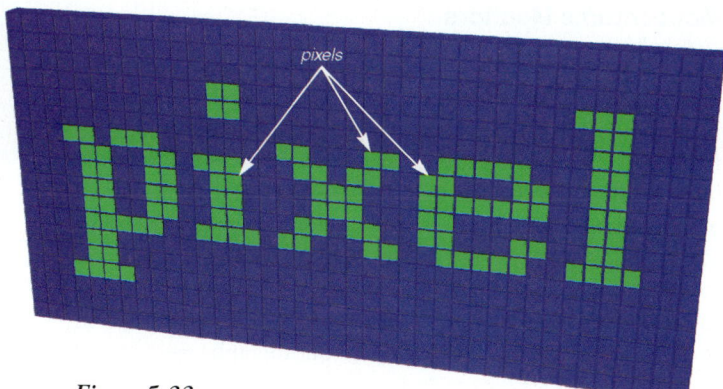

Figure 5-33
The word "pixel" shown here is made up of individual picture elements (pixels) as they would be displayed on a bit-mapped screen. Each pixel can be turned on or off to form an image on the screen.

Monitors used for graphics are called **dot-addressable displays** or **bit-mapped displays**. On these monitors, the number of addressable locations on the monitor corresponds to the number of pixels, or dots, that can be illuminated. The number of pixels that is actually displayed is determined by a combination of the software in the computer, the capability of the video adapter board in the computer, and the monitor itself. High-resolution display devices can produce an image that is almost equivalent to the quality of a photograph *(Figure 5-34)*.

Several video graphics standards have been developed, including CGA (Color Graphics Adapter), EGA (Enhanced Graphics Adapter), VGA (Video Graphics Array), and super VGA (SVGA). The term super VGA is often used for any resolution beyond 640 x 480. As shown in *Figure 5-35*, each standard provides for a different number of pixels and colors. Some manufacturers offer even higher resolution monitors. The resolution of most monitors sold for personal computer systems is SVGA.

Figure 5-34
High-resolution display devices can produce images that are equivalent to the quality of a photograph. These devices are often used in graphic arts, engineering, and scientific applications.

Standard	Year	Resolution (W x H)	Available Colors	Maximum Displayed Colors
CGA	1981	640 x 200	16	4
Hercules	1982	720 x 348	None	None
EGA	1984	640 x 480	64	16
VGA	1986	640 x 480	262,144	256
Super VGA	1988	800 x 600 to 1600 x 1200	16.7 million	16.7 million

Figure 5-35
A summary of the more widely used video graphics standards for display screens.

Each of the video graphics standards have a specific frequency or rate at which the video signals are sent to the monitor. Some monitors are designed to only work at a particular frequency and video standard. Other monitors, called **multiscanning** or **multisync monitors**, are designed to work within a range of frequencies and thus can work with different standards and video adapters.

Color Monitors

A **color monitor** can display text or graphics in color *(Figure 5-36)*. Color monitors are widely used with all types of computers because of reduced prices and because much of today's software is written to display information in color. Although some color monitors are capabable of displaying millions of colors, the human eye cannot distinguish the differences. Most PC color monitors display up to 256 colors at one time.

Monochrome Monitors

Monochrome monitors display a single color such as white, green, or amber characters on a black background *(Figure 5-37)* or black characters on a white background. Monochrome monitors are less expensive than color monitors and are often used by businesses for word processing, order entry, and other applications that do not require color. Using a technique known as gray scaling, some monochrome monitors can display good-quality graphic images. **Gray scaling** involves converting an image into pixels that are different shades of gray like a black and white photograph.

Flat Panel Displays

A **flat panel display** is a thin display screen that does not use cathode ray tube (CRT) technology. Flat panel displays are most often used in portable computers but larger units that can mount on a wall or other structure are also available.

Figure 5-36
Color monitors are widely used because most of today's software is written to display information in color.

DISPLAY DEVICES

Two common types of technology used for flat panel displays are liquid crystal display (LCD) and gas plasma *(Figure 5-38)*.

In a **liquid crystal display** (**LCD**), a liquid crystal is deposited between two sheets of polarizing material. When an electrical current passes between crossing wires, the liquid crystals are aligned so light cannot shine through, producing an image on the screen. LCD technology is also commonly used in digital watches, clocks, and calculators. **Active matrix** LCD screens use individual transistors to control each crystal cell. **Passive matrix** LCD screens use fewer transistors; one for each row and column. Active matrix displays cost more but display a sharper, brighter picture (Figure 5-39).

Gas plasma screens substitute a neon gas for the liquid crystal material. Any locations on a grid of horizontal and vertical electrodes can be turned on to cause the neon gas to glow and produce the pixels that form an image. Gas plasma screens offer better resolution than LCD screens but are more expensive.

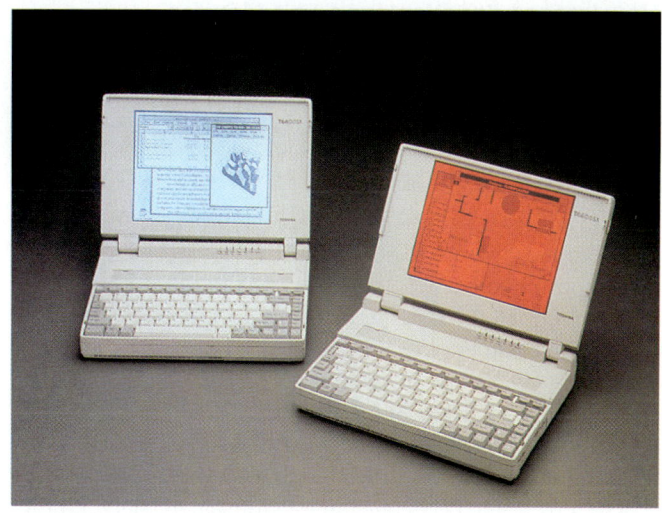

Figure 5-38
Flat panel displays are most often used on portable computers. The system on the left uses a liquid crystal display (LCD) and the system on the right uses a gas plasma display.

Figure 5-37
Monochrome monitors display a single color against a solid background.

Figure 5-39
Active matrix LCD screens produce the best color resolution by using individual transistors to control each crystal cell.

How Images Are Displayed on a Monitor

Most monitors used with personal computers and terminals use cathode ray tube (CRT) technology. When these monitors produce an image, the following steps occur (Figure 5-40):

1. The image to be displayed on the monitor is sent electronically from the CPU to the video circuits to the cathode ray tube.
2. An electron gun at the rear of the tube generates an electron beam towards the screen. The beam passes through holes in a metal screen called the *shadow mask*. The shadow mask helps align the beam so it hits the correct dot on the screen. The screen is coated with phosphor, a substance that glows when it is struck by the electron beam.
3. The yoke, which generates an electromagnetic field, moves the electron beam across and down the screen. **Interlaced monitors** illuminate every other line and then return to the top to illuminate the lines they skipped. **Noninterlaced monitors** illuminate the entire screen more quickly in a single pass. The speed at which the entire screen is redrawn is called the **refresh rate**.
4. The illuminated phosphors create an image on the screen.

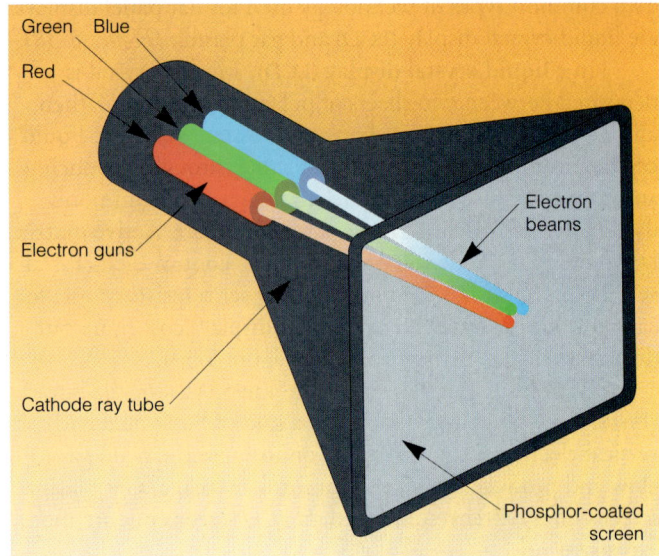

Figure 5-41
Each pixel on a color monitor screen is made up of three colored (red, green, and blue) phosphor dots. These dots can be turned on individually or in combinations to display a wide range of colors.

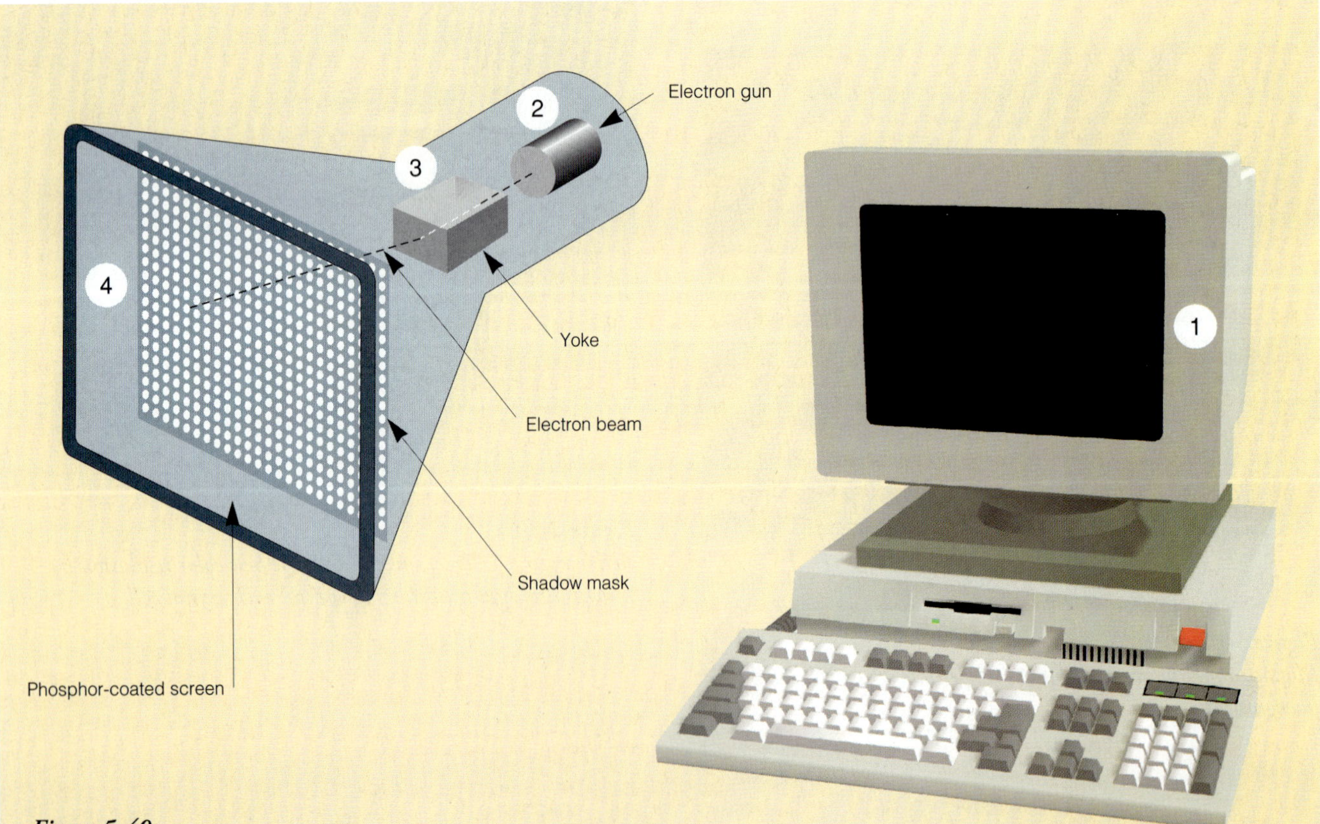

Figure 5-40
How an image is displayed on a monochrome cathode ray tube monitor.

How Color Is Produced

To show color on a screen, each pixel must have three colored phosphor dots. These dots are the additive primary colors red, green, and blue *(Figure 5-41)*. A separate electron gun is used for each color. In the simplest combinations, eight colors can be generated – black (no color), red only, blue only, green only, magenta (red and blue), yellow (red and green), blue-green (blue and green), and white (red, blue, and green together). By varying the intensity of the electron beam striking the phosphors, and making some colored dots glow more than others, many more colors can be generated.

Other Output Devices

Although printers and display devices provide the majority of computer output, other devices are available for particular uses and applications. These include data projectors, plotters, computer output microfilm devices, and voice output devices.

Data Projectors

A variety of devices are available to take the image that displays on a computer screen and project it so it can be clearly seen by a room full of people. Smaller, lower cost units, called **projection panels**, use liquid crystal display (LCD) technology and are designed to be placed on top of an overhead projector *(Figure 5-42)*.

Larger, more expensive units use technology similar to large-screen projection TV sets; separate red, green, and blue beams of light are focused onto the screen (*Figure 5-43* on the next page). The projection panels are easily portable and, depending on the overhead projector with which they are used, can be located at different distances from the projection screen. The three-beam projectors must be focused and aligned for a specific distance and thus once installed, are usually not moved.

Figure 5-42
Projection panels are used together with overhead projectors to display computer screen images to a room full of people.

Plotters

A **plotter** is an output device used to produce high-quality line drawings such as building plans, charts, or circuit diagrams. These drawings can be quite large; some plotters are designed to handle paper up to 40 inches by 48 inches, much larger than would fit in a standard printer. Plotters can be classified by the way they create the drawing. The two types are pen plotters and electrostatic plotters.

As the name implies, **pen plotters** create images on a sheet of paper by moving one or more pens over the surface of the paper or by moving the paper under the tip of the pens.

Two different kinds of pen plotters are flatbed plotters and drum plotters. When a **flatbed plotter** is used to plot, or draw, the pen or pens are instructed by the software to move to the down position so the pen contacts the flat surface of the paper. Further instructions then direct the movement of the pens to create the image. Most flatbed plotters have one or more pens of varying colors or widths. The plotter shown in *Figure 5-44* is a flatbed plotter used to create color drawings.

A **drum plotter** uses a rotating drum, or cylinder, over which drawing pens are mounted. The pens can move to the left and right as the drum rotates, creating an image *(Figure 5-45)*. An advantage of the drum plotter is that the length of the plot is virtually unlimited because roll paper can be used. The width of the plot is limited by the width of the drum.

With an **electrostatic plotter,** the paper moves under a row of wires (called styli) that can be turned on to create an electrostatic charge on the paper. The paper then passes through a developer and the drawing emerges where the charged wires touched the paper. The electrostatic printer image is composed of a series of very small dots, resulting in relatively high-quality output. In addition, the speed of electrostatic plotting is faster than with pen plotters.

Computer Output Microfilm

Computer output microfilm (COM) is an output technique that records output from a computer as microscopic images on roll or sheet film *(Figure 5-46)*. The images stored on COM are the same as the images that would be printed on paper. The COM recording process reduces characters 24, 42,

Figure 5-43
The data projector uses three separate red, green, and blue beams to project data onto a screen. Single beam projectors are also available.

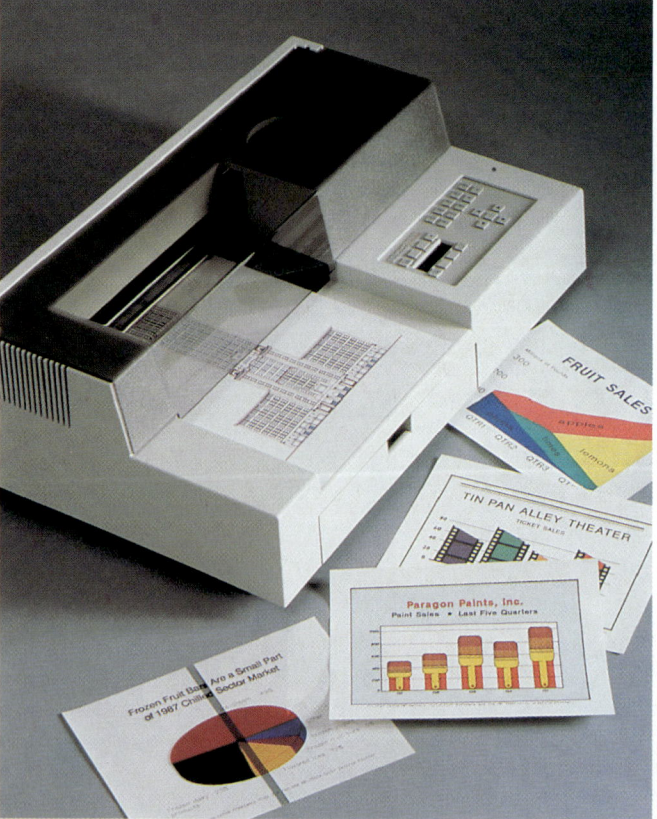

Figure 5-44
A color flatbed plotter.

or 48 times smaller than would be produced on a printer. The information is then recorded on sheet film called **microfiche** or on 16mm, 35mm, or 105mm roll film.

Microfilm has several advantages over printed reports or other storage media for certain applications. Some of these advantages are:

1. Data can be recorded on the film faster than printers; up to 30,000 lines per minute.
2. Costs for recording the data are lower. Studies have shown that microfilm can be as little as one-tenth the cost of printing a report.
3. Less space is required to store microfilm than printed materials. Microfilm that weighs one ounce can store the equivalent of 10 pounds of paper.
4. The cost to store a megabyte of information is less on microfilm than it is on disk.

To access data stored on microfilm, a variety of readers are available. They utilize indexing techniques to provide a quick reference to the data. Some microfilm readers can perform automatic data lookup, called **computer-assisted retrieval** (**CAR**), under the control of an attached computer. With the indexing software and hardware now available for microfilm, a user can usually locate any piece of data in a database in less than 10 seconds, at a far lower cost per inquiry than using an online inquiry system consisting of a computer system that stores the data on a hard disk.

Voice Output

Another important means of generating output from a computer is voice output. **Voice output** consists of spoken words that are conveyed to the user from the computer. Thus, instead of reading words on a printed report or monitor, the user hears the words over earphones, the telephone, or other devices from which sound can be generated.

The data that produces voice output is usually created in one of two ways. First, a person can talk into a device that will encode the words in a digital pattern. For example, the words, *The number is,* can be spoken into a microphone, and the computer software can assign a digital pattern to the words. The digital data is then stored on a disk. At a later time, the data can be retrieved from the disk and translated back from digital data into voice, so the person listening will actually hear the words.

Figure 5-45
A drum plotter can handle larger paper sizes than a flatbed plotter.

Figure 5-46
Microfilm is often used for reports that must be kept on file but do not have to be referred to frequently.

A second type of voice generation is called voice synthesis. **Voice synthesis** can transform words stored in main memory into speech. The words are analyzed by a program that examines the letters stored in memory and generates sounds for the letter combinations. The software can apply rules of intonation and stress to make it sound as though a person were speaking. The speech is then projected over speakers attached to the computer.

You may have heard voice output used by the telephone company for giving number information. Automobile and vending machine manufacturers are also incorporating voice output into their products. The potential for this type of output is great and it will continue to be incorporated in products and services in the future.

Summary of Output from the Computer

The output step of the information processing cycle uses a variety of devices to provide users with information. The equipment discussed in this chapter, including printers, display devices, and other output devices are summarized in *Figure 5-47*.

OUTPUT DEVICE		DESCRIPTION
Speakers		Used for audio (sound) output.
Printers – Impact	Dot matrix	Prints text and graphics using small dots.
	Band	High-speed rotating band text-only printer.
	Chain	High-speed rotating chain text-only printer.
Printers – Nonimpact	Ink-jet	Sprays tiny drops of ink onto a page to form text and graphics. Prints quietly. Inexpensive color printer.
	Page (laser)	Works like a copying machine. Produces very high quality text and graphics.
	Thermal	Uses heat to produce high-quality color output.
Display Devices	Color monitors	Can display multiple colors to enhance information.
	Monochrome monitors	Displays one color on solid background. Less expensive than color.
	LCD	Flat panel liquid crystal display used for laptops. Available in color.
	Gas plasma	High-resolution flat panel display.
Data Projectors		Projects display screen image to a group.
Plotters		Produces hard-copy graphic output. Some can handle large paper sizes.
COM		Stores reduced-size image on sheet or roll film.
Voice		Communicates information to user in the form of speech.

Figure 5-47
A summary of the more common output devices.

COMPUTERS AT WORK

NoteStation – The Key to Getting the Right Music

Musicians and vocalists who purchase sheet music often have a problem finding music in the key that matches their instruments or vocal ranges. Traditionally printed sheet music usually comes in only one key. If the key is not right, the music must be transposed (converted) into another key. Transposing takes additional time and usually costs money if done by someone else. However, a company in California, using computers and multimedia software, appears to have solved the problem.

In combination with computer maker IBM, MusicWriter, Inc. of Los Gatos, California has developed NoteStation, a stand-alone multimedia kiosk that can generate sheet music in any key for more than 3,000 song titles. The potential sheet music buyer uses the NoteStation touch screen display to browse through the available songs by title, artist, style, or composer *(Figure 5-48)*. The system can even find songs if only a portion of the title is known. Once a song is selected, the sheet music is displayed on the screen. If desired, the customer can play a portion of the song. If the key is not right, it can be changed and the song played again. When the customer is happy with the music in his or her chosen key, the sheet music is printed on a laser printer or saved as a MIDI file on a diskette.

The advantages of NoteStation to musicians and vocalists are obvious. They can get their music in the key they want and listen to it before they buy it. If they are not exactly sure of what they want, using the computer to search through the song titles is much easier than leafing through pages of sheet music or a printed catalog. For the music stores where most NoteStations are installed, there are also numerous advantages. The music stores no longer have to order, stock, and inventory individual pieces of sheet music. Unless they run out of printer paper, they are never out of stock of any piece of music. The NoteStation kiosk takes a fraction of the space previously devoted to sheet music. The number of song titles available increases each month when the stores receive a new CD-ROM to load in the kiosk.

The NoteStation kiosk has significance beyond music publishing. The NoteStation is one of the first examples of what is called **point-of-sale manufacturing**; allowing the customer to design, manufacture, and purchase the product on the spot. The kiosk has become the showroom, warehouse, and manufacturing plant all rolled into a single unit that takes up fewer than 10 square feet of floor space. Eventually, this concept will be applied to many consumer products.

Figure 5-48

IN THE FUTURE

Virtual Reality — Beyond Entertainment

Most articles on virtual reality quickly move to discussions of games and rides designed to thrill the participants. Clearly, entertainment is the driving force behind most of today's VR applications. Many believe that VR will eventually have numerous practical applications that go beyond using a simulated laser gun to blast your opponent before he or she blasts you. The following discusses some of the probable future VR applications in training, medicine, and manufacturing.

Training

For some time, virtual reality like simulations have been used to train operators of expensive equipment such as airplanes and ships. In recent years, VR simulators have been developed for less expensive and complicated equipment such as trucks and construction equipment. The logical progression of this trend is that eventually, all products will come with VR training material that will help the user quickly and safely learn to use the equipment. For example, power tools such as a circular saw or electric drill could come with VR training materials that will enable the owner to saw or drill wood and build a project before attempting to use the real equipment.

Medicine

Medicine is another area where VR development work now being done may eventually be used on a widespread basis. To date, most of the VR work in medicine has involved learning systems. Different parts of the human anatomy have been digitized so students can use computer images to explore the body. Some work is already being done on using VR to simulate surgery. Portions of virtual bodies with internal organs and body fluids have been developed for these applications. Eventually, complete virtual patients will be developed to train medical personnel on all aspects of health care from initial consultation to post-operative recovery.

Manufacturing

Manufacturing companies are also experimenting with VR to improve design, production, and maintenance activities. VR prototypes will enable companies and prospective customers to evaluate designs before actual models are built. VR prototypes can also be used for repeated product testing. Manufacturing processes from welding to installing a nut and bolt can be tested for feasibility before production lines are built. Boeing is currently using a process closely related to VR called *augmented reality* to assist in manufacturing jumbo jets. Unlike VR, which creates a simulated scene, **augmented reality** superimposes information on a real scene. In Boeing's case, manufacturing procedures such as how to connect electrical wires in a plane are projected onto special glasses worn by the worker. The worker can see both the wiring diagram and the actual area of the plane where the wires are to be connected. Eventually, all equipment repair manuals might be available for such projected display as you work on the equipment.

All of the probable commercial applications of VR just discussed are either in limited use or under development. However, it may take years before they are widely used. In the meantime, there is this great VR game that you really should experience. Each player has a laser gun and the object of the game is . . .

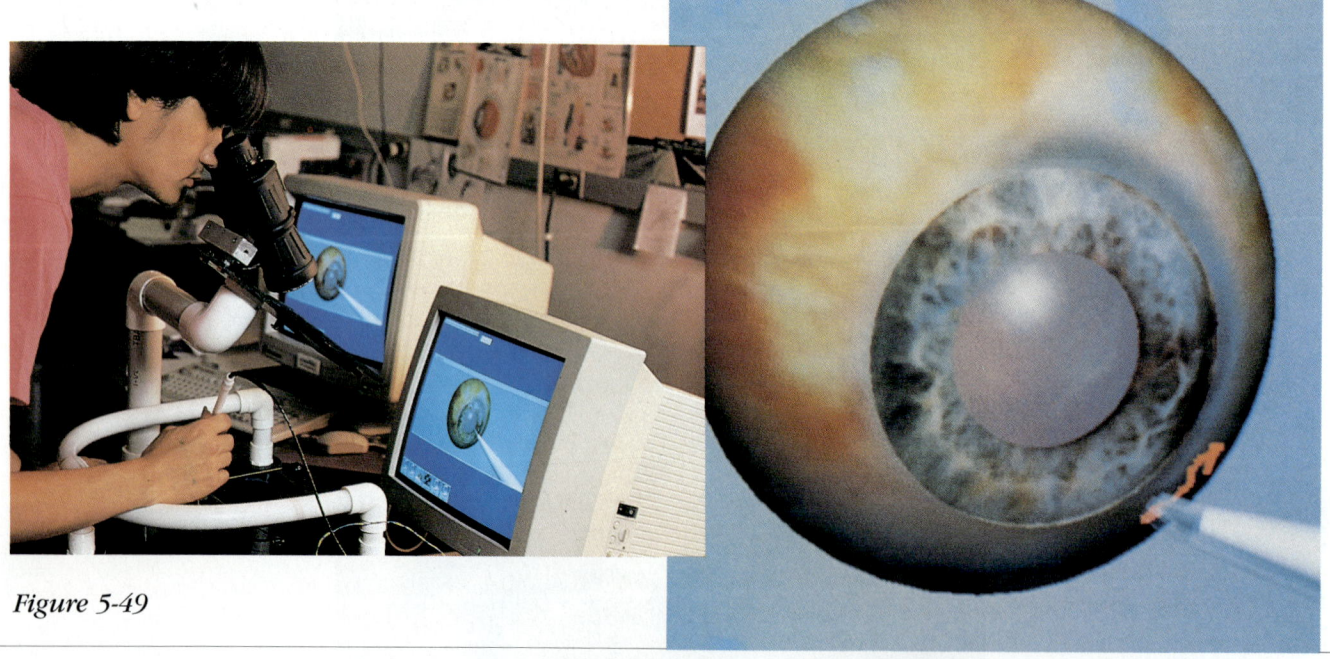

Figure 5-49

What You Should Know

1. **Output** is data that has been processed into a useful form called information that can be used by a person or a machine. Output that is printed is called **hard copy**, and output that is displayed on a screen is called **soft copy**.

2. A **report** is information presented in an organized form. An **internal report** is used by individuals in the performance of their jobs. An **external report** is used outside the organization. The four common types of reports are: **narrative reports**, **detail reports**, **summary reports**, and **exception reports**. **Periodic reports**, also called **scheduled reports**, are produced on a regular basis. **On-demand reports** are created whenever they are needed for information that is not required on a scheduled basis.

3. **Computer graphics** are any non-text pictorial information. **Computer drawing programs** and **computer paint programs** allow an artistic user to create stunning looking works of art.

4. **Audio output**, sometimes called **audio response**, consists of sounds, including words and music, produced by the computer.

5. **Video output** consists of visual images that have been captured with a video input device, such as a VCR or camera, digitized, and directed to an output device such as a computer monitor. **High definition television** (HDTV) sets are designed for digital signals and may eventually replace computer monitors.

6. **Multimedia** is the combination of text, graphics, video, and sound. Most multimedia presentations use a technique called **hypermedia** that allows the user to quickly move to related subject areas. Because of the large amounts of data that multimedia applications require, most multimedia products available today are stored on CD-ROM disks.

7. **Virtual reality** (VR) refers to the use of a computer to create an artificial environment that can be experienced by the computer user. In its simplest form, VR software can display what appears to be a three-dimensional view of a place that can be explored by the user. In more advanced forms, VR software requires the user to wear specialized headgear, gloves, and body suits to enhance the experience of the artificial environment.

8. Generally, printers can be classified into two groups, impact or nonimpact, based on how they transfer characters to the paper.

9. **Impact printers** transfer the image onto paper by some type of printing mechanism striking the paper, ribbon, and character together. Most impact printers use **continuous-form paper**, which has pages that are connected together for a continuous flow through the printer.

10. A **dot matrix printer** produces printed images by striking wire pins against an inked ribbon. Most dot matrix printers used with personal computers have a single print head that moves across the page. Dot matrix printers used with larger computers have fixed print mechanisms at each print position and can print an entire line at a time.

11. The speed of impact printers with movable print heads is rated in **characters per second** (cps). The speed of impact printers that print one line at a time is rated in **lines per minute** (lpm). The speeds quoted by dot matrix printer manufacturers are usually for draft-quality printing. **Draft-quality** printing uses the minimum number of dots to form a character and achieve the fastest printing speed. To achieve a sharper, higher quality look, called **letter quality** (LQ) or **near letter quality** (NLQ), the printer overlaps printed dots.

12. Dot matrix printers with movable print heads are designed to print in a **bidirectional** manner; that is, the print head can print as it moves from left to right, and from right to left. Two types of paper feed mechanisms found on dot matrix printers are **tractor feed mechanisms** and **friction feed mechanisms**.

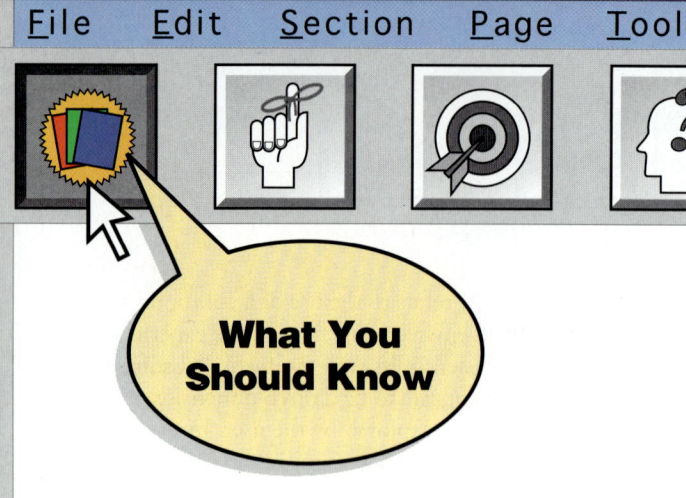

13. Some dot matrix printers can print in multiple colors. Most dot matrix printers are available for less than $1,000.

14. Band and chain printers are impact printers used for high-volume output on large computer systems. **Band printers** use a horizontal, rotating band containing numbers, letters of the alphabet, and selected special characters. The **chain printer** is similar to a band printer and contains characters on a rotating chain.

15. **Nonimpact printing** means that printing occurs without having a mechanism striking against a sheet of paper.

16. An **ink-jet printer** sprays tiny drops of ink onto the paper. The **page printer** is a nonimpact printer that operates similar to a copying machine. Data is converted into light that is directed to a revolving drum. Each position on the drum touched by light attracts the toner (powdered ink) that is transferred onto the paper and then fused to the paper by heat and pressure. **Laser printers** use a laser beam aimed at the drum by a spinning mirror.

17. Page printers are rated by their speed and resolution. Speed is measured in **pages per minute (ppm)**. Page printer resolution is measured by the number of **dots per inch (dpi)** that can be printed.

18. **Thermal printers**, sometimes called **thermal transfer printers**, use heat to transfer colored inks from ink sheets onto the printing surface. A special type of thermal printer using a method called **dye diffusion** uses chemically treated paper to obtain color print quality equal to glossy magazines.

19. A number of printers have been developed for special purposes, including single label printers, bar code label printers, and portable printers.

20. A **display device** is the visual output device of a computer. A **monitor** looks like a television and consists of a display surface, called a screen, and a plastic or metal case to house the electrical components. The term **screen** is used to refer to both the surface of any display device and to any type of display device. A **video display terminal (VDT)** is a type of display device that also includes a keyboard. **CRT**, which stands for **cathode ray tube**, is an older term sometimes used to refer to monitor or VDT display devices. CRT is actually the large tube inside a monitor or VDT.

21. **The resolution**, or clarity, of the image on a monitor depends on the number of individual dots that are displayed on the monitor and the distance between each dot. Each dot that can be illuminated is called a **picture element**, or **pixel**. The distance between each pixel is called the **dot pitch**.

22. Monitors used for graphics are called **dot-addressable displays** or **bit-mapped displays**. Several video graphics standards have been developed, including CGA (Color Graphics Adapter), EGA (Enhanced Graphics Adapter), VGA (Video Graphics Array), and super VGA (SVGA). Some monitors are designed to only work with a particular frequency and video standard. Other monitors, called **multiscanning** or **multisync monitors**, are designed to work within a range of frequencies and thus can work with different standards and video adapters.

23. A **color monitor** can display text or graphics in color. **Monochrome monitors** display a single color such as white, green, or amber characters on a black background, or black characters on a white background. Using a technique known as **gray scaling**, which involves converting an image into pixels that are different shades of gray like a black and white photograph, some monochrome monitors can display good quality graphic images.

24. A **flat panel display** is a thin display screen that does not use cathode ray tube (CRT) technology. In a **liquid crystal display** (LCD), a liquid crystal is deposited between two sheets of polarizing material. When an electrical current passes between crossing wires, the liquid crystals are aligned so light cannot shine through, producing an image on the screen. **Active matrix** LCD screens use individual transistors to control each crystal cell. **Passive matrix** LCD screens use fewer transistors; one for each row and column. **Gas plasma** screens substitute a neon gas for the liquid crystal material.

25. Most monitors used with personal computers and terminals use cathode ray tube (CRT) technology. An electron gun at the rear of the tube generates an electron beam toward the phosphor-coated screen, which glows when it is struck by the electron beam. **Interlaced monitors** illuminate every other line and then return to the top of the screen to illuminate the lines they skipped. **Noninterlaced monitors** illuminate the entire screen in a single pass. The speed at which the entire screen is redrawn is called the **refresh rate**. To show color on a screen, each pixel must have three colored phosphor dots (red, green, and blue). By varying the intensity of the electron beam striking the phosphors, many colors can be generated.

26. **Projection panels** use liquid crystal display (LCD) technology and are designed to be placed on top of an overhead projector.

27. A **plotter** is an output device used to produce high-quality line drawings such as building plans, charts, or circuit diagrams. **Pen plotters** create images on a sheet of paper by moving one or more pens over the surface of the paper or by moving the paper under the tip of the pens. When a **flatbed plotter** is used to plot, or draw, the pen or pens are instructed by the software to move to the down position so the pen contacts the flat surface of the paper. A **drum plotter** uses a rotating drum, or cylinder, over which drawing pens are mounted. With an **electrostatic plotter**, the paper moves under a row of wires (called styli) that can be turned on to create an electrostatic charge on the paper.

28. **Computer output microfilm** (COM) is an output technique that records output from a computer as microscopic images on sheet film, called **microfiche** or on rolls of film. Some microfilm readers can perform automatic data lookup, called **computer-assisted retrieval** (CAR).

29. **Voice output** consists of spoken words that are conveyed to the user from the computer. **Voice synthesis** can transform words stored in main memory into speech.

Terms to Remember

active matrix (5.21)
audio output (5.4)
audio response (5.4)
augmented reality (5.28)

band printers (5.12)
bidirectional (5.11)
bit-mapped displays (5.19)

cathode ray tube (CRT) (5.18)
chain printers (5.13)
characters per second (cps) (5.10)
color monitor (5.20)
computer-assisted retrieval
 (CAR) (5.25)
computer drawing programs (5.4)
computer graphics (5.4)
computer output microfilm
 (COM) (5.24)
computer paint programs (5.4)
continuous-form paper (5.9)
CRT (5.18)

detail report (5.3)
display device (5.18)
dot matrix printer (5.10)
dot pitch (5.18)
dot-addressable displays (5.19)
dots per inch (dpi) (5.15)
draft quality (5.10)
drum plotter (5.24)
dye diffusion (5.15)

electronic plotter (5.24)
exception report (5.3)
external report (5.3)

flat panel display (5.20)
flatbed plotters (5.24)
friction feed mechanisms (5.12)

gas plasma (5.21)
gray scaling (5.20)

hard copy (5.2)
high definition television
 (HDTV) (5.5)
hypermedia (5.5)

impact printers (5.9)
ink-jet printer (5.13)
interlaced monitors (5.22)
internal report (5.2)

laser printers (5.14)
letter quality (5.11)
lines per minute (lpm) (5.10)
liquid crystal display (LCD) (5.21)

microfiche (5.25)
monitor (5.18)
monochrome monitors (5.20)
multimedia (5.5)
multiscanning (5.20)
multisync monitors (5.20)

narrative reports (5.3)
near letter quality (5.11)
nonimpact printing (5.13)
noninterlaced monitors (5.22)

on-demand reports (5.4)
output (5.2)

page printer (5.14)
pages per minute (ppm) (5.15)
passive matrix (5.21)
pen plotters (5.24)
periodic reports (5.4)
picture element (5.18)
pixel (5.18)
plotter (5.24)
point-of-sale manufacturing (5.27)
projection panels (5.23)

refresh rate (5.22)
report (5.2)
resolution (5.18)

scheduled reports (5.4)
screen (5.18)
soft copy (5.2)
summary report (5.3)

thermal printers (5.15)
thermal transfer printers (5.15)
tractor feed mechanisms (5.12)

video display terminal (VDT) (5.18)
video output (5.5)
virtual reality (VR) (5.7)
voice output (5.25)
voice synthesis (5.26)

Test Your Knowledge 5.33

Fill in the Blanks

1. _____ is data that has been processed into a useful form called information that can be used by a person or a machine.

2. Output that is printed is called _____, and output that is displayed on the screen is called _____.

3. _____ is the combination of text, graphics, video, and sound; most presentations of this type use a technique called _____ that allows the user to quickly move to related subject areas.

4. Generally, printers can be classified into two groups, _____ or _____, based on how they transfer characters to the paper.

5. Three different types of display devices are: _____, which display text and graphics in color; _____, which display a single color on a black or white background; and _____, which are thin display screens that do not use cathode ray tube (CRT) technology.

Short Answer

1. What is a report? How is an internal report different from an external report? How is a periodic report different from an on-demand report?

2. How is multimedia more than just a combination of traditional text-based computers and television? Why are most multimedia products available today stored on CD-ROM disks? In what four areas are multimedia applications primarily used?

3. How are impact printers different from nonimpact printers? Give at least two examples of each type of printer. What are the advantages and disadvantages of each printing method?

4. How are images displayed on a monitor that uses cathode ray tube (CRT) technology? How is color produced?

5. Although printers and display devices provide the majority of computer output, other devices are available for particular uses and applications. List at least three output devices other than printers or display devices. Briefly describe each.

Label the Figure

Instructions: Identify the parts of the monochrome cathode ray tube monitor shown in the figure below.

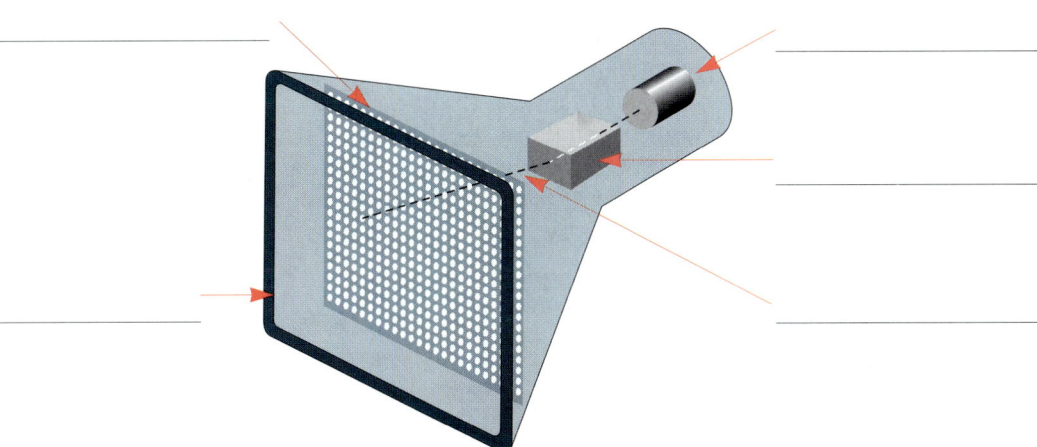

1

Reports can be classified by the way they present information. The four common types of reports are narrative reports, detail reports, summary reports, and exception reports. During your lifetime, you have probably given all of these reports, in either written or oral form. Describe a circumstance in which you offered each type of report.

2

Computer graphics and audio output are assuming increasingly important roles in art and music. Computer drawing programs and computer paint programs make it easy to draw perfect circles, three-dimensional figures, and arresting images. Electronic music technology enables a single person to produce sounds that once required a room full of musicians. What changes, if any, do you foresee in art or music as a result of these technologies? Do you think people who use computers to create graphic images or musical pieces should be called artists or musicians? Why or why not?

3

Some people believe that multimedia will revolutionize the way information is presented and the way people learn. It has even been predicted that eventually books will only be found in museums and antique stores. Do you think that multimedia will eventually replace all books, or certain types of books? Why or why not? What advantages, if any, do books have over multimedia?

4

Virtual reality (VR) software is currently being used to show clients proposed architectural changes, to allow customers to wander among available products in a virtual showroom or virtual office, and in three-dimensional electronic games. As computing power increases, and VR applications are able to run on lower cost computers, even more VR applications and VR technology will be available for a wider number of users. Think of at least three areas in which you think virtual reality software could be effectively employed. Describe how VR applications could be used in each.

5

When computers were first used in business, some people predicted the paperless office; a place where most documents would only exist electronically in the computer database. Many people now feel, however, that the widespread use of computers has actually elevated the quantity of paper used. Why do you think word processing software, spreadsheet programs, and low-cost printers might have increased the paperwork in the typical office? What steps could be taken to decrease the amount of paperwork?

6

Today, nearly all personal computers use two output devices – a monitor and a printer. Do you think these two output devices will still be the most popular twenty-five years from now? Why or why not? What other types of output devices do you think many personal computers will utilize? Why?

Out and About   5.35

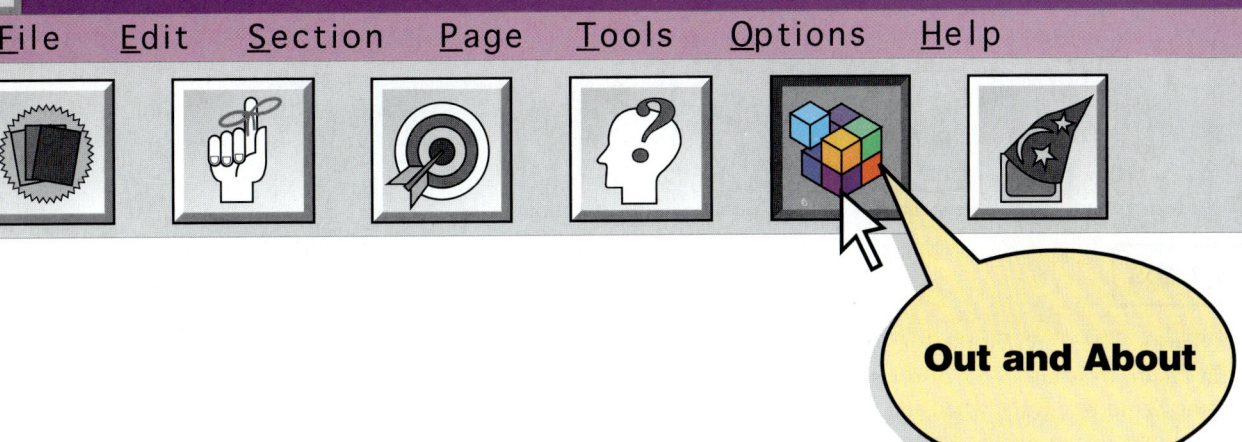

1. Figure 5-31 on page 5.17 offers several questions to be considered when choosing a printer. List the questions posed in Figure 5-31 and answer each according to your current needs. Then, visit a computer store and find at least two printers that fit your requirements. Write down the name of each printer and note its advantages and disadvantages. If you were going to purchase one of these printers, which would you buy? Why?

2. Unlike ordinary television, which uses analog signals, high definition television (HDTV) sets are designed for digital signals. This results in clearer, sharper pictures and makes HDTV sets compatible with other digital technologies such as computers. Visit a library and research HDTV. How is analog technology different from digital technology? Will the development of HDTV be as significant as the introduction of color television approximately thirty years ago? What effect will the evolution of HDTV have on the computer industry?

3. Locate an organization that uses plotters. Possible users include architectural firms, electrical contractors, and a city planning department. Arrange to interview someone in the organization. Find out the purposes for which the plotter is used, what kind of plotter is used, and the advantages (or disadvantages) of using a plotter over creating a drawing by hand. If possible, ask to see a demonstration of the plotter's capabilities.

4. Examine the classified advertisement section of a newspaper or computer magazine. List all of the used computer output devices available. Which type of output device is most prevalent? Why? Choose two output devices in which you might be interested. Note the features and price of each. Would you consider purchasing either of these devices? Why or why not?

5. Contact a library or business that uses computer output microfilm (COM). Interview someone in the library or business to find out why COM is used. What advantages does computer output microfilm have over printed storage media? What are the disadvantages? How is the information accessed? Is the system capable of performing computer-assisted retrieval (CAR)?

6. Visit a computer vendor and obtain information about the highest and lowest priced monitors. Record the names of the monitors, their costs, and the features available with each. Do you think the more expensive monitor is worth the difference in price? Why or why not? Examine a portable computer that uses a flat panel display. What type of screen is it (LCD or gas plasma)? How does its image compare with the least expensive CRT monitor? How does it compare with the most expensive CRT monitor?

 In the Lab

File Edit Section Page Tools Options Help

 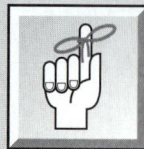   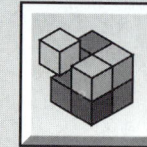

In the Lab

Windows Labs

1 Using a Screen Saver A screen saver, such as those shown in *Figures 5-50* and *5-51,* displays when you are not actively using Windows. Later, when you press a key on the keyboard or move the mouse, the screen saver disappears from the screen. To activate or modify a screen saver, make sure Program Manager displays on the screen. Then, double-click the Main group icon. In the Main group window, double-click the Control Panel program-item icon. In the Control Panel window, double-click the Desktop icon. Perform the following tasks: (1) Click the Help button. Obtain and write down the definition of screen saver. (2) Select the Screen Savers Help topic. Read and print the information. (3) Close the Help window. (4) In the Screen Saver area, click the Name drop-down list box arrow. Select Flying Windows. Click the Test button to display a sample of the screen saver *(Figure 5-50)*. Click the left mouse button. (5) Select Mystify. Click the Test button to display a sample of the screen saver *(Figure 5-51)*. Click the left mouse button. Choose the OK button. (6) Close the Control Panel window by double-clicking its Control-menu box.

2 Changing Desktop Colors With Program Manager on the screen, double-click the Main group icon. In the Main group window, double-click the Control Panel program-item icon. In the Control Panel window, double-click the Color icon. In the Color dialog box, perform the following tasks: (1) Click the Help button. Click the Color Schemes and Sample Screen buttons and write down the definitions. Close the Help window. (2) Click the Color Schemes drop-down list box arrow. Select Hotdog Stand. Notice the Sample Screen displays the Hotdog Stand color *(Figure 5-52)*. (3) Practice selecting other color schemes. Choose the OK button.

in the Color dialog box. (4) Close the Control Panel window by double-clicking its Control-menu box.

3 Shelly Cashman Series Printer Lab Follow the instructions in Windows Lab 2 in Chapter 1 on page 1.30 to display the Shelly Cashman Series Labs window. Select Setting Up to Print and choose the Start Lab button. When the initial screen displays, carefully read the objectives. With your printer turned on, point to the Print Questions button and click the left mouse button. Fill out the top of the Questions sheet and answer the questions as you step through the Lab.

4 Shelly Cashman Series Monitor Lab Follow the instructions in Windows Lab 2 in Chapter 1 on page 1.30 to display the Shelly Cashman Series Labs window. Select Configuring Your Display and choose the Start Lab button. When the initial screen displays, carefully read the objectives. With your printer turned on, point to the Print Questions button and click the left mouse button. Fill out the top of the Questions sheet and answer the questions as you step through the Lab.

5 Printing a Document Using File Manager and Print Manager With Program Manager on the screen, double-click the Main group icon. In the Main group window, double-click the Print Manager program-item icon. Perform the

Figure 5-50

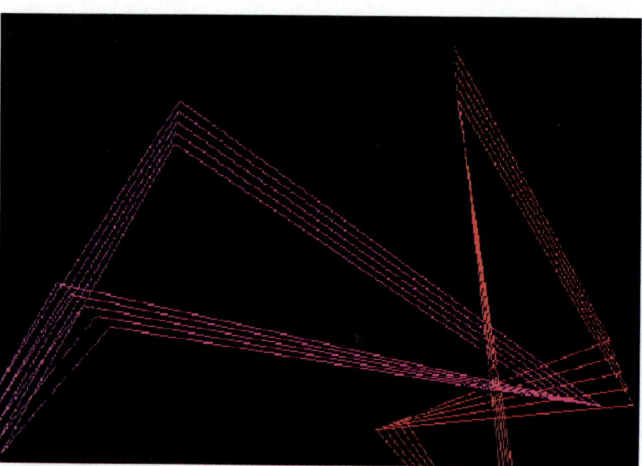

Figure 5-51

following tasks: (1) Minimize the Print Manager window by clicking the Minimize button in the upper right corner of the window. In the Main group window, double-click the File Manager program-item icon. If the File Manager window is maximized, restore it. If necessary, resize the File Manager window so you can see the Print Manager icon at the bottom of your desktop. (2) Insert your diskette with the file win2-2.wri into drive A. Click the drive A icon in the File Manager window to display files on drive A in the directory window. If you do not see the file win2-2.wri, obtain a copy of it from your instructor. (3) Select the file win2-2.wri by clicking it *(Figure 5-53)*. To print the selected file, drag it down to the Print Manager icon and release the mouse button when the mouse pointer changes to a sheet of paper. Choose the OK button in the Print dialog box. (4) Close File Manager. Click the Print Manager program-item icon and choose Close from the Control menu.

6 Using Help to Understand Print Manager With Program Manager on the screen, double-click the Main group icon. In the Main group window, double-click the Print Manager program-item icon. Perform the following tasks: (1) Select the Print Manager Help menu and choose the Contents command. Read and print the information. (2) Select the What Is Print Manager? Help topic. Read and print the information. (3) Click the Back button. Select the Print Your Documents Help topic. Read and print this Help topic and all associated topics on this screen. Close the Help window. Close Print Manager.

DOS Labs

1 Displaying File Contents Insert your diskette containing DOS Lab 2-1 into drive A. At the DOS prompt, type type a:dos2-1 | more and press the ENTER key. Press the PRINT SCREEN key. Press ENTER to see the next screen.

2 Printing File Contents Insert your diskette containing DOS Lab 2-1 into drive A. At the DOS prompt, type print a:dos2-1 and press the ENTER key twice to print it.

3 Redirecting Output Insert a formatted diskette into drive A. At the DOS prompt, type dir > a:dos5-3.txt and press the ENTER key. Did the directory display on the screen? At the DOS prompt, type print a:dos5-3.txt and press the ENTER key. What is the function of the > symbol?

4 Using Help At the DOS prompt, type help and press the ENTER key. Type t to move the cursor to the Help topics beginning with the letter T. Use the arrow keys to move the cursor to <Type> and press the ENTER key. Read and then print the information by pressing ALT, F, P, ENTER.

Online Lab

1 Perusing Advice Columns Using one of the two online services you selected in Chapter 1, connect to the service and perform the following tasks: (1) Search the online service for Advice columns. (2) Write down the names of the available Advice columnists. (3) Read and print three Advice columns.

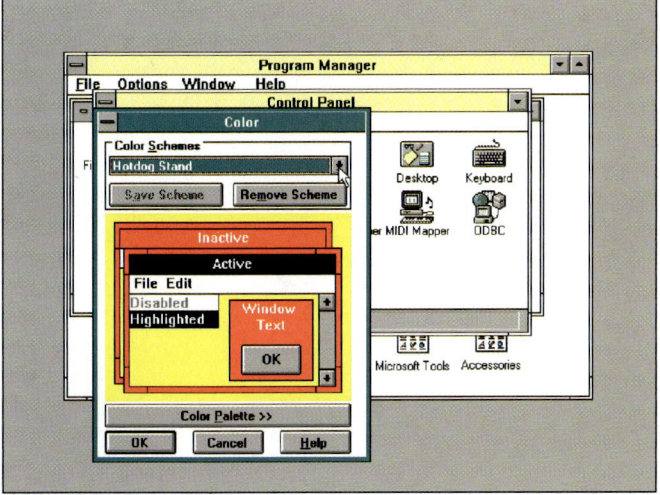

Figure 5-52

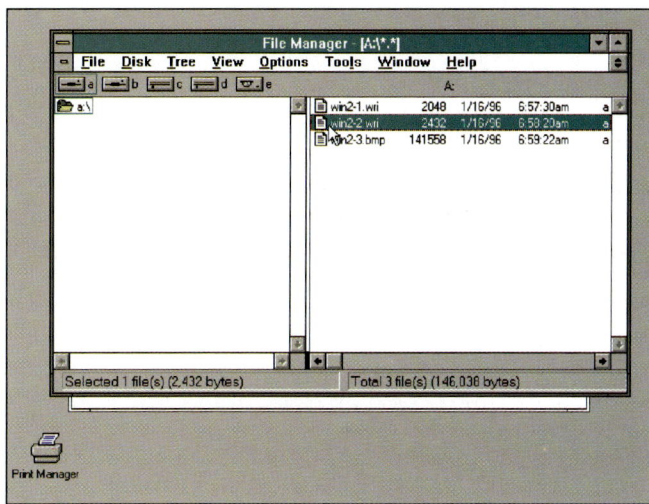

Figure 5-53

CHAPTER SIX

Secondary Storage

Objectives

After completing this chapter, you will be able to:

- Define secondary storage

- Identify the primary devices used for secondary storage

- Explain how data is stored on diskettes and hard disks

- Describe how data stored on diskettes can be protected

- Explain how magnetic tape storage is used with computers

- Describe four other forms of secondary storage: PC cards, optical disks, solid-state devices, and mass storage devices

- Describe how special-purpose storage devices such as smart cards are used

Storage is the fourth and final operation in the information processing cycle. Chapter 6 explains storage operations and the various types of secondary storage devices used with computers. Combining what you learn about storage with your knowledge of input, processing, and output will allow you to complete your understanding of the information processing cycle.

What Is Secondary Storage?

It is important to understand the difference between how a computer uses main memory and how it uses secondary storage. As you have seen, main memory, also called primary storage or ram, temporarily stores programs and data that are being processed. **Secondary storage**, also called **auxiliary storage**, stores programs and data when they are not being processed, just as a filing cabinet is used in an office to store records. Records that are not being used are kept in the filing cabinet until they are needed. In the same way, data and programs that are not being used on a computer are kept in secondary storage until they are needed.

Most secondary storage devices provide a more permanent form of storage than main memory because they are nonvolatile, that is, data and programs stored on secondary storage devices are retained when the power is turned off. Main memory is volatile, which means that when power is turned off, whatever is stored in main memory is erased.

Secondary storage devices can be used as both input and output devices. When they are used to receive data processed by the computer, they are functioning as output devices. When some of their stored data is transferred to the computer for processing, they are functioning as input devices.

User secondary storage needs can vary greatly. Personal computer users may find the amount of data to be stored to be relatively small. For example, the names, addresses, and telephone numbers of several hundred friends or customers of a small business might require only 20,000 bytes of secondary storage (200 records x 100 characters per record). Users of large computers, such as banks or insurance companies, however, may need secondary storage devices that can store billions of characters. To meet the different needs of users, a variety of storage devices are available. *Figure 6-1* shows how different types of storage devices compare in terms of cost and speed. The secondary storage devices named in the pyramid are discussed in this chapter.

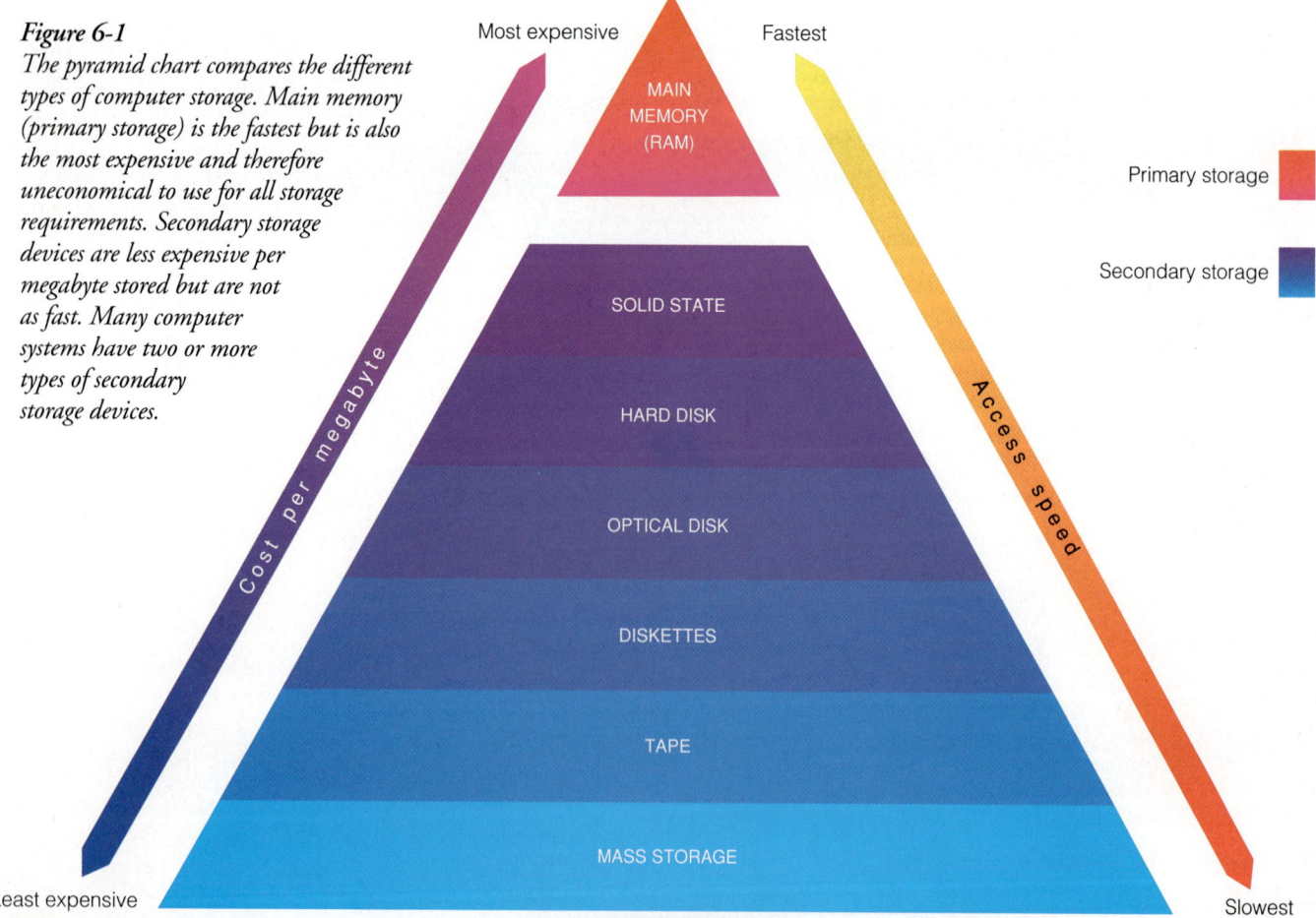

Figure 6-1
The pyramid chart compares the different types of computer storage. Main memory (primary storage) is the fastest but is also the most expensive and therefore uneconomical to use for all storage requirements. Secondary storage devices are less expensive per megabyte stored but are not as fast. Many computer systems have two or more types of secondary storage devices.

Magnetic Disk Storage

Magnetic disk is the most widely used storage medium for all types of computers. A **magnetic disk** consists of a round platter whose surface is covered with a magnetic material. Information can be recorded on or read from the magnetic surface. Magnetic disk offers high storage capacity, reliability, and the capability to directly access stored data. Magnetic disk types include diskettes, hard disks, and removable disk cartridges.

Diskettes

A **diskette** consists of a circular piece of thin mylar plastic (the actual disk), which is coated with an oxide material similar to that used on recording tape. In the early 1970s, IBM introduced the diskette as a new type of secondary storage. These diskettes were eight inches in diameter and were thin and flexible. Because they were flexible, they were often called **floppy disks**, or *floppies,* terms that are still used. Today, diskettes are used as a principal secondary storage medium for personal computers. This type of storage is convenient, reliable, and inexpensive.

Diskettes are available in two different sizes; $3^1/2$ inch and $5^1/4$ inch *(Figure 6-2)*. The size indicates the diameter (width) of the diskette.

Figure 6-2
The most commonly used diskettes are the 3 $^1/2$" (above) and the 5 $^1/4$" (left).

On a 3 1/2-inch diskette, the circular piece of plastic is enclosed in a rigid plastic shell and a piece of metal called the shutter covers the reading and writing area. Paper liners help keep the recording surfaces clean *(Figure 6-3)*. When the 3 1/2-inch diskette is inserted into a disk drive *(Figure 6-4)*, the drive slides the shutter to the side to expose a portion of both sides of the recording surface.

On a 5 1/4-inch diskette, the circular piece of plastic is enclosed in a flexible, square protective jacket. The jacket has an opening on each side so that a portion of the diskette's surfaces are exposed for reading and writing as shown in *Figure 6-5*.

FORMATTING: PREPARING A DISKETTE FOR USE

Before a diskette can be used for secondary storage, it must be formatted. The **formatting** process prepares the diskette so it can store data and includes defining the tracks, cylinders, and sectors on the surfaces of a diskette *(Figure 6-6)*.

A **track** is a narrow recording band forming a full circle around the diskette. A **cylinder** is defined as all tracks of the same number. For example, track 0 on side 1 of the diskette and track 0 on side 2 of the diskette would be called cylinder 0. A **sector** is a pie-shaped section of the diskette. The term sector is more frequently used to refer to a track sector, a section of track within a sector. Each track sector holds 512 bytes. For reading and writing purposes, track sectors are grouped into clusters. A **cluster** consists of two to eight track sectors (the number varies depending on the operating system). A cluster is the smallest unit of diskette space used to store data. Even if a file consisted of only a few characters, one cluster would be used for storage. Each cluster can only hold data from one file, but a file can be made up of many clusters. The number of tracks and sectors created on a

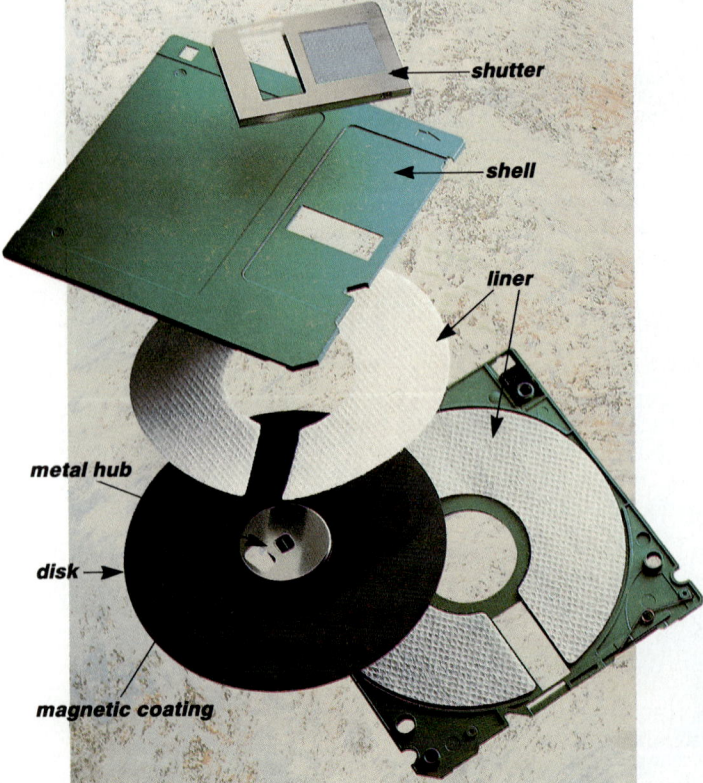

Figure 6-3
In a 3 1/2" diskette, the flexible plastic disk is enclosed between two liners that clean the disk surface of any microscopic debris and help to disperse static electricity. The outside cover is made of a rigid plastic material, and the recording window is covered by a metal shutter that slides to the side when the disk is inserted into the disk drive.

Figure 6-4
A user inserts a diskette into the disk drive of an IBM personal computer.

diskette when it is formatted varies based on the capacity of the diskette, the capabilities of the diskette drive being used, and the specifications in the operating system software that does the formatting. 5 1/4-inch diskettes are formatted with 40 or 80 tracks and 9 or 15 sectors on the surface of the diskette. 3 1/2-inch diskettes are usually formatted with 80 tracks and either 9, 18, or 36 sectors on each side.

In addition to defining the diskette surface, the formatting process erases any data that is on the diskette, analyzes the diskette surface for any defective spots, and establishes a directory that will be used to record information about files stored on the diskette. On personal computers using the DOS operating system, the directory is called the file allocation table. The **file allocation table** (**FAT**) file stores the filename, file size, the time and date the file was last changed, and the cluster number where the file begins. The FAT file also keeps track of unused clusters and is used when the computer writes new files to the diskette. When you instruct the computer to list the files on a diskette, the information comes from the FAT file.

To protect data from being accidentally erased during formatting or other writing operations, diskettes have write-protection features. A 5 1/4-inch diskette has a write-protect notch. This notch is located on the side of the diskette. To prevent writing to a diskette, you cover this notch with a small piece of removable tape. Before writing data onto a diskette, the diskette drive checks the notch. If the notch is open, the drive will proceed to write on the diskette. If the

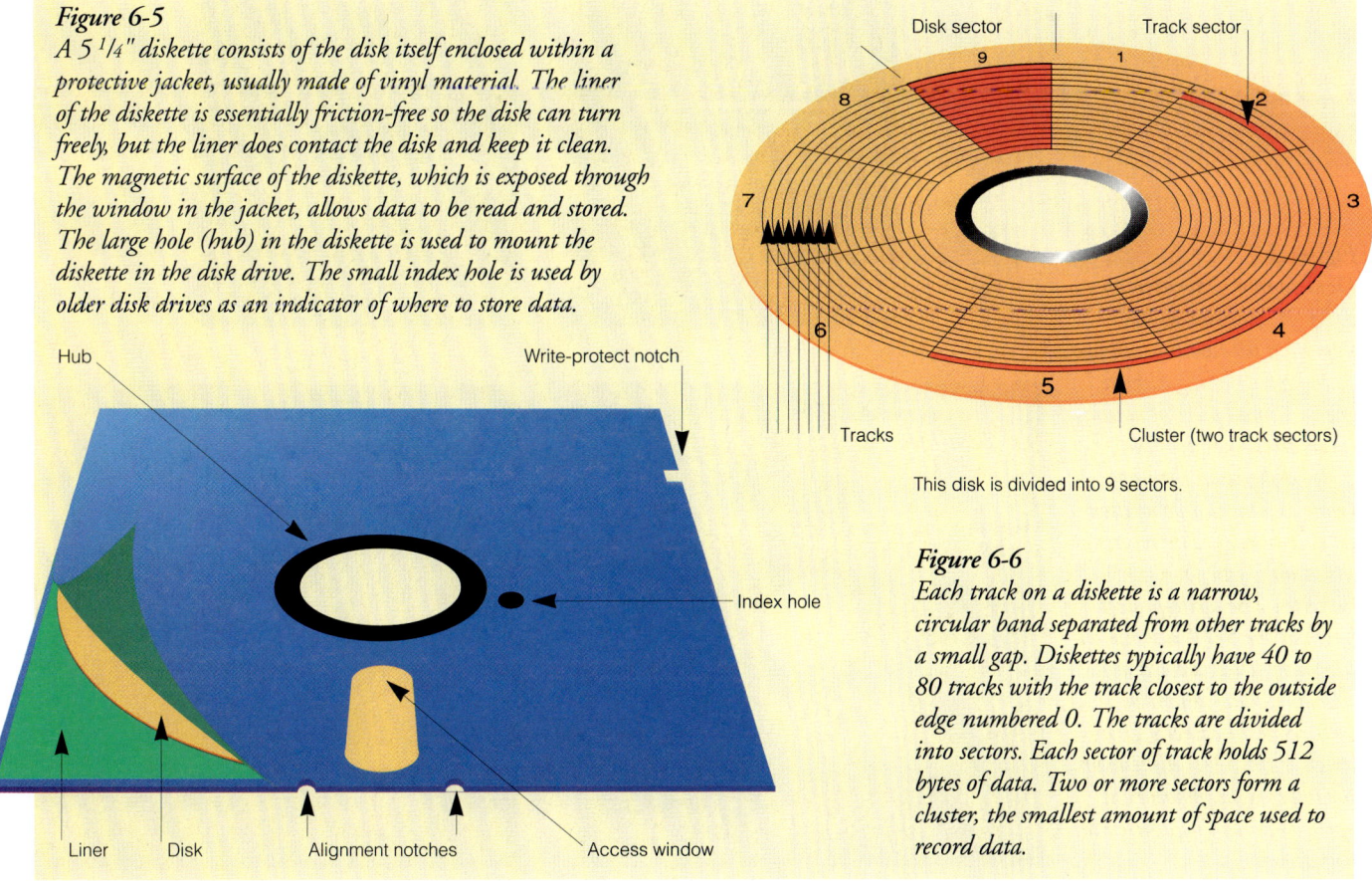

Figure 6-5
A 5 1/4" diskette consists of the disk itself enclosed within a protective jacket, usually made of vinyl material. The liner of the diskette is essentially friction-free so the disk can turn freely, but the liner does contact the disk and keep it clean. The magnetic surface of the diskette, which is exposed through the window in the jacket, allows data to be read and stored. The large hole (hub) in the diskette is used to mount the diskette in the disk drive. The small index hole is used by older disk drives as an indicator of where to store data.

This disk is divided into 9 sectors.

Figure 6-6
Each track on a diskette is a narrow, circular band separated from other tracks by a small gap. Diskettes typically have 40 to 80 tracks with the track closest to the outside edge numbered 0. The tracks are divided into sectors. Each sector of track holds 512 bytes of data. Two or more sectors form a cluster, the smallest amount of space used to record data.

notch is covered, the diskette drive will not write on the diskette *(Figure 6-7)*. On 3¹/₂-inch diskettes, the situation is reversed. Instead of a write-protect notch, there is a small window in the corner of the diskette. A piece of plastic in the window can be moved to open and close the window. If the write-protect window is closed, the drive can write on the diskette. If the window is open, the drive will not write on the diskette.

DISKETTE STORAGE CAPACITY

The amount of data you can store on a diskette depends on two factors: (1) the recording density; and (2) the number of tracks on the diskette.

The **recording density** is the number of bits that can be recorded on one inch of track on the diskette. This measurement is referred to as **bits per inch (bpi)**. The higher the recording density, the higher the storage capacity of the diskette. Most drives store the same amount of data on the longer outside tracks as they do on the shorter inside tracks. Thus, the bpi is measured on the innermost track where it is highest. Some newer drives use a different method. **Multiple zone recording (MZR)** records data at the same density on all tracks. This means that the longer tracks closer to the outside edge of the disk can contain extra sectors. Each time a track becomes long enough to accept it, another sector is added.

The second factor that influences the amount of data that can be stored on a diskette is the number of tracks onto which data can be recorded. This measurement is referred to as **tracks per inch (tpi)**. As you learned earlier in this chapter, the number of tracks depends on the size of the diskette, the drive being used, and how the diskette was formatted.

The capacity of diskettes varies and increases every two or three years as manufacturers develop new ways of recording data more densely. Commonly used diskettes are referred to as either double-density or high-density. Older **single-density** diskettes that could only be written on one side are no longer used. **Double-density (DD) diskettes** can store 360K for a 5¹/₄-inch diskette and 720K for a 3¹/₂-inch diskette. **High-density (HD) diskettes** can store 1.2 megabytes (million characters) on a 5¹/₄-inch diskette and 1.44 megabytes on a 3¹/₂-inch diskette. **Extended-density (ED)** 3¹/₂-inch diskettes that can store 2.88 megabytes are also starting to be used. Even though it is smaller in size, a 3¹/₂-inch diskette can hold more data than a 5¹/₄-inch diskette because it has a higher recording density.

Figure 6-7
Data cannot be written on the 3 1/2" diskette on the upper left because the window in the corner of the diskette is open. A small piece of plastic covers the window of the 3 1/2" diskette on the upper right, so data can be written on this diskette. The reverse situation is true for the 5 1/4" diskettes. The write-protect notch of the 5 1/4" diskette on the lower left is covered and, therefore, data cannot be written to the diskette. The notch of the 5 1/4" diskette on the lower right, however, is open. Data can be written to this diskette.

MAGNETIC DISK STORAGE

A special type of diskette, called a **floptical** diskette, combines optical and magnetic technology to achieve even higher storage rates (currently up to 21 megabytes) on what is basically a 3½-inch diskette. A floptical disk drive uses a low-power laser to read grooves that have been permanently engraved in the diskette recording surface. The grooves allow closely spaced recording and higher bpi and tpi densities. Another advantage of a floptical drive is that it can also read double- and high-density 3½-inch diskettes.

STORING DATA ON A DISKETTE

Regardless of the type of diskette or how it is formatted, the method of storing data on a diskette is essentially the same. When a 3½-inch diskette is inserted into a diskette drive, the notches in the metal hub are engaged by a shaft connected to the drive motor *(Figure 6-8)*.

When you read from or write to a diskette, the motor spins the circular plastic recording surface at approximately 360 revolutions per minute. When you are not reading or writing, the disk does not spin. A lever opens the shutter to expose a portion of the plastic recording surface. Data is stored on tracks of the disk, using the same code, such as ASCII, that is used to store the data in main memory. To do this, a recording mechanism in the drive called the **read/write head** rests on the top and bottom surface of the rotating diskette, generating electronic impulses. The electronic impulses change the magnetic polarity, or alignment, of magnetic areas along a track on the disk. The plus or minus polarity represents the 1 or 0 bits being recorded. To access different tracks on the diskette, the drive moves the read/write head from track to track. When reading data from the diskette, the read/write head senses the magnetic areas that are recorded on the diskette along the various tracks and transfers the data to main memory. When writing data to the diskette, the read/write head transfers data from main memory and stores it as magnetic areas on the tracks on the recording surface.

Data stored in sectors on a diskette must be retrieved and placed in main memory to be processed. The time required to access and retrieve the data is called the **access time**.

The access time for a diskette drive depends on three factors:

1. **Seek time**, the time it takes to position the read/write head over the proper track.

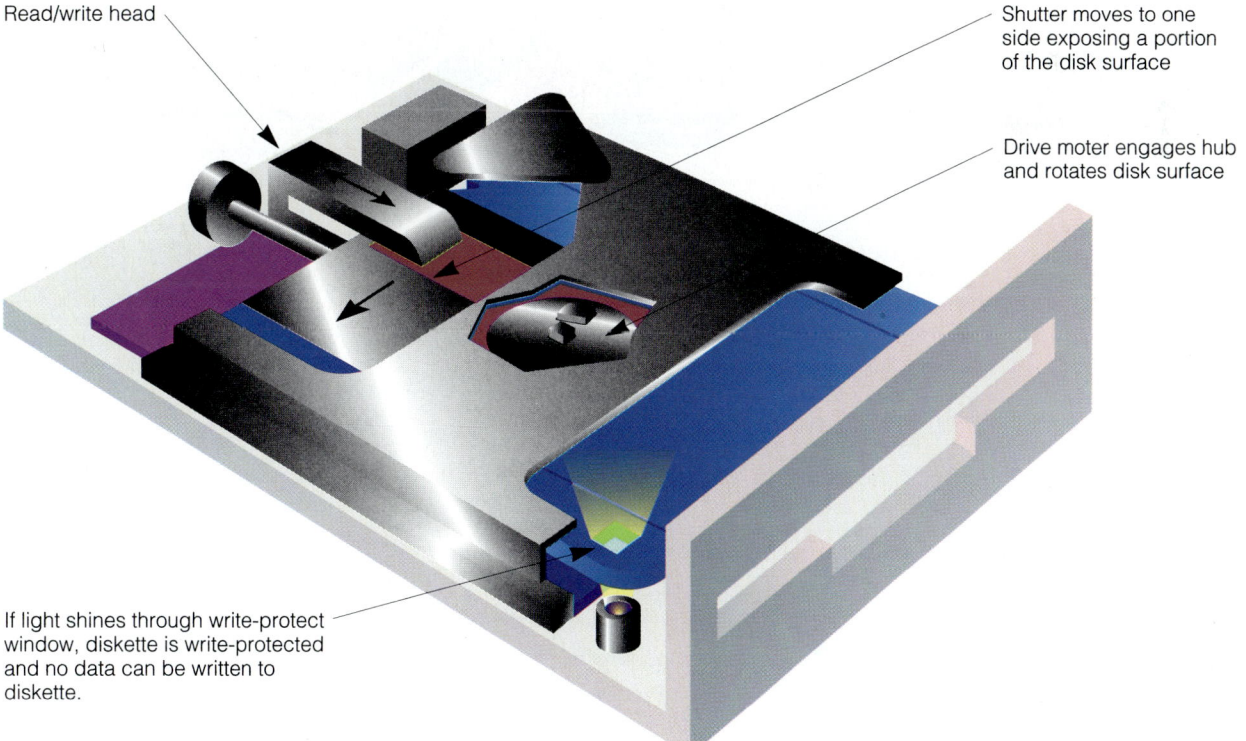

Figure 6-8
When you insert a 3 ½" diskette in a drive, the notches in the metal hub are engaged by a drive motor shaft. A lever moves the shutter to one side so a portion of the disk surfaces are exposed. When you read from or write to a diskette, the shaft spins the disk at approximately 360 rpm. Read/write heads above and below the recording surface move in and out to read or write data.

2. **Rotational delay** (also called **latency**), the time it takes for the sector containing the data to rotate under the read/write head.
3. **Data transfer rate**, the time required to transfer the data from the disk to main memory.

The access time for diskettes varies from about 175 milliseconds (one millisecond equals $1/1000$ of one second) to approximately 300 milliseconds. What this means to the user is that, on the average, data stored in a single sector on a diskette can be retrieved in approximately $1/5$ to $1/3$ of one second.

THE CARE OF DISKETTES

With reasonable care, diskettes provide an inexpensive and reliable form of storage. In handling diskettes, you should take care to avoid exposing them to heat, cold, magnetic fields, and contaminated environments such as dust, smoke, or salt air. One advantage of the $3^1/_2$-inch diskette is that its rigid plastic cover provides more protection for the data stored on the plastic disk inside than the flexible cover on a $5^1/_4$-inch diskette. *Figure 6-9* shows you ways to properly care for your diskettes. Because the read/write head actually comes in contact with the diskette surface, wear takes place and the diskette will eventually become unreadable. To protect against loss, you should copy data onto other diskettes.

Hard Disks

Hard disks provide larger and faster secondary storage capabilities than diskettes. **Hard disks** consist of one or more rigid platters coated with an oxide material that allows data to be magnetically recorded on the surface of the platters *(Figure 6-10)*. The platters are usually made of aluminum but some newer disks use glass or ceramic materials. Most hard disks are permanently mounted inside the computer and are not removable like diskettes. On hard disks, the platters, the read/write heads, and the mechanism for moving the heads across the surface of the disk are enclosed in an airtight, sealed case. This helps to ensure a clean environment for the disk.

Figure 6-9
Guidelines for the proper care of diskettes.

MAGNETIC DISK STORAGE

On minicomputers and mainframes, hard disks are sometimes called **fixed disks** because they cannot be removed like diskettes. They are also referred to as **direct-access storage devices** (**DASD**). These hard disks are often larger versions of the hard disks used on personal computers and can be either mounted in the same cabinet as the computer or enclosed in their own stand-alone cabinet *(Figure 6-11)*.

While most personal computers are limited to two to four disk drives, minicomputers can support 8 to 16 disk devices, and mainframe computers can support more than 100 high-speed disk devices.

HARD DISK STORAGE CAPACITY

Hard disks contain a spindle on which one or more disk platters are mounted *(Figure 6-12* on the next page). Each surface of a platter can be used to store data. Thus, if one platter is used in the drive, two surfaces are available for data. If two platters are used, four surfaces are available for data, and so on. Naturally, the more platters, the more data that can be stored on the drive. Like a diskette, hard disks must be formatted before they can be used to store data. Before a hard disk is formatted, it can be divided into separate areas called **partitions.** Each partition can function as if it were a separate disk. Partitions are sometimes used to separate different types or classes of items such as programs and data or data from different organizations such as subsidiary companies. Separate partitions are also sometimes used for different operating systems. On personal computers, hard disk partitions are usually given letter identifiers, starting with the letter C. The letters A and B are reserved for diskette drives.

Access time for a hard disk is between ten and twenty milliseconds. This is significantly faster than for a diskette because of two reasons. First, a hard disk spins ten to twenty times faster than a diskette drive. Second, a hard disk is always spinning, whereas a diskette only starts spinning when a read or write command is received.

The storage capacity of hard drives is measured in megabytes or millions of bytes of storage. Common sizes for personal computers range from 100MB to 500MB of storage and even larger sizes are available. Each 10MB of storage is equivalent to approximately 5,000 printed pages, assuming approximately 2,000 characters per page.

Figure 6-10
A hard disk consists of one or more disk platters. Each side of the platter is coated with an oxide substance that allows data to be magnetically stored.

Figure 6-11
A high-speed, high-capacity fixed disk drive in a stand-alone cabinet.

Some disk devices used on large computers can store billions of bytes of information *(Figure 6-13)*. A billion bytes of information is called a **gigabyte**.

STORING DATA ON A HARD DISK

Storing data on hard disks is similar to storing data on diskettes. Hard disks rotate at a high rate of speed, usually 3,600 to 7,200 revolutions per minute. Hard disk read/write heads are attached to **access arms** that swing out over the disk surface to the correct track. The read/write heads float on a cushion of air and do not actually touch the surface of the disk. The distance between the head and the surface varies from approximately ten to twenty millionths of an inch. As shown in *Figure 6-14,* the close tolerance leaves no room for any type of contamination. If some form of contamination is introduced or if the alignment of the read/write heads is altered by something accidentally jarring the computer, the disk head can collide with and damage the disk surface, causing a loss of data. This event is known as a **head crash**. Because of the time needed to repair the disk and to reconstruct the data that was lost, head crashes can be extremely costly to users in terms of both time and money.

Depending on the type of disk drive, data is physically organized in one of two ways. One way is the sector method and the other is the cylinder method.

The **sector method** for physically organizing data on hard disks is similar to the method used for diskettes. Each track on the disk surface is divided into sectors. Each sector can contain a specified number of bytes. Data is referenced by indicating the surface, track, and sector where the data is stored.

With the **cylinder method**, all tracks of the same number on each recording surface are considered part of the same cylinder *(Figure 6-15)*. For example, the fifth track on all surfaces would be considered part of cylinder five. All twentieth tracks would be part of cylinder twenty, and so on. When the computer requests data from a disk using the cylinder method, it must specify the cylinder, recording surface, and record number. Because the access arms containing the read/write heads all move together, they are always over the same track on all surfaces. Thus, using the cylinder method to record data *down* the disk surfaces reduces the movement of the read/write head during both reading and writing of data.

Figure 6-13
The IBM 3390 disk drive is used on mainframe computer systems. Each drive, shown here being assembled during manufacturing, can hold 22.7 billion bytes of data.

Figure 6-12
A hard disk with its protective cover removed. The access arm and read/write head over the top platter can be clearly seen. Each platter surface, top and bottom, has an access arm and read/write head.

Some computers improve the apparent speed at which data is transferred to and from a disk by using disk cache. Similar in concept to the RAM cache memory described in Chapter 4, **disk cache** is an area of memory set aside for data most often read from the disk. Every time the computer requests data from the disk, disk cache software looks first for the data in the disk cache memory area. If the requested data is in disk cache, it is immediately transferred to the CPU and the slower disk read operation is avoided. Disk cache memory is updated every time a disk read takes place. In addition to the data requested from the disk, disk cache software also reads adjacent clusters on the assumption that they may be needed next. Disk cache software also makes disk write operations more efficient by temporarily holding data to be written until the CPU is not busy. Microsoft includes a disk cache program called SMARTDrive with the Windows and the DOS operating systems.

The flow of data to and from the hard disk is managed by electronic circuits called the hard disk controller. Sometimes the controller is a separate board in an expansion slot and sometimes the controller is part of the disk drive itself.

On personal computers, two types of controllers are most common, IDE and SCSI. **Integrated Drive Electronics** (IDE) controllers can operate one or two hard disk drives. Most motherboards have built-in IDE connectors that use a cable to attach directly to the disk drive. IDE controllers can transfer data to the disk at a rate of up to 8MB per second. SCSI, pronounced *scuzzy*, stands for **Small Computer System Interface**. SCSI controllers can support seven disk drives or any mix up to seven SCSI devices. SCSI devices are connected to each other in a chain with a cable between each device. SCSI controllers are faster than IDE controllers and can support up to 100MB per second transfer rates. SCSI controllers usually consist of a circuit board mounted in an expansion slot.

Data Compression

One way of storing more data on a disk is to use data compression. **Data compression** reduces the storage requirements of data by substituting codes for repeating patterns of data. For example, consider the familiar Ben Franklin saying, "Early to bed, early to rise, makes a man healthy, wealthy,

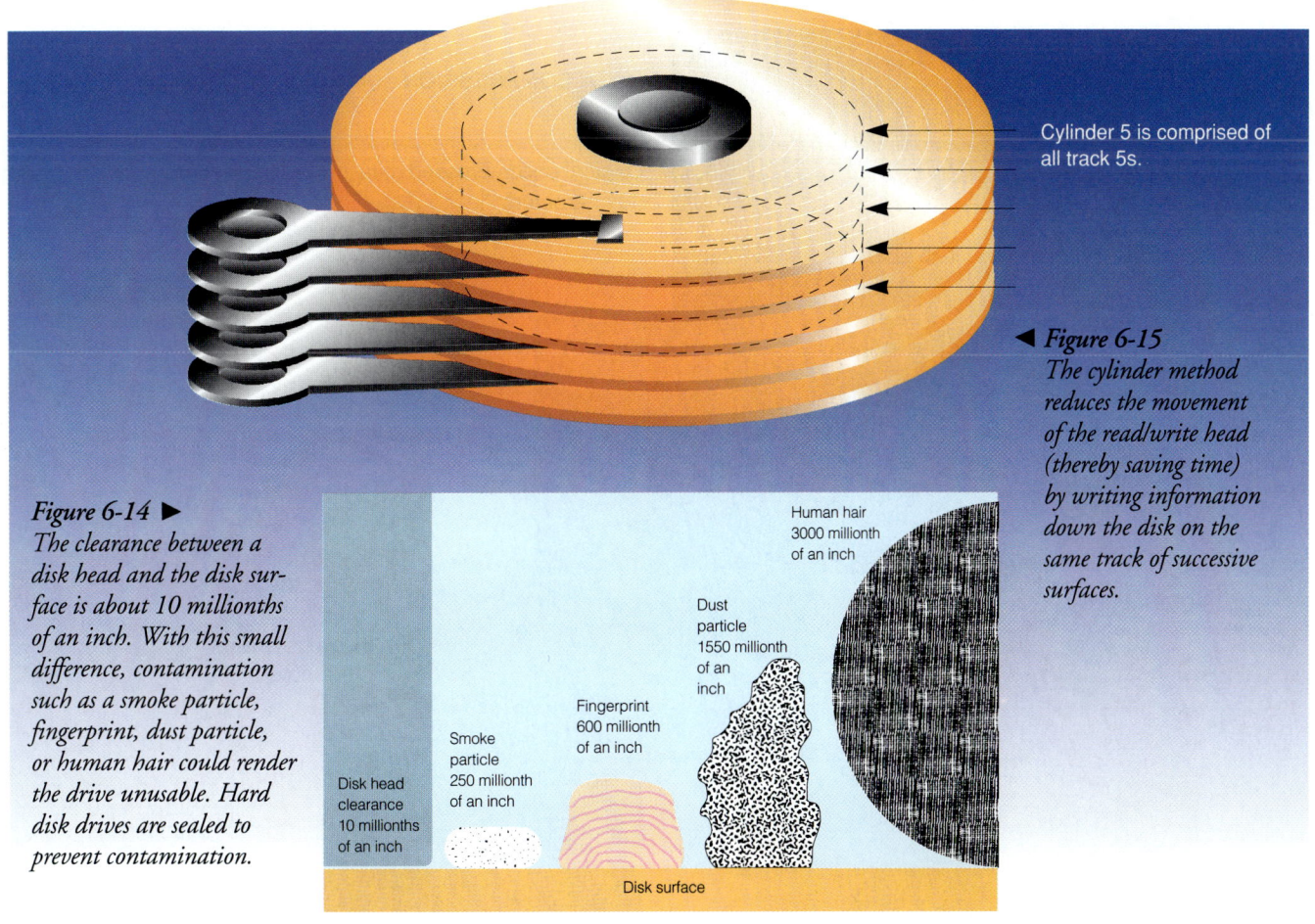

◀ *Figure 6-15*
The cylinder method reduces the movement of the read/write head (thereby saving time) by writing information down the disk on the same track of successive surfaces.

Figure 6-14 ▶
The clearance between a disk head and the disk surface is about 10 millionths of an inch. With this small difference, contamination such as a smoke particle, fingerprint, dust particle, or human hair could render the drive unusable. Hard disk drives are sealed to prevent contamination.

and wise." Including punctuation, this phrase includes 56 characters. As shown in *Figure 6-16,* by substituting special characters for repeating patterns, the original phrase can be compressed to only 30 characters; a reduction of 46%. Compression is most often stated as a ratio of the size of the original uncompressed data divided by the size of the compressed data. In the *Figure 6-16* example, this would be a compression ratio of 1.9 to 1 (56 divided by 30). The codes substituted for the repeating patterns are filed in a table when the data is compressed. This substitution table is used to restore the compressed data to its original form when necessary.

The type of compression just described is called *lossless compression* because no data is lost in the process. Lossless compression works best for text and numeric data that cannot afford to lose any data. Compression ratios for lossless compression average 2 to 1 (the size of the data is reduced 50%). Other compression methods, called *lossy compression,* give up some accuracy for higher compression ratios (up to 200 to 1). Lossy compression methods are typically used to compress video images and sound. Video and sound can both have data removed without a noticeable reduction in the overall quality of the output. Lossy compression is usually accomplished with special hardware such as a video or sound expansion board.

Many manufacturers of complex software programs, such as word processing and spreadsheets, use compression methods to reduce the number of disks that are needed to distribute their products. Utility programs loaded with the software expand the software files as they are loaded on the user's system.

Some file compression programs, such as PKZIP, compress and uncompress data as directed by the user. Disk compression programs, such as Stacker, can be installed to automatically keep all files on a hard disk compressed until they are needed for processing.

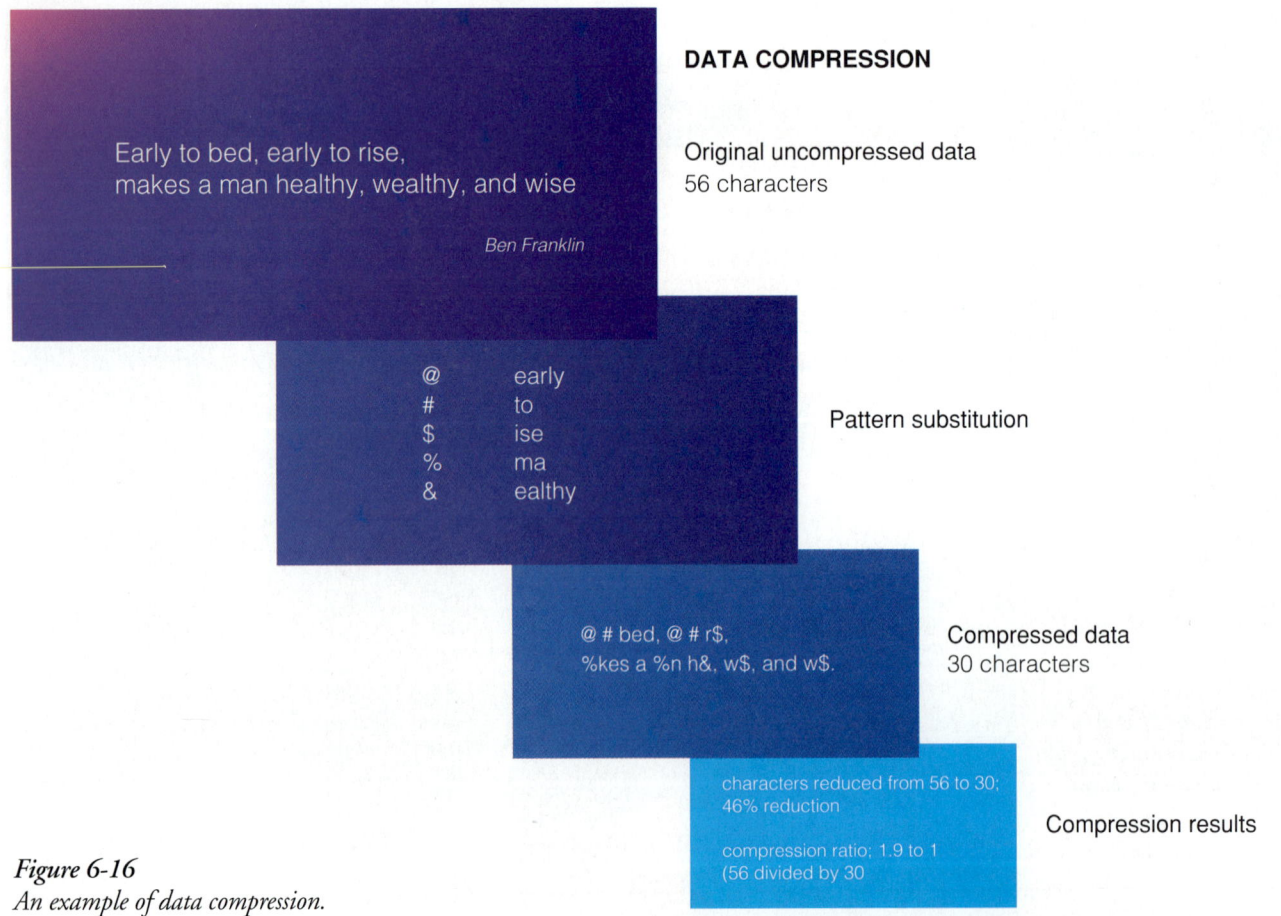

Figure 6-16
An example of data compression.

RAID

As computers became faster, writing data to and reading data from increasingly larger disks became a bottleneck. Computers spent a large percentage of time waiting for data to go to or come from the disk drive. Rather than trying to build even larger and faster disk drives, some disk manufacturers began to connect multiple smaller disks into an integrated unit that acted like it was a single large disk drive. A group of integrated small disks is called a **RAID**, which stands for **redundant array of inexpensive disks**. RAID technology can be implemented in several ways called *RAID levels*.

In the simplest RAID method, called RAID level 1, one backup disk exists for each data disk *(Figure 6-17)*. Each backup disk contains the same information as its corresponding data disk. If the data disk fails, the backup disk becomes the data disk. Because the disks contain duplicate information, RAID level 1 is sometimes called **disk mirroring**.

RAID levels beyond level 1 all spread data across more than one drive. Dividing a logical piece of data, such as a record, word, or character, into smaller parts and writing those parts on multiple drives is called **striping** *(Figure 6-18)*. Some RAID levels call for a separate disk, called a parity or check disk, to keep track of information that can be used to recreate data if one of the data disks malfunctions. Other RAID levels store the parity information on the data disk. This parity information is an important part of RAID technology. It allows the system to rebuild, sometimes automatically, any information that is damaged on one of the data disks.

RAID disks offer a number of advantages over single large disks (called SLEDs for single large expensive disks). Because multiple read or write operations can take place at the same time, data can be read from or written to RAID disks faster. The biggest advantage, however, is the reduced risk of losing data. The capability to rebuild any damaged data is important to organizations that cannot afford to be without the information stored on their disks.

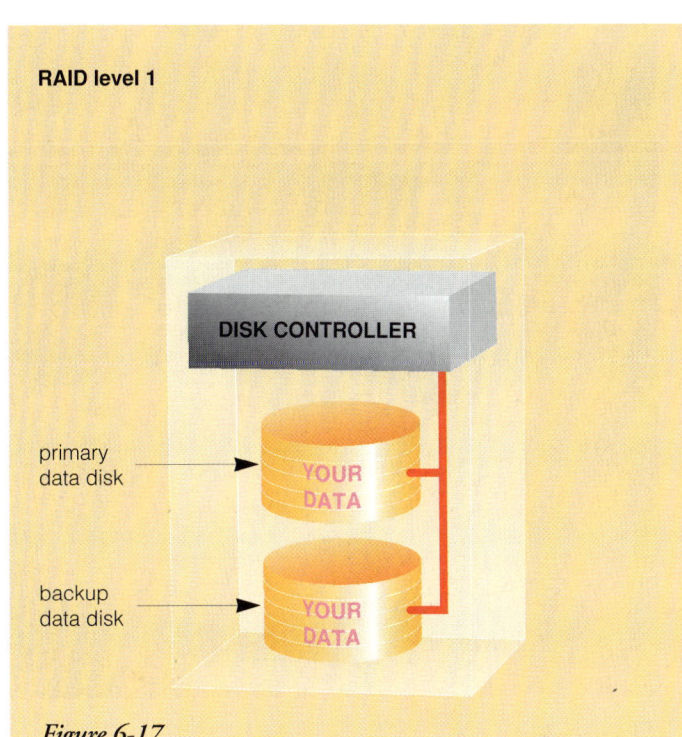

Figure 6-17
In RAID level 1, called disk mirroring, a backup disk exists for each data disk.

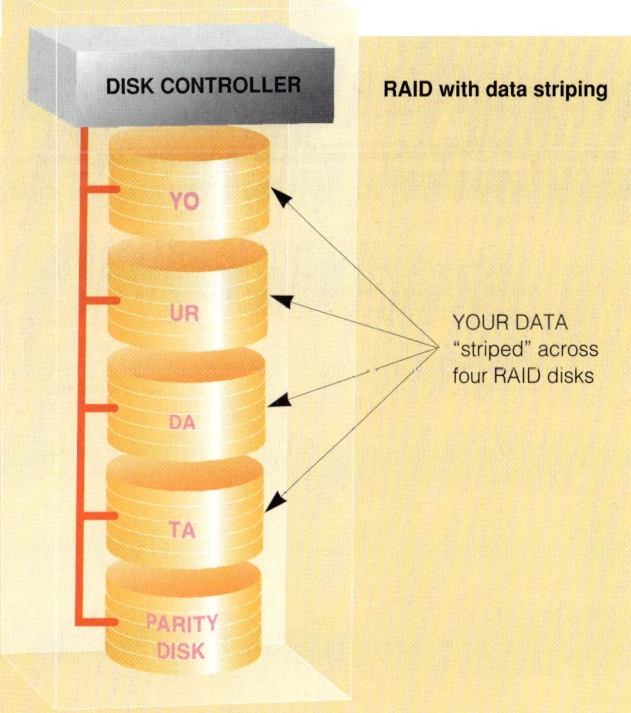

Figure 6-18
In RAID levels beyond level 1, data to be stored is divided into parts and written across several disks. This process is called striping. Some RAID levels call for additional parity disks that keep track of information to be used to recreate information if one of the data disks malfunctions.

Other Types of Hard Disks

Other devices that use hard disk technology are presented in this section. These include disk cartridges, hard cards, and removable disks.

DISK CARTRIDGES

Another variation of disk storage available for use with personal computers is the removable disk cartridge. **Disk cartridges**, which can be inserted and removed from a computer *(Figure 6-19)*, offer the storage and fast access features of hard disks and the portability of diskettes. Disk cartridges are often used when data security is an issue. At the end of a work session, the disk cartridge can be removed and locked up, leaving no data on the computer.

One unique type of disk cartridge is called a Bernoulli disk. The **Bernoulli disk cartridge** works with a special drive unit that uses a cushion of air to keep the flexible disk surface from touching the read/write head. The flexible disk surface reduces the chance of a head crash but does cause the cartridges to eventually wear out.

HARD CARDS

One option for installing a hard disk in a personal computer is a hard card. The **hard card** is a circuit board that has a hard disk built onto it. Hard cards provide an easy way to expand the storage capacity of a personal computer because the board can be installed into an expansion slot of the computer *(Figure 6-20)*. Because of lower prices on larger capacity disk drives, hard cards are not used as much as they once were.

REMOVABLE DISKS

Removable disk devices consist of the drive unit, which is usually in its own cabinet, and the removable recording media, called a **disk pack**. Removable disk packs consist of multiple metal platters that could record from 10 to 300 megabytes of data. Removable disk units were introduced in

Figure 6-19
A removable hard disk cartridge allows a user to remove and transport the entire hard disk from computer to computer or to lock it up in a safe.

Figure 6-20
A hard card is a hard disk drive on a circuit board that can be mounted in a computer's expansion slot.

the early 1960s and for nearly 20 years were the most prevalent type of disk storage on minicomputers and mainframes. During the 1980s, however, removable disks began to be replaced by hard fixed disks that offered larger storage capacities and higher reliability.

Maintaining Data Stored on a Disk

To prevent the loss of disk data, two procedures should be performed on a regular basis; backup and defragmentation.

BACKUP

Backup means creating a copy of important programs and data. To backup diskettes, simply copy the data on one diskette to another diskette. Diskettes are also commonly used to backup at least some of the data stored on a hard disk of a personal computer. Because hard disks can store large quantities of data (up to a gigabyte) diskettes are often used just to backup important files. Magnetic tape, another form of secondary storage, is commonly used to backup data stored on large-capacity hard disks.

DEFRAGMENTATION

When data is stored on a disk, it is placed in the first available clusters. The computer tries to place the data in clusters that are *contiguous* (all in a row), but contiguous clusters may not be available. When a file is stored in clusters that are not next to each other, the file is said to be **fragmented**. The term fragmented is also used to describe the condition of a disk drive that has many files stored in non-contiguous clusters *(Figure 6-21)*. Fragmentation causes the computer to run slower because reading data from the disk takes longer than if the data were all in one location. To solve this problem, the disk must be defragmented. **Defragmentation** reorganizes the data stored on the disk so files are located in contiguous clusters. Defragmentation programs are available as separate programs or as part of system utility packages. Some operating systems also contain defragmentation programs.

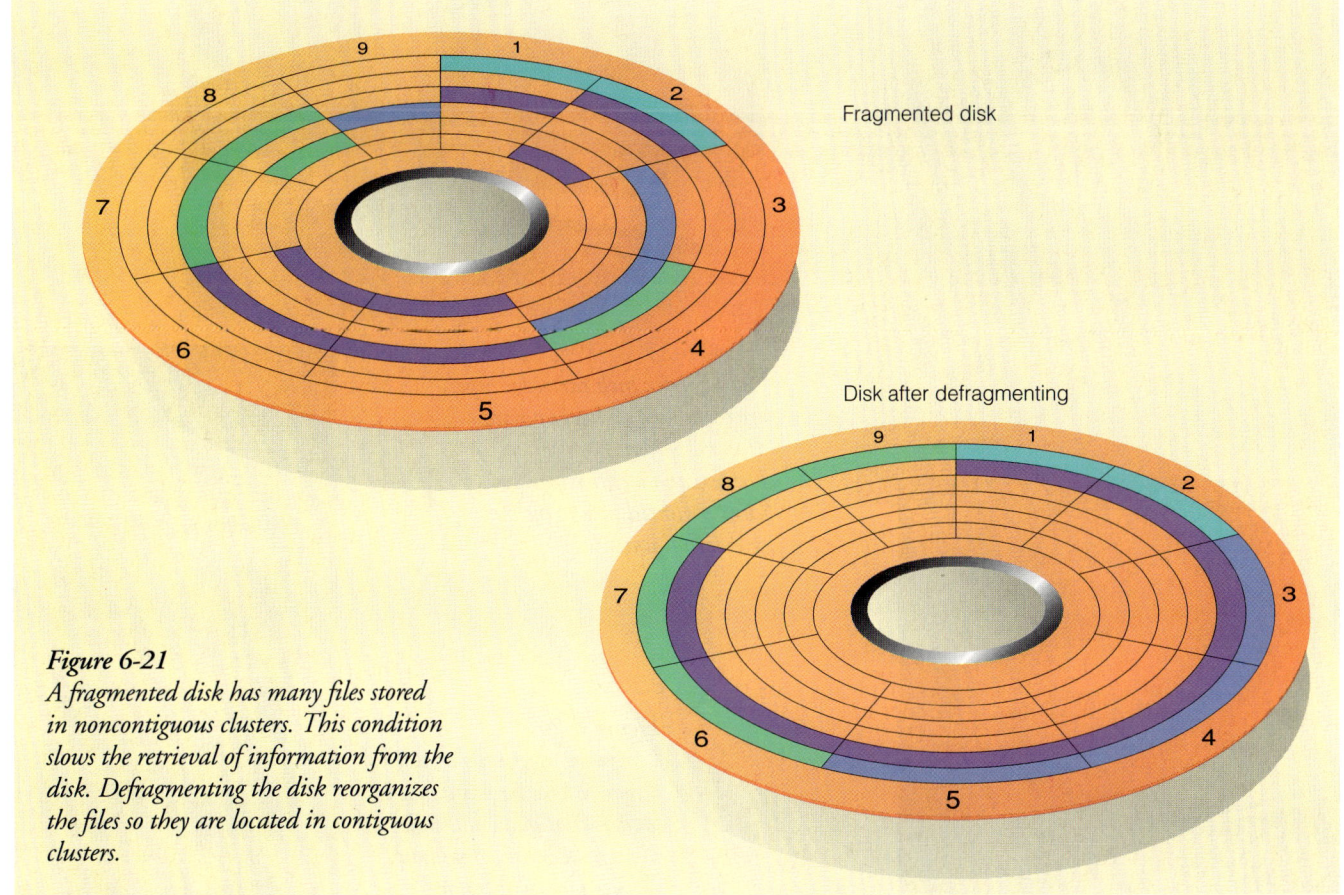

Figure 6-21
A fragmented disk has many files stored in noncontiguous clusters. This condition slows the retrieval of information from the disk. Defragmenting the disk reorganizes the files so they are located in contiguous clusters.

Magnetic Tape

During the 1950s and early 1960s, prior to the introduction of removable disk pack drives, magnetic tape was the primary method of storing large amounts of data. Today, even though tape is no longer used as the primary method of secondary storage, it still functions as a cost-effective way to store data that does not have to be accessed immediately. In addition, tape serves as the primary means of backup for most medium and large systems and is often used to transfer data from one system to another.

Magnetic tape consists of a thin ribbon of plastic. The tape is coated on one side with a material that can be magnetized to record the bit patterns that represent data. The most common types of magnetic tape devices are cartridge and reel-to-reel. Cartridge tape varies from $1/4$- or $1/2$-inch wide, and reel-to-reel tape is $1/2$-inch wide *(Figure 6-22)*.

Cartridge Tape Devices

A **cartridge tape** contains magnetic recording tape in a small rectangular plastic housing. One quarter-inch wide tape in cartridges slightly larger than audio tapes are frequently used for backup on personal computers. Faster and higher storage capacity $1/2$-inch cartridge tapes are increasingly replacing reel-to-reel tape devices on minicomputers and mainframes. For personal computers, cartridge tape units are designed to be internally mounted in a bay or in a separate external cabinet *(Figure 6-23)*.

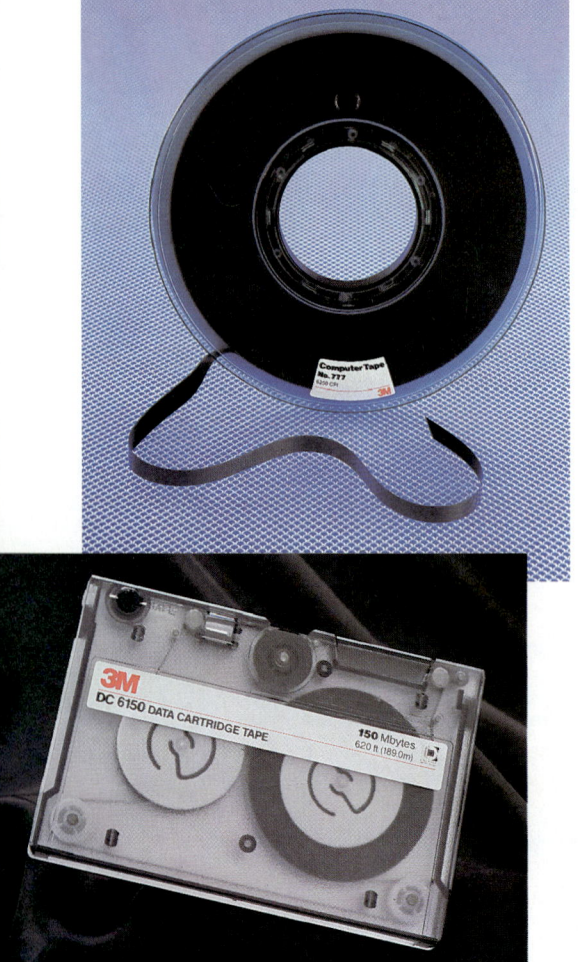

Figure 6-22
One-half inch reel tape (top) and magnetic tape cartridge (bottom).

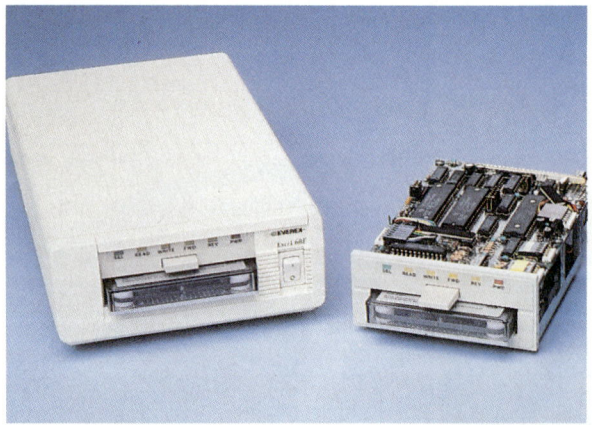

Figure 6-23
One-quarter inch cartridge tapes are often used to backup hard disks on personal computers. Drives can be either internal units mounted in a drive bay or external units.

Figure 6-24
Cartridge tape units used for larger systems have automatic loaders that allow multiple tapes to be recorded without the need of an operator.

For larger systems, cartridge tapes are usually mounted in their own cabinet. Cartridge tapes for larger systems are designed so multiple tapes can be automatically loaded and unloaded, allowing tape storage operations to take place unattended *(Figure 6-24)*.

Reel-to-Reel Tape Devices

Reel-to-reel tape devices use two reels: a supply reel to hold the tape that will be read from or written to, and the take-up reel to temporarily hold portions of the supply reel tape as it is being processed. As the tape moves from one reel to another, it passes over a read/write head, an electromagnetic device that can read or write data on the tape. At the completion of processing, tape on the take-up reel is wound back onto the supply reel.

Older style tape units used vertical cabinets with vacuum columns that held five or six feet of slack tape to prevent breaking during sudden start or stop operations.

Newer style tape units *(Figure 6-25)* allow a tape to be inserted through a slot opening similar to the way videotapes are loaded in a videocassette recorder. This front-loading tape drive takes less space and can be cabinet mounted. The drive automatically threads the end of the tape onto an internal take-up reel. Because of their size and cost, reel-to-reel tape drives are used almost exclusively on minicomputer and mainframe systems.

Reels of tape usually come in lengths of 300 to 3,600 feet and can store up to 200 megabytes of data.

Storing Data on Magnetic Tape

Tape is considered a **sequential storage** media because the computer must record and read tape records one after another. For example, to read the 1,000th record on a tape, the tape drive must first pass over the previous 999 records.

Figure 6-25
Newer style $1/2$" inch tape drives allow the user to slide the tape into a slot at the front of the unit. The drive automatically threads the tape onto an internal take-up reel.

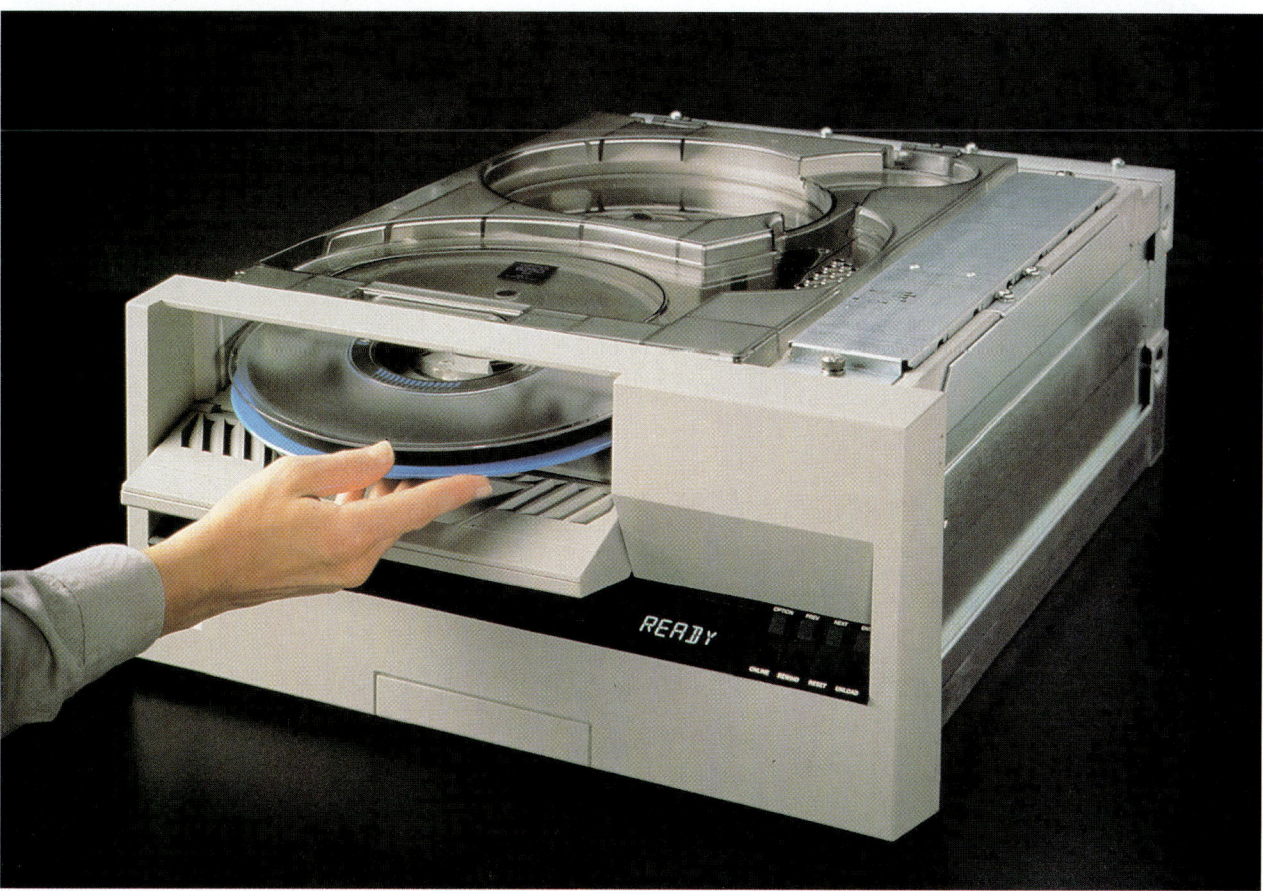

Binary codes, such as ASCII and EBCDIC, are used to represent data stored on magnetic tape. Within a code, each character is represented by a unique combination of bits. The bits are stored on tape in the form of magnetic areas *(Figure 6-26)*. The magnetic areas are organized into rows, called channels, that run the length of the tape. A combination of bits in a vertical column (one from each channel) is used to represent a character. An additional bit is used as a parity bit for error checking.

Tape density is the number of bits that can be stored on an inch of tape. As on disk drives, tape density is expressed in bits per inch, or bpi. Commonly used tape densities are 800, 1,600, 3,200 and 6,250 bpi. Some of the newer cartridge tape devices can record at densities higher than 60,000 bpi. The higher the density, the more data that can be stored on a tape.

Some tape drives can operate in a high-speed streaming mode used to backup and restore hard disk drives. In the **streaming mode**, the tape records data in exactly the same byte-by-byte order as it appears on the hard disk. When used to restore a hard disk, the data recorded on the tape in the streaming mode is used to recreate all the data on the hard disk. The advantage of streaming is that it is faster than normal tape operations and thus data can be recorded in less time. The disadvantage is that the streaming method cannot be used to selectively record or restore an individual file.

Another method of storing large amounts of data on tape is **digital audio tape** (DAT). DAT uses **helical scan technology** to write data at much higher densities across the tape at an angle instead of down the length of the tape *(Figure 6-27)*. Using this method, tape densities can be as high as 61,000 bpi.

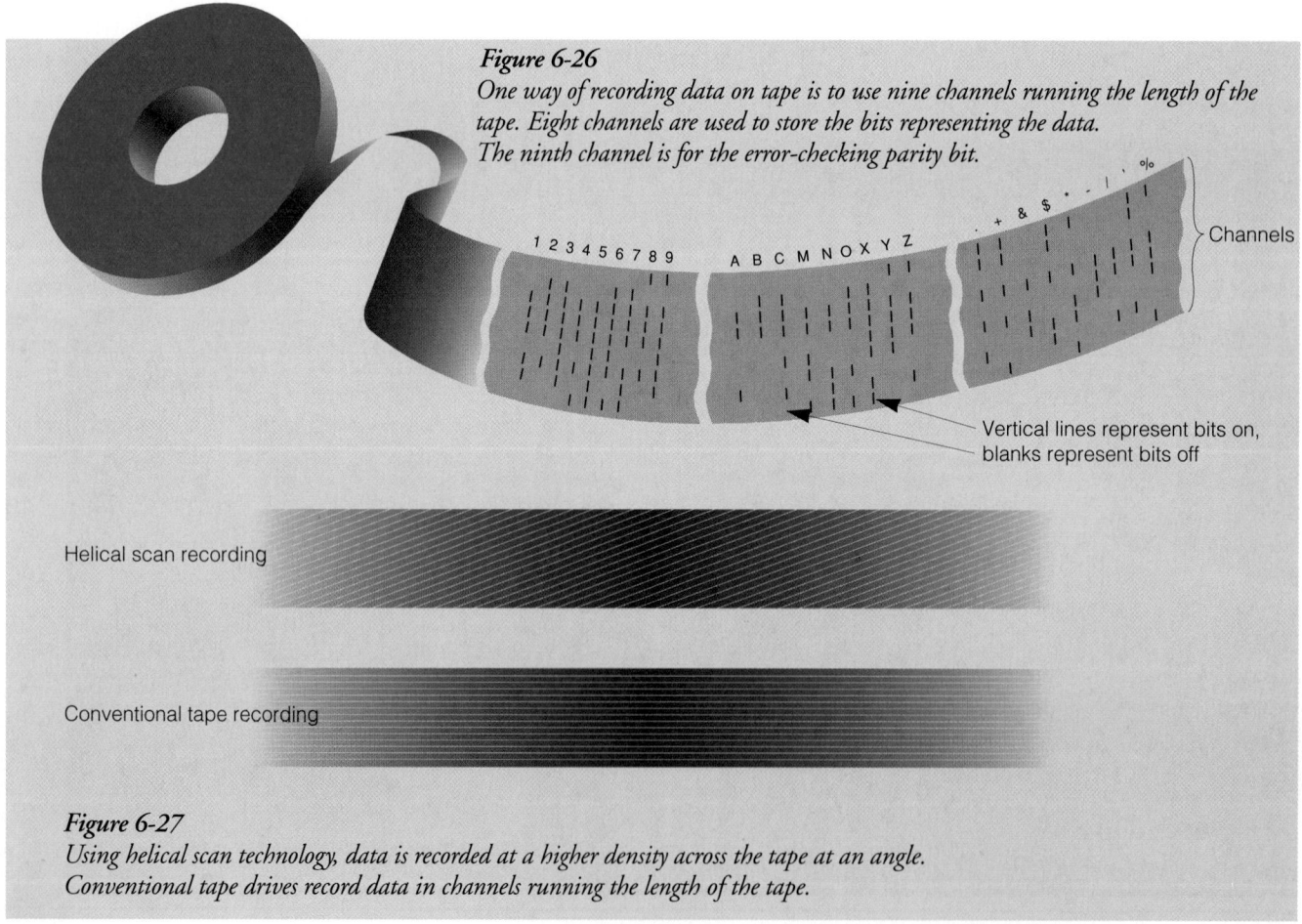

Figure 6-26
One way of recording data on tape is to use nine channels running the length of the tape. Eight channels are used to store the bits representing the data. The ninth channel is for the error-checking parity bit.

Figure 6-27
Using helical scan technology, data is recorded at a higher density across the tape at an angle. Conventional tape drives record data in channels running the length of the tape.

Other Forms of Secondary Storage

The conventional disk and tape devices just described comprise the majority of secondary storage devices and media, but other means for storing data are sometimes used. These include PC cards, optical disks, solid-state devices, and mass storage devices.

PC Cards

PC cards are small, credit card-sized cards that fit into PCMCIA expansion slots. You may recall from Chapter 4 that PCMCIA stands for the Personal Computer Memory Card International Association, the group that develops standards for the cards. Different versions and sizes of the cards are used for storage, communications, and additional memory.

Most often, PC cards are used on portable computers, but they can be incorporated into desktop systems as well. Although they are only 10.5mm thick (about .4 inch), PC cards used for storage contain small rotating disk drives 1.3 inches in diameter that can contain more than 200 megabytes of data *(Figure 6-28)*.

The storage cards can be useful for people who work with more than one computer or who have to share a computer with others. Their data can be maintained on a PC storage card and kept with them.

Optical Disks

Enormous quantities of information are stored on **optical disks** by using a laser to burn microscopic holes on the surface of a hard plastic disk.

A lower power laser reads the disk by reflecting light off the disk surface. The reflected light is converted into a series of bits that the computer can process *(Figure 6-29)*.

Figure 6-28
Type III PC cards are used for small removable disk drives that can hold over 200 megabytes of data.

Figure 6-29
To record data on an optical disk, a high-power laser heats the surface and makes a microscopic pit. To read data, a low-power laser light is reflected from the smooth unpitted areas and is interpreted as 1 bit. The pitted areas do not reflect the laser beam and are interpreted as 0 bits.

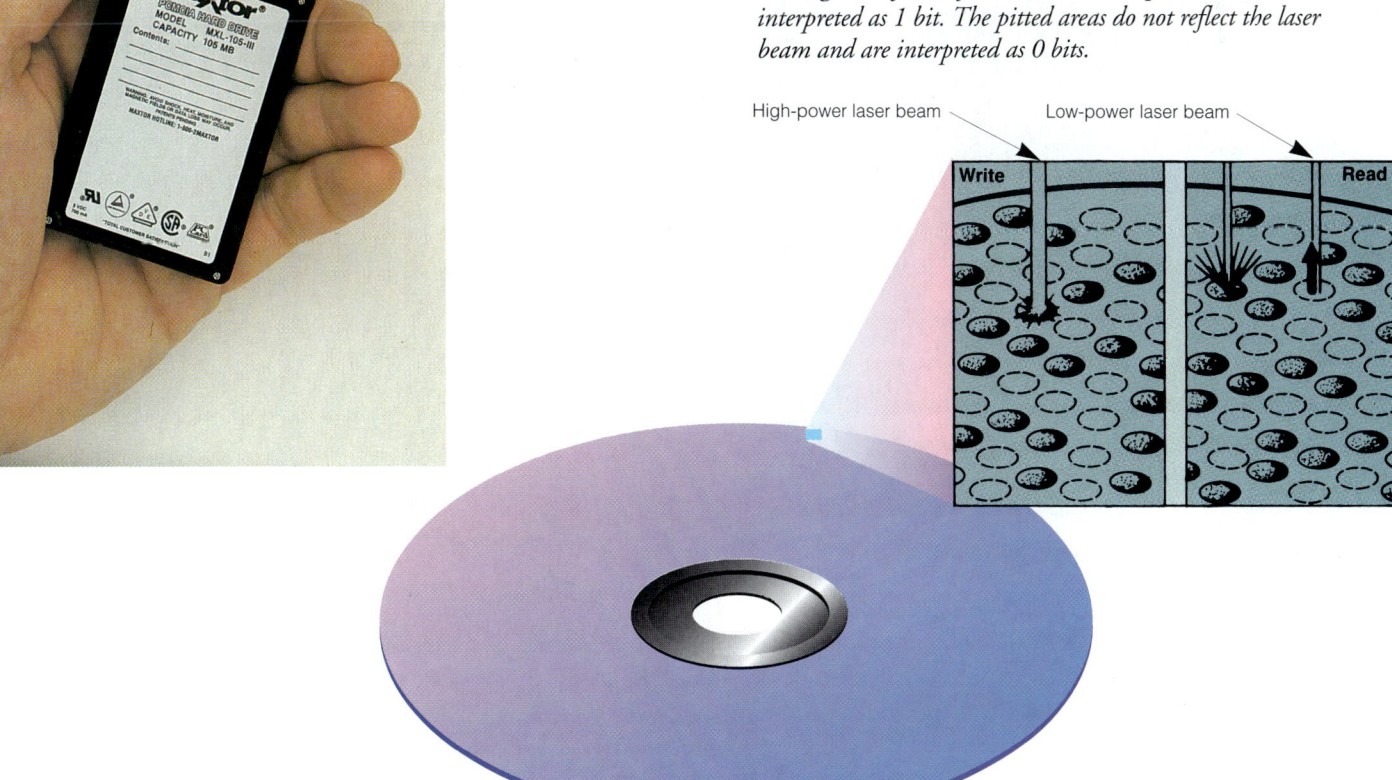

A full-size, 14-inch optical disk can store 6.8 billion bytes of information. Up to 150 of these disks can be installed in automated disk library systems (called jukeboxes) that provide more than one trillion bytes (called a **terabyte**) of online storage. The smaller disks, just under five inches in diameter, can store more than 800 million bytes, or approximately 550 times the data that can be stored on a high-density $3^1/_2$-inch diskette. That is enough space to store approximately 400,000 pages of typed data.

The smaller optical disk is called a **CD-ROM**, an acronym for compact disk read-only memory *(Figure 6-30)*. They use the same laser technology used for the CD-ROM disks that have become popular for recorded music. In fact, if a computer is equipped with a CD-ROM drive, a sound card, and speakers, audio CD-ROM disks can be played.

CD-ROM drives are often advertised as double-, triple-, or quadruple-speed drives. The ratings refer to how fast the drive can transfer data in relation to a standard established for CD-ROM drives used for multimedia applications. The original standard established a minimum transfer rate of 150 kilobytes per second (kbps). A double-speed drive can transfer data at 300 kbps, a triple-speed drive at 450 kbps, and a quadruple-speed drive at 600 kbps.

Most optical disks are prerecorded and cannot be modified by the user. These disks are used for applications such as an auto parts catalog where the information is changed only occasionally, such as once a month, and a new updated optical disk is created. Optical disk devices that provide for one-time recording are called **WORM** devices, an acronym for *write once, read many.* Erasable optical disk drives are just starting to be used. The most common erasable optical drives use **magneto-optical technology**, in which a magnetic field changes the polarity of a spot on the disk that has been heated by a laser.

Figure 6-30
A CD-ROM can store hundreds of times the information as can be stored on a diskette of similar size. Many reference materials, such as encyclopedias, catalogs, and even phone books, are now published on CD-ROM instead of paper.

Figure 6-31
Solid-state storage devices use rows of RAM chips to emulate a conventional rotating disk drive. This solid-state device can transfer data 15 to 20 times faster than a rotating disk system.

Because of their tremendous storage capacities, entire catalogs or reference materials can be stored on a single optical disk. Some people predict that optical disks will someday replace data now stored on film such as microfiche.

Solid-State Storage Devices

To the computer, solid-state storage devices act just like disk drives, only faster. As their name suggests, they contain no moving parts, only electronic circuits. **Solid-state storage devices** *(Figure 6-31)* use the latest in random access memory (RAM) technology to provide high-speed data access and retrieval. Rows of RAM chips provide megabytes of memory that can be accessed much faster than the fastest conventional disk drives. Solid-state storage devices are significantly more expensive than conventional disk drives offering the same storage capacity. Unlike disk or tape systems, solid-state storage devices are volatile; if they lose power their contents are lost. For this reason, these devices are usually attached to emergency power backup systems.

Mass Storage Devices

Mass storage devices provide automated retrieval of data from a library of storage media such as tape or data cartridges. Mass storage is ideal for extremely large databases that require all information to be readily accessible even though any one portion of the database may be infrequently required. Mass storage systems take less room than conventional tape storage and can retrieve and begin accessing records within seconds. *Figure 6-32* shows a mass storage system that uses tape cartridges.

Figure 6-32
The inside of an automated mass storage system that uses tape cartridges. A robot arm with a camera mounted on top accesses and loads any one of thousands of tape cartridges in an average of 11 seconds. Each cartridge is a 4" x 4" square and about 1" thick and can hold up to 200 megabytes of data. The tapes are stored in a circular cabinet referred to as a silo.

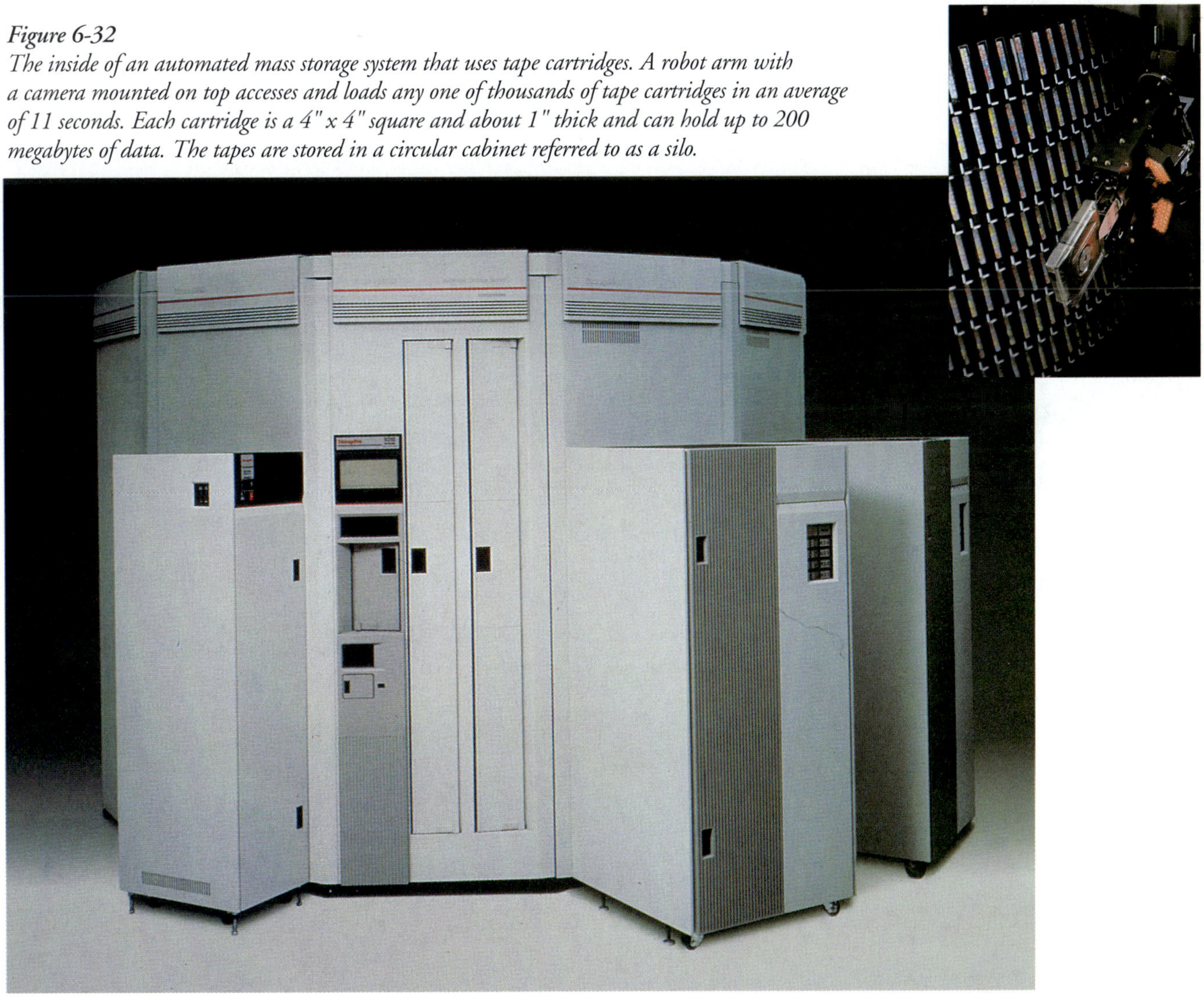

Special-Purpose Storage Devices

Several devices have been developed for special-purpose storage applications. Three of these are memory buttons, smart cards, and optical memory cards.

Memory buttons are small storage devices about the size of a dime that look like watch batteries *(Figure 6-33)*. The buttons can currently hold up to 8,000 characters of information but storage capacities are increasing rapidly. To read or update information in the button, the user touches the button with a small, pen-like probe attached to a hand-held terminal. An audible sound is generated to indicate that the read or write operation has been completed. The buttons are used in applications where information about an item must travel with the item. Examples are laboratory samples, shipping containers, and rental equipment.

Figure 6-34
Smart cards are credit card-sized devices that contain a microprocessor in the left center of the card. The microprocessor can store up to 128,000 bits of information.

Figure 6-33
Memory buttons can hold up to 8,000 characters of information. The buttons are used in applications where information about an item must travel with the item. The buttons can be read or updated using a hand-held device.

Figure 6-35
The optical card can store up to 1,600 pages of information and images. It is the size and thickness of a credit card.

Summary of Secondary Storage

Secondary storage is used to store programs and data that are not currently being processed by the computer. This chapter discussed the various types of secondary storage used with computers. The chart in *Figure 6-36* provides a summary of the secondary storage devices covered. What you have learned about these devices and storage operations in general can now be added to what you have learned about the input, processing, and output operations to complete your understanding of the information processing cycle.

Smart cards are the same size and thickness of a credit card and contain a thin microprocessor capable of storing recorded information *(Figure 6-34)*. When it is inserted into compatible equipment, the information on the smart card can be read and, if necessary, updated. A current user of smart cards is the U. S. Marine Corps, who issues the cards to recruits instead of cash. Each time a recruit uses the card, the transaction amount is subtracted from the previous balance. Other uses of the card include employee time and attendance tracking (instead of time cards) and security applications where detailed information about the card holder is stored in the card.

Optical memory cards can store up to 1,600 pages of text or images on a device the size of a credit card *(Figure 6-35)*. Applications include automobile records and the recording of personal and health-care data.

TYPE	DEVICE	DESCRIPTION
Magnetic Disk	Diskette	Thin, portable plastic storage media that is reliable and low cost.
	Hard disk	Fixed platter storage media that provides large storage capacity and fast access.
	RAID	Multiple small disks integrated into a single unit.
	Disk cartridge	Portable disk unit that provides security.
	Hard card	Hard disk on expansion slot circuit board.
	Removable disk	Older style disk unit with removable disk packs.
Magnetic Tape	Cartridge tape	Tape enclosed in rectangular plastic housing.
	Reel tape	$1/2$-inch tape on 300 to 3,600 foot reel.
Other Storage Devices	PC card	Removable 1.3-inch disks used on portable computers.
	Optical disk	High capacity disks use laser to read and record data.
	Solid-state	Simulate disks using RAM chips to provide high-speed access.
	Mass storage	Automated retrieval of storage media such as tape or data cartridges.
Special-Purpose Devices	Memory button	Stores data on chip in small metal cannister.
	Smart card	Thin microprocessor stores data in credit card-sized holder.
	Optical card	Text and images stored in credit card-sized holder.

Figure 6-36
A summary of secondary storage devices.

COMPUTERS AT WORK

American Express Opts for Optical Storage

American Express' billing operation was once drowning in a sea of paperwork. The AMEX Travel Related Services Company (TRS) was one of the last large credit card operations that still included the actual charge receipts with the monthly statement sent to the cardholder. That meant that each day, several million charge documents had to be processed and temporarily stored until the card holder's bill was prepared. The paper system was prone to errors and at one time, nearly 200 people were assigned to tracking down missing receipts. TRS could have eliminated the receipts like most charge card processors, but they felt that including the receipts was a service to their cardholders.

TRS solved their paperwork problem by implementing the world's largest transaction processing system using optical storage. With the new system, paper charge slips are handled only once when an image of the receipt is captured and stored on a write-once read-many (WORM) optical disk. After they are recorded, the paper receipts are destroyed. Each 12-inch disk can store 100,000 images; the equivalent of six filing cabinets of paper. In a typical year, more than 5,000 WORM disks are used. At the time the image is captured, billing information is also recorded. When it is time to prepare a cardholder's monthly billing statement, the images are electronically sorted and printed along with the statement giving the cardholder written proof of the charge.

Not only does the system offer a unique service to the cardholders, but it costs TRS less than their previous way of processing receipts; nearly 25% less, according to TRS estimates. As their slogan says about their card, "don't leave home without it;" but as far as charge receipts go, don't worry, they'll send them to you in the mail.

Figure 6-37

IN THE FUTURE

Memory Cubes

In the not-too-distant future, you may be able to fit the equivalent of a small library in the palm of your hand. Professor Peter Rentzepis at the University of California Irvine campus has patented a laser device capable of recording 6.5 trillion bits of information on a piece of plastic the size of a sugar cube. That is roughly equal to one million novels.

The plastic cube is made of commercially available polystyrene plastic that has been chemically treated *(Figure 6-38)*. To record data, a single laser beam is split in two and directed toward the cube at right angles. Where the laser beams meet, the plastic molecules are altered and the color changes from clear to blue. Blue molecules are considered 1 bit and the clear, unaltered plastic molecules are considered 0 bits. To read information, a different colored laser beam is used. The reading laser beam only interacts with the blue molecules making them briefly emit a red light. Sensors read the red light and transmit a 1 bit to the computer.

Several obstacles need to be overcome before the memory cubes become commercially feasible. The first challenge is the size of the equipment necessary to record and read the cubes.

The smallest size so far is approximately one foot square. This may not seem that big but it is still much too large for the fastest growing segment of the computer market; personal computers. The second challenge is even more formidable; heat. Currently, the cubes need to stay at very low temperatures to retain their stored information. If the cubes are left at room temperature, they lose their information in a few hours. Even when they are cooled with liquid nitrogen, they only retain their data for a few months. These challenges are worth pursuing however, because of the memory cube's potential. In addition to storing tremendous amounts of data in a small space, the cubes are inexpensive and, unlike disk drives, have no moving parts.

Figure 6-38

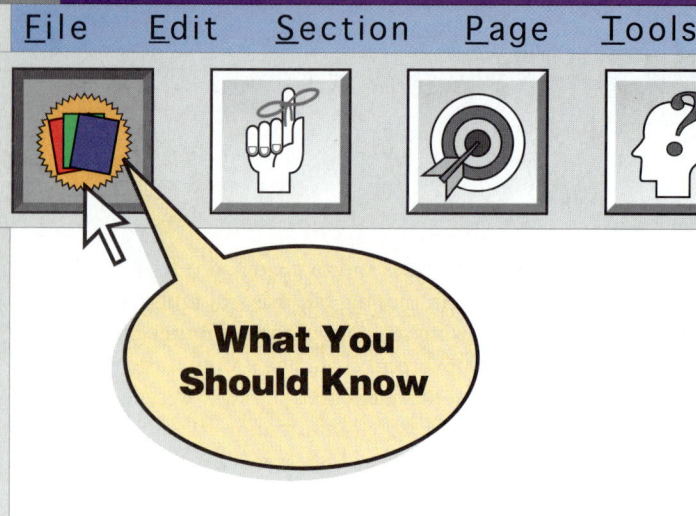

What You Should Know

1. **Main memory**, also called **primary storage**, temporarily stores programs and data that are being processed. **Secondary storage**, also called **auxiliary storage**, stores programs and data when they are not being processed.

2. Most secondary storage devices provide a more permanent form of storage than main memory because they are nonvolatile; that is, data and programs stored on secondary storage devices are retained when the power is turned off. Secondary storage devices are used as both input and output devices. To meet the different needs of users, a variety of secondary storage devices are available.

3. A **magnetic disk** consists of a round platter whose surface is covered with a magnetic material. Magnetic disk offers high storage capacity, reliability, and the capability to directly access stored data. Several types of magnetic disk include diskettes, hard disks, and removable disk cartridges.

4. A **diskette** consists of a circular piece of thin mylar plastic (the actual disk), which is coated with an oxide material similar to that used on recording tape. Because the original diskettes were flexible, they were often called **floppy disks**, or *floppies,* terms that are still used. Because they are convenient, reliable, and inexpensive, diskettes are used as a principal secondary storage medium for personal computers. Diskettes are available in two different sizes (diameters); 3 1/2 inches and 5 1/4 inches.

5. Before a diskette can be used for secondary storage, it must be formatted. The **formatting** process prepares the diskette so that it can store data and includes defining the tracks, cylinders, and sectors on the surfaces of a diskette. A **track** is a narrow recording band forming a full circle around the diskette. A **cylinder** is defined as all tracks of the same number. A **sector** is a pie-shaped section of the diskette. A **cluster**, the smallest unit of diskette space used to hold data, consists of two to eight track sectors. The formatting process also erases any data on the diskette, analyzes the diskette surface for any defective spots, and establishes a directory that will be used to record information about files stored on the diskette. On personal computers using the DOS operating system, the directory is called the **file allocation table** (**FAT**).

6. The amount of data you can store on a diskette depends on two factors: (1) the recording density; and (2) the number of tracks on the diskette.

7. The **recording density** is the number of bits that can be recorded on one inch of track on the diskette. This measurement is referred to as **bits per inch** (**bpi**). Most drives store the same amount of data on the longer outside tracks as they do on the shorter inside tracks. Some newer drives, however, use **multiple zone recording** (**MZR**), which records data at the same density on all tracks, so the longer tracks can contain extra sectors.

8. The measurement of the number of tracks onto which data can be recorded is referred to as **tracks per inch** (**tpi**). This number depends on the size of the diskette, the drive being used, and how the diskette was formatted.

9. Older **single-density** diskettes that could only be written on one side are no longer used. **Double-density** (**DD**) **diskettes** can store 360K for a 5 1/4-inch diskette and 720K for a 3 1/2-inch diskette. **High-density** (**HD**) **diskettes** can store 1.2 megabytes (million characters) on a 5 1/4-inch diskette and 1.44 megabytes on a 3 1/2-inch diskette. **Extended-density** (**ED**) 3 1/2-inch diskettes that can store 2.88 megabytes are also starting to be used. A **floptical diskette** combines optical and magnetic technology to achieve even higher storage rates.

10. When you read from or write to a diskette, a motor spins the circular plastic recording surface at approximately 360 revolutions per minute. A recording mechanism in the drive called the **read/write head** rests on the top and bottom surface of the rotating diskette, generating electronic impulses. The electronic impulses change the polarity, or alignment, of magnetic areas along a track on the disk.

What You Should Know

11. When reading data from a diskette, the read/write head senses the magnetic areas that are recorded on the diskette along various tracks and transfers the data into main memory. The time required to access and retrieve data is called the access time. The access time for a diskette depends on three factors: **seek time**, **rotational delay** (also called **latency**), and **data transfer rate**.

12. With reasonable care, diskettes provide an inexpensive and reliable form of storage. Wear does take place, however, and a diskette will eventually become unreadable. To protect against loss, data should be copied onto other diskettes.

13. Hard disks provide larger and faster secondary storage capabilities than diskettes. **Hard disks** consist of rigid platters coated with an oxide material that allows data to be magnetically recorded on the surface of the platters. Most hard disks are permanently mounted inside the computer and are not removable like diskettes.

14. On minicomputers and mainframes, hard disks are sometimes called **fixed disks** because they cannot be removed like diskettes. They are also referred to as **direct-access storage devices** (DASD).

15. Hard disks contain a spindle on which one or more disk platters are mounted. Like a diskette, hard disks must be formatted before they can be used to store data. Before a hard disk is formatted, it can be divided into separate areas called **partitions**, each of which can function as if it were a separate disk.

16. The storage capacity of hard drives is measured in megabytes, or millions of bytes, of storage. Some disk devices can store billions of bytes of information, called a **gigabyte**.

17. Storing data on hard disks is similar to storing data on diskettes. Hard disk read/write heads are attached to **access arms** that swing out over the disk surface to the correct track. The read/write heads float on a cushion of air and do not actually touch the surface of the disk. If some form of contamination is introduced or if the alignment of the read/write head is altered by something jarring the computer, the disk head can collide with and damage the surface of the disk. This event is known as a **head crash** and causes a loss of data.

18. Depending on the type of disk drive, data is physically organized in two ways. The **sector method** for physically organizing data on hard disks is similar to the method used for diskettes. With the **cylinder method**, all tracks of the same number on each recording surface are considered part of the same cylinder.

19. Some computers improve the apparent speed at which data is transferred to and from a disk by using a **disk cache**, an area of memory set aside for data most often read from the disk.

20. The flow of data to and from the hard disk is managed by electronic circuits called the hard disk controller. **Integrated Drive Electronics** (IDE) controllers can operate one or two disk drives. SCSI (**Small Computer System Interface**) controllers can support seven disk drives or any mix of up to seven SCSI devices.

21. **Data compression** reduces the storage requirements of data by substituting codes for repeating patterns of data. Compression ratios for *lossless compression,* in which no data is lost, average 2 to 1. *Lossy compression* gives up some accuracy for higher compression ratios (up to 200 to 1).

22. A group of integrated small disks is called a RAID, which stands for **redundant array of inexpensive disks**. In the simplest RAID method, called RAID level 1, one backup disk exists for each data disk. Because disks contain duplicate information, RAID level 1 is sometimes called **disk mirroring**. RAID levels beyond level 1 all spread data across more than one drive. Dividing a logical piece of data into smaller parts and writing those parts on multiple drives is called **striping**.

23. **Disk cartridges**, which can be inserted and removed from a computer, offer the storage and fast access features of hard disks and the portability of diskettes. The **Bernoulli disk cartridge** works with a special drive unit that uses a cushion of air to keep the flexible disk surface from touching the read/write head.

24. The **hard card** is a circuit board that has a hard disk built onto it. Hard cards provide an easy way to expand the storage capacity of a personal computer because the board can be installed into an expansion slot of the computer.

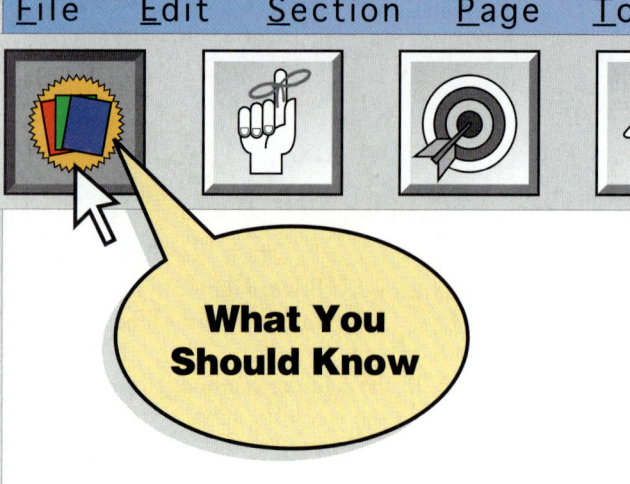

What You Should Know

25. **Removable disk devices** consist of the drive unit, which is usually in its own cabinet, and the removable recording media, called a **disk pack**.

26. To prevent the loss of disk data, two procedures should be performed on a regular basis; backup and defragmentation. **Backup** means creating a copy of important programs and data. When a file is stored in clusters that are not next to each other, the file is said to be **fragmented**. **Defragmentation** reorganizes the data stored on the disk so files are located in contiguous clusters.

27. **Magnetic tape** consists of a thin ribbon of plastic coated on one side with a material that can be magnetized to record the bit patterns that represent data. At one time the primary method of storing large amounts of data, magnetic tape still functions as a cost-effective way to store data that does not have to be accessed immediately, serves as the primary means of backup for most medium and large systems, and is often used to transfer data from one system to another.

28. A **cartridge tape** contains magnetic recording tape in a small, rectangular plastic housing. **Reel-to-reel tape devices** use two reels: a supply reel to hold the tape that will be read from or written to, and the take-up reel to temporarily hold portions of the supply reel tape as it is being processed.

29. Tape is considered a **sequential storage** media because the computer must record and read tape records one after another. **Tape density** is the number of bits that can be stored on an inch of tape. Some tape drives can operate in a high-speed streaming mode used to backup and restore hard disk drives. In the **streaming mode**, the tape records data in exactly the same byte-by-byte order as it appears on the hard disk. Another method of storing large amounts of data on tape is **digital audio tape (DAT)**. DAT uses **helical scan technology** to write data at much higher densities across the tape at an angle instead of down the length of the tape.

30. **PC cards** are small, credit card-sized cards that fit into PCMCIA expansion slots. Although they are only 10.5mm thick (about .4 inch), PC cards used for storage contain small rotating disk drives 1.3 inches in diameter that can contain over 200 megabytes of data.

31. Enormous quantities of information are stored on **optical disks** by using a laser to burn microscopic holes on the surface of a hard plastic disk. Up to 150 of these disks can be installed in automated disk libraries (called jukeboxes) that provide more than one trillion bytes (called a **terabyte**) of online storage. A smaller optical disk is called a **CD-ROM**, an acronym for compact disk-read only memory. Most optical disks are prerecorded and cannot be modified by the user. Optical disk devices that provide for one-time recording are called **WORM** devices, an acronym for write once, read many. The most common erasable optical devices use **magneto-optical technology**, in which a magnetic field changes the polarity of a spot on the disk that has been heated by a laser.

32. Solid-state storage devices contain no moving parts, only electronic circuits. **Solid-state storage devices** use the latest in random access memory (RAM) technology to provide high-speed data access and retrieval.

33. **Mass storage devices** provide automated retrieval of data from a library of storage media such as tape or data cartridges.

34. Several devices have been developed for special-purpose storage applications. **Memory buttons** are small storage devices about the size of a dime that look like watch batteries. The buttons are used in applications where information about an item must travel with the item. **Smart cards** are the same size and thickness of a credit card and contain a thin microprocessor capable of storing recorded information. Smart cards are used for employee time and attendance tracking and security applications where detailed information about the card holder is stored in the card. **Optical memory cards** can store up to 1,600 pages of text or images on a device the size of a credit card. Applications include automobile records and the recording of personal and health-care data.

Terms to Remember

access arms (6.10)
access time (6.7)
auxiliary storage (6.2)

backup (6.15)
Bernoulli disk cartridge (6.14)
bits per inch (bpi) (6.6)

cartridge tape (6.16)
CD-ROM (6.20)
cluster (6.4)
cylinder (6.4)
cylinder method (610)

data compression (6.11)
data transfer rate (6.8)
defragmentation (6.15)
digital audio tape (DAT) (6.18)
direct-access storage devices (DASD) (6.9)
disk cache (6.11)
disk cartridges (6.14)
disk mirroring (6.13)
disk pack (6.14)
diskette (6.3)
double-density (DD) diskettes (6.6)

extended-density (ED) diskettes (6.6)

file allocation table (FAT) (6.5)
fixed disks (6.9)
floppy disks (6.3)
floptical (6.7)
formatting (6.4)
fragmented (6.15)

gigabyte (6.10)

hard card (6.14)
hard disks (6.8)
head crash (6.10)
helical scan technology (6.18)
high-density (HD) diskettes (6.6)

Integrated Drive Electronics (IDE) (6.11)

latency (6.8)

magnetic disk (6.3)
magnetic tape (6.16)
magneto-optical technology (6.20)
mass storage devices (6.21)
memory buttons (6.21)
multiple zone recording (MZR) (6.6)

optical disks (6.19)
optical memory cards (6.22)

partitions (6.9)
PC cards (6.19)

RAID (6.13)
read/write head (6.7)
recording density (6.6)
redundant array of inexpensive disks (RAID) (6.13)
reel-to-reel tape devices (6.17)
removable disk (6.14)
rotational delay (6.8)

SCSI (6.11)
secondary storage (6.2)
sector (6.4)
sector method (6.10)
seek time (6.7)
sequential storage (6.17)
single-density (6.6)
Small Computer System Interface (SCSI) (6.11)
smart cards (6.22)
solid-state storage (6.21)
streaming mode (6.18)
striping (6.13)

tape density (6.18)
terabyte (6.20)
track (6.4)
tracks per inch (tpi) (6.6)

WORM (6.20)

Test Your Knowledge

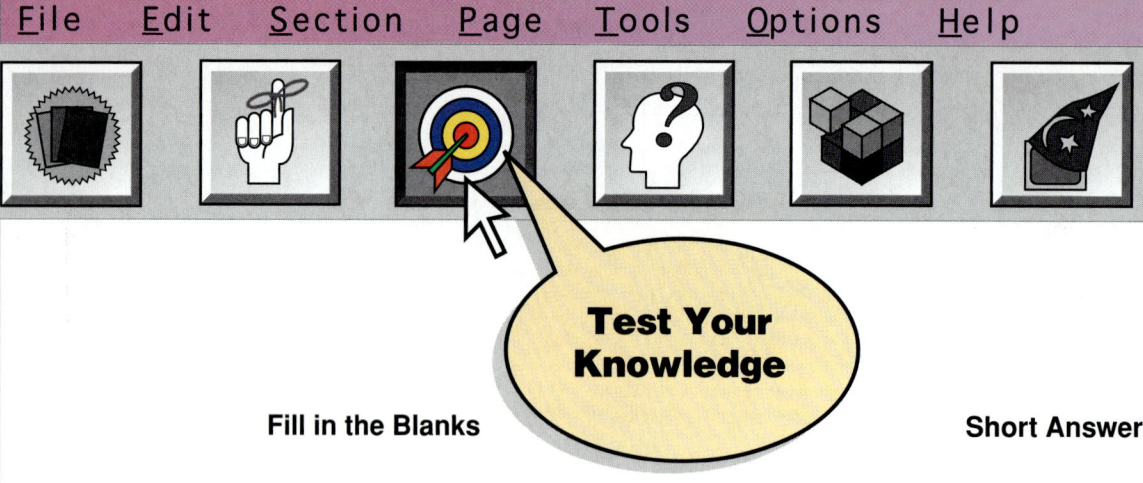

Fill in the Blanks

1. _____ stores programs and data when they are not being processed.

2. A(n) _____ the most widely used storage medium for all types of computers, consists of a round platter whose surface is covered with a magnetic material.

3. _____, which consists of a thin ribbon of plastic, functions as a cost-effective way to store data that does not have to be accessed immediately.

4. Enormous quantities of information are stored on _____ by using a laser to burn microscopic holes on the surface of a hard plastic disk.

5. _____, which contain only electronic circuits, use the latest in random access memory (RAM) technology to provide megabytes of memory that can be accessed much faster than conventional disk drives.

Short Answer

1. How is data written to and read from a diskette?

2. What is access time? On what three factors does access time depend? Briefly explain each. Why is access time significantly faster for a hard disk than for a diskette?

3. What is data compression? How is lossless compression different from lossy compression? For what kind of data is each type of compression used?

4. What two procedures should be performed on a regular basis to prevent the loss of disk data? Explain each.

5. What do memory buttons, smart cards, and optical memory cards have in common? How are they different? For what purpose is each used?

Label the Figure

Instructions: Write the appropriate secondary storage device in each level of the pyramid chart shown below.

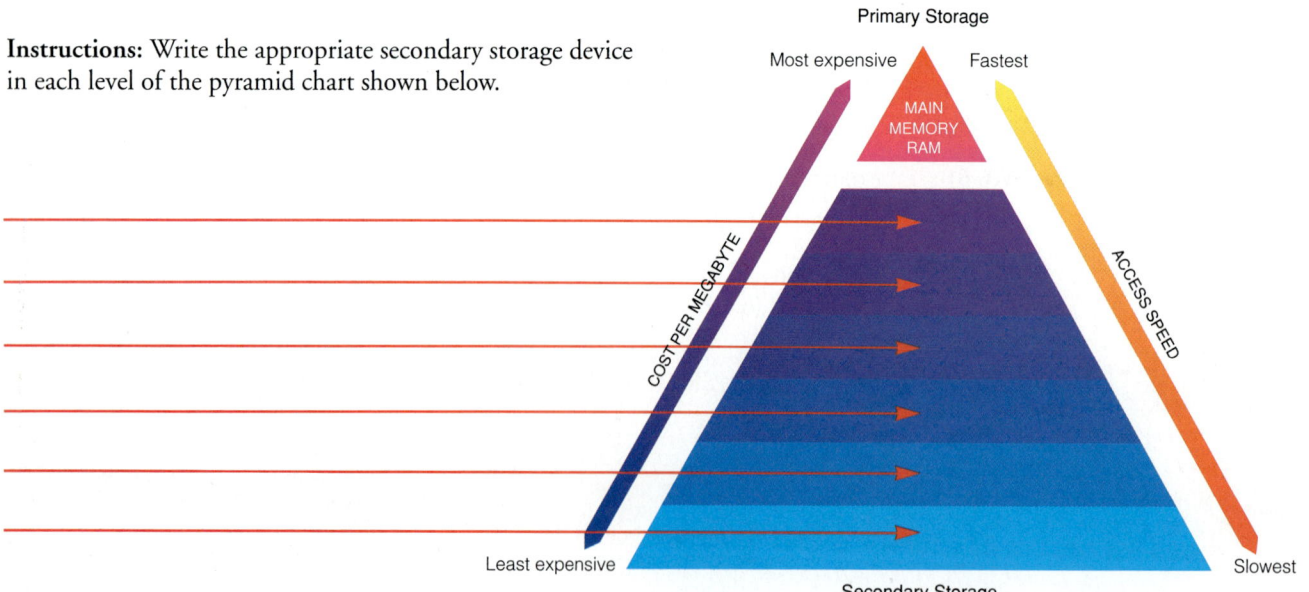

Points to Ponder

1
Magnetic disks are called direct-access storage devices because a computer system can go directly to a desired piece of data. Magnetic tape, on the other hand, is called a sequential access storage device because data must be read in sequence, one piece of data after another. Although magnetic tape is slower than magnetic disks, it is less expensive and well-suited for certain applications such as providing a backup. Think of at least one other business application for which a sequential access storage device, such as magnetic tape, is ideal. Explain why magnetic tape is appropriate for the application. Think of at least one business application for which magnetic tape is unsuitable. Explain why.

2
Instead of supplying potential customers with printed brochures, a few companies now provide a marketing diskette or CD-ROM that can be used by customers with personal computers. Some automobile manufacturers provide a marketing diskette or CD-ROM that lets PC users "walk around and kick the tires" of a vehicle by furnishing photographs, statistics, option packages, and pricing information. A personal computer video game is even supplied that allows buyers to "test drive" a vehicle by participating in a wildlife photo safari. Think of another product that you could market. What kind of information would you provide? Do you think potential sales of the product would justify the cost of producing the diskette or CD-ROM? Why or why not?

3
Some CD-ROM disks contain interactive children's "books." Using these disks, a computer can read the story in several different languages, reread selected passages, show the book's illustrations, allow children to ask questions about what is on the screen, and even reveal surprises when children use a mouse to click some part of a picture. Discuss the advantages and disadvantages of these CD-ROM disks compared to watching a television program or hearing a story read by someone else.

4
The National Gallery of Art in Washington, D.C. has recorded its entire collection on an optical disk, including works that, because of space limitations, are not normally displayed. The images on the disk offer startling clarity — even brush strokes are visible. Users of the disk can almost instantaneously display any work in the collection, locate works based on a wide range of criteria (artist, nationality, period, and so on), and magnify portions of a work on the screen. The optical disk is being made available to schools around the country. Why do you think optical disk was chosen to store the gallery's collection instead of some other secondary storage medium such as magnetic disk or magnetic tape? In what school classes do you think the disk will be used? How? As more museums take advantage of optical disk technology, do you think museum attendance will decline? Why or why not?

5
Despite the risk of data loss, a study has shown that less than 35 percent of all companies, and less than 20 percent of small companies, have backup policies. Of companies that do have backup policies, more than one-quarter had experienced a computer crash in the past. It is estimated that data loss costs American companies approximately $4 billion each year. Why do you think so few companies backup their data? If you were the CEO of a large company, what backup policy would you establish? How would you make sure your policy was carried out?

6
Recently out of college, you have just been hired by Wiley's Widgets, LTD. Although Wiley's Widgets uses computers to produce letters, memorandums, and spreadsheets, much to your surprise, you find that all of the employee, customer, and inventory records are stored on paper in file cabinets. Your coworkers tell you that this is the way Wiley's Widgets has kept its records since the company was founded in 1865, and that old Mr. Wiley hates change. One day as you are riding the elevator up to your office, you bump into Mr. Wiley and mention the benefits of saving records using some form of computer secondary storage. Mr. Wiley is intrigued and wants to hear more. Write a memo to Mr. Wiley describing the advantages and, because Mr. Wiley is no fool, any disadvantages in using some type of secondary storage to store company records. What form of secondary storage would you recommend? Why?

Out and About

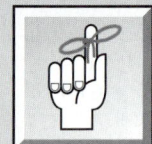

1. Some organizations, such as insurance companies, banks, libraries, and college registrars, are *information-intensive,* meaning that they must keep track of and manipulate large amounts of data. Visit an information-intensive organization and interview someone responsible for maintaining the organization's data. What are the organization's storage requirements? What type of secondary storage medium is used? Why? Have there ever been any problems with secondary storage? If so, how were the problems remedied? What type of backup procedures are employed?

2. The price of diskettes varies depending on such things as diskette size, recording density, the diskette manufacturer, and whether or not the diskette is already formatted for an Apple or IBM-compatible personal computer. Visit a store that sells computer supplies and compare the price of the least expensive diskettes to the price of the most expensive diskettes. What factors account for the difference in price? Which diskettes are recommended by the store's salesperson? Why? If you were buying diskettes for your own personal computer, which ones would you purchase? Why?

3. Because many companies store large amounts of information on hard disks that are permanently mounted inside the computer, the problem of data security has become an important issue. No companies can afford to have sensitive information on customers or product development stolen by industrial spies or dissatisfied employees. Visit a large firm and interview an employee on data security. How are records protected? Who has access to sensitive data? Have there ever been problems with data security? If so, what measures have been taken to make sure the problems do not recur?

4. As a result of the expanding storage requirements of some software and graphic files, new technologies are being developed that offer even greater secondary storage. These technologies include flash memory cards, glass disks, glass-ceramic disks, and "wet" hard drives. Using current computer magazines, prepare a report on one or more of these new technologies. What does the technology entail? What benefits does it offer? Why? When is the technology likely to be available for general use?

5. Visit a computer store and obtain information on the different types of hard disk drives available for personal computers. Summarize your findings and include data on price, storage capacity, and access speed. Calculate the cost per megabyte of storage for each drive. If you have a personal computer, which type of hard disk drive do you think is best suited for your current needs? Do you think the same disk drive will be adequate five years from now? Why or why not?

6. Many people feel that we have only begun to take advantage of smart card technology. In addition to the uses described in this chapter, smart cards that store the medical histories of the cardholders are being tested in New York, and smart cards have taken the place of food stamps for some residents of Dayton, Ohio. Visit a library and research smart cards. How much information can they contain? How do they work? In what applications have they been used? Why? How may smart cards be used in the future?

In the Lab   6.33

 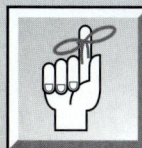    

Windows Labs

1 Formatting a Diskette With Program Manager on the screen, double-click the Main group icon. Double-click the File Manager program-item icon. Click the Maximize button to maximize the window. Insert a diskette into drive A other than the one you used in earlier Labs. (*Caution:* Formatting erases all information on a diskette.) Select the Disk menu and choose Format Disk. If necessary, change the displayed capacity of the diskette (see page 6.6) by clicking the Capacity drop-down list box arrow and selecting the appropriate capacity from the list. Choose the OK button. If a confirmation dialog box displays, choose the Yes button. As Windows formats the diskette, it displays a percentage complete message *(Figure 6-39)*. When the formatting process is complete, Windows displays a Format Complete dialog box. Choose the No button in this dialog box. Remove the diskette from drive A. Put your name on a label and place it on the diskette. Close File Manager by clicking its Control-menu box.

2 Managing Files on a Disk Open the File Manager window as described above in Windows Lab 1. Maximize the File Manager window. Perform the following tasks: (1) Insert the diskette containing your Windows Labs from previous chapters into drive A. Click the drive A icon in the File Manager window to display files on drive A in the directory window. If you do not see your windows labs, click the subdirectory name containing these files. Select the file win2-2.wri by clicking it. If you do not have a copy of win2-2.wri, ask your instructor for a copy. (2) Select the File menu and choose the Copy command. In the Copy dialog box, type win2-2a.wri and choose the OK button. Notice that win2-2a.wri, an exact copy of win2-2.wri, now displays in the directory window *(Figure 6-40)*. (3) Select the file win2-2a.wri by clicking it. Select the File menu and choose the Rename command. In the Rename dialog box, type win6-2.wri and choose the OK button. Notice that the name of win2-2a.wri has changed to win6-2.wri in the directory window *(Figure 6-41 on the next page)*. (4) Select the file win6-2.wri by clicking it. Select the File menu and choose the Print command. Choose the OK button in each Print dialog box that displays. (5) Select the file win6-2.wri by clicking it. Select the File menu and choose the Delete command. In the Delete dialog box, choose the OK button. Choose the Yes button in the Confirm File Delete dialog box. Notice that the file win6-2.wri is no longer in the directory window. (6) Select the File menu and choose the Undelete command to display the Microsoft Undelete dialog box. Click the filename ?IN6-2.WRI to select it *(Figure 6-42 on the next page)*. Click the Undelete button . Type w as the first character of the filename and choose the OK button. Close the Microsoft Undelete dialog box. Notice that the file win6-2.wri once again displays in the directory window. Close File Manager by clicking its Control-menu box.

3 Shelly Cashman Series Secondary Storage Lab Follow the instructions in Windows Lab 2 in Chapter 1 on page 1.30 to display the Shelly Cashman Series Labs screen.

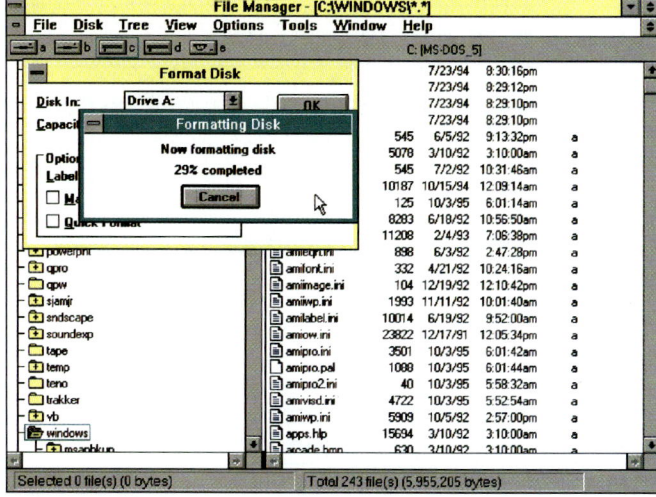

Figure 6-39

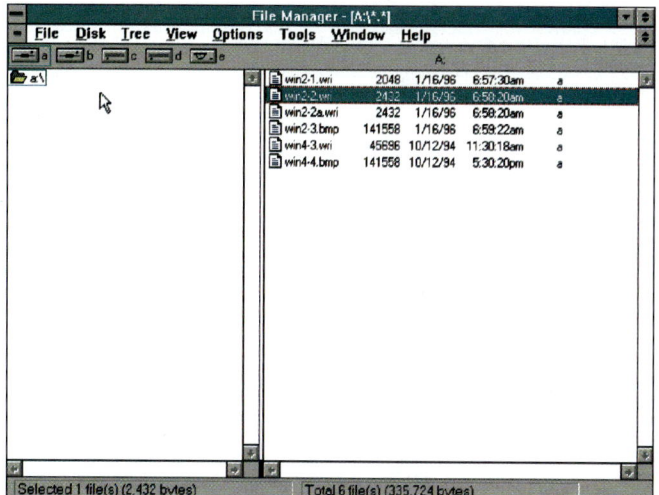

Figure 6-40

6.34 In the Lab

File Edit Section Page Tools Options Help

 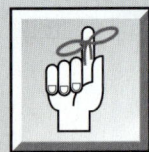    

In the Lab (continued)

Select Secondary Storage by pointing to it and clicking the left mouse button. When the initial Secondary Storage Lab screen displays, carefully read the objectives. With your printer turned on, point to the Print Questions button and click the left mouse button. Fill out the top of the Questions sheet and answer the questions as you step through the Secondary Storage Lab.

4 Using File Manager Help Open File Manager and maximize its window as described in Windows Lab 1 on the previous page. Select the Help menu and choose the Search for Help on command. Perform the following tasks: (1) Type changing drives and press the ENTER key twice. Read and print the information. Choose the Search button. (2) Repeat the procedure in Step 1 for these topics: selecting files, copying files, renaming files, deleting files, and formatting disks. Close the Help window. Close File Manager.

DOS Labs

1 Formatting a Diskette Determine the byte capacity of your diskette; that is, it is either 360K, 720K, 1.2M, or 1.44M (see page 6.6). At the DOS prompt, type format a:/f:nnnn, where nnnn is the capacity of the diskette in kilobytes or megabytes. Press the ENTER key. Insert a diskette into drive A other than the one you used in earlier Labs and press the ENTER key. (*Caution:* Formatting erases all information on a diskette.) As DOS formats the diskette, it displays a percent complete message. Enter your last name as the volume label. When prompted to format another diskette, type n and press the ENTER key. Remove the diskette, put your name on a label and place it on the diskette.

2 Managing Files on a Disk Insert the diskette containing your DOS Labs into drive A. At the DOS prompt, perform the following tasks: (1) Type a: and press the ENTER key to change the default to drive A. (2) Type dir and press the ENTER key. Press PRINT SCREEN to print the screen. (3) Type copy dos2-1 dos 2-1a and press the ENTER key to make a copy of the source file. If you do not have a copy of dos2-1, ask your instructor for a copy. (4) Type ren dos2-1a dos6-2 and press the ENTER key to rename the file. (5) Print the file dos6-2 by typing print dos6-2 and pressing the ENTER key twice. (6) Type del dos6-2 and press the ENTER key to remove the file. Type dir and press ENTER to view the file names. (7) Type undelete and press ENTER. At the Undelete prompt for the file ?OS6-2, type y and then type d as the first character of the filename. Type dir and press the ENTER key to view the file names. Press the PRINT SCREEN key.

3 Using the Question Mark to Obtain Help Clear the screen. Type copy /? and press the ENTER key to display help on the COPY command. Press PRINT SCREEN. Use this same technique to obtain help on: REN, DEL, UNDELETE, and FORMAT. Print each command's help.

Online Lab

1 Using an Electronic Encyclopedia Using one of the two online services you selected in Chapter 1, connect to the service and perform the following tasks: (1) Search the online service for the Encyclopedia section. (2) Select a topic related to computers or the use of computers in your field of study and print the information.

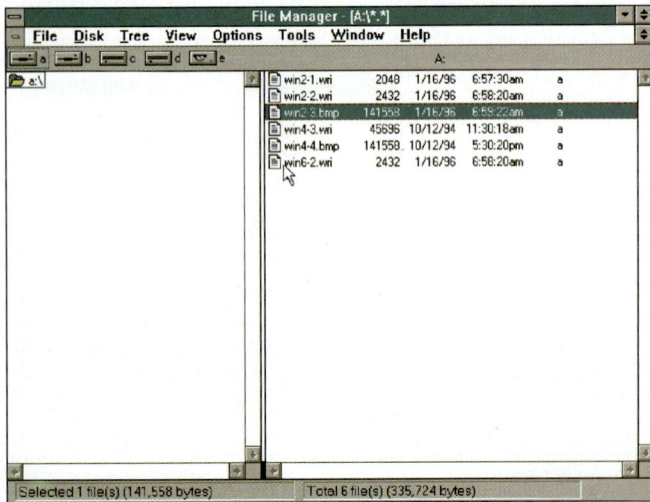

Figure 6-41

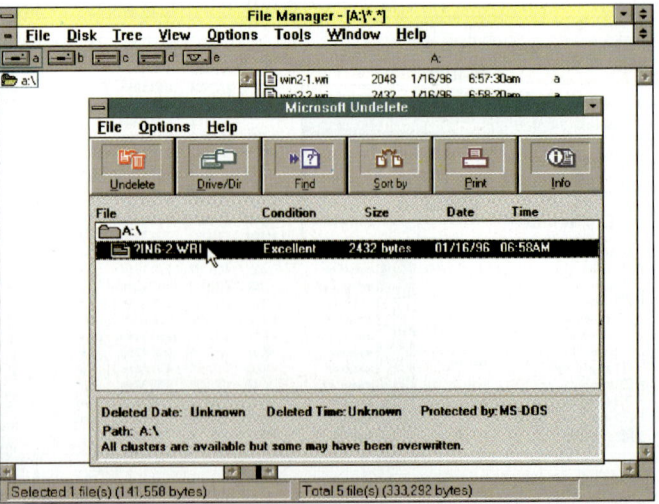

Figure 6-42

CHAPTER SEVEN

Communications and Networks

7

Objectives

After completing this chapter, you will be able to:

- Describe several examples of how communications technology is used

- Define the term communications

- Describe the basic components of a communications system

- Describe the various transmission media used for communications channels

- Describe the different types of line configurations

- Describe how data is transmitted

- Identify and explain the communications equipment used in a communications system

- Describe the functions performed by communications software

- Explain the two major categories of networks, and describe three common network configurations

- Describe how bridges and gateways are used to connect networks

Computers are well recognized as important computing devices. They should also be recognized as important communications devices. It is now possible for a computer to communicate with other computers anywhere in the world. This capability, sometimes referred to as connectivity, allows users to quickly and directly access data and information that otherwise would have been unavailable or that probably would have taken considerable time to acquire. Banks, retail stores, airlines, hotels, and many other businesses use computers for communications purposes. Personal computer users communicate with other personal computer users. They can also access special databases available on larger computers to quickly and conveniently obtain information such as weather reports, stock market data, airline schedules, news stories, or even theater and movie reviews.

This chapter provides an overview of communications with an emphasis on the communication of data and information. The chapter explains some of the terminology, equipment, procedures, and applications that relate to computers and their use as communications devices. How computers can be joined together into computer networks is discussed. Networks multiply the power of individual computers by allowing users to communicate and share hardware, software, and information.

7.2 Examples of How Communications Is Used

The ability to instantly and accurately communicate information is changing the way people do business and interact with each other. Advances in communications software and hardware now allow people to easily transmit voice and data communications around the world. The following applications rely on communications technology:

- Electronic mail
- Voice mail
- Teleconferencing
- FAX
- Groupware
- Telecommuting
- Electronic data interchange (EDI)
- Global positioning systems (GPS)
- Bulletin board systems (BBS)
- Online services

Electronic Mail

Electronic mail, also described in detail in Chapter 2, is the capability to use computers to transmit messages to and receive messages from other computer users. The other users may be on the same computer network or on a separate computer system reached through the use of communications equipment. Each E-mail user has an address to which mail can be sent. The address acts as a mailbox and accumulates messages. Most E-mail programs support distribution lists that send messages to several individuals at the same time.

Many organizations with internal computer networks provide E-mail for employees. Online service providers such as Prodigy and America Online also offer E-mail capabilities.

Voice Mail

Voice mail can be considered verbal electronic mail. Made possible by the latest computerized telephone systems, voice mail reduces the problem of telephone tag, where two people trying to reach each other wind up leaving a series of messages to please call back. With voice mail, the caller can leave a message, similar to leaving a message on an answering machine. The difference between voice mail and an answering machine is that with a voice mail system the caller's message is digitized so it can be stored on a disk like other computer data. This allows the party who was called to hear the message later (by converting it to an audio form) and also, if desired, add a reply or additional comments and forward the message to someone else who has access to the system.

Teleconferencing

Teleconferencing once meant three or more people sharing a phone conversation. Today, however, **teleconferencing** usually means video conferencing, the use of computers and television cameras to transmit video images and the sound of the participant(s) to a remote location that has compatible equipment *(Figure 7-1)*. Special software and equipment is used to digitize and compress the video image so it can be transmitted along with the audio over standard communications channels. Although the video image is not as clear for moving objects as commercial television, it does contribute to the discussion and is adequate for nonmoving objects such as charts and graphs. Video conferencing was originally developed for larger groups of people who had to use a room specially outfitted with video conferencing equipment. More recently, desktop video equipment has been developed to allow individual users to visually communicate with other people within their building or at remote locations *(Figure 7-2)*.

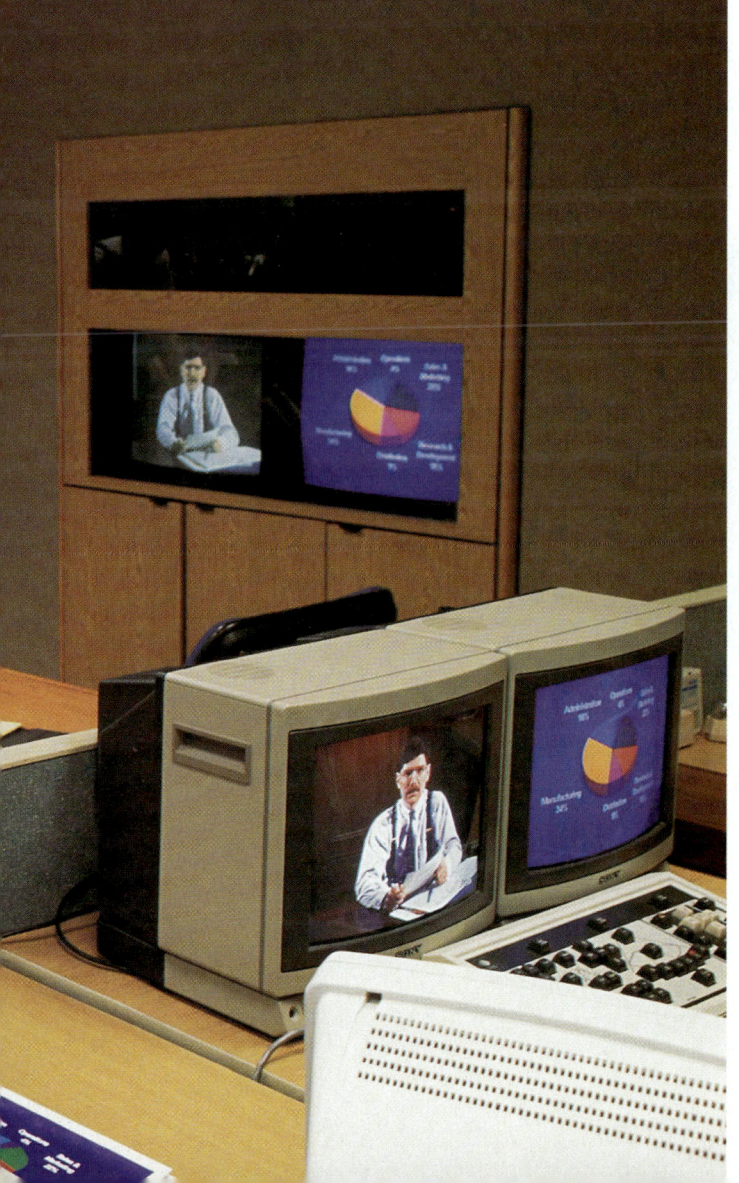

Figure 7-1
Video conferencing is used to transmit and receive video and audio signals over standard communications channels. This meeting is being transmitted to a video conference center at another location. The people at the other location are also being recorded and transmitted and can be seen on the TV monitor.

Figure 7-2
Desktop video conferencing equipment allows individual users to communicate with other employees on their computer network. Some systems can also connect to remote locations.

FAX

Facsimile, or **FAX,** equipment is used to transmit a reproduced image of a document over phone lines *(Figure 7-3)*. The document can contain text or graphics, can be handwritten, or be a photograph. FAX machines optically scan the document and convert the image into digitized data that is transmitted over a phone line. A FAX machine at the receiving end converts the digitized data back into its original image. FAX equipment is available as stand-alone machines or as part of data communications equipment called modems that are discussed later in this chapter. Using FAX software, the FAX modems can directly transmit computer-prepared documents or documents that have been digitized with the use of a scanner. FAX equipment is having an increasing impact on the way people transmit documents. Many documents that were previously sent through the mail are now sent by FAX. With the speed and convenience of a phone call, a document sent by FAX can be transmitted anywhere in the world.

Groupware

Groupware is a loosely defined term applied to software that helps multiple users work together by sharing information. Groupware is part of a broad concept called **workgroup technology** that includes equipment and software that help group members communicate and manage their activities.

Some software applications discussed separately in this section, including E-mail and video conferencing, can also be considered groupware. Other groupware applications include:

- **Group Editing**   The capability for multiple users to revise a document with each set of revisions separately identified.
- **Group Scheduling**   A group calendar that tracks the time commitments of multiple users and helps schedule meetings when necessary.
- **Group Decision Support**   A decision support system that relies on the input of multiple users.
- **Workflow Software**   Software that automates repetitive processes such as processing an insurance claim, in which multiple persons must review and approve a document.

One of the more widely used groupware packages is Lotus Notes *(Figure 7-4)*. Notes uses a shared database approach to groupware. In addition, Notes offers E-mail and a programming language that can be used to develop customized groupware applications.

Figure 7-3
A facsimile (FAX) machine can send and receive copies of documents to and from any location where there is phone service and another FAX machine.

Figure 7-4
Notes from Lotus Corporation is one of the most widely used groupware packages. Notes allows users to share information and work together on documents. Notes also includes E-mail capabilities.

Groupware and workgroup technology are still relatively new ideas and, other than E-mail, are not yet widely used. The need for small staffs to work quickly and efficiently on changing job assignments will, however, increase the use of groupware.

Telecommuting

Telecommuting refers to the capability of individuals to work at home and communicate with their offices by using personal computers and communications channels. With a personal computer, an employee can access the main computer at the office. He or she can read and answer electronic mail. An employee can access databases and can transmit completed projects. Some predict that by the year 2000, ten percent of the work force will be telecommuters. Telecommuting provides flexibility, allowing companies and employees to increase productivity and, at the same time, meet the needs of individual employees. Some of the advantages of telecommuting include reducing the time used to commute to the office each week; eliminating the need to travel during poor weather conditions; providing a convenient and comfortable work environment for disabled employees or workers recovering from injuries or illnesses; and allowing employees to combine work with personal responsibilities such as child care.

Electronic Data Interchange (EDI)

Electronic data interchange (EDI) is the capability to electronically transfer documents from one business to another. EDI is frequently used by large companies for routine transactions such as purchase orders and billing. In some businesses, such as the automotive industry, EDI is the standard way of doing repeat business with suppliers. EDI offers a number of

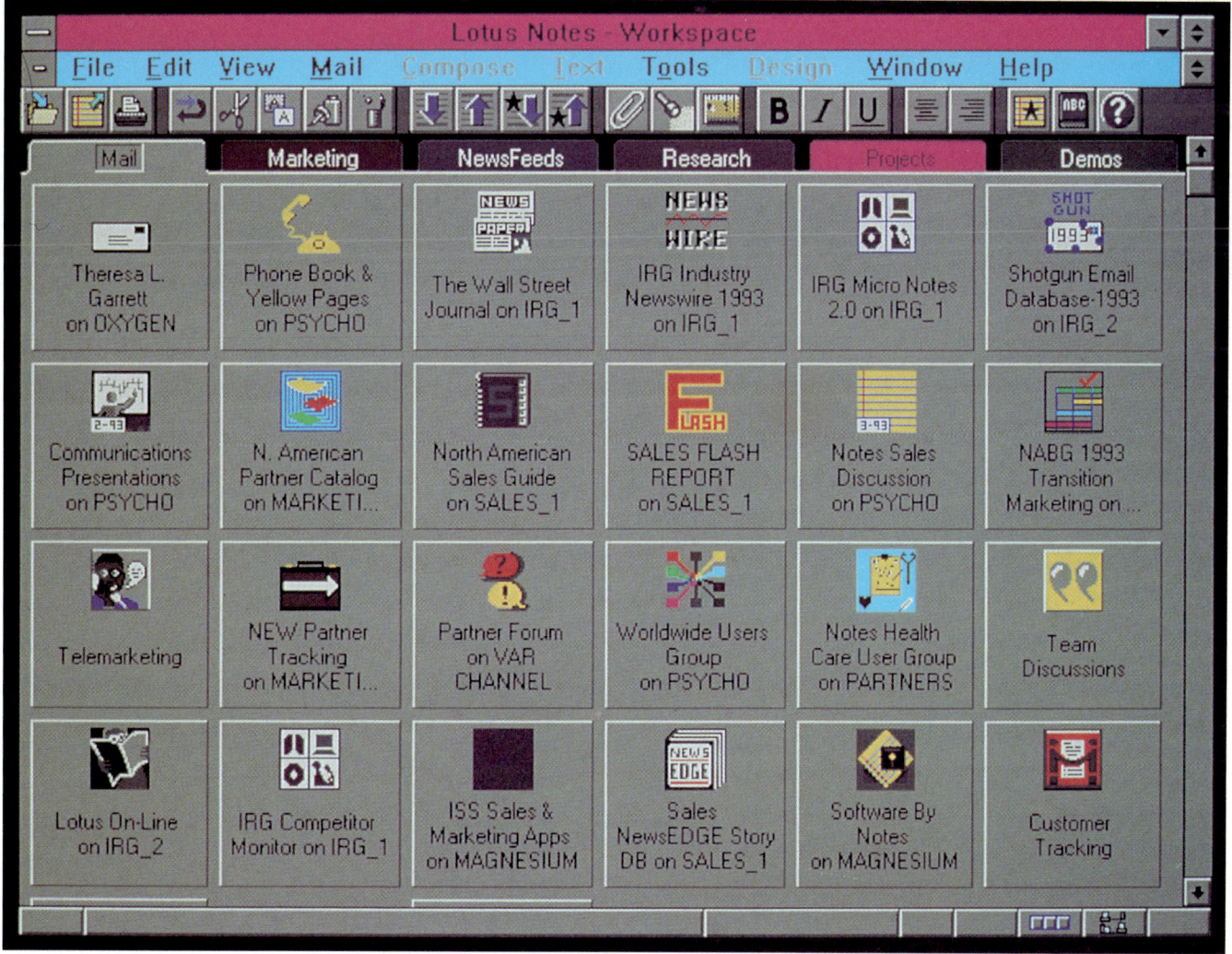

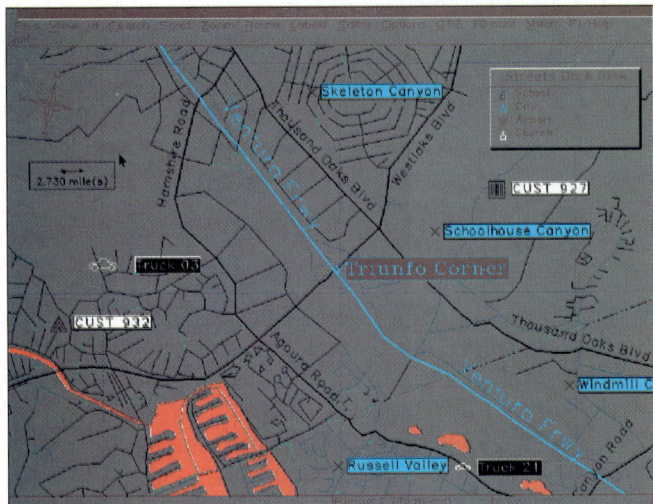

Figure 7-5
Satellite mapping software works with global positioning system (GPS) equipment to help users locate their exact location on a displayed map. Maps are available for most metropolitan areas.

advantages over paper documents, including the following:
- Lower transaction costs
- Reduced time to transmit documents
- Reduced data entry errors because data need not be reentered at the receiving end
- Reduced paper flow

Some companies have developed sophisticated EDI applications where orders from a customer are automatically created based on sales or inventory levels, transmitted to a vendor electronically, and shipped to the customer without any human intervention.

Global Positioning Systems (GPS)

A **global positioning system** (GPS) uses satellites to determine the geographic location of earth-based GPS equipment. Depending on the equipment used, a GPS system can be accurate up to 100 feet. GPS systems are often used for tracking and navigation of all types of vehicles; cars, trucks,

BBS	MODEM NUMBER	DESCRIPTION	LOCATION
America's Suggestion Box	516-471-8625	Collects and distributes consumer feedback	Ronkonkoma, NY
Automobile Consumer Services	513-624-0552	New and used car pricing reports	Cincinnati, OH
Boardwatch	303-973-4222	Lists of BBSs maintained by Boardwatch magazine	Denver, CO
BMUG BBS	510-849-2684	Macintosh support and information	Berkeley, CA
Exec PC	414-789-4210	Largest BBS in United States	Elm Grove, WI
FEDLINK ALIXII	202-707-4888	US government information	Washington, D.C.
NASA Spacelink	205-895-0028	NASA space information and history	Huntsville, AL
SBA Online	800-697-4636	Advice for small business owners	Washington, D.C.
The Well	415-332-6106	Whole Earth conferencing system	Sausalito, CA
WeatherBank	800-827-2727	Weather forecasts for any city	SaltLake City, UT

Figure 7-6
A partial list of the major bulletin boards in the United States.

boats, and planes. Small GPS systems have even been designed for use in portable personal computers. A number of companies have developed map software to work with GPS systems *(Figure 7-5)*. The map software can either be used by itself to find locations or to measure distances between two points. When the software is used with GPS equipment, the user's exact location and direction of travel is displayed on the map.

Bulletin Board Systems (BBS)

A **bulletin board system** (**BBS**) allows users to communicate with one another and share information *(Figure 7-6)*. While some bulletin boards provide specific services such as buying and selling used computer equipment, many bulletin boards function as electronic clubs for special-interest groups and are used to share information about hobbies as diverse as stamp collecting, music, genealogy, and astronomy. Some BBSs are strictly social; users meet new friends and conduct conversations by entering messages through their keyboards. Many hardware and software vendors have set up BBSs to provide online support for their products.

Online Services

Online services, sometimes called **information services**, include information and services provided to users who subscribe to the service for a fee. Typically, the user accesses the services by using communications equipment and software to temporarily connect to the service provider's computer. Services that are available include electronic banking, shopping, news, weather, hotel and airline reservations, and investment information. Some online services provide very specific information such as stock market data. Other online services, such as Prodigy *(Figure 7-7)* and America Online, provide a wide variety of information. *Figure 7-8* is a list of major online service providers.

Figure 7-7
The Prodigy online information service offers the latest news, weather, sports, and financial information along with shopping, entertainment, and electronic mail.

NAME	DESCRIPTION	PHONE
America Online	Fastest growing provider; news, weather, shopping, finance, travel, and more	800-827-6364
Prodigy	Largest online provider; news, weather, shopping, finance, travel, and more	800-776-3449
CompuServe	Most comprehensive of all services; business oriented	800-848-8199
Delphi	Internet access and services	800-695-4005
GEnie	News plus professional and technical databases	800-638-9636
Imagination	Games and entertainment	800-743-7721
eWorld	General-interest service started by Apple	800-775-4556
Dow Jones	Finance and business news	800-522-3567

Figure 7-8
The names and information phone numbers of major online information service providers.

What Is Communications?

Communications, sometimes called **data communications**, refers to the transmission of data and information over a communications channel, such as a standard telephone line, between one computer or terminal and another computer. Other terms such as telecommunications and teleprocessing are also used to describe communications.

Telecommunications describes any type of long-distance communications including television signals. **Teleprocessing** refers to the use of a terminal or a computer and communications equipment to access computers and computer files located elsewhere. As communications technology continues to advance, the distinction between these terms is blurred. Therefore, most people refer to the process of transmitting data or information of any type as data communications, or simply communications.

A Communications System Model

Figure 7-9 shows the basic model for a communications system. This model consists of the following equipment:
- A computer or a terminal
- Communications equipment that sends (and can usually receive) data
- The communications channel over which the data is sent
- Communications equipment that receives (and can usually send) data
- Another computer

The basic model also includes communications software. If two computers are communicating with each other, compatible communications software is required on each system. If a computer is communicating with a terminal, communications are directed either by a separate program running on the computer or by the computer operating system. A **communications channel**, also called a **communications line**, **communications link**, or **data link**, is the path the data follows as it is transmitted from the sending equipment to the receiving equipment in a communications system. These channels are made up of one or more transmission media.

Figure 7-9
The basic model of a communications system. In addition to the equipment, communications software is also required.

Transmission Media

Transmission media are the materials or technologies that are used to establish the communications channel. Two types of transmission media include those that use some type of physical cabling and those that use wireless technology. Cabling media include twisted pair wire, coaxial cable, and fiber-optics cable. Wireless technology includes microwaves, radio waves, or light waves.

Twisted Pair Wire

Twisted pair wire *(Figure 7-10)* consists of pairs of copper wires that are twisted together. To insulate and identify the wires, each wire is covered with a thin layer of colored plastic. Twisted pair wire is commonly used for telephone lines and to connect personal computers with one another. It is an inexpensive transmission medium, and it can be easily strung from one location to another. A disadvantage of twisted pair wire is that it can be affected by outside electrical interference generated by machines such as fans or air conditioners. While this interference may be acceptable on a voice call, it can garble the data as it is sent over the line, causing transmission errors to occur.

Coaxial Cable

A **coaxial cable** is a high-quality communications line used in offices, and it can be laid underground or underwater. Coaxial cable consists of a copper wire conductor surrounded by a nonconducting insulator that is in turn surrounded by a woven metal outer conductor, and finally a plastic outer coating *(Figure 7-11)*. Because of its more heavily insulated construction, coaxial cable is not susceptible to electrical interference and can transmit data at higher data rates over longer distances than twisted pair wire.

The two types of coaxial cable, named for the transmission techniques they support, are baseband and broadband. **Baseband** coaxial cable carries one signal at a time. The signal, however, can travel very fast – in the area of ten million bits per second for the first 1,000 feet. The speed drops significantly as the length of the cable increases, and special equipment is needed to amplify (boost) the signal if it is transmitted more than approximately one mile.

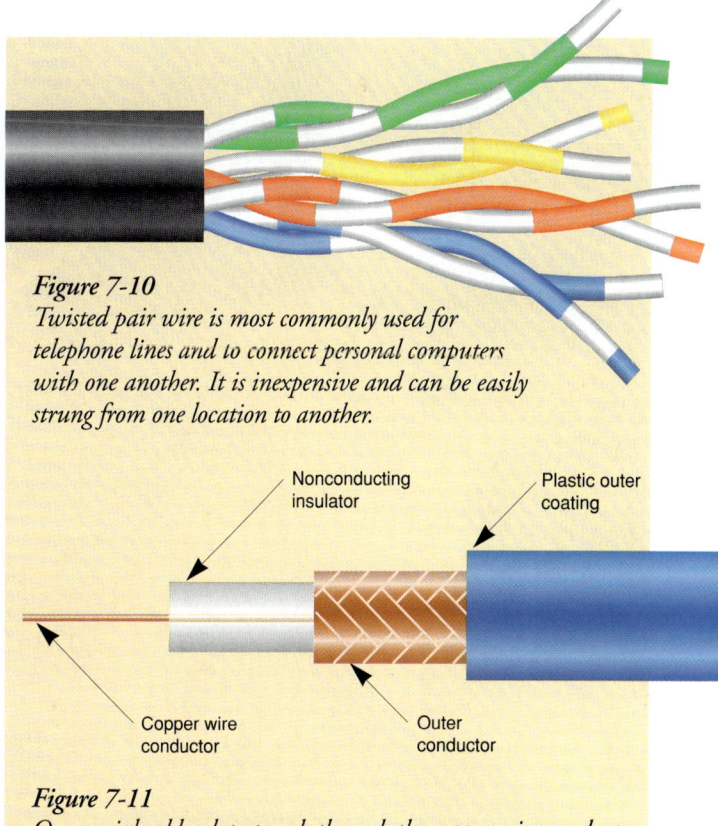

Figure 7-10
Twisted pair wire is most commonly used for telephone lines and to connect personal computers with one another. It is inexpensive and can be easily strung from one location to another.

Figure 7-11
On coaxial cable, data travels through the copper wire conductor. The outer conductor is made of woven metal mesh that acts as an electrical ground.

Broadband coaxial cable can carry multiple signals at one time. It is similar to cable TV where a single cable offers a number of channels to the user. A particular advantage of broadband channels is that data, audio, and video transmission can occur over the same line.

Fiber Optics

Fiber-optics cable uses smooth, hair-thin strands of glass to conduct light with high efficiency *(Figure 7-12)*. The major advantages of fiber optics over wire cables include substantial weight and size savings and increased speed of transmission. Another advantage is that fiber-optic cable is not affected by electrical and magnetic fields. A single fiber-optic cable can carry several hundred thousand voice communications simultaneously. The disadvantages of fiber-optic cable are that it is more expensive than twisted pair or coaxial cable and it is more difficult to install and modify than metal wiring. Fiber optics is frequently being used in new voice and data installations.

Figure 7-12
The fiber-optic cable (right) can transmit as much information as the 1,500-pair copper-wire cable (left).

Figure 7-13
The round antenna on this tower is used for microwave transmission. Microwave transmission is limited to line-of-sight. Antennas are usually placed 25 to 75 miles apart.

Microwave Transmission

Microwaves are radio waves that can be used to provide high-speed transmission of both voice and data. Data is transmitted through the air from one microwave station to another in a manner similar to the way radio signals are transmitted (Figure 7-13). A disadvantage of microwaves is that they are limited to line-of-sight transmission. This means that microwaves must be transmitted in a straight line and that there can be no obstructions, such as buildings or mountains, between microwave stations. For this reason, microwave stations are characterized by antennas positioned on tops of buildings, towers, or mountains.

Satellite Transmission

Communications satellites receive microwave signals from earth, amplify the signals, and retransmit the signals back to earth. The microwave signals used by satellites are generally of a higher frequency than the signals used by terrestrial (earth-based) microwave equipment. **Earth stations** (Figure 7-14) are communications facilities that use large, dish-shaped antennas to transmit and receive data from satellites. The transmission *to* the satellite is called an **uplink** and the transmission *from* the satellite to a receiving earth station is called a **downlink**.

Many businesses with operations in multiple locations are now using private satellite systems to communicate information. If only a limited amount of information needs to be transmitted each day, such as daily sales results from a retail store, a small dish-shaped antenna can be used. **Very small aperture terminal** (VSAT) antenna measuring only one to three meters in size can transmit up to 19,200 bits per second. Higher speeds require larger antenna. The use of a private satellite using a VSAT antenna can be as low as $200 per month.

Communications satellites are usually placed about 22,300 miles above the earth in a **geosynchronous orbit** (Figure 7-15). This means that the satellite is placed in an orbit where it rotates with the earth, so the same antennas on earth that are used to send and receive signals can remain fixed on the satellite at all times.

Figure 7-14
Earth stations use large, dish-shaped antennas to communicate with satellites.

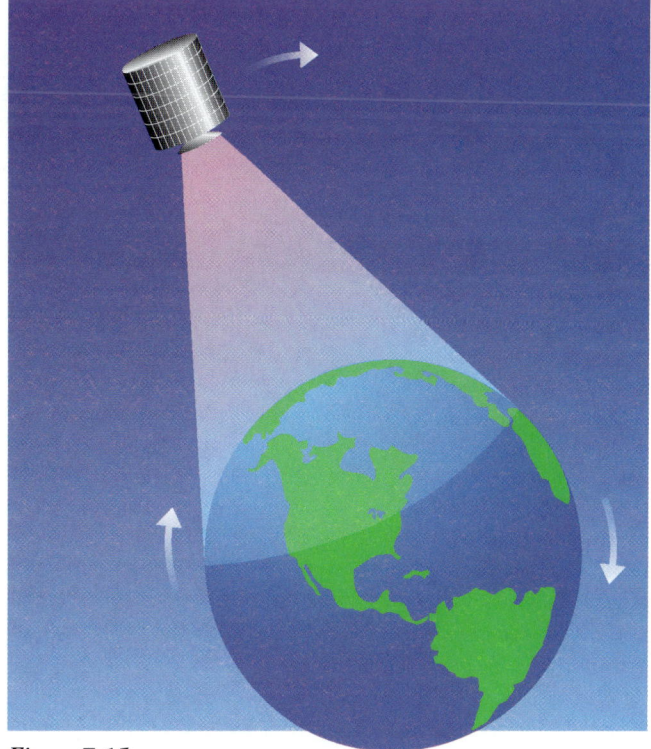

Figure 7-15
Communications satellites are placed in geosynchronous orbits approximately 22,300 miles above the earth. Geosynchronous means that the orbit of the satellite matches the rotation of the earth so the satellite is always above the same spot on the earth.

Several groups are planning on launching a series of low earth orbit (LEO) satellites between 1996 and 1998. For example, Motorola plans on launching 66 satellites as part of their Iridium system that will offer inexpensive, two-way voice and data communications from any spot on the globe. Because they will orbit only 400 to 500 miles above the earth, the LEO satellites will not be as expensive to build or launch as geosynchronous satellites. The closer distance will also mean that earth-based phones and other satellite communications equipment will not have to be as powerful.

Wireless Transmission

Wireless transmission uses one of three techniques to transmit data: light beams, radio waves, or carrier-connect radio, which uses the existing electrical wiring of a building to act as an antenna. These methods are sometimes used by companies to connect devices that are in the same general area such as an office or business park. For example, the unit shown in *Figure 7-16* uses light beams to transmit or receive data over a distance up to 70 feet. Local wireless systems offer design flexibility and portability but provide slower transmission speed than wired connections.

For longer distances, radio-wave wireless systems are becoming widely used. Motorola sells time on its ARDIS network that contains more than 1,100 base radio stations serving more than 8,000 cities in 50 states. Potential users include companies with large numbers of service personnel who need access to their company's computer data when they are at a customer site. For example, a repair technician may need to know the nearest location of a particular part. Using a portable radio data terminal *(Figure 7-17)* the technician could access the company's inventory database and obtain information about the availability of the required part.

A wireless device available to the general public that offers many of the same advantages as private radio networks is a cellular telephone. A **cellular telephone** uses radio waves to communicate with a local antenna assigned to a specific geographic area called a cell *(Figure 7-18)*. Cellular phones are often used in automobiles. As a cellular telephone user travels

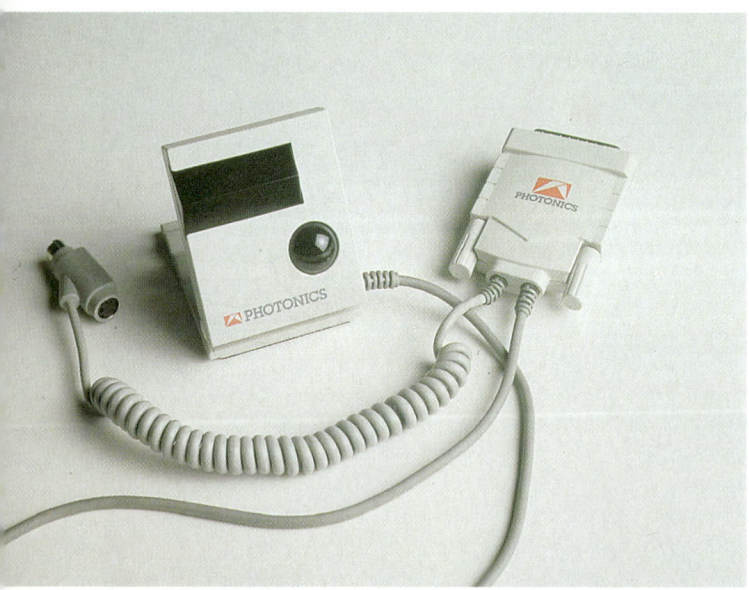

Figure 7-16
This wireless communication device from Photonics Corp. transmits data by bouncing infrared light beams off reflective surfaces such as a ceiling or a wall. The unit can also receive reflected light signals and convert them back to data. The device can transmit one million bits of data per second and has a range of thirty feet.

Figure 7-17
The portable terminal uses radio waves to communicate with a base radio station that is connected to a host computer. Using such a terminal, service technicians can instantly inquire as to the availability of repair parts.

from one cell to another, a computer that monitors the activity in each cell switches the conversation from one radio channel to another. By switching channels in this manner, the same channel can be used by another caller in a nonadjacent cell. Individual cells range from one to ten miles in width and use between 50 and 75 radio channels. Cellular telephone channels can be used for both voice and data transmission.

An Example of a Communications Channel

When data is transmitted over long distances, several different transmission media are generally used to make a complete communications channel. *Figure 7-19* on the next page illustrates how some of the various transmission media could be used to transmit data from a personal computer on the West Coast of the United States to a large computer on the East Coast. An example of the steps that could occur are as follows:

1. An entry is made on the personal computer. The data is sent over telephone lines from the computer to a microwave station.
2. The data is then transmitted from one microwave station to another.
3. The data is transmitted from the last microwave station to an earth station.
4. The earth station transmits the data to the communications satellite.
5. The satellite relays the data to another earth station on the other side of the country.
6. The data received at the earth station is transmitted to microwave stations.
7. The data is sent by telephone lines to the large computer.

This entire transmission process would take less than one second. Not all data transmission is as complex as this example, but such sophisticated communications systems do exist to meet the needs of some users.

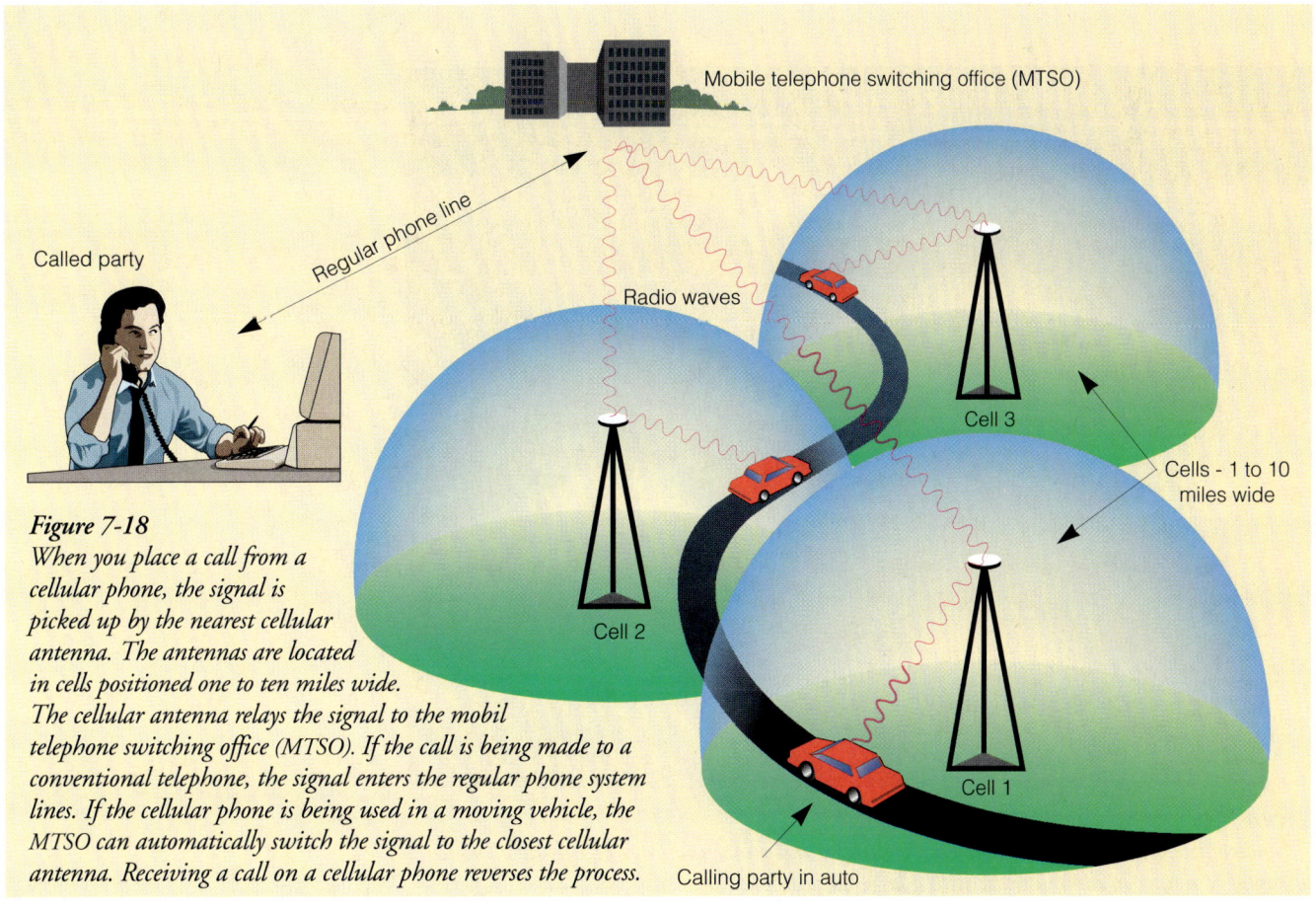

Figure 7-18
When you place a call from a cellular phone, the signal is picked up by the nearest cellular antenna. The antennas are located in cells positioned one to ten miles wide. The cellular antenna relays the signal to the mobil telephone switching office (MTSO). If the call is being made to a conventional telephone, the signal enters the regular phone system lines. If the cellular phone is being used in a moving vehicle, the MTSO can automatically switch the signal to the closest cellular antenna. Receiving a call on a cellular phone reverses the process.

Line Configurations

Two major **line configurations** (types of line connections) commonly used in communications are point-to-point lines and multidrop, or multipoint, lines.

Point-to-Point Lines

A **point-to-point line** is a direct line between a sending and a receiving device. It may be one of two types: a switched line or a dedicated line *(Figure 7-20)*.

SWITCHED LINE

A **switched line** uses a regular telephone line to establish a communications connection. Each time a connection is made, the line to be used for the call is selected by the telephone company switching stations (hence the name switched line). Using a switched line for communicating data is the same process as one person using a telephone to call another person. The communications equipment at the sending end dials the telephone number of the communications equipment at the receiving end. When the communications equipment at the receiving end answers the call, a connection is established and data can be transmitted. The process of establishing the communications connection is sometimes referred to as the **handshake**. When the transmission of data is complete, the communications equipment at either end terminates the call by hanging up and the line is disconnected.

An advantage of using switched lines is that a connection can be made between any two locations that have telephone service and communications equipment. For example, a personal computer could dial one computer to get information about the weather and then hang up and place a second call to another computer to get information about the stock market. A disadvantage of a switched line is that the quality of the line cannot be controlled because the line is chosen at random by the telephone company switching equipment. The cost of a switched line is the same for data communications as for a regular telephone call.

DEDICATED LINE

A **dedicated line** is a line connection that is always established (unlike the switched line where the line connection is reestablished each time it is used). The communications device at one end is always connected to the device at the other end. A user can create his or her own dedicated line connection by running a wire or cable between two points, such as between two offices or buildings, or the dedicated line can be provided

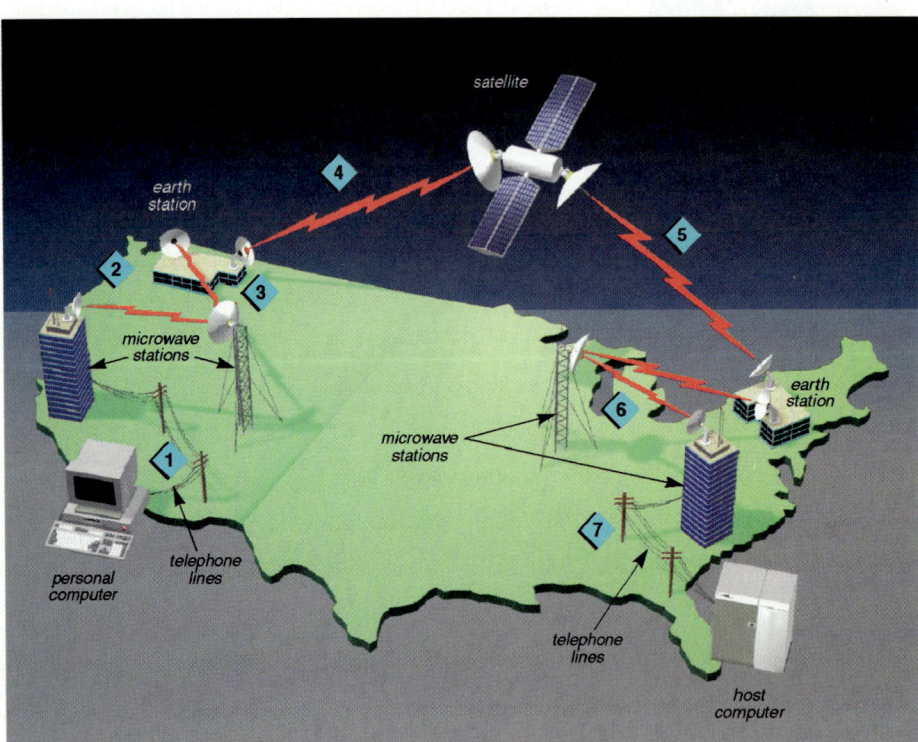

Figure 7-19
The use of telephone wires, microwave transmission, and a communications satellite allows a personal computer to communicate with a large host computer.

by an outside organization such as a telephone company or some other communications service company. If the dedicated line is provided by an outside organization, it is sometimes called a **leased line**, or a **private line**. The quality and consistency of the connection is better than on a switched line because a dedicated line is always established. Use of dedicated lines provided by outside organizations are usually charged on a flat-fee basis, which is a fixed amount each month regardless of how much time the line is actually used to transmit data. The cost of dedicated lines varies based on the distance between the two connected points and, sometimes, the speed at which data will be transmitted.

Multidrop Lines

The second major line configuration is called a **multidrop line**, or **multipoint line**. This type of line configuration is commonly used to connect multiple devices, such as terminals or personal computers, on a single line to a main computer, sometimes called a **host computer** *(Figure 7-21).*

For example, a ticket agent could use a terminal to enter an inquiry requesting flight information from a database stored on a main computer. While the request is being transmitted to the main computer, other terminals on the line are not able to transmit data. The time required for the data to be transmitted to the main computer, however, is short — most likely less than one second. As soon as the inquiry is received by the computer, a second terminal can send an inquiry. With such short delays, it appears to the users that no other terminals are using the line, even though multiple terminals may be sharing the same line.

The number of terminals to be placed on one line is a decision made by the designer of the system based on the anticipated amount of traffic on the line. For example, 100 or more terminals could be contained on a single line, provided each one would send only short messages, such as inquiries, and each terminal would use the communications line only a few hours per day. But if longer messages, such as reports, were required and if the terminals were to be used almost continuously, the number of terminals on one line would have to be smaller.

A leased line is almost always used for multidrop line configurations. The use of multidrop lines can decrease line costs considerably because one line is used by many terminals.

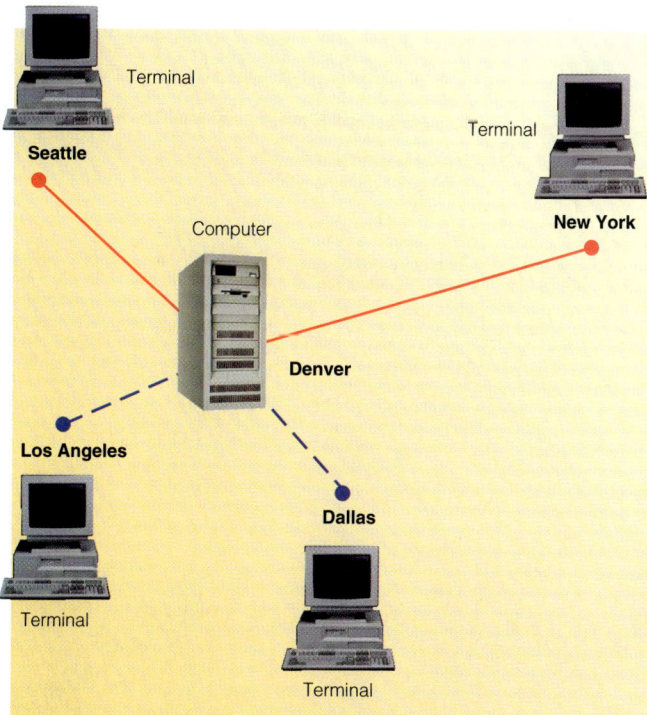

Figure 7-20
A point-to-point line configuration using both switched telephone (dial-up) lines (– – – –) and dedicated lines (———) are connected to a computer in Denver. The dedicated lines are always connected, whereas the switched lines have to be connected each time they are used.

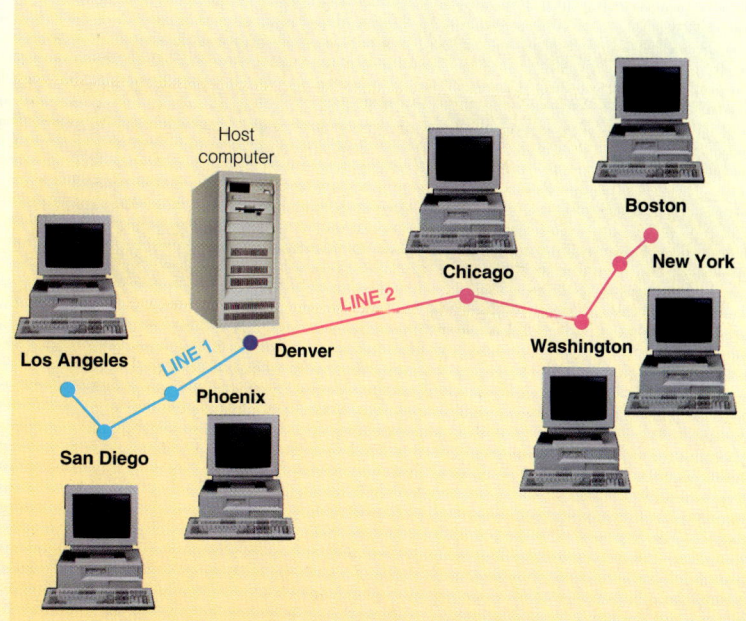

Figure 7-21
Two multidrop lines connect several cities with a computer in Denver. Each line is shared by terminals at several locations. Multidrop line configurations are less expensive than individual lines to each remote location.

Characteristics of Communications Channels

The communications channels just described can be categorized by a number of characteristics including the type of signal, transmission mode, transmission direction, and transmission rate.

Types of Signals: Digital and Analog

Computer equipment is designed to process data as **digital signals**, which are individual electrical pulses that represent the bits that are grouped together to form characters. Telephone equipment was originally designed to carry only voice transmission, which is comprised of a continuous electrical wave called an **analog signal** *(Figure 7-22)*. Thus, a special piece of equipment called a *modem* is required to convert the digital signals to analog signals so telephone lines can carry data. Modems are discussed in more detail later in this chapter.

To provide better communications services, telephone companies are now offering **digital data service**, communications channels specifically designed to carry digital instead of voice signals. Digital data service is available within and between all major metropolitan areas and provides higher speed and lower error rates than voice lines. Modems are not needed with digital data service; instead, users connect to the communications line through a device called a **digital service unit** (DSU).

Transmission Modes: Asynchronous and Synchronous

In **asynchronous transmission mode** *(Figure 7-23)*, individual bytes (made up of bits) are transmitted at irregular intervals, such as when a user enters data. To distinguish where one byte stops and another starts, the asynchronous transmission mode uses a start and a stop bit. An additional bit, called a *parity bit,* is sometimes included at the end of each byte. As you learned in the discussion of memory in Chapter 4, parity bits are used for error checking and they detect if one of the data bits has been changed during transmission. The asynchronous transmission mode is used for lower speed data transmission and is used with most communications equipment designed for personal computers.

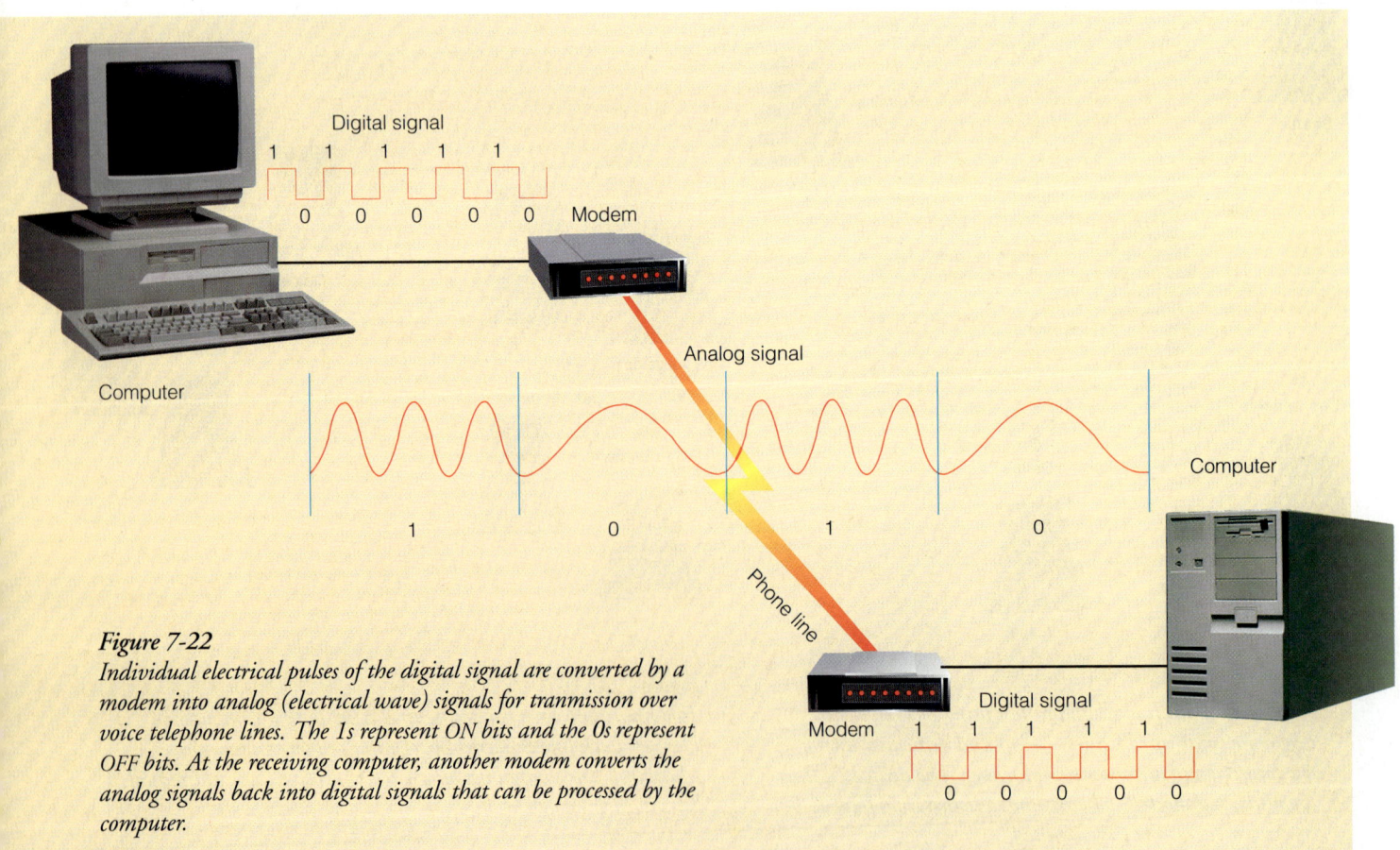

Figure 7-22
Individual electrical pulses of the digital signal are converted by a modem into analog (electrical wave) signals for tranmission over voice telephone lines. The 1s represent ON bits and the 0s represent OFF bits. At the receiving computer, another modem converts the analog signals back into digital signals that can be processed by the computer.

CHARACTERISTICS OF COMMUNICATIONS CHANNELS

In the **synchronous transmission mode** (Figure 7-23), large blocks of data are transmitted at regular intervals. Timing signals synchronize the communications equipment at both the sending and receiving ends and eliminate the need for start and stop bits for each byte. Error-check bits and start and stop bytes, called sync bytes, are also transmitted. Synchronous transmission requires more sophisticated and expensive equipment but it does give much higher speeds and accuracy than asynchronous transmission.

Direction of Transmission: Simplex, Half-Duplex, and Full-Duplex

The direction of data transmission is classified as either simplex, half-duplex, or full-duplex (Figure 7-24). In **simplex transmission**, data flows in one direction only. Simplex is used only when the sending device, such as a temperature sensor, never requires a response from the computer. For example, if a computer is used to control the temperature of a building, numerous sensors are placed throughout it. Each sensor is connected to the computer with a simplex transmission line because the computer only needs to receive data from the temperature sensors and does not need to send data back to the sensors.

In **half-duplex transmission**, data can flow in both directions but in only one direction at a time. An example is a citizens band radio. The user can talk or listen but not do both at the same time.

In **full-duplex transmission**, data can be sent in both directions at the same time. A normal telephone line is an example of full-duplex transmission. Both parties can talk at the same time. Full-duplex transmission is used for most interactive computer applications and for computer-to-computer data transmission.

Transmission Rate

The transmission rate of a communications channel is determined by its bandwidth and its speed. The **bandwidth** is the range of frequencies that a channel can carry. Because transmitted data can be assigned to different frequencies, the wider the bandwidth, the more frequencies. Thus, more data can be transmitted at the same time.

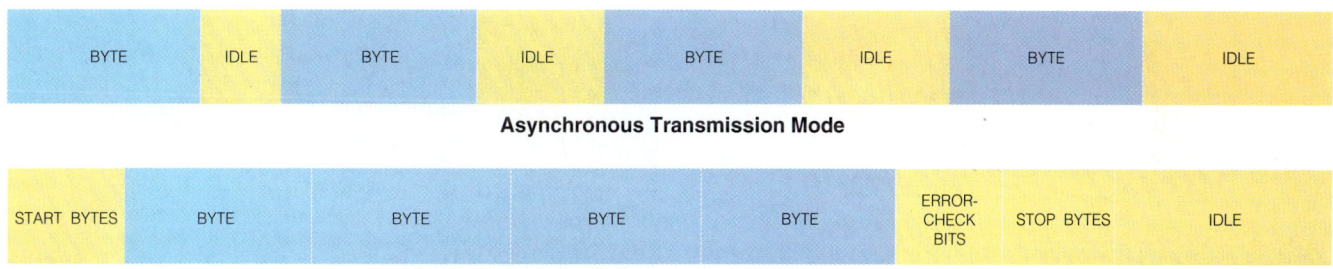

Figure 7-23
In asynchronous transmission mode, individual bytes are transmitted. Each byte has start, stop, and error-check bits. In synchronous transmission mode, multiple bytes are sent in a block with start bytes at the beginning of the block and error-check bits and stop bytes at the end of the block. Synchronous transmission is faster and more accurate.

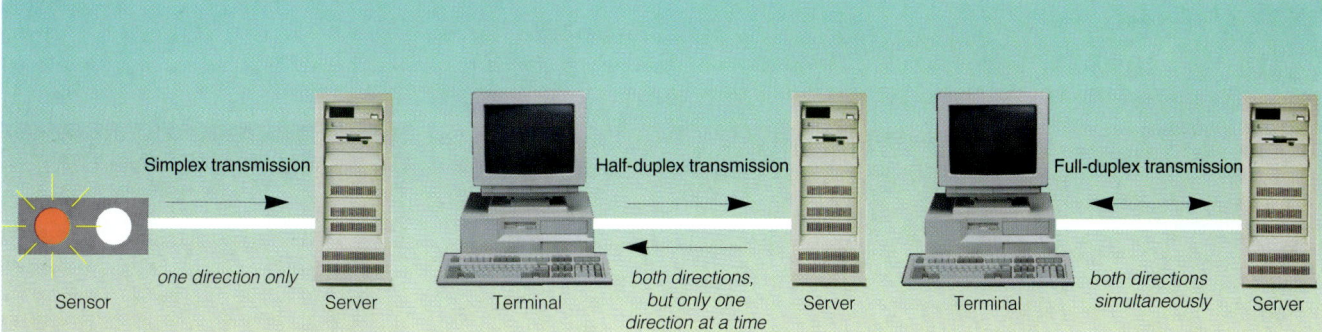

Figure 7-24
Simplex transmission allows data to flow in one direction only. Half-duplex transmission allows data to flow in both directions but not at the same time. Full-duplex transmission allows data to flow in both directions simultaneously.

The speed at which data is transmitted is usually expressed as bits per second or as a baud rate. **Bits per second (bps)** is the number of bits that can be transmitted in one second. Using a 10-bit byte to represent a character (7 data bits, 1 start, 1 stop, and 1 parity bit), a 9,600 bps transmission would transmit 960 characters per second. At this rate, a 20-page, single-spaced report that has an average of 3,000 characters per page would be transmitted in a little more than one minute. The **baud rate** is the number of times per second that the signal being transmitted changes. With each change, one or more bits can be transmitted. At speeds up to 2,400 bps, usually only one bit is transmitted per signal change and, thus, the bits per second and the baud rate are the same. To achieve speeds in excess of 2,400 bps, more than one bit is transmitted with each signal change and, thus, the bps will exceed the baud rate. *Figure 7-25* shows the range of transmission rates that can be achieved with different media. Each year, communications companies invent ways to increase these rates.

Communications Equipment

If a terminal or a personal computer is within approximately 1,000 feet of another computer, the two devices can usually be directly connected by a cable. At distances of more than 1,000 feet, however, the electrical signal weakens to the point that some type of special communications equipment is required to increase or change the signal to transmit it farther. A variety of communications equipment exists to perform this task, but the equipment that a user is most likely to encounter is a modem, a multiplexor, and a front-end processor. Computers that are connected to a network, which are discussed later in this chapter, usually require a network interface card.

Modems

A **modem** converts the digital signals of a terminal or computer to analog signals that are transmitted over a communications channel. It also converts analog signals it receives into digital signals that are used by a terminal or computer. The word modem comes from a combination of the words *mo*dulate, which means to change into a sound or analog signal, and *dem*odulate, which means to convert an analog signal into a digital signal. A modem is needed at both the sending and receiving ends of a communications channel.

MEDIA	RATE*
Twisted pair wire (voice-grade phone line)	300 bps to 28.8 Kbps
Twisted pair wire (direct connection)	1 to 10 Mbps
Coaxial cable	1 to 20 Mbps
Fiber-optic cable	up to 200 Mbps
Terrestial microwave	1.544 Mbps
Satellite microwave	64 to 512 Kbps
Wireless (radio wave)	4.8 to 19.2 Kbps

*RATE: bps — bits per second
Kbps — kilo (thousand) bits per second
Mbps — mega (million) bits per second

Figure 7-25
Transmission rates of different media.

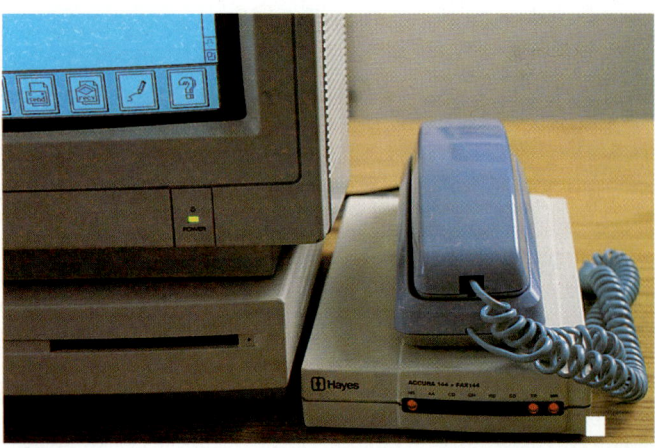

Figure 7-26
An external modem is connected to a terminal or computer and to a telephone outlet.

Figure 7-27
An internal modem is mounted inside a personal computer.

An **external modem** *(Figure 7-26)* is a separate, or stand-alone, device that is attached to the computer or terminal by a cable and to the telephone outlet by a standard telephone cord. An advantage of an external modem is that it can be easily moved from one terminal or computer to another.

An **internal modem** *(Figure 7-27)* is a circuit board installed inside a computer or terminal. Internal modems are generally less expensive than comparable external modems but once installed, they are not as easy to move.

Modems can transmit data at rates from 300 to 38,400 bits per second (bps). Most personal computers would use a modem between 2,400 and 14,400 bps. Business or heavier volume users would use faster and more expensive modems.

Multiplexors

A **multiplexor**, sometimes referred to as a MUX, combines more than one input signal into a single stream of data that can be transmitted over a communications channel *(Figure 7-28)*. The multiplexor at the sending end codes each character it receives with an identifier that is used by the multiplexor at the receiving end to separate the combined data stream into its original parts. A multiplexor may be connected to a separate modem or may have a modem built in. By combining the individual data streams into one, a multiplexor increases the efficiency of communications and saves the cost of individual communications channels.

Front-End Processors

A **front-end processor** is a computer that is dedicated to handling the communications requirements of a larger computer. Relieved of these tasks, the larger computer is then dedicated to processing data, while the front-end processor communicates the data. Tasks that the front-end processor would handle include **polling** (checking the connected terminals or computers to see if they have data to send), error checking and correction, and access security to make sure that a connected device or the user of the connected device is authorized to access the computer.

Network Interface Cards

A **network interface card** (NIC) fits in an expansion slot of a computer and attaches to the cable or wireless technology used to connect the devices in the network. The NIC has circuits that coordinate the transmission, receipt, and error checking of transmitted data.

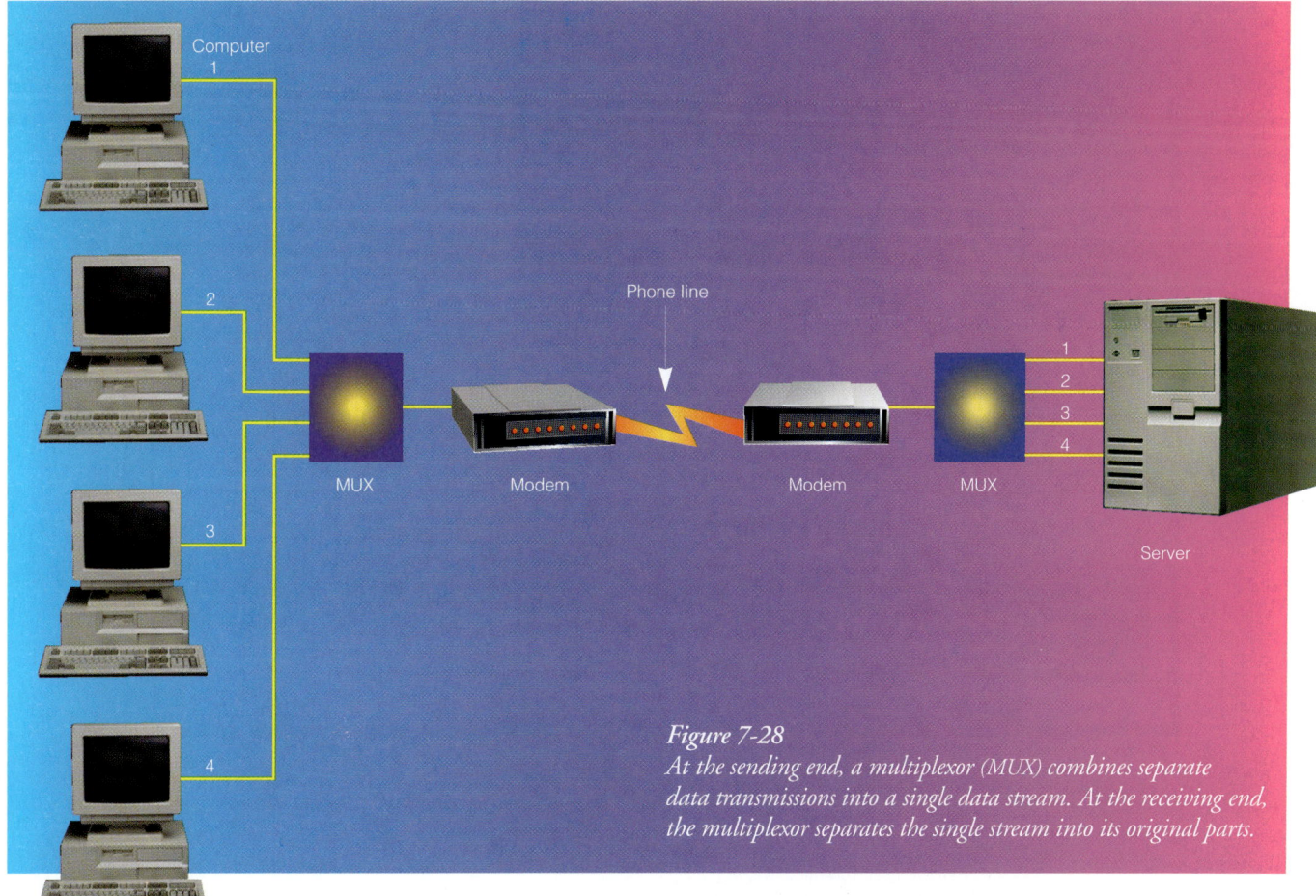

Figure 7-28
At the sending end, a multiplexor (MUX) combines separate data transmissions into a single data stream. At the receiving end, the multiplexor separates the single stream into its original parts.

Communications Software

Sometimes communications equipment is preprogrammed to accomplish its designed communications tasks. Other times, the user must load a program before transmitting data. These programs, referred to as **communications software**, can perform a number of tasks including dialing (if a switched telephone line is used), file transfer, terminal emulation, and data encryption.

Dialing software allows you to store, review, select, and dial telephone numbers of computers that can be called. The software provides a variety of meaningful messages to assist you in establishing a connection before transmitting data. For example, a person using a personal computer and a modem at home to communicate with a computer at the office could use dialing software to establish the communications connection. The software would display the office computer's telephone number on the user's personal computer screen. The user would enter the appropriate command for the dialing software to begin dialing the office computer and to establish a connection. During the 10 or 15 seconds of this process, the software would display messages to indicate specifically what was happening, such as "DIALING," "CARRIER DETECT" (which means that the office computer has answered), and "CONNECTED" (to indicate that the communications connection has been established and data transmission can begin).

File transfer software allows you to move one or more files from one system to another. Generally, you have to load the file transfer software on both the sending and receiving computers.

Terminal emulation software allows a personal computer to imitate or appear to be a specific type of terminal, so the personal computer can connect to another, usually larger, computer *(Figure 7-29)*. Most minicomputers and mainframes are designed to work with terminals that have specific characteristics such as speed and parity. Terminal emulation software performs the necessary speed and parity conversion.

Data encryption protects confidential data during transmission. **Data encryption** is the conversion of data at the sending end into an unrecognizable string of characters or bits and the reconversion of the data at the receiving end. Without knowing how the data was encrypted, someone who intercepted the transmitted data would have a difficult time determining what the data meant.

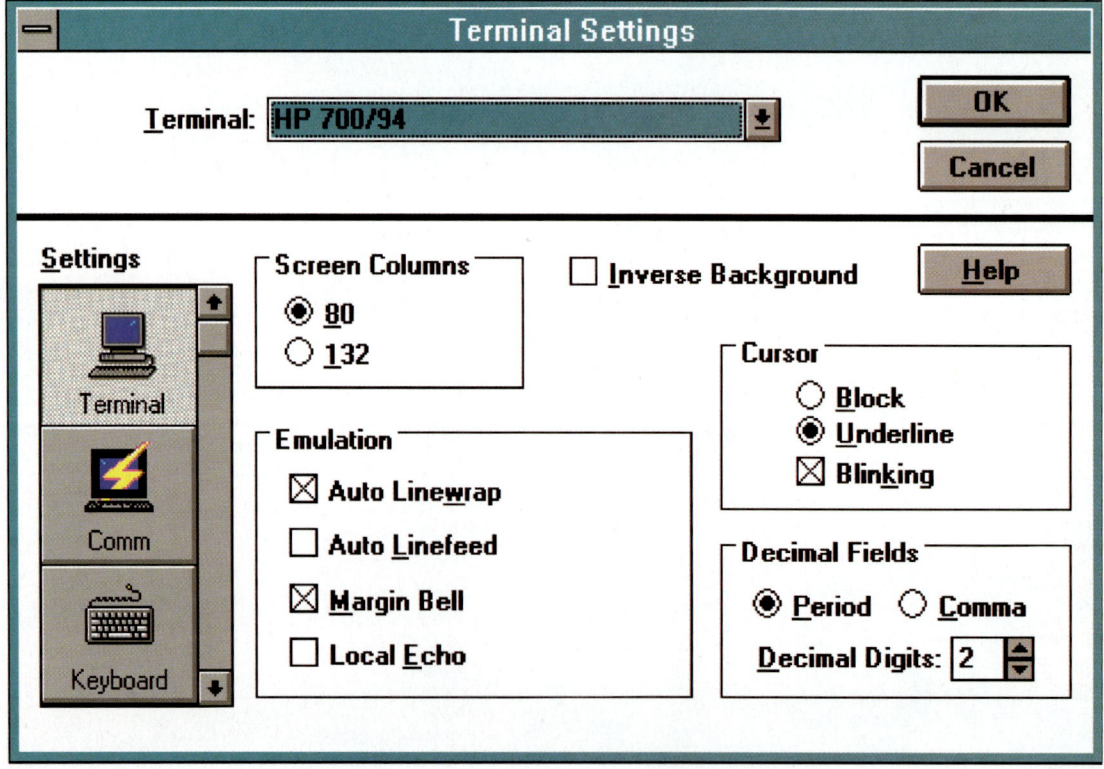

Figure 7-29
Terminal emulation software makes a personal computer function as if it were a particular type of terminal. Terminal emulation software is often used to allow PCs to communicate with larger systems such as minicomputers or mainframes. This screen, from Crosstalk for Windows, shows how a personal computer is set up to emulate a Hewlett-Packard (HP) model 700/94 terminal.

Communications Protocols

Communications software is written to work with one or more protocols. A **protocol** is a set of rules and procedures for exchanging information between computers. Protocols define how the communications link is established, how information is transmitted, and how errors are detected and corrected. Using the same protocol, different types and makes of computers can communicate with each other. Over the years, numerous protocols have been developed. The table shown in *Figure 7-30* lists some of the more widely used protocols. Today, however, there are strong efforts to establish standards that all computer and communications equipment manufacturers will follow. The International Standards Organization (ISO) based in Geneva, Switzerland has defined a set of communications protocols called the **Open Systems Interconnection** (OSI) model. The OSI model has been endorsed by the United Nations.

Communications Networks

A communications **network** is a collection of terminals, computers, and other equipment that uses communications channels to share data, information, hardware, and software. Networks can be classified as either local area networks or wide area networks.

Local Area Networks (LANs)

A **local area network,** or LAN, is a privately owned communications network that covers a limited geographic area such as a school computer laboratory, an office, a building, or a group of buildings.

The LAN consists of a communications channel that connects either a series of computer terminals together with a minicomputer or, more commonly, a group of personal computers to one another. Very sophisticated LANs can connect a variety of office devices such as word processing equipment, computer terminals, video equipment, and personal computers.

Three common applications of local area networks are hardware, software, and information resource sharing. **Hardware resource sharing** allows each personal computer in the network to access and use devices that would be too expensive to provide for each user or would not be justified for each

PROTOCOL	DESCRIPTION
Ethernet	One of the most widely used protocols for LANS
Token ring	Uses an electronic token to avoid transmission conflict by only allowing one device to transmit at at time
PowerTalk	Links Apple Macintosh computers
FDDI	Fiber Distributed Data Interface; high-speed fiber-optic protocol
SNA	System Network Architecture; primarily used to link large systems
TCP/IP	Transmission Control Protocol/Internet Protocol; used on the Internet
X.25	International standard for packet switching
ATM	Asynchronous Transfer Mode; recently developed protocol for transmitting voice, data, and video over any type of media
IPX	Used on Novell Netware networks
Xmodem	PC protocol that uses 128-byte blocks
Ymodem	PC protocol that uses 1,024-byte blocks
Zmodem	PC protocol that uses 512-byte blocks
Kermit	PC protocol that uses variable-length blocks

Figure 7-30
Some of the more commonly used communications protocols. Protocols specify the procedures that are used during transmission.

user because of only occasional use. For example, when a number of personal computers are used on the network, each may need to use a laser printer. Using a LAN, a laser printer could be purchased and made a part of the network. Whenever a user of a personal computer on the network needed the laser printer, it could be accessed over the network. *Figure 7-31* depicts a simple local area network consisting of four personal computers linked together by a cable. Three of the personal computers (computer 1 in the sales and marketing department, computer 2 in the accounting department, and computer 3 in the personnel department) are available for use at all times. Computer 4 is used as a **server**, a computer dedicated to handling the communications needs of the other computers in the network. The users of this LAN have connected the laser printer to the server. Using the LAN, all computers and the server can use the printer. In small networks, the server computer can also be used to run applications, along with the other computers on the network. In large networks, the server is usually dedicated to providing network services such as hardware, software, and information resource sharing.

Software resource sharing consists of storing frequently used software on the hard disk of the server so the software can be accessed by multiple users. Sharing software is a common practice for both in-house and commercial software. Many software vendors now sell a network version of their software. When a commercial software package is accessed by many users, it is sometimes necessary to obtain a special agreement from the software vendor called a **site license**. The site license fee is usually based on the number of computers on the network and is less than if individual copies of the software package were purchased for each computer.

Information resource sharing allows anyone using a personal computer on the local area network to access data stored on any other computer in the network. In actual practice, hardware resource sharing and information resource sharing are often combined. For example, in *Figure 7-31*, the daily sales records could be stored on the hard disk associated with the server unit personal computer. Anyone needing access to the sales records could use this information resource. The capability to access and store data on common secondary storage is an important feature of many local area networks.

Information resource sharing is usually provided by using either the file-server or client-server method. Using the

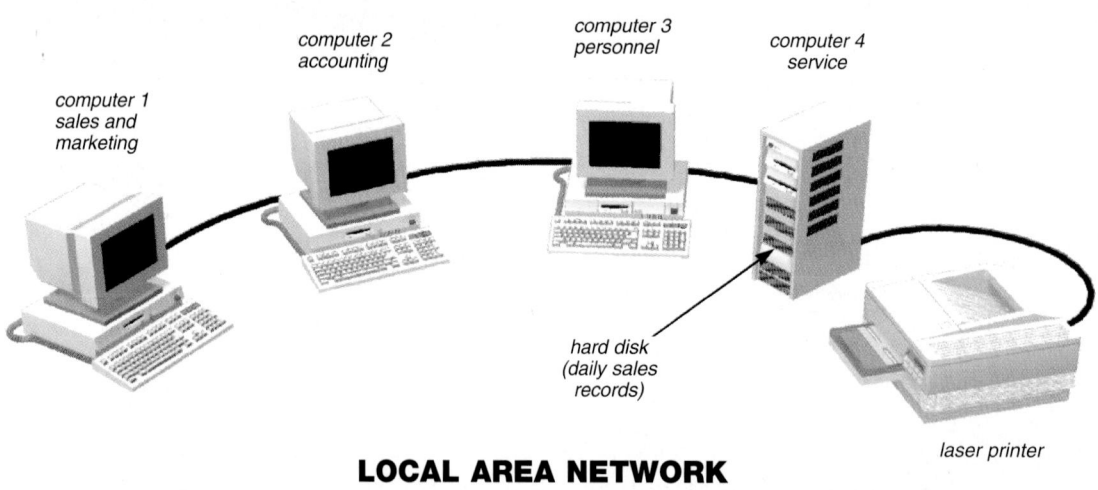

Figure 7-31
A local area network (LAN) consists of multiple personal computers or terminals connected to one another. The LAN allows users to share hardware and information.

file-server method, the server sends an entire file at a time. The requesting computer then performs the processing. With the **client-server** method, as much processing as possible is done on the server system before data is transmitted.

Figure 7-32 illustrates how the two methods would process a request for information stored on the server system for customers with balances over $1,000. With the file-server method, the user transmits a request for the customer file to the server unit (1). The server unit locates the customer file (2) and transmits the entire file to the requesting computer (3). The requesting computer selects customers with balances over $1,000 and prepares the report (4).

With the client-server method, the user transmits a request for customers with a balance over $1,000 to the server unit (1). The server unit selects the customer records that meet the criteria (2) and transmits the selected records to the requesting computer (3). The requesting computer prepares the report (4). The client-server method greatly reduces the amount of data sent over a network but requires a more powerful server system.

A local area network does not have to use a single server computer. A **peer-to-peer network** allows any computer to share the software, data, or hardware (such as a printer) located on any other computer in the network. Peer-to-peer networks are appropriate for a small number of users who primarily work on their own computers and only occasionally need to use the resources of other computers.

Simple peer-to-peer networks need a minimum amount of software to manage their activities. Often the necessary software is provided by the manufacturer of the network interface cards or other hardware used to link the networked systems. Artisoft's LANtastic, Microsoft's Windows for Workgroups, and Apple's AppleTalk are examples of peer-to-peer network software. Client-server networks, however, need more sophisticated software, called a network operating system, to keep them running efficiently. A **network operating system (NOS)** is software that allows a user to manage the resources of a computer network. The NOS runs on the server computer in addition to the client operating systems, such as DOS, Windows, or OS/2, that run on the individual computers that make up the network. A NOS usually provides the following capabilities:

- **Administration** Adding, deleting, and organizing client users and performing maintenance tasks such as backup.

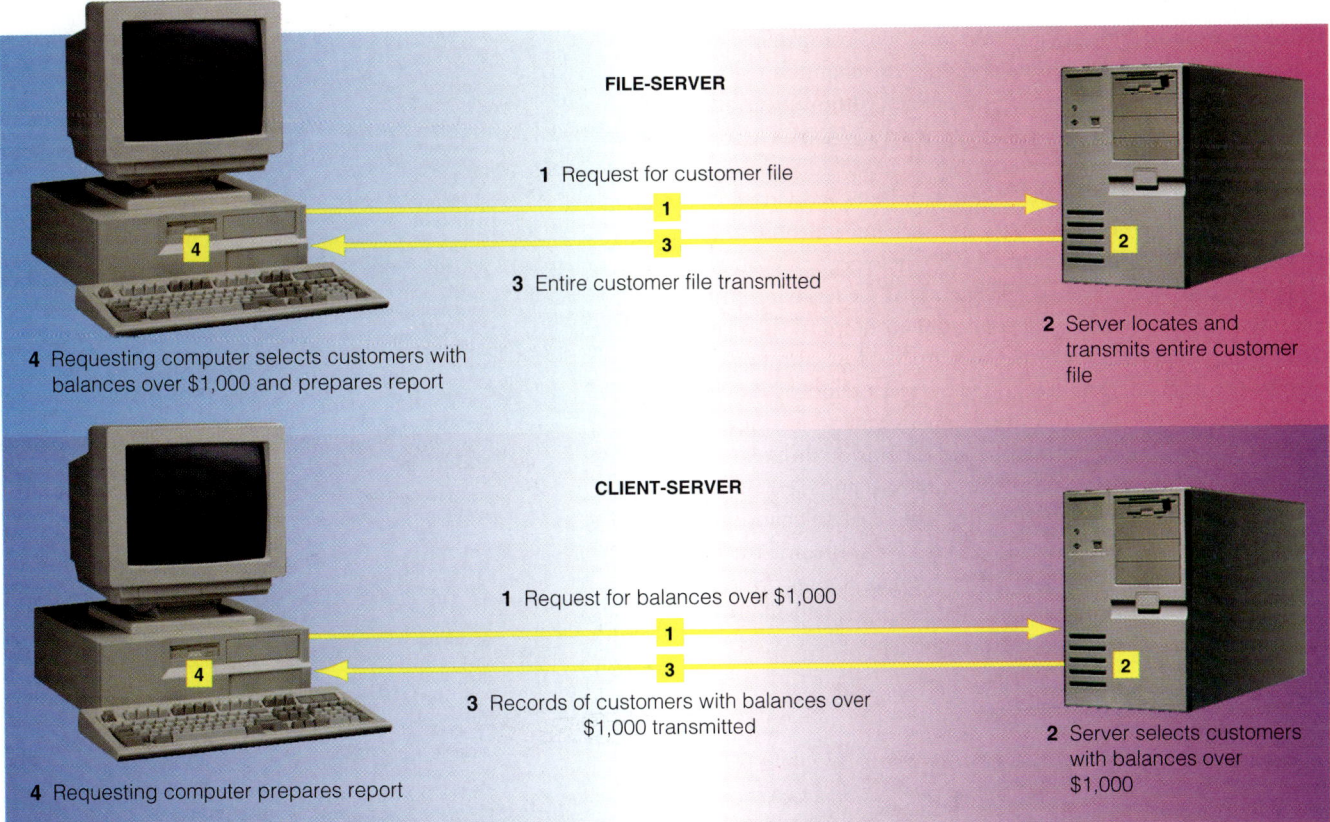

Figure 7-32
A request for information about customers with balances over $1,000 would be processed differently by file-server and client-server networks.

- **File Management** The capability to quickly locate and transfer files from the server to the client computers.
- **Printer Management** The capability to prioritize print jobs and direct reports to specific printers on the network.
- **Security** The capability to restrict access to network resources. Novell's Netware, Microsoft's Advanced NT Server, and IBM's LAN Server are examples of network operating systems.

Wide Area Networks (WANs)

A **wide area network**, or WAN, is geographic in scope (as opposed to local) and uses telephone lines, microwaves, satellites, or a combination of communications channels. A wide area network limited to the area surrounding a city is sometimes referred to as a **metropolitan area network**, or MAN. Public wide area network companies include so-called **common carriers** such as the telephone companies. Telephone company deregulation has encouraged a number of companies to build their own wide area networks. For example, EDS has built one of the larger private communications networks (Figure 7-33) to handle the needs of its computer services business and the needs of its parent company, General Motors.

Communications companies, such as MCI, have built WANs to compete with other communications companies. Companies called **value-added carriers** lease channels from the common carriers to provide specialized communications services referred to as **value-added networks** (VANs). For example, Tymnet, Inc. operates a VAN that provides packet-switching services. **Packet-switching** combines individual packets of information from various users and transmits them together over a high-speed channel. The messages are separated and distributed over lower speed channels at the receiving end. Sharing the high-speed channel is more economical than each user having their own high-speed channel. Most common carriers are now offering **Integrated Services Digital Network** (ISDN) services. ISDN is an international standard for the digital transmission of both voice and data using different channels and communications companies. Using ISDN lines, data can be transmitted over one or more separate channels at 64,000 bits per second. Future plans for ISDN include the use of fiber-optic cable that will allow transmission rates up to 2.2 billion bits per second. These higher speeds will allow full-motion video images to be transmitted.

Figure 7-33
The control room for EDSNET, the private communications network of Electronic Data Systems Corporation (EDS). The network was built by EDS spanning a three-year period and with a cost of more than $1 billion. The network provides communications for EDS, its computer services customers, and its parent company, General Motors.

The Internet

The largest and best known wide area network is the Internet. The **Internet** is a worldwide network of computer networks. It is difficult to give numbers for the size of the Internet because of its rapid growth. In late 1994, it was estimated that the Internet consisted of the following:
- 30 million users worldwide
- Users located in 100 countries
- 20,000 member organizations
- 21,000 connected networks
- 2 million connected computers

Because of its tremendous size and number of users, some have called the Internet a "virtual community." The Internet was originally started in 1969 as a way of linking government researchers at four universities. Other university and private research sites were added over the years. The Internet really started to grow in the late 1980s when a number of public and private networks were joined together with the National Science Foundation network. Since 1988, the Internet has doubled in size every year. Some of the services and resources available on the Internet include the following:

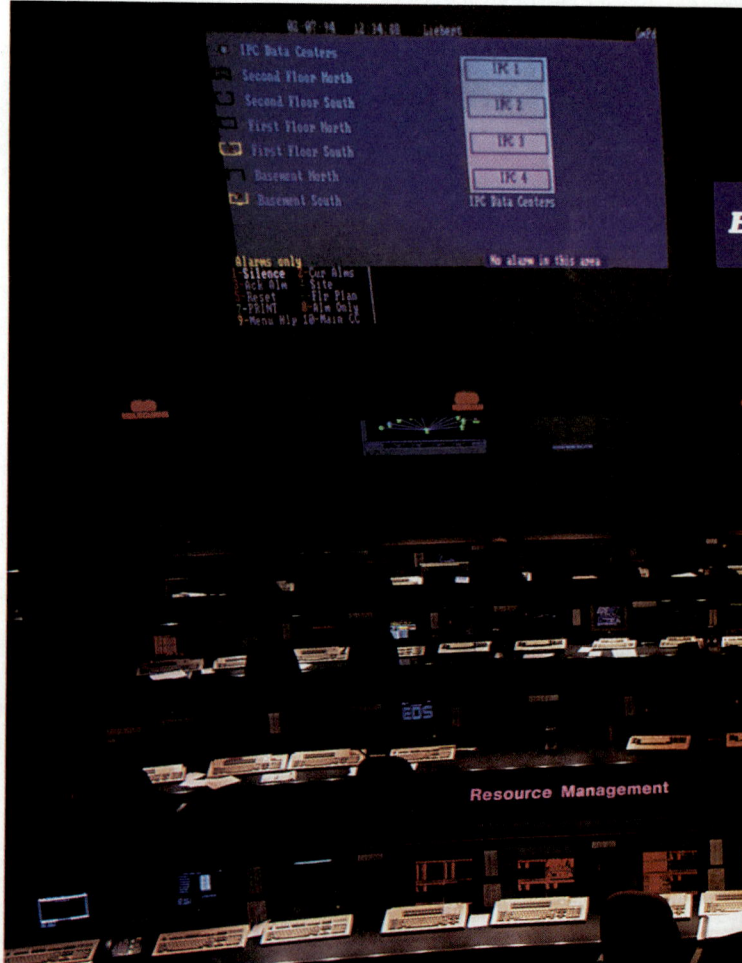

- **Electronic mail** E-mail can be sent anywhere in the world to users with an Internet address. Addresses can be obtained free of charge.
- **File transfer** Thousands of files on countless subjects are available for transfer.
- **Database search** More than 200 universities and several public libraries have their databases online and available for review. Internet offers several tools for finding information on a particular subject.
- **Remote logon** The capability to run a program located on another computer.
- **Discussion and news groups** Thousands of discussion topics currently exist, or you can start your own on a subject of interest.
- **Games** A variety of single and multiple player games.

Students can usually gain access to the Internet through one of their school's computer systems. Most colleges and universities have access. Individuals can gain access through many of the online service providers. Businesses or other organizations that want to regularly use the Internet can obtain direct connection rights. For further examples of using the Internet, see page 7.43.

Network Configurations

The configuration, or physical layout, of the equipment in a communications network is called **topology**. Communications networks are usually configured in one or a combination of three patterns. These configurations are star, bus, and ring networks. Although these configurations can be used with wide area networks, they are illustrated here with local area networks. Devices connected to a network, such as terminals, printers, or other computers, are referred to as **nodes**.

Star Network

A **star network** contains a central computer and one or more terminals or personal computers connected to it, forming a star. A pure star network consists of only point-to-point lines between the terminals and the computer, but most star networks, such as the one shown on the next page in *Figure 7-34,* include both point-to-point lines and multidrop lines. A star network configuration is often used when the central

computer contains all the data required to process the input from the terminals, such as an airline reservation system. For example, if inquiries are being processed in the star network, all the data to answer the inquiry would be contained in the database stored on the central computer.

A star network can be relatively efficient and close control can be kept over the data processed on the network. Its major disadvantage is that the entire network is dependent on the central computer and the associated hardware and software. If any of these elements fail, the entire network is disabled. Therefore, in most large star networks, backup computer systems are available in case the primary system fails.

Bus Network

When a **bus network** is used, all the devices in the network are connected to and share a single cable. Information is transmitted in either direction from any one personal computer to another. Any message can be directed to a specific device. An advantage of the bus network is that devices can be attached or detached from the network at any point without disturbing the rest of the network. In addition, if one computer on the network fails, this does not affect the other users of the network. *Figure 7-31* on page 7.22 illustrates a simple bus network.

Ring Network

A **ring network** does not use a centralized host computer. Instead, a circle of computers communicate with one another *(Figure 7-35)*. A ring network can be useful when the processing is not done at a central site, but at local sites. For example, computers could be located in three departments: accounting, personnel, and shipping and receiving. The computers in each of these departments could perform the processing required for each of the departments. On occasion, however, the computer in the shipping and receiving department could communicate with the computer in the accounting department to update certain data stored on the accounting department computer. Data travels around a ring network in one direction

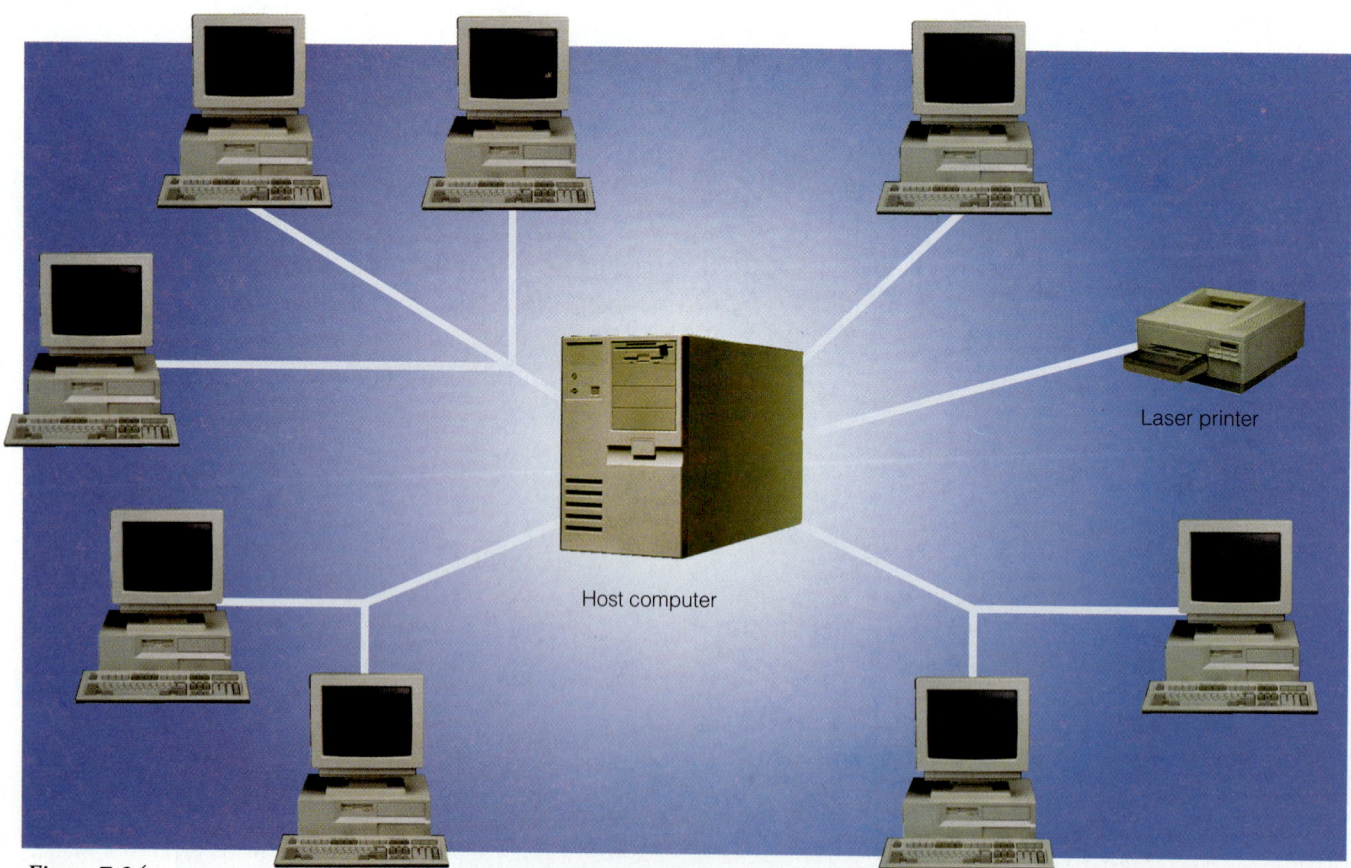

Figure 7-34
A star network contains a single, centralized host computer with which all the terminals or personal computers in the network communicate. Both point-to-point and multidrop lines can be used in a star network.

only and passes through each node. Thus, one disadvantage of a ring network is that if one node fails, the entire network fails because the data does not get past the failed node. An advantage of a ring network is that less cable is usually needed than for a star network and therefore network cabling costs are lower.

A common type of ring network is called a token ring network. A **token ring network** constantly circulates an electronic signal, called a token, around the network. Devices on the network that want to send a message take the token and attach it to their data. When it is attached to data, the token is not available for other devices to use. When data is delivered to its destination, the data is replaced with an acknowledgment that the data was received. When the original sending device receives the token and the acknowledgment, the token is again made available for other devices to use.

Connecting Networks

Certain circumstances require you to connect separate networks. You do this by using gateways, bridges, and routers. A **gateway** is a combination of hardware and software that allows users on one network to access the resources on a *different* type of network. For example, a gateway could be used to connect a local area network of personal computers to a mainframe computer network. A **bridge** is a combination of hardware and software used to connect *similar* networks. For example, if a company had similar but separate local area networks of personal computers in its accounting and marketing departments, the networks could be connected with a bridge. In this example, using a bridge makes more sense than joining all the personal computers together in one large network because the individual departments only occasionally need to access information on the other network. A router is used when several networks are connected together. A **router** is an intelligent network-connecting device that can route communications traffic directly to the appropriate network. In the case of a partial network failure, routers are smart enough to determine alternate routes.

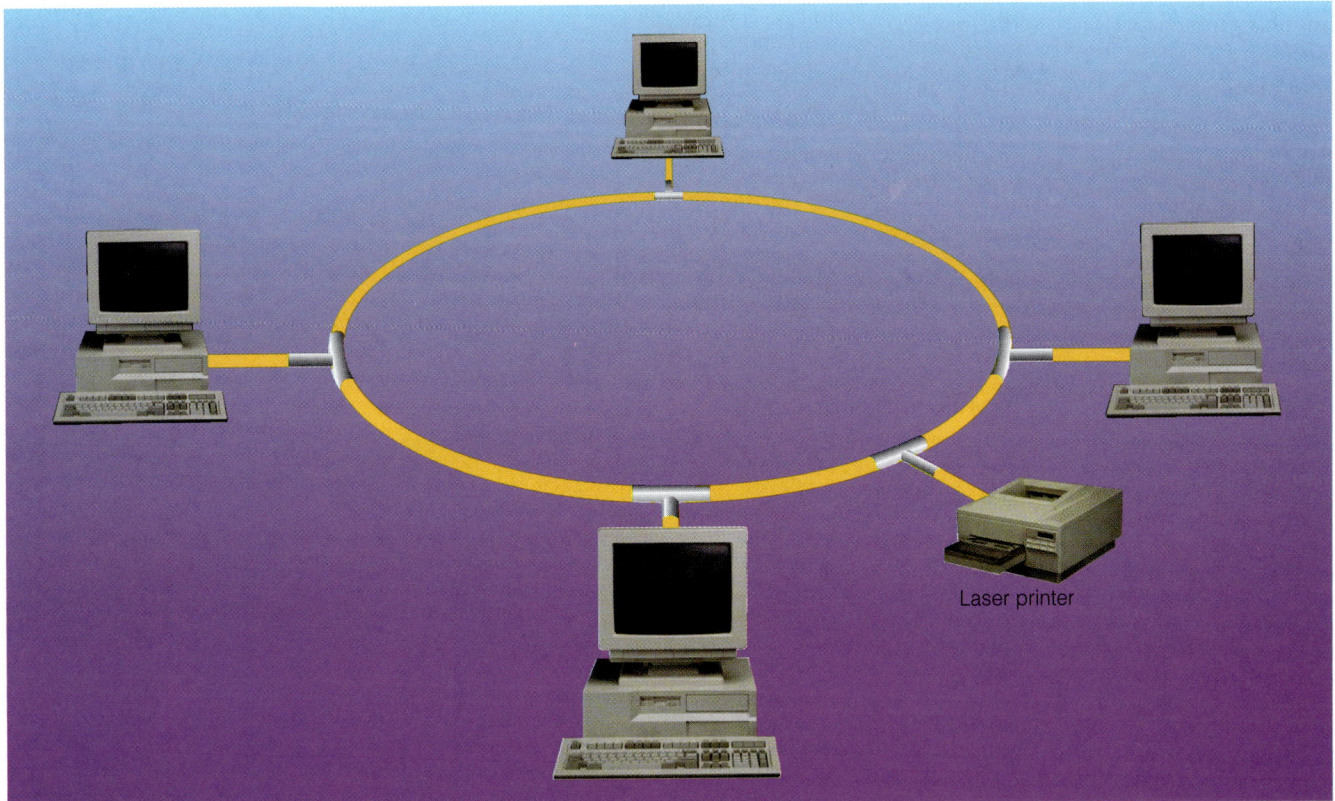

Figure 7-35
In a ring network, all computers are connected in a continous loop. Data flows around the ring in one direction only.

An Example of a Communications Network

The diagram in *Figure 7-36* illustrates how two personal computer networks and a mainframe computer can be connected to share information with each other and with outside sources.

The marketing department operates a bus network of four personal computers (1). Frequently used marketing data and programs are stored in the server unit (2). The personal computers in the marketing department share a laser printer (3). A modem (4) is attached to the marketing server unit so outside sales representatives can use a dial telephone line (5) to call the marketing system and obtain product price information.

The administration department operates a bus network of three personal computers (6). As with the marketing network, common data and programs are stored on a server unit (7) and the administration personal computers share a laser printer (8). Because the administration department sometimes needs information from the marketing system, the two similar networks are connected with a LAN bridge (9). The bridge allows users on either network to access data or programs on the other network.

Administration department users sometimes need information from the company's mainframe computer system (10). They can access the mainframe through the use of a gateway (11) that allows different types of network systems to be connected. All communications with the mainframe computer are controlled by a front-end processor (12). A dial telephone line (13) connected to a modem (14) allows remote users to call the mainframe and allows mainframe users to call other computers. A leased telephone line (15) and a modem (16) are used for a permanent connection to

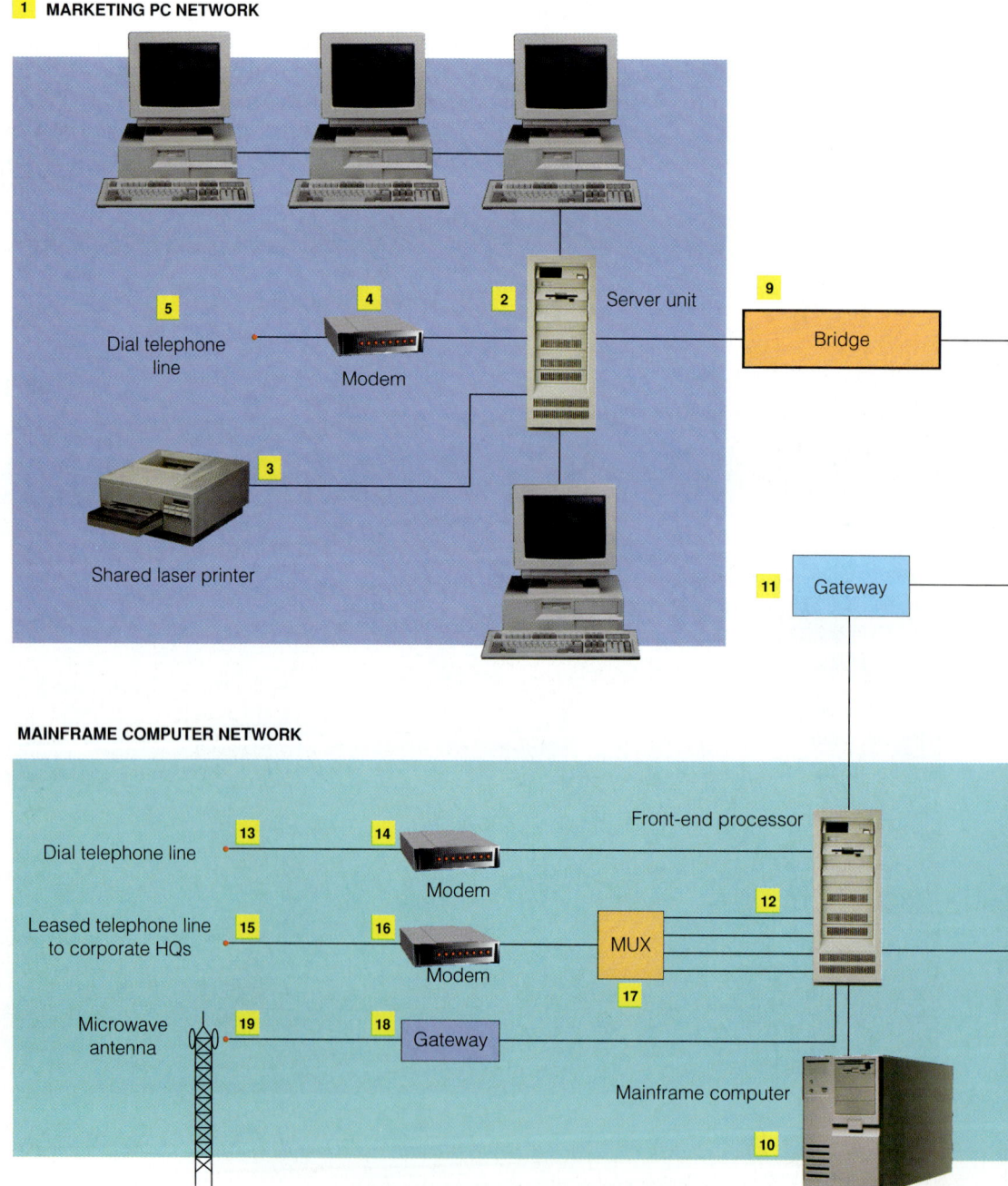

Summary of Communications and Networks

the computer at the corporate headquarters, several hundred miles away. The leased line can carry the signals of up to four different users. The signals are separated by the use of a multiplexor (MUX) (17). A gateway (18) connects the front-end processor and mainframe system to a microwave antenna (19) on the roof of the building. The microwave antenna sends and receives data from a computer at the manufacturing plant located two miles away. The front-end processor also controls mainframe computer terminals located throughout the company (20).

Communications will continue to affect how people work and how they use computers. Individuals and organizations are no longer limited to local data resources but instead, with communications capabilities, they can obtain information from anywhere in the world at electronic speed. With communications technology rapidly changing, today's businesses are challenged to find ways to adapt the technology to provide better products and services for their customers and make their operations more efficient. Networks are one way that organizations are making individual computers more powerful. By joining individual computers into networks, computing resources are expanded and the ability of individuals to communicate with each other is increased. For individuals, the new technology offers increased access to worldwide information and services and provides new opportunities in business and education.

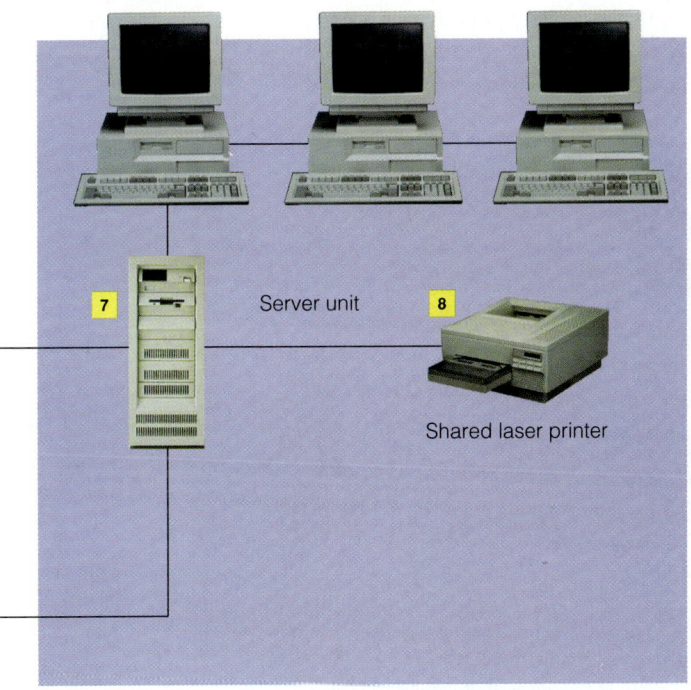

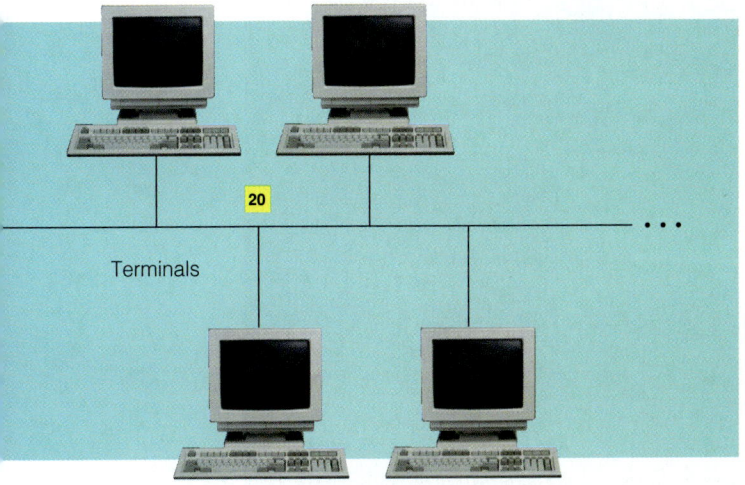

Figure 7-36
The two personal computer networks are connected together with a bridge. A gateway is used to connect the administration personal computer network with the mainframe. All communications with the mainframe are controlled by a separate computer called a front-end processor. Modems are used to connect the networks to leased and dial telephone lines.

COMPUTERS AT WORK

Satellites Help Track Moving Vans

Have you ever stayed around the house or apartment all day waiting for an item to be delivered by truck? When you call the trucking company, all they can tell you is, "the truck is on the way!" This is not the case with North American Van Lines. If you ship your items with North American, they can tell you the exact location of their trucks within 1,000 feet. North American, the fifth largest trucking company in the United States, has outfitted its trucks with a two-way satellite communications system manufactured by Qualcomm of San Diego, California. Besides being able to pinpoint the location of its trucks, North American can instantly communicate with the drivers. There is no longer a wait until the driver pulls off the road to call in. The two-way communication feature allows North American to direct its drivers to pick up additional cargo as they pass through an area. Before they had the systems, drivers might have driven through an area not knowing that a load was waiting. The system offers benefits to the drivers, as well. If a driver runs into trouble because of bad weather or a mechanical breakdown, he or she can send a message to the home office in Indiana *(Figure 7-36)*. Even if the truck is in the middle of a snow storm on a stretch of deserted highway, the message will get through instantly. The system has even been used to dispatch emergency help to the scenes of accidents. Like many other business systems that have been computerized, the benefits of the North American Van Lines system may one day be made directly available to North American customers. North American is considering allowing its regular customers who frequently ship high-tech cargo such as computers and medical equipment to directly access the tracking system.

Figure 7-36

IN THE FUTURE

The Information Superhighway

Many believe that the path to the future may be along what has been called the **Information Superhighway**; a nationwide and eventually worldwide network of information and services. Originally proposed as part of the 1991 High Performance Computing and Communications (HPCC) initiative, the scope of the U.S. network was expanded in 1993 as part of the **National Information Infrastructure** (NII). The NII is envisioned as a high-speed digital network that will make information services, training, education, medical services, and government data available to everyone, including individuals as well as businesses and larger organizations. Universal access is one of the key principles of NII.

Some of the preliminary work on a nationwide network is already being accomplished by private organizations such as cable TV and telephone companies. This is consistent with the NII plan to allow private companies to construct and operate much of the network. The U.S. government's challenge is to provide guidelines, standards, and incentives to make sure that separately constructed parts of the network can communicate with each other and that all individuals have access to the network at a reasonable price. Several other countries have similar nationwide networks planned or under development. Eventually, all these networks could be linked together using software that automatically translates one language into another.

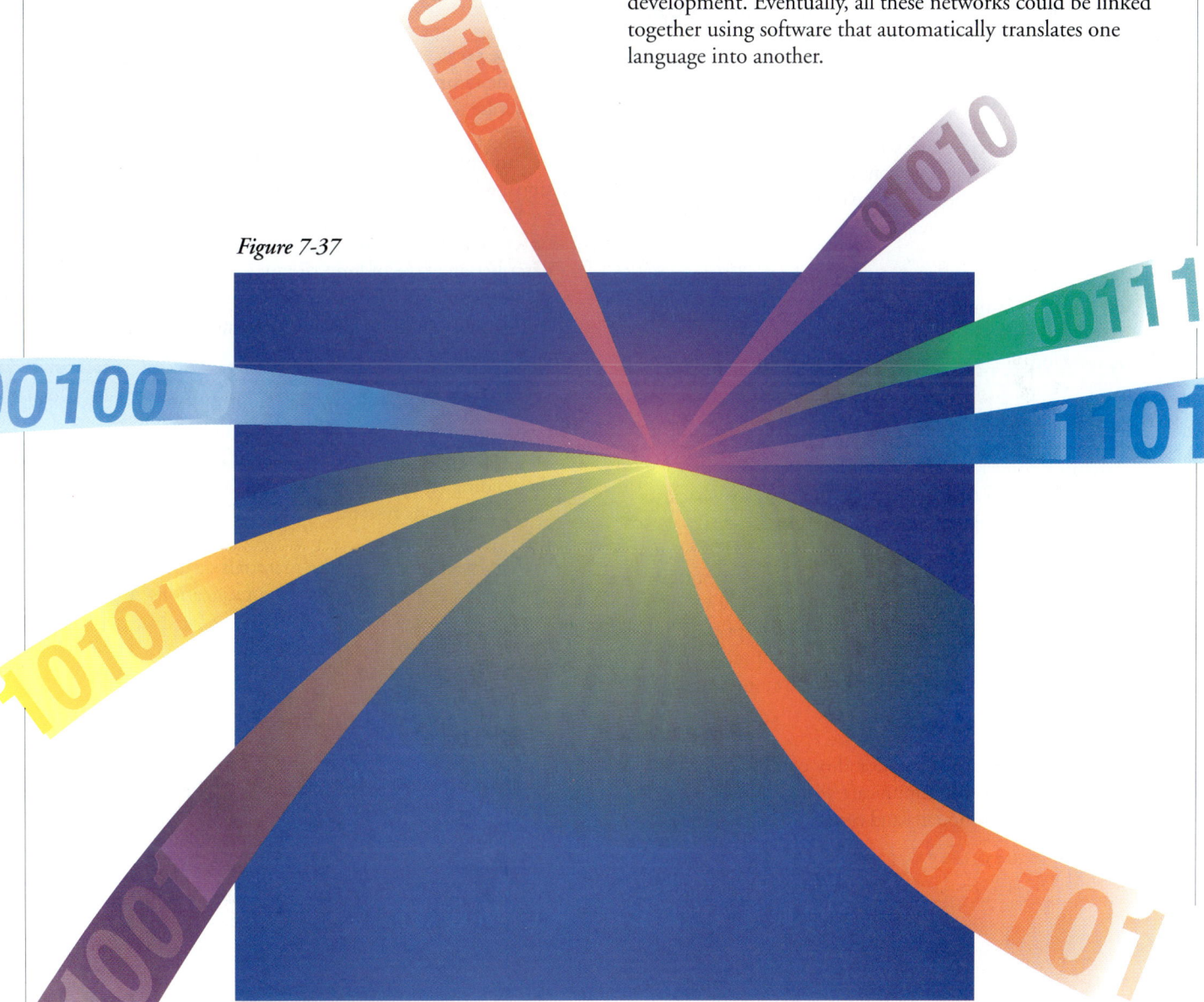

Figure 7-37

What You Should Know

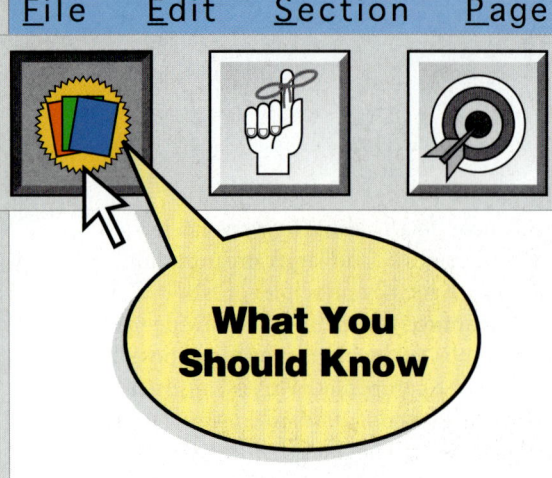

1. The capability of a computer to communicate with other computers, sometimes called connectivity, allows users to quickly and directly access data and information that otherwise would have been unavailable or that probably would have taken considerable time to acquire.

2. **Electronic mail** is the capability to use computers to transmit messages and receive messages from other computer users.

3. **Voice mail,** which can be considered verbal electronic mail, digitizes a caller's message so it can be stored on disk like other computer data.

4. Today, **teleconferencing** usually means video conferencing, the use of computers and television cameras to transmit video images and the sound of the participant(s) to a remote location that has compatible equipment.

5. **Facsimile,** or FAX, equipment is used to transmit a reproduced image of a document over phone lines. FAX machines convert the image into digitized data that is transmitted and then convert the digitized data back into its original image at the receiving end.

6. **Groupware** is a loosely defined term applied to software that helps multiple users work together by sharing information. Groupware is part of a broad concept called **workgroup technology** that includes equipment and software that help group members communicate and manage their activities.

7. **Telecommuting** refers to the ability of individuals to work at home and communicate with their offices by using personal computers and communications channels.

8. **Electronic data interchange** (EDI) is the capability to electronically transfer documents from one business to another. EDI is frequently used by large companies for routine transactions such as purchase orders and billing.

9. A **global positioning system** (GPS) uses satellites to determine the geographic location of earthbased GPS equipment. GPS systems are often used for tracking and navigation of all types of vehicles.

10. A **bulletin board system** (BBS) allows users to communicate with one another and share information.

11. **Online services,** sometimes called **information services**, include information and services provided to users who subscribe to the service for a fee.

12. **Communications**, sometimes called **data communications**, refers to the transmission of data and information over a communications channel between one computer or terminal and another computer. **Telecommunications** describes any type of long-distance communications including television signals. **Teleprocessing** refers to the use of computers and communications equipment to access computers and computer files located elsewhere.

13. A **communications channel**, also called a **communications line**, **communications link**, or **data link**, is the path the data follows as it is transmitted from the sending equipment to the receiving equipment in a communications system.

14. **Transmission media** are the materials or technologies that are used to establish the communications channel. Two types of transmission media are those that use some type of physical cabling (including twisted pair wire, coaxial cable, and fiber-optics cable) and those that use wireless technology (including microwaves, radio waves, or light waves).

15. **Twisted pair wire** consists of pairs of copper wires that are twisted together. Twisted pair wire is commonly used for telephone lines and to connect personal computers with one another.

What You Should Know

16. A **coaxial cable** is a high-quality, heavily insulated communications line that is used in offices and can be laid underground or underwater. **Baseband** coaxial cable carries one signal at a time. **Broadband** coaxial cable can carry multiple signals at one time.

17. **Fiber-optic** cable uses smooth, hair-thin strands of glass to conduct light with high efficiency. Fiber optics is frequently being used in new voice and data installations.

18. **Microwaves** are radio waves that can be used to provide high-speed transmission of both voice and data. Data is transmitted through the air from one microwave station to another in a manner similar to the way radio signals are transmitted.

19. **Communications satellites** receive microwave signals from earth, amplify the signals, and retransmit the signals back to earth. **Earth stations** are communications facilities that use large, dish-shaped antennas to transmit and receive data from satellites. The transmission *to* the satellite is called an **uplink** and the transmission *from* the satellite to a receiving earth station is called a **downlink**. To transmit a limited amount of information, a small satellite dish can be used. **Very small aperture terminal** (VSAT) antenna measuring only one to three meters in size can transmit up to 19,200 bits per second. Communications satellites are usually positioned about 22,300 miles above the earth in a **geosynchonous orbit**, meaning that the satellite is placed in an orbit where it rotates with the earth.

20. **Wireless transmission** uses one of three techniques to transmit data: light beams, radio waves, or carrier-connect radio. A **cellular telephone** uses radio waves to communicate with a local antenna assigned to a specific geographic area called a cell.

21. Two major **line configurations** (types of line connections) commonly used in communications are point-to-point lines and multidrop, or multipoint, lines.

22. A **point-to-point** line is a direct line between a sending and a receiving device. A **switched line** uses a regular telephone line to establish a communications connection. The process of establishing the communications connection is sometimes referred to as the **handshake**. A **dedicated line** is a line connection that is always established (unlike the switched line where the line connection is reestablished each time it is used). If the dedicated line is provided by an outside organization, it is sometimes called a **leased line**, or a **private line**.

23. The second major line configuration is called a **multidrop**, or **multipoint**, **line**. This type of line configuration is commonly used to connect multiple devices on a single line to a main computer, sometimes called a **host computer**.

24. Communications channels can be categorized by a number of characteristics including the type of signal, transmission mode, transmission direction, and transmission rate.

25. Computer equipment is designed to process data as **digital signals**, which are individual electrical pulses that represent the bits that are grouped together to form characters. Telephone equipment was originally designed to carry only voice transmission, which is comprised of a continuous electrical wave called an **analog signal**. A special piece of equipment called a modem is used to convert between the digital signals and analog signals so that telephone lines can carry data. To provide better communication services, telephone companies are now offering **digital data service** communications channels, which are specifically designed to carry digital instead of voice signals. Modems are not needed with digital data service; instead, users connect to the communications line through a device called a **digital service unit** (DSU).

26. In **asynchronous transmission mode**, individual bytes (made up of bits) are transmitted at irregular intervals, such as when a user enters data. In the **synchronous transmission mode**, large blocks of data are transmitted at regular intervals.

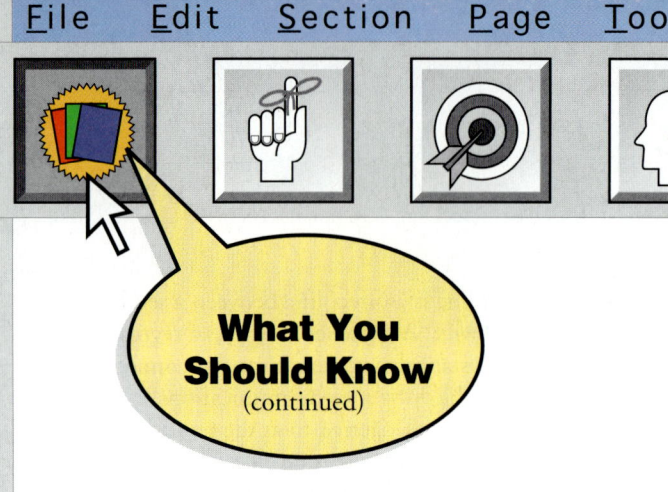

27. In **simplex transmission**, data flows in one direction only. In **half-duplex transmission**, data can flow in both directions but in only one direction at a time. In **full-duplex transmission**, data can be sent in both directions at the same time.

28. The transmission rate of a communications channel is determined by its bandwidth and its speed. The **bandwidth** is the range of frequencies that a channel can carry. The speed at which data is transmitted is usually expressed as **bits per second (bps)**, the number of bits that can be transmitted in one second, or as **baud rate**, the number of times per second the signal being transmitted changes.

29. A variety of communications equipment exists to increase or change a signal to transmit it farther, but the equipment a user is most likely to encounter is a modem, a multiplexor, and a front-end processor. Computers that are connected to a network usually require a network interface card.

30. A **modem** converts the digital signals of a terminal or computer to analog signals that are transmitted over a communications channel. An **external modem** is a separate, or stand-alone, device that is attached to the computer or terminal by a cable and to the telephone outlet by a standard telephone cord. An **internal modem** is a circuit board that is installed inside a computer or terminal.

31. A **multiplexor**, sometimes referred to as a MUX, combines more than one input signal into a single stream of data that can be transmitted over a communications channel, thus increasing the efficiency of communications and saving on the cost of individual communications channels.

32. A **front-end processor** is a computer that is dedicated to handling the communications requirements of a larger computer. Tasks that the front-end processor would handle include **polling** (checking the connected terminals or computers to see if they have data to send), error checking and correction, and access security.

33. A **network interface card** (NIC) fits in an expansion slot of a computer and attaches to the cable or wireless technology used to connect the devices in the network.

34. Programs that a user must load before transmitting data, referred to as **communications software**, can perform a number of tasks. **Dialing software** allows you to store, review, select, and dial telephone numbers of computers that can be called. **File transfer software** allows you to move one or more files from one system to another. **Terminal emulation software** allows a personal computer to imitate or appear to be a specific type of terminal so the personal computer can connect to another usually larger computer. **Data encryption** protects confidential data through the conversion of data at the sending end into an unrecognizable string of characters or bits and the reconversion of the data at the receiving end.

35. A **protocol** is a set of rules and procedures for exchanging information between computers. The International Standards Organization (ISO) based in Geneva, Switzerland has defined a set of communications protocols, called the **Open Systems Interconnection** (OSI) model, which has been endorsed by the United Nations.

36. A communications **network** is a collection of terminals, computers, and other equipment that uses communications channels to share data, information, hardware, and software.

37. A **local area network,** or LAN, is a privately owned communications network that covers a limited geographic area. Three common applications of local area networks are hardware, software, and information resource sharing.

38. **Hardware resource sharing** allows each personal computer in the network to access and use devices that would be too expensive to provide for each user or would not be justified for each user because of only occasional use. A **server** is a computer dedicated to handling the communications needs of the other computers in a network.

39. **Software resource sharing** consists of storing frequently used software on the hard disk of the server so the software can be accessed by multiple users. When a commercial software package is accessed by many users, it is sometimes necessary to obtain a special agreement from the software vendor called a **site license**.

40. **Information resource sharing** allows anyone using a personal computer on the local area network to access data stored on any other computer in the network. Using the **file-server** method, the server sends an entire file at a time and the requesting computer then performs the processing. With the **client-server** method, as much processing as possible is done on the server system before the data is transmitted.

41. A **peer-to-peer network** allows any computer to share software, data, or hardware located on any other computer in the network. A **network operating system** (NOS) is software that allows a user to manage the resources of a computer network.

42. A **wide area network**, or WAN, is geographic in scope (as opposed to local) and uses telephone lines, microwaves, satellites, or a combination of communications channels. A wide area network limited to the area surrounding a city is sometimes referred to as a **metropolitan area network**, or MAN. Public wide area network companies include so-called **common carriers** such as the telephone companies. Companies called **value-added carriers** lease channels from the common carriers to provide specialized communications services referred to as **value-added networks** (VANs). **Packet-switching** combines individual packets of information from various users and transmits them together over a high-speed channel. Most common carriers are now offering **Integrated Services Digital Network** (ISDN) services. ISDN is an international standard for the digital transmission of both voice and data using different channels and communications companies.

43. The largest and best known wide area network is the Internet. The **Internet** is a worldwide network of computer networks.

44. The configuration, or physical layout, of the equipment in a communications network is called **topology**. Devices connected to a network, such as terminals, printers, or other computers, are referred to as **nodes**.

45. A **star network** contains a central computer and one or more terminals or personal computers connected to it, forming a star. A star network configuration is often used when the central computer contains all the data required to process the input from the terminals.

46. When a **bus network** is used, all the devices in the network are connected to and share a single cable. Information is transmitted in either direction from any one personal computer to another.

47. A **ring network** does not use a centralized host computer. Data travels around a ring network in one direction only and passes through each node. A **token ring network** constantly circulates an electronic signal, called a token, around the network. If a device has the token, a message can be sent.

48. A **gateway** is a combination of hardware and software that allows users on one network access to the resources on a *different* type of network. A **bridge** is a combination of hardware and software that is used to connect *similar* networks. A **router** is an intelligent network connecting device that can route communications traffic directly to the appropriate network.

7.36 Terms to Remember

analog signal (7.16)
asynchronous transmission mode (7.16)

bandwidth (7.17)
baseband (7.9)
baud rate (7.18)
bits per second (bps) (7.18)
bridge (7.27)
broadband (7.10)
bulletin board system (BBS) (7.7)
bus network (7.26)

cellular telephone (7.12)
client-server (7.23)
coaxial cable (7.9)
common carriers (7.24)
communications (7.8)
communications channel (7.8)
communications line (7.8)
communications link (7.8)
communications satellites (7.11)
communications software (7.20)

data communications (7.8)
data encryption (7.20)
data link (7.8)
dedicated line (7.14)
dialing software (7.20)
digital data service (7.16)
digital service unit (DSU) (7.16)
digital signals (7.16)
downlink (7.11)

earth stations (7.11)
electronic data interchange (EDI) (7.5)
electronic mail (7.2)
external modem (7.19)

facsimile (7.4)
FAX (7.4)
fiber optics (7.10)

file-server (7.23)
file transfer software (7.20)
front-end processor (7.19)
full-duplex transmission (7.17)

gateway (7.27)
geosynchronous orbit (7.11)
global positioning system (GPS) (7.6)
groupware (7.4)

half-duplex transmission (7.17)
handshake (7.14)
hardware resource sharing (7.21)
host computer (7.15)

information resource sharing (7.22)
information services (7.7)
information superhighway (7.31)
Integrated Services Digital Network (ISDN) (7.24)
internal modem (7.19)
Internet (7.25)

LAN (7.21)
leased line (7.15)
line configurations (7.14)
local area network (LAN) (7.21)

MAN (7.24)
metropolitan area network (MAN) (7.24)
microwaves (7.11)
modem (7.18)
multidrop line (7.15)
multiplexor (7.19)
multipoint line (7.15)

National Information Infrastructure (NII) (7.31)
network (7.21)
network interface card (NIC) (7.19)
network operating system (NOS) (7.23)
nodes (7.26)

online services (7.7)
Open Systems Interconnection (OSI) (7.21)

packet-switching (7.24)
peer-to-peer network (7.23)
point-to-point line (7.14)
polling (7.19)
private line (7.15)
protocol (7.21)

ring network (7.27)
router (7.27)

server (7.22)
simplex transmission (7.17)
site license (7.22)
software resource sharing (7.22)
star network (7.26)
switched line (7.14)
synchronous transmission mode (7.17)

telecommunications (7.8)
telecommuting (7.5)
teleconferencing (7.3)
teleprocessing (7.8)
terminal emulation software (7.20)
token ring network (7.27)
topology (7.26)
transmission media (7.9)
twisted pair wire (7.9)

uplink (7.11)

value-added carriers (7.24)
value-added networks (VANs) (7.24)
very small aperture terminal (VSAT) (7.11)
voice mail (7.3)

WAN (7.24)
wide area network (WAN) (7.24)
wireless transmission (7.12)
workgroup technology (7.4)

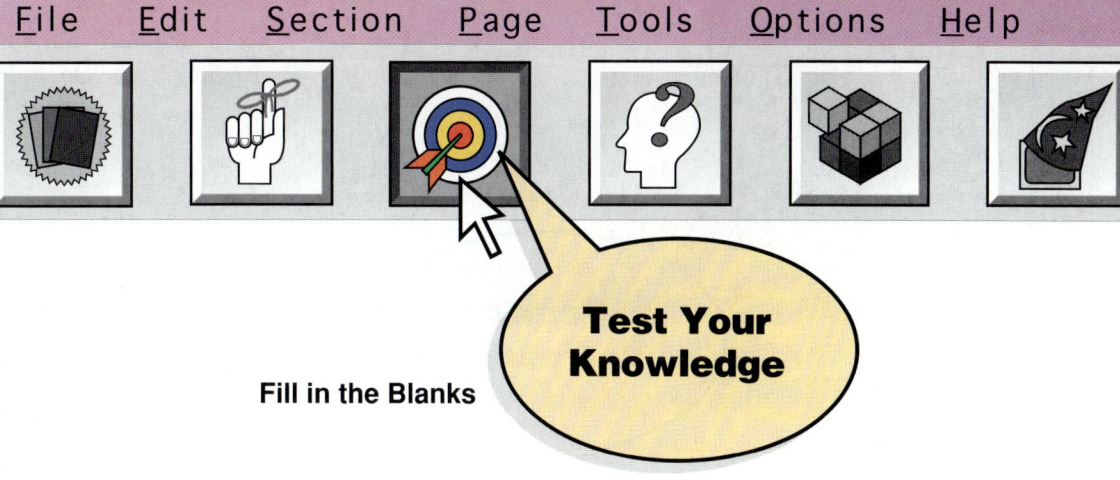

Test Your Knowledge

Fill in the Blanks

1. _____ refers to the transmission of data and information over a channel such as a telephone line, between one computer and another computer.

2. In _____ transmission mode, individual bytes (made up of bits) are transmitted at irregular intervals, while in _____ transmission mode, large blocks of data are transmitted at regular intervals.

3. The direction of data transmission is classified as either _____ (data flows in one direction only), _____ (data can flow in both directions but in only one direction at a time), or _____ (data can be sent in both directions at the same time).

4. Communications equipment includes a(n) _____, which converts the digital signals of a terminal or computer to analog signals, a(n) _____, which combines more than one input signal into a single stream of data, a(n) _____, which is a computer dedicated to handling the communications requirements of a larger computer, and a(n) _____ that fits in an expansion slot of a computer and attaches to the cable or wireless technology used to connect the devices in a network.

5. A(n) _____ is a combination of hardware and software that allows users on one network to access the resources on a different network, while a(n) _____ is a combination of hardware and software that is used to connect similar networks.

Short Answer

1. List seven examples of how communications technology is used. Briefly describe each.

2. Name three transmission media that use some type of physical cabling. How are they different? Name three transmission media that use wireless technology. How are they different?

3. Two major line configurations commonly used in communications are point-to-point lines and multidrop lines. What are point-to-point lines? How is a switched line different from a dedicated line? What are multidrop lines?

4. What is communications software? Describe four tasks that can be performed by communications software.

5. What is a network? How is a local area network (LAN) different from a wide area network (WAN)? Briefly describe three common network topologies.

Label the Figure

Instructions: Identify the basic components of a communications system shown in the figure below.

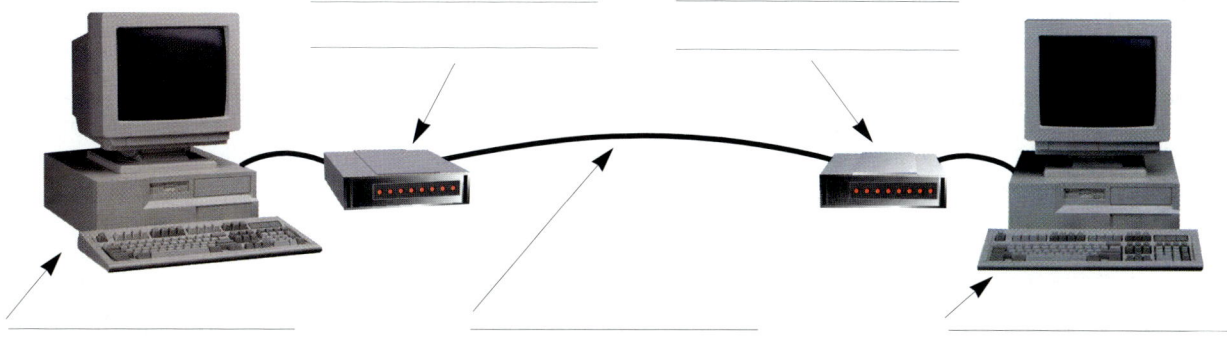

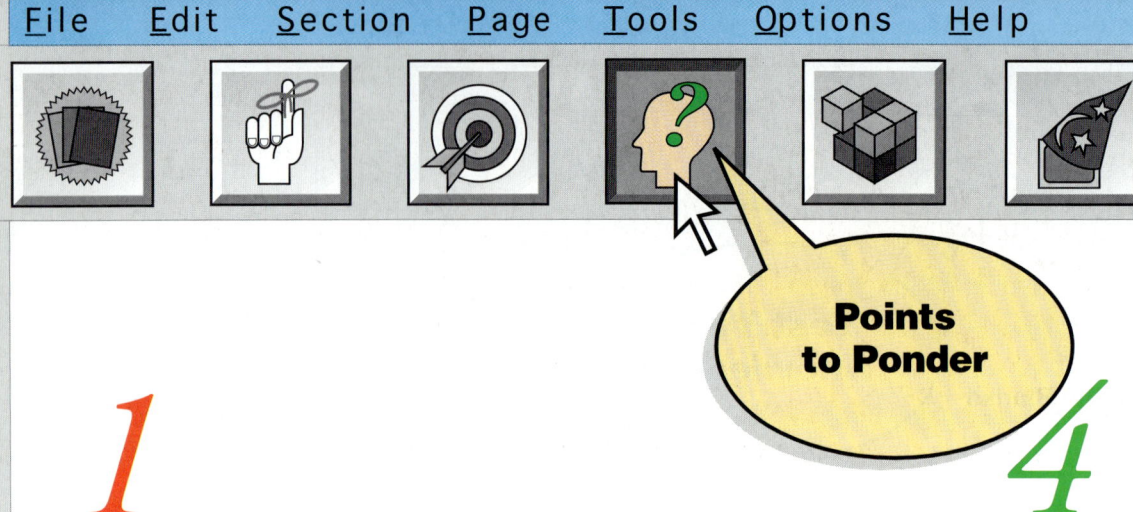

Points to Ponder

1

This chapter describes several applications that rely on communications technology. Which of these applications would you be most likely to use as a college student? Which application do you think you would use in your career? Which application would you be most likely to use for social reasons? Which application do you think will have the greatest impact on society over the next twenty-five years? Explain why you answered each part of this question as you did.

2

Plagiarism is the act of stealing someone else's ideas or words and passing them off as one's own. In ancient Greece, however, "plagiarism" often worked in reverse; in an effort to give his thoughts a wider audience, an unknown author would pass off his own ideas or words as the work of someone famous. Some people feel that the anonymity provided by electronic mail and computerized bulletin board systems will also lead to a wider dissemination of ideas by eliminating biases based on age, gender, race, social class, or cultural origin. Others believe, however, that the high cost of the necessary computer equipment will continue to keep a large percentage of the population silent. What do you think? Will these applications give more people the opportunity to express their views? Why or why not?

3

Computer bulletin board systems (BBSs) have led to some controversies related to the issue of free speech. Police have closed bulletin board systems providing information that could be used to commit crimes, such as telephone codes that can be employed to make free long-distance telephone calls. It is more difficult, however, to control the posting of confidential material, hate messages, and discriminatory correspondence. Bulletin board systems are often available to a large geographic area, and statutes and standards vary from state to state and community to community. Some BBS operators have pulled communications they considered objectionable, but many feel this amounts to censorship. Do you think a bulletin board system operator has the right to control what information is presented? Why or why not? What regulations, if any, do you think should be passed to control the type of material that can be posted on a bulletin board system? Why?

4

The number of employees telecommuting either full or part time in the United States more than doubled from 1988 to 1991 and is expected to double again by 1996. Studies have shown that telecommuting workers are 10 to 20 percent more productive than their office-bound brethren. There are disadvantages to telecommuting, however, including the inability of office managers to oversee workers, the difficulty in conducting spontaneous staff meetings, and a potential loss of "team spirit." Whether or not telecommuting is a success seems to depend primarily on the employee's personality and the employer's ability to make adjustments. What type of personality do you think is necessary for someone to telecommute successfully? What types of adjustments must be made by employers? Given your personality and the career you intend to pursue, do you think you would be a successful telecommuter? Why or why not?

5

During a typical day, you probably encounter communication situations that have distinct directions of transmission. Describe three circumstances you have experienced with different directions of transmission; one in which the direction of communication was comparable to simplex transmission, another in which the direction

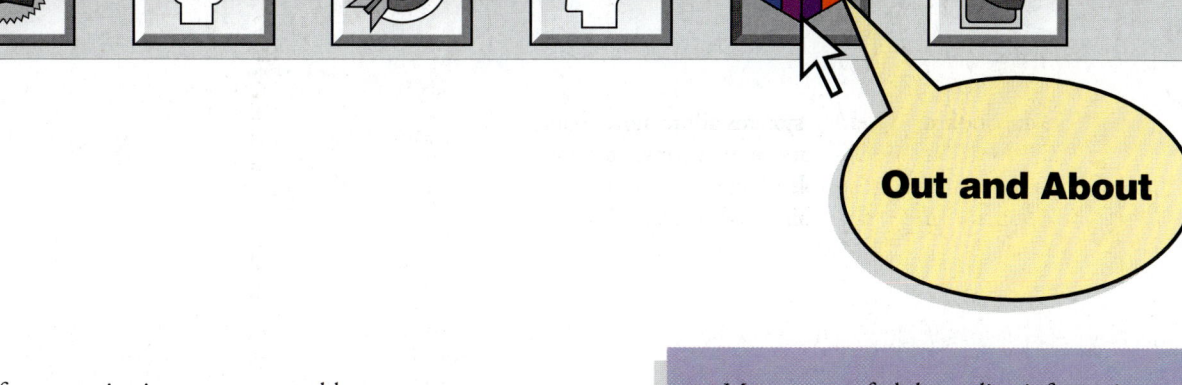

Out and About

of communication was comparable to half-duplex transmission, and a third in which the direction of communication was comparable to full-duplex transmission. Why did you classify each situation as you did? Do you think communication would have been improved if the direction of transmission had been different? Why or why not?

6

Although analog telephone transmissions can be tapped fairly easily, data encryption can make digital telephone transmissions very difficult to tap. So that police can gather the evidence necessary to convict some criminals, the FBI has proposed legislation that would require all providers of electronic communications to use equipment capable of being wiretapped. An encryption standard, the details of which would be available only to law enforcement agencies, has also been presented that would eventually eliminate all other standards. Some businesses and civil liberties groups have objected to the proposals, insisting that wiretapping would become too easy, and there is no guarantee unauthorized government eavesdropping would not take place. What do you think? Should government be allowed to regulate data communications? Why or why not?

1. Many experts feel that online information services will eventually be as much a part of our lives as newspapers, radio, and television are today. Figure 7-8 on page 7.7 furnishes the names of major online information service providers and offers a brief description of each. Call the phone numbers for at least three of the services listed to obtain additional information. What services are offered? Does the service require a particular type of user interface? What is the membership fee? Are there other fees (such as a minimum monthly charge, hourly access fee, or added cost for certain services)? From the information supplied, in which online information service are you most interested? Why?

2. Questions have been raised regarding concerns that cellular telephones cause brain tumors or other health problems. A Florida man has filed a lawsuit, claiming that his wife's death resulted from a brain tumor induced by radiation from her cellular telephone. Although the Cellular Telecommunications Industry Association maintains thousands of studies have been done showing the phones are not hazardous, an advisory group that has reviewed the studies feels they contain data gaps and insufficient evidence. Visit a library and, using current newspapers and periodicals, prepare a report on the health issues related to cellular telephone use. On the basis of your findings, do you think the use of cellular telephones is safe? Why or why not? What additional studies, if any, do you think should be done?

Out and About

3. Many schools and offices have a network connecting their computers. Locate a school or office that uses a network and talk to someone connected to it about how the network works. What are the advantages of having a network? What are the disadvantages? Find out what type of network (star, bus, ring, or token ring) it is and draw a simple diagram of the network. Why is that network topology used? Have there ever been any problems with the network? If so, would the problems have been avoided with a different network configuration? Is the network connected to another network? If so, how?

4. To take advantage of computerized telecommunications over analog phone lines, a modem is an essential piece of equipment. Visit a computer vendor and compare several modems. List the characteristics of each, including such items as the transmission rate, the cost, and whether it is an internal or external modem. If you have a personal computer, or know what type of personal computer you would like to have, ask a salesperson to recommend a modem for your personal computer. On the basis of the information you have gathered, which modem would you be most likely to purchase? Why?

5. Regardless of your interests, a computer bulletin board system (BBS) probably exists that is tailor-made for you. Currently, there are more than 50,000 public-access bulletin boards in the United States dealing with a wide range of topics, including politics, the environment, sports, religion, alternative lifestyles, music, and business opportunities. Make a list of at least three areas of interest to you. Then, by using a personal computer magazine, contacting a local computer users' group, or telephoning an online information service that offers a BBS, discover the name of a bulletin board system that fits each of your interests. If possible, find out the answers to such questions as: How do you connect to the BBS? Are any fees required? Are electronic mail services offered? Are public domain software and shareware provided that can be downloaded (copied from the BBS) to a personal computer system?

6. Facsimile equipment has become incredibly popular. FAX machines are now an essential piece of equipment for even small businesses, and many people have FAX machines in their homes. As a result, FAX machines are now available at a variety of stores including computer stores, office supply stores, discount stores, electronics stores, and catalog stores. Visit three different types of stores and find FAX machines that offer similar features. Write down the brand name of each machine, the available features, in what store the machine was found, and the cost of each. Ask a salesperson to explain the machine's warranty and the store's service policy. From what you have learned, in which store would you be most likely to purchase a FAX machine? Why?

Windows Labs

1 Understanding the Terminal Window With Program Manager on the screen, double-click the Accessories group icon. Double-click the Terminal program-item icon. Maximize the Terminal window.

Select the Settings menu and choose the Communications command. If all the options are ghosted (dimmed) in the Communications dialog box, select a connector in the Connector list box *(Figure 7-38)*. Answer the following questions: (1) What are the baud rate options? (2) What are the options for data and stop bits? (3) What are the parity options? (4) What connectors are in the scrollable list? Choose the Cancel button. Close Terminal.

2 Shelly Cashman Series Communications Lab Follow the instructions in Windows Lab 2 in Chapter 1 on page 1.30 to display the Shelly Cashman Series Labs screen. Select Connecting to the Internet by pointing to it and clicking the left mouse button. When the initial screen displays, carefully read the objectives. With your printer turned on, point to the Print Questions button and click the left mouse button. Fill out the top of the Questions sheet and answer the questions as you step through the Communications Lab.

3 Creating a Text File for File Transfer Text files (also called ASCII files) are often used in online file transfer operations because they can be read by any word processing package or editor. Many Windows users use Notepad to create files to upload to a bulletin board or a friend's computer through the Terminal program.

With Program Manager on the screen, double-click the Accessories group icon. In the Accessories group window, double-click the Notepad program-item icon. Maximize the Notepad window. Type the first paragraph on page 7.8 under the heading, What Is Communications?, as shown in *Figure 7-39*. To indent the first line of the paragraph, press the SPACEBAR five times. Press the ENTER key at the end of each line on page 7.8. Use the same error-correction techniques in Notepad as you used in Write (see Windows Lab 1 in Chapter 2 on page 2.36). When your document is correct, save it by choosing the Save command from the File menu, typing a:win7-3 and choosing the OK button. With your printer turned on, print the document by choosing the Print command from the File menu. Close Notepad.

4 Connecting to a Bulletin Board System Turn on your modem. Open the Terminal window as described in Windows Lab 1 above. Maximize the Terminal window. Select the Settings menu and choose the Communications command. If a connector is not specified, select the appropriate connector (port). Choose the OK button. Select the Settings menu and choose the Terminal Preferences command. In the Terminal Font area of the Terminal Preferences dialog box, enlarge the font size to 14. Choose the OK button. Select the Settings menu and choose the Phone Number command. In the Phone Number dialog box, type 1-800-697-4636 and choose the OK button. Select the Phone menu

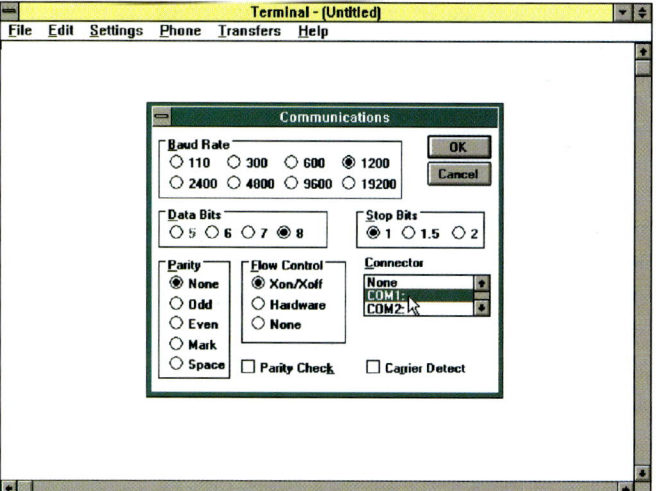

Figure 7-38

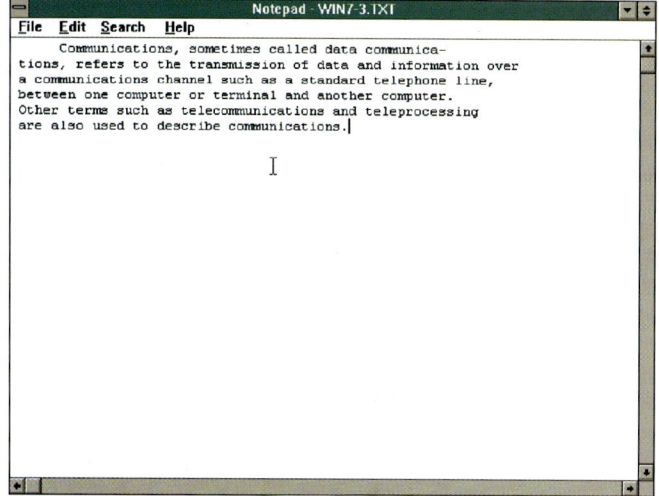

Figure 7-39

 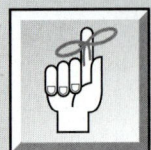    

In the Lab (continued)

and choose the Dial command. While the connection is being established, your computer displays a series of messages *(Figure 7-40)*. What does your system display?

Once you are connected to SBA Online *(Figure 7-41)*, write down your caller number, register yourself, and then use SBA Online to obtain the following information: (1) Identify the purpose of SBA. (2) Discuss one of SBA's programs. (3) List three federal bulletin board systems, along with their Federal Agency, telephone number, and communication speed. (4) List the names and addresses of the senators and representatives in your state. Quit SBA Online. Select the Phone menu and choose Hangup. Close Terminal. Choose the No button to not save settings. Close Accessories.

5 Using Help With Program Manager on the screen, double-click the Main group icon. In the Main group window, double-click the Windows Setup program-item icon. If your system has a network installed, write down its name. Select the Windows Setup Help menu and choose the Contents command. One by one, click the green items below the How To Help topic. Read and print the contents of the windows. After printing each window, click the Back button to return to the Contents window. Close Help. Close Windows Setup.

DOS Labs

1 Understanding Your System's Configuration At the DOS prompt, type msd and press the ENTER key to display the Microsoft Diagnostics (MSD) program. If your system displays a Microsoft Windows message, press the ENTER key.

If your system has a network installed, write down its name. Press N to display the Network window. Write down your station number. Press ENTER. How many COM Ports does your system have? Press C to display the COM Ports window. For each COM port listed, identify its baud rate, number of data bits, and number of stop bits. Press ENTER to return to the MSD screen. Press F3 to exit MSD.

2 Creating a Brief ASCII File for File Transfer At the DOS prompt, type copy con a:dos7-2.txt and press the ENTER key. Type your name and press the ENTER key. Type your course name and press the ENTER key. Press F6. Press the ENTER key. Display the file by typing type a:dos7-2.txt and pressing the ENTER key. Print the file by typing print a:dos7-2.txt and pressing the ENTER key twice.

3 Using Help At the DOS prompt, type help msd and press the ENTER key to display help on the Microsoft Diagnostics program. Read and print the information on the Notes and Examples jump topics. Exit the Help window.

Online Lab

1 Corresponding via Electronic Mail Using one of the two online services you selected in Chapter 1, connect to the service and perform the following tasks: (1) Obtain the account number of a friend or someone on the service who has the same interests as you. (2) Search the service for the Electronic Mail section. Read the policy on electronic mail. (3) Send a message to the person you selected and ask him or her to respond to your message. (4) Later, check for mail. Display and print the message sent back to you.

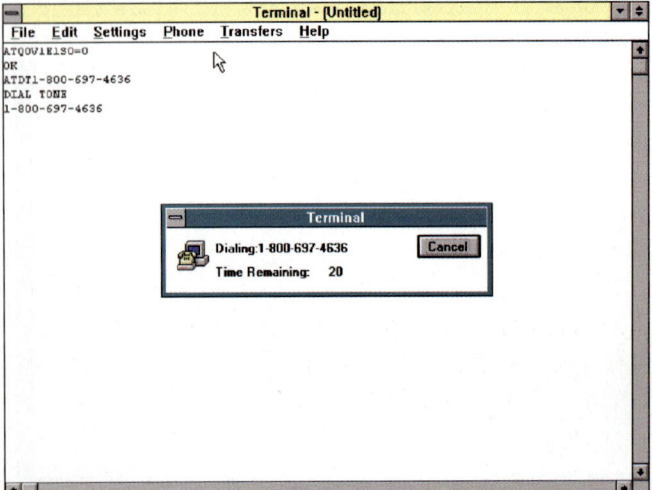

Figure 7-40

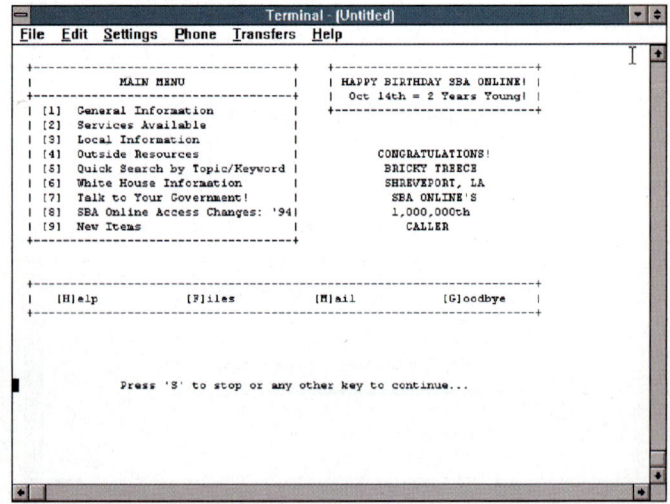

Figure 7-41

The Internet

The Internet is a network of networks. It links approximately 30 million people and thousands of organizations worldwide. The number of people using the Internet is growing 5% each month. The Internet is a vast resource of information and services. Some of the things you can do on the Internet are listed on the right.

- Send and receive electronic mail
- Transfer files
- Search databases
- Participate in discussions on particular subjects
- Play games
- Run programs on remote computers
- Order products and services

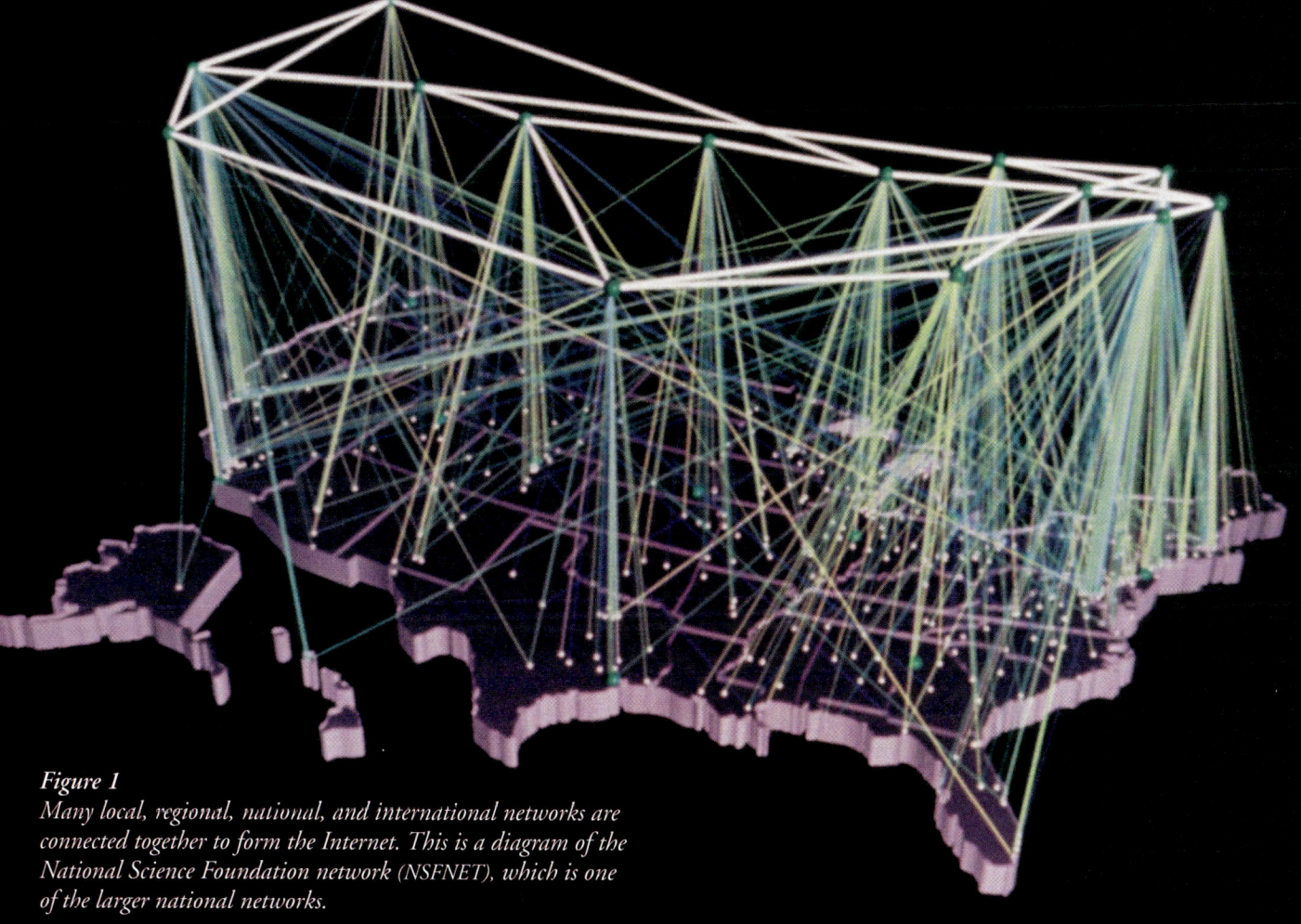

Figure 1
Many local, regional, national, and international networks are connected together to form the Internet. This is a diagram of the National Science Foundation network (NSFNET), which is one of the larger national networks.

- 30 million users
- Users located in more than 100 countries
- 20,000 member organizations
- 21,000 connected networks
- 2 million networked computers
- Number of users growing at 5% per month

INTERNET TERMS

ARCHIE	A method of locating files on the Net.
FAQ	Frequently Asked Question. Lists of FAQs help users learn about a particular topic on the Net.
FLAME	Slang term for an aggressive or rude message.
FTP	File Transfer Protocol. Method of transferring files from one computer to another.
GOPHER	A menu-based system for exploring the Net.
IRC	Internet Relay Chat. Interactive discussion among multiple users.
MOSAIC	Graphical user interface that uses hypertext links.
NET	Abbreviation for the Internet.
NEWSGROUPS	Discussion groups on various topics.
PPP	Point-to-Point Protocol. A type of Internet connection.
SLIP	Serial Line Internet Protocol. A type of Internet connection.
SURFING	Slang term for browsing the Net.
TCP/IP	Transmission Control Protocol/Internet Protocol. Primary communications protocol used on the Net.
TELNET	A terminal emulation communications protocol that allows users to login to other computer systems.
URL	Uniform Resource Locator. The Internet address where a document can be found.
USENET	An informal group of systems that exchange news on a variety of topics.
VERONICA	A search tool used with Gopher.
WAIS	Wide Area Information Service. A system for finding information in Net databases.
WWW	World Wide Web. A linked hypertext system used for accessing Net resources.

Figure 2
Common Internet terms.

Figure 3
A quick and easy way to get connected to the Internet is to buy a starter kit such as Internet In A Box. Internet In A Box provides the necessary communications and utility software as well as a guide book of Internet resources.

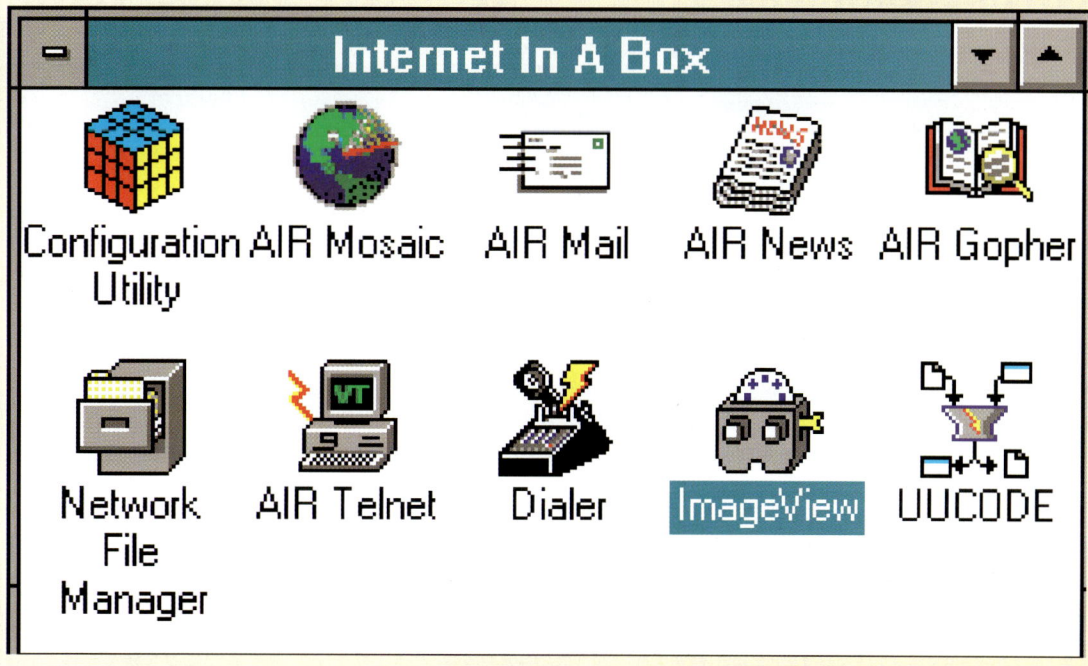

Figure 4
Some portions of the Internet are administered by private companies that provide Internet access and services. This photograph shows the control center of Nearnet, an Internet access provider that serves the northeastern United States.

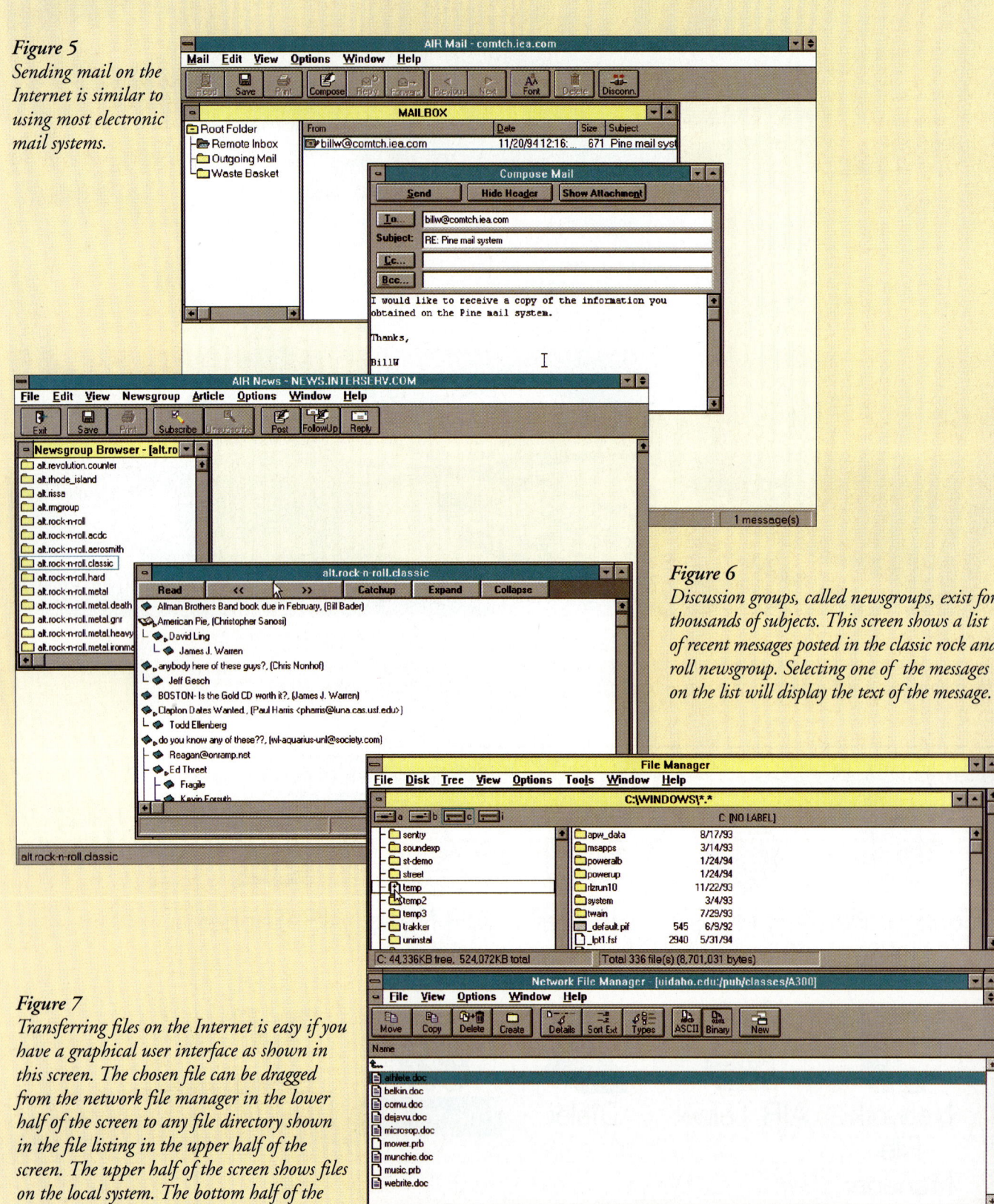

Figure 5
Sending mail on the Internet is similar to using most electronic mail systems.

Figure 6
Discussion groups, called newsgroups, exist for thousands of subjects. This screen shows a list of recent messages posted in the classic rock and roll newsgroup. Selecting one of the messages on the list will display the text of the message.

Figure 7
Transferring files on the Internet is easy if you have a graphical user interface as shown in this screen. The chosen file can be dragged from the network file manager in the lower half of the screen to any file directory shown in the file listing in the upper half of the screen. The upper half of the screen shows files on the local system. The bottom half of the screen shows files at the remote Internet location; in this case, the University of Idaho.

Figure 8
A wide variey of information is available on the Internet from government and educational organizations. This screen shows population estimates that are updated monthly by the U.S. Census Bureau.

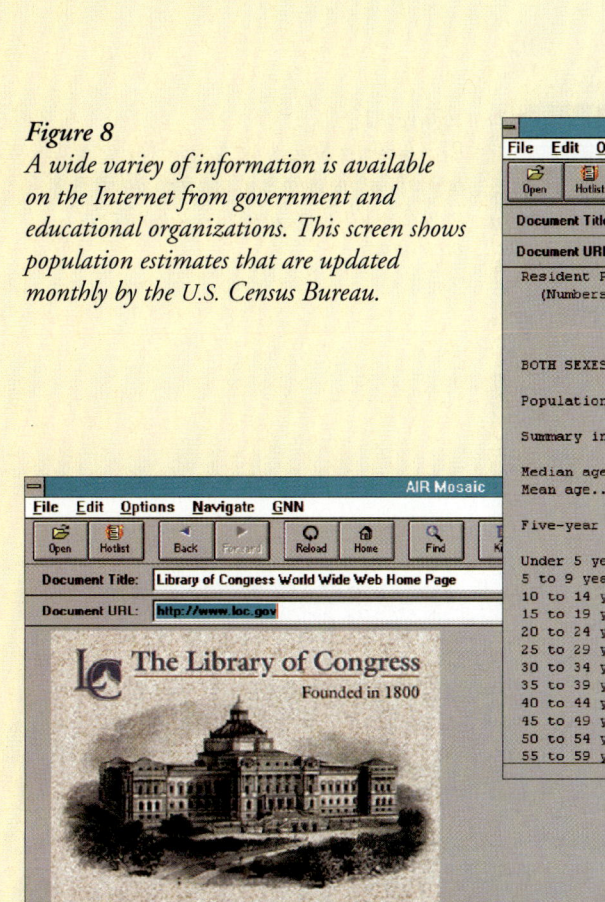

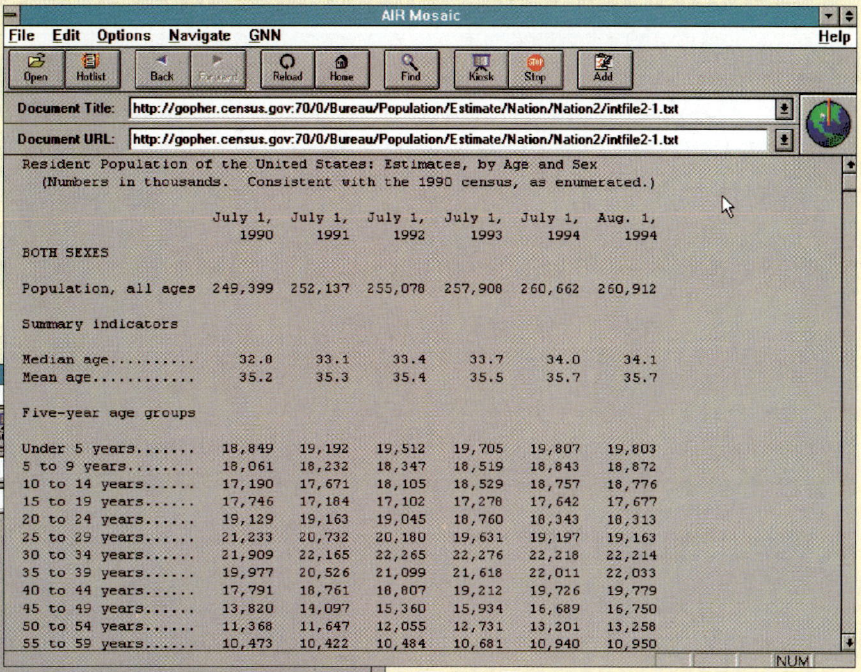

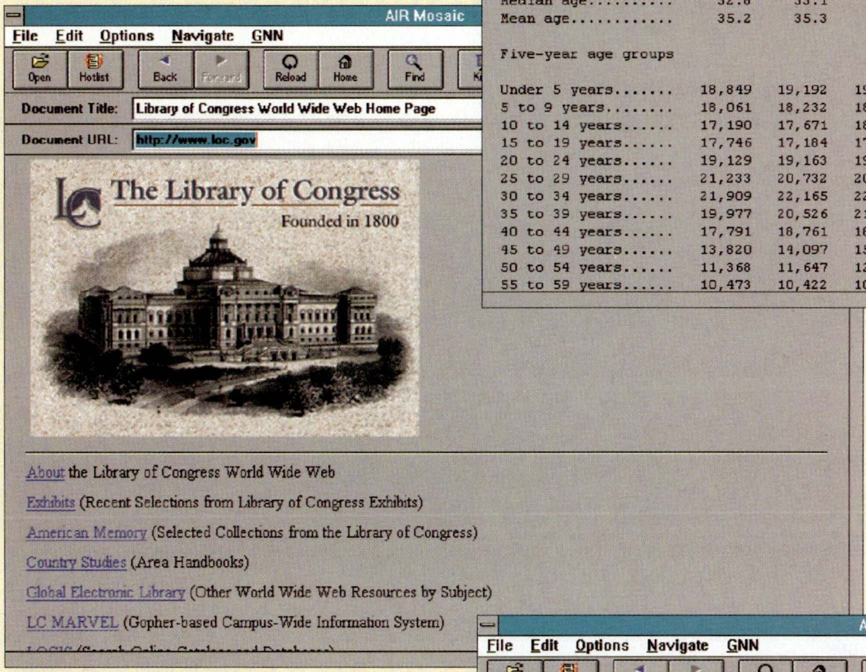

Figure 9
The Library of Congress is another source of research information on many subjects.

Figure 10
A number of employers are now listing job openings and information about their companies on the Internet.

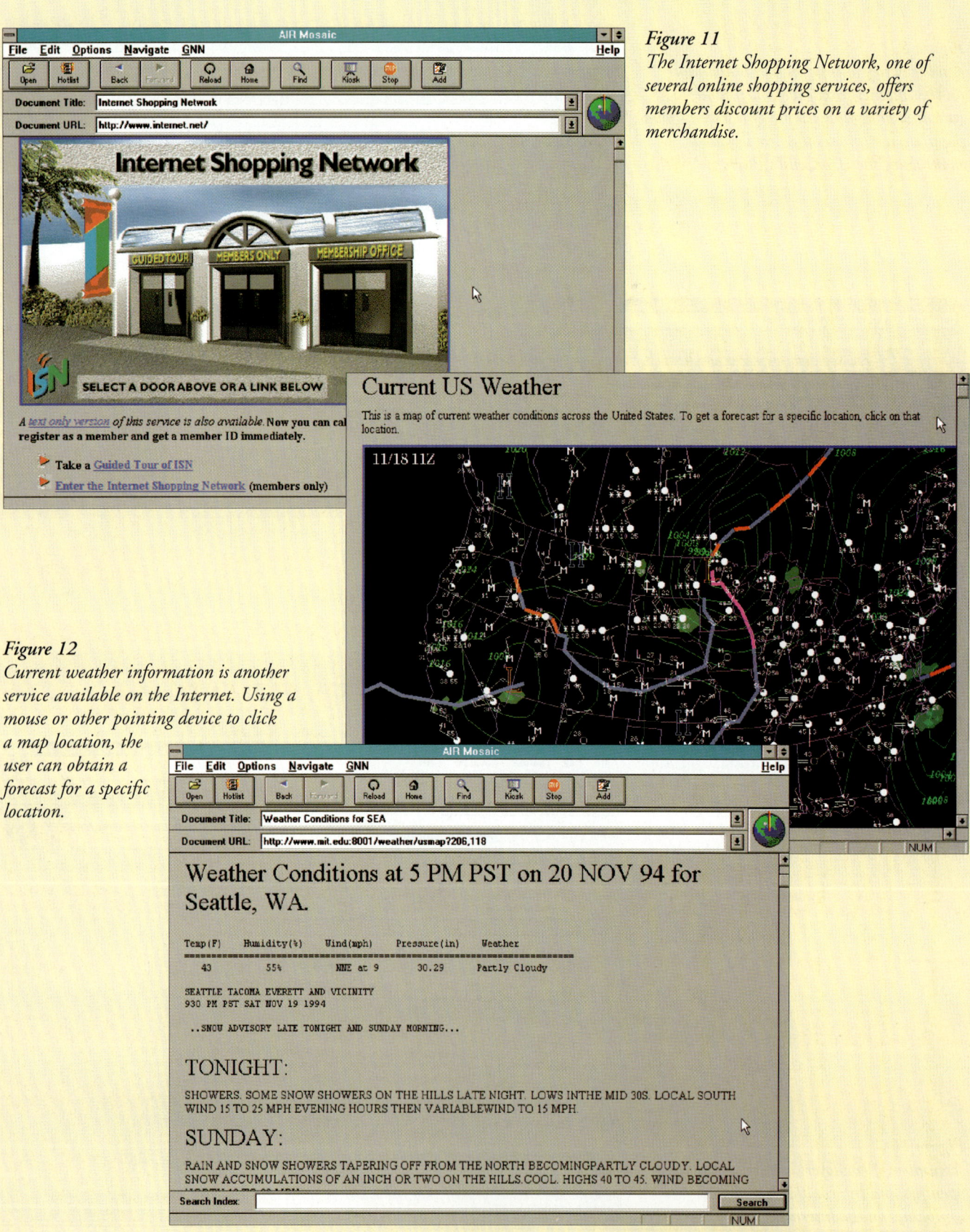

Figure 11
The Internet Shopping Network, one of several online shopping services, offers members discount prices on a variety of merchandise.

Figure 12
Current weather information is another service available on the Internet. Using a mouse or other pointing device to click a map location, the user can obtain a forecast for a specific location.

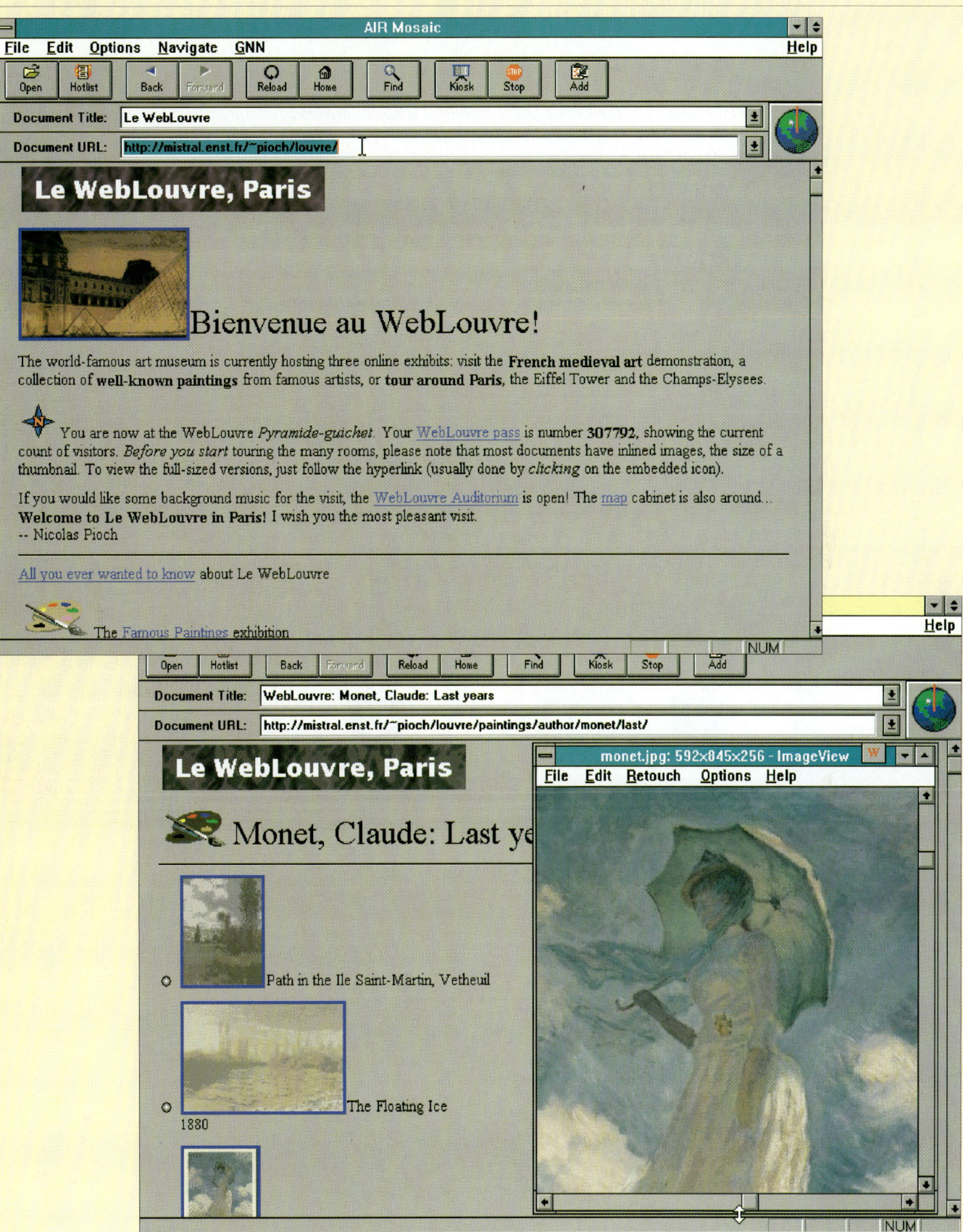

Figure 13
A number of international locations have English language services. These screens above show information on the Louve Museum in Paris, France. This service resides on a computer in Paris connected to the Internet. The information includes details on current exhibits and information on famous painters. Digital images of many of the paintings can be displayed and downloaded.

Figure 14
The White House, home of the United States President, is also connected to the Internet. Electronic visitors can sign the guest book, listen to messages from the President and Vice President, and take a tour.

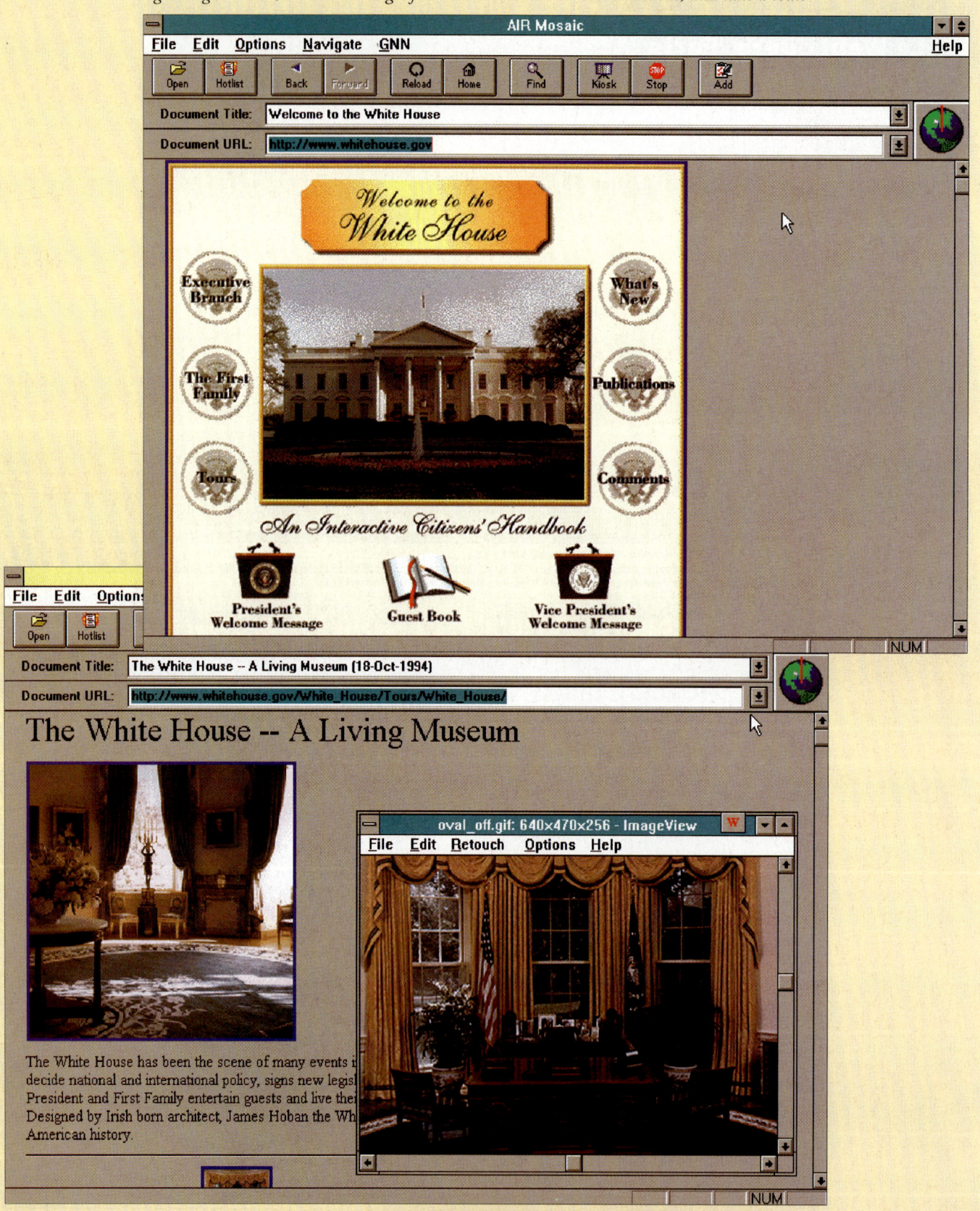

CHAPTER EIGHT

Operating Systems and System Software

8

Objectives

After completing this chapter, you will be able to:

- Describe the three major categories of system software

- Define the term operating system

- Describe the various types of operating systems and explain the differences in their capabilities

- Describe the functions of an operating system, including allocating system resources, monitoring system activities, and disk and file management

- Explain the difference between proprietary and portable operating systems

- Name and briefly describe the major operating systems that are being used today

- Discuss utilities and language translators

When most people think of software they think of application software such as word processing, spreadsheet, and database software. For application software to run on a computer, however, another type of software is needed to interface between the user, the application software, and the equipment. This software consists of programs referred to as the operating system. The operating system is part of what is called system software.

This chapter discusses operating system features of both large and small computer systems. It is important to understand the features of large computer operating systems because these features are steadily being implemented on small systems such as personal computers.

What Is System Software?

System software consists of all the programs including the operating system that are related to controlling the operations of the computer equipment. Some of the functions that system software perform include: starting up the computer; loading, executing, and storing application programs; storing and retrieving files; and performing a variety of functions such as formatting disks, sorting data files, and translating program instructions into machine language. System software can be classified into three major categories; operating systems, utilities, and language translators.

What Is an Operating System?

An **operating system** (OS) consists of one or more programs that control the allocation and usage of hardware resources such as memory, CPU time, disk space, and peripheral devices. These programs function as an interface between the user, the application programs, and the computer equipment (Figure 8-1).

The operating system is usually stored on disk. For a computer to operate, the essential and most frequently used instructions in the operating system must be copied from the disk and stored in the main memory of the computer. This *resident* portion of the operating system is called by many different names: the **supervisor**, **monitor**, **executive**, **master program**, **control program**, or **kernel**. Commands that are included in the resident portion of the operating system are called **internal commands**. The *nonresident* portions of the operating system are called **external commands**. The nonresident portions of the operating system remain on the disk and are available to be loaded into main memory whenever they are needed.

Most operating systems allow the user to give specific instructions to the computer, such as to list all the files on a diskette or to copy a file from one diskette to another. These instructions are called the **command language**. The portion of the operating system that carries out the command language instructions is called the **command language interpreter**.

Figure 8-1
The operating system and other system software programs act as an interface between the user, the application software, and the computer.

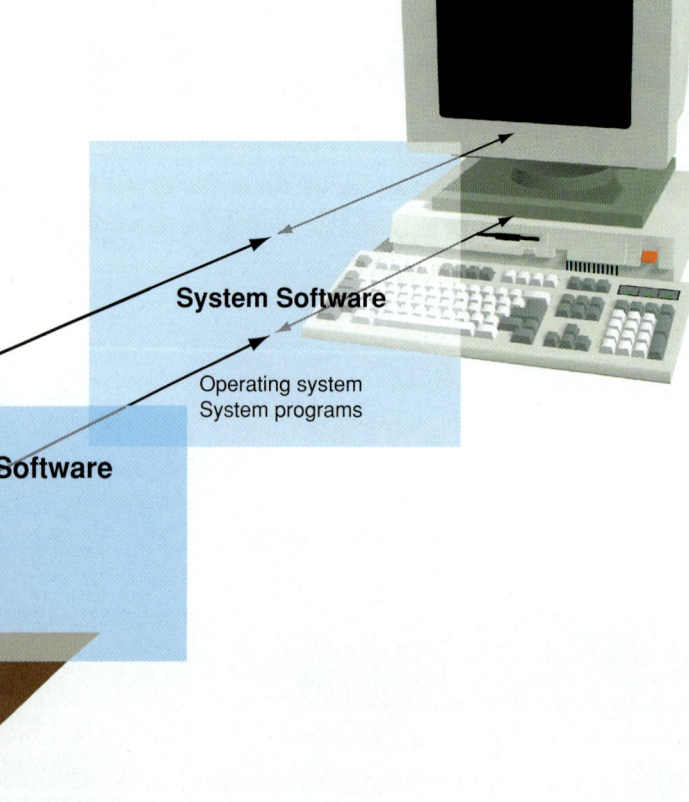

Loading an Operating System

The process of loading an operating system into main memory is called **booting** the system. *Figure 8-2* shows information that is displayed during this process. The actual information displayed will vary depending on the make of the computer and the equipment installed. The following steps explain what happens during the boot process on an IBM compatible personal computer that operates using DOS (Disk Operating System).

1. When you turn on your computer, the power supply distributes current to the motherboard and the other devices located in the system unit case.
2. The surge of electricity causes the CPU chip to reset itself and look to the BIOS chip for instructions on how to proceed. **BIOS** stands for **Basic Input/Output System**. The BIOS is a set of instructions that provides the interface between the operating system and the hardware devices. The BIOS is stored in a read-only memory (ROM) chip.
3. The BIOS chip begins a set of tests to make sure the equipment is working correctly. The tests, called the **POST**, for **Power On Self Test**, check the memory, keyboard, buses, and expansion cards. After some of the early tests are completed, the BIOS instructions are copied into memory where they can be executed faster than in ROM.
4. After the POST tests are successfully completed, the BIOS begins looking for the operating system. Usually, it first looks in diskette drive A. If an operating system disk is not loaded in drive A, the BIOS looks on drive C, the drive letter usually given to the first hard drive.
5. When the BIOS finds the operating system, it begins loading the *resident* portion into memory. For personal computers using a version of DOS, the resident portion is called the *DOS kernel*.
6. The kernel then loads system configuration information. The configuration information is contained in a file called **CONFIG.SYS**. This file tells the computer what devices you are using, such as a mouse, a CD-ROM, a scanner, or other devices. For each of these devices, a device driver program is usually loaded. Device driver programs tell the computer how to communicate with a device.
7. The kernel loads the command language interpreter. On DOS computers, the command language interpreter is called **COMMAND.COM**.
8. COMMAND.COM loads a batch file named **AUTOEXEC.BAT** that performs optional tasks such as telling the system where to look for files (PATH command) and loading programs that you want to run every time you turn on your system, such as certain utility programs.
9. If you haven't specified that the computer immediately start a particular application program, the system displays a **command language prompt** that indicates the system is ready to accept a command from the user. If you always want a particular application program to automatically start during the boot process, such as a word processing program or Microsoft Windows, you include the name of the program as the last line in the AUTOEXEC.BAT file.

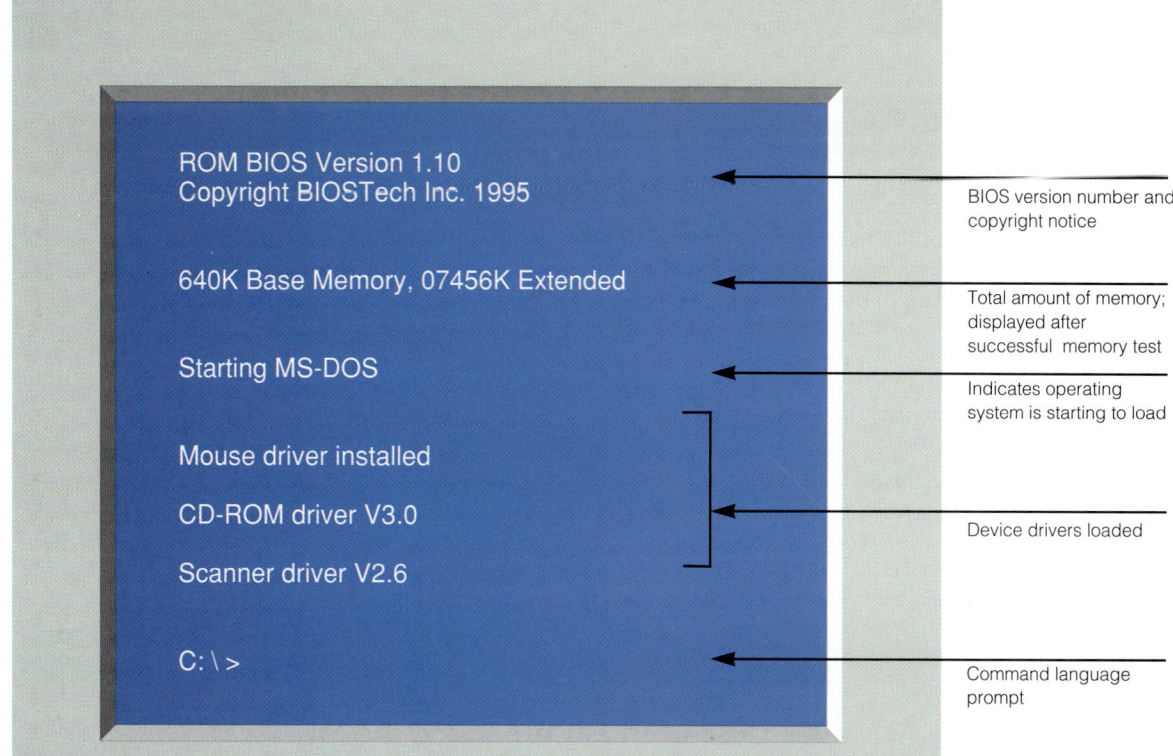

Figure 8-2 *An example of information that is displayed during the boot process.*

Types of Operating Systems

The types of operating systems include single program, multitasking, multiprocessing, and virtual machine operating systems. These operating systems can be classified by two criteria: (1) whether they allow more than one user to use the computer at the same time and (2) whether they allow more than one program to run at the same time *(Figure 8-3)*.

Single Program

Single program operating systems allow only a single user to run a single program at one time. This was the first type of operating system developed. Older personal computers used this type of operating system. For example, a single program operating system allowed you to load only one application, such as a spreadsheet, into main memory. To work on another application, such as word processing, you would exit the spreadsheet application and load the word processing program into memory.

Multitasking

Multitasking operating systems allow more than one program to run at the same time on one computer. Even though the CPU is only capable of working on one program instruction at a time, its capability to switch back and forth between programs makes it appear as though all programs are running at the same time. For example, with a multitasking operating system, the computer could be performing a complex spreadsheet calculation and at the same time be downloading a file from another computer while the user is writing a memo with the word processing program.

Multitasking operating systems on personal computers can usually support a single user running multiple programs. Multitasking operating systems on some personal computers and most minicomputers and mainframes can support more than one user running more than one program. This version of a multitasking operating system is sometimes called a **timesharing** or **multiuser** operating system. These operating systems also allow more than one user to run the same program. For example, a wholesale distributor may have dozens of terminal operators entering sales orders using the same order entry program on the same computer.

	SINGLE PROGRAM	MULTITASKING	MULTIPROCESSING	VIRTUAL MACHINE
NUMBER OF PROGRAMS RUNNING	One program	More than one program	More than one program each CPU	More than one program on each operating system
NUMBER OF USERS	One user	One or more than one user (timesharing)	More than one user each CPU	More than one user on each operating system

Figure 8-3
Operating systems can be classified by whether they allow more than one user and whether they allow more than one program to be operating at the same time.

Multiprocessing

Computers that have more than one CPU are called **multiprocessors**. A **multiprocessing** operating system coordinates the operations of computers with more than one CPU. Because each CPU in a multiprocessor computer can be executing one program instruction, more than one instruction can be executed simultaneously. Besides providing an increase in performance, most multiprocessors offer another advantage. If one CPU fails, work can be shifted to the remaining CPUs. There are two ways to implement multiprocessing *(Figure 8-4)*. In **asymmetric multiprocessing**, application tasks are assigned to a specific CPU. Each CPU has its own amount of memory. In **symmetric multiprocessing**, application tasks may be assigned to whatever CPU is available. Memory, as needed, is shared among the CPUs. Symmetric multiprocessing is more complex but achieves a higher processing rate because the operating system has more flexibility in assigning tasks to available CPUs.

As mentioned in Chapter 4, some microprocessors have multiple CPUs designed into a single chip. Other multiprocessor systems use physically separate CPUs. Some of the systems with separate CPUs are designed to keep operating even if one of the CPUs fails. **Fault-tolerant computers** are built with redundant components such as memory, input and output controllers, and disk drives. If any one of the components fail, the system can continue to operate with the duplicate component. Fault-tolerant systems are used for airline reservation systems, communications networks, bank teller machines, and other applications where it is important to keep the computer operating at all times.

Virtual Machine

A **virtual machine** (VM) operating system allows a single computer to run two or more different operating systems. The VM operating system allocates system resources such as memory and processing time to each operating system. To users, it appears that they are working on separate systems, hence the term virtual machine. The advantage of this approach is that an organization can run different operating systems (at the same time) that are best suited to different tasks. For example, some operating systems are best for interactive processing and others are best for batch processing. With a VM operating system, both types of operating systems can be run concurrently.

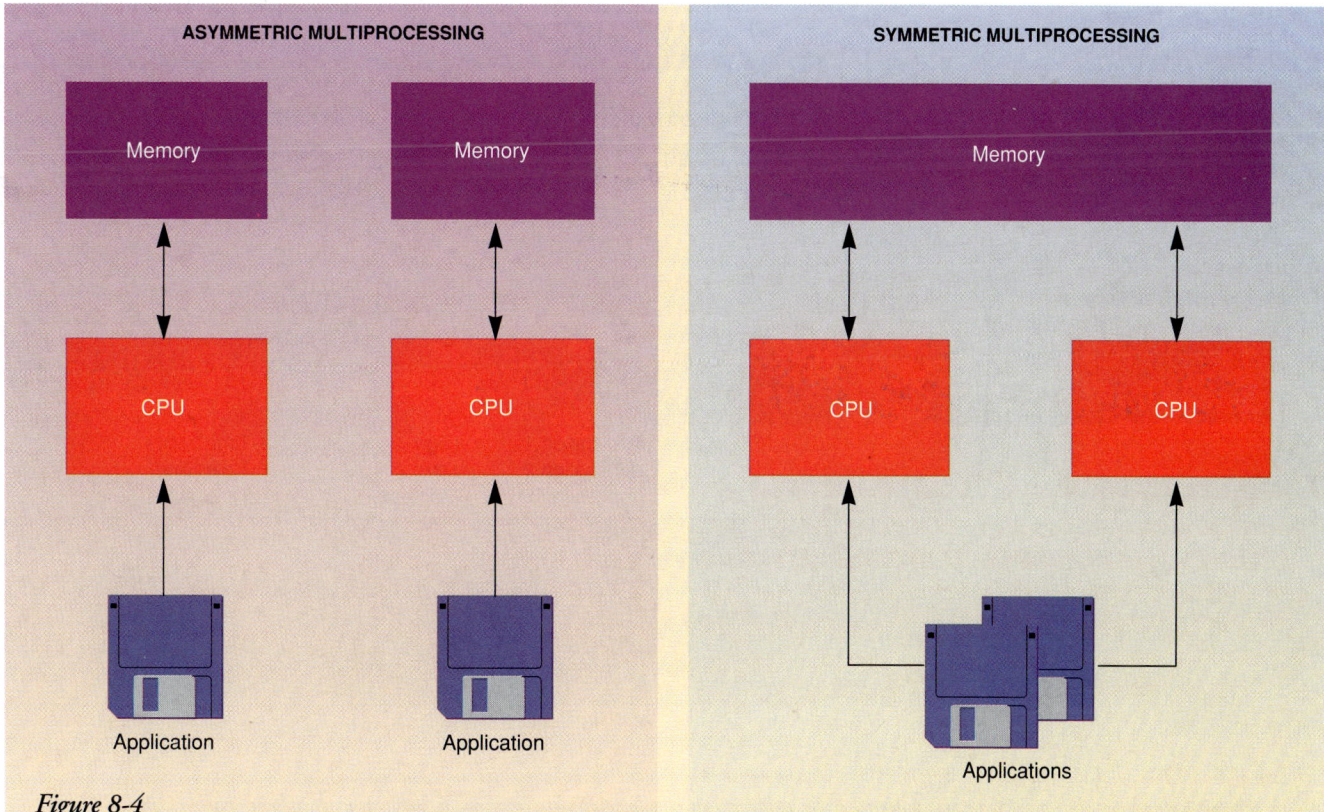

Figure 8-4
In asymmetric multiprocessing, application tasks are assigned to a specific CPU that has its own memory.
In symmetric multiprocessing, application tasks are assigned to any available CPU that shares memory with the other CPUs.

Functions of Operating Systems

The operating system performs a number of functions that allow the user and the application software to interact with the computer. These functions apply to all operating systems but become more complex for operating systems that allow more than one program to run at a time. The functions can be grouped into three types: allocating system resources, monitoring system activities, and disk and file management *(Figure 8-5)*.

Allocating System Resources

The primary function of the operating system is to allocate, or assign, the resources of the computer system. That is, just as a police officer directs traffic, the operating system decides what resource will currently be used and for how long. These resources include the CPU, main memory, and the input and output devices such as disk and tape drives and printers.

CPU MANAGEMENT

Because a CPU can only work on one program instruction at a time, a multitasking operating system must keep switching the CPU among the different instructions of the programs that are waiting to be performed. A common way of allocating CPU processing is time slicing. A **time slice** is a fixed amount of CPU processing time, usually measured in milliseconds (thousandths of a second). With this technique, each user in turn receives a time slice. Because some instructions take less time to execute than others, some users may have more instructions completed in their time slice than other users. When a user's time slice has expired, the operating system directs the CPU to work on another user's program instructions, and the most recent user moves to the end of the line to await the next time slice *(Figure 8-6)*. Unless the system has a heavy work load, however, users may not even be aware that their program has been temporarily set aside. Before they notice a delay, the operating system has allocated them another time slice and their processing continues.

Because some work has a higher priority or is more important than other work, most operating systems have ways to adjust the amount of time slices a user receives, either automatically or based on user-specified criteria. One technique for modifying the number of time slices is to have different priorities assigned to each user. For each time slice received by the lowest priority, the highest priority would receive several consecutive time slices. For example, it would be logical to assign a higher priority to a program that processes

ALLOCATING RESOURCES	MONITORING ACTIVITIES	DISK AND FILE MANAGEMENT
CPU management	System performance	Formatting
Memory management	System security	Copying
Input/output management		Deleting

Figure 8-5
Operating system functions.

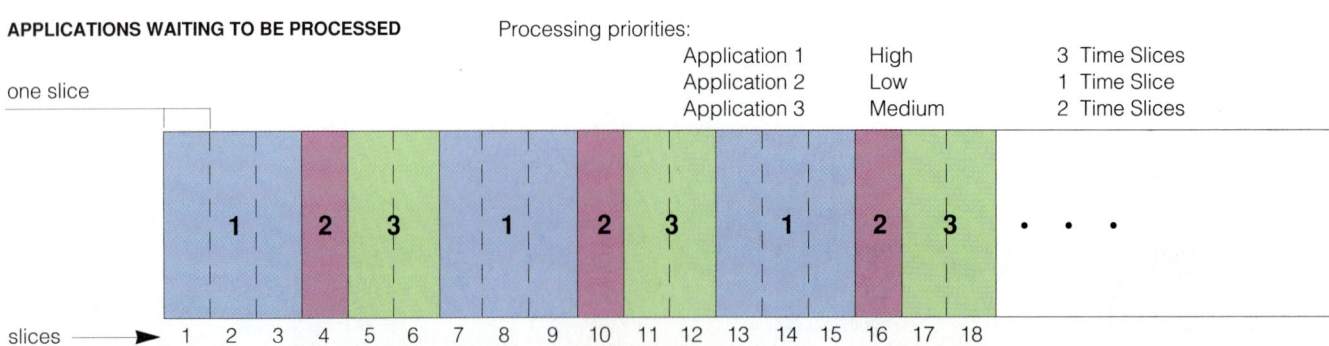

Figure 8-6
With the time slice method of CPU management, each application is allocated one or more fixed amounts of time called slices. Higher priority (more important) applications receive more consecutive slices than lower priority applications. When its processing time has expired, an application goes to the end of the line until all other applications have received at least one time slice. Here, application 2 is the lowest priority and so receives only one time slice. Application 1 is the highest priority and receives three time slices.

orders and records sales than to an accounting program that could be run at a later time. Another way to allocate time slices is based on the type of work being performed. For example, some operating systems automatically allocate more time slices to interactive processes such as keyboard entry than they do to CPU-only processes such as calculations. This gives a higher priority to users entering data than to a report being printed.

Another way of assigning processing priorities is to designate each job as either foreground or background. **Foreground** jobs receive a higher processing priority and more CPU time. Data entry would be an example of a job that would be classified as a foreground job. **Background** jobs receive a lower processing priority and less CPU time. Printing a report or calculating payroll are examples of jobs that could be classified as background jobs.

MEMORY MANAGEMENT

During processing, items such as the operating system, application program instructions, data waiting to be processed, and work space used for calculations, sorting, and other temporary tasks are stored in main memory. It is the operating system's job to allocate, or assign, each of these items to areas of main memory. Data that has just been read into main memory from an input device or is waiting to be sent to an output device is stored in areas of main memory called **buffers**. The operating system assigns the location of the buffers in main memory and manages the data that is stored in them.

Operating systems allocate at least some portion of memory into fixed areas called **partitions** *(Figure 8-7)*. Some operating systems allocate all memory on this basis while others use partitions only for the operating system instructions and buffers.

Another way of allocating memory is called virtual memory management, or virtual storage. **Virtual memory management** increases the effective (or *virtual*) limits of memory by expanding the amount of main memory to include disk space. Without virtual memory management, an entire program must be loaded into main memory during execution. With virtual memory management, only the portion of the program that is currently being used is required to be in main memory. Virtual memory management is used with multitasking operating systems to maximize the number of programs using memory at the same time. The operating system performs

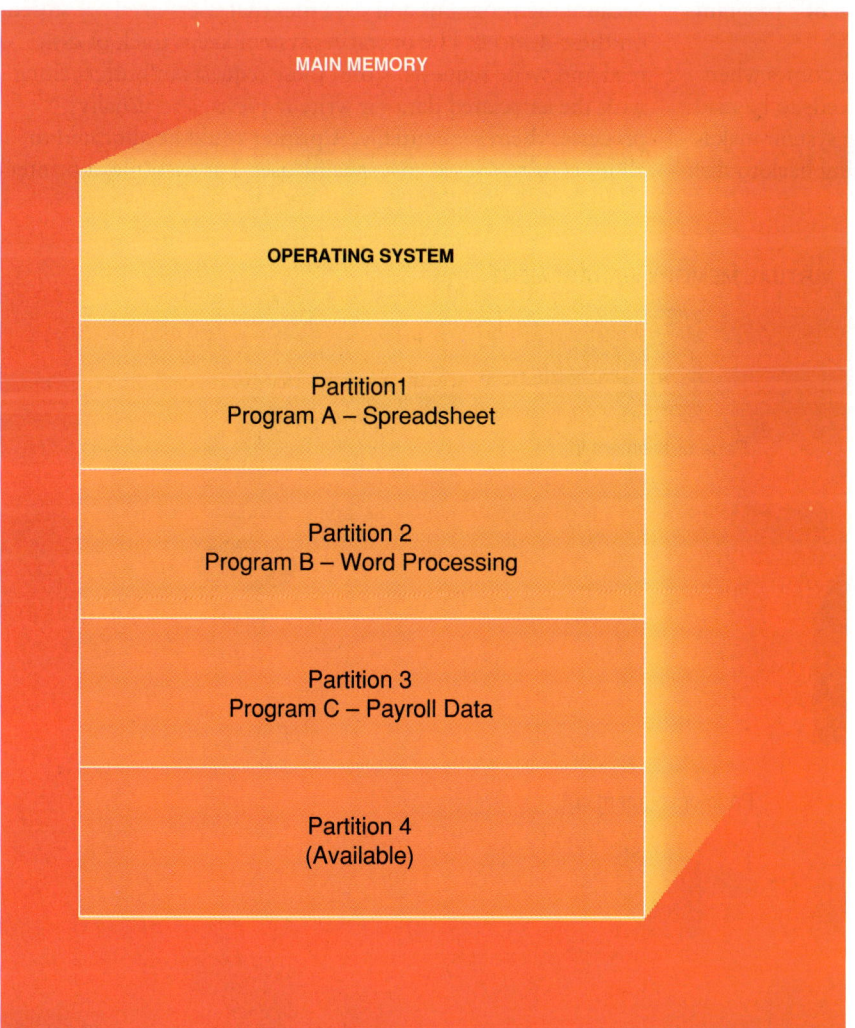

Figure 8-7
Some computer systems allocate memory into fixed blocks called partitions. The CPU then keeps track of programs and data by assigning them to a specific partition.

virtual memory management by transferring data and instructions to and from memory and the disk by using one or both of the two methods, segmentation and paging.

In **segmentation**, programs are divided into logical portions called **segments**. For example, one segment of a program may edit data and another segment may perform a calculation. Because the segments are based on logical portions of a program, some segments are larger than others. When a particular program instruction is required, the segment containing that instruction is transferred from the disk into main memory.

In **paging**, a fixed number of bytes is transferred from the disk each time data or program instructions are required. This fixed amount of data is called a **page**, or a **frame**. The size of a page, generally from 512 to 4,000 bytes, is determined by the operating system. Because a page is a fixed number of bytes, it may not correspond to a logical division of a program like a segment.

In both segmentation and paging, a time comes when memory is full but another page or segment needs to be read into memory. When this occurs, the operating system makes room for the new data or instructions by writing back to disk one or more of the pages or segments currently in memory. This process is referred to as **swapping** *(Figure 8-8)*. The operating system usually chooses the least recently used page or segment to transfer back to disk.

INPUT AND OUTPUT MANAGEMENT

At any given time, more than one input device can be sending data to the computer. At the same time, the CPU could be ready to send data to an output device such as a terminal or printer or a storage device such as a disk. The operating system is responsible for managing these input and output processes.

Some devices, such as a tape drive, are usually allocated to a specific user or application program. This is because tape is a sequential storage medium, and generally it would not make sense to have more than one application writing records to a single tape. Disk drives are usually allocated to all users because the programs and data files that users need are stored on these devices. The operating system keeps track of disk read and write requests, stores these requests in buffers along with the associated data for write requests, and usually processes them sequentially. A printer could be allocated to all users or restricted to a specific user. For example, a printer

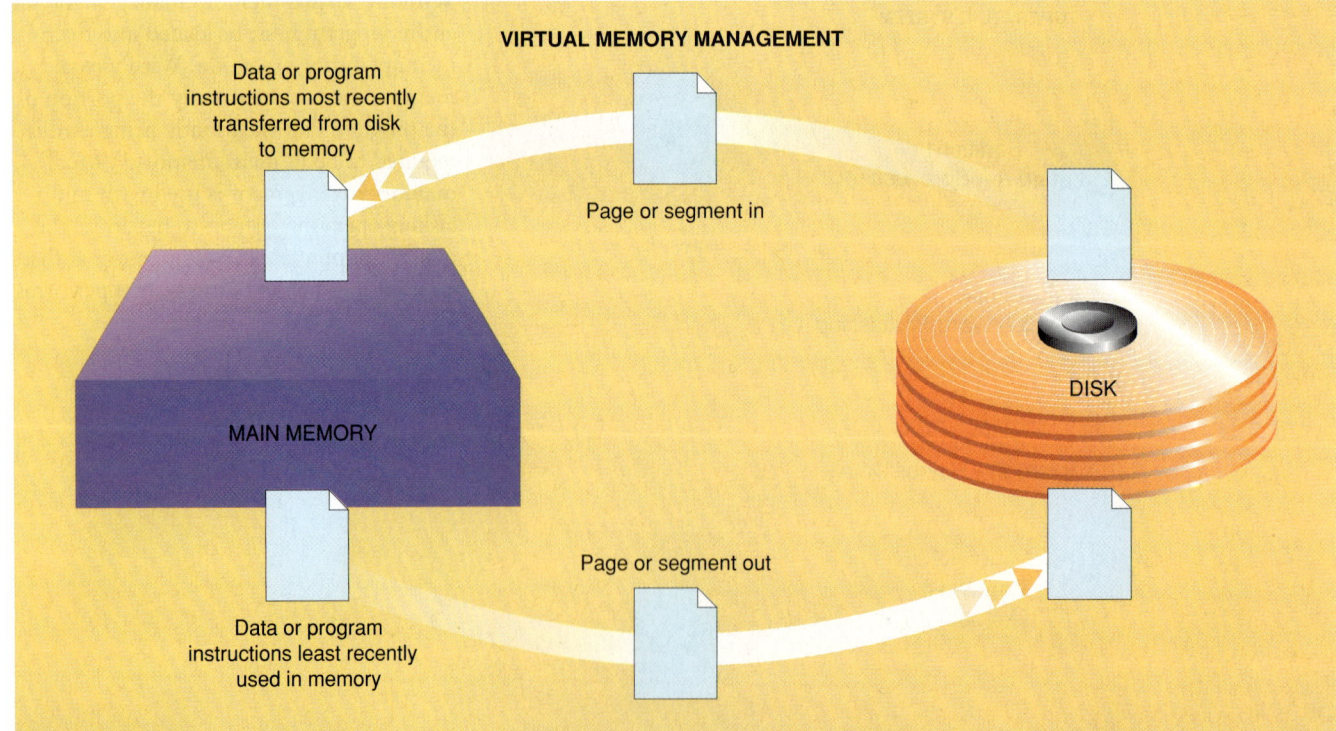

Figure 8-8
With virtual memory management, the operating system expands the amount of main memory to include available disk space. Data and program instructions are transferred to and from memory and disk as required. The segmentation technique transfers logical portions of programs that may be different sizes. The paging technique transfers pages of the same size. To make room for the new page or segment, the least recently used page or segment is swapped, or written back to the disk.

FUNCTIONS OF OPERATING SYSTEMS

would be restricted to a specific user if the printer was going to be used with preprinted forms such as payroll checks.

Because the printer is a relatively slow device compared to other computer system devices, the technique of spooling is used to increase printer efficiency and reduce the number of printers required. With **spooling** *(Figure 8-9)*, a report is first written (saved) to the disk before it is printed. Writing to the disk is much faster than writing to the printer. For example, a report that may take one-half hour to print (depending on the speed of the printer) may take only one minute to write to the disk. After the report is written to the disk, the CPU is available to process other programs. The report saved on the disk can be printed at a later time or, in a multitasking operating system, a print program can be run (at the same time other programs are running) to process the **print spool** (the reports on the disk waiting to be printed).

Because many input and output devices use different commands and control codes to transmit and receive data, programs called **device drivers** are used by the operating system to control these devices. For example, a different device driver would be required for a high-resolution color monitor than for a standard-resolution monochrome monitor. Device drivers are usually supplied with the operating system or by the device manufacturers.

Monitoring System Activities

Another function of the operating system is monitoring the system activity. This includes monitoring system performance and system security.

SYSTEM PERFORMANCE

System performance can be measured in a number of ways but is usually gauged by the user in terms of response time. **Response time** is the amount of time from the moment a user enters data until the computer responds.

Response time can vary based on what the user has entered. If the user is simply entering data into a file, the response time is usually within a second or two. However, if the user has just completed a request for a display of sorted data from several files, the response time could be minutes.

A more precise way of measuring performance is to run a program that is designed to record and report system activity.

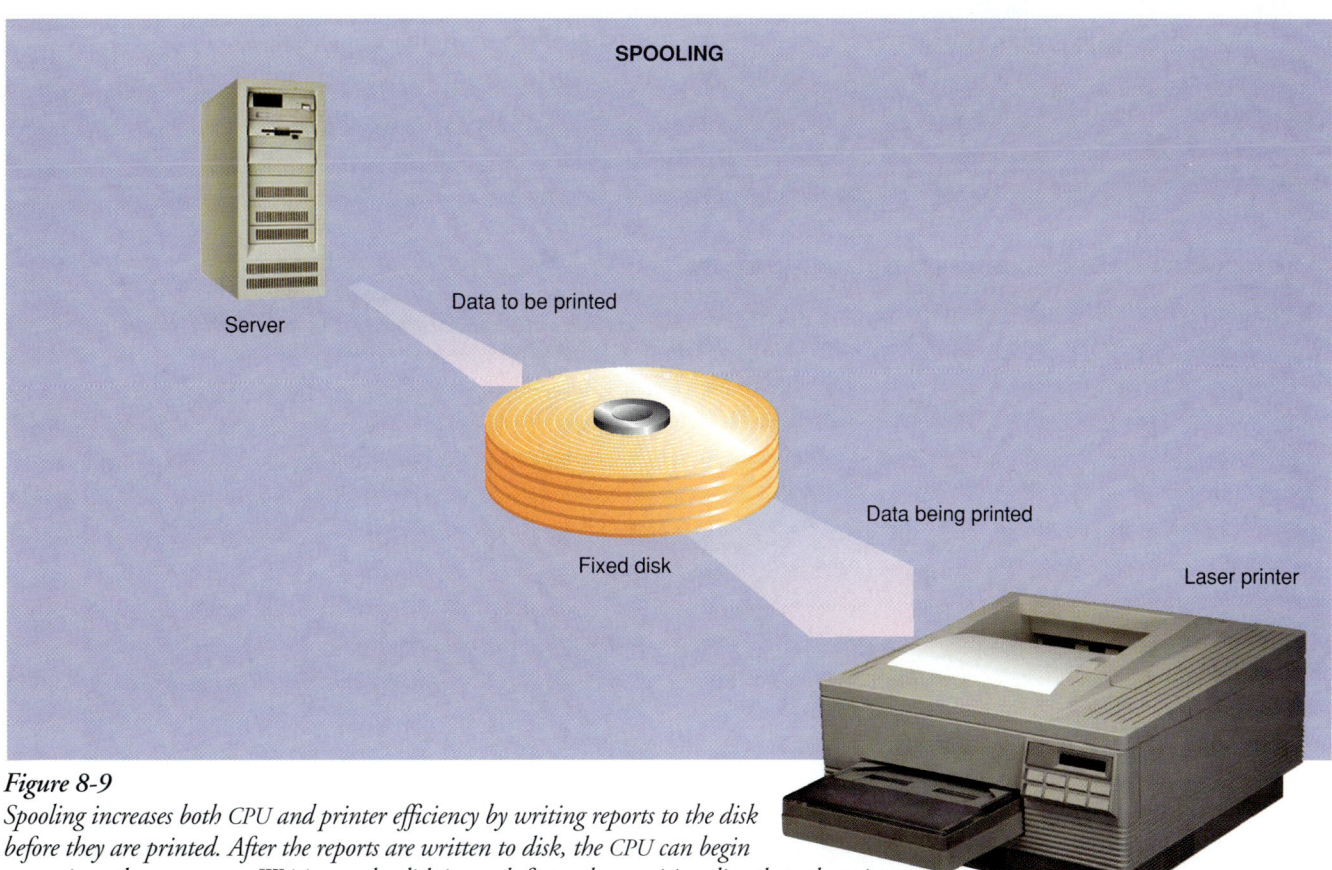

Figure 8-9
Spooling increases both CPU and printer efficiency by writing reports to the disk before they are printed. After the reports are written to disk, the CPU can begin processing other programs. Writing to the disk is much faster than writing directly to the printer.

Among other information, these programs usually report CPU **utilization,** the amount of time that the CPU is working and not idle, waiting for data to process. *Figure 8-10* shows a CPU performance measurement report.

Another measure of performance is to compare the CPU utilization with the disk input and output rate, referred to as disk I/O. How a virtual memory management operating system swaps pages or segments from disk to memory as they are needed was previously discussed. Systems with heavy work loads and insufficient memory or CPU power can get into a situation called **thrashing,** where the system is spending more time moving pages to and from the disk than processing the data. System performance reporting can alert the computer user to this problem.

System Security

Most multiuser operating systems provide for a logon code, a user ID, and a password that must all be entered correctly before a user is allowed to use an application program *(Figure 8-11)*. Each is a word or series of characters. A **logon code** usually identifies the application that will be used, such as accounting, sales, or manufacturing. A **user ID** identifies the user, such as Jeffrey Ryan or Mary Gonzales. The **password** is usually confidential; often it is known only to the user and the computer system administrator. The logon code, user ID, and password must match entries in an authorization file. If they do not match, the user is denied access to the system. Both successful and unsuccessful logon attempts are often recorded in a file so management can review who is using or attempting to use the system. These logs can also be used to allocate computing expenses based on the percentage of system use by an organization's various departments.

Disk and File Management

In addition to allocating system resources and monitoring system activities, most operating systems contain programs that can perform functions related to disk and file management. Some of these functions include formatting disks and diskettes, deleting files from a disk, copying files from one secondary storage device to another, and renaming stored files.

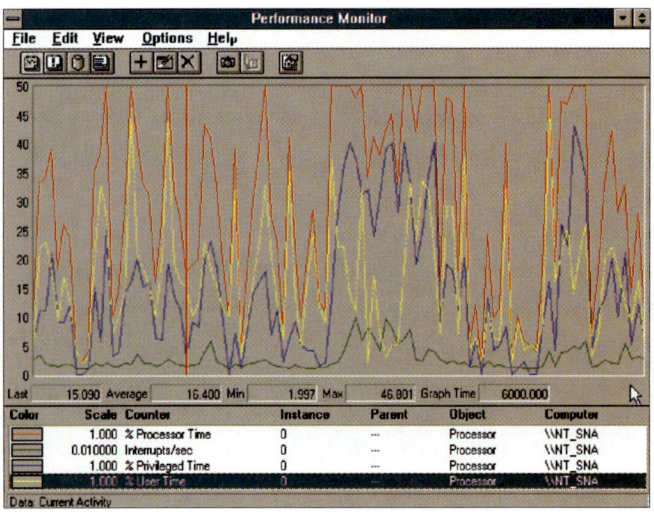

Figure 8-10
System performance measurement programs report the amount of time the CPU is actually working and not waiting to process data.

Figure 8-11
The logon code, user ID, and password must all be entered correctly before the user is allowed to use the computer. Because the password is confidential, it is usually not displayed on the screen when the user enters it.

Logon code; usually specifies application to be used

User ID; usually name of user

Password; unique word or combination of characters known only to user

Popular Operating Systems

The first operating systems were developed by manufacturers for the computers in their product line. When the manufacturers came out with another computer or model, they often produced an improved and different operating system. Because programs are designed to be used with a particular operating system, this meant that users who wanted to switch computers, either from one vendor to another or to a different model from the same vendor, would have to convert their existing programs to run under the new operating system. Today, however, the trend is away from operating systems limited to a specific model and toward operating systems that will run on any model by a particular manufacturer.

Going even further, many computer users are supporting the move away from **proprietary operating systems** (meaning privately owned) and toward **portable operating systems** that will run on many manufacturers' computers. The advantage of portable operating systems is that the user is not tied to a particular manufacturer. Using a portable operating system, a user could change computer systems, yet retain existing software and data files, which usually represent a sizable investment in time and money. For example, consider a small business that purchases a computer system to handle their immediate needs and to provide for several years of anticipated growth. Five years later, the business has reached the capacity of the computer; no more memory or terminals can be added. In addition, the manufacturer of the five-year-old computer does not make a larger or more powerful model. Because the business originally chose a computer that used a portable operating system, it can purchase a more powerful computer from another manufacturer that offers the same portable operating system and continue to use the existing software and data files.

One of the most popular portable operating systems is DOS, which is discussed along with the several other computer operating systems in this section.

DOS

DOS stands for **Disk Operating System,** the most widely used operating system on personal computers. Several slightly different but compatible versions of DOS exist. The two most widely used, MS-DOS and PC-DOS, were both originally developed by Microsoft Corporation in 1981.

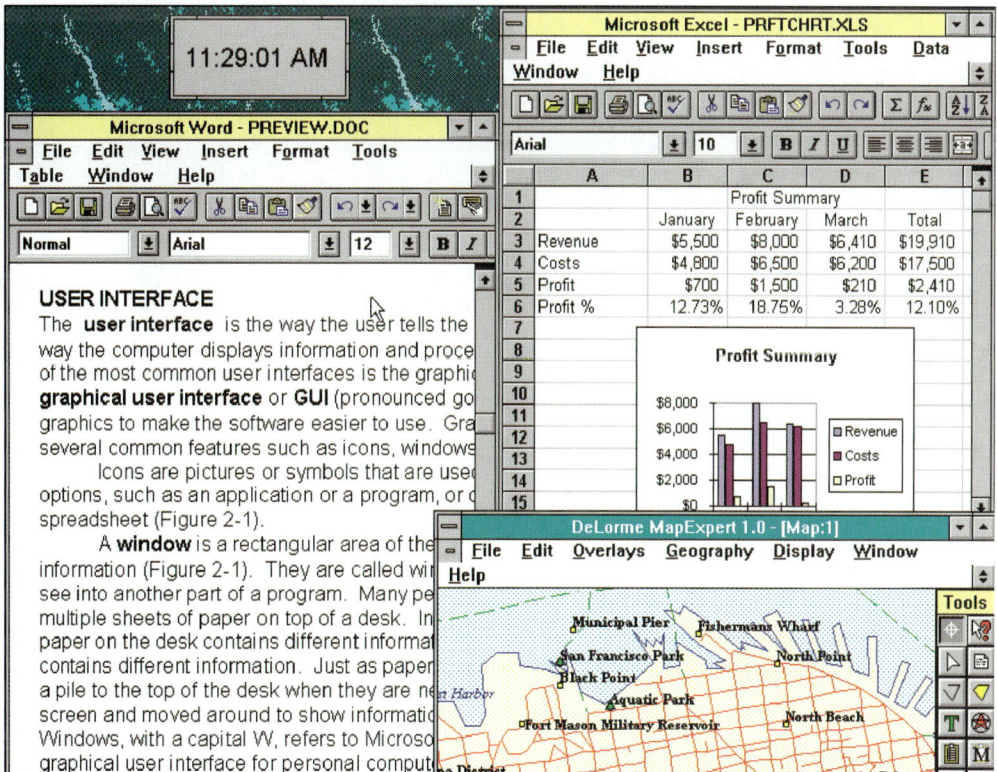

Figure 8-12
The Microsoft Windows operating system provides a graphical user interface that makes computers easy to use. This screen shows three different applications; word processing, spreadsheet, and a map program. Each application is displayed in a window. A digital clock is displayed in the upper left corner.

MS-DOS is marketed directly by Microsoft and is installed on most IBM-compatible personal computer systems. PC-DOS was developed by Microsoft for IBM and is installed by IBM on systems that IBM sells. Through the years, DOS has been improved many times. Each new version, called a *release,* has added new features and capabilities. However, DOS remains primarily a single user, single program operating system. Most importantly, DOS is unable to take full advantage of the newer 32-bit microprocessors, but DOS does have a large installed base, estimated at more than 100 million users.

Windows

Microsoft Windows is the most widely used graphical user interface for personal computers (*Figure 8-12* on the previous page). Windows version number 3.1 or below is not technically an operating system, but rather, is a multitasking graphical user interface **operating environment** that runs on DOS-based computers.

Common features of an operating environment (and Windows) include support for use of a mouse, icons, pull-down menus, the capability to have several applications open at the same time, and the capability to easily move data from one application to another. Closely related to operating environments are operating system shell programs. Like an operating environment, a **shell** program acts as an interface between the user and the operating system. Shell programs, however, usually offer a limited number of utility functions such as file maintenance and do not offer application windowing or graphics.

The most recent version of Windows, called Windows 95, does not require DOS and is a true multitasking operating system designed to take advantage of 32-bit microprocessors. Application programs written for prior versions of Windows and DOS can still run under the newer 32-bit version of Windows.

Windows NT

Microsoft Windows NT is a sophisticated version of Windows that is designed for use on client-server computer systems. Like the latest version of Windows, Windows NT is a complete operating system that does not require DOS. Unique features of Windows NT include the following:

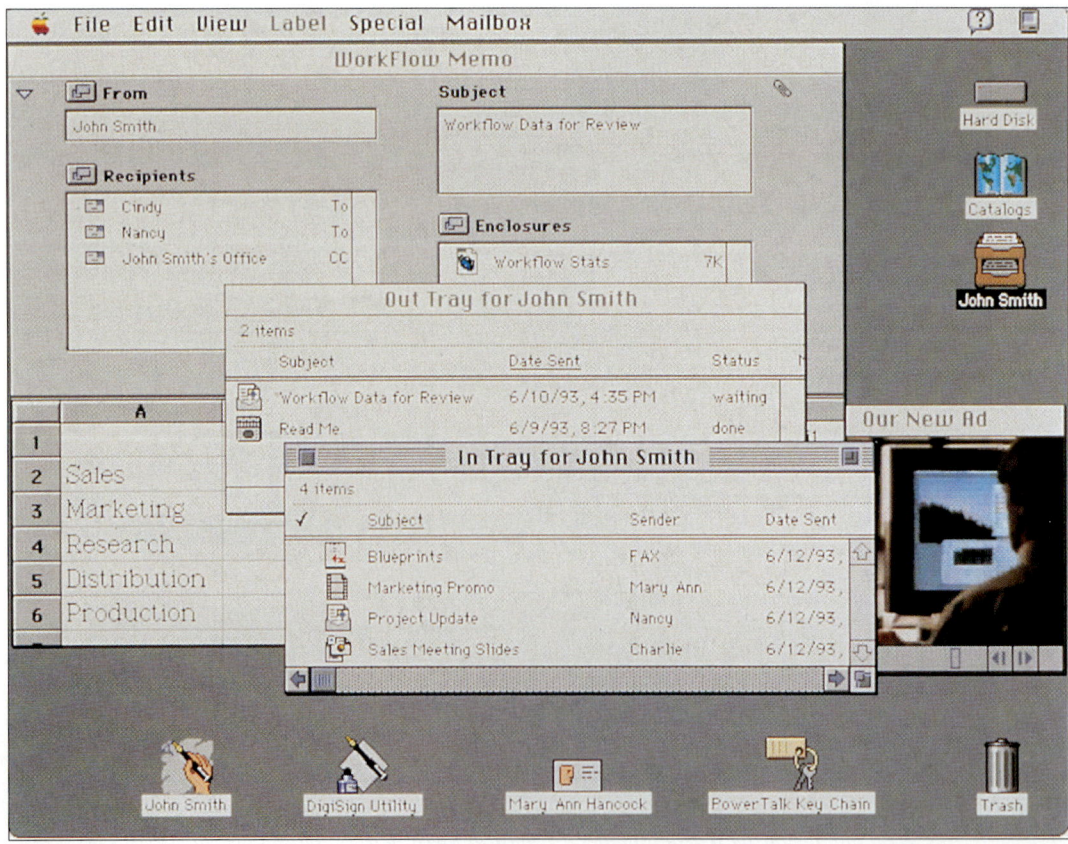

Figure 8-13
Apple's Macintosh operating system offers a graphical user interface and the capability to display information in separate windows.

- Support for most major networking communications protocols
- The capability to run 32-bit application programs
- *User Manager,* a program that creates user accounts and manages system security
- *Performance Monitor,* a program that measures network performance

Because it is more complex than Windows, Windows NT requires significant system resources including 12 to 16 MB of memory and 75 to 100 MB of disk space.

Macintosh

The Apple **Macintosh** multitasking operating system used the first commercially successful graphical user interface when it was released with Macintosh computers in 1984 *(Figure 8-13).* Since then, it has set the standard for operating system ease of use and has been the model for most of the new graphical user interfaces developed for non-Macintosh systems. Distinctive features of the latest version of the operating system, called System 7.5, include built-in networking support, electronic mail, and an extensive step-by-step help system called Apple Guide.

OS/2

OS/2 is IBM's operating system designed to work with 32-bit microprocessors *(Figure 8-14).* Besides being able to run programs written specifically for OS/2, the operating system can also run programs written for DOS or Windows. Like Windows, OS/2 has a graphical user interface. OS/2 is popular with businesses that need a sophisticated operating system to use for day-to-day operations. Several different versions of OS/2 exist, including an entry-level version designed to work on systems with only 4 MB of memory and a more complex version designed to work on servers with multiple processors. The latest version of OS/2 is called OS/2 Warp, version 3.

UNIX

The **UNIX** operating system was developed in the early 1970s by scientists at Bell Laboratories. It was specifically designed to provide a way to manage a variety of scientific and specialized computer applications. Because of federal regulations, Bell Labs (a subsidiary of AT&T) was prohibited from actively promoting UNIX in the commercial marketplace.

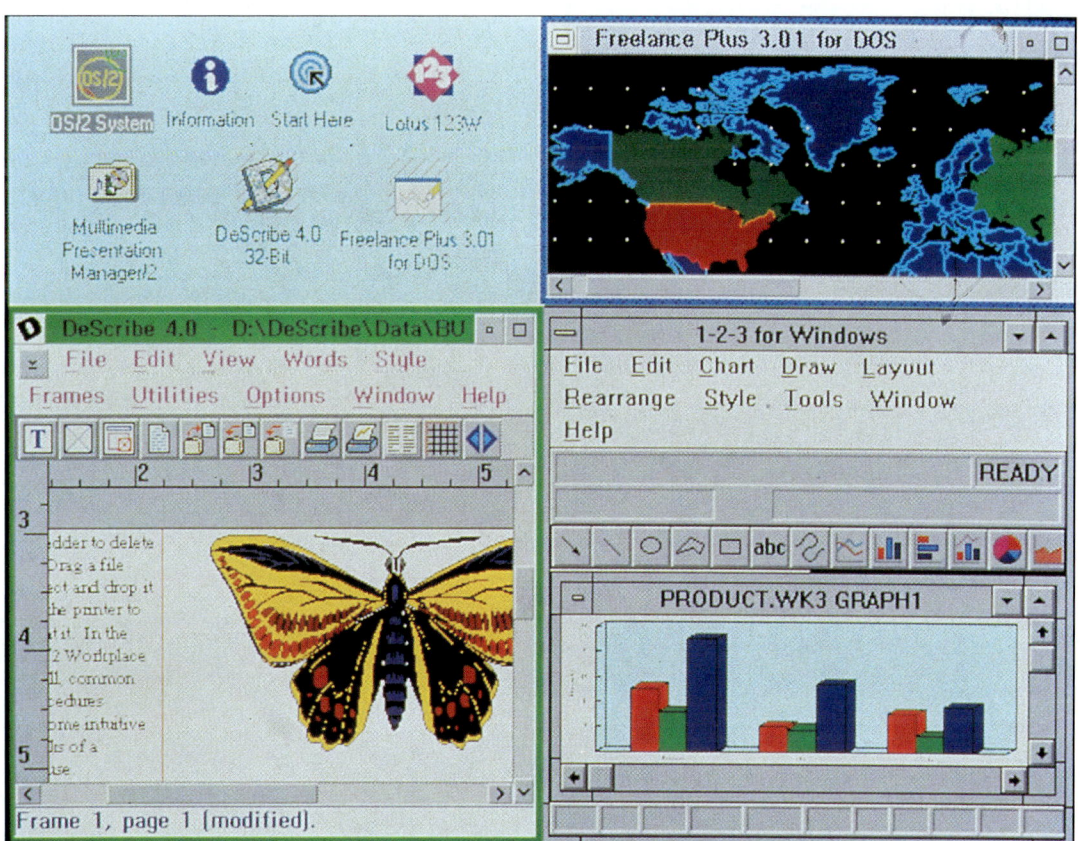

Figure 8-14
IBM's OS/2 operating system takes advantage of the increased processing power of the latest 32-bit microprocessors.

Instead, for a low fee, Bell Labs licensed UNIX to numerous colleges and universities where it obtained a wide following. With the deregulation of the telephone companies in the 1980s, AT&T was allowed to enter the computer system marketplace. With increased promotion and the trend toward portable operating systems, UNIX has aroused tremendous interest. One of the advantages of UNIX is its extensive library of more than 400 instruction modules that can be linked together to perform almost any programming task. Today, most major computer manufacturers offer a multiuser version of the UNIX operating system to run on their computers.

With all its strengths, however, UNIX has not yet obtained success in the commercial business systems marketplace. Some people attribute this to the fact that UNIX has never been considered user friendly. For example, most of the UNIX program modules are identified by obscure names such as MAUS, SHMOP, and BRK. Other critics contend that UNIX lacks the file management capabilities to support the online interactive databases that increasingly more businesses are implementing. With the support of most major computer manufacturers, however, these problems are being worked on, and UNIX may become one of the major operating systems of the coming years.

Figure 8-15
The NextStep operating system from NeXT Computer is designed to help software developers create new applications in significantly less time than using traditional methods and operating systems.

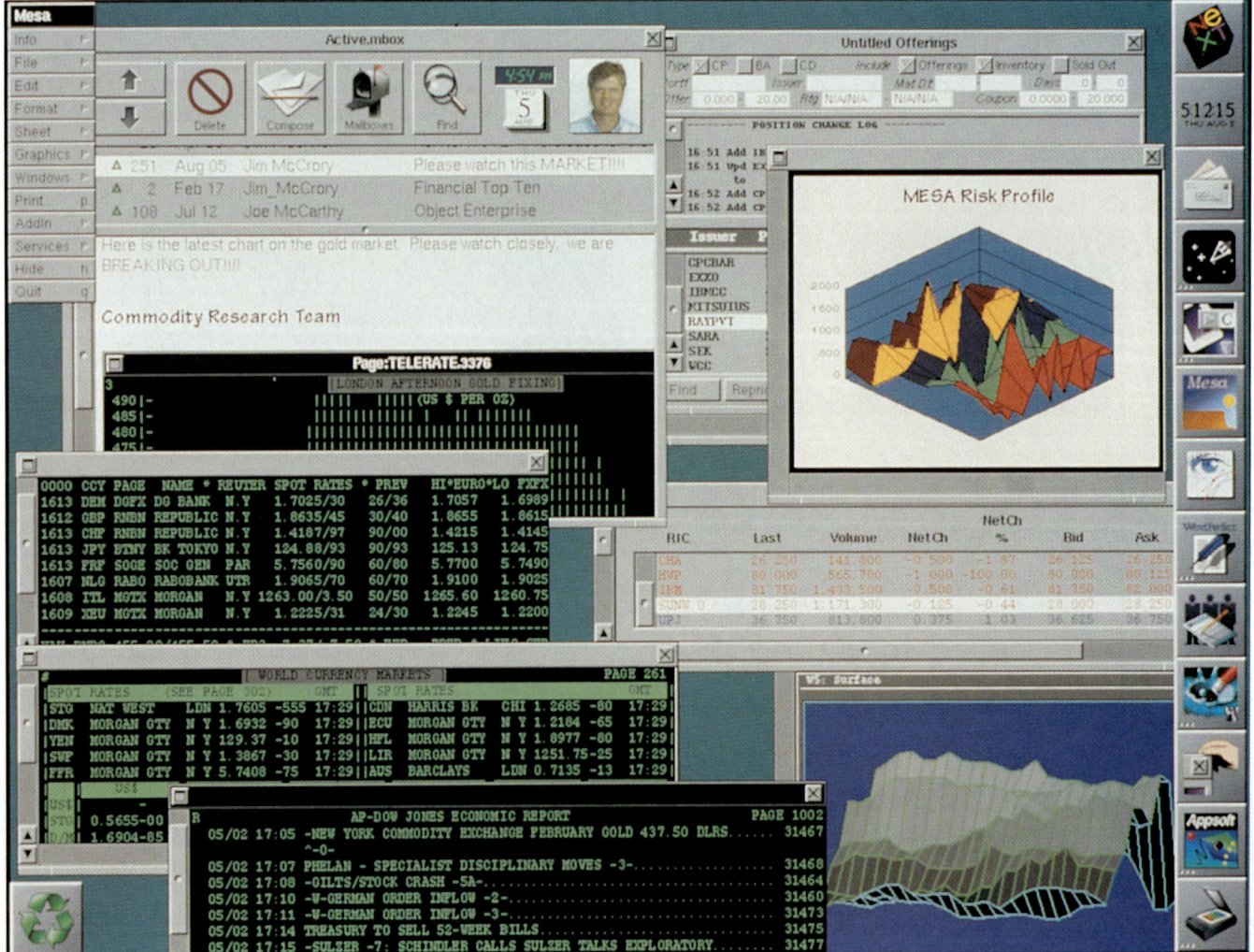

NextStep

The NextStep operating system from NeXT Computer was originally written to operate on the computers they manufactured. In recent years, NeXT has rewritten the operating system to run on Intel and other microprocessors and has stopped manufacturing computers to concentrate on NextStep development and marketing. NextStep is fundamentally different because it is the only object-oriented operating system *(Figure 8-15)*. Objects are a combination of the separate procedures and data that are used by most programs and operating systems. The main impact of object-oriented technology is that programs can be developed in much less time; some say in as little as one-tenth the time of traditional methods. NeXT hopes that NextStep, which has been designed to support object-oriented programming, will appeal to businesses that must develop new applications quickly.

Other Operating Systems

Other popular operating systems exist in addition to those just discussed. Most mainframe operating systems are unique to a particular make of computer or are designed to be compatible with one of IBM's operating systems such as DOS/VS, MVS, or VM, IBM's virtual machine operating system.

Although not yet widely used, the MACH operating system has been called a possible replacement for the increasingly popular UNIX operating system and possibly the standard operating system of the future. Considered a streamlined version of UNIX, MACH has the support of several large governmental and educational organizations. Currently being developed by Carnegie Mellon University, MACH has also been chosen by the Open Software Foundation (OSF), a 170-member organization that is trying to establish an industry-wide operating system standard.

Utilities

Utility programs perform specific tasks related to managing computer resources or files. Many utility programs are included with the operating system. These utility programs usually handle frequently performed tasks such as copying and moving files and formatting disks. Other utility programs are sold separately or in a group with other utility programs that are designed to work together. A brief description of some of the tasks addressed by utility programs follows:

- **File Management**   Listing, editing, copying, moving, and deleting files and directories.
- **Disk Management**   Formatting and defragmenting disks.
- **Memory Management**   Configuring a system to make the most memory available for running application programs. Memory managers do this by moving certain programs, such as device drivers, to other areas of RAM.
- **Backup and Restore**   Backup software allows the user to select one or more files for copying to diskettes or tape. The backup software monitors the copying process and alerts the user if an additional diskette or tape is needed. Restore software reverses the process and allows the user to reinstate files that have been previously copied to disk or tape.
- **Data Recovery**   Data recovery software assists the user in rebuilding files that have been deleted or files that have been damaged.
- **Data Compression**   Reduces the amount of space that a file requires. See Chapter 6 for a discussion on how data compression works.
- **Virus Protection**   A virus is a computer program that is designed to copy itself into other programs and spread through multiple computer systems. Most virus programs cause damage to files on the system where the virus is present. Virus protection programs use a number of methods to prevent virus programs from being loaded on a computer.

Another type of utility program is a screen saver. If the same image is displayed on a monitor for long periods of time, a very dim version of the image can be permanently etched on the monitor screen. A **screen saver** program prevents this problem, called *ghosting,* by dimming the brightness of the screen or displays moving images on the screen. The screen saver program automatically starts if the image on a screen does not change for a certain period of time that can be set by the user. The moving image screen savers are often quite entertaining and allow the user to choose from a variety of images. *Figure 8-16* is an example of a screen saver display.

Language Translators

Special-purpose system software programs called **language translators** are used to convert the programming instructions written by programmers into the machine instructions that a computer can understand. Language translators are written for specific programming languages and computer systems.

Summary of Operating Systems and System Software

System software, including the operating system, utilities, and language translators, are essential parts of a computer system and should be understood by users who want to obtain the maximum benefits from their computers. This is especially true for the latest personal computer operating systems that include features such as virtual memory management and multitasking. Understanding and being able to use these and other features will give users more control over their computer resources.

Figure 8-16
The After Dark screen saver utility program from Berkeley Systems prevents an image from being permanently etched on a monitor screen by displaying entertaining images that move across the screen.

COMPUTERS AT WORK

NextStep: Objects May Be Closer Than They Appear

NeXT Computer believes that its NextStep operating system has a significant advantage that business users will want. So far, the businesses that have tried NextStep think that NeXT is right. NextStep is the only operating system designed to support object-oriented computing. Objects are combinations of data and procedures that are treated separately by traditional operating systems. One advantage of objects is that they are *smart*. Because they contain procedures that specify how they behave in certain situations, much less programming code is required and applications can be developed in a fraction of the time. An example of an object would be an invoice that knows how to print itself. Instead of using a program to specify exactly how to print the invoice data, an invoice object merely has to be sent a message saying, print. Another advantage of objects is that they are reusable. Over time, the user builds a library of objects that can be used to quickly create applications. NeXT claims that with NextStep, applications can be developed in one-fifth to one-tenth the time. Many of their customers have found this to be true.

Chrysler Financial, the financing subsidiary of the Chrysler automobile company, used NextStep to create a system for processing all car loans. They developed their first five applications in four months, less time than it takes to even design most programs. In the next four months, Chrysler Financial developed nineteen more applications. These applications are being used by approximately 3,000 people at 100 financial centers. Another NextStep user, Swiss Bank Corporation, developed a sophisticated options trading system in only two and one-half months.

NeXT believes that three trends will help NextStep become successful in the corporate market:
- The move to client/server computing
- The move to object-oriented computing
- The continued reengineering of major businesses that requires them to develop new ways of processing information

If NeXT is correct, the widespread use of objects may be closer that some people think.

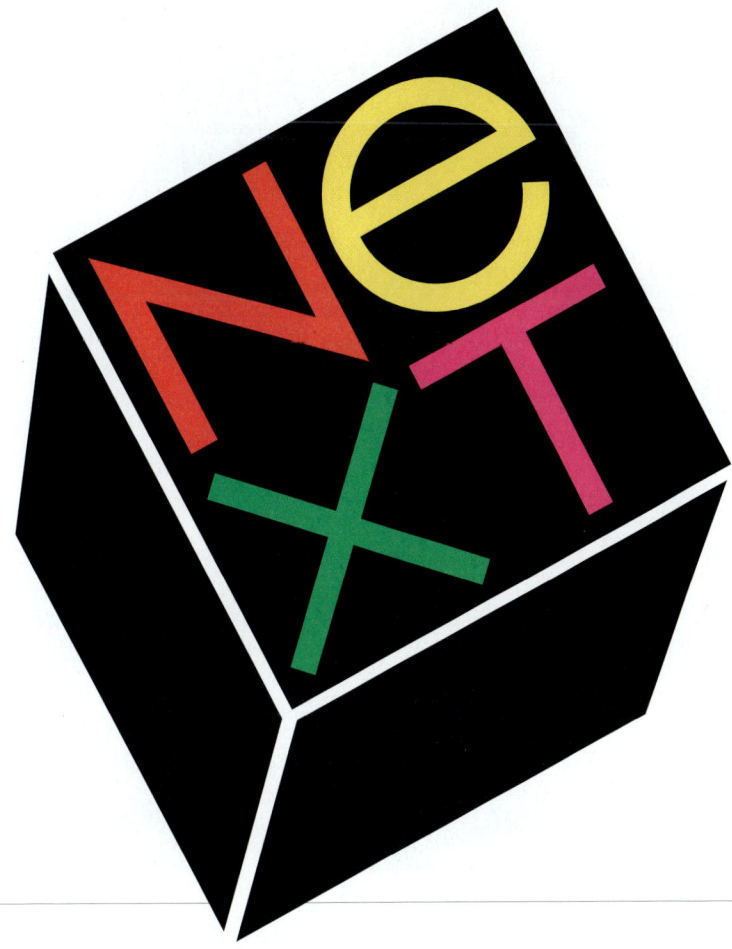

Figure 8-17

IN THE FUTURE

Is There a Future for Utility Software?

Some utility software developers worry about the future of their type of software. Recently, it seems that every time a good utility program is developed, it is not long before a similar utility program shows up as part of one of the major operating systems. When users upgrade to the new version of an operating system and obtain the additional utility programs, they have little, if any, incentive to pay for the utilities separately. Examples of utilities that started out as separate programs but have wound up as part of the operating system include the following:
- Communications
- Memory management
- File management
- Backup and restore
- Disk compression
- Virus protection
- Performance monitoring

To better support the increased use of computer networks, several developers have plans to include features such as network configuration management, network security, and electronic mail in future versions of their operating systems.

As with the consolidation in the application software industry, some worry that the trend of moving utilities into the operating system will lead to less competition and less innovation. Optimistic and confident developers point out that good utility programs will always find a market. Still others suggest that moving utilities into the operating system is a natural evolution with several advantages. They claim that users want to minimize the number of companies they buy products from and, perhaps more importantly, want to minimize the number of companies they have to talk with if something goes wrong.

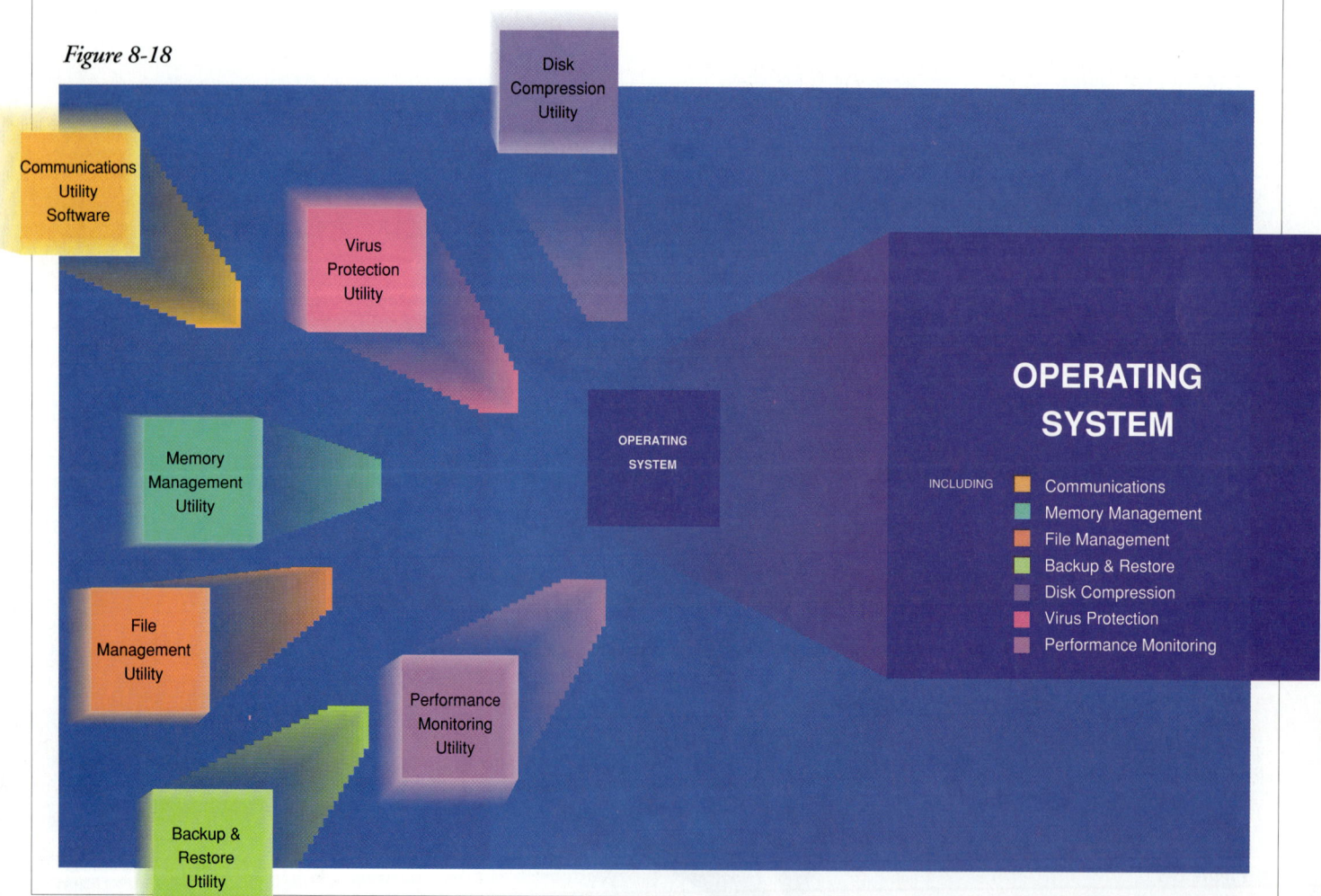

Figure 8-18

What You Should Know

1. **System software** consists of all the programs, including the operating system, that are related to controlling the operations of the computer equipment. System software can be classified into three major categories; operating systems, utilities, and language translators.

2. An **operating system** (OS) consists of one or more programs that control the allocation of hardware resources such as memory, CPU time, disk space, and peripheral devices. These programs function as an interface between the user, the application programs, and the computer equipment.

3. For a computer to operate, the essential and most frequently used instructions in the operating system must be copied from disk and stored in the main memory of the computer. This *resident* portion of the operating system is called by many different names: the **supervisor**, **monitor**, **executive**, **master program**, **control program**, or **kernel**. Commands that are included in the resident portion of the operating system are called **internal commands**. The *nonresident* portions of the operating system are called **external commands** that remain on disk and are available to be loaded into main memory when needed.

4. Most operating systems allow the user to give specific instructions to the computer. These instructions are called the **command language**. The **command language interpreter** is the portion of the operating system that carries out the command language instructions.

5. The process of loading an operating system into main memory is called **booting** the system. When the computer is turned on, the power supply distributes current to the devices in the system unit. The CPU chip resets itself and looks to the BIOS chip for instructions on how to proceed. The BIOS, which stands for **Basic Input/Output System**, is a set of instructions that provides the interface between the operating system and the hardware devices. The BIOS chip runs a series of tests, called the POST, for **Power On Self Test**, to make sure the equipment is working correctly. After the POST tests are completed, the BIOS looks for the operating system and begins loading the *resident* portion, called the kernel, into main memory. The kernel then loads the system configuration information, which is contained in a file called **CONFIG.SYS**, that tells the computer what devices you are using. For each device, a device driver program is usually loaded that tells the computer how to communicate with the device. The kernel loads the command language interpreter, called **COMMAND.COM** on DOS computers. COMMAND.COM loads a batch file named **AUTOEXEC.BAT** that performs optional tasks. If you haven't specified that the computer immediately start a particular application program, the system displays a **command language prompt** that indicates the system is ready to accept a command from the user.

6. Operating systems can be classified by two criteria: (1) whether they allow more than one user to use the computer at the same time; and (2) whether they allow more than one program to run at the same time.

7. **Single program** operating systems allow only a single user to run a single program at one time.

8. **Multitasking** operating systems allow more than one program to be run at the same time on one computer. Multitasking operating systems on some personal computers and most minicomputers and mainframes that can support more than one user running multiple programs, are called **timesharing** or **multiuser** operating systems.

9. Computers that have more than one CPU are called **multiprocessors**. A multiprocessing operating system coordinates the operations of computers with more than one CPU. In **asymmetric multiprocessing**, application tasks are assigned to a specific CPU. In **symmetric multiprocessing**, application tasks may be assigned to whatever CPU is available. **Fault-tolerant computers** are built with redundant components and can continue to operate with duplicate components if one of the components fails.

10. A **virtual machine** (VM) operating system allows a single computer to run two or more different operating systems.

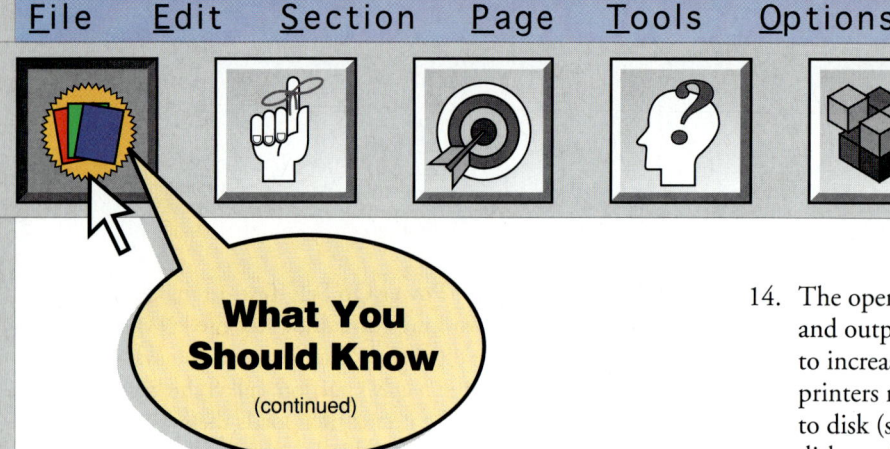

What You Should Know (continued)

11. The primary function of the operating system is to allocate, or assign, the resources of the computer system. These resources include the CPU, main memory, and the input and output devices.

12. A common way a multitasking operating system allocates CPU processing time is time slicing. A **time slice** is a fixed amount of CPU processing time, usually measured in milliseconds (thousandths of a second). Processing priorities can be assigned by designating each job as either a **foreground** job, which receives a higher priority and more CPU time, or a **background** job, which receives a lower priority and less processing time.

13. It is the operating system's job to allocate, or assign, items to areas of main memory. Data that has just been read into main memory from an input device or is waiting to be sent to an output device is stored in areas of main memory called **buffers**. Operating systems allocate at least some portion of main memory into fixed areas called **partitions**. The effective (or virtual) limits of memory can be increased by **virtual memory management**, which expands the amount of main memory to include disk space. With virtual memory management, only the portion of the program currently being used is required in main memory. In **segmentation**, the operating system performs virtual memory management by dividing programs into logical portions called **segments**. In **paging**, virtual memory management is performed by transferring a fixed number of bytes, called a **page** or a **frame**, from the disk each time data or program instructions are required. The process of making room for new data or instructions by writing back to disk one or more of the segments or pages currently in memory is referred to as **swapping**.

14. The operating system is responsible for managing input and output processes. The technique of spooling is used to increase printer efficiency and reduce the number of printers required. With **spooling**, a report is first written to disk (saved) before it is printed. The report saved on disk can be printed at a later time or, on a multitasking operating system, a print program can be run at the same time other programs are running to process the **print spool** (the reports on the disk waiting to be printed). Because many input and output devices use different commands and control codes to transmit and receive data, programs called **device drivers** are used by the operating system to control these devices.

15. Another function of the operating system is monitoring system activity. This includes monitoring system performance and system security.

16. System performance is usually gauged by the user in terms of **response time**, the amount of time from the moment a user enters data until the computer responds. **CPU utilization** is the amount of time that the CPU is working and not idle, waiting for data to process. Systems with heavy work loads and insufficient memory or CPU power can get into a situation called **thrashing**, where the system is spending more time moving pages to and from the disk than processing data.

17. Most multiuser operating systems monitor system security by providing for a logon code, a user ID, and a password that must all be entered correctly before a user is allowed to use the application program. A **logon code** usually identifies the application that will be used. A **user ID** identifies the user. The **password** is usually confidential; often it is known only to the user and the computer system administrator.

18. In addition to allocating system resources and monitoring system activities, most operating systems contain programs that can perform functions related to disk and file management.

19. Although the first operating systems were developed by manufacturers for computers in their product lines, today the trend is away from operating systems limited to a specific model and toward operating systems that will run on any model by a particular manufacturer. Going even further, many computer users are supporting the move away from **proprietary operating systems** (meaning privately owned) and toward **portable operating systems** that will run on many manufacturers' computers.

20. **DOS** stands for **Disk Operating System**, the most widely used operating system on personal computers. **MS-DOS** is marketed by Microsoft and is installed on most IBM-compatible personal computer systems. **PC-DOS** was developed by Microsoft for IBM and is installed by IBM on systems that IBM sells. Each new version of DOS, called a *release*, has added new features and capabilities.

21. Microsoft Windows is the most widely used graphical user interface for personal computers. Prior versions of Windows (version numbers 3.1 and below) were not technically an operating system, but were actually an **operating environment**, a graphical user interface designed to work in combination with an operating system. Like an operating environment, a **shell** program acts as an interface between the user and the operating system.

22. **Microsoft Windows NT** is a sophisticated version of Windows that is designed for use on client-server computer systems. Like the latest version of Windows (Windows 95), Windows NT is a complete operating system that does not require DOS.

23. The Apple **Macintosh** multitasking operating system used the first commercially successful graphical user interface. It has set the standard for operating system ease of use and has been the model for most of the new graphical user interfaces designed for non-Macintosh systems.

24. **OS/2** is IBM's operating system designed to work with 32-bit microprocessors. The operating system can run programs written for OS/2, DOS, or Windows. OS/2 has a graphical user interface (like Windows).

25. The **UNIX** operating system was developed in the early 1970s by scientists at Bell Laboratories to provide a way to manage a variety of scientific and specialized computer applications. Today, most major computer manufacturers offer a multiuser version of the UNIX operating system to run on their computers.

26. The NextStep operating system, from NeXT Computer, is the only object-oriented operating system. The main impact of object-oriented technology is that programs can be developed in much less time.

27. Other operating systems include mainframe operating systems (unique to a particular machine or designed to be compatible with one of IBM's operating systems) and MACH (considered a streamlined version of UNIX).

28. **Utility programs** perform specific tasks related to managing computer resources or files. These tasks include: file management, disk management, memory management, backup and restore, data recovery, data compression, and virus protection. A **screen saver** program prevents a problem called *ghosting* (having a dim version of a long-displayed image etched on the monitor screen) by dimming the brightness of the screen or displays moving images on the screen.

29. Special-purpose system software programs called **language translators** are used to convert the programming instructions written by programmers into the machine language instructions that a computer can understand.

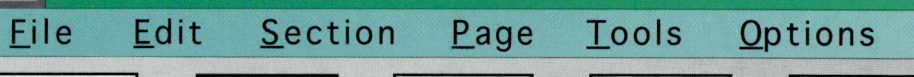

Terms to Remember

asymmetric multiprocessing (8.5)
AUTOEXEC.BAT (8.3)

background (8.7)
Basic Input/Output System (BIOS) (8.3)
BIOS (8.3)
booting (8.3)
buffers (8.7)

command language (8.2)
command language interpreter (8.2)
command language prompt (8.3)
COMMAND.COM (8.3)
CONFIG.SYS (8.3)
control program (8.2)
CPU utilization (8.10)

device driver (8.9)
Disk Operating System (DOS) (8.11)
DOS (8.11)

executive (8.2)
external commands (8.2)

fault-tolerant computers (8.5)
foreground (8.7)
frame (8.8)

internal commands (8.2)

kernel (8.2)

language translators (8.16)
logon code (8.10)

Macintosh (8.13)
master program (8.2)
Microsoft Windows NT (8.12)
monitor (8.2)
MS-DOS (8.12)
multiprocessing (8.5)
multiprocessors (8.5)
multitasking (8.4)
multiuser (8.4)

operating environment (8.12)
operating system (8.2)
OS/2 (8.13)

page (8.8)
paging (8.8)
partitions (8.7)
password (8.10)
PC-DOS (8.12)
portable operating systems (8.11)
POST (8.3)
Power On Self Test (POST) (8.3)
print spool (8.9)
proprietary operating systems (8.11)

response time (8.9)

screen saver (8.16)
segmentation (8.8)
segments (8.8)
shell (8.12)
single program (8.4)
spooling (8.9)
supervisor (8.2)
swapping (8.8)
symmetric multiprocessing (8.5)
system software (8.2)

thrashing (8.10)
time slice (8.6)
timesharing (8.4)

UNIX (8.13)
user ID (8.10)
utility programs (8.15)

virtual machine (VM) (8.5)
virtual memory management (8.7)

Test Your Knowledge

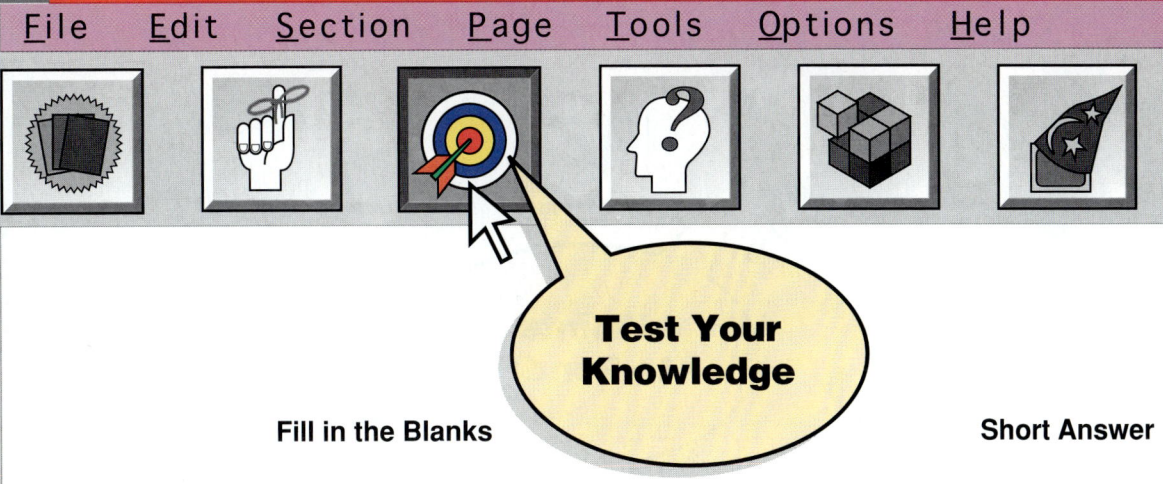

Fill in the Blanks

1. System software can be classified into three major categories; _____, _____, and _____.

2. A(n) _____ consists of one or more programs that manage the operations of a computer.

3. _____ is the most widely used operating system on personal computers.

4. The _____ operating system, developed by scientists at Bell Laboratories, was specifically designed to provide a way to manage a variety of scientific and specialized computer applications.

5. Special-purpose system software programs called _____ are used to convert the programming instructions written by programmers into machine instructions that a computer can understand.

Short Answer

1. What is a single program operating system? How is a multitasking operating system different from a multi-processing operation system? What is a virtual machine OS?

2. What is virtual memory management? With what types of operating systems is virtual memory management used? Why? How is segmentation different from paging? What is thrashing?

3. How are proprietary operating systems different from portable operating systems? What is the advantage of portable operating systems?

4. What do Microsoft Windows, Windows NT, Macintosh, and OS/2 have in common? How are they different? Why are earlier versions of Windows called operating environments?

5. What are utility programs? What are some of the tasks addressed by utility programs? What is the purpose of a screen saver?

Label the Figure

Instructions: Complete the diagrams to show the two ways in which multiprocessing is implemented.

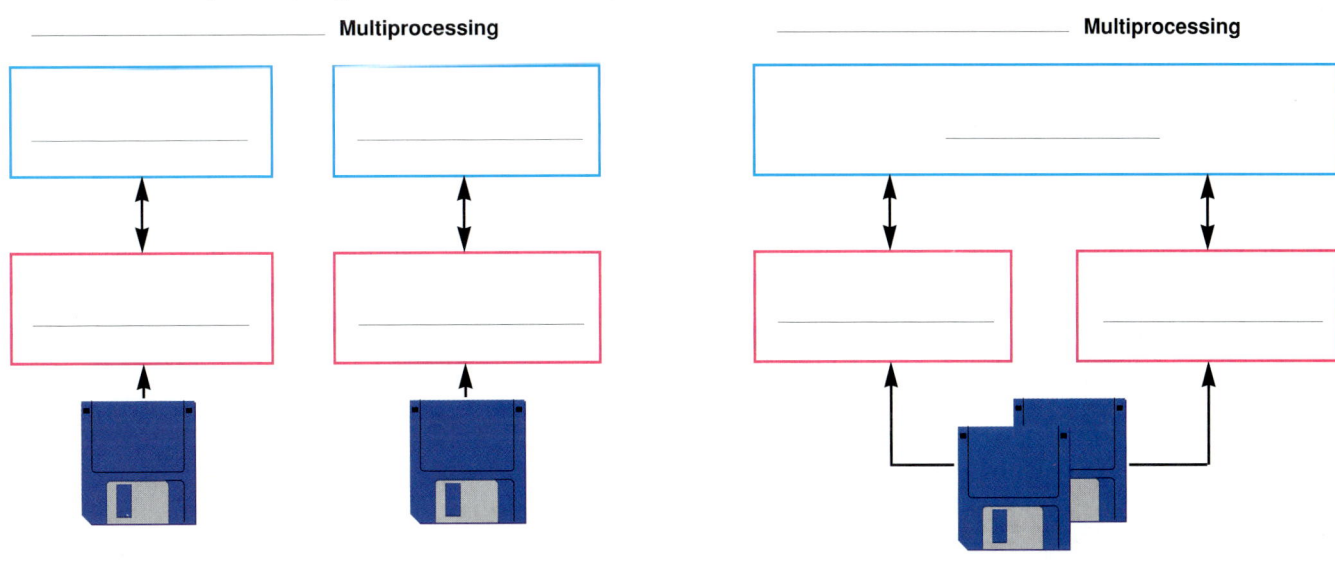

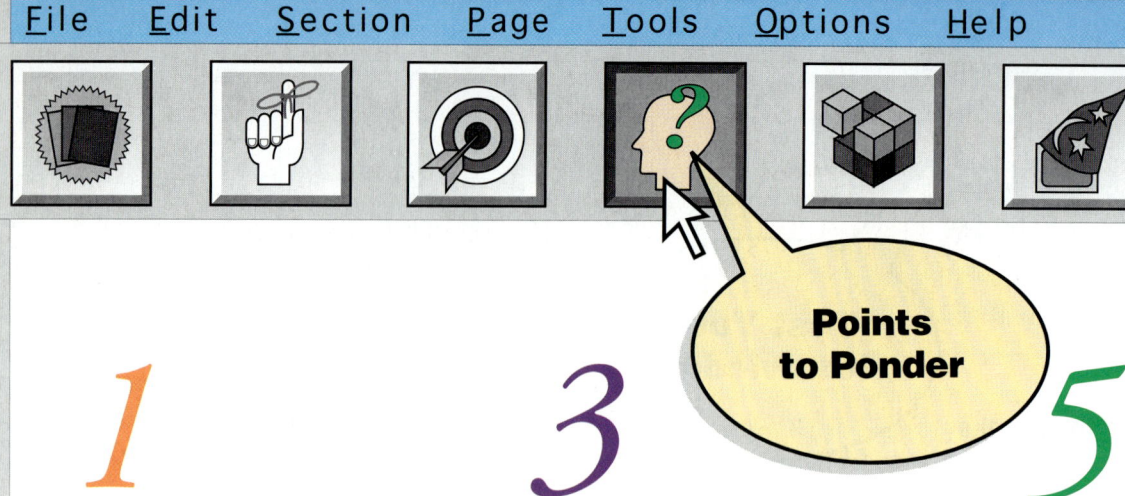

Points to Ponder

1

In its role as an interface between application programs and computer hardware, one of the things an operating system does is provide a common set of computer functions. Some basic tasks need to be accomplished by almost all application programs, such as getting input from the keyboard. The operating system converts an application program's simple instruction to perform a task to the more complex set of instructions the hardware needs to complete the task. Make a list of at least six functions you think must be performed by almost all application programs. Rank your list from the function that you believe is performed most to the function that you believe is performed least. Briefly explain why you ranked the functions as you did.

2

You are the team leader of a group developing a new operating system. As team leader, you are responsible for providing a "vision" of the ideal operating system. Write a description of the perfect operating system. Answer such questions as: What type of operating system (single program, multitasking, multiprocessing, or virtual machine) is it? How does the operating system allocate system resources, monitor system activities, and manage disks and files? What kind of interface does the operating system use? Explain why you think each of the features of your ideal operating system is important.

3

You are the CEO of Computers and Advanced Technology (CAT), a company that specializes in the manufacture of laptop computers (company slogan: "Life is better with a CAT on your lap"). Your research department has just developed a new operating system, the features of which promise to make most other operating systems seem antiquated. Although the operating system was designed specifically to work with CAT laptop computers, your programmers assure you that it can be adapted to work with other personal computers. As CEO, you now have a decision to make. Should the new operating system remain proprietary, possibly enhancing the sale of CAT computers, or should you instruct your programmers to make it portable, thus making it marketable to a wider spectrum of users? Explain your decision.

4

You have been hired as a consultant by a small, family-run printing business that wants to purchase its first personal computers. The company intends to buy twelve PCs and does not plan to obtain any more computers for about five years. Your job is to make a recommendation regarding the type of personal computers the company should purchase and the operating system (DOS, Windows, Windows NT, Macintosh, OS/2, UNIX, or NextStep) it should buy to work with the computers. Write a report to the company giving your recommendations and explaining the reasons behind them.

5

Some of the tasks described in this chapter that are addressed by utility programs include file management, disk management, memory management, backup and restore, data recovery, data compression, virus protection, and screen saver. If you could afford to purchase only four of these utility programs for your personal computer, which would you buy? Why? If you were purchasing utility programs for an entire company, which four do you think are most important? Why? If the utility programs you would buy for your personal computer are not the same as the utility programs you think are most important for a company, briefly explain why the lists are different.

6

The latest in utility programs are intelligent utilities. These utility programs can be customized to fit your needs and will perform a task until you tell it to stop. For example, intelligent utilities can be programmed to turn on your computer at a certain time, automatically backup files you've changed, examine the latest stock prices and advise you when to buy or sell, or even check your calendar and remind you to buy a birthday or anniversary gift for your spouse! If you had an intelligent utility, what types of tasks would you program it to do? What tasks could you program it to do in your chosen career field? As intelligent utilities continue to develop, what effect do you think they will have on an individual's personal and professional life in the future?

Out and About

1. Using current computer magazines and business publications, research the ways in which one of the operating systems described in this chapter is being used today. What kinds of businesses are using the operating system? Why? How much is the operating system being used by individuals on personal computers? What are the advantages of the operating system? What are the disadvantages? What are the system requirements and price of the operating system? From your research, what do you think is the future of the operating system?

2. Find out the operating system that is used on your, or a friend's, personal computer. What company manufactures the operating system? What type of interface does the operating system use? Does the operating system support multitasking? Refer to the documentation that accompanied the computer or operating system to determine the operating system's version and release number, and the year it was produced. Try to find out when the first version of the operating system was introduced, when the next version is expected, and how much the company charges for upgrades.

3. Locate a department in your school or a local company that uses a mainframe computer. Interview an administrator in charge of the mainframe about the computer's operating system. What operating system is used? How was the operating system chosen? What are the advantages of the operating system? What are the disadvantages? Have there ever been any problems with the operating system? Has the operating system been changed to meet specific needs of the department or company? If so, how? Does the administrator anticipate using the same operating system five years from now? Why or why not?

4. Bill Gates, the founder of Microsoft Corporation, is a modern legend. Gates is one of the wealthiest men in America, and Microsoft is one of the most influential companies in the computer industry. The fascinating story of Bill Gates and Microsoft is told in several books, including: *Hard Drive: Bill Gates and the Making of the Microsoft Empire* (by James Wallace), *Gates* (by Stephen Manes), and *Accidental Empires: How the Boys of Silicon Valley Make Their Millions, Battle Foreign Competition, and Still Can't Get a Date* (by Robert X. Cringely). Read one of these books, or another book on Gates and Microsoft, and write a report on the qualities you think led to the success of Bill Gates and Microsoft.

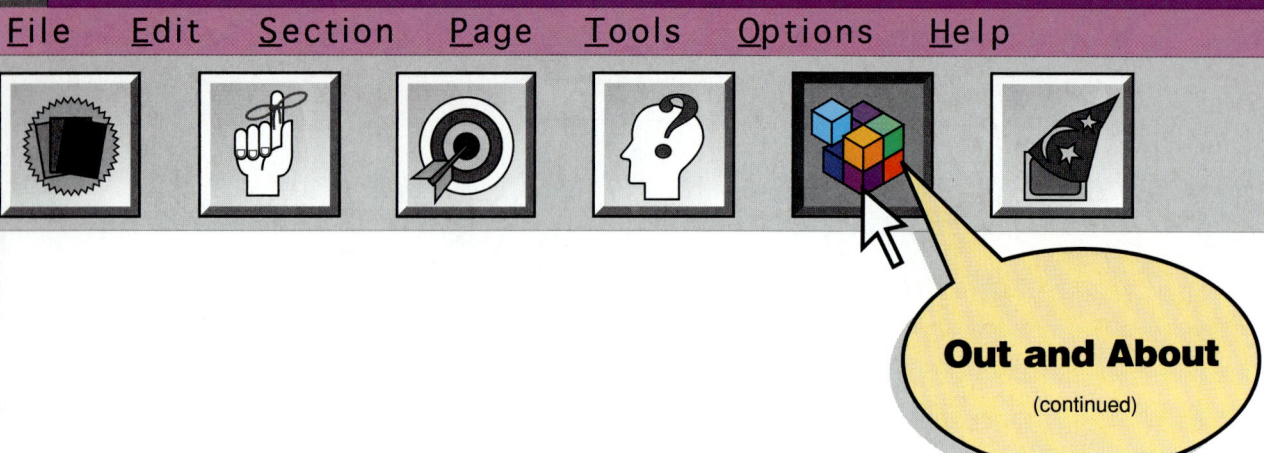

Out and About
(continued)

5. Application programs are designed to be used with specific operating systems. When you purchase software, it is important to read the program's packaging to determine if it is compatible with the operating system on your personal computer. Operating systems undergo frequent revisions, each of which is designated by a version number. A higher version number means a more recent revision (DOS 6.0 is a newer version than DOS 5.0). Usually, operating systems are downwardly compatible, meaning that an application program written for an earlier version of an operating system will work with a later version of the same operating system. Often, however, an application program written for a later version of an operating system will not work correctly with an earlier version. Visit a computer software vendor and find four application programs in which you are interested that require the DOS operating system. Which of the programs could you run on your personal computer if you had DOS 3.3? DOS 5.0? DOS 6.0?

6. Many utility programs are available for users of personal computers. Visit a computer store, or read a computer magazine, and choose two utility programs in which you are interested. Write a review of the two programs. What is the function of each? What are the system requirements? How easy is the program to use? How much does the program cost? In your opinion, is the utility worth the price? Why or why not? If you could buy only one of the utility programs, which would you purchase? Why?

In the Lab 8.27

File Edit Section Page Tools Options Help

Windows Labs

1 Searching for System Files With Program Manager on the screen, double-click the Main group icon. In the Main group window, double-click the File Manager program-item icon. Maximize the File Manager window. Be sure the directory window in NOT maximized. Select the View menu and choose the By File Type command. If it is not already selected, click the Show Hidden/System Files check box in the By File Type dialog box. Choose the OK button.

Select the File menu and choose the Search command. In the Search dialog box, type *.sys in the Search For text box, type c:\ in the Start From text box, be sure the Search All Subdirectories check box is selected, and choose the OK button to display the Search Results window *(Figure 8-19)*. Scroll through the list of files. Write down the filenames that have a red exclamation point (!) in their icons. Write down the path where the file config.sys is located. Close the Search Results window.

Use the same procedure to search for the filename autoexec.bat, and write down the path where this file is located. Close the Search Results window. Close File Manager.

2 Shelly Cashman Series System Software Lab Follow the instructions in Windows Lab 2 in Chapter 1 on page 1.30 to display the Shelly Cashman Series Labs screen. Select Evaluating Operating Systems and choose the Start Lab button. When the initial screen displays, carefully read the objectives. With your printer turned on, point to the Print Questions button and click the left mouse button. Fill out the top of the Questions sheet and answer the questions as you step through the System Software Lab.

3 Shelly Cashman Series Ergonomics Lab Follow the instructions in Windows Lab 2 in Chapter 1 on page 1.30 to display the Shelly Cashman Series Labs screen. Select Working at Your Computer and choose the Start Lab button. When the initial screen displays, carefully read the objectives. With your printer turned on, point to the Print Questions button and click the left mouse button. Fill out the top of the Questions sheet and answer the questions as you step through the Ergonomics Lab.

4 Performing Calculations With Program Manager on the screen, double-click the Accessories group icon. Double-click the Calculator program-item icon. Select the View menu and choose Standard. Press NUM LOCK. Using the numeric keypad, type 23.65+98.42 and press the ENTER key. The result displays in the Calculator window *(Figure 8-20)*. Press ESC to clear the calculation. You can also use the mouse to enter expressions. Type 4624 and click the sqrt button. Write down the result. Press ESC to clear the calculation. Write down the results of each of these calculations: 2489 divided by 8; 54 multiplied by 78; and 65 minus 423.5. Close Calculator.

5 Keeping Track of Appointments With Program Manager on the screen, double-click the Accessories group icon. In the Accessories group window, double-click

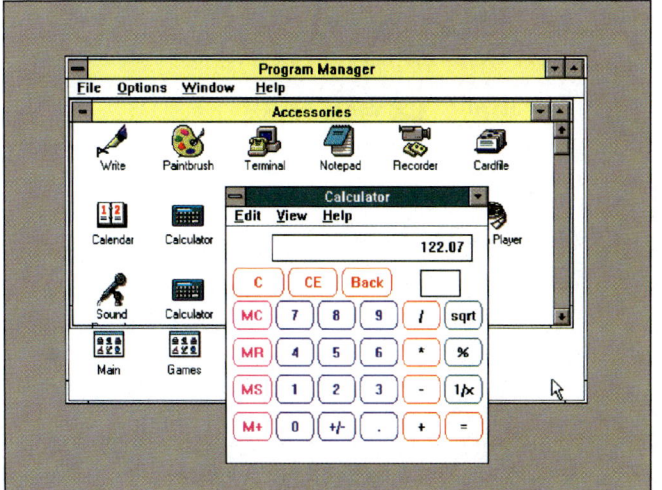

Figure 8-19

Figure 8-20

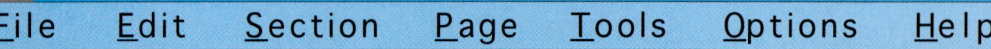

 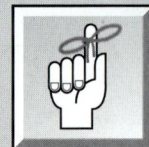    

In the Lab (continued)

the Calendar program-item icon. Maximize the Calendar window. Select the Show menu and choose the Date command. In the Show Date dialog box, type 2-15-96 in the Show Date text box and choose the OK button. Under AM times, click 8:00 and type ENGL 104; click 10:00 and type COM 115; click 12:00 PM and type Meet Sue in Cafeteria (Figure 8-21). Select the Options menu and choose the Special Time command. In the Special Time dialog box, type 3:30 in the Special Time text box and click the PM option button. Choose the Insert button. Type CIS 204. Click the right arrow in the status line, the line below the menu bar, to display 2-16-96. Click 10:00 and type Meet John in Library; click 5:00 and type Pizza Party at Gino's. Click the left arrow in the status line.

Save the appointment book by choosing the Save command from the File menu. Use the filename WIN8-5. Select the File menu and choose the Print command. With 2/15/96 in the From text box, press the TAB key, type 2/16/96 in the To text box and choose the OK button. From the View menu, choose the Month command to display the calendar in month view *(Figure 8-22)*. Close Calendar.

6 Using Help to Switch Between Open Applications
With Program Manager on the screen, select the Help menu and choose the Contents command. Select the Switch Between Applications topic. Read and print the topic contents. With the Help screen still open, click in the Program Manager window to make it active. Open the Write application in the Accessories group. With the Program Manager, Write, and Help windows all open, practice the techniques listed on the Switch Between Applications Help topic. Close the Help window. Close Write.

DOS Labs

1 Displaying the DOS Version and Disk Volume
At the DOS prompt, type cls and press the ENTER key. Type ver and press the ENTER key to display the version of DOS currently loaded into memory. What version of DOS are you using? Type vol and press the ENTER key to display the volume information for the default disk drive. What is the volume label and serial number of the default disk drive? Press the PRINT SCREEN key.

2 Optimizing Your Computer's Memory Before starting this Lab, check with your instructor. At the DOS prompt, type memmaker and press the ENTER key. Read the welcome screen and press the ENTER key. Choose Express Setup and follow the remaining instructions. When the MemMaker program is finished, write down the free conventional memory both before and after MemMaker. Press the ESC key to undo MemMaker's changes. Press the ENTER key twice.

Online Lab

1 Reviewing Entertainment Using one of the two online services you selected in Chapter 1, connect to the service and perform the following tasks: (1) Search the online service for the Entertainment section. (2) Locate, display, and print the five best-selling: video movies, nonfiction books, fiction books, and CD albums. (3) Locate, display, and print two Broadway reviews.

Figure 8-21

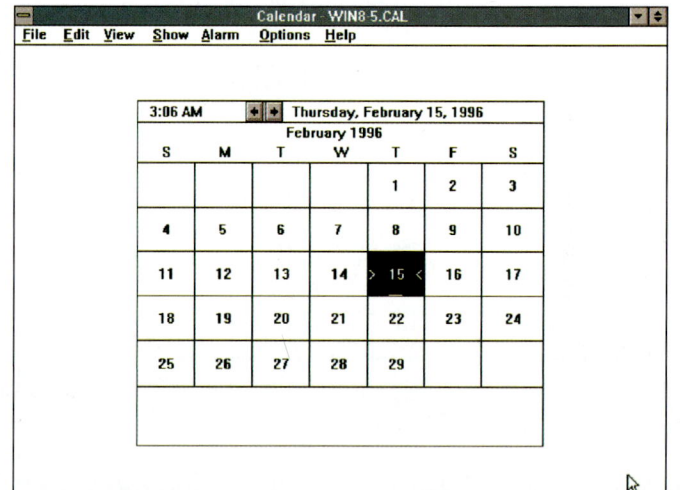

Figure 8-22

How to Purchase, Install, and Maintain a Personal Computer

At some point in time, perhaps during this course, you may decide to buy a computer system. It could be your first system or a replacement system. The decision is an important one and will require an investment of both time and money. The following guidelines are presented to help you purchase, install, and maintain your system. The guidelines assume you are purchasing a desktop personal computer, often referred to as a PC. It is further assumed that the computer will be used for home or small business use. Because it is the most widely purchased type of system, some of the guidelines assume an IBM-compatible computer is being purchased. Most of the guidelines however, may be applied to the purchase of any personal computer, including a Macintosh or other non-DOS or non-Windows system. The type of system you purchase should be determined by your software requirements and the need to be compatible with other systems with which you work. Many of the guidelines can also be applied to purchasing a portable computer such as a laptop. A laptop computer may be an appropriate choice if you need computing capability when you travel. Keep in mind, though, that many laptop computer users also have larger capacity desktop systems at home and/or at work. The laptop systems are commonly used for applications such as word processing and electronic mail that the user needs when he or she is traveling.

How to Purchase a Computer System

1 **Determine what applications you will use on your computer.** This decision will guide you as to the type and size of computer. Artists and others who work with graphics will need a larger, better quality monitor and additional disk space.

2 **Choose your software first.** Some packages only run on Macintosh computers, others only on a PC. Certain packages only run under the Windows operating system. In addition, some software requires more memory and disk space than other packages. Most users will want at least word processing and spreadsheet packages. For the most software for the money, consider purchasing an integrated package or a software suite that offers reduced pricing on several applications purchased at the same time. Be sure the software contains the features that are necessary for the work you will be performing.

3 **Be aware of *hidden costs*.** Realize there will be additional costs associated with buying a computer. Such costs may include the following: an additional phone line or outlet to use a modem; computer furniture; consumable supplies such as diskettes and paper; diskette holders; reference manuals on specific software packages; and special training classes you may want to take. Depending on where you buy your computer, the seller may be willing to include some or all of these in the system purchase price.

4 **Buy equipment that meets the *Energy Star* power consumption guidelines.** These guidelines require that computer systems, monitors, and printers reduce electrical consumption if they have not been used for some period of time, usually several minutes. Equipment meeting the guidelines can display the *Energy Star* logo.

5 **Consider buying from local computer dealers, retail stores, or direct mail companies.** Each has certain advantages. The local dealer or retail store can more easily provide hands-on support, if necessary. With a mail-order company, you are usually limited to speaking to someone over the phone. Mail-order companies usually, but not always, offer the lowest prices. The important thing to do when you are shopping for a system is to make sure you are comparing identical or similar configurations. Local companies can be found in the phone book. Call first to see if they sell to individual customers; some sell only or primarily sell to businesses. Phone numbers for mail-order companies can be found in their advertisements that run in PC periodicals. Most libraries subscribe to several of the major PC magazines. If you call a mail-order firm, ask if it has a catalog that can be sent to you. If you do not buy a system right away, call for another catalog; prices and configurations change frequently.

6 **Use a spreadsheet, like the one shown in Figure 1, to compare purchase alternatives.** Use a separate sheet of paper to take notes on each vendor's system and then summarize the information on the spreadsheet.

Figure 1
A spreadsheet is an effective way to summarize and compare the prices and equipment offered by different system vendors. List your desired system in the column labeled Desired. Place descriptions on the lines and enter prices in the boxes.

SYSTEM COST COMPARISON WORKSHEET

		Desired	#1	#2	#3	#4
Base System	Mfr					
	Model					
	Processor	486DX2				
	Speed	66 MHz				
	Power supply	200 watts				
	Expansion slots	5				
	Local bus video	yes				
	Operating System	Windows				
	Price					
Memory	Amount	8 MB				
	Price					
Disk	Mfr					
	Size	>500 MB				
	Price					
Diskette	3 1/2					
	5 1/4					
	Combination	Combo				
Color Monitor	Mfr					
	Model					
	Size	15 inch				
	Resolution	SVGA				
	Dot Pitch	0.28 mm				
	Price					
Sound Card	Mfr					
	Model					
	Price					
Speakers	Mfr					
	Model					
	Size	2 inch				
	Price					
CD-ROM	Mfr					
	Speed	300 kbps				
	Price					
Mouse	Mfr					
	Price					
Fax Modem	Mfr					
	Speeds	14.4/14.4				
	Price					
Printer	Mfr					
	Model					
	Type	ink jet				
	Speed	6 ppm				
	Price					
Surge Protector	Mfr					
	Price					
Tape Backup	Mfr					
	Price					
UPS	Mfr					
	Price					
Other	Sales Tax					
	Shipping					
	1 YR Warranty	standard				
	1 YR On-Site Svc					
	3 YR On-Site Svc					
	TOTAL					
Software	List free software					

7. Consider more than just price.
Do not necessarily buy the lowest priced system. Consider intangibles such as how long the vendor has been in business, its reputation for quality, and reputation for support.

8. Do some research.
Talk to friends, coworkers, and teachers. Ask what type of system and software they bought and why. Would they recommend their systems and the companies they bought from? Are they satisfied with their software? Spend some time at the library reviewing computer periodicals. Most have frequent articles that rate systems and software on cost, performance, and support issues.

9. Look for free software.
Many system vendors now include free software with their systems. Some even let you choose which software you want. Free software only has value, however, if you would have purchased it if it had not come with the computer.

10. Buy a system compatible with the one you use elsewhere.
If you use a personal computer at work or at some other organization, make sure the computer you buy is compatible. That way, if you need or want to, you can work on projects at home.

11. Consider purchasing an on-site service agreement.

If you use your system for business or otherwise cannot afford to be without your computer, consider purchasing an on-site service agreement. Many of the mail-order vendors offer such support through third-party companies. Agreements usually state that a technician will be on-site within 24 hours. Some systems include on-site service for only the first year. It is usually less expensive to extend the service for two or three years when you buy the computer instead of waiting to buy the service agreement later.

12. Use a credit card to purchase your system, if possible.

Many credit cards now have purchase-protection benefits that cover you in case of loss or damage to purchased goods. Some also extend the warranty of any products purchased with the card. Paying by credit card also gives you time to install and use the system before you have to pay for it. Finally, if you're dissatisfied with the system and cannot reach an agreement with the seller, paying by credit card gives you certain rights regarding withholding payment until the dispute is resolved. Check your credit card agreement for specific details.

13. Avoid buying the smallest system available.

Studies show that many users become dissatisfied because they did not buy a powerful enough system. Plan on buying a system that will last you for at least three years. If you have to buy a smaller system, be sure it can be upgraded with additional memory and devices as your system requirements grow. Consider the entries in the box below as a minimum recommended system. Each of the components are discussed separately in the box to the right.

Base System Components

- 486DX2 Processor, 66 megahertz
- 200 watt power supply
- 340 to 540 MB hard disk drive
- 8 MB of RAM
- 3 expansion slots
- 1 open expansion bay
- local bus video card
- 1 parallel and 2 serial ports
- 3.5" diskette drive
- 14" or 15" SVGA color monitor
- mouse or other pointing device
- enhanced keyboard
- ink-jet or dot matrix printer
- surge protector
- latest version of operating system
- FCC Class B approved

Optional Components

- 5.25" diskette
- 14.4 fax modem
- laser printer
- sound card and speakers
- CD-ROM drive
- tape backup
- uninterruptable power supply (UPS)

Processor:
A 486DX2 processor with a speed rating of at least 66 megahertz is needed for today's more sophisticated software, even word processing software.

Power Supply:
200 watts. If the power supply is too small, it will not be able to support additional expansion cards that you may want to add in the future. The power supply should be UL (Underwriters Laboratory) approved.

Hard Disk:
340 to 540 megabytes (MB). Each new release of software requires more hard disk space. Even with disk compression programs, disk space is used up fast. Start with more disk than you ever think you'll need.

Memory (RAM):
8 megabytes (MB). Like disk space, the new applications demand more memory. It is easier and less expensive to obtain the memory when you buy the system than if you wait until later.

Expansion Slots:
At least three open slots. Expansion slots are needed for scanners, tape drives, video capture boards, and other equipment you may want to add in the future as your needs change and the price of this equipment becomes lower.

Expansion Bay:
At least one open bay. An expansion (drive) bay will let you add another disk or diskette drive, a tape drive, or a CD-ROM drive.

Local Bus Video Card:
Local bus video cards provide faster video performance than video cards that use the slower expansion bus. Make sure the video card has at least 1 MB of memory.

Ports:
At least one parallel and two serial ports. The parallel port is used for your printer. The serial ports can be used for additional printers, external modems, joysticks, a mouse, and some network connections.

Diskette Drives:
Most software is now distributed on 3.5-inch disks. As an option, consider adding

a 5.25-inch diskette to read data and programs stored on that format. The best way to achieve this is to buy a combination diskette drive which is only slightly more expensive than a single 3.5-inch diskette drive. The combination device has both 3.5- and 5.25-inch diskette drives in a single unit.

Color Monitor:
14 or 15 inch. This is one device where it pays to spend a little more money. A 15-inch super VGA (SVGA) monitor with a dot pitch of 0.28 mm or less will display graphics better than a 14-inch model. For health reasons, make sure you pick a low- radiation model. Also, look for a monitor with an antiglare coating on the screen or consider buying an antiglare filter that mounts on the front of the screen.

Pointing Device:
Most systems include a mouse as part of the base package. Some people prefer to use a trackball.

Enhanced Keyboard:
Almost always included with the system. Check to make sure the keyboard is the *enhanced* and not the older *standard* model. The enhanced keyboard is also sometimes called the *101 keyboard* because it has 101 keys (some enhanced keyboards have even more keys).

Printer:
Dot matrix are the lowest cost and most reliable types of printers. However, they do not print graphics as well as an ink-jet printer, which is only slightly more expensive. If you are going to be frequently working with graphics or want the best quality output, choose a laser or other type of page printer.

Surge Protector
A voltage spike can literally destroy your system. It is low-cost insurance to protect

yourself with a surge protector. Do not merely buy a fused multiple-plug outlet from the local hardware store. Buy a surge protector designed for computers with a separate protected jack for your phone (modem) line.

Operating System:
Almost all new systems come with an operating system, but it is not always the most current. Make sure the operating system is the one you want and is the latest version.

FCC Class B approved
The Federal Communications Commission (FCC) provides radio frequency emission standards that computer manufacturers must meet. If a computer does not meet the FCC standards, it could cause interference with radio and television reception. Class B standards apply to computers used in a home. Class A standards apply to a business installation.

Fax Modem:
14.4K speed for both the modem and FAX. Volumes of information are available via online databases. In addition, many software vendors provide assistance and free software upgrades via bulletin boards. For the speed they provide, 14.4K modems are worth the extra money. Facsimile (FAX) capability costs only a few dollars more and gives you more communication options.

Sound Card and Speakers:
Increasingly more software and support materials are incorporating sound.

CD-ROM Drive:
Multimedia is the wave of the future and it requires a CD-ROM drive. Buy a double-speed or faster.

Tape Backup
Larger hard disks make backing up data on diskettes impractical. Internal or external tape backup systems are the most common solution. Some portable units, great if you have more than one system, are designed to connect to your printer port. The small tapes can store the equivalent of hundreds of diskettes.

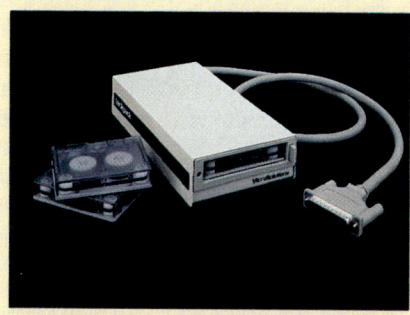

Uninterruptable Power Supply (UPS):
A UPS uses batteries to start or keep your system running if the main electrical power is turned off. The length of time they provide depends on the size of the batteries and the electrical requirements of your system but is usually at least 10 minutes. The idea of a UPS is to give you enough time to save your work. Get a UPS that is rated for your size system.

Remember that the types of applications you want to use on your system will guide you as to the type and size of computer that is right for you. The ideal computer system you choose may differ from the general recommendation presented here. Determine your needs and buy the best system your budget will allow.

How to Install a Computer System

1. **Read the installation manuals *before* you start to install your equipment.** Many manufacturers include separate installation instructions with their equipment that contain important information. Take the time to read them.

2. **Allow for adequate workspace around the computer.** A work space of at least two feet by four feet is recommended.

3. **Install bookshelves.** Bookshelves above and/or to the side of the computer area are useful for keeping manuals and other reference materials handy.

4. **Install your computer in a well-designed work area.** An applied science called **ergonomics** is devoted to making the equipment people use and the surrounding work area safer and more efficient. Ergonomic studies have shown that the height of your chair, keyboard, monitor, and work surface is important and can affect your health. See *Figure 2* for specific work area guidelines.

5. **Use a document holder.** To minimize neck and eye strain, obtain a document holder that holds documents at the same height and distance as your computer screen.

6. **Provide adequate lighting.** Use nonglare bulbs that illuminate your entire work area.

7. **While working at your computer, be aware of health issues.** See *Figure 3* for a list of computer user health guidelines.

8. **Have a phone nearby that can be used while you are sitting at the computer.** Having a phone near the computer really helps if you need to call a vendor about a hardware or software problem. Often the vendor support person can talk you through the correction while you are on the phone. To avoid data loss, however, do not place diskettes on the phone or near any other electrical or electronic equipment.

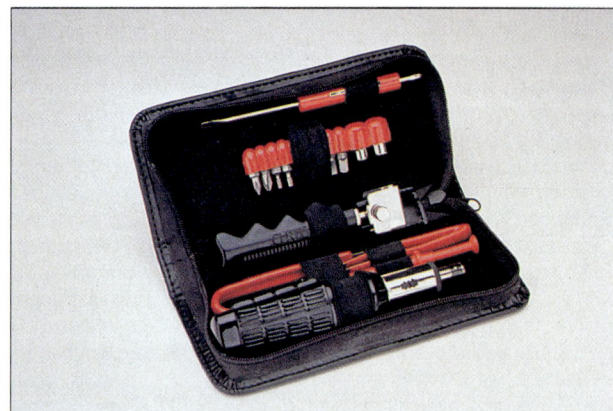

9. **Obtain a computer tool set.** Computer tool sets are available from computer dealers, office supply stores, and mail-order companies. These sets will have the right size screwdrivers and other tools to work on your system. Get one that comes in a zippered carrying case to keep all the tools together.

10. **Save all the paperwork that comes with your system.** Keep it in an accessible place with the paperwork from your other computer-related purchases. To keep different-sized documents together, consider putting them in a sealable plastic bag.

11. **Record the serial numbers of all your equipment and software.** Write the serial numbers on the outside of the manuals that came with the equipment as well as in a single list that contains the serial numbers of all your equipment and software.

12. **Keep the shipping containers and packing materials for all your equipment.** This material will come in handy if you have to return your equipment for servicing or have to move it to another location.

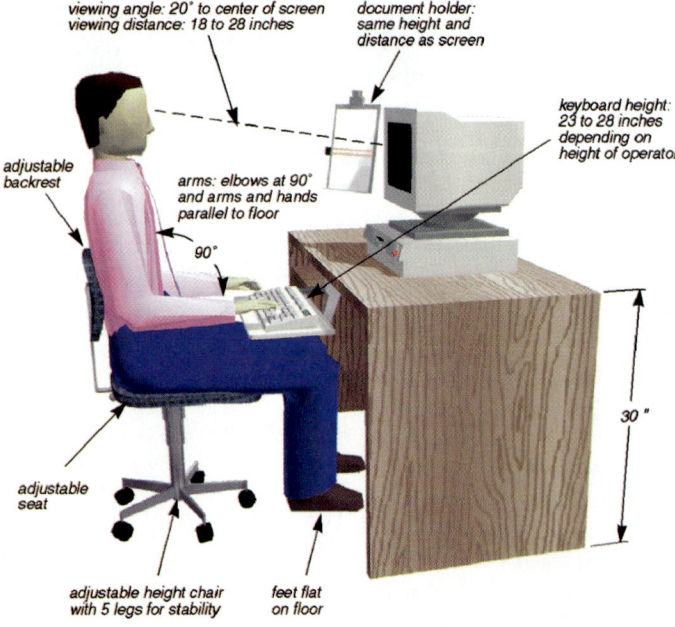

Figure 2
More than anything else, a well-designed work area should be flexible to allow adjustment to the height and build of different individuals. Good lighting and air quality should also be considered

Figure 3
All computer users should follow the guidelines below to maintain their health.

Computer User Health Guidelines

1. Work in a well-designed work area. See Figure 2 for guidelines.
2. Alternate work activities to prevent physical and mental fatigue. If possible, change the order of your work to provide some variety.
3. Take frequent breaks. Every 15 minutes look away from the screen to give your eyes a break. At least once per hour, get out of your chair and move around. Every two hours, take at least a 15 minute break.
4. Incorporate hand, arm, and body stretching exercises into your breaks. At lunch, try to get outside and walk.
5. Make sure your computer monitor is designed to minimize electromagnetic radiation (EMR). If it is an older model, consider adding EMR reducing accessories.
6. Try to eliminate or minimize surrounding noise. Noisy environments contribute to stress and tension.
7. If you frequently have to use the phone and the computer at the same time, consider using a telephone headset. Cradling the phone between your head and shoulder can cause muscle strain.
8. Be aware of symptoms of repetitive strain injuries; soreness, pain, numbness, or weakness in neck, shoulders, arms, wrists, and hands. Do not ignore early signs; seek medical advice.

Static electricity can permanently damage the microprocessor chips on the circuit boards. Before you replace the cover, take several photographs of the computer showing the location of the circuit boards. These photos may save you from taking the cover off in the future if you or a vendor has a question about which equipment controller card is installed in which expansion slot. If you don't feel comfortable performing this step by yourself, ask a more experienced computer user to help. If you buy your system from a local dealer, have the dealer perform this step with you.

14. **Identify device connectors.** At the back of your system there are a number of connectors for the printer, the monitor, the mouse, a phone line, and so on. If they are not already identified by the manufacturer, use a marking pen to write the purpose of each connector on the back of the computer case.

15. **Complete and send in your equipment and software registration cards right away.** If you are already entered in the vendors user database, it can save you time when you call in with a support question. Being a registered user also makes you eligible for special pricing on software upgrades.

16. **Install your system in an area where the temperature and humidity can be maintained.** Try to maintain a constant temperature between 60 and 80 degrees Fahrenheit when the computer is operating. High temperatures and humidity can damage electronic components. Be careful when using space heaters; their hot, dry air has been known to cause disk problems.

17. **Keep your computer area clean.** Avoid eating and drinking around the computer. Smoking should be avoided also. Cigarette smoke can quickly cause damage to the diskette drives and diskette surfaces.

18. **Check your home or renters insurance policy.** Some policies have limits on the amount of computer equipment they cover. Other policies do not cover computer equipment at all if it is used for a business (a separate policy is required).

13. **Look at the inside of your computer.** Before you connect power to your system, remove the computer case cover and visually inspect the internal components. The user manual usually identifies what each component does. Look for any disconnected wires, loose screws or washers, or any other obvious signs of trouble. Be careful not to touch anything inside the case unless you are grounded.

How to Maintain a Computer System

1. **Start a notebook that includes information on your system.** This notebook should be a single source of information about your entire system, both hardware and software. Each time you make a change to your system, adding or removing hardware or software, or when you change system parameters, record the change. Include the following items:

   - Serial numbers of all equipment and software.
   - Vendor support phone numbers. These numbers are often buried in user manuals. Look up these numbers once and record all of them on a single sheet of paper at the front of your notebook.
   - Date and vendor for each equipment and software purchase.
   - Print outs for key system files (e.g., autoexec.bat and config.sys).
   - Trouble log; a chronological history of any equipment or software problems. This history can be helpful if the problem persists and you have to call for support.
   - Notes on discussions with vendor support personnel (can be combined with trouble log). *(Figure 4.)*

2. **Periodically review disk directories and delete unneeded files.** Files have a way of building up and can quickly use up your disk space. If you think you may need a file in the future, back it up to a diskette.

3. **Any time you work inside your computer turn off the power and disconnect the equipment from the power source.** In addition, before you touch anything inside the computer, touch an unpainted metal surface such as the power supply. This will help to discharge any static electricity that could damage internal components.

4. **Reduce the need to clean the inside of your system by keeping the surrounding area dirt and dust free.** Diskette cleaners are available but should be used sparingly (some owners never use them unless they experience diskette problems). If dust builds up inside the computer it should be carefully removed with compressed air and a small vacuum. Don't touch the components with the vacuum.

5. **Back up key files and data.** At a minimum, you should have a system diskette with your **command.com**, **autoexec.bat**, and **config.sys** files. If your system crashes, these files will help you get going again. In addition, back up any files with a file extension of **.sys**. For Windows systems, all files with a file extension of **.ini** and **.grp** should also be backed up.

6. **Periodically, defragment your hard disk.** Defragmenting your hard disk reorganizes files so they are in contiguous (adjacent) clusters and makes disk operations faster. Defragmentation programs have been known to damage files so make sure your disk is backed up first.

7. **Protect your system from computer viruses.** Computer viruses are programs designed to *infect* computer systems by copying themselves into other computer files. The virus program spreads when the infected files are used by or copied to another system. Virus programs are dangerous because they are often designed to damage the files of the infected system. You can protect yourself from viruses by installing an anti-virus program.

8. **Learn to use system diagnostic programs.** If they did not come with your system, obtain a set. These programs help you identify and possibly solve problems before you call for technical assistance. Some system manufacturers now include diagnostic programs with their systems and ask that you run the programs before you call for help.

PC OWNER'S NOTEBOOK OUTLINE

1. Vendor phone numbers
   Vendor
   City/State
   Product
   Phone #

2. Serial numbers
   Product
   Manufacturer
   Serial #

3. Purchase history
   Date
   Product
   Manufacturer
   Vendor
   Cost

4. Key file listings
   autoexec.bat
   config.sys
   win.ini
   system.ini

5. Trouble log
   Date
   Time
   Problem
   Resolution

6. Support calls
   Date
   Time
   Company
   Contact
   Problem
   Comments

7. Vendor paperwork

Figure 4
This suggested notebook outline to organize important information about your computer should be kept on hand.

CHAPTER NINE

Information Management: Files and Databases

9

Objectives

After completing this chapter, you will be able to:

- Discuss data management and explain why it is needed

- Describe sequential files, indexed files, and direct files

- Explain the difference between sequential retrieval and random retrieval of records from a file

- Describe the data maintenance procedures for updating data including adding, changing and deleting

- Discuss the advantages of a database management system (DBMS)

- Describe hierarchical, network, and relational database systems

- Explain the use of query language

- Describe the responsibilities of a database administrator (DBA)

- Explain several guidelines for creating database files

- Discuss personal computer database systems

To provide maximum benefit to a company, data must be carefully managed, organized, and used. The purpose of this chapter is to explain the need for data management, how files on secondary storage are organized and maintained (kept current), and the advantages, organization, and use of databases. Learning this information will help you better understand how data and information is stored and managed on a computer.

9.2 CHAPTER 9 – INFORMATION MANAGEMENT: FILES AND DATABASES

Data Management

For data to be useful, it must be accurate and timely. **Data management** refers to procedures that are used to keep data accurate and timely and provide for the security and maintenance of data. The purpose of data management is to ensure that data required for an application will be available in the correct form and at the proper time for processing. Both data processing professionals and users share the responsibility for data management.

To illustrate the need for data management, *Figure 9-1* uses an example of a credit bureau. A summary of the application follows.

- Data entered into the database of the credit bureau is acquired from numerous sources such as banks and stores. The data includes facts such as income, history of paying debts, bankruptcies, and certain personal information.
- When the data is entered into the computer, it becomes a part of the database. The database is stored on a secondary storage device such as a hard disk.
- Customers of the credit bureau can call and request information about an individual. The credit bureau employee uses a terminal to retrieve information from the database and gives the caller a brief credit history of the person in question. The system also generates a record that causes a complete credit history to be printed that is mailed to the credit bureau customer.

Data Accuracy

For a user, such as a credit bureau customer, to have confidence in the information provided by a computer system, he or she first must be confident that the data used to create the information is accurate. **Data accuracy**, sometimes called **data integrity**, means that the source of the data is reliable and the data is correctly reported and entered. For example, if someone incorrectly reports to the credit bureau that an individual did not pay a bill and this information becomes part of the database, a customer could be denied credit unjustly. Users must be confident that the people and organizations providing data to the credit bureau provide accurate data. In addition, the data they obtain must be entered into the computer correctly. This is called reliable data entry. In the credit bureau example, if a bank reports that the balance on a credit card account is $200, but the balance is incorrectly entered as $2,000, the information passed on to a credit bureau customer would be invalid.

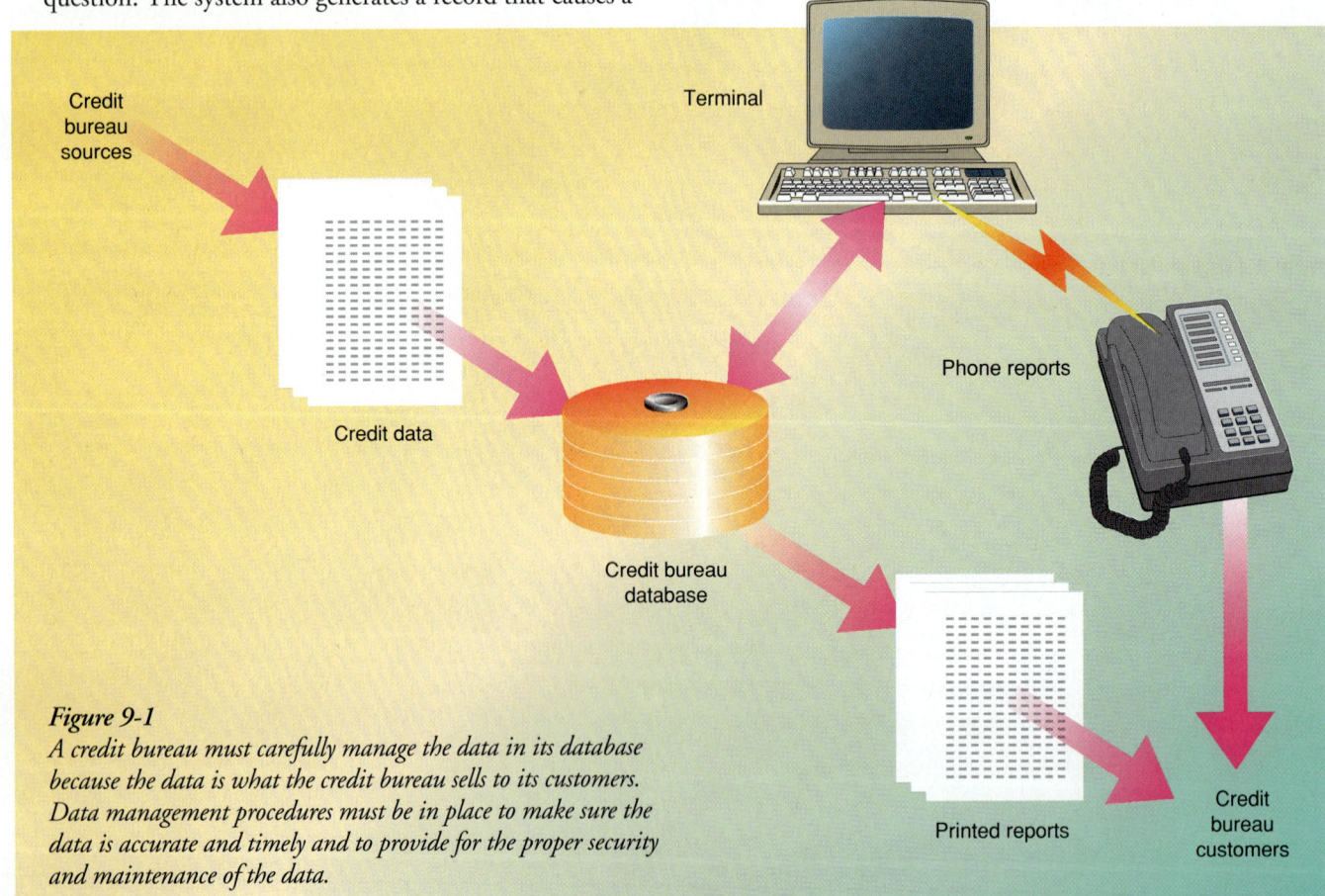

Figure 9-1
A credit bureau must carefully manage the data in its database because the data is what the credit bureau sells to its customers. Data management procedures must be in place to make sure the data is accurate and timely and to provide for the proper security and maintenance of the data.

Accurate data must also be timely. Timely data means the data has not lost its usefulness because time has passed. For example, assume that five years ago a salary of $20,000 was entered for an individual. Today, that data is not timely because five years have passed and the person may be earning either less or more.

Data Security

Data management also includes managing data security. **Data security** refers to protecting data to keep it from being misused or lost. This is important because misuse or loss of data can have serious consequences. In the credit bureau example, a person's credit rating and history of financial transactions are confidential. People do not want their credit information made available to unauthorized persons. Therefore, the credit bureau must develop systems and procedures that allow only authorized personnel to access the data stored in the database. In addition, if the data in the database should be lost or destroyed, the credit bureau must have a way to recover the correct data. Therefore, data in an information system is periodically copied, or backed up. **Backup** refers to making copies of data files so if data is lost or destroyed, a timely recovery can be made and processing can continue. Backup copies are normally kept in fireproof safes or in a separate building to ensure that a single disaster, such as a fire, will not destroy both the primary and the backup copy of the data.

Data Maintenance

Data maintenance, another aspect of data management, refers to the procedures used to keep data current. When data is maintained it is called **updating** and includes procedures for **adding** new data, such as creating a record for a new person to include in the credit bureau database; **changing** existing data, such as posting a change of address to an existing record; and **deleting** obsolete data, such as removing inactive records.

Summary of Data Management

Data management includes managing data accuracy, data security, and data maintenance *(Figure 9-2)*. If data management procedures are inadequate, the information processing system will not perform as intended and the output will have little value.

The data accumulated by organizations is stored in files. The next section discusses files and how they are organized and maintained.

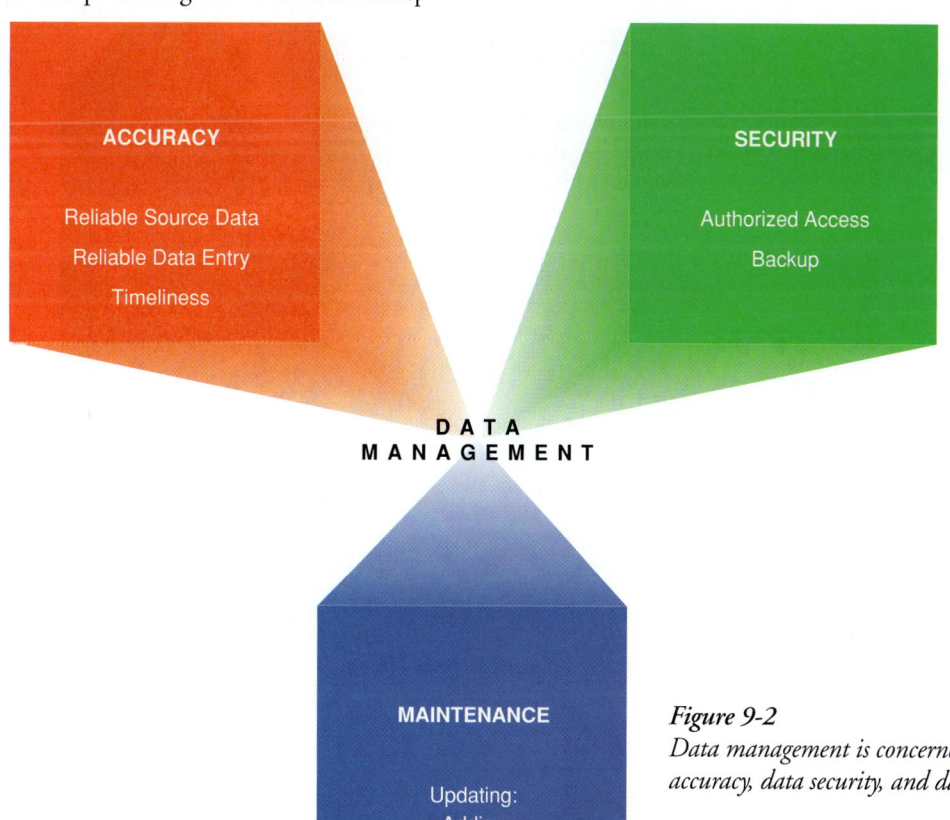

Figure 9-2
Data management is concerned with data accuracy, data security, and data maintenance.

What Is a File?

A **file** is a collection of related data or information stored under a single name. For many types of files, such as text, graphics, or sound, the data is relatively unstructured. For example, a word processing text file consists of variable-length words, sentences, and paragraphs. For database applications, however, files are made up of structured groups of related facts called **records**. The same type of facts recorded for one record are also recorded for all other records in the same file. The individual facts that make up the records are called **fields**. *Figure 9-3* shows an example of a payroll file. Individual records exist for each employee. Each record contains fields for Social Security number, employee name, and paycheck amount. Files contain data that relates to one subject. For example, a business can have separate files that contain data related to payroll, personnel, inventory, customers, vendors, and so forth. Most companies have hundreds, sometimes thousands, of files that store the data pertaining to their business. Files that are stored on secondary storage devices can be organized in several different ways, and there are advantages and disadvantages to each of these types of file organization.

Types of File Organization

Three types of file organization are used on secondary storage devices. These are sequential, indexed, and direct or relative, file organization. Files stored on tape are processed as sequential files. Files on disk are usually indexed or direct.

Sequential File Organization

Sequential file organization means that records are stored one after the other, normally in ascending or descending order, based on a value in each record called the key. The **key**, also called the key field, is a field that contains unique data, such as a Social Security number, part number, or customer number that is used to identify the records in a file *(Figure 9-4)*. The key is a different value for each record.

Records stored using sequential file organization are also retrieved sequentially. **Sequential retrieval**, also called **sequential access**, means the records in a file are retrieved one record after another in the same order as the records are stored. For example, in *Figure 9-4*, the file contains student records stored in sequence by student identification number. The data in the file is retrieved one record after another in the same sequence as it is stored in the file.

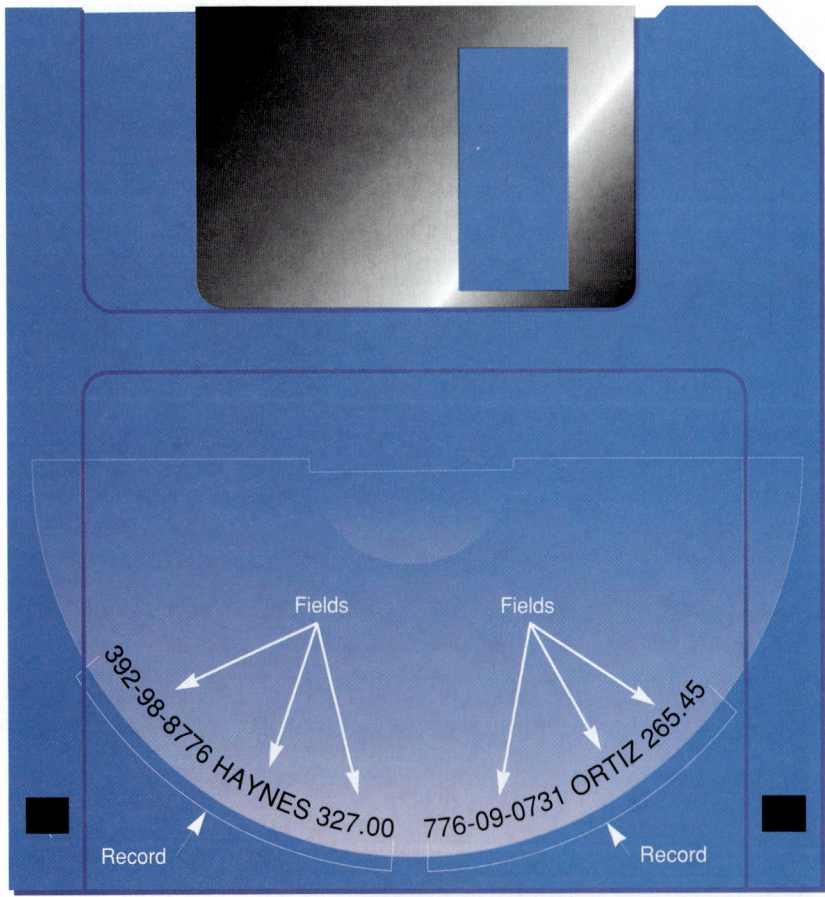

Figure 9-3
This payroll file stored on a diskette contains payroll records. Each payroll record contains a Social Security number field, a name field, and a paycheck amount field.

Sequential retrieval has a major disadvantage – because records must be retrieved one after another in the same sequence as they are stored, the only way to retrieve a record is to read all preceding records first. Therefore, in *Figure 9-4,* if the record for Joan Schwartz must be retrieved, the records for Tom Lee and Ray Ochoa must be read before retrieving the Joan Schwartz record. Because of this, sequential retrieval is not used when fast access to a particular record is required. However, sequential retrieval is appropriate when records are processed one after another. An example is a weekly payroll application where employee records are processed sequentially one after another.

A common use of sequential files is as backup files, where data from a disk is copied onto a tape or another disk so that if the original data becomes unusable, the original file can be restored from the backup file.

Indexed File Organization

A second type of file organization is called **indexed file organization**. Just as in a sequential file, records are stored in an indexed file in an ascending or descending sequence based on the value in the key field of the record.

An indexed file, however, also has an index that itself is a file. An **index** consists of a list containing the values of a key field and the corresponding disk address for each record in a file (*Figure 9-5* on the next page). In the same way that an index for a book points to the page where a particular topic is covered, the index for a file points to the place on a disk where a particular record is located. The index is updated each time a record is added to or deleted from the file. The index is retrieved from the disk and placed in main memory when the file is to be processed.

Records can be accessed in an indexed file both sequentially and randomly. As previously discussed, sequential retrieval means that the records in a file are retrieved one record after another in the same order as the records are stored. **Random access**, also called **direct access**, means the

Figure 9-4
The student records in this file are stored sequentially in ascending order using the student identification number as the key field. The records in this file will be retrieved sequentially.

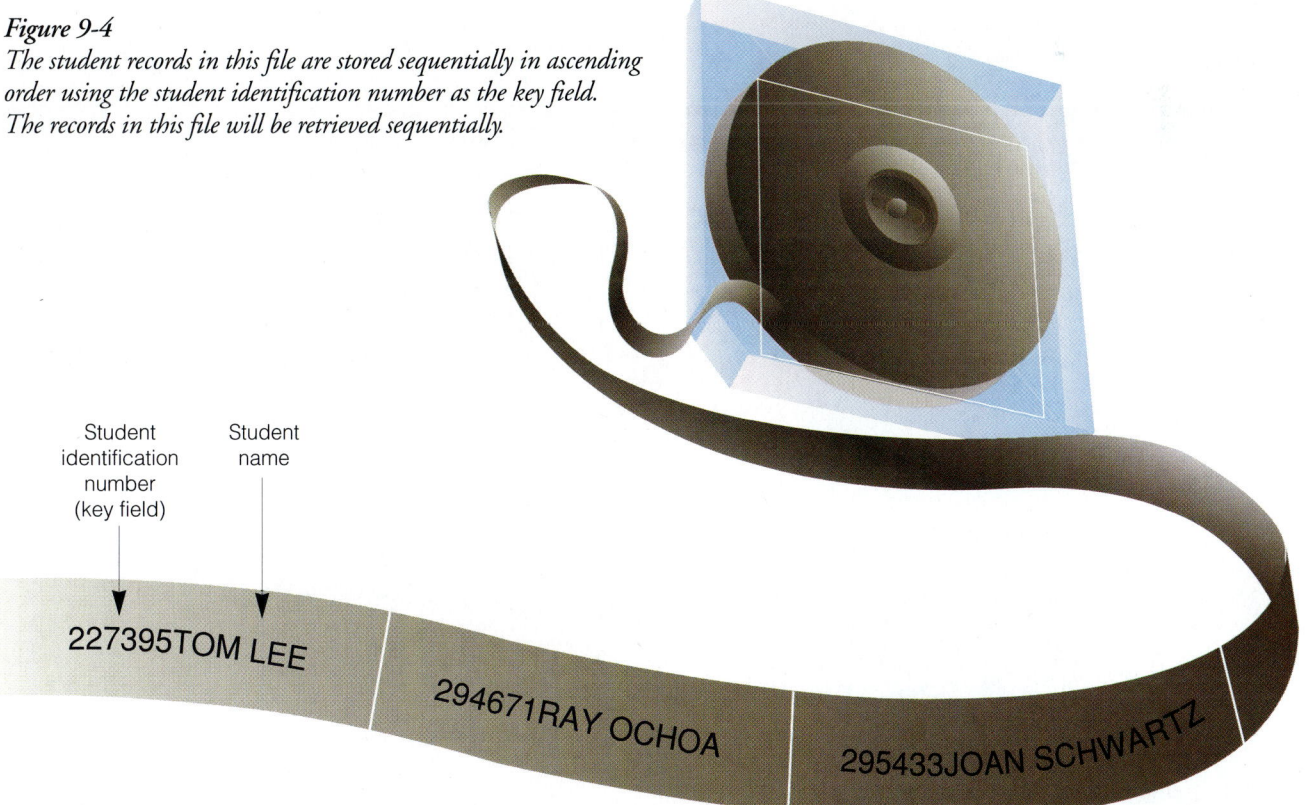

system can go directly to a record without having to read the preceding records. For example, with sequential retrieval, to read the fiftieth record in a file, records 1 through 49 would be read first. With random access, the system can go directly to the fiftieth record. To directly access a record in an indexed file, the index is searched until the key of the record to be retrieved is found. The address of the record (also stored in the index) is then used to retrieve the record directly from the file without reading any other records. An advantage of indexed files is that usually more than one index can be maintained. Each index can be used to access records in a particular order. For example, an employee file might have three separate indexes; one for employee number, a second for employee name, and a third for Social Security number. A disadvantage of indexed files is that searching an index for a record in a large file can take a long time. In addition, maintaining one or more indexes adds to the processing time whenever a record is added or deleted.

Direct File Organization

A **direct file** (sometimes called a relative or random file) uses the key value of a record to determine the location on the disk where the record is or will be stored. For example, a program could establish a file that has nine locations where records can be stored. These locations are sometimes called **buckets**. If the key in the record is a one-digit value (1-9), then the value in the key would specify the relative location within the file where the record was stored. For example, the record with key 3 would be placed in relative location, or bucket, 3, the record with key 6 would be placed in relative location 6, and so on. A bucket can also contain multiple records.

Usually, the storage of records in a file is not so simple. For instance, what if the maximum number of records to be stored in a direct file is 100 and the key for the record is a four-digit number? In this case, the key of the record could not be

Figure 9-5
The index in an indexed file contains the key field and the corresponding disk address for each record in the file. Here, the index contains the employee number, which is the key for the employee file, and the disk address for the corresponding employee record.

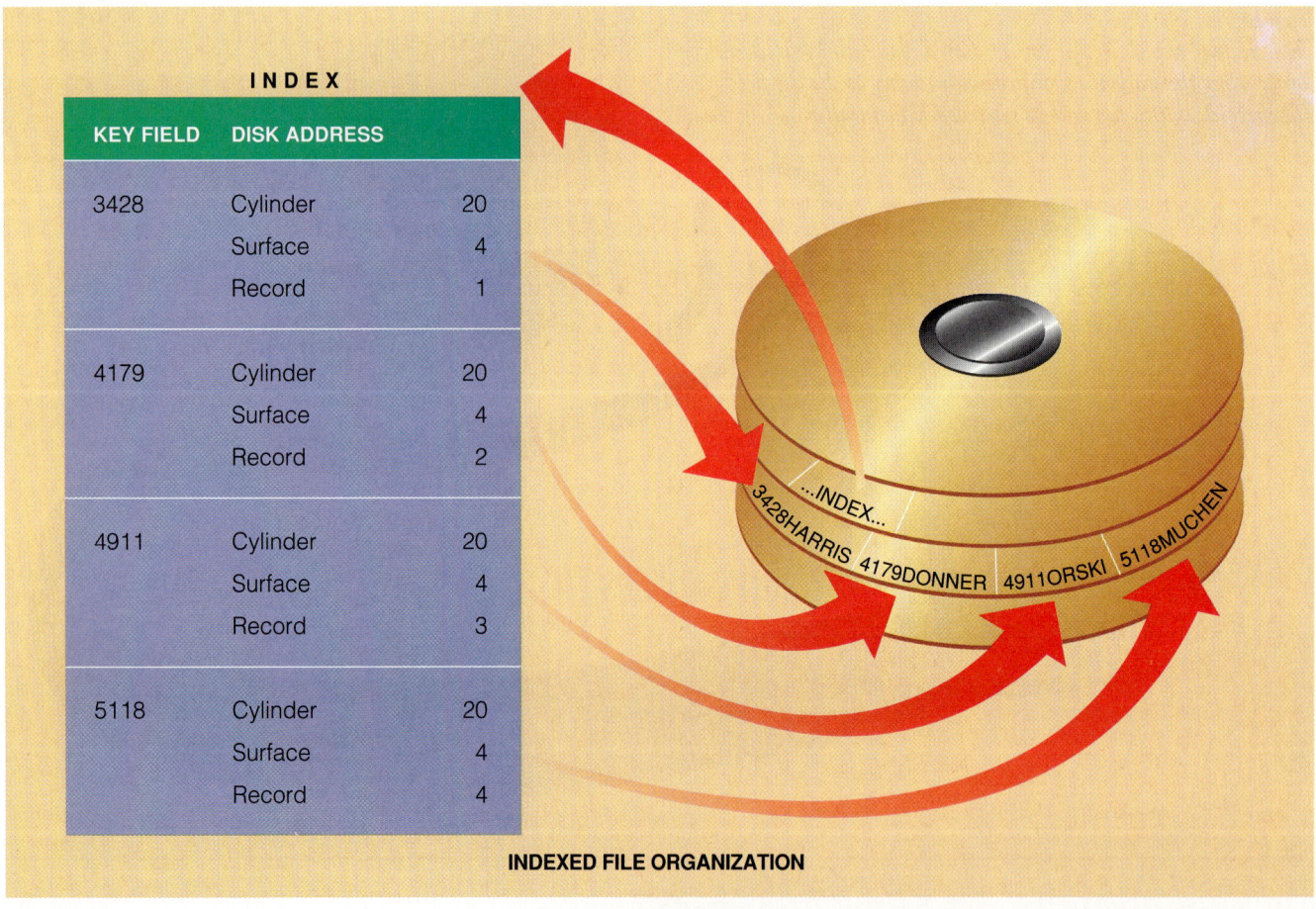

INDEXED FILE ORGANIZATION

used to specify the relative or actual location of the record because the four-digit key could result in up to 9,999 records. In cases such as these, an arithmetic formula is used to calculate the relative or actual location in the file where the record is stored. The process of using a formula and performing the calculation to determine the location of a record is called **hashing**.

One hashing method is the division/remainder method. With this method, the computer uses a prime number close to but not greater than the number of records to be stored in the file. A **prime number** is a number divisible by only itself and 1. For example, suppose you have 100 records. The number 97 is the closest prime number to 100 without being greater than 100. The key of the record is then divided by 97 and the remainder from the division operation is the relative location where the record is stored. For example, if the record key is 3428, the relative location where the record will be stored in the file is location 33 *(Figure 9-6)*.

Direct files present one problem you do not encounter with sequential or indexed files. In all three file organization methods, the key in the record must be unique so it can uniquely identify the record. For example, the employee number, when acting as the key in an employee file, must be unique. No two employees can have the same number. When a hashing technique is used to calculate a disk address, however, it is possible that two different keys could identify the same location on disk. For example, employee number 3331 generates the same relative location (33) as employee number 3428. When the locations generated from the different keys are the same, they are called **synonyms**. The occurrence of this event is called a **collision**. A method that is often used to resolve collisions is to place the record that caused the collision in the next available storage location. This location may be in the same bucket (if multiple records are stored in a bucket) or in the next bucket *(Figure 9-7)*.

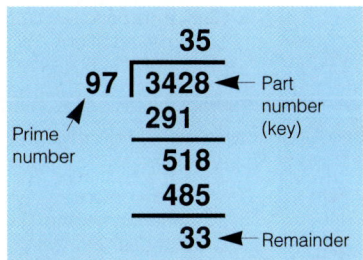

Figure 9-6
When the value 3428 is divided by the prime number 97, the remainder is 33. This remainder is used as the bucket where the record with key 3428 is stored in the direct file.

Figure 9-7
Sometimes the hashing computation produces synonyms, or records that have the same relative address. In this example, both records have a relative address of 33. When the computer tries to store the second record and finds that location 33 is already full, it stores the second record at the next available location. Here, record 3331 is stored in location 34.

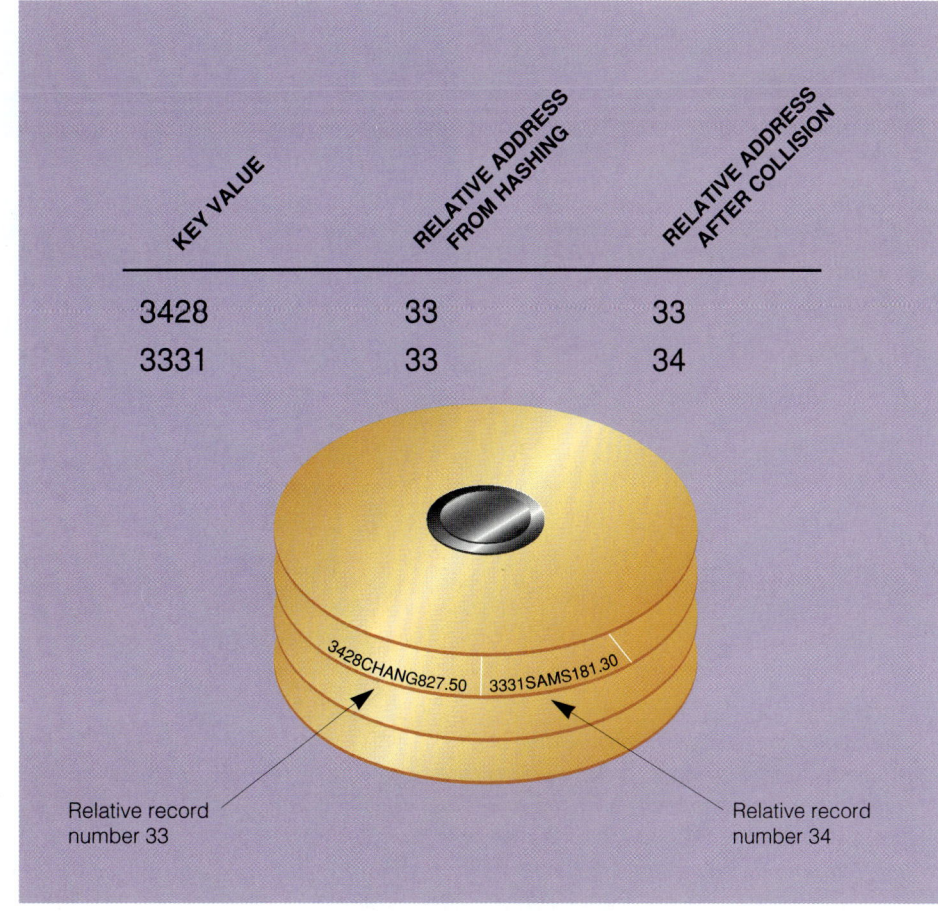

Once a record is stored in its relative location within a direct file, it can be retrieved either randomly or sequentially. The method normally used with direct files is random retrieval. A record is retrieved from a direct file by performing three steps.

1. The program obtains the key of the record to be retrieved. The value of the key, such as an employee number, is entered by the user or is read from another file.
2. The program determines the location of the record to be retrieved by performing the same hashing process as when the record was initially stored. Thus, to retrieve the record with key 3428, the key value would be divided by the prime number 97. The remainder, 33, specifies the location of the bucket where the record is stored.
3. The software directs the computer to bucket 33 to retrieve the record.

Sequential retrieval from a direct file can be accomplished by indicating that the record from the first relative location is to be retrieved, followed by the record from the second relative location, and so on. All the records in the file are retrieved based on their relative location in the file.

Summary of File Organization Concepts

Files are organized as either sequential, indexed, or direct files. Sequential file organization is used on tape and requires that the records in the file be retrieved sequentially. Indexed and direct files are stored on disk and the records are accessed either sequentially or randomly.

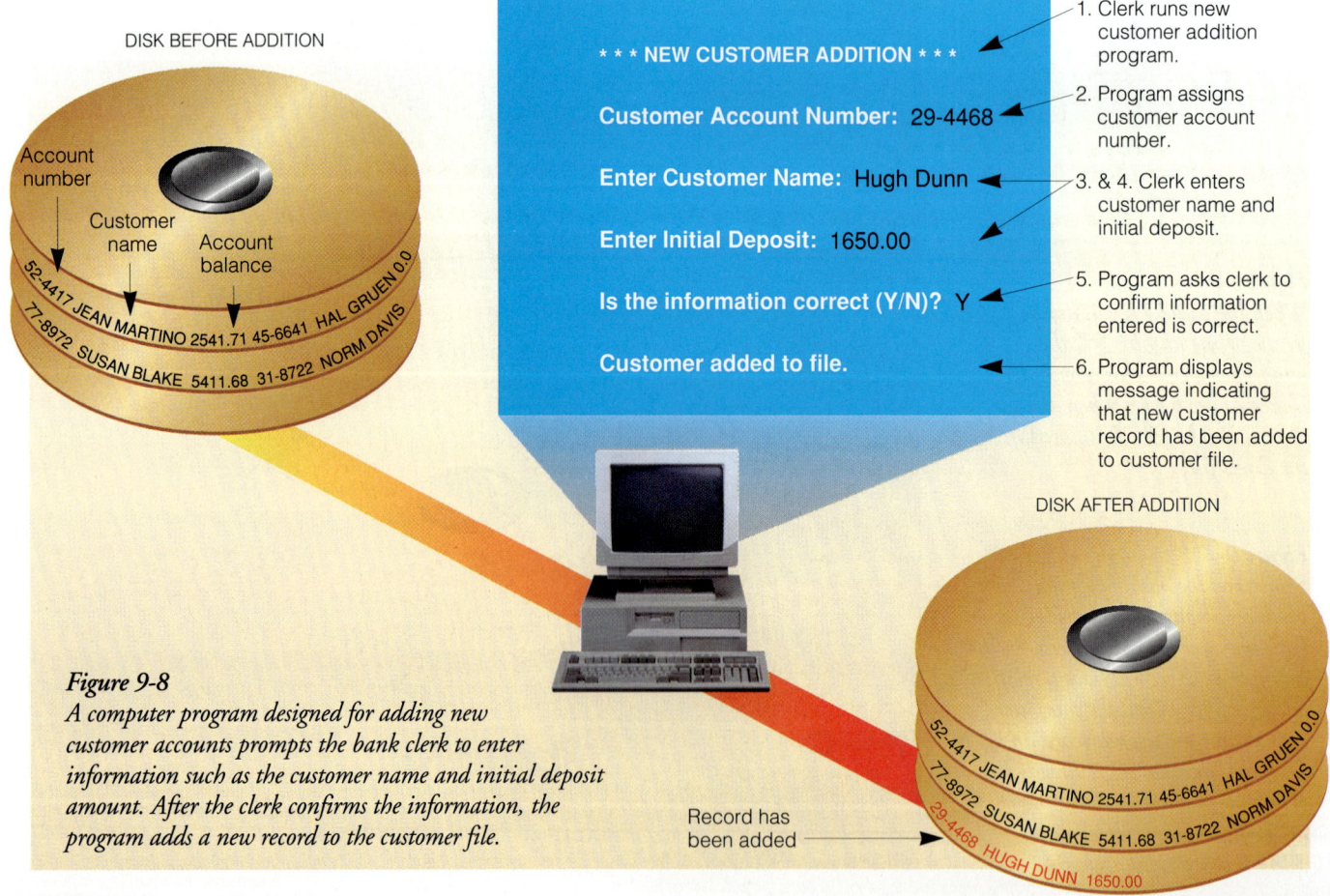

Figure 9-8
A computer program designed for adding new customer accounts prompts the bank clerk to enter information such as the customer name and initial deposit amount. After the clerk confirms the information, the program adds a new record to the customer file.

How Is Data in Files Maintained?

Data stored on secondary storage must be kept current to ensure it will produce accurate results when it is processed. To keep the data current, the records in the files must be updated. Updating records within a file means adding records to the file, changing records within the file, and deleting records from the file.

Adding Records

Records are added to a file when additional data is needed to make the file current. For example, if a customer opens a new account at a bank, a record containing the data for the new account must be added to the bank's account file. The process that would take place to add this record to the file is detailed in the steps below and shown in *Figure 9-8*.

1. The bank clerk runs a program designed for adding new customer accounts.
2. The computer program assigns a new customer number.
3. The clerk enters personal information about the customer. For purposes of this example, the only personal information entered is the customer name.
4. The clerk enters the initial deposit amount.
5. The program asks the clerk to confirm that the information entered is correct.
6. The update program writes the new customer record to the file. The location on the disk where the record is written will be determined by the program that manages the disk. In some cases, a new record will be written between other records in the file. In other cases, such as illustrated in *Figure 9-8,* the new record will be added to the end of the file.

Whenever data is stored on secondary storage for later use, the capability to add records must be present to keep the data current.

Changing Records

Changing data takes place for two primary reasons: (1) to correct data that is known to be incorrect, and (2) to update data when new data becomes available *(Figure 9-8)*.

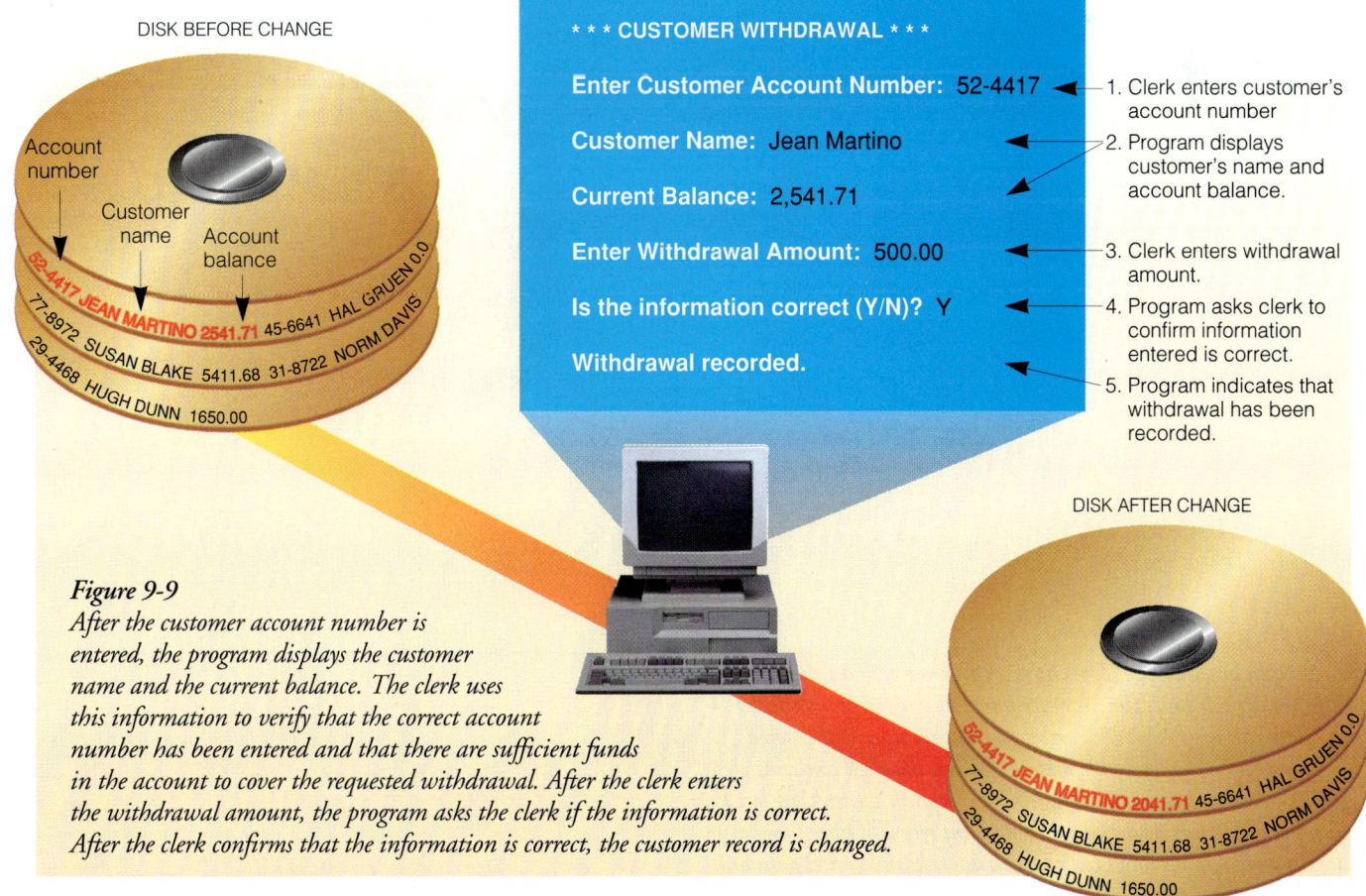

Figure 9-9
After the customer account number is entered, the program displays the customer name and the current balance. The clerk uses this information to verify that the correct account number has been entered and that there are sufficient funds in the account to cover the requested withdrawal. After the clerk enters the withdrawal amount, the program asks the clerk if the information is correct. After the clerk confirms that the information is correct, the customer record is changed.

As an example of the first type of change, assume in *Figure 9-8* that instead of entering Hugh Dunn as the name for the customer, the bank clerk enters Hugh Done. The error is not noticed and the customer leaves the bank. When the customer receives his statement, he notices the error and contacts the bank to request that the spelling of his name be corrected. To do this, the bank clerk would enter Hugh Dunn as a change to the name field in the record. This change replaces data known to be incorrect with data known to be correct.

A bank account example can also be used to illustrate the second reason for change – to update data when new data becomes available. This type of change is made when a customer deposits or withdraws money. In *Figure 9-9* on the prevous page, Jean Martino withdraws $500. The following steps occur when the record for Jean Martino must be changed to reflect her withdrawal.

1. The bank clerk enters Jean Martino's account number, 52-4417.
2. The program displays Ms. Martino's name and account balance. This information allows the clerk to verify that the correct account number was entered and that the account contains sufficient funds to cover the withdrawal.
3. The clerk enters the withdrawal amount of $500.
4. The program asks the clerk to confirm the transaction.
5. After the transaction is confirmed, the customer record on the disk is changed. After the change, the record stored on the disk contains the new account balance.

Changing data stored on secondary storage to reflect the correct and current data is an important part of the updating process required for data.

Deleting Records

Records are deleted when they are no longer needed as data. *Figure 9-10* shows the updating procedures to delete a record for Hal Gruen, who has closed his account. The following steps occur to delete the record.

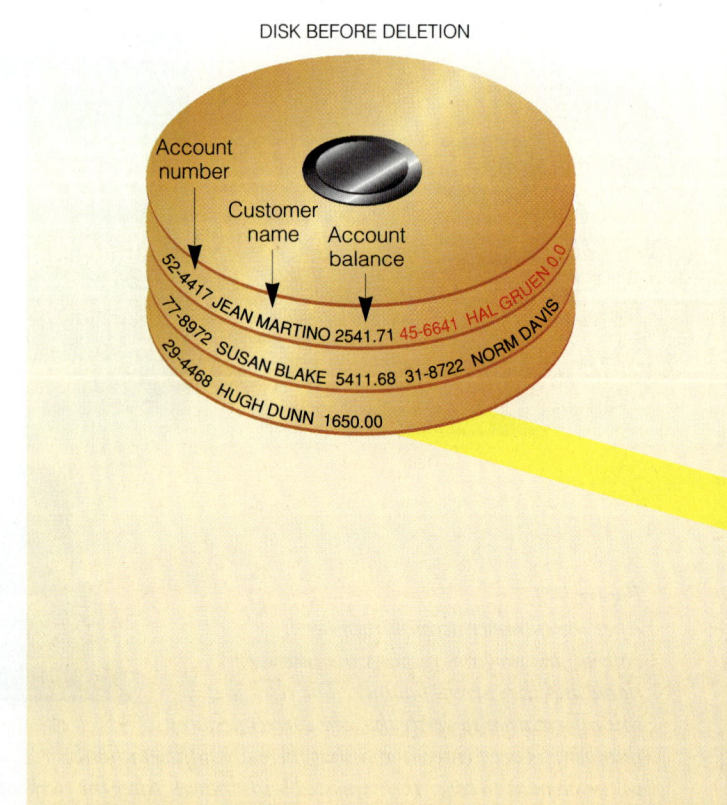

Figure 9-10
To close an account, the clerk enters a customer account number. The program displays the customer name and account balance so the clerk can verify that the correct account number was entered and there is no money in the account. When the clerk confirms that the correct account is displayed, the program writes an asterisk in the first position of the customer account record. Other programs are designed to not process records with asterisks in the first position.

HOW IS DATA IN FILES MAINTAINED?   9.11

1. The bank clerk enters Hal Gruen's account number, 45-6641.
2. The program displays Hal Gruen's name and account balance.
3. The program asks the clerk to confirm that the correct account is displayed.
4. The actual processing that occurs to delete a record from a file depends on the type of file organization being used and the processing requirements of the application. Sometimes, the record is removed from the file. Other times, as in this example, the record is not removed from the file. Instead, the record is *flagged*, or marked in some manner, so it will not be processed again. In this example, an asterisk (*) is added at the beginning of the record.
5. The program displays a message indicating that the account has been closed.

Application programs for bank transactions such as deposits and withdrawals are designed to not process records that begin with an asterisk. Even though the record is still physically stored on the disk, it is effectively deleted because it will not be retrieved for processing.

Flagged records are used in applications where data should no longer be processed but must be maintained for some period of time, such as until the end of the year. Periodically, the user can run a utility program that reorganizes the current records and removes the flagged records. Deleting records that are no longer necessary reduces the size of files and makes additional disk space available for other applications.

Summary of How Data Is Maintained

Data maintenance is updating, or adding, changing, and deleting data stored on secondary storage. The maintenance of data is essential for information derived from the processing of that data to be reliable. When updating data, it does not matter if the data is stored as a single file or if it is part of a series of files organized into a database. The concept of adding, changing, and deleting data to keep it current remains the same.

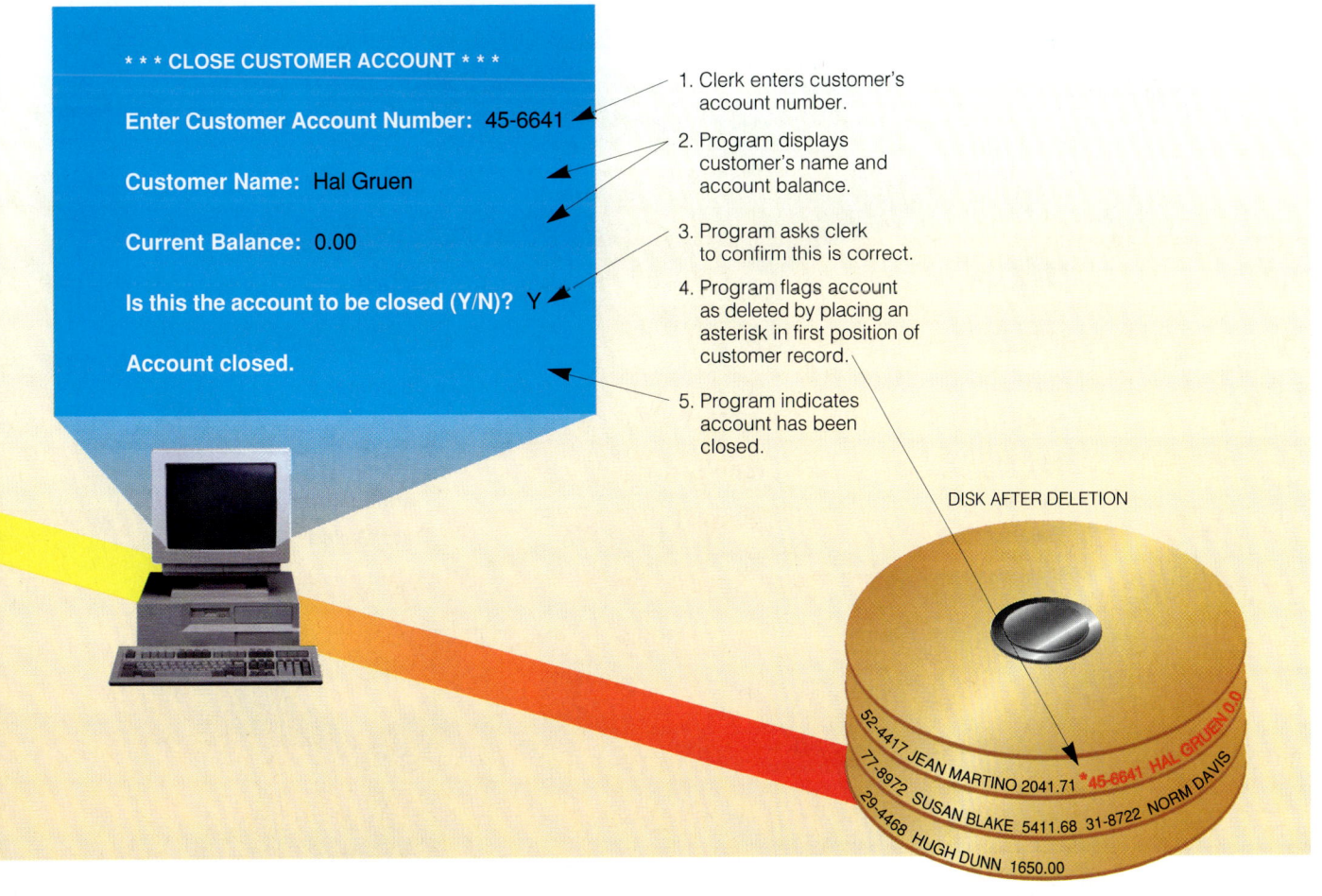

Databases: A Better Way to Manage and Organize Data

Most business people realize that next to the skills of their employees, data (and the information it represents) is one of a company's more valuable assets. They recognize that the information accumulated on sales trends, competitors' products and services, employee skills, and production processes is a valuable resource that would be difficult, if not impossible, to replace.

Unfortunately, in many cases, this resource is located in different files in different departments throughout the organization, often known only to the individuals who work with their specific portion of the total information. In these cases, the potential value of the information goes unrealized because it is not known to people in other departments who may need it or because it cannot be accessed efficiently. In an attempt to organize their information resources and provide for timely and efficient access, many companies have implemented databases.

What Is a Database?

This chapter has previously presented how data elements (characters, fields, and records) can be organized in files. In file-oriented systems, a **flat file** is independent and contains all the information necessary to process the records in that file. Although technically a flat file can be considered a database because it is a collection of data, the term **database** usually means multiple related files. Because these files are related, users can access data in multiple files at one time. A **database management system** (DBMS) is the software that allows the user to create, maintain, and report the data and file relationships. By contrast, a **file management system**, sometimes called a flat-file management system, is software that allows the user to create, maintain, and access one file at a time.

Figure 9-11
In a file-oriented system, each file contains the customer name and address. In the database system, only the customer file contains the name and address. Other files, such as the catalog file, use the customer number to retrieve the customer name and address when it is needed for processing.

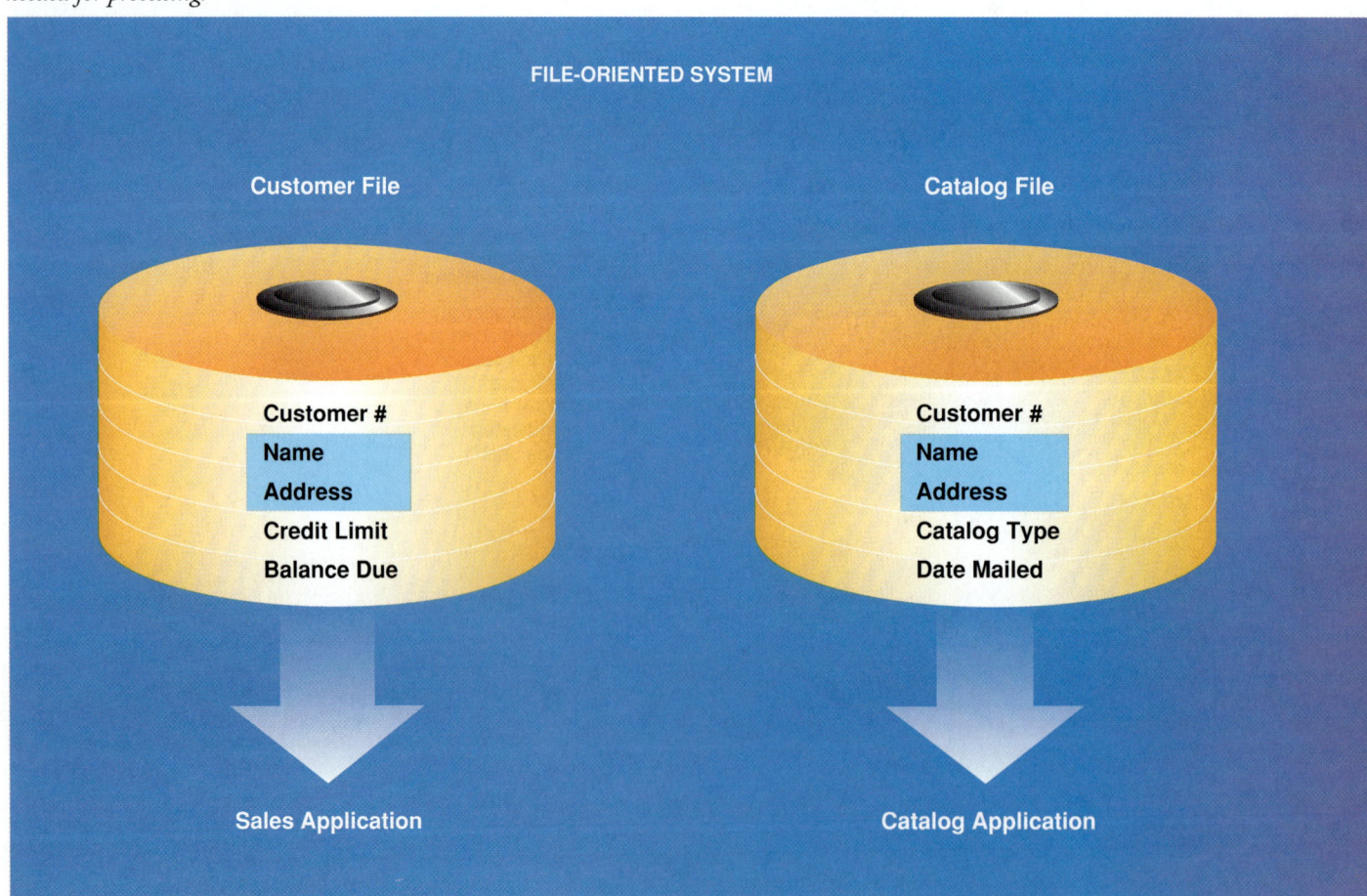

Why Use a Database?

The following example *(Figure 9-11)* illustrates some of the advantages of a database system as compared to a file-oriented system. Assume that a business periodically mails catalogs to its customers. If the business is using a file-oriented system, it would probably have a file used for the catalog mailing application that contains information about the catalog plus customer information such as customer account number, name, and address. Files that are used in a file-oriented system are independent of one another. Therefore, other applications, such as the sales application, which also need customer information would each have files that contain the same customer information that is stored in the catalog mailing file. Thus, in a file-oriented system, the customer data would be duplicated several times in different files. This duplication of data wastes secondary storage space. In addition, it makes maintaining the data difficult because when a customer record must be updated, all files containing that data must be individually updated.

In a database system, however, only one of the applications would have a file containing the customer name and address data. That is because in a database system, files are integrated; that is, related files are linked together by the database management system either through predefined relationships or through common data fields. In this example, the link could be the customer account number. If the sales file contained the customer account number, name, and address, the catalog mailing file would only need to contain the customer's account number plus the other catalog information. When the catalog application program is executed, the customer's name and address would be obtained from the sales file. The advantage of the database is that because the files are integrated, the customer name and address would only be stored once. This saves secondary storage space. It also allows data to be maintained more easily because update information need only be entered once.

As the previous example illustrates, a database system offers a number of advantages over a file-oriented system. These advantages and several others are summarized as follows:

- **Reduced data redundancy**   Redundant, or duplicate, data is greatly reduced in a database system. Frequently used data elements such as names, addresses, and descriptions are stored in one location. Having such items in one instead of many locations lowers the cost of maintaining the data.
- **Improved data integrity**   Closely related to reduced data redundancy is the database advantage of improved data integrity. Because data is only stored in one place, it is more

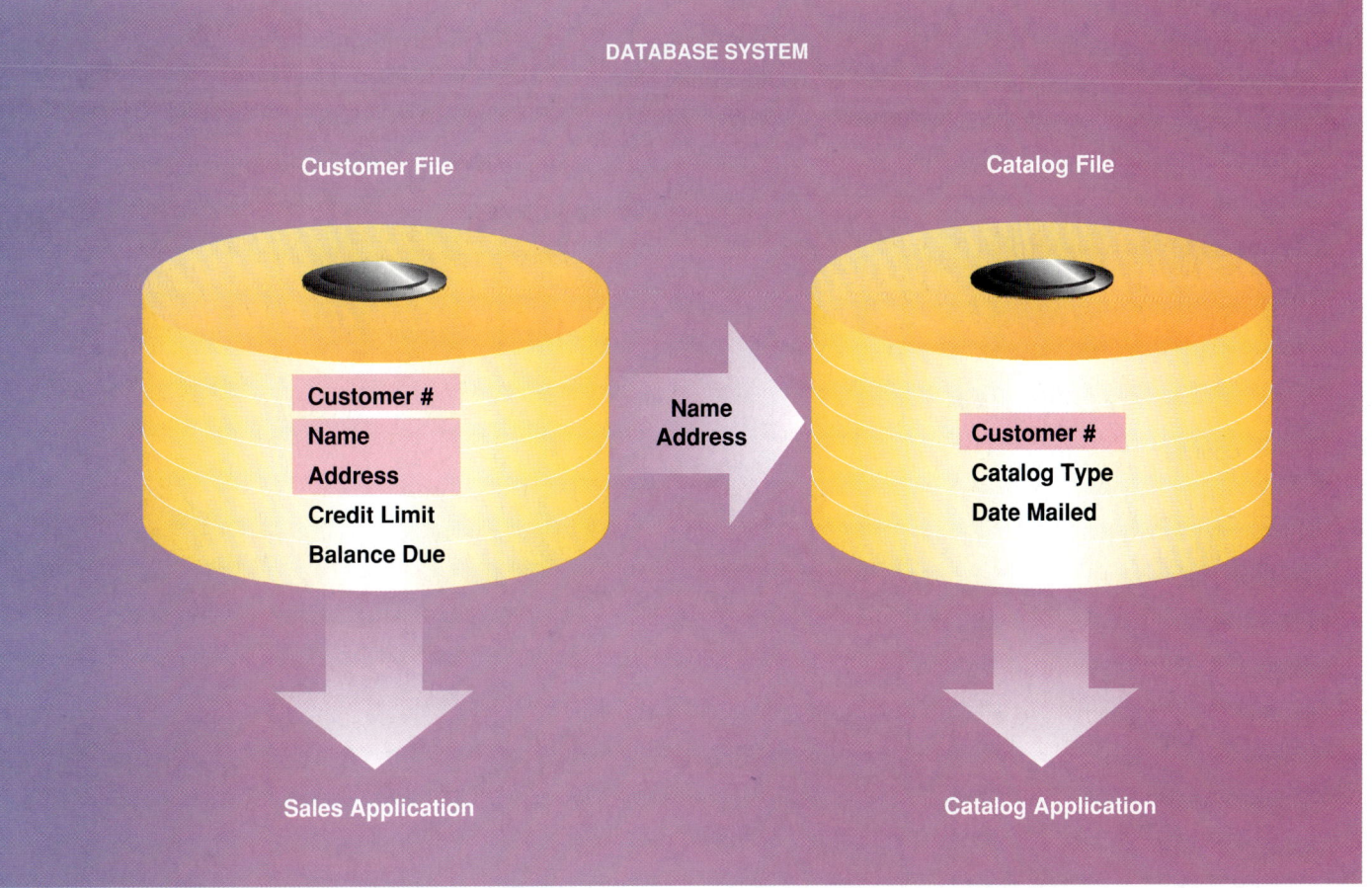

likely to be accurate. When it is updated, all applications that use the data will be using the most current version.
- **Easier reporting**   The capability to extract data from multiple files at one time makes it easier to produce meaningful inquiries and reports.
- **Improved data security**   Most database management systems allow the user to establish different levels of security over information in the database. For example, a department manager may have *read only* privileges on certain payroll data, which means the manager could inquire about the data but not change it. The payroll supervisor would have *full update* privileges, meaning the supervisor not only could inquire about the data but also could make changes. A nonmanagement employee would probably have no access privileges to the payroll data and could neither inquire about nor change the data.
- **Reduced development time**   Because data is better organized in a database, development of programs that use this data is more efficient and takes less time. The need to create new files is reduced. Instead, new attributes are added to existing files.

The following section discusses the ways databases can be organized.

Types of Database Organization

The four types of database organization are: hierarchical, network, relational, and object-oriented.

Hierarchical Database

In a **hierarchical database** *(Figure 9-12)*, data is organized in a series like a family tree or organization chart (the term hierarchy means an organized series). Like a family tree, the hierarchical database has branches made up of parent and child records. Each **parent record** can have multiple child records. However, each **child record** can have only one parent. The parent record at the top of the database is referred to as the **root record**.

Hierarchical databases are the oldest form of database organization and reflect the fact that they were developed when the disk and memory capacity of computers was limited and most processing was done in batches of transactions. Data access is sequential in the sense that an inquiry begins at the root record and proceeds down the branch until the requested data is found. All parent-child relationships are

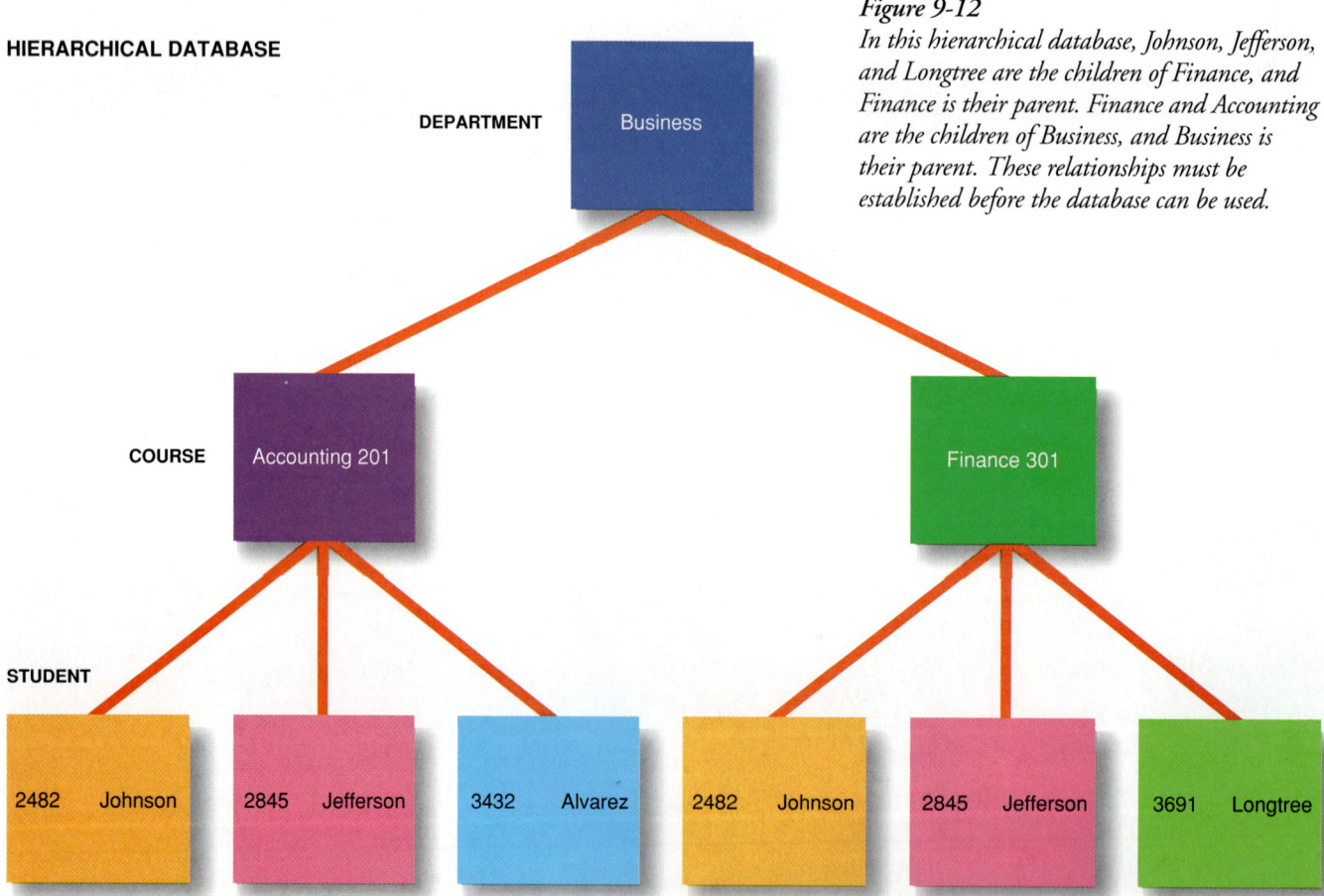

Figure 9-12
In this hierarchical database, Johnson, Jefferson, and Longtree are the children of Finance, and Finance is their parent. Finance and Accounting are the children of Business, and Business is their parent. These relationships must be established before the database can be used.

established when the database is created in a separate process that is sometimes called *generating* the database.

After the database is created, access must be made through the established relationships. This points out two disadvantages of hierarchical databases. First, records located in separate branches of the database cannot be accessed easily at the same time. Second, adding new fields to database records or modifying existing fields, such as adding the four-digit ZIP code extension, requires the redefinition of the entire database. Depending on the size of the database, this redefinition process can take a considerable amount of time. The advantage of a hierarchical database is that because the data relationships are predefined, access to and updating of data is very fast.

Network Database

A **network database** *(Figure 9-13)* is similar to a hierarchical database except that each child record can have more than one parent. In network database terminology, a child record is referred to as a **member** and a parent record is referred to as an **owner.** Unlike the hierarchical database, the network database is able to establish relationships between different branches of the data and thus offers increased access capability for the user. However, like the hierarchical database, these data relationships must be established prior to the use of the database and must be redefined if fields are added or modified.

Relational Database

The relational database structure takes advantage of large-capacity, direct-access storage devices that were not available when the hierarchical and network methods were developed. In a **relational database**, data is organized in tables that in database terminology are called **relations**. The tables are further divided into rows (called **tuples**) and fields (called **attributes**). The tables can be thought of as files and the rows as records. The range of values that an attribute can have is called a **domain**.

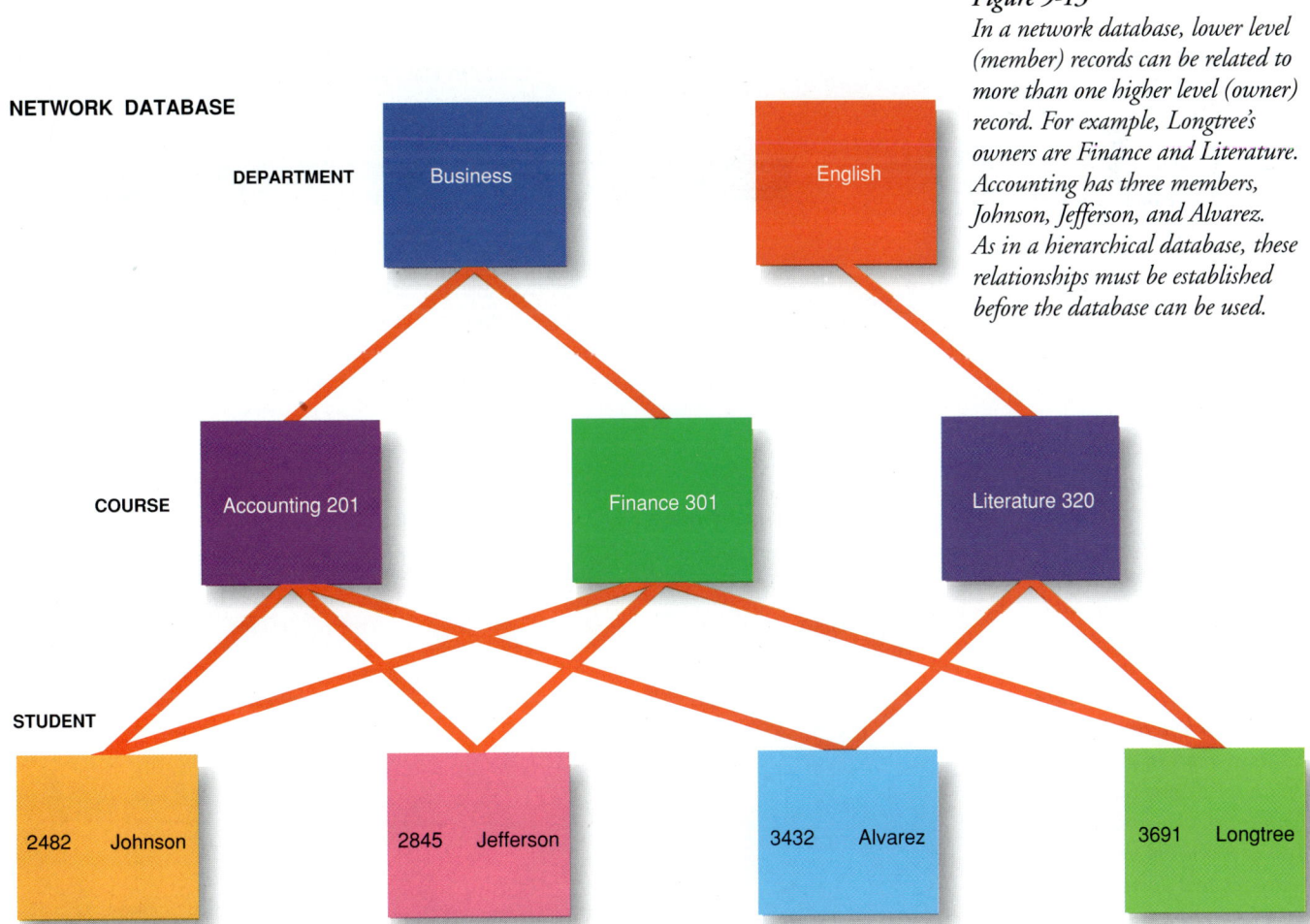

Figure 9-13
In a network database, lower level (member) records can be related to more than one higher level (owner) record. For example, Longtree's owners are Finance and Literature. Accounting has three members, Johnson, Jefferson, and Alvarez. As in a hierarchical database, these relationships must be established before the database can be used.

These terms with a Student Master Table are illustrated in *Figure 9-14*.

Recall that a key advantage of a database is its capability to link multiple files together. A relational database accomplishes this by using a common field that exists in each file. For example, in a database for a college, the link between files containing student information could be the student identification number. Hierarchical and network databases can also extract data from multiple files, but in these database structures, the data relationships that will enable the multiple file combination must be defined when the database is created. The advantage of a relational database is that the data relationships do not have to be predefined. The relational database needs only a common field in both data files to make a relationship between them *(Figure 9-15)*. Because it is sometimes difficult to know ahead of time how data will be used, the flexibility provided by a relational database is an important advantage.

Another advantage of a relational database is its capability to add new fields. All that need be done is to define the fields in the appropriate table. With hierarchical and network database systems, the entire database has to be *redefined*; existing relationships have to be reestablished to include the new fields. A disadvantage of a relational database is that its more complex software requires more powerful computers to provide acceptable performance.

Object-Oriented Database

In recent years, another type of database structure has been developed based on object-oriented technology. An **object-oriented database** keeps track of objects, entities that contain both data and the action that can be taken on the data. For example, a nonobject-oriented database employee record would contain only data about the employee; information such as employee number, name, address, department, pay rate, and so on. An object-oriented database employee record would contain the same data but would also include information on how to display or print the employee record and how to calculate the employee's pay. Object-oriented databases are also designed to contain nontext data such as photographs, graphics, and sound. Some relational databases can also contain nontext data. Object-oriented technology is discussed in more detail in Chapter 12.

RELATIONAL DATABASE STRUCTURE

Figure 9-14
This example shows the terms used with relational databases.

Figure 9-15
In a relational database, files (called tables) do not require predefined relationships as they do with hierarchical or network databases. Instead, common fields are used to link one table to another. For example, Student ID# could be used to link the Student Master Table in Figure 9-14 with the Course-Student Table (a). Department ID could be used to link the Department Table (b) with the Course-Master Table (c).

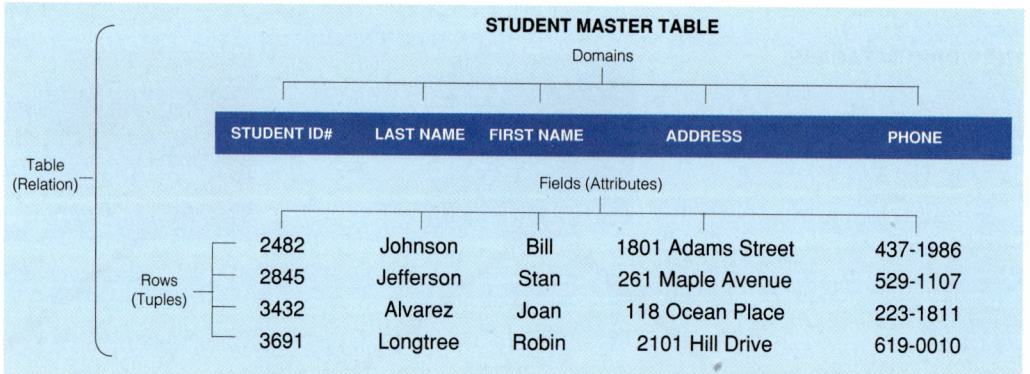

Database Management Systems

A number of common database management system features are available, including the following described in *Figure 9-16*.

- **Data dictionary** The data dictionary defines each data field that will be contained in the database files. Information stored in the dictionary includes field name, field size, description, type of data (e. g., text, numeric, or date), default value, validation rules, and the relationship to other data elements.
- **Utilities** Database management system utility programs provide for a number of maintenance tasks including creating files and dictionaries, monitoring performance, copying data, and deleting unwanted records.
- **Security** Most database management systems allow the user to specify different levels of user access privileges. The privileges can be established for each user for each type of access (retrieve, update, and delete) to each data field. Be aware that without some type of access security, the data in a database is more subject to unauthorized access than in a decentralized system of individual files.
- **Query language** The query language is one of the most valuable features of a database management system. It allows the user to retrieve information from the database based on the criteria and in the format specified.
- **Recovery** More sophisticated database management systems keep a log that records what the record looked like before and after a change is made (called the before and after *image*). This log is used to restore the database in the event of a hardware or software malfunction. Using **forward recovery**, also called **rollforward**, the log is used to automatically reenter transactions from the last time the system was backed up. Using **backward recovery**, also called **rollback**, the log is used to reverse transactions that took place during a certain period of time, such as an hour. The transactions for this period of time then have to be reentered.

Figure 9-16
A summary of common database management system features.

FEATURE	DESCRIPTION
Data Dictionary	Defines data files and fields
Utility Program	Creates files and dictionaries, monitors performance, copies data and deletes unwanted records
Security	Controls different levels of access to a database
Query Language	Allows user to specify report content and format
Recovery	Helps restore database after an equipment or software malfunction

C COURSE-MASTER TABLE

COURSE	COURSE NAME	DEPARTMENT ID	UNITS	MAX ENROLLMENT
ACC201	Advanced Accounting	BUS	4	50
FIN301	Investments	BUS	2	30
LIT320	Modern Literature	ENG	3	20

Query Languages: Access to the Database

A **query language** is a simple English-like language that allows users to specify what data they want to see on a report or screen display. Although each query language has its own grammar, syntax, and vocabulary, these languages can generally be learned in a short time by persons without a programming background.

Most database management systems include a feature called query by example. **Query by example** (**QBE**) helps the user construct a query by displaying a list of fields that are available in the files from which the query will be made. In addition, the user can specify selection criteria to limit the number of records displayed. *Figure 9-17* shows a query by example screen from the Microsoft Access for Windows database.

A Query Example

Figure 9-18 shows how a user might query a relational database. This example illustrates the relational operations that might be performed when a relational database inquiry is made. These three **relational operations** are select, project, and join. They allow the user to manipulate the data from one or more files to create a unique **view**, or subset, of the total data.

The **select relational operation** selects certain records (rows or tuples) based on user-supplied criteria. In the example, the user queries the database to select records from the sales order file that contain part number C-143. Selection criteria can be applied to more than one field and can include tests to determine if a field is greater than, less than, equal to, or not equal to a value specified by the user. Connectors such as AND and OR can also be used.

The **project relational operation** specifies the fields (attributes) that appear on the query output. In the example, the user wants to see the names of the customers who placed orders for part number C-143.

The **join relational operation** is used to combine two files (relations or tables). In the example, the customer number, a field contained in each file, is used to join the two files. After the query is executed, most query languages allow the user to give the query a unique name and save it for future use.

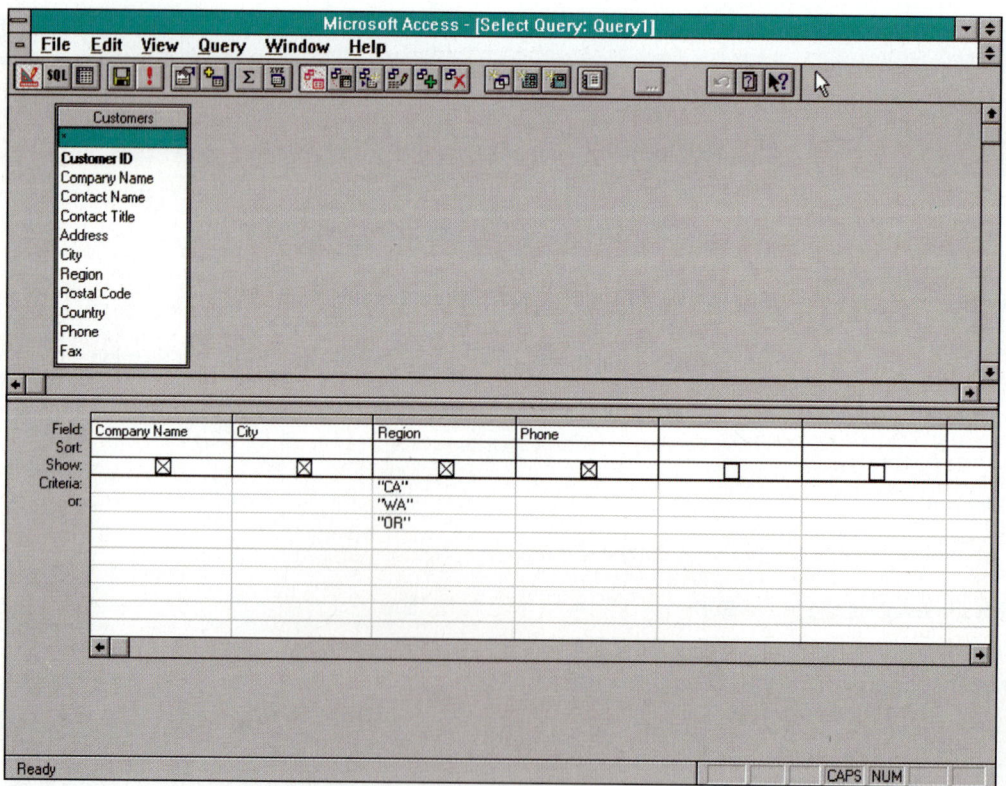

Figure 9-17
Query by example (QBE) helps a user construct a query. In this example from Microsoft Access for Windows, four fields have been chosen from the list of fields in the Customers file. Selection criteria under the Region field will limit the query to customers from California, Washington, or Oregon.

Structured Query Language

One of the most widely used query languages is **Structured Query Language**, often referred to as **SQL** (sometimes pronounced *sequel*). SQL received increased support as the emerging relational database management system query language when, in 1985, the American National Standards Institute formed a committee to develop industry standards for SQL. The standards were issued in 1987. Today, most database software vendors have incorporated SQL into their products. The standardization of SQL will further accelerate its implementation on a wide range of computer systems from personal computers to supercomputers. This action, coupled with the increasing dominance of relational databases, will mean that SQL will be available to many computer users. *Figure 9-19* shows an example of the SQL statements that would be used to create the response (view) shown in *Figure 9-18*.

```
SELECT ORDNO, CUSTNO, CUSTNAME, PARTNO, QTYORD
FROM SALESORDERS, CUSTOMERS
WHERE SALESORDERS.PARTNO = "C-143" AND
      SALESORDERS.CUSTNO = CUSTOMERS.CUSTNO
ORDER BY ORDNO
```

Figure 9-19 ▲
These Structured Query Language (SQL) statements will generate the response (view) shown in Figure 9-18. The statements specify that the sales order number (ORDNO), customer number (CUSTNO), part number (PARTNO), and quantity ordered (QTYORD) appear on the report. The report information will be taken from records in the SALESORDERS file where the part number is C-143 and from records in the CUSTOMERS file where the customer number matches the customer number in the records selected from the SALESORDERS file (the records with a C-143 part number). Information on the report will be listed in sales order number (ORDNO) sequence.

Figure 9-18 ▼
The three relational operations (select, project, and join) are used to produce a response to the query. The query response is referred to as a view.

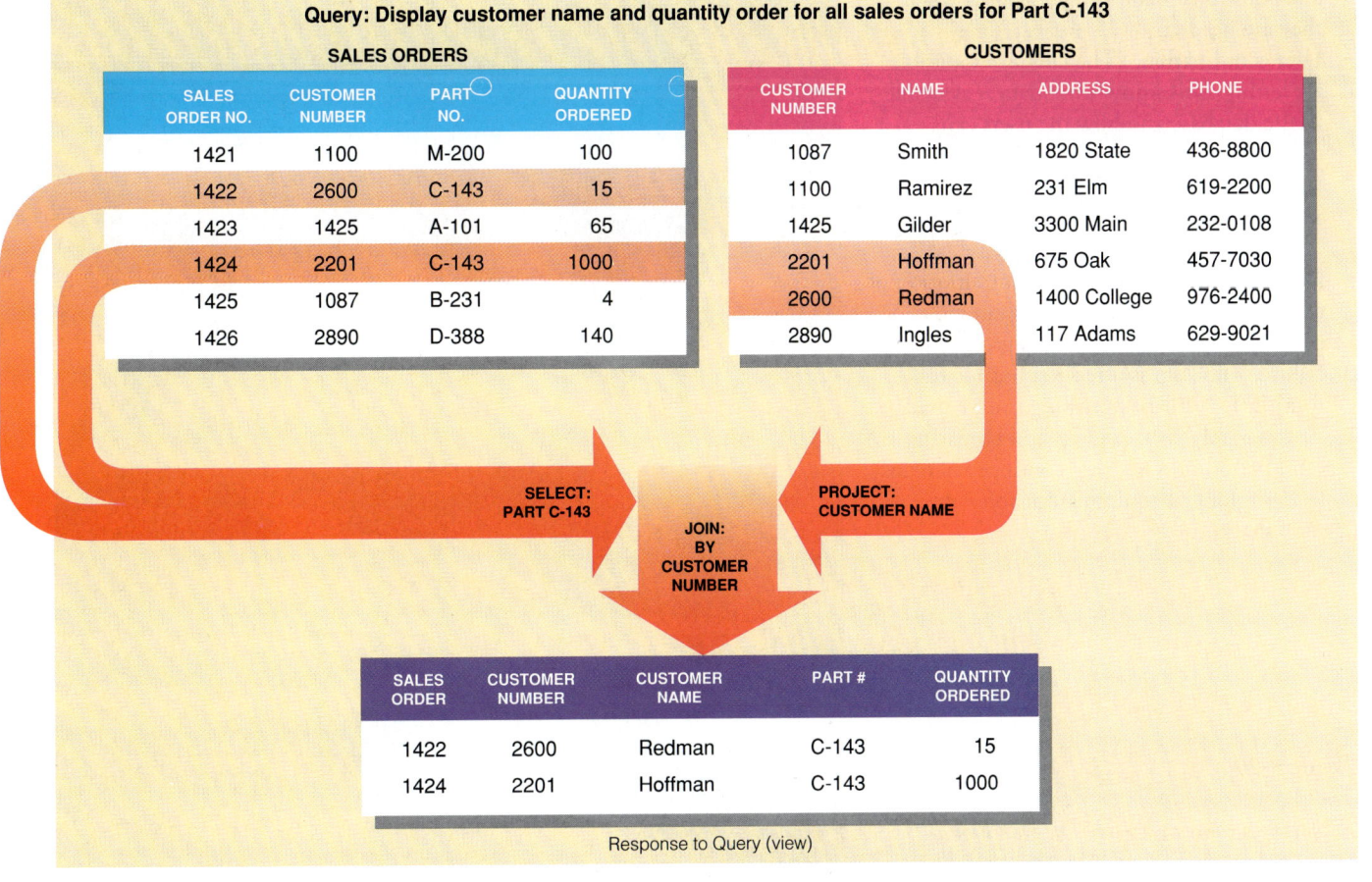

Database Administration

The centralization of an organization's data into a database requires much cooperation and coordination on the part of the database users. In file-oriented systems, if a user wanted to keep track of some data, he or she would just create another file, often duplicating some data that was already being tracked by someone else. In a database system, the user must first check to see if some or all of the data is already on file and if not, how it can be added to the system. The role of coordinating the use of the database belongs to the database administrator.

The Database Administrator

The **database administrator,** or **DBA**, is the person responsible for managing all database activities *(Figure 9-20)*. In small organizations, this person usually has other responsibilities such as the overall management of the computer resources. In medium and large organizations, the role of the DBA is a full-time job for one or more people. The job of the DBA usually includes the following responsibilities:

- **Database design** The DBA determines the design of the database and specifies where to add additional data file and records when they are needed.
- **User coordination** The DBA is responsible for letting users know what data is available in the database and how the users can retrieve it. The DBA also reviews user requests for additions to the database and helps establish priorities for their implementation.
- **Backup and recovery** The centralization of data in a database makes an organization particularly vulnerable to a computer system failure. The DBA is often responsible for minimizing this risk, making sure that all data is regularly backed up and preparing (and periodically testing) contingency plans for a prolonged equipment or software malfunction.
- **System security** The DBA is responsible for establishing and monitoring system access privileges to prevent the unauthorized use of an organization's data.
- **Performance monitoring** The performance of the database, usually measured in terms of response time to a user request, can be affected by a number of factors such as file sizes and the types and frequency of inquiries during the day. Most database management systems have utility programs that enable the DBA to monitor these factors and make adjustments to provide for more efficient database use.

In addition to the DBA, the user also has a role in a database management system.

Figure 9-20
The database administrator plays a key role in managing a company's data. The DBA should possess good technical and management skills.

The Responsibility of the User in a Database Management System

One of the user's first responsibilities is to become familiar with the data in the existing database. First time database users are often amazed at the wealth of information available to help them perform their jobs more effectively.

Another responsibility of the user, in organizations of any size, is to play an active part in the specification of additions to the database. The maintenance of an organization's database is an ongoing task that must be constantly measured against the overall goals of the organization. Therefore, users must participate in designing the database that will be used to help them achieve those goals and measure their progress.

Guidelines for Designing Database Files

Carefully designed database files can make it easy for a user to query and report on database information. For relational database files a process called **normalization** is used to organize data into the most efficient and logical file relationships. For flat files, formal rules do not exist but the common sense guidelines shown in *Figure 9-21* can be applied to both relational and flat files.

Personal Computer Database Systems

A variety of software packages are available for personal computers, ranging from simple file management programs to full relational database management systems. Some of the popular database packages designed for personal computers include Microsoft Access, dBASE 5, Paradox, and FoxPro.

As with large system packages, many personal computer software vendors have developed or modified existing packages to support Structured Query Language (SQL). The advantage of SQL packages for personal computers is that they can directly query mainframe databases that support SQL.

With so many software packages available (a recent survey included 43), it is difficult to decide which one to choose. If you have simple requirements, a file management package is probably all you need. If you need the capability of a database, one of the more popular database management systems will offer you increased capability and growth potential.

Summary of File and Database Management

Understanding the data management, file, and database concepts presented in this chapter gives you a knowledge of how data is stored and managed on a computer. This information will be useful to you, whether you are a home computer user who wants to store personal data or a computer user accessing the database of a company.

DATABASE FILE GUIDELINES

Design your file on paper first.
Write down everything you want to keep track of in the database. Organize the data into logical groups. Large groups of data should probably be separate files.

Include a unique key field.
Database systems need a unique field to identify each record. If one is not specified, database systems usually assign a sequential number to each record. That may be fine for a list of personal friends, but it is not efficient for large files or files that are frequently accessed. For some data, the choice is obvious such as the Social Security number for an employee file. If a unique field has to be established, avoid creating one that has built-in *significance* such as a combination of customer's address and name (e.g., 1813WILL). Significant key fields make sense at first but eventually break down when duplicates are encountered.

Use separate fields for logically distinct items.
If an item will ever need to be referred to separately, it should be stored in a separate field. A person's name is a good example. To be thorough, you need at least six fields: Salutation (Mr., Mrs., Ms.), First Name, Middle Name or Initial, Last Name, Suffix (Jr.), and Nickname.

Do not create fields for information that can be derived from entries in other fields.
For example, in an employee file, do not include a field for age. Instead, store the employee's birth date. That way, the employee's age can always be accurately calculated.

Allow enough space for each field.
Think about the type of data that will be stored and allow sufficient but not unnecessary space. If foreign names and addresses are going to be stored, allow extra room. Numeric fields should be equal to the largest total that may be displayed or printed from the data.

Set default values for frequently entered data.
Some database programs let you set a field value for use during data entry. Unless you override it, the value is entered as part of the record. An example would be a state code in a name and address file. If most of the entries in a name and address file will be from the same state, say Oregon, a default value of OR can be assigned to the state code. The value OR will be automatically displayed during data entry. If the new entry is from Oregon, the state code does not have to be entered. If the new entry is not from Oregon, the user enters the correct two-letter state code.

Figure 9-21
Guidelines for creating database files.

COMPUTERS AT WORK

Finding Information Among the Data

Relational database software is helping many organizations find information among the millions of facts that they process each day. Once the information is found, database software keeps the information readily available for future use.

For example, Whirlpool Corporation, a manufacturer of home appliances, uses data on 15 million customers and 20 million installed appliances as a source of information for marketing, sales, product design, and customer service. Recently, database access to information on installed products allowed Whirlpool to replace a defective part on hundreds of washers *before* they broke and caused damage to customer's homes and Whirlpool's reputation. Database information on the frequency of repairs has also helped Whirlpool lower spare parts inventories.

Viewlogic, a developer of sophisticated circuit design software, is another company that is using relational database software to manage a critical customer-related operation. Viewlogic customer service representatives use database software to search for answers to questions from an average of 200 customers per day. An exact match of the reported problem and the answers on file is not necessary. Using a relevance scoring system based on key words, the search process looks for answers that are related to the problem. Whenever a new problem is encountered, its solution is added to the database.

Database applications like the ones used at Whirlpool and Viewlogic have not been used in the past because the data was unorganized or too voluminous to access efficiently. But relational database software, larger capacity hard disk drives, and faster computers have overcome these obstacles for many organizations.

Figure 9-22

IN THE FUTURE

Nontext Databases

As shown by the tremendous interest in multimedia, computers are being used for much more than traditional text processing. Database applications are moving in a similar direction. Sounds, graphics, and video are more frequently being incorporated into stand-alone documents and will soon be part of database files as well. Although not yet widely used, some database developers have already added capabilities for keeping track of nontext data. Several of the leading database packages can incorporate graphic images including photographs into the actual database files.

One of the most promising nontext database applications is geographic information systems (GIS). GIS systems take traditional data and merge it with geographic information to produce a map that graphically displays the data. The maps are used to show existing or potential customers and the location of particular types of businesses or services. Any information that can be tied to a geographic reference such as a street address, ZIP code, or county name can be converted to a graphical map display. One early use of GIS is in site selection for retail stores. Western Auto, an auto parts retailer, uses GIS software not only to help select the locations for its stores but also to determine what inventory items should be stocked. Using census and market research data, Western Auto creates a detailed demographic profile of a potential store site. The information helps them decide if the area is likely to have do-it-yourselfers who need a selection of repair parts or mechanically challenged individuals who are more likely to buy polishes and accessories.

Nontext databases will grow rapidly but probably not as stand-alone products. Instead, nontext information will just be one more option that you can process on your computer. Visual and audio data items are being incorporated now. How long will it be before taste, touch, and smell elements can be added to a database?

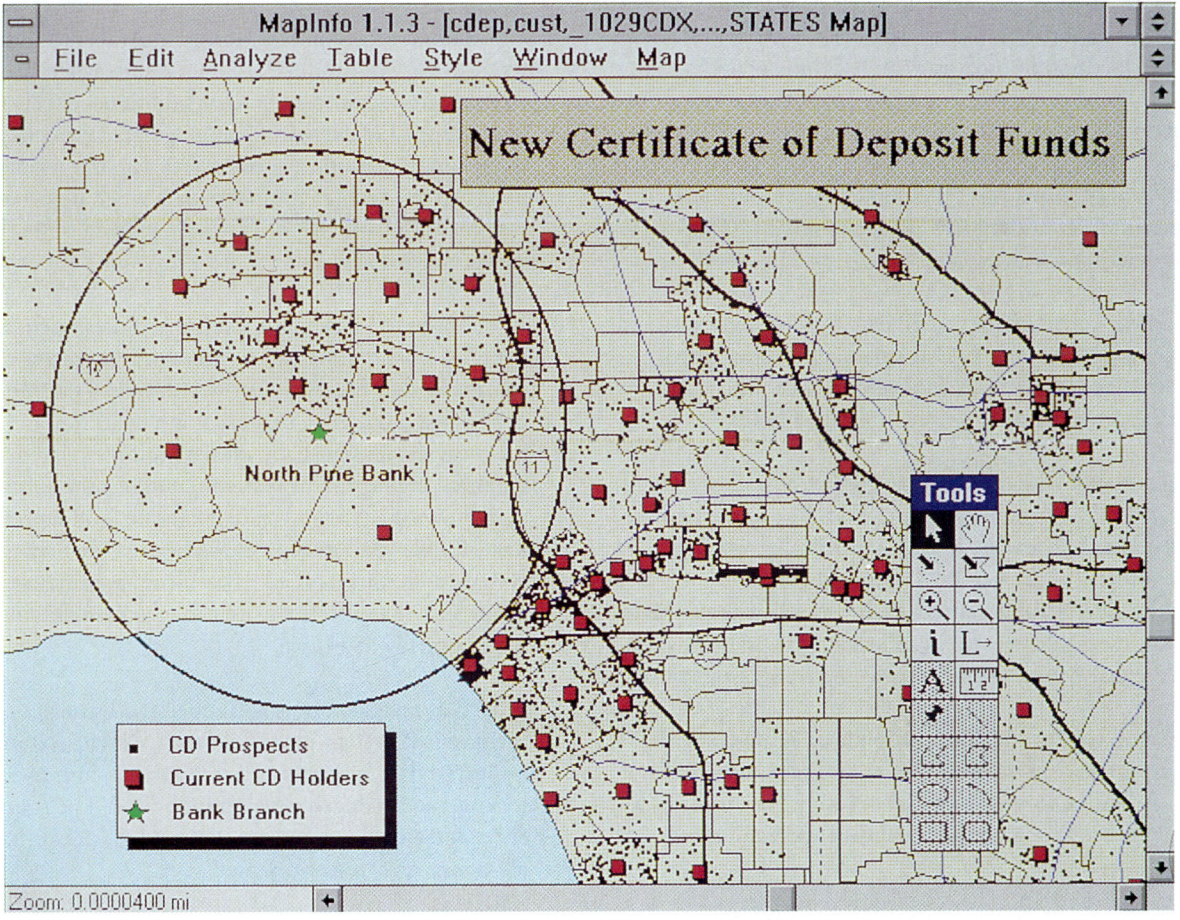

Figure 9-23

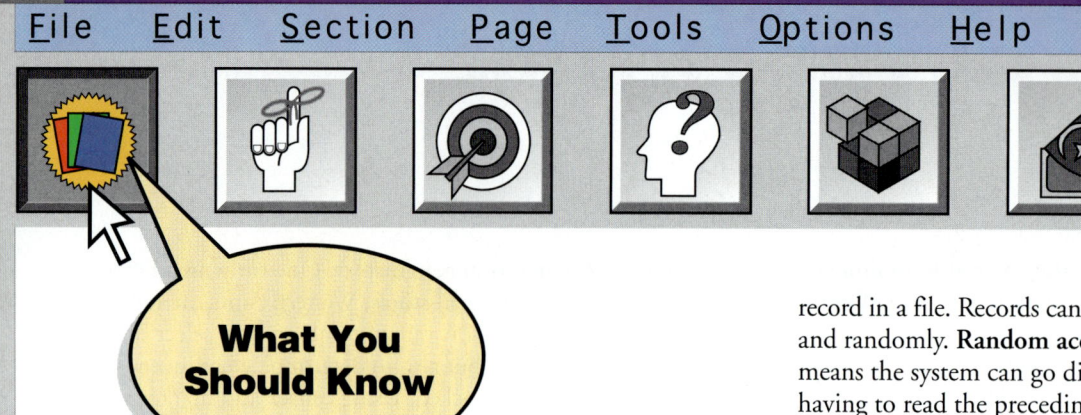

1. **Data management** refers to procedures that are used to keep data accurate and timely and provide for the security and maintenance of data.

2. **Data accuracy**, sometimes called **data integrity**, means that the source of the data is reliable and the data is correctly reported and entered. Accurate data must also be timely.

3. **Data security** refers to protecting data to keep it from being misused or lost. **Backup** refers to making copies of data files so if data is lost or destroyed, a timely recovery can be made and processing can continue.

4. **Data maintenance**, another aspect of data management, refers to the procedures used to keep data current. When data is maintained it is called **updating** and includes procedures for **adding** new data, **changing** existing data, and **deleting** obsolete data.

5. A **file** is a collection of related data or information stored under a single name. Files are made up of structured groups of related facts called **records**. The individual facts that make up the records are called **fields**.

6. **Sequential file organization** means that records are stored one after the other, normally in ascending or descending order, based on a value in each record called the key. The **key**, also called the **key field**, is a field that contains unique data. **Sequential retrieval**, also called **sequential access**, means the records in a file are retrieved one record after another in the same order as the records are stored.

7. A second type of file organization is called **indexed file organization**. An indexed file has an index that itself is a file. An **index** consists of a list containing the value of a key field and the corresponding disk address for each record in a file. Records can be accessed both sequentially and randomly. **Random access**, also called **direct access**, means the system can go directly to a record without having to read the preceding records.

8. A **direct file** (sometimes called a relative or random file) uses the key value of a record to determine the location on the disk where the record is stored. These locations are sometimes called **buckets**. The process of using a formula and performing the calculation to determine the location of a record is called **hashing**. One hashing method is the division/remainder method, in which the computer uses a **prime number** (a number divisible by only itself and 1) to determine the relative location where the record is stored. When locations generated from different keys are the same, they are called **synonyms**. The occurrence of this event is called a **collision**.

9. Data stored on secondary storage must be kept current to ensure it will produce accurate results when processed. Records are added to a file when additional data is needed to make the file current. Changing data takes place for two primary reasons: (1) to correct data that is known to be incorrect, and (2) to update data when new data becomes available. Records are deleted when they are no longer needed as data.

10. In file-oriented systems, a **flat file** is independent and contains all the information necessary to process the records in that file. Although technically a flat file can be considered a database because it is a collection of data, the term **database** usually means multiple related files. A **database management system** (DBMS) is the software that allows the user to create, maintain, and report the data and file relationships. By contrast, a **file management system**, sometimes called a flat-file management system, is software that allows the user to create, maintain, and access one file at a time.

11. A database system offers a number of advantages over a file-oriented system including: reduced data redundancy, improved data integrity, easier reporting, improved data security, and reduced development time. The four types of database organization are hierarchical, network, relational, and object-oriented.

12. In a **hierarchical database**, data is organized in a series like a family tree or organization chart (the term hierarchy means an organized series). Each **parent record** can have multiple child records. However, each **child record** can have only one parent. The parent record at the top of the database is referred to as the **root record**. Because data relationships are predefined, access to and updating of data is very fast.

13. A **network database** is similar to a hierarchical database except that each child record can have more than one parent. In network database terminology, a child record is referred to as a **member** and a parent record is referred to as an **owner**. The network database is able to establish relationships between different branches of data and thus offers increased access capability.

14. In a **relational database**, data is organized in tables that in database terminology are called **relations**. The tables are further divided into rows (called **tuples**) and fields (called **attributes**). The range of values that an attribute can have is called a **domain**. Data relationships do not have to be predefined.

15. An **object-oriented database** keeps track of objects, which are entities that contain both data and the action that can be taken on the data. Object-oriented databases are also designed to contain nontext data.

16. Common database management system features include: a data dictionary, utilities, security, query language, and recovery. Using **forward recovery**, also called **rollforward**, a log that records what the record looked like before and after a change is made is used to automatically reenter transactions from the last time the system was backed up. Using **backward recovery**, also called **rollback**, the log is used to reverse transactions that took place during a certain period of time.

17. A **query language** is a simple, English-like language that allows users to specify what data they want to see on a report or screen display. **Query by example** (**QBE**) helps the user construct a query by displaying a list of fields that are available in the file from which the query will be made.

18. Three **relational operations** that might be performed when a user queries a relational database are select, project, and join. They allow the user to create a unique **view**, or subset, of the total data. The **select relational operation** selects certain records (rows or tuples) based on user-supplied criteria. The **project relational operation** specifies the fields (attributes) that appear on the query output. The **join relational operation** is used to combine two or more files (relations or tables).

19. One of the most widely used query languages is **Structured Query Language**, often referred to as **SQL** (sometimes pronounced sequel).

20. The centralization of an organization's data into a database requires much cooperation and organization on the part of the database users. The **database administrator**, or **DBA**, is the person responsible for managing all database activities. The job usually includes the following responsibilities: database design, user coordination, backup and recovery, system security, and performance monitoring. The user is responsible for becoming familiar with the data in the existing database and playing an active part in the specification of additions to the database.

21. For relational database files, a process called **normalization** is used to organize data into the most efficient and logical file relationships.

22. A variety of software packages are available for personal computers, ranging from simple file management programs to full relational database management systems.

Terms to Remember

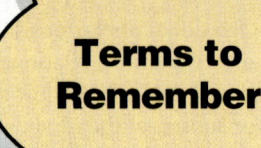

adding (9.3)
attributes (9.15)

backup (9.3)
backward recovery (9.17)
buckets (9.6)

changing (9.3)
child record (9.14)
collision (9.7)

data accuracy (9.2)
data integrity (9.2)
data maintenance (9.3)
data management (9.2)
data security (9.3)
database (9.12)
database administrator (DBA) (9.20)
database management system (DBMS) (9.12)
DBA (9.20)
deleting (9.3)
direct access (9.5)
direct file (9.6)
domain (9.15)

fields (9.4)
file (9.4)
file management system (9.12)
flat file (9.12)
forward recovery (9.17)

hashing (9.7)
hierarchical database (9.14)

index (9.5)
indexed file organization (9.5)

join relational operation (9.18)

key (9.4)
key field (9.4)

member (9.15)

network database (9.15)
normalization (9.21)

object-oriented database (9.16)
owner (9.15)

parent record (9.14)
prime number (9.7)
project relational operation (9.18)

query by example (QBE) (9.18)
query language (9.18)

random access (9.5)
records (9.4)
relational database (9.15)
relational operations (9.18)
relations (9.15)
rollback (9.17)
rollforward (9.17)
root record (9.14)

select relational operation (9.18)
sequential access (9.4)
sequential file organization (9.4)
sequential retrieval (9.4)
SQL (9.19)
Structured Query Language (SQL) (9.19)
synonyms (9.7)

tuples (9.15)

updating (9.3)

view (9.18)

Test Your Knowledge 9.27

File   Edit   Section   Page   Tools   Options   Help

Test Your Knowledge

Fill in the Blanks

1. _____ refers to procedures that are used to keep data accurate and timely and provide for the security and maintenance of data.

2. _____ means the records in a file are retrieved one record after another in the same order as the records are stored, while _____ means the system can go directly to a record without having to read the preceding records.

3. Updating records within a file means _____ records to the file, _____ records within the file, and _____ records from the file.

4. A(n) _____ is a simple, English like language that allows users to specify what data they want to see on a report or screen display.

5. The responsibilities of a database administrator (DBA) include: _____, _____, _____, _____, and _____.

Short Answer

1. How are sequential file organization, indexed file organization, and direct file organization different? What storage medium is used with each type of file organization?

2. What advantages does a database management system (DBMS) offer over a file-oriented system? Briefly explain each.

3. How are hierarchical database, network database, and relational database systems different? What are the advantages of each system?

4. Why is it important that database files be carefully designed? What are some guidelines for creating database files?

5. List some popular database packages designed for personal computers. What is the advantage of SQL packages for personal computers? How should you choose a database software package?

Label the Figure

Instructions: Complete the following table to show the concerns of data management.

DATA MANAGEMENT		
ACCURACY	**SECURITY**	**MAINTENANCE**
_____ _____ _____	_____ _____ _____	Updating: _____ _____

Points to Ponder

1
Data management includes managing data security. One of the ways in which this is done is to restrict access and update privileges for different levels of data to certain groups of individuals. Consider your student file. In addition to your name, address, and grades, this file may contain information on your ethnicity, gender, family, financial status, health, extra-curricular activities, disciplinary record, and so on. Using this file as an example, list what data, if any, each of the following groups should be able to access: you, other students, faculty, administrators, and outside organizations. Which groups, if any, should have update privileges, and what data should they be able to update? Explain your answers.

2
Imagine if, instead of using a central database, your school used a file-oriented system to handle student records. Basic data (such as your name, address, and telephone number) might be kept in a central office file; financial data might be kept in the school business office file; and data concerning your grades and the credits you have earned might be kept in a file by each individual instructor or department from which you have taken a class. How would such a system affect your life as a student? What would be the disadvantages of a file-oriented system for student records? Can you think of any advantages a file-oriented system would have over a database system? If so, what?

3
Every week you probably have contact with a database. This contact may be direct, such as the query of a library database for a specific book, or indirect, such as the purchase of a scanned item whose price is determined from a database. Make a list of all your database contacts during the past two weeks, either direct or indirect. If databases did not exist, how would the two weeks have been different? Overall, do you think your life is easier or more difficult because of databases? Why?

4
Many companies now have computerized personnel databases. These databases generally contain data on employment status, salary, employment history, attendance, and job performance. They may also contain personal information (health, age, family, interests, and so on), opinion ("Mary tends to be overly aggressive"), rumors ("John seems to be romantically involved with a coworker"), and even a picture. Personnel records have always been a key factor in deciding job promotion or termination, and they have sometimes been misused. Some people feel, however, that the information in a personnel record is given additional merit when part of a computer file or printout. What information do you think should be in a personnel file? Why? What information do you think should not be included in a personnel file? Why?

5
The type of database organization employed depends on such factors as the kind of data in the database, how frequently the data needs to be updated, and how the data is used. Consider some information that you would want to store in a database on your personal computer. On the basis of the factors mentioned, what type of database organization (hierarchical, network, or relational) would you use? Why? What type of database organization would be least appropriate for your data? Why?

6
This chapter outlines some of the job responsibilities of a database administrator (DBA). Starting salaries of $50,000 for database administrators are common, and senior DBAs can earn as much as $100,000. Database administrators typically have taken courses in computer science, programming or systems analysis, and business. In addition, classes that deal with problem solving (such as mathematics, philosophy, or related subjects) are suggested. Database administrators must be aware of new technologies, able to resolve conflicts, curious and tenacious, and have a wide range of interests. Create a resume that you could use in applying for a position as database administrator. Include courses you have taken and, using your college catalog, courses you may take. Describe any work experiences in which you had responsibilities similar to those of a DBA. Give examples of situations in which you demonstrated some of the qualities required of a database administrator.

1. Visit a computer store and obtain information on a file management system and a database management system. Compare the features, processing requirements, and prices of the two packages. On the basis of your comparison, which system of managing data files is more appropriate for your current needs? Why? Do you think the same system would still be best five years from now? If you were choosing a system of managing data files for a small business, would your decision be different? Why or why not?

2. Automobile dealers frequently use databases that contain information about both cars in their own inventories and cars in the inventories of other dealers who sell the same make. Salespeople use these databases to find a car that meets a customer's requirements and then, if the car is in another dealer's inventory, they "dealer trade" for the desired car. Visit an automobile dealership that uses a computerized database and ask a salesperson for a demonstration. How many dealers are represented in the database? How is the database used? What criteria can be employed when querying the database? How often is the database updated? What are the advantages and disadvantages offered by using the database?

3. In 1991, the U.S. Supreme Court decision in *Feist v. Rural Telephone* removed much of the protection corporate databases had previously enjoyed. This decision held that, despite the effort involved in creating a database, publishers did not deserve copyright protection and the facts compiled could be copied, even by competitors. Visit a library and, using law books and periodicals, find out more about the *Feist v. Rural Telephone* decision and the protection of corporate databases. Why did the court decide as it did? Can some databases, especially those dealing with proprietary data, be protected in other ways (such as with trade-secrets law or by arranging data in a creative manner)? What effect has the Supreme Court's decision had on American business?

4. Most libraries use computerized databases to keep track of their collections. A library database often contains not only titles on its own shelves, but also titles in other libraries where an individual has borrowing privileges. Visit a public or school library that uses a database. Interview the person in charge or a librarian. How often is the database updated? What are the benefits of using a database? What are the drawbacks?

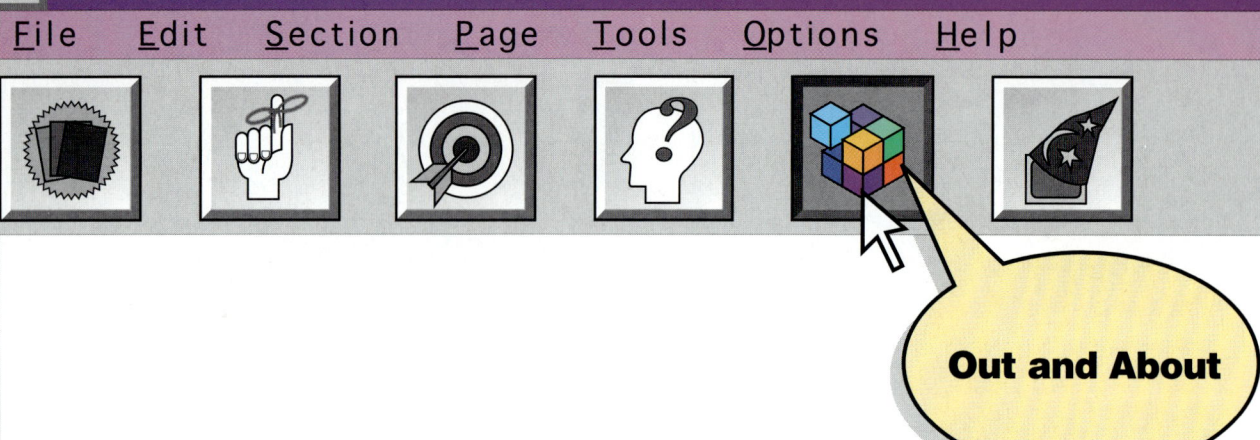

5. One of the most interesting applications of computerized databases is in the sports arena. Some database programs help individual athletes, such as the Sport Sight program that studies pitchers' motions and the Sport Technology program that analyzes golf swings. Other programs, such as one from Sports-Tech International, are used by several college and professional teams to compare game tapes and determine how opponents tend to handle particular situations. The Indiana Pacers credit their database program in the draft selection of basketball star Kenny Williams and their defeat of Michael Jordan and the Chicago Bulls in the first six games the teams played after starting the system. Using current computer magazines, research the relationship between computerized databases and sports. How are databases currently being used? How could they be used in the future? What impact will computerized databases have on individual and team sports?

6. Law enforcement agencies are some of the most extensive users of databases. Visit your local police department to find out about the role computerized databases play in law enforcement. Does the department maintain its own database? To what other databases does the department have access? How are databases used? Do any problems ever result from the use of databases (for example, what happens if an individual pulled over for a traffic violation has the same name as a wanted felon)? What are the advantages and disadvantages of police use of computerized databases for law-abiding citizens?

 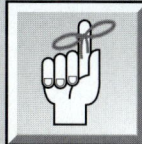    

Windows Labs

1 Working with Subdirectories With Program Manager on the screen, double-click the Main group icon. In the Main group window, double-click the File Manager program-item icon. Maximize the File Manager window.

Insert the diskette with your Windows Labs into drive A. Click the drive A icon. Select the File menu and choose the Create Directory command. Type winlabs and choose the OK button *(Figure 9-24)*. Follow the same procedure to create a subdirectory with your first name as its name. Does the subdirectory of your first name display above or below the winlabs directory? Click the winlabs subdirectory. How many files are in this subdirectory? Click the directory of your first name. Select the File menu and choose the Rename command. In the Rename dialog box, type your last name in the To text box and choose the OK button. Select the File menu and choose the Delete command. Choose the OK or Yes button in each Delete dialog box that displays. Close File Manager.

2 Shelly Cashman Series Database Lab Follow the instructions in Windows Lab 2 in Chapter 1 on page 1.30 to display the Shelly Cashman Series Labs screen. Select Designing a Database and choose the Start Lab button. When the initial screen displays, carefully read the objectives. With your printer turned on, point to the Print Questions button and click the left mouse button. Fill out the top of the Questions sheet and answer the questions as you step through the Database Lab.

3 Working with Files in Subdirectories Open File Manager as discussed in Windows Lab 1 above. Maximize the File Manager window. With your Windows Labs disk in drive A, click the drive A icon.

With the root directory selected, click the first file in the list (win2-1.wri) to select it. While holding down the SHIFT key, click the last file in the list; then release the SHIFT key. All files between the first and last, inclusive, are selected *(Figure 9-25)*. Select the File menu and choose the Move command. In the Move dialog box, type winlabs in the To Text box and choose the OK button. Click the winlabs directory. How many files are in the winlabs directory?

With the winlabs directory selected, click the filename win2-2.wri to select it. While holding down the CTRL key, click the filename win6-2.wri to select this noncontiguous file. Select the File menu and choose the Copy command. In the Copy dialog box, type a backslash in the To text box and choose the OK button. Click the root directory of your diskette in drive A. How many files are there?

Select the two files in the root directory. From the File menu, choose the Delete command. Choose the OK or Yes button in each Delete dialog box that displays. Close File Manager. Close the Main group window.

4 Organizing and Managing Information With Program Manager on the screen, double-click the Accessories group icon. In the Accessories group window, double-click the Cardfile program-item icon. Maximize the Cardfile window. Select the Edit menu and choose the

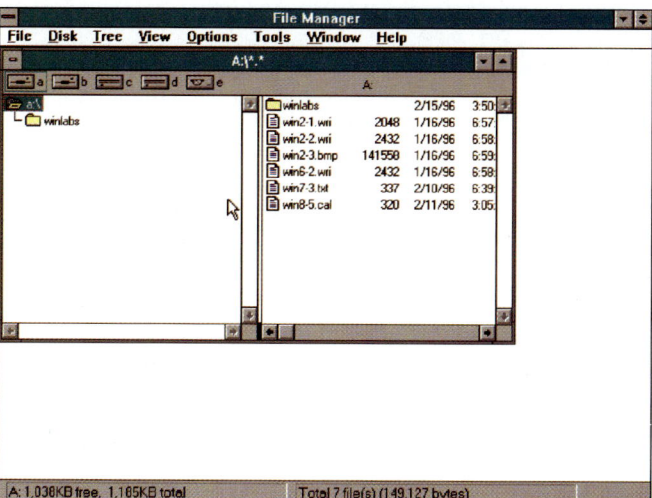

Figure 9-24

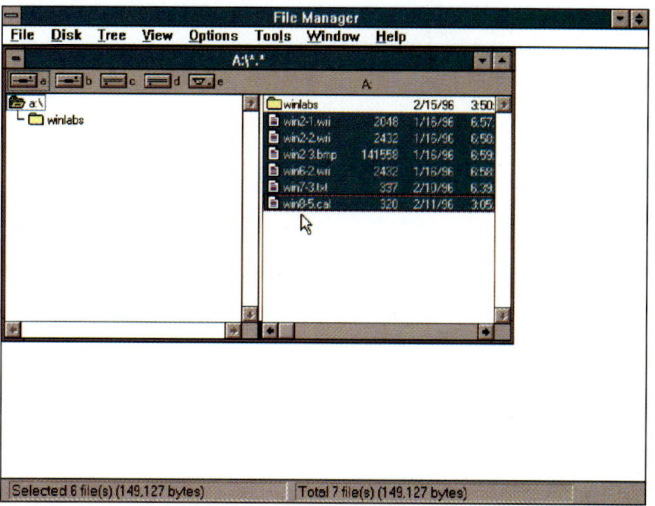

Figure 9-25

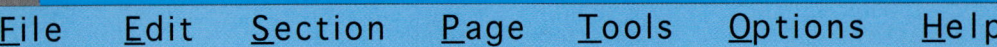
 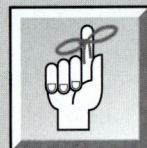    

In the Lab (continued)

Index command. In the Index dialog box, type **Pender, Mary** in the Index Line text box and choose the OK button. With the insertion point in the information area of the index card, type **123 Seventh Place** and press the ENTER key. Type **Chicago, IL 60606**. Select the Card menu and choose the Add command. In the Add dialog box, type **Baker, Greg** in the Add text box and choose the OK button. In the information area, type **17 Grace Avenue** and press the ENTER key. Type **Hammond, IN 46323** *(Figure 9-26)*. Add another card for yourself.

    Select the Search menu and choose the Go To command. Type **Pender** in the Go To text box and choose the OK button. What happened to Pender's card? Select the Search menu and choose the Find command. In the Find dialog box, type **Grace** in the Find What text box and choose the Find Next button; choose the Cancel button. Whose card is now in front?

    Save the file using the Save command on the File menu. Assign the filename win9-4. Select the File menu and choose the Print All command. Select the View menu and choose the List command *(Figure 9-27)*. Click your name in the list. Select the View menu and choose the Card command. Close Cardfile. Close the Accessories group window.

5 Using Help   Open the Cardfile window as described in Windows Lab 4 above. Select the Help menu and choose the Contents command. Read and print the information for each of these Help topics: Add or Change Text in the Index Line, Delete Cards, Find Text, Move Through a Card File, and Select Cards. Close the Help window. Close Cardfile. Close the Accessories group window.

DOS Labs

1 Working with Subdirectories   Insert the diskette with your DOS Labs into drive A. At the DOS prompt, type **a:** and press the ENTER key. Type **md \doslabs** and press the ENTER key to create a subdirectory. Type **dir > prn** and press the ENTER key to print a directory listing. Type **cd \doslabs** and press the ENTER key to change to the doslabs subdirectory. Print the directory listing. Type **cd** and press the ENTER key to return to the root directory.

2 Working with Files in Subdirectories   At the DOS prompt, type **move *.* \doslabs** and press the ENTER key to move the files from the root to the doslabs subdirectory. Print the directory listing. Type **cd \doslabs** and press the ENTER key. Print the directory listing. Type **cd** and press the ENTER key. Print the directory listing.

3 Using Help   At the DOS prompt, type **help** and press the ENTER key. Print all help information regarding these commands: MD, CD, RD, and MOVE. Exit Help.

Online Lab

1 Travel Guide   Using one of the two online services you selected in Chapter 1, connect to the service and perform the following tasks: (1) Search the online service for the Travel Guide section. (2) Locate, display, and print the list of sights to see in Atlanta, GA; Nashville, TN; and New Orleans, LA.

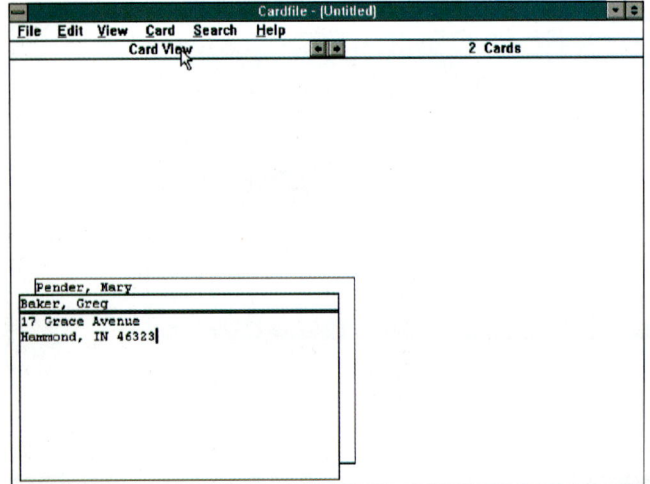

Figure 9-26

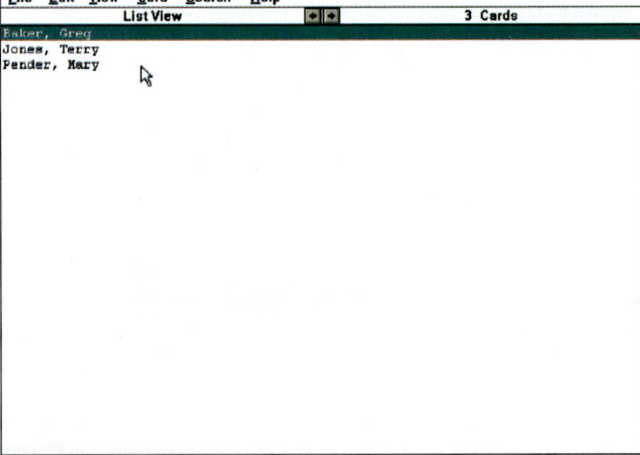

Figure 9-27

CHAPTER TEN

Information Systems

10

Objectives

After completing this chapter, you will be able to:

- Define the term information system and identify the six elements of an information system

- Describe why information is important to an organization

- Explain how managers use information by describing the four managerial tasks

- Discuss the different levels in an organization and how the information requirements differ for each level

- Explain the qualities of information

- Describe the different types of information systems and the trend toward integration

- Explain how personal computers are used in information systems

An **information system** is a collection of elements that provides accurate, timely, and useful information. As discussed in Chapter 1, all information systems that are implemented on a computer are comprised of the six elements: equipment, software, accurate data, trained information systems personnel, knowledgeable users, and documented procedures (Figure 10-1 on the next page). Each element contributes to a successful information system, and conversely, a weakness in any of these elements can cause an information system to fail. People who create, use, or change any type of information system should consider all six elements to ensure success.

10.2

Why Is Information Important to an Organization?

Increasingly more organizations are realizing that the information in their databases is an important asset that must be protected. Like more tangible assets such as buildings and equipment, an organization's information assets have a present and future value and have costs associated with their acquisition, maintenance, and storage. Information is no longer thought of as a by-product of doing business, but rather as a key ingredient in both short- and long-range decision making. Just as many companies have consistently utilized product strategies, some companies are now developing *information strategies* that specify the types of information they want available for decision making *(Figure 10-2)*.

Several factors have contributed to the increased need for timely and accurate information. Among these factors are expanded markets, increased competition, shorter product life cycles, and government regulation.

Expanded markets means that to be successful today, businesses must sell their products in as many markets as possible. Often this means national as well as international distribution of a product. Companies that produce a product for local or regional use are at a disadvantage against companies that produce larger volumes of products for a wider distribution. When companies expand their markets, they must have more information about a larger number of potential selling areas (markets) and the different ways of getting their products to those markets. Automobiles are an example of this trend. The number of automobile producers has decreased, and the surviving companies have moved to worldwide distribution of their products.

Increased competition means that competing companies are financially stronger and better organized. To compete successfully, it is important for an organization to have current information on how competitors are selling their products. Many companies now maintain large databases that include information on competitive product features, prices, and methods of distribution. For consumer product companies, this information often includes sales and the percent of the total market. This information is important in measuring the impact of advertising campaigns. For example, many companies will measure the impact of a new advertising campaign

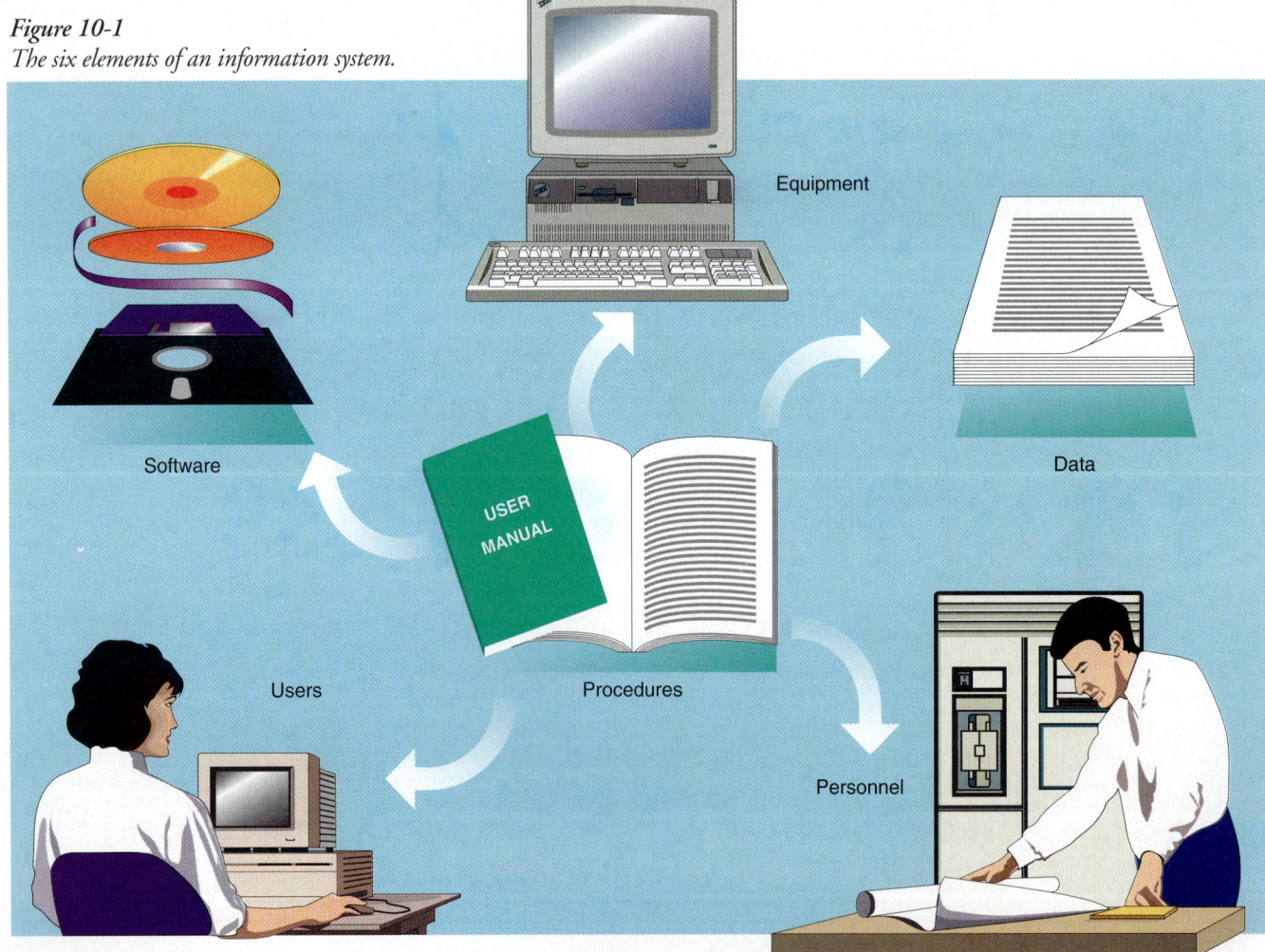

Figure 10-1
The six elements of an information system.

How Do Managers Use Information?

All employees in an organization need information to effectively perform their jobs, but the primary users of information are managers. **Managers** of an organization are the men and women responsible for directing the use of resources such as people, money, materials, and information so the organization can operate efficiently and prosper. Managers work toward this goal by performing the four management tasks of planning, organizing, leading, and controlling.

1. *Planning* involves establishing goals and objectives. Upper-level management plans by establishing the strategies of the organization to help meet these goals and objectives. For example, upper-level management often prepares a three- to five-year plan that includes strategies on how to enter new markets or increase existing market share. Lower-level management plans by establishing specific policies and procedures to implement the strategies. A lower-level management plan might include a specific inventory quantity to be maintained for a part.

in a limited geographic area such as a large metropolitan city before they use the advertising nationwide.

Shorter product life cycles mean that companies have less time to perfect a product. More often than not, the product has to be successful when it is first introduced because companies have less time to make corrections after a product is introduced. This means that before they introduce products, they must have accurate information about what potential customers want. Shorter product life cycles have led to the increased use of test marketing. Company managers use the results of tests to decide advertising, packaging, and product features. Shorter product life cycles have also required companies to begin work earlier on next-generation products. To do this, managers must have information about existing product features that customers want changed and new features they want added.

Government regulation has also contributed to the need for more information. One good example of this is in human resource management. To comply with equal employment opportunity (EEO) guidelines and laws, organizations must keep detailed records on employee testing, hiring, and promotion practices. The employee database, once used almost exclusively for payroll purposes, has now been expanded to include valuable information on employee skill and education levels as well as the results of performance reviews. With this information, companies can document their compliance with government regulations and guidelines.

INFORMATION STRATEGY:

1. What internal and external factors will affect the future sucess of the organization?

    Examples: interest rates, labor costs, raw material prices, government regulation, consumer trends, competive products.

2. What sources of information are available to monitor these factors?

    Examples: Newspapers, trade journals, government studies, private research.

3. How often should each of these factors be monitored? Daily, weekly, monthly, quarterly, annually?

4. What form should reports on these factors take? Written, oral, statistical, graphic, on-site visits?

5. Who should receive these reports?

Figure 10-2
Questions organizations must address when developing an information strategy.

2. *Organizing* includes identifying and bringing together the resources necessary to achieve the plans of an organization. Resources include people, money, materials (facilities, equipment, raw materials), and information. Organizing also involves establishing the management structure of an organization such as the departments and reporting relationships. For example, to introduce a new product, a company can assign responsibility to an existing department or form a new team whose sole responsibility is the new product.

3. *Leading,* sometimes referred to as *directing,* involves instructing and authorizing individuals to perform the necessary work. To lead effectively, managers must be able to communicate what needs to be done and motivate people to do the work. Leadership often takes place at daily or weekly meetings where managers meet with their employees to discuss job priorities.

4. *Controlling* involves measuring performance and, if necessary, taking corrective action. Daily production reports are a control device that give managers the information they need to make any necessary adjustments in production rate or product mix.

The four management tasks shown in *Figure 10-3* are usually performed in a sequence that becomes a recurring cycle. Actual performance is measured against a previously established plan as part of the control task; this often results in a revised plan. The revised plan may result in additional organizational and leadership activities, and so the cycle repeats itself. The four tasks are related and a change in one task usually affects one or more of the other tasks.

All managers perform these management tasks, but their area of focus, such as finance or production, and the information they need to perform the tasks is influenced by their level in the organization.

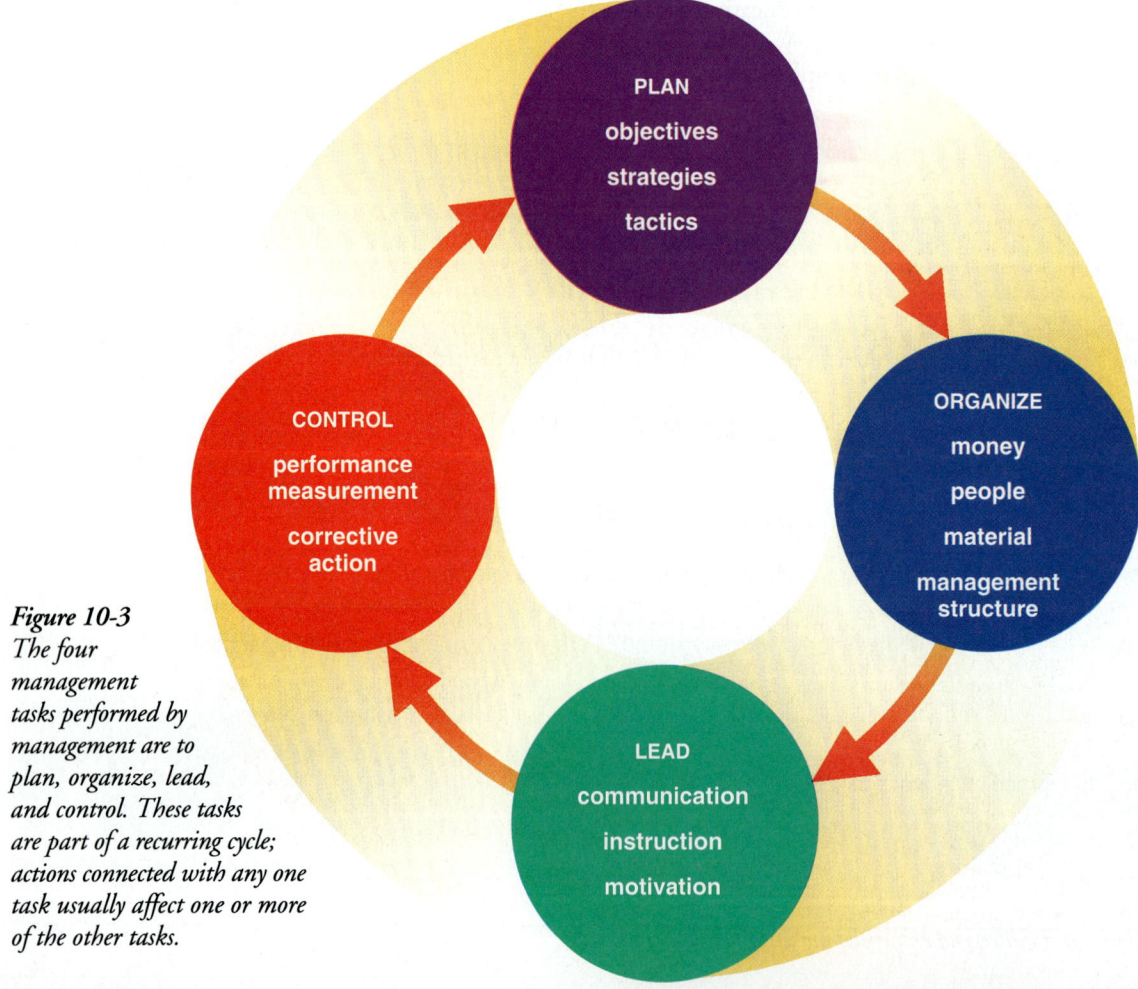

Figure 10-3
The four management tasks performed by management are to plan, organize, lead, and control. These tasks are part of a recurring cycle; actions connected with any one task usually affect one or more of the other tasks.

Management Levels in an Organization

Management is usually classified into three levels; senior management, middle management, and operational management. The names for these levels can vary. As shown in *Figure 10-4*, these three levels of management are above a fourth level of the organization consisting of the production, clerical, and nonmanagement staff. Together, these four levels make up the entire organization. The following sections discuss these levels and their different informational requirements.

Senior Management – Strategic Decisions

Senior management, also referred to as executive or top management, includes the highest management positions in an organization. Senior management is concerned with the long-range direction of the organization. Senior managers are primarily responsible for **strategic decisions** that deal with the overall goals and objectives of an organization. Examples of strategic decisions are whether to add or discontinue a product line or whether to diversify into a new business. The time frame for such decisions is usually long range, starting one or more years in the future and continuing for several years or indefinitely. Senior management decisions often involve factors that cannot be directly controlled by the organization such as the changing trends of society. An example of such a trend is the increasing average age of the population. Senior management decisions often require information from outside the company such as industry statistics, consumer surveys, or broad economic indicators, such as the change in personal income or the number of new houses being built.

Senior management is also responsible for monitoring how current operations are meeting the objectives of previously made strategic decisions. For example, are sales of a new product meeting previously forecasted levels? Because senior management is concerned with all areas of an organization, it must rely on summarized information to review all operations in a timely manner. Often information on current operations is presented only if it is significantly above or below what was planned. This helps senior management to focus on only the variations that require its involvement.

Another senior management responsibility is to supervise middle management personnel.

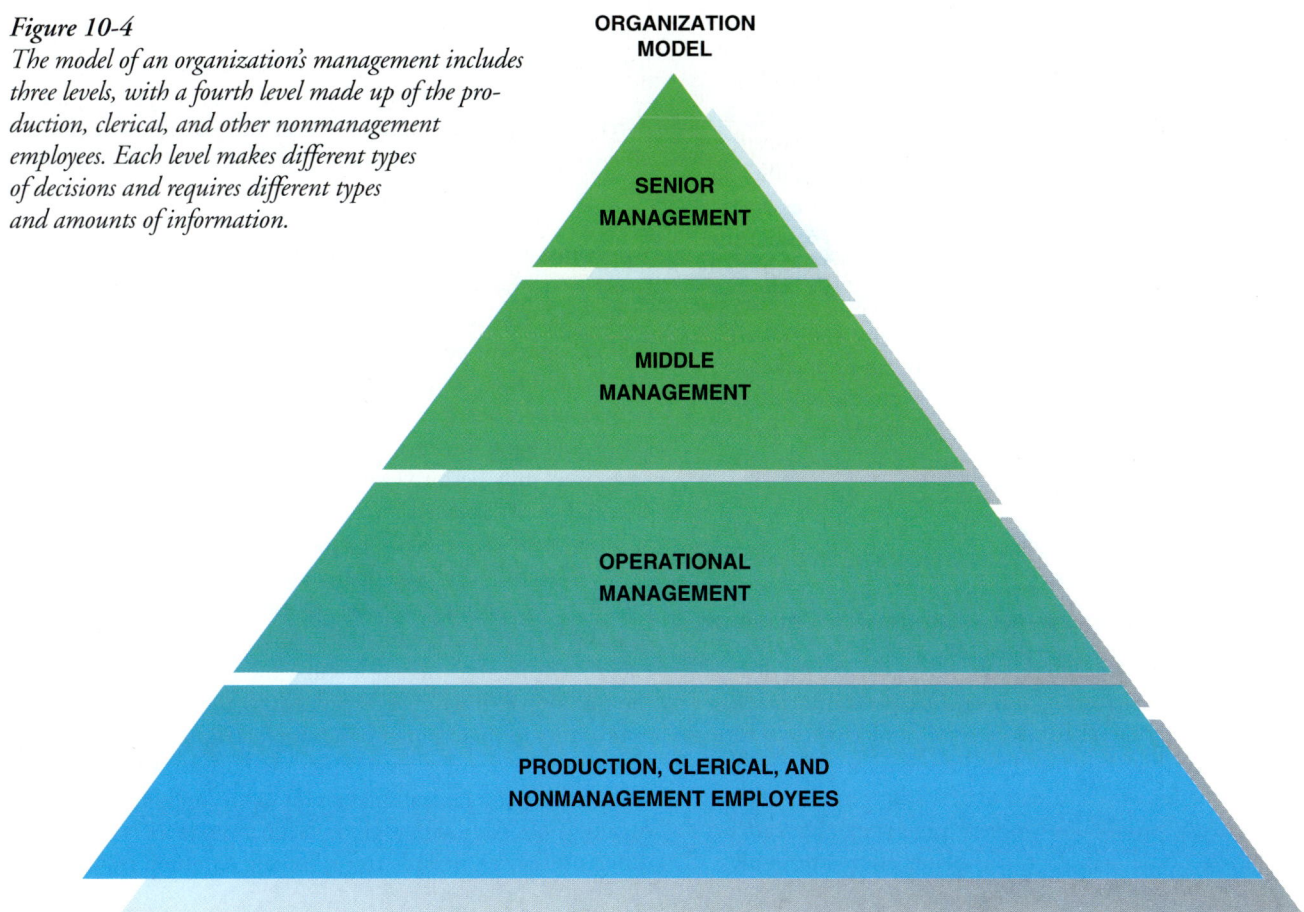

Figure 10-4
The model of an organization's management includes three levels, with a fourth level made up of the production, clerical, and other nonmanagement employees. Each level makes different types of decisions and requires different types and amounts of information.

Middle Management – Tactical Decisions

Middle management is responsible for implementing the strategic decisions of senior management. To do this, middle managers make **tactical decisions** that implement specific programs and plans necessary to accomplish the stated objectives. Tactical decisions could include how to best advertise and promote a company's products. Such decisions usually involve a shorter time frame than strategic decisions but often cover an entire year. Although they are interested in external events that may influence their work, middle managers are more concerned with the internal operations of the organization and, therefore, rely on information generated by the organization. Middle management also uses summarized and exception-oriented reports although not to the extent of senior management. Middle management sometimes must review detailed information to understand performance variances.

Middle management is also responsible for supervising operational management.

Operational Management – Operational Decisions

Operational management supervises the production, clerical, and nonmanagement staff of an organization. In performing their duties, operational managers make **operational decisions** that usually involve an immediate action such as accepting or rejecting an inventory delivery or approving a purchase order. The operational decisions should be consistent with and support the tactical decisions made by middle management. The decision time frame of operational managers tasks is usually very short, such as a day, a week, or a month. Operational managers directly supervise the production and support of an organization's product or service; thus, they need detailed information telling them what was produced. Summary and exception reporting, always an important tool for senior- and middle-level managers, is increasingly being used by operational managers. There are two reasons for this change. First, upper levels of management are allowing lower levels of management to make more decisions. Second, because of computerized systems, the information necessary to make decisions at lower levels is more readily available.

Nonmanagement Employees – On-the-Job Decisions

Nonmanagement employees, which include production, clerical, and staff personnel, also need frequent information to perform their jobs. The trend toward flexible manufacturing systems has increased the need for information to be available to the production worker. Instead of working at the same task repeatedly, production workers often work as a team on related tasks. Some manufacturing plants allow a team of workers to move with the product from the beginning of production to the end. Such changes require production workers to understand more about the production process than ever before. Often, this information is made available to the workers through the use of production-floor terminals that can be used to inquire on the next production process or tool required. Some systems tell the workers which job they should work on next.

Today, clerical and nonproduction workers also have more information available to them than in the past. For example, more documentation of administrative systems is being placed online for immediate access. As previously mentioned, this is part of a trend toward giving lower level, nonmanagement employees the information they need to make decisions made formerly by managers.

Other Approaches to Management Organization

Most organizations are structured into levels as shown in *Figure 10-4* on page 10.5. Across these four levels, management and employees are usually divided into *functional* groups such as finance, manufacturing, marketing, and so on. Each functional group usually includes employees from each level; senior, middle, and operational management, and nonmanagement employees *(Figure 10-5)*. Within each level there may be several layers of management.

Sometimes a functional organization can prove to be a barrier to employee communication and getting work done efficiently. For example, before a middle manager in marketing can ask an operational manager in finance to perform a task, a finance middle manager must first approve the request. Sometimes the marketing middle manager might even have to ask his or her top management marketing person to ask his or her counter-part in finance (meaning the corresponding top management person in finance) to first approve the request and then pass the request *down the line* to the finance person who is being requested to do the work. This process is called following the *chain of command,* which means that employees only perform work approved by their immediate supervisors. As you can imagine, this formal request and approval process can significantly delay action being taken.

To improve intercompany communication, increase productivity, and decrease the amount of time it takes to respond to problems, many companies have adopted or are experimenting with management structures different from the traditional functional organization. Some of these new approaches to management and organization structure include reengineering, cross-functional organization, core competencies, organizational architecture, and horizontal organization. Although each of these approaches is slightly different, they all include the following common features:

MANAGEMENT LEVELS IN AN ORGANIZATION

- **Fewer levels of management.** Older established companies sometimes have as many as ten to fifteen layers of management between a nonmanagement employee and the top executive. Progressive companies are eliminating as many layers of management as possible so remaining managers can work more closely with nonmanagement employees and customers. All layers of management have been affected by this trend, but middle managers have lost the most jobs.
- **Employees are organized by process not function.** A process, such as order fulfillment or product development, typically involves several functional areas such as sales, manufacturing, engineering, and finance. Some companies are now placing all employees involved with a process into a single group dedicated to efficiently carrying out the process tasks. The person responsible for managing the process group is sometimes called the *process owner.*
- **Self-managed teams are used wherever possible.** Although they have long been used for one-time projects, teams of employees with different functional backgrounds are now being given ongoing responsibilities and being told to manage themselves. An important requirement for this approach is to give the team a well-defined purpose and measurable performance goals.

The impact of these new management methods and structures on information systems has been significant. Task and process teams often require information that was previously prepared by separate functional departments. With fewer levels of management, managers are required to rely more on exception reports to help them allocate their limited time to the most important areas. With the increasing pressure to reduce costs, information system managers have been encouraged to **downsize** operations by moving applications from mainframe and minicomputer systems to networks of personal computers. Some companies have eliminated their in-house information system departments altogether. In a process called **outsourcing**, companies hire outside firms to provide information systems support for a contracted fee.

Whatever form of organization companies adopt, they realize that they must develop an *information architecture* that matches their *organization architecture.*

With the importance of information to an organization and how it is used by various levels clearly outlined, the characteristics, or qualities, that all information should have will be explained.

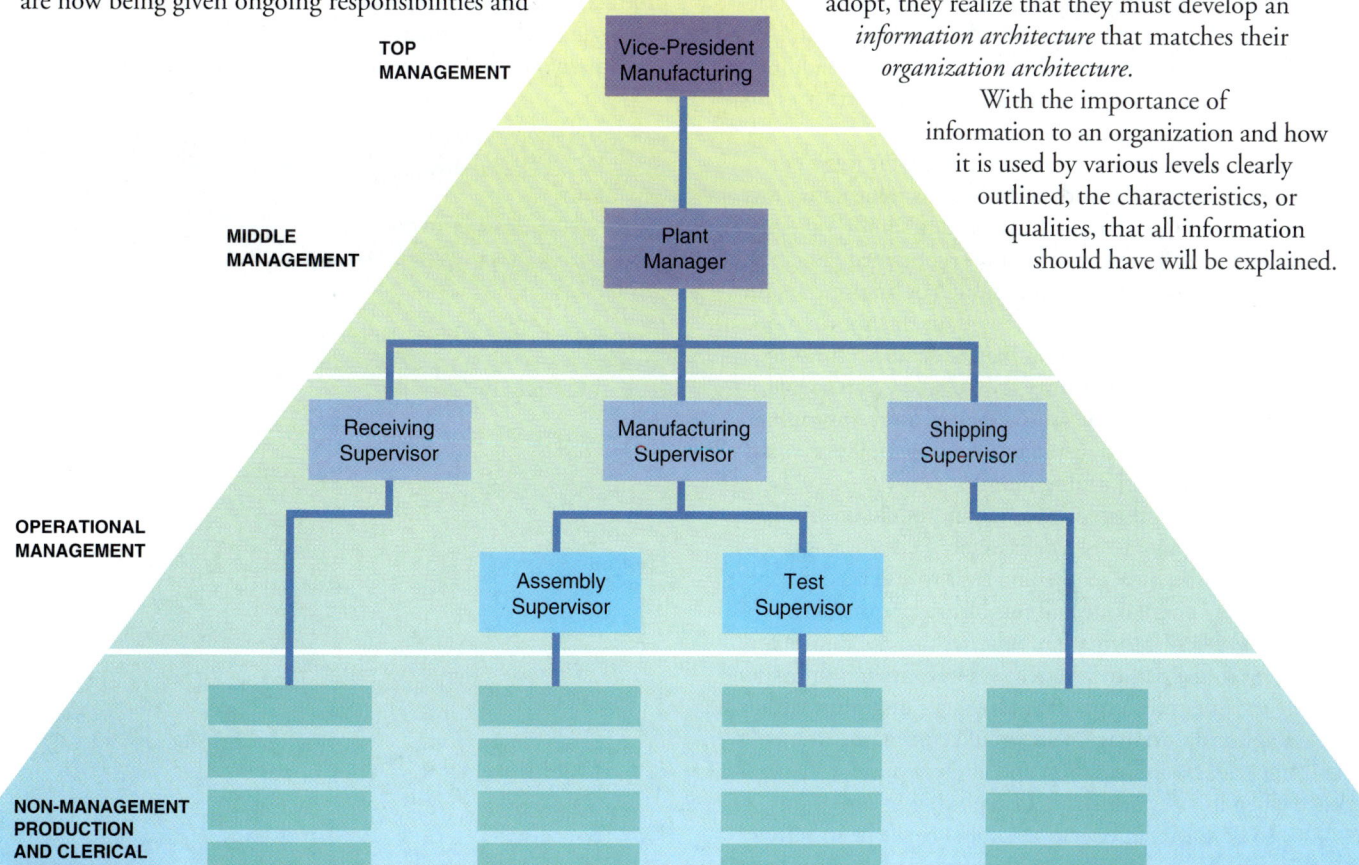

Figure 10-5
Most organizations are divided into functional groups such as finance, manufacturing, marketing, and administration. As shown in this organization chart, functional groups usually have employees at each level of the organization. Within a level, there are sometimes two or more layers of management as shown in the operational management level.

Qualities of Information

As previously mentioned, the purpose of processing data is to create information. Just as data should have certain characteristics, so too should information. These characteristics are often called the qualities of information *(Figure 10-6)*. Terms used to describe these qualities include: accurate, verifiable, timely, organized, meaningful, useful, and cost effective.

Although it may seem obvious, the first quality of information is that it should be *accurate*. Inaccurate information is often worse than no information at all. Accuracy is also a characteristic of data. Although accurate data does not guarantee accurate information, it is impossible to produce accurate information from erroneous data. Remember the term GIGO introduced earlier; it stands for *Garbage In, Garbage Out*.

Closely related to accuracy is that information be *verifiable*. This means that if necessary, the user can confirm the information. For example, before relying on the amounts in a summary report, an accountant would want to know that the totals could be supported by details of the transactions. The accountant could verify the accuracy of the report totals by testing some or all of the totals by adding up the supporting detail records and comparing the results to the report.

Another quality of information is that it must be *timely*. Although most information loses its value with time, some information, such as trends, becomes more valuable as time passes and more information is obtained. The point to remember is that the timeliness must be appropriate for any decisions that will be made based on the information. Up-to-the-minute information may be required for some decisions such as the inventory level of a key part, while older information may be satisfactory or more appropriate for other decisions such as the number of employees planning vacations in the coming month.

To be most valuable, information should be *organized* to suit users' requirements. For example, a sales manager who assigns territories on a geographic basis would need prospect lists sorted by postal code and not by prospect name.

Meaningful information indicates that the information is relevant to the person who receives it. Certain information is only meaningful to specific individuals or groups within an organization. Management should eliminate extraneous and unnecessary information and always consider the audience when it is accumulating or reporting information.

To be *useful*, information should result in an action being taken or specifically not being taken, depending on the situation. Often, this quality can be improved through exception reporting, which focuses only on the information that exceeds certain limits. An example of exception reporting is an inventory report showing items whose balance on hand is less than a predetermined minimum quantity. Instead of the manager having to look through an entire inventory report to find such items, the exception report would quickly bring these items to the attention of the managers responsible for maintaining the inventory.

Last, but not least, information must be *cost effective*. That is, the cost to produce the information must be less than the value of the information. This can sometimes be hard to determine. If the value of the information cannot be determined, perhaps the information should be produced only as managers require it, instead of on a regular basis. Many organizations periodically review the information they produce in reports to determine if the reports maintain the qualities of information just described. The cost of producing these reports can, therefore, still be justified or possibly reduced.

Although the qualities of information have been discussed in combination with computer systems, these qualities apply to all information regardless of how it is produced. Being knowledgeable of these qualities will help you evaluate the information you receive and provide every day, whether or not it is generated by a computer.

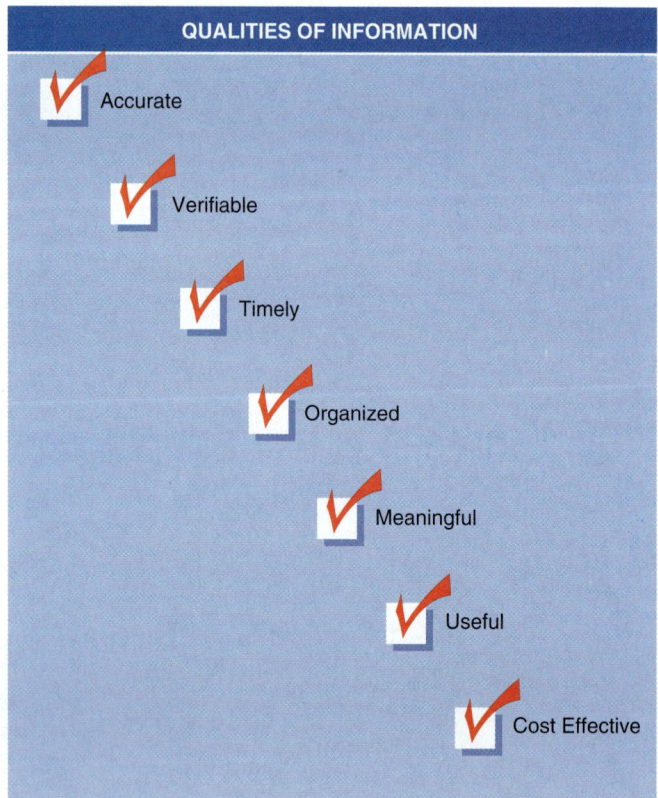

Figure 10-6
The qualities of information are characteristics that all information should have, whether or not it is produced by a computer.

Types of Information Systems

Information systems that are implemented on a computer are generally classified into four categories: (1) transaction processing systems; (2) management information systems; (3) decision support systems; and (4) expert systems.

Transaction Processing Systems

A **transaction processing system** (TPS) processes data generated by the day-to-day transactions of an organization *(Figure 10-7)*. Some examples of a TPS are billing systems, inventory control systems, accounts payable systems, and order entry systems.

When computers were first used for processing business applications, the information systems developed were primarily TPSs. Usually, the purpose was to computerize an existing manual system. This approach often resulted in faster processing, reduced clerical costs, and improved customer service. The first TPSs were usually batch processing systems. In **batch processing**, transaction data is collected and, at a later time, all transactions are processed as a *batch*. As computers became more powerful, online transaction processing systems were developed. With **online transaction processing** (OLTP), transactions are processed as they are entered. All related records are updated at the same time. Today, most TPSs use online transaction processing. However, some processing tasks, such as calculating payroll checks or printing invoices, are most efficiently performed on a batch basis.

Although the TPS was originally designed to process daily transactions, it was modified over time to provide summaries, trends, and exception data useful to management. Today, TPSs are often a part of management information systems, which are discussed in the next section.

Management Information Systems

The concept of management information systems evolved as managers realized that computer processing could be used for more than just day-to-day transaction processing and that the computer's capability to perform rapid calculations and compare data could be used to produce meaningful information for management. A **management information system** (MIS) refers to a computer-based system that generates timely and accurate information for managing an organization. Frequently, a management information system is integrated with a transaction processing system. For example, to process

Figure 10-7
Transaction processing systems (TPSs) process the day-to-day transactions of an organization.

a sales order, the transaction processing system would record the sale, update the customer's accounts receivable balance, and make a deduction from the inventory. In the related management information system, reports would be produced that show slow- or fast-selling products, customers with past due accounts receivable balances, and inventory items that need reordering. In the management information system, the focus is on the information that management needs to do its job *(Figure 10-8)*.

A special type of management information system is the executive information system. **Executive information systems** (EIS) are management information systems that have been designed for the information needs of senior management. Company-wide management information systems usually address the information needs of all levels of management. Because senior managers may not be familiar with (or comfortable with) computer systems, the EIS features make them easier for executives to use. The EIS user interface often uses a mouse or a touch screen to help executives unfamiliar with using a keyboard. One leading system uses a remote control device similar to those used to control a television set.

Another aspect of the EIS user interface is the graphic presentation of information. The EIS relies heavily on graphic presentation of both the processing options *(Figure 10-9)* and data. Again, this is designed to make the system easier to use.

Because executives focus on strategic issues, the EIS often has access to external databases such as the Dow Jones News/Retrieval service. Such external sources of information can provide current information on interest rates, commodity prices, and other leading economic indicators.

Although they offer great promise, many EISs have not been successfully implemented and many executives have stopped using them. A common reason cited in several failed attempts is the mistake of not modifying the system to the specific needs of the individual executives who will use the system. For example, many executives prefer to have information presented in a particular sequence with the option of seeing different levels of supporting detail information such as cost data on a spreadsheet. The desired sequence and level of detail varies for each executive. It appears that an EIS must

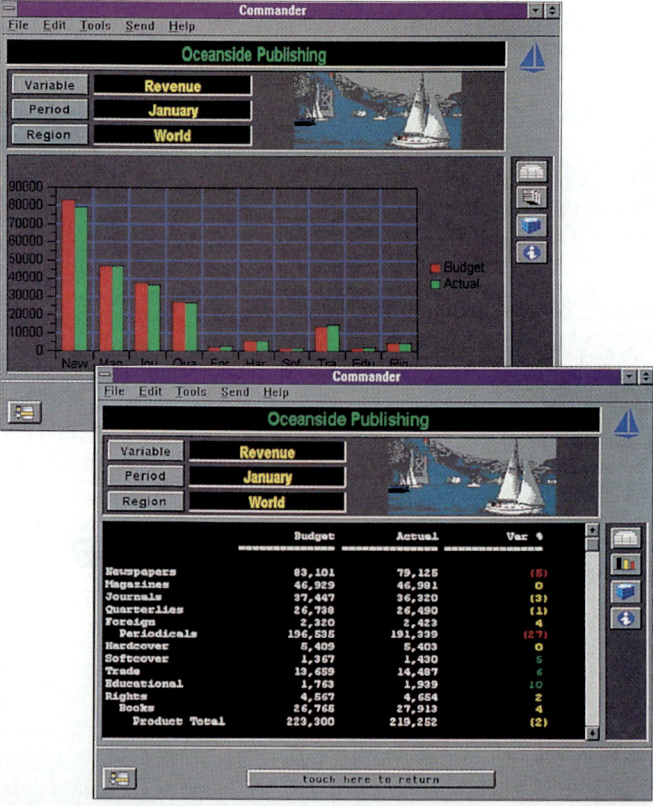

Figure 10-8
Management information systems (MIS) focus on the summary information and exceptions that managers use to perform their jobs.

Figure 10-9
Executive information systems (EIS) often use graphics and touch screens to make the systems easier to use by executives who may not be familiar with computers.

be tailored to the executives' requirements or the executives will continue to manage with information they have obtained through previously established methods.

Decision Support Systems

Frequently, management needs information that is not routinely provided by transaction processing systems and management information systems. For example, a vice president of finance may want to know the net effect on company profits if interest rates on borrowed money increase and raw material prices decrease. Transaction processing systems and management information systems do not usually provide this type of information. Decision support systems have been developed to provide this information.

A **decision support system** (DSS) is a system designed to help someone reach a decision by summarizing or comparing data from either or both internal and external sources. Internal sources include data from an organization's database such as sales, manufacturing, or financial data. Data from external sources could include information on interest rates, population trends, new housing construction, or raw material pricing. Frito Lay, for example, collects and reports sales data on its own and competitors' products every day *(Figure 10-10)*. The information is part of a decision support system that allows Frito Lay to analyze important trends in days or weeks instead of the months that it used to take.

Decision support systems often include query languages, statistical analysis capabilities, spreadsheets, and graphics to help the user evaluate the decision data. More advanced decision support systems also include capabilities that allow users to create a model of the variables affecting a decision. With a **model**, users can ask *what-if* questions by changing one or more of the variables and seeing what the projected results would be. A simple model for determining the best product price would include factors for the expected sales volume at each price level. Many people use electronic spreadsheets for simple modeling tasks. A decision support system is sometimes combined with executive information systems (EIS).

Figure 10-10
Frito Lay, a major producer of snack foods, has developed a decision support system that uses sales information collected daily on hand-held terminals by more than 10,000 salespeople. The system helps Frito Lay spot sales trends in days or weeks instead of the months it used to take.

Generally speaking, a decision support system is more analytical and is designed to work on unstructured problems that do not have a predefined number of variables. For example, a problem involving how to finance a company's growth would involve estimates of sales, income, depreciation, interest rates, and other variables that would best be handled by a decision support system. An executive information system is primarily oriented toward collecting and presenting meaningful information from a variety of sources.

Expert Systems

Expert systems, sometimes called **knowledge systems**, combine the knowledge on a given subject of one or more human experts into a computerized system that simulates the human experts' reasoning and decision-making processes (Figure 10-11). Thus, the computer also becomes an *expert* on the subject.

Expert systems are made up of the combined subject knowledge of the human experts, called the **knowledge base**, and the **inference rules** that determine how the knowledge is used to reach decisions. Although they may appear to *think*, the current expert systems actually operate within narrow preprogrammed limits and cannot make decisions based on common sense or on information outside their knowledge base. An example of how a simple expert system uses rules to identify an animal is shown in *Figure 10-12*.

A more practical application of an expert system has been implemented by Ford Motor Company to help its

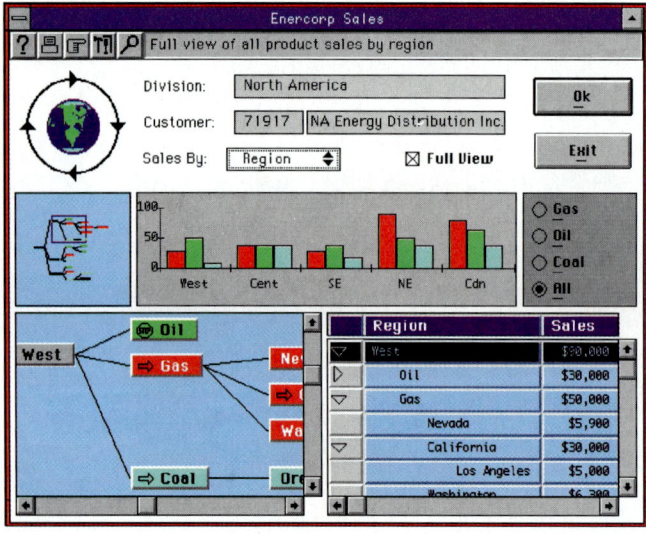

Figure 10-11
Nexpert Object is a powerful expert system that provides a highly visual presentation of its data, rules, and conclusions.

dealers diagnose engine repair problems. Previously, when they encountered an engine problem they could not solve, dealers would call Dearborn, Michigan to talk with a Ford engine expert. Now dealers can access a nationwide computer system that Ford has developed to duplicate the reasoning that Kujawski uses when trouble-shooting a problem (*Figure 10-13* on the next page).

Although expert systems can be used at any level in an organization, to date they have been primarily used by non-management employees for job-related decisions. Expert systems have also been successfully applied to problems as diverse as diagnosing illnesses, searching for oil, and making soup. These systems are part of an exciting branch of computer science called **artificial intelligence**, the application of human intelligence to computer systems. Artificial intelligence is discussed further in Chapter 14.

Integrated Information Systems

With today's sophisticated software, it can be difficult to classify a system as belonging uniquely to one of the four types of information systems previously discussed. For example, much of today's application software provides both transaction and MIS information, and some of the more advanced software even includes some decision support capabilities. Although expert systems still operate primarily as separate systems, the trend is clear: combine all of an organization's information needs into a single, integrated information system.

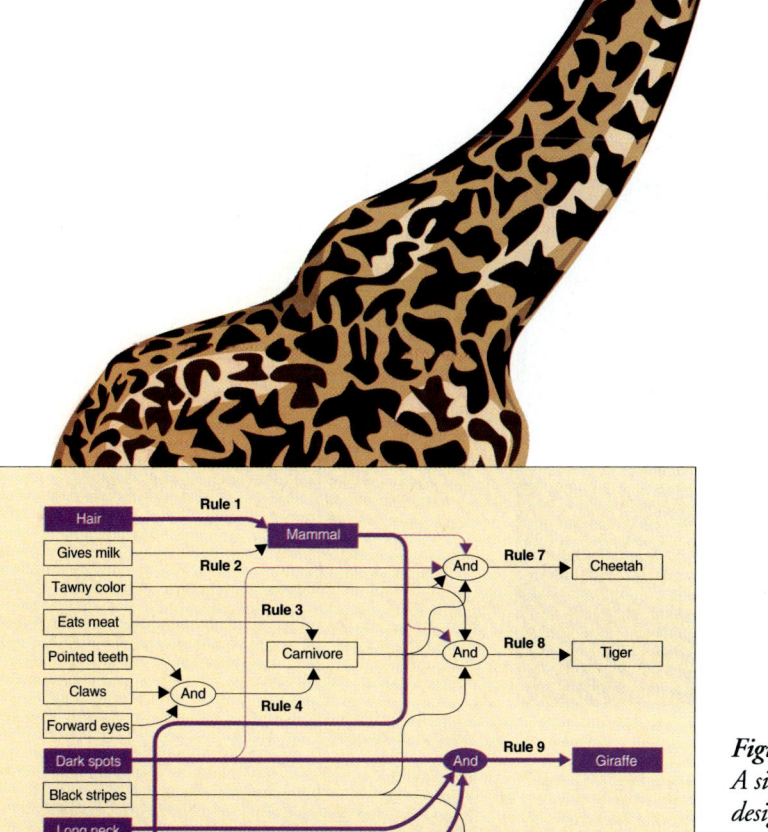

Figure 10-12
A simulated dialog between a user and a simple expert system is designed to identify an animal based on observations about the animal provided by the user. Notice how answers to certain questions result in other questions that narrow the possible conclusions. Once a conclusion is reached, the expert system can display or print the rules upon which the conclusion was based.

The Role of Personal Computers in Information Systems

The personal computer is playing an increasingly significant role in modern information systems. As organizations have moved toward decentralizing decision making, personal computers have given managers access to the information they need to make their decisions. Nonmanagement employees also benefit from having information available through networked personal computers on their desk or in the production area. For many applications, personal computers are more cost effective than larger systems.

One study estimated that the cost to process a million transactions on a mainframe is fifty times more expensive than on a personal computer. Flexibility is another advantage of personal computers. Individual or networks of personal computers can often be added more quickly than the corresponding amount of equipment that would be needed with minicomputer or mainframe systems. Many professionals believe the ideal information system involves a network of personal computers attached to a server, minicomputer, or mainframe that stores the common information that many users can access. This centralized data and decentralized computing arrangement allows users and organizations the most flexibility over controlling their information resources.

Summary of Information Systems

Numerous factors have combined to make information an increasingly important asset for most organizations. Organizations manage this asset using information systems, computer-based systems that provide the information necessary to manage the activities of the organization. Information systems provide different types of information based on the users' needs, which is often related to the users' level in the organization. New approaches to management organization are requiring corresponding changes in information systems.

The trend of information systems is to combine and integrate transaction, MIS, decision support, and expert systems that previously operated independently.

Figure 10-13
Ford Motor Company has developed an expert system that incorporates the knowledge of engine repair expert Gordy Kujawski. Instead of calling Kujawski, Ford dealers can now access the expert system when they are trying to diagnose engine problems.

COMPUTERS AT WORK

Computers at Work: Expert Systems Capture and Apply Knowledge

Many organizations now use the power of the computer to make decisions based on complex rules and the intuition, judgment, and experience of veteran workers. Expert systems, also called knowledge systems, combine these elements into a set of computer-based rules used to make a decision. Thus, the computer becomes the expert. The following are several examples of expert systems in use.

Lockheed Missile & Space Co. uses an expert system to help speed the purchase of materials ranging from industrial coolant to satellite and rocket parts. The problem with the old system was a complicated purchasing request form that required the user to answer 104 questions. Less than one-quarter of the old forms were properly completed, causing them to be returned, sometimes several times, for corrections. The expert system now in place leads the user through the purchase request form. Based on the type and cost of the material being purchased, the expert system asks relevant questions and skips sections of the purchasing request that do not apply. With the old system, completing a purchasing request could take up to six weeks. With the expert system, most requests are completed in two days.

British Columbia Telephone (BCTel), Canada's second largest telephone company, uses expert systems in several applications. In its Business division, the company uses an expert system to suggest the type of phone service for business customers. The expert system evaluates calling patterns and the amount of voice and data communications to recommend a specific mix of phone services. The expert system even estimates the expected costs of the service. BCTel uses another expert system to reroute calls during peak periods such as holidays. The expert system analyzes the telephone network traffic every five minutes and suggests alternate routes if the main lines become overloaded.

Successful applications such as the ones just described encourage other organizations to apply expert systems software to a wide variety of decision-making problems. Knowledge is perhaps the most underused asset organizations have. Expert systems help capture that knowledge and make it available to the entire organization.

Figure 10-14

IN THE FUTURE

The Virtual Corporation

In discussing how companies will function in the future, many management theorists describe what has been termed the **virtual corporation**, which is a temporary network of companies that join together to provide goods and services. Virtual corporations form quickly and stay together only as long as the opportunity remains profitable.

The term virtual corporation comes from the concept of virtual memory, not virtual reality. As discussed in Chapter 4, with virtual memory management, computers can increase the amount of memory by temporarily using available disk space. In a virtual corporation, the capabilities of one company are increased by adding the capabilities of one or more other companies. In a virtual corporation, each partner contributes it **core competencies**; what it does best. One company may be responsible for product design, another for manufacturing, and a third for sales. The initial idea for a product may have come from another company. This partnering approach has been used in the past for one-time projects such as motion pictures and construction projects but now is being applied to consumer products and services as well.

For example, because they lacked manufacturing capacity, Apple Computer, Inc. asked Sony Corporation to produce one model of its PowerBook line of computers. The arrangement allowed Apple to get the PowerBook model to market faster than if Apple tried to make the unit itself.

As the virtual corporation extends its boundaries to include separate businesses, its information systems must expand also. *Interenterprise information systems* will have to be developed. Each virtual corporation partner must be part of a network that allows them to efficiently communicate a wide variety of information such as designs, costs, and plans. The networks and software applications necessary to handle this information flow must be established quickly with the thought that they may exist for only as long as the joint product or service is in demand.

Many legal and organizational problems will have to be worked out before virtual corporations can operate as well as described by management theorists. When they are in operation, it will be the information systems that hold them together. In fact, it may be that information will be the only inventory that a virtual corporation owns.

Figure 10-15

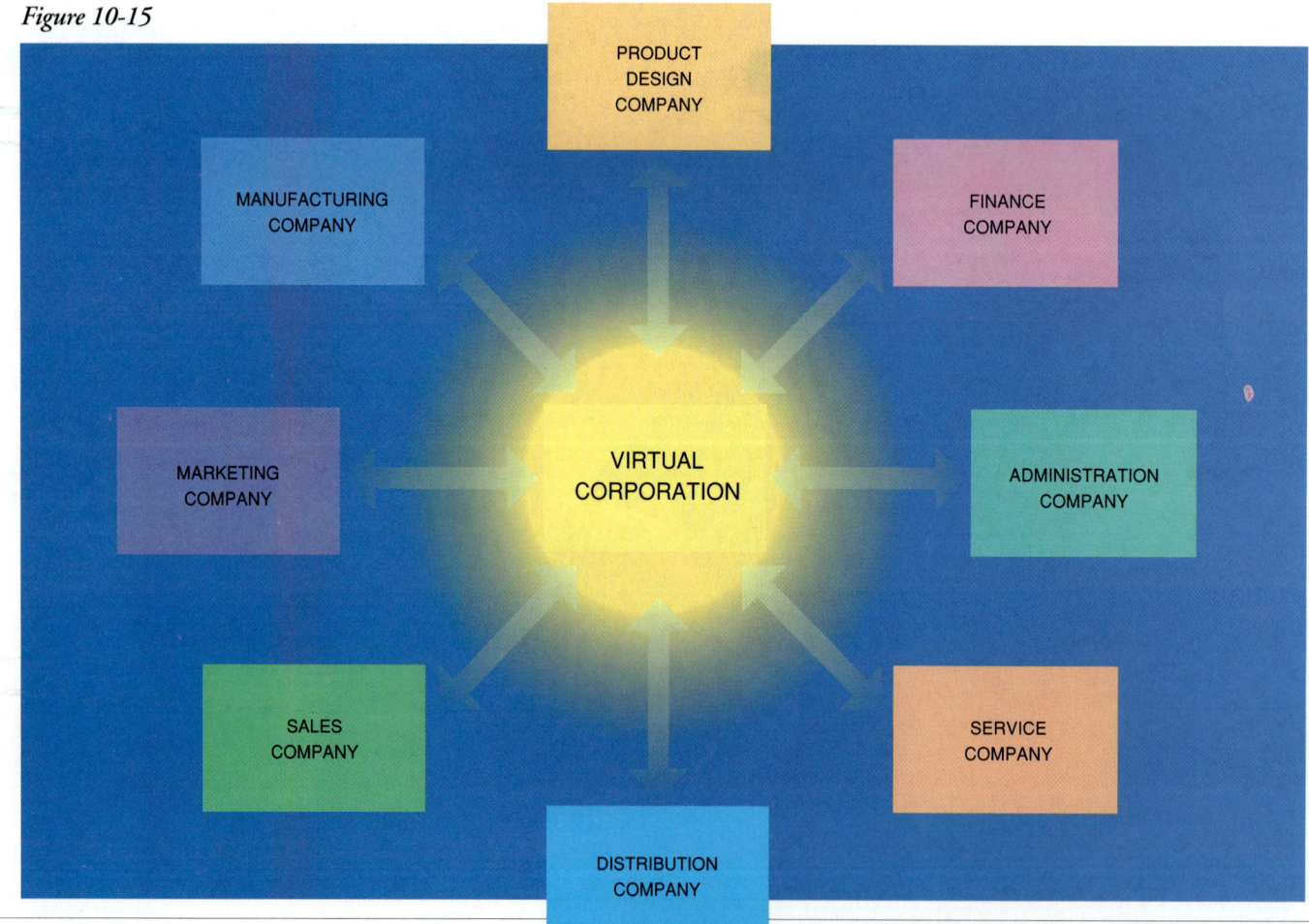

1. An **information system** is a collection of elements that provides accurate, timely, and useful information. All information systems that are implemented on a computer are comprised of six elements: equipment, software, accurate data, trained information systems personnel, knowledgeable users, and documented procedures.

2. Several factors have contributed to the increased need for timely and accurate information. Among these factors are expanded markets, increased competition, shorter product life cycles, and government regulations.

3. **Managers** of an organization are the men and women responsible for directing the use of resources such as people, materials, and information so the organization can operate efficiently and prosper. Managers work toward this goal by performing the four management tasks of planning, organizing, leading, and controlling.

4. **Senior management**, also referred to as executive or top management, includes the highest management positions in an organization. Senior managers are primarily responsible for **strategic decisions** that deal with the overall goals and objectives of an organization.

5. **Middle management** is responsible for implementing the strategic decisions of senior management. To do this, middle managers make **tactical decisions** that implement specific programs and plans necessary to accomplish the stated objectives.

6. **Operational management** supervises the production, clerical, and nonmanagement staff of an organization. In performing their duties, operational managers make **operational decisions** that usually involve an immediate action.

7. **Nonmanagement employees**, which include production, clerical, and staff personnel, also need frequent information to perform their jobs.

8. Across the four levels of an organization, management and employees are usually divided into *functional groups*. Because a functional organization can prove to be a barrier to employee communication and getting work done efficiently, many companies have adopted or are experimenting with other management structures. Although each of these approaches is slightly different, they all include some common features: fewer levels of management, employees organized by process not function, and the use of self-managed teams wherever possible.

9. With the increasing pressure to reduce costs, information systems managers have been encouraged to **downsize** operations by moving applications from mainframe and minicomputer systems to networks of personal computers. In a process called **outsourcing**, companies hire outside firms for a contracted fee to provide information systems support.

10. Characteristics that information should have are often called the qualities of information. Terms used to describe these qualities include: accurate, verifiable, timely, organized, meaningful, useful, and cost effective.

11. Information systems that are implemented on a computer are generally classified into four categories: (1) transaction processing systems; (2) management information systems; (3) decision support systems; and (4) expert systems.

12. A **transaction processing system** (TPS) processes data generated by the day-to-day transactions of an organization. In **batch processing**, transaction data is collected and, at a later time, all transactions are processed as a *batch*. With **online transaction processing** (OLTP), transactions are processed as they are entered.

13. A **management information system** (MIS) refers to a computer-based system that generates timely and accurate information for managing an organization. An **executive information system** (EIS) is a management information system designed for the information needs of senior management.

14. A **decision support system** (DSS) is a system designed to help the user reach a decision by summarizing or comparing data from either or both internal and external sources. More advanced decision support systems also include capabilities that allow users to create a model of the variables affecting a decision. With a **model**, users can ask what-if questions by changing one or more of the variables and seeing what the projected results would be.

15. **Expert systems**, sometimes called **knowledge systems**, combine knowledge on a given subject of one or more human experts into a computer system that simulates human experts' reasoning and decision making processes. Expert systems are made up of the combined subject knowledge of the human experts, called the **knowledge base**, and the **inference rules** that determine how the knowledge is used to reach decisions. An exciting branch of computer science called **artificial intelligence** is the application of human intelligence to computer systems.

16. With today's sophisticated software, it can be difficult to classify a system as belonging uniquely to one of the four types of information systems. Although expert systems still operate primarily as separate systems, the trend is clear: combine all of an organization's informational needs into a single, integrated information system.

17. The personal computer is playing an increasing role in modern information systems. Personal computers give managers and nonmanagement employees access to information, are more cost effective than larger systems, and provide increased flexibility.

Terms to Remember

artificial intelligence (10.13)

batch processing (10.9)

core competencies (10.16)

decision support system (DSS) (10.11)
downsize (10.7)

executive information systems (EIS) (10.10)
expert systems (10.12)

inference rules (10.12)
information system (10.1)

knowledge base (10.12)
knowledge systems (10.12)

management information system (MIS) (10.9)
managers (10.3)
middle management (10.6)
model (10.11)

nonmanagement employees (10.6)

online transaction processing (OLTP) (10.9)
operational decisions (10.6)
operational management (10.6)
outsourcing (10.7)

senior management (10.5)
strategic decisions (10.5)

tactical decisions (10.6)
transaction processing system (TPS) (10.9)

virtual corporation (10.16)

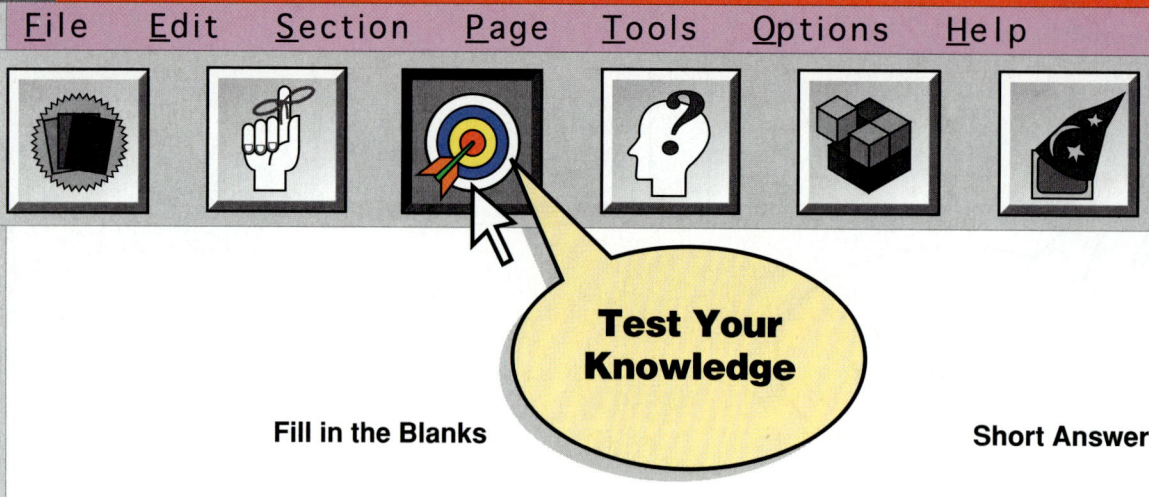

Test Your Knowledge

Fill in the Blanks

1. A(n) _____ is a collection of elements that provides accurate, timely, and useful information.
2. All information systems that are implemented on a computer are comprised of six elements: _____, _____, _____, _____, _____, and _____.
3. The managerial task of _____ involves establishing goals and objectives, while the task of _____ includes identifying and bringing together the resources necessary to achieve these goals and objectives.
4. _____, which include production, clerical, and staff personnel, need frequent information to perform their jobs.
5. Today, _____, which process data generated by an organization's day-to-day transactions, are often a part of _____, which generate timely and accurate information for managing an organization.

Short Answer

1. Why is information important to an organization? List some factors that have contributed to the increased need for timely and accurate information.
2. How are the information requirements of senior management, middle management, and operational management different?
3. What are the qualities that all information should have? Briefly explain each.
4. What are the four categories into which information systems are generally classified? Briefly explain each. Why is there a trend toward integrated information systems?
5. Why are personal computers playing an increasing role in information systems? What do many professionals believe is the ideal information system? Why?

Label the Figure

Instructions: Complete the following model to show the levels in an organization.

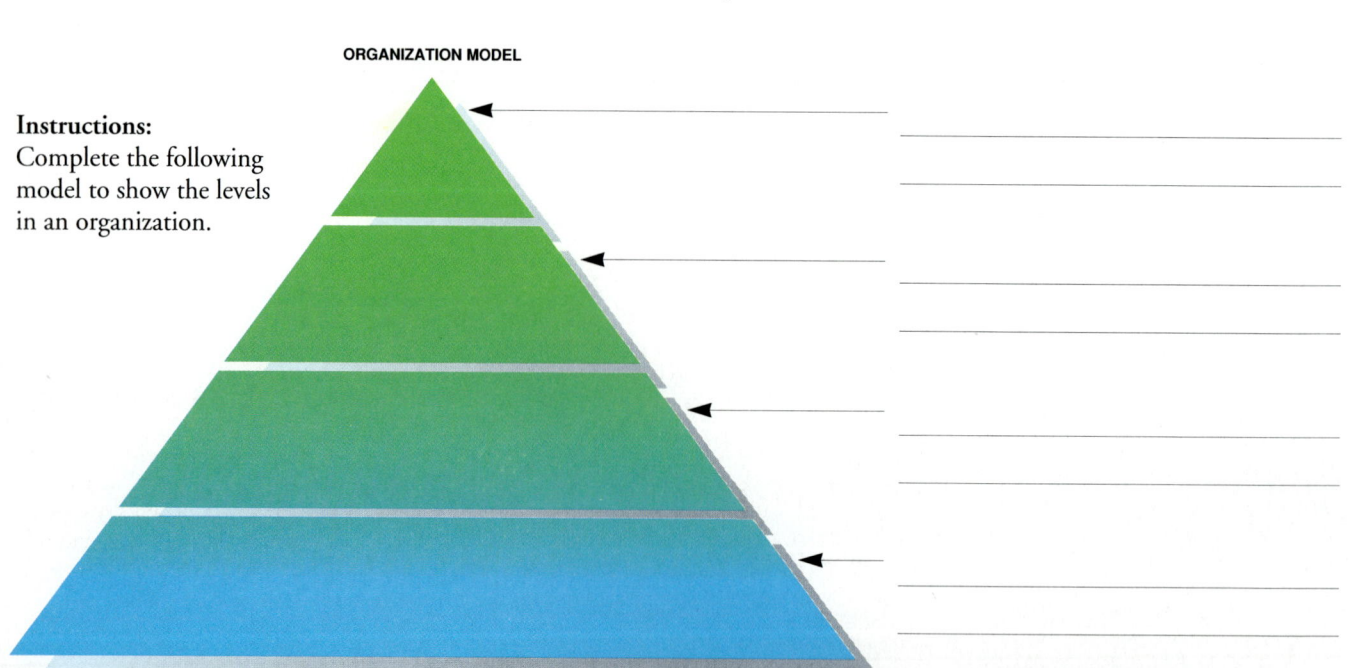

Points to Ponder

1

It is difficult to deny the importance of information to a business. Ironically, however, some people believe that while 50 years ago managers had too little information, now they may have too much. Managers can be overwhelmed by the information available through increasingly effective information systems, online public databases used by business (currently there are more than 5,000), expanding media coverage, and improved communications. Some business consultants feel the flood of information has added to managerial stress and forced managers to spend more time sifting information than making crucial business decisions. To address this dilemma, software products have been developed to sort through information sources on the basis of a manager's criteria, and a few businesses are turning to outside firms to preprocess information, checking it for relevance. Can an individual ever have too much information? Why or why not? If so, what do you think can be done about this problem?

2

This chapter describes two kinds of processing used by transaction processing systems: batch processing and online transaction processing. Consider the student records at your school. Identify three types of information that could be updated (or processed) using batch processing. Identify three types of information that could be updated (or processed) using online transaction processing. Explain why each form of processing would be appropriate. Is there any type of information that you feel must be dealt with using a specific kind of processing? Why or why not?

3

Health care in the United States has been an important topic during the past few years. The cost of health care is more than $800 billion and is growing at about 13 percent per year, more than twice the rate of economic growth. Some people believe information technology could reduce health care costs. One of the country's largest health maintenance organizations uses a computerized system that maintains medical records, orders and reports the results of lab tests, sends prescriptions to the center's pharmacy, and even helps doctors make a diagnosis on the basis of reported symptoms. A similar system guides doctors toward more cost-effective decisions when ordering medicines and tests. How could these systems lower the cost of health care? What effect would they have on the quality of health care? What could be some disadvantages of applying information technology to health care?

4

According to this chapter, information should be accurate, verifiable, timely, organized, meaningful, useful, and cost effective. Think of some information you acquired that had a significant impact on your life. What was the information and how did it affect you? Which of the qualities of information did it have? Why? Would the information have been as important if it lacked any of these qualities? Why or why not?

5

Information systems are intended to help businesses be more productive. Yet, some studies indicate that computers have resulted in only a marginal increase in productivity. According to one study of companies that introduced new office systems, approximately 40 percent failed to achieve their intended goals. Several reasons have been suggested for this failure. Some feel workers are spending too much time on relatively unimportant tasks (such as sorting through irrelevant information, polishing memos on a word processor, or adding unnecessary graphics to a spreadsheet). Others think rapid developments in software mean workers must be frequently retrained, preventing them from pursuing more productive activities. Still others maintain that the power of computers has raised people's goals, making it appear as though productivity has suffered when the new goals are not met. What do you think? If you were a manager, what steps would you take to ensure that information systems and computers enhanced your company's productivity?

6

This chapter outlines four levels in an organization. At each level, a different type of decision is made and different information is required. Using your school as a sample organization, identify what school personnel you would categorize at each level. Justify your classification on the basis of the kind of decisions made by the personnel and/or the information each requires.

Out and About

 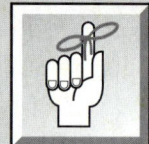    

1. As pointed out in this chapter, information systems are used not only by managers but by nonmanagement employees as well. Interview a nonmanagement employee who uses an information system, or consider a nonmanagement job you have held that uses an information system. What type of information system is it? How is the system used? What information does it provide? How does the organization benefit from the information? In what ways was the job different before the system was used? Is the job easier or more difficult as a result of the information system? Why?

2. Expert systems have occasionally been a source of controversy. Recently, a British doctor created a medical uproar with a computer program that determines whether a patient is likely to live or die. The program assesses a patient's chances based on his or her medical condition and history. If the patient is unlikely to survive ninety days of treatment, a black coffin with a white cross lights up on the screen. The doctor maintains a lot of money can be saved by withdrawing treatment earlier from patients who are hopelessly ill. Using library resources, prepare a report on this or another controversial expert system. For what purpose is the expert system used? What advantages does it offer? Why is the system controversial? Is your overall reaction to the expert system positive or negative? Why?

3. Most organizations are divided into functional groups, perhaps even your school. Visit an organization that uses functional groups and interview someone about the organization's structure. Draw a detailed diagram (similar to *Figure 10-5* on page 10.7) showing the specific job titles at various levels within each functional group. What are the advantages and disadvantages of a functional grouping? What steps could be taken to overcome the disadvantages? Has any other approach to management and organization structure ever been considered? If so, what?

4. Interview a manager at a local company. Find out the level of management at which the individual serves by determining the kinds of decisions he or she makes and what information is used to reach those decisions. What type of information system does the manager use? How does the information system influence the manager's decisions? Is any information necessary that is not provided by the system? What? Could the information by provided by an information system?

5. Visit a large supermarket or department store and speak to a manager about how transaction processing systems are used. How does the system help in processing orders, authorizing credit, recording sales data, or performing market analysis? What advantages does a transaction processing system provide for the retailer? What advantages does the system provide for the consumer? Are there any disadvantages to using a transaction processing system? If so, what?

6. A recent development in information systems is communication and data sharing among different organizations. An interorganizational information system (IOIS) is a technological or social system used to help in the collection, analysis, and relay of information among organizations. Some companies, such as Wal-Mart, are already using electronic data interchange, a procedure that facilitates the exchange of data from one organization's computer to the computer system of another organization. Using recent computer magazines, prepare a report on interorganizational information systems. How can these systems be used? What tools will be needed to manage these systems? What are the possible benefits of interorganizational systems? What are the potential disadvantages?

In the Lab   10.23

 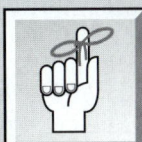   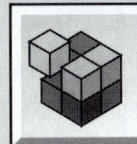 

In the Lab

Windows Labs

1 Changing Desktop Patterns and Wallpaper With Program Manager on the screen, double-click the Main group icon. In the Main group window, double-click the Control Panel program-item icon. In the Control Panel window, double-click the Desktop icon. Click the Help button. Read and print the information on the screen. Close Help.

In the Pattern area, click the Name drop-down list box arrow to display the list of available patterns. Select Boxes from the list. Choose the OK button. Notice the desktop now displays the boxes pattern *(Figure 10-16)*.

Display the Desktop dialog box. In the Wallpaper area of the Desktop dialog box, click the File drop-down list box arrow to display the list of available wallpaper files. Scroll through the list and select leaves.bmp. Choose the OK button. Notice the desktop now displays leaves *(Figure 10-17)*. If you select Wallpaper, it overrides any patterns or colors you have selected. To turn off the Pattern and/or Wallpaper, select (None) in each list in the Desktop dialog box. Close Control Panel.

2 Movie Box Office Simulation Obtain information from your instructor on the location (path) of the file MOVIES.EXE. With Program Manager on the screen, select the File menu and choose the Run command. In the Command Line text box, type the path and filename movies. For example, type c:\sclabs\movies. Press the ENTER key. The Movie Box Office window displays on the screen *(Figure 10-18 on the next page)*. Use the options to simulate a ticket vending operation at a movie theater. Enter the following data and determine the amount due for all transactions: (1) *Psycho*, matinee, 3 tickets; (2) *Jaws*, no matinee, 1 ticket; (3) *Gone With The Wind*, matinee, 3 tickets; (4) *North By Northwest*, matinee, 4 tickets; (5) *Jaws*, no matinee, 2 tickets.

Write down the summary lines that display in the Transaction Record list box. Close Movie Box Office.

3 Working with Group and Program-item Icons With Program Manager on the screen, select the File menu and choose the New command. Select the Program Group option button in the New Program Object dialog box. Choose the OK button. In the Program Group Properties dialog box, type LAB 10-3 in the Description text box and choose the OK button. Windows creates a group window called LAB 10-3. With this group window active, select the File menu and choose the New command. Select the Program Item option button in the New Program Object dialog box. Choose the OK button. In the Program Item Properties dialog box, type DOS Editor in the Description text box; type edit in the Command Line text box; and choose the OK button. Windows creates a program-item icon inside the group window *(Figure 10-19 on the next page)*. Double-click the DOS Editor program-item icon to start the MS-DOS Editor. Press the ESC key to clear the dialog box. Select the File menu and choose the Exit command. Close the LAB 10-3 group window. Select the LAB 10-3 group icon by clicking it. Select the File menu and choose the Delete command. If a confirmation dialog box displays, choose the Yes button to delete the group icon and its contents.

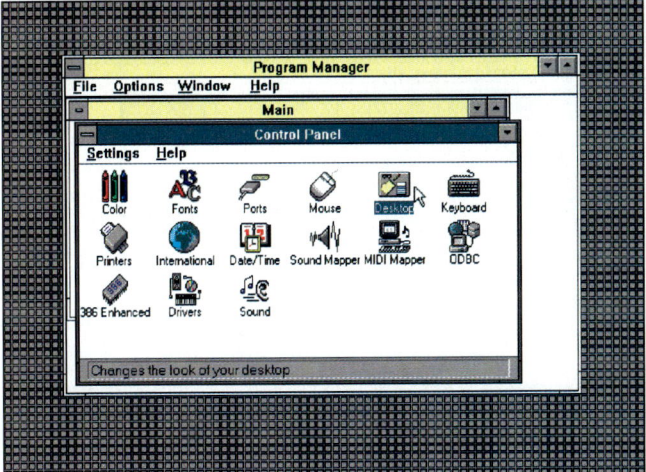

Figure 10-16

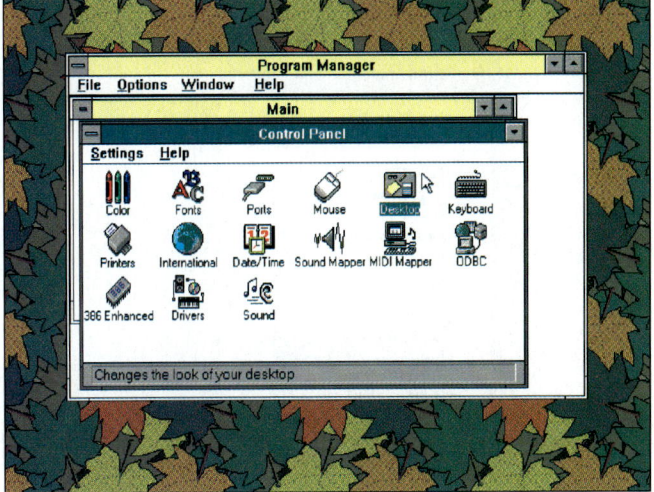

Figure 10-17

In the Lab (continued)

4 Using the Clipboard to Capture Screen Images With Program Manager on the screen, press ALT+PRINT SCREEN to place a copy of the active window on the Clipboard. Double-click the Main group icon. In the Main group window, double-click the Clipboard Viewer program-item icon . Maximize the Clipboard Viewer window to display the screen image of the Program Manager window. Close the Clipboard Viewer window. Open the Accessories group window. Start Paintbrush. Maximize the Paintbrush window. Select the Edit menu and choose the Paste command to paste the image of the Program Manager window into the Paintbrush application. Save the image using the filename WIN10-4. Print the screen image. Close Paintbrush.

5 Using Help on Clipboard Viewer Open Clipboard Viewer as discussed in Windows Lab 4 above. From the Help menu, choose Contents. Read and print the Help topics about Clipboard Viewer. Close Help. Close Clipboard Viewer.

DOS Labs

1 Changing a File's Attributes Insert your diskette with the DOS Labs in drive A. Change to drive A by typing a: and pressing the ENTER key. Type dir dos*.* and press the ENTER key. How many DOS Labs are there? Type attrib +h dos2-1 and press the ENTER key. Display a directory listing. How many files are there? Type attrib -h dos2-1 and press the ENTER key. Display a directory listing. What is the function of the h attribute?

Type attrib +r dos2-1 and press the ENTER key. Display a directory listing. Type del dos2-1 and press the ENTER key. What message displays? What is the function of the r attribute? Type attrib -r dos2-1 and press the ENTER key.

2 Comparing the Contents of Two Files Type comp dos2-1 dos6-2 and press the ENTER key. What message displays? Type N and press the ENTER key. Type comp dos5-3.txt dos7-2.txt and press the ENTER key. What message displays? Type N and press the ENTER key.

3 Using Help Type comp /? and press the ENTER key. What parameters are available for the comp command? Type help attrib and press the ENTER key. Read and print the Help contents. Choose the Notes jump topic; read and print the information. Choose the Examples jump topic; read and print the information. Exit Help.

Online Lab

1 Stock Market Information Lookup Using one of the two online services you selected in Chapter 1, connect to the service and perform the following tasks: (1) Search the online service for Stock Market information. (2) Display and write down the most recent indexes for: Dow Jones 30 Industrials; S&P 500; Amex; and Nasdaq Composite. Include the date of the indexes. (3) Display and write down the most recent High, Low, and Close prices for Apple, Compaq, IBM, Microsoft, and Novell. Include the date of the prices. (4) Display and print two investor advice columns.

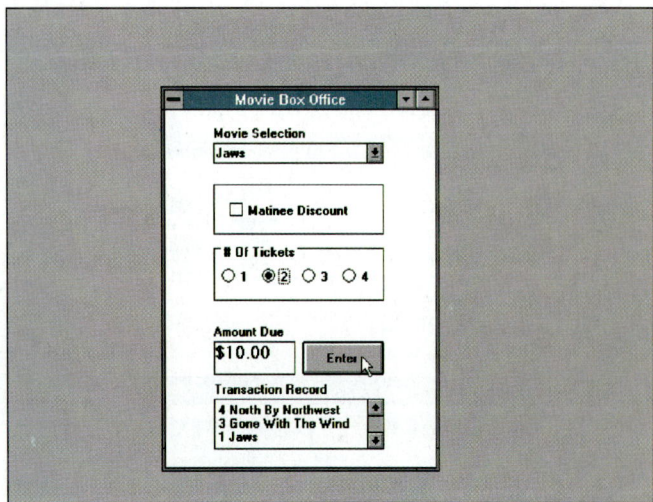

Figure 10-18

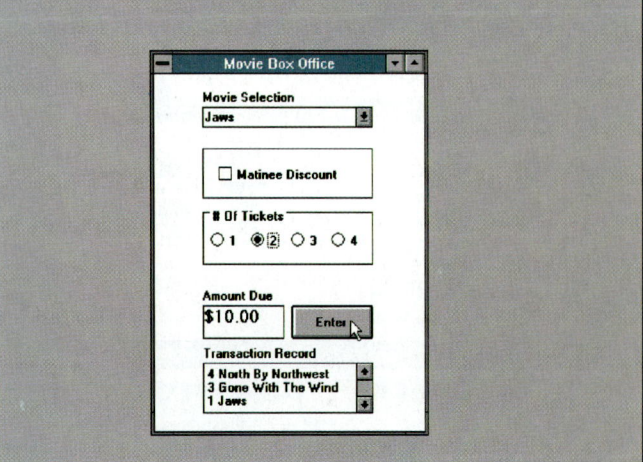

Figure 10-19

CHAPTER ELEVEN

Information System Development

11

Objectives

After completing this chapter, you will be able to:

- Explain the phases and paths of the system development life cycle

- Explain the importance of project management and documentation

- Define commercial application software and describe the difference between horizontal and vertical applications

- Discuss each of the steps of acquiring commercial application software

- Discuss the reasons for developing custom software

- Describe how various analysis and design tools, such as data flow diagrams, are used

- Explain how program development is part of the system development life cycle

- Explain several methods used for conversion to a new system

- Discuss the installation and maintenance of an information system

Every day, competition, government regulations, and other such influences cause people to face new challenges as they try to obtain the information they need to perform their jobs. A new product, a new sales commission plan, or a change in tax rates are just three examples of why an organization must change the way it processes information. Sometimes, these challenges can be met by existing methods but other times, meeting the challenge requires an entirely new way of processing data. In these cases, a new or modified information system is needed. As a computer user, either as an individual or within your organization, it is possible you will someday participate in acquiring, developing, or modifying a system. Creating an information system can be described by phases known as the system development life cycle. This chapter illustrates each phase of this process by using a case study about the wholesale auto parts division of the Sutherland Company.

What Is the System Development Life Cycle?

The **system development life cycle** (SDLC) is an organized approach for obtaining an information system. Regardless of the type or complexity of an information system, the structured process of the SDLC should be followed whenever an information system is acquired or developed. The activities of the SDLC can be grouped into distinct phases.

The Phases of the System Development Life Cycle

As shown in *Figure 11-1*, the phases of the system development life cycle are:
- Analysis
- Acquisition or Design
- Customizing or Development
- Implementation
- Maintenance

Each of the phases includes important activities relating to the acquisition or development of an information system.

As *Figure 11-1* also shows, there is an *acquisition path* and a *development path* in the system development life cycle. After the analysis phase, an organization can either choose to acquire a system by purchasing software or develop one by writing its own software. If an organization does not find a suitable system during the acquisition phase, it will move to the design phase of the development path. All system projects have analysis, implementation, and maintenance phases.

Before explaining each of the phases, project management and documentation will be discussed because these two activities are ongoing processes performed throughout the cycle. The information system specialists and users who participate in the various phases of the SDLC will also be identified.

Project Management

Project management involves planning, scheduling, reporting, and controlling the individual activities that make up the system development life cycle. These activities are usually recorded in a **project plan** on a week-by-week basis that includes an estimate of the time to complete the activity and the start and finish dates. As you might expect, the start of many activities depends on the successful completion of other activities. For example, implementation activities cannot begin until you have completed at least some, if not all, of the development activities. An effective way of showing the relationship of project activities is with a graphic display called a Gantt chart *(Figure 11-2)*. A Gantt chart, named after the developer, shows time across the top of the chart and a list of activities to be completed down the left side. Marks on the

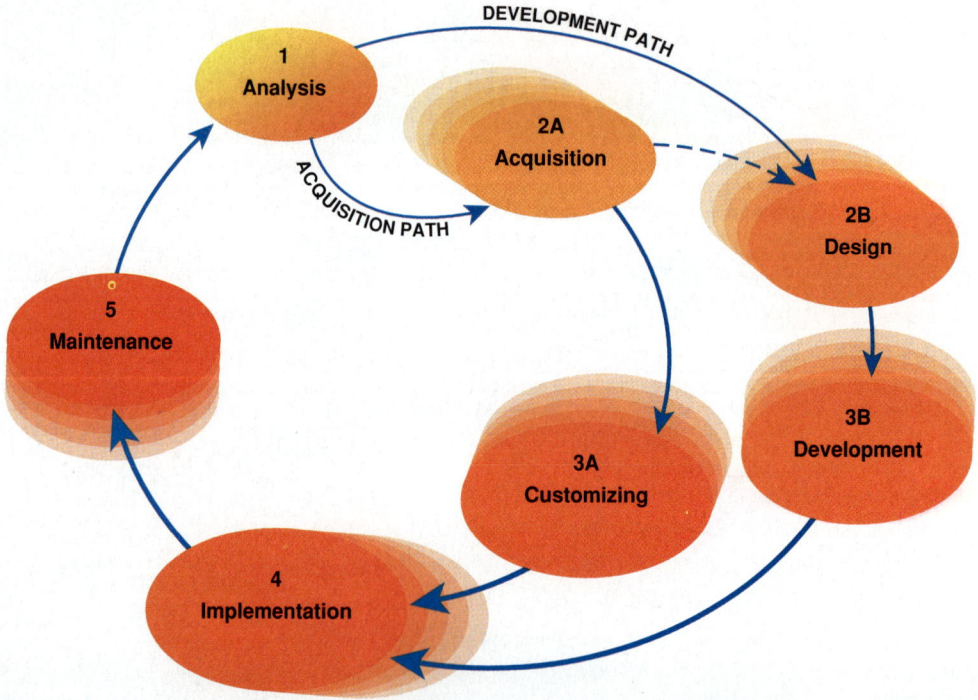

Figure 11-1
The system development life cycle consists of five phases along one of two paths that depend on whether software is acquired or developed.

chart indicate when an activity begins and is completed. Lines or bars between the marks indicate progress toward completing the task.

The importance of maintaining a realistic schedule for project management cannot be overstated. Without a realistic schedule, the success of a project is in jeopardy from the start. If project members do not believe the schedule is realistic, they may not participate to the full extent of their abilities. Project management is a place for realistic, not wishful, thinking.

Project management should be practiced throughout the development process. In most projects, activities need frequent rescheduling. Some activities will take less time than originally planned and others will take longer. To measure the impact of the actual results and revised estimates, they should be recorded regularly and a revised project plan issued. Project management software provides an efficient method of recording results and revising project plans.

Documentation

Documentation refers to written materials produced as part of the system development life cycle such as a report describing the overall purpose of the system or layout forms used to design reports and screens. Documentation should be identified and agreed on prior to beginning the project. Well-written, thorough documentation makes it easier for users and others to understand why particular decisions are made. Too often, documentation is put off until the completion of a project and is never adequately finished. Documentation should be an ongoing part of the entire development process and should not be thought of as a separate phase. Well-written, thorough documentation can also extend the useful life of a system. Unfortunately, systems are sometimes replaced simply because no one understands how they work.

Who Participates in the System Development Life Cycle?

Every person who will be affected by the new system should have the opportunity to participate in its development. The participants fall into two categories: users and information system personnel such as systems analysts and computer programmers. Systems analysts work closely both with the users and the programmers to define the system. The systems analyst's job is challenging, requiring good communication, analytical, and leadership skills to keep the development process on track and on schedule. Good communication skills are especially important during analysis, the first phase of the system development life cycle.

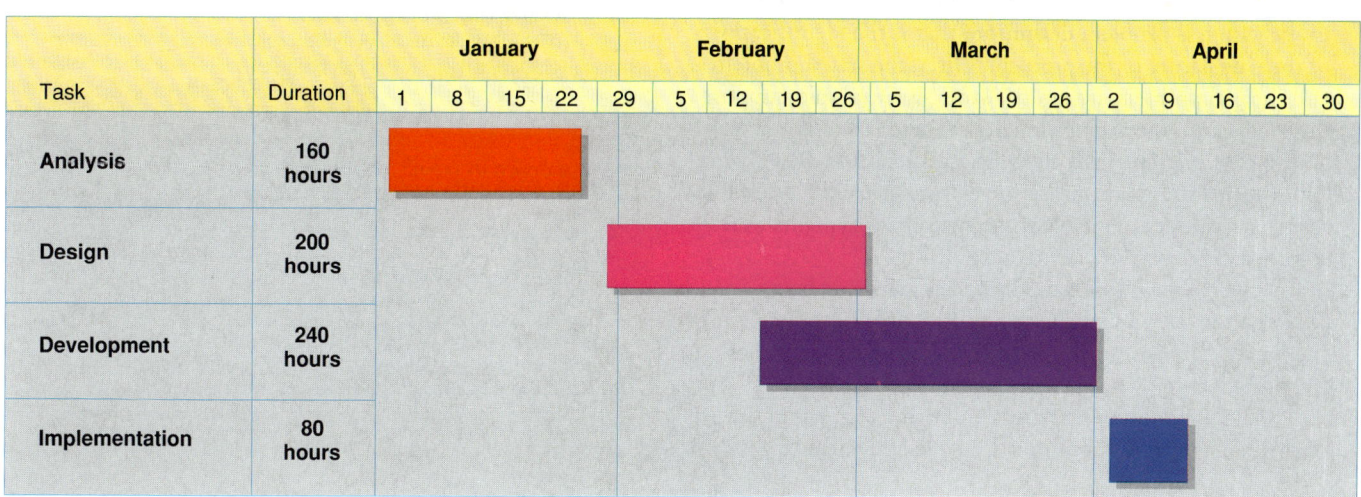

Figure 11-2
A Gantt chart is an effective way of showing the time relationships of the project activities.

Analysis Phase

Analysis is the separation of a system into its parts to determine how the system works. In addition, the analysis phase of a project also includes the identification of a proposed solution to the problems identified in the current system. A system project can originate in several ways, but a common way is for the manager of a user department, such as accounting or personnel, to contact the information systems department with a request for assistance. The initial request may be verbal, but it is eventually written on a standard form that becomes the first item of documentation *(Figure 11-3).* In most organizations, requests for new system projects exceed the capacity of the information systems department to implement them. Therefore, the manager of the information systems department must review each request and make a preliminary determination as to the potential benefit for the company. Requests for large development projects, such as an entirely new system, are often reviewed by committees made up of users, information systems department personnel, and representatives of top management. When the managers of the user and information systems departments determine a request warrants further review, one or more systems analysts will be assigned to begin a preliminary investigation, which is the first step in the analysis phase.

The Preliminary Investigation

The purpose of the **preliminary investigation** is to determine if a request justifies further detailed investigation and analysis. The most important aspect of the preliminary investigation is **problem definition**, that is the identification of the true nature of the problem. Often the stated problem and the real problem are not the same. For example, suppose the manager of the accounting department requests a new accounts receivable report showing recent customer payments. An investigation might reveal the existing accounts receivable reports would be acceptable if the customer payments were recorded daily instead of once a week.

The real problem is customer payments are being recorded too late to be included in the existing reports. Thus, the preliminary investigation determines the real source of the problem.

The preliminary investigation begins with an interview of the manager who submitted the request. Depending on the request, other users can be interviewed as well. For example, a request might involve data or a process affecting morethan one department, or clerical workers may have to be interviewed to obtain detail information.

The preliminary investigation is usually quite short when compared to the remainder of the project. At the end of the investigation, the systems analyst presents the findings to management of both the user department and information systems department and recommends the next action. Sometimes the results of a preliminary investigation indicate an obvious solution that can be implemented at minimal cost. Other times, however, the only thing the preliminary investigation does is confirm there is a problem needing further study. In these cases, detailed system analysis is recommended. Managers of the user department, the information systems department, and the systems analyst work together to decide how to proceed.

Detailed System Analysis

Detailed system analysis involves both a thorough study of the current system and at least one proposed solution to the problems found.

SUTHERLAND COMPANY
REQUEST FOR SYSTEM SERVICES

ISD CONTROL #: 2143

I. To Be Completed By Person Requesting Services
SUBMITTED BY: MIKE CHARLES DEPT: AUTO PARTS SALES DATE: 1/23/95

REQUEST TYPE: ☐ MODIFICATION ☑ NEW SYSTEM

NEED: ☐ ASAP ☑ IMMEDIATE ☐ LONG RANGE

BRIEF STATEMENT OF REQUEST (attach additional material, if necessary)
NEED ORDER ENTRY AND INVOICING CAPABILITY.
EXISTING SYSTEM CAN NO LONGER KEEP UP WITH INCREASED SALES VOLUME.

☐ ADDITIONAL MATERIAL ATTACHED

II. To Be Completed By Information Systems Department
REQUEST INVESTIGATED BY: FRANK PEACOCK DATE: 2/3/95
COMMENTS: INVOICING RUNNING 3 DAYS BEHIND SHIPMENTS.
RECOMMEND DETAILED SYSTEM ANALYSIS

III. Disposition
☑ REQUEST APPROVED FOR IMMEDIATE IMPLEMENTATION
☑ ANALYST ASSIGNED: MARY RUIZ
☐ REQUEST APPROVED FOR IMPLEMENTATION AS SOON AS POSSIBLE
☐ REQUEST REJECTED
COMMENTS:

SIGNED: George Lucey DATE: 2/15/95

Figure 11-3
The system development project usually starts with a request from a user. The request should be documented on a form such as this one to provide a record of the action taken.

The study of the current system is important for two reasons. First, it helps increase the systems analyst's understanding of the activities a new system would perform. Second, and perhaps most important, studying the current system builds a relationship between the systems analyst and the user. The systems analyst will have much more credibility with users if he or she understands how the users currently perform their job responsibilities. This may seem an obvious point, but surprisingly, many systems are created or modified without studying the current system or without adequately involving the users.

The basic fact-gathering techniques used during the detailed system analysis are: (1) interviews, (2) questionnaires, (3) reviewing current system documentation, and (4) observing current procedures. During this phase of the system study, the systems analyst must develop a critical, questioning approach to each procedure within the current system to determine what is actually taking place. Often systems analysts find operations are being performed not because they are efficient or effective, but because they have always been done that way.

Information gathered during this phase includes: (1) the output of the current system, (2) the input to the current system, and (3) the procedures used to produce the output.

An effective method for documenting this information is called structured analysis. **Structured analysis** is the use of analysis and design tools such as data flow diagrams, data dictionaries, process specifications, structured English, decision tables, and decision trees to document the specifications of an information system.

DATA FLOW DIAGRAMS

One of the difficulties in analyzing any system is how to document the findings in a way that can be understood by users, programmers, and other systems analysts. Structured analysis addresses this problem by using graphics to represent the flow of data. These graphics are called data flow diagrams.

A **data flow diagram** (DFD) graphically shows the flow of data through a system. The key elements of a DFD *(Figure 11-4)* are arrows, or vectors, called data flows that represent data; circles (also called bubbles) that represent processes such

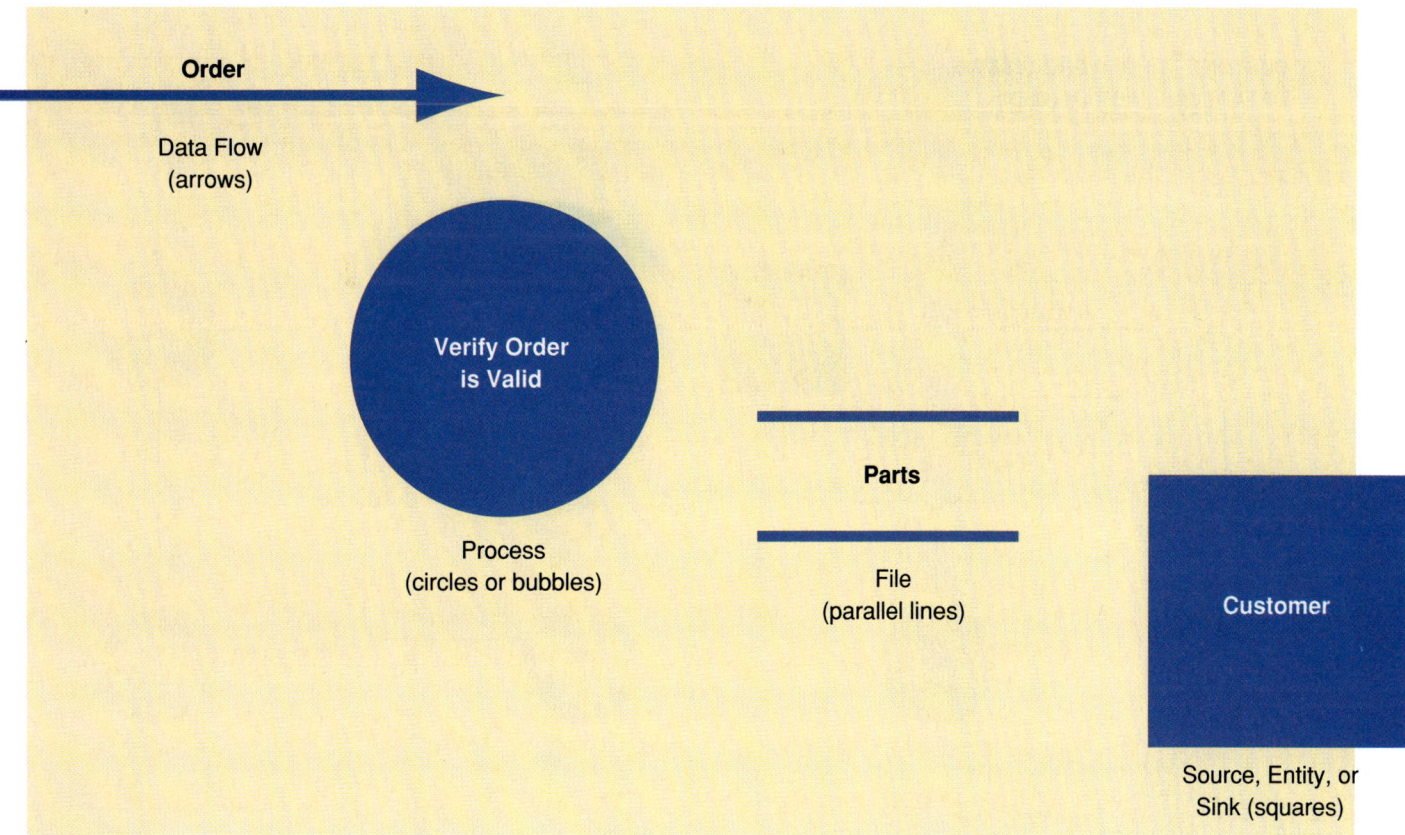

Figure 11-4
The symbols used to create data flow diagrams.

as verifying an order or creating an invoice; parallel lines that represent data files; and squares, called entities, sources, or sinks, that represent either or both an originator or a receiver of data such as a customer.

Because they are visual, DFDs are particularly useful for reviewing the existing or proposed system with the user *(Figure 11-5)*. DFDs are prepared on a level-by-level basis. The top level only identifies major processes. Lower levels further define the higher levels. For example, in *Figure 11-5,* the Apply Invoice Payment process in the lower left corner could have its own separate DFD to define subprocesses that take place.

DATA DICTIONARIES

The **data dictionary** describes the elements making up the data flow. Each element can be thought of as equivalent to a field in a record. The data dictionary also includes information about the attributes of each element such as length, where the element is used (which files and data flows include the element), and any values or ranges the element might have, such as the value 002 in *Figure 11-6* for a credit limit code to indicate a $5,000 credit line. The data dictionary is created by the systems analyst in the analysis phase and is used in all subsequent phases of the system development life cycle.

STRUCTURED ENGLISH

Process specifications describe and document what happens to a data flow when it reaches a process circle. For example in *Figure 11-5,* process specifications describe what happens in each of the circles. One way of writing process specifications is to use **structured English**, a style of writing and presentation that describes the alternatives and actions that are part of the process. *Figure 11-7* shows an example of a structured English process specification describing a policy for order processing.

DECISION TABLES AND DECISION TREES

Another way of documenting the system during the analysis phase is with a decision table or decision tree. A **decision table** or a **decision tree** identifies the actions that should be taken under different conditions. *Figures 11-8* and *11-9* show a decision table and decision tree for the order processing policy described with structured English in *Figure 11-7*. Decision tables and trees are an excellent way of showing the desired action when the action depends on multiple conditions.

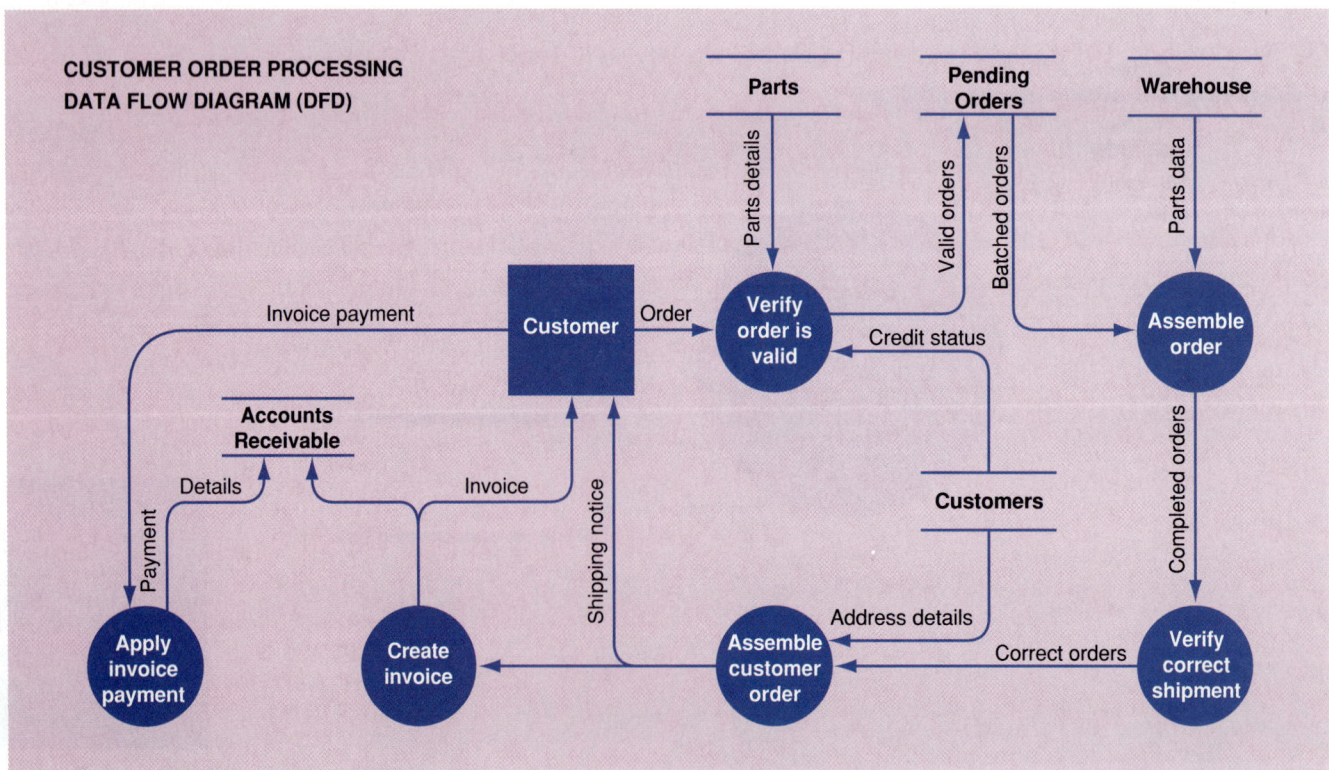

Figure 11-5
Data flow diagrams (DFDs) are used to graphically illustrate the flow of data through a system. The customer (box in diagram) both originates and receives data (represented by arrows). The circles indicate where actions take place on the data. Files are shown as parallel lines.

DATA DICTIONARY - DATA ELEMENT	
Data Element Name:	limit
Aliases:	credit-code, limit-code, credit-limit
Description:	Code indicating customer's credit limit used in order processing and credit management
Length:	3 characters
Type:	alphanumeric
Values and Meanings:	CSH — cash or check in advance COD — collect on delivery 001 — $1 to $1,000 credit line 002 — $1,001 to $5,000 credit line 003 — $5,001 to $10,000 credit line 004 — $10,001 to $20,000 credit line *(Credit Limit Code)*
Default Value:	COD - collect on delivery
Validation Rules:	1. Must be one of established values 2. Null value not allowed
Files Containing Element:	Customer-Master, Credit-Limits

Figure 11-6
A data dictionary records information about each of the data elements that make up a data flow.

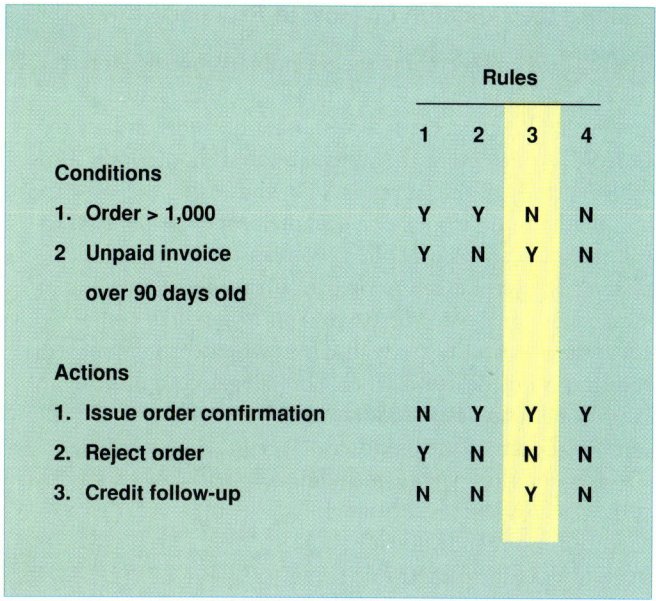

Figure 11-8
Decision tables help a user quickly determine the course of action based on two or more conditions. This decision table is based on the order processing policy described in Figure 11-7. For example, if an order is $1,000 or less and the customer has an unpaid invoice over 90 days old, the policy (Rule 3) is to issue an order confirmation and perform a credit follow-up on the past due invoice.

STRUCTURED ENGLISH

If order amount exceeds $1,000
    If customer has an unpaid invoice over 90 days old
        Do not issue order confimation
        Write message on order reject report
    Otherwise (account is in good standing)
        Issue order confirmation
Otherwise (order is $1,000 or less)
    If customer has an unpaid invoice over 90 days old
        Issue order confirmation
        Write message on credit follow-up report
    Otherwise (account is in good standing)
        Issue order confirmation

Figure 11-7
Structured English is an organized way of describing what actions are taken on data. This structured English example describes an order processing policy.

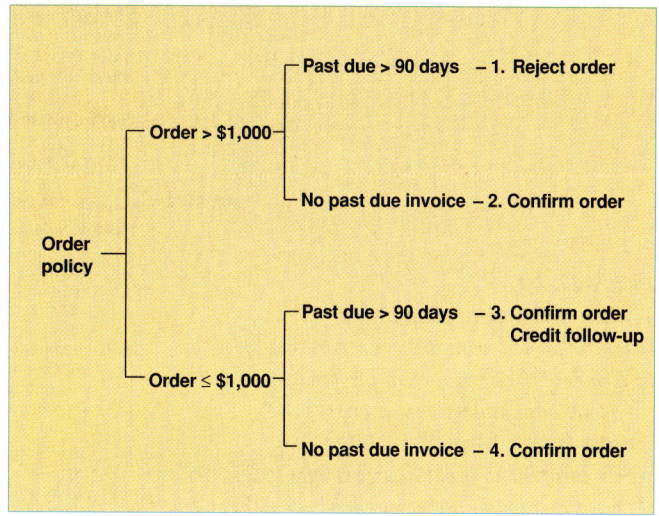

Figure 11-9
Like a decision table, a decision tree illustrates the action to be taken based on the given conditions but presents it graphically. This decision tree is based on the order processing policy described in Figure 11-7.

Making the Decision on How to Proceed

Just as at the completion of the preliminary investigation, at the completion of the analysis phase, the user, systems analyst, and management face another decision on how to proceed. At this point the systems analyst should have completed a study of the current system and, using the same tools and methods, developed one or more proposed solutions to the current system's identified problems. Sometimes, the systems analyst is asked to prepare a feasibility study and a cost/benefit analysis. These two reports are often combined.

The **feasibility study** discusses whether the proposed solution is practical and capable of being accomplished. The **cost/ benefit analysis** identifies the estimated costs of the proposed solution and the benefits (including potential cost savings) expected. If there are strong indications at the beginning of the project that some type of new system will likely be developed, the feasibility study and cost/benefit analysis are sometimes performed as part of the preliminary investigation.

The systems analyst presents the results of his or her work in a written report *(Figure 11-10)* to both user and information systems department management who consider the alternatives and the resources, such as time, people, and money of the organization. The end of the analysis phase is usually when the organization faces a **make-or-buy decision** and has to decide to either acquire a commercial software package from an outside source, develop the software themselves, or have a third party develop the software. If a decision is made to proceed, the project enters the acquisition phase if a software package is going to be obtained or the design phase if software is going to be developed. If a suitable software package cannot be found, an organization will shift to the design phase of the development path.

SUTHERLAND COMPANY

MEMORANDUM

TO: Management Review Committee
FROM: George Lacey, Information Systems Manager
DATE: April 3, 1995
SUBJECT: Detailed Investigation and Analysis of Order Entry System

Introduction

A detailed system investigation and analysis of the order entry system was conducted as a result of approval given by the management review committee on March 1. The findings of the investigation are presented below.

Objectives of Detailed Investigation and Analysis

The study investigated reported problems of the wholesale auto parts order entry system. We have received complaints that orders were not being shipped promptly and that customers were not notified about out-of-stock parts when they placed their orders. In addition, invoices are not sent to customers until twelve to sixteen days after orders are shipped. The objective of this study was to determine where the problems existed and to develop alternative solutions.

Findings of the Detailed Investigation and Analysis

The following problems appear to exist within the order entry system:

Possible Solutions:

1. Acquire a separate personal computer LAN system and order entry software. Estimated costs: LAN server, $50,000. Software license, $50,000. Training, $12,000. Annual maintenance, $20,000.

2. Obtain commercial application software for auto parts order entry and invoicing that would run on the main computer. Estimated costs: Software license, $50,000 to $100,000. Annual software maintenance, 10% of license fee. Training, $10,000.

3. Internally develop necessary order entry software to run on main computer. Estimated costs:
   (1) System analysis and design, $26,000; (2) Programming and implementation, $40,000;
   (3) Training, $7,000; (4) Terminal emulation software (ten users), $2,000.

Recommended Action

The information systems department recommends alternative 2, the investigation of existing commercial application software that could run on the main computer. If suitable software cannot be found, we recommend the design of a computerized order entry and invoicing system utilizing alternative 3.

George Lacey

Figure 11-10
Written reports summarizing the systems analyst's work are an important part of the development project. Two portions of such a report are shown. The top portion shows the report introduction that describes why the investigation of the order entry system was performed. The middle portion of the report (not shown) describes the problems that were found during the investigation. The bottom portion shows three possible solutions and the action recommended by the information systems manager.

Analysis at Sutherland

The Sutherland Company is a large corporation with three separate divisions selling tools, electric motors, and auto parts. Although the tool and electric motor divisions have been computerized for some time, the auto parts division, started just a year ago, has been small enough that it has relied on personal computers with spreadsheet, word processing, and database packages. In the last six months, however, auto parts sales doubled and the order entry and invoicing systems are now incapable of keeping up with the increased work load.

Mike Charles, the auto parts sales manager, decides to submit a request for system services to the information systems department that provides computer services for the other Sutherland divisions. George Lacey, the head of the information systems department, assigns Frank Peacock, a senior systems analyst, to investigate Mike's request.

As part of the preliminary investigation, Frank interviews Mike to try to determine the problem. During his interview with Mike and a subsequent tour of the auto parts sales department, Frank discovers invoices are not being sent to customers until twelve to sixteen days after their parts orders have shipped. In addition, Frank discovers customers complain about shipments being late and about not being notified when parts they ordered are not available. To quantify the expected increases in sales volume, Frank has Mike prepare the transaction volume summary shown in *Figure 11-11*. As a result of his preliminary investigation, Frank recommends a detailed system analysis. George Lacey agrees with Frank's recommendation and assigns systems analyst Mary Ruiz to perform a detailed analysis.

Mary reviews Frank's notes and begins to perform a detailed analysis of the auto parts order entry and invoicing systems. As part of her study, Mary interviews several people in the auto parts division and prepares several documents including a data flow diagram (see *Figure 11-5* on page 11.6), a data dictionary definition for the different credit limits assigned to customers (see *Figure 11-6* on page 11.7), and a structured English statement of the order processing policy (see *Figure 11-7* on page 11.7).

After studying the manual procedures for a week, Mary discusses her findings with George Lacey. Based on Mary's work, George writes a report to the management review committee recommending the order entry and invoicing systems be computerized *(Figure 11-10)*. The report contains three possible solutions: (1) obtain a separate PC LAN using a server, (2) obtain a commercial application software package to run on the main computer, and (3) internally develop the necessary software for the main computer.

Before proceeding to develop the necessary software internally, George recommends Sutherland try to find a suitable commercial software package that can run on Sutherland's main computer. The management review committee meets every month to review requests for additional computer equipment and software. The committee is made up of top management representatives from each division, the finance department, and the information systems department. Based on George's report, the management review committee authorizes the information systems department to find a commercial package to satisfy the auto parts division's order entry and invoicing requirements.

TRANSACTION VOLUME SUMMARY

	LAST YEAR	CURRENT	1 YEAR ESTIMATE	3 YEAR ESTIMATE
Number of Customers	175	300	400	600
Orders per Month	525	950	1250	1900
Invoices per Month	600	1100	1375	2100

Figure 11-11
A transaction volume summary was prepared to estimate the projected growth at Sutherland Company. Systems should be designed to handle the projected volume of transactions, not just the current volume.

Acquisition Phase

Once the analysis phase has been completed, the **acquisition** phase begins. It has four steps: (1) summarizing the application requirements, (2) identifying potential software vendors, (3) evaluating software alternatives, and (4) making the purchase. Before describing these steps, commercial application software will be discussed.

What Is Commercial Application Software?

Commercial application software is already-developed software available for purchase. Prewritten software is available for computers of all sizes. Most users know about the numerous application packages available for personal computers. In addition, users should be aware that numerous packages are available for larger computers. This section discusses the categories of commercial application software available, how to determine software requirements, and how to acquire the software. This information is important to know because it is possible you will someday either acquire application software for yourself or participate in software selection for your organization.

It's probably safe to say at least some part of every type of business, government branch, or recreational pastime has been computerized. *Figure 11-12* is an excerpt from a category listing from an application software catalog. Within each category, numerous programs are available to perform different types of tasks. This catalog contains listings for more than 20,000 individual software packages. Notice this list is divided into two parts: nonindustry specific and industry specific. The more commonly used terms are horizontal and vertical applications.

Horizontal application software is software used by many different types of organizations. Accounting packages are a good example of horizontal applications because they apply to most organizations. If, however, an organization has a unique way of doing business, then it requires a package developed specifically for that job. Software developed for a unique way of doing business, usually within a specific industry, is called **vertical application software**. Examples of specific industries using vertical software include food service, construction, and real estate. Each of these industries has unique information processing requirements.

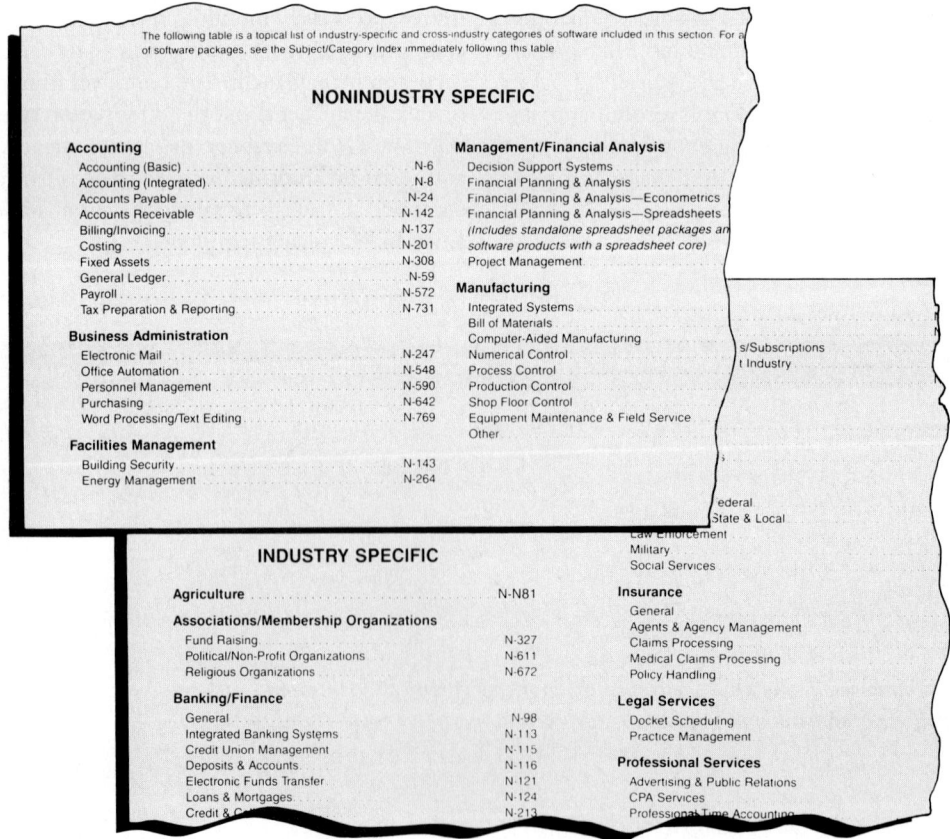

Figure 11-12
An excerpt from a category listing in an application software catalog that contains information on more than 20,000 individual software packages.

The difference between horizontal and vertical application software is important to understand. If you become involved in selecting software, one of the first things you will have to decide is how unique is the task for which you are trying to obtain software. If the task is not unique to your business, you will probably be able to use a horizontal application package. Horizontal application packages tend to be widely available (because they can be used by a greater number of organizations) and less expensive. If your task is unique to your type of organization, you will probably have to search for a vertical software solution. Often an organization's total software requirements are made up of a combination of unique and common requirements.

Now that you understand what commercial application software is, the steps used to acquire it will be discussed.

Summarizing the Application Requirements

One way organizations summarize their software requirements is in a request for proposal. A **request for proposal**, or **RFP**, is a written list of an organization's software requirements. This list is given to prospective software vendors to help the vendors determine if they have a product that is a possible software solution. Just as the depth of application evaluations varies, so do RFPs. RFPs for simple applications may be only a single page consisting of the key features and a transaction volume summary. Other RFPs for large systems could consist of more than a hundred pages that identify desired key and secondary features. An example of a page from an RFP is shown in *Figure 11-13*.

If an organization wants to acquire a specific piece of software (or hardware) that is available from several vendors, an RFQ can be used. **A request for quotation** (**RFQ**) is a request for a written price quotation on an item to be purchased. A RFQ is an organized way to compare price, delivery, and other purchasing terms offered by different vendors.

Identifying Potential Software Vendors

After you have an idea of the software features you want, your next step is to locate potential vendors selling the type of software you are interested in buying. If the software will be implemented on a personal computer, a good place to start looking for software is a local computer store. Most computer stores have a wide selection of application software.

SUTHERLAND COMPANY
REQUEST FOR PROPOSAL
ACCOUNTS PAYABLE

Features	Standard Feature	Comments
1. Interface to general ledger	✔	
2. Matching to receiving documents	✔	
3. Matching to purchasing documents	✔	
4. Automatic check printing	✔	
5. Recurring payments		PLANNED FOR NEXT RELEASE
6. Flexible payment selection	✔	
7. Checking statement reconciliation		WILL DO ON CUSTOM BASIS
8. Consolidated check preparation	✔	
9. Duplicate invoice check		NO PLANS FOR THIS FEATURE
10. Manual check processing	✔	

Reports		
1. Vendor listing	✔	BY NAME, BUYER
2. Invoice register	✔	
3. Check register	✔	
4. Cash requirements	✔	WEEKLY & MONTHLY
5. Detail aging	✔	30, 60, 90, 120 + DAYS
6. Form 1099 reports		PLANNED FOR NEXT RELEASE
7. Account distribution	✔	
8. Bank statement reconciliation		WILL DO ON CUSTOM BASIS

Figure 11-13
A request for proposal (RFP) documents the features users want in a software package.

and can suggest several packages for you to consider. If you have prepared an RFP, even a simple one, it will help the store representative to narrow the choices. If you require software for a minicomputer or mainframe, you won't find it at the local personal computer store. For this type of software, which can cost tens to hundreds of thousands of dollars, the best place to start is the computer manufacturer. In addition to having some software themselves, most manufacturers have a list of software companies with which they work – companies specializing in developing software for the manufacturer's equipment. **Software houses** are businesses specializing in developing software for sale. **Value-added resellers** (**VARs**), also called **system houses**, not only sell software but also sell the computer equipment. VARs have resale agreements with one or more computer manufacturers and take full responsibility for equipment, software, installation, and training. Sometimes, they even provide equipment maintenance, although this is usually left to the equipment manufacturer or a separate service organization. The advantage of dealing with a VAR is the user deals with only a single company for the entire system. VARs often specialize in a particular application area such as law offices, manufacturing, or hotel systems.

System integrators are similar to VARs in that they can offer a total system solution but they generally do not limit themselves to one or two types of computers as VARs do.

Another place to find software suppliers, especially for vertical applications, is to look in trade publications, which are magazines written for specific businesses or industries. Companies and individuals who have written software for these industries often advertise in the trade publications. Some industry trade groups also maintain lists of companies providing specific software solutions.

For horizontal applications, many computer magazines publish regular reviews of individual packages and often have annual reviews of several packages of the same type. *Figure 11-14* shows a software review of an accounting package.

Another way to identify software suppliers is to hire a knowledgeable consultant. Although the fee paid to a consultant increases your software costs, it may be worth it, considering the real cost of making a bad decision. Many consultants specialize in assisting organizations of all sizes to identify and implement software packages. A good place to start looking for a consultant would be to contact professional organizations in your industry. Your accountant may also be able to recommend a possible software solution or a consultant.

PC MAGAZINE EDITORS' CHOICE

FACT FILE

Macola Progression, Version 6.0

Macola Inc., 333 East Center St., Marion, OH 43301-0485; 800-468-0834; fax, 614-382-0239.

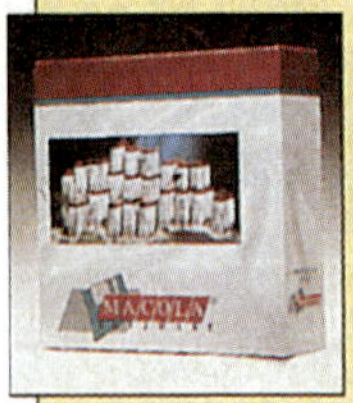

List price: $995 per module; 5-user system manager, $995; $995 for each additional 5 users.
Requires: Server: 8MB RAM, 300MB hard disk space, NetWare 3.1 or later. DOS workstation: 640K RAM, 1MB hard disk space, DOS 3.1. Windows workstation: 4MB RAM, 1MB hard disk space, Windows 3.1
In short: Macola's distribution modules (Inventory Management, Customer Order Processing, Purchase Order and Receiving, and Bill of Materials) are the heart of its accounting software library. They are well complemented by Macola's financial and manufacturing modules and a host of third-party applications.
497 ON READER SERVICE CARD

SUITABILITY TO TASK

Macola Progression

	POOR	FAIR	GOOD	EXCELLENT
Financial accounting	●	●	●	○
Managing orders and inventory	●	●	●	●
Reporting	●	●	●	○
Customization and implementation	●	●	●	●
Auditing and securing data	●	●	●	●

Figure 11-14
Many publications regularly evaluate applications software. This review also included a narrative discussion of the package.

ACQUISITION PHASE

Evaluating Software Alternatives

After you have identified several possible software solutions, you must evaluate them and choose one. First, match each choice against your original requirements list. Be as objective as possible–try not to be influenced by the salesperson or representative demonstrating the software or the appeal of the marketing literature. Match each package against your list or RFP and give each package a score. Take into consideration that some features are probably more important than others. Try to complete this rating in writing either during or immediately after a demonstration of the package while the features are still fresh in your mind *(Figure 11-15)*.

The next step is to talk to existing users of the software. For vertical application software packages, software vendors routinely provide user references. User references are important because if a software package does (or does not) work for an organization like yours, it probably will (or will not) work for you.

Finally, try the software yourself. For a small application, this may be as simple as entering a few sample transactions using a demonstration copy of the software at the computer store. For large applications, it may require one or more days of testing at the vendor's office or on your existing computer to be sure the software meets your needs.

If you are concerned about whether the software can handle a certain transaction volume efficiently, you may want to perform a benchmark test. A **benchmark test** measures the time it takes to process a set number of transactions. For example, a benchmark test could consist of measuring the time it takes a particular software package to produce a sales summary report using 1,000 sales transactions. Comparing the time it takes different packages to perform the same task using the same data and the same equipment is one way of measuring the packages' relative performance.

Figure 11-15
You should ask to see a demonstration of any program you are considering purchasing. During or after the demonstration, you should rate how well the package meets your requirements.

Making the Purchase

When you purchase software, you usually do not own it. What you are actually purchasing is a **software license** *(Figure 11-16)*, which is the right to use the software under certain terms and conditions. One of the usual terms and conditions of a software license is that you can use the software on a single computer only. In fact, some software is licensed to a specific computer and the serial number of the computer is recorded in the license agreement. Other license restrictions include prohibitions against making the software available to others (for example, renting it or leasing it) and modifying or translating the software into another language. These restrictions are designed to protect the rights of the software developer, who does not want someone else to benefit unfairly from the developer's work.

For personal computer users, software license terms and conditions usually cannot be modified. But for larger computer users, terms of the license agreements can sometimes be modified and, therefore, should be carefully reviewed and considered a part of the overall software selection process. Modifications to the software license are generally easier to obtain before the sale is made than after.

Acquisition at Sutherland

Based on the directions of the management review committee, a software selection committee is formed with Mike Charles as the chairperson. Mary Ruiz and Frank Peacock from the information systems department are also members, as are the order entry and billing supervisors from the auto parts division. Also asked to participate is Bill Comer, computer systems specialist with Sutherland's CPA firm. Mary and Frank take the information developed during the analysis phase and summarize it into a request for proposal (RFP). The RFP is sent to ten software vendors that Bill Comer has identified. Eight of the ten vendors send a response to the RFP within the one month deadline set by Sutherland. Most of the vendors had contacted and visited the auto parts operation to gather information necessary for their responses.

Of the eight replies, Sutherland chooses three vendors for further discussions. The committee eliminates five of the vendors because they believe these systems do not meet the requirements of an auto parts distributor. The software selection committee visits the offices of all three remaining software vendors for a thorough demonstration of their respective packages. In addition, the committee visits a customer of each of the three vendors. The vendor and customer site visits are conducted during a one-month period.

At this point, Sutherland faces a difficult choice. None of the commercial software packages is significantly better than the other and all three have areas needing substantial modifications to meet Sutherland's way of doing business. The software selection committee summarizes its findings in a report to the management review committee. After discussing the report, the management review committee authorizes the information services department to begin development of an order entry and invoicing system to run on Sutherland's existing computer system.

Figure 11-16
A software license grants the purchaser the right to use the software but does not include ownership rights.

Commercial Applications Versus Custom Software

Each year, the number of application software packages increases. With so much software available, why would an organization choose to develop its own applications?

There could be several reasons. The most common reason is the organization's software requirements are so unique it is unable to find a package meeting its needs. In such a case, the organization would choose to develop the software itself or have it developed specifically for them. Application software developed by the user or at the user's request is called **custom software**. An example of a requirement for custom software might be a government agency implementing a new health care service. If the service has new forms and procedures and is different from previous services, it is unlikely any appropriate software exists.

Another reason to develop rather than buy software is that new software must work with existing custom software. This is an important point to keep in mind; once an organization chooses to use custom software, it will usually choose custom software for future applications as well. This is because it is often difficult to make custom software work with purchased software. The following example illustrates this point.

Suppose a company has previously developed a custom inventory control software system and now wants to computerize its order entry function. Order entry software packages allow the user to sell merchandise from stock and, therefore, must work closely with the inventory files. In fact, many order entry systems are sold together with inventory control systems. If the company wants to retain its existing inventory control application, it would probably have a hard time finding a commercial order entry package capable of working with its custom inventory files. This is because the software and the database structures used in the commercial package will not be the same as the existing software. For this reason, the company would probably decide to develop a custom order entry application.

Both custom and commercial software have their advantages and disadvantages. The advantage of custom software is if it is correctly developed, it will match an organization's exact requirements. The disadvantages of custom software are it is one of a kind, difficult to change, often poorly documented, and usually more expensive than commercial software. In addition, custom software projects are often difficult to manage and complete on time.

The advantage of commercial software is that it is ready to install immediately. After sufficient training, usually provided by the vendor who developed or sold the software, people can begin using the software for productive work. The disadvantage of commercial software is that an organization will probably have to change some of its methods and procedures to adapt to the way the commercial software functions.

A good guideline for evaluating an organization's need for custom or commercial software is to look for a package with an 80% or better fit with the requirements. If there is less than an 80% fit, an organization should either consider custom software or reevaluate its requirements. *Figure 11-17* shows the most likely software solutions for different application requirements.

APPLICATION CHARACTERISTICS	APPLICATION EXAMPLE	MOST LIKELY SOFTWARE SOLUTION
Applicable to many different types or organizations	Accounts receivable	Horizontal application package
Specific to a particular type of business or organization	Hotel room reservations	Vertical application package
Unique to a specific organization or business	Space shuttle launch program	Custom software

Figure 11-17
Software guidelines for different types of applications.

Customizing Phase

Ideally, acquired commercial application software will meet 80% or more of an organization's requirements. But what about the other 20% or so? For these requirements, the organization has two choices: change its way of doing business to match the way the software works, or modify the way the software works to match its organization. Usually, it will choose a combination of the two alternatives.

Modifying a commercial application package is usually referred to as **customizing**, or **tailoring**. The process of customizing a commercial package involves the following four steps:

1. Identify potential modifications.
2. Determine the impact of changing current operations to match the software and thus avoid making a modification.
3. Specify the amount of work required to make the modifications and the corresponding cost.
4. Choose which modifications will be made. If possible, the modifications should be made prior to the system being implemented. This avoids users having to relearn how the system works.

Some software vendors do not recommend or support modifications to their packages. Other vendors facilitate modifications by providing copies of the programs or by doing the modifications themselves, usually for a fee. Generally speaking, the larger and more expensive the application package, the more likely modifications will be required and will be permitted.

Customizing at Sutherland

Because the software selection committee does not choose a commercial application software package, the customizing phase does not take place at Sutherland.

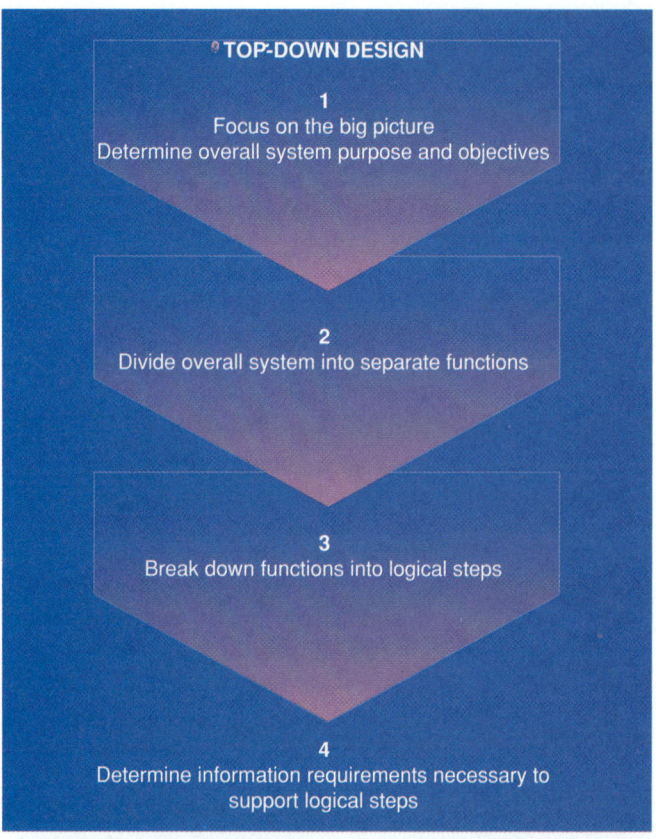

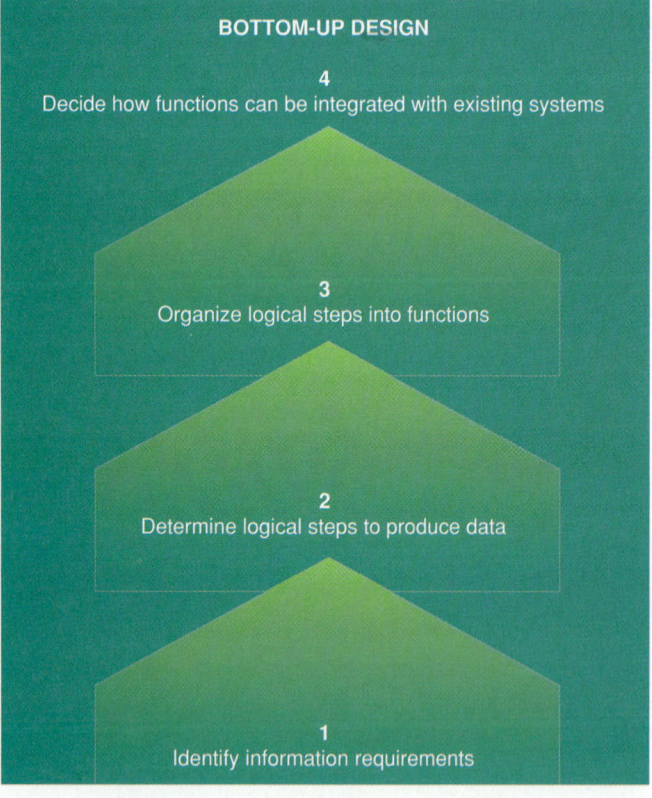

Figure 11-18
Top-down design is appropriate for large projects and the design of entire systems. Bottom-up design is used when a specific output must be produced, such as a new report, from an existing system.

Design Phase

The proposed solution developed as part of the analysis phase usually consists of what is called a **logical design**, which means the design was deliberately developed without regard to a specific computer or programming language and no attempt was made to identify which procedures should be automated and which procedures should be manual. This approach avoids early assumptions that may limit the possible solutions.

During the **design** phase the logical design will be transformed into a **physical design** that identifies the procedures to be automated. The physical design also specifies the programming language that will be used and the equipment needed for the system.

Structured Design Methods

The system design usually follows one of two methods, top-down design or bottom-up design *(Figure 11-18)*.

TOP-DOWN DESIGN

Top-down design, also called **structured design**, focuses on the major functions of the system, such as recording a sale or generating an invoice, and keeps breaking down those functions into smaller and smaller activities, sometimes called modules, that can eventually be programmed. Top-down design is a popular method because it focuses on the total requirements and helps users and systems analysts reach an early agreement on what the major functions of the new system are.

BOTTOM-UP DESIGN

Bottom-up design focuses on the required information. The approach used determines what output is needed and moves up to the processes needed to produce the output.

In practice, most systems analysts use a combination of the top-down and bottom-up designs. Some information requirements, such as payroll checks, for example, have required data elements that correspond to bottom-up design. Other requirements, such as management-oriented exception reports based on the needs of a particular user, are better suited to a top-down design. Regardless of the design method used, the systems analyst will eventually need to complete the design activities.

Design Activities

Design activities include individual tasks a systems analyst performs to design an information system. These include designs for the output, input, database, processes, system controls, and testing.

OUTPUT DESIGN

The design of the output is critical to the successful implementation of the system. Output provides information to the users, and information is the basis for the justification of most computerized systems. For example, most users do not know (or necessarily care) how the data will be processed, but they usually do have clear ideas on how they want the information output to look. Often, requests for new or modified systems begin with a user-prepared draft of a report the current system does not produce. During **output design**, the systems analyst and the user document specific screen and report layouts to display or report information from the new system.

INPUT DESIGN

During **input design**, the systems analyst and the user identify what data needs to be entered into the system to produce the desired output and where and how the data will be entered. The systems analyst and the user determine the sequence of inputs and computer responses, called a **dialogue**, the user will encounter when he or she enters data.

DATABASE DESIGN

During **database design**, the systems analyst uses the data dictionary information developed during the analysis phase and merges it into new or existing system files. During this phase of the design, the systems analyst works closely with the database administrator to identify existing database elements that can be used to satisfy design requirements.

Efficient file design can be a challenging task, especially with relational database systems that stress minimum data redundancy (duplicate data). The systems analyst must also consider the volume of database activity. For example, large, frequently accessed files may need a separate index file to allow inquiries to be processed in an amount of time acceptable to the user.

PROCESS DESIGN

During **process design**, the systems analyst specifies exactly what actions will be taken on the input data to create output information. Decisions on the timing of actions are added to the logical processes the systems analyst identified in the analysis phase. For example, the systems analyst might have found in the analysis phase that an exception report should be produced if inventory balances fall below a certain level. During the process design phase, the frequency of the report will be determined.

One way to document the relationship of different processes is with a **system flowchart** *(Figure 11-19)*. The system flowchart shows the major processes (each of which may require one or more programs), reports (including their distribution), data files, and the types of input devices, such as terminals, that will provide data to the system.

Some of the special symbols used in a system flowchart are shown in *Figure 11-20*.

During process design the systems analyst, the user, and the other members of the development project sometimes meet to conduct a **structured walkthrough**, a step-by-step review of the process design. The purpose of these sessions is to identify any design logic errors and to continue the communication between the systems analyst and the user. Structured walk-throughs are also used to review work during other phases of the system development life cycle.

SYSTEM CONTROLS

An important aspect of the design phase is the establishment of a comprehensive set of system controls. **System controls** ensure only valid data is accepted and processed by authorized users. Adequate controls must be established for two reasons: (1) to ensure the accuracy of the processing and the information generated from the system, and (2) to prevent computer-related fraud.

There are five types of controls considered by the systems analyst. These controls are: (1) source document controls, (2) input controls, (3) processing controls, (4) accounting controls, and (5) access controls.

1. **Source document controls** include serial numbering of certain input documents such as invoices, credit memos, and paychecks.
2. **Input controls** are established to assure the complete and accurate conversion of data from the source documents or other sources to a machine-processable form. Editing data as it enters the system is the most important form of input controls.
3. **Processing controls** refer to procedures established to determine the accuracy of data after it has been input to the system. For example, the accuracy of the total accounts receivable could be verified by taking the prior day's total, adding the current day's sales invoices, and subtracting the current day's payments.

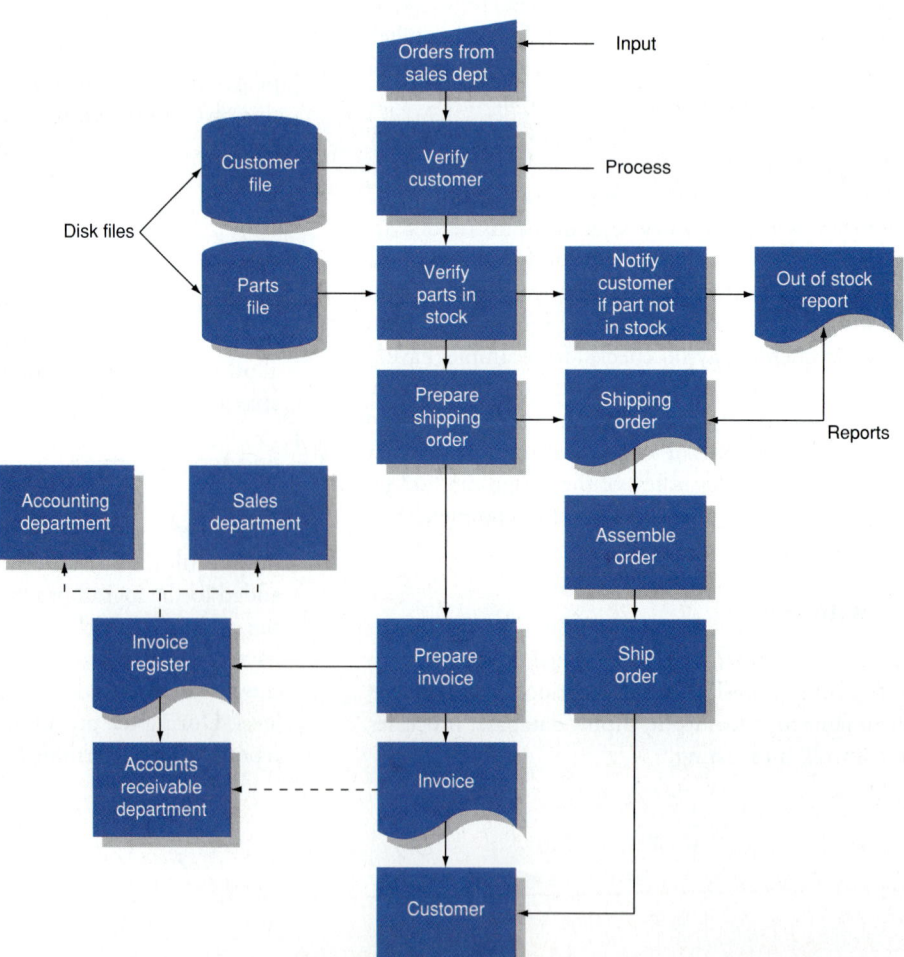

Figure 11-19
The system flowchart documents the equipment used to enter data, such as the terminals for the salespeople and the order department, the processes that will take place, such as the Verify Customer process, the files that will be used, such as the Parts and Customer files, and the reports that will be produced, such as the Shipping Order. Dotted lines indicate additional copies of reports, such as the copy of the Invoice that is sent to the Accounts Receivable Department.

4. **Accounting controls** provide assurance that dollar amounts recorded in the accounting records are correct. One type of accounting control is making sure detail reports are created to support the summary reports used to make entries in an organization's financial system. For example, many companies record sales by product line based on a summary report showing product line totals. In addition to this summary report, a detail report showing individual product sales should also be prepared and agreed to the summary report.
5. **Access controls** specify what levels of security are required for different processes. For example, in a payroll system, the capability to change pay rates would have a more restricted level of security than the capability to make changes to an employee's address.

TESTING DESIGN

During the design phase, test specifications are developed. The exact tests to be performed should be specified by someone other than the user or the systems analyst, although both should be consulted. Users and systems analysts have a tendency to test only what has been designed. An impartial third party, who has not been actively involved in the design, is more likely to design a test for, and therefore discover, a procedure or type of data overlooked in the design. Sometimes organizations avoid test design and test their systems with actual transactions. While such *live testing* is valuable, it may not test all conditions the system is designed to process. This is especially true of error or exception conditions that do not occur regularly. For example, payroll systems are usually designed to reject input for hours worked over some limit, say 60 hours in a week. If only actual data is used to test the system, this limit may not be tested. Thus, it is important to design testing specifications that test each system control by using both valid and invalid data. Types of tests include the following:

- **Unit testing**   Tests individual programs.
- **System testing**   Tests all programs in an application.
- **Integration testing**   Tests a new application to make sure it works with other applications.
- **Acceptance testing**   Demonstrates to the users that the system can meet user-designed test criteria.

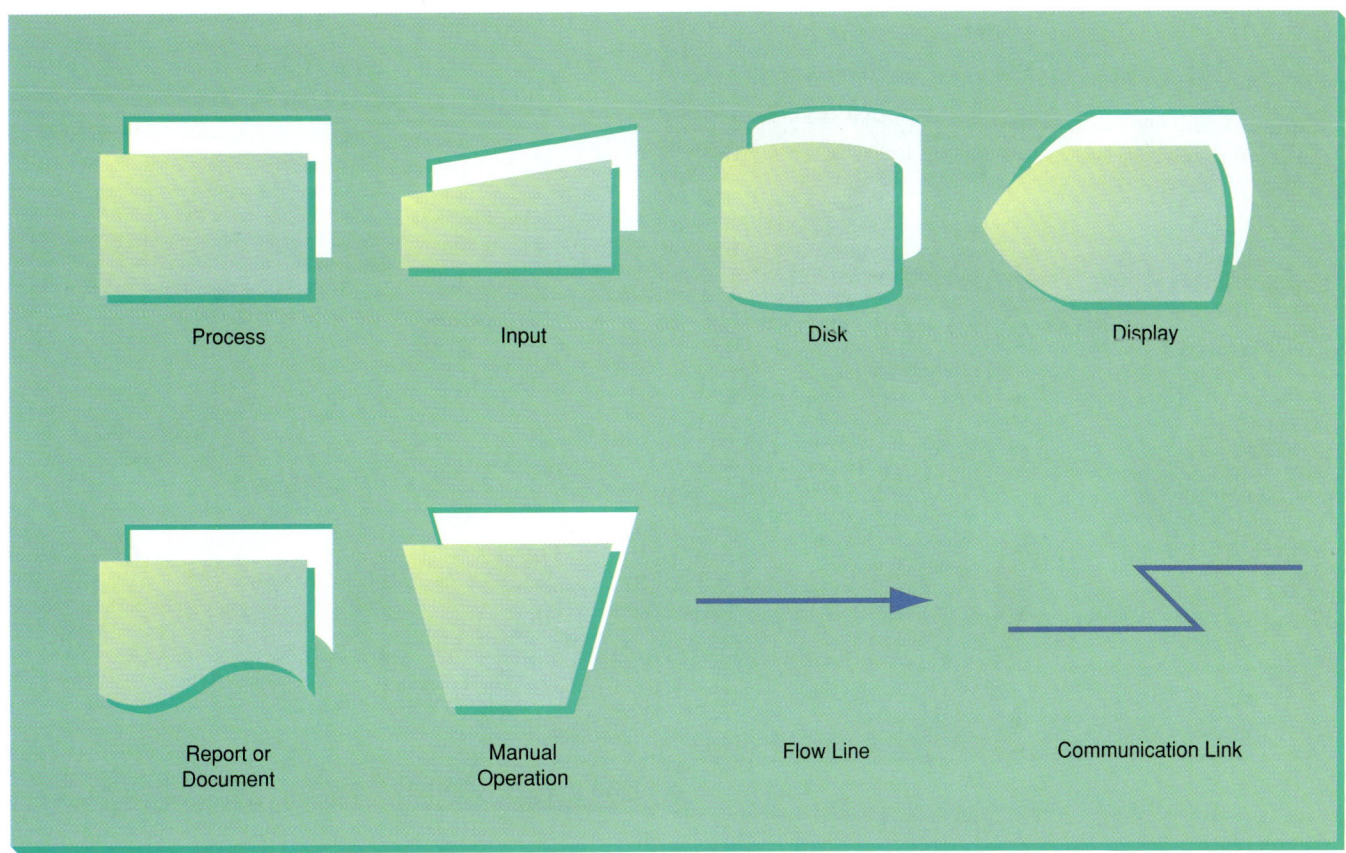

Figure 11-20
Symbols used for preparing a system flowchart.

Design Review

At the end of the design phase, management performs a **design review** and evaluates the work completed so far to determine whether to proceed *(Figure 11-21)*. This is a critical point in any development project, and all parties must take equal responsibility for the decision.

Usually, the design review will only result in requests for clarification of a few items. But sometimes an entire project will be terminated. Although canceling or restarting a project from the beginning is a difficult decision, in the long run it is less costly than implementing an inadequate or wrong solution. If management decides to proceed, the project enters the development phase.

Before discussing the development phase, prototyping and computer-aided software engineering are discussed. Prototyping is a development method that can be used in several phases of system development. Computer-aided software engineering is an automated approach to system design.

Prototyping

Prototyping is building a working model of the new system. The advantage of prototyping is it lets the user actually experience the system before it is completed. Some organizations use prototyping during the analysis phase, while others use it during the design phase. Still other companies use prototyping to go directly from the preliminary investigation to an implemented system. These companies continue refining the prototype until the user says it is acceptable. Another advantage of prototyping is that because the system is built in small steps, it requires end users and developers to have frequent meetings to discuss how the system should operate.

A disadvantage of such an accelerated approach is that key features of a new system, especially exception conditions, may be overlooked. Another disadvantage is that documentation, an important part of any system development effort, is usually not as well or as thoroughly prepared. Used as a tool to show the user how the system will operate, prototyping can be an important system development tool.

Computer-Aided Software Engineering (CASE)

Many organizations are now using computer software specifically developed to aid the system development life cycle

Figure 11-21
The design review is a critical point in the development process. Representatives from the user information systems departments and top management meet to determine if the system should be developed as designed or if additional design work is necessary.

process. **Computer-aided software engineering** (**CASE**) refers to the use of automated computer-based tools to design and manage a software system *(Figure 11-22)*. Sometimes these tools, such as a data dictionary, exist separately. Other CASE vendors have combined several tools into an integrated package referred to as a **CASE workbench**. CASE workbench tools might include:

- *Analysis and design tools* such as data dictionaries, decision tables, or data flow diagram builders
- *Prototyping tools* used to create models of the proposed system
- *Code generators* that create actual computer programs
- An *information repository* that cross references and organizes all information about a system
- *Management tools* that assist in the management of a systems project

In addition to the benefits of increased productivity, CASE tools promote the completion of the design work before development begins. Starting the development work before the design is completed often results in work that has to be redone. A disadvantage of CASE tools is that it can take a long time to learn how to use them.

Design at Sutherland

Upon approval by the management review committee, Mary Ruiz begins designing the order entry and invoicing system. After she studies existing documents and talks to users, Mary designs printed reports and screen displays. Mary reviews the sample output and screen displays with Mike Charles and the employees who will be doing the order entry. To graphically show how the overall system will work, Mary prepares a system flowchart (see *Figure 11-19* on page 11.18). The system flowchart shows that auto parts orders will be entered on terminals in the sales department and will use data in the Parts and Customer files to verify the orders are valid. Shipping orders and invoices are two of the reports produced. An important part of Mary's design time involves specifying the system controls to be used during processing. These controls include verifying the customer number before processing the order and checking to see if the ordered part is in stock. If the ordered part is not in stock, the customer is notified immediately.

After completing her design work, Mary meets with representatives from the user and information systems departments and top management to review her design. After Mary explains the design, the committee agrees to develop the system.

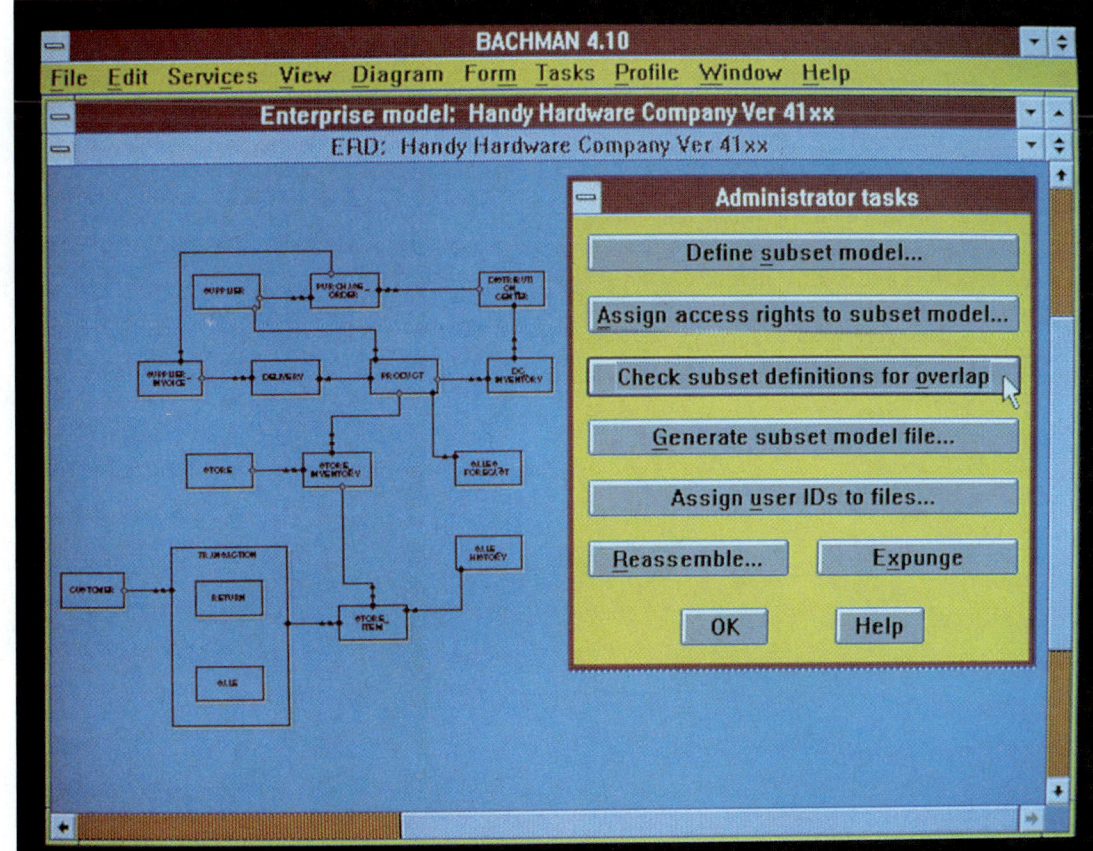

Figure 11-22
Computer-aided software engineering (CASE) packages help users design complex systems. Excelerator by Intersolv allows users to create and revise data flow diagrams, data dictionary elements, screens, reports, and process specifications.

Development Phase

Once the system design phase has been completed, the project enters the system development phase. There are two parts to the **development phase**: program development and equipment acquisition.

Program Development

The process of developing the software, or programs, required for a system is called **program development** and includes the following steps: (1) reviewing the program specifications, (2) designing the program, (3) coding the program, (4) testing the program, and (5) finalizing the program documentation. The primary responsibility for completing these tasks is assumed by computer programmers who work closely with the systems analyst who designed the system. Chapter 12 explains program development in depth. The important concepts to understand now are that this process is a part of the development phase of the system development life cycle and its purpose is to develop the software required by the system.

Equipment Acquisition

During the development phase, final decisions will be made on what additional equipment, if any, will be required for the new system. A preliminary review of the equipment requirements would have been done during the analysis phase and included in the written report prepared by the systems analyst. Making the equipment acquisition prior to the development phase would be premature because any equipment selected should be based on the requirements specified in the design phase. Equipment selection is affected by factors such as the number of users who will require personal computers or terminals and the disk storage required for new files and data elements. In some cases, a new or upgraded computer is required. If an organization chose to acquire a commercial software package instead of developing software, the equipment acquisition would take place during the acquisition phase.

Development at Sutherland

During the development phase, Mary works closely with the two programmers who are assigned to the project. She regularly meets with the programmers to answer questions about the design and to check on the progress of their work. Prior to starting the programming, Mary arranges for the programmers to meet with the auto parts sales employees so the programmers will have a better understanding of the purpose of the new system.

Because the sales department already has personal computers, no additional input devices are required. Terminal emulation software is installed on the PCs to enable them to communicate with Sutherland's central computer.

Figure 11-23
All users should be trained on the system before they use it to process actual transactions. Training should include both classroom and hands-on sessions.

Implementation Phase

Implementation is the phase of the system development life cycle when people actually begin using the new system. This critical phase of the project usually requires careful timing and the coordination of all the project participants. Important parts of this phase contributing to the success of the new system are training and education, conversion, and post-implementation evaluation.

Training and Education

Someone once said, "If you think education is expensive, you should consider the cost without it." The point is that untrained users can prevent the estimated benefits of a new system from ever being obtained or, worse, contribute to less efficiency and more costs than when the old system was operational. *Training* consists of showing people exactly how they will use the new system *(Figure 11-23)*. This training can include classroom-style lectures and should include hands-on sessions using realistic sample data on the equipment the individuals will be using. *Education* consists of learning new principles or theories that help people understand and use the system. For example, before implementing a manufacturing system, many companies require their manufacturing personnel to attend classes on material requirements planning (MRP), shop floor control, and other essential manufacturing topics.

Conversion

Conversion refers to the process of changing from the old system to the new system. A number of different methods of conversion can be used including direct, parallel, phased, and pilot *(Figure 11-24 on the next page)*.

With **direct conversion**, the user stops using the old system one day and begins using the new system the next. The advantage of this approach is it is fast and efficient. The disadvantage is it is risky and can seriously disrupt operations if the new system does not work correctly the first time.

Parallel conversion consists of continuing to process data on the old system while some or all of the data is also processed on the new system. Results from both systems are compared, and if they agree, all data is switched to the new system. Parallel conversion requires the most effort because two systems are operating simultaneously.

Phased conversion is used with larger systems that can be broken down into individual modules that can be implemented separately at different times. An example would be a complete business system that could have the accounts receivable, inventory, and accounts payable modules implemented separately in phases. Phased conversions can be direct, parallel, or a combination of both.

Pilot conversion means the new system will be used first by only a portion of the organization, often at a separate location such as a plant or an office.

At the beginning of conversion, existing data must be made ready for the new system. Converting existing manual and computer-based files so they can be used by a new system is called **data conversion**.

Post-Implementation Evaluation

After a system is implemented, it is important to conduct a **post-implementation evaluation** to determine if the system is performing as designed, if operating costs are as anticipated, and if any modifications are necessary to make the system operate more effectively.

Implementation at Sutherland

Before they begin to use the new system to enter real transactions, the users participate in several training sessions. Because this is the first application in the auto parts division to use the main system, Mary begins the training sessions with an overview of how the main computer system processes data.

Before the system can be used, the Parts and Customer files have to be converted from the files on the PCs. Separate conversion programs are written for each file. After the files are converted, they are carefully reviewed by Mike Charles and other department employees.

Although he knows it means extra work, Mike decides a parallel conversion is the safest way to implement the new system. Using this method, Mike verifies the results of the new system with those of the existing system. Actual use of the system begins on the first business day of the month so transaction totals can be balanced to accounting reports.

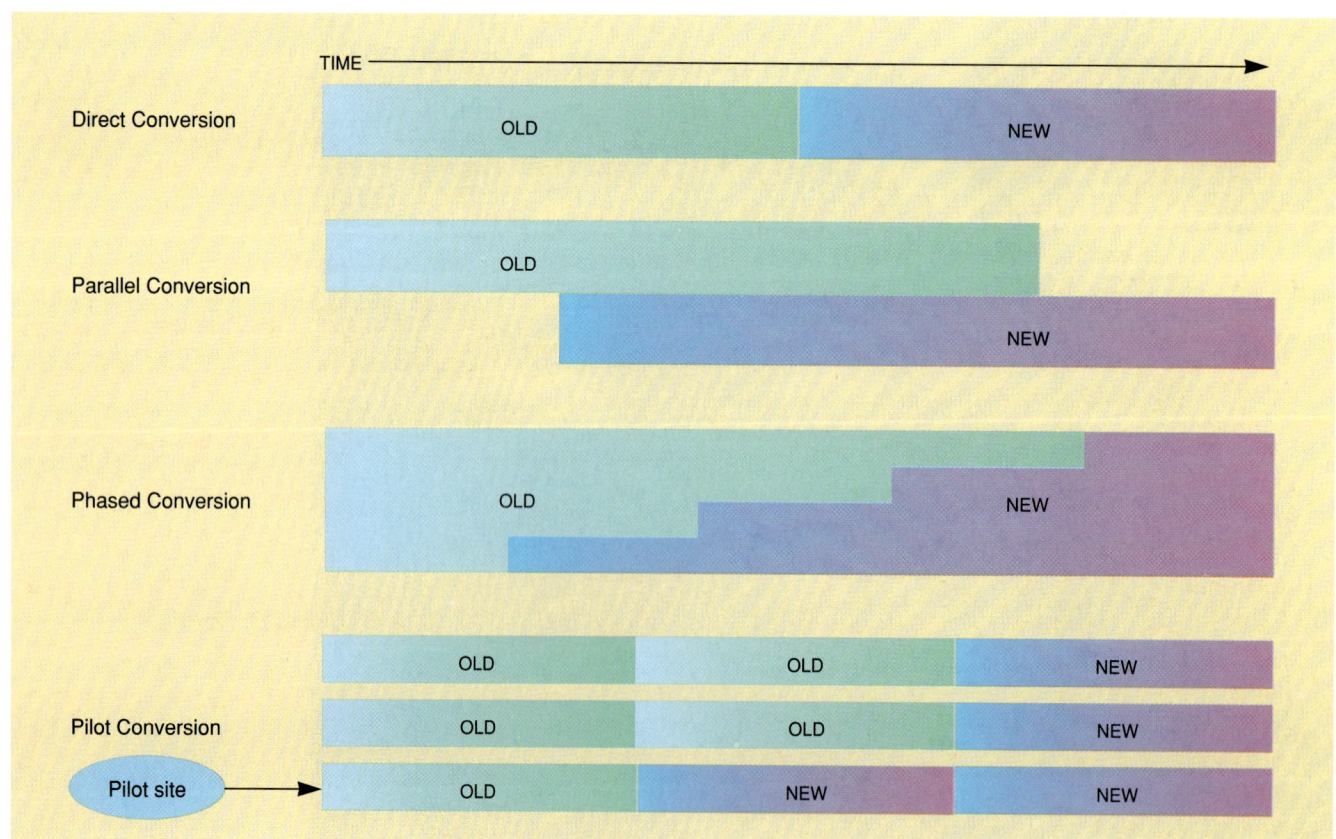

Figure 11-24
Different methods of converting from an old to a new system

Because they are thoroughly trained, the order clerks feel comfortable when they begin entering real orders. They encounter a few minor problems, such as orders for special parts not in the parts file. These problems become less frequent and at the end of the month, after Mike compares the old system and the new system report totals, he decides to discontinue the use of the old system.

During the post-implementation review, Mike and Mary discover nine out of ten customer orders are now shipped the same day as the order is received. Before the new system was implemented, less than half the orders were shipped within two days of receipt. Invoices, which once lagged twelve to sixteen days behind shipments, are now mailed on the same day. Perhaps the most positive benefit of the new system is that customer complaints about order processing are practically eliminated.

Maintenance Phase

Maintenance is the process of supporting the system after it is implemented. Maintenance consists of three activities: performance monitoring, change management, and error correction.

Performance Monitoring

Performance monitoring is the ongoing process of comparing response times, file sizes, and other system performance measures against the estimates prepared during the analysis, design, and implementation phases. Variances from these estimates may indicate the system requires additional equipment resources, such as more memory or faster disk drives.

Change Management

Change is an inevitable part of any system; thus, all users of the system should be familiar with methods and procedures that provide for change. Sometimes, changes are required because existing requirements were overlooked. Other times, new information requirements caused by external sources such as government regulations will force change. Or perhaps someone has an idea for improving the system.

A key part of change management is documentation. The same documentation standards that were followed during the analysis and design phases should also be used to record changes. In fact, in many organizations, the same document used to request new systems (see *Figure 11-3* on page 11.4) is used to request changes to an existing system. Thus, the system development life cycle continues as the analysis phase begins on the change request.

Error Correction

Error correction deals with problems caused by programming and design errors discovered after the system is implemented. Often these errors are minor problems, such as the ZIP code not appearing on a name and address report, and can be quickly fixed by a programmer. Other times, however, the error requires more serious investigation by the systems analyst before a correction can be determined. Design errors not found until after a system is implemented are much more expensive to correct than had they been found earlier.

Maintenance at Sutherland

During the months following the system implementation, users discover a number of minor errors in the system. The programming staff quickly corrects most of these errors, but in one case involving special credit terms for a large customer, Mary Ruiz becomes involved and prepares specifications for the necessary program changes.

Approximately one year after Mike Charles submits his original request for a computerized order entry and invoicing system, he submits another request *(Figure 11-25)* for a change to the system to provide for a new county sales tax. This type of request does not require a preliminary investigation and is assigned to Mary Ruiz as soon as she is available. Mike submits his request five months before the tax is scheduled to go into effect, which allows ample time for the necessary program changes to be implemented.

Summary of the System Development Life Cycle

Although the system development life cycle may appear to be a straightforward series of steps, in practice it is a challenging activity calling for the skills and cooperation of all involved. New development tools have made the process more efficient but the success of any project always depends on the commitment of the project participants. The understanding you have gained from this chapter will help you participate in information system development projects and give you an appreciation for the importance of each phase.

SUTHERLAND COMPANY
REQUEST FOR SYSTEM SERVICES

ISD CONTROL #: __4703__

I. To Be Completed By Person Requesting Services
SUBMITTED BY: __MIKE CHARLES__ DEPT: __AUTO PARTS SALES__ DATE: __2/1/96__

REQUEST TYPE: ☑ MODIFICATION ☐ NEW SYSTEM

NEED: ☑ ASAP ☐ IMMEDIATE ☐ LONG RANGE

BRIEF STATEMENT OF REQUEST (attach additional material, if necessary)
__SALES INVOICE PROGRAM NEEDS TO PROVIDE FOR__
__1% COUNTY TAX THAT WILL GO INTO EFFECT JULY 1, 1996__

☑ ADDITIONAL MATERIAL ATTACHED __COUNTY TAX RATE SCHEDULE__

II. To Be Completed By Information Systems Department
REQUEST INVESTIGATED BY: _____ DATE: _____
COMMENTS: _____

III. Disposition
☐ REQUEST APPROVED FOR IMMEDIATE IMPLEMENTATION
☐ ANALYST ASSIGNED: _____
☐ REQUEST APPROVED FOR IMPLEMENTATION AS SOON AS POSSIBLE
☐ REQUEST REJECTED
COMMENTS: _____

SIGNED: _____ DATE: _____

Figure 11-25
The same form used to request a new system (see Figure 11-3) is also used to request a modification to an existing system.

COMPUTERS AT WORK

The Case for CASE

Like many new technologies, when Computer-Aided Software Engineering (CASE) was first promoted, its backers claimed it was the *silver bullet* that would kill the monster backlog of applications waiting to be developed. And, like most technologies, the actual results did not live up to the early claims.

The move from mainframes to client/server LANs has also slowed the use of CASE because CASE software vendors have had to scramble to adapt their products that were originally developed for use on and development of larger systems. But CASE has adapted to the new system architectures and many organizations now use it to speed development of new applications.

The City of Phoenix, Arizona Police Department used CASE tools from Unisys Corporation to develop a system that has helped solve several crimes. The system, called PACE, which stands for Police Automated Computer Entry, keeps track of information recorded by field officers, even when someone is not arrested. The information results in a database of activity that took place at a particular time and location. The database has proved helpful in identifying both witnesses and suspects for crimes that were later reported.

Federated Department Stores has chosen CASE tools from Seer Technologies to move mainframe applications to client/server networks. Before choosing a totally integrated CASE approach, Federated experimented with PC-based application development tools. Federated found that the application development tools were great for building stand-alone desktop applications but did not work well with their overall plans to reengineer most of the company's business processes. They decided they needed a more comprehensive set of tools that addressed the entire system development life cycle and not just the development phase. The CASE software met those needs.

Despite these and other notable successes, many users are still hesitant to implement CASE software. For some, the view of CASE has changed from an easy-to-use wonder tool to a hard-to-learn, hard-to-use tool. But for others who have invested the time and effort, CASE has more than proved its value as an organized and efficient way of developing applications.

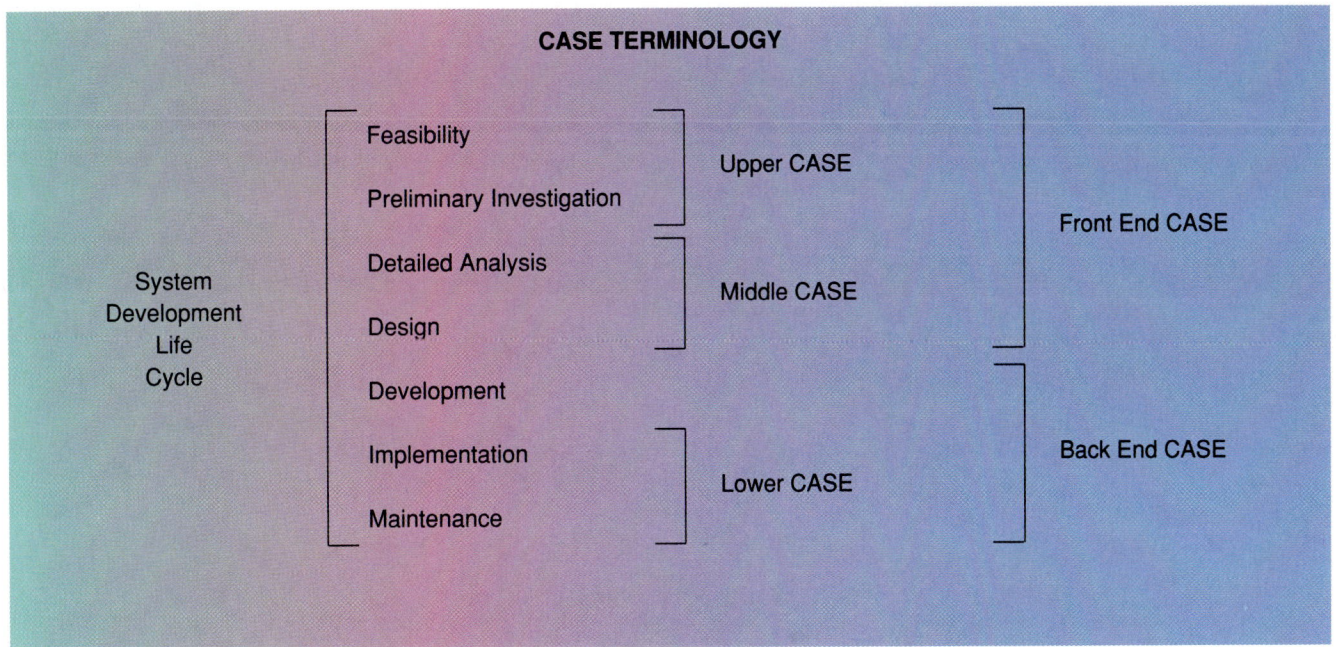

Figure 11-26

IN THE FUTURE

A RADical New Way to Develop Applications

In an attempt to decrease the amount of time it takes to develop a new application, some companies are trying a new approach called rapid application development (RAD).

With RAD, less time is spent on the traditionally separate phases of analysis and design. Using a RAD approach, analysis, design, and development are combined into a single process. Users work closely with developers using prototyping tools to create portions of the new application. Frequent user feedback helps refine the prototype until it becomes a usable system.

Instead of delivering an entire system at one time, RAD applications are usually delivered in modules as they are completed. The average development time for a module is three to four months and no module should take longer than six months. This is considerably less time than the 18 to 36 month development times that are common for business applications.

In order for a RAD approach to be successful, its supporters recommend the following:

- Both user and developer must have a firm understanding of the system's purpose and how it fits into the overall organization.
- The contents of key files should be determined before the RAD project begins. Other file contents can wait because they will become apparent as the system is developed.
- The overall project should be divided into manageable modules that can be developed in several months.
- Upon completion, individual modules should be implemented as soon as possible.
- Teamwork is critical. Teams must include people who will eventually use the system.

Ultimately, the success of RAD will depend less on state-of-the-art software tools and more on the ability of the user and the developer to efficiently cooperate and work together. And when that happens, it really will be RAD.

Figure 11-27

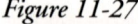

What You Should Know

1. The **system development life cycle** (SDLC) is an organized approach for obtaining an information system. The activities of the SDLC can be grouped into distinct phases: analysis, acquisition or design, customizing or development, implementation, and maintenance.

2. Project management and documentation are ongoing processes performed throughout the system development life cycle. **Project management** involves planning, scheduling, reporting, and controlling the individual activities that make up the SDLC. These activities are usually recorded in a project plan on a week-by-week basis that includes an estimate of the time to complete the activity and start and finish dates. **Documentation** refers to written materials produced as part of the system development life cycle.

3. Every person who will be affected by the new system should have the opportunity to participate in its development. The participants fall into two categories: users and information systems personnel.

4. **Analysis** is the separation of a system into its parts to determine how the system works. The analysis phase of a project also includes the identification of a proposed solution to the problems identified in the current system.

5. The purpose of the **preliminary investigation** is to determine if a request for a new system project justifies further detailed investigation and analysis. The most important aspect of the preliminary investigation is problem definition, which is the identification of the true nature of the problem.

6. **Detailed system analysis** involves both a thorough study of the current system and at least one proposed solution to the problems found. **Structured analysis** is the use of analysis and design tools such as **data flow diagrams**, **data dictionaries**, **process specification**, **structured English**, **decision tables**, and **decision trees** to document specifications of an information system.

7. Sometimes the systems analyst is asked to prepare a feasibility study and a cost/benefit analysis. The **feasibility study** discusses whether the proposed solution is practical and capable of being accomplished. The **cost/benefit analysis** identifies the estimated costs of the proposed solution and the benefits expected.

8. The end of the analysis phase is usually when organizations face a **make or buy decision** and have to decide either to acquire a commercial software package from an outside vendor, develop software themselves, or contract with a third party to develop software.

9. Once the analysis phase has been completed, the **acquisition** phase begins. It has four steps: (1) summarizing the application requirements, (2) identifying potential software vendors, (3) evaluating software alternatives, and (4) making the purchase.

10. **Commercial application software** is already developed software available for purchase. **Horizontal application software** is software used by many different types of organizations. Software developed for a unique way of doing business, usually within a specific industry, is called **vertical application software**.

11. A **request for proposal**, or **RFP**, is a written list of an organization's software requirements. A **request for quotation** (RFQ) is a request for a written price quotation on an item to be purchased.

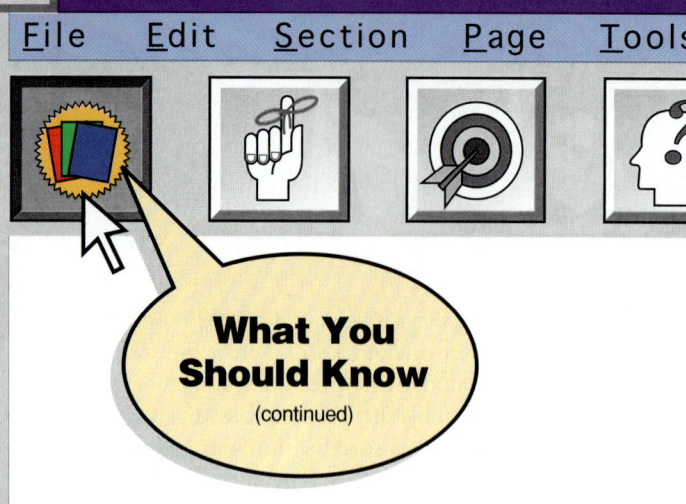

What You Should Know (continued)

12. Most computer stores have a wide selection of application software for personal computers. **Software houses** are businesses specializing in developing software for sale. **Value added resellers** (VARs), also called **system houses**, not only sell software but also sell computer equipment. **System integrators** are similar to VARs in that they can offer a total system solution, but they generally do not limit themselves to one or two types of omputers as do VARs.

13. Evaluating software alternatives involves matching each choice against the requirements list, talking to other users of the software, and trying the software. A **benchmark test** measures the time it takes to process a set number of transactions.

14. When software is purchased, it is not usually owned. What is actually purchased is a **software license**, which is the right to use the software under certain terms and conditions.

15. Application software developed by the user or at the user's request is called **custom software**. Modifying a commercial application package is usually referred to as **customizing**, or **tailoring**.

16. The proposed solution developed as part of the analysis phase usually consists of what is called a **logical design**. During the **design** phase, the logical design will be transformed into a **physical design** that identifies the procedures to be automated.

17. The system design usually follows one of two methods: top-down design or bottom-up design. **Top-down design**, also called **structured design**, focuses on the major functions of the system and keeps breaking those functions down into smaller and smaller activities. **Bottom-up design** focuses on the required information.

18. During **output design**, the systems analyst and the user document specific screen and report layouts to display or report information from the new system.

19. During **input design**, the systems analyst and the user identify what data needs to be entered into the system to produce the desired output. The systems analyst and the user determine the sequence of inputs and computer responses, called a **dialogue**, the user will encounter when he or she enters data.

20. During **database design**, the systems analyst uses the data dictionary information developed during the analysis phase and merges it into the new or existing system files.

21. During **process design**, the systems analyst specifies exactly what actions will be taken on the input data to create output information. One way to document the relationship of different processes is with a **system flowchart**. During process design, the systems analyst, the user, and other members of the development project sometimes meet to conduct **structured walk-throughs**, a step-by-step review of the process design.

22. **System controls** ensure only valid data is accepted and processed. The five types of controls considered by the systems analyst are: (1) **source document controls**, (2) **input controls**, (3) **processing controls**, (4) **accounting controls**, and (5) **access controls**.

23. Types of tests include the following: **unit testing** (testing individual programs), **system testing** (testing all programs in an application), **integration testing** (testing a new application) to make sure it works with other applications, and **acceptance testing** (demonstrating to the users that the system can meet user designed test criteria).

24. At the end of the design phase, management performs a **design review** and evaluates the work completed so far to determine whether to proceed.

25. **Prototyping** is building a working model of the new system. **Computer-aided software engineering** (**CASE**) refers to the use of automated computer-based tools to design and manage a software system. A **CASE workbench** is an integrated package that combines several tools, which may include: *analysis and design tools, prototyping tools, code generators, an information repository, and management tools.*

26. The two parts to the **development phase** are: program development and equipment acquisition. The process of developing the software, or programs, required for a system is called **program development**. During the development phase, final decisions are made on what additional equipment, if any, must be acquired for the new system.

27. **Implementation** is the phase of the system development life cycle when people actually begin using the new system. Training and education is an important part of this phase.

28. **Conversion** refers to the process of changing from the old system to the new system. With **direct conversion**, the user stops using the old system one day and begins using the new system the next. **Parallel conversion** consists of continuing to process data on the old system while some or all of the data is also processed on the new system. **Phased conversion**, used with larger systems, can be broken down into individual modules that can be implemented separately at different times. **Pilot conversion** means the new system will be used first by only a portion of the organization. Converting existing manual and computer-based files so they can be used by a new system is called **data conversion**.

29. After a system is implemented, it is important to conduct a **post-implementation evaluation** to determine if the system is performing as designed.

30. **Maintenance** is the process of supporting the system after it is implemented. Maintenance consists of three activities: performance monitoring, change management, and error correction.

31. **Performance monitoring** is the ongoing process of comparing system performance measures against the estimates prepared during the analysis, design, and implementation phases. Change is an inevitable part of any system. A key part of change management is documentation. Error correction deals with problems caused by programming and design errors after the system is implemented.

Terms to Remember

acceptance testing (11.19)
access controls (11.19)
accounting controls (11.19)
acquisition (11.10)
analysis (11.4)

benchmark test (11.13)
bottom-up design (11.17)

CASE workbench (11.21)
commercial application software (11.10)
computer-aided software engineering (CASE) (11.21)
conversion (11.23)
cost/benefit analysis (11.8)
custom software (11.15)
customizing (11.16)

database design (11.17)
data conversion (11.24)
data dictionary (11.6)
data flow diagram (DFD) (11.15)
decision table (11.6)
decision tree (11.6)
design (11.17)
design review (11.20)
detailed system analysis (11.4)
development phase (11.22)
dialogue (11.17)
direct conversion (11.23)
documentation (11.3)

feasibility study (11.8)

horizontal application software (11.10)

implementation (11.23)
input controls (11.18)
input design (11.17)
integration testing (11.19)

logical design (11.17)

maintenance (11.25)
make-or-buy decision (11.8)

output design (11.17)

parallel conversion (11.23)
performance monitoring (11.25)
phased conversion (11.24)
physical design (11.17)
pilot conversion (11.24)
post-implementation evaluation (11.24)
preliminary investigation (11.4)
problem definition (11.4)
process design (11.17)
processing controls (11.18)
process specifications (11.16)
program development (11.22)
project management (11.2)
project plan (11.2)
prototyping (11.20)

request for proposal (RFP) (11.11)
request for quotation (RFQ) (11.11)
RFP (11.11)
RFQ (11.11)

software houses (11.12)
software license (11.14)
source document controls (11.18)
structured analysis (11.5)
structured design (11.17)
structured English (11.6)
structured walkthrough (11.18)
system controls (11.18)
system development life cycle (SDLC) (11.2)
system flowchart (11.18)
system houses (11.12)
system integrators (11.12)
system testing (11.19)

tailoring (11.16)
top-down design (11.17)

unit testing (11.19)

value-added resellers (VARs) (11.12)
vertical application software (11.10)

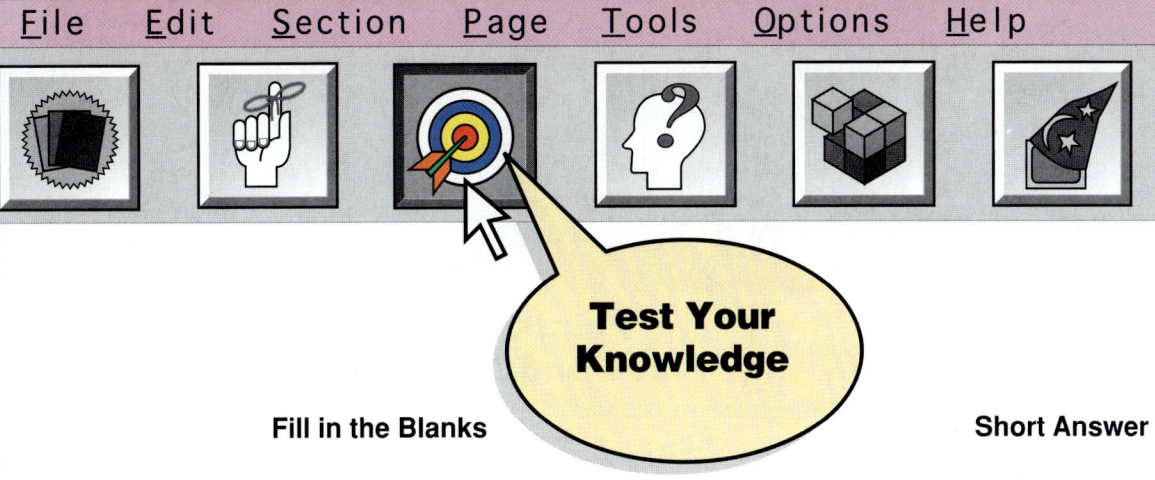

Test Your Knowledge

Fill in the Blanks

1. The _____ is an organized approach to obtaining an information system.

2. _____ involves planning, scheduling, reporting, and controlling the individual activities that make up the system development life cycle; while _____ refers to written materials produced as part of the system development life cycle describing the overall purpose of the system.

3. _____ is already developed software available for purchase.

4. Three analysis and design tools are: a(n) _____, which graphically shows the flow of data through a system; the_____, which describes the elements making up the data flow; and a(n) _____, which identifies the actions that should be taken under different conditions.

5. Unlike _____ conversion, in which the user stops using the old system one day and begins using the new system the next, _____ conversion consists of continuing to process data on the old system while some or all of the data is also processed on the new system.

Short Answer

1. How is horizontal application software different from vertical application software? Why is it important to understand the difference between the two types of application software?

2. What are the four steps in the acquisition phase? Briefly explain each.

3. Why would an organization choose to develop custom software? What guidelines can be used for evaluating the need for custom software versus commercial application software?

4. What is program development? List the five steps in program development. Who is responsible for program development?

5. What is maintenance? What three activities are part of maintenance? Briefly describe each.

Label the Figure

Instructions: Identify the phases in the system development life cycle.

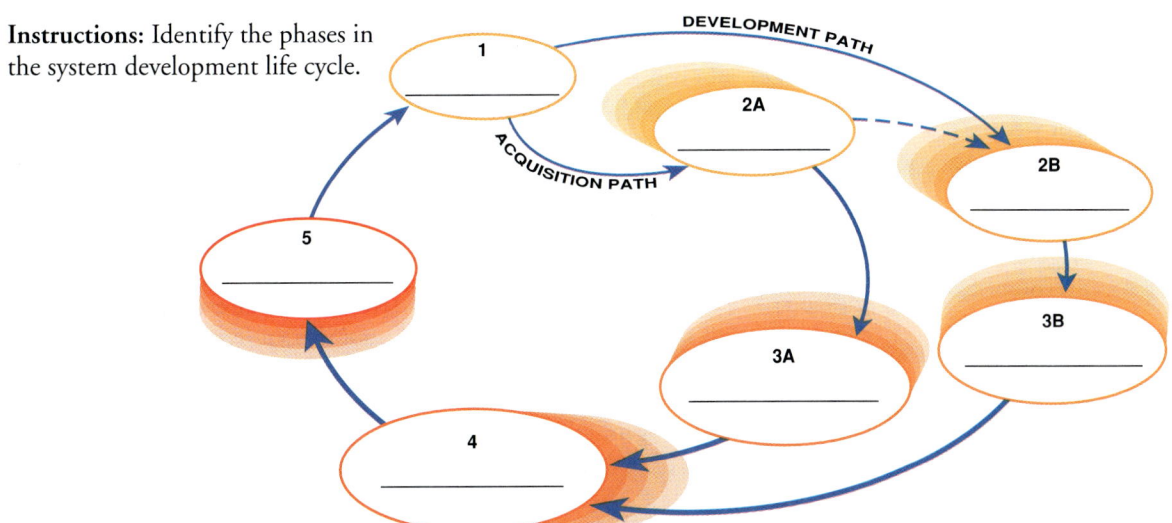

Points to Ponder

1

The system development life cycle may be undertaken in response to a problem, or problems, that an organization is experiencing. Think of a difficult problem you had and were able to solve. List, in the order in which they were taken, all of the steps you followed to solve the problem. Using the system development life cycle as a guide, in which phase (analysis, acquisition or design, customizing or development, implementation, or maintenance) would you place each step in your solution to the problem? Why? Which phase do you think was most crucial in solving your problem? Why? Which phase do you think was least important? Why?

2

Upon completion of the analysis phase of the SDLC, a written report is submitted by the systems analyst. This report explains why an investigation of the current system was performed, describes the problems that were found, and outlines possible solutions and the action recommended. Some authorities have found that in most instances, any changes suggested by the user after this report is completed are resisted. Why do you think this is true? Under what circumstances should user changes be considered? Why? Should suggested changes ever be ignored? Why or why not?

3

Prepare one of the following:

a. A data flow diagram illustrating the flow of information through your school's computer system during class registration.

b. A decision table or decision tree showing whether or not you will register for a class given at least two conditions.

c. A system flowchart documenting the data you enter, processes you perform, files you use, and reports you produce in registering for a specific class.

4

Occasionally organizations hire an outside consultant to identify software suppliers. Although some organizations feel these consultants have saved them considerable sums of money, others insist they would have been better off not hiring a consultant. Under what circumstances do you think a company would hire a consultant? What advantages, if any, could a consultant have in locating software suppliers, choosing appropriate software packages, and helping to implement those packages? What problems, if any, could an outside consultant encounter? To be most effective, what sort of cooperation would a consultant need from the organization?

5

Imagine you are the head of the information systems department for a small manufacturing firm. Several department managers have contacted your office complaining that the current information system is outdated (it is almost eight years old) and is no longer meeting their needs, so you have organized a committee to investigate the problem. At your first meeting, George, a department manager, suggests a representative from Colonial Computing, the vendor that supplied the current computer system, be made a part of the system development team. Martha, another department manager, strongly disagrees. In fact, she maintains that if it is necessary to acquire a new system, the firm should consider using several different vendors instead of a single supplier. What are the strengths and weaknesses of the suggestions made by each department manager? As head of the committee, how would you resolve the conflict?

6

Problems encountered during system development are easier and less expensive to remedy at some phases in the system development life cycle than at others. At what phase of the system development life cycle would it be easiest to identify problems? At what phase would it be most difficult? At what phase would it be easiest and least expensive to solve problems? At what phase would it be most difficult and most expensive? Explain your answers.

Out and About

1. Is the system development life cycle always the best method of creating solutions to information systems problems? Some systems analysts feel that prototyping, used from preliminary investigation to system implementation, results in greater user satisfaction and increased likelihood that users will be able to work with the final system. Interview a systems analyst at a company, or from the computer department or information systems department in your school, about his or her opinion of the system development life cycle versus prototyping. What does he or she feel is the best approach to developing information systems? What are the advantages and disadvantages of the SDLC? What are the advantages and disadvantages of prototyping? Under what circumstances would he or she choose to use each approach? Can either the system development life cycle or prototyping be used when solving noncomputer related problems? Why or why not?

2. Identify a problem on campus, or a problem you have, that could be solved using a personal computer and application software. Write a request for proposal (RFP), similar to that shown in *Figure 11-13* on page 11.11, documenting the features you think would be necessary in the application software. Visit a software vendor and, using your RFP, attempt to find at least two software packages that meet most of your requirements. Evaluate the software by scoring each package against your list of requirements, talking to people who use the software (if possible), and trying the software yourself. On the basis of your evaluation, which software package, if any, would you choose? Why?

3. Using trade publications or computer magazines, find advertisements for or articles on at least three examples of vertical application software. Who makes each software package? For what industry is the software designed? What is its function? What capabilities does it have that cannot be found in horizontal application software? How much does the software cost?

4. Locate a computer consultant by using the yellow pages, newspapers, or computer store references. Arrange to interview the consultant about his or her job. What services does the consultant provide? What advantages does the consultant offer a company? What tools does he or she use? What kind of education, experience, and personality is required to be an effective computer consultant? What is the most difficult part of a consultant's job? What is the most rewarding aspect of being a consultant?

5. Occasionally we hear stories about computer errors that cost individuals or organizations a great deal of money and trouble. Locate a newspaper or magazine article on such an error. Describe the error. After reading the article, do you think it was really a computer error or was it a mistake made in some phase of the system development life cycle? Why? If you believe a mistake was made in a phase of the SDLC, in which phase was it made? How? What could have been done to prevent the "computer error?"

6. In 1994, the median salary for systems analysts was $45,000, and top systems analysts were making as much as $75,000. Some authorities believe that soon all types of businesses, including software companies, manufacturing firms, and brokerage houses, will need systems analysts to monitor the information systems essential to modern companies. It is expected that more than 20,000 systems analyst positions will be added by the year 2000. Using want ads from newspapers, computer publications, or trade journals, and possibly calling some prospective employers, find out what qualities employers are looking for in a systems analyst. Describe the type of education, experience, achievements, and personality that make an individual a successful candidate for a systems analyst position.

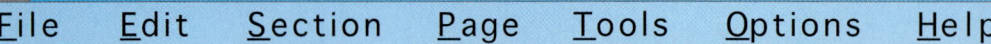

<u>F</u>ile <u>E</u>dit <u>S</u>ection <u>P</u>age <u>T</u>ools <u>O</u>ptions <u>H</u>elp

  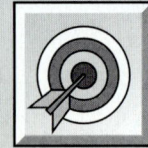  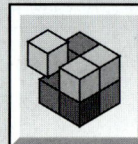 

Windows Labs

1 Arranging Windows on Your Desktop Maximize the Program Manager window. Double-click the Main group icon. Double-click the Accessories group icon. Select the Window menu and choose the Tile command to tile the two group windows *(Figure 11-28)*. What do tiled windows look like? Select the Window menu and choose the Cascade command to cascade the two group windows. What do cascaded windows look like? In the Accessories group window, double-click the Paintbrush program-item icon. Press CTRL+ESC to display the Task List window. In the Task List window, click the Tile button to tile the application windows. Press CTRL+ESC. In the Task List window, click the Cascade button to cascade the application windows *(Figure 11-29)*. Close Paintbrush. Close the Accessories and Main group windows. Select the Window menu and choose the Arrange Icons command.

2 Traffic Sign Tutorial Obtain information from your instructor on the location (path) of the file TRAFFIC.EXE. With Program Manager on the screen, select the File menu and choose the Run command. In the Command Line text box, type the path and filename traffic. For example, type c:\sclabs\traffic. Press the ENTER key. The Traffic Sign Tutorial window displays on the screen *(Figure 11-30)*. Drag the signs to their correct containers. If you drag a sign to the wrong container, it will snap back to its original location.

Select the Options menu and choose the Clear command to initialize the tutorial. Select the Options menu and choose the Show command to show the answers. Choose the Clear command from the Options menu to initialize the tutorial. Select the Options menu and choose the Quiz command. Answer the quiz questions. Close the Traffic Sign Tutorial window.

3 Specifying International Settings With Program Manager on the screen, double-click the Main group icon. In the Main group window, double-click the Control Panel program-item icon. In the Control Panel window, double-click the International icon. In the International dialog box *(Figure 11-31)*, click the Help button. Read and print the information on the screen. Select the Help topic in green. Read and print the information. Close the Help window.

Click the Country drop-down list box arrow to display the list of countries. How many countries are listed? Click the Country drop-down list box arrow again to remove the list. Repeat this procedure for the remaining drop-down list box arrows in the International dialog box. Write down the languages available. How many keyboard layouts are available? List the available measurements.

In each of the format areas at the bottom of the International dialog box, click the Change button, read any available help information, and then choose the Cancel button to return to the International dialog box. What is the current short date format? long date format? How many ways can negative values be displayed? What is the 1000 separator? What is the time separator? Choose the Cancel button in the International dialog box. Close Control Panel.

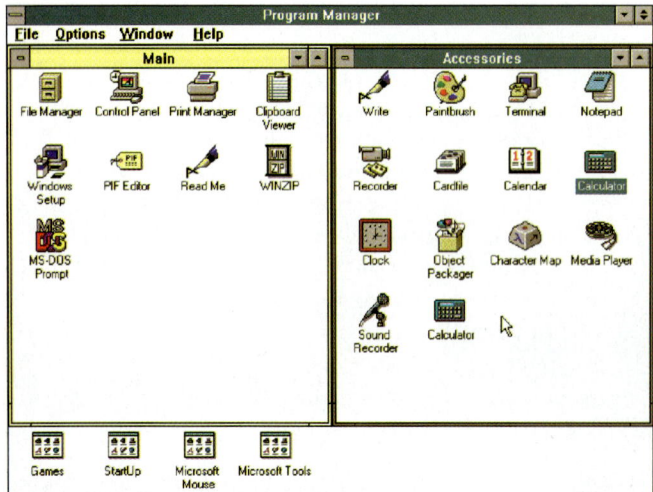

Figure 11-28

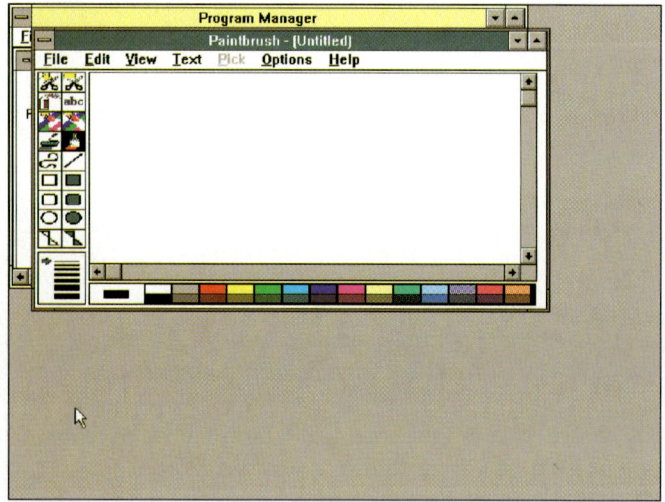

Figure 11-29

In the Lab   11.37

4 Using the Clipboard to Transfer Information Between Applications
With Program Manager on the screen, double-click the Accessories group icon. Start Paintbrush and maximize the window. Select the File menu and choose Open. In the Open dialog box, select tartan.bmp. Choose the OK button to display the TARTAN.BMP file.

Select the Help menu and choose the Search for Help On command. In the Search dialog box, type pick tool and press the ENTER key twice. Read and print the information. Close the Help window. Select the Pick tool. Drag the mouse from the upper left corner of the tartan picture to its lower right corner to select it. With the picture selected, select the Edit menu and choose the Copy command to copy your selection to the Clipboard. Close Paintbrush. Do not save changes.

Start the Write application in the Accessories group window. Maximize the Write window. Select the Edit menu and choose the Paste command to copy the tartan picture from the Clipboard. In Write, beneath the picture, enter a few sentences to describe the procedure you just followed to place the Paintbrush picture in the Write application. Save the file with the name WIN11-4. Print the file. Close Write.

5 Using Calculator Help
With Program Manager on the screen, double-click the Accessories group icon. In the Accessories group window, double-click the Calculator program-item icon. Select the Help menu and choose Search for Help On. Type memory functions and press the ENTER key twice. Read and print the information. Choose the Search button. Type clipboard and press the ENTER key twice. Read and print the information. Close Help. Close Calculator.

DOS Labs

1 Changing the System Prompt
At the DOS prompt, type prompt doslab11-1$g and press the ENTER key. What is the new DOS prompt? What is the purpose of $g? Type prompt dg and press the ENTER key. What is the new DOS prompt? Type prompt vg and press the ENTER key. What is the new DOS prompt? Type prompt pg and press the ENTER key to return to the original DOS prompt.

2 Scanning a Disk
Insert your diskette in drive A. At the DOS prompt, type scandisk a: and press the ENTER key. When you are prompted, type n to not perform a surface scan. Did ScanDisk find any problems? Press the ENTER key to view the log. What areas did ScanDisk check? Press the ENTER key and type x to exit ScanDisk.

3 Using Help
At the DOS prompt, type help chkdsk and press the ENTER key. Read and print the information on this screen and on the Notes and the Examples screens. Exit the MS-DOS Help window.

Online Lab

1 Playing Games Online
Using one of the two online services you selected in Chapter 1, connect to the service and perform the following tasks: (1) Search the online service for Games. (2) Choose a game, read the instructions, and play the game.

Figure 11-30

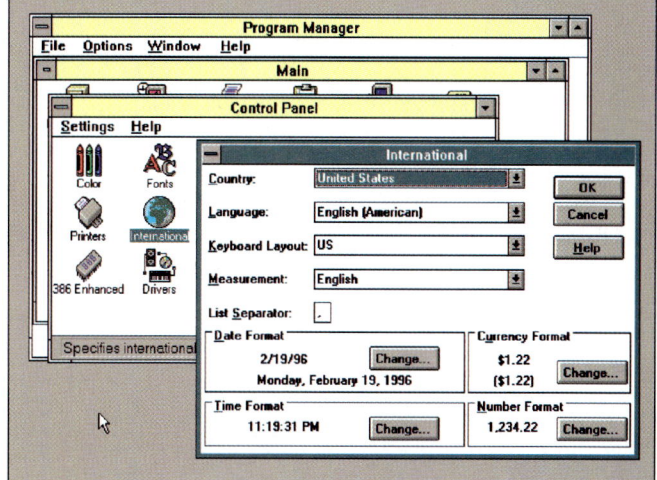

Figure 11-31

CHAPTER TWELVE

Program Development and Programming Languages

12

Objectives

After completing this chapter, you will be able to:

- Define the term computer program

- Describe the five steps in program development

- Explain the concepts of structured program design

- Explain and illustrate the sequence, selection, and iteration control structures used in structured programming

- Define the term programming language and discuss the various categories of programming languages

- Explain and discuss application generators

- Explain and discuss object-oriented programming

- Discuss the programming languages that are commonly used today

- Explain the factors that should be considered when choosing a programming language

The system development life cycle covers the entire process of taking a plan for processing data through various phases until it becomes a functioning information system. During the development phase of this cycle, computer programs are written. The purpose of these programs is to process data and produce information as specified in the information system design. This chapter focuses on the steps taken to write a program and the available tools that make the program development process more efficient. This chapter also discusses the different languages used to write programs.

Although you may never write a program yourself, you may someday request information that will require a program to be written or modified; thus, you should understand how a computer program is developed.

What Is a Computer Program?

A **computer program** is a detailed set of instructions that directs a computer to perform the tasks necessary to process data into information. These instructions, usually written by a computer programmer, can be coded (written) in a variety of programming languages discussed later in this chapter. To create programs that are correct (produce accurate information) and maintainable (easy to modify), programmers follow a process called program development.

What Is Program Development?

Program development is the process of producing one or more programs to perform specific tasks on a computer. The process of program development has evolved into a series of five steps most experts agree should take place when any program is developed *(Figure 12-1)*.

1. *Review specifications.* The programmer reviews the specifications created by the systems analyst during the system design phase.
2. *Design.* The programmer determines and documents the specific actions the computer will take to accomplish the desired tasks.
3. *Code.* The programmer writes the actual program instructions.
4. *Test.* The written programs are tested to make sure they perform as intended.
5. *Finalize documentation.* Throughout the program development process, the programmer documents, or writes, explanatory information about the program. In this final step, the documentation produced during steps 1 through 4 is brought together and organized.

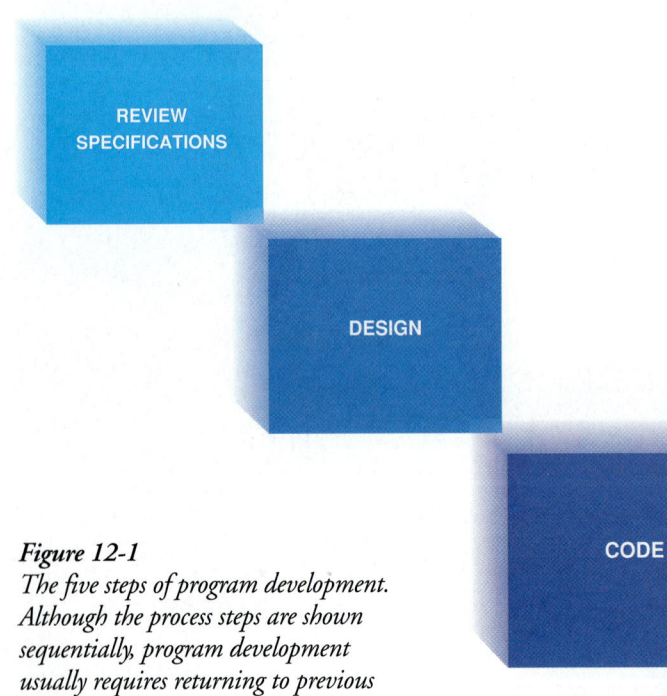

Figure 12-1
The five steps of program development. Although the process steps are shown sequentially, program development usually requires returning to previous steps to correct errors.

Step 1 – Reviewing the Program Specifications

The first step in the program development process is a review of the program specifications. **Program specifications** can consist of data flow diagrams, system flowcharts, process specifications that indicate the action to be taken on the data, a data dictionary identifying the data elements that will be used, screen formats, report layouts, and actual documents such as invoices or checks. These documents help the programmer understand the work that needs to be done by the program. Also, the programmer meets with the user and the systems analyst who designed the system to understand the purpose of the program from the user's point of view.

If the programmer believes some aspect of the design should be changed, such as a screen layout, he or she discusses it with the systems analyst and the user. If the change is agreed on, the written design specification is changed. The programmer, however, should not change the specified system without the agreement of the systems analyst and the user. If a change is authorized, it should be recorded in the system design. The systems analyst and the user, through the system design, have specified what is to be done. It is the programmer's job to determine *how* to do it.

Large programming jobs are usually assigned to more than one programmer. In these situations, a good system design is essential so each programmer can be given a logical portion of the system to be programmed.

Although these five steps are listed sequentially, the program development process usually requires returning to previous steps to correct errors that are discovered.

To better understand how the steps in the program development process relate to the overall development of an information system, the phases of the system development life cycle are shown in *Figure 12-2*. Program development is a phase on the development path of the system development life cycle. If, after the analysis phase, an organization is unable to acquire commercial software that meets its needs, it shifts to the design phase. The development phase, which includes program development, follows the design phase and is made up of the five steps shown in *Figure 12-1* on the previous page.

Figure 12-2
Program development occurs during the development phase of the system development life cycle.

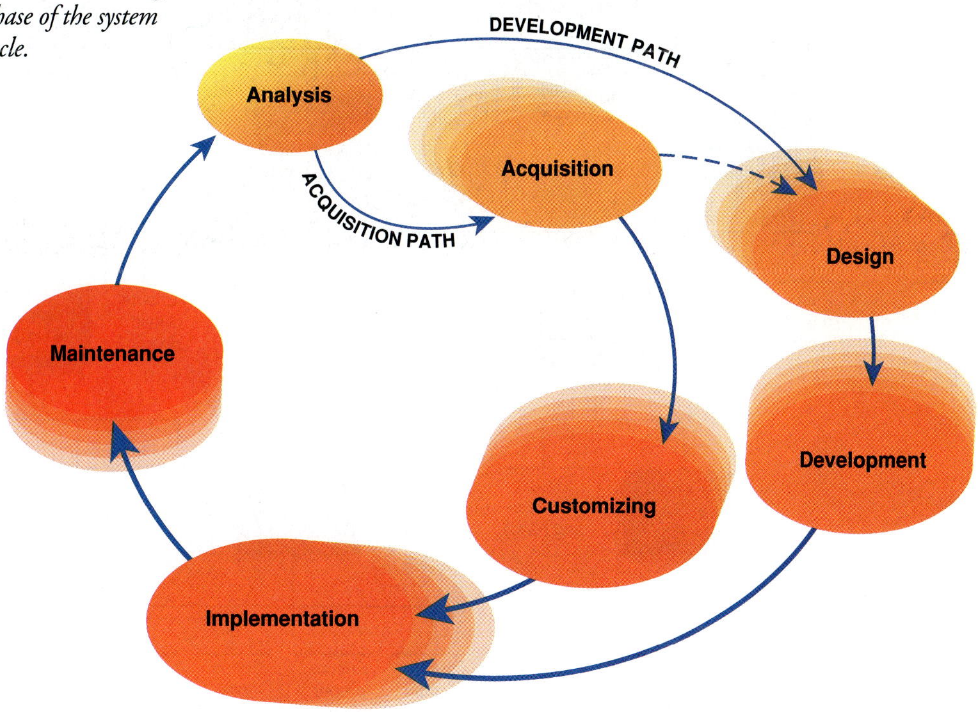

Step 2 – Designing the Program

After the programmer has carefully reviewed the specifications, program design begins. During **program design**, a logical solution to the programming task is developed and documented. The solution is broken down into a step-by-step procedure called an **algorithm**. Determining the logic for a computer program can be an extremely complex task. To aid in program design and development, a method called structured program design is commonly used.

Structured Program Design

Structured program design is a methodology emphasizing three main program design concepts: modules, control structures, and single entry/single exit. Use of these concepts helps create programs that are easy to write, read, understand, check for errors, and modify.

MODULES

With structured design, programming problems are *decomposed* (separated) into smaller parts called modules. Each **module**, sometimes referred to as a **subroutine**, performs a given task within the program. The major benefit of this technique is it simplifies program development because each module of a program can be developed individually. When the modules are combined, they form a complete program that accomplishes the desired result.

Structure charts, also called **hierarchy charts**, are often used to decompose and represent the modules of a program. When the program decomposition is completed, the entire structure of a program is illustrated by the hierarchy chart *(Figure 12-3)*, which shows the relationship of the modules within the program.

CONTROL STRUCTURES

In structured program design, three basic **control structures** are used to form the logic of a program. All logic problems can be solved by a combination of these structures. The three basic control structures are: sequence, selection, and iteration.

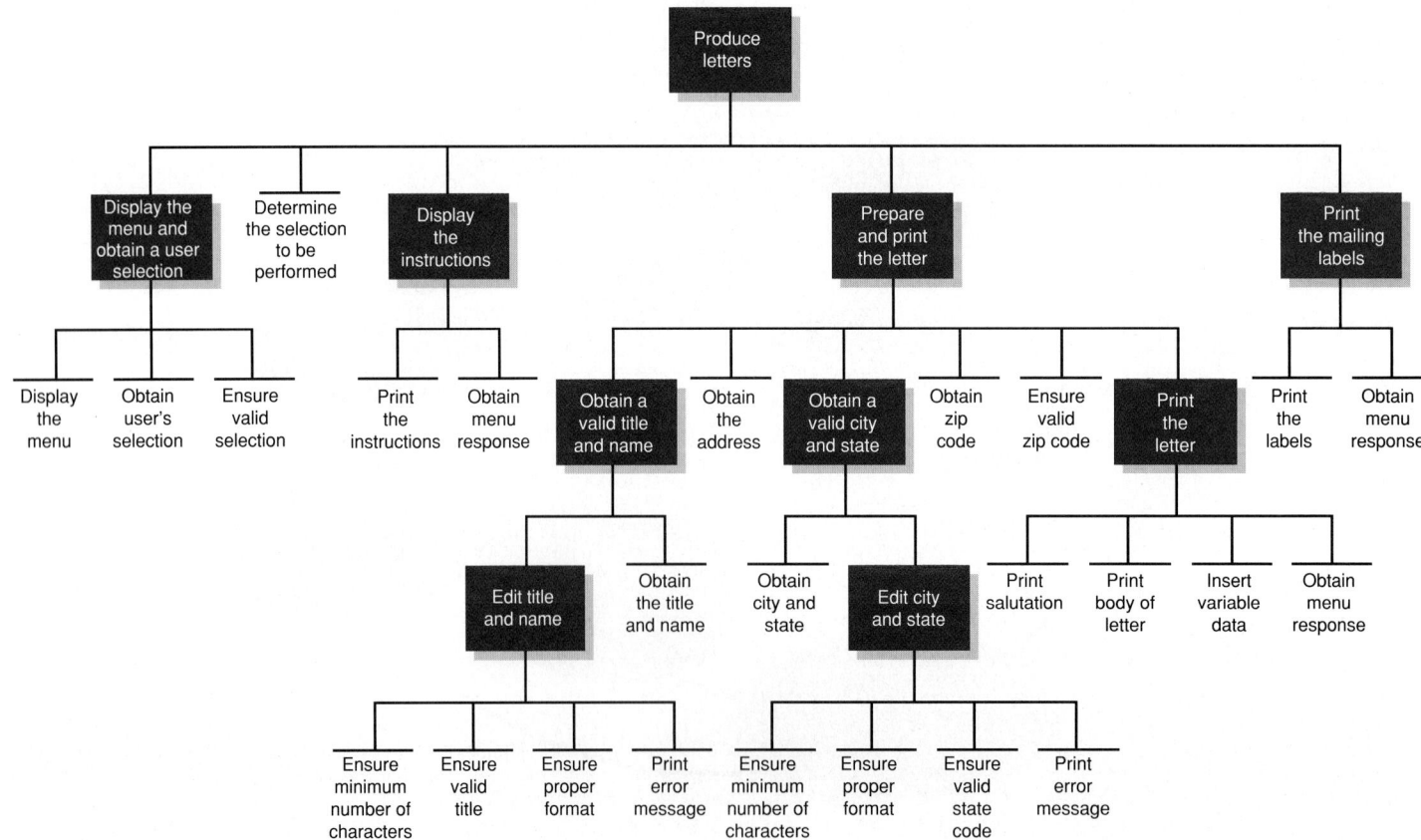

Figure 12-3
In this structure chart, the relationship of individual program modules is graphically shown as boxes. The text below each box indicates the processing steps that would be performed.

1. In the **sequence structure**, one process occurs immediately after another. In *Figure 12-4*, each rectangular box represents a particular process that is to occur. For example, a process could be a computer instruction to multiply two numbers. Each process occurs in the exact sequence specified, one process followed by the next.
2. The second control structure, called the **selection structure**, or **if-then-else structure**, gives programmers a way to represent conditional program logic (*Figure 12-5*). Conditional program logic can be expressed in the following way: *If* the condition is true, *then* perform the true condition processing, *else* perform the false condition processing. When the if-then-else structure is used, the *if* portion of the structure tests a given condition. The true portion of the statement is executed if the condition tested is true, and the false portion of the statement is executed if the condition is false. An if-then-else structure might be used to determine if an employee is hourly or salaried and then process the employee accordingly. To do this, an employee code might be tested to determine if an employee is hourly. If the employee is hourly, the true portion of the structure would be executed and hourly pay would be calculated. If the employee is not hourly, the false portion of the structure would be executed and salary pay would be calculated. The selection, or if-then-else, structure is used by programmers to represent conditional logic problems.

    A variation of the selection structure is the case structure. The **case structure** is used when a condition being tested can lead to more than two alternatives (*Figure 12-6*). In a program, a menu is an example of a case structure because it provides multiple processing options.
3. The third control structure, called the **iteration structure**, or **looping structure**, means one or more processes continue to occur as long as a given condition remains true. There are two forms of this control structure: the **do-while structure** and the **do-until structure** (*Figure 12-7* on the next page). In the do-while structure, a condition is tested.

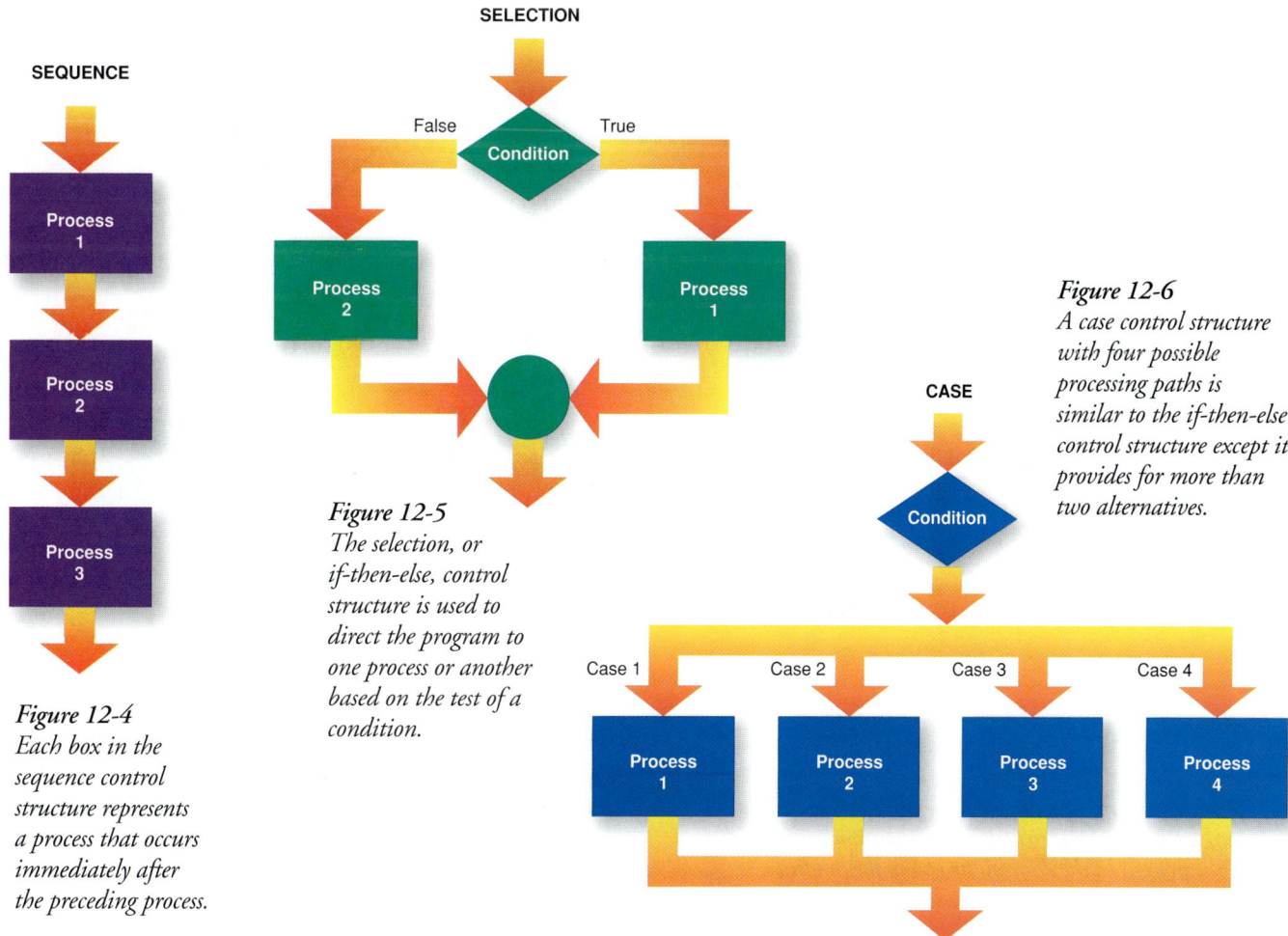

Figure 12-4
Each box in the sequence control structure represents a process that occurs immediately after the preceding process.

Figure 12-5
The selection, or if-then-else, control structure is used to direct the program to one process or another based on the test of a condition.

Figure 12-6
A case control structure with four possible processing paths is similar to the if-then-else control structure except it provides for more than two alternatives.

If the condition is true, the process is performed. The program then *loops* back and tests the condition again. If the condition is still true, the process is performed again. This looping continues until the condition being tested is false. At that time, the program exits the loop, moves to another section of the program, and performs some other processing. An example of this type of testing would be a check to see if all records have been processed.

The do-until control structure is similar to the do-while except the condition tested is at the end instead of the beginning of the loop. Processing continues *until* the condition is met.

Programmers combine these three control structures—sequence, selection, and iteration—to create program logic solutions. A structured program design rule that applies to these control structures and how they are combined is the single entry/single exit rule.

SINGLE ENTRY/SINGLE EXIT

An important concept in structured programming is **single entry/single exit**, meaning there is only one entry point and one exit point for each of the three control structures. An **entry point** is the point where a control structure is entered. An **exit point** is the point where the control structure is exited. For example, in *Figure 12-8*, when the if-then-else structure is used, the control structure is entered at the point where the condition is tested. When the condition is tested, one set of instructions will be executed if the condition is true and another set will be executed if the condition is false. Regardless of the result of the test, however, the structure is exited at the single exit point.

This feature substantially improves the logic of a program because, when reading the program, the programmer can be assured that whatever happens within the if-then-else structure, the control structure will always be exited at a common point. Prior to the use of structured programming, many programmers would transfer control to other parts of

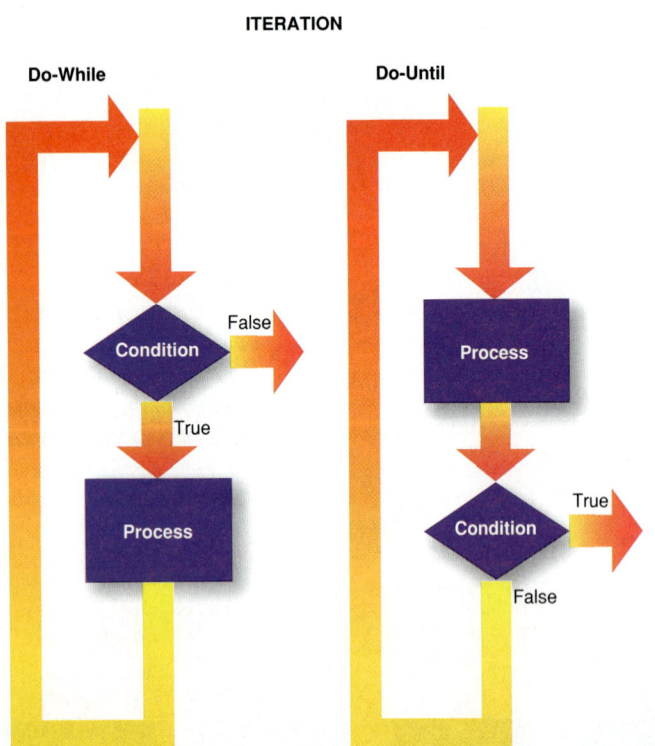

Figure 12-7
The iteration control structure has two forms, do-while and do-until. In the do-while structure, the condition is tested before the process. In the do-until structure, the condition is tested after the process.

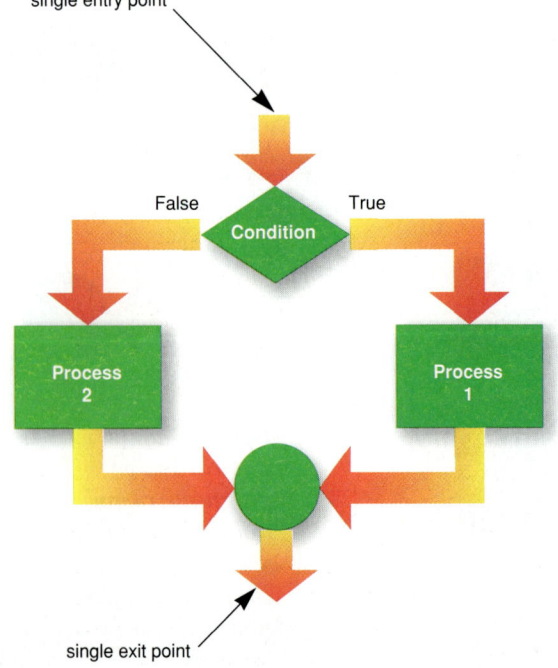

Figure 12-8
Structured programming concepts require all control structures to have a single entry point and a single exit point. This contributes to programs that are easier to understand and maintain.

a program without following the single entry/single exit rule. This practice led to poorly designed programs that were extremely difficult to read, check for errors, and modify. Because the logic path of such programs jumps from one section of the program to another, the programs are sometimes referred to as *spaghetti code*.

Program Design Tools

Programmers use several popular program design tools to develop and document the logical solutions to the problems they are programming. Two commonly used design tools are program flowcharts and pseudocode.

PROGRAM FLOWCHARTS

Program flowcharts were one of the first program design tools. *Figure 12-9* shows a flowchart drawn in the late 1940s by Dr. John von Neumann, a computer scientist and one of the first computer programmers. In a **program flowchart,** all the logical steps of a program are represented by a combination of symbols and text.

A set of standards for program flowcharts was published in the early 1960s by the American National Standards Institute (ANSI). These standards, which are still used today, specify symbols, such as rectangles and diamonds, used to represent the various operations performed on a computer *(Figure 12-10)*. Program flowcharts were used as the primary means of program design for many years prior to the introduction of structured program design. During these years, programmers designed programs by focusing on the detailed steps required for a program and creating logical solutions for each new combination of conditions as it was encountered. Developing programs in this manner led to poorly designed programs.

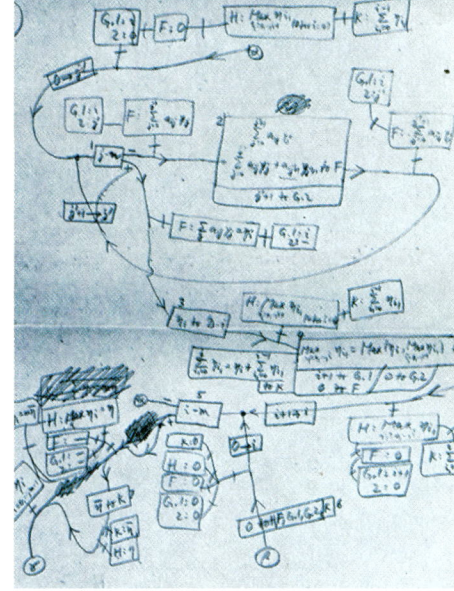

Figure 12-9
An example of an early flowchart developed by computer scientist Dr. John von Neumann in the 1940s to solve a problem involving game theory. This flowchart was drawn prior to the standardization of flowchart symbols and the development of structured design techniques.

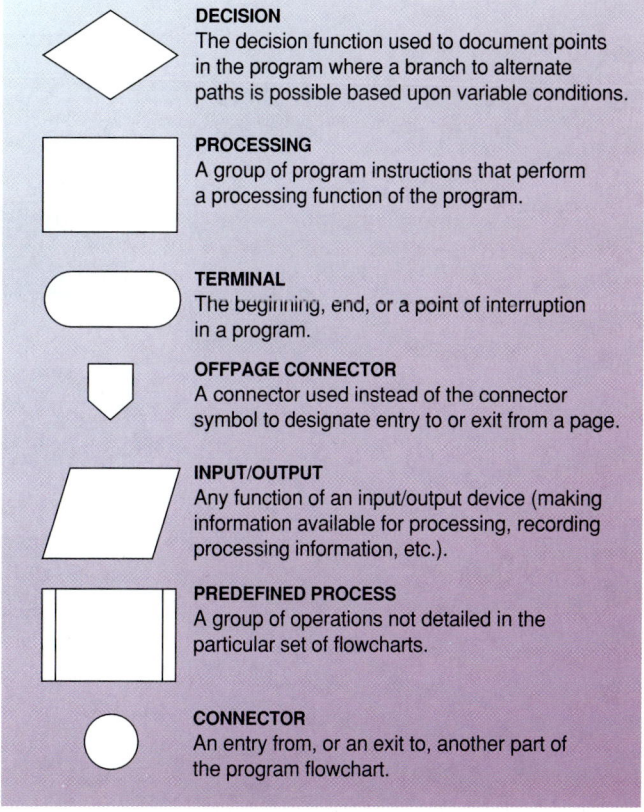

Figure 12-10
Standard symbols used to create program flowcharts.

Today, programmers are taught to apply the structured design concepts when they create program flowcharts *(Figure 12-11)*. When they use basic control structures, program flowcharts are a valuable program design tool.

PSEUDOCODE

Some experts in program design advocate the use of pseudocode when designing the logic for a program. In **pseudocode**, the logical steps in the solution of a problem are written as English statements and indentations are used to represent the control structures *(Figure 12-12)*. An advantage of pseudocode is it eliminates the time spent with flowcharting to draw and arrange symbols while attempting to determine the program logic. The major disadvantage is that, unlike flowcharting, pseudocode does not provide a graphic representation, which some people find easier to interpret when they examine programming logic.

To ensure that the program design is efficient and correct, many development teams use structured walkthroughs.

Structured Walkthrough

After a program has been designed, the programmer schedules a structured walkthrough of the program. The **structured walkthrough** is a review of the program logic by

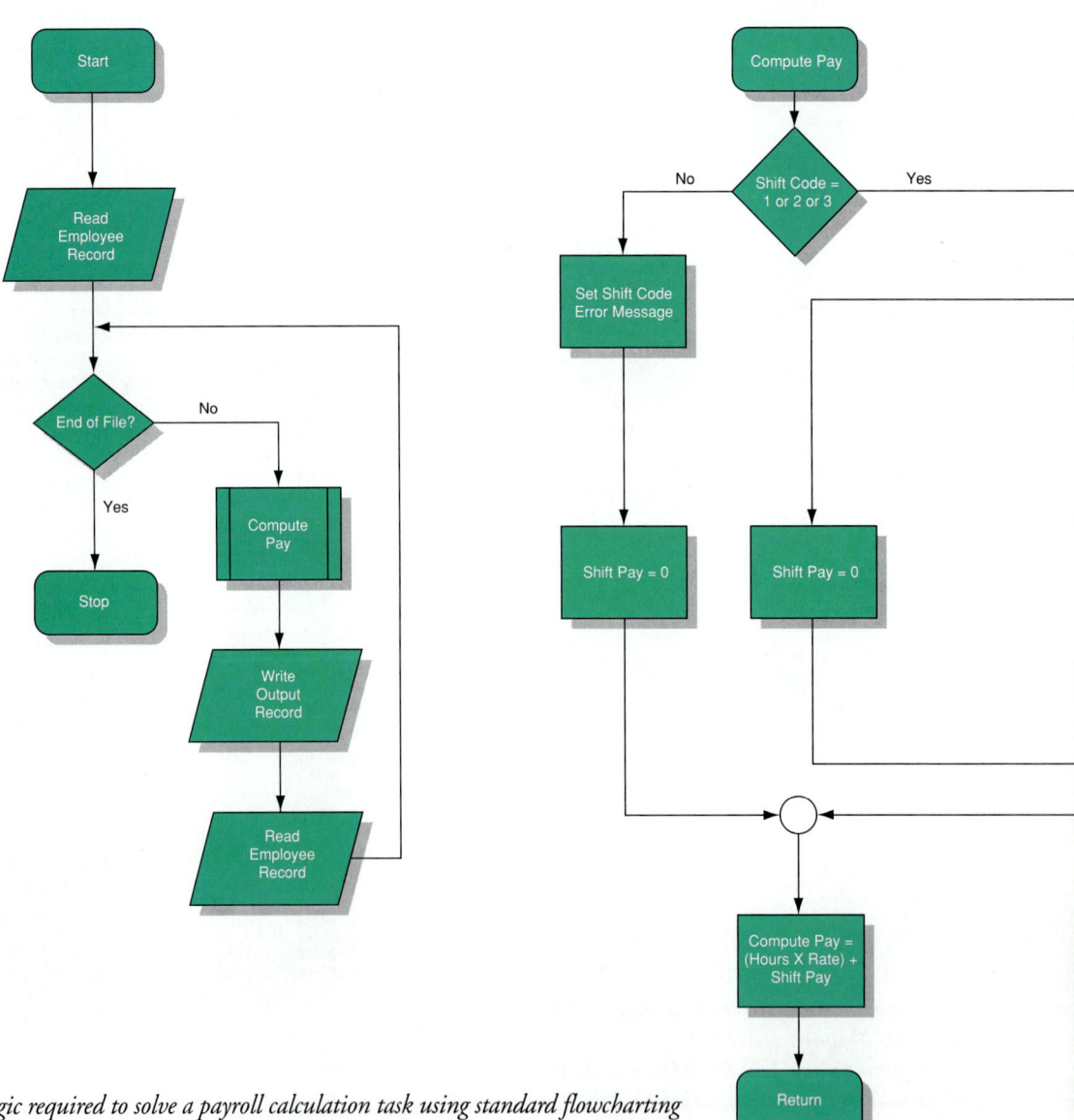

Figure 12-11
This flowchart displays the logic required to solve a payroll calculation task using standard flowcharting symbols and the three control structures of structured programming.

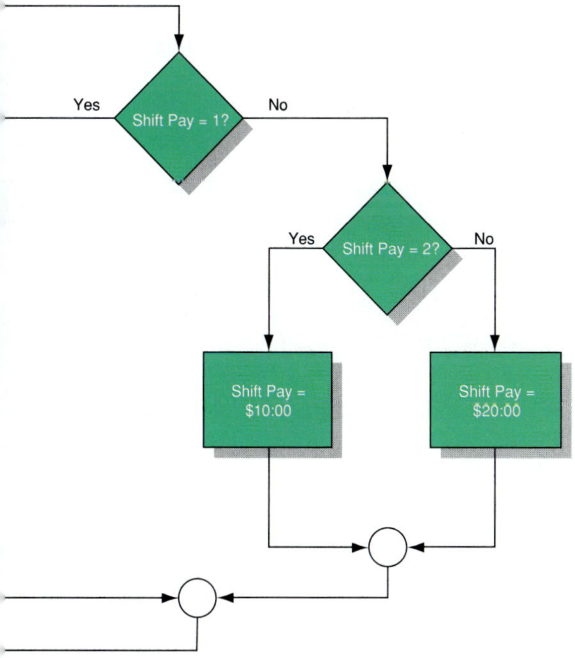

Step 3 – Coding the Program

Coding the program refers to the process of writing the program instructions that process the data and produce the output specified in the program design. As previously mentioned, programs are written in different languages, each of which has particular rules on how to instruct the computer to perform specific tasks such as read a record or multiply two numbers. Fortunately, most of the commonly used languages adhere to code standards established by the American National Standards Institute (ANSI). **Code standards** enable the same program to work on different types of computers.

If the program design is thorough, logical, and well structured, the coding process is greatly simplified and can sometimes be a one-for-one translation of a design step into a program step. Coding language is explained in detail later in this chapter. The amount of time it takes to code a program can be shortened if an organization maintains a code library. A **code library** stores partial or complete programs written to solve a particular problem such as calculating city, county, and state sales taxes. Before starting a new program, a programmer checks the code library to see if any existing code can be reused.

other members of the development team. During the walkthrough, the person who designed the program explains the program logic. The purpose of the design walkthrough is to review the logic of the program for errors, and if possible, improve program design. Early detection of errors and approval of program design improvements reduces the overall development time and therefore the cost of the program. It is much better to find errors and make needed changes to the program during the design step than to make them later in the program development process. Structured walkthroughs are also used to review work in other phases of the system development life cycle.

Once the program design is complete, the programmer can begin to code the program.

```
MAIN PROCESSING MODULE;

Read employee record
DO WHILE not end of file
    Compute pay
    Write output record
    Read employee record
ENDDO
Stop

COMPUTE PAY MODULE;

IF shift code = 1 or 2 or 3
    IF shift code = 1
        Set shift pay = 0
    ELSE
        IF shift code = 2
            Set shift pay = $10.00
        ELSE
            Set shift pay = $20.00
        ENDIF
    ENDIF
ELSE
    Set shift code error message
    Set shift pay = 0
ENDIF
Compute pay = (hours X rate) + shift pay
RETURN
```

Figure 12-12
This pseudocode is another way of documenting the logic shown in the flowchart in Figure 12-11.

Step 4 – Testing the Program

Before a program is used to process real data and produce information people rely on, it should be thoroughly tested to make sure it is functioning correctly. A programmer can perform several different types of tests.

Desk checking is the process of reading the program and mentally reviewing its logic. This is a simple process performed by the programmer who wrote the program or by another programmer. This process can be compared to proofreading a letter before you mail it. Desk checking can also uncover **syntax errors**, which are violations of the grammar rules of the language in which the program was written. An example of a syntax error would be the program command READ being misspelled REED. Syntax errors missed by the programmer during desk checking are identified by the computer when it decodes the program instructions.

Logic testing is what most programmers think of when the term testing is used. During **logic testing**, the sequence of program instructions is tested to make sure it provides the correct result. Logic errors may be the result of a programming oversight such as using the wrong data to perform a calculation or a design error such as forgetting to specify that some customers do not have to pay sales tax when they purchase merchandise.

Logic testing is performed with **test data**, which is data that simulates real data the program will process when it is implemented. To obtain an independent and unbiased test of the program, test data and the review of test results should be the responsibility of someone other than the programmer who wrote the program. The test data should be developed by referring to the system design, but it should also try to *break* or *crash* the program by including data outside the range of data found during normal operations. For example, if the specifications of a payroll program stated that an employee should never work in excess of 60 hours per week, the program should be designed, coded, and tested to display an error message if the hours exceed 60. If such an error is found, the program should display an error message or in some other way indicate an invalid number of hours has been entered.

One of the more colorful terms of the computer industry is **debugging**, which refers to the process of locating and correcting program errors, called **bugs**, found during testing. A popular story is that the term bug was first used when the failure of one of the first computers was traced to a moth lodged in the electronic components *(Figure 12-13)*. Most programming languages include a **debugger** program that identifies syntax errors and allows the programmer to stop the program while it is running to examine program values such as the result of a calculation.

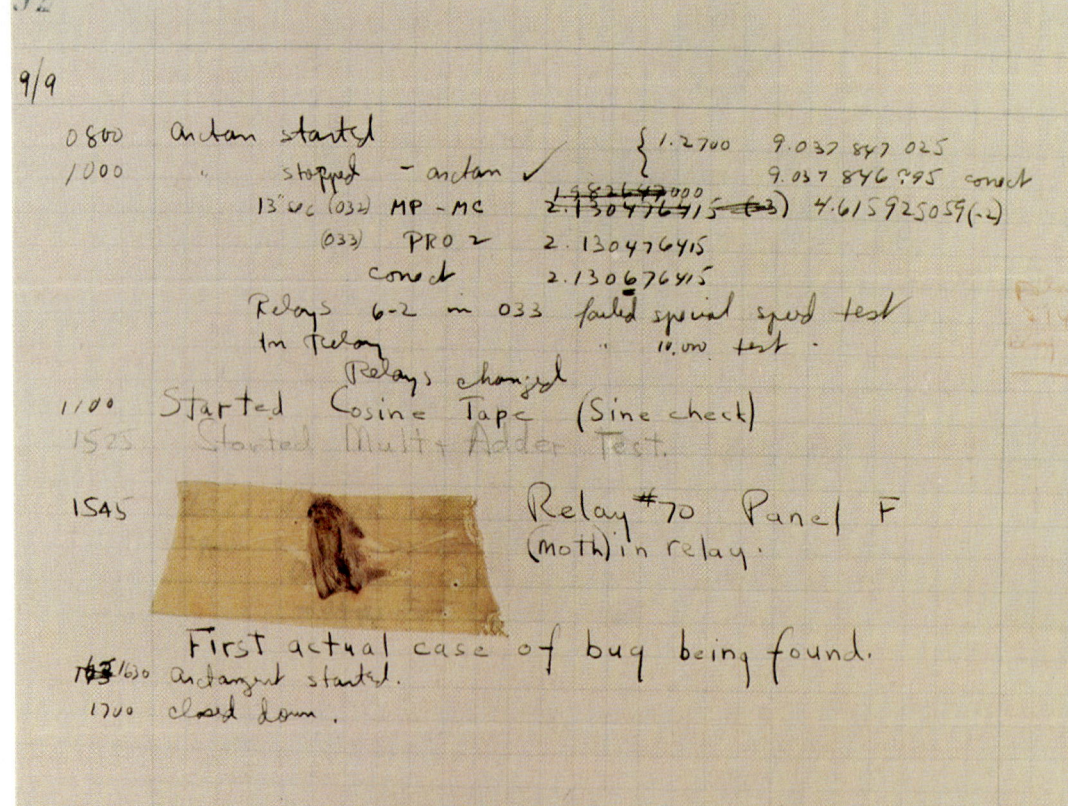

Figure 12-13
In 1945, the cause of the temporary failure of the world's first electro-mechanical computer, the Mark 1, was traced to a dead moth (shown taped to the log book) caught in the electrical components. Some say this event is the origin of the term bug, meaning a computer error.

Step 5 – Finalizing Program Documentation

Documentation, which is the preparation of documents explaining the program, is an essential but sometimes neglected part of the programming process. Documentation should be an ongoing part of developing a program and should only be finalized, meaning organized and brought together, after the program is successfully tested and ready for implementation. Documentation developed during the programming process should include a narrative description of the program, program design documents such as flowcharts or pseudocode, program listings, and test results. Comments in the program itself are also an important part of program documentation *(Figure 12-14)*. Data entry and computer operations procedures should also be documented prior to implementation.

In addition to helping programmers develop programs, documentation is valuable because it helps the next programmer who is asked, six months or one year later, to make a change to the program. Proper documentation can substantially reduce the amount of time the new programmer will have to spend learning enough about the program to know how best to make the change.

Program Maintenance

Program maintenance includes all changes to a program once it is implemented and processing real transactions. Sometimes, maintenance is required to correct errors not found during the testing step. Other times, maintenance is required to make changes resulting from new information requirements. It may surprise you to learn that the majority of all business programming today consists of maintaining existing programs, not writing new programs.

Because so much time is spent on maintenance programming, it should be subject to the same policies and procedures, such as design, testing, and documentation, required for new programs. Unfortunately, this is not always the case. Because maintenance tasks are usually shorter than new programming efforts, they often are not held to the same standards. The result is that over time, programs can become unrecognizable when compared with their original documentation. Maintaining high standards for program maintenance not only can lower overall programming costs, but also lengthen the useful life of a program.

Summary of Program Development

The key to developing quality programs for an information system is to follow the steps of the program development process. Program specifications must be carefully reviewed and understood. Programmers should use structured concepts to design programs that are modular, use the three control structures, and follow the single entry/single exit rule. Programmers should carefully code and test the program and finalize documentation. If each of these steps is followed, programmers will create quality programs that are correct and can be easily read, understood, and maintained.

```
REM Program 12-14
REM Determining a Salesperson's Commission
REM Dave Brame, CIS 204, Div. 01
REM September 30, 1996
REM **************************************
REM Clear Screen
CLS
REM Request Data from Operator
INPUT "Commission rate =====> ", Rate
INPUT "Week 1 sales ========> ", Week1
INPUT "Week 2 sales ========> ", Week2
INPUT "Return sales ========> ", Returns
```

Figure 12-14
Most programming languages allow programmers to place explanatory comments directly in the program. This is an effective way of documenting the program. In this QuickBASIC program, comment lines are identified by the letters REM, which is an abbreviation for REMARK.

What Is a Programming Language?

As mentioned at the beginning of this chapter, computer programs can be written in a variety of programming languages. People communicate with one another through language, established patterns of words and sounds. A similar definition can also be applied to a **programming language**, which is a set of written words and symbols that allow the programmer or user to communicate with the computer. As with English, Spanish, Chinese, or other spoken languages, programming languages have rules, called syntax, that govern their use.

Categories of Programming Languages

Hundreds of programming languages are available, each with its own syntax. Some languages were developed for specific computers and others, because of their success, have been standardized and adapted to a wide range of computers. Programming languages can be classified into one of four categories: machine language, assembly language, high-level languages, and fourth-generation languages.

Machine Language

Machine language is the fundamental language of the computer's processor. Programs written in all other categories of languages are eventually translated into machine language before they are executed. Individual machine language instructions exist for each of the commands in the computer's instruction set (the operations such as add, move, or read that are specific to each computer). Because the instruction set is unique for a particular processor, machine languages are different for computers that have different processors.

(a) MACHINE LANGUAGE
9b df 46 0c
9b d9 c0
9b db 7e f2
9b d9 46 04
9b d8 c9
9b d9 5e fc
9b d9 c0
9b dc 16 ac 00
9b dd d8
9b dd 7e f0
90 9b
8a 66 f1
9e
9b dd c0
76 19
9b d9 46 fc
9b dc 0e b4 00
9b de e9
9b d9 5e 08
90 9b
eb 0d
90
8b 46 fc
8b 56 fe
89 46 08
89 56 0a

Figure 12-15
Program instruction chart for: (a) machine language (printed in a hexadecimal form), (b) assembly language, and (c) a high-level language called C. The machine language and assembly language instructions correspond to the high-level instructions and were generated when the high-level language statements were translated into machine language. As you can see, the high-level language requires fewer program instructions and is easier to read.

CATEGORIES OF PROGRAMMING LANGUAGES

Most microprocessor manufacturers, however, design their new microprocessors so they will run programs written for earlier generations within the same *family* (product line) of microprocessors.

The advantage of writing a program in machine language is the programmer can control the computer directly and accomplish exactly what needs to be done. Therefore, well-written machine language programs are very efficient. The disadvantages of machine language programs are they take a long time to write and they are difficult to review if the programmer is trying to find an error. In addition, because they are written using the instruction set of a particular processor, the programs will only run on computers with the same type of processor. Because they are written for specific processors, machine languages are also called **low-level languages**. *Figure 12-15(a)* shows an example of machine language instructions.

Assembly Language

To make it easier for programmers to remember the specific machine instruction codes, assembly languages were developed. An **assembly language** is similar to a machine language, but uses abbreviations called **mnemonics** or **symbolic operation codes** to represent the machine operation code. Another difference is assembly languages usually allow **symbolic addressing**, which means a specific computer memory location can be referenced by a name or symbol, such as TOTAL, instead of by its actual address as it would have to be referenced in machine language. Assembly language programs can also include **macroinstructions** that generate more than one machine language instruction.

Assembly language programs are converted into machine language instructions by a special program called an **assembler**. Even though assembly languages are easier to use than machine languages, they are still considered a low-level language because they are so closely related to the specific design of the computer. *Figure 12-15(b)* shows an example of assembly language instructions.

(b) ASSEMBLY LANGUAGE	(c) HIGH-LEVEL LANGUAGE
| ```
    fld  WORD PTR [bp+12];qty
fld ST(0)
    fstp TBYTE PTR [bp-14]
    fld  DWORD PTR [bp+4];price
fmul ST(0),ST(1)
    fstp DWORD PTR [bp-4];gross
``` | `gross = qty * price;` |
| ```
    fld  ST(0)
         fcom QWORD PTR $T20002
fstp ST(0)
    fstsw    WORD PTR [bp-16]
    fwait
mov ah,BYTE PTR [bp-15]
    sahf
ffreeST(0)
    jbe $I193
``` | `if (qty > ceiling)` |
| ```
    fld  DWORD PTR [bp-4];gross
    fmul QWORD PTR $T20003
fsub
    fstp DWORD PTR [bp+8];net
    fwait
``` | `net = gross - (gross * discount_rate);` |
| ```
    jmp SHORT $I194
    nop
``` | `else` |
| ```
    $I193:
mov ax,WORD PTR [bp-4];gross
mov dx,WORD PTR [bp-2]
mov WORD PTR [bp+8],ax ;net
mov WORD PTR [bp+10],dx
    $I194:
``` | `net = gross;` |
```

High-Level Languages

High-level languages were developed in the late 1950s and 1960s. **High-level languages** more closely resemble what most people would think of as a language because they contain nouns, verbs, and mathematical, relational, and logical operators that can be grouped together to form what appear to be sentences (*Figure 12-15(c)* on the previous page). These sentences are called **program statements**. Because of these characteristics, high-level languages can be read by programmers and are thus easier to learn and use than machine or assembly languages. Another important advantage over low-level languages is high-level languages are usually machine independent, which means they can run on different types of computers.

As mentioned previously, all languages must be translated into machine language before they can be executed. High-level languages are translated in one of two ways: with a compiler or an interpreter.

A **compiler** converts an entire program into machine language that is usually stored on a disk for later execution. The program to be converted is called the **source program** and the machine language produced is called the **object program** or **object code**. Compilers check the program syntax, perform limited logic checking, and make sure that data to be used in comparisons or calculations, such as a discount rate, is properly defined somewhere in the program. An important feature of compilers is they produce an error listing of all program statements not meeting the program language rules. This listing helps the programmer make the necessary changes to debug or correct the program. *Figure 12-16* illustrates the process of compiling a program.

Because machine language is unique to each processor, different computers require different compilers for the same language. For example, a mainframe, minicomputer, and personal computer would each have different compilers that would translate the same source language program into the specific machine language for each computer.

While a compiler translates an entire program, an **interpreter** translates one program statement at a time and

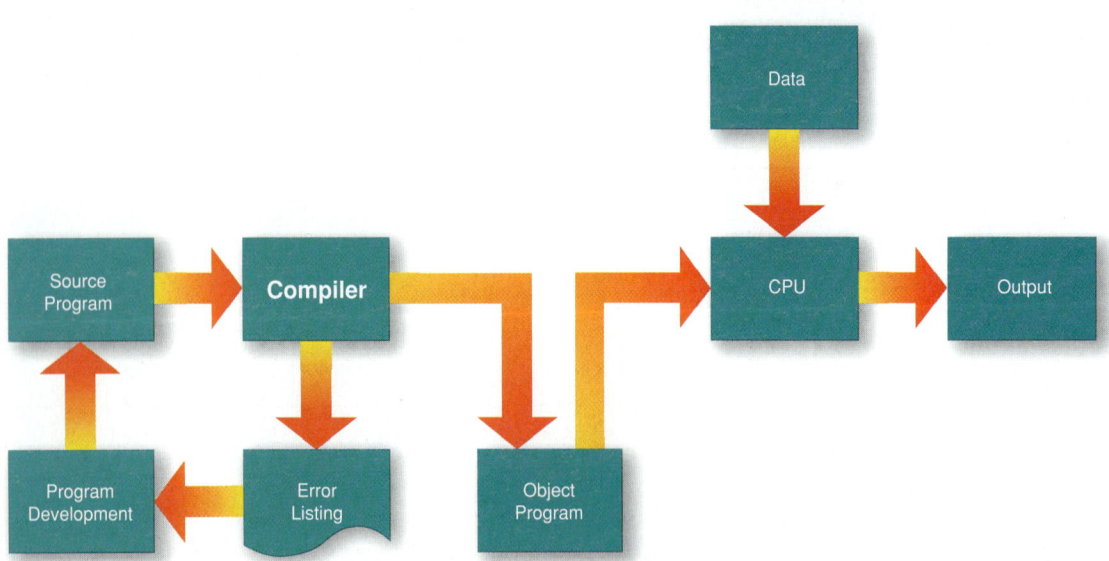

Figure 12-16
When a compiler is used, a source language program is compiled into a machine language object program. When the user wants to run the program, the object program is loaded into the main memory of the CPU and the program instructions begin executing. As instructed by the program, the CPU processes data and creates output. Errors in the source program identified during compilation are shown on an error listing that is used to make the necessary corrections during program development.

then executes the resulting machine language before translating the next program statement. When using an interpreter, each time the program is run, the source program is interpreted into machine language and executed. No object program is produced. *Figure 12-17* illustrates this process.

The advantage of interpreters is the compiling process is not necessary before program changes can be tested. The disadvantage of interpreters is interpreted programs do not run as fast as compiled programs because the translation to machine language occurs each time the program is run. Interpreted languages were once common on personal computers because early PCs did not have the memory or computing power required by compilers. Compilers for most high-level languages are now available for the newer and more powerful personal computers.

Fourth-Generation Languages

The evolution of computer languages is sometimes described in terms of generations with machine, assembly, and high-level languages considered the first, second, and third generations, respectively. Each generation offered significant improvements in ease of use and programming flexibility over the previous generation. Although a clear definition does not yet exist, **fourth-generation languages** (4GLs), sometimes called **very high level languages**, continue the programming language evolution by being even easier to use than high-level languages for both the programmer and the nonprogramming user.

A term commonly used to describe fourth-generation languages is **nonprocedural**, which means the programmer does not specify the procedures to be used to accomplish a task as is done with lower procedural language generations. Instead of telling the computer how to do the task, the programmer tells the computer *what* is to be done, usually by describing the desired output. A database query language *(Figure 12-18)* is an example of a nonprocedural fourth-generation language.

The advantage of fourth-generation languages is they are *results* oriented (*what* is to be done, not *how*), and they

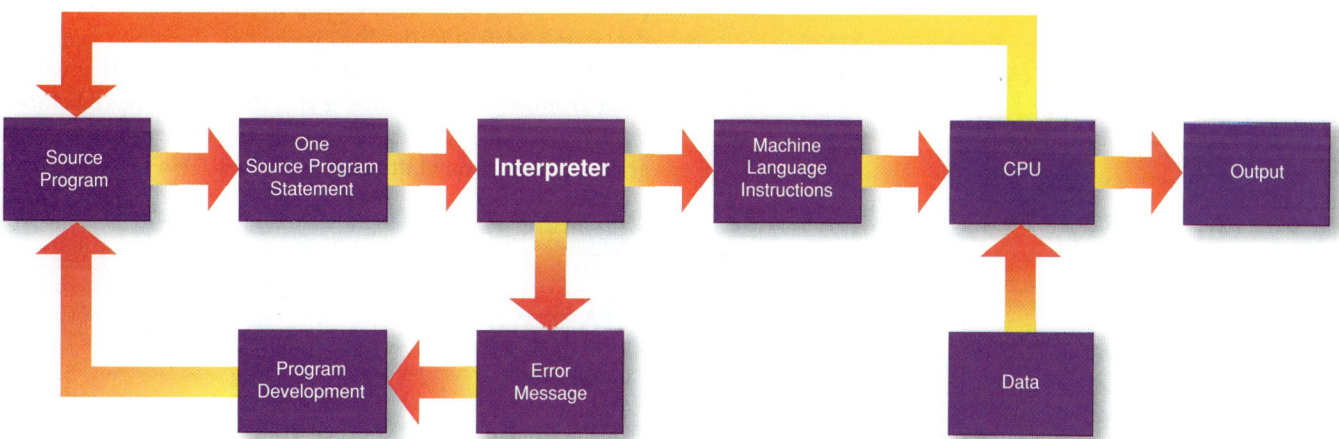

Figure 12-17
When an interpreter is used, one source language statement at a time is interpreted into machine language instructions that are executed immediately by the CPU. As instructed by the machine language instructions, the CPU processes data and creates output. Error messages indicating an invalid source language statement are produced as each source program statement is interpreted and are used to make the necessary corrections during program development.

LIST CUSTOMERS CUSTOMER.NAME WITH BALANCE.DUE>1000

Figure 12-18
This database query is considered an example of a fourth-generation language because it tells the computer what the user wants, not how to perform the processing. The query will produce a list of customers with balances greater than $1,000.

can be used by nonprogramming personnel. The disadvantage of fourth-generation languages is they do not provide as many processing options to the programmer as other language generations and they require more computer processing power than other language generations. Most experts, however, believe their ease of use far outweighs these disadvantages and they predict fourth-generation languages will continue to be more widely used.

An extension of fourth-generation languages is a natural language. A **natural language**, sometimes called a **fifth generation language**, is a type of query language that allows the user to enter a question as if he or she were speaking to another person. For example, a fourth-generation query might be stated as LIST SALESPERSON TOTAL-SALES BY REGION. A natural language version of that same query might be TELL ME THE NAME OF EACH SALESPERSON AND THE TOTAL SALES FOR EACH REGION. The natural language allows the user more flexibility in the structure of the query and can even ask the user a question if it does not understand what is meant by the initial query statement. A few natural languages are available today but they are not yet widely used.

Application Generators

Application generators, also called **program generators**, are programs that produce source-language programs, such as BASIC or COBOL, based on input, output, and processing specifications entered by the user. Application generators are available as stand-alone programs or as part of other software such as CASE and database packages. Application generators can greatly reduce the amount of time required to develop a program. They are designed on the basis that most programs are comprised of standard processing modules, such as routines to read, write, or compare records, that can be combined together to create unique programs. These standard processing modules are stored in a library and are selected and grouped together based on user specifications. Application generators often use menu and screen generators to assist in developing an application.

A **menu generator** lets the user specify a menu (list) of processing options that can be selected. The resulting menu is automatically formatted with heading, footing, and prompt line text.

A **screen generator**, sometimes called a **screen painter**, allows the user to design an input or output screen by entering the names and descriptions of the input and output data directly on the screen. The advantage is the user enters the data exactly as it will appear after the program is created. As each data name, such as Order No., is entered, the screen generator asks the user to specify the length and type of data that will be entered and what processing, if any, should take place before or after the data is entered. As shown in *Figure 12-19*, screen generators can create both GUI and character-based screens.

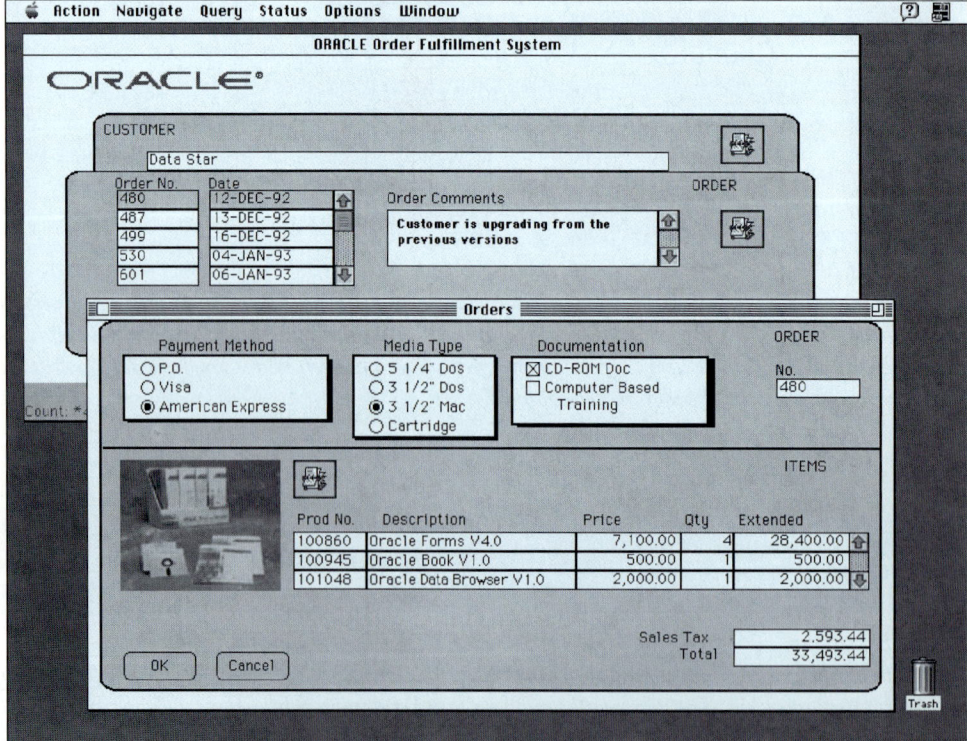

Object-oriented Programming

Object-oriented programming (OOP) is a new approach to developing software that allows programmers to create **objects**, a combination of data and program instructions. Traditional programming methods keep data, such as files, independent of the programs that work with the data. Each traditional program, therefore, must define how the data will be used for that particular program. This often results in redundant programming code that must be changed every time the structure of the data is changed, such as when a new field is added to a file. With OOP, the program instructions and data are combined into objects that can be used repeatedly by programmers whenever they need them. Specific instructions, called **methods**, define how the object acts when it is used by a program. The capability to combine methods (instructions) with objects (data) is called **encapsulation**. The following example, illustrated in *Figure 12-20* on the next page, describes how OOP minimizes the number of instructions that must be defined.

With OOP, programmers define classes of objects. Each **class** contains the methods unique to that class. As shown in *Figure 12-20,* the class of animals could contain methods on how animals eat, sleep, and breathe. Each class can have one or more subclasses. Each subclass contains the methods of its higher level classes plus whatever methods are unique to the subclass. For example, the subclass Humans contains the method Talk. The subclass Dogs contains the method Bark. Both subclasses, Humans and Dogs, also contain the Eat, Sleep, and Breathe methods of the higher class, Animals. The OOP capability to pass methods to lower levels is called **inheritance**. A specific **instance** of an object contains all methods from its higher level classes plus any methods unique to the object. For example, the object Anne contains a method on how to play the violin. The object Anne also inherits the Eat, Sleep, Breathe, and Talk methods from the higher levels. The object Bowser contains methods on how Bowser bites and chases cars. Although these methods may be shared by other humans and dogs, respectively, they cannot be placed at higher levels because they are not shared by all humans or dogs. When an OOP object is sent an instruction to do something, called a **message**, unlike a traditional program, the message does not have to tell the OOP object exactly what to do. *What to do* is defined by the methods the OOP object

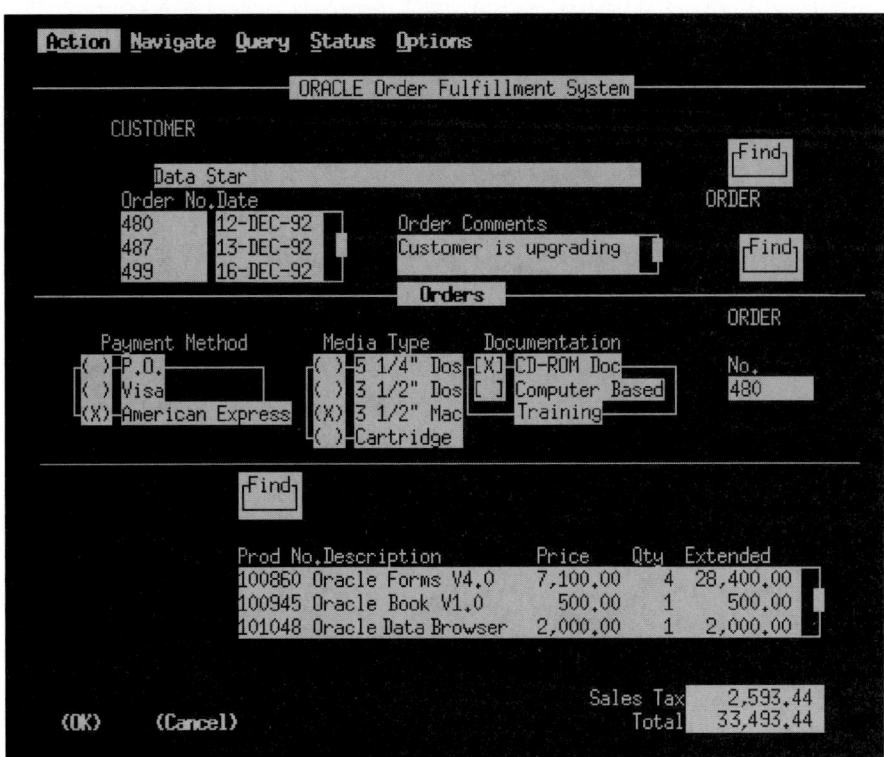

Figure 12-19
Oracle Forms from Oracle Corporation can generate either graphical user interface (GUI) screens such as the one on the left or character-based screens such as the one on the right.

contains or has inherited. For example, in *Figure 12-20*, if the object Bowser was sent a message to bark, the method of barking would be defined by the bark method in the subclass Dogs. However, if the object Butch was sent the same message to bark, its actions would be defined by the bark (perhaps a growl) associated with Butch. This illustrates that higher level methods can be overridden to define actions unique to a particular object or class.

A business example of an object might include a class called Invoices. With traditional programming, each time an invoice is displayed on a screen, specific programming instructions are included in the program. With OOP, a method called Display could be part of the object Invoice. An OOP program would only have to send a message identifying the object (Invoice) and stating the desired method (Display). How to display the invoice would be defined as part of the Invoice object.

As OOP is used by an organization, the organization builds a library of OOP objects and classes that can be reused. The more extensive the library, the more powerful and efficient OOP becomes. OOP development systems allow programmers to access such libraries and link objects to quickly build programs. Popular OOP languages include C++, Visual Basic, Turbo Pascal, SmallTalk, and HyperTalk (used on Apple Macintosh computers).

OOP languages are often described as being event-driven instead of procedural. **Event-driven** means that the program is designed to respond to events that take place when an application is run. An event can be pressing a particular key, using the mouse, or entering a particular value in response to a prompt. Events can take place at any time or in any sequence. Procedural programs, on the other hand, usually assume that processing continues from beginning to end in a linear manner.

Closely related to OOP are object-oriented software and object-oriented operating systems. **Object-oriented software** means applications developed using OOP programming techniques. **Object-oriented operating systems** are operating systems specifically designed to run OOP applications.

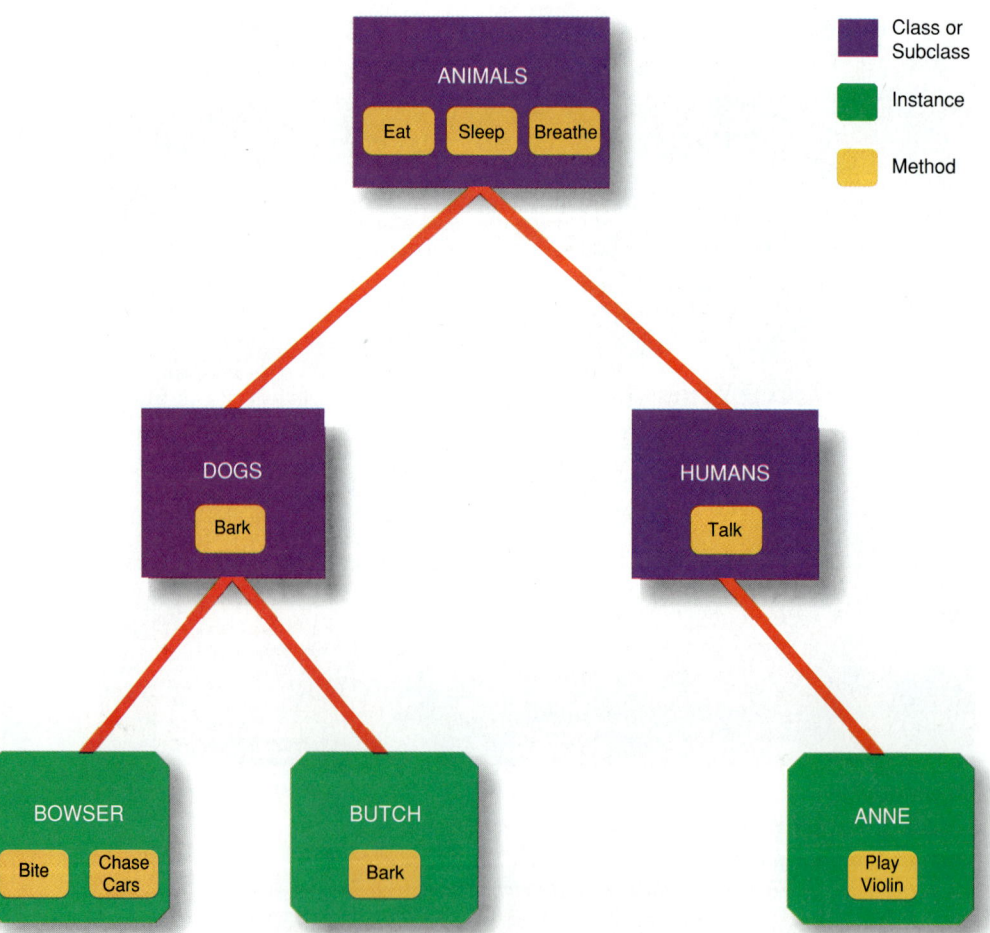

Figure 12-20
Object-oriented programming (OOP) allows procedures (called methods) to be combined with data to form objects. In traditional programming, procedures are defined by the program instructions that are separate from the data. In OOP, the methods define how the object will act when it is referenced and how it can be inherited from higher levels, called classes. For example, the method BARK can be inherited by BOWSER from the class DOGS. Objects can also have unique methods that differ from higher level methods. Thus, BUTCH can have a different BARK than BOWSER. The capability to inherit methods from higher levels makes programming more efficient because only methods unique to the specific object need to be defined. A specific occurrence of an object is called an instance.

Programming Languages Used Today

Although hundreds of programming languages have been developed, only a few are used extensively enough to be recognized as industry standards. Most of these are high-level programming languages that can be used on a variety of computers. This section discusses commonly used programming languages, their origins, and their primary purpose.

To help illustrate the differences, program code for the languages is shown. Except for the code shown for the Visual Basic language, the programming code solves the problem of computing the net sale of a transaction by multiplying the quantity sold times the sales price. A discount of 5% is calculated if the gross sale is more than $100.00.

BASIC

BASIC, which stands for **B**eginner's **A**ll-purpose **S**ymbolic **I**nstruction **C**ode, was developed by John Kemeny and Thomas Kurtz in 1964 at Dartmouth College *(Figure 12-21)*. They originally designed BASIC to be a simple, interactive programming language for college students to learn and use. Since then, other versions of BASIC have been developed including Microsoft **QuickBASIC** (also referred to as **QBASIC**). BASIC is widely used on both PCs and minicomputers to develop business applications. Versions of BASIC are also used as macro languages in some application software.

```
5010 REM ****************P R O C E S S   A N D   D I S P L A Y********
5040 GROSS = QTY * SLSPR
5050 IF GROSS > CEILING THEN NET = GROSS - (GROSS * DISC) ELSE NET = GROSS
5070 PRINT "THE NET SALES IS ";
5080 PRINT USING "$$#,###.##"; NET
5090 RETURN
```

Figure 12-21
An excerpt from a BASIC program.

Visual Basic

Visual Basic, developed by Microsoft Corporation in the early 1990s, is an object-oriented extension of the BASIC programming language. Visual Basic has a number of features that assist the user in designing a Windows-compatible graphical user interface (GUI). Once the GUI is designed, programming code is written to specify what happens when GUI features are used, such as selecting a button, or when data is entered. *Figure 12-22* shows a simple currency conversion program developed with Visual Basic. The first screen shows the design of the graphical user interface. The second screen shows the program code that will execute when the Command1 (CONVERT) button is chosen. The third screen shows the finished application.

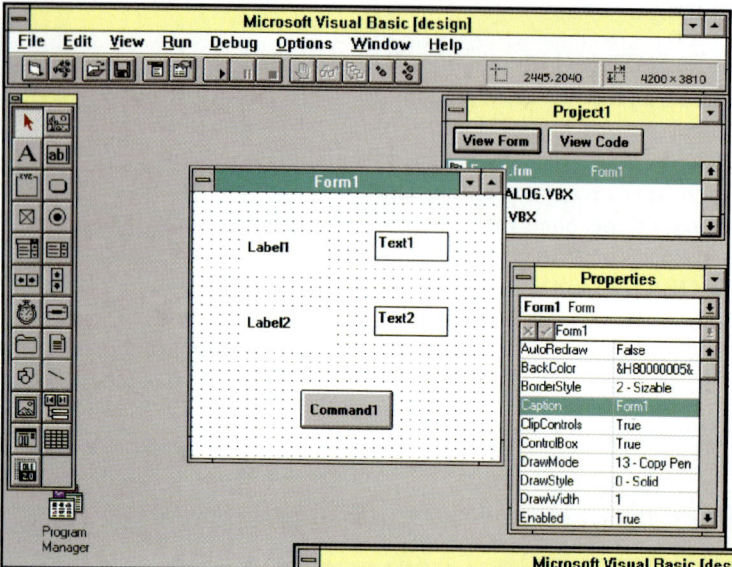
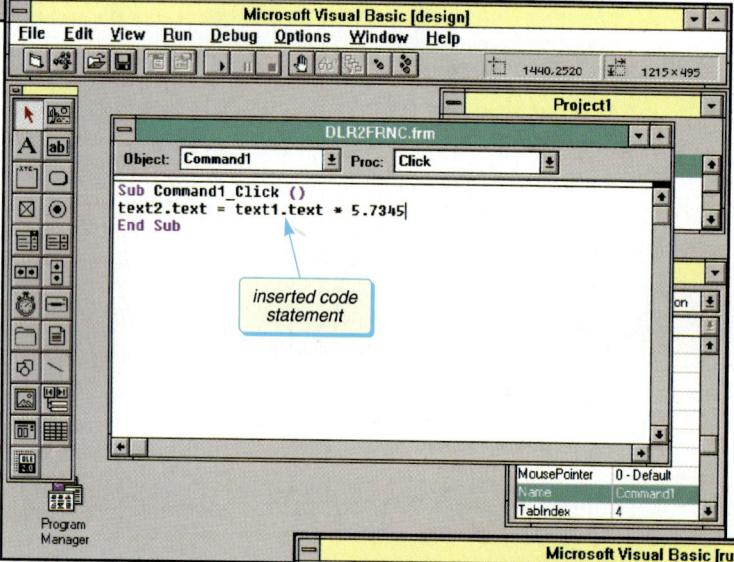

Figure 12-22
This figure shows how the Microsoft Visual Basic programming language is used to develop an application to convert dollars to French francs. The first screen shows how the programmer builds the user interface. Text1 will be entered by the user. Text2 will display the result after the user chooses the Command1 button. The second screen shows the program code that is associated with the screen. When the user chooses the Command1 button (shown as Command1_Click in the program code), the value in Text1 is multiplied by 5.7345 (the francs to dollars exchange rate) and displayed in the Text2 box. The third screen shows the finished application.

COBOL

COBOL (COmmon Business Oriented Language) was introduced in 1960. Backed by the U. S. Department of Defense, COBOL was developed by a committee of representatives from both government and industry. Rear Admiral Grace M. Hopper was a key person on the committee and is recognized as a prime developer of the COBOL language. COBOL is one of the more widely used programming languages for business applications *(Figure 12-23)*. Using an English-like format, COBOL instructions are arranged in sentences and grouped into paragraphs. The English format makes COBOL easy to write and read, but also makes it a wordy language that produces lengthy program code. COBOL is very good for processing large files and performing relatively simple business calculations. Other languages are better suited to performing complex mathematical formulas and functions.

C

The **C** programming language *(Figure 12-24)* was developed at Bell Laboratories in 1972 by Dennis Ritchie. It was originally designed as a programming language for writing systems software, but is now considered a general-purpose programming language and is widely used on personal computers. C is a powerful programming language that requires professional programming skills to be used effectively. The C programming language is used to develop a wide variety of software, including operating systems, application programs such as word processors and spreadsheets, and business applications. C programs are often used with the UNIX operating system (most of the UNIX operating system is written in C).

```
00100     016200  C010-PROCESS-AND-DISPLAY.
00101     016400**********************************************************
00102     016600* FUNCTION:              CALCULATE NET SALES AMOUNT    *
00103     016700*                        AND DISPLAY RESULTS           *
00104     016800* ENTRY/EXIT:            B000-LOOP-CONTROL             *
00105     016900* CALLS:                 NONE                          *
00106     017100**********************************************************
00107     017300      COMPUTE GROSS-SALES-WRK = QUANTITY-SOLD-WRK * SALES-PRICE-WRK.
00108     017500      IF GROSS-SALES-WRK IS GREATER THAN CEILING
00109     017600          COMPUTE NET-SALES-WRK = GROSS-SALES-WRK -
00110     017700              (GROSS-SALES-WRK * DISCOUNT-RATE)
00111     017800      ELSE
00112     017900          MOVE GROSS-SALES-WRK TO NET-SALES-WRK.
00113     018100      MOVE NET-SALES-WRK TO NET-SALES-OUTPUT.
00114     018300      DISPLAY CLEAR-SCREEN.
00115     018500      WRITE PRINT-LINE FROM DETAIL-LINE
00116     018600          AFTER ADVANCING 2.
```

Figure 12-23
An excerpt from a COBOL program. Notice the additional words in the COBOL program compared to the BASIC program in Figure 12-21 on page 12.19. Although the extra words increase the time it takes to write a COBOL program, they also make the program easier to read and understand.

```
float gross;
gross = qty * price;
if (gross > ceiling)
    net = gross - (gross * discount_rate);
else
    net = gross;
return(net);
```

Figure 12-24
An excerpt from a C program.

C++

C++ (pronounced C plus plus) is an object-oriented extension of the C programming language. Developed by Bjarne Stroustrup at Bell Laboratories in the 1980s, C++ includes all of the standard C language plus additional features for working with objects, classes, and other object-oriented programming concepts. Like C, C++ is a powerful and efficient language but can be difficult to learn. C++ is frequently used to develop application software.

FORTRAN

FORTRAN (FORmula TRANslator) was developed by a team of IBM programmers led by John Backus. Released in 1957, FORTRAN was designed as a programming language to be used by scientists, engineers, and mathematicians *(Figure 12-25)*. FORTRAN is considered the first high-level language developed and is noted for its capability to easily express and efficiently calculate mathematical equations.

```
 1    67.000          SUBROUTINE CALC(QTY,SALES,DISC,MAX,GROSS,NET)
 2    68.000          REAL SALES, DISC, MAX, GROSS, NET
 3    69.000          INTEGER QTY
 4    70.000          GROSS = QTY * SALES
 5    71.000          IF(GROSS .GT. MAX) THEN
 6    72.000    1        NET = GROSS - (GROSS * DISC)
 7    73.000    1     ELSE
 8    74.000    1        NET = GROSS
 9    75.000    1     ENDIF
10    76.000          PRINT *, "   "
11    77.000          RETURN
```

Figure 12-25
An excerpt from a FORTRAN program.

```
BEGIN                                      (* Begin procedure *)
   GROSS := SALES * QTY;
   IF GROSS > CEILING
      THEN NET := GROSS - (GROSS * DISCOUNT_RATE)
      ELSE NET := GROSS;
   WRITELN('THE NET SALES IS $',NET:6:2);
END;                                       (* End of procedure *)
```

Figure 12-26
An excerpt from a Pascal program.

Pascal

The **Pascal** language was developed in 1968 by Niklaus Wirth, a computer scientist at the Institut für Informatik in Zurich, Switzerland. It was developed for teaching programming. The name Pascal is not an abbreviation or acronym, but rather the name of a mathematician, Blaise Pascal (1623-1662), who developed one of the earliest calculating machines. Pascal is available for use on both personal and large computers and was one of the first programming languages developed where the instructions in the language were designed and written so programmers would be encouraged to develop programs that follow structured program design principles *(Figure 12-26)*. An object-oriented version of Pascal called Turbo Pascal has been developed by Borland Corporation.

Ada

The programming language **Ada** is named for Augusta Ada Byron, Countess of Lovelace, a mathematician in the 1800s, who is thought to have written the first computer program. The development of Ada, which is based on Pascal, was supported by the U. S. Department of Defense, which requires its use on all U. S. government military projects. Ada was introduced in 1980 and designed to facilitate the writing and maintenance of large programs used over a long period of time. The language encourages coding of readable programs that are also portable, allowing them to be transferred from computer to computer *(Figure 12-27)*.

```
31    GROSS_SALES_PRICE := FLOAT(QUANTITY * SALES_PRICE);
32    if GROSS_SALES_PRICE > 100.0 then
33       NET_SALES_PRICE := GROSS_SALES_PRICE - (GROSS_SALES_PRICE * 0.05)
34    else
35       NET_SALES_PRICE := GROSS_SALES_PRICE
36    end if;
```

Figure 12-27
An excerpt from an Ada program.

Other Programming Languages

In addition to the commonly used programming languages just discussed, a number of other languages are sometimes used. *Figure 12-28* lists some of these languages and their primary uses.

How to Choose a Programming Language

Although each programming language has its own unique characteristics, selecting a language for a programming task can be a difficult decision. Factors to be considered include the following:

1. *The programming standards of the organization.* Many organizations have programming standards specifying that a particular language is used for all applications.
2. *The need to interface with other programs.* If a program is going to work with other existing or future programs, ideally it should be written in the same language as the other programs.
3. *The suitability of a language to the application to be programmed.* As discussed, most languages are best suited to a particular type of application. For example, FORTRAN works well with applications requiring many complex calculations.
4. *The expertise of the available programmers.* Unless another language is far superior, you should choose the language used by the existing programmers.
5. *The need for the application to be portable.* If the application will run on different systems, a language common to the different systems should be chosen.

Summary of Program Development and Programming Languages

Because of their large installed base, procedural languages such as COBOL and BASIC will continue to be used for many years. A clear trend exists toward the creation of programs using nonprocedural tools, such as object-oriented, fourth-generation, and natural languages. These tools allow developers and users to concentrate more on *what* they want done than *how* they want it done. Your knowledge of the program development process and programming languages will help you to understand how the computer converts data into information and help you to obtain better results if you directly participate in the programming process.

ALGOL	**ALGO**rithmic **L**anguage – The first structured procedural language
APL	**A P**rograming **L**anguage – Uses special symbols to manipulate tables of numbers
FORTH	Similar to C – Creates fast and efficient program code; originally developed to control astronomical telescopes
HYPERTALK	Object-oriented language – Developed by Apple to manipulate cards that can contain text, graphics, and sound
LISP	**LIS**t **P**rocessing – Used for artificial intelligence applications
LOGO	Primarily known as an educational tool – Used to teach programming and problem-solving to children
MODULA-2	A successor to Pascal – Used for developing systems software
PILOT	**P**rogrammed **I**nquiry **L**earning **O**r **T**eaching – Used to write computer-aided instruction programs
PL/1	**P**rogramming **L**anguage One – Business and scientific language that combines many of the features of FORTRAN and COBOL
PROLOG	**PRO**gramming **LOG**ic – Used for artificial intelligence applications
RPG	**R**eport **P**rogram **G**enerator – Uses special forms to help user specify input, output, and calculation requirements of a program
SMALLTALK	Considered the first of the object-oriented programming languages

Figure 12-28
Other computer languages.

COMPUTERS AT WORK

COBOL: The Language That Keeps Marching On

Starting in the 1970s, the BASIC programming language was being widely used on minicomputers, and many predicted the demise of COBOL. In the 1980s, the most talked about language was C and again, many predicted that COBOL's days were over. Now in the 1990s, object-oriented languages such as Visual Basic and C++ are the hot topic and people are still predicting the end of COBOL. How is it that COBOL, after 35 years, is still being used by thousands of organizations around the world and new COBOL applications are being developed every day?

For one reason, it is because of the tremendous number of COBOL programs that were written in the past. One study estimated more than 70 *billion lines* of COBOL code are in existence. COBOL was used almost exclusively for business system development in the 1960s and early 1970s when many businesses first installed computers. The self-documenting nature of COBOL has also contributed to its continued use. Because COBOL code is easy to read, it is not difficult for maintenance programmers to figure out how a program works and make necessary changes. Some believe that other languages, such as C++, are not only more difficult to learn but are also more difficult to maintain because of their more concise and sometimes cryptic coding structure.

One company that decided to stick with COBOL was NCH Chemical of Irving, Texas. When NCH decided to replace their mainframe and minicomputers with a PC LAN, they did not want to rewrite more than 500 existing COBOL applications that were essential to their business. Instead of converting to another language, they chose a version of COBOL specifically developed for PCs called Micro Focus COBOL from Micro Focus Inc. Using Micro Focus COBOL, most of NCH's programs were directly converted to the LAN. Some programs that had been extensively modified over the years were rewritten using Micro Focus development tools.

The advantages of modern programming languages have not been overlooked by Micro Focus and existing COBOL users. Micro Focus COBOL includes some object-oriented features, and specifications for a standardized version of object-oriented COBOL are under development by the American National Standards Institute (ANSI).

Object-oriented COBOL! Who would have thought that after 35 years COBOL would still be around and would be borrowing the latest concepts from other languages?

Figure 12-29

IN THE FUTURE

Computing Naturally

Although query languages, such as SQL, have made accessing information much easier than in the past, many users, especially those who only make an occasional query, still find them difficult to use. The problem is that most query languages require the user to know the name of the file they want to access and the name of the data fields they want to display or print.

The solution to this problem is the use of a **natural language** that translates the user's plain English statements into file and field names and logical operators the computer can understand and process. With a natural language, questions like "What projects are over budget?" or "What's up in sales?" can be converted into standard SQL commands. Users do not need to know how to form a SQL statement or what the database structure looks like. All they need to know is how to ask a question in English. It sounds simple enough, but the actual process that takes place is quite complex. Here is what happens when using Natural Language, from Natural Language, Inc., a software product that interprets whole English sentences into SQL statements.

1. The user enters a request for information in the form of a question.
2. The software identifies the individual words in the request. Each word is matched against a 100,000-word dictionary and, if necessary, spelling is corrected. Words are identified by type, such as verbs and nouns.
3. The request is rebuilt in the best grammatical structure.
4. A first attempt is made to interpret the sentence into a database query.
5. Ambiguous references (what the software does not understand) are resolved by comparing the references with three sources; previous questions from the user, a library of concepts, and a library of rules that are specific to the user's organization. Previous questions can help identify pronouns such as who, or they, or it. For example, if two questions were asked, "Who are the top three salespersons?" and "What are they paid?", the *they* in the second sentence would be identified with the *salespersons* in the first sentence. The concepts library enables the system to understand a statement such as, "Turn the stew down", because its common-sense knowledge base tells it that things that are turned down are burners on stoves, and stew goes on a stove burner. The rules library contains a knowledge base that is specific to the user's organization.
6. The question is echoed back to the user in English.
7. A SQL statement is built and sent to the database manager.
8. The answer to the SQL statement is presented as a table, graph, or English sentence.

Although not yet widely used, natural language interfaces are estimated to become part of approximately 25% of all relational database management systems by 1996. Eventually, they will be part of all database systems and most, if not all, application packages as well. A logical evolution of the natural language interface is its integration with voice recognition. Already under development, a voice recognition natural language interface would be ideal for information inquiry applications such as airline reservations and hotel availability.

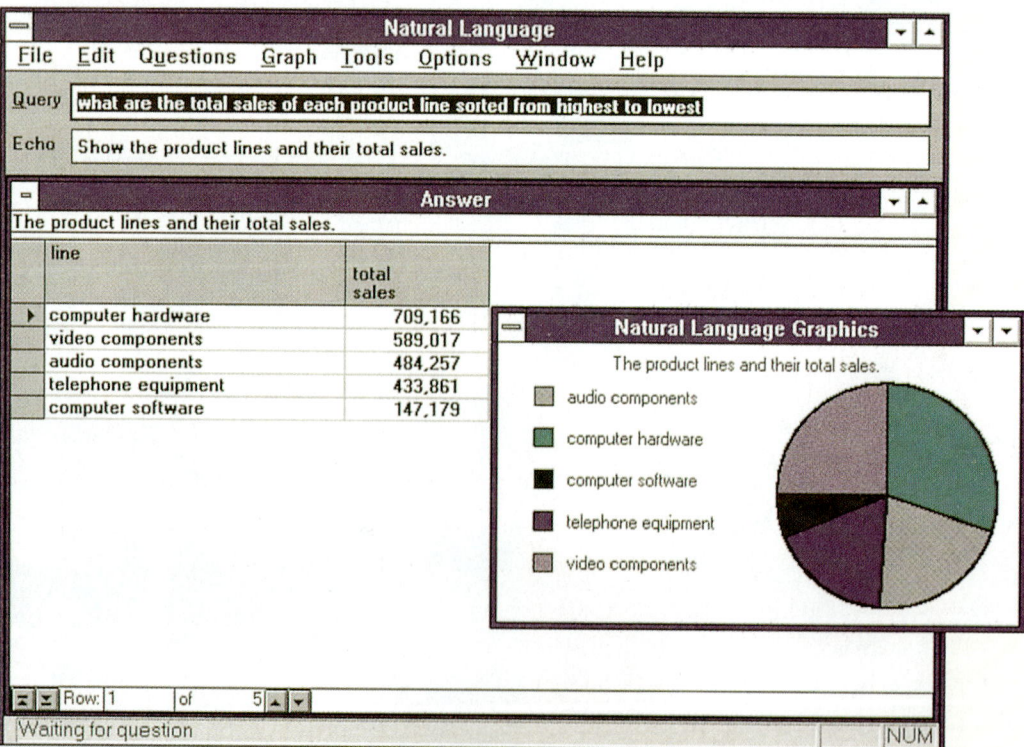

Figure 12-30

What You Should Know

1. A **computer program** is a detailed set of instructions that directs a computer to perform the tasks necessary to process data into information. **Program development** is the process of producing one or more programs to perform specific tasks on a computer. The process of program development has evolved into a series of five steps most experts agree should take place when any program is developed: (1) review of program specifications, (2) program design, (3) coding, (4) testing, and (5) finalizing documentation.

2. **Program specifications** can consist of data flow diagrams, system flowcharts, process specifications that indicate the action to be taken on the data, a data dictionary identifying the data elements that will be used, screen formats, report layouts, and actual documents. These documents help the programmer understand the work that needs to be done by the program.

3. During **program design**, a logical solution to the programming task is developed and documented. The solution is broken down into a step-by-step procedure called an **algorithm**. A methodology called **structured program design** emphasizes three main program concepts: modules, control structures, and single entry/single exit.

4. Each **module**, sometimes referred to as a **subroutine** in programming, performs a given task within the program. **Structure charts**, also called hierarchy charts, are often used to decompose and represent the modules of a program.

5. In structured program design, three basic **control structures** are used to form the logic of a program. In the **sequence structure**, one process occurs immediately after another. The **selection structure**, or **if-then-else structure**, gives programmers a way to represent conditional program logic. A variation of the selection structure, the **case structure**, is used when a condition being tested can lead to more than two alternatives. The **iteration structure**, or **looping structure**, means one or more processes continue to occur as long as a given condition remains true. There are two forms of this control structure: the **do-while structure** and the **do-until structure**.

6. An important concept in structured programming is **single entry/single exit**, meaning there is only one entry point and one exit point for each of the three control structures. An **entry point** is the point where a control structure is entered. An **exit point** is the point where the control structure is exited.

7. Two commonly used design tools are program flowcharts and pseudocode. In a **program flowchart**, all the logical steps of a program are represented by a combination of symbols and text. In **pseudocode**, the logical steps in the solution of a problem are written as English statements, and indentations are used to represent the control structures. To ensure that the program design is efficient and correct, many organizations use a **structured walkthrough**, which is a review of the program logic by other members of the development team.

8. **Coding** the program refers to the process of writing the program instructions that process data and produce the output specified in the program design. **Code standards** enable the same program to work on different types of computers. A **code library** stores partial or complete programs written to solve a particular problem.

9. Before a program is used to process real data and produce information, it should be thoroughly tested. **Desk checking** is the process of reading the program and mentally reviewing its logic. Desk checking can also uncover **syntax errors**, which are violations of the grammar rules of the language in which the program is written. During **logic testing**, the sequence of program instructions is tested to make sure it provides the correct result. Logic testing is done with **test data**, which is data that simulates the type of input the program will process when it is implemented. **Debugging** refers to the process of locating and correcting program errors, called **bugs**, found during testing. Most programming languages include a **debugger**, a program that identifies syntax errors and allows the programmer to stop the program while it is running to examine values.

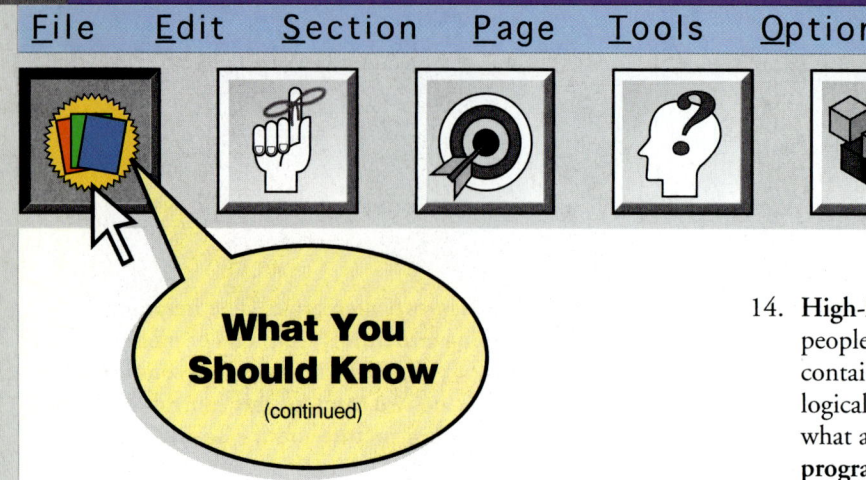

10. Documentation, the preparation of documents explaining the program, should be an ongoing part of developing a program and should only be finalized (organized and brought together) after the program is successfully tested and ready for implementation. **Program maintenance** includes all changes to a program once it is implemented and processing real transactions.

11. A **programming language** is a set of written words and symbols that allows the programmer or user to communicate with the computer. Programming languages can be classified into one of four categories: machine language, assembly language, high-level languages, and fourth-generation languages.

12. **Machine language** is the fundamental language of the computer's processor. Programs written in all other categories of languages are eventually converted into machine language before they are executed. Because they are written for specific processors, machine languages are also called **low-level languages**.

13. An **assembly language** is similar to a machine language, but uses abbreviations called **mnemonics** or **symbolic operation codes** to represent the machine operation code. Assembly languages usually allow **symbolic addressing**, which means a specific computer memory location can be referenced by a name or symbol instead of its actual address. Assembly language programs can also include **macroinstructions** that generate more than one machine instruction. Assembly language programs are converted into machine language instructions by a special program called an **assembler**.

14. **High-level languages** more closely resemble what most people would think of as a language because they contain nouns, verbs, and mathematical, relational, and logical operators that can be grouped together to form what appear to be sentences. These sentences are called **program statements**.

15. A **compiler** converts an entire high-level language program into machine language that is usually stored on a disk for later execution. The program to be converted is called the **source program** and the machine language produced is called the **object program** or **object code**. While a compiler translates an entire program, an **interpreter** translates one program statement at a time and then executes the resulting machine language before translating the next program statement.

16. Although a clear definition does not yet exist, **fourth-generation languages** (4GLs), sometimes called very high level languages, continue the programming language development by being even easier to use than high-level languages for both the programmer and nonprogramming user. A term commonly used to describe fourth-generation languages is **nonprocedural**, which means the programmer does not specify the procedures to be used to accomplish a task as is done with lower procedural language generations.

17. An extension of fourth-generation languages is a natural language. A **natural language**, sometimes called a **fifth generation language**, is a type of query language that allows the user to enter a question as if he or she were speaking directly to another person.

18. **Application generators**, also called **program generators**, are programs that produce source-language programs. A **menu generator** lets the user specify a menu (list) of processing options that can be selected. A **screen generator**, sometimes called a **screen painter**, allows the user to design an input or output screen by entering the names and descriptions of the input and output data directly on the screen.

19. **Object-oriented programming (OOP)** is a new approach to developing software that allows programmers to create **objects**, a combination of data and program instructions. Specific instructions, called **methods**, define how the object acts when it is used by a program. The capability to combine methods (instructions) with objects (data) is called **encapsulation**.

20. With OOP, programmers define classes of objects. Each **class** contains the methods unique to that class. The OOP capability to pass methods to lower levels is called **inheritance**. A specific **instance** of an object contains all methods from its higher level classes plus any methods unique to the object. When an OOP object is sent an instruction to do something, called a **message**, the message does not have to tell the OOP object exactly what to do, because *what to do* is defined by the methods the OOP object contains or has inherited.

21. OOP languages are often described as being event-driven instead of procedural. **Event-driven** means the program is designed to respond to events that can take place when an application is run. Closely related to OOP are **object-oriented software**, applications that are developed using OOP programming techniques, and **object-oriented operating systems**, which are operating systems specifically designed to run OOP applications.

22. Although hundreds of programming languages have been developed, only a few are used extensively enough to be recognized as industry standards.

23. **BASIC**, which stands for **B**eginner's **A**ll-purpose **S**ymbolic **I**nstruction **C**ode, was originally designed to be a simple, interactive programming language and is widely used on both PCs and minicomputers to develop business applications. Other versions of BASIC have been developed including Microsoft **QuickBASIC** (also referred to as **QBASIC**). Microsoft **Visual Basic** is an object-oriented extension of the BASIC programming language.

24. **COBOL** (**CO**mmon **B**usiness **O**riented **L**anguage), developed by a committee of representatives from both government and industry, is one of the most widely used programming languages for business applications.

25. The C programming language was originally designed for writing systems software, but is now considered a general-purpose programming language and is widely used on PCs. **C++** is an object-oriented extension of the C programming language.

26. **FORTRAN** (**FOR**mula **TRAN**slator) is considered the first high-level language developed and is noted for its capability to easily express and efficiently calculate mathematical equations. The **Pascal** language, available for use on both personal and large computers, was developed for teaching programming and fosters the development of programs that follow structured program design. The programming language **Ada**, designed to facilitate the writing and maintenance of large programs used over a long period of time, encourages coding of readable programs that are also portable.

27. Factors to be considered when choosing a programming language include: (1) the programming standards of the organization, (2) the need to interface with other programs, (3) the suitability of a language to the application to be programmed, (4) the expertise of the available programmers, and (5) the need for the application to be portable.

Terms to Remember

Ada (12.23)
algorithm (12.4)
application generators (12.16)
assembler (12.14)
assembly language (12.13)

BASIC (12.19)
bugs (12.10)

C (12.21)
C++ (12.22)
case structure (12.5)
class (12.17)
COBOL (12.21)
code library (12.9)
code standards (12.9)
coding (12.9)
compiler (12.14)
computer program (12.2)
control structures (12.4)

debugger (12.10)
debugging (12.10)
desk checking (12.10)
do-until structure (12.5)
do-while structure (12.5)

encapsulation (12.17)
entry point (12.6)
event-driven (12.18)
exit point (12.6)

fifth-generation language (12.16)
FORTRAN (12.22)
fourth-generation languages (4GLs) (12.15)

hierarchy charts (12.4)
high-level languages (12.14)

if-then-else structure (12.5)
inheritance (12.17)
instance (12.17)
interpreter (12.15)
iteration structure (12.5)

logic testing (12.10)
looping structure (12.5)
low-level languages (12.13)

machine language (12.13)
macroinstructions (12.14)
menu generator (12.16)
message (12.17)
methods (12.17)
mnemonics (12.13)
module (12.4)

natural language (12.16)
nonprocedural (12.15)

object code (12.14)
object program (12.14)
object-oriented operating systems (12.18)
object-oriented programming (OOP) (12.17)
object-oriented software (12.18)
objects (12.17)

Pascal (12.23)
program design (12.4)
program development (12.2)
program flowchart (12.7)
program generators (12.16)
program maintenance (12.11)
program specifications (12.3)
program statements (12.14)
programming language (12.12)
pseudocode (12.8)

QBASIC (12.19)
QuickBASIC (12.19)

screen generator (12.16)
screen painter (12.16)
selection structure (12.5)
sequence structure (12.5)
single entry/single exit (12.6)
source program (12.14)
structure charts (12.4)
structured program design (12.4)
structured walkthrough (12.8)
subroutine (12.4)
symbolic addressing (12.13)
symbolic operation code (12.13)
syntax errors (12.10)

test data (12.10)

very high level languages (12.15)
Visual Basic (12.20)

Test Your Knowledge

Fill in the Blanks

1. A(n) _____ is a detailed set of instructions that directs a computer to perform the tasks necessary to process data into information.
2. Structured program design is a methodology emphasizing three main program design concepts: _____, which perform a given task within the program; _____, which form the logic of the program; and _____, meaning there is only one entry point and one exit point for each control structure.
3. A(n) _____ is a set of written words and symbols that allows the programmer or user to communicate with the computer.
4. _____ are programs that produce source-oriented programs based on input, output, and processing specifications entered by the user.
5. _____, an interactive programming language originally designed for college students, is widely used on both PCs and minicomputers to develop business applications; while _____, one of the more widely used programming languages for business applications, is very good for processing large files and performing relatively simple calculations.

Short Answer

1. What are the five steps in program development? Briefly describe each.
2. What do the sequence structure, selection structure, and iteration structure have in common? How are they different?
3. How are machine languages and assembly languages different? Why are they both considered low-level languages? In what way are low-level languages different from high-level languages?
4. What is object-oriented programming (OOP)? How are traditional programming methods different from object-oriented programming? Why are OOP languages often described as being event-driven, instead of procedural?
5. What factors should be considered when choosing a programming language? Briefly explain the importance of each.

Label the Figure

Instructions: In the following figure, identify each of the standard symbols used to create program flowcharts.

Points to Ponder

1

When computers were first introduced in schools, computer programming was routinely taught to students at the college, high school, and even elementary school levels. As time passed, however, the emphasis turned toward learning to use productivity software. Some educators feel programming should still be an integral part of computer education. They point out that many new applications include a programming language with which users can write programs to work in the application. They also maintain that knowledge of programming helps people recognize the kinds of problems that computers can, and cannot, be used to solve. Teachers also point out that programming improves logical and critical thinking skills. How important do you think it is to learn programming? Why? Who should be taught computer programming? Should programming in some form be a part of computer education at every level? Why or why not?

2

Using structured program design concepts and the flowchart symbols shown in *Figure 12-10* on page 12.7, prepare a program flowchart showing the logical steps in performing a common task such as balancing a checkbook or changing the oil in a car. Be as detailed and accurate as possible. When you are finished, ask a classmate to check the logic of your flowchart by performing a structured walk-through.

3

One programmer describes his job as being a combination of engineer and artist. What do you think he meant by this? Is computer programming a science, a skill, a craft, or an art? Why? Computer programmers in small organizations are generally responsible for all five steps in program development, while programmers in large organizations often divide up program development and take part in only one or two steps. If you were a programmer, would you prefer to work in a small or a large organization? Why? If you did work in a large company, in what step of program development would you be most interested? Why?

4

One day in 1990, a software bug prevented the AT&T Long Distance Network from completing almost one-third of the long distance calls attempted, and it lost half of its 800-number service. The telephone system depends on more than two million lines of code. Given these numbers, do you think it is possible to remove all bugs from software programs? Why or why not? What can be done to reduce the number of software bugs? If software bugs are inevitable, or at least to be expected, what steps can people relying on computer programs take to deal with them?

5

Machine language programs tend to be lengthy, difficult to code, and time-consuming to write. Despite this, some U.S. Department of Defense programming is done in machine language because of the speed with which these programs can be executed. Using the four categories into which programming languages can be classified, describe an application you feel would be ideal for a language in each category. Tell why a language in that category would be an appropriate choice for the applications you describe.

6

Because each programming language has its strengths and weaknesses, different languages are used for different applications. Some authorities believe, however, it would be best to develop a single programming language that could be used for all applications. What would be the advantages of writing all applications using the same programming language? What would be the disadvantages? Do you think such a "generic" programming language will ever be developed? Why or why not?

Out and About

1. Some sophisticated application packages come with programming languages (sometimes called macro languages) that can be used to write programs within the application. For example, Microsoft Excel, a spreadsheet program, includes Visual Basic, and Microsoft Word, a word processing program, includes WordBasic. Visit a software vendor and find an application package that contains a programming language. What is the name of the application? What is the name of the programming language? For what purpose is the programming language used? If possible, ask to see a demonstration of the programming language. Does the language appear difficult to use? Why or why not? Would the inclusion of a programming language in the application package be a significant factor in your decision whether or not to purchase the package? Why or why not?

2. Just a few decades ago, computer programs consisting of 3,000 lines of code were thought to be long. Current word processing programs, however, might be as many as several hundred thousand lines long! What will computer programming be like in the future? Some experts see such trends as continued movement toward natural languages, greater participation in programming by computer users, and computers taking a more active part in their own programming. Using computer magazines and library resources, prepare a report on what programming will be like in ten years. How will programming be different from what it is today? Who will be doing the programming? How will they be doing it? What effect could developments in computer hardware have on programming?

3. Some organizations are forced to spend a great deal of time maintaining old, poorly written, badly documented programs that are nevertheless essential to the organization's business. Special software tools, such as Renaissance from Viasoft, have been developed to handle this problem. These software tools can convert cumbersome, disorganized programs into structured code. Using current computer magazines, research this or another software programming tool. How does it work? How much can it do? What does it not do? What are the advantages of using this tool? What are the disadvantages?

4. Visit the computer center at your school and talk to one of the individuals in charge about the most widely used applications. Choose at least two applications and find out the programming language in which they are written. Why do you think that language was chosen? Can you think of any other languages that might have been appropriate? Ask for a partial print out of each program. Circle and identify any program code related to the material in this chapter. If you think you can figure out the purpose of any program statements, underline the statement and explain it.

5. Programming languages can be classified as procedural (concerned with *how* something is done) or nonprocedural (concerned with *what* is to be done), business-oriented (capable of handling large data files and executing basic computations) or scientific-oriented (capable of performing sophisticated calculations), and general-purpose (designed to solve different types of problems) or special-purpose (designed to deal with one specific type of problem or application). Visit a library and prepare a report on one of the languages listed in *Figure 12-28* on page 12.24. Describe the history, intent, and use of the language. Then, categorize the language according to the classifications suggested above. Explain why you classified the language as you did.

6. While enrollment in computer science programs has dropped, estimates anticipate an almost 50 percent increase in the number of new programmer positions between 1988 and the year 2000. What knowledge and skills are required to land one of these jobs? Using classified ads from newspapers, computer magazines, and trade journals, try to determine what employers are looking for in prospective programmers. What programming languages are most in demand? What other course work is required? What kind of experience is helpful? What are the programmer's responsibilities? What salary can be expected? What are the opportunities for advancement?

In the Lab

 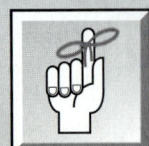    

Windows Labs

1 Adjusting Keyboard Speed With Program Manager on the screen, double-click the Main group icon. Double-click the Control Panel program-item icon. In the Control Panel window, double-click the Keyboard icon. In the Keyboard dialog box *(Figure 12-31)*, click the Help button. Read and print the information on the screen. Close the Help window. On the Delay Before First Repeat scroll bar, drag the scroll box to Short. Click the Test text box. Press and hold down any letter on the keyboard until it begins repeating. Drag the scroll box to Long. Test this adjustment. Which setting do you prefer? Set the scroll box to your desired adjustment. Repeat this procedure on the Repeat Rate scroll bar. Which setting do you prefer? Choose the OK button.

2 Shelly Cashman Series Programming Language Lab Follow the instructions in Windows Lab 2 in Chapter 1 on page 1.30 to display the Shelly Cashman Series Labs screen. Select Choosing a Programming Language and choose the Start Lab button. When the initial screen displays, carefully read the objectives. With your printer turned on, point to the Print Questions button and click the left mouse button. Fill out the top of the Questions sheet and answer the questions as you step through the Programming Language Lab.

3 Associating Files With Program Manager on the screen, double-click the Main group icon. Double-click the File Manager program-item icon. Maximize the File Manager window. Obtain a copy of the file WIN12-3 from your instructor. Place the diskette with this file into drive A. Click the drive A icon in the File Manager window.

Select the Help menu and choose the Contents command. Click the Glossary button. In the glossary window, click the word associate. What is the definition of associate? Close the glossary and File Manager Help windows.

Copy WIN12-3 by selecting it, selecting the File menu, choosing the Copy command, typing win12-3.abc and choosing the OK button. Double-click the file WIN12-3.ABC. What happens? Choose the OK button. Select the File menu and choose the Associate command. In the Associate dialog box, scroll through the files in the Associate With list box and select Text File (notepad.exe). Choose the OK button. Select the File menu and choose the Print command. Choose the OK button. Double-click the filename WIN12-3.ABC in the directory window *(Figure 12-32)*. What happens? With which application is WIN12-3.ABC associated? Close Notepad. Close File Manager.

4 Creating a Macro for Printing in Write Be sure Program Manager is not maximized. Double-click the Accessories group icon. In the Accessories group window, double-click the Recorder program-item icon. Minimize the Recorder window and double-click the Write program-item icon *(Figure 12-33)*. Double-click the Recorder icon at the bottom of the screen to open the Recorder-(Untitled) window. Select the Macro menu and choose the Record command. In the Record Macro dialog box, type print a file in the Record Macro Name text box, press the TAB key, and type p in the

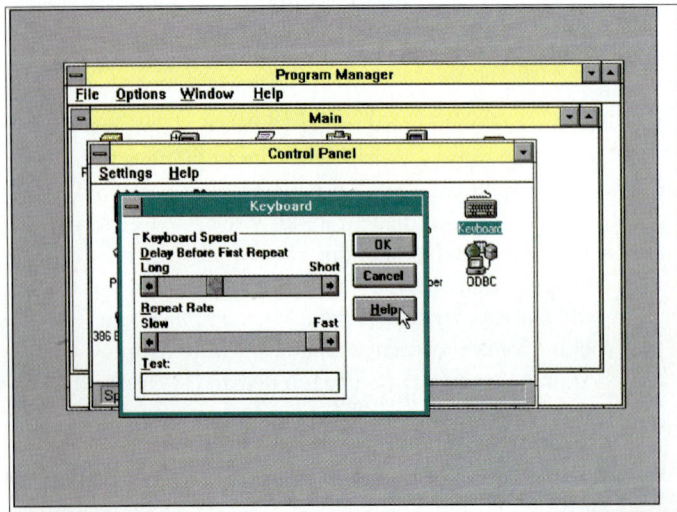

Figure 12-31

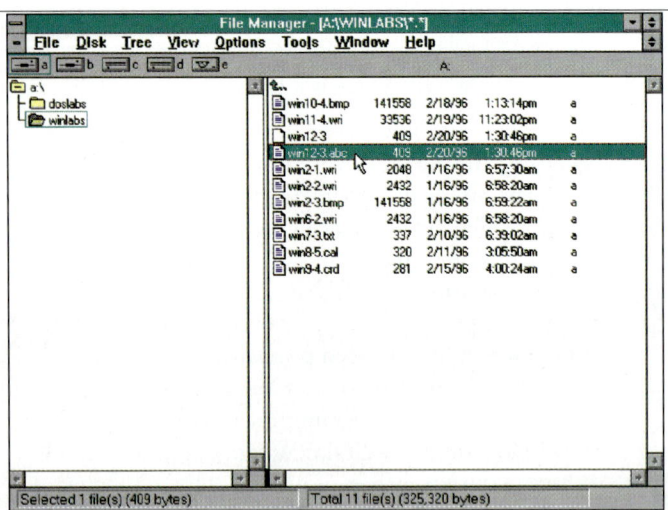

Figure 12-32

Shortcut Key text box *(Figure 12-34)*. Choose the Start button. What is the Recorder icon at the bottom of the screen doing now? In the Write window, select the File menu and choose the Print command. Choose the OK button. Click the Recorder icon at the bottom of the screen to display the Recorder dialog box. Be sure the Save Macro option button is selected, and choose the OK button.

In the Write window, type a few sentences explaining macros and type your name. Save the file using the filename WIN12-4. Press CTRL+P to execute the macro that prints the file. Close Write. Double-click the Recorder icon at the bottom of the screen. Save the macro using the Save command on the File menu. Use the filename WRITE. Close Recorder.

5 Using Recorder Help Open Recorder as described in Windows Lab 4 above. Select the Help menu and choose Contents. Read and print information on these Recorder Help screens: Record Simple Macros, Replay Macros, and Modify Macro Settings. Close Recorder Help. Close Recorder.

DOS Labs

1 Modifying a Program Obtain a copy of the file DOS12-1.BAS from your instructor. Insert the diskette containing this file into drive A. At the DOS prompt, type qbasic a:dos12-1.bas and press the ENTER key. Press SHIFT+F5 to run the program. At the Miles prompt, type 2 and press the ENTER key. At the Yards prompt, type 2 and press the ENTER key. At the Feet prompt, type 2 and press the ENTER key. At the Inches prompt, type 6 and press the ENTER key. Press the PRINT SCREEN key. What displays at the top of the screen? Press the ENTER key.

In the QBasic program, press the DOWN ARROW key four times to position the cursor on the P in the first PRINT statement. Press the ENTER key. Press the UP ARROW key. Type cls to clear the screen at this point in the program. Save the revised file by selecting the File menu, choosing the Save As command, typing dos12-1a and pressing the ENTER key. Press SHIFT+F5. Enter the same values as before. Print the screen. Exit QBasic by selecting the File menu and choosing the Exit command.

2 Creating a Batch File At the DOS prompt, type copy con dos12-2.bat and press the ENTER key. Type echo off and press the ENTER key. Type cls and press the ENTER key. Type echo HELLO and press the ENTER key. Press F6. Press the ENTER key. Type dos12-2 and press the ENTER key. What happens? Press the PRINT SCREEN key.

3 Using Help At the DOS prompt, type help and press the ENTER key. Obtain and print help on the topics: Qbasic and Batch commands. Exit Help.

Online Lab

1 Consumer Information Using one of the two online services you selected in Chapter 1, connect to the service and perform the following tasks: (1) Search the online service for Consumer Information. (2) Display and print product reviews for VCRs, automobiles, and computers.

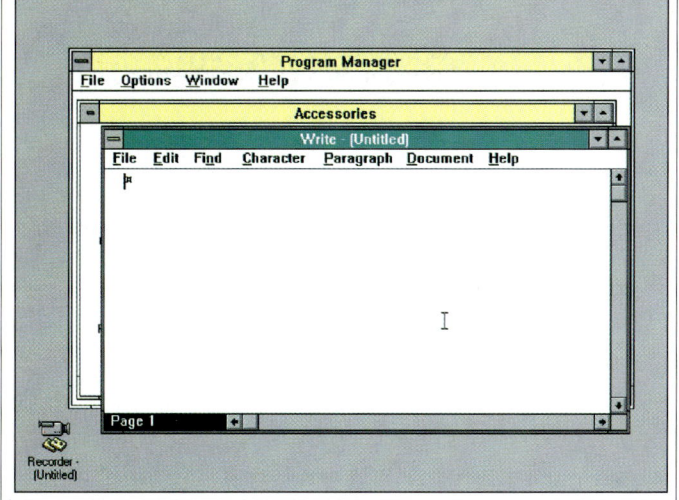

Figure 12-33

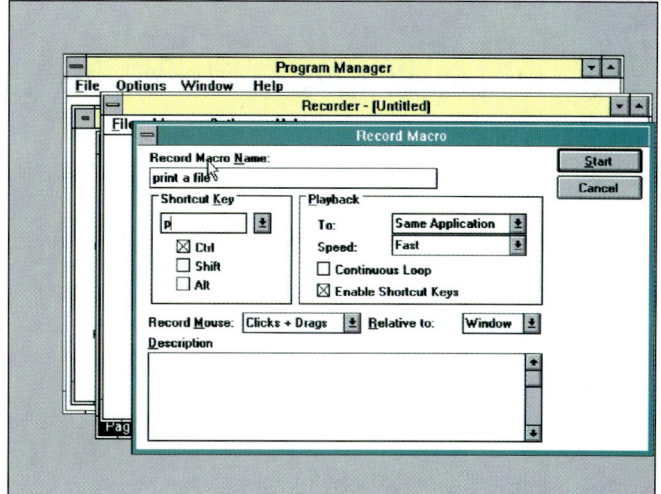

Figure 12-34

Multimedia

Multimedia is the combination of sound, images, graphics, and text. These elements are controlled by a computer system that allows a user to interact with the multimedia presentation. This interaction is one of the key features of multimedia. Unlike television, which can also combine the same elements, multimedia allows the user to choose what material will be presented and in what sequence. The following figures illustrate just some of the thousands of multimedia applications.

Figure 1 **MULTIMEDIA PC**
To run multimedia applications on your PC, it should be equipped with a sound card, a color monitor, and speakers. Because most multimedia applications are available on a CD-ROM, you should also have a CD-ROM drive. To record sounds, you need a microphone. Many PCs now come equipped with these components. Multimedia upgrade kits that contain these items can also be purchased.

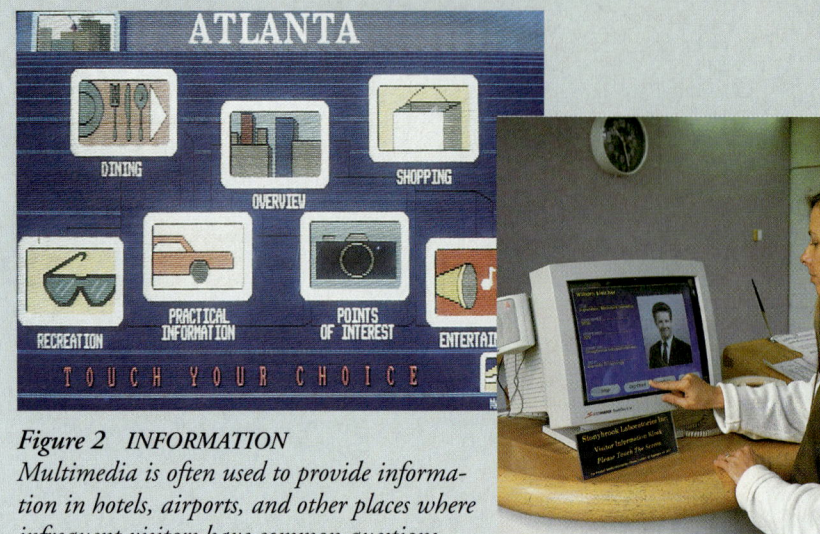

Figure 2 **INFORMATION**
Multimedia is often used to provide information in hotels, airports, and other places where infrequent visitors have common questions.
The touch screen on the left is available in many locations in Atlanta, Georgia to help visitors find their way around the city. The touch screen on the right is used to help visitors to Stonybrook Laboratories find the name and phone number of the person they have come to see.

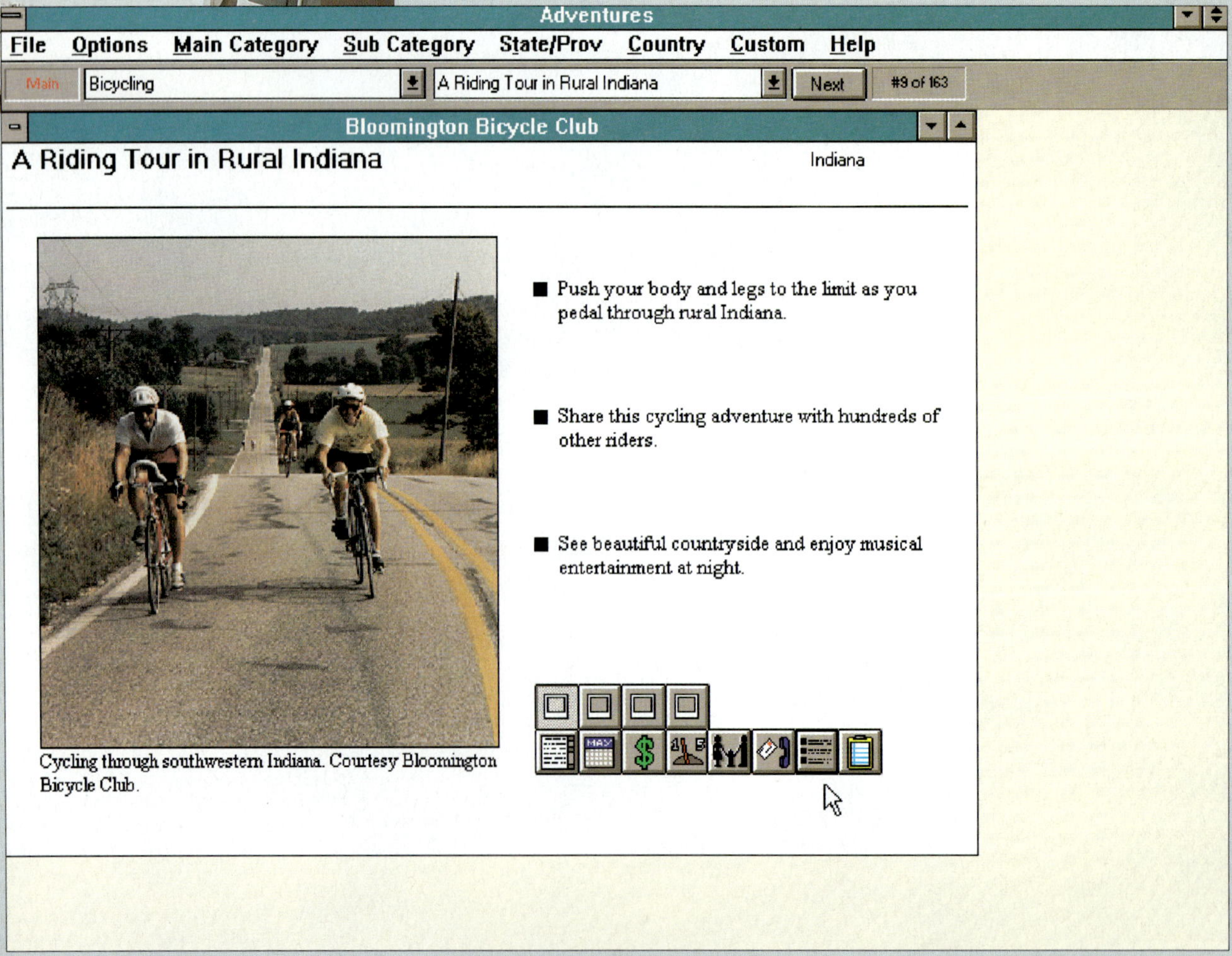

Figure 3 **TRAVEL**
Travel destination is a popular multimedia subject. Some focus on specific locations, such as Hawaii, and others include information on multiple sites. The Complete Adventures CD-ROM from Deep River Publishing includes information on hundreds of travel activities around the world. Besides photos and video segments, the package provides specific information on costs, the best time to visit, and whether or not the activity is suitable for children.

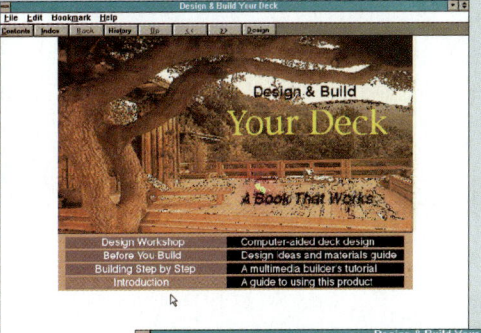

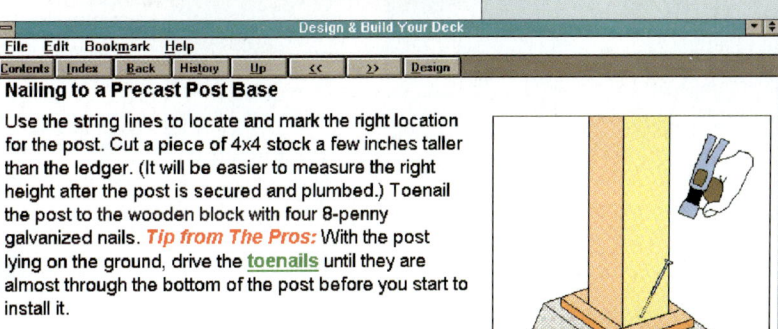
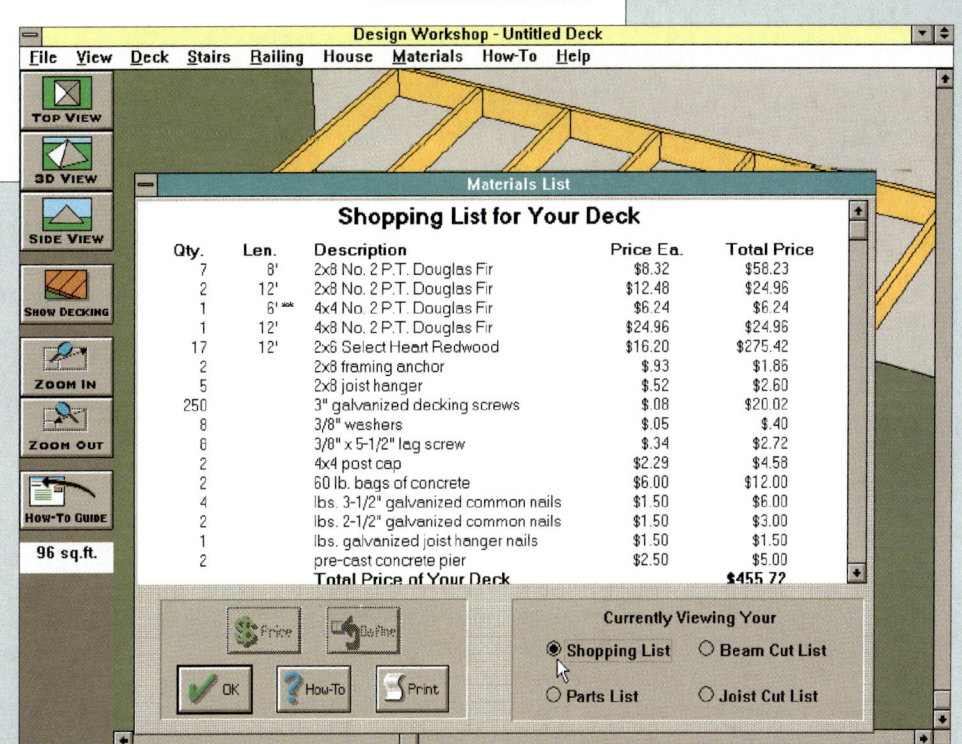

Figure 5 TRAINING
Many organizations use multimedia for employee training. The interactive nature of multimedia lets employees proceed at their own pace and review material in the sequence they determine.

Figure 4 DO-IT-YOURSELF
This multimedia software from Books That Work helps users plan and build a deck. The software includes actual deck photographs and standard designs that can be modified. Construction notes include animations that show how to cut, nail, and install various deck components. After the deck is designed, the package creates a detailed shopping list that includes estimated prices for each item.

Figure 6 REFERENCE
Encyclopedias are one of the more widely used multimedia reference materials. This screen shows information from the Microsoft Encarta interactive multimedia encyclopedia. The speaker-shaped icons at the top of the text indicate that audio segments can be listened to.

Figure 7 REFERENCE
Video segments are often included in multimedia packages. This figure shows a video clip of an eagle catching a fish that can be viewed in the Microsoft Encarta multimedia encyclopedia.

Figure 8 MAGAZINES
Several multimedia magazines are now available and more are planned. Medio Magazine includes regular sections on entertainment, living, news, finance, sports, kidstuff, and technology. Audio and video clips are included for recent movies, TV shows, and recordings.

MULTIMEDIA

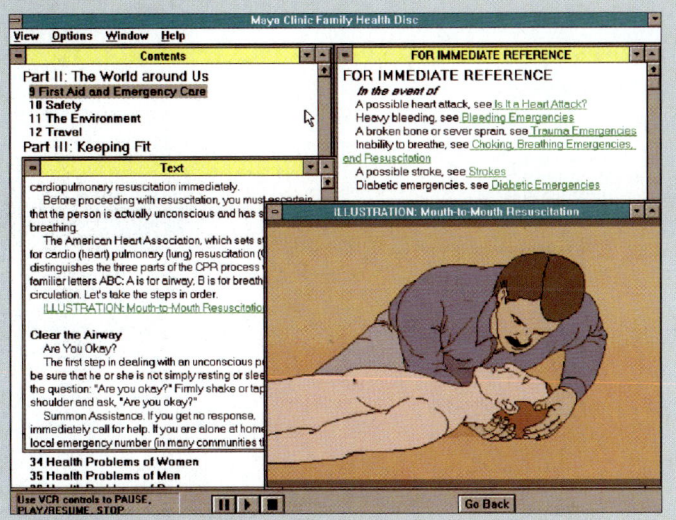
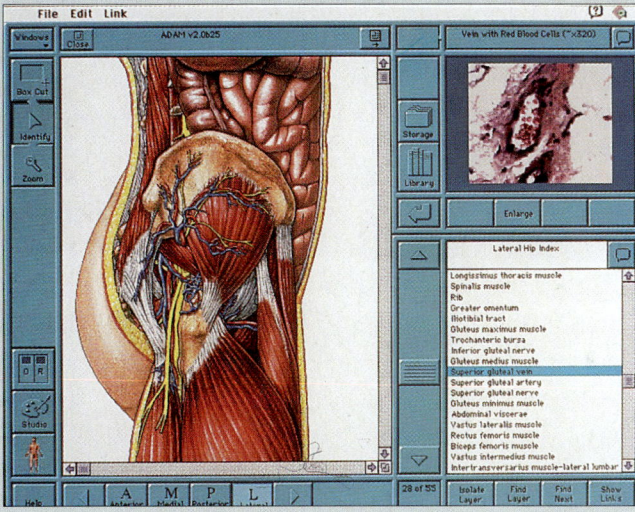

Figure 9 **HEALTH and MEDICINE**
The Mayo Clinic helped develop the multimedia family health reference shown on the left. Illustrations, animations, and actual photographs are included on hundreds of health and first aid topics. The A.D.A.M. (Animated Dissection of Anatomy for Medicine) multimedia software, shown on the right, is used by medical students to learn about the body and by practicing physicians to communicate information to their patients.

Figure 10 **MUSIC**
Multimedia software has been specifically developed to aid musicians in recording. Software exists that will automatically translate input from an instrument into sheet music. Once the music is recorded, it can be edited in a manner similar to editing a word processing document; sections of the music can be cut, copied, or changed to a different instrument. The tempo can be changed and special effects, such as fade and echo, can be added. After each change, the user can play back all or a part of the piece.

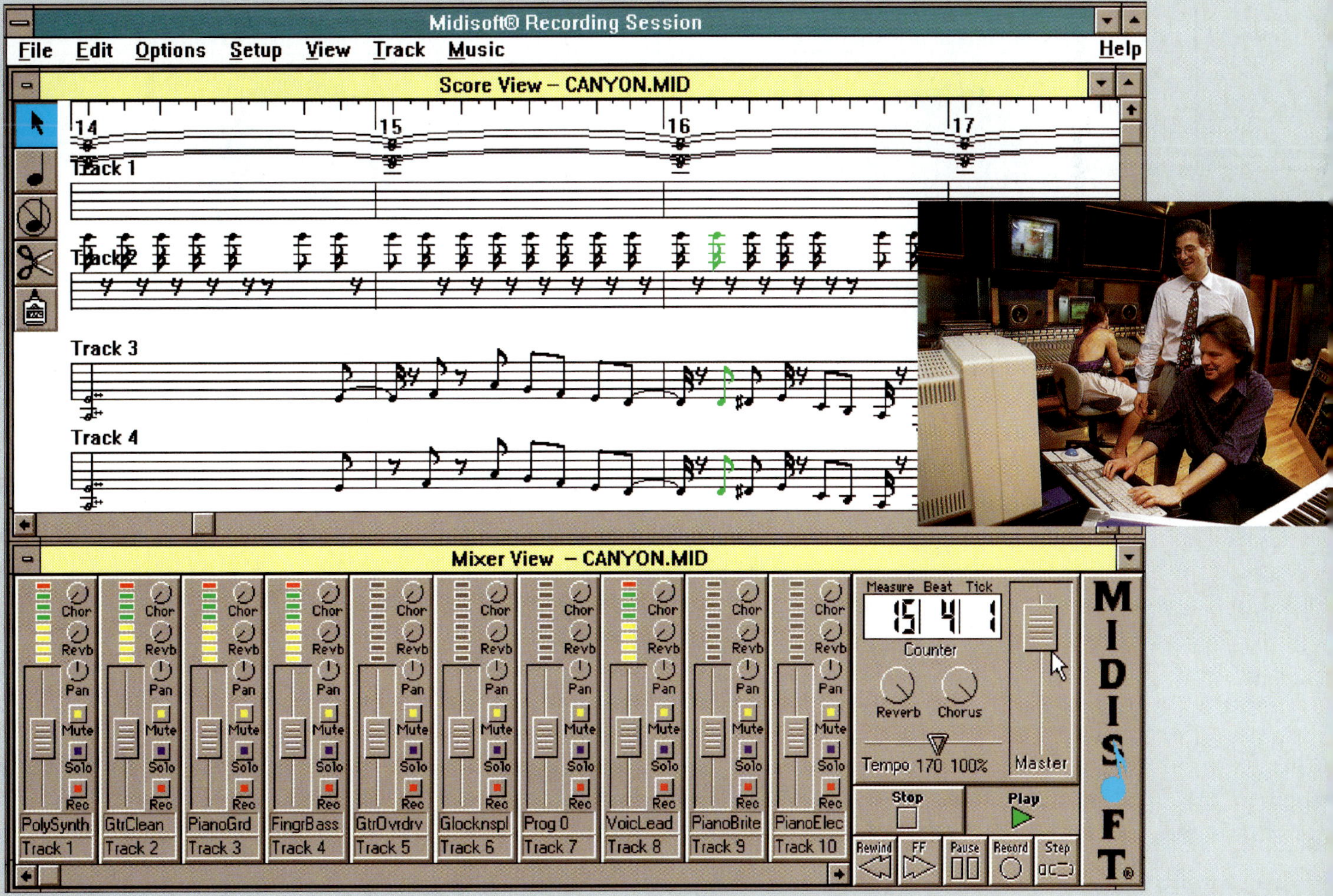

Figure 11 MORPHING
Morphing is an animation technique sometimes seen in multimedia presentations. It involves blending two images together. In the first screen, the image of the man on the left will be combined with the woman on the right. The lines and dots shown in the second screen help the software align the images. The morphed image is shown at the bottom of the second screen.

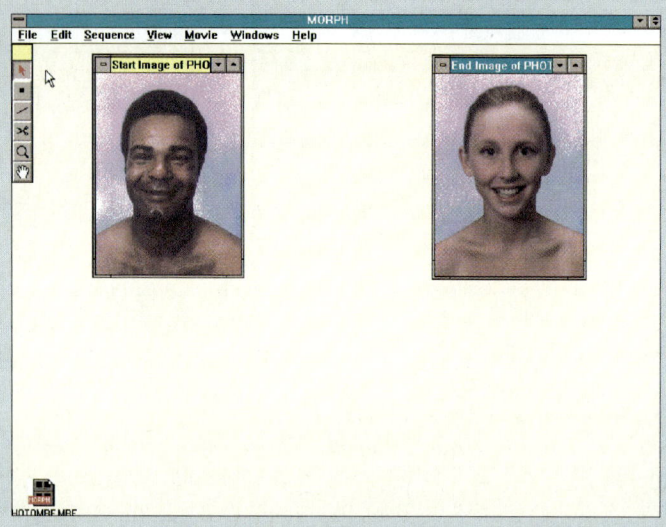

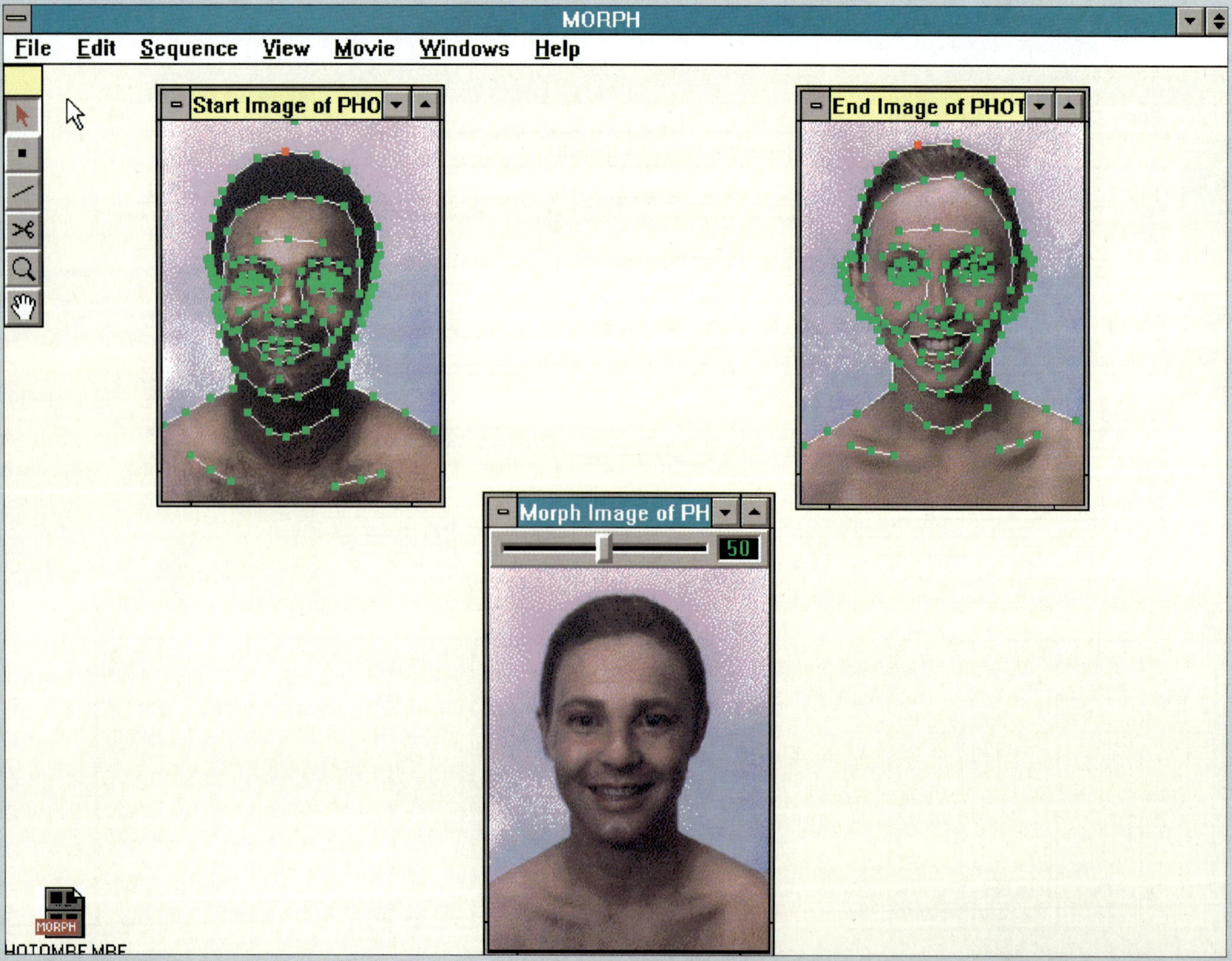

CHAPTER THIRTEEN

Security, Ethics, and Privacy

13

Objectives

After completing this chapter, you will be able to:

- Understand the different types of security risks that can threaten computer systems

- Describe different ways computer systems can be safeguarded

- Describe how a computer virus works and steps that can be taken to prevent viruses

- Explain why computer backup is important and how it is accomplished

- Discuss the steps in a disaster recovery plan

- Discuss ethical issues with respect to the information age

- Discuss issues relating to information privacy

The more people depend on computers in their work and daily lives, the more important it is to make sure the systems they use are protected from damage and misuse. People and organizations have come to rely on computers and some require their systems to be available 24 hours a day. For this reason, this chapter identifies the risks to a computer system and the safeguards that can be taken to minimize these risks.

In addition, society is becoming more concerned about the ethical use of computer systems and the difference between what is right, what is wrong, and what is criminal. Finally, the issue of information privacy is discussed including the current laws that are designed to keep certain data confidential.

Computer Security: Risks and Safeguards

A computer **security risk** is defined as any event or action that could cause a loss to computer equipment, software, information, or processing capability. The following section describes some of the more common computer security risks and what can be done to minimize or prevent their consequences. This section concludes with a discussion on how to develop an overall computer security plan.

Computer Viruses

A computer **virus** is an illegal and potentially damaging computer program designed to *infect* other software by attaching itself to the software with which it comes in contact. Usually, virus programs are designed to maliciously damage computer systems by destroying or corrupting data. If infected software is transferred to or accessed by another computer system, the virus will spread to the other system. *Figure 13-1* shows how a virus can spread from one system to another. Viruses have become a serious problem in recent years and currently there are thousands of known virus programs.

Three main types of viruses exist: a boot sector virus, a file virus, and a Trojan horse virus. A **boot sector virus** replaces the program that is used to start the system (the boot program) with a modified version of the program. When the infected boot program is run, it loads the virus into the computer's memory. Once a virus is in memory, it can spread to any diskette inserted into the computer. A **file virus** inserts virus code into program files. The virus then spreads to any program that accesses the infected file. A **Trojan horse virus** (named after the Greek myth) is a virus that hides within or is designed to look like a legitimate program.

Some viruses interrupt processing by freezing a computer system temporarily and displaying sounds or messages. For example, when the Stoned boot sector virus is triggered, it causes the infected computer to display a message saying "Your computer is now stoned" *(Figure 13-2)*. Other viruses contain time bombs or logic bombs. A **time bomb** is a program that performs an activity on a particular date. A well-known time bomb is the Michelangelo virus, which destroys data on a user's hard disk on March 6, Michelangelo's birthday. A logic

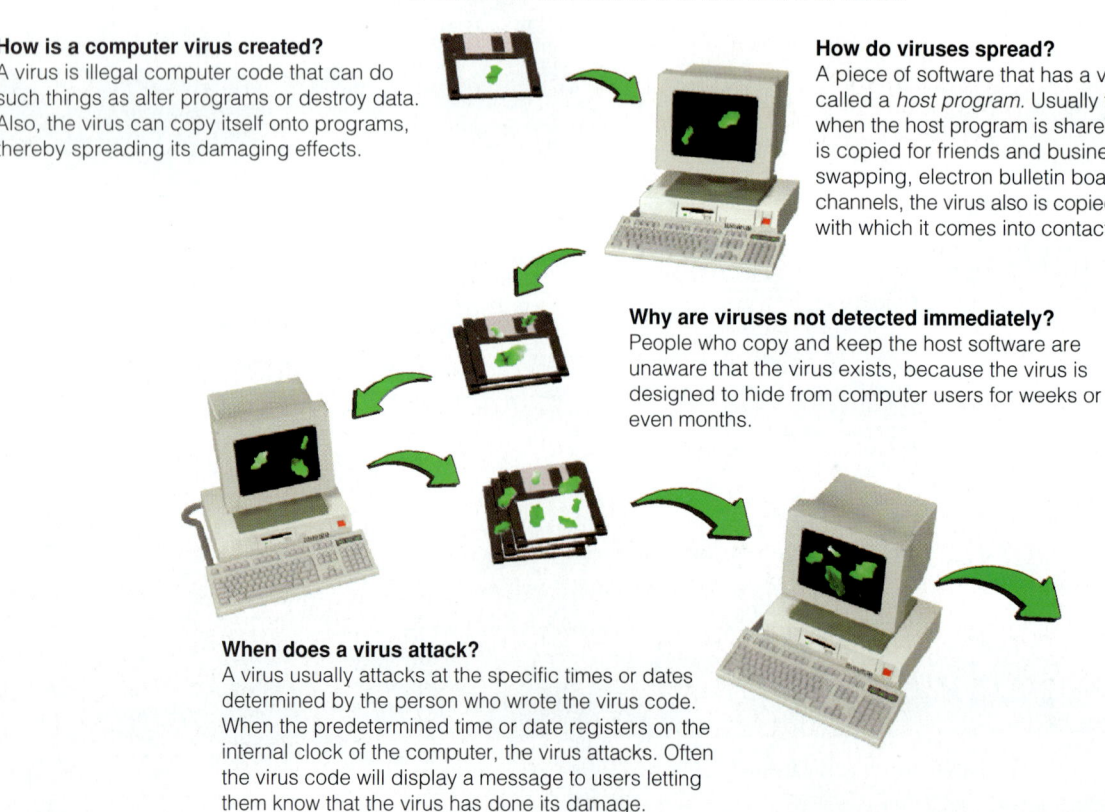

A COMPUTER VIRUS: WHAT IT IS AND HOW IT SPREADS

How is a computer virus created?
A virus is illegal computer code that can do such things as alter programs or destroy data. Also, the virus can copy itself onto programs, thereby spreading its damaging effects.

How do viruses spread?
A piece of software that has a virus attached to it is called a *host program*. Usually the virus is spread when the host program is shared. As the host program is copied for friends and business associates through swapping, electron bulletin boards, and other usual channels, the virus also is copied. It infects the software with which it comes into contact.

Why are viruses not detected immediately?
People who copy and keep the host software are unaware that the virus exists, because the virus is designed to hide from computer users for weeks or even months.

When does a virus attack?
A virus usually attacks at the specific times or dates determined by the person who wrote the virus code. When the predetermined time or date registers on the internal clock of the computer, the virus attacks. Often the virus code will display a message to users letting them know that the virus has done its damage.

Figure 13-1
This figure shows how a virus can spread from one computer system to another.

bomb is a program that performs an activity when a certain action has occurred, such as an employee being terminated.

Another type of malicious program is a worm. Although it is often called a virus, a worm, unlike a virus, does not attach itself to another program. Instead, a **worm** program is designed to repeatedly copy itself in memory or on a disk drive until no memory or disk space remains. When no memory or disk space remains, the computer stops working.

Virus Detection and Removal

To protect against computer viruses, **anti-virus programs**, called **vaccines**, have been developed. Most anti-virus programs, however, only protect against viruses written before the vaccine was released. Anti-virus programs work by looking for viruses that attempt to modify the boot program, the operating system, and other programs that are normally read from but not written to (*Figure 13-3* on the next page). Anti-virus programs also look for specific patterns of known virus code called a **virus signature**. Virus signature files need to be frequently updated to include newly discovered viruses.

One type of virus that is extremely difficult to detect is called a polymorphic virus. A **polymorphic virus** is designed to modify its program code each time it attaches itself to another program or file. Because it never looks the same, a polymorphic virus cannot be detected with a virus signature.

Another way vaccine programs prevent viruses is by *inoculating* existing program files. When a program file is **inoculated**, information such as the file size and file creation date is recorded in a separate inoculation file. Using this information, the vaccine program can tell if a virus program has tampered with the program file.

Besides detecting viruses, anti-virus programs also have utilities to remove or repair infected programs and files. Before attempting to remove or repair files, however, the anti-virus programs usually require the user to restart the computer using a rescue disk (actually a diskette). The **rescue disk** contains an uninfected copy of certain operating system commands and essential information about the computer that enables the computer to restart correctly. Once the computer has been *cleanly* restarted, the repair and removal programs can be run.

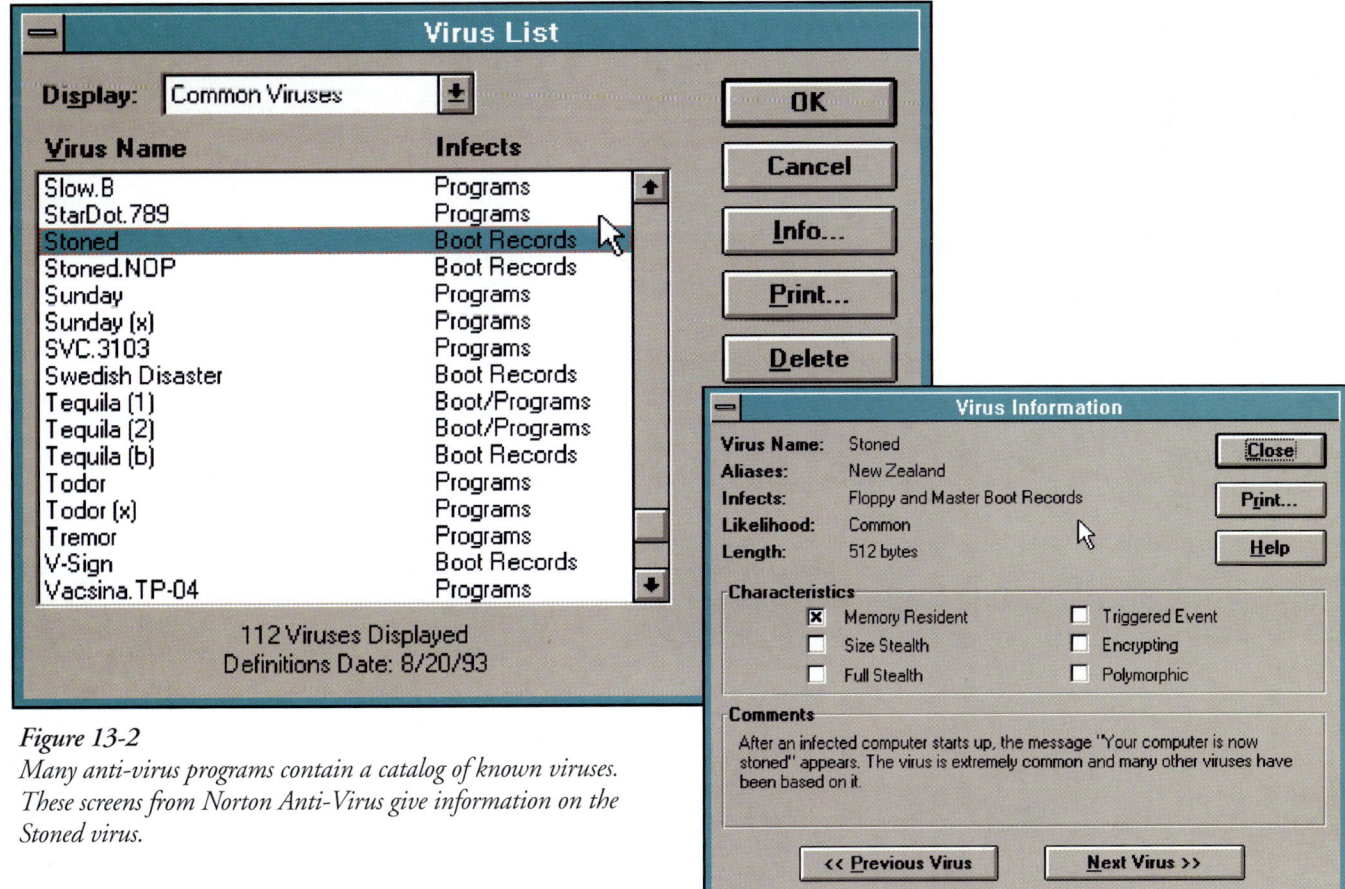

Figure 13-2
Many anti-virus programs contain a catalog of known viruses. These screens from Norton Anti-Virus give information on the Stoned virus.

To protect against being infected by a computer virus, experts recommend the following:
- Install virus protection software *(Figure 13-3)* on every system you work on. Most businesses and large organizations have adopted this policy. The cost of anti-virus software is much less than the cost of rebuilding damaged files.
- Before using any diskette, use a virus scan program to check for viruses. This is true even for shrink-wrapped software from major developers. Even commercial software has been infected and distributed to unsuspecting users.
- Check all programs downloaded from bulletin boards. Viruses are often first placed in seemingly innocent programs on bulletin boards so they will affect a large number of users.

Sometimes damaged files cannot be repaired and must be replaced with uninfected backup copies. The process of making backup copies of programs and files is discussed later in this chapter.

Companies and individuals that need help with virus-infected PCs can contact The National Computer Security Association (NCSA) at 900-555-NCSA for low-cost assistance.

Unauthorized Access and Use

Unauthorized access can be defined as computer trespassing or using a computer system without permission. Persons who deliberately try to illegally access computer systems, usually by using a modem, are called **crackers**. The term **hacker**, although originally a positive term, also has become associated with persons who try to break into computer systems. Some intruders do not do any damage; they merely wander around the accessed system before logging off. Other intruders leave some evidence of their presence by either leaving a message or deliberately altering data.

Unauthorized use is the use of a computer system or computer data for unapproved or possibly illegal activities. Unauthorized use may range from an employee using a computer for keeping his or her child's soccer league scores to someone gaining access to a bank funds system and creating an unauthorized transfer.

The key to preventing both unauthorized access and unauthorized use is computer security that controls who can access the computer, when they can access it, and what actions they can perform while accessing the computer. Many commercial software packages are designed to implement

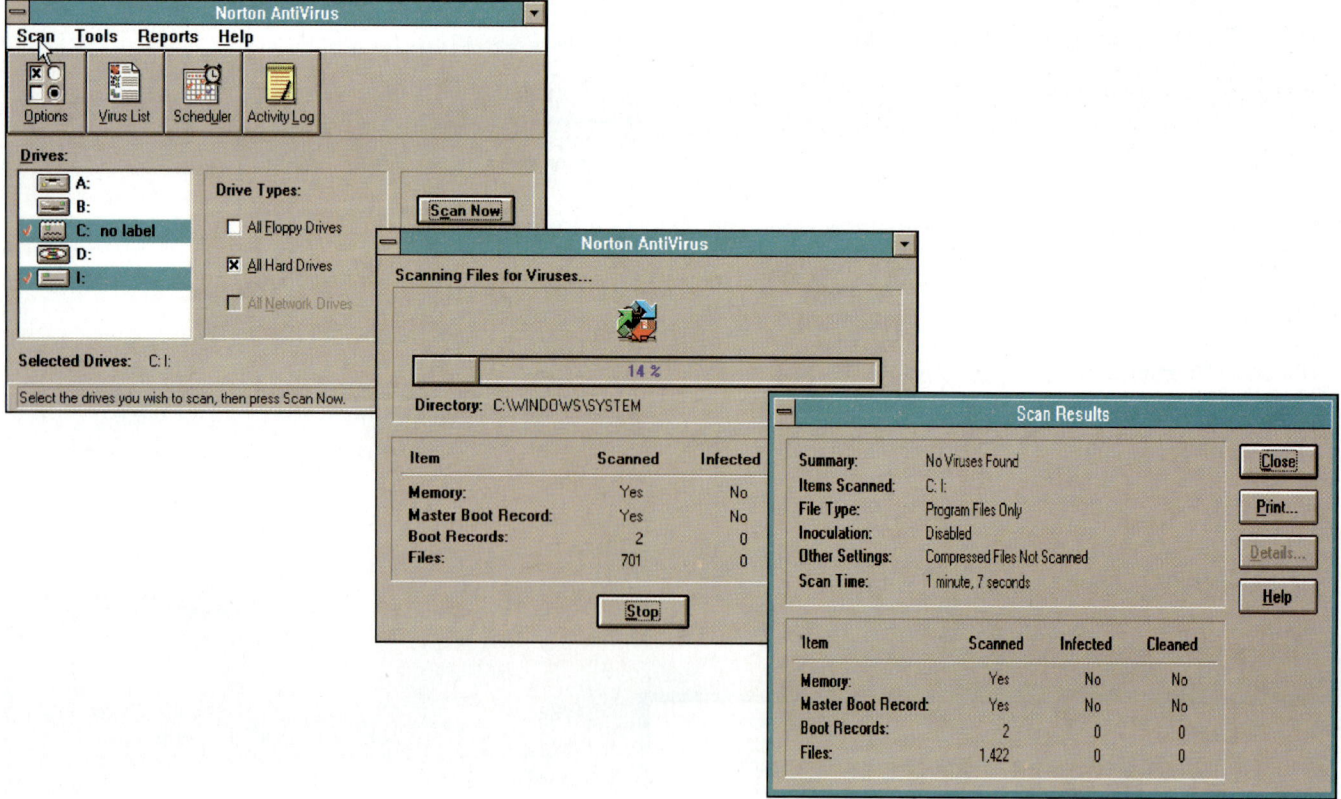

Figure 13-3
Anti-virus programs check disk drives and memory for computer viruses. The top screen allows the user to select the drives to be scanned. The middle screen displays the status during the scan, and the bottom screen shows the results.

these types of **access controls** through a process called identification and authentication. **Identification** verifies that the user is a valid user, and **authentication** verifies that the user is who he or she claims to be. The authentication technique used should match the degree of risk associated with the unauthorized access. An organization should regularly review the levels of authorization for users to determine if the levels are still appropriate. Three methods of authentication exist: remembered information, possessed objects, and biometric devices.

With **remembered information** authentication, a user is required to enter a word or series of characters that matches an entry in a security file in the computer. Most multi-user operating systems provide for a logon code, a user ID, and a password (all forms of remembered information) that must all be entered correctly before a user is allowed to use an application program. A **logon code** usually identifies the application that will be used, such as accounting, sales, or manufacturing. A **user ID** is a code that identifies the user. User ID's are usually assigned by the organization and are often a version of the user's name or initials. For example, a user ID for employee Mary Beth Gonzales may be GONZALMB; that is, the first six letters of her last name followed by her first and middle initials.

A **password** is usually confidential; often it is known only by the user and the computer system administrator. The logon code, user ID, and password must match entries in an authorization file. If they don't match, the user is denied access to the system.

Users usually select their own passwords. Often, they try to choose a word or series of characters that will be easy to remember. The problem is that if it is too simple, such as a persons initials or birthday, it can be easily guessed. As shown in *Figure 13-4*, each character added to a password significantly increases the number of possible combinations and the length of time it would take for someone to guess the password. Some techniques users can follow to create passwords are:
- Choose names of obscure places in other countries
- Join two words together
- Mix initials and dates together
- Choose words from other languages
- Choose family names far back in your family tree
- Add letters to or subtract letters from an existing word

PASSWORD PROTECTION

Number of Characters	Possible Combinations	Average Time to Discover	
		Human	Computer
1	36	3 minutes	.000018 seconds
2	1,300	2 hours	.00065 seconds
3	47,000	3 days	.02 second
4	1,700,000	3 months	1 second
5	60,000,000	10 years	30 seconds
10	3,700,000,000,000,000	580 million years	59 years

- Possible characters include the letters A-Z and numbers 0-9
- Human discovery assumes one try every 10 seconds
- Computer discovery assumes one million tries per second
- Average time assumes password would be discovered in approximately half the time it would take to try all possible combinations

Figure 13-4
This table shows the effect of increasing the length of a password made up of letters and numbers. The longer the password, the more difficult it is to discover. Long passwords, however, are more difficult for users to remember. Even long passwords do not provide complete protection against unauthorized access. So called "sniffer" programs have been used to copy passwords as they are entered by authorized users. The copied passwords are later retrieved and used to logon to the computer. Because the password used is valid, the unauthorized access is difficult to discover.

The more creative a user is when assigning a password, the more difficult it is for someone to discover. Many software programs now incorporate rules when users create their passwords. For example, a minimum length of 6 characters is common, and a mixture of numbers and letters is often required. One software package requires between 6 and 10 characters, 2 of which must be numeric. Following these guidelines, the password SUE04 is invalid because it is too short, but SUE0412 is valid. This password is also easy for the user to remember because SUE is her daughter's name and April 12 is her son's birthday (04/12).

A variation of remembered information authentication is called dialog. With **dialog** authentication, one of several possible items of personal information, such as a spouse's first name, a birth date, or a mother's maiden name, is randomly chosen from information on file and asked of the user. Like a password, the dialog response must match information already on file or access is denied.

A **possessed object** is any item that a user must carry to gain access to the computer facility. Examples of possessed objects are badges, cards, and keys. Possessed objects are often used in conjunction with personal identification numbers. A **personal identification number** (PIN) is a numeric password, either assigned by the issuing organization or selected by a user. An example of a PIN is the number that must be entered when using an automated teller machine (ATM) card.

A **biometric device** is one that verifies personal characteristics to authenticate a user. Examples of personal characteristics are fingerprints, voice pattern, signature, hand size, and retinal (eye) patterns.

A biometric device translates a user's personal characteristic into a digital code that is compared to a digital code stored in the computer. If the digital code in the computer does not match the user's code, access is denied.

Biometric security is gaining in popularity because it is a virtually foolproof method of authentication. Passwords can be copied and possessed objects can be duplicated, but personal characteristics like fingerprints cannot be lost; they

Figure 13-5
This retinal scanner identifies a user by reading the tiny blood vessel patterns in the back of the eye.

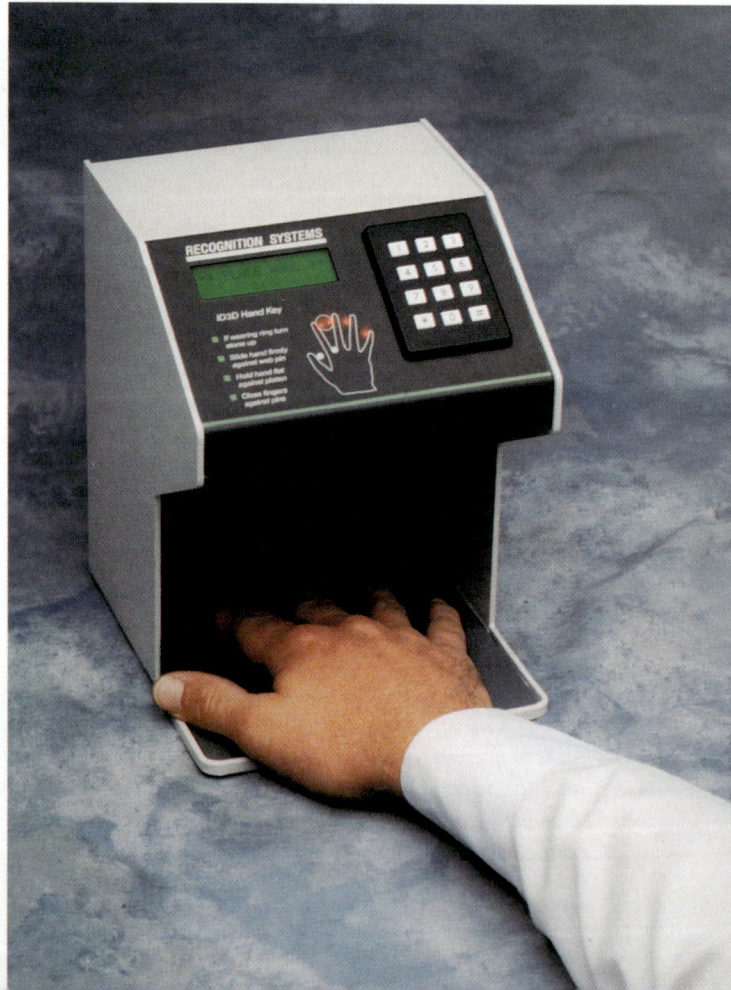

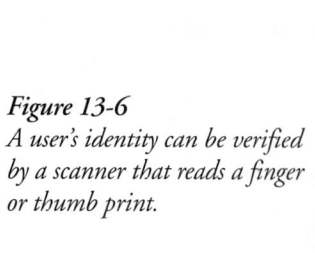

Figure 13-6
A user's identity can be verified by a scanner that reads a finger or thumb print.

are always with the user. Because they can be expensive, biometric devices are most often used with highly sensitive data by government security organizations, the military, and financial institutions.

Many types of biometric security devices are currently in use. Retinal scanners *(Figure 13-5)* read the tiny blood vessels in the back of the eye. These blood vessel patterns are as unique as a fingerprint, which also can be tested by a finger or thumb print scanner *(Figure 13-6)*. A biometric pen measures the pressure a person exerts and the motion used to write a signature *(Figure 13-7)*. Typing patterns and rhythms can be measured with keystroke analysis devices. The shape, size, and other characteristics of a person's hand can be measured using hand geometry systems. Finally, biometric devices can verify a person's speaking voice.

Although the advantages of biometric devices are clear, they do have some disadvantages. For example, if someone cuts his or her thumb, a finger or thumb print scanner may reject a valid user. If a user is nervous, a voice, signature, or typing pattern may not match. Some people also question the health safety of retinal scanners. However, because access security is becoming more important, these problems will be addressed and the use of biometric security devices is likely to increase.

An access control method sometimes used to authenticate remote users is the callback system. With a **callback system**, remote users can only be connected to the computer system after the computer calls them back at a previously established telephone number. To initiate the callback system, the user calls the computer and enters a logon code, user ID, and password. If these entries are valid, the computer instructs the user to hang up the telephone connection. The computer then calls the user back at the previously established number. This prevents access to the computer by a person who has stolen or guessed the logon code, user ID, and password. Unless that person is also at the authorized phone number, they will not get on the system.

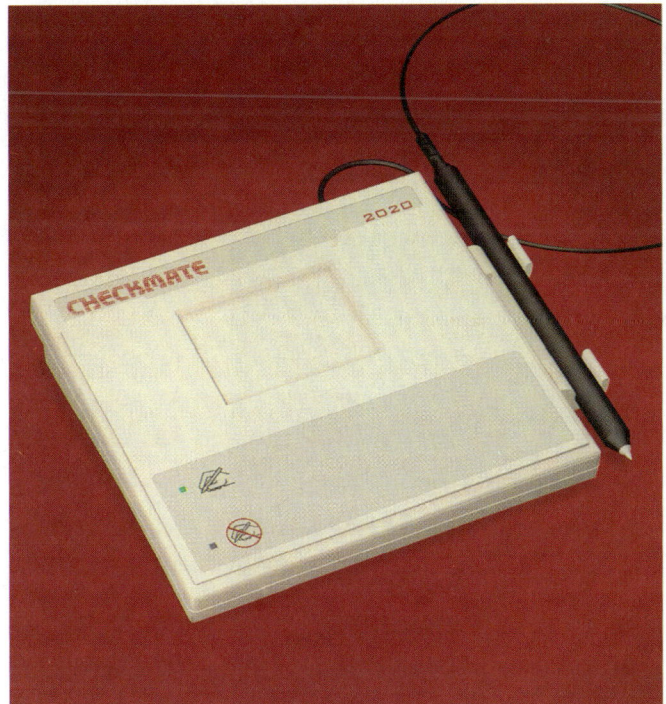

Figure 13-7
A biometric pen device can measure the characteristics of a person's signature.

CHAPTER 13 – SECURITY, ETHICS, AND PRIVACY

The callback system only works for users who regularly work away from the computer at the same location, such as from home or a remote office. The callback system does not work for employees who travel and need to access the computer from different locations and therefore different phone numbers.

No matter what type of identification and authentication is used, the computer system should record both successful and unsuccessful access attempts. Unsuccessful access attempts should be investigated immediately. Successful access should be reviewed for irregularities such as use of the system after normal working hours or by remote terminals. Records of system usage also can be used to allocate information processing expenses based on the percentage of system use by various departments. In addition, organizations should have written policies regarding the personal use of computers by employees. Some organizations prohibit such use entirely. Others permit personal use on the employee's own time, before or after work. Most organizations have informal policies decided on a case-by-case basis. Whatever the policy, it should be made clear to employees and any personal use should be approved in advance.

Hardware Theft

Hardware theft of most desktop and larger computer systems is generally not a problem. Physical access controls such as locked doors and windows are usually adequate to protect the equipment in a home or office. Most offices and some homes also install alarm systems. School computer labs and other similar areas that have a large number of irregular users often install additional physical security such as cables or other devices that lock the equipment to a desk or floor *(Figure 13-8)*.

Portable equipment such as notebook computers or personal digital assistants (PDAs) do pose serious theft risks. A fully configured high-end notebook computer may cost $6,000 or more and yet weigh less than seven pounds. Such a device can be a tempting target to a thief who can sell the stolen computer for a fraction of its cost and still make thousands of dollars.

Common sense and a constant awareness of the risk are the best preventive measures against portable computer theft. Physical devices, such as cables that can temporarily lock a portable to a desk or table, also can be used. Portable

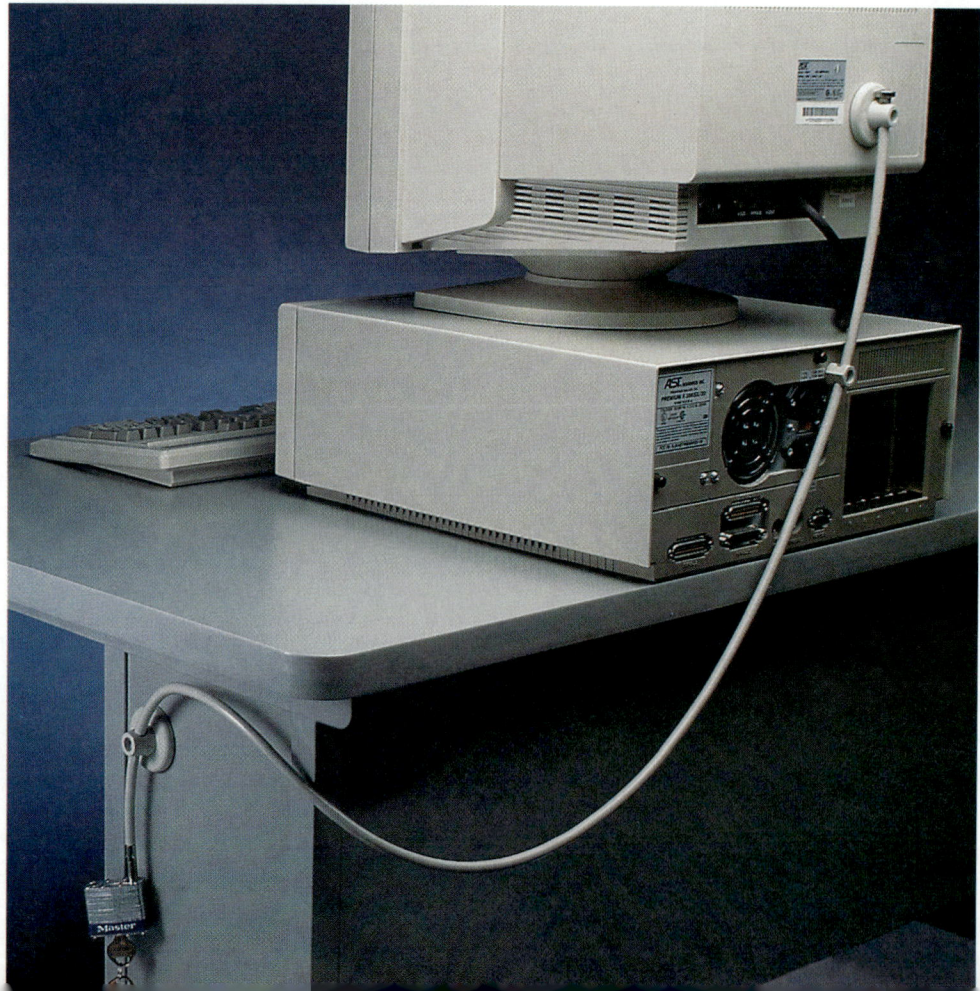

Figure 13-8
Cable locking devices can be used to prevent the theft of desktop and portable computer equipment.

computing devices should not be left out in the open, such as on the seat of a car, or be left unattended in a public place, such as in an airport or a restaurant. All information on portable computers should be regularly backed up.

Software Theft

With the increased use of personal computers, software theft, often called **software piracy**, has become a major problem. Some people have difficulty understanding why they should pay hundreds, perhaps thousands, of dollars for what appears to be an inexpensive diskette or tape. Perhaps they don't understand that ownership rights are not acquired when software is purchased. Users generally do not have the right to copy, loan, rent, or in any way, distribute the software. Estimates are that for every authorized copy of a commercial program, there is at least one illegal copy. One study reported that software piracy resulted in worldwide losses of more than $12 billion per year. Software piracy is a violation of copyright law and is a federal crime. Software companies take illegal copying seriously, and in some cases offenders who have been caught have been vigorously prosecuted. Penalties can include fines up to $250,000 and up to five years in jail. Many organizations and businesses have written policies prohibiting the copying and use of copyrighted software. Some of these organizations enforce the policy by periodically checking to make sure that all software is properly licensed. In order to promote a better understanding of piracy problems and, if necessary, to take legal action, a number of major U.S. software companies formed the Business Software Alliance (BSA). BSA operates anti-piracy hotlines in the United States and 24 countries *(Figure 13-9)*.

To reduce the cost for organizations with large numbers of users, software vendors often offer special discount pricing. The more copies of a program an organization purchases, the greater the discount. Network versions of many software packages also are available. These packages allow network users to share a single copy of the software that resides on the network server computer. Network software can be priced based on a fixed fee for an unlimited number of users, a maximum

Figure 13-9
The Business Software Alliance fights against software piracy by operating anti-piracy hotlines in the United States and 24 other countries.

number of users, or on a per user basis. Sometimes organizations will purchase a software site license. A **site license** gives an organization the right to install the software on multiple computers at a single site. The site license fee is less than if individual copies of the software package were purchased for each computer.

In addition to purchasing commercial software, an organization or individual also can consider acquiring shareware and public domain software. **Shareware** is software that users may try out on their own systems before paying a fee. If the users decide to keep and use the software, they send in a registration fee to the software publisher (Figure 13-10). **Public domain software** is free software that is not copyrighted and can therefore be distributed among users. The quality of shareware and public domain software varies greatly. Both shareware and public domain software can be obtained from BBSs and also from public domain software libraries.

Information Theft

There can be several reasons for the deliberate theft of information from a computer system. Organizations may steal or buy stolen information to learn about a competitor. Other information that has value includes credit card and telephone charge card numbers. Both types of numbers are frequently stored in an accounting or administrative department file on the computer.

Most organizations prevent information theft by implementing the user identification and authentication controls discussed in the previous section of this chapter on Unauthorized Access and Use. These controls work well to prevent the theft of information that resides on computers located on an organization's premises. Information transmitted over communications channels, however, offers a higher degree of risk because it can be intercepted. Portable computers that may contain sensitive company information generally do not have the same level of access controls and therefore also carry a higher risk of information theft.

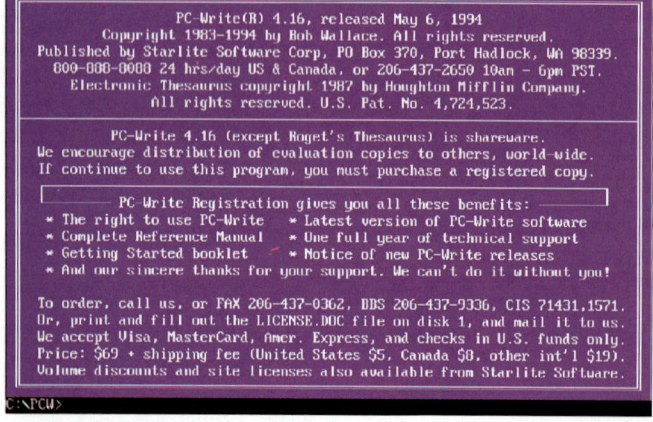

Figure 13-10
PC-Write is a shareware word processing program for the DOS operating system. Users can try the program for free. If they want to continue using the program, and receive a reference manual and support, they are given instructions on how to register the program. The registration form is included in the program as a document.

One way to protect sensitive data is to use encryption. **Encryption** is the process of converting readable data, called **plaintext**, into unreadable characters, called **ciphertext**. The conversion is accomplished with a formula that uses a code, called an **encryption key**, to modify the plaintext. The encryption key also is used by the person who receives the ciphertext message to **decrypt** (or **decipher**) the data back into the original plaintext.

Many methods exist for encrypting data. *Figure 13-11* shows examples of some simple encryption methods. Often, an encryption formula will use more than one technique, such as a combination of transposition and substitution. Some organizations develop their own encryption methods but most use available software packages. An encryption method widely used by the U.S. government is the **data encryption standard** (DES). *Figure 13-12* on the next page illustrates the Gettysburg Address encrypted with the DES.

Most data encryption is accomplished using software. In a controversial announcement made in 1993, the U.S. government proposed establishing a federal standard for voice and data encryption that would use a hardware approach.

The proposed standard called for the use of an encryption formula called **Skipjack** implemented in a tamper-resistant microprocessor called the **Clipper chip**. The idea was to have the Clipper chip built into voice, data, and fax communication devices. Since many computers now offer all three communications capabilities, Clipper chips also would be directly installed in PCs. Government security agencies such as the National Security Agency and the Federal Bureau of Investigation have stated they want a single hardware-based encryption method like the Clipper chip so they can, if necessary and, if authorized, monitor private communications. Because of widespread opposition to the government's proposal, plans to implement the Clipper chip have been put on indefinite hold.

System Failure

A **system failure** is defined as a prolonged malfunction of a computer system. System failures are caused by natural disasters such as fires, floods, storms, or by events such as

ENCRYPTION METHODS

NAME	METHOD	PLAINTEXT	CIPHERTEXT	EXPLANATION
Transposition	Switch the order of characters	COMPUTER	OCPMTURE	Adjacent characters swapped
Substitution	Replace characters with others	PRINTER	EOJLZRO	Each letter replaced with another
Expansion	Insert characters between existing characters	TAPE	TYAYPYEY	Letter Y inserted after each character
Compaction	Characters removed and stored elseware	HARDWARE	HADWRE	Every third letter removed (R and A)

Figure 13-11
This table shows four methods of encryption; or translating plaintext into ciphertext. Most encryption programs use a combination of methods.

electrical power problems that are discussed in this section. Two ways of minimizing the impact of a system failure, backup and disaster recovery planning, also are discussed.

One of the most common causes of system failures is electrical power variations. Electrical power variations can cause loss of data or loss of equipment. If the computer equipment is connected to a network, multiple systems can be damaged with a single power disturbance. Electrical disturbances include undervoltages, overvoltages, and noise.

An **undervoltage** occurs when there is a drop in the electrical supply. In North America, electricity normally flows at approximately 120 volts through the wall plug. Any significant drop below 120 volts is considered an undervoltage. A **brownout** is a prolonged drop in power and a **blackout** is a complete power failure. Undervoltages can cause a loss of data but generally do not damage equipment. An **overvoltage** occurs when the incoming electrical power increases significantly above the normal 120 volts. Overvoltages, or **power surges**, can cause immediate and permanent damage to hardware. A momentary overvoltage, called a **spike**, occurs when the power increase lasts for less than one millisecond (one thousandth of a second). Spikes are caused by uncontrollable disturbances, such as lightning bolts, or controllable disturbances, such as turning on a piece of equipment that is on the same electrical circuit. **Noise** is any unwanted signal, usually varying quickly, that is mixed with the normal voltage entering the computer. Noise is caused from external devices such as fluorescent lighting, radios, and televisions, as well as from components within the computer itself. Computer power supplies are designed to filter out noise and noise is generally not a risk to hardware or data.

To protect against overvoltages, surge protectors are used. A **surge protector**, also called a **surge suppressor**, uses special electrical components to keep an overvoltage from reaching the computer equipment *(Figure 13-13)*. Small overvoltages are absorbed by the surge protector without damage. Large overvoltages, such as those caused by a lightning strike, will cause the surge protector to fail in order to

Four score and seven years ago our fathers brought forth on this continent, a new nation, conceived in liberty, and dedicated to the proposition that all men are created equal.

Now we are engaged in a great civil war, testing whether that nation or any nation so conceived and so dedicated, can long endure. We are met on a great battle field of that war. We have come to dedicate a portion of that field as a final resting place for those who here gave their lives that the nation might live. It is altogether fitting and proper that we should do this.

“˜ÌÛ_»)…_¤.™ô$Éª|×æ[^ª1ÞjÖQ´ŸèÓk,\âÿÎ.ô
_|¦›ú{RÁ__sÜY&Ñ[‰5Ç_UiUÀ_µÓûT]È:ôdĂ&,
Ÿ__7ø+Y□{~]•dYôs□¦□Ū_¬èþ…këâ>äUzZ×"1-
â`·ƒ|K_uâ-\re—xé-¡-
ƒ_□%±êý°êÞþzvº[)ƒˉÑKcû3$ĭKÜâ¹ê‰“_3|ÑË_
"¢×*ö□¦Cpš7¿|_ÏÀû@·□ƒr"óG_¹-þ'Ðtøĩ<ô¢00
âÐ?+@§ĺò2_ÏĂ_x_êUÊêØO,"□Á)Q«¢)BŐÜ¨0□
åĂk°ÖÀ¹³_ÿ0¼ÞJ†<p6¨_ò_ŒÊÁÙK_WƒÊ__+ñ
osSŒSCGWT_+·ø|¾/M£D6u9uÕÛ•¼ôk□□0¼
#7,{Îé˙KŇ_.ôò›7ÛYur□w×Hi¶)Ç®ŐHÁ+□ô_SÚ
“»ˉ~û"□.£‹Ý¥ÒWm?²§Á□¢`_q¹f+ĭ¦ØSYÆ□Aè
å(¯U,6_Ë_BûMô@_Îá¿□'¬ôóyN…×s_¦‘~JZ□
Öe;MÙê_ÞxWÐ@£f…•(¨×Ë_¿Ê8_¼+¡À¶e²¨9°
HW_ì§À›¼ô□s¶ñâ1s§ŸìUn¦ò□V_pmOù×Ô…nì
EIQ_ÎÐç=›pU¿e±_P"Dgˆô9Ė¢I“_¯_œÛ_´ÉÐ[{
Õû¤ç˚…ĭ_ã/fœâ1k¡ûo«Ësʘ¤□_y¢_£©"

Figure 13-12
This figure shows the first two paragraphs of the Gettysburg Address in plaintext and ciphertext. It was encrypted using a software package that employs the DES encryption formula.

protect the computer equipment. Surge protectors are not 100% effective; large power surges can bypass the protector and repeated small overvoltages can permanently weaken a surge protector. Some experts recommend replacing surge protectors every two to three years.

For additional electrical protection, many users connect an uninterruptable power supply to the computer. An **uninterruptable power supply** (UPS) is a device that contains surge protection circuits and one or more batteries that can provide power during a temporary or permanent loss of power. The amount of time a UPS allows a user to continue working depends on the electrical requirements of the computer system and the size of the batteries in the UPS. A UPS for a PC should provide from ten to thirty minutes of use in the case of a total power loss. This should be enough time to save work currently being worked on and to properly shut down the computer.

Backup Procedures

To prevent against data loss caused by a system failure, computer users should have backup procedures. A **backup** is a copy of information stored on a computer. Used as a verb, to *back up* a file means to make a copy. **Backup procedures** specify a regular plan of copying and storing key data and program files. In the case of a system failure or the discovery of corrupted files, backup copies can be used to **restore** the files (reload the files on the computer). Backup copies are normally kept in fireproof safes or vaults or **offsite**, in a building different from the computer site. Offsite storage is used so a single disaster, such as a fire, will not destroy both the primary and the backup copy of the data.

An installation can perform three types of backup: full, differential, or incremental. A **full backup** includes all files in the computer. A full backup provides the best protection because all program and data files are copied. Because a full backup can take a long time, however, it is often used in conjunction with differential and incremental backups. A **differential backup** duplicates only the files that have changed *since the last full backup*. An **incremental backup** duplicates

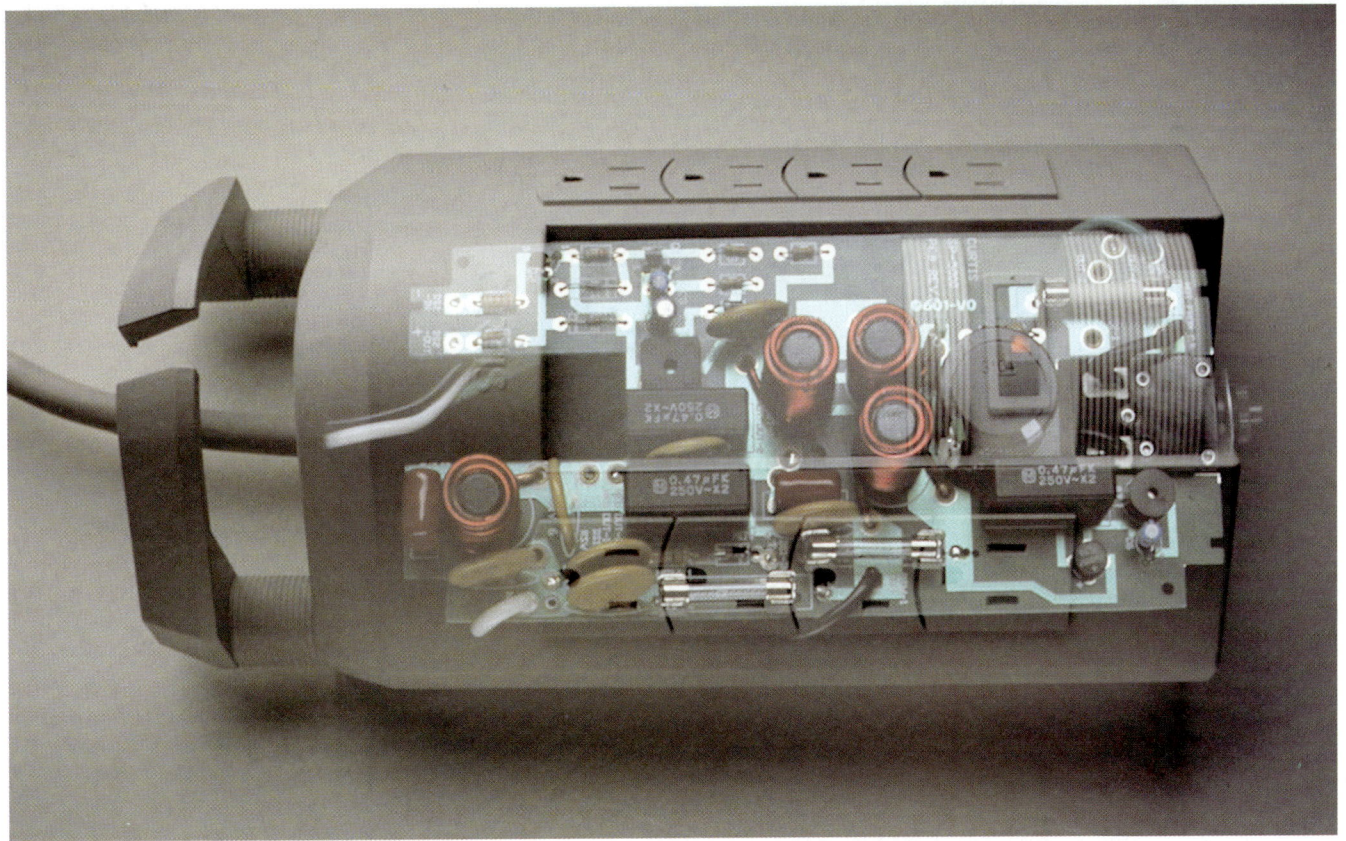

Figure 13-13
Circuits inside a surge protector protect against overvoltages.

only the files that have changed since the last full *or incremental backup*. The following will clarify the difference between a differential backup and an incremental backup. With a differential backup, you always have two backups; the full backup and the differential backup of all changes since the last full backup. With incremental backups, you may have several incremental backup copies. The first incremental backup copies all changes since the last full backup. Subsequent incremental backups only copy changes since the last incremental backup. Differential backups may be appropriate if there are relatively few changes in relation to the total amount of data to be backed up. If there are many changes, incremental backups will take less time. *Figure 13-14* outlines the advantages and disadvantages of each type of backup.

Generally, an organization develops a policy where a full backup is performed at regular intervals, such as at the end of each week and at the end of the month. Between full backups, differential or incremental backups are performed. *Figure 13-15* shows an approach for backing up a system for one month. This mixture of full and incremental backups provides an efficient way of protecting data and provides several restore starting points if a problem is found with incorrect data. Whatever backup procedures an organization adopts, they should be clearly stated, in writing, and be consistently followed.

Sometimes important individual files are backed up separately and a *three generation backup* policy is often used. The oldest copy of the file is called the **grandfather**. The second oldest copy of the file is called the **father**. The most recent copy of the file is called the **son**.

Backup and restore programs are available from many sources including most developers of anti-virus programs and developers of utility software. Backup and restore programs also are included with most operating systems and with backup devices such as cartridge tape drives.

Disaster Recovery Plan

Because the prolonged loss of computing capability could seriously damage an organization's ability to function, a disaster recovery plan should be developed. A **disaster recovery**

TYPE OF BACKUP	ADVANTAGES	DISADVANTAGES
Full	Fastest recovery method. All files are saved.	Longest backup time.
Differential	Fast backup method. Requires minimal space to backup.	Recovery is time consuming because need last full backup plus the differential backup.
Incremental	Fastest backup method. Requires minimal space to backup. Only most recent changes saved.	Recovery is most time consuming because need last full backup and all incremental backups since last full backup.

Figure 13-14
The advantages and disadvantages of different backup methods.

COMPUTER SECURITY: RISKS AND SAFEGUARDS

plan is a written plan describing the steps an organization would take to restore computer operations in the event of a disaster. A disaster recovery plan contains four major components: the emergency plan, the backup plan, the recovery plan, and the test plan *(Figure 13-16)*.

THE EMERGENCY PLAN

An **emergency plan** specifies the steps to be taken immediately after a disaster strikes. The emergency plan is usually organized by type of disaster, such as fire, flood, or earthquake. Depending on the nature and extent of the disaster, some emergency procedures will differ. All emergency plans should contain the following information:

- Names and phone numbers of people and organizations to be notified (e.g., management, fire department, police department)
- Procedures to be followed with the computer equipment (e.g., equipment shutdown, power shutoff, file removal)
- Employee evacuation procedures
- Return procedures; that is, who can reenter the facility and what actions are they to perform

THE BACKUP PLAN

Once the procedures in the emergency plan have been followed, the next step is to follow the backup plan. The **backup plan** specifies how an organization will use backup files and equipment to resume information processing. Because an organization's normal location may be destroyed or unusable, the backup plan should include an alternate computer facility. The backup plan identifies these items:

- The location of backup data, supplies, and equipment
- The personnel responsible for gathering backup resources and transporting them to the alternate computer facility
- A schedule indicating the order and approximate time each application should be up and running

For a backup plan to be successful, it is crucial that an installation back up all critical resources; that is, hardware, software, data, facilities, supplies, and documentation. Because personnel could be injured in a disaster, it is also crucial that multiple people, including possibly non-employees, are trained in the backup and recovery procedures.

The location of the alternate computer facility is also important. It should be close enough to be convenient, yet

DAY	TYPE OF BACKUP
Each Monday	Incremental or Differential
Each Tuesday	Incremental or Differential
Each Wednesday	Incremental or Differential
Each Thursday	Incremental or Differential
1st Friday	Full
2nd Friday	Full
3rd Friday	Full
End of Month	Full

Figure 13-15
This table shows a backup strategy that can be used each month. The tapes used for Monday, Tuesday, Wednesday, and Thursday backups would be the same each week. The tapes used for Friday backups would be used again the following month. A new tape would be used each month for the end of month backup. End of month backup tapes are usually kept for at least one year.

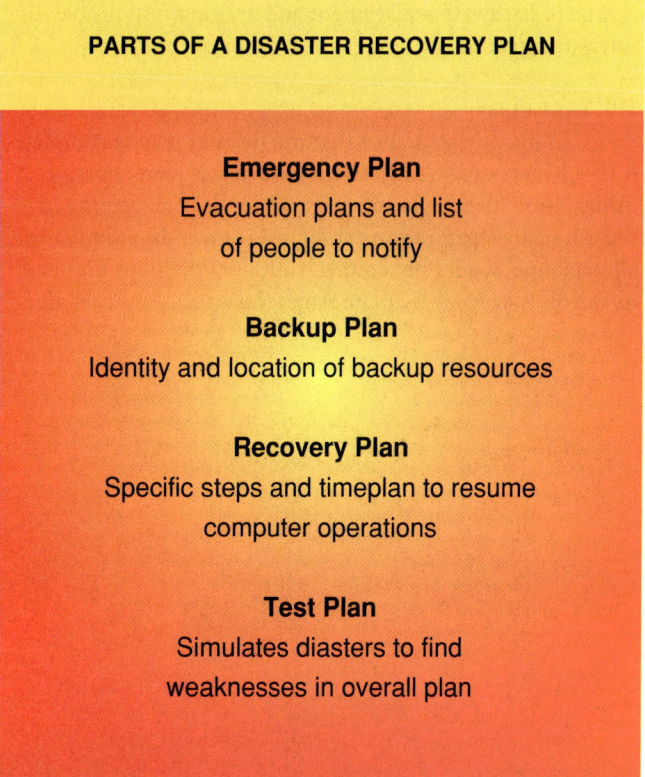

Figure 13-16
A summary of the four parts of a disaster recovery plan.

not too close that a single disaster, such as an earthquake, could destroy both the main and alternate computer facility. Two types of alternate computer facilities exist: a hot site and a cold site. A **hot site** is an alternate computer facility that has compatible computer resources; that is, it already has installed the necessary hardware, software, and communications equipment. Because installing and maintaining a hot site is quite expensive, many organizations instead use a cold site as their alternate computer facility. A **cold site** is an empty facility that can accommodate the necessary computer resources. A cold site requires immediate installation of computer equipment and software in case of disaster. Instead of using a hot or cold site as the alternate computer facility, some organizations enter into **reciprocal backup relationships** with other firms; that is, in case of disaster, one firm provides space, and sometimes equipment, to the other.

THE RECOVERY PLAN

The **recovery plan** specifies the actions to be taken to restore full information processing operations. Like the emergency plan, the recovery plan will differ for each type of disaster. To plan for disaster recovery, committees should be established, with each responsible for different forms of recovery. For example, one committee may be designated in charge of hardware replacement and another responsible for software replacement.

THE TEST PLAN

To provide assurance that the disaster plan is complete, it should be tested. A **disaster recovery test plan** contains information for simulating different levels of disasters and recording an organization's ability to recover. In a simulation, all personnel would be required to follow the steps outlined in the disaster recovery plan. Any recovery actions that are required but are not in the plan should be added to the plan. Although simulations can be scheduled, the best test of the plan is to simulate a disaster without advance notice.

Developing a Computer Security Plan

The individual risks and safeguards previously mentioned and the disaster recovery plan should all be incorporated into an overall computer security plan. A **computer security plan** summarizes in writing the safeguards that are in place to protect an organization's information assets. A computer security plan should do the following:

- Identify all information assets of an organization, including equipment, software, documentation, procedures, people, data, facilities, and supplies.
- Identify all security risks that may cause an information asset loss. Risks should be ranked from most likely to occur to least likely. An estimated value should be placed on each risk, including the value of lost business. For example, what is the estimated loss if customers cannot place orders for one hour, one day, or one week.
- For each risk, identify the safeguards that exist to detect, prevent, and recover from a loss.

The computer security plan should be updated annually or more frequently for major changes in information assets, such as the addition of a new computer or the implementation of a new application. In developing the plan, it should be kept in mind that some degree of risk is unavoidable. The more secure a system is, the more difficult it is for everyone to use. The goal of a computer security plan is to match an appropriate level of safeguards against the identified risks. Fortunately, most organizations will never experience a major information system disaster. Because many organizations and individuals rely heavily on computers, however, disaster recovery must be planned for.

Ethics and the Information Age

Like any powerful technology, computers can be used for both good and bad actions. The standards that determine whether an action is good or bad are called ethics. **Computer ethics** are the moral guidelines that govern the use of computers and information systems. Five areas of computer ethics that are frequently discussed are software theft (piracy), unauthorized use of computer systems, the accuracy of computer information, codes of conduct, and the privacy of computerized information. Software piracy and unauthorized use were covered earlier in this chapter during the discussion of computer risks and safeguards. Privacy of computerized information is discussed in a separate section at the end of this chapter. The following sections deal with the accuracy of computer information and codes of conduct.

Information Accuracy

Organizations have long been concerned about the accuracy of computer input. Inaccurate input can result in erroneous information and incorrect decisions based on that information. Information accuracy is even more of an issue today because many users access information maintained by other organizations, such as online service providers. Often, the organization providing access to the information did not create the information. An example is the airline flight schedules available from several online service providers. The question that arises is "Who is responsible for the accuracy of the information?" Does the responsibility rest solely with the original creator of the information or does the service that passes along the information also have some responsibility to verify its accuracy? Legally, these questions have not been resolved.

In addition to concerns about the accuracy of computer input, some people have raised questions about the ethics of using computers to alter output, primarily graphic output such as retouched photographs. Using graphics equipment and software, photographs can be digitized and edited to add, change, or remove images *(Figure 13-17)*. One group who is opposed to any manipulation of an image is the National Press Photographers Association. They believe that allowing even the slightest alteration could eventually lead to deliberately misleading photographs. Others believe that digital photo retouching is acceptable as long as the significant

Figure 13-17
This digitally altered photograph shows sports star Michael Jordan (born 1963) meeting famous scientist Albert Einstein (deceased since 1955).

content or meaning of the photograph is not changed. Digital retouching is another area where legal precedents have not yet been established.

Codes of Conduct

Recognizing that individuals and organizations need specific standards for the ethical use of computers and information systems, a number of computer related organizations have established **codes of conduct**, which are written guidelines that help determine whether a specific computer action is ethical or unethical *(Figure 13-18)*. Many businesses have adopted similar codes of conduct and made them known to their employees.

One of the problems with ethical issues in business is that some people believe ethical decisions are the responsibility of management, not employees. This is often true in service departments, such as information processing or accounting, whose organization function is sometimes interpreted to be providing whatever information upper-level management wants. Codes of conduct that apply to an entire organization can help in this area by giving all employees, management included, a standard against which they can measure their actions.

Information Privacy

Information privacy has to do with the rights of individuals and organizations to deny or restrict the collection and use of information about them. In the past, it was easier to maintain privacy because information tended to be kept in separate locations; individual stores had their own credit files, government agencies had separate records, doctors had separate files, and so on. It is now technically and economically feasible, however, to store large amounts of related data about individuals in one database. Some people believe this increases the possibility for unauthorized use. Many people also are concerned that their privacy is violated when computers are used to monitor their activities. Both of these issues, unauthorized collection and use of information and employee monitoring, are discussed in the following sections.

Unauthorized Collection and Use of Information

Many individuals are surprised to learn that information provided for magazine subscriptions, product warranty registration cards, contest entry forms, and other separate

---

CODE OF CONDUCT

1. Computers may not be used to harm other people.
2. Employees may not interfere with other's computer work.
3. Employees may not snoop in other's computer files.
4. Computers may not be used to steal.
5. Computers may not be used to bear false witness.
6. Employees may not use other's computer resources without authorization.
7. Employees may not illegally copy or use software.
8. Employees may not use other's output.

Figure 13-18
An example of a code of conduct that an employer may distribute to employees.

documents is often sold to national marketing organizations. The national marketing organizations combine this acquired data with other information obtained from public sources, such as driver license and vehicle registration information, to create an electronic profile of an individual. The combined information is then sold to organizations who want to send information on their product, service, or cause to a specific group of individuals, such as all sports car owners, over 40 years of age, living in the southeastern United States. Direct marketing supporters say that the use of information in this way lowers overall selling costs and therefore product prices as well. Critics of the electronic profiles contend that the combined information may reveal more about individuals than anyone has a right to know. Critics contend that, at a minimum, individuals should be informed the information they furnish may be provided to others and have the right to deny the transfer.

The concern about privacy has led to federal and state laws regarding the storage and disclosure of personal data (Figure 13-19). Common points in some of these laws include the following:

1. Information collected and stored about individuals should be limited to what is necessary to carry out the function of the business or government agency collecting the data.
2. Once collected, provisions should be made to restrict access to the data to those employees within the organization who need access to it to perform their job duties.
3. Personal information should be released outside the organization collecting the data only when the person has agreed to its disclosure.
4. When information is collected about an individual, the individual should know that the data is being collected and have the opportunity to determine the accuracy of the data.

DATE	LAW NAME	PURPOSE
1994	Computer Abuse Amendments Act	Amends 1984 act to outlaw transmission of harmful computer code such as viruses.
1992	Cable Act	Extends privacy of Cable Communications Policy Act of 1984 to include cellular and other wireless services.
1991	Telephone Consumer Protection Act	Restricts activities of telemarketers.
1988	Computer Matching and Privacy Protection Act	Regulates the use of government data to determine the eligibility of persons for federal benefits.
1988	Video Privacy Protection Act	Forbids retailers from releasing or selling video-rental records without customer consent or a court order.
1986	Electronic Communications Privacy Act (ECPA)	Provides the same right of privacy protection for the postal delivery service and telephone companies to the new forms of electronic communications, such as voice mail, E-mail, and cellular telephones.
1984	Cable Communications Policy Act	Regulates disclosure of cable TV subscriber records.
1984	Computer Fraud and Abuse Act	Outlaws unauthorized access of federal government computers.
1978	Right to Financial Privacy Act	Strictly outlines procedures federal agencies must follow when looking at customer records in banks.
1974	Privacy Act	Forbids federal agencies from allowing information to be used for a reason other than which it was collected.
1974	Family Educational Rights and Privacy Act	Gives students and parents access to school records and limits disclosure of records to unauthorized parties.
1970	Fair Credit Reporting Act	Prohibts credit reporting agencies from releasing credit information to unauthorized people and allows consumers to review their credit records.

Figure 13-19
A summary of the major U.S. government laws concerning privacy.

Several federal laws deal specifically with computers. The 1986 Electronic Communications Privacy Act (ECPA) provides the same protection that covers mail and telephone communications to new forms of electronic communications such as voice mail. The 1988 Computer Matching and Privacy Protection Act regulates the use of government data to determine the eligibility of persons for federal benefits. The 1984 and 1994 Computer Fraud and Abuse Acts outlaw unauthorized access to federal government computers and the transmission of harmful computer code such as viruses.

One law with an apparent legal loophole is in the Fair Credit Reporting Act. Although the act limits the rights of others viewing a credit report to those with a *legitimate business need*, a legitimate business need is not defined. The result is that just about anyone can say they have a legitimate business need and gain access to someone's credit report.

Credit reports contain much more than just balance and payment information on mortgages and credit cards. The largest credit bureaus maintain information on family income, number of dependents, employment history, bank balances, driving records, and social security numbers. In total, these credit bureaus have more than 400 million records on more than 160 million people. Some credit bureaus sell combinations of the data they have stored in their database to direct marketing organizations. Because of continuing complaints about credit report errors and the invasion of privacy, the U.S. Congress is considering a major revision of the Fair Credit Reporting Act.

Employee Monitoring

Employee monitoring involves the use of computers to observe, record, and review employee communications and keyboard activity. The most frequently discussed issue is whether or not an employer has the right to read employee E-mail messages. Actual policies vary widely, with some organizations declaring E-mail messages will be regularly reviewed and others stating E-mail is considered private. Most organizations, estimated in one study to be approximately 75%, do not have formal E-mail policies, which, in effect, means that E-mail could be read without notifying employees.

At present, no laws exist relating to E-mail. The 1986 Electronic Communications Privacy Act does not cover communications within an organization. Because many believe that such internal communications should be private, several lawsuits have been filed against employers. In response to the issue of workplace privacy, the U.S. Congress proposed the Privacy for Consumers and Workers Act, which entitles employees to be notified if their employer is monitoring electronic communications. Supporters of the legislation hope that it will also restrict the types and amount of monitoring that employers can legally conduct.

Summary of Security, Ethics, and Privacy

Increased reliance on computer systems and computerized information makes it essential that steps are taken to protect the systems and information from known risks. The livelihood of many organizations and individuals depends on the computer systems they use every day. Both society and individuals, however, have an obligation to use computer systems responsibly and not abuse the power they provide. This presents constant challenges that sometimes weigh the rights of the individual against increased efficiency and productivity. The computer must be thought of as a tool whose effectiveness is determined by the skill and experience of the user. With the computer knowledge you have acquired you will be better able to participate in decisions on how to ethically and efficiently use computerized information systems. To measure your ethical views, answer the ethics questionnaire in *Figure 13-20*.

COMPUTER ETHICS

	Ethical	Unethical	Crime
1. An employee installs a new upgraded version of a word processing program on his office computer. Because no one will be using the old version of the program, the employee takes it home to use on his personal computer so his children can use it to write school papers.	☐	☐	☐
2. While reviewing her employee's E-mail messages, a department manager discovers that one of her employees is using the E-mail system to operate a weekly football betting pool.			
employee	☐	☐	☐
manager	☐	☐	☐
3. A company hires a consultant to develop a custom program. After completing the program, the consultant tries to license the program to other companies.	☐	☐	☐
4. An employee learns the password to the personnel system and uses it to review the salaries of the corporate officers. No use is made of the information. "I was just curious" is the individual's response when caught.	☐	☐	☐
5. A bank employee electronically transfers money from an inactive customer account to his own personal account. After pay day, the employee transfers the money plus interest back to the inactive account.	☐	☐	☐
6. While reviewing a list of available programs on a bulletin board, a user notices the name of a program that is similar to a popular spreadsheet package. After downloading the program, the user discovers that the program appears to be a test version of the popular spreadsheet program that sells for $200 in computer stores. The user keeps and uses the program.	☐	☐	☐
7. A programmer is asked to write a program that she knows will generate inaccurate financial information. When she questions her manager about the program, she is told to write the program or risk losing her job. She writes the program.			
programmer	☐	☐	☐
manager	☐	☐	☐
8. As a practical joke, an employee enters a program on the company computer. Each time an employee uses a diskette on the company network, the program is copied to the diskette. The first time the diskette is used after January 1, a "Happy New Year" message is displayed.	☐	☐	☐
9. A newspaper uses photo retouching software to remove a billboard advertisement for a competitive newspaper from the background of a front-page photo.	☐	☐	☐
10. A company occasionally uses software to monitor the productivity of its staff. It only uses the software to monitor an employee thought to be repeatedly goofing off.	☐	☐	☐

Figure 13-20
Indicate whether you think the described situation is ethical, unethical, or a crime. Discuss your answers with your instructor and other students.

COMPUTERS AT WORK

Active Badges Help Locate Users

Tired of missing phone calls because you were away from your desk? Frustrated by not being able to find a co-worker you know is in the building? These and similar employee location problems are being solved by **active badge systems** developed by Olivetti Research Limited of Cambridge, England.

The active badge contains a small transmitter and is worn on the outside of clothing. Every fifteen seconds the badge emits an infrared signal that is picked up by sensors in offices and hallways. Infrared signals are used because they do not penetrate walls and therefore can be traced to a specific location. The sensors are connected to a computer that updates a database of locations and users. The computer used for the sensors is connected to an organization's main computer or computer network so users can display location information.

If a user is in a meeting or otherwise does not want to be disturbed, he or she can press a button on the badge twice. This results in a busy message on the location display. The busy status remains until the user changes locations. If a user does not want to be located at all, they can place their badge in a pocket, purse, or drawer. The badges have a light sensor that shuts them off in the dark.

Advanced versions of the devices called Authentication Badges are currently under development. Authentication badges contain small microprocessors that can be programmed. One anticipated use of authentication badges is as security devices that will let authorized users enter restricted areas.

Active Badges are just one type of device called a Portable Interactive Computing Object (PiCO). Olivetti has plans for an entire family of smart PiCO devices that can be attached to persons or things. Olivetti believes the increased productivity achieved from the use of the devices will more than offset any concerns about worker privacy.

Figure 13-21

IN THE FUTURE

Who Will Set The Standards and Methods of Information Privacy?

One positive result of the U.S. government's Clipper chip proposal was that it stimulated a lot of debate over how information should be protected and who should set the standards. Although the proposed plan was voluntary, many objected to the government's plan to have encryption chips imbedded in voice, data, and fax machines, including computers. Opponents of the plan were worried that the government-controlled encryption standard would make it easier for government agencies to eavesdrop on electronic communications. It should be noted that numerous laws and procedures currently in effect supposedly prevent this type of abuse.

Opponents also complained that the encryption formula would be kept by the National Security Agency (NSA), the highly secret international intelligence organization. In the past, NSA has been criticized for operating independently with little government supervision. Other arguments against the Clipper chip were that foreign companies and governments would not use an encryption device controlled by the U.S. government and that serious criminals could easily bypass the chip by using a different software-based encryption method.

Judging by the number of articles that dealt with the government's proposal, many people apparently believe the government should stay out of the electronic privacy standards and methods business. Part of this opinion is undoubtedly just a conservative view that the government should involve itself as little as possible in the activities of businesses and individuals. Others firmly believe that the use of many different encryption methods, instead of just one government-approved method, provides the best protection against widespread information theft and the invasion of electronic privacy.

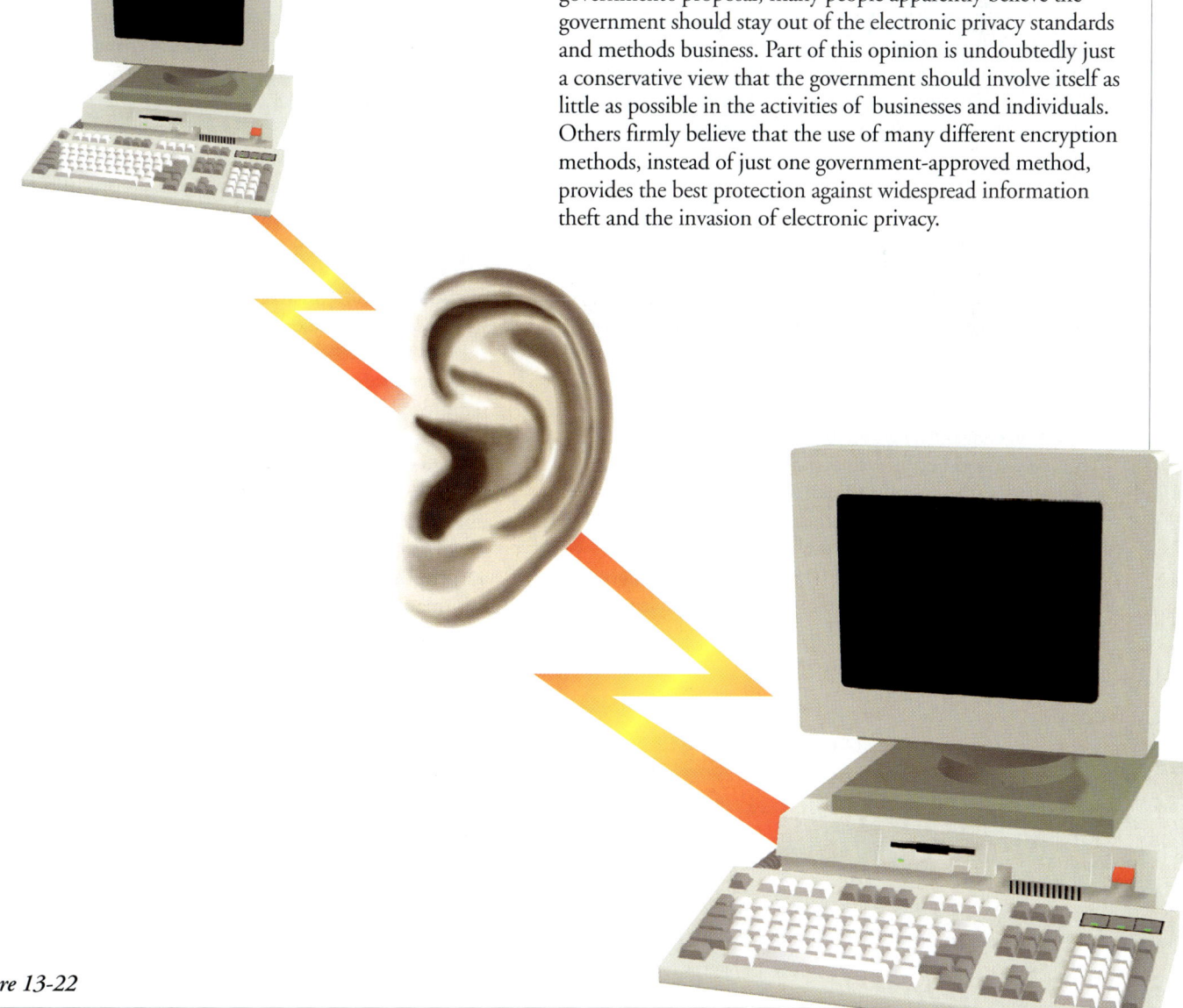

Figure 13-22

What You Should Know

1. A **computer security risk** is defined as any event or action that could cause a loss to computer equipment, software, information, or processing capability.

2. A computer **virus** is an illegal and potentially damaging computer program designed to *infect* other software by attaching itself to the software with which it comes in contact. A **boot sector virus** replaces the program that is used to start the system with a modified version of the program. A **file virus** inserts virus code into program files. A **Trojan horse virus** is a virus that hides within or is designed to look like a traditional program.

3. Some viruses contain time bombs or logic bombs. A **time bomb** is a program that performs an activity on a particular date. A **logic bomb** is a program that performs an activity when a certain action has occurred. A **worm**, unlike a virus, does not attach itself to a program, but instead is designed to repeatedly copy itself in memory or on a disk drive until there is no memory or disk space remaining.

4. To protect against viruses, **anti-virus programs**, called **vaccines**, have been developed. Anti-virus programs look for viruses that attempt to modify the boot program, the operating system, and other programs that are normally read from but not written to. Anti-virus programs also look for specific patterns of known virus code called a **virus signature**. A **polymorphic virus**, which is designed to modify its program code each time it attaches itself to another program or file, is extremely difficult to detect.

5. When a program file is **inoculated**, information such as the file size and file creation date is recorded in a separate inoculation file. Using this information, a vaccine program can tell if a virus program has tampered with the program file. A **rescue disk** contains an uninfected copy of certain operating system commands and essential information about the computer that enables the computer to restart correctly.

6. **Unauthorized access** can be defined as computer trespassing; in other words, using a computer system without permission. Persons who deliberately try to illegally access computer systems, usually by using a modem, are called **crackers**. The term **hacker**, although originally a positive term, also has become associated with persons who try to break into computer systems. **Unauthorized use** is the use of a computer system or computer data for unapproved or possibly illegal activities.

7. Many commercial software packages are designed to implement **access controls** through a process called identification and authentication. **Identification** verifies that the user is a valid user, and **authentication** verifies that the user is who he or she claims to be. Three methods of authentication exist: remembered information, possessed objects, and biometric devices.

8. With **remembered information** authentication, a user is required to enter a word or series of characters that matches an entry in a security file in the computer. Most multiuser operating systems provide for a **logon code**, a **user ID**, and a **password** (all forms of remembered information) that must be entered correctly before a user is allowed to use an application program. With **dialog** authentication, which is a variation of remembered information authentication, one of several possible items of personal information is randomly chosen from information on file and asked of the user.

9. A **possessed object** is any item that a user must carry to gain access to the computer facility. A possessed object is often used in combination with a **personal identification number** (PIN), which is a numeric password either assigned by the issuing organization or selected by a user.

10. A **biometric device** is one that verifies personal characteristics to authenticate a user. Examples of personal characteristics are fingerprints, voice pattern, signature, hand size, and retinal (eye) patterns.

11. A **callback system**, which is an access control method sometimes used to authenticate remote users, connects users to the computer system only after the computer calls them back at a previously established telephone number.

12. Hardware theft of most desktop and larger computer systems is generally not a problem. Portable equipment, however, such as notebook computers or personal digital assistants (PDAs), do pose serious theft risks. Common sense and a constant awareness of the risk are the best preventive measures.

13. With the increased use of personal computers, software theft, often called **software piracy**, has become a major problem. Users generally do not have the right to copy, loan, rent, or in any way distribute software when it is purchased. A **site license** gives an organization the right to install software on multiple computers at a single site. **Shareware** is software that users may try out on their own systems before paying a fee. **Public domain software** is free software that is not copyrighted and can therefore be distributed among users.

14. Most organizations prevent information theft by implementing user identification and authentication controls. One way to protect sensitive data is to use encryption.

15. **Encryption** is the process of converting readable data, called **plaintext**, into unreadable characters, called **ciphertext**. The conversion is accomplished with a formula that uses a code, called an **encryption key**, to modify the plaintext. The encryption key is also used by the person who receives the ciphertext message to **decrypt** (or **decipher**) the data back into the original plaintext. An encryption method widely used by the U.S. government is the **data encryption standard** (DES). A proposed federal standard for voice and data encryption requires the use of an encryption formula named **Skipjack** implemented in a tamper-resistant microprocessor called the **Clipper chip**.

16. A **system failure** is defined as a prolonged malfunction of a computer system. System failures are caused by natural disasters or events such as electrical power problems. An **undervoltage** occurs when there is a drop in the electrical supply. A **brownout** is a prolonged drop in power and a **blackout** is a complete power failure. An **overvoltage**, or **power surge**, occurs when the incoming electrical power increases above the normal 120 volts. A momentary overvoltage, called a **spike**, occurs when the power increase lasts for less than one millisecond. **Noise** is any unwanted signal that is mixed with the normal voltage entering the computer.

17. A **surge protector**, also called a **surge suppressor**, uses special electrical components to keep an overvoltage from reaching the computer equipment. An **uninterruptable power supply** (UPS) is a device that contains surge protection circuits and one or more batteries that can provide power during a temporary or permanent loss of power.

18. A **backup** is a copy of information stored on a computer. **Backup procedures** specify a regular plan of copying and storing key data and program files. In the case of a system failure or the discovery of corrupted files, backup copies can be used to **restore** the files (reload the files on the computer). Backup copies are normally kept in fireproof safes or vaults or **offsite**, in a building different from the computer site. An installation can perform three types of backup: **full backup**, **differential backup**, or **incremental backup**.

19. Sometimes important individual files are backed up separately, and a *three-generation* backup policy is often used. The oldest copy of the file is called the **grandfather**, the second oldest copy is called the **father**, and the most recent copy is called the **son**.

20. A **disaster recovery plan** is a written plan describing the steps an organization would take to restore computer operation in the event of a disaster. A disaster recovery plan contains four major components: the emergency plan, the backup plan, the recovery plan, and the test plan.

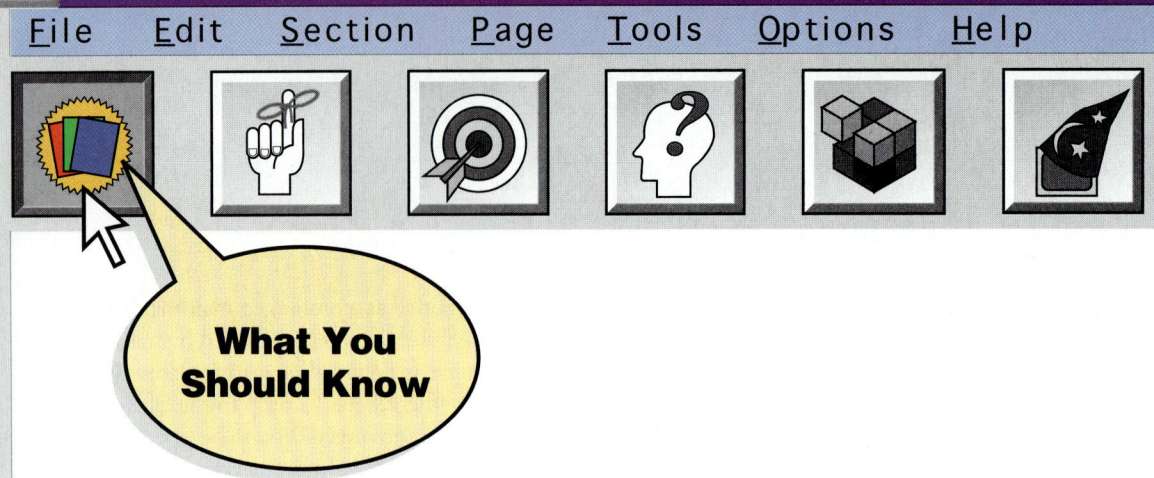

21. The **emergency plan** specifies the steps to be taken immediately after a disaster strikes. The **backup plan** specifies how an organization will use backup files and equipment to resume information processing. Two types of alternate computer facilities exist: a **hot site** and a **cold site**. Some organizations enter into **reciprocal backup relationships** with other firms; that is, in case of disaster one firm provides space, and sometimes equipment, to the other.

22. The **recovery plan** specifies the actions to be taken to restore full information processing operations. The **disaster recovery test plan** contains information for simulating different levels of disasters and recording an organization's capability to recover.

23. A **computer security plan** summarizes in writing the safeguards that are in place to protect an organization's information assets.

24. **Computer ethics** are the moral guidelines that govern the use of computers and information systems. In addition to software theft (piracy) and unauthorized use of computer systems, other areas of computer ethics frequently discussed are the accuracy of information, codes of conduct, and the privacy of computerized information.

25. Inaccurate input can result in erroneous information and incorrect decisions based on the information. Information accuracy is even more of an issue today because many users access information maintained by other organizations. Some people also have raised questions about the ethics of using computers to alter output.

26. Recognizing that individuals and organizations need specific standards for the ethical use of computers and information systems, a number of computer-related organizations have established **codes of conduct**, which are written guidelines that help determine whether a specific computer action is ethical or unethical.

27. **Information privacy** has to do with the rights of individuals and organizations to deny or restrict the collection and use of information about them. Concern with the unauthorized collection and use of information has led to federal and state laws regarding the storage and disclosure of personal data. A second information privacy issue is **employee monitoring**, which involves the use of computers to observe, record, and review employee communications and keyboard activity.

Terms to Remember

access controls (13.5)
active badge systems (13.22)
anti-virus programs (13.3)
authentication (13.5)

backup (13.13)
backup plan (13.15)
backup procedures (13.13)
biometric device (13.6)
blackout (13.12)
boot sector virus (13.2)
brownout (13.12)

callback system (13.7)
ciphertext (13.11)
Clipper chip (13.11)
codes of conduct (13.18)
cold site (13.16)
computer ethics (13.17)
computer security plan (13.16)
computer security risk (13.2)
crackers (13.4)

data encryption standard (13.11)
decipher (13.11)
decrypt (13.11)
dialog (13.6)
differential backup (13.13)
disaster recovery plan (13.14)
disaster recovery test plan (13.16)

emergency plan (13.15)
employee monitoring (xx)
encryption (13.11)
encryption key (13.11)

father (13.14)
file virus (13.2)
full backup (13.13)

grandfather (13.14)

hacker (13.4)
hot site (13.16)

identification (13.5)
incremental backup (13.13)
information privacy (13.8)
inoculated (13.3)

logic bomb (13.2)
logon code (13.5)

noise (13.12)

offsite (13.13)
overvoltage (13.12)

password (13.5)
personal identification number (PIN) (13.6)
plaintext (13.1)
polymorphic virus (13.3)
possessed object (13.6)
power surges (13.2)
public domain software (13.10)

reciprocal backup relationships (13.16)
recovery plan (13.16)
remembered information (13.5)
rescue disk (13.3)
restore (13.13)

shareware (13.10)
site license (13.10)
Skipjack (13.11)
software piracy (13.9)
son (13.14)
spike (13.12)
surge protector (13.12)
system failure (13.11)

time bomb (13.2)
Trojan horse (13.2)

unauthorized access (13.4)
unauthorized use (13.4)
under voltage (13.12)
uninterruptable power supply (UPS) (13.13)
user ID (13.5)

vaccines (13.3)
virus (13.2)
virus signature (13.3)

Test Your Knowledge

Fill in the Blanks

1. A(n) _____ is defined as any event or action that could cause a loss to computer equipment, software, information, or processing capability.

2. A(n) _____ is an illegal and potentially damaging computer program designed to *infect* other software by attaching itself to the software with which it comes in contact.

3. In the case of a system failure or the discovery of corrupted files, _____ copies of information stored on a computer can be used to _____ files (reload the files on the computer).

4. A(n) _____ is a written scheme describing the steps an organization would take to restore computer operations in the event of a catastrophe.

5. _____ has to do with the rights of individuals and organizations to deny or restrict the collection and use of knowledge about them.

Short Answer

1. What is a computer security plan? What should a computer security plan do? How often should a computer security plan be updated?

2. How are a boot sector virus, a file virus, and a Trojan horse virus different? What is the purpose of an anti-virus program? What do experts recommend to protect against being infected by a computer virus?

3. What is software piracy? Why is software piracy a crime? In addition to purchasing commercial software, in what other ways can an individual legally acquire software?

4. How are a full backup, differential backup, and incremental backup different? Where are backup copies normally kept? Why?

5. What are computer ethics? What five areas of computer ethics are frequently discussed? Briefly explain each.

Label the Figure

Instructions: Identify the four parts of a disaster recovery plan in the following figure.

PARTS OF A DISASTER RECOVERY PLAN	
_____	Evacuation plans and list of people to notify
_____	Identity and location of backup resources
_____	Specific steps and timeplan to resume computer operations
_____	Simulates disasters to find weaknesses in overall plan

1

In a famous case, Robert Morris was found guilty of infecting a computer network with a virus that damaged data and files for more than 6,000 users. Morris's sentence was 400 hours of community service, a three-year probation, and a $10,000 fine. Some people feel this sentence was too lenient, given the extent of harm the virus caused. Others believe Morris actually did the network a favor by demonstrating the limitations of its security system. Was the punishment appropriate? Why or why not? Would this punishment serve as a deterrent to other potential computer criminals?

2

Some companies are unwilling to prosecute hackers after they are caught. This decision is usually a result of the youth of most hackers and the organization's reluctance to publicize its vulnerability. Many authorities argue that hackers will not stop until they are brought to trial and their crimes are made public. What are the advantages and disadvantages of publicizing the misdeeds of known hackers? Should all hackers be openly prosecuted? Why or why not?

3

In 1990, Lotus Development Corporation created a database of consumer information called Marketplace that it intended to sell to small and medium businesses. After thousands of consumers asked that their names be removed from the database, Lotus withdrew the product. Nevertheless, other databases are routinely bought and sold. Although there are certain benefits to shared databases, such as faster decisions on credit applications and access to products which would otherwise be unfamiliar, the problem with selling databases is twofold: accuracy and privacy. A study of 1,500 reports from three large credit bureaus discovered mistakes in 43 percent of the files, and it is generally agreed that some personal information should not be made public. What measures can be taken to solve these problems? What restrictions, if any, should be placed on selling or sharing databases? Should some databases not be shared under any circumstances?

4

As databases become more complete and widely accessed, it has become possible to learn about almost any individual. Information garnered from credit card purchases, warranty cards, voting records, opinion polls, telephone records, and so on can be used to form a picture of a person's habits, likes, and interests. Make a list of information you have supplied over the past year that might be recorded in a database. If someone was able to combine all of this information, how do you think you would be described? Is the description accurate? Why or why not?

5

Recently, a photograph of a public figure accused of murder was run on the cover of a national news magazine. Using a computer, the photograph had been retouched to give the person a more sinister appearance. Many people objected to the photograph, arguing that it distorted the facts and could lead people to believe in the individual's guilt before being tried. Other people claimed the photograph was not offered as an exact representation and was only enhanced to graphically point out the seriousness of the crime. What do you think? Under what circumstances, if any, is it all right to enhance a photograph using a computer? Should any, or all, retouched photographs include a written disclaimer indicating the photograph has been modified?

6

Using computerized employee monitoring systems, employers can keep track of every keystroke an employee makes, determine the efficiency with which an employee works, record the files an employee has accessed, and note how many breaks an employee takes. Some managers keep copies of E-mail sent between employees. Employers insist these systems protect the security and enhance the productivity of the organization. Many employees, however, find these practices dehumanizing and an invasion of privacy. Who is right? Do these systems place undo stress on employees? What limits, if any, should be placed on employee monitoring?

13.30 Points to Ponder

Out and About

1. What motivates hackers? Are they simply intellectual adventurers, thrilled by the challenge of entering other computer systems, or are they selfish, sometimes malicious, busybodies intent on accessing information to which they have no right? Are their motivations different from those who create computer viruses? What, if anything, should be done to deter hackers? Prepare a report on a hacker-related book to answer these and some of your own questions about hackers. Suggested titles include: *Cyberpunk–Outlaws and Hackers on the Computer Frontier* (Katie Hafner and John Markoff), *Hackers: Heroes of the Computer Revolution* (Steven Levy), and *The Hacker Crackdown: Law and Disorder on the Electronic Frontier* (Bruce Sterling).

2. An issue related to computer ethics is the effect of computers on the environment, particularly in terms of the power they deplete. An Environmental Protection Agency survey indicates that 30 to 40 percent of personal computer users leave their personal computer systems running all the time. The EPA estimates that personal computers and computer peripherals squander about two billion dollars worth of electricity annually! To combat this, the EPA has initiated the Energy Star program. Computer system components that use less than 30 watts when idle are awarded an "Energy Star" label. Visit a computer vendor and make a list of computer components that have the Energy Star designation. Which components are most likely to meet the Energy Star requirements? Which components are least likely to meet the requirements? Is there a significant difference in price between components with an Energy Star and those without an Energy Star?

3. With today's global markets, privacy and computer security have become international issues. The International Association of Computer Crime Investigators has been formed to look into computer-related crimes worldwide. Several countries, including France, Spain, and Sweden, have laws concerning the transmission of data across their borders, and transborder data flow is becoming an increasingly complex issue. Visit a library and prepare a report on the international transmission of data. What are some of the laws with which organizations should be familiar when doing business in the world market?

4. Visit a local business, or the computer center at your school, and interview the individual in charge of computer security. What does he or she perceive as the gravest security threats? What security measures are in place to handle these threats? Are these measures adequate? Is there a code of conduct or policy regarding computer use? If so, to whom does it apply? What activities are prohibited? How does the organization deal with violators?

5. Find out as much information as you can about your student file. What type of information is stored in the file? Who has access to the file? What information in the file are you allowed to see? What information are others (students or faculty) allowed to see? How is the accuracy of the information in the file verified? Who can change information in the file? What information security measures are in force? Can you get a list of the individuals who see your file? How long is the file retained after you graduate?

6. Computer software can be protected through a patent or a copyright. A patent provides an owner, under certain conditions, with a monopoly on the ideas behind the software for 17 years. A copyright protects the expression of an idea, but not the idea itself. The Software Protection Law, enacted by Congress in 1980, prohibits the literal copying of a program or its component parts, but does not prevent copying the ideas behind the software. Each of these measures involves subtle distinctions that have resulted in several lawsuits. Some software creators, such as Lotus Development Corporation, have been successful in their litigation, while others, such as Apple, have not. Using law books or current periodicals, prepare a report on at least two court cases, one in which the software developer won and one in which the software developer lost. Describe each case and explain how they were different. Do you think the decision was correct in each case? Why or why not?

In the Lab   13.31

 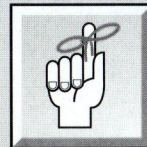   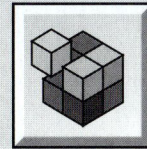

Windows Labs

1 Checking for Viruses With Program Manager on the screen, double-click the Microsoft Tools group icon. In the Microsoft Tools group window, double-click the Anti-Virus program-item icon. In the Microsoft Anti-Virus window, select the Scan menu and choose Virus List to display the Virus List dialog box containing known viruses *(Figure 13-23)*. Print the list by clicking the Print button.

Insert the diskette containing your Windows Labs into drive A. Click the drive A icon. Click the Detect and Clean button. While searching for viruses in memory and on your disk, a percentage complete message displays *(Figure 13-24)*. When finished, a Statistics dialog box displays. Were any of your files infected? What was your scan time? Choose the OK button. Close the Microsoft Anti-Virus window.

2 Shelly Cashman Series Anti-Virus Lab Follow the instructions in Windows Lab 2 in Chapter 1 on page 1.30 to display the Shelly Cashman Series Labs screen. Select Keeping Your Computer Virus Free and choose the Start Lab button. When the initial screen displays, carefully read the objectives. With your printer turned on, point to the Print Questions button and click the left mouse button. Fill out the top of the Questions sheet and answer the questions as you step through the Anti-Virus Lab.

3 Understanding Backing Up With Program Manager on the screen, double-click the Microsoft Tools group icon. In the Microsoft Tools group window, double-click the Backup program-item icon. If it not already selected, click drive C in the Backup From area. What other drives are available for backup on your computer? Click the Backup Type drop-down list box arrow. What types of backups can be performed? Click the box arrow again. Click the Backup To box arrow. Select drive A. Note the statistics that display in the bottom right corner of the screen *(Figure 13-25* on the next page). How many files will be backed up on your computer? How long will it take to perform the backup? Choose the Quit button to exit Microsoft Backup.

4 Managing Files on Multiple Disks With Program Manager on the screen, double-click the Main group icon. In the Main group window, double-click the File Manager program-item icon. Maximize the File Manager window. Be sure the directory window is NOT maximized. Insert the diskette with your Windows Labs into drive A. Click the drive A icon in the File Manager window. Insert a formatted disk into drive B. Double-click the drive B icon to open a second window that displays the files on the disk in drive B. Select the Window menu and choose Tile.

Suppose you want to make a copy of all your Write files on the disk in drive A to the disk in drive B. Click within the drive A window, and if necessary, double-click the subdirectory containing the Write files. Select the File menu and choose Select Files. In the Select Files dialog box, type *.wri and choose the Select button. Choose the Close button. Select the File menu and choose Copy. In the Copy dialog box, type b: and choose the OK button. Windows copies the selected files

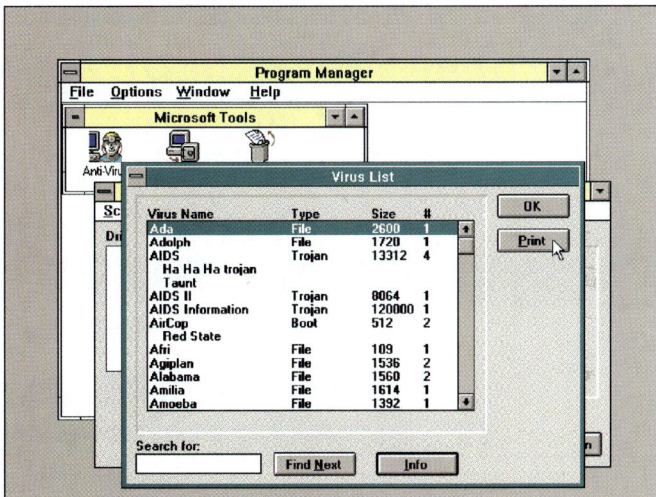

Figure 13-23

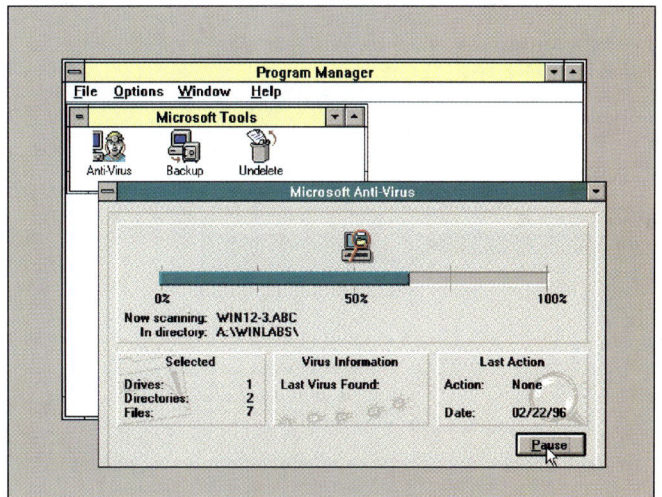

Figure 13-24

13.32 In the Lab

 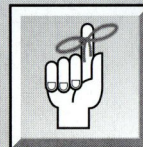    

File Edit Section Page Tools Options Help

In the Lab (continued)

from drive A to drive B *(Figure 13-26)*. Close the drive B window by double-clicking its Control-menu box. Select the Window menu and choose Cascade. Close File Manager.

5 Using Help Open Microsoft Backup as described in Windows Lab 3 on the previous page. Select the Help menu and choose Glossary. Write down the definition of copy-protected files and hidden attribute by clicking each topic. In the Help window, select the Help menu and choose About Help. Who is this product licensed to? Who has the copyright? Choose the OK button. Close Help. In the Microsoft Backup window, select the Help menu and choose About Windows Backup. Who is this product licensed to? Who has the copyright? Choose the OK button. Close Microsoft Backup.

DOS Labs

1 Checking for Viruses This exercise requires MS-DOS 6.0 or higher, and Microsoft Anti-Virus must be installed for DOS. At the DOS prompt, type msav and press the ENTER key. Press F9 to display the list of known viruses. Print the list by pressing ALT+P, followed by ALT+P again. Close the Virus List by pressing ALT+O.

Insert the diskette containing your DOS Labs into drive A. Press ALT+S, followed by typing a. Select Detect and Clean by pressing ALT+C. While searching for viruses in memory and on your disk, a percentage complete message displays. When finished, a Statistics box displays. Were any of your files infected? What was your scan time? Press ALT+O. Exit Microsoft Anti-Virus by pressing F3, followed by ALT+O.

2 Understanding Back Up This exercise requires MS-DOS 6.0 or higher, and Microsoft Backup must be installed for DOS. At the DOS prompt, type msbackup and press the ENTER key. Press ALT+B to select backup. What drives are available for backup on your computer? Which drive is selected? Press ALT+Y. What types of backups can be performed? Press the ESC key. What drive is selected as the drive to backup to? Note the statistics that display in the bottom right corner of the screen. How many files will be backed up on your computer? How many disks will be required? Press the ESC key. Press ALT+Q to exit Microsoft Backup.

3 Using Help This exercise requires MS-DOS 6.0 or higher. At the DOS prompt, type help and press the ENTER key. Display and print Help information on the topics Msav and Msbackup. Exit Help.

Online Lab

1 Visiting a Chat Room Using one of the two online services you selected in Chapter 1, connect to the service and perform the following tasks: (1) Search the online service for Chat Room information. (2) Read the instructions on how to visit a Chat Room and the conduct expected of you. (3) Visit a Chat Room and participate in the conversation by sending messages back and forth. (4) **Extra Credit**: Start your own Chat Room on a subject that would interest service users.

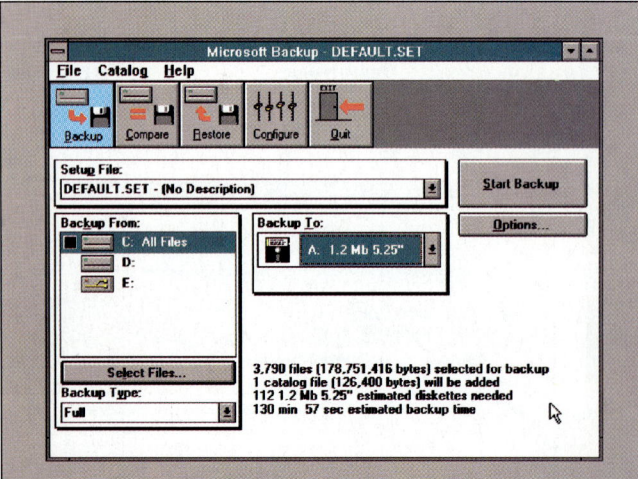

Figure 13-25

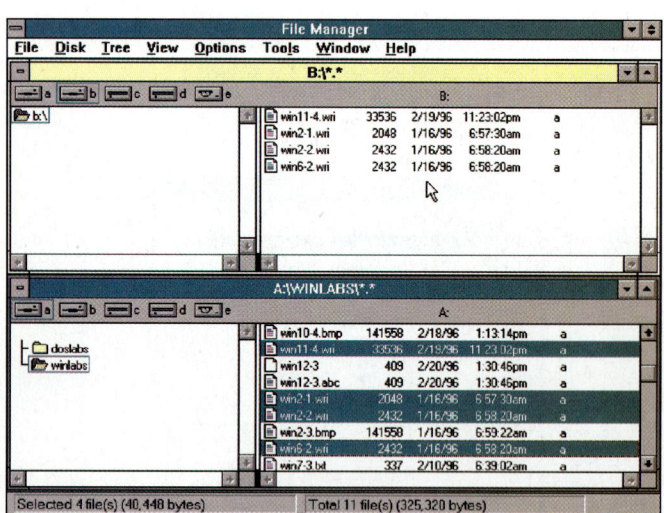

Figure 13-26

CHAPTER FOURTEEN

Your Future in the Information Age

14

Objectives

After completing this chapter, you will be able to:

- Discuss the areas that provide the majority of computer-related jobs

- Describe the career positions available in the information processing industry

- Discuss the compensation and growth trends for information processing careers

- Describe different ways to develop a career in the information processing industry

- Discuss trends affecting computers and the information processing industry

- Describe how business information systems are likely to change in the future

- Describe how computers are, and will be, used in the home

After reading the preceding chapters, you may be interested enough in computers to consider a career in the information processing industry. The information processing industry is growing rapidly and offers many rewarding jobs. The first part of this chapter discusses the types of positions available, how much they currently pay, and how to prepare for a job.

Even if you do not work in the information processing industry, computers will undoubtedly affect your work and leisure activities. The second half of this chapter discusses trends in information processing that will affect these areas.

14.2

The Information Processing Industry

The information processing industry is one of the largest industries in the world with annual sales close to $200 billion. Approximately two-thirds of this total is related to equipment sales and the remainder comes from software and services sales. Job opportunities in the industry come primarily from three areas: the companies that manufacture computer-related equipment; the companies that develop software; and the companies that hire information processing professionals to work with these products. As in any major industry, many service companies support each of these three areas. Examples are companies that sell computer supplies and companies that consult on communication networks.

The Computer Equipment Industry

The computer equipment, or hardware, industry includes all manufacturers and distributors of computers *(Figure 14-1)* and computer-related equipment such as disk and tape drives, monitors, printers, and communications equipment.

The five largest minicomputer and mainframe manufacturers in the United States – IBM, Digital Equipment Corporation, UNISYS, Hewlett-Packard, and AT&T GIS – are large organizations with tens of thousands of employees worldwide. Major personal computer manufacturers include Compaq, Apple, Packard Bell, IBM, and Gateway. The largest computer company, IBM, has annual sales of over $60 billion. In addition to the major companies, the computer equipment industry also is known for the many new start-up companies that appear each year. These new companies take advantage of rapid changes in equipment technology, such as wireless communications, networking, multimedia, and fiber optics, to create new products and new job opportunities.

Besides the companies that make end user equipment, thousands of companies make components that most users never see. These companies manufacture chips (CPU, memory, and special purpose), power supplies, wiring, and the hundreds of other parts that go into computer equipment.

Figure 14-1
Personal computers are assembled and tested on production lines.

What Are the Career Opportunities in Information Processing?

The use of computers in so many aspects of life has created thousands of new jobs. Because of rapid changes in technology, many of the current jobs did not even exist ten years ago. The following section describes some of the current career opportunities.

The Computer Software Industry

The computer software industry includes all the developers and distributors of applications and system software. Thousands of companies provide a wide range of software from operating systems to complete business systems. Software is a huge industry with annual sales exceeding $50 billion. Leading companies include Microsoft, Oracle, Computer Associates, Novell, and Lotus. Most software companies specialize in one particular type of software product, such as business application software, or productivity tools, such as word processing or spreadsheets. The largest companies, however, have multiple products.

Information Processing Professionals

Information processing professionals are the people who put the equipment and software to work to produce information for the end user *(Figure 14-2)*. This includes people such as programmers and systems analysts who are hired by companies to work in an information systems department.

Working in an Information Systems Department

The people in the information systems department work together as a team to meet the information demands of their organizations. Several job positions already have been discussed, including database administrator (Chapter 9), systems analysts (Chapter 11), and programmers (Chapter 12). In addition to these jobs, many other positions exist. These positions can be divided into four main groups:
1. Operations
2. System Development
3. Technical Services
4. End User Computing

Figure 14-2
Computer professionals must be able to understand the end user's point of view and often meet with the user to review his or her information processing requirements.

The chart in *Figure 14-3* shows some of the management and nonmanagement positions in each of these groups that are described in the following section.

OPERATIONS

The **operations group** is responsible for operating the centralized (computer center) equipment and network administration including both data and voice communications. The **computer operator** performs equipment related activities such as monitoring performance, running jobs, and backup and restore. A **communications specialist** evaluates, installs, and monitors data and/or voice communications equipment and software. A **PC network specialist** installs and maintains local area networks. A **control clerk** accounts for all input and output processed by the computer center. A **data entry operator** uses a data entry device, such as a terminal or PC, to transcribe data from source documents into a computer. The **data librarian** maintains the collection of production and backup tapes and disks.

SYSTEM DEVELOPMENT

The **system development group** is responsible for analyzing, designing, developing, and implementing new information systems and maintaining and improving existing systems. The **systems analyst** works closely with users to analyze their requirements and design an information system solution. The **application programmer** converts the system design into the appropriate computer language. The **technical writer** works with the analyst, programmer, and user to create program and system documentation, and user manuals.

TECNICAL SERVICES

The **technical services group** is responsible for the evaluation and integration of new technologies, the administration of the organization's data resources, and support of the central computer operating system. A **technical evaluator** researches new technologies, such as wireless communications, and recommends how such technologies can be used by the organization. The **database analyst** is familiar with the organization's database structure and assists systems analysts and programmers in developing or modifying applications that use the database. The **system programmer** installs and maintains operating system software and provides technical support to other staff. The **quality assurance specialist** reviews programs and documentation to make sure they meet the organization's standards.

GROUP	MANAGEMENT	NONMANAGEMENT
Operations	Computer Operations Manager	Computer Operator
	Network Administration Manager	Communications Specialist
	Voice Communications Manager	PC Network Specialist
		Control Clerk
		Data Entry Operator
		Data Librarian
System Development	System Development Manager	Systems Analyst
	Programming Manager	Application Programmer
	Project Manager	Technical Writer
Technical Services	Technical Support Manager	Technical Evaluator
	Database Administrator	Database Analyst
	Systems Software Manager	System Programmer
	Quality Assurance Manager	Quality Assurance Specialist
End User Computing	End User Computing Manager	PC Support Specialist
	Information Center Manager	Information Center Specialist
	Office Automation Manager	Office Automation Specialist
	Training Manager	Trainer
		EIS Specialist

Figure 14-3
This table shows some of the management and nonmanagement jobs available within an information systems department.

END USER COMPUTING

The **end user computing group** is responsible for assisting end users in working with existing systems and in using productivity software and query languages to obtain the information necessary to perform their jobs. The **PC support specialist** installs and supports personal computer equipment and software. The **information center specialist** assists users in obtaining information from an organization's existing database and putting it in a form that they can use, such as presentation graphics. The **office automation specialist** assists users in implementing both computerized and noncomputerized office automation technologies. A **trainer** develops education and training materials to teach users how to use existing and new applications. The **executive information system (EIS) specialist** works with senior management to develop reports and systems to meet their information requirements.

As you can see, an information systems department provides career opportunities for people with a variety of skills and talents. Other information industry jobs are found in the areas of sales, service and repair, education and training, and consulting.

Sales

Sales representatives must have a general understanding of computers and a specific knowledge of the product they are selling. Strong interpersonal, or people, skills are important, including listening ability and strong oral and written communication skills. Sales representatives are usually paid based on the amount of product they sell, and top sales representatives are often the most highly compensated employees in a computer company.

Some sales representatives work directly for equipment and software manufacturers and others work for resellers. Many personal computer products are sold through dealers *(Figure 14-4)*. Some dealers, such as Egghead Discount Software, specialize in selling popular software products.

Service and Repair

Being a **service and repair technician** is a challenging job for individuals who like to troubleshoot and solve problems and who have a strong background in electronics *(Figure 14-5)*. In the early days of computers, repairs were often made

Figure 14-4
Computer retailers need sales people who understand personal computers and have good people skills.

Figure 14-5
Computer service and repair requires a knowledge of electronics.

at the site of the computer equipment. Today, however, malfunctioning components, such as circuit boards, are usually replaced and taken back to the service technician's office or sent to a special facility for repair. Many equipment manufacturers include special diagnostic software with their computer equipment that helps the service technician identify the problem. Using a modem, some computer systems can automatically telephone another computer at the service technician's office and leave a message that a malfunction has been detected.

Education and Training

The increased sophistication and complexity of today's computer products has opened wide opportunities in computer education and training *(Figure 14-6)*. Qualified instructors are needed in schools, colleges, universities, and in private industry. In fact, the high demand for teachers has created a shortage at the university level, where many instructors have been lured into private industry because of higher pay. This shortage probably will not be filled in the near future; the supply of Ph.D.s, usually required at the university level, is not keeping up with the demand.

Consulting

After building experience in one or more areas, some individuals become **consultants**, who are people that draw upon their experience to give advice to others. Consultants must have not only strong technical skills in their area of expertise, but also must have the people skills to effectively communicate their suggestions to their clients. Qualified consultants are in high demand for such tasks as computer system selection, system design, and communications network design and installation.

Compensation and Growth Trends for Information Processing Careers

Compensation is a function of experience and demand for a particular skill. Demand is influenced by geographic location, with metropolitan areas usually having higher pay than rural areas. *Figure 14-7* shows the result of a salary survey of over 85,000 computer professionals across the United States and Canada.

As shown in *Figure 14-8,* some industries pay higher than others for the same job. According to the survey, financial services companies pay the highest salaries. These companies have many challenging applications and pay the highest rate to obtain the best qualified employees.

According to the U. S. Bureau of Labor Statistics, the fastest growing computer career positions through the year 2005 will be systems analyst, programmer, and computer repair technician *(Figure 14-9)*.

Figure 14-6
A high demand in schools and industry exists for qualified instructors who can teach information processing subjects.

PROGRAMMING (Commercial):	Median Salary ($000)
Mainframe	
Junior Programmer	32
Programmer/Analyst	37
Senior Programmer/Analyst	42
Midrange	
Junior Programmer	30
Programmer/Analyst	35
Senior Programmer/Analyst	40
Microcomputer	
Junior Programmer	32
Programmer/Analyst	40
Senior Programmer/Analyst	45
Software Engineer	
Junior Software Engineer	35
Software Engineer	45
Senior Software Engineer	50
BUSINESS SYSTEMS:	
Systems Analyst	45
Consultant	46
EIS Analyst	46

Figure 14-7
Salary levels (in thousands of dollars) for different computer industry positions. (Source: *Source EDP, 1994 Computer Salary Survey*)

SPECIALISTS:	Median Salary ($000)
Data Base Management	
Data Base Analyst	45
Data Base Administrator	50
LAN Administrator	40
End User Support	
PC Support Specialist	35
PC Analyst	41
System Administrator/Mgr.	42
Telecommunications	
Voice Analyst	37
Data Communications Analyst	45
System Programmer	46
EDP Auditing	
EDP Auditor	37
Senior EDP Auditor	45
Technical Writing	
Writer	30
Editor	38
System Integrator	46
MANAGEMENT:	
MIS Director/CIO	
Small/Medium Shop	58
Large Shop	70
Applications Development	61
Technical Services	59
Project Manager	58
Project Leader	50
SALES:	
Account Representative	57
Pre/Post Sales Support Rep.	41
Management	74
DATA CENTER:	
Data Center Manager	46
Computer Operations	
Operator	22
Senior Operator	27
Operations Support	
Technician	30
Senior Technician	33
Communications/Network	
Operator	32
Senior Operator	38

PROGRAMMER COMPENSATION BY INDUSTRY

	Salary	% of Average
Financial Services	$38,913	115.6%
Other Services	37,715	112.0%
Manufacturing	36,431	108.2%
Government	36,108	107.2%
Information Services	34,865	103.5%
Transportation /Utilities	33,806	100.4%
Retail	32,744	97.2%
Education	30,926	91.8%
Medical/Legal Services	30,457	90.5%
Construction/Mining/ Agriculture	30,000	89.1%
Average	**$33,672**	**100.0%**

Figure 14-8
Some industries tend to pay more for the same job position. This table shows the average 1994 salary for a programmer.
(Source: *Datamation Magazine 1994 Salary Survey*)

PROJECTED GROWTH 1992 - 2005
(thousands of jobs)

	1992	2005	Change	% Change
Systems Analysts	455	956	501	110%
Programmers	555	723	168	30%
Computer Repair	83	120	37	45%

Figure 14-9
The table above shows the projected growth rates for computer-related careers as compiled by the U. S. Bureau of Labor Statistics.

Preparing for a Career in Information Processing

To prepare for a career in the information processing industry, individuals must decide what computer field they are interested in and obtain education in the field they choose. The three major computer fields and some of the opportunities for obtaining education in those fields are described below.

What Are the Fields in the Information Processing Industry?

While this book has focused primarily on the use of computers in business, three broad fields actually exist in the information processing industry: computer information systems; computer science; and computer engineering. **Computer information systems** (CIS) refers to the use of computers to provide the information needed to operate businesses and other organizations. The field of **computer science** includes the technical and theoretical aspects of computers and system software. **Computer engineering** deals with the design and manufacturing of electronic computer components and computer hardware. Each field provides unique career opportunities and has specialized requirements.

Obtaining Education for Information Processing Careers

Trade schools, technical schools, community colleges, colleges, and universities all offer formal education and certification or degree programs in computer information systems, computer science, and computer engineering. Usually, schools have separate programs for each area.

With the wide variety of career opportunities that exist in information processing, it is difficult to make anything other than broad general statements when it comes to discussing degree requirements for employment in the industry. As in most other industries, the more advanced degree an individual has in a chosen field, the better that individual's chances are for success. While not having a degree may limit a person's opportunities for securing a top position, it will neither prevent entry nor preclude success in an information processing career.

Career Development in the Information Processing Industry

People employed in the information processing industry have several ways to develop their skills and increase recognition among their peers. These include professional organizations, certification, and professional growth and continuing education activities. Numerous publications also can help an individual keep up with changes in the information processing industry.

Professional Organizations

Computer-related organizations have been formed by people who have common interests and a desire to share their knowledge. Two of the organizations that have been influential in the industry are the Association for Computing Machinery (ACM) and the Data Processing Management Association (DPMA). The **Association for Computing Machinery** (ACM) is composed of persons interested in computer science and computer science education. A large number of college and university computer educators are members. The **Data Processing Management Association** (DPMA) is a professional association of programmers, systems analysts, and information processing managers. Both ACM and DPMA offer the following benefits:
- chapters throughout the United States and in several foreign countries
- monthly meetings
- workshops, seminars, and conventions
- journals and articles
- special interest groups (SIGs)
- continuing education material
- student chapters

Attending professional meetings provides an excellent opportunity for students to learn about the information processing industry and to meet and talk with professionals in the field.

In addition to these and other professional organizations, user groups exist for most makes of computers. A **user group** is a group of people with common computer equipment or software interests that meet regularly to share information. Most metropolitan areas have one or more local computer societies that meet monthly to discuss topics of common interest about personal computers. For anyone employed or interested in the computer industry, these groups can be an effective and rewarding way to learn and continue career development.

Certification

Many professions offer certification programs to encourage and recognize the efforts of their members to attain a level of knowledge about their professions. Some computer industry companies, such as Novell, Microsoft, and IBM, offer certification programs on their hardware and software products. Although no states require that computer professionals be certified or licensed, it has been proposed by some groups.

The most widely recognized certification program in the information processing industry is administered by the **Institute for the Certification of Computer Professionals** (ICCP). The Institute is sponsored and supported by several professional organizations including ACM and DPMA. Prior to 1994, the ICCP offered four different certification designations. The best known of these was the Certified Data Processor (CDP). Other designations were Certified Computer Programmer (CCP), Certified Systems Professional (CSP), and Associate Computer Professional (ACP). Starting in 1994, the first three designations were combined under one standard title: **Certified Computing Professional** (CCP). The **Associate Computing Professional** (ACP) still exists for entry level personnel. To become certified, a CCP candidate must pass a core examination and any two specialty examinations. ACP candidates must pass the core examination and at least one computer language test. *Figure 14-10* summarizes the requirements for the certifications.

Professional Growth and Continuing Education

Because of rapid changes in technology, staying aware of new products and services in the information processing industry can be a challenging task. One way of keeping up is by participating in professional growth and continuing education activities. This broad category includes events such as

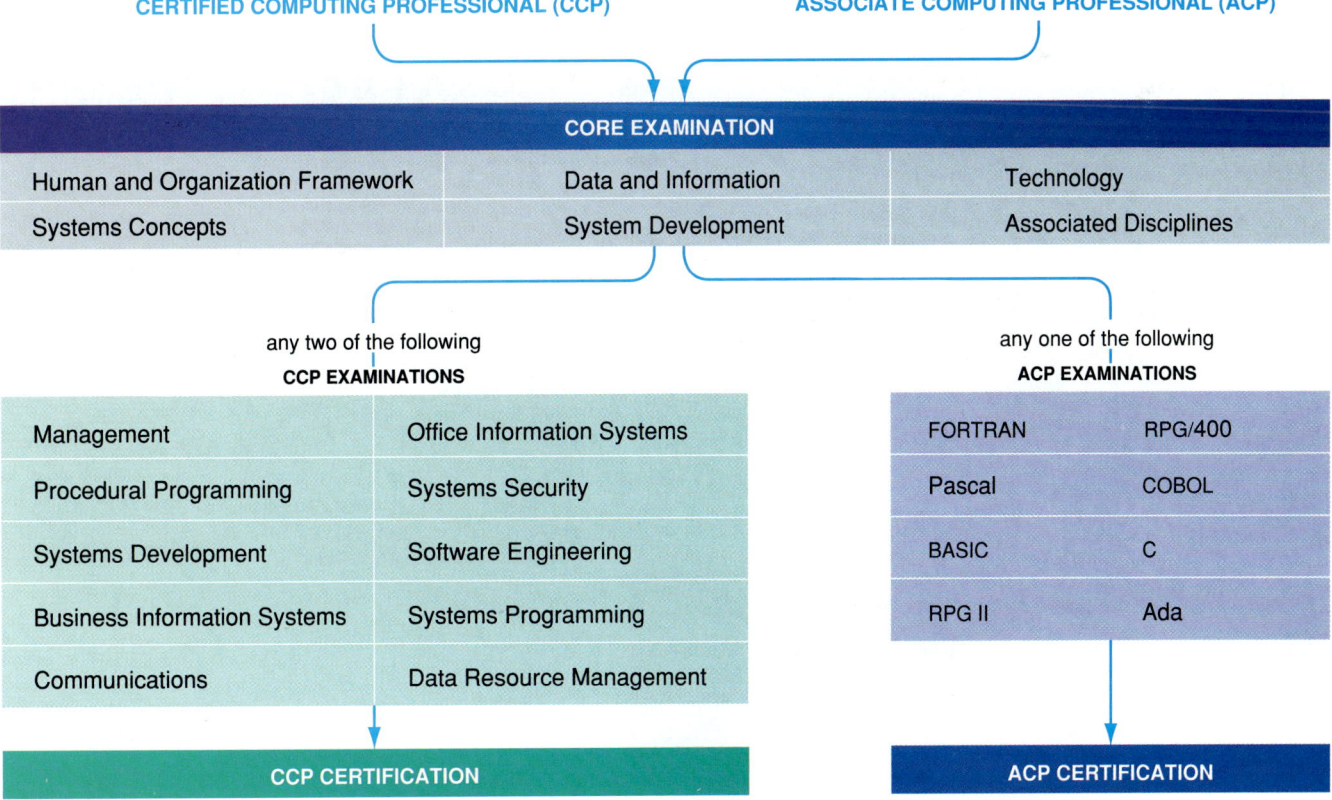

Figure 14-10
The Institute for the Certification of Computer Professionals (ICCP) offers two certification programs. This chart summarizes the examination requirements for each program.

workshops, seminars, conferences, conventions, and trade shows that provide both general and specific information on equipment, software, services, and issues affecting the industry. Workshops and seminars usually last a day or two, while conferences, conventions, and trade shows often last a week. The largest trade show in the United States, **COMDEX**, brings together over 2,000 vendors to display their newest products and services to 200,000 attendees *(Figure 14-11)*.

Computer Publications

Another way of keeping informed about what is going on in the computer industry is to regularly read one or more computer industry publications *(Figure 14-12)*. You can choose from hundreds of publications. Some publications, such as *Computerworld, InfoWorld,* and *PC Week,* are like newspapers and cover a wide range of issues. Other publications are oriented toward a particular topic area such as communications, personal computers, or a specific equipment manufacturer. Many of the more popular publications can be found in public or school libraries.

Summary of Computer Career Opportunities

With the increased use of computers, the prospects for computer-related career opportunities are excellent. Not only are the numbers of traditional information processing jobs, such as programmer and systems analyst, expected to increase, but the application of the computer to existing occupations will create additional job opportunities. Regardless of an individual's career choice, a basic understanding of computers should be an essential part of any employee's job skills.

As discussed in the remainder of this chapter, computers will continue to have an important impact on work and leisure activities.

Figure 14-11
COMDEX is one of the largest computer product trade shows in the world. More than 2,000 vendors display their newest products and services to 200,000 attendees.

Trends in Computers and Information Processing

The features titled In the Future at the end of each chapter highlight computer-related developments that may take place in the near future. The following section discusses additional changes that are likely to happen in the workplace and at home based on current trends. Before discussing these changes, however, two trends that will have a widespread influence will be reviewed; digital convergence and the application of artificial intelligence.

Digital Convergence

Digital convergence describes the merging of technologies and products from the communications, entertainment, publishing, and computing industries. What is making this merger possible is the conversion of the information transmitted by each of these industries into a digital form that can be processed, stored, and distributed by computers. The conversion of non-computer information into a digital form has been going on for some time but has been limited by hardware and software. For example, digital phone service has been available for a number of years but digitized video, which requires tremendous amounts of data, has not been widely implemented. Recent advances in both hardware and software, however, make it clear that high-quality digitized video and audio will eventually be widely available. The following section will discuss some of the changes that will take place in the areas of communications, entertainment, and publishing.

In the area of communications, wider use of fiber optic cabling will allow data to be transmitted at higher speeds. The higher volume transmission will enable data-intensive

Figure 14-12
Numerous computer industry publications are available at bookstores, libraries, or by subscription.

applications such as video and graphics to be transmitted over phone equipment. Video will become a more common component of transmitted information such as electronic mail. Another probable application of video will allow customer service representatives to show customers how to use or repair their products while they are talking to them.

Wireless communications will also become more common. Personal digital assistants (PDAs), the small hand-held computing devices that are used by mobile workers, usually have a wireless capability to send and receive data.

In the entertainment area, the digitization will mean that entertainment products such as movies and television programming can be distributed in ways not previously possible. For example, in the future, a user could choose a personalized selection of previously recorded shows, movies, or events and have them down loaded into their digital entertainment system to be viewed at the user's convenience. It will certainly be more convenient than trying to program a VCR to record multiple events!

In the area of publishing, significant changes already are underway. For example, every picture and every drawing in this book is digitized. These digitized images are placed into position on each page by a designer using a computer application called QuarkXpress. Then, through the use of specialized equipment, the digitized book is transformed to film from which printing plates are made.

Several major newspapers and magazines now offer online versions of their publications.

Another available service allows a user to choose any number of topics on which they want to receive information. The service company, which reviews and classifies articles from numerous sources, provides the user with a summary of the articles that meet the user's area of interest. Full versions of the articles also can be provided. Digitized electronic versions of traditional books also are becoming increasingly available.

Eventually, all forms of communications (written, visual, and audio) will be digitized and will be able to be stored, modified, and communicated by computers.

Figure 14-13
Robots are often used in situations requiring repetitive actions and where it would be unsafe or unhealthy for a human to perform the same task.

Artificial Intelligence

Artificial intelligence (AI) is the application of human intelligence to computers. Stated another way, it is the attempt to make computers imitate human actions and thinking. Experts predict that eventually some form of AI will be incorporated into most products and services. Several AI applications have been previously discussed; voice input and speech recognition (Chapter 3), expert systems (Chapter 10), and a natural language interface (Chapter 12). The following sections discuss four other applications of AI: robotics, vision systems, fuzzy logic, and agent software.

Robotics

Robotics deals with the development of **robots**, which are devices that mimic human actions and appear to function with some degree of intelligence. Robots are commonly used in manufacturing and in other situations where it would be unsafe or unhealthy for a human to perform the same task *(Figure 14-13)*.

Vision Systems

A **vision system** uses a camera and a computer to identify objects by digitizing their image and then comparing the image against a database of known shapes. Based on the identity of the object, the computer can be programmed to take a specific action. Vision systems are currently used to inspect products for manufacturing errors such as missing or broken parts. The U.S. Army has an experimental driver-less vehicle that uses a vision system to avoid obstacles such as boulders or ditches while driving over rough terrain.

Fuzzy Logic

Fuzzy logic, a type of mathematics, deals with values that are not precise and values that have a degree of uncertainty. For example, consider the following simplified situation. A production manager is trying to estimate the number of products a new assembly line will be able to produce. His best guess is 60 units per hour. Under the worst conditions, he believes the assembly line can produce at least 40 units per hour and under the best conditions perhaps as many as 100 units per hour. Assigning a weight of 1.0 to his most likely guess and zero to his best and worst case estimates, a diagram like the one shown in *Figure 14-14* is produced. This fuzzy logic diagram graphically represents the degree of certainty associated with the estimated range of assembly line

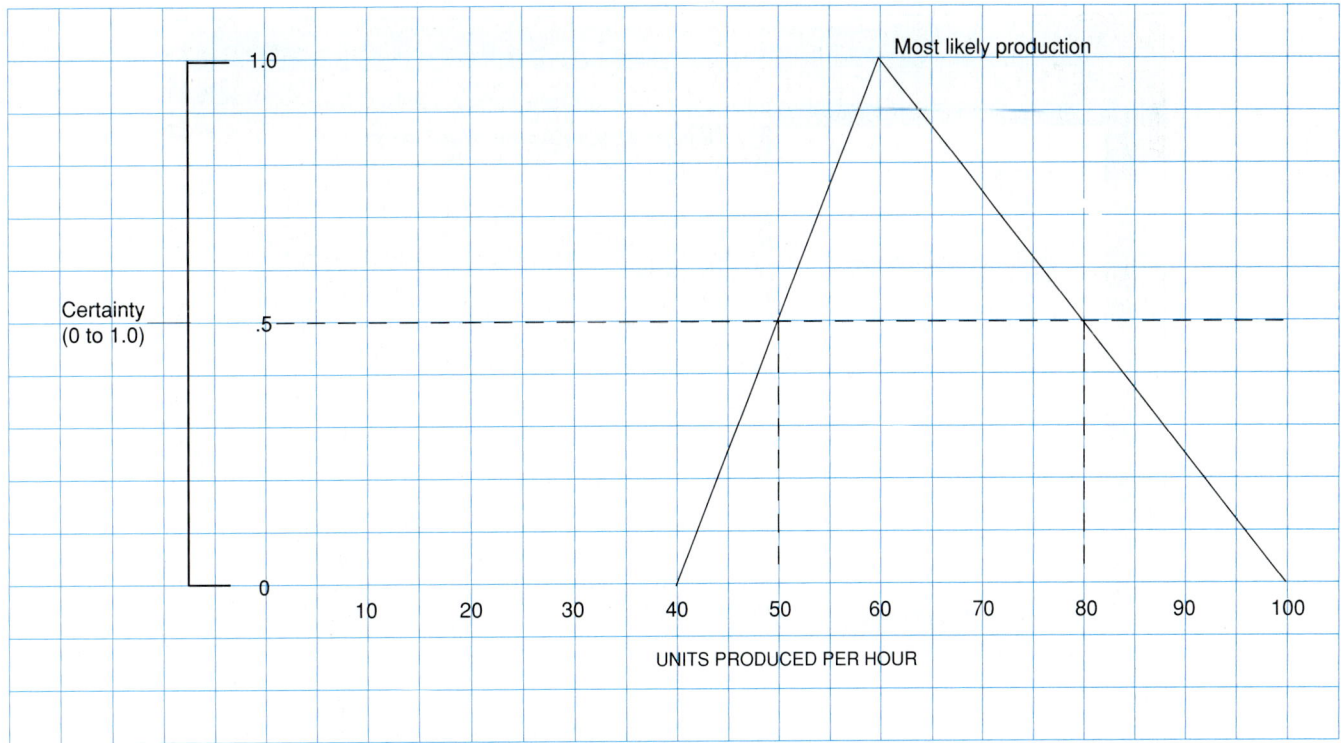

Figure 14-14
Fuzzy logic deals with imprecise numbers and degrees of certainty and uncertainty. This fuzzy logic diagram represents the number of units a production manager thinks a new assembly line will produce each hour. The production manager's confidence level, from a low of zero to a high of 1.0, is shown on the left side of the chart. The chart shows the production manager is 50% certain that production will be between 50 and 80 units per hour.

output. For example, the diagram shows there is a 50% certainty the output will be between 50 and 80 units per hour.

To date, applications of fuzzy logic primarily have been in controllers for consumer products such as video cameras, air conditioners, and washing machines. In these products, fuzzy logic is used to make continuous small adjustments instead of merely switching a feature on or off. Wider use of fuzzy logic is expected as fuzzy logic software tools are developed.

Agent Software

For more than 40 years, AI experts have talked about the advantages of *smart software;* that is, software with built-in intelligence. In recent years, this concept has become known as agent software. Although not precisely defined, the term **agent** has come to mean a software program that can independently carry out tasks on behalf of a user. Some agents perform work within a single program and other agents, sometimes called *network agents,* perform tasks on remote computers before bringing the results back to the user.

An example of agents that work within single programs are the *wizards* included with Microsoft Corporation's productivity software applications, such as Word and Excel. Wizards take you step-by-step through a process such as creating a document. Wizards prompt the user to answer questions and then use the answers to complete the task. *Figure 14-15* shows a wizard screen used to create a memorandum. Other software developers have incorporated smart software similar to wizards.

Network agents are generally more intelligent than wizards because they perform their work on remote computers and cannot prompt the user for information on how to continue. A common use of a network agent is gathering information on a particular subject. For example, a network agent might be directed to research all references to Civil War battles in the state of Virginia. Some network agents require specific instructions but others can be given general instructions such as "book a flight from New York to Boston on the morning of June 20." The agent software would then choose which airline and a specific flight from the flights available. Agent software already has been incorporated into several E-mail packages that allow the user to filter incoming messages and be immediately notified of messages from specific individuals or on specific subjects.

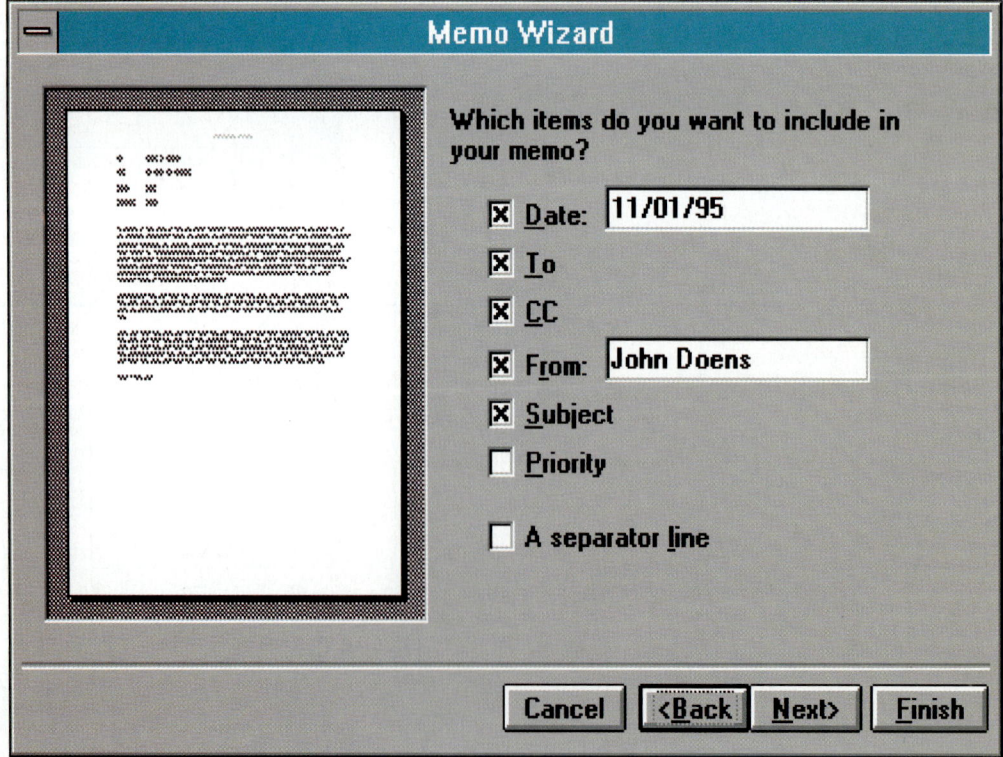

Figure 14-15
Microsoft Word word processing software includes wizards, which are software agents that help a user complete tasks. The wizards ask the user to fill in information or accept the default values. The answers are then used to automatically complete the task, in this case, creating a memorandum document.

Information Systems in Business

The largest use of computers is in business. Millions of systems ranging from mainframes to personal computers are installed and used for applications such as inventory control, billing, and accounting. This section discusses how these traditional applications will be affected by changes in technology and methods.

How Will Existing Information Systems Change?

Existing business information systems will continue to undergo profound changes as new technology, software, and methods are applied to the huge installed base of traditional business system users. The expansion of networks and the increased use of digitized information means that users will have a wider variety of data and information available for decision making, and more flexibility presenting information on reports and displays. The increased number of people using computers will make the computer-user interface even more important. These and other trends that will affect the information systems of tomorrow are shown in *Figure 14-16* on this and the next page.

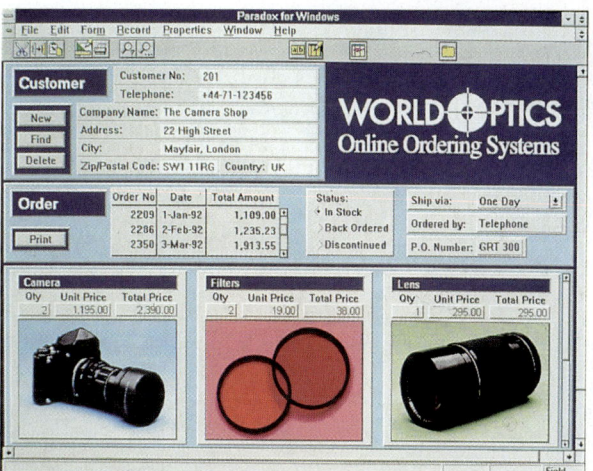

SOFTWARE
- Fourth-generation and natural languages will enable the user to communicate with the computer in a more conversational manner
- Object orientation will combine processes and methods with data
- Computer aided software engineering (CASE) and rapid application development (RAD) will shorten the system development time frame
- Increased use of decision support and artificial intelligence systems will help users make decisions
- Easier access to networks such as the Internet
- Operating systems available for multiplatform use
- Integrated applications will eliminate the need for separate programs for word processing, spreadsheets, graphics, telecommunications, and other applications
- Virtual reality will be common for training and recreation

EQUIPMENT
- Increased use of personal computers networked to other PCs and to server computers
- World-wide communication networks will allow users to access data or send messages from any location
- Larger systems will be used as central storehouses of data with processing done on a decentralized basis by powerful personal computers
- Increased use of page printers that can print high quality graphics and text
- Reduced instruction set computers (RISC) and parallel processing that will greatly increase the number of instructions that can be processed at one time
- Increased use of portable computing equipment such as notebook computers and personal digital assistants
- Increased competition among processor manufacturers will lead to much faster and less expensive computers
- Plug and play components will enable additional features to be easily added to systems

Figure 14-16
Trends affecting information systems of tomorrow.

DATA
- Automatic input of data at the source where it is created
- Compound documents that combine text, numbers, and non-text data such as voice, image, and full motion video
- Digital cash will facilitate online commercial transactions

Figure 14-16 (continued)

USERS
- Most people will be "computer literate," with a basic understanding of how computers work, and how to use them in their jobs
- Increased responsibility for design, operation, and maintenance of information processing systems
- Users will increasingly rely on computers to manage the continuing proliferation of information (the worldwide volume of printed information doubles every eight years)
- Will use computers to collaborate with other workers
- Will use computers and online databases to obtain information and update skills and knowledge

INFORMATION SYSTEMS PERSONNEL
- Increased interface with users
- Shift from machine and software orientation to user application orientation
- Emphasis will change from how to capture and process data to how to more effectively use the data available and create information
- Reduced staff levels will have to handle increased processing workloads
- Some processing operations will be "outsourced" to independent contractors
- Continuous need for retraining and education to keep up with new technology

The Automated Office

The **automated office**, sometimes referred to as the **electronic office**, makes use of electronic devices such as computers, facsimile machines, and computerized telephone systems to make office work more productive. Automated office applications, such as word processing, electronic mail, voice mail, desktop publishing, facsimile, image processing, and teleconferencing, started out as separate, stand-alone applications. In recent years, however, the trend has been to integrate these applications into a network of devices and services that can share information. According to surveys, over one-half of the U.S. workforce has access to a PC and half of the PCs used in business are connected to some type of network. Eventually all applications will be integrated and users will be able to combine tasks that are now performed separately.

Stand-alone office machines also will become part of the same networks used to link computers *(Figure 14-17)*. In

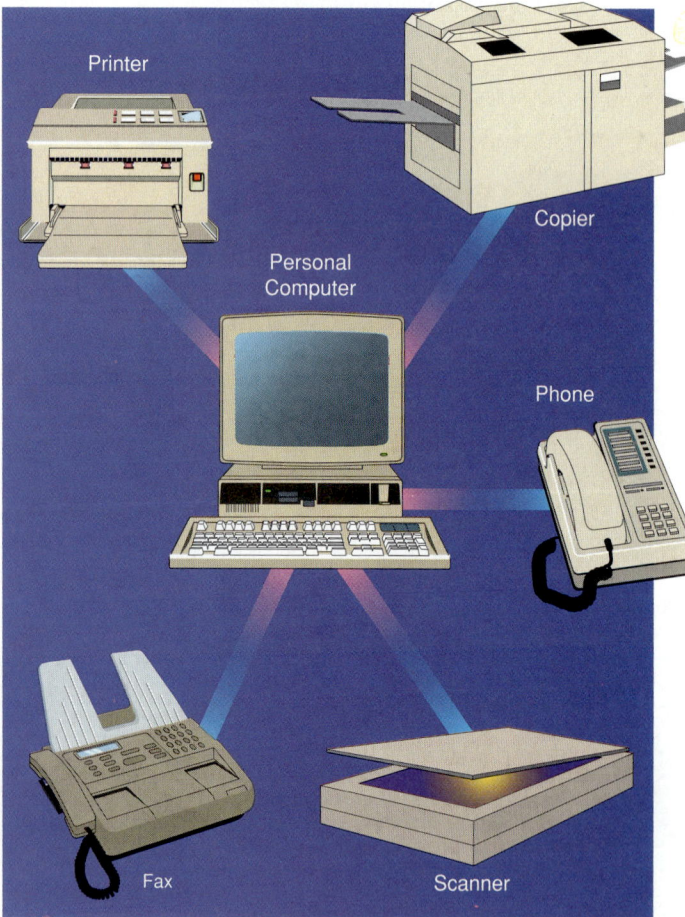

Figure 14-17
Eventually, most office machines will be connected to computer networks and share information with other devices.

a concept called **Microsoft At Work**, Microsoft Corporation has proposed a standardized intelligent graphical user interface that will be built into all office machines such as copiers, printers, and fax machines. The interface will allow data to be sent to or received from any device on the network. The office phone system also will become part of an organization's network. Microphones and speakers will be incorporated into desktop computer systems and automatic dialing will be a utility program that can be accessed from any application. Incoming calls, including the name and photo of the caller (if on file), will be displayed on a user's screen.

Another condition that will be affected by technology improvements is the amount of paper used in the office. A goal of having a *paperless* office may not be realistic but the increasing use of electronic documents will result in the *less-paper* office. One advantage of electronic documents is that they can incorporate video and sound data elements.

In the future, office equipment and tasks will be automated and *smart*.

The Digital Factory

As with automated office applications, the goal of the **digital factory** is to increase productivity through the use of networked, computer-controlled equipment. Technologies used in the digital factory include computer-aided design, computer-aided engineering, and computer-aided manufacturing. Once thought of as stand-alone processes, these technologies now are being linked together into what is called computer-integrated manufacturing. A brief review of these technologies follows.

COMPUTER-AIDED DESIGN (CAD)

Computer-aided design (CAD) uses a computer and special graphics software to aid in product design *(Figure 14-18)*. The CAD software eliminates the laborious drafting that used to be required and allows the designer to dynamically change the size of some or all of the product and view the design from different angles. The capability to store the design electronically offers several advantages over traditional manual methods. One advantage is that the designs can be changed more easily than before. Another is that the design database can be reviewed more easily by other design engineers.

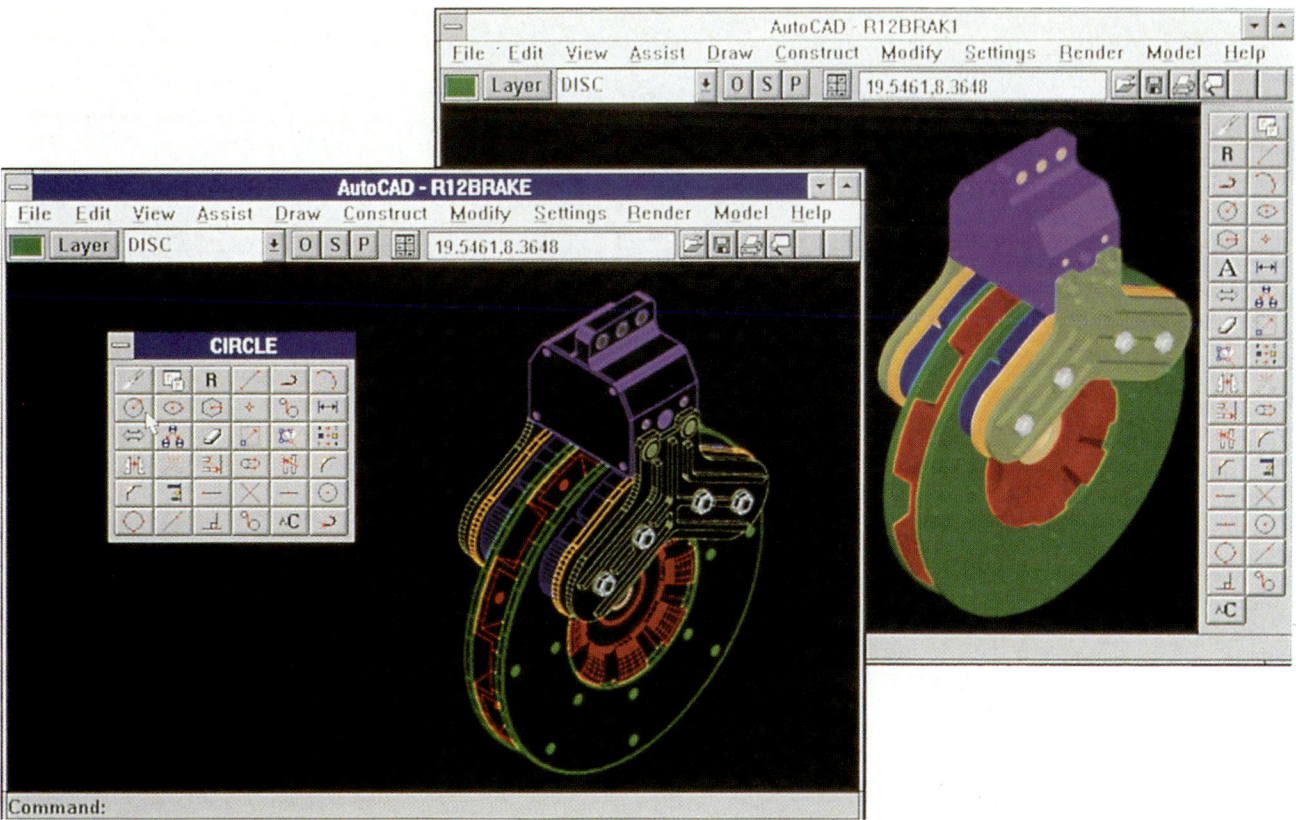

Figure 14-18
Computer-aided design (CAD) is an efficient way to develop plans for new products.

This increases the likelihood that an existing part will be used in a product instead of a new part designed. For example, if a support bracket was required for a new product, the design engineer could review the design database to see if any existing products used a support bracket that would be appropriate for the new product. This not only decreases the overall design time but increases the reliability of the new product by using proven parts.

COMPUTER-AIDED ENGINEERING (CAE)

Computer-aided engineering (CAE) is the use of computers to test product designs. Using CAE, engineers can test the design of a car or a bridge before it is built *(Figure 14-19)*. Sophisticated programs simulate the effects of wind, temperature, weight, and stress on product shapes and materials. Before the use of CAE, prototypes of products had to be built and subjected to testing that often destroyed the prototype. CAE allows engineers to create a computer prototype that can be tested under a variety of conditions. CAE allows products to be tested in some conditions, such as earthquakes, that could not previously be simulated.

COMPUTER-AIDED MANUFACTURING (CAM)

Computer-aided manufacturing (CAM) is the use of computers to control production equipment. CAM production equipment includes software-controlled drilling, lathe, welding, and milling machines.

COMPUTER-INTEGRATED MANUFACTURING (CIM)

Computer-integrated manufacturing (CIM) is the total integration of the manufacturing process using computers *(Figure 14-20)*. Using CIM concepts, individual production processes are linked so that the production flow is balanced and optimized and products flow at an even rate through the factory. In a CIM factory, automated design processes are linked to automated machining processes that are linked to automated assembly processes that are linked to automated testing and packaging. Under ideal CIM conditions, a product will move through the entire production process under computer control. Many companies may never fully implement CIM because it is so complex. But CIM's related concepts of minimum inventory and efficient demand-driven production are valid and will be incorporated into many manufacturers' business plans.

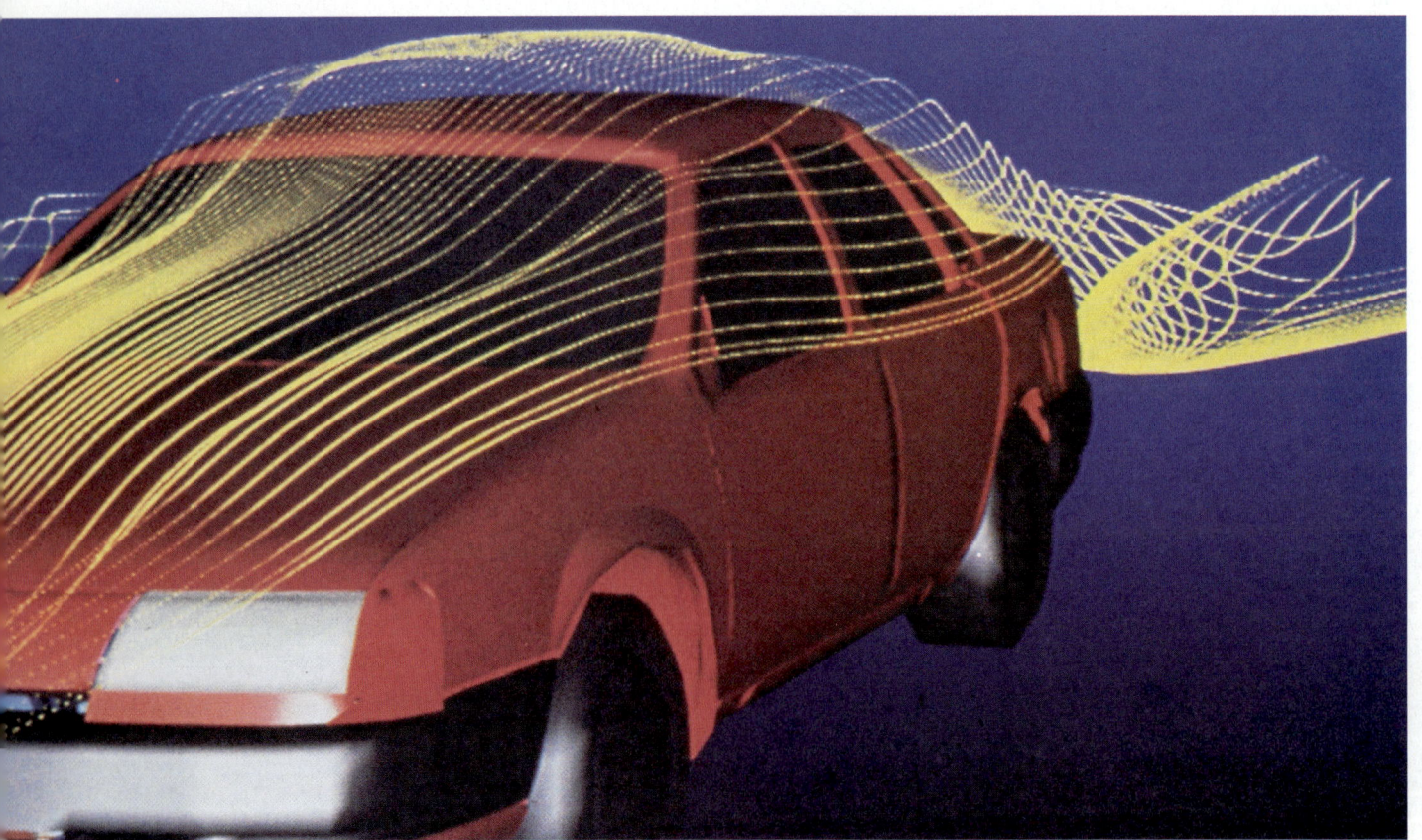

Figure 14-19
Computer-aided engineering (CAE) allows the user to test a product design before the product is built.

The Computer-Integrated Enterprise

Although in the previous sections we discuss the office and factory separately, the trend is the **computer-integrated enterprise** – an organization in which all information storage and processing is performed by a network of computers and intelligent devices. In a computer-integrated enterprise, all office, factory, warehouse, and communications systems are linked using a common interface allowing authorized users in any functional area of the organization to access and use data stored anywhere in the organization. Instead of being machine- or software-oriented as today's systems, future systems will be document- or information-oriented. The user will not need to separately start a word processing, spreadsheet, or communications program. Instead, users will be able to create and distribute compound documents that contain text, graphics, numbers, and full-motion video. They will be able to record, in their own voice, comments or questions about the document before it is stored or routed to someone else in the organization. For example, a new product marketing plan could contain a text description of the product, a spreadsheet showing projected sales, and a narrated video showing the product in use. If the president of a company had questions about the plan, he or she could add questions to the plan in his or her own voice, and route the plan to the appropriate person for a response.

Bringing the Information Age Home

Millions of personal computers have been purchased for home use, and the use of personal computers in the home is expected to increase. Currently, approximately one in three homes have at least one personal computer. In 1994, for the first time, the sales of PCs for home use equaled the purchases of PCs for business use. Just as the use of computers in the workplace has changed how people work, the use of computers in homes is changing family life.

The Use of Personal Computers in the Home

People use personal computers in their homes in a variety of ways. These ways usually fall into five general categories: (1) personal services, (2) control of home systems, (3) telecommuting, (4) education, and (5) entertainment.

PERSONAL SERVICES

In many ways, running a home is similar to running a small business. The productivity tools you use in the office, such as word processing, spreadsheet, and database, also can be used in the home to help you with creating documents,

Figure 14-20
The concept of computer-integrated manufacturing (CIM) is to use computers to integrate all phases of the manufacturing process from planning and design to manufacturing and distribution.

with financial planning and analysis, and with filing and organizing data. Personal computer software also is available to assist you with home accounting applications such as balancing checkbooks, making household budgets, and preparing tax returns *(Figure 14-21)*. In addition, using a personal computer to transmit and receive data over telephone lines allows home users to access a wealth of information and services from online service providers such as America Online and Prodigy. Stock brokerage firms such as Charles Schwab & Co. have developed software that allows users to buy and sell stock online and manage their investments. Eventually, most if not all financial services will be able to be performed from home using a computer.

CONTROL OF HOME SYSTEMS

Another use of computers in the home is to control home systems such as security, environment, lighting, and landscape sprinkler systems. Personal computers used in this manner are usually linked to special devices such as alarms for security; thermostats for temperature control; and timing devices for lighting and sprinkler systems. For example, if the personal computer system has communications capabilities, a homeowner who is away can use a telephone or another computer to call home and change the operation of one of the control systems. Suppose a homeowner is on vacation in Texas and learns that heavy rains have been falling at home in Pennsylvania. He or she could call the computer and use the keys of a touch-tone telephone to instruct the computer to turn off the garden sprinkler system.

Most existing home control systems were installed after the home was built and often consist of separate systems to control each set of devices. This will change in the future. The Electronic Industries Association has issued a wiring standard called the Consumer Electronics Bus (CEBus). The CEBus sets standards for sending information throughout a home using existing electrical wiring, phone lines, TV cable, and nonwired techniques such as radio waves. In a related effort, Echelon Corporation is designing chips to be used in consumer electronics and building products. The chips will allow appliances, lighting systems, and other home products to be networked together and controlled by a single system using a consistent set of commands *(Figure 14-22)*. Although they are not yet widely implemented, these changes will result in what many refer to as the intelligent

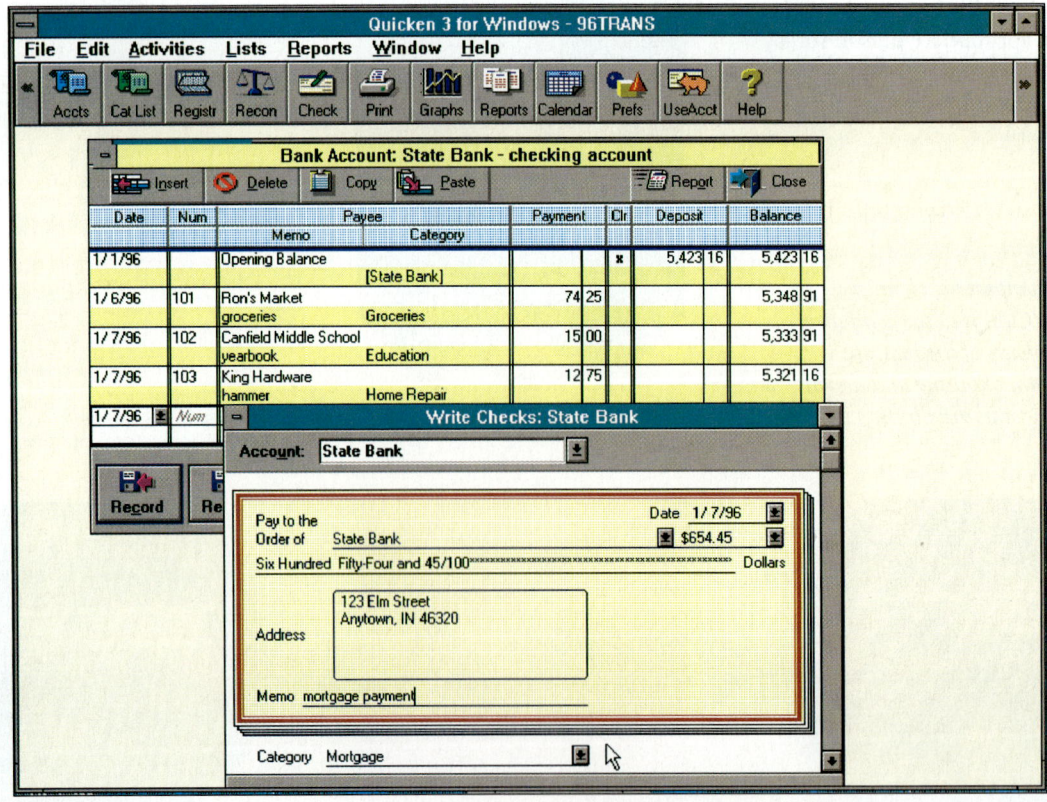

Figure 14-21
A number of personal finance programs, such as Quicken for Windows shown here, help keep track of personal expenditures and allow you to produce computer-prepared checks.

home or smart house. Smart home products are expected to be a $2 billion a year business by the year 2000.

TELECOMMUTING

Telecommuting refers to the ability of individuals to work away from the office, often at home and communicate by using personal computers and communications lines. Many companies have found that employees can do their jobs just as well on the road or at home. According to one survey, nearly 10 million people telecommute to work at least two times a week. Some cities such as Telluride, Colorado and Pullman, Washington have implemented programs to upgrade local communications capabilities in order to attract telecommuters. The number of telecommuters increases about 20% each year and is expected to include as many as 20 million workers by the year 2000.

EDUCATION

The use of personal computers for education, called **computer-aided instruction** (CAI), is another rapidly growing area. Whereas CAI is frequently used to describe software that is developed and used in schools, much of the same software is available for home users. CAI software can be classified into three types: drill and practice, tutorials, and simulations.

Drill and practice software uses a flash-card approach to teaching by allowing users to practice skills in subjects such as math and language. A problem or word appears on the computer screen and the user enters the answer. The computer accepts the answer and responds by telling the student whether the answer is correct or incorrect. Sometimes the user gets second and third chances to select the correct answer before the computer software reveals the correct answer.

With **tutorial software**, the computer software uses text, graphics, and sometimes sound to teach a user concepts about subjects such as chemistry, music theory, or computer literacy. Following the instruction, tutorial software might present true/false or multiple choice questions to help the user ensure that he or she understands the concepts.

The third type of CAI, **simulation software**, is designed to teach a user by creating a model of a real-life situation. For example, many simulation packages are available to teach business concepts.

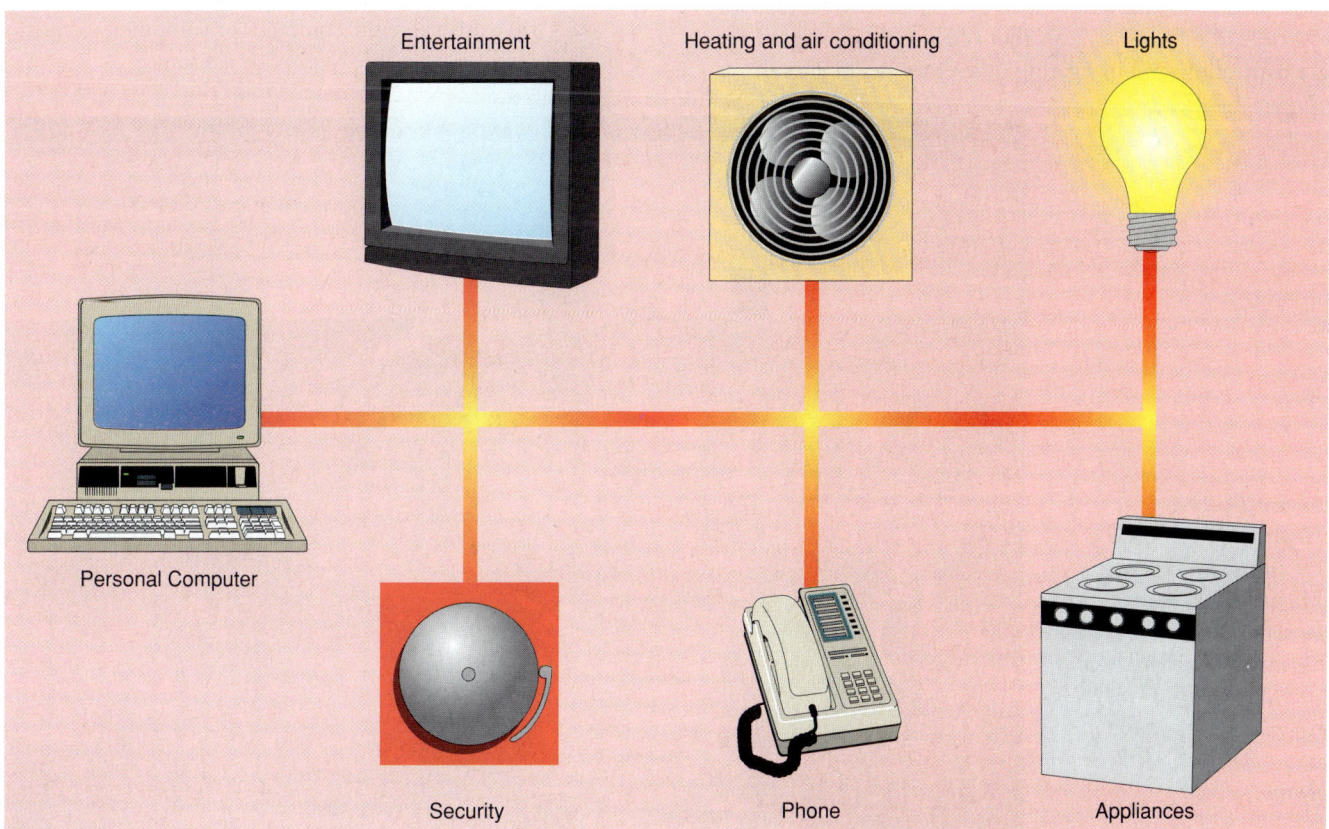

Figure 14-22
Eventually, many homes will contain networks that will enable household devices to be connected to a central computer.

In an approach that is sometimes called **remote learning**, some trade schools, colleges and universities now offer students with personal computers the opportunity to take electronic correspondence courses in their homes. Lessons and assignments for classes are transmitted between the student and the school over communications lines.

Education in the home through CAI or electronic correspondence courses allows home users to learn at their own pace, in the convenience of their home, and at a time that fits into their personal schedule. Well-written educational software can be so entertaining that it is sometimes difficult to distinguish between it and entertainment software.

ENTERTAINMENT

Entertainment software, or game playing, on home computers always has had a large following among the younger members of the family. Many adults, however, are surprised to find that entertainment software also can provide them with hours of enjoyment. Popular types of entertainment software include arcade games, board games, simulations, and interactive graphics programs. Most people are familiar with the arcade-type games (similar to video games) that are available for computers. A popular board game is computer chess. Simulations include games such as baseball and football and a variety of flight simulators that allow users to pretend they are controlling and navigating different types of aircraft (Figure 14-23).

Also available are a wide variety of interactive graphic adventure games that range from rescuing a princess from a castle's dungeon to solving a murder mystery. Some games can be played in groups using a network. The software usually allows players to adjust the level of play to match their abilities, that is, beginner through advanced. With entertainment software, the computer becomes a fun, skillful, and challenging game partner.

In addition to playing games, some personal computer users use their home computer as a tool for personal hobbies. Computers are used by hobbyists to design quilt and stained glass patterns, run model trains, organize stamp, doll, and photography collections, and write, transpose, play, and print musical scores.

Summary of Your Future in the Information Age

Based on current and planned developments, the impact of computers and the information age will be even greater in the future than it has been to date. Individual PCs, in the workplace and the home, will increasingly be connected to networks that will provide access to information and services. Few tasks will exist where the computer or computer accessed information will not be able to provide assistance.

Figure 14-23
Flight simulators, such as the one shown here from Microsoft Corporation, can be both fun and educational. Some simulators offer realistic instrument consoles and regional flight patterns that help teach the user about flying.

COMPUTERS AT WORK

Rapid Prototyping Using Stereolithography

Using a process called stereolithography, manufacturers can now produce prototype parts directly from engineering drawings. **Stereolithography** (SL) uses a computer, a laser, and photochemistry to build a three dimensional model of a part one thin layer at a time.

The process starts with special software that converts a computer-aided design (CAD) drawing into horizontal slices 0.0025 inches thick. This information is used to direct an ultraviolet laser beam towards a vat of a liquid plastic called photopolymer. Wherever the liquid plastic is exposed to the laser, it hardens. After each pass of the laser, a platform in the liquid is lowered, submerging the hardened material just under the surface of the liquid plastic. Each pass of the laser adds another layer of hardened plastic that bonds with the previously created material. Layer by layer, the part is formed. After the part is completely formed, it is removed from the vat and exposed to ultraviolet radiation to finish hardening. The finished part can then be sanded, painted, or sprayed with a metal coating.

Because three dimensional prototypes are a common requirement for most industrial and consumer products, stereolithography has a large potential marketplace. More than 80% of the world's auto manufacturers and 75% of the major aerospace and aircraft manufacturers use stereolithography in their engineering and manufacturing operations. Without using stereolithography or some other rapid prototyping technology, prototypes have to be made the traditional way; by hand or by using machine tools to cut, grind, and drill a part into shape. Stereolithography is a much faster and more precise process and can be used several times in the same amount of time it would take with traditional methods. Users of stereolithography systems have reported cost and time savings of approximately 50%. Although full stereolithography systems can cost up to $500,000, 3D Systems of California, the leading stereolithography system supplier, is developing a desktop system that could eventually sell for as little as $5,000.

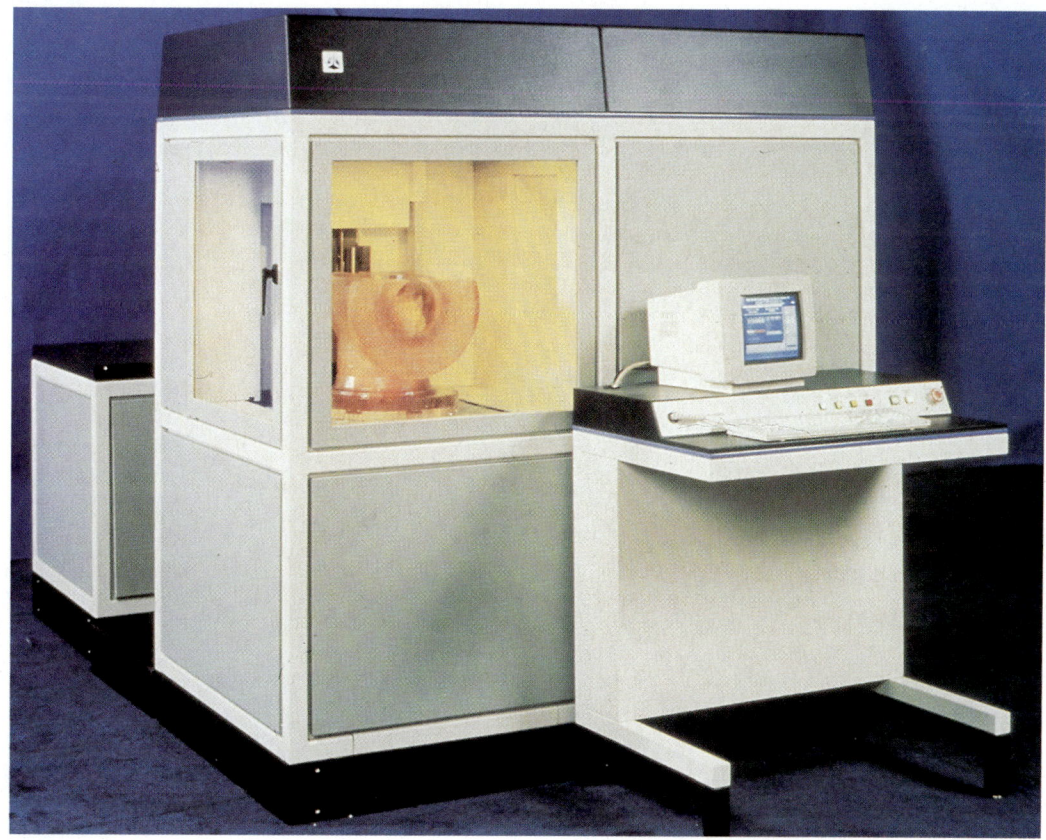

Figure 14-24

IN THE FUTURE

Human Computer Integration

Microprocessors have rapidly spread from the desktop PC to many, if not most of the appliances people use everyday. Televisions, VCRs, stereos, phones, copiers, fax machines, microwaves, refrigerators, coffee makers, bread machines, alarm clocks, bathroom scales, and automobiles all contain one or more chips that monitor their operations and enable people to control some of the device's functions. Some believe that eventually the microprocessor will become an integral part of the most complex device known—the human body.

An early phase of this process will involve implanting chips to assist the body in performing its functions. For example, a microprocessor could be used to regulate the release of hormones in the same way that microprocessors regulate the fuel mixture in modern autos. An even more futuristic use of embedded microprocessors is called CyberSight, an application conceived by Canadian futurist Frank Ogden. With CyberSight, a microprocessor would interface with a person's optic nerve and allow him or her to see information transmitted over a wireless link. A firefighter, for example, could have the floor plans of a burning building transmitted from a computer database and displayed in his or her mind before deciding to enter. Or a police officer could download mug shots of suspected criminals from a criminal database without arousing suspicion or returning to the police car.

A further phase of human computer integration could involve downloading a person's intelligence into a microprocessor. The best estimates are that the human brain stores about 10^{18} bits of information, or a billion billion bits. The brain processes those bits at 10^{16} bits per second. Based on current chip densities, it would take a chip the size of a large house to store the amount of information the brain keeps track of. But if chip densities keep doubling every two years, as they have for the last twenty years, a chip that could fit in your hand (or your head) could hold 10^{18} bits by the year 2020. This potential technical possibility raises all sorts of challenging ethical questions. For example, if memories were recorded in a chip could they or should they be edited? Could they be used to prove or disprove someone's innocence or guilt? Could someone's silicon consciousness make legally binding decisions? These are just some of the questions that will have to be answered.

Figure 14-25

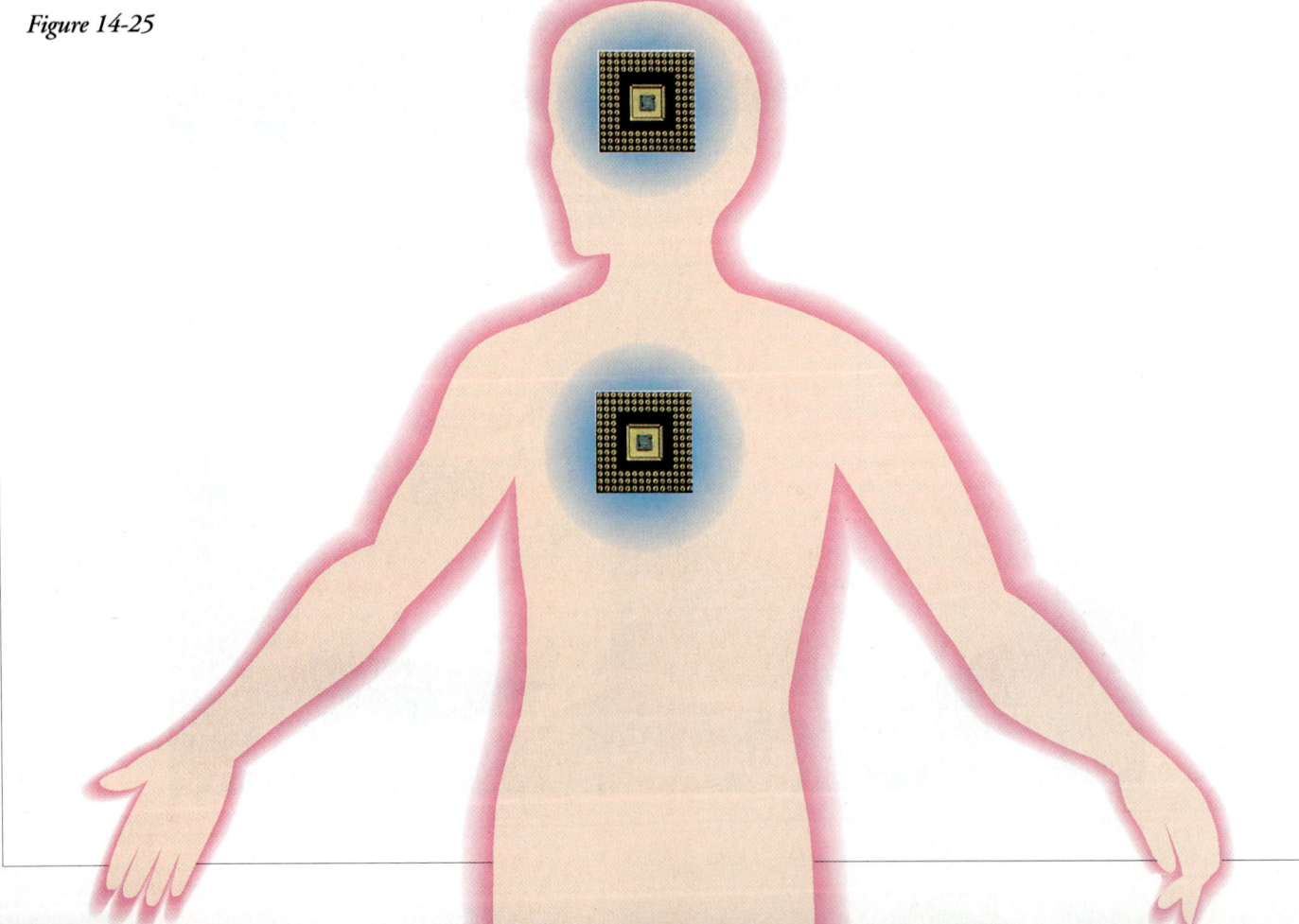

What You Should Know

1. The **information processing industry** is one of the largest industries in the world with annual sales of close to $200 billion. Job opportunities in the industry come primarily from three areas: the companies that manufacture computer-related equipment; the companies that develop software; and the companies that hire information processing professionals to work with these products.

2. The people in the **information systems department** work together as a team to meet the information demands of their organizations. Positions in an information systems department can be divided into four main groups.

3. The **operations group** is responsible for operating the centralized (computer center) equipment and network administration including both data and voice communications. Positions in the operations group include **computer operator**, **communications specialist**, **PC network specialist**, **control clerk**, **data entry operator**, and **data librarian**.

4. The **system development group** is responsible for analyzing, designing, developing, and implementing information systems and maintaining and improving existing systems. Positions in the system development group include **systems analyst**, **application programmer**, and **technical writer**.

5. The **technical services group** is responsible for the evaluation and integration of new technologies, the administration of the organization's data resources, and support of the central computer operating system. Positions in the technical services group include **technical evaluator**, **database analyst**, **system programmer**, and **quality assurance specialist**.

6. The **end user computing group** is responsible for assisting end users in working with existing systems and in using productivity software and query languages to obtain the information necessary to perform their jobs. Positions in the end user computing group include **PC support specialist**, **information center specialist**, **office automation specialist**, **trainer**, and **executive information system (EIS) specialist**.

7. Other information industry jobs are found in the areas of sales, service and repair, education and training, and consulting. **Sales representatives** must have a general understanding of computers and a specific knowledge of the product they are selling. Being a **service and repair technician** is a challenging job for individuals who like to troubleshoot and solve problems and have a strong background in electronics. The increased sophistication and complexity of today's computer products has opened wide opportunities in computer education and training. After building experience in one or more areas, some individuals become **consultants**, who are people that draw upon their experience to give advice to others.

8. Compensation is a function of experience and demand for a particular skill. To prepare for a skill in the information processing industry, individuals must decide what computer field they are interested in and obtain education in the field they choose.

9. Three broad fields exist in the information processing industry. **Computer information systems** (CIS) refers to the use of computers to provide the information needed to operate businesses and other organizations. The field of **computer science** includes the technical and theoretical aspects of computers and system software. **Computer engineering** deals with the design and manufacturing of electronic computer components and computer hardware.

10. Trade schools, technical schools, community colleges, colleges, and universities all offer formal education and certification or degree programs in computer information systems, computer science, and computer engineering.

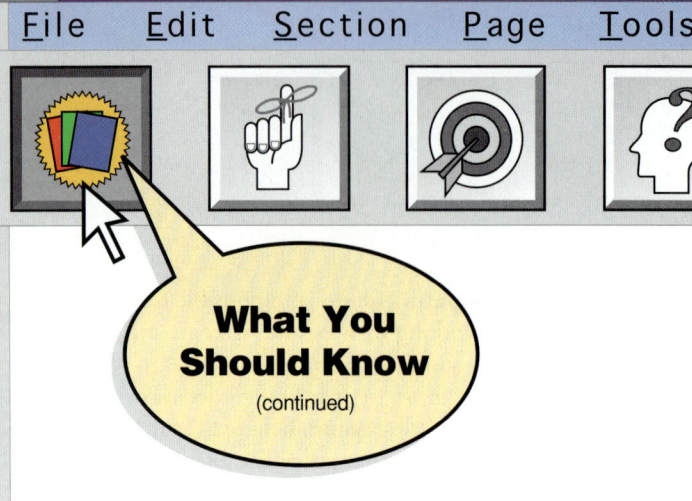

What You Should Know (continued)

11. Persons employed in the information processing industry can develop their skills through professional organizations, certification, and professional growth and continuing education activities.

12. The **Association for Computing Machinery** (ACM) is composed of persons interested in computer science and computer science education. The **Data Processing Management Association** (DPMA) is a professional association of programmers, systems analysts, and information processing managers. A **user group** is a group of people with common computer equipment or software interests who meets regularly to share information.

13. The most widely recognized certification program in the information processing industry is administered by the **Institute for the Certification of Computer Professionals** (ICCP). Two certification designations are **Certified Computing Professional** (CCP) and **Associate Computing Professional** (ACP).

14. One way of keeping up with new products and services in the information processing industry is by participating in professional growth and continuing education activities. The largest trade show in the United States, **COMDEX**, brings together more than 2,000 vendors to display their newest products and services to 200,000 attendees. Hundreds of computer industry publications also are available.

15. Two trends that will have a widespread influence are digital convergence and the application of artificial intelligence. **Digital convergence** describes the merging of technologies and products from the communications, entertainment, publishing, and computing industries. **Artificial intelligence** (AI) is the application of human intelligence to computers. Voice input and speech recognition, expert systems, and natural language interfaces are all applications of AI. Other AI applications include robotics, vision systems, fuzzy logic, and agent software.

16. **Robotics** deals with the development of **robots**, which are devices that mimic human actions and appear to function with some degree of intelligence. A **vision system** uses a camera and a computer to identify objects by digitizing their images and then comparing the images against a database of known shapes. **Fuzzy logic**, a type of mathematics, deals with values that are not precise and values that have a degree of uncertainty. Although not precisely defined, the term **agent** has come to mean a software program that can independently carry out tasks on behalf of a user.

17. The largest use of computers is in business. Existing business information systems will continue to undergo profound changes as new technology, software, and methods are applied to the huge installed base of computer users.

18. The **automated office**, sometimes referred to as the **electronic office**, makes use of electronic devices such as computers, facsimile machines, and computerized telephone systems to make work more productive. In a concept called **Microsoft At Work**, Microsoft Corporation has proposed a standardized intelligent graphical user interface that will be built into all office machines allowing data to be sent to or received from any device on the network.

19. As with automated office applications, the goal of the **digital factory** is to increase productivity through the use of networked, computer-controlled equipment. Technologies used in the digital factory include **computer-aided design (CAD)**, **computer-aided engineering (CAE)**, and **computer-aided manufacturing (CAM)**.

20. **Computer-integrated manufacturing** (CIM) is the total integration of the manufacturing process using computers. The current trend is toward the **computer-integrated enterprise** – an organization in which all information storage and processing is performed by a network of computers and intelligent devices – allowing authorized users in any functional area of the organization to access and use data stored anywhere in the organization.

21. Millions of personal computers have been purchased for home use, and the use of personal computers in the home is expected to increase. The ways people use personal computers in their homes usually fall into five general categories: (1) personal services, (2) control of home systems, (3) telecommuting, (4) education, and (5) entertainment.

22. Personal services includes the use of computers in the home for creating documents, financial planning and analysis, and filing and organizing data. Personal computer software also is available to assist with home accounting applications and to transmit and receive data over telephone lines, allowing home users to access a wealth of information and services.

23. Another use of computers in the home is to control home systems such as security, environment, lighting, and landscape sprinkler systems. Telecommuting refers to the ability of individuals to work at home and communicate with their offices by using personal computers and communications lines.

24. The use of personal computers for education, called **computer-aided instruction** (CAI), is another rapidly growing area. CAI software can be classified into three types: **drill and practice software**, **tutorial software**, and **simulation software**. In an approach that is sometimes called **remote learning**, some trade schools, colleges, and universities now offer students with personal computers the opportunity to take electronic correspondence courses in their homes.

25. Entertainment software, or game playing, on home computers always has had a large following among the younger members of the family, but it also can provide adults with hours of enjoyment. Popular types of entertainment software include arcade games, board games, simulations, and interactive graphics programs.

Terms to Remember

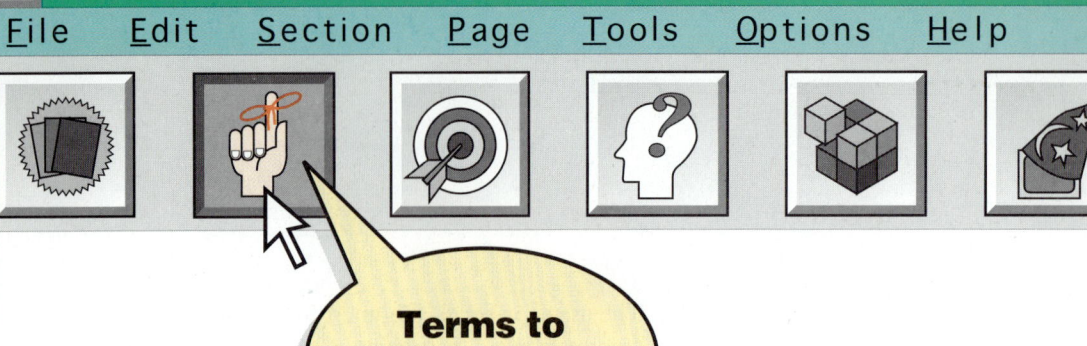

agent (14.14)
application programmer (14.14)
artificial intelligence (AI) (14.13)
Associate Computing Professional (ACP) (14.9)
Association for Computing Machinery (ACM) (14.8)
automated office (14.16)

Certified Computing Professional (CCP) (14.9)
COMDEX (14.10)
communications specialist (14.4)
computer engineering (14.8)
computer information systems (CIS) (14.8)
computer operator (14.4)
computer science (14.8)
computer-aided design (CAD) (14.17)
computer-aided engineering (CAE) (14.18)
computer-aided instruction (CAI) (14.21)
computer-aided manufacturing (CAM) (14.18)
computer-integrated enterprise (14.19)
computer-integrated manufacturing (CIM) (14.18)
consultants (14.6)
control clerk (14.4)

data entry operator (14.4)
data librarian (14.4)
Data Processing Management Association (DPMA) (14.8)
database analyst (14.4)
digital convergence (14.11)
digital factory (14.17)
drill and practice software (14.21)

electronic office (14.16)
end user computing group (14.5)
executive information system (EIS) specialist (14.5)

fuzzy logic (14.13)

information center specialist (14.5)
Institute for the Certification of Computer Professionals (ICCP) (14.9)

Microsoft At Work (14.17)

office automation specialist (14.5)
operations group (14.4)

PC network specialist (14.4)
PC support specialist (14.5)

quality assurance specialist (14.4)

remote learning (14.21)
robotics (14.13)
robots (14.13)

sales representatives (14.5)
service and repair technician (14.5)
simulation software (14.21)
stereolithography (SL) (14.23)
system development group (14.4)
system programmer (14.4)
systems analyst (14.4)

technical evaluator (14.4)
technical services group (14.4)
technical writer (14.4)
trainer (14.5)
tutorial software (14.21)

user group (14.9)

vision system (14.13)

Test Your Knowledge

Fill in the Blanks

1. Job opportunities in the information processing industry come primarily from three areas: _____, _____, and _____.

2. Two positions in the systems development group of an information systems department are the _____, who works closely with users to analyze their requirements and design an information systems solution, and the _____, who converts the system design into the appropriate computer language.

3. The most widely recognized certification program in the information processing industry is administered by the _____, which is sponsored and supported by several professional organizations including the ACM and DPMA.

4. _____ describes the merging of technologies and products from the communications, entertainment, publishing, and computing industries.

5. Although the use of computers in the office and the factory can be discussed separately, the trend is the _____ – an organization in which all information storage and processing is performed by a network of computers and intelligent devices.

Short Answer

1. What are the four groups into which positions in an information systems department can be divided? What are the responsibilities of each group?

2. Upon what factors does compensation for information processing careers depend? What industries pay the highest salaries? Why? According to the U.S. Bureau of Labor Statistics, what will be the fastest growing computer career positions through the year 2005?

3. How is the Association for Computing Machinery (ACM) different from the Data Processing Management Association (DPMA)? What benefits are offered by both associations? What is a user group?

4. What is the goal of the digital factory? What are some of the technologies used in the digital factory? Briefly describe each.

5. What is computer-aided instruction (CAI)? How are drill and practice software, tutorial software, and simulation software different? What advantages does education in the home through CAI or electronic correspondence courses offer?

Label the Figure

Instructions: Label the following figure to show how computer-integrated manufacturing (CIM) integrates all phases of the manufacturing process.

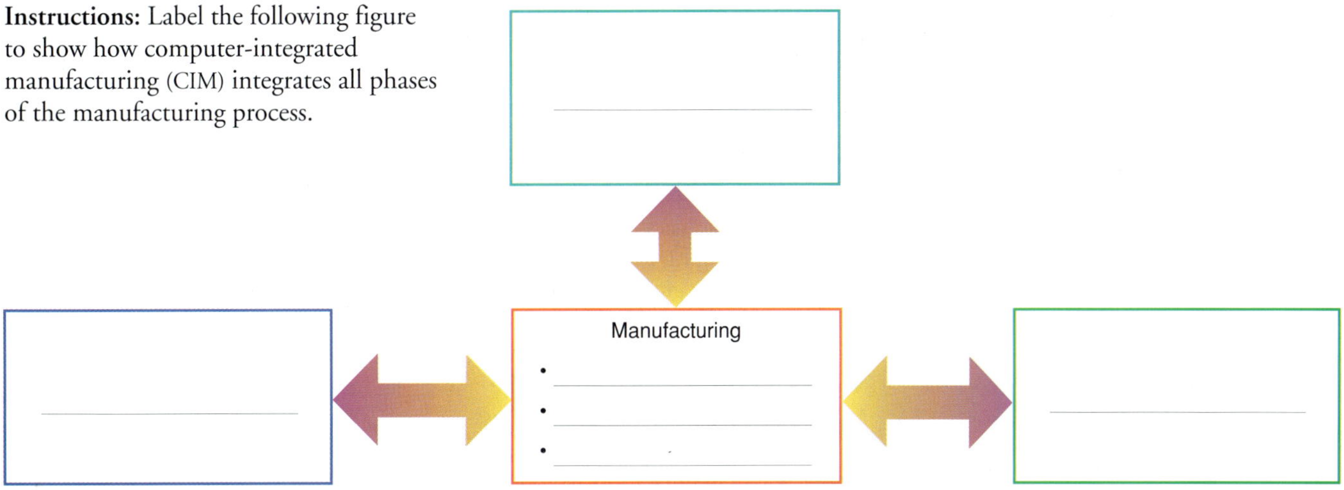

Manufacturing

1

A researcher from International Resource Development, Inc. reported that about one-fourth of the work force may have emotional problems related to the use of computers. Many established workers expressed feelings of incompetence, loss of control, job insecurity, and anticipated demotion with the introduction of personal computers in the workplace. Some experts believe these feelings, which are occasionally called compuphobia, could lead frustrated workers to sabotage computer systems and equipment. Why are established workers more apt to experience compuphobia than new employees? Are the fears of these workers justified? Why or why not? If you were the manager of a department in which computers were being introduced, what would you do to prevent compuphobia?

2

This chapter describes many current career opportunities in information processing. Choose the four positions in which you are most interested and explain why. What do the four positions you have chosen have in common? What personal qualities and experiences do you have that would help you be successful in any of the four positions? What types of classes do you think you should take to prepare for a career in these positions? Why?

3

With the introduction of information technology, a group of life insurance companies was able to reduce their administrative staff by 45 percent and at the same time expand their business by 25 percent. While experts feel information technology will result in a net increase in the number of available jobs, most admit that many people without computer skills will be displaced. What responsibilities, if any, does an organization have to displaced workers? Why? What steps, if any, should government take to prepare displaced workers for a changing workplace?

4

Some companies offer employees discount programs on purchasing personal computers. Although this may simply seem to be a generous perk, a few people wonder if it is really intended as a means of getting additional work out of employees. It was once thought that computers would shorten the length of the work day, but the introduction of such items as portable computers, facsimile machines, modems, cellular telephones, and paging devices, along with increasingly global markets that know no time zones, has blurred the boundary between office and home. While some individuals applaud the added flexibility, others regret the loss of "personal" time. How do you feel? Under what circumstances would you be willing to work beyond normal office hours? Why? What effects do you think extended working hours will have on society as a whole? Does all work and no play truly make Jack a dull boy?

5

Imagine you have been given fifteen days to write a ten-page paper. Your teacher has promised to give extra credit for each day the paper is turned in early and to deduct credit for each day the paper is submitted after the deadline. On graph paper, construct a fuzzy logic diagram similar to that shown in *Figure 14-14* on page 14.13, illustrating your degree of certainty regarding the completion date. Indicate the days on the horizontal axis and the certainty (0, 0.5, 1.0) on the vertical axis. Mark the number of days it will take you to complete the paper under the best conditions (the topic is familiar, the library has the necessary resources, your other course work is light, and so on), your most likely guess of the number of days it will take you to complete the paper, and the number of days it will take you to complete the paper under the worst conditions (the demands on your time are heavy, the materials you need are unavailable, your word processor breaks down, and so on), and then connect the marks.

Out and About

6

It has been argued that American education lags far behind technological developments. Children still spend years learning skills such as long division, an operation that can be performed in seconds on a five-dollar calculator. Many urge that curriculums be totally reexamined; teaching procedures that are performed more efficiently using a computer can be abandoned, and instead students could be taught to take advantage of a computer's capabilities. Others insist, however, that unless people are familiar with skills like long division they will not know when, perhaps because of an input error, the information supplied by a computer or calculator is incorrect. Some teachers also feel that these computational skills help to develop the rigorous thought processes necessary in the information age. Consider your own education. In terms of technology, do you think that education was adequate? What skills or concepts, if any, did you spend time learning that now, because of computers, you feel are unnecessary? At what age should students be introduced to computers? What computer-related topics should students be taught in elementary school and secondary school? Explain your answers.

1. How would you like to work in an information systems department? Choose a position in *Figure 14-3* on page 14.4 in which you are interested, contact an individual who works in that position in a local organization, and arrange to interview that individual about his or her job. What are the individual's responsibilities? What are the most difficult aspects of the job? To what professional organizations does he or she belong? What certification, if any, is required? What type of educational background does the individual have? Approximately how much does the position pay? What are the opportunities for advancement? After receiving answers to these and other questions, is this a career into which you would like to enter? Why or why not?

2. Digital convergence is expected to have an impact in several areas, including communications, entertainment, and publishing. Choose an area in which you are interested and, using library resources and current computer magazines, prepare a report on the anticipated effect of digital convergence. What changes will probably result in the area? What types of hardware and software will be necessary? How is the area likely to look when digital convergence is realized? Will anything that you think is valuable be lost? How will people's lives be different? When is it expected that the effects of digital convergence will be realized?

14.32 Out and About

 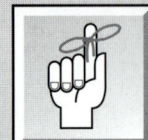   

Out and About
(continued)

3. Try out a software application that includes an agent, or wizard, such as Microsoft Word or Microsoft Excel. For what purpose is the wizard used? What are the advantages of using a wizard to complete the task over simply performing the task on your own? What are the disadvantages? Is the final result created by the wizard more or less attractive, creative, or distinctive than what you could have done on your own? Why? Would you be more likely to purchase an application with an agent than one that did not have one? Why or why not?

4. Arrange for a tour of a factory. What digital technologies are used in the factory? How are they used? What advantages are offered by these technologies? Does the factory use robots? If so, how and why? How have the factory's workers been affected by the new technologies? What kind of training did they undergo? Where any positions lost as a result of the technologies introduced? Where any new positions created?

5. Visit a software vendor and locate at least two different packages that can be used to assist with home accounting, such as balancing checkbooks, making household budgets, or preparing tax returns. What is the name of each package? What is the cost? What are the hardware requirements? If possible, test the packages and perform the same task with each. Is one package easier to use? If so, why? Does either package provide more capabilities than the other? What? On the basis of your examination, which package, if any, would you be most inclined to purchase? Why?

6. Volunteer to help out in a primary or secondary school class while it is using computer-aided instruction (CAI). What type of software is being used? Is it effective? Do you think the same topic could be taught more effectively using a different type of software? Why or why not? Could the topic be taught better by a teacher? Why? How do the students respond to CAI? From your observation, what do you think are the advantages of CAI? What are the disadvantages? In general, are your feelings about computer-aided instruction positive or negative? Why?

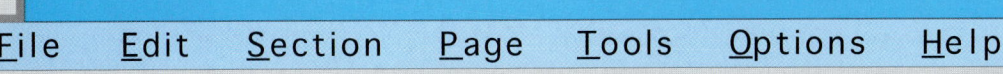

In the Lab   14.33

<u>F</u>ile   <u>E</u>dit   <u>S</u>ection   <u>P</u>age   <u>T</u>ools   <u>O</u>ptions   <u>H</u>elp

 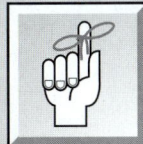   

In the Lab

Windows Labs

1 Starting an Application from Program Manager or File Manager   With Program Manager on the screen, select the File menu and choose the Run command. In the Run dialog box, type edit in the Command Line text box and choose the OK button to open the MS-DOS Editor and display it on the screen. Press the ESC key. Exit the Editor by selecting its File menu and choosing the Exit command.

With Program Manager on the screen, double-click the Main group icon. In the Main group window, double-click the File Manager program-item icon. Maximize the File Manager window. Select the Help menu and choose the Search for Help on command. In the Search dialog box, type starting applications and press the ENTER key twice. Read and print the information. Close Help. In the directory window, click the dos subdirectory. Scroll through the list of files in the dos subdirectory and locate the file edit.com *(Figure 14-26)*. (If you cannot find edit.com, use the Search command as discussed in Windows Lab 8-1 in Chapter 8 on page 8.27 to identify which directory it is in.) Double-click edit.com to open the MS-DOS Editor and display it on the screen. Press ESC. Exit the Editor. Close File Manager.

2 Shelly Cashman Series Computers of the Future Lab   Follow the instructions in Windows Lab 2 in Chapter 1 on page 1.30 to display the Shelly Cashman Series screen. Select Exploring the Computers of the Future and choose the Start Lab button. When the initial screen displays, carefully read the objectives. With your printer turned on, point to the Print Questions button and click the left mouse button. Fill out the top of the Questions sheet and answer the questions as you step through the Computers of the Future Lab.

3 Linking an Object   With Program Manager on the screen, double-click the Accessories group icon. Start Paintbrush and maximize its window. Select the File menu and choose the Open command. In the Open dialog box, scroll through the files, select marble.bmp and choose the OK button to display the MARBLE.BMP file *(Figure 14-27)*.

Select the Pick tool. Drag the mouse from the upper left corner of the marble picture to its lower right corner to select it. With the picture selected, select the Edit menu and choose the Copy command to copy your selection to the Clipboard. Press CTRL+ESC to display the Task List window. Select Program Manager and choose the Switch To button.

Start Write and maximize its window. Select the Edit menu and choose the Paste Link command to copy the marble picture from the Clipboard into Write and establish a link between the picture in Write and the picture in Paintbrush. Press CTRL+ESC. Select Paintbrush - MARBLE.BMP and choose the Switch To button. Use the Pick tool to select a rectangle in the middle of the marble picture; then, select the Edit menu and choose the Cut command. Click the Text tool. Click inside the cutout and type your name. Use CTRL+ESC to switch back to Write *(Figure 14-28* on the next page). Save the Write file with the name WIN14-3. Print the file. Close Write. Close Paintbrush without saving. Close Accessories.

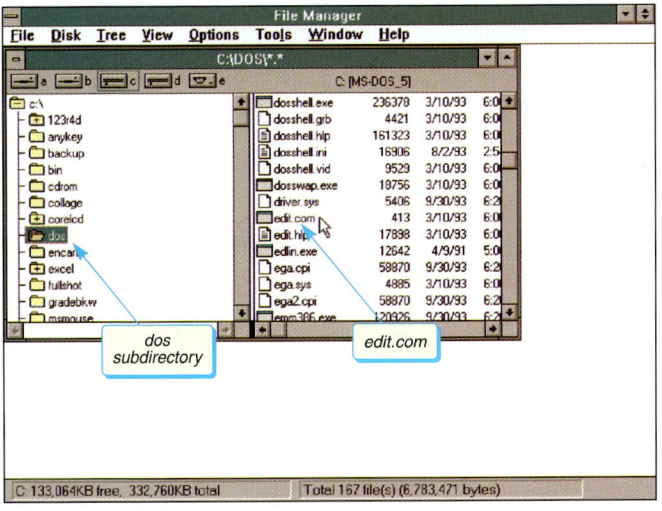

Figure 14-26

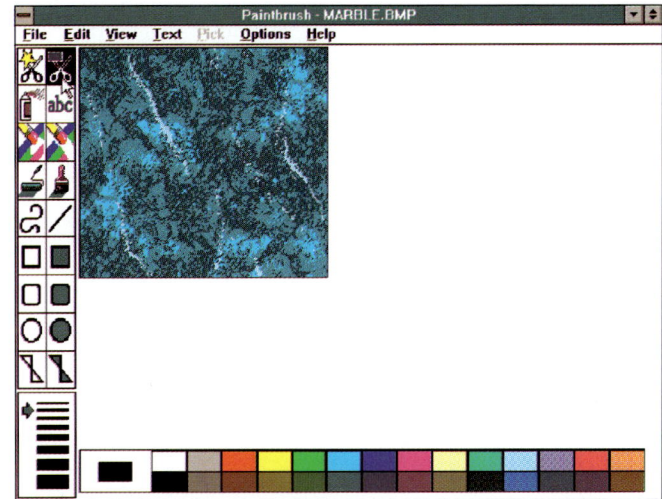

Figure 14-27

14.34 In the Lab

File Edit Section Page Tools Options Help

 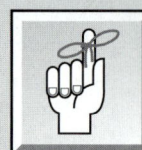    

In the Lab (continued)

4 Understanding How to Set Up a Printer With Program Manager on the screen, double-click the Main group icon. In the Main group window, double-click the Print Manager program-item icon. Maximize the Print Manager window. Select the Options menu and choose the Printer Setup command. What printers are currently installed on your computer? What is the default printer? Choose the Add button to display a list of printers *(Figure 14-29)*. In the List of Printers, click a printer not currently installed on your computer. Choose the Install button. What happens? Choose the Cancel button in the Install Driver dialog box. Be sure the default printer is selected in the Installed Printers area and choose the Setup button. What paper sizes are available for your printer? Choose the Help button to display help on your printer driver. Read and print the information on the screen. Close Help. Choose the Cancel button. Choose the Close button in the Printers dialog box. Close Print Manager. Close the Main group window.

5 Using Help With Program Manager on the screen, select the Help menu and choose the Search for Help on command. In the Search dialog box, type starting applications and press the ENTER key. In the list, select Starting an Application When You Start Windows and choose the Go To button. Read and print the information on the screen. Close Help. Double-click the StartUp group icon. What icons are in your StartUp group window? Close the StartUp group window.

DOS Labs

1 Copying an Entire Diskette At the DOS prompt, type diskcopy a: a: and press the ENTER key. When prompted, insert the diskette containing your DOS Labs and press the ENTER key. When prompted, remove the diskette containing your DOS Labs; insert a new diskette (**any files on this diskette will be erased**); and press the ENTER key. Depending on your DOS version, you may be requested to switch the diskettes again. When the copy is complete, type n and press the ENTER key.

2 Displaying Directories on a Disk At the DOS prompt, type tree /a >prn and press the ENTER key to print a list of directories on the default drive. Type tree /f /a >prn and press the ENTER key to print a list of all files in all directories on the default drive. Insert the diskette containing your DOS Labs, type tree a: /f /a >prn and press the ENTER key.

3 Using Help At the DOS prompt, type help and press the ENTER key. Obtain and print help information on each of these topics: Diskcopy, Xcopy, and Tree. Exit Help.

Online Lab

1 Scanning the Latest News Using one of the two online services you selected in Chapter 1, connect to the service and perform the following tasks: (1) Search the online service for the Latest News. (2) Read five of today's top news stories and log each one's date and headline.

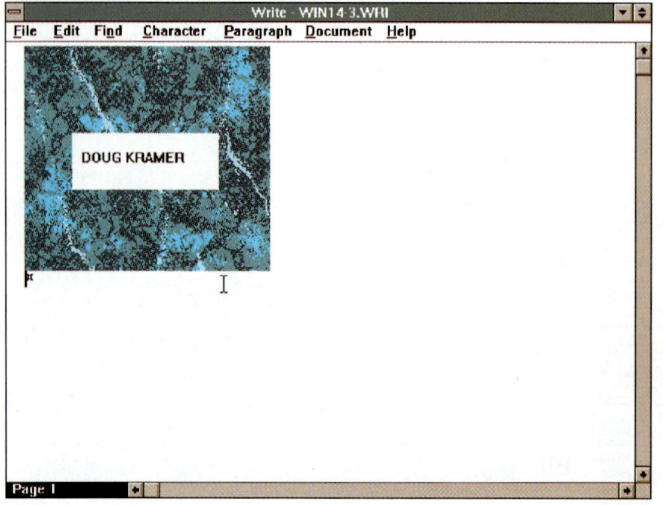

Figure 14-28

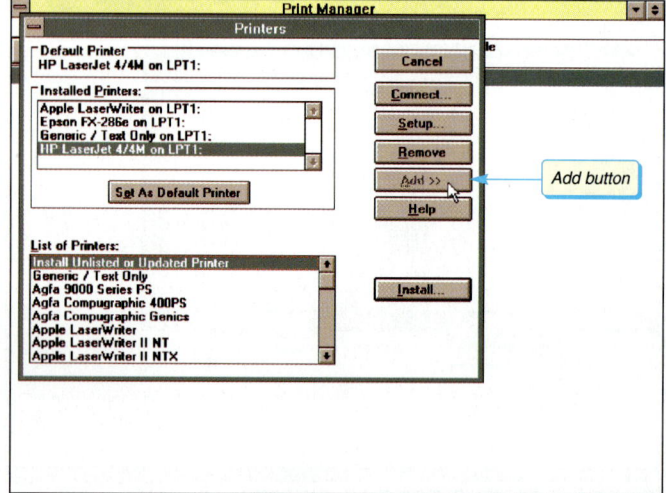

Figure 14-29

Virtual Reality

Virtual reality (VR) is the use of a computer to create an artificial environment that can be experienced by the user. The reality of the artificial environment and the extent the user can interact with it depends on the software and type of hardware used. Desktop virtual reality uses personal computers to display what appears to be a three-dimensional view of an environment such as an office or a home. Using a pointing device, such as a mouse or joystick, the user can simulate moving through the environment; for example, from room to room.

Immersion virtual reality uses additional equipment that makes the user feel as though he or she is actually in the simulated environment. This additional equipment includes a head-mounted display and may also include data gloves or complete body suits.

The following figures illustrate software and hardware used in virtual reality and some of the current applications.

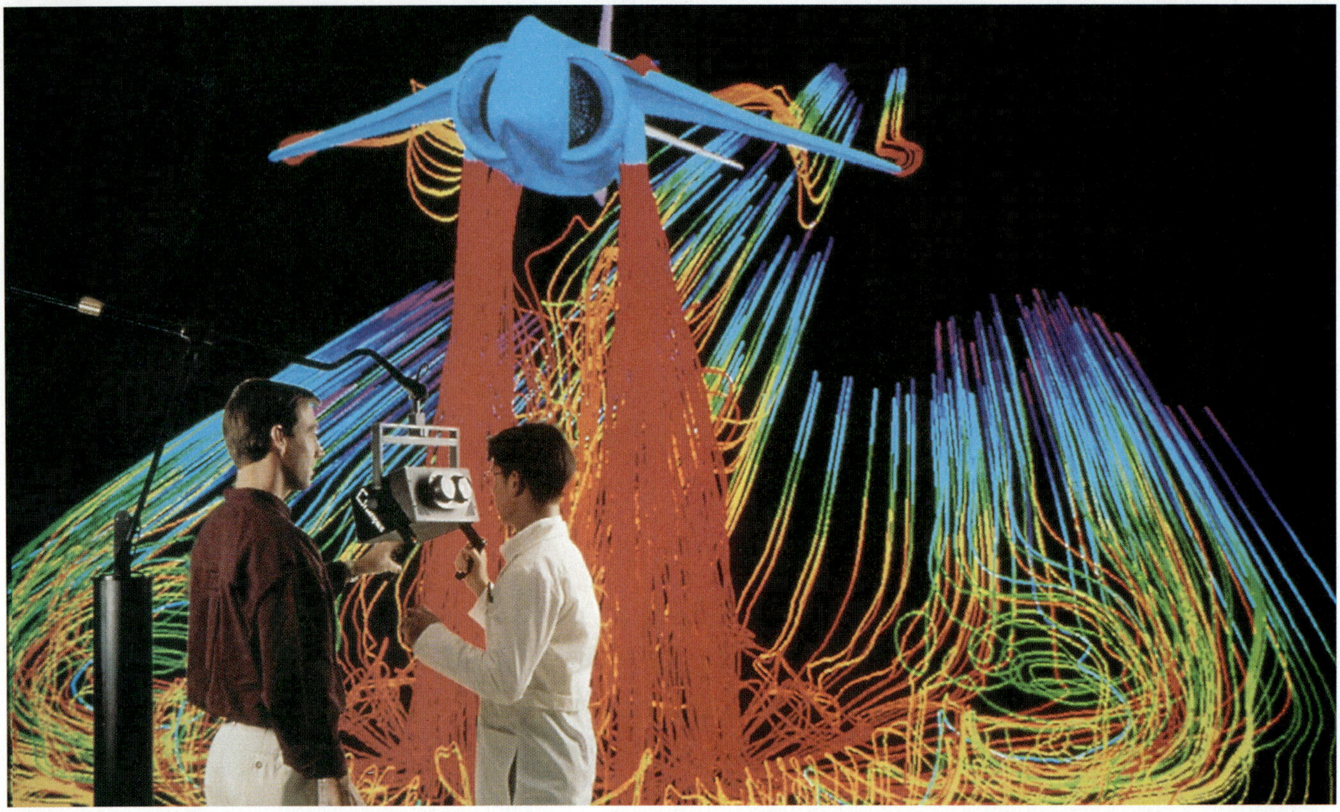

Figure 1
The Virtual Windtunnel Project at NASA Ames Research Center uses a three-dimensional virtual reality display of aircraft and air flows. Different colors indicate different temperatures. Using the stereoscopic boom display from Fakespace Labs, shown in the lower left corner, the user can simulate walking around the aircraft to view the air flows from different angles.

Figure 2
Doctors at Kaiser-Permanente Medical Group worked with engineers at Division Inc. to develop a virtual reality method of helping people overcome a fear of heights. At the start of a Virtual Therapy session, the patient sees the display shown in the photograph. Using a hand-held device to indicate direction, patients can move from the patio, across a plank, and walk along a suspension bridge over a deep gorge. At any time they can look down and experience a sensation of height. Patients that have completed the virtual therapy have been able to more quickly complete their real world treatment, which includes a 15-story ride in a glass enclosed elevator.

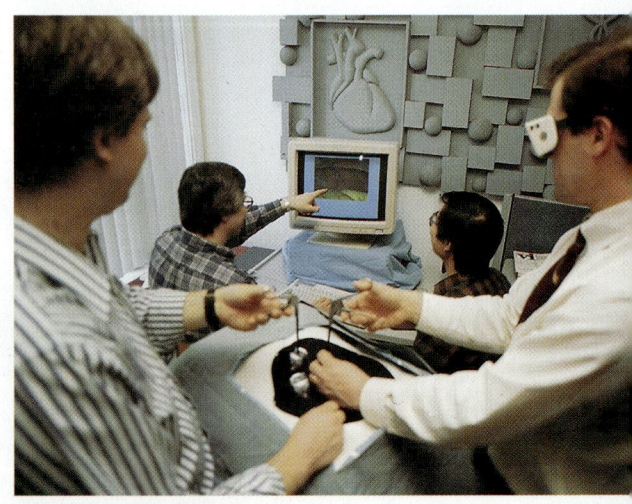

Figure 3
Ciné-Med is one of several companies that have created virtual reality systems allowing doctors and medical students to practice surgery on a virtual patient. Ciné-Med's Virtual Clinic includes a fiberglass torso into which surgical instruments can be inserted. The progress of the operation is displayed on a monitor, just as it would be in real surgery.

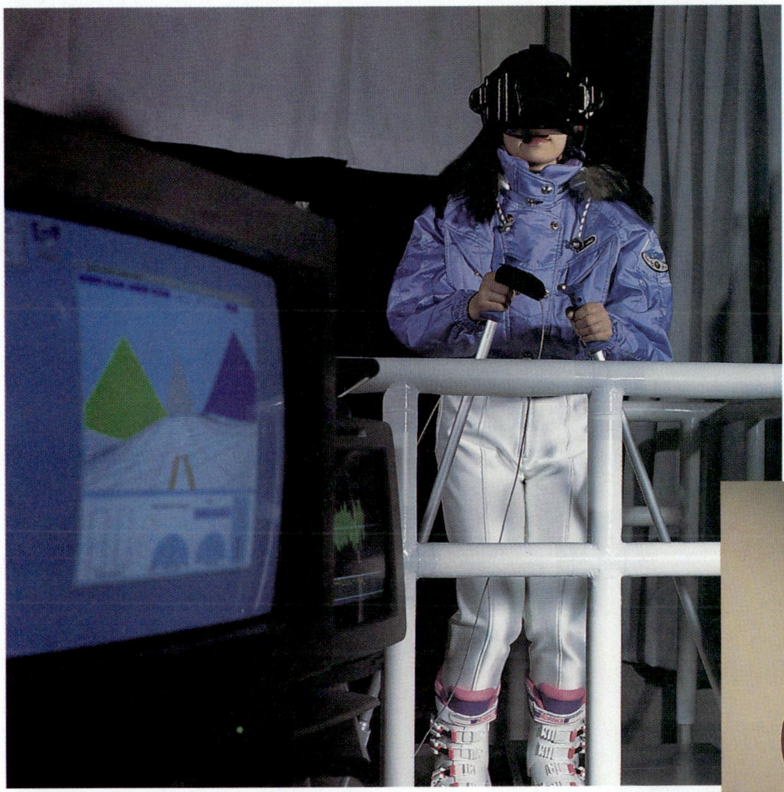

VIRTUAL REALITY

Figure 4
Virtual reality systems have been developed for several sports. The skier on the left can race a simulated course without fear of breaking a leg. The person below is playing a game of racquetball.

Figure 5
The force feedback virtual reality system, developed at the University of North Carolina, allows the user to examine chemical structures and search for places where other molecules could be joined.

14.38 VIRTUAL REALITY

Figure 6
Using data collected by the Voyager space probe on the planet Mars, NASA has created a simulated environment of the planet's surface.

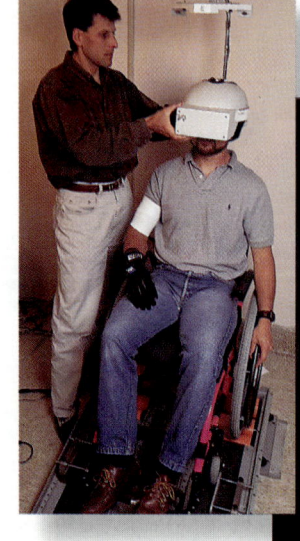

Figure 7
This virtual reality system was developed by the Hines Illinois Veterans Administration Hospital to help design apartments for people who use wheelchairs.

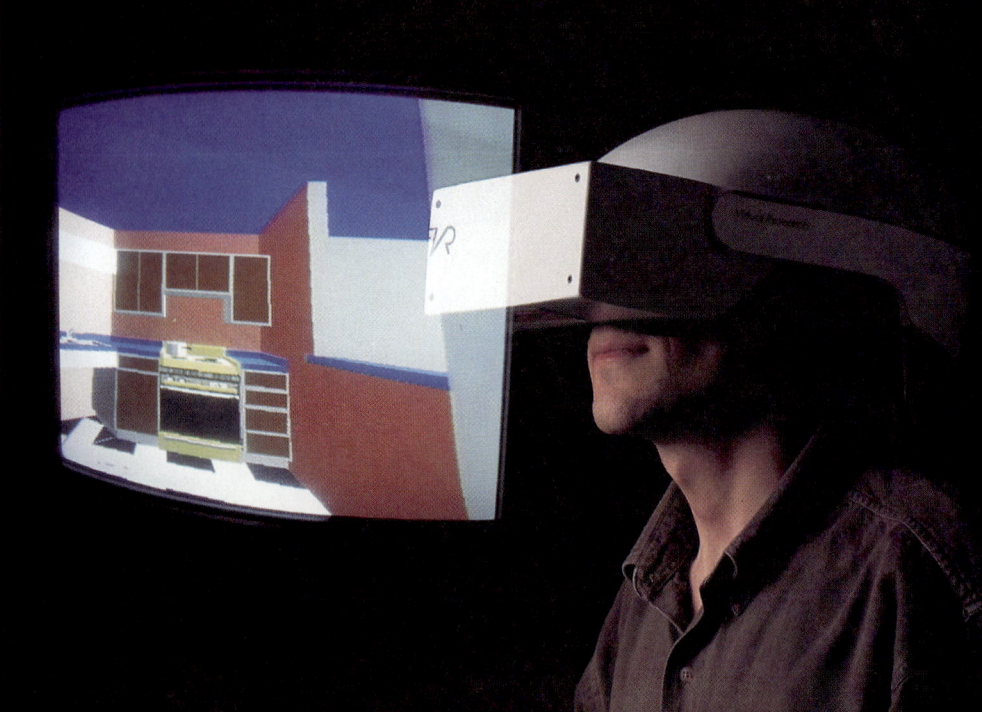

Figure 8
Architects and space planners use virtual reality systems to allow clients to view offices and homes before they are built.

Figure 9
In this virtual kitchen, created for British Gas using software from Sense8 Corporation, cupboards can be opened and closed, cooking pots moved, and the stove's burners turned on.

Figure 10
WalkThrough is a three-dimensional software package from Virtus Corporation that allows a user to create and then explore a virtual environment.

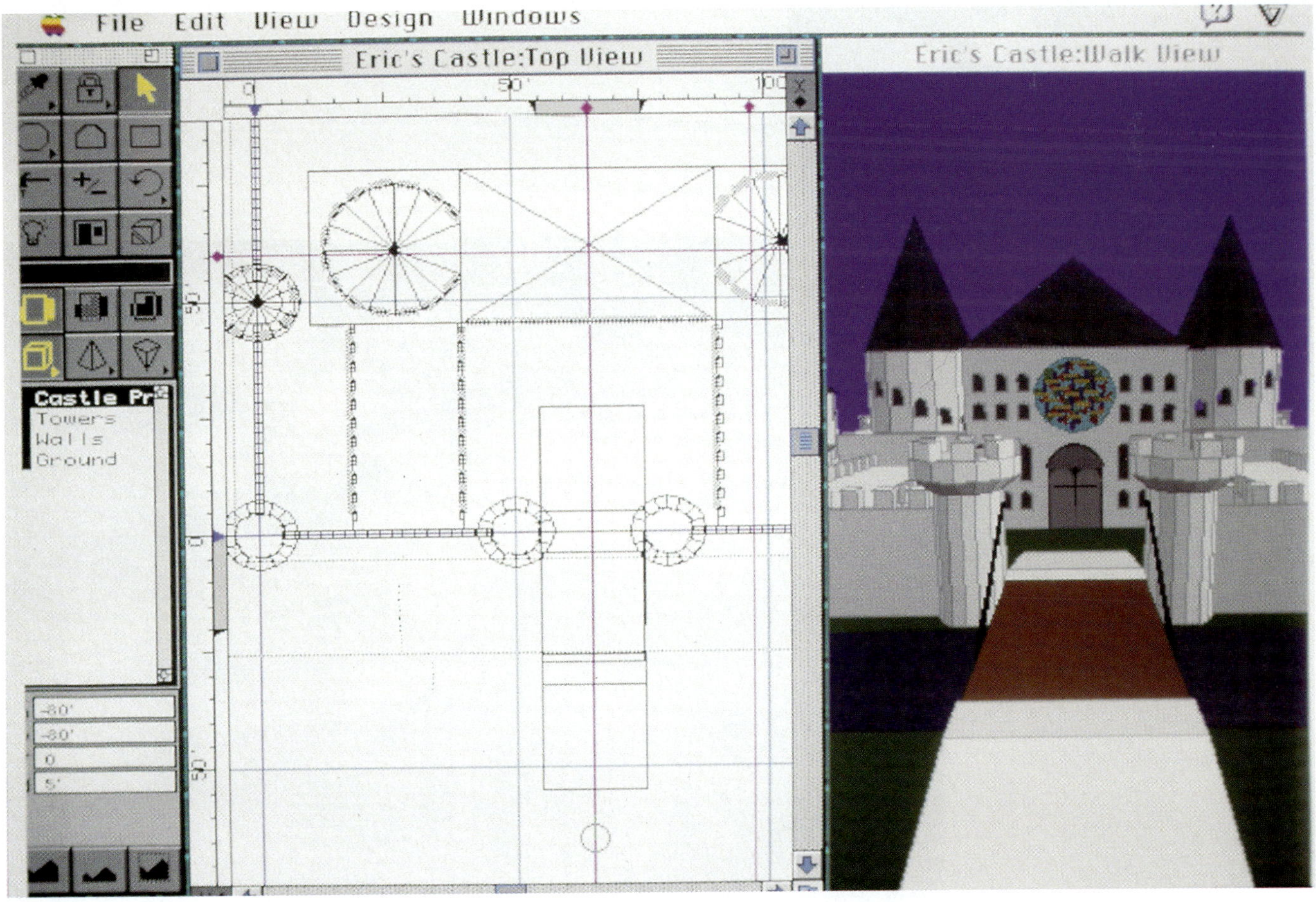

Figure 11
Hanging on the wall are some of the many data gloves and body suits that can be worn to transmit a user's motion to a virtual reality system.

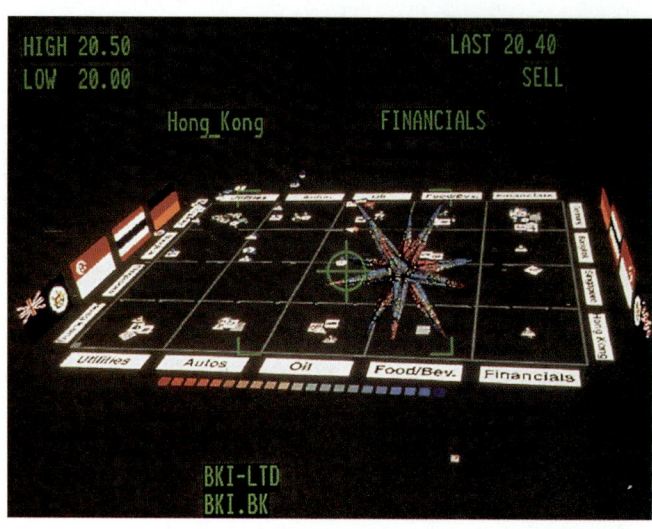

Figure 12
This picture shows a virtual reality financial application designed to track the movement of stocks in several international markets. Each grid represents an industry group, such as oil or autos, in a particular financial market, such as Hong Kong. The small chips within the grids represent individual stocks. The chips spin and blink to indicate buy or sell opportunities. The color of the chip indicates whether the stock has gone up or down from the day before. The distance a chip rises above the surface shows its relative performance to other chips.

Figure 13
Software from Worldesign was used to create these views of the Seattle, Washington harbor area showing the before and after views of a development project. The software allows users to drive or fly through the simulated environment.

Index

Absolute referencing: In spreadsheet programs, when a formula is copied to another cell, the formula continues to refer to the same cell locations. **2.15**
Acceptance testing: During design phase of information systems development, acceptance testing demonstrates to the users that the system can meet user-designed test criteria. **11.19**
Access arm: Contains the read/write heads and moves the heads across the surface of the disk. **6.10**
Access controls: Controls established during design phase of information systems development that specify what levels of security are required for different processes. **11.19, 13.5**
Access privileges, DBMS, 9.17
Access time: The time required to access and retrieve data stored in sectors on a diskette. **6.7**
Accounting controls: System controls to provide assurance that the dollar amounts recorded in the accounting records are correct. **11.19**
Acquisition: Phase in the information system life cycle after the analysis phase. The acquisition phase has four steps:(1) summarizing the application requirements, (2) identifying potential software vendors, (3) evaluating software alternatives, and (4) making the purchase. **11.2, 11.10-14**
  equipment, 11.22
  software, 11.14
Acquisition path, 11.2
Active badge systems: System for locating employees developed by Olivetti Research Limited. The badge contains a small transmitter and is worn on the outside of clothing. The badge emits an infrared signal that is picked up by sensors in offices and hallways, identifying to a computer the location of the employee. **13.22**
Active matrix: LCD screens that use individual transistors to control each crystal cell. **5.21**
Ada: A programming language supported by the U.S. Department of Defense. Its use is required on all U.S. government military projects. Ada was designed to facilitate the writing and maintenance of large programs that would be used over a long period of time. **12.23**
Adapter cards, *see* **Expansion board**
Adaptive technology, 3.22
Adding data: Updating data, such as creating a record for a new employee to include in a file or database. **9.3, 9.9**
Agent: Software that can independently carry out tasks on behalf of a user. **14.14**
Algorithm: During program design, the step-by-step procedure of the logical solution to a programming task. **12.4**
Alignment: Formatting text so characters line up with a margin or tab. **2.8**
American Express, 6.24
American National Standards Institute (ANSI)
  code standards and, 12.9
  object-oriented COBOL and, 12.25
  program flowcharts and, 12.7
American Standard Code for Information Interchange (ASCII): The most widely used coding system to represent data, primarily on personal computers and many minicomputers. **4.3**
Analog computer: Computer designed to process continuously variable data, such as electrical voltage. **4.2**
Analog signal: A signal used on communications lines that consists of a continuous electrical wave. **7.16**
Analysis: Phase in the information life cycle where the system is separated into its parts in order to determine how the system works. This phase consists of the preliminary investigation, detailed system analysis, and making the decision to proceed. **11.2, 11.4-9**
Analytical graphics: The charts provided by spreadsheet packages. **2.16**
Anti-virus programs: Programs that protect against computer viruses by looking for viruses that attempt to modify the boot program, the operating system, and other programs that are normally read from but not written to, and also look for specific patterns of known virus code. **13.3**
Apple computers, 1.35, 14.2. *See also* **Macintosh**

Application generators: Programs that produce source-language programs, such as BASIC or COBOL, based on input, output, and processing specifications entered by the user. Also called program generators. **12.16**
Application programmer: Programmer that converts the system design into the appropriate computer language. **14.4**
Application software: Programs that tell a computer how to produce information. **1.15**
  horizontal, 11.10-11
  purchasing, 8.30
  user tools, 2.1-32
  vertical, 11.10-11
Application software packages: Programs purchased from computer stores or software vendors. **1.15**
  early development of, 1.36
  integrated, 2.25-26
  registering, 8.35
  superapplications and, 2.29
  See also Software
Arithmetic/logic unit (ALU): Part of the CPU that performs arithmetic and logical operations. **1.8, 4.7**
Arithmetic operations: Numeric calculations performed by the arithmetic/logic unit in the CPU. That include addition, subtraction, multiplication, and division. **1.9, 4.7**
Arrow keys: Keys on a keyboard that move the cursor up, down, left, or right on the screen. **3.4**
Artificial intelligence: A branch of computer science applying human intelligence to computer systems. **10.13, 14.13-14**
ASCII, *see* **American Standard Code for Information Interchange**
Assistive technology, 3.22
Assembler: A special program that converts assembly language programs into machine language instructions. **12.14**
Assembly language: A low-level language that is similar to machine language, but uses abbreviations called mnemonics or symbolic operation code to represent the machine operation code. **12.13-14**
Associate Computing Professional (ACP): Professional certification for entry-level personnel offered by the Institute for the Certification of Computer Professionals. To become certified, an ACP candidate must pass a core examination and at least one computer language test. **14.9**
Association for Computing Machinery (ACM): Professional organization composed of persons interested in computer science and computer science education. **14.8**
Asymmetric multiprocessing: Type of processing whereby application tasks are assigned to a specific CPU in computers that have more than one CPU. **8.5**
Asynchronous transmission mode: Data communication method that transmits one character at a time at irregular intervals using start and stop bits. **7.16**
Atanasoff, John V., 1.32
Attributes: Fields in a relational database. **9.15**
Audio output: Consists of sounds, including words and music, produced by the computer;sometimes called audio response. **5.4-5**
Audio response, *see* **Audio output**
Augmented reality: Used by manufacturing companies; virtual reality simulation that superimposes computer design information on a real scene. The worker wears a special pair of glasses that allow the design to be seen, superimposed on the actual work area. **5.28**
Authentication: Access control techniques that verifies the user is who he or she claims to be. **13.5**
AUTOEXEC.BAT: A batch file loaded by the DOS kernel when the computer is turned on that performs tasks such as telling the system where to look for files (PATH command) and loading programs that the user wants to run every time the system is turned on, such as certain utility programs. **8.3**
  backup of, 8.37
  printout of, 8.36
Automated office: The use of electronic devices such as phone systems to make office work more productive; also known as electronic office. **14.16-17**
Auxiliary storage devices: Devices that store instructions and data when they are not being used by the system unit. **1.9, 6.2**
  computer output microfilm and, 5.24-25
  See also Storage

Background: Jobs assigned a lower processing priority and less CPU time. Compare with foreground jobs. **8.7**
Backup: Procedures that provide for storing copies of program and data files so in the event the files are lost or destroyed, they can be recovered. **6.15, 9.3, 13.13**
  database administrator and, 9.20
  data librarian and, 14.4
  differential, 13.13
  full, 13.13
  incremental, 13.13
  need for, 8.37
  reciprocal relationships, 13.16
  sequential files and, 9.5
  utilities and, 8.15
Backup plan: Disaster recovery plan that specifies how an organization will use backup files and equipment to resume information processing. **13.15**
Backup procedures: Procedures used by organizations that specify a regular plan of copying and storing key data and program files. **13.13**
Backus, John, 12.22
Backward recovery: In DBMS recovery operations, a log is kept showing changes made to the database, which is used to reverse transactions that took place during a certain period of time, such as an hour;also call rollback. **9.17**
Band printers: Impact printers that use a horizontal, rotating band and can print in the range of 600 to 2,000 lines per minute. **5.12**
Bandwidth: The range of frequencies that a communications channel can carry. **7.17**
Bar chart: Chart that displays relationships among data with blocks or bars. **2.16**
Bar code: A type of optical code found on most grocery and retail items, usually scanned to produce price and inventory information about the product. **3.11**
Bar code label printers, 5.16
Base of a number system, 4.21
Baseband: Coaxial cable that can carry one signal at a time at very high rates of speed. **7.9**
BASIC (Beginners All-purpose Symbolic Instruction Code): A simple interactive programming language. BASIC is one of the more commonly used programming languages on microcomputers and minicomputers. **12.19**
  development of, 1.34
  minicomputer use, 12.25
Basic Input/Output System (BIOS): When the computer is turned on, the CPU chip looks to the BIOS chip for instructions on how to proceed. The instructions provide the interface between the operating system and the hardware devices. **8.3**
Batch processing: Data is collected, and at some later time, all the data that has been gathered is processed as a group, or batch. **10.9**
Baud rate: The number of times per second that a data communications signal being transmitted changes; with each change, one or more bits can be transmitted. **7.18**
Bay: An open area inside the system unit used to install additional equipment. **4.6, 4.16**
  purchasing computers and, 8.32
Bell Laboratories, 8.13
Benchmark test: Test on software that measures the time it takes to process a set number of transactions. **11.13**
Bernoulli disk cartridge: Disk storage device that works with a special drive unit that uses a cushion of air to keep the flexible disk surface from touching the read/write head. The flexible disk surface reduces the chance of a head crash but does cause the cartridges to eventually wear out. **6.14**
Bidirectional printing: Printing method of dot matrix printers, in which the print head can print while moving in either direction. **5.11**
Binary number system, 4.2, 4.22
Biometric device: Security device that verifies personal characteristics such as fingerprints, voice pattern, signature, hand size, and retinal (eye) patterns, to authenticate a user. **13.6**
BIOS, *see* **Basic Input/Output System**
Bit(s): An element of a byte that can represent one of two values, on or off. There are 8 bits in a byte. **4.2**
  parity, 4.4

I.1

INDEX

Bit-mapped displays, *see* **Dot-addressable displays**
Bits per inch (bpi): Number of bits that can be recorded on one inch of track on a diskette. **6.6**
Bits per second (bps): A measure of the speed of data transmission; the number of bits transmitted in one second. **7.18**
Blackout: A complete electrical power failure. **13.12**
Bold: Formatting text so characters appear thicker and more distinct than surrounding text. **2.7**
Booting: The process of loading an operating system into main memory. **8.3**
Boot sector virus: Computer virus that works by replacing the program that is used to start the system (the boot program) with a modified version of the program. When the infected boot program is run, it loads the virus into the computer's memory and can spread to any diskette inserted into the computer. **13.2**
Border: A line or lines around text or graphics to distinguish it from the rest of the document. **2.8**
Borland Corporation, 12.23
Bottom-up design: Design approach that focuses on the data, particularly the output of the system. **11.17**
Break program, 12.10
Bricklin, Dan, 1.35
Bridge: A combination of hardware and software that is used to connect similar networks. **7.28**
Broadband: Coaxial cable that can carry multiple signals at one time. **7.10**
Brownout: A prolonged drop in electrical power supply. **13.12**
Buckets: The location on a disk where records in a direct file can be stored. **9.6**
Buffers: Areas of memory used to store data that has been read or is waiting to be sent to sent to an output device. **8.7**
Bugs: Program errors. **12.10**
Bulletin board systems (BBSs): Allows users to communicate electronically with one another and share information using personal computers. **7.7**
Bus: Any line that transmits bits between the memory and the input/output devices, and between memory and the CPU. **4.12**
comparison of widths, 4.8
expansion, 4.12
local, 4.13
Business, information systems in, 14.15-19
Business graphics, *see* **Analytical graphics**
Business Software Alliance, 13.9
Bus network: A communications network in which all the devices are connected to and share a single cable. **7.26**
Button: An icon that, when selected, causes a specific action to take place. **2.3**
Byron, Augusta Ada, 12.23
Byte: Each storage location within main memory, identified with a memory address. **4.2**

C: A programming language originally designed for writing systems software, but it is now considered a general-purpose programming language. C requires professional programming skills to be used effectively. **12.21**
C++: An object-oriented extension of the C programming language, developed at Bell Laboratories, frequently used to develop application software. **12.22**, 12.25
Cache memory: High-speed RAM memory between the CPU and the main memory that increases processing efficiency. **4.10**. *See also* **Disk cache**
Cage: Two or more bays together. **4.16**
Callback system: An access control method that authenticates remote users; users can only be connected to the computer system after the computer calls them back at a previously established telephone number. **13.7**
Career opportunities, 14.3-10
Cartridge tape: Frequently used storage medium for backup on personal computers. **6.16**
purchasing computers and, 8.33
CASE (computer-aided software engineering): The use of automated computer-based tools to design and manage a software system. **11.21**, 11.27
Case structure: Variation of the selection structure, used when a condition is being tested that can lead to two or more alternatives. **12.5**

CASE workbench: Integrated package of several CASE tools. These tools might include (1) analysis and design tools, (2) prototyping tools, (3) code generators, (4) an information repository, and (5) management tools. **11.21**
Cathode ray tube (CRT): An output device; monitor. **1.8**, **5.18**
CD-ROM (compact disk read-only memory): A small optical disk that uses the same laser technology as audio compact disks. **6.20**
purchasing, 8.33
Cell: The intersection where a row and a column meet on a spreadsheet. **2.12**
Cellular telephone: A wireless telephone available to the general public that uses radio waves to communicate with a local antenna assigned to a specific geographic area called a cell. **7.12**
Central processing unit (CPU): Processing unit containing a control unit that executes program instructions, and an arithmetic/logic unit (ALU) that performs math and logic operations. **1.8**, **4.6**
operating system management of, 8.6-7
performance of, 8.9-10
utilization, 8.10
Certification programs, 14.9
Certified Computing Professional (CCP): Professional certification offered by the Institute for the Certification of Computer Professionals; offered to candidates who pass a core examination and any two specialty examinations. **14.9**
Chain of command, 10.6
Chain printers: High-speed impact printers that use a rotating chain to print up to 3,000 lines per minute of good print quality. **5.13**
Changing: Updating data, such as posting a change of address to an existing record. **9.3**, 9.9-10
Characters per second (cps): Speed measurement of impact printers that have movable print heads. **5.10**
Chart: In a spreadsheet program, a graphic representation of the relationship of numeric data. **2.16**
Child record: In a hierarchical database, a record that is below the parent record. Each child record can have only one parent. **9.14**
Chip, *see* **Integrated circuit**
Ciphertext: Unreadable characters used by encryption process to protect sensitive data. **13.11**
CISC (complex instruction set computing): Computers that have hundreds of commands in their instruction sets; describes most computers. **4.18**
Class: In object-oriented programming, programmers define classes of objects. Each class contains the methods that are unique to that class. **12.17**
Client-server: In information resource sharing on a network, as much processing as possible is done on the server system before data is transmitted to the requesting computer. **7.23**
Clip art: Collections of art that are stored on disks and are designed for use with desktop publishing packages. **2.11**
Clipboard: Temporary storage place for text during cut operations. **2.6**
Clock, *see* **System clock**
Clipper chip: A tamper-resistant microprocessor that contains an encryption formula called Skipjack. **13.11**, 13.23
Cluster: Two to 8 track sectors on a diskette; the smallest unit of diskette space used to store data. **6.4**
contiguous, 6.15
Coaxial cable: A high-quality communications line that is used in offices and laid underground and laid underneath the ocean. Coaxial cable consists of a copper wire conductor surrounded by a nonconducting insulator that is in turn surrounded by a woven metal mesh outer conductor, and finally a plastic outer coating. **7.9**
COBOL (COmmon Business Oriented Language): One of the more widely used programming languages for business applications, which uses an English-type format. 1.32, **12.21**, 12.25
Code generators, CASE and, 11.21
Codes of conduct: Written guidelines that help determine whether a specific computer action is ethical or unethical; established by a number of computer-related organizations. **13.18**

Coding: The process of writing the program instructions that will process the data and produce the output specified in the program design. **12.9**
object, 12.14
Cold site: In case of a disaster that destroys the computer facility, an empty facility is established that can accommodate the necessary computer resources. **13.16**
Collision: Occurs with direct files when a hashing program generates the same disk location (called synonyms) for records with different key values. **9.7**
Color monitor: Monitor that can display text or graphics in color. **5.20**
method of producing color, 5.23
purchasing, 8.33
Color printers, 5.14, 5.15
Columns: Data that is organized vertically on a spreadsheet. **2.12**
COMDEX: The largest computer trade show in the United States. **14.10**
Command(s): In a graphical user interface, instructions for menus that cause the software to perform specific actions. **2.3**, **3.2**
COMMAND.COM: The DOS command language interpreter. **8.3**
backup of, 8.37
Command language: Instructions that the operating system allows the user to give to the computer, such as to list all the files on a diskette, or to copy a file from one diskette to another. **8.2**
Command language interpreter: The portion of the operating system that carries out the command language instructions. **8.2**
Command language prompt: Prompt displayed when the computer is turned on that indicates the system is ready to accept a command from the user. **8.3**
Commercial application software: Software that has been already developed and is available for purchase. **11.10**
custom software versus, 11.15
Common carriers: Public wide area network companies such as the telephone companies. **7.24**
Communications: The transmission of data and information over a communications channel, such as a standard telephone line, between one computer terminal and another computer. **7.1**, **7.8**
bulletin board systems and, 7.6
digital convergence and, 14.11-12
electronic data interchange and, 7.5-6
electronic mail, 7.2
equipment, 7.18-19
examples of use, 7.2
fax, 7.4
global positioning systems and, 7.6-7
groupware and, 7.4-5
line configurations and, 7.14-15
networks, 7.21-29
online services and, 7.7
protocols, 7.21
software, 7.20
system model, 7.8
telecommuting and, 7.5
teleconferencing, 7.3
transmission media and, 7.8-13
voice mail, 7.3
wireless, 14.12
Communications channel: The link, or path, that the data follows as it is transmitted from the sending equipment to the receiving equipment in a communications system. **7.8**
characteristics of, 7.16-18
example of, 7.13
Communications line, *see* **Communications channel**
Communications link, *see* **Communications channel**
Communications network, *see* **Network**
Communications satellites: Man-made space devices that receive, amplify, and retransmit signals from earth. **7.11**
Communications software: Programs that perform data communications tasks such as dialing, file transfer, terminal emulation, and data encryption. **2.22**, **7.20**
Communications specialist: Information processing employee who evaluates, installs, and monitors data and/or voice communications equipment and software. **14.4**

Compaq, 14.2
Competition, importance of information and, 10.2
Compiler: A program that translates high-level source programs into machine language object code. **12.14**
Computer(s): An electronic device, operating under the control of instructions stored in its own memory unit, that can accept data (input), that process data arithmetically and logically, produce output from the processing, and store the results for future use. **1.4**
  categories of, 1.9-13
  components of, 1.7-9
  diagnostic programs, 8.37
  evolution of industry, 1.32-38
  example of use, 1.17-21
  fourth-generation, 1.34
  host, 7.15
  installing, 8.34-35
  maintenance of, 8.36-37
  operations, 1.4-5
  performance of, 8.9-10
  purchasing, 8.30-33
  reliability, 1.6
  speed, 1.5
  storage, *see* Storage
  third-generation, 1.34
  tool set for, 8.34
  trends in, 14.11
  See also Personal computer(s)
Computer-aided design (CAD): Design method that uses a computer and special graphics software to aid in product design. 1.20, **14.17**-18, 14.23
Computer-aided engineering (CAE): The use of computers to test product designs. **14.18**
Computer-aided instruction (CAI): The use of computers for education. **14.21**
Computer-aided manufacturing (CAM): The use of computers to control production equipment. **14.18**
Computer-aided software engineering (CASE), *see* CASE
Computer-assisted retrieval (CAR): Process in which microfilm readers perform automatic data lookup. **5.25**
Computer Associates, 14.3
Computer concepts, overview of, 1.1-26
Computer drawing programs: Graphics programs that allow an artistic user to create works of art. **5.4**
Computer engineering: Information processing career field that deals with the design and manufacture of electronic computer components and computer hardware. **14.8**
Computer equipment, *see* Hardware
Computer ethics: The moral guidelines that govern the use of computers and information systems. **13.17**
Computer graphics: Any nontext pictorial information. **5.4**
Computer information systems (CIS) The use of computers to provide the information needed to operate businesses and other organizations. **14.8**
Computer-integrated enterprise (CIE): An organization in which all information storage and processing is performed by a network of computers and intelligent devices. **14.19**
Computer-integrated manufacturing (CIM): The total integration of the manufacturing process using computers. **14.18**
Computer literacy: Knowing how to use a computer. **1.2**, 2.1, 14.16
Computer operator: Person who works in the computer room and is responsible for running the computer equipment and monitoring processing operations. **14.4**
Computer-output microfilm (COM): An output technique that records output from a computer as microscopic images on roll or sheet film. **5.24**
Computer paint programs, *see* **Computer drawing programs**
Computer program, *see* **Program(s)**
Computer programmers: Persons who design, write, test, and implement programs necessary to direct the computer to process data into information. **1.14**
  career growth, 14.6
  choosing programming language and, 12.24
  system development life cycle and, 11.3
  Computer publications, 14.10
  Computer-related organizations, 14.8-9

Computer science: Includes the technical aspects of computers such as hardware operation and systems software. **14.8**
Computer security plan: Summary in writing of the safeguards that are in place to protect an organization's information assets. **13.16**
Computer security risk: Any event or action that could cause a loss to computer equipment, software, information, or processing capability. **13.2**-16
Computer software, *see* **Software**
Computer system: The equipment that performs the four operations of the information processing cycle. **1.9**
Computer tool set, 8.34
Computer users, *see* **User(s)**
Computer virus, *see* **Virus(es)**
CONFIG.SYS: File containing configuration information that tells the computer what devices are being used, such as a mouse or CD-ROM disk; this file is read during the system booting phase. **8.3**
  backup of, 8.37
  printout of, 8.36
Connectivity: The capability to connect a computer to other computers. **1.17**
Connectors: Couplers contained in ports, used to attach cables to peripheral devices. **4.14**
Consultants: People who draw upon their experience to give advice to others. They must have not only strong technical skills in their area of expertise, but also have the people skills to effectively communicate with clients. **14.6**
Continuous-form paper: A type of paper that is connected together for a continuous flow through the printer. **5.9**
Continuous speech recognition: Voice input system that allows the user to speak in a flowing conversational tone. **3.19**
Control clerk: Information processing employee that accounts for all input and output processed by the computer center. **14.4**
Controller cards, *see* **Expansion board**
Controlling, management function, 10.4
Control program: The resident portion of the operating system. **8.2**
Control structures: In structured program design, used to form the logic of a program. The three control structures are: the sequence structure, selection structure, and iteration structure. **12.4**-6
Control unit: Part of the CPU that repeatedly executes the fetching, decoding, executing, and storing operations, called the machine cycle. **1.8**, **4.6**
Conventional memory: Memory located in the first 640K of RAM used for the operating system, programs, and data. **4.10**
Conversion: During the implementation phase of the system development process, conversion refers to the process of changing from the old system to the new system. **11.23**
Coprocessors: A special microprocessor chip or circuit board designed to perform a specific task, such as numeric calculations. **4.12**
Copy: Makes a copy of the marked text, but leaves marked text where it was. **2.6**
Core competencies: In a virtual corporation, describes what each partner does best. **10.16**
Core memory, 1.32
Cost/benefit analysis: During the analysis phase of the information processing life cycle, identifies the estimated costs of the proposed solution and the benefits (including potential cost savings) that are expected. **11.8**
Cost effective information, 10.8
CPU, *see* Central processing unit
CPU utilization: The amount of time that the CPU is working and not idle, waiting for data to process. **8.10**
Crackers: Persons who deliberately try to illegally access computer systems, usually by using a modem. **13.4**
Crash program, 12.10
CRT, *see* Cathode ray tube
Currency: A type of database field. **2.19**
Cursor: A symbol such as an underline character or an arrow that indicates where you are working on the screen. **2.5**, **3.4**
Cursor control keys: Keys that move the cursor. **3.4**
Customizing: Modification of a commercial application software package. 11.2, **11.16**

Custom software: Applications software that is developed by the user or at the user's request. **11.15**, 11.17-21
Cut: Removing text from an area of a word processing document. **2.6**
CyberSight, 14.24
Cylinder: All the tracks on a diskette or hard disk that have the same number. **6.4**
Cylinder method: The physical organization of data on a disk, where the data is stored down the disk surfaces reducing movement of the read/write head during both reading and writing operations. **6.10**

Data: The raw facts, including numbers, words, images, and sounds, given to a computer during the input operation, which is processed to produce information. **1.4**, **3.3**
  backup of, *see* Backup
  current, 9.3
  electronic representation of, 4.2-3
  fragmented, 6.15
  future of information systems and, 14.15
  maintenance of stored, 6.15
  meaningful, 10.8
  recovery of, 8.15
  redundant, 9.13, 11.17
  timely, 9.2-3, 10.1, 10.2, 10.9
  unauthorized use of, 13.18-20
  useful, 10.1, 10.9
  verifiable, 10.8
Data accuracy: The source of the data is reliable and the data is correctly reported and entered. Also called data integrity. 3.20-21, **9.2**, 9.13-14
  ethics and, 13.17-18
  information system and, 10.1, 10.2, 10.8, 10.9
  system design and, 11.18
Database: Collection of data that is stored in related files. **2.18**, **9.12**-23
  competitive information and, 10.2
  external, 10.10
  generating, 9.15
  hierarchical, 9.14-15
  information center specialist and, 14.5
  Internet and, 7.25
  network, 9.15
  nontext, 9.23
  object-oriented, 9.16
  organization of, 9.14-16
  querying, 9.18-19
  reasons for using, 9.13-14
  relational, 9.15, 9.22
Database administration, 9.20-21
Database administrator (DBA): The person responsible for managing an organization's computerized data and all database activities. **9.20**
Database analyst: Information processing employee who is familiar with the organization's database structure and assists systems analysts and programmers in developing or modifying applications that use the database. **14.4**
Database design: In information system design, the data dictionary information developed during the analysis phase is merged into new or existing system files. **11.17**
  database administrator and, 9.20
Database management system (DBMS): The software that allows the user to create, maintain, and report the data and file relationships. **9.12**
  features of, 9.17
  file-oriented system versus, 9.13
  personal computer, 9.21
Database software: Software that allows the user to create a database and to retrieve, manipulate, and update the data that is stored in it. **2.18**-19
Data collection devices: Input devices designed and used for obtaining data at the site where the transaction or event being reported takes place. **3.14**
Data communications, *see* **Communications**
Data communications software: Used to transmit data from one computer to another. **2.22**
Data compression: Method of storing data on a disk that reduces storage requirements by substituting codes for repeating patterns of data. **6.11**
Data conversion: During conversion phase of information systems development, the process of converting existing manual and computer-based files so they can be used by a new system. **11.24**

Data dictionary: The data dictionary defines each data field, or element, to be used in the database. **9.17, 11.6,** 11.17
CASE and, 11.21
Data encryption: Communications software that protects confidential data during transmission. The data is converted at the sending end into an unrecognizable string of characters or bits and reconverted at the receiving end. **7.20**
Data encryption standard: An encryption method widely used by the U.S. government. **13.11**
Data entry, reliable, 9.2
Data entry operator: Persons responsible for entering large volumes of data into the computer system. **14.4**
Data flow diagram (DFD): Graphic representation of the flow of data through a system. **11.5-6**
CASE and, 11.21
Data integrity, *see* **Data accuracy**
Data librarian: Information processing employee that maintains the collection of production and backup tapes and disks. **14.4**
Data link, *see* **Communications channel**
Data maintenance: The procedures used to keep data current, called updating. **9.3,** 9.9-11
Data management: Procedures that are used to keep data accurate and timely and provide for the security and maintenance of data. **9.2-3**
Data processing: The production of information by processing data on a computer. Also called information processing. **1.5**
Data Processing Management Association (DPMA): Professional association of programmers, systems analysts, and information processing managers. **14.8**
Data projectors, 5.23
Data security: Protection of data to keep it from being misused or lost. **9.3,** 9.14
Data transfer rate: The time required to transfer data from disk to main memory. **6.8**
Date: Type of database field. **2.19**
DBA, *see* **Database administrator**
DBMS, *see* **Database management system**
Debugger: An error-correction feature included with programming languages that identifies syntax errors and allows the programmer to stop the program while it is running to examine the program values such as the results of a calculation. **12.10**
Debugging: The process of locating and correcting program errors, or bugs, found during testing. **12.10**
Decimal number system, 4.21-22
Decipher, *see* **Decrypt**
Decision making, information system and, 10.2
on-the-job, 10.6
operational, 10.6
strategic, 10.5
tactical, 10.6
Decision support system (DDS): A system designed to help someone reach a decision by summarizing or comparing data from either or both internal and external sources. **10.11**
Decision tables: A way of documenting the system during the analysis phase; identifies the actions that should be taken under different conditions. **11.6**
CASE and, 11.21
Decision trees: Like a decision table, illustrates the action to be taken based on given conditions, but presents it graphically. **11.6**
Decoding: Control unit operation that translates the program instruction into the commands that the computer can process. **4.7**
Decomposed programming problems, 12.4
Decrypt: Process of converting unreadable ciphertext message back into readable characters (plaintext). **13.11**
Dedicated line: A communications line connection between devices that is always established. **7.14**
Dedicated word processing systems: Computers that are used only for word processing. **2.4**
Defragmentation: Storage method that reorganizes stored data so files are located in contiguous clusters, improving the speed of the computer. **6.15**
Delete: Removing text from a word processing document. **2.6**
Deleting data: Update procedure for getting rid of obsolete information, such as removing inactive records. **9.3,** 9.10-11

Design: Second phase in the information system life cycle, where the logical design that was created in the analysis phase is transformed into a physical design. 11.2, **11.17**-21, **12.4**-9
structured, 12.4-7
structured walk through and, 12.8-9
tools, 12.7-8
Design review: Performed by management at the end of the design phase to evaluate the work completed thus far to determine whether to proceed. **11.20**
Desk checking: The process of reading the program and mentally reviewing its logic, before the program is used to process real data. **12.10**
Desktop computer, *see* **Personal computer(s)**
Desktop publishing (DTP) software: Allows users to design and produce professional looking documents that contain both text and graphics. **2.10-11**
Detailed system analysis: Involves both a thorough study of the current system and at least one proposed solution to any problems found. **11.4**-7
Detail report: A report in which each line usually corresponds to one input record. **5.3**
Development: Phase three in the information system life cycle, performed after the design phase. The development phase consists of program development and equipment acquisition. 11.2, 11.15, **11.22, 12.2**
database and, 9.14
personnel and, 14.4
programming and, 12.1-30
steps in, 12.2-11
Development path, 11.2
Device drivers: Programs used by the operating system to control input and output devices. **8.9**
Diagnostic programs, 8.37
Dialing software: Communications software that stores, selects, and dials telephone numbers. **7.20**
Dialog: Authentication procedure that requires users to enter one of several possible items of personal information randomly chosen by the computer, such as a spouse's first name, a birth date, or a mother's maiden name, in order to access a computer system. **13.6**
Dialogue: The sequence of inputs and computer responses that a user will encounter when he or she enters data on an interactive system. **11.17**
Differential backup: Backup procedure that duplicates only the files that have changed since the last full backup. **13.13**
Digital audio tape (DAT): A method of storing large amounts of data on tape. It uses helical scan technology to write data at much higher densities across the tape at an angle instead of down the length of the tape. **6.18**
Digital cameras: Cameras that record photographs in the form of digital data that can be stored on a computer. **3.19**
Digital computer: Computer that processes data, whether it be text, sound, graphics, or video, into a digital (numeric) value; describes most computers. **4.2**
Digital convergence: The merging of technologies and products from the communications, entertainment, publishing, and computing industries. **14.11**
Digital data service: Offered by telephone companies, communications channels specifically designed to carry digital instead of voice signals. **7.16**
Digital Equipment Corporation (DEC), 1.35, 14.2
Digital factory: Manufacturing technologies to increase productivity through the use of networked, computer-controlled equipment. Technologies used in the digital factory include computer-aided design, computer-aided engineering, and computer-aided manufacturing. **14.17**
Digital service unit (DSU): Device used to connect to a communications line. **7.16**
Digital signal processing (DSP): In voice input systems, a board that is added to the computer to convert the voice into digital form. **3.18**
Digital signals: A type of signal for computer processing in which individual electronic pulses represent bits that are grouped together to form characters. **7.16**
Digitizer: Converts points, lines, and curves from a sketch, drawing, or photograph to digital impulses, and transmits them to a computer. **3.9**
Digitizing: The process a computer uses to convert data into a digital form. **4.2**

Direct access, *see* **Random access**
Direct access storage devices, *see* **Fixed disks**
Direct conversion: The user stops using the old system one day and begins using the new system the next. **11.23**
Direct file: File organization that uses the key value of a record to determine the location on the disk where the record is or will be stored. Also called relative file, or random file. **9.6-8**
Directing, management function, 10.4
Disabled persons, computers and, 3.22
Disaster recovery plan: Written plan describing the steps an organization would take to restore computer operations in the event of a disaster. **13.14-15**
Disaster recovery test plan: Test of the disaster plan that contains information for simulating different levels of disasters and recording and organization's capability of recovering. **13.16**
Discrete speech recognition: Voice input system that requires the user to pause slightly between each word spoken to the computer. **3.19**
Discussion groups, the Internet and, 7.25
Disks, *see* Hard disk; Magnetic disk
Disk cache: An area of memory set aside for data most often read from the disk. **6.11**
Disk cartridges: Disk storage available for use with personal computers, which can be inserted and removed, and offer the storage and fast access features of hard disks and the portability of diskettes. **6.14**
Disk directories, reviewing and maintaining, 8.36
Diskettes: Used as a principal auxiliary storage medium for personal computers. **1.9, 6.3**
care of, 6.8
preparing for use, 6.4-6
storage capacity, 6.6-7
types of, 6.6
Diskette drives, purchasing, 8.32
Disk input and output (I/O) rate, 8.10
Disk management
operating system and, 8.10
utilities and, 8.15
Disk mirroring, *see* **Redundant array of inexpensive disks (RAID)**
Disk Operating System (DOS): The most widely used operating system on personal computers, developed by Microsoft Corporation. **8.12**
Disk pack: A removable recording media, consisting of metal platters that are used on both sides for recording data. **6.14**
Display device: The visual output device of a computer, such as a monitor. **5.18**
color monitors, 5.20, 5.23
flat panel displays, 5.20-21
method of displays and, 5.22-23
monochrome monitors, 5.20
resolution of, 5.18-20
Display terminals: A keyboard and a screen. **3.15**
Document(s)
desktop publishing and, 2.10-11
electronic data interchange and, 7.5-6
word processing, 2.4-9
See also **Source document**
Documentation: Written materials that are produced as part of the information system life cycle. **11.3**
program, 12.11
quality assurance specialist and, 14.4
reviewing current, 11.5
technical writer and, 14.4
Document holder, using when entering data, 8.34
Domain: The range of values an attribute can have in a relational database. **9.15**
DOS, *see* **Disk Operating System**
Dot-addressable displays: Screens used for graphics in which the number of addressable locations corresponds to the number of dots (pixels) that can be illuminated. Also called bit-mapped displays. **5.19**
Dot matrix printers: An impact printer in which the print head consists of a series of small tubes containing pins that, when pressed against ribbon and paper, print small dots closely together to form characters. **5.10**
Dot pitch: The distance between each pixel on the computer screen. **5.18**
Dots per inch (dpi): Measurement of page printer resolution. **5.15**

INDEX

Double-density diskettes: Diskettes that can store 360K for a 5 1/4-inch diskette, and 720K for a 3-1/2 inch diskette. **6.6**
Do-until structure: Control structure where a condition is tested at the end of a loop. Processing continues until the condition is met. **12.5**
Do-while structure: Control structure where a condition is tested at the beginning of a loop. If the condition is true, the process is performed. The program then loops back and tests the condition again. This looping continues until the condition being tested is false. **12.5**
Downlink: The transmission from a satellite to a receiving earth station. **7.11**
Downsize: In the information system department, a money-saving process that reduces the size of operations by moving applications from mainframe and mini-computer systems to networks of personal computers; some companies have eliminated their in-house information system departments altogether. **10.7**
DP, *see* Data processing
Draft quality: Printer output that a business would use for internal purposes and not for correspondence. **5.10**
Drill and practice software: Educational software that uses a flash-card approach to teaching by allowing users to practice skills in subjects such as math and languages. **14.21**
Drive bay, *see* Bay
Drum plotter: Plotter that uses a rotating drum, or cylinder, over which drawing pens are mounted. **5.24**
Dumb terminal: A keyboard and a display screen that can be used to enter and transmit data to, or receive and display data from, a computer to which it is connected. A dumb terminal has no independent processing capability or auxiliary storage. **3.15**
Dye diffusion: Used by a special type of thermal printer; chemically treated paper is used to obtain color print quality equal to glossy magazines. **5.15**
Dynamic RAM (DRAM) chips: A type of RAM memory that has access speeds of 50 to 100 nanoseconds. **4.11**

Earth stations: Communications facilities that contain large, dish-shaped antennas used to transmit data to and receive data from communications satellites. **7.11**
EBCDIC, *see* **Extended Binary Coded Decimal Interchange Code**
Eckert, J. Presper, Jr., 1.32, 1.33
Editing: Making changes and corrections to electronic text. **2.6**
Education
 career opportunities, 14.6
 career requirements, 14.8
 information system implementation and, 11.23
 personal computers for, 14.21
 professional, 14.9-10
Electronic data interchange (EDI): The capability to electronically transfer documents from one business to another. **7.5**
Electronic mail, the Internet and, 7.25, 7.46
Electronic mail software: Software that allows users to send messages to and receive messages from other computer users. 2.22, **2.23**
 example of use, 7.2
Electronic office, *see* **Automated office**
Electronic spreadsheet, *see* **Spreadsheet**
Electrostatic plotter: Plotter in which the paper moves under a row of wires (styli) that can be turned on to create an electrostatic charge on the paper. **5.24**
E-mail, *see* **Electronic mail software**
Emergency plan: Organization plan that specifies the steps to be taken immediately after a disaster strikes. The plan is usually organized by type of disaster, such as fire, flood, or earthquake. **13.15**
Encapsulation: In object-oriented programming, the capability to combine methods (instructions) with objects (data). **12.17**
Encryption: Protecting sensitive data by converting readable data into unreadable characters. **13.11**
Encryption chip, 13.23
Encryption key: Code used by a formula that converts readable data into unreadable data to protect sensitive information. **13.11**
Encyclopedia, multimedia, 5.6

End user(s), *see* User(s)
End user computing group: Information processing employees who are responsible for assisting end users in working with existing systems and in using productivity software and query languages to obtain the information necessary to perform their jobs. **14.5**
Energy Star power consumption guidelines, 1.38, 8.30
ENIAC (Electronic Numerical Integrator and Computer), 1.32
Entertainment software, 14.22
Entry point: The point where a control structure is entered. **12.6**
Equipment, *see* Hardware
Ergonomics: The science of making the equipment that people use and the surrounding work area safer and more efficient. **8.34**
Error correction, system maintenance and, 11.25
Escape key, 3.4
ETHERNET, 1.34
Ethics, information age and, 13.17-18
Evaluation, post-implementation, 11.24
Even parity: The total number of on bits in the byte (including the parity bit) must be an even number. **4.4**
Event-driven: Description of object-oriented programming languages meaning that the program is designed to respond to events that can take place when an application is run. Events can take place at any time or in any sequence. **12.18**
Exception report: A report that contains information that is outside of normal user-specified values or conditions, called the exception criteria. **5.3**
Executing: Control unit operation that processes the computer demands. **4.7**
Executive: The resident portion of the operating system. **8.2**
Executive information systems (EIS): Management information systems that have been designed for the information needs of senior management. **10.10**
Executive information system (EIS) specialist: Employee who works with senior management to develop reports and systems to meet its information requirements. **14.5**
Exit point: The point where the control structure is exited. **12.6**
Expanded markets, 10.2
Expanded memory: Up to 32MB of memory on a memory expansion board. A separate program called an expanded memory manager is used to access this memory 16K at a time. **4.10**
Expansion bay, *see* Bay
Expansion board: Circuit board for add-on devices. **4.13**
Expansion bus: Bus that carries data to and from the expansion slots. **4.12**
Expansion cards, *see* **Expansion board**
Expansion slot: A socket designed to hold the circuit board for a device, such as a tape drive or sound card, that adds capability to the computer system. **4.13**
 purchasing computers and, 8.32
Expert system: Combines the knowledge on a given subject of one or more human experts into a computerized system that simulates the human experts' reasoning and decision-making processes. **10.12**, 10.15
Extended Binary Coded Decimal Interchange Code (EBCDIC): A coding system used to represent data, primarily on mainframes. **4.3**
Extended density (ED): 3-1/2 inch diskettes that can store 2.88 megabytes. **6.6**
Extended memory: All memory above 1MB, used for programs and data. **4.10**
External commands: Instructions to the computer in the nonresident portion of the operating system. **8.2**
External modem: A separate, or stand-alone, device attached to the computer or terminal by a cable and to the telephone outlet by a standard telephone cord. **7.19**
External report: A report used outside the organization. **5.3**

Facsimile, *see* **Fax**
Father: The second oldest copy of a file. **13.14**
Fault-tolerant computers: Computers built with redundant components to allow processing to continue if any single component fails. **8.5**

Fax (facsimile): Communications method in which equipment is used to transmit a reproduced image of a document over phone lines. The image is scanned and converted into digitized data that is transmitted to a receiving fax machine that converts the digitized data back into its original image. **7.4**
 purchasing, 8.33
Feasibility study: During the analysis phase of the information system life cycle, the feasibility study discusses whether the proposed solution is practical and capable of being accomplished. **11.8**
Federal Communications Commission, 8.33
Fetching: Control unit operation that obtains the next program instruction from main memory. **4.6**
Fiber optics: A technology based on the capability of smooth, hair-thin strands of glass that conduct light waves to rapidly and efficiently transmit data. **7.10**
Fields: A specific item of information, such as a name or Social Security number, in a record of a database file. **2.18**, **9.4**
 relational database and, 9.16
Fifth-generation language, *see* **Natural language**
File(s): A collection of related records. **2.18**, **9.4**
 database versus file-oriented system and, 9.13
 defragmentation of, 6.15
 fragmented, 6.15
 operating system management of, 8.10
 organization of, *see* File organization
 utilities managing, 8.15
File allocation table: On personal computers using the DOS operating system, the file that stores information such as the filename, file size, the time and date the file was last changed, and the cluster numbers where the file begins. **6.5**
File management system: Software that allows the user to create, maintain, and access one file at a time. **9.12**
File organization
 direct, 9.6-8
 indexed, 9.5-6
 sequential, 9.4-5
File-oriented system, database system versus, 9.13
File-server: In information resource sharing on a network, allows an entire file to be sent at a time, on request. The requesting computer then performs the processing. **7.23**
File transfer, the Internet and, 7.25, 7.46
File transfer software: Communications software that allows the user to move one or more files from one system to another. The software generally has to be loaded on both the sending and receiving computers. **7.20**
File virus: Virus that works by inserting virus code into program files. The virus then spreads to any program that accesses the infected file. **13.2**
Firmware: Instructions that are stored in ROM memory. Also called microcode. **4.11**
Fixed disks: Hard disks on minicomputers and mainframes. Also called direct-access storage devices. **6.9**
Flagged record, 9.11
Flash memory: Type of RAM that can retain data even when power is turned off. **4.10**
Flash RAM, *see* **Flash memory**
Flatbed plotter: Plotter in which the pens are instructed by the software to move to the down position so the pen contacts the flat surface of the paper. **5.24**
Flat file: In file-oriented systems, a file that is independent and contains all the information necessary to process the records in that file. **9.12**
Flat panel display: Plasma and LCD screens, which do not use the conventional cathode ray tube technology, and are relatively flat. **5.20**
Floppy disks, *see* **Diskettes**
Floptical: Diskette that combines optical and magnetic technology to achieve high-storage rates (currently up to 21 megabytes) on what is basically a 3-1/2 inch diskette. **6.6**
Fonts: A specific combination of typeface and point size. **2.7**, 5.14
Footer: In word processing documents, text that is printed at the bottom of every page. **2.9**
Foreground jobs: Assignment of a higher processing priority and more CPU time. Compare with background jobs. **8.7**
Format: Changing the appearance of a document. **2.7**
 desktop publishing, 2.10-11
 spreadsheet, 2.17
 word processing document, 2.7

Formatting: Process that prepares a diskette so it can store data and includes defining the tracks, cylinders, and sectors on the surfaces of the diskette. **6.4**

Formulas: Perform calculations on the data on a spreadsheet. **2.12**

FORTRAN (FORmula TRANslator): A programming language designed to be used by scientists, engineers, and mathematicians. FORTRAN is noted for its capability to easily express and efficiently calculate mathematical equations. 1.33, **12.22**

Fourth-generation computers, 1.34

Fourth-generation languages (4GLs): Programming languages that are easy to use, both for programmers and nonprogrammers, because the user tells the computer what is to be done, not how to do it. Also called very high level languages. **12.15-**16

Forward recovery: In DBMS recovery operations, a log is kept showing changes made to the database, which is used to automatically reenter transactions from the last time the system was backed up; also called rollforward. **9.17**

Fragmented: File stored in clusters that are not next to each other; also used to describe the condition of a disk drive that has many files stored in non-contiguous clusters, slowing down the computer's speed. **6.15**

Frame, *see* Page

Frankston, Bob, 1.35

Friction feed mechanism: Printing mechanisms that move paper through a printer by pressure between the paper and the carriage. **5.12**

Front-end processor: A computer that is dedicated to handling the communications requirements of a larger computer. **7.19**

Full backup: Backup procedure that includes all files in the computer. **13.13**

Full-duplex transmission: Data transmission method in which data can be sent both directions at the same time. **7.17**

Full justification: Text is aligned with both the left and right margins. **2.8**

Full update privileges, 9.14

Function(s): Stored formulas that perform common calculations in a spreadsheet. **2.12**

Functional organization, 10.6-7

Function keys: A set of numerical keys preceded by an "F", included on computer keyboards as a type of user interface. Pressing a function key in an applications program is a shortcut that takes the place of entering a command. **3.4**

Fuzzy logic: A type of mathematics that deals with values that are not precise and values that have a degree of uncertainty, used in artificial intelligence applications. **14.13**

Games, 14.22
  Internet and, 7.25
  virtual reality and, 5.8

Gantt chart, 11.2

Garbage In, Garbage Out (GIGO): Describes inaccurate information caused by inaccurate data. **3.20**, 10.8

Gas plasma: Screens that use neon gas deposited between two sheets of polarizing material. **5.21**

Gates, Bill, 1.36

Gateway, 14.2

Gateway: A combination of hardware and software that allows users on one network to access the resources on a different type of network. **7.28**

Generating the database, 9.15

Geographic information systems (GIS), 9.23

Geosynchronous orbit: Orbit about 22,300 miles above the earth that communications satellites are placed in. The satellite rotates with the earth, so the same dish antennas on earth that are used to send and receive signals can remain fixed on the satellite at all times. **7.11**

Gestures: Special symbols made with a pen input device that issue commands to the computer. **3.7**

Gigabyte (GB): A measurement of memory space, equal to a billion bytes. **6.10**

Gigaflops (GFLOPS): Billions of floating-point operations per second. **4.19**

GIGO, *see* Garbage In, Garbage Out

Global positioning system (GPS): Communications system that uses satellites to determine the geographic location of earth-based GPS equipment; often used for tracking and navigation of all types of vehicles. **7.6-**7

Government regulation, 10.3

Grammar checker: Software used to check for grammar, writing style and sentence structure errors. **2.7**

Grandfather: The oldest copy of a file. **13.14**

Graphic(s), multimedia and, 5.5-6

Graphical user interface (GUI): A user interface that provides visual clues, such as symbols called icons, to help the user when entering data or running programs. **1.15**, **2.2**

Graphics tablet: Converts points, lines, and curves from a sketch, drawing, or photograph to digital impulses and transmits them to a computer. It also contains unique characters and commands that can be automatically generated by the person using the tablet. **3.9**

Gray scaling: Used by monochrome monitors to convert an image into pixels that are different shades of gray, like a black and white photograph. **5.20**

Groupware: Software that helps multiple users work together by sharing information. **7.4-**5

GRP file extension, 8.37

GUI, *see* Graphical user interface

Hacker: Person who tries to break into computer systems. **13.4**

Half-duplex transmission: Data transmission method in which data can flow in both directions, but in only one direction at a time. **7.17**

Hand-held computers: Small computers used by workers who are on their feet instead of sitting at a desk, such as meter readers or inventory counters. **1.10**

Handouts, presentation graphics and, 2.21

Handshake: The process of establishing the communications connection on a switched line. **7.14**

Handwriting recognition software: Software that can be taught to recognize an individual's unique style of writing. **3.7**

Hard card: A circuit board that has a hard disk built onto it. The board can be installed into an expansion slot of a personal computer. **6.14**

Hard copy: Output that is printed. **5.2**

Hard disk/drive: Secondary storage device containing nonremovable disks. **1.9**, **6.8**
  disk cartridges, 6.14
  hard cards, 6.14
  maintenance and, 6.15
  purchasing computers and, 8.32
  removable disks, 6.14
  storage capacity, 6.9-10
  streaming mode and, 6.18

Hardware: Equipment that processes data, consisting of input devices, a processor unit, output devices, and secondary storage units. **1.7**
  communications, 7.9-15, 7.18-19
  disabled persons and, 3.22
  front-end processors, 7.19
  future changes, 14.15
  industry, 14.2
  input devices, 1.7-9, 3.2-22
  installing, 8.34-35
  keyboard, 3.3-4
  line configurations and, 7.14-15
  maintenance of, 8.36
  modems, 7.18-19
  multimedia, 3.16-20
  multiplexors, 7.19
  network interface cards, 7.19
  output devices, 1.8
  PC support specialist and, 14.5
  pointing devices, 3.5-9
  purchasing, 11.22
  registering, 8.35
  repair and, 14.5-6
  secondary storage devices, 1.9, 6.1-25
  source data automation and, 3.10-14
  system unit, 1.8, 4.5
  terminals, 3.15
  theft, 13.8-9
  wireless, 7.12

Hardware resource sharing: Used in local area networks, allowing all network users to access a single piece of equipment rather than each user having to be connected to their own device. **7.21**

Hashing: The program managing the disk uses a formula or performs a calculation to determine the location (position) where a record will be placed on a disk. **9.7**

Head crash: The disk head collides with and damages the surface of a hard disk, causing a loss of data. The collision is caused if some form of contamination is introduced, or if the alignment of the read/write heads is altered. **6.10**

Header: In word processing documents, text that is printed at the top of every page. **2.9**

Health, multimedia and, 12.41

Health guidelines, 8.35

Helical scan technology: Used by digital audio tape to write data at high densities across the tape at an angle instead of down the length of the tape. **6.18**

Hewlett-Packard, 14.2

Hexadecimal (base 16): Number system which represents binary in a more compact form. Hexadecimal is used to represent the electronic status of bits in main memory, and addressing the memory locations. **4.21**, 4.22

Hierarchical database: Database in which data is organized in a top to bottom series like a family tree or organization chart, having branches made up of parent and child records. **9.14-**15

Hierarchy charts, *see* Structure charts

High definition television (HDTV): Television sets designed to handle a computer's digital signals; may eventually replace computer screens. **5.5**

High-density (HD) diskettes: Diskettes that can store 1.2 megabytes on a 5 1/4 inch diskette and 1.44 megabytes on a 3 1/2 inch diskette. **6.6**

High-level languages: Computer languages that are easier to learn and use than low-level languages, and contain nouns, verbs, and mathematical, relational, and logical operators that can be grouped together in what appear to be sentences. These sentences are called program statements. **12.14-**15

High Performance Computing and Communications (HPCC), 1.38

Hoff, Ted, 1.35

Home
  personal computers in, 14.19-22
  working at, 7.5

Home systems, computers controlling, 14.20

Hopper, Grace, 1.32, 12.21

Horizontal application software: Software packages that can be used by many different types of organizations, such as accounting packages. **11.10**

Host computer: In a data communications system, a main computer that is connected to several devices (such as terminals or personal computers). **7.15**

Hot site: In case of a disaster that destroys the computer facility, an alternate computer facility that has compatible computer resources; that is, it already has installed the necessary hardware, software, and communications equipment. **13.16**

Hypermedia: Technique used in multimedia presentations that allows the user to quickly move among screens to related subject area, such as pictures, sounds, animation, or maps in computerized encyclopedias. **5.5**

IBM (International Business Machines), 14.2
  early computer development, 1.32, 1.34
  operating systems and, 8.12
  personal computers development, 1.36
  third-generation computers and, 1.34
  virtual machine operating system, 8.15

IC, *see* Integrated circuit

Icons: On screen pictures that represent processing options. **1.15**, **2.3**

If-then-else structure, *see* Selection structure

Image, before and after, 9.17

Image on screen, resolution of, 5.18-20

Image processing systems: Use scanners to input and store an image of the source document. These systems are like electronic filing systems. **3.10**

Image scanner, *see* Page scanner

Impact printers: Printers that transfer the image onto paper by some type of printing mechanism striking the paper, ribbon, and character together. **5.9**
  band, 5.12-13
  chain, 5.13
  dot matrix, 5.10-12

Implementation: The phase of the system development process when people actually begin using the new system. This phase includes training and education, conversion, and the post-implementation evaluation. **11.23**

Incremental backup: Backup procedure that duplicates only the files that have changed since the last full or incremental backup. **13.13-14**

Index: A file that consists of a list containing the key field and the corresponding disk address for each record in a file. **9.5**

Indexed file organization: Records are stored on disk in an index file in ascending or descending sequence based on a key field. An index is used to retrieve records. **9.5-6**

Inference rules: In expert systems, rules that determine how the knowledge is used to make decisions. **10.12**

Information: Data that has been processed into a form that has meaning and is useful. **1.4**
 importance of, 10.2-3
 management of, 9.1-25
 managers using, 10.3-4
 multimedia used for, 12.38
 privacy and, 13.18-20
 qualities of, 10.8
 theft of, 13.10-11
 unauthorized collection and use of, 13.18-20
 See also Data
Information age
 ethics and, 13.17-18
 future in, 14.1-27
 at home, 14.99-22
Information appliances, 1.23
Information architecture, 10.7

Information center specialist: Employee that assists users in obtaining information from an organization's existing database and putting it in a form that they can use, such as presentation graphics. **14.5**

Information literacy: Knowing how to find, analyze, and use information. **1.2**

Information privacy: The rights of individuals and organizations to deny or restrict the collection and use of information about them. **13.18-20**

Information processing: The production of information by processing data on a computer, also called data processing (DP). **1.5**
 career opportunities in, 14.3-10

Information processing cycle: Input, process, output, and storage operations. Collectively, these operations describe the procedures that a computer performs to process data into information and store it for future use. **1.4**, **1.7**
 input and, *see* Input
 output and, *see* Output
 overview of, 3.2
 processing and, 1.7
 storage and, *see* Storage
Information processing industry, 14.2-10
Information processing professionals, 14.3-10

Information resource sharing: Allows local area network users to access the data stored on any other computer in the network. **7.22**

Information services, *see* Online services
Information strategies, 10.2, 10.3

Information superhighway: A nationwide and eventually worldwide network of information and services. **7.31**

Information system: A collection of elements that provides accurate, timely, and useful information. These elements include: equipment, software, accurate data, trained information systems personnel, knowledgeable users, and documented procedures. **1.16**, **10.1-19**
 in business, 14.15-19
 change management and, 11.25
 development of, 11.1-31
 executive, 10.10
 expert, 10.12-13, 10.15
 future changes, 14.15
 integrated, 10.13
 interenterprise, 10.16
 personal computers and, 10.14
 types of, 10.9-13
 See also **Management information system; System development life cycle**
Information systems department, 1.21, 14.3-5

Inheritance: In object-oriented programming, the capability to pass methods to lower levels of classes or objects. **12.17**
INI file extension, 8.37
Ink: Describes the darkened location on screen when a pen input device touches it. **3.7**

Ink jet printer: Nonimpact printer that forms characters by using a nozzle that shoots droplets of ink onto the page, producing high-quality print and graphics. **5.13**-14

Inoculated: Vaccine programs prevent viruses by inoculating program files. When a program file is inoculated, information such as the file size and file creation date is recorded in a separate inoculation file. **13.3**

Input: The process of entering programs, commands, user responses, and data into main memory. Input can also refer to the media (such as disks, tapes, and documents) that contain these input types. **1.7**, **3.2-26**
 data accuracy and, 3.20-21
 disabled persons and, 3.22
 keyboard, 3.3-4
 multimedia, 3.16-20
 operating system managing, 8.8
 pointing devices, 3.5-9
 source data automation, 3.10-14
 terminals, 3.15

Input controls: System controls established to assure the complete and accurate conversion of data from the source documents or other sources to a machine-processable form. **11.18**

Input design: The identification of what information needs to be entered into the system to produce the desired output, and where and how the data will be entered. **11.17**

Input devices: Hardware used to enter data into a computer. **1.7**
Insert mode, 2.6

Insert text: Add characters to existing text in a word processing document. **2.6**

Instance: In object-oriented programming, a specific instance of an object contains all methods from its higher level classes plus any methods that are unique to the object. **12.17**

Institute for the Certification of Computer Professionals (ICCP): Offers four certification programs, as a way of encouraging and recognizing the efforts of its members to attain a level of knowledge about their profession. **14.9**

Instruction set: The collection of commands, such as ADD or MOVE, that the computer's circuits can directly perform. **4.18**

Integrated circuit (IC): A complete electronic circuit that has been etched on a small chip of nonconducting material such as silicon. Also called chip or microchip. **1.5**, **4.6**
 encryption, 13.23
 future development plans, 4.24-25
 history of, 1.34-38
 large-scale, 1.34
 making of, 4.35-38
 static electricity and, 8.35

Integrated Drive Electronics (IDE): Controllers that can operate 1 or 2 hard disk drives. **6.11**

Integrated Services Digital Network (ISDN): An international standard for the digital transmission of both voice and data using different channels and communications companies. **7.24**

Integrated software: Software packages that combine applications such as word processing, electronic spreadsheet, database, graphics, and data communications into a single, easy-to use set of programs. **2.25**

Integration testing: During design phase of information systems development, process of testing a new application to make sure it works with other applications. **11.19**
Intel microprocessors
 evolution of, 1.35, 1.37, 1.38
 parallel processing and, 4.24-25
 types of, 4.8

Intelligent terminal: Terminal that contains not only a keyboard and a screen, but also has built-in processing capabilities, disk drives, and printers. **3.15**

Interface cards, *see* Expansion board
Interlaced monitors: Monitors that display images by illuminating every other line and then returning to the top to illuminate lines that were skipped. **5.22**

Internal commands: Instructions to the computer included in the resident portion of the operating system. **8.2**

Internal modem: A circuit board containing a modem that is installed inside a computer or terminal. **7.19**

Internal report: A report used by individuals in the performance of their jobs and only by personnel within an organization. **5.2**

Internet: The largest and best known wide area network; a worldwide network of computer networks. **7.25**, 7.43-50

Interpreter: Translates a program in a high-level language one program statement at a time to machine language and then executes the resulting machine language before translating the next program statement. **12.15**

Iteration structure: Control structure where one or more processes continue to occur as long as a given condition remains true, also called looping structure. Two forms of this structure are the do-while structure, and the do-until structure. **12.5**

Jobs, Steve, 1.35
Join relational operation: In a relational database query, used to combine two files (relations or tables). **9.18**

Joystick: Pointing device that uses the movement of a vertical stem to direct the pointer. **3.6**
Justification, *see* Alignment

Kapor, Mitch, 1.37
Kemeny, John, 1.34
Kernel: The resident portion of the operating system. **8.2**

Key: A field that contains unique data, such as Social Security number, that is used to identify the records in a file. **9.4**
 hashing and, 9.7

Keyboard: An input device that contains alphabetic, numeric, cursor control, and function keys. Used to enter data. **1.7**, **3.3-4**

Keyboard templates: Plastic sheets that fit around a portion of the keyboard. The template details keyboard commands. **2.27**
Key field, *see* Key

Kilobyte (K or KB): A measure of memory equal to 1,024 bytes. **4.9**

Knowledge base: In expert systems, the combined subject knowledge of human experts. **10.12**
Knowledge system, *see* Expert system

Label printers, 5.16
Labels: Text that is entered in the cell of a spreadsheet. **2.12**
LAN, *see* Local area network
Landscape orientation: Printing orientation that is wider than it is tall. **2.9**

Language translators: Special-purpose systems software programs that are used to convert the programming instructions written by programmers into the machine instructions that a computer can understand. **8.16**

Laptop computers: Larger versions of notebook computers that weigh between 8 and 15 pounds. **1.11**

Laser printers: Nonimpact page printers that use a laser beam aimed at a photosensitive drum to create the image to be transferred to paper. **5.14**
Latency, *see* Rotational delay
LCD, *see* Liquid crystal display
Leading, management function, 10.4
Learning
 aids for application users, 2.27
 Internet and, 7.25
 multimedia and, 5.25

Leased line: A dedicated communications line provided by an outside organization. Also called private line. **7.15**

Letter quality (LQ): High-quality printer output in which the printer character is a fully formed, solid character like those made by a typewriter, used for business or legal correspondence. **5.11**
Light emitting diode arrays, printers and, 5.14

Light pen: Pen used as input device by touching it on the display screen to create or modify graphics. **3.9**

Line chart: Graphic chart that indicates a trend by use of a rising or falling line. **2.16**

INDEX

Line configurations: The types of line connections used in communications systems. The major line configurations are point-to-point lines and multidrop, or multipoint lines. **7.14**

Line spacing: In word processing document, the distance from the bottom of one line to the bottom of the next line. **2.8**

Lines per minute (lpm): Measurement for the rate of printing of line printers. **5.10**

Liquid crystal display (LCD): Type of flat panel display screen that has liquid crystal deposited between 2 sheets of polarizing material. When an electrical current passes between crossing wires, the liquid crystals are aligned so light cannot shine through, producing an image on the screen. **5.21**

Liquid crystal shutters, printers and, 5.14

Live testing, 11.19

Local area network (LAN): A privately owned communications network that covers a limited geographical area such as a school computer laboratory, an office, a building, or a group of buildings. **7.21**
  development of first, 1.34

Local bus: An expansion bus that connects directly to the CPU. **4.13**

Local bus video card, purchasing, 8.32

Logical design: In the analysis phase of the information life cycle, a design that offers a solution to an existing problem without regard to a specific computer or programming language. **11.17**

Logical operations: Comparisons of data by the arithmetic/logic unit of the central processing unit, to see if one value is greater than, equal to or less than another. **1.8**, **4.7**

Logic bomb: Virus program that performs an activity (such as destroying data) when a certain action has occurred, such as an employee being terminated. **13.2-3**

Logic testing: The sequence of program instructions is tested for incorrect results using test data. **12.10**

Logon code: In multiuser operating systems, a logon code, consisting of a word or series of characters, must be entered correctly before a user is allowed to use an application program. **8.10**, **13.5**
  Internet and, 7.25

Looping structure, see **Iteration structure**

Lossless data compression, 6.12

Lossy data compression, 6.12

Lotus 1-2-3, 1.37, 14.3

Lotus Notes, 7.5

Low-level language, see **Machine language**

Machine cycle: The four steps which the CPU carries out for each machine language instruction: fetch, decode, execute, and store. **4.6**

Machine language: The fundamental language of the computer's processor, also called low-level language. All programs are converted into machine language before they can be executed. **12.13**

Machine language instructions: Program instructions written by users are translated into a form that the electronic circuits in the CPU can interpret and convert into one or more of the commands in the computer's instruction set. **4.18**-19

MACH operating system, 8.15

Macintosh: Multitasking operating system first released with Macintosh computers in 1984; the first commer-cially successful graphical user interface. **8.13**
  development of, 1.36

Macroinstructions: Instructions in assembly language programs that generate more than one machine language instruction. **12.14**

Magazines, multimedia and, 12.40

Magnetic disk: The most widely used storage medium for computers, in which data is recorded on a platter (the disk) as a series of magnetic spots. Magnetic disks offer high storage capacity, reliability, and capability to directly access stored data. **6.3**
  data compression and, 6.11-12
  diskettes, 6.3-8
  hard disks, 6.8-11, 6.14
  RAID and, 6.13

Magnetic ink character recognition (MICR): Software that recognizes characters using a special ink that is magnetized during processing; used primarily by the banking industry for processing checks. **3.13**

Magnetic tape: A thin ribbon of plastic, coated on one side with a material that can be magnetized to record the bit patterns that represent data. The primary means of backup for most medium and large systems. **6.16**
  cartridge, 6.16
  purchasing computers and, 8.33
  reel-to-reel, 6.17
  storing data on, 6.17-18

Magneto-optical technology: Used by erasable optical disk drives, in which a magnetic field changes the polarity of a spot on the disk that is heated by a laser. **6.20**

Main board, see **Motherboard**

Mainframe computers: Large systems that can handle hundreds of users, store large amounts of data, and process transactions at a very high rate. **1.13**
  manufacturers of, 14.2
  operating systems, 8.15

Main memory: Contained in the processor unit of the computer; temporarily stores data and program instructions when they are being processed. Also called RAM. **1.8**, **4.9**-10
  amount needed, 8.32
  solid-state storage and, 6.21

Maintenance: The final phase in the information system life cycle. The process of supporting the system after it is implemented, consisting of three activities: performance monitoring, change management, and error correction. 11.2, **11.25**-26, **12.11**
  COBOL and, 12.25
  of computer system, 8.36-37
  of stored data, 6.15

Make-or-buy decision: Decision made at the end of the analysis phase of information systems development when organizations have to decide to either acquire a commercial software package from an outside source, develop the software themselves, or have a third party develop the software. **11.8**

MAN, see **Metropolitan area network**

Management information systems (MIS): Any computer-based system that provides timely and accurate information for managing an organization. **10.9**

Managers/management: The men and women responsible for directing the use of resources such as people, money, materials, and information so the organization can operate efficiently and prosper. Managers are responsible for the tasks of planning, organizing, directing, and controlling. **10.3**
  information use and, 10.3-4
  levels of, 10.5-7

Manufacturing, virtual reality applications, 5.28

Margins: The space in the border of a page. **2.8**

Massively parallel processors (MPPs): Processors that use hundreds or thousands of microprocessor CPUs to perform calculations. **4.20**

Mass storage: Storage devices that provide automated retrieval of data from a library of storage media such as tape or data cartridges. **6.21**

Master program: The resident portion of the operating system. **8.2**

Mauchly, John W., 1.32

Medicine
  multimedia and, 12.41
  virtual reality systems and, 5.28

Megabytes (MB): A measure of memory equal to one million bytes. **4.9**

Megaflops (MFLOPS): Millions of floating-point operations per second. **4.19**

Megahertz: A measurement used to describe the speed of the system clock: it is equal to one million cycles (or pulses) per second. **4.7**, **4.25**

Member: A low level record in a network database that is related to one or more higher level (owner) records. **9.15**

Memo: Type of database field. **2.19**

Memory
  buffers, 8.7
  core, 1.32
  flash, 4.10
  main, see Main memory
  operating system managing, 8.7-8
  RAM, see Main memory
  ROM, see Read only memory
  speed, 4.11
  utilities managing, 8.15
  virtual management, 8.7

Memory address: The location of a byte in memory. **4.9**

Memory buttons: Small storage devices about the size of a dime that look like watch batteries, and can be read or updated using a pen-like probe attached to a hand-held terminal. **6.21**

Memory cubes, 6.25

Menu(s): A screen display that provides a list of processing options for the user and allows the user to make a selection. **2.3**

Menu generator: Software that lets a user specify a menu (list) of processing options that can be selected. The resulting menu is automatically formatted. **12.16**

Message: In object-oriented programming, the instruction to do something that is sent to an object. **12.17**

Metcalfe, Robert, 1.34

Methods: In object-oriented programming, specific instructions that define how the object acts when it is used by a program. **12.17**

Metropolitan area network (MAN): A wide area network limited to the area surrounding a city. **7.24**

Micro(s), see **Personal computer(s)**

Micro, see **Personal computer(s)**

Microcode, see **Firmware**

Microcomputer(s), see **Personal computer(s)**

Microfiche: The sheet film used by computer output microfilm. **5.25**

Micro Focus COBOL, 12.25

Microprocessor: The smallest processor, which is a single integrated circuit that contains the CPU and sometimes memory, located on the motherboard. **4.6**-8
  comparison of, 4.8
  everyday appliances and, 14.24
  evolution of, 1.35-38
  purchasing computers and, 8.32

Microsoft At Work: Proposed by Microsoft Corporation, a standardized intelligent graphical user interface that will be built into all office machines such as copiers, printers, and fax machines. The interface will allow data to be sent to or received from any device on the network. **14.17**

Microsoft Corporation, 14.3
  agent software and, 14.14
  founding of, 1.36
  MS-DOS development, 8.12

Microsoft QuickBASIC, 12.19

Microsoft Visual Basic, 12.20

Microsoft Windows: The most popular graphical user interface for personal computers. **2.3**
  evolution of, 1.37
  Windows NT and, 8.12-13
  Windows 95 and, 8.12

Microsoft Windows NT: A sophisticated version of Windows that is designed for use on client-server computer systems. **8.12**

Microwaves: Radio waves that can be used to provide high-speed transmission of both voice and data. **7.11**
  satellites and, 7.11

Middle management: Makes tactical decisions and is responsible for implementing the strategic decisions of senior management. **10.6**

MIDI (musical instrument digital interface) port: Serial port designed to be connected to a musical device such as an electronic keyboard or a music synthesizer. **4.15**
  sheet music and, 5.27

Millisecond: A thousandth of a second. **4.11**

Minicomputers: More powerful than personal computers and can support a number of users performing different tasks. **1.12**
  manufacturers of, 14.2

MIPS (million instructions per second): Measure of the processing speed of computers. **4.19**
  comparison of microprocessors and, 4.8

Mnemonic: A simple, easily remembered abbreviation used in assembly language programming to represent a machine operation code. Also called symbolic operation code. **12.13**

Models: In decision support systems, models allow users to ask what-if questions by changing one or more of the variables and seeing what the projected results would be. **10.11**

Modem: A communications device that converts data between the digital signals of a terminal or computer and the analog signals that are transmitted over a communications channel. **7.18**
Module: Performs a given task within a program, and can be developed individually and then combined to form a complete program; sometimes called subroutine. **12.4**
Monitor: The resident portion of the operating system. **8.2**
Monitor: The screen (terminal) portion of the computer system; can be color or monochrome. **5.18**
  color, 5.20, 5.23
  flat panel displays, 5.20-21
  how images are displayed on, 5.22
  interlaced, 5.22
  monochrome, 5.20
  multiscanning, 5.20
  noninterlaced, 5.22
  resolution of, 5.18-20
Monochrome monitors: Monitors that display a single color such as white, green, or amber characters on a black background, or black characters on a white background. **5.20**
Monospacing: Each character on a page or screen takes up the same amount of space. **2.8**
Morphing, 12.42
Motherboard: A circuit board that contains most of the electronic components of the system unit, sometimes called the main board or system board. **4.6**
Motorola microprocessors, 4.8
Mouse: Small, lightweight input device used with personal computers and some computer terminals to select processing options or information displayed on the screen. **1.7, 3.5**
Mouse pointer: On-screen symbol controlled by user with mouse pointing device. **1.7, 3.5**
MS-DOS (Microsoft Disk Operating System): A single-user operating system originally developed by Microsoft Corporation for IBM personal computers. The IBM version is called PC-DOS. **1.36, 8.12**
Multidrop line: A communications line configuration using a single line to connect multiple devices, such as terminals or personal computers, to a main computer. Also called multipoint line. **7.15**
Multimedia: The combination of sound and images with text and graphics. To capture sound and image data, special input devices require electronics contained on a sound or video card that is installed in the computer. **3.16-20, 5.5, 12.37-42**
  digital cameras, 3.19-20
  sound input, 3.16
  video input, 3.20
  voice input, 3.16-19
Multimedia PC, 12.38
Multiplexor (MUX): An electronic device that converts multiple input signals into a single stream of data that can be efficiently transmitted over a communications channel. **7.19**
Multiple zone recording (MZR): Storage method that records data at the same density on all tracks. **6.6**
Multipoint line, *see* **Multidrop line**
Multiprocessing: Coordinates the operations of computers with more than one CPU. **8.5**
Multiprocessors: Computers that have more than one CPU. **8.5**
Multiscanning: Monitors that are designed to work within a range of frequencies and thus can work with different standards and video adapters. **5.20**
Multisync monitors, *see* **Multiscanning**
Multitasking: Operating systems that allow more than one program to run at the same time on one computer. **8.4**
  Windows 95 and, 8.12
Multiuser: Operating system that allows more than one user to run the same program. **8.4**
Music, sheet, 5.27
MusicWriter, Inc., 5.27
MUX, *see* **Multiplexor**

Nanosecond: Measure of time equal to one billionth of a second. **4.11**
Narrative reports: Reports that are primarily text-based, but may contain some graphic or numeric information. **5.3**

National Information Infrastructure (NII): A proposed high-speed digital network that will make information services, training, education, medical services, and government data available to everyone. **7.31**
National Security Agency, 13.23
Natural language: A type of query language that allows the user to enter a question as if he or she were speaking to another person. **12.16, 12.26**
Natural Language, Inc., 12.26
Natural language voice interface: Allows the user to ask a question and have the computer not only convert the question to understandable words but interpret the question and give an appropriate response. **3.19**
NCR, 14.2
Near letter quality (NLQ): Printer output that is not fully formed characters, but still offers good print quality. **5.11**
Network: Collection of computers, especially personal computers, that allows users to share data and computer resources. **1.13, 7.21**
  bus, 7.26-27
  configurations, 7.26-27
  example of, 7.28-29
  Internet, 7.25
  local area, 7.21-24
  ring, 7.27
  software, 13.9
  star, 7.26
  topology, 7.26
  wide area, 7.24
Network administrator, 14.4
Network agents, 14.14
Network control unit, *see* **Server**
Network database: Similar to a hierarchical database except that each member can have more than one owner. **9.15**
Network interface card: Communications card that fits in an expansion slot of a computer and attaches to the cable or wireless technology used to connect the devices in the network; the card has circuits that coordinate the transmission, receipt, and error checking of transmitted data. **7.19**
Network operating system (NOS): Software that allows a user to manage the resources of a computer network. **7.23**
Neural network computers: Computers that use specially designed circuits to simulate the way the human brain processes information, learns, and remembers. **4.20**
News groups, Internet and, 7.25
NextStep operating system, 8.14, 8.17
Nodes: Devices connected to a network, such as terminals, printers, or other computers. **7.26**
Noise: Any unwanted signal, usually varying quickly, that is mixed with the normal voltage entering the computer. **13.12**
Nonimpact printing: Printing that occurs without having a mechanism striking against a sheet of paper. **5.13**
  ink-jet printers, 5.13-14
  page printers, 5.14-15
  thermal printers, 5.15
Noninterlaced monitors: Monitors that display images by illuminating the entire screen quickly in a single pass. **5.22**
Nonmanagement employees: Employees who need frequent information to make on-the-job decisions, including production, clerical, and staff personnel. **10.6**
Nonprocedural: Said of fourth-generation languages, because the programmer does not specify the actual procedures that the program must use to solve a problem. **12.15**
Nonvolatile: Type of memory (ROM) that retains its contents even when the computer is turned off. **4.11**
Normalization: In relational databases, a process that is used to organize data into the most efficient and logical file relationships. **9.21**
Notebook computer: Small personal computer that is small enough to be carried in a briefcase but is often transported in its own carrying case; it weighs between 4 and 8 pounds. **1.10**
Notes page, presentation graphics and, 2.20-21
NoteStation, 5.27

Novell, 14.3
Number systems, processing and, 4.2, 4.21-23
  binary, 4.22
  decimal, 4.21-22
  hexadecimal, 4.22
Numeric: Type of database field. **2.19**
Numeric keypad: Numeric keys arranged in an adding machine or calculator format to aid the user with numeric data entry. **3.3**

Object(s): A combination of data and program instructions, used in object-oriented programming. **12.17**
Object code, *see* **Object program**
Object-oriented database: Database that keeps track of objects, entities that contain both data and the action that can be taken on the data, also designed to contain nontext data such as photographs, graphics, and sound. **9.16**
Object-oriented operating systems: Operating systems specifically designed to run object-oriented programming applications. 8.14, 8.17, **12.18**
Object-oriented programming (OOP): A new approach to developing software that allows programmers to create objects, which can be used repeatedly by programmers whenever they need them. **12.17-18, 12.25**
  COBOL and, 12.25
  Pascal version, 12.23
Object-oriented software: Applications that are developed using object-oriented programming techniques. **12.18**
Object program: The machine instructions produced by a compiler from a program originally written in a high-level language. Also called object code. **12.14**
OCR (optical character recognition) devices: Scanners that read typewritten, computer-printed, and in some cases hand-printed characters from ordinary documents. An OCR device scans the shape of a character, compares it with a predefined shape stored in memory, and converts the character into the corresponding computer code. **3.12**
OCR software: Software that is used with image scanners to convert text images into data that can be processed by word processing software. **3.13**
Odd parity: The total number of on bits in the byte (including the parity bit) must be an odd number. **4.4**
Office automation specialist: Employee who assists users in implementing both computerized and non-computerized office automation technologies. **14.5**
Offsite: Location where backup files are kept that is in a building different from the computer site. **13.13**
Ogden, Frank, 14.24
Olivetti Research Limited, 13.22
On-demand reports: Reports created for information that is not required on a scheduled basis, but only when it is requested. **5.4**
Online help: Instructions within an application showing how to use an application. **2.27**
  bulletin board systems providing, 7.7
Online publications, 14.12
Online services: Information and services provided to users who subscribe to the service for a fee; accessed with communications equipment and software. **2.22, 7.7**
Online transaction processing (OLTP): Transactions are processed as they are entered. **10.9**
On-site service agreement, 8.32
Open Software Foundation (OSF), 8.15
Open Systems Interconnection (OSI) model: A set of communications protocols defined by the International Standards Organizations based in Geneva, Switzerland. **7.21**
Operand: Specifies the data or location of the data that will be used by machine language instructions. **4.18**
Operating environment: A graphic interface between the user and the operating system. **1.15, 8.12**
Operating system: One or more programs that manage manage and control the allocation and usage of hardware resources such as memory, CPU time, disk space, and peripheral devices. **1.14, 8.2, 8.17**
  disk and file management and, 8.10
  DOS, 8.11-12
  functions of, 8.6-10
  input and output management, 8.8-9
  loading, 8.3
  Macintosh, 8.13

monitoring system activities, 8.9
multiprocessing, 8.5
multitasking, 8.4
NextStep, 8.14, 8.17
object-oriented, 8.14
popular, 8.11-14
portable, 8.11
proprietary, 8.11
purchasing, 8.33
single program, 8.4
system performance and, 8.9-10
system programmer and, 14.4
system security and, 8.10
types of, 8.4-5
UNIX, 8.13-14
virtual machine, 8.5
viruses and, 13.3
Windows, 8.12

Operational decisions: Decisions made by operational management that involve an immediate action such as accepting or rejecting an inventory delivery or approving a purchase order. **10.6**

Operational management: Management level that makes operational decisions and provides direct supervision over the production, clerical, and non-management staff of an organization. **10.6**

Operation code: A unique value typically stored in the first byte in a machine language instruction that indicates which operation is to be performed. **4.18**

Operations group: Information processing employees responsible for operating the centralized (computer center) equipment and network administration including both data and voice communications. **14.4**

Optical character recognition (OCR), *see* **OCR**

Optical codes: In source data automation, codes that use a pattern or symbol to represent data, such as a bar code. **3.11**

Optical disks: Storage medium that uses lasers to burn microscopic holes on the surface of a hard plastic disk; able to store enormous quantities of information. **6.19**

Optical mark recognition (OMR): Input devices that are often used to process questionnaires or test answer sheets. Carefully placed marks on the form indicate responses to questions that are read and interpreted by a computer program. **3.12**

Optical memory cards: Storage devices that can store up to 1,600 pages of text or images on a device the size of a credit card. **6.22**

Optical recognition: Devices that use a light source to read codes, marks, and characters and convert them into digital data that an be processed by a computer. **3.11**

Oracle, 14.3
Organization(s)
  information systems in, 14.15-19
  virtual corporation and, 10.16
Organization architecture, 10.7
Organization model, 10.5
Organization structure, 10.6-7
Organizing, management function, 10.4

OS/2: IBM's operating system designed to work with 32-bit microprocessors. In addition to running programs written specifically for OS/2, the operating system can also run programs written for DOS or Windows. **8.13**

Outlines, presentation graphics and, 2.20

Output: The data that has been processed into a useful form called information that can be used by a person or machine. **1.7, 5.2-32**
  audio, 5.4-5, 5.25-26
  computer output microfilm, 5.24-25
  data projectors, 1.35, **12.23**
  display devices, 5.18-23
  graphics, 5.4
  multimedia, 5.5-6, 5.27
  operating system managing, 8.8
  plotters, 5.24
  printers and, 5.9-17
  reports, 5.2-4
  types of, 5.2-8
  video, 5.5
  virtual reality, 5.7-8, 5.28
  voice, 5.25-26

Output devices: Most commonly used devices are the printer and the computer screen. **1.8**

Outsourcing: Process in which companies hire outside firms to provide information systems support for a contracted fee. **10.7**

Overtype mode, 2.6

Overvoltage: Occurs when the incoming electrical power increases significantly above the normal 120 volts, which can cause immediate and permanent damage to hardware. **13.12**

Owner: The higher level record in a network database. **9.15**

Packard Bell, 14.2

Packet switching: In communications networks, individual packets of information from various users are combined and transmitted over a high-speed channel. **7.24**

Page: In virtual memory management, the fixed number of bytes that are transferred from disk to memory each time new data or program instruction are required. **8.8**

Page composition and layout: In desktop publishing, the process of arranging text and graphics on a document page. **2.10**

Page definition language: In desktop publishing, language describing the document to be printed that the printer can understand. **2.11**

Page makeup, *see* **Page composition and layout**

Page printers: Nonimpact printers that operate similar to a copying machine to produce high-quality text and graphic output. **5.14**

Page scanner: An input device that electronically captures an entire page of text or images such as photography or art work. The scanner converts the text or image on the original document into digital information that can be stored on a disk and processed by the computer. **3.10**

Pages per minute (ppm): Measure of the speed of printers that can produce an entire page at one time. **5.15**

Paging: In virtual memory management, a fixed number of bytes (a page) is transferred from disk to memory each time new data or program instructions are required. **8.8**

Palmtop computer: Small computers that often have several built-in or interchangeable personal information management functions, such as a calendar to keep track of meetings and events, and an address and phone file; they do not have disk storage devices and usually have a nonstandard keyboard. **1.10**

Paperless office, 14.17

Parallel conversion: Continuing to process data on the old system while some or all of the data is also processed on the new system. **11.23**

Parallel ports: Ports most often used to connect devices that send or receive large amounts of data such as printers or disk and tape drives. **4.15**
  purchasing computers and, 8.32

Parallel processing: The use of multiple CPU's, each with their own memory, that work on their assigned portion of a problem simultaneously. **4.20**
  applications of, 4.24

Parent record: In a hierarchical database, a record that has one or more child records. **9.14**

Parity bit: One extra bit for each byte that is used for error checking. **4.4**

Partition(s): Portions of memory allocated by operating system into fixed areas. **8.7**

Partitioned disk: Hard disk is divided into separate areas called partitions before it is formatted. **6.9**

Pascal: A programming language developed for teaching programming. Pascal contains programming statements that encourage the use of structured program design. 1.35, **12.23**

Passive matrix: LCD screens that use fewer transistors; one for each row and column. **5.21**

Password: A value, such as a word or number, which identifies the user. In multiuser operating systems, the password must be entered correctly before a user is allowed to use an application program. The password is usually confidential. **8.10, 13.5**

Paste: In word processing operations, an option used after performing either the cut or the copy command, where the text is placed elsewhere in the document. **2.6**

PC cards: Small, credit-card sized cards that fit into PCMCIA expansion slots, used for storage, communications, and additional memory. **6.19**

PC-DOS: Operating system developed by Microsoft Corporation for IBM and is installed by IBM on systems that IBM sells. **8.12**

PCMCIA (Personal Computer Memory Card International Association) cards: A special type of expansion slot that can be inserted into a personal computer, used for additional memory, storage, and communications. The small fitting into the expansion slot, called PC cards, are the size of credit cards. **4.13**

PC network specialist: Employee who installs and maintains local area networks. **14.4**

PCs, *see* **Personal computer(s)**

PC support specialist: Employee involved with end user computing group who installs and supports personal computer equipment and software. **14.5**

PDA, *see* **Personal digital assistant**

Peer-to-peer network: Local area network that allows any computer to share the software, data, or hardware (such as a printer) located on any other computer in the network. **7.23**

Pen computers: Specialized portable computers that use a pen-like device to enter data. **1.11**

Pen input devices: Allows the user to input hand-printed letters and numbers to record information. **3.7**

Pen plotters: Plotters used to create images on a sheet of paper by moving one or more pens over the surface. **5.24**

Pentium microprocessor, 1.38

Performance monitoring: During the maintenance phase of the information system life cycle, the ongoing process of comparing response times, file sizes, and other system performance measures against the values that were estimated when the system was designed. **11.25**
  database administrator and, 9.20

Periodic reports: Reports that are produced on a regular basis such as daily, weekly, or monthly. Also called scheduled reports. **5.4**

Peripheral devices: The input devices, output devices, and auxiliary storage units that surround the processing unit. **1.9**

Personal communicator, *see* **Personal digital assistant**

Personal computer(s): The small systems that have become so widely used in recent years. Depending on their size and features, personal computer prices range from several hundred to several thousand dollars. **1.10**
  application software packages, 1.15
  evolution of, 1.35-38
  home use, 14.19-22
  information systems and, 10.14
  installation of, 8.34-35
  maintenance of, 8.36-37
  owner's notebook outline, 8.36
  purchasing, 8.30-33
  vendors, 14.5
  See also Computer(s)

Personal Computer Memory Card International Association, *see* **PCMCIA**

Personal digital assistant (PDA): Small pen input device designed for workers on the go; often has built-in communications capabilities that allow the PDA to use voice, fax, or data communications. **1.11**, 1.38, 14.12

Personal identification number (PIN): A numeric password, used to access computer system. **13.6**

Personal information management (PIM) software: Helps users keep track of miscellaneous bits of personal information. Notes to self, phone messages, and appointment scheduling are examples of this type of software. **2.24**

Personal services, home computers and, 14.19-20

Phased conversion: Used with larger systems that can be broken down into individual modules that can be implemented separately at different times. **11.24**

Physical design: In the information system life cycle, the logical design that was created during the analysis phase is transformed into physical design, identifying the procedures to be automated, choosing the programming language, and specifying the equipment needed for the system. **11.17**

Picture elements, *see* **Pixels**

Pie chart: A graphic representation of proportions depicted as slices of a pie. **2.16**

INDEX

Pilot conversion: The new system will be used first by only a portion of the organization, often at a separate location. **11.24**
Pipelining: Describes the CPU starting a new instruction as soon as the preceding instruction moves to the next stage, providing rapid throughput. **4.19**
Pixels (picture elements): On screens, the dots that can be illuminated. **5.18**
 color monitors and, 5.23
Plaintext: Readable data that is converted into ciphertext in the encryption process. **13.11**
Planning, management and, 10.3
Plotters: An output device used to produce high-quality line drawings and diagrams. **5.24**
Point: Measure of character size, equal to 1/72 of one inch. **2.7**, **5.14**
Pointer, *see* **Mouse pointer**
Pointing devices, 3.5-9, 3.16
 digitizer, 3.9
 graphics tablet, 3.9
 joystick, 3.6
 light pen, 3.9
 pen input, 3.7
 purchasing, 8.33
 touchscreen, 3.8
 trackball, 3.6
 See also Mouse
Point-of-sale (POS) manufacturing: Retail purchasing device that allows the customer to design, manufacture, and purchase the product on the spot. **5.27**
Point-of-sale (POS) terminals: Allow data to be entered at the time and place where the transaction with the consumer occurs, such as in fast-food restaurants or hotels. **3.15**
Point-to-point line: A line configuration used in communications which is a direct line between a sending and a receiving device. It may be either a switched line or a dedicated line. **7.14**
Polling: Used by a front-end processor to check the connected terminals or computers to see if they have data to send. **7.19**
Polymorphic virus: Virus designed to modify its program code each time it attaches itself to another program or file. Because it never looks the same, a polymorphic virus cannot be detected with a virus signature. **13.3**
Port: A socket used to connect the system unit to a peripheral device such as a printer or a modem. **4.14**
 parallel, 4.15
 serial, 4.15
Portable computers
 trackball and, 3.6
 See also Laptop computers
Portable interactive computing object, 13.22
Portable operating systems: Operating systems that will run on many manufacturers computers. **8.11**
Portable printers, 5.16
Portrait orientation: Printing orientation that is taller than it is wide. **2.9**
Positional number system, 4.21
Possessed object: Any item that a user must carry to gain access to the computer facility, such as a badge, card, or key. **13.6**
POST (Power On Self Test): Tests run by the BIOS chip when the computer is turned on to make sure the equipment is running correctly. **8.3**
Post-implementation evaluation: Conducted after a system is implemented to determine if the system is performing as designed, if operating costs are as anticipated, and if any modifications are necessary to make the system operate more effectively. **11.24**
Post Script: A page definition language. **2.11**
Power On Self Test, *see* **POST**
Power supply: Converts the wall outlet electricity to the lower voltages used by the computer. **4.16**
 purchasing computers and, 8.32, 8.33
 system failure and, 13.11-12
Power surges, *see* **Overvoltage**
Preliminary investigation: Determines if a request for development or modification of an information system justifies further detailed investigation. **11.4**
Presentation graphics: Software that allows the user to create documents called slides that are used in making presentations before a group to help communicate information more effectively. **2.20-21**

Primary storage, *see* **Main memory**
Prime numbers: A number divisible by only itself and 1, used in a hashing operation. **9.7**
Printers/printing: Output device. **1.8**
 band, 5.12-13
 chain, 5.13
 dot matrix, 5.10-12
 impact, 5.9-13
 ink jet, 5.13-14
 laser, 5.14
 nonimpact, 5.13-15
 page, 5.14-15
 purchasing, 5.17, 8.33
 special purpose, 5.16
 thermal, 5.15
 word processing documents, 2.9
Print preview: Allows the user to see on the screen how a document will look when it is printed. **2.9**
Print spool: The reports stored on disk that are waiting to be printed. **8.9**
Privacy, information, 13.18-20, 13.23
Private line, *see* **Leased line**
Problem definition: Aspect of preliminary investigation, where the true nature of the problem is identified. **11.4**
Process/processing: Part of the information processing cycle;the procedures a computer performs to process data into information. **1.7**, 4.1-29
 batch, 10.9
 online transaction, 10.9
 operating system managing, 8.6-7
 parallel, 4.20
 transaction, 10.9
 types of, 4.19-20
 See also System unit
Process design: In information systems design,the systems analyst specifies exactly what actions will be taken on the input data to create output information. **11.17**
Processing controls: Procedures that are established to determine the accuracy of information after it has been input to the system. **11.18**
Processor(s)
 coprocessors, 4.12
 front-end, 7.19
 massively parallel, 4.20
 multi-, 8.5
 See also Microprocessor
Process owner, 10.7
ProDOS operating system, 8.15
Productivity software: Personal computer software that helps people perform their work more efficiently. **2.2**
 companies using, 2.28
 end user computing and, 14.5
Productivity tools, home computers and, 14.19-20
Product life cycles, 10.3
Professional organizations, 14.8-9
Program(s): The detailed set of instructions that tells the computer exactly what to do, so it can perform the operations in the information processing cycle. Also called program instructions, or software. **3.2**, **12.2**
 applications software, 1.15-16
 coding, 12.9
 documentation, 12.11
 free, 8.31
 interface with other, 12.24
 object, 12.14
 object-oriented, 8.14, 12.17-18
 purchasing, 8.30
 systems software, 1.14-15
 testing, 12.10
Program design, *see* **Design**
Program development, *see* **Development**
Program flowchart: A program design tool in which the logical steps of a program are represented by a combination of symbols and text. **12.7-8**
Program generators, *see* **Application generators**
Program instructions: The detailed set of instructions that tell a computer which operations to perform. **1.6**
Programmable terminals, *see* **Intelligent terminals**
Program maintenance, *see* **Maintenance**
Programmers, *see* **Computer programmers**
Programming language(s): A set of written words and symbols that allow a programmer or user to communicate with the computer. **12.12**-16
 choosing, 12.24

 history of, 1.32, 1.33
 in use today, 12.19-24
Programming standards, 12.24
Program specifications: Can include many documents such as data flow diagrams, system flowcharts, process specifications, a data dictionary, screen formats, and report layouts. **12.3**
Program statements: The sentences of high-level programming language. **12.14**
Projection panels: Projection of the computer screen image that can be clearly seen by a room full of people, using liquid crystal display technology, designed to be placed on top of an overhead projector. **5.23**
Project management: Involves planning, scheduling, reporting, and controlling the individual activities that make up the information system life cycle. **11.2**
 CASE and, 11.21
Project management software: Allows users to plan, schedule, track, and analyze the events, resources, and costs of a project. **2.25**
Project plan: Week-by-week record of individual activities that make up the information system life cycle, and includes an estimate of the time to complete the activity and the start and finish dates. **11.2**
Project relational operation: In a relational database query, specifies the fields (attributes) that appear on the query output. **9.18**
Proportional spacing: On a page or screen, wide characters, such as a W or M are given more space than narrow characters, such as an I. **2.8**
Proprietary operating systems: Operating systems that are privately owned, and limited to a specific computer model. **8.11**
Protocols: In data communications, a set of rules and procedures for exchanging information between computers. **7.21**
Prototyping: In information system development, building a working model of the new system. **11.20**, 11.21
 rapid, 14.23
 users and, 11.28
Pseudocode: The logical steps in the solution of a problem are written as English statements and indentations are used to represent the control structures. **12.8**
Public domain software: Free software that is not copyrighted and can therefore be distributed among users. **13.10**

QBASIC: Version of BASIC programming language developed by Microsoft. **12.19**
Quality assurance specialist: Employee who reviews programs and documentation to make sure they meet the organization's standards. **14.4**
Query: The capability to retrieve database information in a report, based on criteria specified by the user. **2.19**
Query by example (QBE): A feature of DBMS that helps the user construct a query by displaying a list of fields that are available in the files from which the query will be made, and the user can specify selection criteria to limit the number of records displayed. **9.18**
Query language: A single English-like language that allows users to retrieve information from the database based on the criteria and the format specified by the user. **9.17**, 9.18-19
 decision support systems and, 10.11
 end user computing and, 14.5
 natural language, 12.26
QuickBASIC, *see* **QBASIC**

RAID, *see* **Redundant array of inexpensive disks**
Rails: Mounting brackets needed to install a device in a bay inside the system unit. **4.16**
RAM, *see* **Main memory**
Random access: A retrieval method in which the system can go directly to the record without having to read the preceding records. Also called direct access. **9.5-6**
Random access memory (RAM), *see* **Main memory**
Random file, *see* **Direct file**
Rapid application development (RAD), 11.29
Read only memory (ROM): Describes chips that store information or instructions that do not change. Data is permanently recorded in the memory when it is manufactured. ROM memory retains its contents even when the power is turned off. **4.11**
Read-only privileges, 9.14

Read/write head: Recording mechanism in the drive that rests on the top and bottom surface of the rotating diskette, generating electronic impulses that change the polarity, or alignment of magnetic areas along a track on the disk. **6.7**
hard disks, 6.10
Reciprocal backup relationships: Relationships entered into with other organizations in case of a disaster; one firm provides space, and sometimes equipment, to the other. **13.16**
Record(s): A collection of related data items or fields. **2.18, 9.4**
adding, 9.9
before and after image of, 9.17
changing, 9.9-10, 9.17
deleting, 9.10-11
direct file organization and, 9.6-8
flagged, 9.11
random access of, 9.5-6
sequential retrieval of, 9.4-5
Recording density: The number of bits that can be recorded on one inch of track on a disk, referred to as bits per inch. **6.6**
Recovery, DBMS and, 9.17, 9.20
Recovery plan: Specifies the actions to be taken to restore full information processing operations, in case of a disaster that damages computer facilities. **13.16**
Redundant array of inexpensive disks (RAID): Storage technique whereby multiple small disks are connected into an integrated unit that acts like a single large disk drive. **6.13**
Reel-to-reel tape devices: Magnetic storage tape devices that use 2 reels: a supply reel to hold the tape that will be read from or written to, and the take-up reel to temporarily hold portions of the supply reel tape as it is being processed. **6.17**
Reference
Internet used for, 7.47
multimedia used for, 12.40
network agents and, 14.14
Refresh rate: The speed at which the entire screen is redrawn. **5.22**
Registers: Storage locations in the CPU that temporarily store specific data such as the address of the next instruction. **4.7**
Relation(s): In a relational database, data that is organized in tables. **9.15**
Relational database: Database in which data is organized in tables called relations. **9.15-16, 9.22**
designing, 11.17
Relational operations: When a user queries a relational database, the three relational operations are select, project, and join. **9.18**
Relative file, *see* **Direct file**
Relative referencing: In spreadsheet programs, when a formula is copied to another cell, the formula is automatically updated to the new location. **2.15**
Remembered information: Authentication process that requires a user to enter a word or series of characters that matches an entry in a security file in the computer. **13.5**
Remote learning: Describes process in which some trade schools, colleges, and universities are offering students with personal computers the opportunity to take electronic correspondence courses from their homes. Lessons and assignments for classes are transmitted between the student and the school over communications lines. **14.22**
Removable disks: Consist of the drive unit, which is usually in its own cabinet, and the removable recording media, called a disk pack. **6.14**
Rentzep, Peter, 6.25
Replace: Word processing feature, used with search feature, that allows substitution of new letters or words for the old. **2.6**
Report(s): Information presented in an organized form. **5.2**
database, 9.14
detail, 5.3
exception, 5.3-4
external, 5.3
internal, 5.2-3
narrative, 5.3
on-demand, 5.4
periodic, 5.4
summary, 5.3
word processing software and, 2.4

Request for proposal (RFP): A written list of an organization's software requirements that is given to prospective software vendors. **11.11**
Request for quotation (RFQ): During the acquisition phase of information systems development, a request for a written price quotation on an item to be purchased is made to vendors. **11.11**
Rescue disk: Disk that contains an uninfected copy of certain operating system commands and essential information about the computer that enables a computer to restart correctly, so that an anti-virus program can remove or repair files. **13.3**
Resolution: Measure of a screen's image clarity, and depends on the number of individual dots displayed (pixels) on the screen, and the distance between each dot. **5.18**
Response time: The amount of time from the moment a user enters the data until the computer responds. **8.9**
Restore files: Reloading files on computer in case of a system failure or the discovery of corrupted files. **13.13**
RFP, *see* **Request for proposal**
RFQ, *see* **Request for quotation**
Ring network: A communications network that has a series of computers connected to each other in a ring. **7.27**
RISC (reduced instruction set computing): Technology that involves reducing the computer's instruction set to only those instructions that are most frequently used, which allows the computer to operate faster. **4.18**
Ritchie, Dennis, 12.21
Robot(s): Devices that mimic human actions and appear to function with some degree of intelligence; commonly used in manufacturing and other situations where it would be unsafe or unhealthy for a human to perform the same task. **14.13**
Robotics: Artificial intelligence application that deals with the development of robots, which are commonly used in manufacturing environments. **14.13**
Rollback, *see* **Backward recovery**
Rollforward, *see* **Forward recovery**
ROM, *see* **Read only memory**
Root record: In a hierarchical database, the parent record at the top of the hierarchy. **9.14**
Rotational delay: The time it takes for the sector containing the data to rotate under the read/write head. Also called latency. **6.8**
Router: Connection between two computers in personal computer network. **7.29**
Rows: Data which is organized horizontally on a spreadsheet. **2.12**

Sales representatives: Persons that must have a general understanding of computers and a specific knowledge of the product they are selling; often the most highly compensated employees in a computer company. **14.5**
Satellites, communication, 7.11-12
tracking moving vans and, 7.30
Scheduled reports, *see* **Periodic reports**
Scientific research reference materials, 1.22
Screen(s): Output device used to display data on both personal computers and terminals. Also called a monitor, CRT (cathode ray tube), or VDT (video display terminal). **1.8, 5.18**
Screen generator: Software that allows the user to design an input or output screen by entering the names and descriptions of the input and output data directly on the screen. **12.16**
Screen painter, *see* **Screen generator**
Screen saver: A utility program that prevents the problem of ghosting (a dim version of an image is permanently etched on the monitor screen because the same image is displayed for a long time). The screen saver dims the brightness of the screen or displays moving images on the screen, and starts automatically if the image on a screen does not change for a certain period of time. **8.16**
Scrolling: The movement of screen data up or down one line or screen at a time. **2.4**
SCSI (small computer system interface) controllers: Controllers that can support 7 disk drives or any mix up to 7 SCSI devices. **6.11**
SCSI (small computer system interface) port: A special type of parallel port that can be used to attach up to 7 different devices to a single port. **4.15**

Search: Word processing feature that allows user to find all occurrences of a particular character, word, or combination of words. **2.6**
Secondary storage, *see* **Auxiliary storage**
Sector: A pie-shaped section of the disk, also a section of a track; the basic storage units for floppy disks. **6.4**
Sector method: Physical organization and addressing of data stored on disk that divides each track on the disk surface into individual storage areas called sectors. **6.10**
Security, 13.2-16
access controls and, 11.19, 13.4-8
backup and, *see* **Backup**
database, 9.3, 9.14, 9.17
database administrator and, 9.20
data encryption and, 7.20
disaster recovery plan and, 13.14-16
hardware theft and, 13.8-9
information theft and, 13.10-11
logon code and, 8.10
operating system and, 8.10
passwords and, 8.10
software theft and, 13.9-10
speaker recognition and, 3.17
system failure and, 13.11-13
user ID and, 8.10
viruses and, 13.2-4
Seek time: The time it takes to position the read/write head over the proper track. **6.7**
Segmentation: In virtual memory management, programs are divided into logical portions called segments, which are brought into main memory from a disk only when needed. **8.8**
Segments: In virtual memory management, programs are divided into logical portions. **8.8**
Selection structure: Control structure used for conditional program logic, also called if-then-else structure. **12.5**
Select relational operation: In relational database query, selects certain records (rows or tuples) based on user-supplied criteria. **9.18**
Self-managed teams, 10.7
Senior management: The top managers in an organization, who make strategic decisions and are concerned with the long-range direction of the organization. Also called executive and top management. **10.5**
Sequence structure: Control structure where one process occurs immediately after another.
Sequential access, *see* **Sequential retrieval**
Sequential file organization: File organization method in which files are stored one after the other, normally in ascending or descending order, based on a value in each record called the key. **9.4-5**
Sequential retrieval: The records on a tape or disk are retrieved (accessed) one after another in the same order that the records are stored. Also called sequential access. **9.4**
Sequential storage: Magnetic tape is considered a sequential storage media because the computer must record and read tape records one after another. **6.17**
Serial numbers, on equipment, 8.36
Serial port: Port that transmits data one bit at a time and is considerably slower than a parallel port. **4.15**
purchasing computers and, 8.32
Serial processing: Computers that contain one CPU that processes a single instruction at a time. **4.20**
Server: Computer designed to support a computer network that allows users to share files, applications software, and hardware. **1.12, 7.22**
Service and repair technician: A challenging job for individuals who like to troubleshoot and solve problems, and who have a strong background in electronics. **14.5-6**
Shading: Word processing feature that darkens the background area of a section of a document or table. **2.8**
Shareware: Software that users may try out on their own systems before paying a fee. **13.10**
Shell programs: Act as an interface between the user and the operating system, and offer a limited number of utility functions such as file maintenance, but not application windowing or graphics. **8.12**
Shopping, online, 2.22
Signals, communication channels and, 7.16
SIMM (single in-line memory mode): Small circuit board that holds multiple RAM chips. **4.10**

INDEX

Simplex transmission: Data transmission method in which data flows in only one direction. **7.17**
Simulation software: Software designed to teach a user by creating a model of a real-life situation. **14.21**
Single-density: Diskettes that could only be written on one side, and are no longer in use. **6.6**
Single entry/single exit: Means there is only one entry point and one exit point from each of the control structures. **12.6-7**
Single label printers, 5.16
Single program operating systems: Allow only a single user to run a single program at one time. **8.4**
Site license: A special agreement, obtained from the software vendor, that allows a commercial software package to be shared by many users within the same organization. **7.22, 13.10**
Skipjack: A formula used for voice and data encryption that uses a government proposed federal standard. **13.11**
Slides: Documents created by presentation graphics software that are used in making presentations before a group. **2.20**
Small computer system interface controllers, *see* **SCSI controllers**
Smart cards: Special purpose storage devices about the same size and thickness of a credit card that contain a thin microprocessor capable of storing recorded information. **6.22**
Smart terminals, *see* **Intelligent terminals**
Society, impact of computer on, 1.37
Sockets, *see* **Upgrade sockets**
Soft copy: Output displayed on a screen. **5.2**
Software
  agent, 14.14
  alternatives, 11.13
  commercial application versus custom, 11.15
  communications, 2.22, 7.20
  database, 2.18-19, 9.12
  data communications, 2.22, 7.20
  desktop publishing, 2.10-11
  educational, 14.21-22
  electronic mail, 2.23
  entertainment, 14.22
  file transfer, 7.20
  future changes, 14.15
  game playing, 14.22
  handwriting recognition, 3.7
  industry, 14.3
  integrated, 2.25-26
  language translators, 8.16
  learning aids and, 2.27
  personal information management, 2.24
  presentation graphics, 2.20-21
  productivity, 2.2
  project management, 2.25
  purchasing, 11.14
  spreadsheet, 2.12-17
  system, 1.14, 8.2, 8.17-18
  terminal emulation, 7.20
  theft, 13.9-10
  user interface and, 2.2
  utilities, 8.15-16, 8.18
  vendors, 11.11, 14.5
  viruses and, 13.3-4
  word processing, 2.4-9
  See also **Program(s)**
Software houses: Businesses that specialize in developing software for sale. **11.12**
Software industry, development of, 1.35
Software license: A license from the software manufacturer to the buyer that describes the right to use software under certain terms and conditions. **11.14,** 13.9
Software packages, *see* **Application software packages**
Software piracy: Distribution of software to persons that have not legally purchased it by copying, loaning, renting it. **13.9**
Software resource sharing: Frequently used software is stored on the hard disk of the server in a local area network so the software can be accessed by multiple users. **7.22**
Solid-state storage: Use RAM chips to provide fast data access and retrieval. These devices are volatile. **6.21**
Son: The most recent copy of a file. **13.14**
Sound, multimedia and, 3.16, 5.6
Sound boards, 4.17

Sound card: Multimedia device containing electronics that capture sound data input; installed in the computer. **3.16**
  purchasing, 8.33
Source data automation: Procedures and equipment designed to make the input process more efficient by eliminating the manual entry of data; the equipment captures data directly from its original form such as an invoice or inventory tag. **3.10**-14
  data collection devices and, 3.14
  image scanner and, 3.10
  magnetic ink character recognition and, 3.13
  optical recognition and, 3.11-13
Source data collection: Data that is entered as the event or transaction is occurring and at the location where it is occurring. **3.10**
Source document: In source data automation, the original form that data is captured from. **3.10**
Source document control: A system control unit that includes serial numbering of input documents such as invoices and paychecks, document registers in which each input is recorded and time-stamped as it is received, and batch totalling and balancing to predetermined totals to assure the accuracy of processing. **11.18**
Source program: A program written in high-level language, and later converted by a compiler, or interpreter, to machine language. **12.14**
Spacing: Describes how far apart individual letters and lines of text are placed. **2.8**
Speaker dependent: Each person using this voice input system has to train it to recognize the speaker's individual speech pattern. **3.18**
Speaker independent: Voice input system that has voice templates for each word, so the system does not have to be trained to recognized the speaker's individual speech pattern. **3.18**
Speakers, purchasing, 8.33
Spelling checker: Allows the user to enter a command that tells the software to check individual words or entire documents for correct spelling. **2.6**
Spike: A momentary overvoltage that occurs when the power increase lasts for less than one millisecond; caused by uncontrollable disturbances, such as lightning bolts, or controllable disturbances, such as turning on equipment that is on the same electrical circuit. **13.12**
Spooling: A report is first written (saved) to the disk before it is printed; used to increase printer efficiency. **8.9**
Spreadsheet: Organization of numeric data in a worksheet or table format, by electronic spreadsheet software. Data is organized horizontally in rows, and vertically in columns. **2.12**-17
  decision support system and, 10.11
Spreadsheet software: Software that allows the user to organize numeric data in a worksheet or table format called a spreadsheet. **2.12**
  integrated package development, 1.36
SQL, *see* **Structured Query Language**
Star network: A communications network that contains a central computer and one or more terminals or computers connected to it, forming a star. **7.26**
Static electricity, 8.35, 8.36
Static RAM (SRAM) chip: A type of RAM memory chip that is larger than dynamic RAM and has access times of 10 to 50 seconds. **4.11**
Statistical analysis, 10.11
Stereolithography: Use of a computer, a laser, and photochemistry to build a three dimensional model of a part one thin layer at a time, used in manufacturing. **14.23**
Storage: Part of the information processing cycle in which data is saved; also called auxiliary storage or primary storage. **1.7,** 6.1-29
  American Express and, 6.24
  data maintenance and, 9.9
  file organization and, 9.4-8
  magnetic disk, 6.3-15
  magnetic tape, 6.16-18
  mass storage devices, 6.21
  memory cubes and, 6.25
  optical disks, 6.19-21
  PC cards, 6.19
  sequential, 6.17
  solid-state devices, 6.21
  special-purpose, 6.21-22

Storing: Control unit operation that takes place when the result of the instruction is written to main memory. **4.7**
Strategic decisions: Decisions made by senior management that deal with the overall goals and objectives of an organization. **10.5**
Streaming mode: The magnetic tape records data in exactly the same byte-by-byte order that it appears on the hard disk. **6.18**
Striping: Storage technique that divides a logical piece of data, such as a record, word, or character, into smaller parts and writing those parts on multiple drives. **6.13**
Strousrup, Bjarne, 12.22
Structure charts: Charts used to decompose and represent the modules of a program; also called hierarchy charts. **12.4**
Structured analysis: The use of analysis and design tools such as data flow diagrams, data dictionaries, process specifications, structured English, decision tables and decision trees to document the specifications of an information system. **11.5**
Structured design, *see* **Top-down design**
Structured English: One way of writing process specifications; a style of writing and presentation that highlights the alternatives and actions that are part of the process. **11.6**
Structured program design: A methodology that emphasizes three main program design concepts: modules, control structures, and single entry/single exit. **12.4**
Structured Query Language (SQL): A widely used query language. **9.19**
Structured walk through: A step-by-step review performed on the process design to identify any design logic errors, and to continue the communication between the systems analyst and the user. Also used during program development. **11.18, 12.8**-9
Style: Specific combination of features affecting the appearance of a document, such as bold, italic, or underline formatting. **2.7**
Style sheet: Word processing function that allows user to save font and format information so it can be applied to new documents. **2.9**
Subnotebook computer: Smaller versions of notebook computers that weigh less than 4 pounds. **1.10**
Subroutine, *see* **Module**
Suites: Individual applications packaged in the same box and sold for a price that is significantly less than buying the applications individually. **2.26**
Summary report: A report that summarizes data, containing totals from detailed input data. **5.3**
Superapplications, 2.29
Supercomputers: The most powerful category of computers, and the most expensive. They can process hundreds of millions of instructions per second. **1.13**
Supervisor: The resident portion of the operating system. **8.2**
Support tools, for application users, 2.27
Surge protector: Device that uses special electrical components to keep an overvoltage from reaching computer equipment. **13.12**
Surge suppressor, *see* **Surge protector**
Swapping: When using paging or segmentation, the operating system sometimes needs to swap data in memory with new data on disk. **8.8**
Switched line: A point-to-point line using a regular telephone line to establish a communications connection. **7.14**
Symbolic addressing: Assembly language allows a specific computer memory location to be referenced by a name or symbol. **12.13**
Symbolic generation code, *see* **Mnemonic**
Symbolic operation code, *see* **Mnemonic**
Symmetric multiprocessing: Application tasks may be assigned to whatever CPU is available, in computers that have more than one CPU. **8.5**
Synchronous transmission mode: Data communication method which transmits blocks of data at regular intervals using timing signals to synchronize the sending and receiving equipment. **7.17**
Synonyms: The same disk location for records with different key values, in a hashing operation. **9.7**
Syntax errors: Violations of the grammar rules of the language in which the program was written. **12.10**
Sys file extension, 8.37

System board, *see* **Motherboard**
System clock: Used by the control unit to synchronize, or control the timing of, all computer operations, generating electronic pulses at a fixed rate, measured in megahertz. **4.7**
  speed of, 4.8
System controls: During the design phase, system controls are established to (1) ensure that only valid data is accepted and processed, and (2) to prevent computer-related fraud. **11.18**
System development, *see* Development
System development group: Information processing employees that are responsible for analyzing, designing, developing, and implementing new information systems and maintaining and improving existing systems. **14.4**
System development life cycle (SDLC): An organized approach to obtaining an information system. **11.2-3**
  acquisition phase, 11.2, 11.10-14
  analysis phase, 11.2, 11.4-9
  CASE and, 11.20-21
  commercial applications versus custom software and, 11.15
  customizing phase, 11.2, 11.15-16
  design phase, 11.2, 11.17-21
  development phase, 11.2, 11.15, 11.22, 12.1-30
  implementation phase, 11.2, 11.23-25
  maintenance phase, 11.2, 11.25-26
System diagnostic programs, 8.37
System files, printouts of, 8.36
System flowchart: A graphical depiction of the major processes, reports, data files, and types of input devices that provide data to the system. **11.12**
System houses: Software companies that not only sell software but also sell the equipment.
System integrators: Businesses that not only sell software, but also sell different types of equipment so they can offer a total system solution. **11.12**
System performance, operating system and, 8.9-10
System programmer: Person who installs and maintains operating system software and provides technical support to other staff. **14.4**
System resources, operating system allocating, 8.6
Systems analyst: Person that works with both the user and the programmer to determine and design the desired output of a program. **1.14, 14.4**
  career growth, 14.6
  design activities, 11.17
  report on system analysis and, 11.8
  systems development life cycle and, 11.3, 11.8
System failure: A prolonged malfunction of a computer system, caused by disasters such as fires, floods, storms, or by events such as electrical power problems. **13.11**
System software: All the programs including the operating system that are related to controlling the operations of the computer equipment, classified into three major categories: operating systems, utilities, and language translators. **1.14, 8.2, 8.17**
System testing: During design phase of information systems development, process of testing all programs in an application. **11.19**
System unit: Part of the computer that contains the electronic circuits that actually cause the processing of data to occur; includes the central processing unit, main memory, and other electronic components. **1.8, 4.2-29**
  bays and, 4.16
  buses and, 4.12-13
  components of, 4.5
  connectors and, 4.14-15
  coprocessors and, 4.12
  CPU and, 4.6-8
  electronic representation of data and, 4.2-4
  expansion slots and, 4.13
  hardware and, 1.8, 4.5
  machine language instructions and, 4.18-19
  memory and, 4.9-11
  microprocessor and, 4.6-8
  motherboard, 4.6
  number systems and, 4.21-23
  parallel processors and, 4.20, 4.24
  ports and, 4.14-15
  power supply and, 4.16
  speed and, 4.7, 4.25
  sound components, 4.17
  types of processing and, 4.19-20
  upgrade sockets and, 4.8

Tactical decisions: The decisions made by middle management, implementing specific programs and plans necessary to accomplish the strategic objectives of an organization. **10.6**
Tailoring, *see* **Customizing phase**
Tape backup, *see* **Magnetic tape**
Tape density: The number of bits that can be stored on one inch of tape. Commonly used densities are 800, 1,600, 3,200, and 6,250 bpi. **6.18**
Technical evaluator: Person who researches new technologies, such as wireless communications, and recommends how such technologies can be used by the organization. **14.4**
Technical services group: Information processing employees responsible for the evaluation and integration of new technologies, the administration of the organization's data resources, and support of the central computer operating system. **14.4**
Technical writer: Person who works with the analyst, programmer, and user to create program and system documentation, and user manuals. **14.4**
Telecommunications: Any type of long-distance communications including television signals. **7.8**
Telecommuting: The capability of individuals to work at home and communication with their offices by using personal computers and communications channels. **7.5, 14.21**
Teleconferencing: Video conferencing using computers and television cameras to transmit video images and the sound of the participant(s) to a remote location that has compatible reception equipment. **7.3**
Telephone, cellular, 7.12
Teleprocessing: The use of a terminal or a computer and communications equipment to access computers and computer files located elsewhere. **7.8**
Terabyte: One trillion bytes. **6.20**
Terminal emulation software: Communications software that allows a personal computer to imitate or appear to be a specific type of terminal, so that the personal computer can connect to another usually larger computer. **7.20**
Test data: Data that simulates the type of input that the program will process when it is implemented; used during logic testing. **12.10**
Testing program, 12.10
Testing system design, 11.19
Thesaurus software: Allows the user to look up synonyms for words in a document while the word processor is in use. **2.7**
Thermal printers: Printers that use heat to transfer colored inks from ink sheets onto the printing surface. **5.15**
Thermal transfer printers, *see* **Thermal printers**
Third-generation computers, 1.34
Thrashing: A condition where the operating system is spending more time swapping pages to and from the disk than processing data. **8.10**
Time bomb: Virus program that performs an activity (such as destroying data) on a particular date. **13.2**
Timesharing, *see* **Multiuser**
Time slice: A common way for an operating system to allocate CPU processing time. **8.6**
Token ring network: A type of ring network that constantly circulates an electronic signal, called a token, around the network, which allows devices on the network to send messages by taking the token and attaching it to their data. **7.27**
Top-down design: A design approach that focuses on the major functions of an information system, and keeps breaking those functions down into smaller and smaller activities, sometimes called modules, that can eventually be programmed. Also called structured design. **11.17-19**
Topology: The configuration, or physical layout, of the equipment in a communications network. **7.26**
Touch screens: Allow user to touch areas of the screen to enter data. **3.8**
Tower computers: Personal computers in an upright case, which provides room for expanding the system and adding optional equipment. **1.11**
Track: A narrow recording band forming a full circle around the diskette. **6.4**

Trackball: A pointing device like a mouse. To move the cursor with a trackball, the user simply rotates the top mounted ball in the desired direction. **3.6**
  purchasing, 8.33
Tracks per inch (tpi): The number of tracks onto which data can be recorded. **6.6**
Tractor feed mechanisms: Mechanisms that transport continuous-form paper by using sprockets inserted into holes on the sides of the paper. **5.12**
Trade books: Books to help users learn to use the features of an applications package. These books are usually found where software is sold, and are frequently carried in regular bookstores. **2.27**
Trainer: Person in end user computing group who develops education and training materials to teach users how to use existing and new applications. **14.5**
Training
  career opportunities, 14.5, 14.6
  information system development and, 11.23
  multimedia used for, 12.39
  virtual reality used for, 5.28
Transaction processing system (TPS): Information system that processes data generated by the day-to-day transactions of an organization. Some examples of a TPS are billing systems, inventory control systems, accounts payable systems, and order entry systems. **10.9**
Transcription error: During data entry, operator error made in copying the values from a source document. **3.21**
Transistors, 1.33
Transmission
  direction of, 7.17
  rate of, 7.17-18
Transmission media: Communications channels are made up of one or more transmission media, including twisted pair wire, coaxial cable, fiber optics, microwave transmission, satellite transmission, and wireless transmission. **7.9**
  coaxial cable, 7.9-10
  fiber optics, 7.10
  microwave, 7.11
  satellite, 7.11
  twisted pair wire, 7.9
  wireless, 7.12-13
Transmission mode
  asynchronous, 7.16
  synchronous, 7.17
Transposition error: During data entry, operator error made by switching two characters. **3.21**
Travel, multimedia and, 12.38
Trojan horse virus: Virus named after the Greek myth that works by hiding within or is designed to look like a legitimate program. **13.2**
Tuples: Rows in a relational database. **9.15**
Turbo Pascal, 12.23
Turn-around document: A document designed to be returned to the organization in which it was originally issued. When it is returned (turned around), the data on it is read by an OCR device. **3.12**
Tutorial software: Software that uses text, graphics, and sometimes sound to teach users concepts about a subject and follows the instruction with questions to help the user ensure that he or she understands the concepts. **2.27, 14.21**
Twisted pair wire: Pairs of copper wire that are twisted together, commonly used for telephone lines and to connect personal computers with one another for communications and transmission of data. **7.9**
Typeface: A specific set of characters that are designed the same, such as Helvetica or Times New Roman. **2.7, 5.14**
Typeover mode, 2.6

Unauthorized access: Computer trespassing or using a computer system without permission. **13.4**
Unauthorized use: The use of a computer system of computer data for unapproved or possibly illegal activities. **13.4**
Undervoltage: A drop in the electrical power supply, and can cause a loss of data but generally do not damage equipment. **13.12**
Uninterruptable power supply (UPS): For electrical protection, a device that contains surge protection circuits and one or more batteries that can provide power during a temporary or permanent loss of power. **13.13**

Unisys Corporation, 11.27, 14.2
Unit testing: During the design phase of the information systems development, process of testing individual programs. **11.19**
UNIVAC 1, 1.33
Universal product code (UPC): Type of bar code, used for input information about grocery and retail items. **3.11**
Universities, teacher shortages in, 14.6
UNIX: A popular operating system from AT&T that was originally developed to manage a variety of scientific and specialized computer applications. With the deregulation of the phone companies in the 1980s, a multiuser version of UNIX has become available to run on most major computers. **8.13**
Updating: Data maintenance procedures for adding new data, changing existing information, and deleting obsolete information. **9.3,** 9.9-11
Upgrade sockets: Empty sockets in motherboard that can be used to install more powerful CPUs or upgrade memory. **4.8**
Uplink: The transmission to a satellite. **7.11**
Upper memory: Memory located between 640K and 1MB of RAM that is used for programs that control input and output devices and other computer hardware. **4.10**
User(s): The people who either use the computer directly or use the information it provides, also called computer users, or end users. **1.5**
  access privileges, 9.17
  DBMS role, 9.21
  future changes and, 14.16
  health guidelines, 8.35
  learning aids, 2.27
  prototyping tools and, 11.28
  support tools, 2.27
  system development life cycle and, 11.3
  training, 11.23
User coordination, database administrator and, 9.20
User group: A group of people with common computer equipment or software interests that meet regularly to share information. **14.9**
User ID: In multiuser operating systems, a user ID identifies the user, and must be entered correctly before a user is allowed to use an application program. **8.10**
User interface: A combination of hardware and software that allows a user to communicate with a computer system. **2.2**
User responses: The data that a user inputs to respond to a question or message from the software. **3.3**
Utility programs: Programs that perform specific tasks related to managing computer resources or files, and are included with the operating system. Tasks performed include copying and moving files and formatting disks. **8.15**
  DBMS and, 9.17
  future of, 8.18

Vaccines, *see* **Anti-virus programs**
Vacuum tubes, 1.32
Validation: In database programs, the comparison of data entered against a predefined format or value. **2.19**
Value-added carriers: Companies that lease channels from common carriers to provide specialized communications services. **7.24**
Value-added networks: Networks provided by companies that lease channels from common carriers to provide specialized communications services. **7.24**
Value-added resellers (VARs), *see* **System houses**
Values: Numerical data contained in the cells of a spreadsheet. **2.12**
Vendors, 8.30
  information systems development and, 11.11
  personal computer, 14.5
  software, 11.11, 14.5
  support phone numbers, 8.36
Vertical application software: Software developed for a unique way of doing business, usually within a specific industry. **11.10**
Very high-level languages, *see* **Fourth-generation languages**
Very small aperture terminal (VSAT): Satellite antenna measuring only 1 to 3 meters in size than can transmit up to 19,200 bits of data per second. **7.11**
Video, in multimedia, 5.6

Video card: Multimedia device containing electronics that capture and process video data; installed in the computer. **3.16**
  local bus, 8.32
Video display terminals (VDT), *see* **Display terminals; Screen(s)**
Video output: Output that consists of visual images that have been captured with a video input device, such as a VCR or camera, digitized, and directed to an output device such as a computer monitor. Video output can also be directed to a television monitor. **5.5**
View: In a relational database, the data from one or more files the user manipulates for a query. **9.18**
Virtual corporation: A temporary network of companies that join together to provide goods and services to take advantage of new opportunities. Virtual corporations form quickly and stay together only as long as the opportunity remains profitable. **10.16**
Virtual machine (VM) operating system: Allows a single computer to run two or more different operating systems. **8.5,** 8.15
Virtual memory management: Increases the effective (or virtual) limit of memory by expanding the amount of main memory to include disk space. **8.7**
Virtual reality: The use of a computer to create an artificial environment that can be experienced by the computer user. **5.7**
  commercial applications, 5.8, 14.35-40
Virus(es): An illegal and potentially damaging computer program designed to infect other software by attaching itself to the software with which it comes in contact, and often designed to damage computer systems by destroying or corrupting data. 8.37, **13.2**
Virus signature: Specific patterns of known virus code. **13.3**
VisiCalc, 1.35
Visual Basic: Object-oriented extension of the BASIC programming language developed by Microsoft Corporation that has a number of features that assist the user in designing a Windows-compatible graphical user interface. **12.20,** 12.25
Vision system: Artificial intelligence system that uses a camera to identify objects by digitizing their image and then comparing the image against a database of known shapes. **14.13**
Voice, fiber optics and, 7.10
Voice input: Allows the user to enter data and issue commands to the computer with spoken words. **3.16**-20, 3.23, **5.25**
Voice mail: Verbal electronic mail that allows the caller to leave a message via telephone that is digitized so it can be stored on a disk like other computer data, and accessed by the recipient. **7.3**
Voice output: Spoken words that are conveyed to the user from the computer. **5.25**
Voice synthesis: A type of voice generation that can transform words stored in main memory into speech. **5.26**
Voice templates: Used by voice input systems that recognize patterns of sounds. **3.18**
Volatile memory: RAM memory is said to be volatile because the programs and data stored in RAM are erased when the power to the computer is turned off. **4.9**
von Neumann, John, 1.33

WAN, *see* **Wide area network**
What-if analysis: The capability of a spreadsheet to recalculate when data is changed. **2.16,** 10.11
Wide area network (WAN): A communications network that covers a large geographical area, and uses telephone lines, microwaves, satellites, or a combination of communications channels. **7.24**
Window: A rectangular portion of the screen that is used to display information. **2.3**
Windows, *see* **Microsoft Windows**
Wireless transmission: Used to connect devices that are in the same general area such as an office or business park, using one of three transmission techniques: light beams, radio waves, or carrier-connect radio. **7.12**
Wirth, Niklaus, 12.23
Wizards, 14.14

Word processing: Computer software used to produce or modify documents that consist primarily of text. **2.4**-9
Word recognition, 3.23
Word size: The number of bits that the CPU can process at one time. **4.7**
Word wrap: An automatic line return that occurs when text reaches a certain position on the word processing document. **2.5**
Workgroup technology: Equipment and software that help group members communicate and manage their activities. **7.4**
Workstations: Expensive high-end personal computers that have powerful calculating and graphics capabilities; frequently used by engineers. **1.11**
Worm: Virus program that works by repeatedly copy itself in memory or on a disk drive until no memory or disk space remains, causing the computer to stop working. **13.3**
WORM (write once, read many): Optical disk devices that provide for one-time recording. **6.20**
WYSIWYG: An acronym for What You See Is What You Get. A feature that allows the user to design on screen an exact image of what a printed page will look like. **2.11**

Zero insertion force socket, 4.8

PHOTO CREDITS

CHAPTER 1 *Figure 1-1*, (top) International Business Machines Corp.; (center) International Business Machines Corp.; (bottom left) International Business Machines Corp.; *Figure 1-3*, © Henry Blackham:*Figure 1-4*, International Business Machines Corp.; *Figure 1-5*, International Business Machines Corp.; *Figure 1-7*, © Henry Blackham; *Figure 1-9*, (a) Omnidata; (b) Hewlett-Packard Co.; (c) Toshiba America Information Systems, Inc.; (d) Zeos International Ltd.; (e) International Business Machines Corp.; (f) EO Inc.; (g) © Frank Pryor/Apple Computer Inc.; (h) © Mosgrove Photo/Apple Computer Inc.; (i) International Business Machines Corp.; (j) International Business Machines Corp.; *Figure 1-10*, Dell Computer Corp.; *Figure 1-11*, International Business Machines Corp.; *Figure 1-12*, International Business Machines Corp.; *Figure 1-13*, Cray Computer Corp.; *Figure 1-14*, Cray Research; *Figure 1-17*, CompUSA Inc.; *Figure 1-21*, Hewlett-Packard Co.; *Figure 1-22*, Hewlett-Packard Co.; *Figure 1-24*, International Business Machines Corp.; *Figure 1-25*, International Business Machines Corp.; *Figure 1-26*, International Business Machines Corp.; *Figure 1-27*, International Business Machines Corp.; *Figure 1-28*, Stock/Boston; *Figure 1-29*, Hewlett-Packard Co.; *Figure 1-30*, International Business Machines Corp.; *Figure 1-31*, International Business Machines Corp.; *Figure 1-32*, International Business Machines Corp.; *Figure 1-33*, © Frank Pryor/Apple Computer; **TIMELINE** *Page 1.32*, (top left) Iowa State University, News Service Photo Dept.; (top center left) Iowa State University; (top center right) Iowa State University; (top right) University of Pennsylvania Archives; (bottom left) Harvard University Archives; (bottom center left) Dept. of Navy; (bottom center right) Massachusetts Institute of Technology; (bottom right) Dept of Navy; *Page 1.33*, (top left) Institute for Advanced Studies; (top center) UNISYS Corp.; (top right) UNISYS Corp.; (bottom left) Dept. of Navy; (bottom center); Massachusetts Institute of Technology; (bottom right) International Business Machines Corp.; *Page 1.34*, (top left) International Business Machines Corp.; (top right) © Stuart Bratesman; (bottom left) Integrated Circuit Corporation; (bottom center left) International Business Machines Corp.; (bottom center right) Computer Museum; (bottom right) InfoWorld; *Page 1.35*, (top left) Digital Equipment Corporation; (top center left) © Shelly R.Harrison; (top center right) Intel Corp.; (top right) Intel Corp.; (botom left) Apple Computer, Inc.; (bottom center left) Apple Computer, Inc.; (bottom center right) Apple Computer, Inc.; (bottom right) VisiCalc; *Page 1.36*, (top left) Microsoft Corp.; (top right) International Business Machines Corp.; (bottom left) Apple Computer, Inc.(bottom right) Compaq Computer Corp.; *Page 1.37*, (top left) Time Magazine; (top center left) Lotus Development Corp.; (top center right) Lotus Development Corporation; (top right) International Business Machines Corp.; (bottom left) Intel Corp.; (bottom right) Microsoft Corp.; *Page 1.38*, (top left) Apple Computer, Inc.; (top center) Apple Computer, Inc.; (top right) Intel Corp.; (bottom) Environmental Protection Agency (EPA). **CHAPTER 2** *Figure 2-10*, © Fredrik D.Bodin; *Figure 2-25*, © Curtis Fukuda; *Figure 2-38*, (c) © Fredrik D.Bodin; (d) © Fredrik D.Bodin. **CHAPTER 3** *Figure 3-1*, © Henry Blackham; *Figure 3-2*, (a) International Business Machines Corp.; (b) International Business Machines Corp.; *Figure 3-3*, (a) Microsoft Corp.; (b) © Phil Matt; *Figure 3-5*, International Business Machines Corp.; *Figure 3-6*, Texas Instruments Inc./Temelin McClain PR; *Figure 3-7*, Suncom Technologies Inc.; *Figure 3-8*, (a) International Business Machines Corp.; (b) International Business Machines Corp.; *Figure 3-9*, GRID System Corp.; *Figure 3-11*, International Business Machines Corp.; *Figure 3-12*, International Business Machines Corp.; *Figure 3-13*, Compaq Computer Corp.; *Figure 3-14*, Compaq Computer Corp.; *Figure 3-15*, Hewlett-Packard Co.; *Figure 3-16*, Logitech Inc.; *Figure 3-17*, International Business Machines Corp.; *Figure 3-19*, (a) © Ed Kashi/Dell Computer; (b) Hewlett-Packard Co.; (c) © Paul Shambroom/Science; *Figure 3-20*, (right) Scantron Corp.; *Figure 3-23*, © Fredrik D.Bodin; *Figure 3-24*, NCR Corp.; *Figure 3-25*, Cooper Tire; *Figure 3-26*, Cimlinc, Inc.; *Figure 3-27*, International Business Machines Corp.; *Figure 3-29*, Texas Instruments Inc.; *Figure 3-31*, Videolabs Inc.; *Figure 3-32*, © Fredrik D.Bodin; *Figure 3-35*, © Gary Payne/Gamma Liaison; *Figure 3-38*, The Image Bank. **CHAPTER 4** *Figure 4-1*, © Henry Blackham; *Figure 4-8*, © Phil Matt; *Figure 4-9*, Intel Corp.; *Figure 4-10*, International Business Machines Corp.; *Figure 4-13*, © Phil Matt; *Figure 4-15*, © Alan L.Detrick; *Figure 4-20*, © Phil Matt; *Figure 4-21*, MegaHertz Corp.; *Figure 4-22*, © Phil Matt; *Figure 4-26*, © Tom Pantages; *Figure 4-35*, Courtesy of Paul DuBois, Hermes Engineering NV. **MAKING A COMPUTER CHIP** *Page 4.35*, (1) Index Stock Photography; *Page 4.36* (2) © Frank Wing Photographer; (6) Intel Corp.; (7) C-I Photography; *Page 4.37*, (5) Photo Researchers, Inc.; (9) International Business Machines Corp.; (10) © David Scharf; *Page 4.38*, (11) © L.Manning/Westlight; (12) International Business Machines Corp.; (13) C-I Photography; (14) © Chuck O'Rear/West*light*; (15) Dr.Jerry Burgess/Science Photo Library; (16) © Peloton & Associates, Inc./Westlight. **CHAPTER 5** *Figure 5-5*, Radius Computer Corp.; *Figure 5-6*, International Business Machines Corp.; *Figure 5-7*, AT&T; *Figure 5-10*, International Business Machines Corp.; *Figure 5-11*, © Peter Menzel; *Figure 5-12*, © Ed Kashi; *Figure 5-13*, © Gerry Gropp/Sipa Press; *Figure 5-15*, © Eric Futran Photography/Liaison International; *Figure 5-17*, Epson America, Inc.; *Figure 5-18*, Printronix; *Figure 5-24*, Hewlett-Packard Co.; *Figure 5-25*, Lexmark; *Figure 5-27*, Hewlett-Packard Co.; *Figure 5-28*, Siemens Nixdorf Printing Systems; *Figure 5-29*, CalComp Inc.; *Figure 5-30*, (a) Seiko Corporation; (b) Zebra Technologies Corp.; (c) Citizen America Corp.; *Figure 5-32*; Portrait Display Labs; *Figure 5-34*, Evans & Sutherland Computer Corp.; *Figure 5-36*, NEC Technologies Inc.; *Figure 5-37*, International Business Machines Corp.; *Figure 5-38*, Toshiba America Information Systems, Inc.; *Figure 5-39*, NEC Corp.; *Figure 5-42*, TRW Inc.; *Figure 5-43*, Electrohome Corp.; *Figure 5-44*, Hewlett-Packard Co.; *Figure 5-45*, Hewlett-Packard Co.; *Figure 5-46*, Eastman Kodak Co.; *Figure 5-48*, MusicWriter, Inc.; *Figure 5-49*, © Hank Morgan/Science Photo Library. **CHAPTER 6** *Figure 6-2*, © Phil Matt; *Figure 6-7*, © Phil Matt; *Figure 6-10*, Hewlett-Packard Co.; *Figure 6-11*, International Business Machines Corp.; *Figure 6-12*, Quantum Corp.; *Figure 6-13*, International Business Machines Corp.; *Figure 6-19*, © Phil Matt; *Figure 6-20*, MAC USA; *Figure 6-22*, 3M Corp.; *Figure 6-23*, 3M Corp.; *Figure 6-24*, International Business Machines Corp.; *Figure 6-28*, © Phil Matt; *Figure 6-30*, 3M Corporation; *Figure 6-31*, Symmetrix Inc.; *Figure 6-32*, Storage Technology Corp.; *Figure 6-33*, Dallas Semiconductor; *Figure 6-34*, © Phil Matt; *Figure 6-35*, LaserCard Inc.; *Figure 6-37*, © Phil Matt; *Figure 6-38*, © Kerry Klayman/U.C.Irvine; *Figure 6-39*, © Kerry Klayman/U.C.Irvine. **CHAPTER 7** *Figure 7-1*, © HMS Images; *Figure 7-2*, (b) MCI International Inc.; *Figure 7-3*, © Peter Hendrie/The Image Bank; *Figure 7-4*, Lotus Development Corporation; *Figure 7-5*, Klynas Engineering; *Figure 7-9*, © Henry Blackham; *Figure 7-12*, The Image Bank; *Figure 7-13*, © Don Lowe/Tony Stone Images; *Figure 7-14*, © Jim Zuckerman/Westlight; *Figure 7-16*, Photonics Inc.; *Figure 7-24*, Photos © Henry Blackham; *Figure 7-26*, © Fredrik D.Bodin; *Figure 7-27*, Hayes Microcomputer Products Inc.; *Figure 7-28*, Photos © Henry Blackham; *Figure 7-31*, Photos © Henry Blackham; *Figure 7-32*, Photos © Henry Blackham; *Figure 7-33*, EDS Corp.; *Figure 7-34*, Photos © Henry Blackham; *Figure 7-35*, Photos © Henry Blackham; *Figure 7-36*, Photos © Henry Blackham; *Figure 7-37*, North American Van Lines. **THE INTERNET** *Figure 1*, NCSA of University of IL; *Figure 4*, BBN Communications Corp. **CHAPTER 8** *Figure 8-9*, Photos © Henry Blackham; *Figure 8-13*, Apple Computer Inc.; *Figure 8-14*, International Business Machines Corp.; *Figure 8-16*, Berkeley Systems Inc.; *Figure 8-17*, NeXT Computers Inc.; **BUYER'S GUIDE** *Page 8.29*, (a) International Business Machines Corp.; (b) © Phil Matt; (c) © Phil Matt; *Page 8.30*, (a) Environmental Protective Agency (EPA):(b) Dell Computer Corp.:*Page 8.33*, (a) Curtis Inc.; (b) © Phil Matt; (c) American Power Conversion Corp.(APC); (d) MicroSolutions Computer Products, Inc.; *Page 8.34*, Curtis Inc.; *Page 8.35*, © Phil Matt. **CHAPTER 9** *Figure 9-20*, © Jay Freis/The Image Bank; *Figure 9-23*, Bank Marketing Group. **CHAPTER 10** *Figure 10-7*, © David Young-Wolff/Photo Edit; *Figure 10-8*, © Catherine Noren/Stock Boston; *Figure 10-9*, COMSHARE, Inc.; *Figure 10-13*, Ford Motor Co. **CHAPTER 11** *Figure 11-14*, PC Magazine; *Figure 11-15*, © Ed Kashi; *Figure 11-16*, © Phil Matt; *Figure 11-21*, © Richard Pasley; *Figure 11-22*, Bachman Information Systems Inc.; *Figure 11-23*, © Jim Pickerell/West Light. **CHAPTER 12** *Figure 12-13*, U.S.Naval Archives. **MULTIMEDIA** *Opening Page*, © David Wagner/Phototake NYC; *Figure 1*, International Business Machines Corp.; *Figure 2*, (left) International Business Machines Corp.; *Figure 3*, Deep River Publishing; *Figure 4*, Books That Work; *Figure 5*, Books That Work; *Figure 6*, Microsoft Corp.; *Figure 7*, Microsoft Corp.; *Figure 8*, Medio Magazine; *Figure 9*, (left) Mayo Clinic; (right) A.D.A.M.Software; *Figure 10*, (right) © Ed Kashi. **CHAPTER 13** *Figure 13-1*, Photos © Henry Blackham; *Figure 13-6*, Recognition Systems; *Figure 13-7*, Checkmate Software Inc.; *Figure 13-8*, © Moss Warner Communications; *Figure 13-9*, Business Software Alliance; *Figure 13-10*, QuickSoft, Inc.; *Figure 13-13*, Curtis Inc.; *Figure 13-17*, Cynthia Satloff; *Figure 13-21*, Olivetti Research Ltd.; *Figure 13-22*, Photos © Henry Blackham. **CHAPTER 14** *Figure 14-1*, © Ed Kashi; *Figure 14-2*, © Ed Kashi; *Figure 14-4*, © Michael Newman; *Figure 14-5*, © Robert E.Daemmrich; *Figure 14-6*, © Ed Lalio/Liason International; *Figure 14-8*, Datamation; *Figure 14-11*, © Peter B.Young/The Interface Group; *Figure 14-12*, © Phil Matt; *Figure 14-13*, Arcmate; *Figure 14-16*, (a) Toshiba America Information Systems, Inc.; (c) International Business Machines Corp.; (d) Prosignia VS; (e) International Business Machines Corp.; *Figure 14-19*, Ford Motor Company; *Figure 14-23*, Microsoft Corporation; *Figure 14-24*, 3-D Systems; *Figure 14-25*, © Henry Blackham. **VIRTUAL REALITY** *Figure 1*, Fake Space Inc., Photo Court, NASA Ames Research Center; *Figure 2*, Division Incorporated; *Figure 3*, Ciné-Med; *Figure 4*, (upper) Caroline Parsons, The Gamma Liaison Network; (lower) Jack Menzel, Autodesk Inc.; *Figure 5*, (left) Peter Menzel VR, University of North Carolina; (right) Peter Menzel VR, University of North Carolina; *Figure 6*, Peter Menzel, NASA Ames Research, Moffett AFB, CA VR; Mars data from Voyager, Lewis Hitchner; *Figure 7*, David Sutton Picture Group; *Figure 8*, Gamma Liaison; *Figure 9*, Sense8 Corporation; *Figure 10*, Virtus Software; *Figure 11*, Peter Menzel VPL Research Wall; *Figure 12*, VR Financial; *Figure 13*, Worldesign.

Programming in QuickBASIC

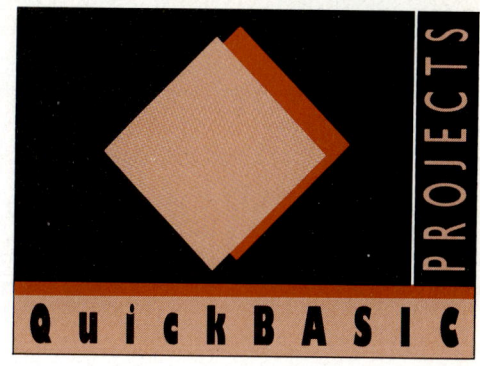

◆ PROJECT 1
An Introduction to Programming in QuickBASIC *QB1*

The Programming Process *QB1*
Sample Program 1—Patient Listing *QB2*
The DATA Statement *QB5*
The CLS, PRINT, and END Statements *QB6*
Variables *QB7*
The READ Statement *QB7*
The DO WHILE and LOOP Statements *QB8*
Try It Yourself Exercises *QB11*
The QB Operating Environment *QB12*
Executing Programs and Hard-Copy Output *QB17*
Saving, Loading, and Erasing Programs *QB20*
The QB Advisor On-Line Help System *QB22*
Try It Yourself Exercises *QB23*
Student Assignments *QB23*

◆ PROJECT 2
Basic Arithmetic Operations and Accumulating Totals *QB25*

The LET Statement *QB25*
Sample Program 2—Auto Expense Report *QB27*
Report Editing *QB33*
Printing a Report on the Printer *QB38*
Try It Yourself Exercises *QB39*
Student Assignments *QB41*

◆ PROJECT 3
Decisions *QB42*

The IF Statement *QB42*
Coding If-Then-Else Structures *QB44*
Sample Program 3—Video Rental Report *QB47*
Logical Operators *QB51*
The SELECT CASE Statement *QB54*
Try It Yourself Exercises *QB56*
Student Assignments *QB59*

◆ PROJECT 4
Interactive Programming, For Loops, and An Introduction to the Top-Down Approach *QB62*

The INPUT Statement *QB62*
The BEEP and LOCATE Statements *QB64*
Editing Data Entered Through the Keyboard *QB65*
Sample Program 4—Item Cost Report *QB66*
The FOR and NEXT Statements *QB68*
An Introduction to the Top-Down Approach *QB72*
The GOSUB and RETURN Statements *QB73*
Try It Yourself Exercises *QB77*
Student Assignments *QB80*

◆ PROJECT 5
Sequential File Processing *QB83*

File Organization *QB83*
Creating a Sequential Data File *QB83*
Sample Program 5A—Creating a Sequential Data File *QB83*
Reading Data From a Sequential Data File *QB91*
Sample Program 5B—Processing a Sequential Data File *QB92*
Try It Yourself Exercises *QB96*
Student Assignments *QB97*

◆ PROJECT 6
Arrays and Functions *QB99*

Arrays *QB99*
The DIM Statement *QB100*
Sample Program 6—Customer Account Table Lookup *QB101*
Functions *QB108*
Try It Yourself Exercises *QB112*
Student Assignments *QB113*

◆ APPENDIX
QuickBASIC Debugging Techniques *QB115*

Examining Values Through the Immediate Window *QB115*
Executing One Statement at a Time *QB115*
Breakpoints *QB116*
Tracing *QB116*
Set Next Statement *QB116*
Recording *QB117*
Watch Variables and Watchpoints *QB117*

◆ REFERENCE CARD *R.1*

PROJECT 1

An Introduction to Programming in QuickBASIC

In Project 1 we provide an introduction to the principles of program design and computer programming using the QuickBASIC programming language. QuickBASIC was developed for the personal computer (PC) by Microsoft Corporation, one of the largest microcomputer software companies in the world. Today, QuickBASIC is one of the most widely used programming languages on PCs.

Our approach in illustrating QuickBASIC is to present a series of applications that can be processed using a PC. We carefully explain the input data, the output to be produced, and the processing. Through the use of a flowchart, we illustrate the program design and logic. The flowchart is followed by an explanation of the QuickBASIC statements required to implement the logic. We then present the complete QuickBASIC program. The program solution, when entered into the PC and executed, will produce the output from the specified input.

THE PROGRAMMING PROCESS

Computer programs can vary significantly in size and complexity. A simple program may contain only a few statements. A complex program can contain hundreds and even thousands of statements. Regardless of the size of the program, it is extremely important that the task of computer programming be approached in a professional manner, as computer programming is one of the most precise of all activities.

Learning computer programming should not be approached as a trial-and-error-type of activity. By carefully reviewing the sample problems, the program design, and the QuickBASIC code we present within these projects, you should be able to write well-designed programs that produce correct output when executed on a PC.

Computer programming is not *naturally* an error-prone activity. Errors enter into the design and coding of the computer program only through carelessness or lack of understanding of the programming process. With careful study and attention to detail, you can avoid errors. Just as it is the job of the accountant, the mathematician, the engineer, and the scientist to produce correct results, so too it is the job of the computer programmer to produce a program that is reliable, easy to read, and produces accurate results.

The actual programming process involves the activities described in Figure 1-1. When you use this careful approach to program design and coding, you can develop programs that are easy to read, efficient, reliable, and execute properly.

STEP	DESCRIPTION
1	Define the problem to be solved precisely in terms of input, processing, and output.
2	Design a detailed logic plan using flowcharts or some other logic tool.
3	Desk check the logic plan as if you are the computer.
4	Code the program.
5	Desk check the code as if you are the computer.
6	Enter the program into the computer.
7	Test the program until it is error free.
8	Run the program using the input data to generate the output results.

FIGURE 1-1 The program development cycle

SAMPLE PROGRAM 1 — PATIENT LISTING

In this first sample program we generate a patient listing on the screen. The input data consists of the series of patient records shown in Figure 1-2. Each record contains a patient name, a doctor name, and a room number.

PATIENT NAME	DOCTOR NAME	ROOM NUMBER
Tim Krel	Nance	112
Mary Lepo	Gold	102
Tom Pep	King	245
Joe Ruiz	Ward	213
EOF	End	0

FIGURE 1-2 The patient records

The data taken as a group is called a **file**. The data about a single individual is called a **record**. Each unit of data within the record is called a **field**, or **data item**. Thus, the input data consists of a file of patient records. Each record contains a patient name field, a doctor name field, and a room number field.

In the list of records in Figure 1-2, the last record contains the patient name EOF, the doctor name End, and the room number 0. This record is called a trailer record, or sentinel record. A **trailer record** is added to the end of the file to indicate when all the valid records have been processed.

The output for this sample program is a listing on the PC screen of each record in the patient file. The output listing is shown in Figure 1-3.

```
        Patient Listing

Room        Patient         Doctor

 112        Tim Krel        Nance
 102        Mary Lepo       Gold
 245        Tom Pep         King
 213        Joe Ruiz        Ward

End of Patient List
```

FIGURE 1-3 The required output for Sample Program 1

The patient list includes the room number, the patient name, and the doctor name for each record. Notice that the sequence of the fields displayed on the screen is different from the sequence of the fields in the input record. Column headings identify each field. After all records have been processed, the message End of Patient List displays.

Program Flowchart

The flowchart, QuickBASIC program, and output for Sample Program 1 are shown in Figure 1-4. The flowchart illustrates a simple looping structure. After the headings are displayed, a record is read. This read statement, prior to the loop, is called a **primary read**, or **lead read**.

Sample Program 1 — Patient Listing   QB 3

A. PROGRAM FLOWCHART

B. PROGRAM LISTING

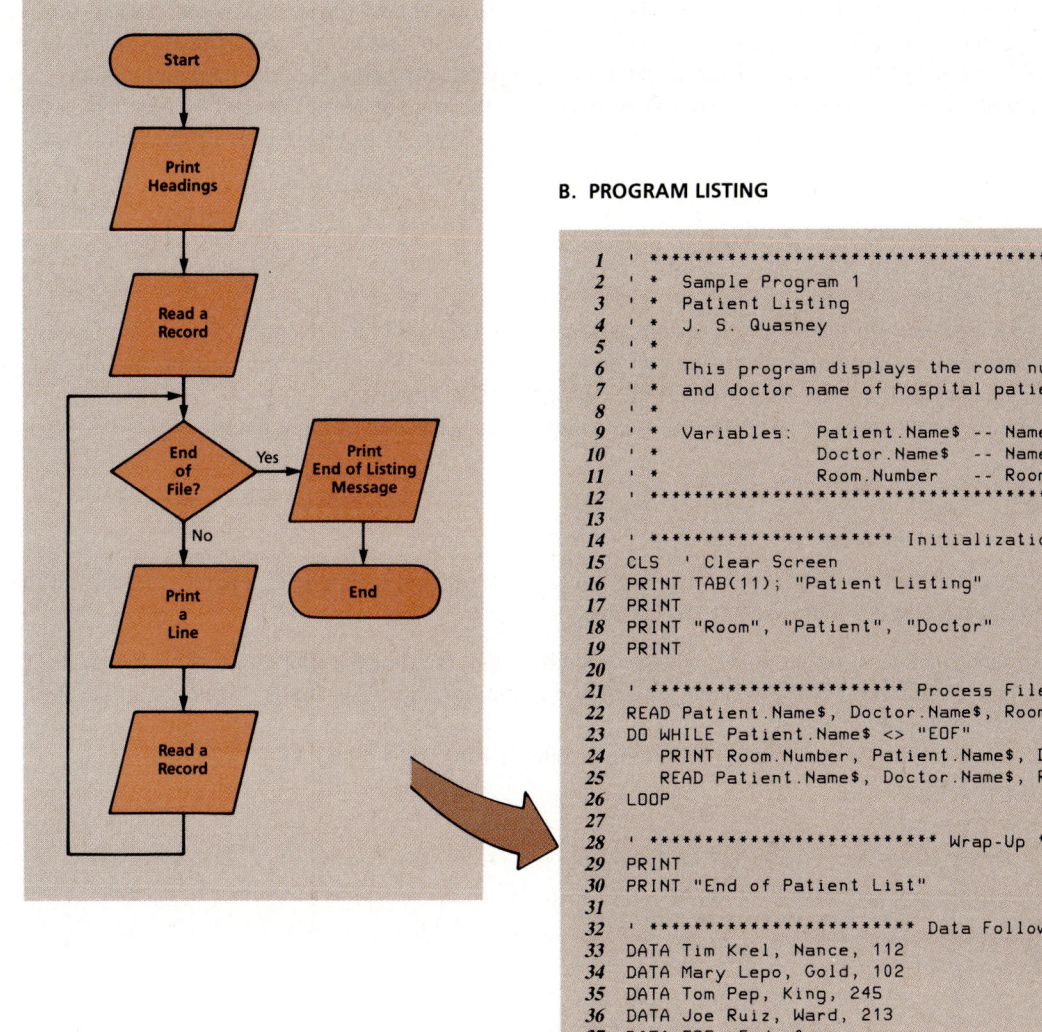

C. OUTPUT RESULTS

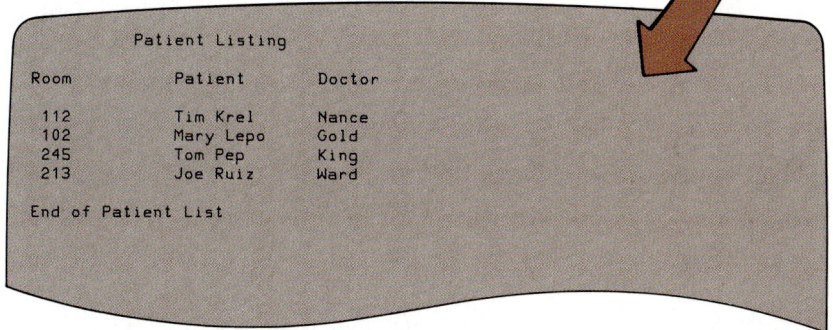

FIGURE 1-4 The program flowchart (A), program listing (B), and output results (C) for Sample Program 1

Following the lead read in the program flowchart in Figure 1-4, a test is performed to determine if the record just read was the trailer record containing the patient name EOF. If so, there are no more records to process. If not, then more records remain to be processed. This decision determines if the loop should be entered. If the end-of-file has not been reached, the loop is entered. Within the loop the previously read record is displayed on the screen and another record is read. Control then returns to the decision symbol at the top of the loop. As long as the trailer record has not been read, the looping continues.

When the trailer record is read, the looping process stops and an end-of-job message displays followed by termination of the program. This basic logic is appropriate for all applications which involve reading records and displaying the fields from the record read on an output device.

The QuickBASIC Program

Programs should be well documented, easy to read, easy to understand, and easy to modify and maintain. For these reasons, programming standards have been developed to guide the beginning programmer in the task of writing programs. We illustrate and explain these standards in all sample programs we present in these programming projects.

A program written using QuickBASIC consists of a series of statements which serve one of three functions:

1. Document the program
2. Cause processing to occur
3. Define data

A quality program is well documented. This means the program contains information which helps a reader understand the program. Documentation within the program should include the following:

- A prologue, including the program name, program title, an author identification, the date the program was written, a brief description of the program, and a description of the variable names used in the program. The first 12 lines of Sample Program 1 (Figure 1-5) contain the prologue.
- Remark lines should come before any major module in a program. In Sample Program 1, lines 14, 21, 28, and 32 are remark lines that precede major modules.

FIGURE 1-5
The prologue for Sample Program 1

```
 1  ' *************************************************************
 2  ' *  Sample Program 1                        September 15, 1994 *
 3  ' *  Patient Listing                                            *
 4  ' *  J. S. Quasney                                              *
 5  ' *                                                             *
 6  ' *  This program displays the room number, patient name,       *
 7  ' *  and doctor name of hospital patients.                      *
 8  ' *                                                             *
 9  ' *  Variables:   Patient.Name$ -- Name of patient              *
10  ' *               Doctor.Name$  -- Name of doctor               *
11  ' *               Room.Number   -- Room number                  *
12  ' *************************************************************
```

Documentation within a QuickBASIC program is accomplished through the use of the REM statement. The general form of the REM statement is shown in Figure 1-6.

FIGURE 1-6
The general form of the REM statement

```
REM comment

   or

' comment
```

The remark statement begins with REM or an apostrophe (') followed by any characters, numbers, or words required to document the program. Notice that in these programming projects, we use the apostrophe (') rather than the keyword REM to initiate a remark line. Asterisks (*) are used in the remark lines to highlight the documentation.

Blank lines, such as lines 13, 20, 27, and 31 of Sample Program 1 (Figure 1-4), are used to end any major module. For example, the Initialization module (Figure 1-7) begins with a remark line and ends with a blank line. The proper use of remark lines, blank lines, and indentations can substantially improve the readability of a program. We suggest that you follow the format illustrated in Sample Program 1 when coding all QuickBASIC programs.

The apostrophe (') can also be used to include in-line remarks as shown following the CLS statement in line 15 of Figure 1-7. All characters that follows the apostrophe in an in-line remark are considered to be part of the documentation.

Remember that remark lines and blank lines can be added before or after any line in a program. In addition, they are strictly for human comprehension and have no effect on the outcome of the program.

FIGURE 1-7
The Initialization module of Sample Program 1

```
14  ' ******************** Initialization ********************
15  CLS   ' Clear Screen
16  PRINT TAB(11); "Patient Listing"
17  PRINT
18  PRINT "Room", "Patient", "Doctor"
19  PRINT
20
```

THE DATA STATEMENT

ample Program 1 employs DATA statements to define the data. The DATA statements for Sample Program 1 are shown in Figure 1-8.

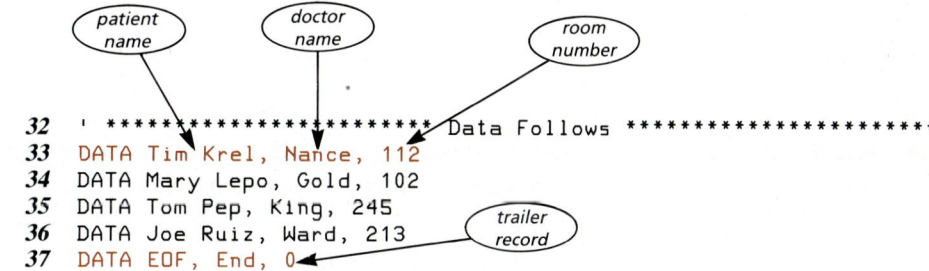

FIGURE 1-8
The data to be processed by Sample Program 1

In Figure 1-8, line 33 defines the first patient record. Line 34 defines the second patient record, and so on. DATA statements begin with the keyword DATA followed by a space and the data. The DATA statement in line 33 contains the patient name (Tim Krel), the doctor name (Nance), and the room number (112). As shown in Figure 1-8, each of the data items must be separated by a comma.

The last DATA statement is the trailer record, when a trailer record is used in this manner, you must include an entry for each field. In line 37, the phrase EOF is included for the patient name, the word End is included in place of the doctor name, and the numeric value 0 is included for the room number. These values, of course, will not be included in the listing generated by the program.

The general form of the DATA statement is shown in Figure 1-9.

FIGURE 1-9
The general form of the DATA statement

> DATA data item, data item, ..., data item
>
> where each data item is a numeric or string value

THE CLS, PRINT, AND END STATEMENTS

Up to this point, we have talked about REM and DATA statements. Both of these statements are classified as nonexecutable. Neither type of statement has anything to do with the logic shown in the flowchart in Figure 1-4. For example, the DATA statements can be moved from the bottom of the program to the top of the program with no effect on the logic of the program.

In this section we discuss the CLS, PRINT, and END statements.

The CLS Statement

The first executable statement in Sample Program 1 is the CLS statement in line 15 (Figure 1-10). The function of this statement is to clear the output screen and move the cursor to the upper left corner. The **output screen** is the one that shows the results due to the execution of a program.

```
14  ' ******************* Initialization *********************
15  CLS   ' Clear Screen
16  PRINT TAB(11); "Patient Listing"
17  PRINT
18  PRINT "Room", "Patient", "Doctor"
19  PRINT
20
```

FIGURE 1-10
The Initialization module of Sample Program 1

The PRINT Statement

The PRINT statement is used to write information on the output screen. It is commonly used to display headings and the values of variables and control spacing in a report. As shown in Figure 1-11, the PRINT statement consists of the keyword PRINT. It may also have an optional list of print items separated by commas and semicolons.

FIGURE 1-11
The general form of the PRINT statement

> PRINT list
>
> where **list** is the items to display separated by semicolons or commas

The list in a PRINT statement includes print items. The **print items** can be any of the following:

- Variables, such as Doctor.Name$, Patient.Name$, and Room.Number
- Constants, such as numeric and string values—string values must be enclosed in quotation marks (")
- Function references, such as the TAB function—the TAB function allows you to move the cursor to the right to a specified column position

Lines 16 through 19 of Sample Program 1 (Figure 1-10) display the report title and column headings. Line 16 displays the report title on line 1. The first print item in line 16 is the TAB function. It causes the cursor to move to column 11. The semicolon following the TAB function instructs the PC to display the next print item (Patient Listing) at the current cursor location (column 11). Hence, the report title Patient Listing displays beginning in column 11 on line 1. After line 16 is executed, the cursor moves down one line on the output screen to line 2.

The PRINT statement in line 17 contains no print items. A PRINT statement with no print items causes the PC to skip a line. Thus, line 2 on the output screen is left blank.

Line 18 displays the three column headings. Each column heading is surrounded by the required quotation marks. Notice that the column headings also are separated by commas. When the print items are separated by commas, the fields are displayed in predefined columns called print zones. There are five print zones per line. Each **print zone** has 14 positions for a total of 70 positions per line as shown in Figure 1-12.

FIGURE 1-12
There are five print zones of 14 positions each for a total of 70 positions

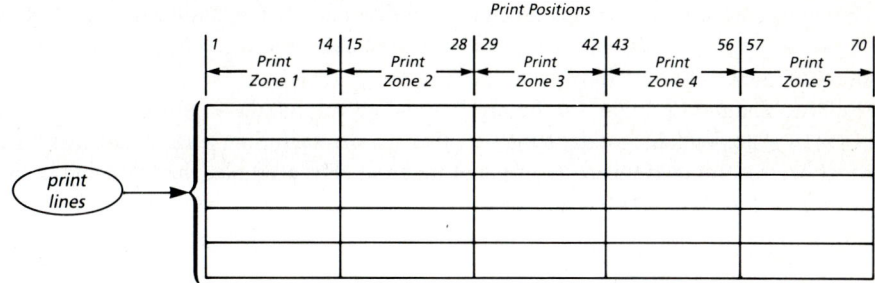

When line 18 in Sample Program 1 executes, Room displays beginning in column 1, Patient displays beginning in column 15, and Doctor displays beginning in column 29. Like line 17, line 19 causes the PC to skip a line on the output screen.

The END Statement

The last line in Sample Program 1 is the END statement. When executed, the END statement instructs the PC to stop executing the program. Although the END statement is not required, it is recommended that you always include one.

VARIABLES

In programming, a **variable** is a location in main memory whose value can change as the program executes. There are two major categories of variables—numeric and string. A **numeric variable** can only be assigned a numeric value. A **string variable** may be assigned a string of characters such as a word, name, phrase, or sentence.

A **variable name** is used to define and reference a variable in main memory. Variable names must conform to certain rules. In QuickBASIC, a variable name begins with a letter and may be followed by up to 39 letters, digits, and decimal points. You may not use a QuickBASIC keyword, such as CLS or PRINT, as a variable name. For a complete list of the QuickBASIC keywords, refer to the last page of the reference card at the back of this book.

String variable names always end with a dollar sign ($). Numeric variable names never end with a dollar sign. For example, in Sample Program 1, Room.Number is a numeric variable and Patient.Name$ and Doctor.Name$ are string variables.

With respect to the variable names used in Sample Program 1, notice how we use the decimal point (.) to better describe what the variables will hold during the execution of the program.

THE READ STATEMENT

To assign the data in the DATA statements to variables, we use the READ statement. As shown in Figure 1-13, the READ statement consists of the keyword READ followed by one or more variable names separated from each other by commas. The variable names must be specified in the READ statement in the order in which the data is recorded in the DATA statements.

FIGURE 1-13
The general form of the READ statement

> READ $variable_1$, $variable_2$, ..., $variable_n$
>
> where each variable is a numeric variable or string variable

When line 22 (Figure 1-14) is executed, the first data item is assigned to the first variable in the READ statement. Thus, Tim Krel is assigned to Patient.Name$. The second data item (Nance) is assigned to Doctor.Name$ and the third data item (112) is assigned to Room.Number.

Refer to Sample Program 1 in Figure 1-4 and notice that the READ statement in line 22 has the same number of variables as the DATA statements have data items. In other words, each time a READ statement is executed, one DATA statement is used. Although we recommend this style, it is not required. For example, the following shows that it is valid to write the READ statement in line 22 as three READ statements:

```
READ Patient.Name$
READ Doctor.Name$
READ Room.Number
DATA Tim Krel, Nance, 112
```

We could have also placed one data item per DATA statement as follows:

```
READ Patient.Name$, Doctor.Name$, Room.Number
DATA Tim Krel
DATA Nance
DATA 112
```

THE DO WHILE AND LOOP STATEMENTS

Following the first READ statement in line 22, lines 23 through 26 establish a **Do loop** (Figure 1-14). The DO WHILE statement in line 23 and the LOOP statement in line 26 cause the range of statements between them to be executed repeatedly as long as Patient.Name$ does not equal the string value EOF. The expression Patient.Name$ <> "EOF" following DO WHILE in line 23 is called a **condition**. A condition can be true or false. In the case of the DO WHILE, the statements within the loop are executed while the condition is true.

```
21  ' ********************* Process File *********************
22  READ Patient.Name$, Doctor.Name$, Room.Number
23  DO WHILE Patient.Name$ <> "EOF"
24     PRINT Room.Number, Patient.Name$, Doctor.Name$
25     READ Patient.Name$, Doctor.Name$, Room.Number
26  LOOP
27
28  ' ********************* Wrap-Up *********************
29  PRINT
30  PRINT "End of Patient List"
31
```

FIGURE 1-14
The Process File and Wrap-Up modules of Sample Program 1

When Patient.Name$ does equal EOF, the condition in line 23 is false. Therefore, the PC skips the statements within the loop and continues execution at the first executable statement following the corresponding LOOP statement. The first executable statement following the LOOP statement is the PRINT statement in line 29.

One execution of a Do loop is called a **pass**. The statements within the loop, lines 24 and 25, are indented by three spaces for the purpose of readability. Collectively, lines 24 and 25 are called the **range** of statements in the Do loop.

Following execution of the lead read in line 22, Patient.Name$ is equal to Tim Krel. Hence, control passes into the Do loop and the first patient record is displayed due to the PRINT statement in line 24. Next, the READ statement in line 25 assigns the variables Patient.Name$, Doctor.Name$, and Room.Number the data items found in the second DATA statement. The LOOP statement in line 26 automatically returns control to the DO WHILE statement in line 23. This process continues while Patient.Name$ does not equal EOF.

The general forms of the DO WHILE and LOOP statements are shown in Figure 1-15.

FIGURE 1-15
The general forms of the DO WHILE and LOOP statements

```
DO WHILE condition
    [range of statements]
LOOP
```

Testing for the End-of-File

Lines 33 through 36 in Sample Program 1 (Figure 1-4) contain data for only four patients. The fifth patient in line 37 is the **trailer record**. It represents the end-of-file and is used to determine when all the valid data has been processed. To incorporate an end-of-file test, a variable must be selected and a trailer record added to the data. We selected the patient name as the test for end-of-file and the data value EOF. Since it guards against reading past end-of-file, the trailer record is also called the **sentinel record**. The value EOF is called the **sentinel value**. The value EOF is clearly distinguishable from all the rest of the data assigned to Patient.Name$. This sentinel value is the same as the string constant found in the condition in line 23.

After the READ statement in line 25 assigns Patient.Name$ the value EOF, the LOOP statement returns control to the DO WHILE statement. Since Patient.Name$ is equal to the value EOF, the DO WHILE statement causes the PC to pass control to line 29 which follows the corresponding LOOP statement. Line 29 skips a line and line 30 displays an end-of-job message. Lines 29 and 30 are referred to as an **end-of-file routine**.

Three other worthy points to consider about establishing a test for end-of-file in a Do loop are:

1. It is important that the trailer record contain enough values for all the variables in the READ statement. In Sample Program 1, if we only added the sentinel value EOF to line 37, there would not be enough data to fulfill the requirements of the three variables in the READ statement. We arbitrarily assigned End and 0 to the second and third variables in the READ statement.
2. The Do loop requires the use of two READ statements. The first READ statement (line 22) reads the first patient record before the PC enters the Do loop. The second READ statement, found at the bottom of the Do loop (line 25), causes the PC to read the next data record. This READ statement reads the remaining data records, one at a time, until there are no more data records left. If the first record contains the patient name EOF, the DO WHILE statement will immediately transfer control to the statement below the corresponding LOOP statement.
3. Sample Program 1 can process any number of patients by placing each in a DATA statement prior to the trailer record.

Conditions

The DO WHILE statement in line 23 (Figure 1-14) contains the condition

    Patient.Name$ <> "EOF"

The condition is made up of two expressions and a **relational operator**. The condition specifies a relationship between expressions that is either true or false. If the condition is true, execution continues with the line following the DO WHILE statement. If the condition is false, then control is transferred to the line following the corresponding LOOP statement.

The PC makes a comparison between the two operators based on the relational operator. Figure 1-16 lists the six valid relational operators.

FIGURE 1-16
Relational operators used in conditions

RELATION	MATH SYMBOL	QuickBASIC SYMBOL	EXAMPLE
Equal To	=	=	Educ$ = "12"
Less Than	<	<	Total < 25
Greater Than	>	>	Disc > .15
Less Than Or Equal To	≤	<= or =<	Deduc <= 10
Greater Than Or Equal To	≥	>= or =>	Code$ >= "A"
Not Equal To	≠	<> or ><	State$ <> "TX"

There are several important points to watch for in the application of conditions. For example, it is invalid to compare a numeric variable to a string value as in the following:

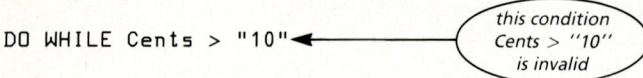
```
DO WHILE Cents > "10"
```
(this condition Cents > "10" is invalid)

Furthermore, the condition should ensure termination of the loop. For example, look at the following logical error:

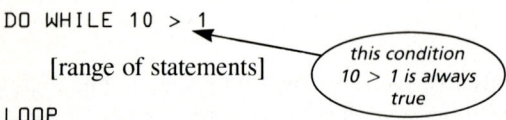
```
DO WHILE 10 > 1
    [range of statements]
LOOP
```
(this condition 10 > 1 is always true)

If such an error is not detected, a never-ending loop develops. There is no way to stop the endless program execution except by manual intervention, such as pressing **Ctrl + Break** on your PC keyboard. (The plus sign between two keys means hold down the first key and press the second key, and then release both keys.)

The complete QuickBASIC program and the output results are again illustrated in Figures 1-17 and 1-18.

FIGURE 1-17
Sample Program 1

```
1  ' ****************************************************************
2  ' *   Sample Program 1                         September 15, 1994 *
3  ' *   Patient Listing                                             *
4  ' *   J. S. Quasney                                               *
5  ' *                                                               *
6  ' *   This program displays the room number, patient name        *
7  ' *   and doctor name of hospital patients.                       *
8  ' *                                                               *
9  ' *   Variables:   Patient.Name$  -- Name of patient              *
10 ' *                Doctor.Name$   -- Name of doctor               *
11 ' *                Room.Number    -- Room number                  *
12 ' ****************************************************************
13
14 ' ********************* Initialization *********************
15 CLS   ' Clear Screen
16 PRINT TAB(11); "Patient Listing"
17 PRINT
18 PRINT "Room", "Patient", "Doctor"
19 PRINT
20
21 ' ********************* Process File *********************
22 READ Patient.Name$, Doctor.Name$, Room.Number
23 DO WHILE Patient.Name$ <> "EOF"
24     PRINT Room.Number, Patient.Name$, Doctor.Name$
25     READ Patient.Name$, Doctor.Name$, Room.Number
26 LOOP
27
28 ' ********************* Wrap-Up *********************
29 PRINT
30 PRINT "End of Patient List"
31
32 ' ********************* Data Follows *********************
33 DATA Tim Krel, Nance, 112
34 DATA Mary Lepo, Gold, 102
35 DATA Tom Pep, King, 245
36 DATA Joe Ruiz, Ward, 213
37 DATA EOF, End, 0
38 END
```

Annotations: prologue (lines 1–12); clear screen and display headings (lines 15–19); process patient file (lines 22–26); end-of-file routine (lines 29–30); patient file (lines 33–37).

FIGURE 1-18
The output results due to the execution of Sample Program 1

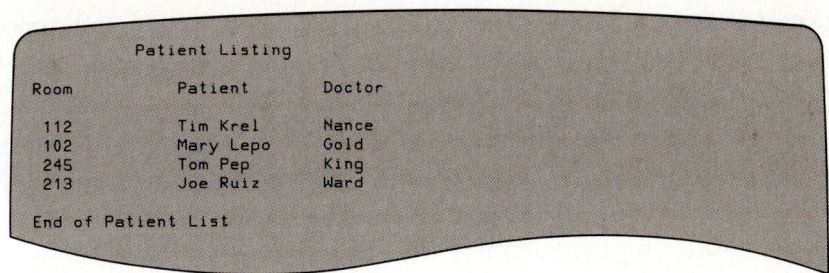

TRY IT YOURSELF EXERCISES

1. Which of the following are valid numeric variables in QuickBASIC?
   a. X$
   b. Account
   c. 8T
   d. Inventory.No

2. Write a CLS statement and a series of PRINT statements that display the value LINE 1 beginning in column 1 of line 1, LINE 3 in column 1 of line 3, and LINE 5 in column 1 of line 5.

3. Write a PRINT statement that displays the string values Name, Account, Balance, Date in print zones 1 through 4 of the current line.

4. Use the TAB function in a PRINT statement to display the string value The answer is beginning in column 42 of the current line.

5. Given the following DATA statement:

   DATA 16723, 12, 56

   Use the variables Inventory.Number, On.Order, and On.Hand to write a READ statement that assigns Inventory.Number the value 16723, On.Order the value 12, and On.Hand the value 56.

6. State the purpose of the LOOP statement.

7. List and describe the six relational operators.

8. Which of the following are invalid DO WHILE statements? Why?
   a. DO WHILE X = 10
   b. DOWHILE Acct$ <> "End"
   c. DO WHILE 5 < Tax
   d. DO WHILE On.Hand LT 25
   e. DO WHILE Volts Equals 37

9. Determine whether the conditions below are true or false, given the following: Hours = 6, Tonnage = 12.5, and Bonus = 1.75
   a. Hours >= 10
   b. Tonnage >= 12
   c. Bonus <> 2
   d. Hours <> 6
   e. Tonnage < 12.5
   f. Bonus = 1.75

10. Write the QuickBASIC code for the Process File and Wrap-Up modules that correspond to the following program flowchart. Use the variable names specified in the Read and Print symbols. Do not include any DATA statements. Start each module with a remark line and end each module with a blank line. For the end-of-file test, assume the trailer record includes the following data items: EOF, 0, 0.

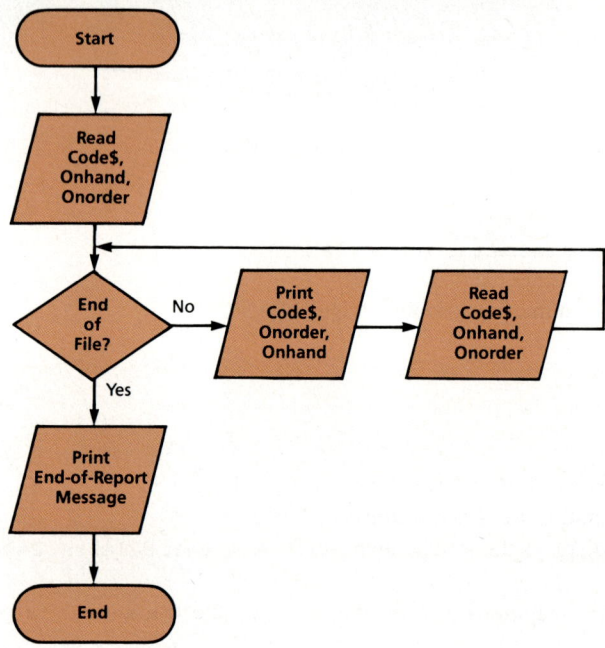

THE QB OPERATING ENVIRONMENT

o enter a program such as Sample Program 1 into the PC and execute it, you must familiarize yourself with the QB operating environment.

Starting a Session

Boot the PC using the steps outlined by your instructor, or those found in the PC's Operations manual. Once the PC is operational, do the following:

1. Place the QuickBASIC program disk in the default drive and your data disk in the other drive.
2. At the DOS prompt, enter QBI if you are using the textbook version of QuickBASIC or QB if you are using the commercial version of QuickBASIC.

Several seconds will elapse while the QuickBASIC program is loaded from the disk into main memory. The red light on the disk drive turns on during this loading process. After the QuickBASIC program is loaded into main storage, it is automatically executed.

The first screen displayed by QuickBASIC includes a Welcome message in the middle of the screen. In the Welcome message, QuickBASIC directs you to press the **Esc key** to begin entering a program or press the **Enter key** to obtain help from the QB Advisor. The **QB Advisor** is an on-line help system that answers your questions about QuickBASIC as fast as you can click the mouse or press the **F1 key**. The QB Advisor is discussed in more detail later in this section.

The QB Screen

There are four parts to the QB screen—the view window, menu bar, immediate window, and the status line. These are shown in Figure 1-19.

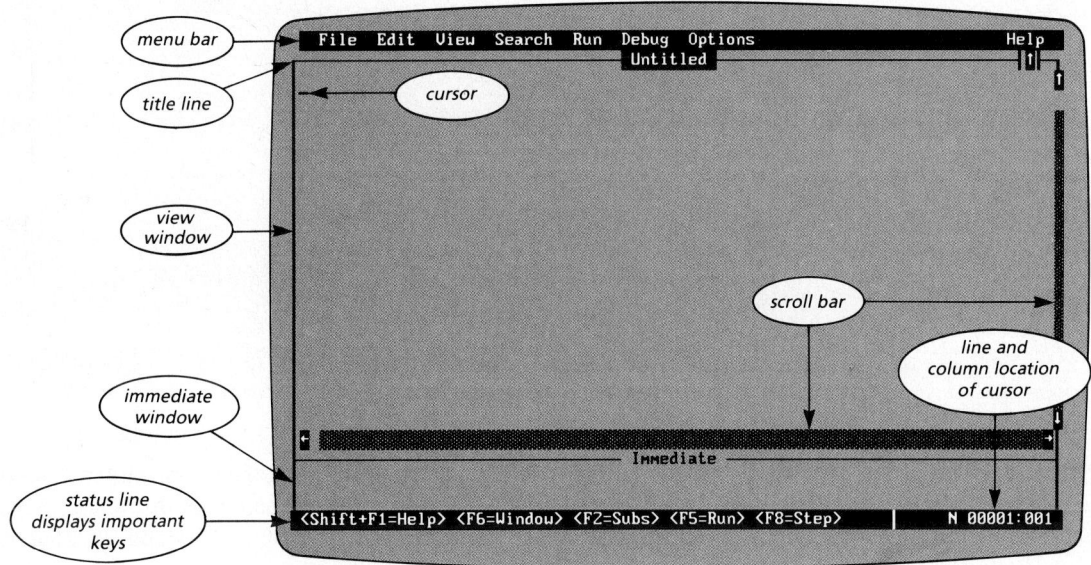

FIGURE 1-19 The QB (QuickBASIC) screen

View Window The **view window** is the largest part of the screen and the one that contains the cursor (Figure 1-19). In the view window you can enter, modify, and display programs. When the QuickBASIC program first executes, the view window is active. That is, if you start typing characters, they will appear on the first line of the view window. At the top of the view window is the title line. The **title line** displays the name of the current program. The program title is highlighted when the view window is active. The program is called "Untitled" until it is given a name. Program names will be discussed shortly.

Along the bottom and the right side of the view window are the **scroll bars**. If you have a mouse, you can move the pointer along the scroll bars and move the window in any direction to see code that does not appear in the view window.

Menu Bar   The **menu bar**, the line at the very top of the QB screen (Figure 1-19), displays a list of menu names. Each menu name has a corresponding menu of commands. These commands are useful when entering and modifying programs.

To activate the menu bar, press the **Alt key**. Next, type the first letter of the name of the menu you want to open. You can also select a menu by using the **Right Arrow key** or the **Left Arrow key** to highlight the menu name. With the menu name highlighted, press the **Enter key**. QuickBASIC immediately displays a *pull-down menu* that lists a series of commands. Figure 1-20 shows the **File menu**, which is superimposed over the display of Sample Program 1. To deactivate the menu bar or any menu and activate the view window, press the **Esc key**.

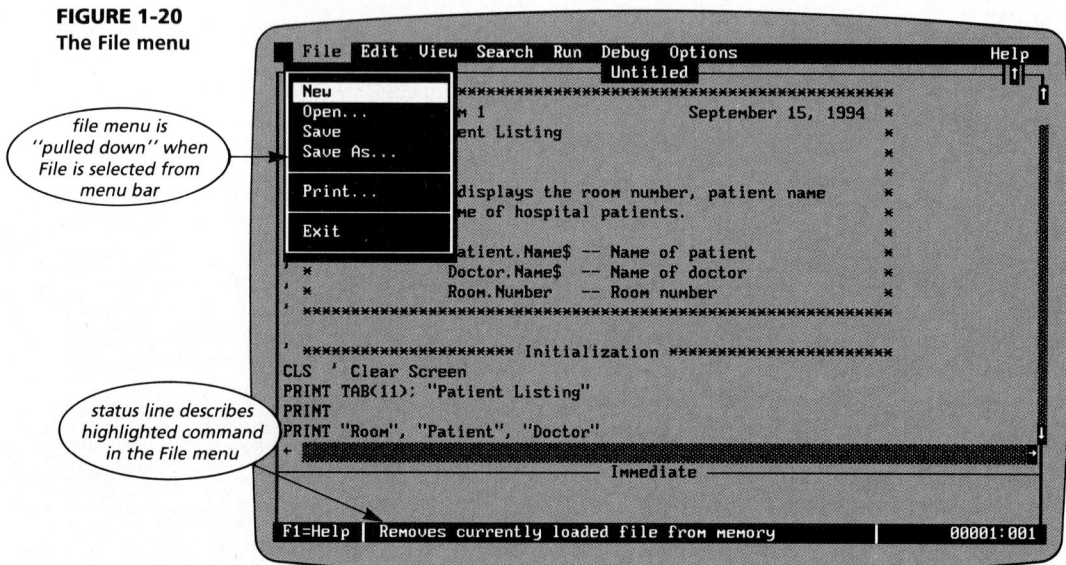

FIGURE 1-20
The File menu

file menu is "pulled down" when File is selected from menu bar

status line describes highlighted command in the File menu

If your PC has a mouse, move the mouse pointer to the desired menu name and click the mouse button. The **mouse pointer** is a character-size, rectangular box on the screen. The **mouse button** is the left button on the mouse. To deactivate the menu bar and reactivate the view window, move the mouse pointer to any part of the view window and click the mouse button.

Immediate Window   The narrow window below the view window is called the **immediate window**. The immediate window is used to execute statements as soon as they are entered. Statements entered in the immediate window are not part of the current program.

At any time, you can activate the immediate window by pressing the function key **F6**. This moves the cursor from the view window to the immediate window. QuickBASIC highlights the word Immediate. The function key **F6** is like a **toggle switch**. Press it once, and the cursor moves from the view window to the immediate window. Press it again, and the cursor moves back to the view window. You may use the immediate window as a calculator and debugging tool. For more information on the use of the immediate window, refer to the section titled Debugging Techniques in the Appendix.

If you have a mouse, move the pointer to the inactive window and click the mouse button.

Status Line   The line at the very bottom of the QB screen (Figure 1-19) is the **status line**. This line contains a list of the most often used function keys and the line and column location of the cursor on the screen. Keyboard indicators, such as C for Caps Lock and N for Num Lock, display immediately to the left of the cursor line and column location counter when these keys are engaged.

If the menu bar is active and one of the menus is selected, then the status line displays the function of the highlighted command in the menu (Figure 1-20).

Dialog Boxes

QuickBASIC uses **dialog boxes** to display messages and request information from you. For example, if you use a keyword for a variable name, such as PRINT LET instead of PRINT BET, QuickBASIC displays a dialog box when you move the cursor off the line containing the invalid variable name LET. You move the cursor off the line by pressing the **Enter key** or the **Up Arrow key** or **Down Arrow key**.

The dialog box shown in Figure 1-21 displays if you attempt to end the QuickBASIC session and return control to DOS without saving the latest changes made to the current program. Dialog boxes list acceptable user responses in buttons and text boxes. **Buttons** are labeled to indicate what they represent. **Text boxes** are used to enter information such as a file name.

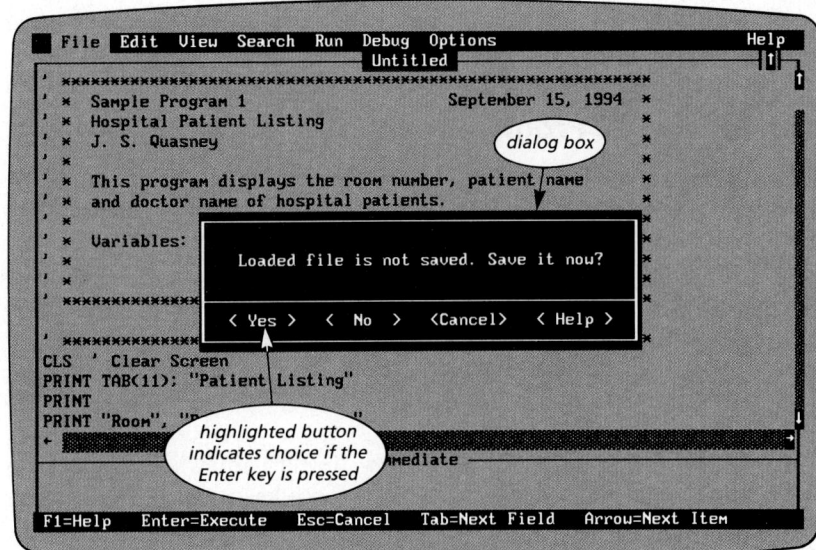

FIGURE 1-21
QuickBASIC displays a dialog box in the middle of the view window when it requires a response from the user before it can continue

In response to the message in the dialog box in Figure 1-21, you can use the **Tab key** or mouse pointer to select one of four buttons—Yes, No, Cancel, or Help. When you press the **Enter key**, the highlighted button, the one with the cursor, is selected. If your PC has a mouse, move the mouse pointer to the desired button or text box and click the mouse button.

Cursor Movement Keys

Several keys on the keyboard are used to move the cursor on the screen. These keys are called the **cursor movement keys**. The arrow keys are used to move the cursor in the windows, menu bar, or menu, one position at a time. Other keys such as the **Home key** and **End key** are used to move the cursor more than one position at a time. The cursor movement keys are summarized on the last page of the reference card at the back of this book.

Function Keys

IBM-type keyboards include a set of ten or twelve **function keys**, which are located to the far left side of the keyboard or along the top of the typewriter keys. The function keys are labeled **F1** through **F10** or **F12**. Pressing these keys instructs QuickBASIC to carry out various tasks. For example, if you press function key **F1** with the cursor in a keyword, QuickBASIC displays a help screen. If you press **Shift + F5**, QuickBASIC executes the current program in the view window. For a complete list of the function keys, refer to the last page of the reference card at the back of this book.

Terminating a QuickBASIC Session

To terminate your QuickBASIC session, press the **Alt key** to activate the menu bar. With the cursor on the word **File**, type the letter **F** or press the **Enter key** to display the **File menu** (Figure 1-20). Next, type the letter **X** for **Exit** or use the arrow keys to move the cursor to the word Exit and press the **Enter key**. Thus, the sequence of keystrokes **Alt**, **F**, **X** instructs the PC to return control to DOS. To quit QuickBASIC using a mouse, click on **File** in the menu bar and click on **Exit** in the **File menu**. The term *click on* means move the mouse pointer to the specified word and click the mouse button.

If you did not save the latest version of the current program, then the dialog box shown earlier in Figure 1-21 appears. QuickBASIC requests that you select one of the buttons before continuing. An alternative to selecting a button is to press the **Esc key**, which cancels the command and returns control to the view window.

When the DOS prompt appears, remove your diskettes from the disk drives. Turn the PC's power switch to Off. Turn the monitor power switch to Off. Finally, if you are using a printer, turn the power switch to Off.

Editing QuickBASIC Programs

QuickBASIC programs are entered one line at a time into the view window. The **Enter key** signals QuickBASIC that a line is complete. During the process of entering a program, you will quickly learn that it is easy to make keyboard errors and grammatical errors because of your inexperience with the QuickBASIC language and your unfamiliarity with the keyboard. Logical errors can also occur in a program if you have not considered all the details associated with the problem.

You can eliminate some of the errors if you carefully review your design and program before you enter it into the view window. Any remaining errors are resolved by editing the program. **Editing** is the process of entering and altering a program.

This section describes the most common types of editing. You will find the editing features of QuickBASIC to be both powerful and easy to use.

Deleting Previously Typed Characters   Use the arrow keys or mouse to position the cursor. Press the **Delete key** to delete the character under the cursor and the **Backspace key** to delete the character to the left of the cursor. To delete a series of adjacent characters in a line, position the cursor on the leftmost character to be deleted. Hold down one of the **Shift keys** and press the **Right Arrow key** until the characters to delete are highlighted. Press the **Delete key**.

If you have a mouse, select the adjacent characters to delete by moving the pointer from the first character to the last while holding down the mouse button.

Changing or Replacing Previously Typed Lines   Move the cursor to the character position where you want to make a change. Begin typing the new characters. QuickBASIC is by default in the insert mode. In the **insert mode**, the cursor is a blinking underline, and the character under the cursor and those to the right are *pushed* to the right as you enter new characters in the line. In the **overtype mode**, the cursor is a blinking box, and the character under the cursor is replaced by the one you type. Use the **Insert key** to toggle between the insert and overtype modes. As you enter new characters in this mode, they replace the old characters.

Adding New Lines   Press the **Enter key** to add a new or blank line. To add a new line above the current line, move the cursor to the first character and press the **Enter key**. To add a new line below the current line, move the cursor immediately to the right of the last character and press the **Enter key**.

You should only press the **Enter key** with the cursor at the beginning or end of a line. If you press the **Enter key** in the middle of a line, it is split. To join the split lines, press the **Backspace key** with the cursor on the first character of the second line.

Deleting A Series of Lines   Position the cursor at the beginning or end of the series of lines to delete. Hold down one of the **Shift keys** and press the **Up Arrow key** or **Down Arrow key** to highlight the series of lines. Press the **Delete key**.

If you have a mouse, highlight the lines to be deleted by holding down the mouse button and moving the pointer from the first character to the last in the series of lines. With the lines highlighted, press the **Delete key**.

Moving Text Moving text from one location to another in a program is called **cut and paste**. To cut and paste text, follow these steps:

1. Use the arrow keys or mouse to move to the beginning of the text you want.
2. Hold down one of the **Shift keys** and use the arrow keys to select the text. If you are using a mouse, click the mouse button and move the pointer to select the text.
3. Hold down one of the **Shift keys** and press the **Delete key** to *cut* the text. The deleted text is placed in the clipboard. The **clipboard** is a temporary storage area that contains the last text deleted through the use of the **Shift key** and **Delete key**.
4. Move the cursor to the new location using the arrow keys or the mouse. Hold down one of the **Shift keys** and press the **Insert key** to *paste* the text.

Copying Lines Copying text from one location to another in a program is called **pasting**. To paste text, follow these steps:

1. Use the arrow keys or mouse to move the cursor to the beginning of the text you want to paste.
2. Hold down one of the **Shift keys** and use the arrow keys to select the text. If you are using a mouse, hold down the mouse button and move the pointer to select the text.
3. Hold down the **Ctrl key** and press the **Insert key** to copy the text into the clipboard.
4. Move the cursor to the new location using the arrow keys or the mouse. Hold down one of the **Shift keys** and press the **Insert key** to *paste* the text.

You will find a summary of the editing keys on the last page of the reference card at the back of this book.

EXECUTING PROGRAMS AND HARD-COPY OUTPUT

The menu bar at the top of the screen contains eight menu names (Figure 1-19). Each menu name has a menu of commands. As we indicated earlier, to activate the menu bar, press the **Alt key**. Next, open a menu in one of two ways: (1) type the first letter in the menu name; or (2) use the **Left Arrow key** or **Right Arrow key** to move the cursor to the menu name and press the **Enter key**.

If you have a mouse, you can activate the menu bar and pull down a menu by moving the pointer to the menu name and clicking the mouse button.

The two most important menu names are Run and File. The **Run menu** is primarily used to execute the current program. The **File menu** contains several important commands. One in particular, the **Print** command, is used to print all or part of the current program.

Executing the Current Program

You execute (run) the current program by selecting the **Start** command in the **Run menu** (Figure 1-22 on the next page). The **Start** command can be selected in any one of the following three ways:

1. Press the **Alt key**, **R** for **Run**, and **S** for **Start**.

    or

2. Press **Shift + F5**.

    or

3. If you have a mouse, click on **Run** in the menu bar and click on **Start** in the Run menu.

If an error message displays within a dialog box when you execute the program, carefully read the message and then press the Enter key or click the OK button in the dialog box. QuickBASIC responds by highlighting the line with the error. Correct the line and execute the program again.

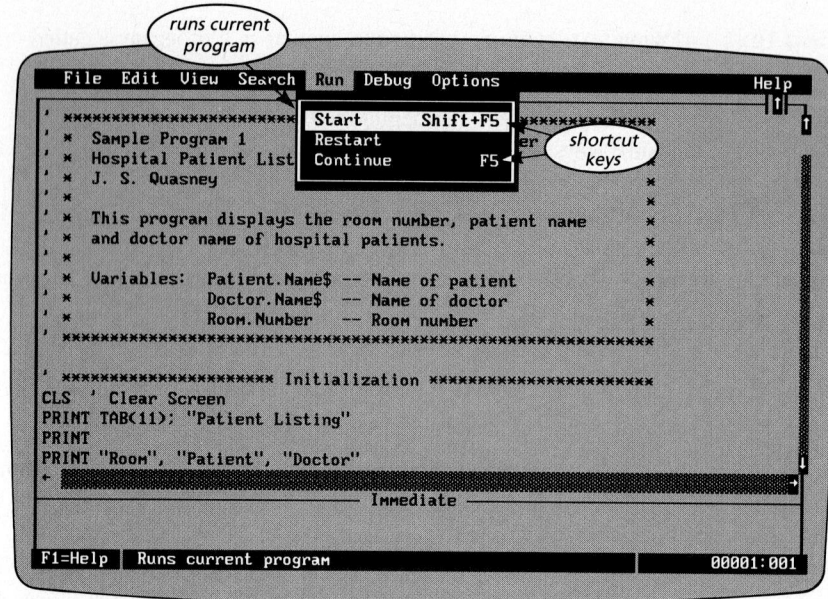

FIGURE 1-22
The Run menu

When the program first executes, QuickBASIC replaces the QB screen with the output screen. As we indicated earlier, the output screen shows the results due to the execution of the current program. Figure 1-23 shows the output screen for Sample Program 1. After you read the output results, you can redisplay the QB screen by pressing any key on the keyboard. This is indicated at the bottom of the output screen. To redisplay the output results, press the function key **F4**.

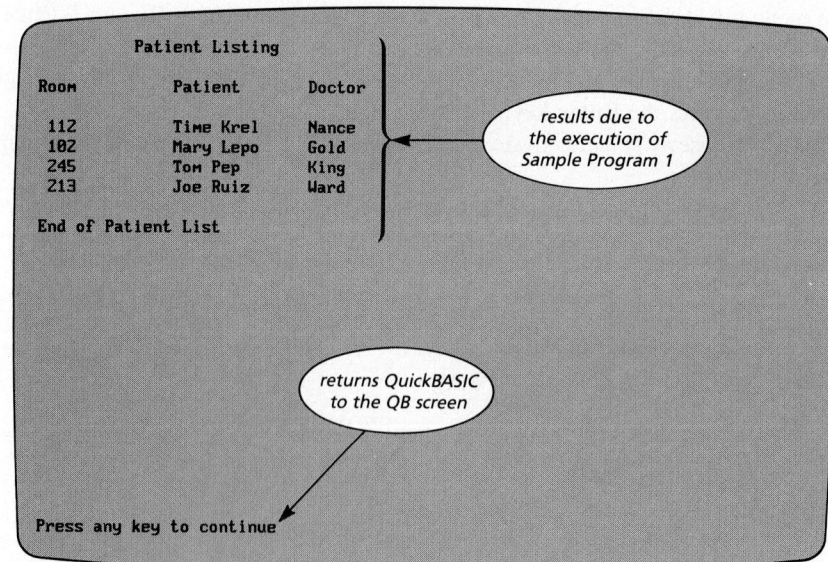

FIGURE 1-23
The output screen

Listing Program Lines to the Printer

Most programmers use a keyboard for input and a monitor (screen) for output. In many instances, it is desirable to list the program and the results on a printer. A listing of this type is called **hard-copy output**.

You can list all or part of the current program to the printer by using the **Print** command in the **File menu**. With the printer in the Ready mode, press the **Alt key** to activate the menu bar and type the letter **F** to pull down the **File menu** (Figure 1-24). Next, type the letter **P** for **Print** to print the current program. The three periods following the **Print** command mean a dialog box will appear requesting additional information. When the Print dialog box appears (Figure 1-25), make sure the bullet is next to the selection Current Module (Entire Program or Document if you are using the textbook version). Finally, press the **Enter key**.

If you have a mouse, click on **File**, click on **Print**, and click on **OK** when the Print dialog box appears.

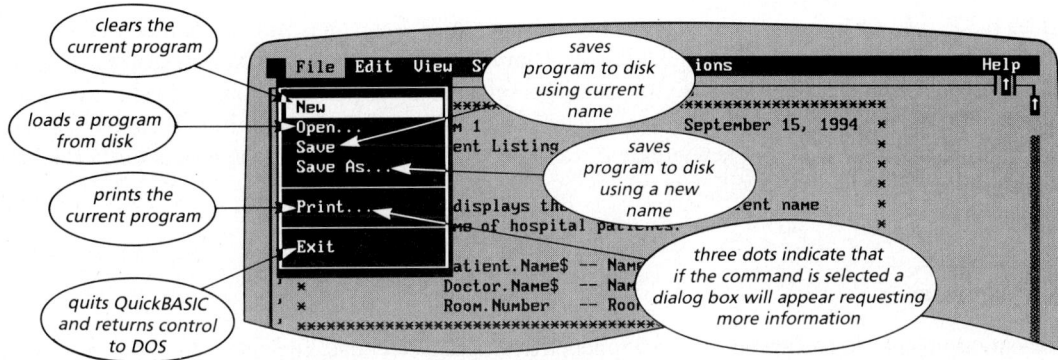

FIGURE 1-24 The File menu

Listing a Portion of the Program to the Printer

To print a portion of the current program, use the **Shift key** and arrow keys (or the mouse) to highlight the lines in the program you want to print. Next, follow the steps outlined in the previous paragraphs for printing the program. When the Print dialog box appears on the screen, the bullet should be in front of Selected Text (Figure 1-25). QuickBASIC automatically assigns the bullet to Selected Text when a series of lines is selected prior to issuing the **Print** command.

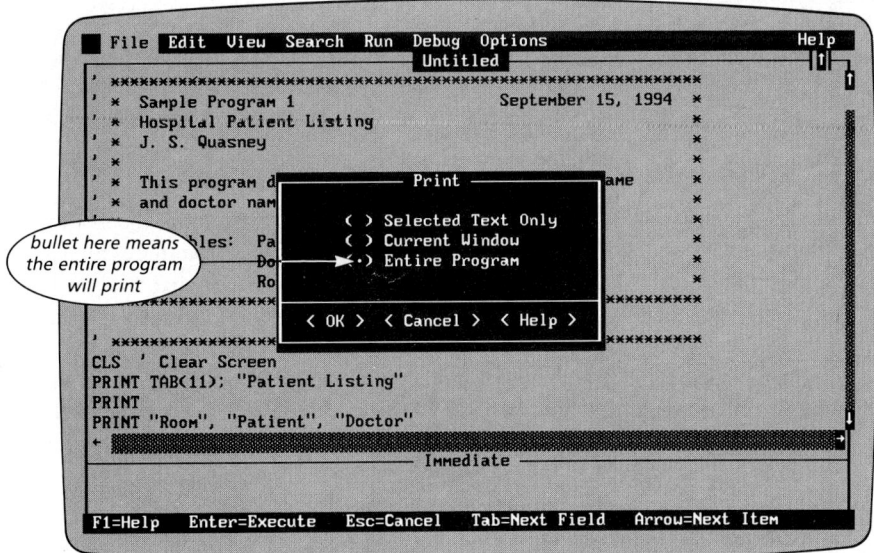

FIGURE 1-25 The dialog box for the Print command

Printing the Results on the Output Screen

To print a copy of the output screen, press **Print Screen** (**Shift + Prt Sc** on older PCs) while the output screen displays on the monitor. Later we discuss the LPRINT statement as an alternative means to generating hard-copy output.

SAVING, LOADING, AND ERASING PROGRAMS

Besides the **Print** and **Exit** commands, there are four additional commands in the **File menu** (Figure 1-24) that are essential for your first session with QuickBASIC—**Save**, **Save As**, **Open**, and **New**. The **Save** and **Save As** commands allow you to store the current program to disk. Later, you use the **Open** command to load the program from disk into main storage to make it the current one. The **New** command erases the current program from main memory. It clears the view window and indicates the beginning of a new program. Before we discuss these three commands further, it is important that you understand the concept of a file specification.

File Specifications

A **file specification**, also called a **filespec**, is used to identify programs and data files placed in auxiliary storage. A filespec is made up of a device name, file name, and extension.

```
              filespec
         ⎴⎴⎴⎴⎴⎴⎴⎴⎴⎴⎴⎴⎴⎴⎴⎴⎴
    device name:file name.extension
```

The **device name** refers to the disk drive. If no device is specified, then the filespec refers to the default drive of the PC. If a device name is included in the filespec, then it must be followed by a colon.

File names can be from 1 to 8 characters in length. Valid characters are uppercase or lowercase A–Z, 0–9, and certain special characters ($ & # @ ! % " ( ) - { } _ / \). If an extension is used, then the file name must be followed by a period.

An **extension** that is up to three characters in length may be used to classify a file. Valid characters are the same as for a file name. With QuickBASIC, the default extension is bas. That is, when you use a command that requires a filespec, QuickBASIC will automatically append an extension of bas if one is not included.

Examples of valid filespecs include b:payroll, b:lab2-1, PAYROLL.BAS, Accounts, and S123. The first two examples reference files on drive B. The latter three examples reference files on the default drive.

Saving the Current Program to Disk

When you enter a program through the keyboard, it is stored in main memory (RAM), and it displays in the view window. When you quit QuickBASIC or turn the computer off, the current program disappears from the screen and, more importantly, from main memory. To save a program to disk for later use, use the **Save** or **Save As** command in the **File menu**. Use the **Save** command to save the program under the same name. Use the **Save As** command to save the program under a new name. Because this is the first time we are saving the program, we will use the **Save As** command.

To select the **Save As** command, press the **Alt key** to activate the menu bar. Type the letter **F** to pull down the **File menu** (Figure 1-24). Type **A** for **Save As**. Here again, the three periods following the **Save As** command in the File menu mean QuickBASIC requires additional information. In this case QuickBASIC needs to know the filespec.

When the Save As dialog box appears (Figure 1-25), enter the file name and press the **Enter key**. In Figure 1-26, we entered the file name prg-1. QuickBASIC stores the current program using the filespec a:prg-1.bas. Notice in Figure 1-26 that the default drive (A:\) is specified below the file name box.

The **dirs/drives box** in the Save As dialog box includes a list of the disk drives and any subdirectories that are part of the current default drive. You may use the **Tab key** or mouse to activate this box and select a different default drive.

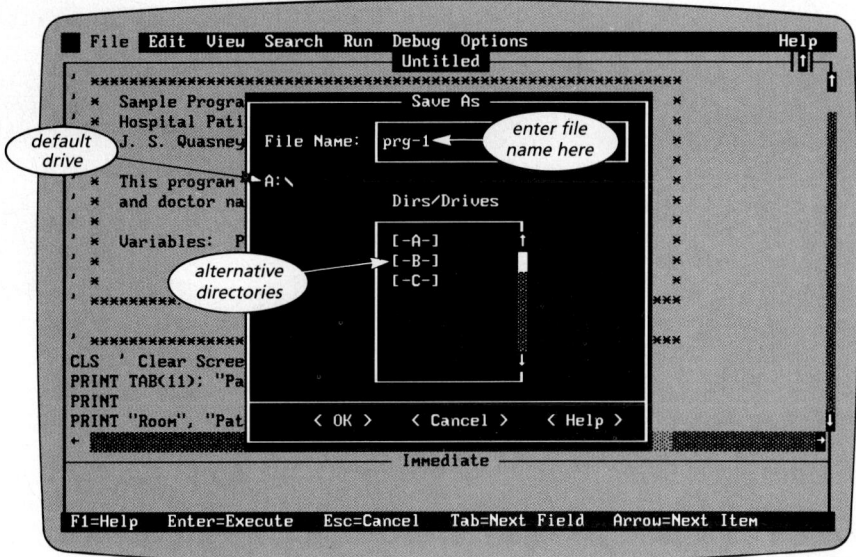

FIGURE 1-26 The dialog box for the Save As command

If you loaded the current program from disk or saved the program earlier, use the **Save** command to save the program under its current name.

To save the current program using a mouse, click on **File** and click on **Save** or **Save As**. If you click on **Save As**, enter the name in the file name box and click on the **OK** button.

Loading a Program from Disk

To load a program stored on disk into main storage, use the **Open** command in the **File menu** (Figure 1-24). This command causes the dialog box shown on the next page in Figure 1-27 to display. In the middle of the dialog box, QuickBASIC displays the files box. The **files box** lists the file names on the default drive that have an extension of bas. The current default drive displays just above the files box. To display any other directory on your PC, enter the disk drive (or path) in the file name box or select one from the dirs/drive box and press the **Enter key**.

In the file name box, enter the name of the program you want to load from auxiliary storage into main storage. In Figure 1-27 we entered the file name prg-1. Enter the file name by typing it on the keyboard or use the **Tab key** and arrow keys to select the file name from the file names box. Each time you press an arrow key, the name of the program under the cursor displays in the file names box. To complete the command, press the **Enter key**.

If you did not save the current program before attempting to load a new one, QuickBASIC will give you the opportunity to save it before it loads the new program into main storage.

To load a program from disk using the mouse, click on **File** and click on **Open**. Double-click on the name of the program in the files box.

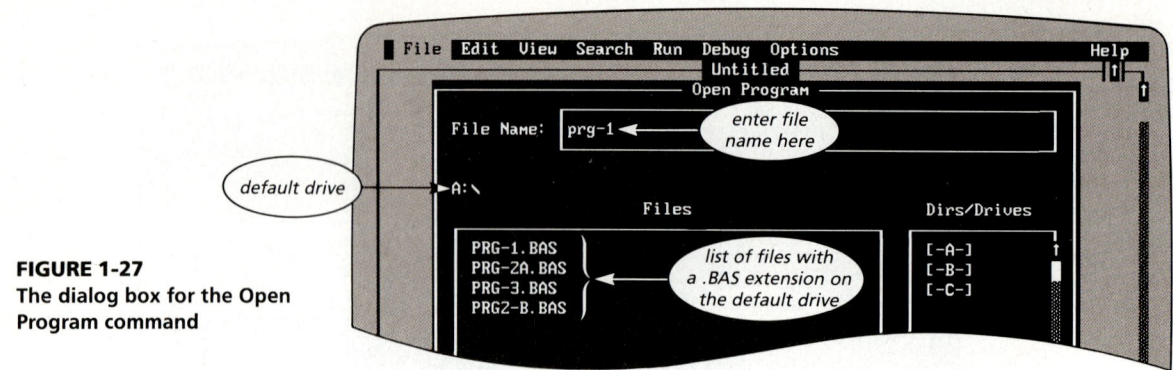

FIGURE 1-27
The dialog box for the Open Program command

Starting a New Program

The **New** command in the **File menu** (Figure 1-24) instructs QuickBASIC to erase the current program from main storage. This also clears the view window. Use this command when you are finished with the current program and wish to start a new one from scratch. Notice that it is not necessary to clear the current program if you are loading a program from disk. The **Open** command clears main storage before it loads the new program.

THE QB ADVISOR ON-LINE HELP SYSTEM

The QB Advisor is a fully integrated, on-line help system with instant access to any QuickBASIC question. You can request immediate help when you first enter QuickBASIC by pressing the **Enter key** rather than the **Esc key**. Thereafter, at any time while you are using QuickBASIC, you can interact with the QB Advisor and display help screens on any QuickBASIC topic using the keys described on the last page of the reference card at the back of this book. For example, if you press **Shift + F1**, the initial help screen shown in Figure 1-28 displays. To return to the view window, press the **Esc key**. If you press **F1**, QuickBASIC displays help for the topic in which the cursor is positioned. The QB Advisor is literally a complete reference manual at your fingertips. The best way to familiarize yourself with the QB Advisor is to use it.

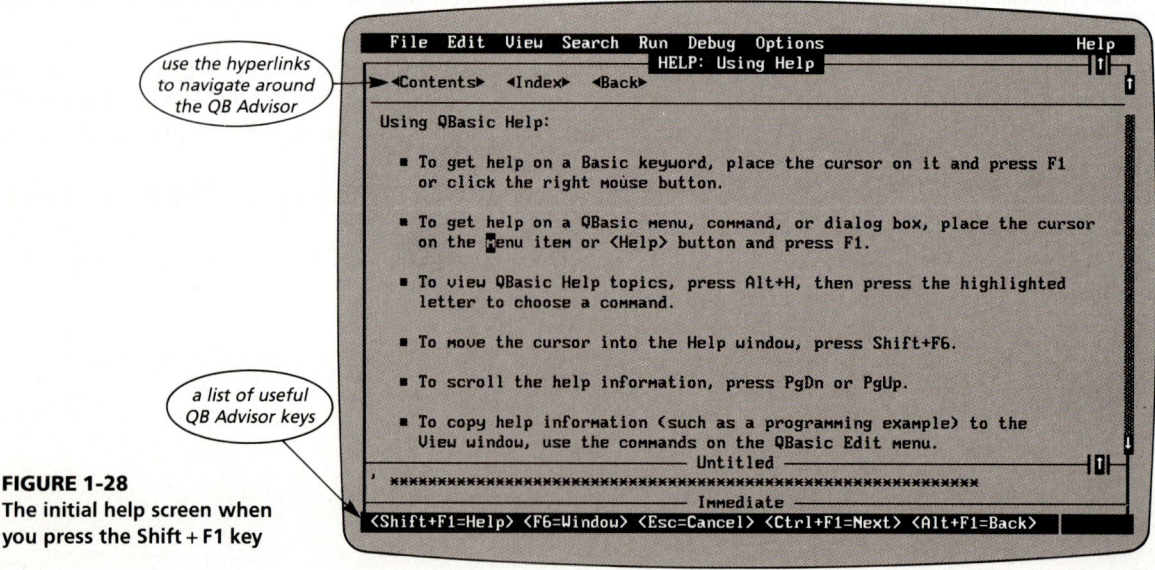

FIGURE 1-28
The initial help screen when you press the Shift + F1 key

TRY IT YOURSELF EXERCISES

1. Identify the 8 major components of the QB screen shown below.

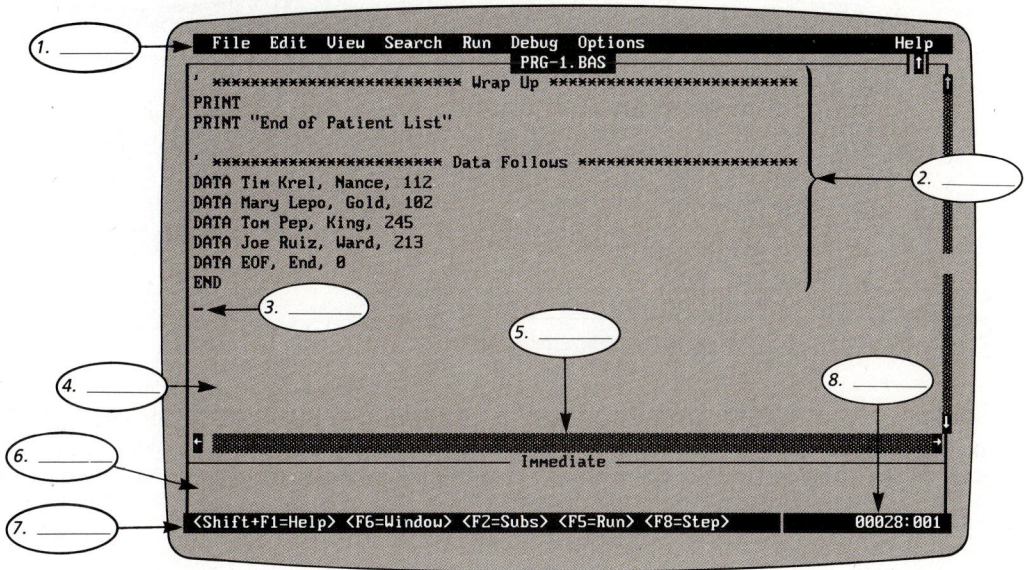

2. List the function of the following keys when a dialog box is active.
   a. Esc
   b. Tab
   c. Enter

3. List the function of the following keys when the view window is active.
   a. Alt
   b. Shift + Delete
   c. Enter
   d. Home
   e. End
   f. Ctrl + Home
   g. Ctrl + Q, X
   h. Shift + F5
   i. F4
   j. F6
   k. Backspace
   l. Delete
   m. Insert
   n. Shift + Insert
   o. Page Up

STUDENT ASSIGNMENTS

STUDENT ASSIGNMENT 1: Personnel Report

Instructions: Design and code a program using QuickBASIC to produce the personnel listing as shown on the next page under OUTPUT. The listing includes the employee name, department number, and pay rate for each employee shown under INPUT. Submit a program flowchart, listing of the program, and a listing of the output results. To obtain a hard copy of the output results, use the Print Screen key.

INPUT: Use the following sample data:

NAME	DEPT. NO.	PAY RATE
Sue Long	10	4.25
Chin Song	12	5.15
Mary Lopez	14	4.75
Jan Honig	14	3.85
EOF	99	9.99

Student Assignment 1 (continued)

OUTPUT: The following results are displayed:

```
            Personnel Report

Dept.           Name            Pay Rate

 10             Sue Long          4.25
 12             Chin Song         5.15
 14             Mary Lopez        4.75
 14             Jan Honig         3.85

End of Personnel Report
```

STUDENT ASSIGNMENT 2: Club Membership Report

Instructions: Design and code a program using QuickBASIC to produce the club membership listing shown under OUTPUT. The listing includes a name, birth date, and age for each member shown under INPUT. Submit a program flowchart, listing of the program, and a listing of the output results. To obtain a hard copy of the output results, use the Print Screen key.

INPUT: Use the following sample data:

BIRTH DATE	AGE	NAME
December 7	41	John Sutherlin
March 16	38	Jim Wachtel
June 9	27	Mary Hathaway
August 6	25	Louise Scott
EOF	99	End

OUTPUT: The following results are displayed:

```
            Membership Listing
Name:           John Sutherlin
Birth Date:     December 7
Age:                 41

Name:           Jim Wachtel
Birth Date:     March 16
Age:                 38

Name:           Mary Hathaway
Birth Date:     June 9
Age:                 27

Name:           Louise Scott
Birth Date:     August 6
Age:                 25

End of Membership Listing
```

PROJECT 2

Basic Arithmetic Operations and Accumulating Totals

Many applications require that arithmetic operations be performed on the input data to produce the required output. QuickBASIC includes the following basic arithmetic operators: addition (+), subtraction (-), multiplication (*), division (/), and raising a value to a power (^). These operators are similar to those used in ordinary mathematics. The operators and an example of their use in a LET statement are illustrated in Figure 2-1.

MATHEMATICAL OPERATION	BASIC ARITHMETIC OPERATOR	EXAMPLE
Addition	+	LET Total = Sub1 + Sub2
Subtraction	-	LET Profit = Price - 5.95
Multiplication	*	LET Gross = Hours * Rate
Division	/	LET Amount = Cost / 5
Raising to a Power	^	LET Discount = Rate ^ 2

FIGURE 2-1 QuickBASIC arithmetic operators

THE LET STATEMENT

The LET statement is used to assign a variable a value. As shown in Figure 2-2, the first entry in a LET statement is the keyword LET. The keyword LET is followed by a variable name, an equal sign, and an expression.

> LET numeric variable = numeric expression
>
> or
>
> LET string variable = string expression

FIGURE 2-2 The general form of the LET statement

Expressions

An **expression** can be numeric or string. A **numeric expression** consists of one or more numeric constants, numeric variables, and numeric function references, all of which are separated from each other by parentheses and arithmetic operators. A **string expression** consists of one or more string constants, string variables, and string functions separated by the concatenation operator (+), which combines two strings into one. A numeric expression can only be assigned to a numeric variable. A string expression can only be assigned to a string variable.

Figure 2-3 illustrates numeric expressions in LET statements. Figure 2-4 illustrates string expressions in LET statements.

VALUE OF	LET STATEMENT	RESULTS IN
A = 15 B = 10	LET F = A + B - 10	F = 15
J = 32 H = 16	LET L = J * 2 - H	L = 48
P = 14 Y = 7	LET Q = P / Y	Q = 2
W = 4 S = 6	LET T = 6 * (S - W)	T = 12

FIGURE 2-3 Numeric expressions in LET statements

VALUE OF	LET STATEMENT	RESULTS IN
X$ = ABC	LET W$ = "DEF" + X$	W$ = DEFABC
F$ = WATER G$ = WINE	LET A$ = F$ + " INTO " + G$	A$ = WATER INTO WINE
S$ = "TOP"	LET S$ = S$ + "IT"	S$ = TOPIT

FIGURE 2-4 String expressions in LET statements

From the examples in Figures 2-3 and 2-4 you can see that when performing arithmetic operations, the calculations are specified to the right of the equal sign. The variable assigned the result of the expression is placed to the left side of the equal sign.

Order of Operations

When multiple arithmetic operations are included in a LET statement, the **order of operations** follows the normal algebraic rules. That is, the operations are completed in the following order:

- First, exponentiation is performed from left to right.
- Next, multiplication and division are performed from left to right.
- Finally, addition and subtraction are performed from left to right.

For example, the expression 27 / 3 ^ 2 + 4 * 3 is evaluated as follows:

$$
\begin{align*}
27 / 3 \wedge 2 + 4 * 3 &= 27 / 9 + 4 * 3 \\
&= 3 + 4 * 3 \\
&= 3 + 12 \\
&= 15
\end{align*}
$$

If you had trouble following the logic behind this evaluation, use the following technique. Whenever a numeric expression is to be evaluated, *scan* from left to right three different times. On the first scan, every time you encounter an ^ operator, you perform exponentiation. In this example, 3 is raised to the power of 2, yielding 9.

On the second scan, moving from left to right again, every time you encounter the operators * and /, perform multiplication and division. Hence, 27 is divided by 9, yielding 3, and 4 and 3 are multiplied, yielding 12.

On the third scan, moving again from left to right, every time you detect the operators + and –, perform addition and subtraction. In this example, 3 and 12 are added to form 15. Thus, the following LET statement

    LET Amount = 27 / 3 ^ 2 + 4 * 3

assigns 15 to the variable Amount.

The expression below yields the value of –19.37, as follows:

$$\begin{aligned}4 - 3 * 4 / 10 \wedge 2 + 5 / 4 * 3 - 3 \wedge 3 &= 4 - 3 * 4 / 100 + 5 / 4 * 3 - 27 \\ &= 4 - 0.12 + 3.75 - 27 \\ &= -19.37\end{aligned}$$

Hence, the following LET statement

    LET Total = 4 - 3 * 4 / 10 ^ 2 + 5 / 4 * 3 - 3 ^ 3

assigns –19.37 to the variable Total.

The Use of Parentheses in an Expression

Parentheses may be used to change the order of operations. In QuickBASIC, parentheses are normally used to avoid ambiguity and to group terms in a numeric expression; they do not imply multiplication. When parentheses are inserted into an expression, the part of the expression within the parentheses is evaluated first, and then the remaining expression is evaluated according to the order of operations.

If the first example contained parentheses, as does (27 / 3) ^ 2 + 4 * 3, then it would be evaluated in the following manner:

$$\begin{aligned}(27 / 3) \wedge 2 + 4 * 3 &= 9 \wedge 2 + 4 * 3 \\ &= 81 + 4 * 3 \\ &= 81 + 12 \\ &= 93\end{aligned}$$

Use parentheses freely when you are in doubt as to the formation and evaluation of a numeric expression. For example, if you want to have the PC divide 9 * Tax by 3 ^ Payment, the expression may correctly be written as 9 * Tax / 3 ^ Payment, but you may also write it as (9 * Tax) / (3 ^ Payment) and feel more certain of the result.

For more complex expressions, QuickBASIC allows parentheses to be contained within other parentheses. When this occurs, the parentheses are said to be **nested**. In this case, QuickBASIC evaluates the innermost parenthetical expression first and then goes on to the outermost parenthetical expression. Thus, (27 / 3) ^ 2 + (5 * (7 + 3)) is broken down in the following manner:

$$\begin{aligned}(27 / 3) \wedge 2 + (5 * (7 + 3)) &= 9 \wedge 2 + (5 * (7 + 3)) \\ &= 81 + (5 * 10) \\ &= 81 + 50 \\ &= 131\end{aligned}$$

SAMPLE PROGRAM 2 — AUTO EXPENSE REPORT

The following sample program generates an auto expense report. The program performs calculations and accumulates totals using LET statements. Input consists of auto expense records that contain an employee name, the license number of the employee's car, the beginning mileage for the employee's car, and the ending mileage for the car.

The auto expense file that will be processed by the sample program is shown in Figure 2-5.

NAME	LICENSE	BEGINNING MILEAGE	ENDING MILEAGE
T. Rowe	HRT-111	19,100	19,224
R. Lopez	GLD-913	21,221	21,332
C. Deck	LIV-193	10,001	10,206
B. Alek	ZRT-904	15,957	16,419
EOF	End	0	0

FIGURE 2-5 The employee auto expense file for Sample Program 2

The output generated by Sample Program 2 is a report displayed on the screen. The report contains the employee name, the automobile license number, the total mileage, and the expense. The total mileage is calculated by subtracting the beginning mileage from the ending mileage. The expense is calculated by multiplying the mileage by twenty-five cents.

The report contains both report headings and column headings. After all records have been processed, the total number of employees and total auto expenses are displayed. In addition, the average expense per employee is calculated by dividing the total auto expense by the total number of employees. The average expense per employee is then displayed followed by an end-of-report message. The format of the output is shown in Figure 2-6.

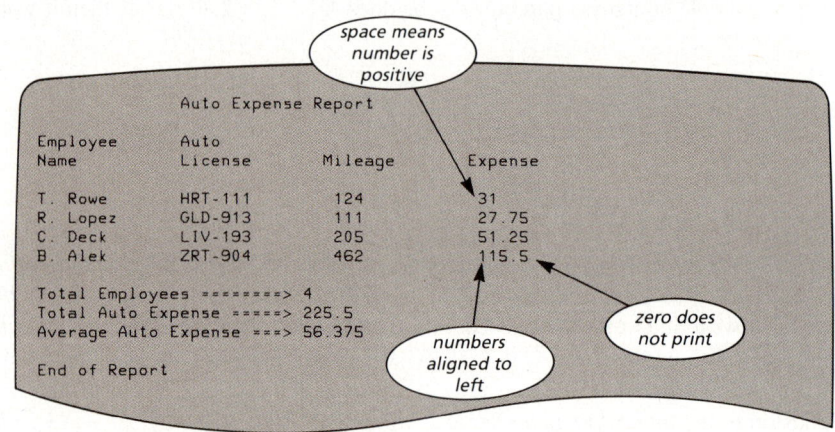

FIGURE 2-6
The report for Sample Program 2

When using the PRINT statement, nonsignificant zeros to the right of a decimal point are not printed. For example, Alek's expense displays as 115.5 rather than 115.50. In addition, when printing decimal numbers, the numbers are left aligned under the column heading rather than right aligned. The single space displayed to the left of each number means that the number is positive. These factors are illustrated in the output in Figure 2-6. Later in this section, we discuss the PRINT USING statement, which allows you to adjust the values displayed to include nonsignificant zeros and right-align numeric values under the column headings.

Accumulators

Most programs require **accumulators**, which are used to develop totals. Accumulators are initialized to a value of zero in the Initialization module, then incremented within the loop in the Process File module, and finally manipulated or displayed in the Wrap-Up module. Although QuickBASIC automatically initializes numeric variables to zero, good programming practice demands that this be done in the program. There are two types of accumulators: counters and running totals.

A **counter** is an accumulator that is used to count the number of times some action or event is performed. For example, appropriately placed within a loop, the statement

    LET Total.Employees = Total.Employees + 1

causes the counter Total.Employees to increment by 1 each time a record is read. Associated with a counter is a statement placed in the Initialization module which initializes the counter to some value. In most cases the counter is initialized to zero.

A **running total** is an accumulator that is used to sum the different values that a variable is assigned during the execution of a program. For example, appropriately placed within a loop, the statement

    LET Total.Expense = Total.Expense + Auto.Expense

causes Total.Expense to increase by the value of Auto.Expense. Total.Expense is called a running total. If a program is processing an employee file and the variable Auto.Expense is assigned the employee's auto expense each time a record is read, then variable Total.Expense represents the running total of the auto expense of all the employees in the file. As with a counter, a running total must be initialized to some predetermined value, such as zero, in the Initialization module.

Program Flowchart

The flowchart for the sample program, which produces an auto expense report and accumulates and prints final totals, is illustrated in Figure 2-7.

Prior to the loop in the flowchart, the accumulators are initialized, the headings are displayed, and the first employee record is read. Within the loop, the employee counter is incremented, the beginning mileage is subtracted from the ending mileage, giving the mileage driven by the employee. The auto expense is then calculated by multiplying the mileage driven times the auto cost per mile (.25). The auto expense is then added to the total auto expense accumulator. Next, a line of information is displayed. At the bottom of the loop another record is read. Control then returns to the top of the loop to determine if the trailer record was read. This looping process continues until there are no more auto expense records.

When the trailer record is read, the total number of employees and total auto expenses are displayed. Next, the total auto expense is divided by the total number of employees to give the average auto expense. Finally, the average and an end-of-report message are displayed.

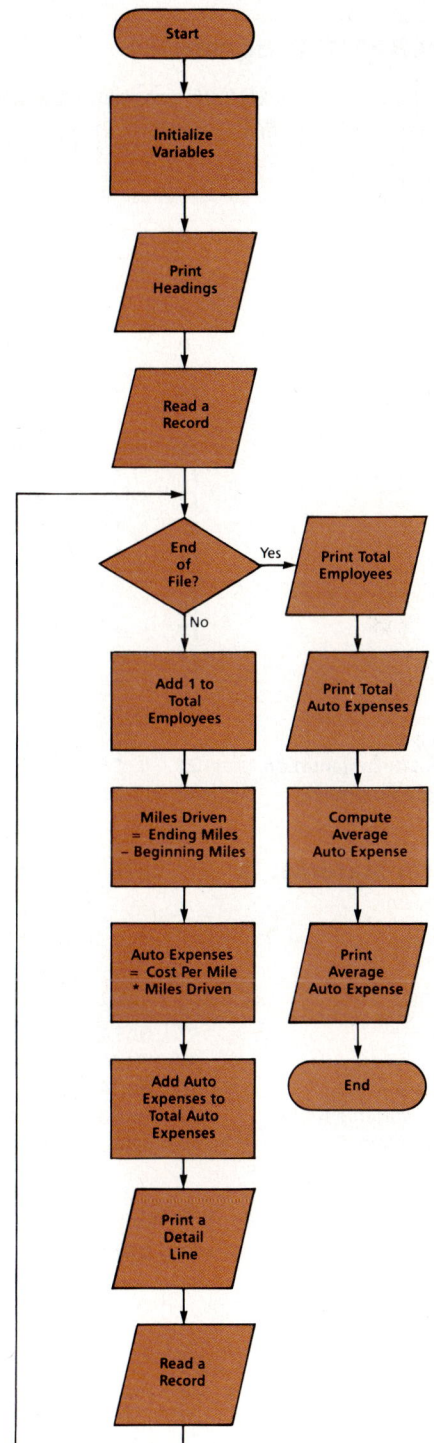

FIGURE 2-7 The flowchart for Sample Program 2

The QuickBASIC Program

The first section of the QuickBASIC program includes the initial documentation. As shown in Figure 2-8, the documentation is similar to Sample Program 1.

```
 1  ' ****************************************************************
 2  ' *  Sample Program 2                          September 15, 1994 *
 3  ' *  Auto Expense Report                                          *
 4  ' *  J. S. Quasney                                                *
 5  ' *                                                               *
 6  ' *  This program displays an auto expense report.  Mileage       *
 7  ' *  expense is calculated on the basis of 25 cents per mile.     *
 8  ' *  As part of the Wrap-Up module, the total number of           *
 9  ' *  employees, total auto expense, and the average expense       *
10  ' *  per employee are displayed.                                  *
11  ' *                                                               *
12  ' *  Variables:  Emp.Name$        -- Name of employee             *
13  ' *              License$         -- Auto license number          *
14  ' *              Begin.Mileage    -- Beginning mileage             *
15  ' *              End.Mileage      -- Ending mileage                *
16  ' *              Miles.Driven     -- Miles driven                  *
17  ' *              Cost.Per.Mile    -- Auto cost per mile            *
18  ' *              Auto.Expense     -- Auto expense                  *
19  ' *              Total.Employees  -- Number of employees           *
20  ' *              Total.Expense    -- Total auto expense            *
21  ' *              Average.Expense  -- Average auto expense          *
22  ' ****************************************************************
23
```

FIGURE 2-8 The initial documentation for Sample Program 2

The DATA Statements The DATA statements in Figure 2-9 correspond to the employee auto expense file described in Figure 2-5.

```
55  ' ********************* Data Follows *********************
56  DATA T. Rowe, HRT-111, 19100, 19224
57  DATA R. Lopez, GLD-913, 21221, 21332
58  DATA C. Deck, LIV-193, 10001, 10206
59  DATA B. Alek, ZRT-904, 15957, 16419
60  DATA EOF, End, 0, 0
61  END
```

FIGURE 2-9 The DATA statements for Sample Program 2

Initialization Module Following the initial program documentation shown in Figure 2-8, the Initialization module initializes the accumulators to zero and displays the report title and column headings. The Initialization module is shown in Figure 2-10.

```
24  ' ********************* Initialization *********************
25  CLS   ' Clear Screen
26  LET Total.Employees = 0
27  LET Total.Expense = 0
28  LET Cost.Per.Mile = .25
29  PRINT TAB(15); "Auto Expense Report"
30  PRINT
31  PRINT "Employee", "Auto"
32  PRINT "Name", "License", "Mileage", "Expense"
33  PRINT
34
```

FIGURE 2-10 The Initialization module for Sample Program 2

Lines 26 and 27 initialize the employee counter (Total.Employees) and total expense running total (Total.Expense) to zero. When these two LET statements are executed, the zeros on the right side of the equal sign are assigned to the variables Total.Employee and Total.Expense. Counters and running totals should always be set to zero at the beginning of a program.

When the LET statement in line 28 is executed, the constant 0.25 on the right side of the equal sign is assigned to Cost.Per.Mile. This variable can then be used later to compute the auto expense. The purpose of assigning 0.25 to a variable is to facilitate future changes to the program. For example, if the auto cost per mile were changed from 0.25 to 0.28, the constant value in line 28 could be changed to 0.28.

Lines 29 through 33 display the report title and column headings. The PRINT statement in line 29 displays the report title beginning in column 15. Line 30 skips a line in the report. Lines 31 and 32 display the column headings. Finally, line 33 skips a line in the report to leave space between the column headings and the first record displayed.

The Process File Module The statements that make up the Process File module for Sample Program 2 are illustrated in Figure 2-11.

```
35  ' ********************* Process File *********************
36  READ Emp.Name$, License$, Begin.Mileage, End.Mileage
37  DO WHILE Emp.Name$ <> "EOF"
38     LET Total.Employees = Total.Employees + 1
39     LET Miles.Driven = End.Mileage - Begin.Mileage
40     LET Auto.Expense = Cost.Per.Mile * Miles.Driven
41     LET Total.Expense = Total.Expense + Auto.Expense
42     PRINT Emp.Name$, License$, Miles.Driven, Auto.Expense
43     READ Emp.Name$, License$, Begin.Mileage, End.Mileage
44  LOOP
45
```

FIGURE 2-11
The Process File module for Sample Program 2

The READ statement in line 36 assigns the data in the first DATA statement (line 56 in Figure 2-9) to Emp.Name$, License$, Begin.Mileage, and End.Mileage. Next, the DO WHILE statement in line 37 tests to see if Emp.Name$ is not equal to EOF. Since Emp.Name$ does not equal EOF, control enters the loop.

The LET statement in line 38 increments the employee counter (Total.Employees). Each time this statement is executed, Total.Employees is incremented by 1. Since Total.Employees was initially set to zero (line 26 in Figure 2-10), it is equal to 1 after line 38 is executed the first time. After the statement is executed a second time, the value of Total.Employees is equal to 2. This counting continues each time through the loop. When the end-of-file is detected, the value of Total.Employees is equal to the number of records processed.

The LET statement in line 39 calculates the mileage the automobile was driven (Miles.Driven) by the employee being processed by subtracting the beginning mileage (Begin.Mileage) from the ending mileage (End.Mileage). Line 40 computes the auto expense (Auto.Expense) by multiplying the miles the automobile was driven (Miles.Driven) by the cost per mile (Cost.Per.Mile). The value 0.25 was assigned to Cost.Per.Mile in line 28 of the Initialization module (Figure 2-10).

The LET statement in line 41 adds the auto expense (Auto.Expense) to the accumulator Total.Expense. Here again, the variable Total.Expense was initialized to zero. When line 41 is executed the first time, the auto expense is added to the value zero. Hence, Auto.Expense is equal to the T. Rowe's auto expense after the first pass on the loop. When line 41 is executed the second time, the auto expense for R. Lopez is added to the auto expense for T. Rowe. Thus, the effect of this LET statement is to accumulate the auto expenses for all the employees.

The PRINT statement in line 42 displays the employee name, license number, miles driven, and the auto expense. Next, the READ statement in line 43 assigns the data for the second employee to Emp.Name$, License$, Begin.Mileage, and End.Mileage. The LOOP statement in line 44 transfers control back up to the DO WHILE statement in line 37. Notice that statements 38 through 43 are indented three spaces to illuminate the statements within the Do loop. The looping process continues until the trailer record is read, at which time control is transferred to the Wrap-Up module (line 47).

End-of-File Processing After all the records are processed, control transfers to the PRINT statement in line 47 (Figure 2-12), which causes the PC to skip a line in the report. The next PRINT statement displays the total number of employees (Total.Employees). Notice the manner in which the PRINT statement is written to display both a constant and a variable. The phrase Total Employees ========> is enclosed within quotation marks ("). The right quotation is followed by a semicolon (;). A semicolon causes the PC to display the value of Total.Employees immediately after the phrase rather than in the next print zone. Recall that if the numeric value is positive, a blank space appears before the numeric value.

After line 49 displays the total expenses, line 50 computes the average expense which is displayed by line 51. Line 52 skips a line and line 53 displays an end-of-report message. Finally, line 61 (Figure 2-9) terminates execution of the program.

FIGURE 2-12
The Wrap-Up module for Sample Program 2

```
46  ' ************************ Wrap-Up ************************
47  PRINT
48  PRINT "Total Employees ========>"; Total.Employees
49  PRINT "Total Auto Expense =====>"; Total.Expense
50  LET Average.Expense = Total.Expense / Total.Employees
51  PRINT "Average Auto Expense ===>"; Average.Expense
52  PRINT
53  PRINT "End of Report"
54
```

The Complete QuickBASIC Program The complete Sample Program 2 is illustrated in Figure 2-13. The report generated by Sample Program 2 is shown in Figure 2-14.

FIGURE 2-13
Sample Program 2

```
1   ' ****************************************************************
2   ' *   Sample Program 2                         September 15, 1994 *
3   ' *   Auto Expense Report                                         *
4   ' *   J. S. Quasney                                               *
5   ' *                                                               *
6   ' *   This program displays an auto expense report.  Mileage     *
7   ' *   expense is calculated on the basis of 25 cents per mile.   *
8   ' *   As part of the Wrap-Up module, the total number of         *
9   ' *   employees, total auto expense, and the average expense     *
10  ' *   per employee are displayed.                                 *
11  ' *                                                               *
12  ' *   Variables:  Emp.Name$        -- Name of employee            *
13  ' *               License$         -- Auto license number         *
14  ' *               Begin.Mileage    -- Beginning mileage           *
15  ' *               End.Mileage      -- Ending mileage              *
16  ' *               Miles.Driven     -- Miles driven                *
17  ' *               Cost.Per.Mile    -- Auto cost per mile          *
18  ' *               Auto.Expense     -- Auto expense                *
19  ' *               Total.Employees  -- Number of employees         *
20  ' *               Total.Expense    -- Total auto expense          *
21  ' *               Average.Expense  -- Average auto expense        *
22  ' ****************************************************************
23
24  ' ******************* Initialization *********************
25  CLS   ' Clear Screen
26  LET Total.Employees = 0
27  LET Total.Expense = 0
28  LET Cost.Per.Mile = .25
29  PRINT TAB(15); "Auto Expense Report"
30  PRINT
31  PRINT "Employee", "Auto"
32  PRINT "Name", "License", "Mileage", "Expense"
33  PRINT
34
```

FIGURE 2-13
(continued)

```
35  ' ********************* Process File *********************
36  READ Emp.Name$, License$, Begin.Mileage, End.Mileage
37  DO WHILE Emp.Name$ <> "EOF"
38     LET Total.Employees = Total.Employees + 1
39     LET Miles.Driven = End.Mileage - Begin.Mileage
40     LET Auto.Expense = Cost.Per.Mile * Miles.Driven
41     LET Total.Expense = Total.Expense + Auto.Expense
42     PRINT Emp.Name$, License$, Miles.Driven, Auto.Expense
43     READ Emp.Name$, License$, Begin.Mileage, End.Mileage
44  LOOP
45
46  ' *********************** Wrap-Up *************************
47  PRINT
48  PRINT "Total Employees ========>"; Total.Employees
49  PRINT "Total Auto Expense ======>"; Total.Expense
50  LET Average.Expense = Total.Expense / Total.Employees
51  PRINT "Average Auto Expense ===>"; Average.Expense
52  PRINT
53  PRINT "End of Report"
54
55  ' ********************* Data Follows **********************
56  DATA T. Rowe, HRT-111, 19100, 19224
57  DATA R. Lopez, GLD-913, 21221, 21332
58  DATA C. Deck, LIV-193, 10001, 10206
59  DATA B. Alek, ZRT-904, 15957, 16419
60  DATA EOF, End, 0, 0
61  END
```

```
                    Auto Expense Report

        Employee       Auto
        Name           License        Mileage        Expense

        T. Rowe        HRT-111          124            31
        R. Lopez       GLD-913          111            27.75
        C. Deck        LIV-193          205            51.25
        B. Alek        ZRT-904          462           115.5

        Total Employees ========> 4
        Total Auto Expense =====> 225.5
        Average Auto Expense ===> 56.375

        End of Report
```

FIGURE 2-14
The output results due to the execution of Sample Program 2

REPORT EDITING

Although the output in Figure 2-14 is readable, it does not conform to the format used by business and industry. For example, a column of numeric values usually has the decimal points aligned and is right-justified under the column heading. Numeric values that represent dollars and cents should include two digits to the right of the decimal point. Placing information in a format such as this is called **report editing**.

QuickBASIC provides for report editing through the use of the PRINT USING statement. This statement allows you to do the following:

- Specify the exact image of a line of output.
- Force decimal-point alignment when displaying numeric tables in columnar format.
- Control the number of digits displayed for a numeric result.

- Specify that commas be inserted into a number. (Starting from the units position of a number and progressing toward the left, digits are separated into groups of 3 by a comma.)
- Specify that the sign status of the number be displayed along with the number (+ or blank if positive, – if negative).
- Assign a fixed or floating dollar sign ($) to the number displayed.
- Force a numeric result to be displayed in exponential form.
- **Left-** or **right-justify** string values in a formatted field (that is, align the leftmost or rightmost characters, respectively).
- Specify that only the first character of a string be displayed.
- Round a value automatically to a specified number of decimal digits.

The general form of the PRINT USING statement is shown in Figure 2-15.

> PRINT USING "format field"; list
>
> or
>
> PRINT USING string variable; list
>
> where **format field** or **string variable** indicates the format and **list** is a variable or a group of variables separated by semicolons.

FIGURE 2-15
The general form of the PRINT USING statement

Report editing with the PRINT USING statement is accomplished using special characters to format the values to be displayed. When grouped together, these special characters form a **format field**. A format field is incorporated in a program as a string constant in the PRINT USING statement or as a string constant assigned to a string variable.

To illustrate the use of the PRINT USING statement, we will modify Sample Program 2. The new, formatted report is illustrated in Figure 2-16.

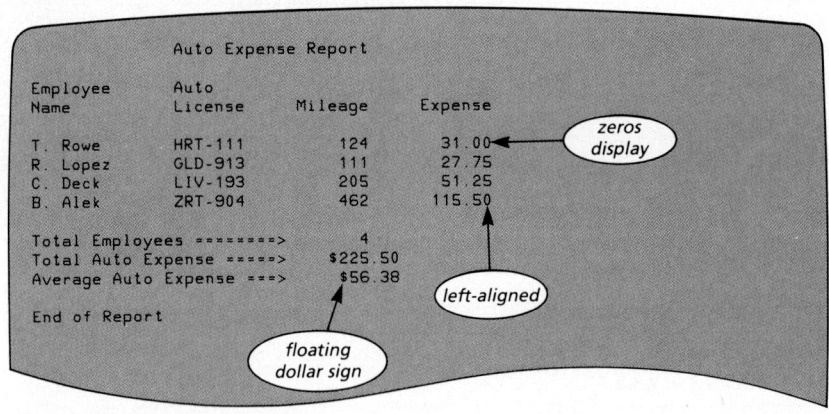

FIGURE 2-16
The formatted auto expense report

Compare the report in Figure 2-16 to the one in Figure 2-14. Notice that the mileage in the third column in Figure 2-16 is right-justified under the column heading. Also, the dollar and cents values in the expense field are right-justified under the column heading, and the decimal points are aligned. In addition, the total auto expense and the average expense per employee values are displayed with the dollar sign immediately adjacent to the leftmost digit in the number. This is known as a **floating dollar sign**.

To control the format of the displayed values, the PRINT USING statement is used in conjunction with a string expression that specifies exactly the image to which the output must conform. The string expression is placed immediately after the words PRINT USING in the form of a string constant or string variable. If the format is described by a string variable, then the string variable must be assigned the format by a LET statement before the PRINT USING statement is executed in the program. In either case, the items to display follow the string constant or string variable in the PRINT USING statement separated by semicolons or commas. The two methods for specifying the format for the PRINT USING statement are shown in Figure 2-17.

Method 1:

```
' Format Specified as a String in the PRINT USING Statement
PRINT USING "Item ### costs $$,###.##"; Item; Cost
```

Method 2:

```
' Format Specified Earlier and Assigned to a String Variable
D1$ = "Item ### cost $$,###.##"
         .
         .
         .
PRINT USING D1$; Item; Cost
```

FIGURE 2-17
The two methods for defining the format for a PRINT USING statement

In Method 1 of Figure 2-17, the string following the keywords PRINT USING instructs the PC to display the values of Item and Cost using the format found in the accompanying string constant. In Method 2, the string constant has been replaced by the string variable D1$ which was assigned the desired format in a previous statement. If Item is equal to 314 and Cost is equal to 2145.50, then the results displayed from the execution of either PRINT USING statement in Method 1 or Method 2 are as follows:

```
Item 314 costs $2,145.50
```

In Method 2 of Figure 2-17, notice that the keyword LET is not part of the LET statement. QuickBASIC considers any statement with an equal sign to be a LET statement. Hence, the keyword LET is optional. When defining format fields, we will not use the keyword LET.

Figure 2-18 illustrates how a LET statement and a PRINT USING statement are used to display the detail line in the report in Figure 2-16.

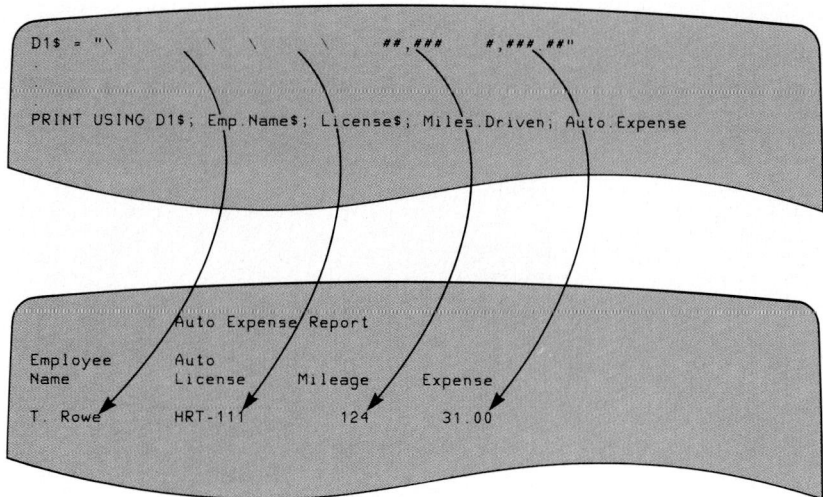

FIGURE 2-18
Using LET and PRINT USING statements to format the output

The backward slash (\) is used to create a format for string fields. The first backward slash indicates the first character position in the string field, and the second backward slash indicates the last character position in the field. Therefore, in the format field for Emp.Name$, eleven characters positions are defined—the two backward slashes and the nine spaces between them.

License$ is also a string variable. It is defined as eight characters in length by the two backward slashes and the six spaces between them. Numeric fields are defined through the use of the number sign (#). Each occurrence of a number sign corresponds to a numeric digit position. Punctuation, such as the comma and decimal point, is placed in the format field where it is to occur in the actual output. The format field for Miles.Driven includes a comma in case the value exceeds 999. Since Miles.Driven in the first line of the report is less than 1,000, the comma does not display. Similarly, a decimal point is placed in the format where it is supposed to print. For Auto.Expense, the format field ###.## specifies three digits to the left of the decimal point and two digits to the right of the decimal point. Thus, the value displays in dollars and cents form.

Notice in Figure 2-18, following the keyword PRINT USING, D1$ identifies the format. This variable name is then followed by a semicolon, and the names of the fields to display are separated by semicolons. The table in Figure 2-19 illustrates additional examples of format fields.

EXAMPLE	DATA	FORMAT FIELD	RESULTS IN
1	125.62	###.##	125.62
2	005.76	###.##	bb5.76
3	.65	###.##	bb0.65
4	1208.78	#,###.##	1,208.78
5	986.05	#,###.##	bb986.05
6	34.87	$$#,###.##	bbbb$34.87
7	3579.75	$$#,###.##	b$3,579.75
8	561.93	$##,###.##	$bbb561.93
9	SALLY	\ \	SALLY
10	EDWARD	\\	ED

FIGURE 2-19 Examples of format fields (b represents a blank character)

You can include constants in a format field. The LET statement in Figure 2-20 illustrates this point.

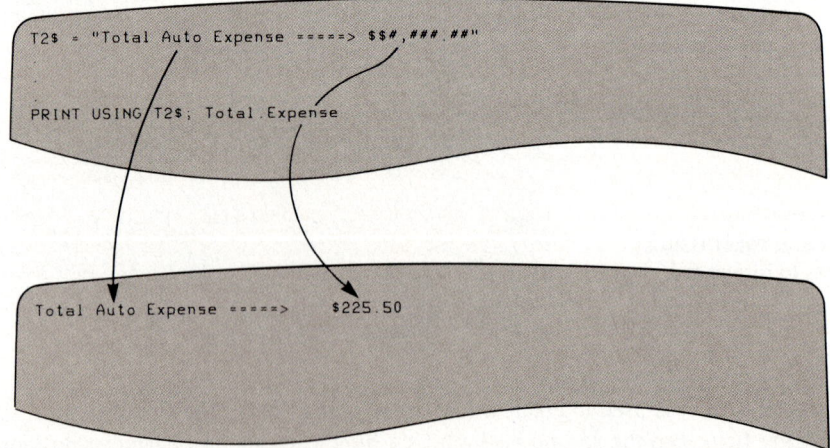

FIGURE 2-20
An example of including a constant in a format field

In Figure 2-20, the constant Total Auto Expense =====> is part of the string expression that includes the format field. When the variable T2$ is referenced by the PRINT USING statement, the constant is displayed exactly as it appears in the string expression. There are additional format symbols available with QuickBASIC. Those we present here, however, are the most widely used.

The coding in Figure 2-21 illustrates the complete program which produces the auto expense report shown on the next page in Figure 2-22. Particular attention should be paid to lines 30 through 39. These lines, when grouped together, show exactly what the report will look like when the program executes. Notice that this group of lines includes PRINT statements that display the report title and column headings and LET statements that define format fields. The column headings are within one string constant, rather than separated by commas, to better control the spacing. The format fields for the detail line (D1$) are immediately below the column headings in line 35.

We did not use the keyword LET in lines 35 through 39 so that all the string constants would begin in the same column in the program.

```
1   ' ***************************************************************
2   ' *   Sample Program 2 Modified            September 15, 1994   *
3   ' *   Auto Expense Report                                       *
4   ' *   J. S. Quasney                                             *
5   ' *                                                             *
6   ' *   This program displays an auto expense report.  Mileage    *
7   ' *   expense is calculated on the basis of 25 cents per mile.  *
8   ' *   As part of the Wrap-Up module, the total number of        *
9   ' *   employees, total auto expense, and the average expense    *
10  ' *   per employee are displayed.                               *
11  ' *                                                             *
12  ' *   Variables:  Emp.Name$        -- Name of employee          *
13  ' *               License$         -- Auto license number       *
14  ' *               Begin.Mileage    -- Beginning mileage         *
15  ' *               End.Mileage      -- Ending mileage            *
16  ' *               Miles.Driven     -- Miles driven              *
17  ' *               Cost.Per.Mile    -- Auto cost per mile        *
18  ' *               Auto.Expense     -- Auto expense              *
19  ' *               Total.Employees  -- Number of employees       *
20  ' *               Total.Expense    -- Total auto expense        *
21  ' *               Average.Expense  -- Average auto expense      *
22  ' *               D1$, T1$, T2$, T3$, T4$   -- Print images     *
23  ' ***************************************************************
24
25  ' ******************* Initialization **********************
26  CLS   ' Clear Screen
27  LET Total.Employees = 0
28  LET Total.Expense = 0
29  LET Cost.Per.Mile = .25
30  PRINT "             Auto Expense Report"
31  PRINT
32  PRINT "Employee         Auto"
33  PRINT "Name             License      Mileage      Expense"
34  PRINT
35  D1$ = "\            \   \       \    ##,###    #,###.##"
36  T1$ = "Total Employees ========>    ###"
37  T2$ = "Total Auto Expense =====> $$#,###.##"
38  T3$ = "Average Auto Expense ===> $$,###.##"
39  T4$ = "End of Report"
40
41  ' ******************** Process File *********************
42  READ Emp.Name$, License$, Begin.Mileage, End.Mileage
43  DO WHILE Emp.Name$ <> "EOF"
44     LET Total.Employees = Total.Employees + 1
45     LET Miles.Driven = End.Mileage - Begin.Mileage
46     LET Auto.Expense = Cost.Per.Mile * Miles.Driven
47     LET Total.Expense = Total.Expense + Auto.Expense
48     PRINT USING D1$; Emp.Name$; License$; Miles.Driven; Auto.Expense
49     READ Emp.Name$, License$, Begin.Mileage, End.Mileage
50  LOOP
51
```

Lines 30–40 bracketed as: image of report

FIGURE 2-21
Sample Program 2 modified to include report editing

(continued)

FIGURE 2-21
(continued)

```
52  ' ************************ Wrap Up ************************
53  PRINT
54  PRINT USING T1$; Total.Employees
55  PRINT USING T2$; Total.Expense
56  LET Average.Expense = Total.Expense / Total.Employees
57  PRINT USING T3$; Average.Expense
58  PRINT
59  PRINT T4$
60
61  ' ********************* Data Follows *********************
62  DATA T. Rowe, HRT-111, 19100, 19224
63  DATA R. Lopez, GLD-913, 21221, 21332
64  DATA C. Deck, LIV-193, 10001, 10206
65  DATA B. Alek, ZRT-904, 15957, 16419
66  DATA EOF, End, 0, 0
67  END
```

```
                Auto Expense Report

Employee       Auto
Name           License      Mileage      Expense

T. Rowe        HRT-111         124        31.00
R. Lopez       GLD-913         111        27.75
C. Deck        LIV-193         205        51.25
B. Alek        ZRT-904         462       115.50

Total Employees   ========>      4
Total Auto Expense =====>    $225.50
Average Auto Expense ===>     $56.38

End of Report
```

FIGURE 2-22
The formatted auto expense report due to the execution of the modified Sample Program 2

PRINTING A REPORT ON THE PRINTER

While the PRINT and PRINT USING statements display results on the screen, the LPRINT and LPRINT USING statements print results on the printer. Everything that has been presented with respect to the PRINT and PRINT USING statements in this section applies to the LPRINT and LPRINT USING statements. Obviously, to use these statements, you must have a printer attached to your PC and it must be in the Ready mode.

Figure 2-23 illustrates the results of the modified Sample Program 2 printed on a printer. To obtain the hard-copy results as shown in Figure 2-23, change all the PRINT and PRINT USING statements in Sample Program 2 (Figure 2-21) to LPRINT and LPRINT USING statements.

```
                Auto Expense Report

Employee       Auto
Name           License      Mileage      Expense

T. Rowe        HRT-111         124        31.00
R. Lopez       GLD-913         111        27.75
C. Deck        LIV-193         205        51.25
B. Alek        ZRT-904         462       115.50

Total Employees   ========>      4
Total Auto Expense =====>    $225.50
Average Auto Expense ===>     $56.38
```

FIGURE 2-23
A printed version of the auto expense report

TRY IT YOURSELF EXERCISES

1. Which arithmetic operation is performed first in the following numeric expressions?
   a. `5 * (Amt + 8)`
   b. `Cost - Sale + Discount`
   c. `8 / 3 * 5`
   d. `(X * (2 + Y)) ^ 2 + Z ^ (2 ^ 2)`
   e. `X + Y / Z`

2. Evaluate each of the following:
   a. `2 * 10 * 6 / 12 - 7 ^ 2 / 7`
   b. `(6 - 8) + 5 ^ 3`
   c. `12 / 6 / 2 + 7 * 3 + 5`

3. Calculate the numeric value for each of the following valid numeric expressions if Amt = 3, Sale = 4, Cost = 5, Discount = 3, S1 = 4, S2 = 1 and S3 = 2.
   a. `(Amt + Sale / 2) + 6.2`
   b. `3 * (Amt ^ Sale) / Cost`
   c. `(Amt / (Cost + 1) * 4 - 5) / 2`
   d. `S2 + 2 * S3 * Discount / 3 - 7 / (S1 - S2 / S3) - Discount ^ S1`

4. Determine the output results for each of the following programs.

   a.
   ```
   ' Exercise 4.a
   X = 2.5
   Y = 4 * X / 2 * X + 10
   PRINT Y
   Y = 4 * X / (2 * X + 10)
   PRINT Y
   X = -X
   PRINT X
   X = -X
   PRINT X
   END
   ```

   b.
   ```
   ' Exercise 4.b
   C = 4
   D = 1
   S = C + D
   PRINT S
   T = D - C
   PRINT T
   C = S + T - C
   PRINT C
   D = 2 * (S + T + C) / 4
   PRINT D
   END
   ```

5. Calculate the numeric value for each of the following numeric expressions if X = 2, Y = 3, and Z = 6.
   a. `X + Y ^ 2`
   b. `Z / Y / X`
   c. `12 / (3 + Z) - X`
   d. `X ^ Y ^ Z`
   e. `X * Y + 2.5 * X + Z`
   f. `(X ^ (2 + Y)) ^ 2 + Z ^ (2 ^ 2)`

6. Insert parentheses so that each of the following results in the value indicated on the right-hand side of the arrow.
   a. `10 / 3 + 2 + 12 ----> 14`
   b. `3 ^ 2 - 1 ----> 3`
   c. `6 / 2 + 1 + 3 * 4 ----> 4`

7. For each of the following format fields and corresponding data, indicate what the PC displays. Use the letter b to indicate the space character. Notice that if a format field does not include enough positions to the left of the decimal point, the PC displays the result preceded by a percent (%) sign. If the format field does not include enough positions to the right of the decimal point, the PC rounds the result to fit the format field.

	Format Field	Data	Result
a.	`####`	15	
b.	`#,###`	345	
c.	`$$,###.##`	1395.54	
d.	`###.##`	12.5675	
e.	`##,###.###`	19412.5	
f.	`##.##`	576.3	
g.	`###.#####`	32.2	
h.	`#.##`	.234	

STUDENT ASSIGNMENTS

STUDENT ASSIGNMENT 1: Payroll Report

Instructions: Design and code a QuickBASIC program to generate the formatted payroll report shown under OUTPUT. The weekly pay is calculated by multiplying the hourly pay by the number of hours. All hours are paid at straight time. As part of the Wrap-Up module, display the total number of employees and the total weekly pay of all employees. Submit a program flowchart, listing of the program, and a listing of the output results.

INPUT: Use the following sample data:

EMPLOYEE NAME	HOURLY PAY RATE	HOURS WORKED
Joe Lomax	7.70	40
Ed Mann	6.05	38.5
Louis Orr	8.10	45
Ted Simms	9.50	39.5
Joan Zang	12.00	92
EOF	0	0

OUTPUT: The following results are displayed:

```
                Payroll Report

Employee        Hourly          Hours           Weekly
Name            Rate            Worked          Pay

Joe Lomax       7.70            40.0            308.00
Ed Mann         6.05            38.5            232.93
Louis Orr       8.10            45.0            364.50
Ted Simms       9.50            39.5            375.25
Joan Zang       12.00           92.0            1,104.00

Total Employees ========>       5
Total Weekly Pay ========>      $2,384.68

End of Report
```

STUDENT ASSIGNMENT 2: Test Score Report

Instructions: Design and code a QuickBASIC program that prints the student test report shown under OUTPUT. In each detail line, include the student's name, test scores, and average test score. The average test score is calculated by adding the score for test 1 and the score for test 2 and dividing by 2. After all records for all students have been processed, print the total number of students and the class average for all tests. To obtain a class average, add all test scores and divide by twice the number of students. Use the `LPRINT` and `LPRINT USING` statements to generate the report on the printer.

INPUT: Use the following sample data:

STUDENT NAME	TEST 1 SCORE	TEST 2 SCORE
Julie Banks	70	78
John Davis	92	93
Joe Gomez	88	84
Sally Katz	78	83
EOF	0	0

OUTPUT: The following results are printed:

```
            Test Score Report

Student
Name            Test 1      Test 2      Average

Julie Banks       70          78          74.0
John Davis        92          93          92.5
Joe Gomez         88          84          86.0
Sally Katz        78          83          80.5

Total Students  ============>    4
Class Average   ============>   83.25

End of Report
```

PROJECT 3

Decisions

QuickBASIC includes the IF and SELECT CASE statements to instruct the PC to select one action or another on the basis of a comparison of numbers or strings. You use the IF statement to implement the **If-Then-Else structure** shown in Figure 3-1. When the structure in a flowchart has more than two alternative paths, you use the SELECT CASE statement. This type of structure is called a **case structure** and is shown in Figure 3-2.

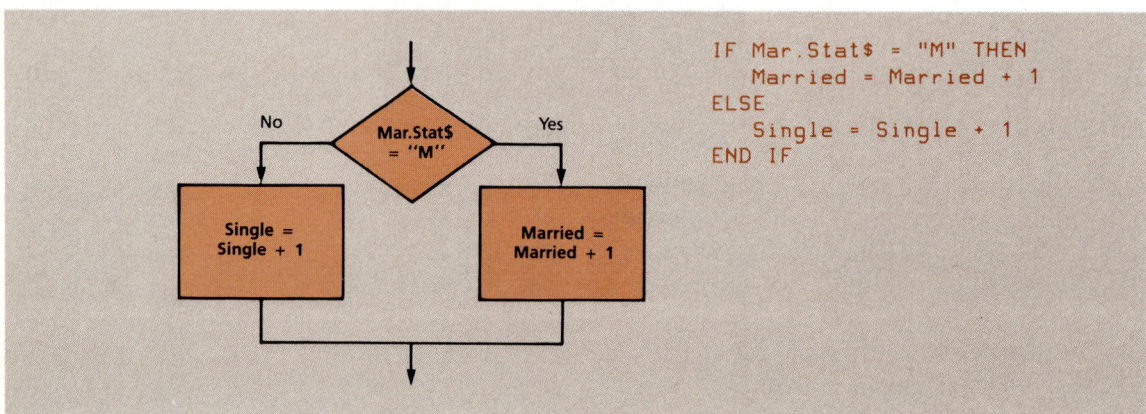

FIGURE 3-1 For the If-Then-Else structure, use the IF statement

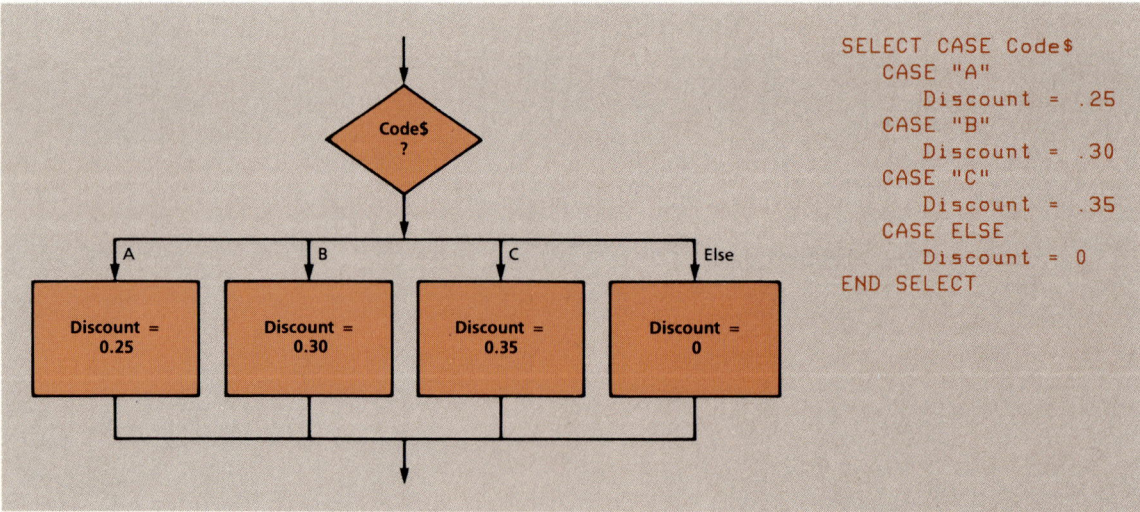

FIGURE 3-2 For a Case structure, use the SELECT CASE statement

THE IF STATEMENT

The IF statement is commonly regarded as the most powerful statement in QuickBASIC. The major function of this statement is to choose between two alternative paths. The IF statement has two general forms as shown in Figure 3-3.

The IF Statement

> **Single-Line IF**
>
> `IF condition THEN true task ELSE false task`
>
> **Block IF**
>
> ```
> IF condition THEN
>    true task
> ELSE
>    false task
> END IF
> ```

FIGURE 3-3 The general form of the IF statement

In Figure 3-3, **condition** is a comparison between two expressions that is either true or false. **True task** and **false task** are statements or series of statements. If the condition is true, the PC executes the true task, also called the `THEN` clause, or **true case**. If the condition is false and an `ELSE` clause is included, the PC executes the false task, also called the `ELSE` clause, or **false case**. After either task is executed, control passes to the statement following the single-line `IF` statement or to the statement following the `END IF` for a block `IF`.

Figure 3-4 illustrates several examples of `IF` statements with conditions made up of numeric and string expressions. For numeric conditions, the PC evaluates not only the magnitude of each resultant expression but also its sign. For string expressions, the PC evaluates the two strings from left to right, one character at a time. With the block `IF` statement, the true and false tasks are indented by three spaces to improve the readability of the code.

Examples 1 through 3 in Figure 3-4 include conditions made up of numeric expressions. Examples 4 and 5 show `IF` statements with conditions made up of string expressions.

EXAMPLE	STATEMENT	VALUE OF VARIABLES	RESULT
1	`IF Amt = 0 THEN Dis = 4`	Amt = 0	The variable Dis is assigned the value 4, and control passes to the line following the IF statement.

2	`IF A < B THEN`
	`   PRINT X`
	`   T = T + 10`
	`ELSE`
	`   PRINT Y`
	`   Tax = Tax + 5`
	`END IF`
		A = 3
		B = 5
			The value of X is displayed; T is incremented by 10, and control passes to the line following the END IF.

3	`IF F < X - Y - 6 THEN`
	`   PRINT S`
	`END IF`
		F = 23
		X = 7
		Y = –8
			Control passes to the line following the END IF.

4	`IF C$ < D$ + E$ THEN`
	`   READ A, B, C`
	`   PRINT Y`
	`END IF`
		C$ = "JIM"
		D$ = "JA"
		E$ = "MES"
			Control passes to the line following the END IF.

5	`IF X$ = "YES" THEN`
	`   PRINT A$`
	`END IF`
		X$ = "yes"	Control passes to the line following the END IF. "YES" and "yes" are not the same string.

FIGURE 3-4 Examples of IF statements

Six types of relations can be used in a condition within an IF statement. These relations include determining if:

1. One value is equal to another (=)
2. One value is less than another (<)
3. One value is greater than another (>)
4. One value is less than or equal to another (< =)
5. One value is greater than or equal to another (> =)
6. One value is not equal to another (< >)

Recall that these are the same six relational operators we discussed earlier with the DO WHILE statement in Project 1 on page QB 9 in Figure 1-16.

CODING IF-THEN-ELSE STRUCTURES

This section describes various forms of the If-Then-Else structure and the use of IF statements to implement them in QuickBASIC.

Simple If-Then-Else Structures

Consider the If-Then-Else structure in Figure 3-5 and the corresponding methods of implementing the logic in QuickBASIC. Assume that the variable Age represents a person's age. If Age is greater than or equal to 18, the person is an adult. If Age is less than 18, the person is a minor. Adult and Minor are counters that are incremented as specified in the flowchart.

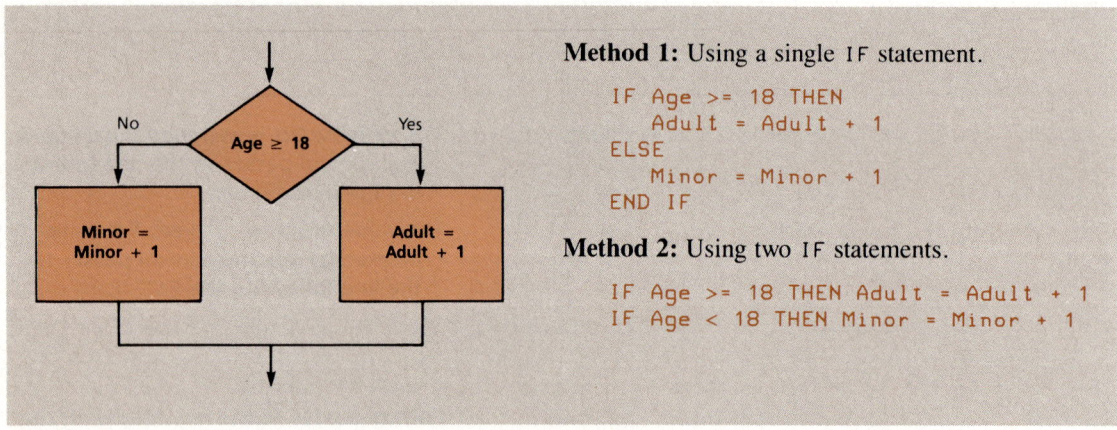

FIGURE 3-5 Coding an If-Then-Else structure with alternative processing for the true and false cases

In the first method shown in Figure 3-5, an IF statement resolves the logic indicated in the partial flowchart. The first line compares Age to 18. If Age is greater than or equal to 18, then Adult is incremented by 1. If Age is less than 18, the false task is carried out and Minor is incremented by 1. Regardless of the counter incremented, control passes to the statement following the END IF.

In Method 2, two single-line IF statements are used. Age is compared to the value 18 twice. In the first IF statement, the counter Adult is incremented by 1 if Age is greater than or equal to 18. In the second IF statement, the counter Minor is incremented by 1 if Age is less than 18.

Although both methods are valid and both satisfy the If-Then-Else structure, the first method is more efficient, as it involves fewer lines of code and less execution time. Therefore, the first method is recommended over the second.

Notice that the first method in Figure 3-5 could have been written as a single-line `IF` statement without the `END IF`. However, for readability purposes we recommend that you use the block `IF` statement as shown in Method 1.

As shown in Figures 3-6, 3-7, and 3-8, the If-Then-Else structure can take on a variety of appearances. In Figure 3-6, there is a task only if the condition is true.

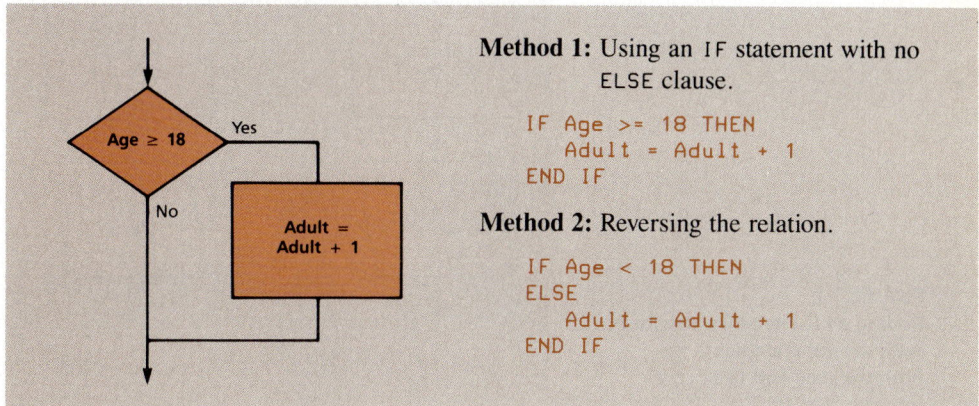

FIGURE 3-6
Coding an If-Then-Else structure with alternative processing for the true case

In Figure 3-6, the first method is preferred over the second since it is more straightforward and less confusing. In Method 2 of Figure 3-6, we reversed the relation. Although this method satisfies the If-Then-Else structure, it is also more difficult to understand. The second method shows that it is valid to have a null `THEN` clause.

The If-Then-Else structure in Figure 3-7 illustrates the incrementation of the counter Minor when the condition is false.

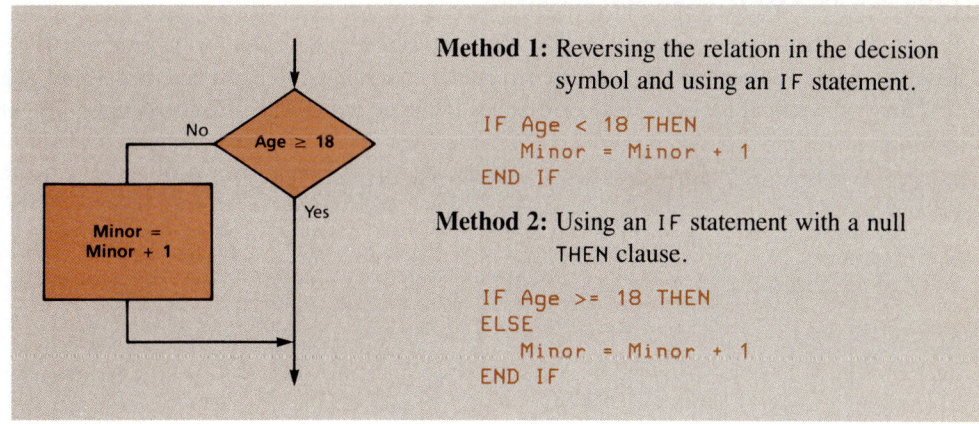

FIGURE 3-7
Coding an If-Then-Else structure with alternative processing for the false case

In Method 1, the relation in the condition that is found in the partial flowchart has been reversed. The condition `Age >= 18` has been modified to read `Age < 18` in the QuickBASIC code. Reversing the relation is usually preferred when additional tasks must be done as a result of the condition being false. In Method 2, the relation is the same as in the decision symbol. When the condition `Age >= 18` is true, the null `THEN` clause simply passes control to the statement following the `END IF`. Either method is acceptable. Some programmers prefer always to include both a `THEN` and an `ELSE` clause, even when one of them is null. On the other hand, some prefer to reverse the relation rather than include a null clause.

On the next page in Figure 3-8, each task in the If-Then-Else structure is made up of multiple statements. We have included a suggested method of implementation.

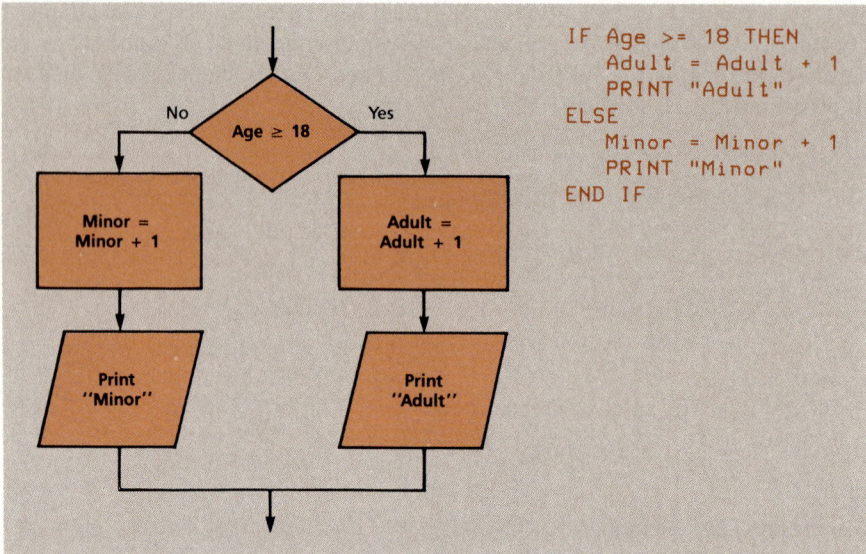

FIGURE 3-8
Coding an If-Then-Else structure with several statements for both the true and false cases

In the code in Figure 3-8, if the condition Age >= 18 is true, the two statements in the THEN clause are executed. If the condition is false, the two statements in the ELSE clause are executed.

Although there are alternative methods for implementing the If-Then-Else structure, the method we have presented is more straightforward and involves fewer lines of code.

Nested If-Then-Else Structures

A nested If-Then-Else structure is one in which the action to be taken for the true or false case includes yet another If-Then-Else structure. The second If-Then-Else structure is considered to be nested, or layered, within the first.

Study the partial program that corresponds to the nested If-Then-Else structure in Figure 3-9.

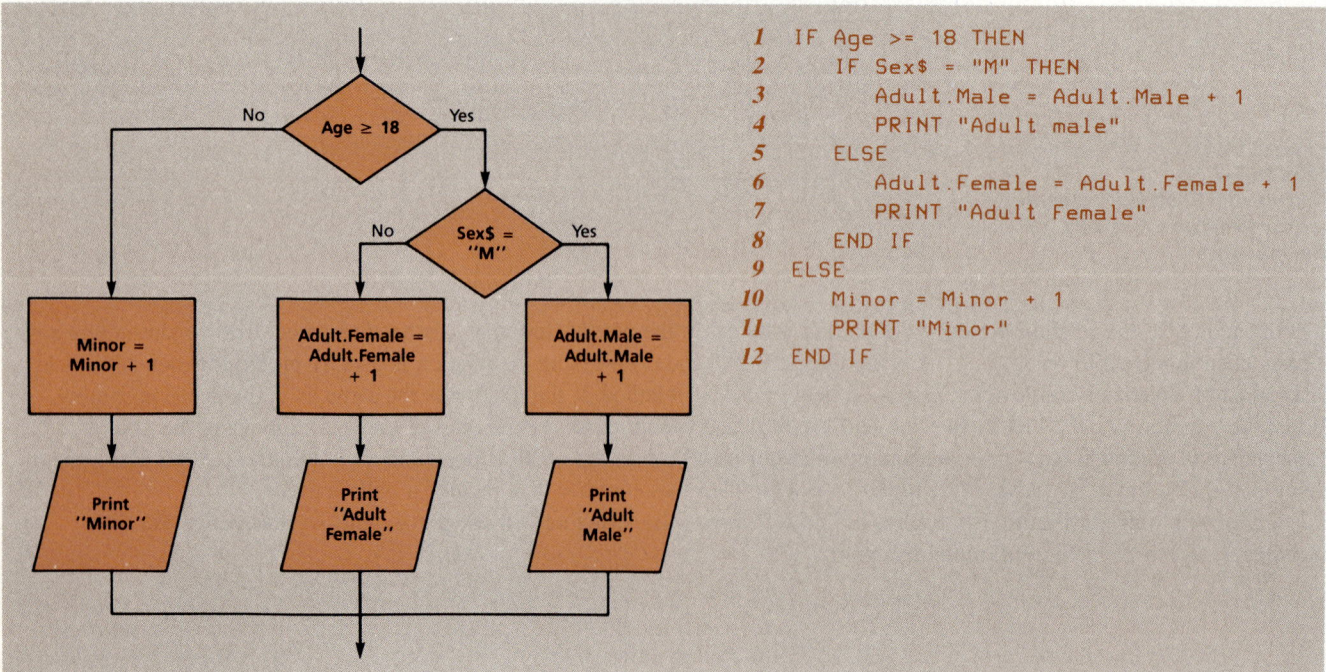

FIGURE 3-9 Coding a nested If-Then-Else structure

In the partial program in Figure 3-9, if the condition `Age >= 18` is true, control passes to the THEN clause beginning with line 2. If the condition is false, the ELSE clause beginning in line 10 is executed. If control does pass to line 2, then a second IF tests to determine if Sex$ equals the value M. If the condition in line 2 is true, lines 3 and 4 are executed. If the condition is false, then the PC executes lines 6 and 7.

QuickBASIC requires that you end each block IF statement with an END IF. Hence, the block IF in line 1 has a corresponding END IF in line 12, and the block IF in line 2 has a corresponding END IF in line 8.

Notice in Figure 3-9 that only one of the three alternative tasks is executed for each record processed. Regardless of the path taken, control eventually passes to the statement immediately following the last END IF in line 12.

SAMPLE PROGRAM 3 — VIDEO RENTAL REPORT

To illustrate a program that uses an IF statement, consider the following video rental problem. In this application, if the video tape is rented for three days or less, the charge is $2.49 per day. There is a one dollar per day discount for each of the first three days for customers who are at least 65 years old. If the video tape is rented for more than three days, the charge is $3.49 per day for each day over three days.

The video records consist of the customer's name, age, video title, and the number of days rented as shown in Figure 3-10.

CUSTOMER NAME	AGE	VIDEO TITLE	DAYS RENTED
Helen Moore	47	Lost in Space	1
Hank Fisher	67	Together Again	3
Joe Frank	34	Three Lives	7
Al Jones	64	The Last Day	5
Shirley Star	65	Monday Morning	4
EOF	0	End	0

FIGURE 3-10 The video rental file for Sample Program 3

The output is a printed video rental summary report that lists the customer name, customer age, title of the video tape rented, the number of days the tape was rented, and the charge for the rental. After all records have been processed, the number of senior citizen customers, the number of tapes rented, and the total charges are printed. The format of the output is illustrated in Figure 3-11.

```
                    Video Rental Report

      Customer              Video           Days
      Name        Age       Title           Rented    Charge

      Helen Moore  47       Lost in Space     1        2.49
      Hank Fisher  67       Together Again    3        4.47
      Joe Frank    34       Three Lives       7       21.43
      Al Jones     64       The Last Day      5       14.45
      Shirley Star 65       Monday Morning    4        7.96

      Senior Citizens ============>      2
      Videos Rented   ============>      5
      Total Charges   ============>    $50.80

      End of Report
```

FIGURE 3-11 The report for Sample Program 3

Program Flowchart

The flowchart in Figure 3-12 illustrates the logic required to produce the video rental report.

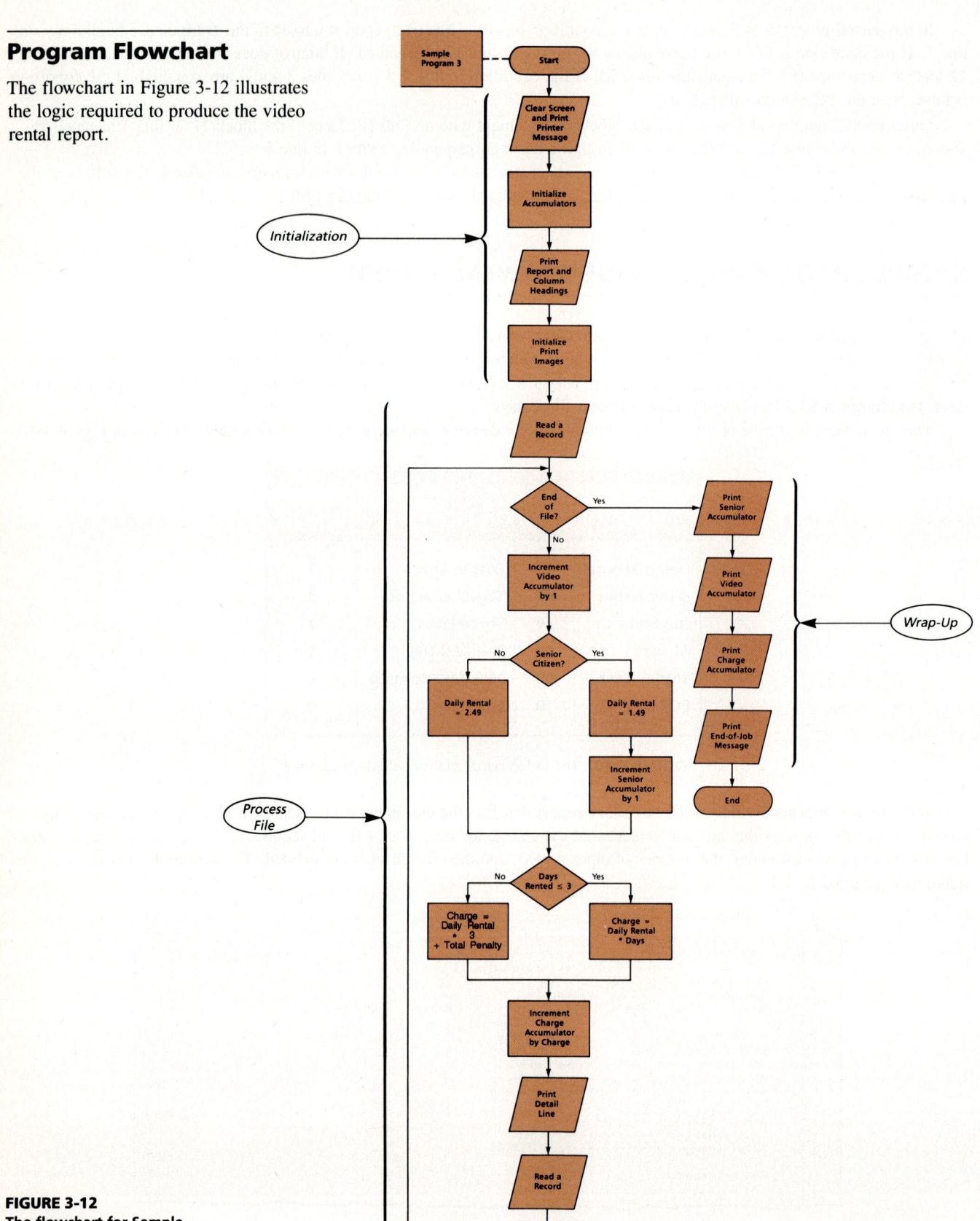

FIGURE 3-12
The flowchart for Sample Program 3

The QuickBASIC Program

The program in Figure 3-13 corresponds to the program flowchart in Figure 3-12.

```
1   '****************************************************************
2   ' *   Sample Program 3                     September 15, 1994    *
3   ' *   Video Rental Report                                        *
4   ' *   J. S. Quasney                                              *
5   ' *                                                              *
6   ' *   This program prints a video rental report.  The charge     *
7   ' *   is based on the number of days the video is rented and     *
8   ' *   the age of the customer.                                   *
9   ' *        As part of the Wrap-Up module, the total number       *
10  ' *   of videos, senior customers, and charges are printed.      *
11  ' *                                                              *
12  ' *   Variables:  Cus.Name$       -- Name of customer            *
13  ' *               Cus.Age         -- Customer age                *
14  ' *               Video.Title$    -- Title of video              *
15  ' *               Days.Rented     -- Days rented                 *
16  ' *               Daily.Rental    -- Cost per day                *
17  ' *               Charge          -- Cost of renting video       *
18  ' *               Penalty         -- Cost per day after 3 days   *
19  ' *               Total.Videos    -- Number of videos rented     *
20  ' *               Total.Seniors   -- Number of senior rentals    *
21  ' *               Total.Charges   -- Total charges               *
22  ' *               DL1$, TL1$, TL2$, TL3$, TL4$ -- Print images   *
23  '****************************************************************
24
25  ' ********************* Initialization *********************
26  CLS   ' Clear Screen
27  PRINT "****** Video Rental Report Printing on Printer ******"
28  LET Total.Videos = 0
29  LET Total.Seniors = 0
30  LET Total.Charges = 0
31  LET Penalty = 3.49
32  LPRINT "                   Video Rental Report"
33  LPRINT
34  LPRINT "Customer                Video                         Days"
35  LPRINT "Name             Age    Title                         Rented    Charge"
36  LPRINT
37  DL1$ = "\            \  ###   \                        \     ###      ###.##"
38  TL1$ = "Senior Citizens ============>    ###"
39  TL2$ = "Videos Rented   ============>    ###"
40  TL3$ = "Total Charges   ============> $$,###.##"
41  TL4$ = "End of Report"
42
```

FIGURE 3-13
Sample Program 3

(continued)

FIGURE 3-13
(continued)

```
43  ' ********************* Process File **********************
44  READ Cus.Name$, Cus.Age, Video.Title$, Days.Rented
45  DO WHILE Cus.Name$ <> "EOF"
46     LET Total.Videos = Total.Videos + 1
47     IF Cus.Age >= 65 THEN
48        LET Daily.Rental = 1.49
49        LET Total.Seniors = Total.Seniors + 1
50     ELSE
51        LET Daily.Rental = 2.49
52     END IF
53     IF Days.Rented <= 3 THEN
54        LET Charge = Daily.Rental * Days.Rented
55     ELSE
56        LET Charge = (Daily.Rental * 3) + Penalty * (Days.Rented - 3)
57     END IF
58     LET Total.Charges = Total.Charges + Charge
59     LPRINT USING DL1$; Cus.Name$; Cus.Age; Video.Title$; Days.Rented; Charge
60     READ Cus.Name$, Cus.Age, Video.Title$, Days.Rented
61  LOOP
62
63  ' *********************** Wrap-Up *************************
64  LPRINT
65  LPRINT USING TL1$; Total.Seniors
66  LPRINT USING TL2$; Total.Videos
67  LPRINT USING TL3$; Total.Charges
68  LPRINT
69  LPRINT TL4$
70
71  ' ********************* Data Follows **********************
72  DATA Helen Moore, 47, Lost in Space, 1
73  DATA Hank Fisher, 67, Together Again, 3
74  DATA Joe Frank, 34, Three Lives, 7
75  DATA Al Jones, 64, The Last Day, 5
76  DATA Shirley Star, 65, Monday Morning, 4
77  DATA EOF, 0, End, 0
78  END
```

Discussion of Sample Program 3

When Sample Program 3 is executed, the report shown in Figure 3-14 prints on the printer. Sample Program 3 includes a few significant points that did not appear in previous programs. They are as follows:

- When executed, line 26 clears the screen and line 27 displays a friendly message informing the user that the report is being printed on the printer.
- LPRINT and LPRINT USING statements are used throughout the program to print the report on the printer rather than display the report on the monitor.
- There are two IF statements that select alternative paths on the basis of the data in the video record being processed. The block IF in lines 47 through 52 determines whether the customer is a senior citizen. If the customer is a senior citizen, the daily rental (Daily.Rental) is set to $1.49 and the senior citizen counter is incremented. If the customer is not a senior citizen, then the daily rental is set to $2.49.

The second block IF statement (lines 53 through 57) determines how much to charge the customer being processed. If the video is rented for three days or less, the charge is determined from the following LET statement:

```
LET Charge = Daily.Rental * Days.Rented
```

If the video is rented for more than three days, the charge is determined from the following LET statement:

```
LET Charge = (Daily.Rental * 3) + Penalty * (Days.Rented - 3)
```

FIGURE 3-14
The report printed when Sample Program 3 is executed

```
                   Video Rental Report

    Customer            Video            Days
    Name        Age     Title            Rented    Charge

    Helen Moore  47     Lost in Space      1        2.49
    Hank Fisher  67     Together Again     3        4.47
    Joe Frank    34     Three Lives        7       21.43
    Al Jones     64     The Last Day       5       14.45
    Shirley Star 65     Monday Morning     4        7.96

    Senior Citizens ===========>    2
    Videos Rented   ===========>    5
    Total Charges   ===========>  $50.80

    End of Report
```

LOGICAL OPERATORS

*I*n many instances, a decision to execute a true task or false task is based upon two or more conditions. In previous examples that involved two or more conditions, we tested each condition in a separate IF statement. In this section, we discuss combining conditions within one IF statement by means of the logical operators AND and OR. When two or more conditions are combined by these logical operators, the expression is called a **compound condition**. The logical operator NOT allows you to write a compound condition in which the truth value of the simple condition following NOT is **complemented**, or reversed.

The NOT Logical Operator

A simple condition that is preceded by the logical operator NOT forms a compound condition that is false when the simple condition is true. If the simple condition is false, then the compound condition is true. Consider the two IF statements in Figure 3-15. Both print the value of Discount if Margin is less than or equal to Cost.

Method 1: Using the NOT logical operator.

```
IF NOT Margin > Cost THEN
    PRINT Discount
END IF
```

Method 2: Reversing the relational operator.

```
IF Margin <= Cost THEN
    PRINT Discount
END IF
```

FIGURE 3-15
Use of the NOT logical operator

   In Method 1 of Figure 3-15, if Margin is greater than Cost (the simple condition is true), then the compound condition NOT Margin > Cost is false. If Margin is less than or equal to Cost (the simple condition is false), then the NOT makes the compound condition true. In Method 2, the relational operator is reversed and, therefore, the NOT is eliminated. Both methods are equivalent.
   Because the logical operator NOT can increase the complexity of the decision statement significantly, use it sparingly. As shown in Figure 3-15, you can always reverse the relational operator in a condition to eliminate the logical operator NOT.

The AND Logical Operator

The AND operator requires that both conditions be true for the compound condition to be true. Consider the two IF statements in Figure 3-16. Both methods read a value for Selling.Price if Margin is greater than 10 and Cost is less than 8.

Method 1: Using the AND logical operator.

```
IF Margin > 10 AND Cost < 8 THEN
    READ Selling.Price
END IF
```

Method 2: Using nested IF statements.

```
IF Margin > 10 THEN
    IF Cost < 8 THEN
        READ Selling.Price
    END IF
END IF
```

FIGURE 3-16 Use of the AND operator

In Method 1 of Figure 3-16, if Margin is greater than 10 and Cost is less than 8, the READ statement assigns a value to Selling.Price before control passes to the line following the END IF. If either one of the conditions is false, then the compound condition is false, and control passes to the line following the END IF without a value being read for Selling.Price. Although both methods are equivalent, Method 1 is more efficient, more compact, and more straightforward than Method 2.

Like a single condition, a compound condition can be only true or false. To determine the truth value of the compound condition, the PC must evaluate and assign a truth value to each individual condition. Then the truth value is determined for the compound condition.

For example, if A equals 4 and C$ equals "X", the PC evaluates the following compound condition in the manner shown:

```
IF A = 3 AND C$ = "X" THEN LET F = F + 1
   1. false      2. true
         3. false
```

The PC first determines the truth value for each condition, then concludes that the compound condition is false because of the AND operator.

The OR Logical Operator

The OR operator requires that only one of the two conditions be true for the compound condition to be true. If both conditions are true, the compound condition is also true. Likewise, if both conditions are false, the compound condition is false. The use of the OR operator is illustrated in Figure 3-17.

> **Method 1:** Using the OR logical operator.
> ```
> IF Code$ = "A" OR Marital.Status$ = "M" THEN
>     END
> END IF
> ```
> **Method 2:** Using two IF statements.
> ```
> IF Code$ = "A" THEN
>     END
> END IF
> IF Marital.Status$ = "M" THEN
>     END
> END IF
> ```

FIGURE 3-17 Use of the OR operator

In Method 1 of Figure 3-17, if either Code$ equals the value A or Marital.Status$ equals the value M, the THEN clause is executed and the program halts execution. If both conditions are true, the THEN clause is also executed. If both conditions are false, the THEN clause is bypassed, and control passes to the line following the END IF. Method 2 employs two IF statements to resolve the same If-Then-Else structure. Again, both methods are equivalent, but, Method 1 is easier to read and understand than Method 2.

As with the logical operator AND, the truth values of the individual conditions in the IF statement are first determined, then the truth values for the conditions containing the logical operator OR are evaluated. For example, if F equals 4 and H equals 5, the following condition is true:

```
IF F = 3 OR H = 5 THEN PRINT "Yes"
   ‾‾‾‾‾   ‾‾‾‾‾
   1. false  2. true
   ‾‾‾‾‾‾‾‾‾‾‾‾‾‾‾
        3. true
```

Combining Logical Operators

Logical operators can be combined in a decision statement to form a compound condition. The formation of compound statements that involve more than one type of logical operator can create problems unless you fully understand the order in which the PC evaluates the entire condition. Unless parentheses dictate otherwise, reading from left to right, conditions containing arithmetic operators are evaluated first; then those containing relational operators; then those containing NOT operators; then those containing AND operators; then those containing OR operators. Refer to the last page of the Reference Card at the back of this book for a summary listing of the order of both arithmetic and logical operators.

For the following compound condition assume, that D = 3, P = 5, R = 3, T = 5, S = 6, and Y = 3:

```
IF S > Y  OR  T = D  AND  P < 5  OR  NOT Y = R  THEN READ L
   ‾‾‾‾‾      ‾‾‾‾‾       ‾‾‾‾‾      ‾‾‾‾‾‾‾‾‾
   1. true    2. false    3. false   4. true
                ‾‾‾‾‾‾‾‾‾‾‾‾‾‾‾‾‾‾    5. false
                    6. false
              ‾‾‾‾‾‾‾‾‾‾‾‾‾‾‾‾‾‾‾‾‾‾‾‾‾‾‾‾‾‾‾
                          7. true
                    ‾‾‾‾‾‾‾‾‾‾‾‾‾‾‾‾‾‾‾‾‾‾‾‾‾‾‾‾‾
                              8. true
```

The Use of Parentheses in Compound Conditions

Parentheses may be used to change the order of precedence. When there are parentheses in a compound condition, the PC evaluates that part of the compound condition within the parentheses first, then continues to evaluate the remaining compound condition according to the order of logical operations. For example, suppose variable J has a value of 2, and E has a value of 6. Consider the following compound condition:

```
IF J = 7   AND   E > 5   OR   J <> 0   THEN LET Cnt = Cnt + 1
   1. false      2. true       3. true
        4. false
             5. true
```

Following the order of logical operations, the compound condition yields a truth value of true. If parentheses surround the last two conditions, then the OR operator is evaluated before the AND condition, and the compound condition yields a truth value of false, as shown:

```
IF J = 7   AND   (E > 5   OR   J <> 0)   THEN LET Cnt = Cnt + 1
   4. false     1. true        2. true
                     3. true
             5. false
```

Parentheses may be used freely when the evaluation of a compound condition is in doubt. For example, if you wish to evaluate the compound condition

    IF C > D AND S = 4 OR X < Y AND T = 5 THEN READ F

you may incorporate it into a decision statement as it stands. You may also write in the following way:

    IF (C > D AND S = 4) OR (X < Y AND T = 5) THEN READ F

and feel more certain of the outcome of the decision statement.

THE SELECT CASE STATEMENT

The SELECT CASE statement is used to implement the case structure. Figure 3-18 illustrates the implementation of a case structure, which determines a letter grade (Letter.Grade$) from a grade point average (GPA) using the following grading scale:

GRADE POINT AVERAGE	LETTER GRADE
GPA ≥ 90	A
80 ≤ GPA < 90	B
70 ≤ GPA < 80	C
60 ≤ GPA < 70	D
0 ≤ GPA < 60	F
GPA < 0	Error

For example, if your GPA is 79.6, your letter grade is a C.

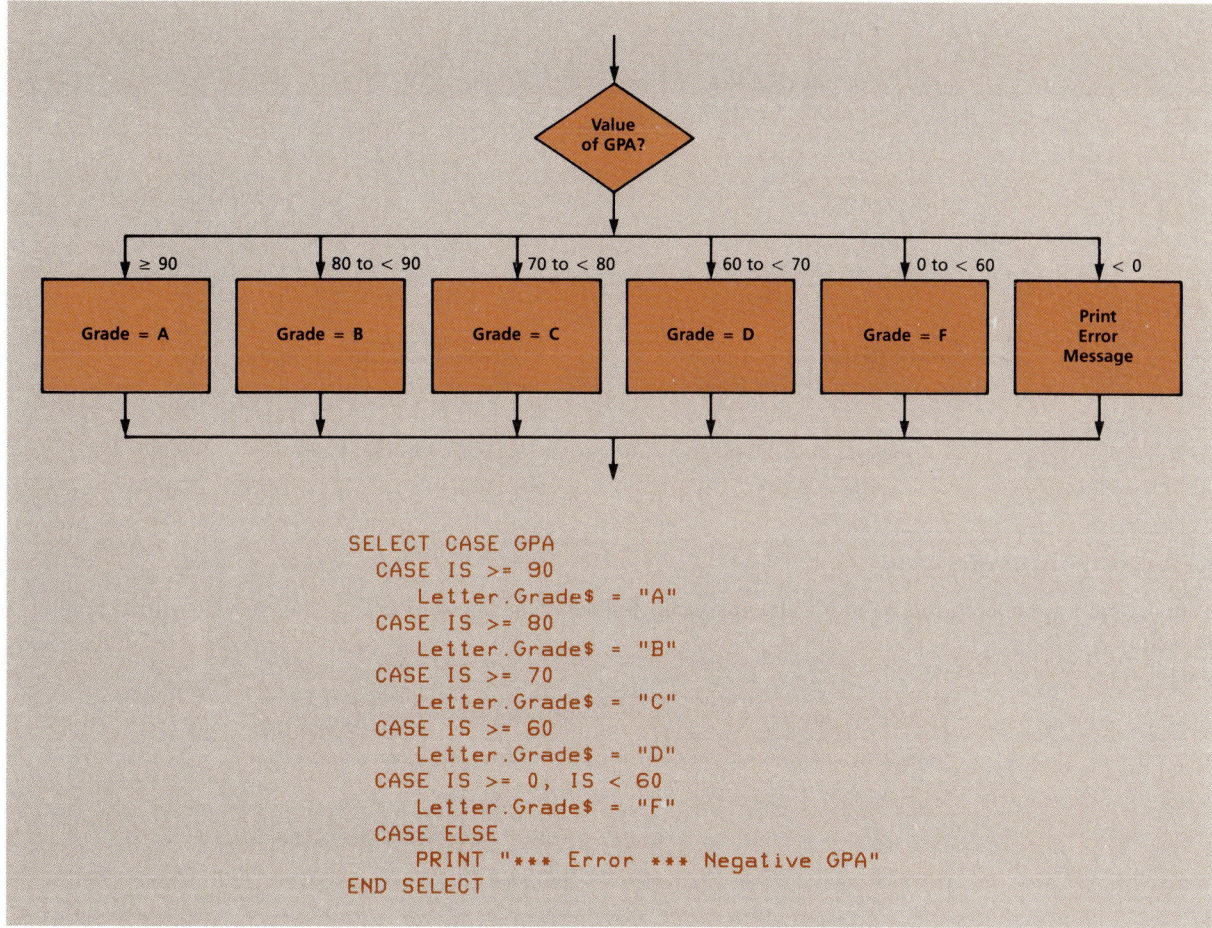

FIGURE 3-18 Implementation of a case structure

The SELECT CASE statement in Figure 3-18 is used to implement the grading scale. When the PC executes the SELECT CASE statement, it compares the variable GPA, which follows the keywords SELECT CASE, to the expressions following the keyword CASE in each CASE clause, also called a **case**. The PC begins the comparison with the first case and continues through the remaining ones until it finds a match. When a match is found, the range of statements immediately following the keyword CASE is executed. Following execution of the case, control immediately transfers to the statement following the END SELECT. The PC does not search for additional matches in the remaining cases.

For example, if GPA is equal to 79.6, then the PC finds a match in the third case. Therefore, it assigns Letter.Grade$ the value C and passes control to the statement following the END SELECT. If GPA equals a negative value, then no match is found, and the PRINT statement following the CASE ELSE is executed.

The CASE ELSE just prior to the END SELECT in Figure 3-18 instructs the PC to use this case if there is no match with any of the previous CASE clauses.

In a SELECT CASE, you place the variable, or expression, also called the **test-expression**, to test after the keywords SELECT CASE. Next, you assign the group of values, also called the **match-expression**, that make each alternative case true after the keyword CASE. Each case contains the range of statements to execute, and you may have as many cases as required. After the last case, end the SELECT CASE with an END SELECT.

The general form of the SELECT CASE statement is shown in Figure 3-19.

```
SELECT CASE test-expression
   CASE match-expression
      [range of statements]
   CASE match-expression
      [range of statements]
      .
      .
      .
   CASE ELSE
      [range of statements]
END SELECT
```

where **test-expression** is a numeric or string expression and **match-expression** indicates the values for which the case is selected.

FIGURE 3-19 The general form of the SELECT CASE statement

Valid Match-Expressions

There are several ways to construct valid match-expressions following the keyword CASE. Consider the match-expressions in Figure 3-20.

EXAMPLE	MATCH-EXPRESSION
1	CASE "F" TO "H", "S", Code$
2	CASE IS = Salary, IS = Max.Salary - 5000
3	CASE IS < 12, 20 TO 30, 48.6, IS > 100

FIGURE 3-20 Valid match-expressions in a SELECT CASE statement

In Example 1 in Figure 3-20, the match-expression is a list made up of the letters F to H, the letter S, and the value of the variable Code$. In Example 2, the match-expression includes Salary and the expression Max.Salary − 5000. If a relational operator is used, then the keyword IS is required. The second value in the list of Example 2 shows that expressions with arithmetic operators are allowed. The third example includes a list that requires the use of the keywords IS and TO. Use the keyword IS before any relational operator, such as = or >. Use the keyword TO to define a range of values.

TRY IT YOURSELF EXERCISES

1. Determine the value of Amt that will cause the condition in the following IF statements to be true:
   a. ```
      IF Amt > 8 OR Amt = 3 THEN
         Z = Z / 10
      END IF
      ```
   b. ```
      IF Amt + 10 >= 7 AND NOT Amt < 0 THEN
         PRINT "The answer is"; A
      END IF
      ```

2. Construct partial programs for each of these structures.
   a.
   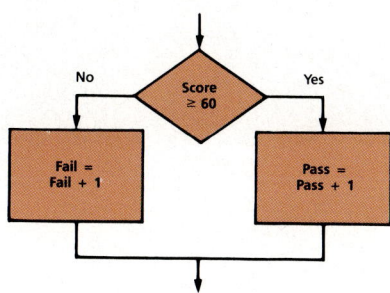
   b.
   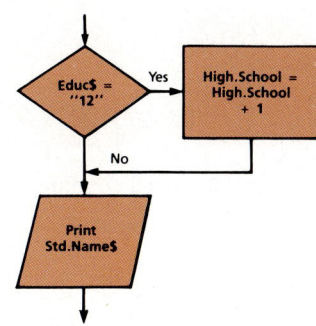

3. Construct partial programs for each of these logic structures.
   a.
   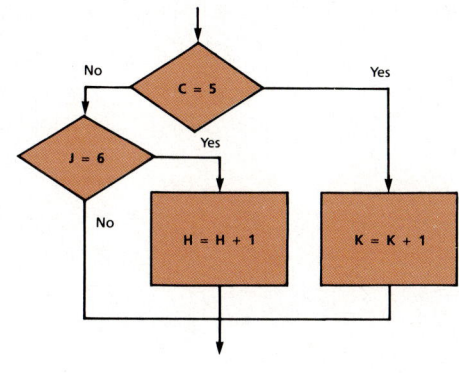
   b.
   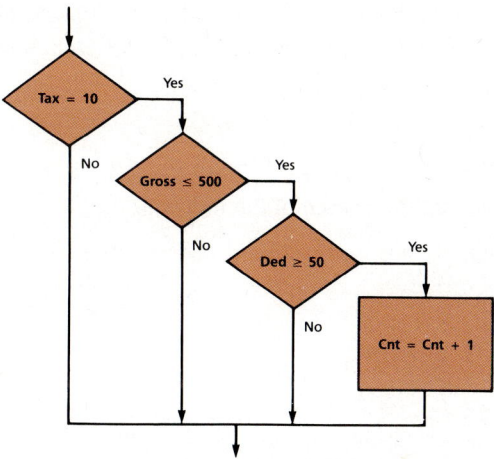

4. What is displayed if the following program is executed?
```
' Exercise 4
READ I
DO WHILE I <> -99
    SELECT CASE I
        CASE 1, 4, 7
            PRINT I, "Case 1"
        CASE IS < 8
            PRINT I, "Case 2"
        CASE 14 TO 21
            PRINT I, "Case 3"
        CASE ELSE
            PRINT I, "Case 4"
    END SELECT
    READ I
LOOP
DATA 1, 4, 7, 2, 21, 20, -99
END
```

5. Given the following:

   Emp.Num = 500
   Salary = $700
   Job.Code$ = "1"
   Tax = $60
   Insurance.Ded = $40

   Determine the truth value of the following compound conditions:

   ```
   a. Emp.Num < 400 OR Job.Code$ = "1"
   b. Salary = 700 AND Tax = 50
   c. Salary - Tax = 640 AND Job.Code$ = "1"
   d. Tax + Insurance.Ded = Salary - 500 OR Job.Code$ = "0"
   e. NOT Job.Code$ < "0"
   f. NOT (Job.Code$ = "1" OR Tax = 60)
   g. Salary < 300 AND Insurance.Ded < 50 OR Job.Code$ = "1"
   h. Salary < 300 AND (Insurance.Ded < 50 OR Job.Code$ = "1")
   i. NOT (NOT Job.Code$ = "1")
   ```

6. Given the following:

   T = 0, V = 4, B = 7, Y = 8, and X = 3

   Determine the action taken for each of the following:

   ```
   a. IF T > 0 THEN
         READ A
      END IF
   b. IF B = 4 OR T > 7 THEN
         IF X > 1 THEN
            READ A
         END IF
      END IF
   c. IF X = 3 OR T > 2 THEN
         IF Y > 7 THEN
            READ A
         END IF
      END IF
   d. IF X + 2 < 5 THEN
         IF B < V + X THEN
            READ A
         END IF
      END IF
   ```

7. Write a program that determines the number of negative values (Negative), number of zero values (Zero) and number of positive values (Positive) in the following data set: 4, 2, 3, –9, 0, 0, –4, –6, –8, 3, 2, 0, 0, 8, –3, 4. Use the –999999 to test for the end-of-file.

8. The values of three variables Num1, Num2, and Num3 are positive and not equal to each other. Using IF statements, determine which has the smallest value and assign this value to Little.

9. The IOU National Bank computes its monthly service charge on checking accounts by adding $0.50 to a value computed from the following:

   $0.21 per check for the first ten checks
   $0.19 per check for the next ten checks
   $0.17 per check for the next ten checks
   $0.15 per check for the remaining checks

   Write a sequence of statements that includes a SELECT CASE statement and a PRINT statement to display the account number (Account), the number of checks cashed (Checks), and the computed monthly charge (Charge). Assume the account number and the number of checks cashed are in DATA statements.

STUDENT ASSIGNMENTS

STUDENT ASSIGNMENT 1: Student Registration Report

Instructions: Design and code a QuickBASIC program to process the data shown under INPUT. Generate the student registration report shown under OUTPUT. A student with less than 12 hours is defined as part-time. The registration fee is determined from the following:

Credits Hours	Fee
Less than 12	$400.00
12 or more	$400.00 plus $30.00 per credit hour in excess of 11 hours

As part of the end-of-job routine, print the total number of part-time students, full-time students, students, and fees.

INPUT: Use the following sample data:

STUDENT NAME	CREDIT HOURS
Joe Franks	14
Ed Crane	9
Susan Lewis	18
Fred Smith	12
Jack North	10
Nikole Hiegh	17
EOF	0

OUTPUT: The following results are printed:

```
             Student Registration

   Student       Credit
   Name          Hours      Fee      Status

   Joe Franks      14       490.00   Full-Time
   Ed Crane         9       400.00   Part-Time
   Susan Lewis     18       610.00   Full-Time
   Fred Smith      12       430.00   Full-Time
   Jack North      10       400.00   Part-Time
   Nikole Hiegh    17       580.00   Full-Time

   Total Part-Time  ====>        2
   Total Full-Time  ====>        4
   Total Students   =====>       6
   Total Fees       =========>  $2,910.00

   End of Report
```

STUDENT ASSIGNMENT 2: Employee Salary Increase Report

Instructions: Design and code a QuickBASIC program to process the data shown under INPUT. Use IF statements with compound conditions to display on the screen the employee salary increase report shown under OUTPUT.

Determine the employee salary increase from the following:
1. All employees get a 4% salary increase
2. All employees get a 0.025% times the number of annual merits salary increase.
3. Employees with more than three annual merits and 10 or more years of service get an additional 2.5% salary increase
4. Employees with four or more annual merits and less than 10 years of service get an additional 1.5% salary increase

INPUT: Use the following sample data. Make sure you enclose the employee names within quotation marks, since each name includes a comma.

EMPLOYEE NAME	ANNUAL MERITS	SERVICE	CURRENT SALARY
Babjack, Bill	9	3	$19,500
Knopf, Louis	0	19	29,200
Taylor, Jane	8	12	26,000
Droopey, Joe	8	4	28,000
Lane, Lyn	2	9	19,800
Lis, Frank	6	1	21,000
Lopez, Hector	10	1	15,000
Braion, Jim	8	19	26,500
EOF	0	0	0

OUTPUT: The following results are displayed:

```
              Employee Salary Increase Report
Employee       Annual    Current                      New
Name           Merits    Salary        Raise          Salary

Babjack, Bill    9       19,500.00     1,116.38       20,616.38
Knopf, Louis     0       29,200.00     1,168.00       30,368.00
Taylor, Jane     8       26,000.00     1,742.00       27,742.00
Droopey, Joe     8       28,000.00     1,596.00       29,596.00
Lane, Lyn        2       19,800.00       801.90       20,601.90
Lis, Frank       6       21,000.00     1,186.50       22,186.50
Lopez, Hector   10       15,000.00       862.50       15,862.50
Braion, Jim      8       26,500.00     1,775.50       28,275.50
                         ==========    ========       ==========
                         185,000.00    10,248.78      195,248.78

Total Employees ============>      8
Average Employee Raise ======>  $1,281.10

End of Report
```

STUDENT ASSIGNMENT 3: Computer Usage Report

Instructions: Design and code a QuickBASIC program to process the data shown under INPUT and prints the report shown under OUTPUT. Use the SELECT CASE statement to determine the computer charges. At the end-of-job, print the total customers, total hours in decimal, and the total charges. The monthly charges can be determined from the following:
  1. $165.00 for one hour or less usage
  2. $240.00 for usage greater than one hour and less than or equal to two hours
  3. $300.00 for usage greater than two hours and less than or equal to three hours
  4. $330.00 for usage greater than three hours and less than or equal to four hours
  5. $375.00 for usage greater than four hours and less than or equal to five hours
  6. $1.25 per minute if the usage is greater than five hours

INPUT: Use the following sample data:

CUSTOMER NAME	HOURS	MINUTES
Acme Inc.	2	0
Hitek	2	50
Floline	5	10
Niki's Food	1	14
Amanda Inc.	6	22
EOF	0	0

OUTPUT: The following results are printed:

```
              Computer Usage Report

   Customer
   Name            Hours      Minutes      Charges

   Acme Inc.         2            0         240.00
   Hitek             2           50         300.00
   Floline           5           10         387.50
   Niki's Food       1           14         240.00
   Amanda Inc.       6           22         477.50

   Total Customers ========>       5
   Total Hours     ============>     17.60
   Total Charges   ==========>  $1,645.00

   End of Report
```

PROJECT 4

Interactive Programming, For Loops, and an Introduction to the Top-Down Approach

One of the major tasks of any program is to integrate the data that is to be processed into the program. In the first three projects, the READ and DATA statements were used to integrate the data into the program. This project introduces you to another method of data integration through the use of the INPUT statement. The INPUT statement is different than the READ and DATA statements, because with the INPUT statement the data is entered *during* execution rather than as *part of the program*.

A second topic covered in this project is alternative methods for implementing loops in QuickBASIC. Through the first three projects, we have consistently created loops using the DO WHILE and LOOP statements. In this project we discuss the creation of loops using the DO and LOOP UNTIL statements and the FOR and NEXT statements. The DO and LOOP UNTIL statements allow you to create loops that test for termination at the bottom of the loop rather than at the top of the loop. The FOR and NEXT statements allow you to more efficiently establish counter-controlled loops. A **counter-controlled loop** is one that exits the loop when a counter has reached a specified number.

Finally, this project presents the top-down approach to solving problems. The top-down approach is a useful methodology for solving large and complex problems. This approach breaks the problem into smaller parts and allows you to solve each part independent of the others.

THE INPUT STATEMENT

The INPUT statement causes a program to temporarily halt execution and accept data through the keyboard as shown in Figure 4-1. After the user enters the required data (1.25 in Figure 4-1) through the keyboard, the program continues to execute.

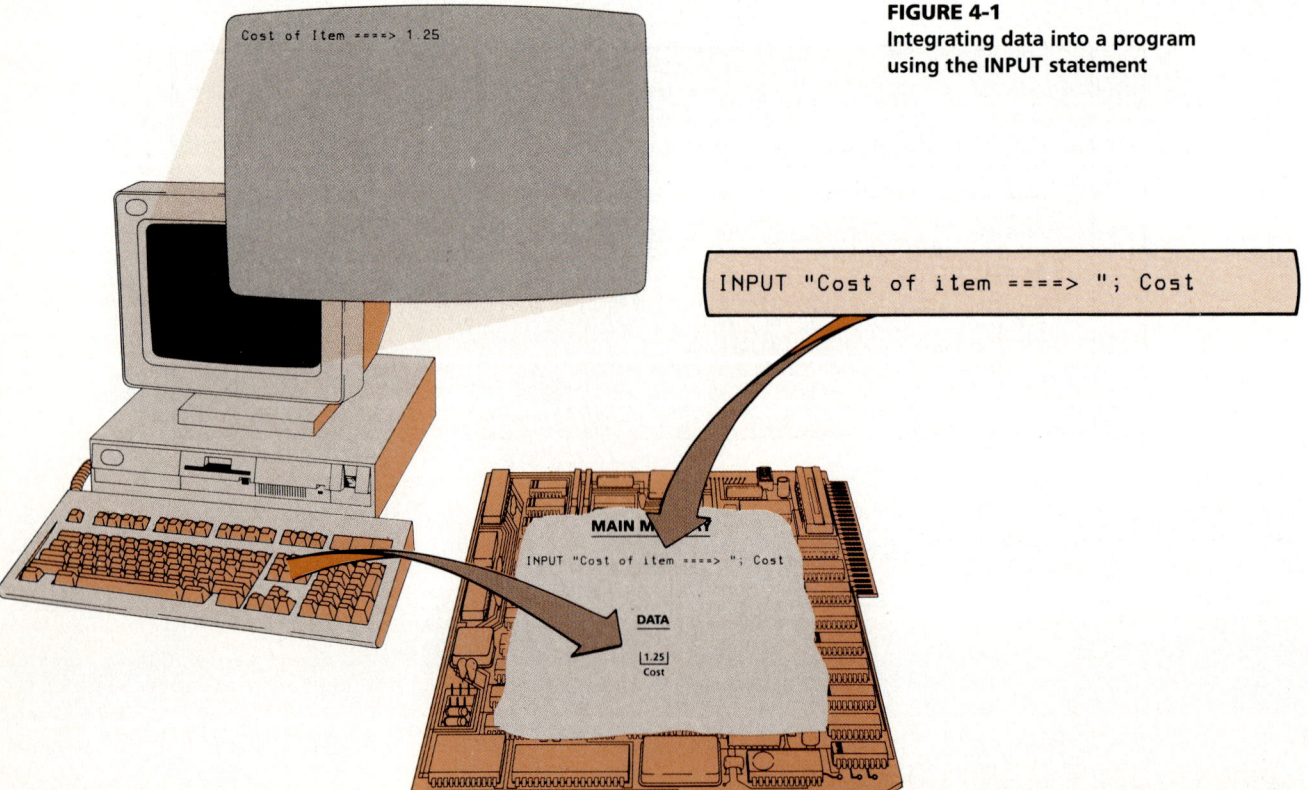

FIGURE 4-1
Integrating data into a program using the INPUT statement

The INPUT statement has two general forms, shown in Figure 4-2. With the first general form, the keyword INPUT is immediately followed by one or more variables separated by commas. When executed, this first form displays a question mark on the screen to indicate that it is waiting for the user to enter data.

The second general form of the INPUT statement shows that the programmer may enter a **prompt message** to inform the user of the required data. In this second and most often used form, the keyword INPUT is followed by the prompt message in quotation marks, a comma or semicolon after the prompt message, and a list of variables separated by commas. A semicolon after a prompt message tells the PC to display a question mark immediately after the prompt message. A comma instructs the PC not to display the question mark. Although this statement may include more than one variable, most programmers place one variable per INPUT statement.

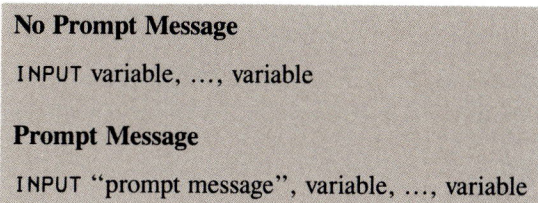

FIGURE 4-2 The general form of the INPUT statement

Figure 4-3 illustrates several examples of INPUT statements.

EXAMPLE	INPUT STATEMENT	DATA ENTERED THROUGH KEYBOARD
1	INPUT Amount, Cost	125.56, 75
2	INPUT Cus.Name$, Age, Deduction	Joe Dac, 57, 25
3	INPUT "Discount =====>", Disc	.25
4	INPUT "What is your name"; User.Name$	Marci Jean
5	PRINT "Do you want to continue?" INPUT "Enter Y for Yes, else N", Control$	Y

FIGURE 4-3 Examples of the INPUT statement

Examples 1 and 2 in Figure 4-3 show that it is not necessary to include a prompt message. When either INPUT statement is executed, a question mark displays on the screen. Examples 3 through 5 include prompt messages. In Example 3, the prompt message

```
Discount =====>
```

displays on the screen at the location of the cursor. Following the display of the prompt, the PC halts execution until the user enters the data (.25) and presses the Enter key.

In Example 4 of Figure 4-3, the following prompt displays:

```
What is your name?
```

Because we ended the prompt message with a semicolon, the PC displays the question mark after the prompt. Example 5 shows how you can utilize the PRINT statement along with the INPUT statement to display prompt messages made up of more than one line.

THE BEEP AND LOCATE STATEMENTS

Two QuickBASIC statements that are often used in tandem with the INPUT statement are the BEEP and LOCATE statements.

The BEEP Statement

When executed, the BEEP statement causes the PC's speaker to beep for a fraction of a second. Several BEEP statements in a row cause the PC to beep for a longer duration. The following line causes the PC to beep for approximately a second:

    BEEP : BEEP : BEEP : BEEP

Notice the colons between the BEEP statements. In QuickBASIC, the colon allows you to place more than one statement per line. The BEEP statement is often used to alert the user that there is a problem with the program or data.

The LOCATE Statement

QuickBASIC defines the output screen as having 25 rows and 80 columns. The LOCATE statement can be used to position the cursor precisely on any one of the two thousand display positions on the screen. For example, the following line causes the PC to move the cursor to row 4, column 15:

    LOCATE 4, 15

It makes no difference whether the cursor is above or below row 4 or to the right or left of column 15. The general form of the LOCATE statement is shown in Figure 4-4.

FIGURE 4-4
The general form of the LOCATE statement

    LOCATE row, column

When executed, the partial program in Figure 4-5 displays the prompt message in the INPUT statement in row 6, column 12.

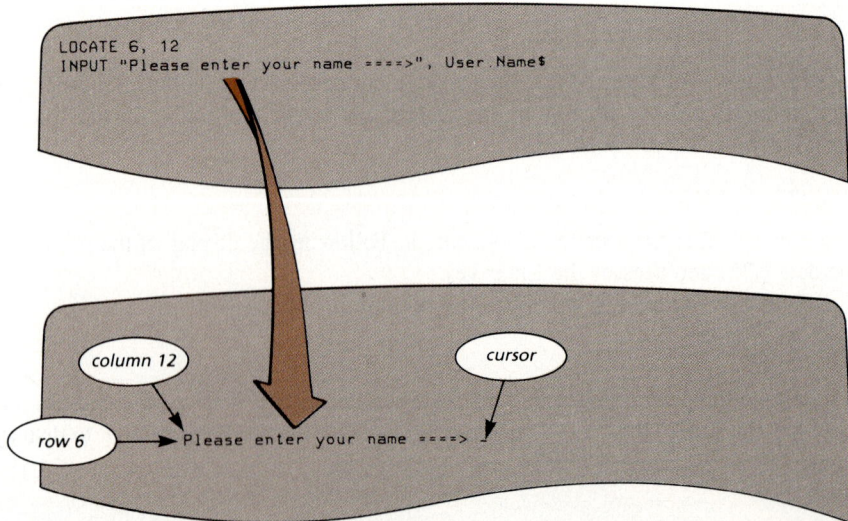

FIGURE 4-5
Use of the LOCATE statement to position the cursor

EDITING DATA ENTERED THROUGH THE KEYBOARD

*I*n most interactive applications it is required that you check the incoming data to be sure that it is reasonable. A **reasonableness check** ensures that the data is legitimate, that is, the data is within a range of acceptable values. If the data is not validated before being used, then the PC can very well generate incorrect information.

The partial program in Figure 4-6 requests that the user enter a value for the variable Item.Cost. Assume that the program specifications state that the value of Cost must be greater than zero and less than 1,000.00.

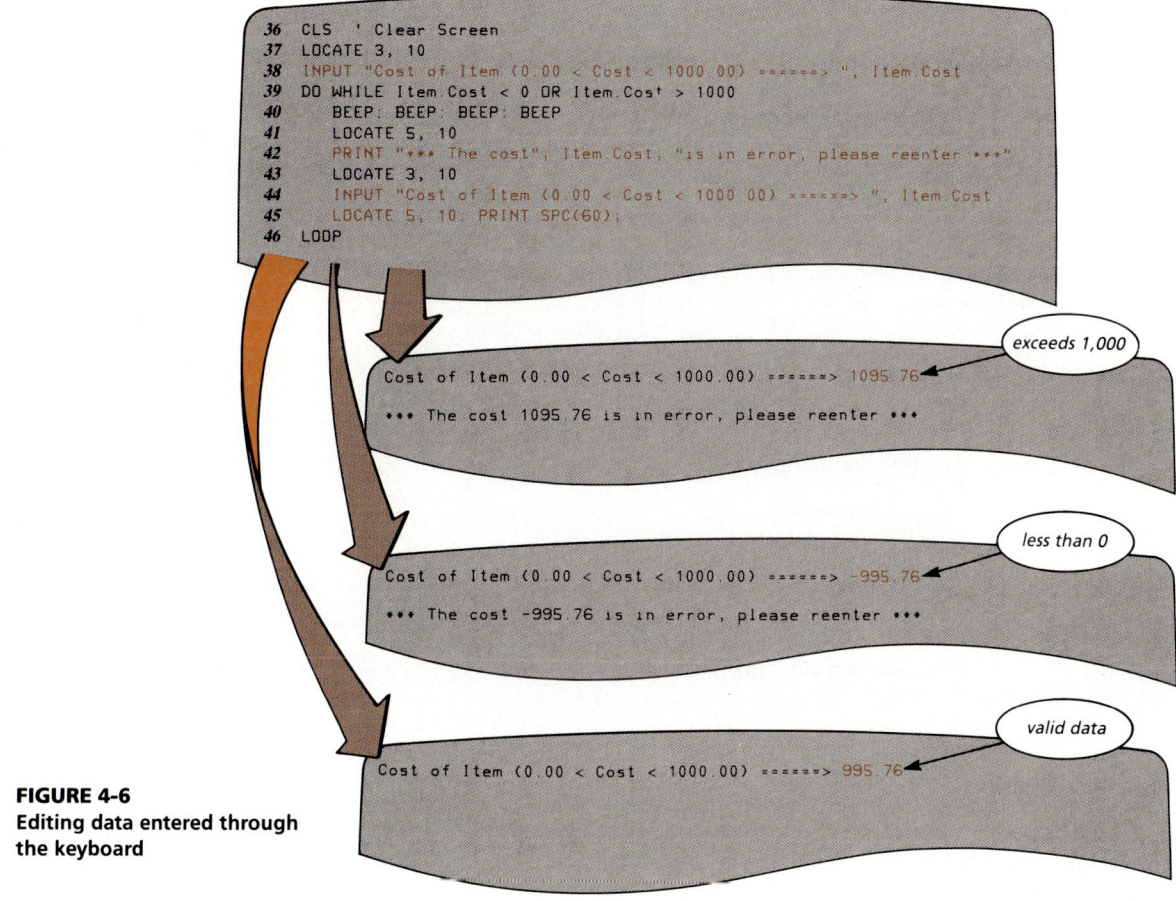

FIGURE 4-6
Editing data entered through the keyboard

When the PC executes the partial program in Figure 4-6, the CLS statement in line 36 clears the output screen. Line 37 moves the cursor to column 10 in row 3. The INPUT statement in line 38 displays the prompt message and halts execution of the program. After the user enters the value 1095.76 and presses the Enter key, the DO WHILE statement in line 39 tests the value of Item.Cost. Since it is greater than 1,000.00, control enters the loop. Line 40 causes the PC speaker to beep for a second. Due to lines 41 and 42, the PC displays an error message beginning at column 10 in row 5.

Lines 43 and 44 again cause the prompt message to display beginning at column 10 in row 3. After the user enters -995.76, the error message in row 5 is erased by the SPC function in the PRINT statement in line 45. The SPC function displays as many spaces as indicated in the parentheses. Thus, SPC(60) displays 60 spaces and in doing so erases the error message in row 5. Since -995.76 is still outside the limits, the PC reexecutes the loop and displays the error message due to line 42. Finally, when the user enters 995.76, the PC exits the loop and continues execution at the line following the LOOP statement.

Data validation is an important part of the programming process. It should be apparent that the information produced by a computer is only as accurate as the data it processes. The term **GIGO** (Garbage In—Garbage Out, pronounced GEE-GOH) is used to describe the generation of inaccurate information from the input of invalid data. Data validation should be incorporated into all programs, especially when the INPUT statement is used.

SAMPLE PROGRAM 4 — ITEM COST REPORT

The sample program in this project illustrates the preparation of an item cost table that contains the cost of one to ten items. The program begins by asking the user to enter the cost of an item. The cost must be greater than zero and less than 1,000.00. After validating the entry, the sample program displays the cost table. Once the table displays, the user is asked if another table should be prepared. The user must enter a Y for yes or an N for no.

If the user enters the letter Y, the loop is executed again and the user is asked to enter the cost of the next item. If the user enters the letter N, the program displays an end-of-job message followed by termination of execution. Figure 4-7 shows the desired output results for Sample Program 4.

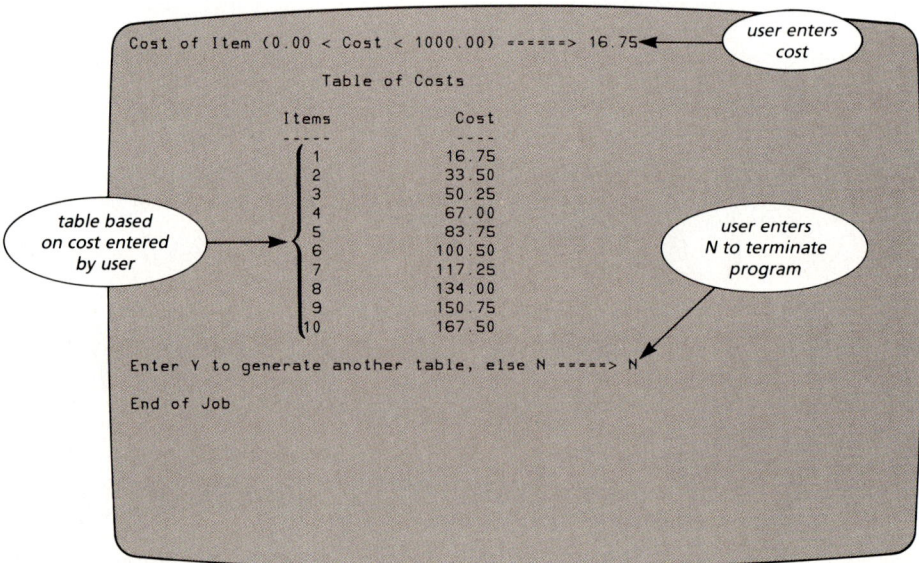

FIGURE 4-7 The desired output results for Sample Program 4

Program Flowchart

The flowchart for Sample Program 4 which produces the item cost table for one to ten items is illustrated in Figure 4-8. At the top of the flowchart, the variable representing the maximum number of items is initialized to 10 and the table format is assigned to string variables.

Control then enters the loop. Notice that this is the first time in this book that a decision symbol is not at the top of the loop. In this flowchart, the decision to terminate the loop is at the bottom. Loops that have the decision to terminate at the top are called **Do-While loops**. Loops that have the decision to terminate at the bottom are called **Do-Until loops**.

Within the major loop, the output screen is cleared and the user is requested to enter the cost of an item. Next, the cost is validated, the table headings are displayed, and a counter is initialized to one. The table is then generated by a looping process that continues while the counter is less than or equal to 10. After the table displays, the user is asked if another is desired. The decision symbol at the bottom of the Do-Until loop determines whether to continue or terminate processing on the basis of the value (Y or N) entered by the user.

Before we can code the logic shown in Figure 4-8 we need to discuss the FOR and NEXT statements.

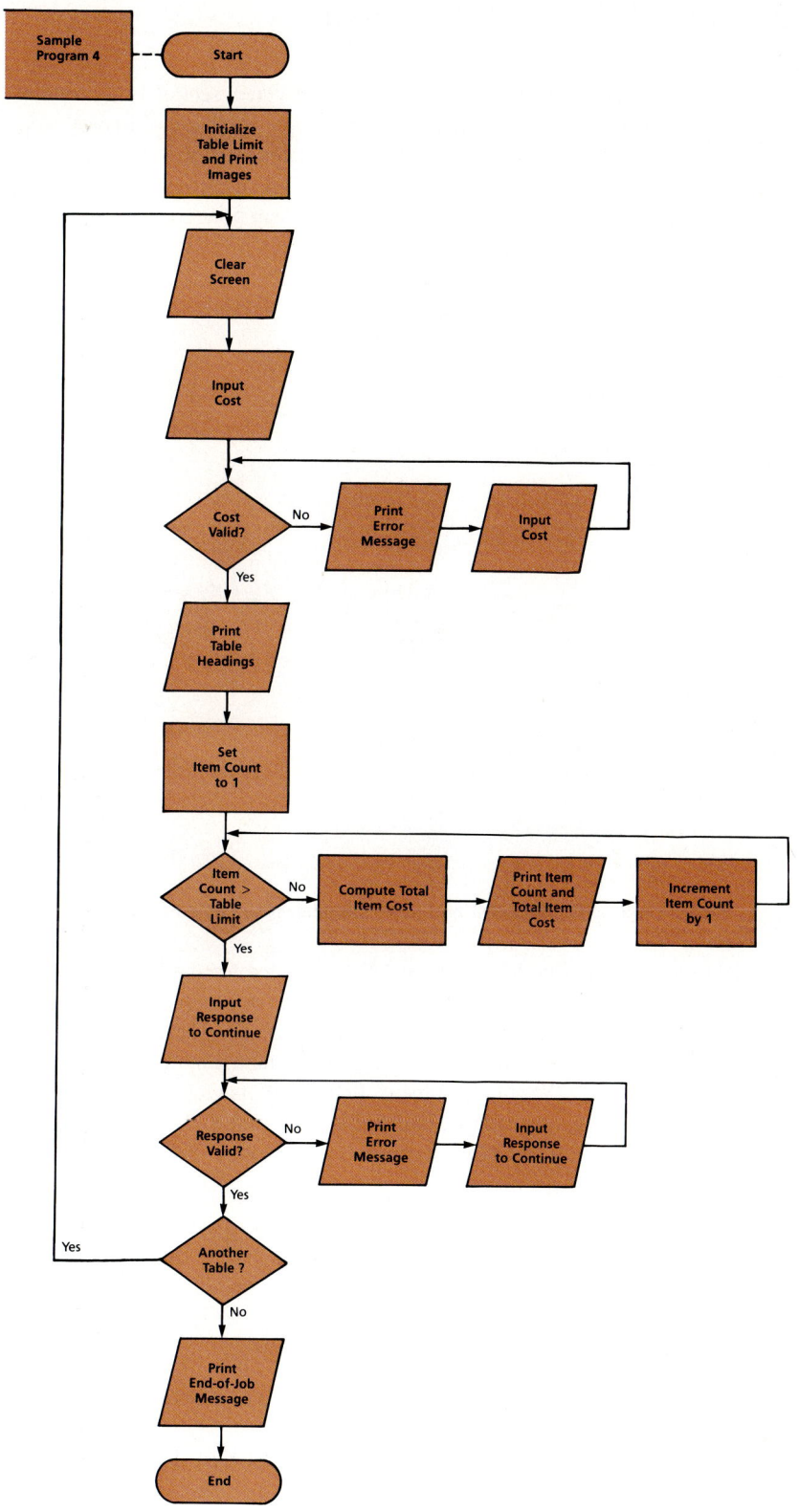

FIGURE 4-8
The flowchart for Sample Program 4

THE FOR AND NEXT STATEMENTS

The FOR and NEXT statements make it possible to execute a section of a program repeatedly, with automatic changes in the value of a variable between repetitions. Whenever you have to develop a counter-controlled loop (a loop that is to be executed a specific number of times based on a counter), the FOR and NEXT statements can be used to develop it. We call such a loop a **For loop**.

Figure 4-9 illustrates how the FOR and NEXT statements can be used to implement the loop that generates the cost table described in the flowchart for Sample Program 4.

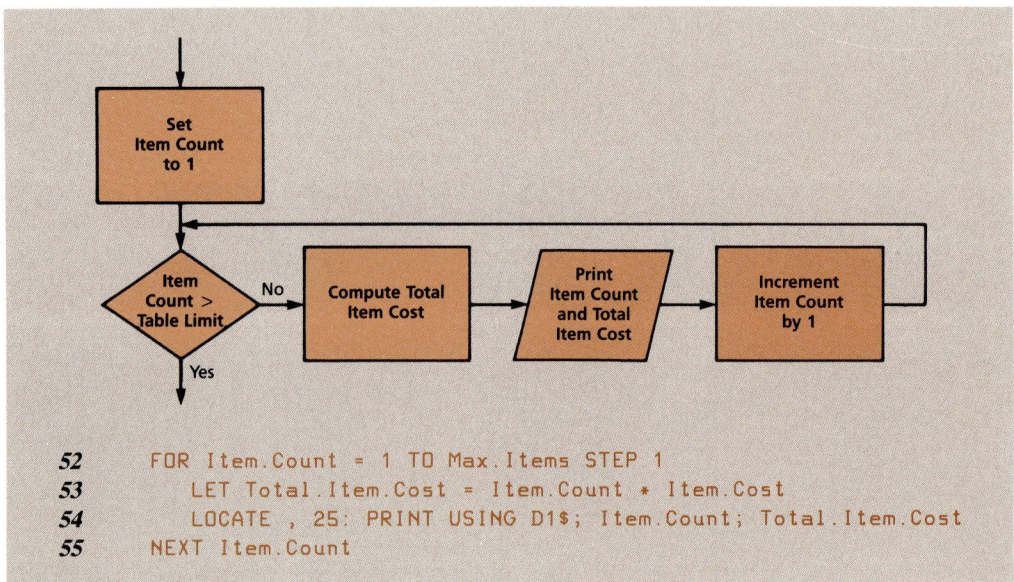

FIGURE 4-9 Using the FOR and NEXT statements to implement the loop that generates the cost table

When the FOR statement in line 52 of Figure 4-9 is executed for the first time, the For loop becomes active and the variable Item.Count is set equal to one. The statements within the For loop, in this case lines 53 and 54, are executed. The NEXT statement in line 55 returns control to the FOR statement in line 52, where the value of Item.Count is incremented by the amount (1), which follows the keyword STEP. If the value of Item.Count is less than or equal to Max.Items (table limit), execution of the For loop continues. When the value of Item.Count is greater than Max.Items, control transfers to the line following NEXT Item.Count. As with other loops, notice that we indent the statements within the loop by three spaces.

The general forms of the FOR and NEXT statements are shown in Figure 4-10.

```
FOR loop-variable = initial TO limit STEP increment

   [range of statements]

NEXT loop-variable
```

FIGURE 4-10 The general forms of the FOR and NEXT statements

In Figure 4-10, the FOR statement indicates the beginning of a For loop and the NEXT statement indicates the end. The range of statements within the For loop is executed repeatedly as long as *loop-variable* is not greater than *limit*. *Loop-variable* is initially assigned the value of *initial*. Each time the range of statements is executed, *loop-variable* is increased by the value of *increment*. When *loop-variable* is greater than *limit*, control passes to the line following the corresponding NEXT statement.

If *increment* is negative, the test to terminate the For loop is reversed. The value of *loop-variable* is decremented each time through the For loop, and the For loop is executed while *loop-variable* is greater than or equal to *limit*. If the keyword STEP is not included in a FOR statement, then the increment value is automatically set to one.

Figure 4-11 illustrates several valid FOR statements.

EXAMPLE	FOR STATEMENT
1	FOR Count = 1 TO 100 STEP 1
2	FOR X = 5 TO Y STEP 3
3	FOR Amount = 1.25 TO 7.35 STEP .05
4	FOR Tax = A TO B STEP C
5	FOR S = 0 TO -35 STEP -3
6	FOR X = 1 TO 10

FIGURE 4-11 Examples of valid FOR statements

In Example 1 of Figure 4-11, the For loop is executed 100 times. Example 2 points out that the initial and increment values can be values other than one. Example 3 initializes Amount to 1.25 for the first pass. Thereafter, the value .05 is added to Amount each time the range of statements is executed. Hence, Amount takes on the values 1.25, 1.30, 1.35, 1.40, and so on, until Amount exceeds 7.35.

Example 4 shows that the initial, limit, and increment values can be variables. Example 5 includes a negative increment (–3). Thus, the test is reversed and S must be less than –35 before the For loop terminates. Finally, Example 6 illustrates a FOR statement without the keyword STEP. In this case, the increment value is automatically set to one.

The QuickBASIC Program

The program in Figure 4-12 corresponds to the program flowchart in Figure 4-8.

FIGURE 4-12
Sample Program 4

```
1   ' ****************************************************************
2   ' *   Sample Program 4                        September 15, 1994  *
3   ' *   Item Cost Report                                            *
4   ' *   J. S. Quasney                                               *
5   ' *                                                               *
6   ' *   This program displays a table of costs of 1 to 10 items.    *
7   ' *   The user enters the cost per item and the program           *
8   ' *   displays the table of costs.                                *
9   ' *        The cost per item entered by the user is validated     *
10  ' *   (greater than zero and less than 1000.00).  After the       *
11  ' *   table is displayed the user is asked if another table       *
12  ' *   should be generated.                                        *
13  ' *        This activity continues until the user indicates       *
14  ' *   that no more tables are to be generated.                    *
15  ' *                                                               *
16  ' *   Variables:  Item.Cost        -- Cost of item                *
17  ' *               Item.Count       -- Item count                  *
18  ' *               Max.Items        -- Maximum number of items     *
19  ' *                                   in table                    *
20  ' *               Total.Item.Cost  -- Cost of items               *
21  ' *               Control$         -- Response to continue        *
22  ' *               H1$, H2$, H3$, D1$, T1$ -- Print images         *
23  ' ****************************************************************
24
```

(continued)

FIGURE 4-12
(continued)

```
25  ' ********************* Initialization **********************
26  LET Max.Items = 10
27  LET H1$ = "    Table of Costs"
28  LET H2$ = "Items          Cost"
29  LET H3$ = "-----          ----"
30  LET D1$ = "   ##        ##,###.##"
31  LET T1$ = "End of Job"
32
33  ' ***************** Generate Cost Table ********************
34  DO
35     ' *********** Accept and Validate Cost of Item ***********
36     CLS  ' Clear Screen
37     LOCATE 3, 10
38     INPUT "Cost of Item (0.00 < Cost < 1000.00) ======> ", Item.Cost
39     DO WHILE Item.Cost < 0 OR Item.Cost > 1000
40        BEEP: BEEP: BEEP: BEEP
41        LOCATE 5, 10
42        PRINT "*** The cost"; Item.Cost; "is in error, please reenter ***"
43        LOCATE 3, 10
44        INPUT "Cost of Item (0.00 < Cost < 1000.00) ======> ", Item.Cost
45        LOCATE 5, 10: PRINT SPC(60);
46     LOOP
47
48     ' *************** Generate Table of Costs ****************
49     LOCATE 5, 25: PRINT H1$
50     LOCATE 7, 25: PRINT H2$
51     LOCATE 8, 25: PRINT H3$
52     FOR Item.Count = 1 TO Max.Items STEP 1
53        LET Total.Item.Cost = Item.Count * Item.Cost
54        LOCATE , 25: PRINT USING D1$; Item.Count; Total.Item.Cost
55     NEXT Item.Count
56
57     ' ******** Accept and Validate Response to Continue ********
58     LOCATE 20, 10
59     INPUT "Enter Y to generate another table, else N =====> ", Control$
60     DO WHILE Control$ <> "N" AND Control$ <> "Y"
61        BEEP: BEEP: BEEP: BEEP
62        LOCATE 22, 10
63        PRINT "*** Response in error, please reenter ***"
64        LOCATE 20, 10
65        INPUT "Enter Y to generate another table, else N =====> ", Control$
66        LOCATE 22, 10: PRINT SPC(50);
67     LOOP
68
69  LOOP UNTIL Control$ = "N"
70
71  ' ********************* Wrap-Up **************************
72  LOCATE 22, 10
73  PRINT T1$
74  END
```

Discussion of Sample Program 4

When Sample Program 4 is executed, the variables in lines 26 through 31 are initialized. Line 26 initializes Max.Items (table limit) to 10. Lines 27 through 31 define the table format. The variables are used later in the PRINT statements in lines 49 through 51, 54, and 73.

The DO statement in line 34 indicates the beginning of a Do-Until loop. With a Do-Until loop, the condition that determines whether the loop should continue is in the LOOP statement (line 69). As shown in Figure 4-13, there are two basic types of loops. The Do-While loop has the decision symbol at the top of the loop. The Do-Until loop has the decision symbol at the bottom of the loop. If the decision is at the top (Figure 4-13A), use the DO WHILE and LOOP statements. If the decision is at the bottom (Figure 4-13B), use the DO and LOOP UNTIL statements.

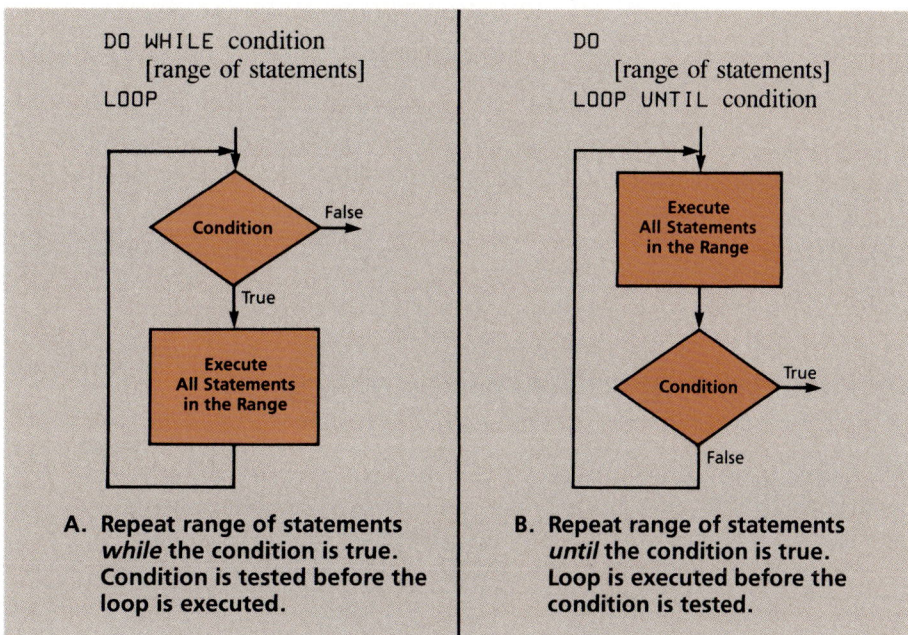

FIGURE 4-13 The two basic types of loops and the statements in QuickBASIC which should be used to implement them

    Upon entering the Do-Until loop, the screen is cleared by line 36. Lines 37 through 46 accept and validate the cost of the item entered by the user. Lines 49 through 51 display the table title and column headings. Lines 52 through 55 compute and display the rows of the table. Notice in line 54 that the LOCATE statement does not include a row number. When the LOCATE statement is written in this fashion, it references the current row, which is one greater than the one referenced by the previously executed PRINT or PRINT USING statement. Hence, each time line 54 is executed in the For loop, the PRINT USING statement begins printing in column 25 of the next row. Notice in lines 49 through 51 and 54 that it is common practice to incorporate both the LOCATE and PRINT statements on the same line. Of course, it is important that you separate the two statements with the colon.

    After the table is displayed on the screen, lines 58 through 67 accept and validate a response from the user that indicates whether the Do-Until loop should continue. In this case, only two values, Y and N, are acceptable (line 60). If the user enters a Y, line 69 causes the PC to continue execution at the top of the loop (line 34). If the user enters the value N, the condition in line 69 is false. Thus, control passes to line 72 and an end-of-job message is displayed followed by termination of execution of the program.

Figure 4-14 shows the display of Sample Program 4 when the value 579.46 is entered as the cost of an item.

```
Cost of Item (0.00 < Cost < 1000.00) ======> 579.46
                Table of Costs
           Items            Cost
           -----            ----
             1            579.46
             2          1,158.92
             3          1,738.38
             4          2,317.84
             5          2,897.30
             6          3,476.76
             7          4,056.22
             8          4,635.68
             9          5,215.14
            10          5,794.60

Enter Y to generate another table, else N ======> N
End of Job
```

FIGURE 4-14
The results displayed due to the execution of Sample Program 4 and a cost per item of $579.46

AN INTRODUCTION TO THE TOP-DOWN APPROACH

op-down programming is a divide and conquer strategy used by programmers to solve large problems. The first step in top-down programming is to divide the task into smaller, more manageable subtasks through the use of a top-down chart. Figure 4-15 illustrates a top-down chart for the problem solved by Sample Program 4.

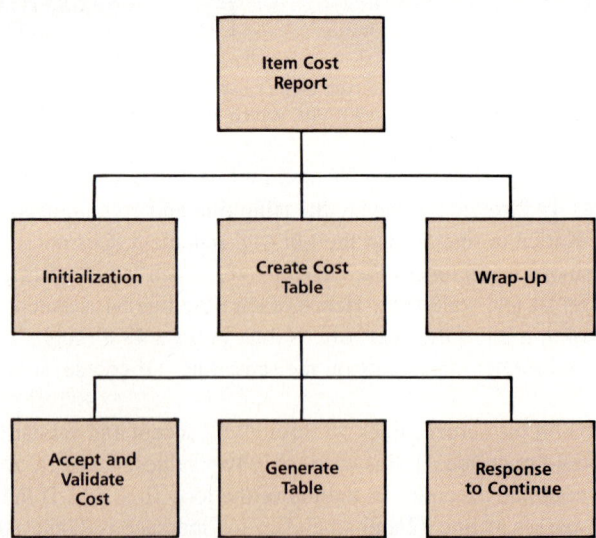

FIGURE 4-15
A top-down chart for the problem solved by Sample Program 4

A top-down chart differs from a program flowchart in that it does not show decision-making logic or flow of control. A program flowchart shows *how* to solve the problem. A top-down chart shows *what* has to be done.

A top-down chart is very similar to a company's organization chart where each lower level subtask carries out a function for its superior task. In Figure 4-15, the top box (Item Cost Report) represents the complete task. The next level of boxes (Initialization, Create Cost Table, and Wrap-Up) shows the subtasks that are required to solve the task of the top box. The lowest level of boxes (Accept and Validate Cost Item, Generate Table, and Response to Continue) indicates the subtasks required to create a table. Usually, a task is divided into lower level subtasks whenever it appears to be too complicated or lengthy to stand by itself.

Implementing the Top-Down Approach

Once the larger, more complex problem has been decomposed into smaller pieces, a solution to each subtask can be designed and coded. We call the group of statements that are associated with a single programming task a **subroutine**, or **module**.

The subroutines that formulate a program solution begin with a name, followed immediately by a colon (:), and end with a RETURN statement. Subroutines are *called* by their superior modules using the GOSUB statement. When a subroutine has completed its task, control returns to the superior module via a RETURN statement. The rules regarding a subroutine name are the same as for a variable name.

THE GOSUB AND RETURN STATEMENTS

The GOSUB statement is used to call a subroutine. As shown in Figure 4-16, the keyword GOSUB is immediately followed by the subroutine name to which control is transferred. Once control transfers, the instructions in the subroutine are executed.

FIGURE 4-16
The general form of the GOSUB statement

`GOSUB subroutine-name`

The RETURN statement (Figure 4-17) at the bottom of the subroutine returns control to the statement following the corresponding GOSUB in the superior module.

FIGURE 4-17
The general form of the RETURN statement

`RETURN`

Consider the partial program on the next page in Figure 4-18 and the following important points regarding the implementation of the top-down approach:

- The END statement is the last statement in the Main module. Control returns to DOS through this statement.
- Indent by three spaces the statements within modules.
- So that lower level modules can easily be located, they should be placed below their superior module and in the order in which they are called.

FIGURE 4-18
Implementing the top-down chart in Figure 4-15

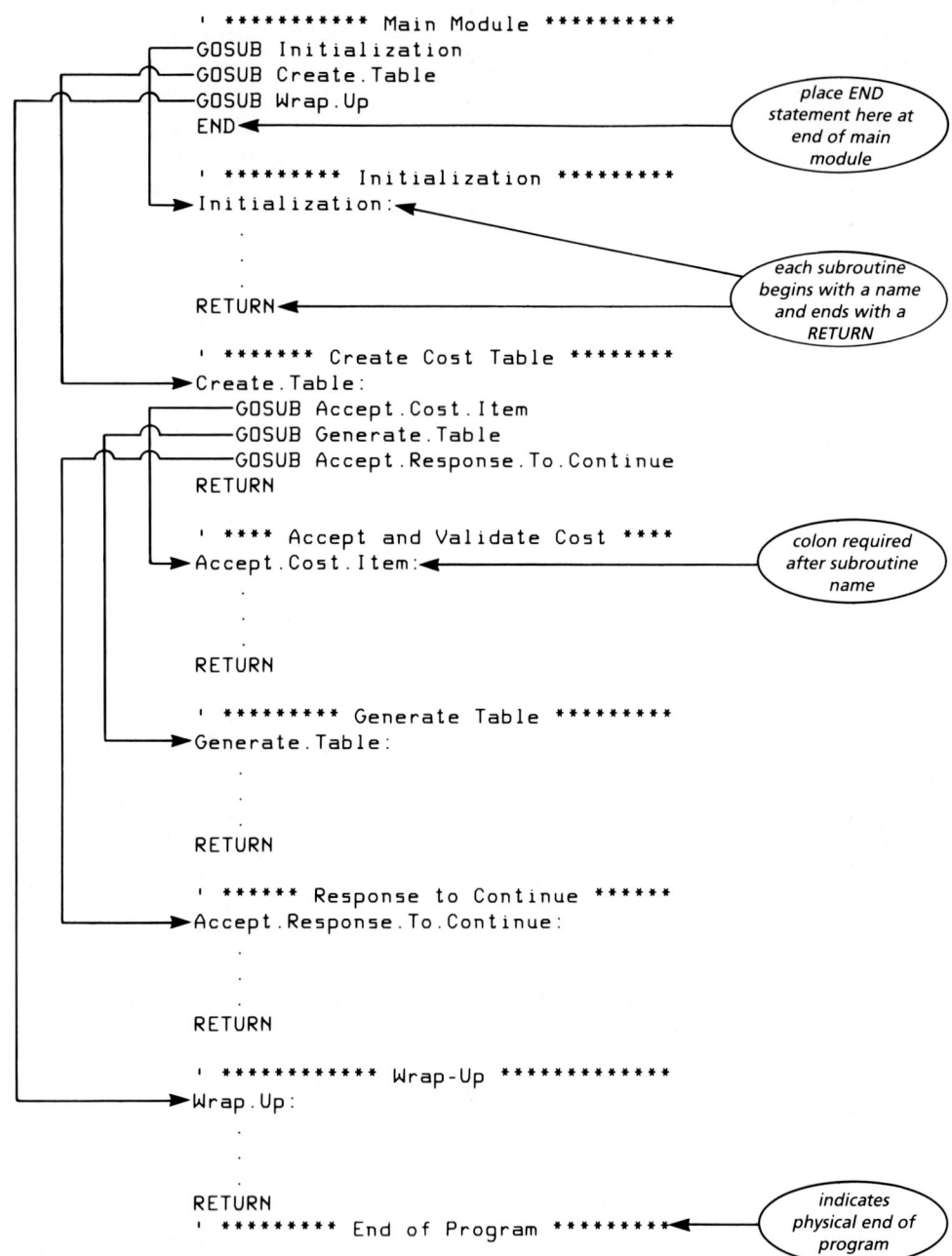

A modified version of Sample Program 4 which utilizes the top-down approach is shown in Figure 4-19. The coding corresponds to the top-down chart in Figure 4-15.

FIGURE 4-19
A top-down version of Sample Program 4

```
1   ' ***************************************************************
2   ' *   Sample Program 4 Modified            September 15, 1994   *
3   ' *   Item Cost Report                                          *
4   ' *   J. S. Quasney                                             *
5   ' *                                                             *
6   ' *   This program displays a table of costs of 1 to 10 items.  *
7   ' *   The user enters the cost per item and the program         *
8   ' *   displays the table of costs.                              *
9   ' *        The cost per item entered by the user is validated   *
10  ' *   (greater than zero and less than 1000.00).  After the     *
11  ' *   table is displayed the user is asked if another table     *
12  ' *   should be generated.                                      *
13  ' *        This activity continues until the user indicates     *
14  ' *   that no more tables are to be generated.                  *
15  ' *                                                             *
16  ' *   Variables:   Item.Cost         -- Cost of item            *
17  ' *                Item.Count        -- Item count              *
18  ' *                Max.Items         -- Maximum number of items *
19  ' *                                     in table                *
20  ' *                Total.Item.Cost   -- Cost of items           *
21  ' *                Control$          -- Response to continue    *
22  ' *                H1$, H2$, H3$, D1$, T1$ -- Print images      *
23  ' ***************************************************************
24
25  ' ***************************************************************
26  ' *                       Main Module                           *
27  ' ***************************************************************
28  GOSUB Initialization
29  GOSUB Create.Table
30  GOSUB Wrap.Up
31  END
32
33  ' ***************************************************************
34  ' *                       Initialization                        *
35  ' ***************************************************************
36  Initialization:
37      LET Max.Items = 10
38      LET H1$ = "     Table of Costs"
39      LET H2$ = "Items           Cost"
40      LET H3$ = "-----           ----"
41      LET D1$ = "  ##         ##,###.##"
42      LET T1$ = "End of Job"
43  RETURN
44
45  ' ***************************************************************
46  ' *                      Create Cost Table                      *
47  ' ***************************************************************
48  Create.Table:
49      DO
50          GOSUB Accept.Cost.Item
51          GOSUB Generate.Table
52          GOSUB Accept.Response.To.Continue
53      LOOP UNTIL Control$ = "N"
54  RETURN
55
```

(continued)

FIGURE 4-19
(continued)

```
56  ' ****************************************************************
57  ' *                 Accept and Validate Cost of Item              *
58  ' ****************************************************************
59  Accept.Cost.Item:
60     CLS  ' Clear Screen
61     LOCATE 3, 10
62     INPUT "Cost of Item (0.00 < Cost < 1000.00) ======> ", Item.Cost
63     DO WHILE Item.Cost < 0 OR Item.Cost > 1000
64        BEEP: BEEP: BEEP: BEEP
65        LOCATE 5, 10
66        PRINT "*** The cost"; Item.Cost; "is in error, please reenter ***"
67        LOCATE 3, 10
68        INPUT "Cost of Item (0.00 < Cost < 1000.00) ======> ", Item.Cost
69        LOCATE 5, 10: PRINT SPC(60);
70     LOOP
71  RETURN
72
73  ' ****************************************************************
74  ' *                    Generate Table of Costs                    *
75  ' ****************************************************************
76  Generate.Table:
77     LOCATE 5, 25: PRINT H1$
78     LOCATE 7, 25: PRINT H2$
79     LOCATE 8, 25: PRINT H3$
80     FOR Item.Count = 1 TO Max.Items STEP 1
81        LET Total.Item.Cost = Item.Count * Item.Cost
82        LOCATE , 25: PRINT USING D1$; Item.Count; Total.Item.Cost
83     NEXT Item.Count
84  RETURN
85
86  ' ****************************************************************
87  ' *              Accept and Validate Response to Continue         *
88  ' ****************************************************************
89  Accept.Response.To.Continue:
90     LOCATE 20, 10
91     INPUT "Enter Y to generate another table, else N =====> ", Control$
92     DO WHILE Control$ <> "N" AND Control$ <> "Y"
93        BEEP: BEEP: BEEP: BEEP
94        LOCATE 22, 10
95        PRINT "*** Response in error, please reenter ***"
96        LOCATE 20, 10
97        INPUT "Enter Y to generate another table, else N =====> ", Control$
98        LOCATE 22, 10: PRINT SPC(50);
99     LOOP
100 RETURN
101
102 ' ****************************************************************
103 ' *                            Wrap-Up                            *
104 ' ****************************************************************
105 Wrap.Up:
106    LOCATE 22, 10
107    PRINT T1$
108 RETURN
109 ' ********************** End of Program **********************
```

Discussion of Sample Program 4 Modified

When the modified version of Sample Program 4 in Figure 4-19 executes, line 28 in the Main module transfers control to the Initialization module which begins at line 36. After lines 37 through 42 are executed, the RETURN statement in line 43 transfers control back to line 29 in the Main module. Next, line 29 transfers control to the Create.Table module (lines 48 through 54). In this module, the Do-Until loop includes three GOSUB statements. Each time through this loop, a cost table such as the one in Figure 4-20 is generated.

When the user enters the letter N in response to the INPUT statement in line 97, control passes back to line 53. Since the condition in line 53 is true, control passes to the RETURN statement in line 54. Line 54 returns control to line 30. Next, line 30 transfers control to the Wrap.Up module which begins at line 105. After the end-of-job message is displayed, control returns to line 31 in the Main module and the program terminates execution.

```
Cost of Item (0.00 < Cost < 1000.00) =======> 67.50
                Table of Costs

            Items           Cost
            -----           ----
              1             67.50
              2            135.00
              3            202.50
              4            270.00
              5            337.50
              6            405.00
              7            472.50
              8            540.00
              9            607.50
             10            675.00

Enter Y to generate another table, else N =====> N

End of Job
```

FIGURE 4-20 The results displayed due to the execution of the modified Sample Program 4 and a cost per item of $67.50

TRY IT YOURSELF EXERCISES

1. What is displayed if each of the following programs are executed?
   a. X is assigned the value 2, and Y is assigned the value 4.

   ```
   ' Exercise 1.a
   INPUT "Enter values for X and Y ===> ", X, Y
   Sum = X + Y
   Diff = Y - X
   Prod = X * Y
   Quot = X / Y
   PRINT Sum, Diff
   PRINT Prod, Quot
   END
   ```

b.
```
' Exercise 1.b
Total = 0
GOSUB Increment.Total
PRINT Total
GOSUB Increment.Total
PRINT Total
GOSUB Increment.Total
PRINT Total
Total = Total - 6
PRINT Total
END
' Increment Total
Increment.Total:
   Total = Total + 2
RETURN
```

c. Selling.Price and Discount.Rate are assigned $30.00 and 25%, respectively.

```
' Exercise 1.c
' ***********************************
' *            Main Module          *
' ***********************************
GOSUB Accept.Data
GOSUB Compute.Discount
GOSUB Display.Discount
END

' ***********************************
' *        Accept Operator Data     *
' ***********************************
Accept.Data:
   CLS   ' Clear Screen
   INPUT "Selling Price ===>", Selling.Price
   INPUT "Discount Rate in % ===>", Discount.Rate
RETURN

' ***********************************
' *         Compute Discount        *
' ***********************************
Compute.Discount:
   Discount.Rate = Discount.Rate / 100
   Discount = Discount.Rate * Selling.Price
RETURN

' ***********************************
' *          Discount Amount        *
' ***********************************
Display.Discount:
   PRINT "Discount ======>"; Discount
RETURN

' *********** End of Program ********
```

2. Is the following partial program invalid? If it is invalid, indicate why.

   ```
   ' Exercise 2
   ' Main Module
       .
       .
       .
   GOSUB Calculate
   ' Calculate Square
   Calculate:
       X = X * X
   RETURN
   END
   ```

3. Write a sequence of LOCATE and PRINT statements that will display the word Retail beginning in column 12 of row 15.
4. Write a series of statements that will display the number 22 in column 22 of row 22.
5. Consider the two following types of loops:
   a. DO WHILE ... LOOP
   b. DO ... LOOP UNTIL

   Answer the following questions for each type of loop:

   (1) Does the loop terminate when the condition is true or false?
   (2) What is the minimum number of times the range of statements in the loop is executed?
   (3) Is the test to terminate the loop made before or after the range of statements is executed?

6. At what column and row is the cursor after the following two statements are executed?

   ```
   LOCATE 15, 34
   LOCATE 17
   ```

7. Identify the syntax and logic error(s), if any, in each of the following:
   a. FOR X = 1 TO 6 STEP -1
   b. FOR Amt = 1 TO Sq
   c. FOR T$ = 0 TO 7
   d. FOR Value = 10 TO 1
   e. FOR H = A TO B STEP -B

8. How many times does the PRINT statement execute when the following program is executed?

   ```
   ' Exercise 8
   FOR J = 1 TO 30
      FOR N = 1 TO 20
         FOR I = 1 TO 3
            PRINT J, N, I
         NEXT I
      NEXT N
   NEXT J
   END
   ```

9. Explain the purpose of the following statement. What are the colons used for?

   ```
   BEEP : BEEP : BEEP : BEEP
   ```

STUDENT ASSIGNMENTS

STUDENT ASSIGNMENT 1: Weekly Pay Rate Table

Instructions: Design and code a top-down QuickBASIC program, such as the one in Figure 4-19, to generate the weekly pay rate table shown under OUTPUT. Request that the user enter through the keyboard an hourly rate between $3.35 and $30.00, inclusive. Validate the entry. Use a For loop to generate a table of 10 hourly rates in increments of $0.50 and the corresponding weekly rates. A weekly rate is equal to 40 times the hourly rate. After the table displays, request the user to enter the letter Y to generate another table or the letter N to terminate the program. Use the following top-down chart as a guide to solving this problem:

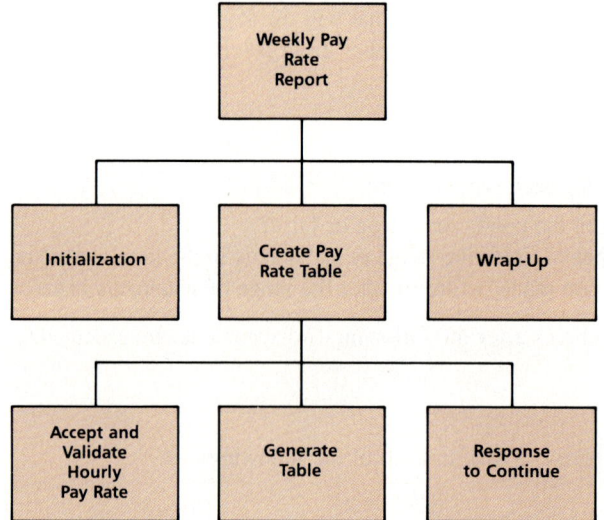

INPUT: Use the following sample data:

Table 1 – Hourly rate $6.75
Table 2 – Hourly rate $22.50

OUTPUT: The following results are displayed for the first table:

```
Initial Pay Rate (3.35 <= Cost <= 30.00) ======> 6.75
      Table of Hourly and Weekly Rates

      Hourly                Weekly
      Rate                  Rate
      ------                ------
       6.75                 270.00
       7.25                 290.00
       7.75                 310.00
       8.25                 330.00
       8.75                 350.00
       9.25                 370.00
       9.75                 390.00
      10.25                 410.00
      10.75                 430.00
      11.25                 450.00

Enter Y to generate another table, else N ======> Y
```

STUDENT ASSIGNMENT 2: Metric Conversion Table

Instructions: Design and code a top-down QuickBASIC program, such as the one in Figure 4-19, to generate a metric conversion table as shown on the next page in the printout. Request that the user enter through the keyboard an initial metric value, a limit metric value, and an increment metric value. Validate each entry. The initial metric value must be between 1 and 1,500, inclusive. The limit metric value must be greater than the initial metric value and less than 2,000. The increment metric value must be greater than zero and less than or equal to 100.

Use a For loop to generate a table of the metric values between the initial metric value and limit metric value. For each metric value, print the equivalent yards, feet, and inches. There are 39.37 inches in a meter, 12 inches in a foot, and 3 feet in a yard. After the table prints, request the user to enter the letter Y to generate another table or the letter N to terminate the program. Use the following top-down chart as a guide to solving this problem:

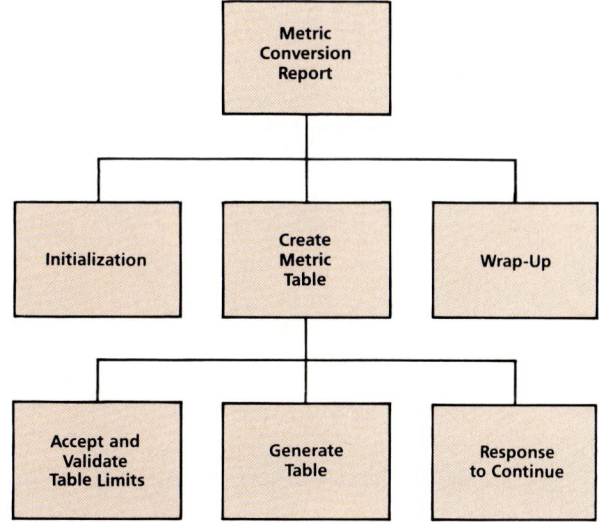

Before you print each table, use the following statement to move the paper in the printer to the top of the next page:

`LPRINT CHR$(12);`

This LPRINT statement prints the value of the function CHR$(12), which is the form feed character.

INPUT: Use the following sample data:

Table 1 – Initial meters 100, Limit meters 200, Increment meters 10
Table 2 – Initial meters 140, Limit meters 160, Increment meters 2

OUTPUT: The following results display on the screen for the Table 1 data:

```
Initial Meter Value (1 <= Initial Meter <= 1500) ==> 100
Limit Meter Value (Initial Meter < Limit Meter < 2,000) ======> 200
Increment Meter Value (0 < Increment Meter <= 100) ======> 10
********* Report Being Printed On Printer *********
Enter Y to generate another table, else N =====> Y
```

Student Assignment 2 (continued)

The following results are printed on the printer for the Table 1 data:

```
          Metric Conversion Table

    Meters      Yards       Feet      Inches
    ------      -----       ----      ------
    100.00     109.36      328.08     3,937.00
    110.00     120.30      360.89     4,330.70
    120.00     131.23      393.70     4,724.40
    130.00     142.17      426.51     5,118.10
    140.00     153.11      459.32     5,511.80
    150.00     164.04      492.13     5,905.50
    160.00     174.98      524.93     6,299.20
    170.00     185.91      557.74     6,692.90
    180.00     196.85      590.55     7,086.60
    190.00     207.79      623.36     7,480.30
    200.00     218.72      656.17     7,874.00

    End of Table
```

PROJECT 5

Sequential File Processing

In the first four projects we emphasized the importance of integrating data into the program. You learned that data may be entered into a program through the use of the INPUT statement or the READ and DATA statements. This project presents a third method for entering data—the use of data files. With data files, the data is stored in auxiliary storage rather than in the program itself. This technique is used primarily for dealing with large amounts of data.

QuickBASIC includes a set of file-handling statements that allow a user to do the following:

- Open a file
- Read data from a file
- Write data to a file
- Test for the end-of-file
- Close a file

FILE ORGANIZATION

QuickBASIC provides for two types of file organization: sequential and random. A file that is organized sequentially is called a **sequential file** and is limited to sequential processing. This means that the records can be processed only in the order in which they are placed in the file. Conceptually, a sequential file is identical to the use of DATA statements within a QuickBASIC program.

The second type of file organization, **random files**, allows you to process the records in the file in any order. If the fifth record is required and it is stored in a random file, then the program may access it without reading the first four records. Random files are not discussed in this project.

CREATING A SEQUENTIAL DATA FILE

This section presents the OPEN, WRITE #n, and CLOSE statements. These statements are used to create a sequential data file. The OPEN statement is used to activate the file. The WRITE #n statement is used to write a record to the file. And the CLOSE statement is used to deactivate the file.

Opening Sequential Files

Before any file can be read from or written to, it must be opened by the OPEN statement. The OPEN statement identifies by name the file to be processed. It indicates whether the file is to be read from or written to. It also assigns the file a filenumber that can be used by statements that need to reference the file in question.

The general form of the OPEN statement is shown in Figure 5-1.

```
OPEN filespec FOR mode AS #filenumber

    where filespec is the name of the file;
         mode is one of the following:
             APPEND opens file so that records can be added to the end of the file;
             INPUT opens file to read beginning with the first record;
             OUTPUT opens file to write records; and
         filenumber is a numeric expression whose value is between 1 and 255.
```

FIGURE 5-1
The general form of the OPEN statement

As described in Figure 5-1, a sequential data file may be opened for input, output, or append. If a file is opened for input, the program can only read records from it. If a file is opened for output, the program can only write records to it. The Append mode allows you to write records to the end of a file that already has records in it. Figure 5-2 illustrates several OPEN statements.

FIGURE 5-2
Examples of OPEN statements

EXAMPLE	STATEMENT
1	OPEN "B:PAYROLL.DAT" FOR OUTPUT AS #4
2	OPEN "ACCOUNT.DAT" FOR APPEND AS #2
3	OPEN Filename$ FOR OUTPUT AS #1
4	OPEN "PART.DAT" FOR INPUT AS #1

The OPEN statement in Example 1 in Figure 5-2 opens PAYROLL.DAT on the B drive for output as filenumber 4. Since it is opened for output, you can only write records to PAYROLL.DAT. If you attempt to read a record, the PC will display a diagnostic message.

Example 2 opens the data file ACCOUNT.DAT for append as filenumber 2. Records can only be written to a data file opened for append. If ACCOUNT.DAT exists, records are written in sequence after the last record. If ACCOUNT.DAT does not exist, the PC creates it and the data file is treated as if it were open for output.

Example 3 in Figure 5-2 shows that in an OPEN statement you can use a string variable as the data file name. The assumption is that you will assign a file name to the string variable before the OPEN statement is executed.

Example 4 opens the data file PART.DAT on the default drive for input as filenumber 1. A file opened for input means we plan to read data from it. Later in this project we will show how data can be read from a data file.

Closing Sequential Files

When a program is finished reading or writing to a file, it must close the file with the CLOSE statement. The CLOSE statement terminates the association between the file and the filenumber assigned in the OPEN statement. If a file is being written to, the CLOSE statement ensures that the last record is written to the data file.

The general form of the CLOSE statement is shown in Figure 5-3.

FIGURE 5-3
The general form of the CLOSE statement

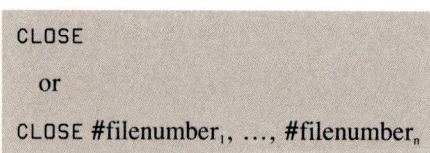

The CLOSE statement terminates access to a data file. For example, CLOSE #1 causes the data file assigned to filenumber 1 to be closed. Any other files previously opened by the program remain open. Following the close of a specified file, the filenumber may be assigned again to the same file or to a different file by an OPEN statement. The keyword CLOSE without any filenumber, closes all opened data files.

Note that when executed, the END statement closes all opened files before terminating execution of the program.

Writing Data to a Sequential File

To write data to a sequential file, we use the WRITE #n statement. The WRITE #n statement writes data in a format required by the INPUT #n statement. The format requirement is similar to that of the READ and DATA statements—all data items are separated by commas. The WRITE #n statement even goes one step further by surrounding all string data items written to the file with quotation marks.

The general form of the WRITE #n statement is shown in Figure 5-4.

FIGURE 5-4
The general form of the
WRITE #n statement

```
WRITE #filenumber, variable₁, variable₂, ..., variableₙ
```

Consider the WRITE #n statement in Figure 5-5. Assume that Part.No$ = 129, Description$ = Hex Bolt, On.Hand = 200, and Wholesale = 1.26. The WRITE #n statement transmits the record shown to the sequential file assigned to filenumber 1. The WRITE #n statement causes a comma to be placed between the data items in the record. Quotation marks are placed around the values of the string variables Part.No$ and Description$, and a carriage return character ↵ is appended to the last data item written to form the record.

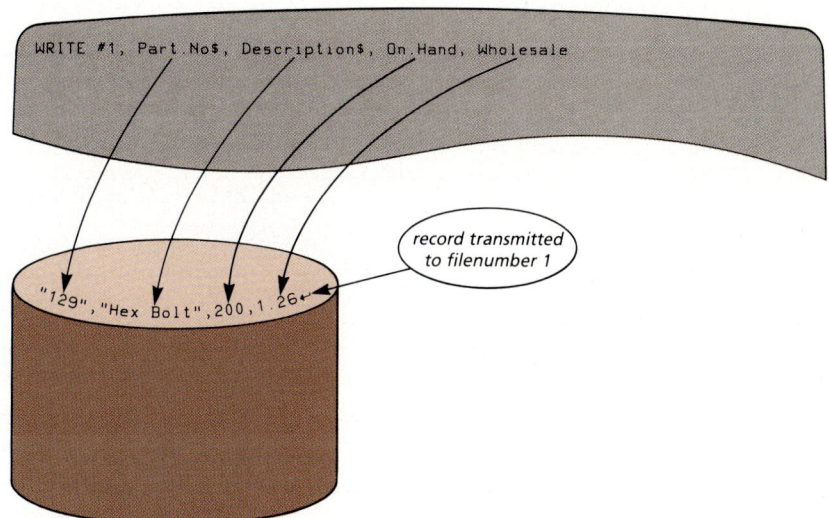

FIGURE 5-5
Writing data to a data file

SAMPLE PROGRAM 5A — CREATING A SEQUENTIAL DATA FILE

In this sample program, we create a sequential data file (PART.DAT) on the B drive from the part data shown in Figure 5-6. The data must be written in a format that is consistent with the INPUT #n statement. We use a series of LOCATE, PRINT, and INPUT statements to display the screen on the screen layout form shown on the next page in Figure 5-7. As part of the Wrap-Up module, the number of records written to PART.DAT is displayed.

PART NUMBER	DESCRIPTION	ON HAND	WHOLESALE PRICE
323	Canon PC-25	12	$799.92
432	Timex Watch	53	27.95
567	12 Inch Monitor	34	50.30
578	Epson Printer	23	179.95
745	6 Inch Frying Pan	17	9.71
812	Mr. Coffee	39	21.90
923	4-Piece Toaster	7	17.57

FIGURE 5-6 The data to be written to the sequential file PART.DAT

Notice that we are not validating the data entered through the keyboard in this sample program so that we can present a clear-cut example of how to create a sequential file. In a production environment, reasonableness checks are always considered for the part number, description, on hand, and wholesale price. Data should always be validated before it is written to a file.

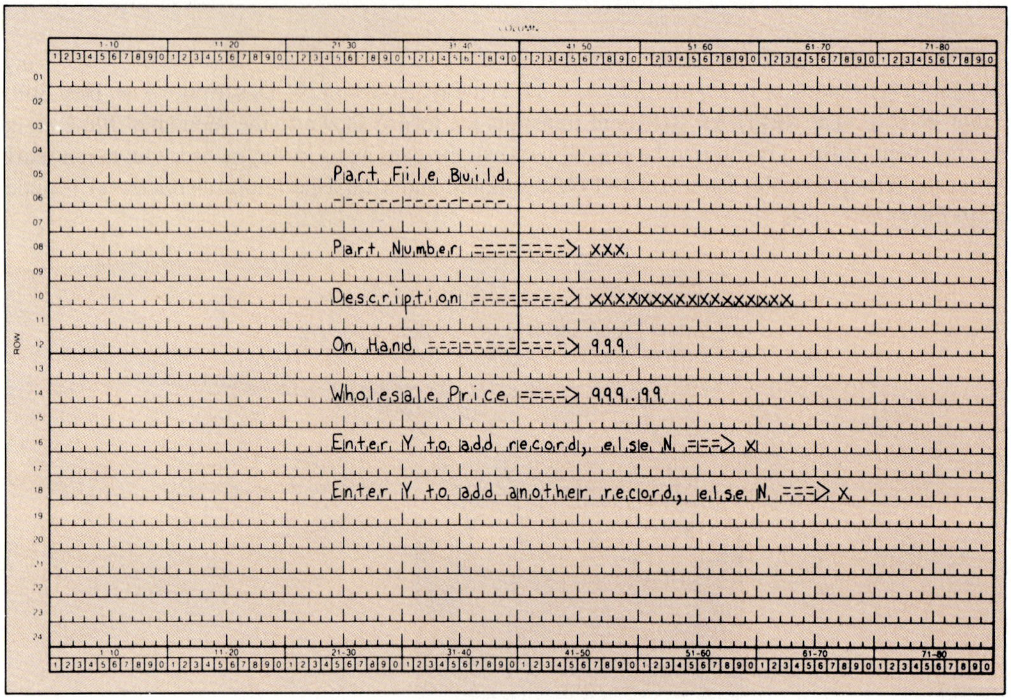

FIGURE 5-7 A screen layout form for Sample Program 5A

A top-down chart, a program flowchart for each module, a program solution, and a discussion of the program solution follow.

Top-Down Chart and Program Flowcharts

Figure 5-8 illustrates the top-down chart and corresponding program flowcharts for each module in Sample Program 5A. In the Initialization module, the record counter is initialized to zero and the data file PART.DAT is opened. The Do-Until loop in the Build File module executes until the user indicates that there are no more records to enter. Within the Do-Until loop, a part record is accepted through the keyboard. After each record is entered, the user must enter the letter Y to add the record. This entry gives the user the opportunity to cancel the record while it is displayed on the screen, but before it is added to PART.DAT. After all the records are entered, the Wrap-Up module displays the number of records written to PART.DAT.

In the program flowcharts, notice that the OPEN, WRITE #n, and CLOSE statements are represented by the Input/Output symbol (parallelogram).

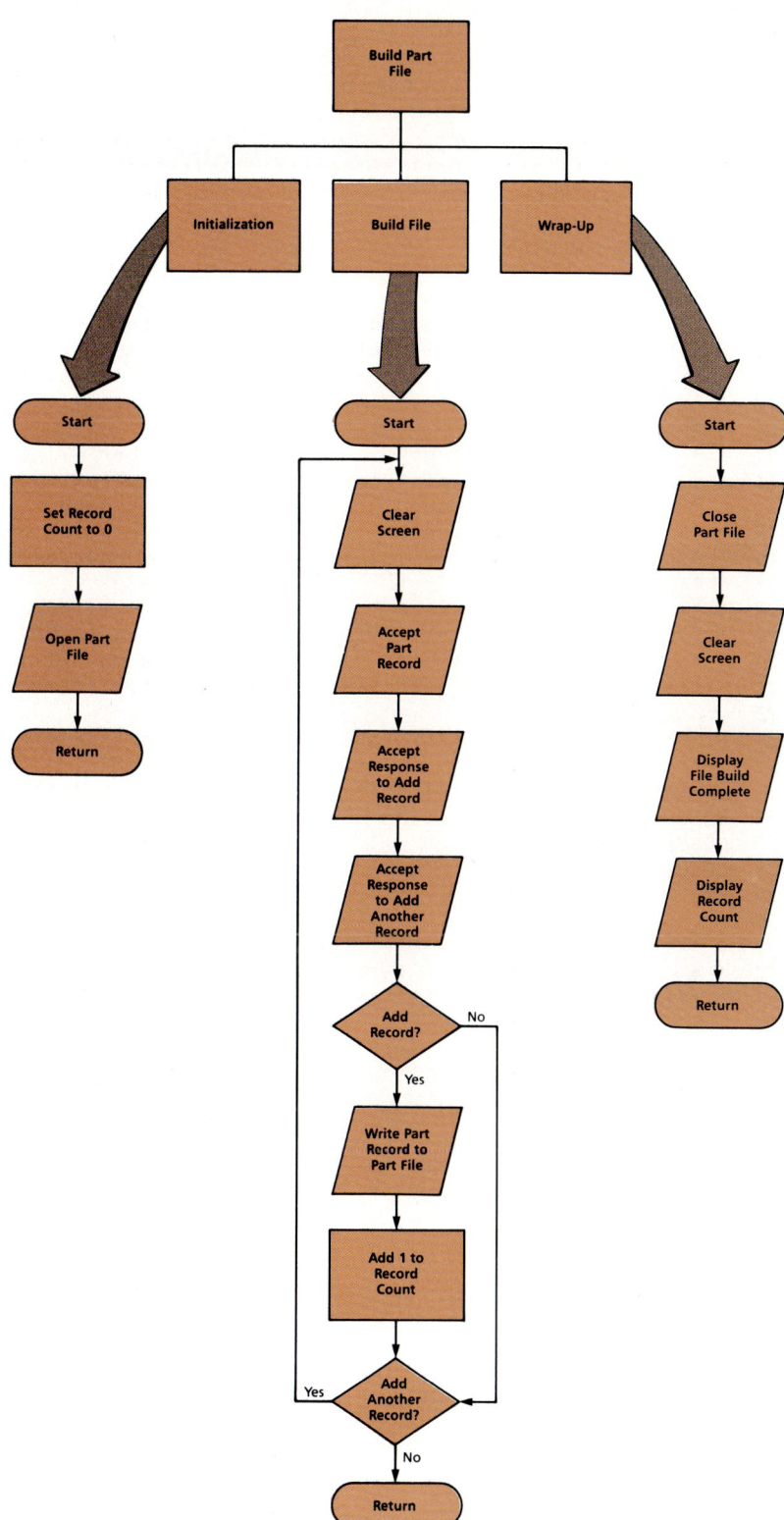

FIGURE 5-8 A top-down chart and corresponding program flowc for Sample Program 5A

The QuickBASIC Program

The program in Figure 5-9 corresponds to the top-down chart and program flowcharts in Figure 5-8.

FIGURE 5-9
Sample Program 5A

```
1  ' ****************************************************************
2  ' *  Sample Program 5A                      September 15, 1994   *
3  ' *  Build Part File                                             *
4  ' *  J. S. Quasney                                               *
5  ' *                                                              *
6  ' *  This program builds the data file PART.DAT.                 *
7  ' *  The user enters each part record through the keyboard.      *
8  ' *  After the record is entered, it is written to PART.DAT.     *
9  ' *      The number of records written to PART.DAT is            *
10 ' *  displayed as part of the Wrap-Up module.                    *
11 ' *                                                              *
12 ' *  Variables:   Part.No$       -- Part number                  *
13 ' *               Description$   -- Part description             *
14 ' *               On.Hand        -- Number on hand               *
15 ' *               Wholesale      -- Wholesale price of part      *
16 ' *               Record.Count   -- Count of records added to    *
17 ' *                                 PART.DAT                     *
18 ' *               Add.Rec$       -- Indicates if record is to    *
19 ' *                                 be written to PART.DAT       *
20 ' *               Control$       -- Controls Do-Until loop       *
21 ' ****************************************************************
22
23 ' ****************************************************************
24 ' *                       Main Module                            *
25 ' ****************************************************************
26 GOSUB Initialization
27 GOSUB Build.File
28 GOSUB Wrap.Up
29 END
30
31 ' ****************************************************************
32 ' *                       Initialization                         *
33 ' ****************************************************************
34 Initialization:
35     Record.Count = 0
36     OPEN "B:PART.DAT" FOR OUTPUT AS #1
37 RETURN
38
```

FIGURE 5-9
(continued)

```
39  ' ****************************************************************
40  ' *                          Build File                          *
41  ' ****************************************************************
42  Build.File:
43     DO
44        CLS  ' Clear Screen
45        LOCATE 5, 25: PRINT "Part File Build"
46        LOCATE 6, 25: PRINT "---------------"
47        LOCATE 8, 25: INPUT "Part Number ========> ", Part.No$
48        LOCATE 10, 25: INPUT "Description ========> ", Description$
49        LOCATE 12, 25: INPUT "On Hand ============> ", On.Hand
50        LOCATE 14, 25: INPUT "Wholesale Price ====> ", Wholesale
51        LOCATE 16, 25: INPUT "Enter Y to add record, else N ===> ", Add.Rec$
52        LOCATE 18, 25
53        INPUT "Enter Y to add another record, else N ===> ", Control$
54        IF Add.Rec$ = "Y" OR Add.Rec$ = "y" THEN
55           WRITE #1, Part.No$, Description$, On.Hand, Wholesale
56           Record.Count = Record.Count + 1
57        END IF
58     LOOP UNTIL Control$ = "N" OR Control$ = "n"
59  RETURN
60
61  ' ****************************************************************
62  ' *                          Wrap-Up                             *
63  ' ****************************************************************
64  Wrap.Up:
65     CLOSE #1
66     CLS  ' Clear Screen
67     LOCATE 10, 15: PRINT "Creation of PART.DAT is Complete"
68     LOCATE 14, 15
69     PRINT "Total Number of Records in PART.DAT ===>"; Record.Count
70  RETURN
71
72  ' ******************** End of Program ********************
```

Discussion of the Program Solution

When Sample Program 5A is executed, line 36 of the Initialization module opens PART.DAT for output on the B drive as filenumber 1. In the Build File module, lines 45 through 53 of the Do-Until loop accepts data values through the keyboard. The display due to the execution of these lines for the first record entered by the operator is shown on the next page in Figure 5-10. Notice the two messages at the bottom of the screen. The first message (displayed due to line 51) gives the operator the opportunity to reject the transaction by assigning Add.Rec$ a value other than Y (or y). The second message (displayed due to line 53) requests that the operator enter a Y (or y) to add another record to the part file.

Owing to line 54, the part record is added by the WRITE #n statement if Add.Rec$ is equal to Y (or y). Line 58 controls the Do-Until loop. If Control$ equals N (or n), then the loop terminates, and control returns to line 28 of the Main module. If Control$ is equal to any other value, then the loop continues.

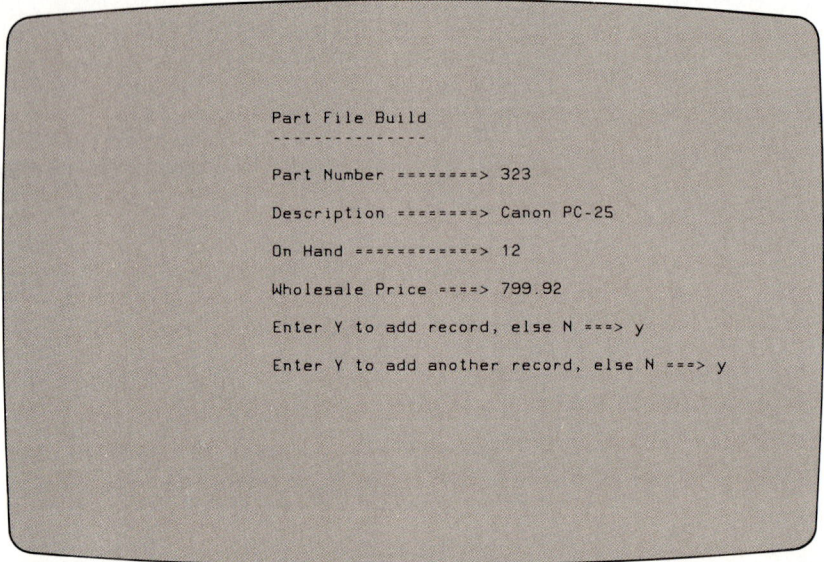

FIGURE 5-10
The display after the first part record is entered due to the execution of Sample Program 5A

The WRITE #n statement in line 55 writes the record to the sequential file PART.DAT in a format that is consistent with the INPUT #n statement. Figure 5-11 shows the format of the data written to PART.DAT by Sample Program 5A.

```
"323","Canon PC-25",12,799.92
"432","Timex Watch",53,27.95
"567","12 Inch Monitor",34,50.3
"578","Epson Printer",23,179.95
"745","6 Inch Frying Pan",17,9.71
"812","Mr. Coffee",39,21.9
"923","4-Piece Toaster",7,17.57
```

FIGURE 5-11
A listing of PART.DAT created by Sample Program 5A

In the Wrap-Up module, line 65 closes PART.DAT. This ensures that the last record entered by the operator is physically written to the data file on auxiliary storage. Figure 5-12 shows the display due to lines 66 through 69 of the Wrap-Up module.

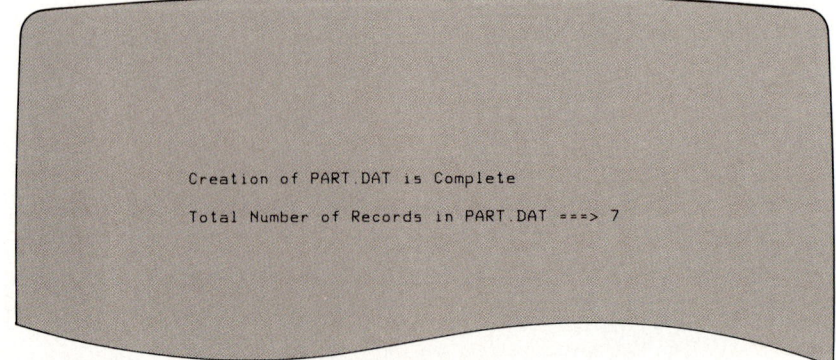

FIGURE 5-12
The display due to the execution of the Wrap-Up module in Sample Program 5A

READING DATA FROM A SEQUENTIAL DATA FILE

The INPUT #n statement is used to read data from a data file that has been created by using the WRITE #n statement. The EOF function is used to determine when all the records have been processed. The following sections describe how the INPUT #n statement and EOF function work.

The INPUT #n Statement

The INPUT #n statement is similar to the READ statement except that it reads data from a data file instead of from DATA statements. In the following partial program,

```
OPEN "PART.DAT" FOR INPUT AS #1
    .
    .
    .
INPUT #1, Part.No$, Description$, On.Hand, Wholesale
```

the PC reads four data items from the sequential file PART.DAT.

The general form of the INPUT #n statement is shown in Figure 5-13.

```
INPUT #filenumber, variable₁, variable₂, ..., variableₙ
```

FIGURE 5-13   The general form of the INPUT #n statement

The EOF Function

When a sequential data file that was opened for output is closed, the PC automatically adds an end-of-file mark after the last record written to the file. Later, when the same sequential file is opened for input, you can use the EOF(n) function to test for the end-of-file mark. The n indicates the filenumber assigned to the file in the OPEN statement.

If the EOF function senses the end-of-file mark, it returns a value of –1 (true). Otherwise, it returns a value of 0 (false). Hence, the EOF function can be used in a DO WHILE statement to control the loop. For example, consider the partial program in Figure 5-14. In the DO WHILE statement, the EOF(1) function is used to control the Do loop. Each time the DO WHILE statement is executed, the PC checks to see whether the data pointer is pointing to the end-of-file mark in PART.DAT.

```
OPEN "PART.DAT" FOR INPUT AS #1
    .
    .
    .
DO WHILE NOT EOF(1)
    INPUT #1, Part.No$, Description$, On.Hand, Wholesale
    LET Record.Count = Record.Count + 1
    LET Total.On.Hand = Total.On.Hand + On.Hand
    LET Part.Cost = On.Hand * Wholesale
    LET Total.Part.Cost = Total.Part.Cost + Part.Cost
    LPRINT USING DL1$; Part.No$; Description$; On.Hand; Wholesale; Part.Cost
LOOP
```

FIGURE 5-14   Using the EOF function to test for end-of-file

When using the EOF function, it is important to organize your program so that the test for the end-of-file precedes the execution of the INPUT #n statement. In Figure 5-14, notice that only one INPUT #n statement is employed, and that this statement is placed inside at the top of the Do loop. This is different from our previous programs which employed two READ statements—one prior to the Do-While loop and one at the bottom of the Do-While loop.

The logic in Figure 5-14 also works when the file is empty (that is, when the file contains no records). If the PART.DAT file is empty, the OPEN statement in the partial program still opens the file for input. However, when the DO WHILE statement is executed, the EOF function immediately detects the end-of-file mark on the empty file, thereby causing control to pass to the statement following the corresponding LOOP statement.

SAMPLE PROGRAM 5B — PROCESSING A SEQUENTIAL DATA FILE

*I*n this sample program we will show how to read data and generate a report using the part file (PART.DAT) built by Sample Program 5A. The display shown in Figure 5-15A instructs the user to prepare the printer to receive the report. The report shown in Figure 5-15B contains a detail line for each part number. The total cost for each part is determined by multiplying the number of on hand by the wholesale price.

As part of the end-of-job routine, the sample program prints the number of part records processed, total number of parts in inventory, and the total cost of all the parts.

A. SCREEN DISPLAY

```
Set the paper in the printer to the top of page.
Press the Enter key when the printer is ready...
End of Job
```

B. PRINTED REPORT

```
                  Part Cost Report

    Part                             Wholesale     Part
    No.    Description      On Hand    Price       Cost
    ----   -----------      -------  ---------   --------
    323    Canon PC-25         12      799.92    9,599.04
    432    Timex Watch         53       27.95    1,481.35
    567    12 Inch Monitor     34       50.30    1,710.20
    578    Epson Printer       23      179.95    4,138.85
    745    6 Inch Frying P     17        9.71      165.07
    812    Mr. Coffee          39       21.90      854.10
    923    4-Piece Toaster      7       17.57      122.99
                              -------              ---------
                                185               18,071.60

    Total Number of Parts =====>    7

    End of Job
```

FIGURE 5-15 The screen display (A) and printed report (B) generated by Sample Program 5B

A top-down chart, a program flowchart for each module, a program solution, and a discussion of the program solution follow.

Top-Down Chart and Program Flowcharts

Figure 5-16 illustrates the top-down chart and corresponding program flowcharts for each module in Sample Program 5B.

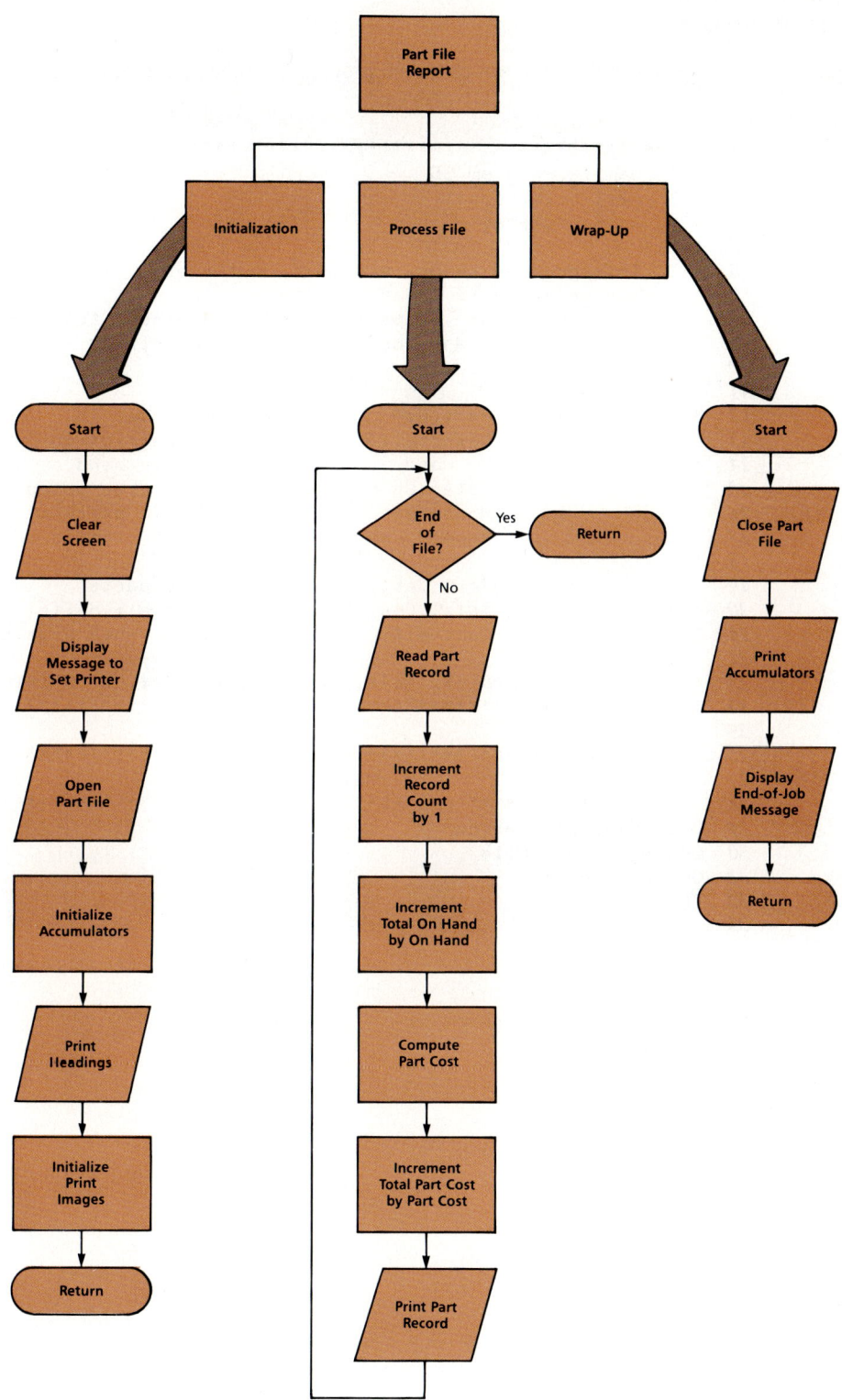

FIGURE 5-16 A top-down chart and corresponding program flowcharts for Sample Program 5B

The QuickBASIC Program

The program in Figure 5-17 corresponds to the top-down chart and program flowcharts in Figure 5-16.

FIGURE 5-17
Sample Program 5B

```
 1   ' ****************************************************************
 2   ' *   Sample Program 5B                          September 15, 1994 *
 3   ' *   Part File Report                                              *
 4   ' *   J. S. Quasney                                                 *
 5   ' *                                                                 *
 6   ' *   This program reads records from the data file PART.DAT        *
 7   ' *   and generates a report on the printer.                        *
 8   ' *      The number of part records processed, total pieces         *
 9   ' *   in inventory, and the total cost are printed as part of       *
10   ' *   the Wrap-Up module.                                           *
11   ' *                                                                 *
12   ' *   Variables:  Part.No$         -- Part number                   *
13   ' *               Description$     -- Part description              *
14   ' *               On.Hand          -- Number on hand                *
15   ' *               Total.On.Hand    -- Total pieces on hand          *
16   ' *               Wholesale        -- Wholesale price of part       *
17   ' *               Record.Count     -- Count of records added to     *
18   ' *                                   PART.DAT                      *
19   ' *               Part.Cost        -- Cost of parts                 *
20   ' *               Total.Cost.Part  -- Cost of all parts             *
21   ' *               Control$         -- Response when printer is      *
22   ' *                                   ready                         *
23   ' *               DL1$, TL1$, TL2$, TL3$, TL4$  -- Print Images     *
24   ' ****************************************************************
25
26   ' ****************************************************************
27   ' *                        Main Module                              *
28   ' ****************************************************************
29   GOSUB Initialization
30   GOSUB Process.File
31   GOSUB Wrap.Up
32   END
33
```

FIGURE 5-17
(continued)

```
34  ' ****************************************************************
35  ' *                        Initialization                         *
36  ' ****************************************************************
37  Initialization:
38      CLS   ' Clear Screen
39      LOCATE 10, 20
40      PRINT "Set the paper in the printer to the top of page."
41      LOCATE 12, 20
42      INPUT "Press the Enter key when the printer is ready...", Control$
43      OPEN "B:PART.DAT" FOR INPUT AS #1
44      Record.Count = 0
45      Total.On.Hand = 0
46      Total.Part.Cost = 0
47      LPRINT "                    Part Cost Report"
48      LPRINT
49      LPRINT "Part                                   Wholesale      Part"
50      LPRINT "No.       Description        On Hand     Price        Cost"
51      LPRINT "----      -----------        -------   ---------      ----"
52      DL1$ = "\  \        \          \     #,###    #,###.##  ##,###.##"
53      TL1$ = "                                -------           ---------"
54      TL2$ = "                                ##,###           ###,###.##"
55      TL3$ = "Total Number of Parts ====>#,###"
56      TL4$ = "End of Job"
57  RETURN
58
59  ' ****************************************************************
60  ' *                        Process File                           *
61  ' ****************************************************************
62  Process.File:
63      DO WHILE NOT EOF(1)
64          INPUT #1, Part.No$, Description$, On.Hand, Wholesale
65          LET Record.Count = Record.Count + 1
66          LET Total.On.Hand = Total.On.Hand + On.Hand
67          LET Part.Cost = On.Hand * Wholesale
68          LET Total.Part.Cost = Total.Part.Cost + Part.Cost
69          LPRINT USING DL1$; Part.No$; Description$; On.Hand; Wholesale; Part.Cost
70      LOOP
71  RETURN
72
73  ' ****************************************************************
74  ' *                           Wrap-Up                             *
75  ' ****************************************************************
76  Wrap.Up:
77      CLOSE #1
78      LPRINT TL1$
79      LPRINT USING TL2$; Total.On.Hand; Total.Part.Cost
80      LPRINT
81      LPRINT USING TL3$; Record.Count
82      LPRINT
83      LPRINT TL4$
84      LOCATE 14, 20
85      PRINT "End of Job"
86  RETURN
87
88  ' ******************* End of Program *********************
```

Discussion of the Program Solution

When Sample Program 5B is executed, the screen display and printed report shown earlier in Figure 5-15 on page QB 92 are generated. The following points should be considered in the program solution represented by Sample Program 5B in Figure 5-17.

- Lines 39 through 42 in the Initialization module display on the screen instructions to the user to set the paper in the printer and press the Enter key when ready. Notice how the INPUT statement in line 42 temporarily halts the program until the user has prepared the printer to receive the report.
- Line 43 opens the data file PART.DAT on the B drive for input as filenumber 1. Hence, the program can read records from B:PART.DAT.
- The DO WHILE statement in line 63 controls the Do-While loop using a condition made up of the EOF function. The loop continues to execute while it is not end-of-file.
- Within the Do-While loop, the INPUT #n statement in line 64 reads a PART.DAT record by referencing filenumber 1 which was specified in the OPEN statement (line 43). After lines 65 through 68 manipulate the data and accumulate totals, line 69 prints the detail line. Line 70 returns control to the DO WHILE statement in line 63 which tests for the end-of-file mark.
- When the end-of-file mark is sensed in line 63, control passes to the RETURN statement in line 71. Line 71 returns control to line 31 in the Main module. Line 31 calls the Wrap-Up module, which prints the accumulators and displays an end-of-job message on the screen. Finally, control returns to the END statement in line 32 and the program terminates execution.

TRY IT YOURSELF EXERCISES

1. Fill in the blanks in the following sentences:
   a. The _____ statement with a mode of _____ must be executed before an INPUT #n statement is executed.
   b. The _____ statement must be executed before a WRITE #n statement is executed.
   c. The _____ function is used to test for the end-of-file mark with a sequential data file.
   d. When records are to be added to the end of a sequential data file, the _____ mode is used in the OPEN statement.

2. Assume Cost = 15, Desc$ = Keyboard, and Code = 4. Using commas, quotation marks, and ↵ for end of record, indicate the makeup of the record written to auxiliary storage by the following WRITE #n statement:

   WRITE #1, Cost, Desc$, Code

3. Explain why the EOF function should be used in a condition controlling the loop before the INPUT #n statement is executed.
4. A program is to read records from one of three sequential data files: PART1.DAT, PART2.DAT, and PART3.DAT. The three files are stored on the diskette in the A drive. Write three OPEN statements that would allow the program to read records from any of the three sequential files.
5. Which of the following are invalid file-handling statements? Why?
   a. OPEN Seq$ FOR OUTPUT AS #1
   b. INPUT #1, Cost,
   c. DO WHILE NOT EOF(#2)
   d. CLOSE #1
   e. WRITE #2, A,
   f. OPEN FOR INPUT "INV.DAT" AS #2
   g. WRITE #1, USING "####.##"; Cost

STUDENT ASSIGNMENTS

STUDENT ASSIGNMENT 1: Payroll File Build

Instructions: Design and code a top-down QuickBASIC program to build the payroll file PAYROLL.DAT. Use the sample data shown under INPUT. Generate a screen to receive the data similar to the one under OUTPUT. At the end-of-job, display the number of records written to the data file.

INPUT: Use the following sample data:

EMPLOYEE NUMBER	EMPLOYEE NAME	DEPENDENTS	PAY RATE	HOURS WORKED
23A5	Linda Frat	3	6.75	40
45K8	Joe Smit	1	12.50	38.5
56T1	Lisa Ann	1	16.25	48
65R4	Jeff Max	5	17.75	42
73E6	Susan Dex	2	13.50	40
87Q2	Jeff Web	0	22.45	50
91W2	Marci Jean	3	13.45	40
92R4	Jodi Lin	9	11.50	56
94Y2	Amanda Jo	12	12.75	20
96Y7	Niki Rai	3	16.00	42.5

OUTPUT: The sequential data file PAYROLL.DAT is created in auxiliary storage. The results for the first payroll record are shown below on the left. The results below on the right are displayed prior to termination of the program.

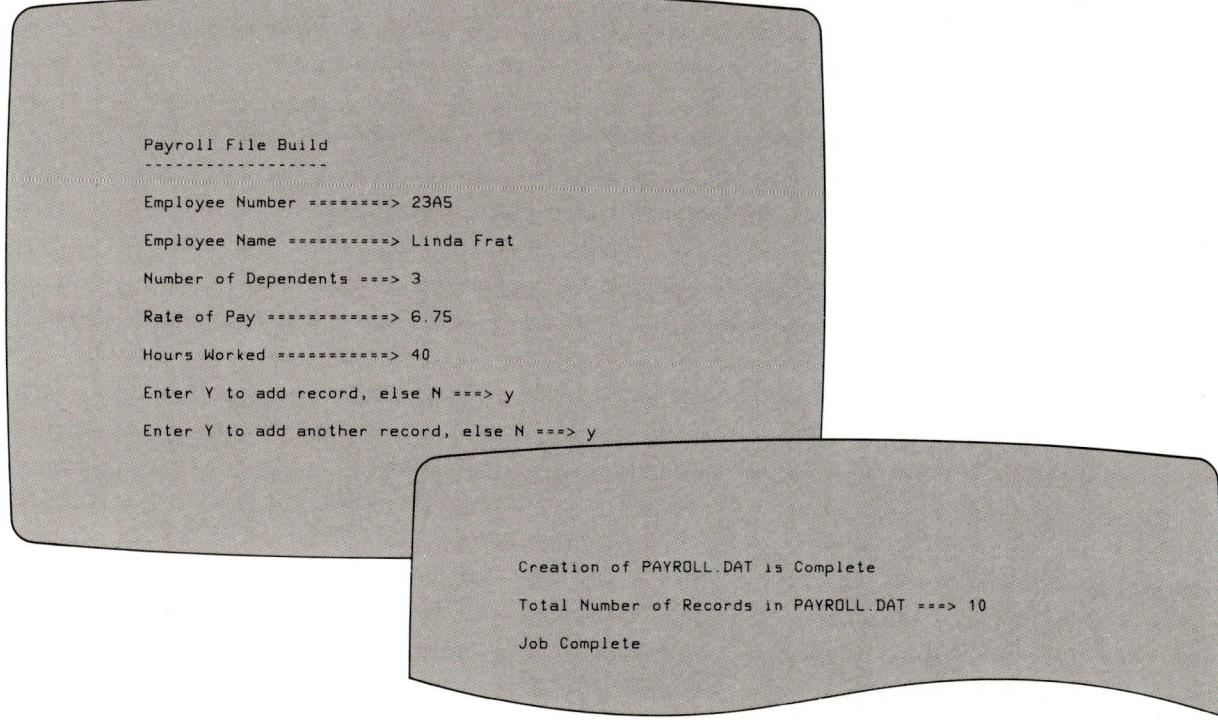

STUDENT ASSIGNMENT 2: Processing a Payroll File

Instructions: Design and code a top-down QuickBASIC program that generates the messages shown on the screen display under OUTPUT and prints the payroll report under OUTPUT. Apply the following conditions:

1. Gross pay = hours worked × hourly rate.
   Overtime (hours worked > 40) are paid at 1.5 times the hourly rate.
2. Federal withholding tax = 0.2 × (gross pay − dependents × 38.46). Assign federal withholding tax a value of zero if the gross pay less the product of the number of dependents and $38.46 is negative.
3. Net pay = gross pay − federal withholding tax.
4. At the end-of-job, print the number of employees processed, total gross pay, total federal withholding tax, and total net pay.
5. Print the report on the printer.

INPUT: Use the sequential data file PAYROLL.DAT created in Student Assignment 1. If you did not do Student Assignment 1, ask your instructor for a copy of PAYROLL.DAT.

OUTPUT: The following screen with messages and prompts is displayed:

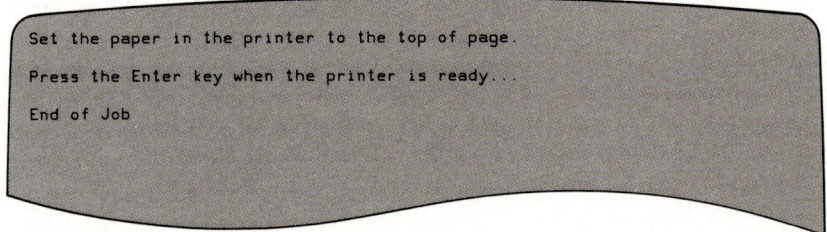

```
Set the paper in the printer to the top of page.
Press the Enter key when the printer is ready...
End of Job
```

The following report prints on the printer:

```
                       Payroll File List

     Emp.                          Pay
     No.    Name       Dep.  Hours Rate  Gross Pay  With. Tax  Net Pay
     ----   ----       ----  ----- ----  ---------  ---------  -------
     23A5   Linda Frat   3   40.0   6.75    270.00      30.92   239.08
     45K8   Joe Smit     1   38.5  12.50    481.25      88.56   392.69
     56T1   Lisa Ann     1   48.0  16.25    845.00     161.31   683.69
     65R4   Jeff Max     5   42.0  17.75    763.25     114.19   649.06
     73E6   Susan Dex    2   40.0  13.50    540.00      92.62   447.38
     87Q2   Jeff Web     0   50.0  22.45  1,234.75     246.95   987.80
     91W2   Marci Jean   3   40.0  13.45    538.00      84.52   453.48
     92R4   Jodi Lin     9   56.0  11.50    736.00      77.97   658.03
     94Y2   Amanda Jo   12   20.0  12.75    255.00       0.00   255.00
     96Y7   Niki Rai     3   42.5  16.00    700.00     116.92   583.08

     Total Employees =======>     10
     Total Gross Pay =======>  6,363.25
     Total Tax =============>  1,013.97
     Total Net Pay =========>  5,349.28

     End of Payroll Report
```

PROJECT 6

Arrays and Functions

*I*n the previous projects we used simple variables such as Count, Emp.Name$, and Balance to store and access data in a program. In this project we discuss variables that can store more than one value under the same name. Variables that can hold more than one value at a time are called **arrays**.

An array is often used to store a **table** of organized data. Income tax tables, insurance tables, or sales tax tables are examples of tables that can be stored in an array for processing purposes. Once the table elements are assigned to an array, the array can be searched to extract the proper values.

Functions are used to handle common mathematical and string operations. For example, it is often necessary in programming to obtain the square root of a number or extract a substring from a string of characters. Without functions, these types of operations would require that you write sophisticated routines in your program. Functions clearly simplify the programming task.

Although we discuss only the most frequently used functions, you should be aware that QuickBASIC has over 70 built-in functions to aid you in your programming. For a summary of all the functions available in QuickBASIC, refer to pages R.4 and R.5 of the reference card in the back of this book.

ARRAYS

*T*he banking application in Figure 6-1 illustrates an example of table processing. The account number, name of the account holder, and account balance of individuals who have savings are stored in arrays. When the teller enters account number 20013, the program searches the account number array to find an equal account number.

When the equal account number is found, the corresponding name (Darla Simmons) and the corresponding balance (932.49) are *pulled* from the table and displayed on the screen.

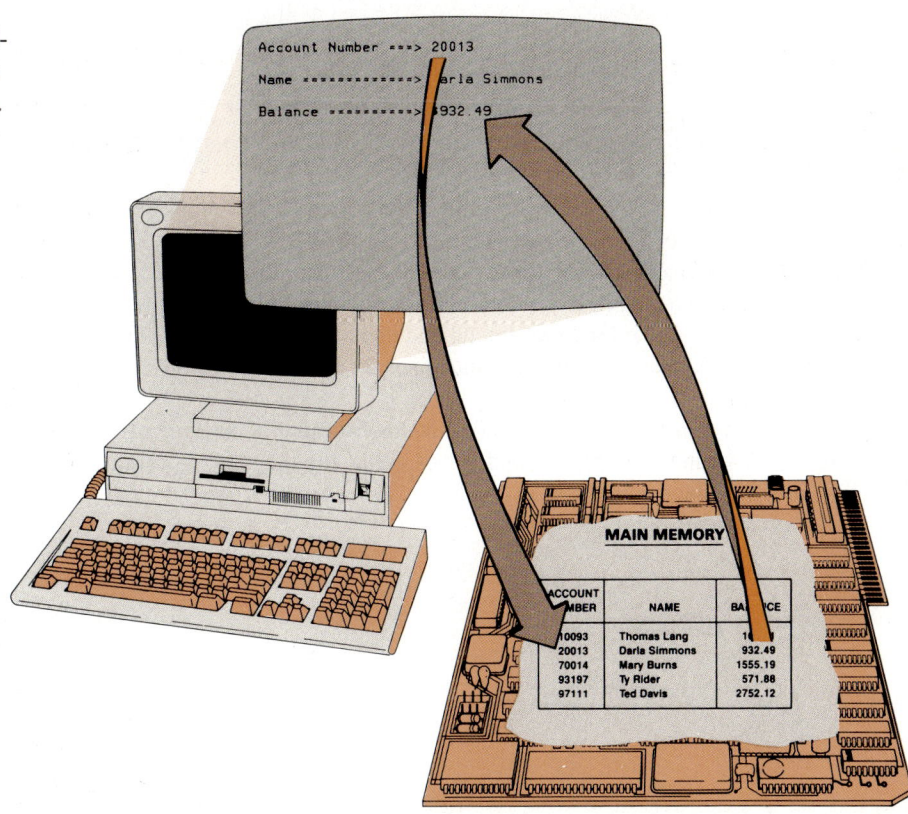

FIGURE 6-1
An example of table processing

THE DIM STATEMENT

efore arrays can be used, they must be declared in a program. This is the purpose of the DIM statement, also called the dimension statement. The general form of the DIM statement is shown in Figure 6-2.

> DIM array-name(lb_1 TO ub_1), ..., array-name(lb_1 TO ub_n)
>
> where **array-name** is a variable name, **lb_1** is a positive or negative integer or numeric variable that serves as the lower-bound value of the array, and **ub_n** is a positive or negative integer or numeric variable that serves as the upper-bound value of the array.

FIGURE 6-2 The general form of the DIM statement

Figure 6-3 illustrates several examples of declaring arrays. Example 1 reserves storage for a one-dimensional numeric array Tax, which consists of 5 elements, or storage locations. These elements—Tax(1), Tax(2), Tax(3), Tax(4), and Tax(5)—can be used in a program the same way in which a simple variable can be used. Notice that the elements of an array are distinguished from one another by **subscripts** that follow the array name within parentheses.

EXAMPLE	DIM STATEMENT
1	DIM Tax(1 TO 5)
2	DIM Job.Code$(1 TO 15), Bonus(1 TO 15)
3	DIM Part.No$(Begin TO Fin), Des(Begin TO Fin)
4	DIM Function.Tax(1 TO 50, 1 TO 25)
5	DIM Inventory.No$(15 TO 35)
6	DIM X(-5 TO 10)

FIGURE 6-3 Examples of the DIM statement

Example 2 in Figure 6-3 declares two arrays—Job.Code$ and Bonus. Both arrays are declared to have 15 elements. Thus, Job.Code$(1) through Job.Code$(15) and Bonus(1) through Bonus(15) can be referenced in the program containing the DIM statement. Job.Code$(0) and Job.Code$(16) do not exist according to the DIM statement, and therefore, should not be referenced. You may declare as many arrays in a DIM statement as required by the program.

Example 3 illustrates that the lower-bound and upper-bound values can be variables that are assigned a value prior to the execution of the DIM statement. Example 4 illustrates a two-dimensional array. QuickBASIC allows an array to have up to 60 dimensions.

Examples 5 and 6 in Figure 6-3 show that the lower-bound of an array can be a value different from 1. It is important to note that the lower-bound and upper-bound values define the range of the array. Any subscript reference that is outside the range will cause a diagnostic message to display.

SAMPLE PROGRAM 6 — CUSTOMER ACCOUNT TABLE LOOKUP

*I*n this sample program we implement the banking application shown on page QB 99 in Figure 6-1. The account number, name of the account holder, and account balance of customers who have savings accounts are shown in Figure 6-4. The table data is stored in the sequential data file ACCOUNTS.DAT. ACCOUNTS.DAT includes a data item (5) prior to the first account record that is equal to the number of records in the data file.

ACCOUNT NUMBER	CUSTOMER NAME	BALANCE
10093	Thomas Lang	$ 100.51
20013	Darla Simmons	932.49
70014	Mary Burns	1,555.19
93197	Ty Rider	571.88
97111	Ted Davis	2,752.12

FIGURE 6-4 The table data stored in ACCOUNTS.DAT

The screen display in Figure 6-5 illustrates the output results when the user enters account number 70014. When the user enters the account number, the program should direct the PC to *look up* and display the corresponding customer name and balance. The message at the bottom of the screen in Figure 6-5 asks the user to enter the letter Y to look up another account or the letter N to terminate the program.

If the account number is not found in the table, a diagnostic error displays.

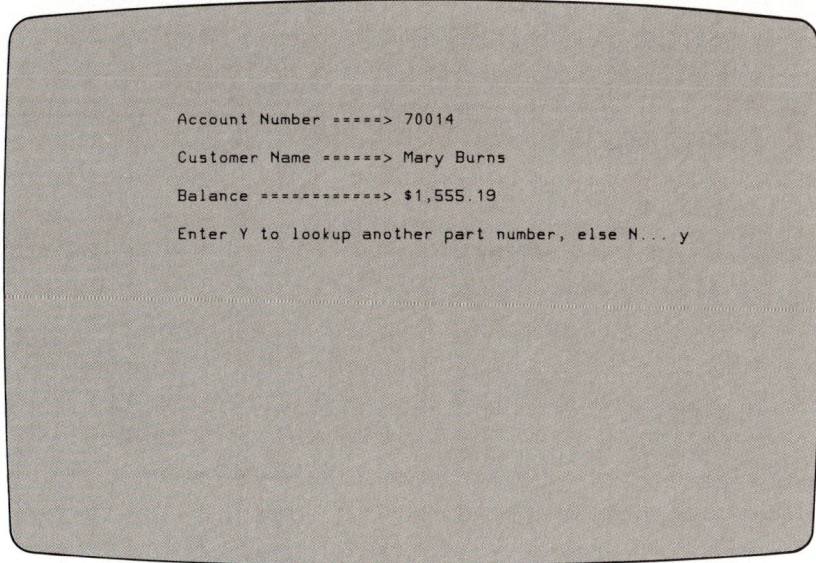

FIGURE 6-5
The display due to the execution of Sample Program 6 and the entering of account number 70014

A top-down chart, a program flowchart for each module, a program solution, and a discussion of the program solution follow.

Top-Down Chart and Program Flowcharts

The top-down chart and corresponding program flowcharts that illustrate the logic for the Sample Program 6 are shown in Figure 6-6.

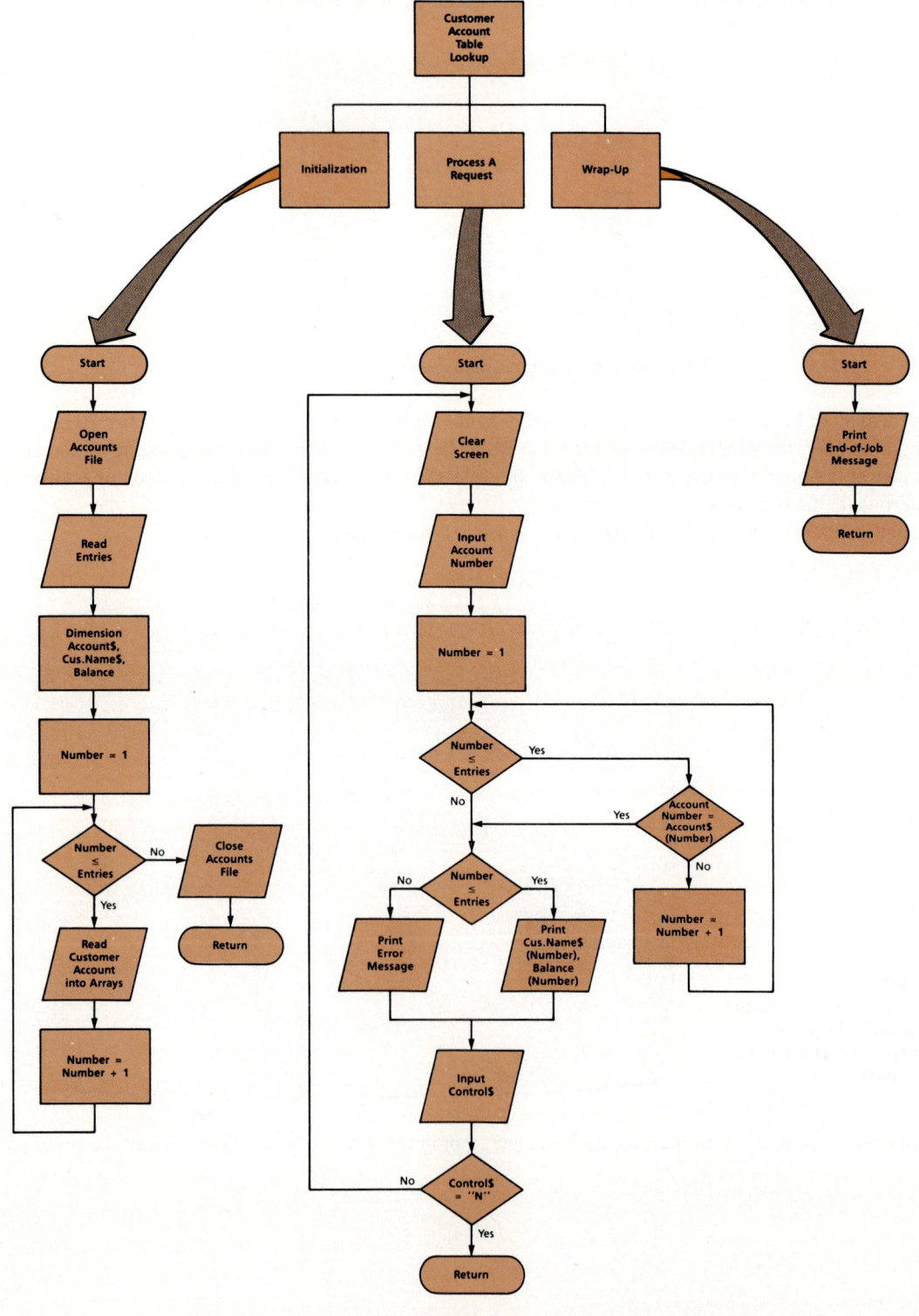

FIGURE 6-6 A top-down chart and corresponding program flowcharts for Sample Program 6

In the Initialization module in Figure 6-6, ACCOUNTS.DAT is opened and the number of records in the account file is read. This value is used to dimension the three arrays that will hold the account information. Next, the same value is used to control a Do-While loop that assigns the account information to the three arrays. After the Do-While loop is finished, ACCOUNTS.DAT is closed.

In the Process A Request module, the program accepts the account number from the user. A Do-While loop is then used to search the array that contains the account numbers. If the search is successful, the customer name and balance display. If the search is unsuccessful, a diagnostic message displays. Finally, the user is asked if he or she wants to enter another account number.

When the user enters the letter N (or n), control returns to the Main module and the Wrap-Up module displays an end-of-job message.

The QuickBASIC Program

The QuickBASIC code in Figure 6-7 corresponds to the top box in the top-down chart in Figure 6-6. The GOSUB statements call the subordinate modules. Following the return of control from the Wrap-Up module, the END statement terminates execution of the program.

```
23  ' **************************************************************
24  ' *                         Main Module                        *
25  ' **************************************************************
26  GOSUB Initialization
27  GOSUB Process.Request
28  GOSUB Wrap.Up
29  END
```

FIGURE 6-7   The Main module for Sample Program 6

Initialization Module The Initialization module for Sample Program 6 is shown in Figure 6-8. The primary objective of this module is to load the data in ACCOUNTS.DAT into the arrays. Line 35 opens ACCOUNTS.DAT on the B drive. Line 36 assigns the first data item in ACCOUNTS.DAT to the variable Entries. Entries is then assigned the value 5. Line 37 dimensions the three arrays with an upper-bound value equal to Entries. The For loop in lines 38 through 40 reads the data in ACCOUNTS.DAT into the three arrays. Arrays Account$, Cus.Name$, and Balance, therefore contain the data in ACCOUNTS.DAT. Since each array contains data that corresponds to the other arrays, we call them **parallel arrays**. Line 41 closes ACCOUNTS.DAT before control is returned to the Main module.

```
31   ' ************************************************************
32   ' *                     Initialization                       *
33   ' ************************************************************
34   Initialization:
35      OPEN "B:ACCOUNTS.DAT" FOR INPUT AS #1
36      INPUT #1, Entries
37      DIM Account$(1 TO Entries), Cus.Name$(1 TO Entries), Balance(1 TO Entries)
38      FOR Number = 1 TO Entries
39         INPUT #1, Account$(Number), Cus.Name$(Number), Balance(Number)
40      NEXT Number
41      CLOSE #1
42   RETURN
```

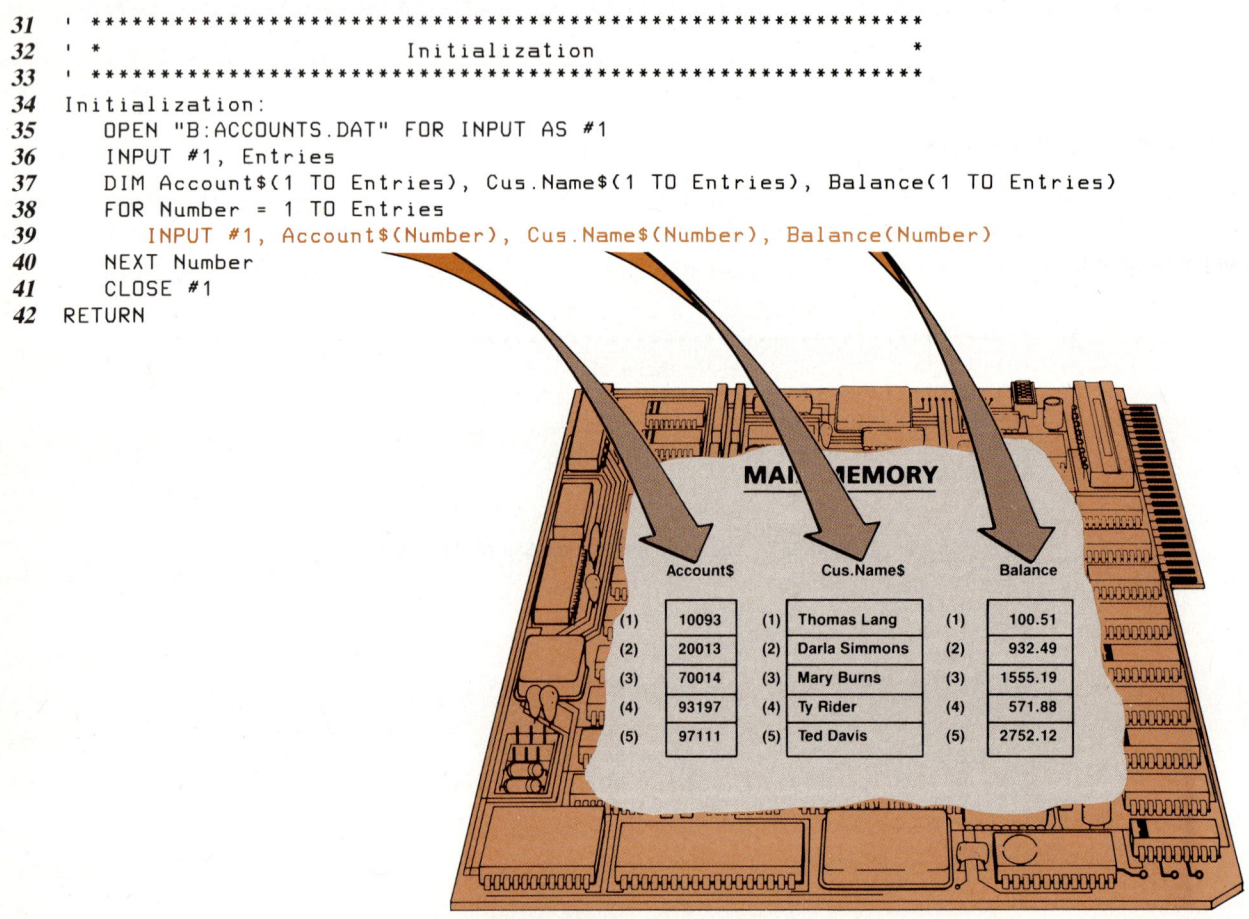

FIGURE 6-8 The Initialization module for Sample Program 6

Process A Request Module After the data in ACCOUNTS.DAT is loaded into the arrays and control passes back to the Main module, line 27 transfers control to the Process A Request module (Figure 6-9). This module begins by clearing the screen and accepting the account number from the user. The account number is assigned to the variable Search.Argument$ (line 51).

```
44  ' ****************************************************************
45  ' *                       Process A Request                      *
46  ' ****************************************************************
47  Process.Request:
48     DO
49        CLS   ' Clear Screen
50        LOCATE 5, 15
51        INPUT "Account Number =====> ", Search.Argument$
52        FOR Number = 1 TO Entries
53           IF Search.Argument$ = Account$(Number) THEN
54              EXIT FOR    ' Process a Table Hit
55           END IF
56        NEXT Number
57        IF Number <= Entries THEN
58           LOCATE 7, 15
59           PRINT "Customer Name ======> "; Cus.Name$(Number)
60           LOCATE 9, 15
61           PRINT USING "Balance =============> $$,###.##"; Balance(Number)
62        ELSE
63           LOCATE 7, 15
64           PRINT "Account Number "; Search.Argument$; " NOT FOUND"
65        END IF
66        LOCATE 11, 15
67        INPUT "Enter Y to lookup another part number, else N... ", Control$
68     LOOP UNTIL Control$ = "N" OR Control$ = "n"
69  RETURN
```

FIGURE 6-9 The Process A Request module for Sample Program 6

The For loop in lines 52 through 56 of Figure 6-9 searches the Account$ array for a match with Search.Argument$. Each time through the loop, the IF statement (line 53) compares Search.Argument$ to the next element in Account$ until a *hit* is made. When a *hit* occurs, the EXIT FOR statement in line 54 causes a premature exit from the For loop and control passes to line 57. If no *hit* occurs, a normal exit from the For loop also passes control to line 57.

Line 57 determines if the search for the account number in Account$ was successful. If the search was successful, then Number is less than or equal to Entries. In this case, the customer number and balance from the two corresponding arrays are displayed using the value of Number for the subscript. Figure 6-10 shows the display due to a successful search.

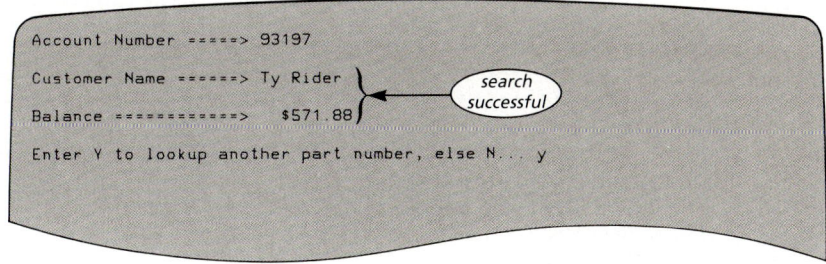

FIGURE 6-10 The display from Sample Program 6 due to entering the account number 93197

If the search is unsuccessful, then Number is greater than Entries and the diagnostic message in line 64 displays as shown in Figure 6-11. Note that if there is a premature exit from the For loop, the search is successful. If the For loop ends normally, the search is unsuccessful.

FIGURE 6-11
The display from Sample Program 6 due to entering the invalid account number 12123

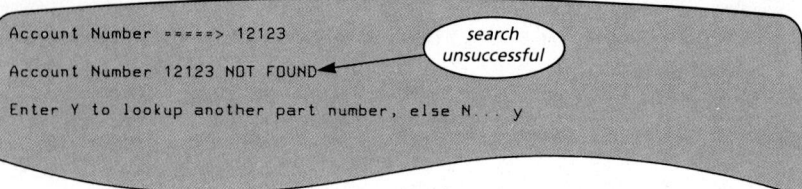

After the true or false task in the IF statement (lines 57 through 65) is executed, line 67 requests that the user enter the letter Y to process another account number or the letter N to terminate execution of the program.

The complete QuickBASIC program is shown in Figure 6-12.

FIGURE 6-12
Sample Program 6

```
1   ' ***************************************************************
2   ' *   Sample Program 6                        September 15, 1994 *
3   ' *   Customer Account Table Lookup                              *
4   ' *   J. S. Quasney                                              *
5   ' *                                                              *
6   ' *   This program loads the data in ACCOUNTS.DAT into arrays.   *
7   ' *   The user enters the account number and the program looks   *
8   ' *   up and displays the customer number and account balance.   *
9   ' *        If the account number is not found, then a            *
10  ' *   diagnostic message is displayed.  After processing a       *
11  ' *   request, the user is asked if he or she wishes to          *
12  ' *   display information of another account or terminate the    *
13  ' *   program.                                                   *
14  ' *                                                              *
15  ' *   Variables: Account$           -- Account number array      *
16  ' *              Cus.Name$          -- Customer name array       *
17  ' *              Balance            -- Customer balance array    *
18  ' *              Search.Argument$   -- Account number requested  *
19  ' *              Control$           -- Response to continue      *
20  ' *              Entries            -- Number of customers       *
21  ' ***************************************************************
22
23  ' ***************************************************************
24  ' *                       Main Module                            *
25  ' ***************************************************************
26  GOSUB Initialization
27  GOSUB Process.Request
28  GOSUB Wrap.Up
29  END
30
```

FIGURE 6-12
(continued)

```
31  ' ****************************************************************
32  ' *                        Initialization                         *
33  ' ****************************************************************
34  Initialization:
35     OPEN "B:ACCOUNTS.DAT" FOR INPUT AS #1
36     INPUT #1, Entries
37     DIM Account$(1 TO Entries), Cus.Name$(1 TO Entries), Balance(1 TO Entries)
38     FOR Number = 1 TO Entries
39        INPUT #1, Account$(Number), Cus.Name$(Number), Balance(Number)
40     NEXT Number
41     CLOSE #1
42  RETURN
43
44  ' ****************************************************************
45  ' *                       Process A Request                       *
46  ' ****************************************************************
47  Process.Request:
48     DO
49        CLS   ' Clear Screen
50        LOCATE 5, 15
51        INPUT "Account Number =====> ", Search.Argument$
52        FOR Number = 1 TO Entries
53           IF Search.Argument$ = Account$(Number) THEN
54              EXIT FOR    ' Process a Table Hit
55           END IF
56        NEXT Number
57        IF Number <= Entries THEN
58           LOCATE 7, 15
59           PRINT "Customer Name ======> "; Cus.Name$(Number)
60           LOCATE 9, 15
61           PRINT USING "Balance ============> $$,###.##"; Balance(Number)
62        ELSE
63           LOCATE 7, 15
64           PRINT "Account Number "; Search.Argument$; " NOT FOUND"
65        END IF
66        LOCATE 11, 15
67        INPUT "Enter Y to lookup another part number, else N... ", Control$
68     LOOP UNTIL Control$ = "N" OR Control$ = "n"
69  RETURN
70
71  ' ****************************************************************
72  ' *                           Wrap-Up                             *
73  ' ****************************************************************
74  Wrap.Up:
75     LOCATE 13, 15
76     PRINT "Job Complete"
77  RETURN
78  ' ********************** End of Program ********************
```

FUNCTIONS

QuickBASIC includes over 70 numeric and string functions. Numeric functions are used to handle common mathematical calculations. String functions are used to manipulate strings of characters.

Numeric Functions

Three of the most frequently used numeric functions are the INT, SQR, and RND functions. The purpose of these functions is summarized in Figure 6-13.

FUNCTION	FUNCTION VALUE
INT(X)	Returns the largest integer that is less than or equal to the argument X.
SQR(X)	Returns the square root of the argument X.
RND	Returns a random number greater than or equal to zero and less than 1.

FIGURE 6-13 Frequently used numeric functions

INT Function The INT function returns a whole number that is less than or equal to the argument. Figure 6-14 shows several examples of the INT function.

VALUE OF VARIABLE	QuickBASIC STATEMENT	RESULT
X = 12.45	LET Y = INT(X)	Y = 12
H = 27.89	LET G = INT(H + 10)	G = 37
J = -15.67	LET K = INT(J)	K = -16

FIGURE 6-14 Examples of the INT function

SQR Function The SQR function computes the square root of the argument. Figure 6-15 illustrates several examples of the SQR function. Note that the argument for the SQR function must be a non-negative value.

VALUE OF VARIABLE	QuickBASIC STATEMENT	RESULT
Y = 4	LET X = SQR(Y)	X = 2
D = 27	LET P = SQR(D * 3)	P = 9
E = -16	LET U = SQR(E)	Illegal Function Call

FIGURE 6-15 Examples of the SQR function

RND Function   The RND function returns an unpredictable number that is greater than or equal to zero and less than 1. The partial program in Figure 6-16 uses a For loop and the RND function to generate three random numbers — .7132002, .6291881, and .3409873.

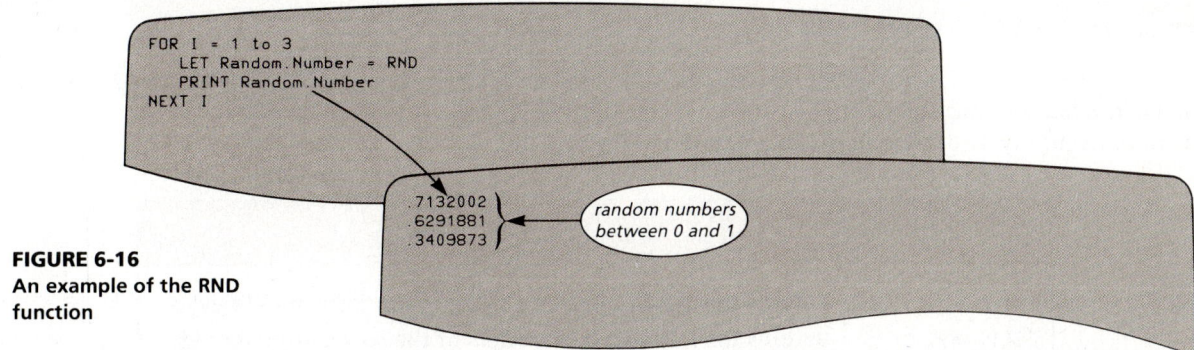

FIGURE 6-16
An example of the RND function

The INT and RND functions can be used to generate random digits over any range. The following expression generates random numbers between L and U:

INT((U - L + 1) * RND + L)

For example, to simulate the roll of a six-sided die, we can write the following:

LET Die = INT((6 - 1 + 1) * RND + 1)

   or

LET Die = INT(6 * RND + 1)

In Figure 6-17, the For loop generates five rolls of two dice. The first LET statement represents the roll of one die and the second LET statement represents the roll of the second die.

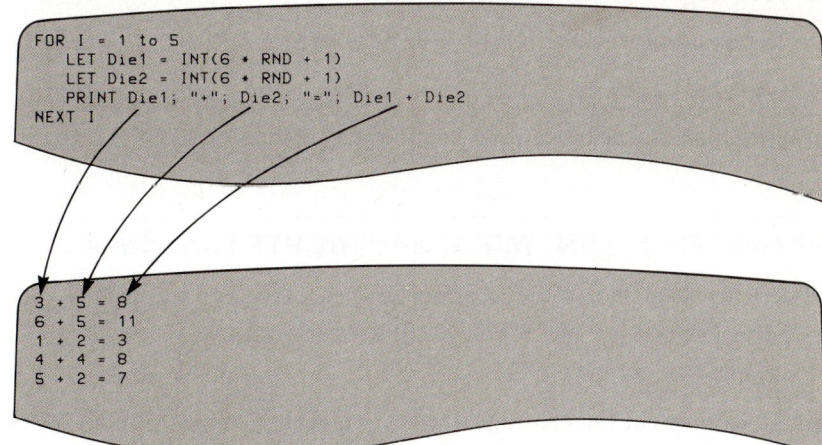

FIGURE 6-17
An example of a partial program that simulates five rolls of two dice

Each time you run the program in Figure 6-17, it generates the same sequence of random numbers. To generate a new sequence of random numbers each time you execute the program, insert the RANDOMIZE statement at the top of the program. When executed, the RANDOMIZE statement requests that you enter a number between −32768 and 32767. The value you enter is used by the PC to develop a new set of random numbers.

String Functions

The capability to process strings is important in business applications. In QuickBASIC, you can join two strings together through the use of the concatenation operator (+). For example, the following LET statement:

```
LET Join$ = "ABC" + "DEF"
```

assigns the variable Join$ the value ABCDEF. Besides the concatenation operator, QuickBASIC includes over 25 functions that allow you to manipulate string values.

The most frequently used string functions are shown in Figure 6-18.

FUNCTION	FUNCTION VALUE
DATE$	Returns the system date as a string in the form mm-dd-yyyy.
LEFT$(S$, X)	Returns the leftmost X characters of the string argument S$.
LEN(S$)	Returns the number of characters in the string argument S$.
MID$(S$, P, X)	Returns X characters from the string argument S$ beginning at position P.
RIGHT$(S$, X)	Returns the rightmost X characters of the string argument S$.
TIME$	Returns the system time of day as a string in the form HH:MM:SS.

FIGURE 6-18 Frequently used string functions

The DATE$ and TIME$ Functions The DATE$ and TIME$ functions return the DOS system date and time. For example, if the system date is initialized to September 15, 1994, then the statement PRINT "The date is "; DATE$ displays the following result:

```
The date is 09-15-1994
```

If the system time is equal to 11:44:42, then the statement PRINT "The time is "; TIME$ displays the following result:

```
The time is 11:44:42
```

The system time is maintained in 24-hour notation. That is, 1:30 P.M. displays as 13:30:00.

Use of the LEFT$, LEN, MID$, and RIGHT$ Functions

The LEN(S$) function returns the number of characters in S$. For example, the following LET statement assigns Length the value 5 because there are 5 characters in the string BASIC:

```
LET Length = LEN("BASIC")
```

The LET statement LET Number = LEN(DATE$) assigns Number the value 10 because there are 10 characters in the system date (mm/dd/yyyy).

The LEFT$, MID$, and RIGHT$ functions are used to extract substrings from a string. Figure 6-19 illustrates several examples of these functions.

VALUE OF VARIABLE	QuickBASIC STATEMENT	RESULT
Assume S$ is equal to GOTO is a four-letter word		
1	LET Q$ = LEFT$(S$, 7)	Q$ = GOTO is
2	LET W$ = LEFT$(S$, 4)	W$ = GOTO
3	LET D$ = RIGHT$(S$, 11)	D$ = letter word
4	LET K$ = RIGHT$(S$, 1)	K$ = d
5	LET M$ = MID$(S$, 6, 2)	M$ = is
6	LET T$ = MID$(S$, 16, 6)	T$ = letter

FIGURE 6-19 Examples of the LEFT$, RIGHT$, and MID$ functions

QuickBASIC also allows the argument to include a function. For example, if the system date is 9/15/94, then the LET statement LET Day$ = MID$(DATE$, 4, 2) assigns Day$ the string value 15. If the system time is equal to 10:32:52, then the LET statement LET Second$ = MID$(Time$, 7, 2) assigns Second$ the string value 52.

Consider the partial program in Figure 6-20 and the corresponding output results. Lines 1 and 2 display the system date and time. Lines 4 through 6 display on separate lines the substrings month, day, and year. Lines 8 through 10 display on separate lines the substrings hour, minute, and second.

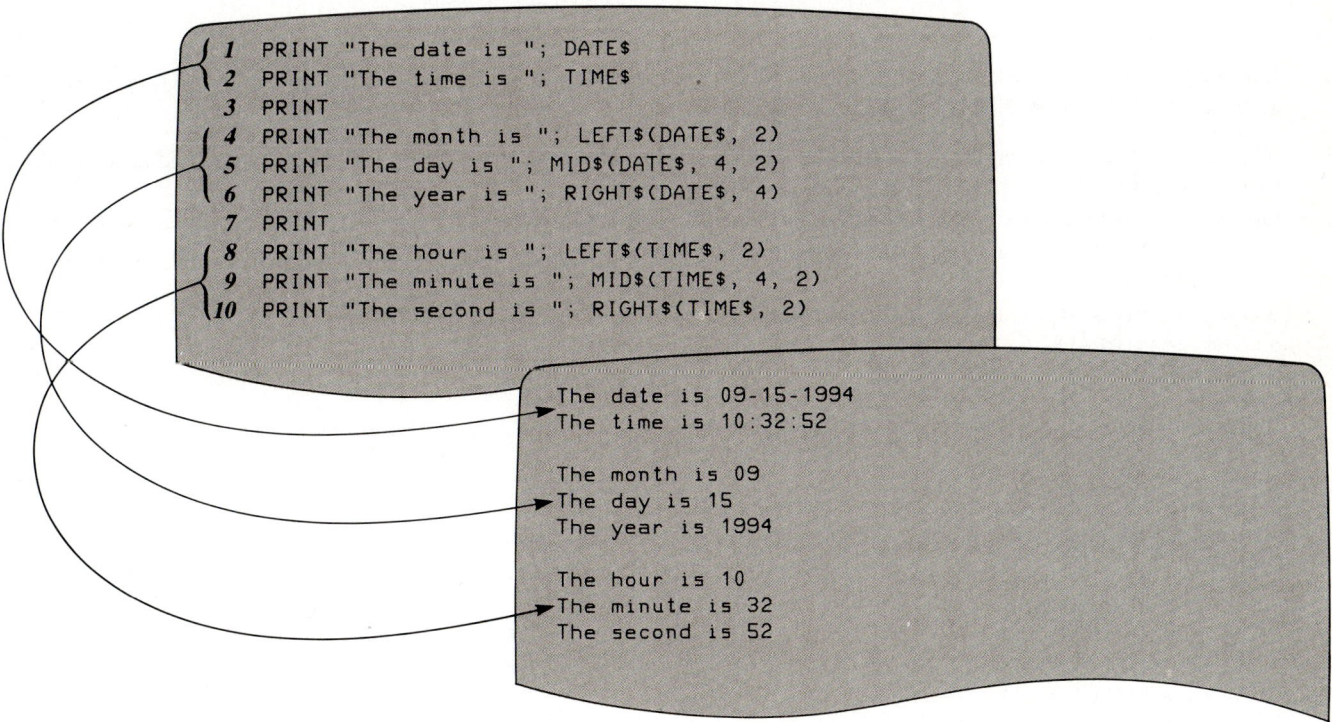

FIGURE 6-20 An example of a partial program that uses string functions. Assume system date is 9/15/94 and system time is 10:32:52

TRY IT YOURSELF EXERCISES

1. What is displayed when the following programs are executed?
   a. ```
      ' Exercise 1.a
      City$ = "Los Angeles"
      PRINT LEFT$(City$, 1) + MID$(City$, 5, 1) + " LAW"
      END
      ```
   b. ```
      ' Exercise 1.b
      PRINT "Number", "Square", "Square Root"
      FOR I = 1 TO 10
         PRINT I, I ^ 2, SQR(I)
      NEXT I
      END
      ```

2. Assume arrays Part and Cost are dimensioned by the statement `DIM Part(1 TO 5), Cost(1 TO 5)`. Assume that the two arrays were loaded with the following values:

ARRAY PART	ARRAY COST
15	1.23
71	2.34
92	.25
94	1.37
99	5.25

   Indicate how you would reference the following values using subscripts. For example, .25 can be referenced by Cost(3).
   a. 71   b. 5.25   c. 2.34   d. 15   e. 1.37   f. 1.23   g. 99

3. Write a `DIM` statement to minimally dimension array X so that subscripts in the range 1 to 900 are valid and array Y so that subscripts in the range –5 to 22 are valid.

4. Given that array G has been declared to have 10 elements (1 to 10), assume that each element of G has a value. Write a partial program that includes a `DIM` statement to shift all the values up one location. That is, assign G(1) to G(2), G(2) to G(3), and G(10) to G(1).

5. Identify the errors, if any, in each of the following:
   a. `DIM Amt(1 TO -1)`   b. `DIM Bal (1 TOO 10)`
   c. `DIM Sales`   d. `DIM (1 TO 35)X`

6. Indicate what each of the following are equal to. Assume Phrase$ is equal to `Aim the arrow carefully`.
   a. `LEN(Phrase$)`   b. `MID$(Phrase$, 4, 3)`
   c. `LEFT$(Phrase$, 13)`   d. `RIGHT$(Phrase$, 5)`

7. Assume that the system date is equal to December 25, 1994 and the system time is equal to 11:12:15. Evaluate the following:
   a. `X$ = TIME$`
   b. `X$ = MID$(TIME$, 4, 1)`
   c. `X$ = RIGHT$(DATE$, 2)`
   d. `X$ = LEFT$(DATE$, 2)`

8. Write a LET statement that assigns Number a random value between 1 and 52.
9. Explain the purpose of the RANDOMIZE statement.
10. What does each of the following equal?
    a. INT(23.46)
    b. SQR(121)
    c. LEN("ABC")
    d. INT(-12.43)
    e. SQR(SQR(81))
    f. SQR(INT(36.57))

STUDENT ASSIGNMENTS

STUDENT ASSIGNMENT 1: Phone Number Lookup

Instructions: Design and code a top-down QuickBASIC program that requests a person's last name and displays the person's telephone number.

Read the data shown in the phone number table under INPUT into parallel arrays from a sequential data file or DATA statements. If you plan to use a sequential data file, ask your instructor for a copy of PHONE.DAT.

Accept a person's last name in lowercase from the user. Search the last name array. If the search is successful, display the corresponding telephone number. If the search is unsuccessful, display a diagnostic message. After the search, ask the user if he or she wants to look up another telephone number. The output results should be similar to the displayed results shown under OUTPUT.

INPUT: Use the following phone number table data. Include a value at the beginning of the file which indicates the number of elements required in the parallel arrays that will hold the names and phone numbers.

Look up the phone numbers of the following individuals: fuqua, bingle, smith, and course.

NAME	PHONE NUMBER
miller	(213) 430-2865
flaming	(213) 866-9082
fuqua	(714) 925-3391
bingle	(805) 402-3376
course	(213) 423-7765

OUTPUT: The following results are displayed for bingle and smith:

```
Person's Name =====> bingle
Phone Number ======> (805) 402-3376
Enter Y to lookup another phone number, Else N... y
```

```
Person's Name =====> smith
The Name smith NOT FOUND
Enter Y to lookup another phone number, Else N... y
```

STUDENT ASSIGNMENT 2: Weight Table Lookup

Instructions: Design and code a top-down QuickBASIC program that accepts a male or female height and displays the average weight ranges for a small-framed, medium-framed, and large-framed person. If the search is unsuccessful, display an error message. The table entries are shown in the height and weight table data under INPUT. The output results are shown under OUTPUT.

INPUT: Use the following height and weight table data. Read the table data into two separate sets of parallel arrays, one for the male weights and one for the female weights, by means of a data file or DATA statements. If you plan to use a sequential data file, ask your instructor for a copy of WEIGHT.DAT. Initialize a variable to nine (the number of different heights for males and for females prior to the DIM statement). Use this variable to dimension the arrays and control any loops that search for heights. Look up the following:

Sex – Male, Height – 72
Sex – Female, Height – 64
Sex – Male, Height – 76
Sex – Female, Height – 72
Sex – Male, Height – 70

MEN

HEIGHT	SMALL FRAME	MEDIUM FRAME	LARGE FRAME
66	124–133	130–143	138–156
67	128–136	134–147	142–161
68	132–141	138–152	147–168
69	136–145	142–156	151–170
70	140–150	146–160	155–174
71	144–154	150–165	159–179
72	148–158	154–170	164–184
73	152–162	158–175	168–189
74	156–167	162–180	173–194

WOMEN

HEIGHT	SMALL FRAME	MEDIUM FRAME	LARGE FRAME
62	102–110	107–119	115–131
63	105–113	110–122	118–134
64	108–116	113–126	121–138
65	111–119	116–130	125–142
66	114–123	120–135	129–148
67	118–127	124–139	133–150
68	122–131	128–43	137–154
69	126–135	132–147	141–158
70	130–140	136–151	145–163

OUTPUT: The following screen displays for the first set of data under INPUT:

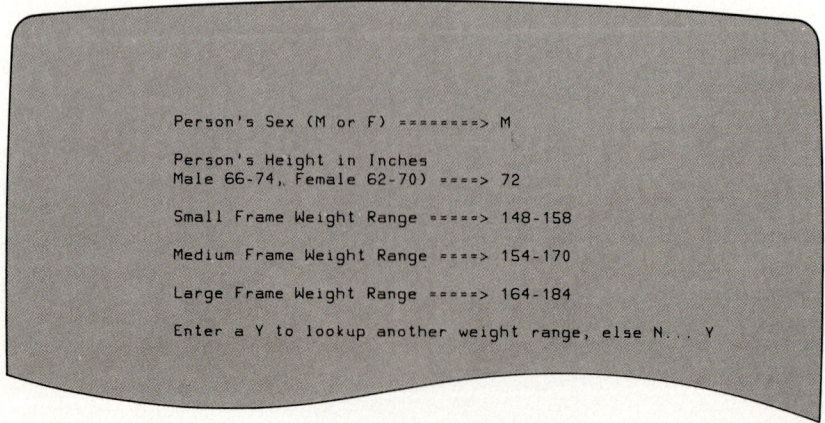

```
Person's Sex (M or F) ========> M

Person's Height in Inches
Male 66-74, Female 62-70) ====> 72

Small Frame Weight Range  =====> 148-158

Medium Frame Weight Range =====> 154-170

Large Frame Weight Range  =====> 164-184

Enter a Y to lookup another weight range, else N... Y
```

APPENDIX

QuickBASIC Debugging Techniques

Although the top-down approach and structured programming techniques help minimize errors, they by no means guarantee error-free programs. Owing to carelessness or insufficient thought, program portions can be constructed which do not work as anticipated and give erroneous results. When such problems occur, you need techniques to isolate the errors and correct the erroneous program statements.

QuickBASIC can detect many different **grammatical errors** and display appropriate diagnostic messages. However, there is no BASIC system that can detect all errors. Some of these errors can go undetected by QuickBASIC until either an abnormal end occurs during execution or the program terminates with the results in error.

There are several techniques you can use for attempting to discover the portion of the program that is in error. These methods are **debugging techniques**. The errors themselves are **bugs**, and the activity involved in their detection is **debugging**. QuickBASIC has a fully integrated debugger which pinpoints errors by tracing, or highlighting, through the QuickBASIC source code. The QuickBASIC debugging features include the following:

- Examining values through the immediate window
- Executing one statement at a time
- Breakpoints
- Tracing
- Set next statement
- Recording
- Watch variables and watchpoints

EXAMINING VALUES THROUGH THE IMMEDIATE WINDOW

Following the termination of execution of a program, the program's variables remain equal to the latest values assigned. Through the immediate window, you can examine their values. This is an easy-to-use, and yet, powerful debugging tool.

To activate the immediate window, press F6. You may then display the value of any variables in the program by using the PRINT statement and the names of the variables. Recall that when a statement is entered in the immediate window, it is executed immediately. After viewing the values, press F6 to deactivate the immediate window and activate the view window.

If you have a mouse, move the pointer to the inactive window and click the mouse button.

EXECUTING ONE STATEMENT AT A TIME

Another debugging tool is the Step mode. In the **Step mode**, the PC executes the program one statement at a time. To activate this mode, press the F8 key. The first time you press the F8 key, the PC displays the first executable statement in reverse video. Thereafter, each time you press the F8 key, the PC executes the statement in reverse video and displays the next executable statement in reverse video. Hence, the PC steps through the program one statement at a time as you press the F8 key.

While the PC is in the Step mode and before you press the F8 key again, you can do any of the following to better understand what the program is doing:

- Activate the immediate window and use the PRINT statement to display the values of variables.
- Use the F4 key to toggle between displaying the program and the output screen.
- Modify any statement in the program. If you modify the statement in reverse video, the reverse video disappears. It reappears as soon as you move the cursor off the line.

To exit the Step mode, press the F5 key. The F5 key continues normal execution of the program. If you want to halt the program again, press Ctrl + Break. To continue execution after pressing Ctrl + Break, you can do one of the following:

- Press F5 to continue normal execution
- Press Shift + F5 to start execution from the beginning of the program
- Press F8 to activate the Step mode

BREAKPOINTS

A **breakpoint** is a line in the program where you want execution to halt. Breakpoints are established by moving the cursor to the line in question, followed by pressing the F9 key or selecting the Toggle Breakpoint command in the Debug menu. When you execute the program after setting one or more breakpoints, the PC halts execution at the next breakpoint and displays it in reverse video. Once the program halts at a breakpoint, you can do one of the following:

- Press the F8 key to enter the Step mode and execute from the one statement at a time to the next breakpoint
- Display the values of variables in the immediate window
- Edit the program
- Delete or add new breakpoints
- Press F5 to continue execution of the program

To toggle off a breakpoint, move the cursor to the breakpoint and press the F9 key. An alternative method for clearing breakpoints is to select the command Clear All Breakpoints in the Debug menu. This latter method can be useful, especially when you have set a number of breakpoints and cannot remember where they are located in the program. A breakpoint only displays in reverse video when it halts execution of the program.

To save time, you should carefully select breakpoints. Commonly used breakpoints include lines immediately following input, calculations, and decision statements.

TRACING

The Trace On command in the Debug menu causes the PC to trace the program. **Tracing** means that the program will execute in slow motion. As the program executes in slow motion, the PC highlights each statement as it executes it. With the Trace On command you can quickly get an idea as to flow of control in your program. This activity must be observed to be appreciated.

The Trace On command works like a toggle switch. Select it once and the PC will trace the flow of control. Select it again, and you turn tracing off. You know that tracing is on when there is a bullet in front of the command in the Debug menu. If you are using the commercial version of QuickBASIC, note that you must toggle on Full Menus in the Option menu for the Trace On command to display in the Debug menu.

Two QuickBASIC statements that carry out the same function as the Trace On command are TRON and TROFF. The TRON statement turns on tracing for all future statements executed. The TROFF statement turns tracing off. Although most QuickBASIC programmers use the Trace On command to trace a program, some find the TRON and TROFF statements useful for tracing small sections of a program.

SET NEXT STATEMENT

The Set Next Statement command in the Debug menu allows you to establish with the cursor where execution will continue following a program halt. For example, assume that you have set a breakpoint in a program. When the PC halts execution at the statement, you can move the cursor to any line in the program and select the Set Next Statement command. When execution resumes, it will begin at the cursor rather than at the statement in reverse video. The Set Next Statement command works much like the infamous GOTO statement. Use caution when evaluating the program results following the use of this command since skipping over code can produce unexpected results. If you are using the commercial version of QuickBASIC, note that you must toggle on Full Menus in the Option menu for the Trace On command to display in the Debug menu.

RECORDING

The History On command in the Debug menu is often used in conjunction with breakpoints. When you select the History On command, the PC records the last 20 lines executed by the program. When the program halts at a breakpoint, you can use the Shift + F8 to go back through the last 20 lines executed. You can use the Shift + F10 to go forward through the last 20 lines executed.

Stepping through the last 20 lines can also be useful when your program halts due to a logic error. If you select History On prior to execution, then you can step through the last 20 lines executed before the program's premature termination.

To stop recording the last 20 lines, select History On. This command acts like a toggle switch. Select it once and it's on. Select it again and it's off. You know that the History On command is active when there is a bullet in front of the command in the Debug menu. (Full Menus in the Option menu must be active for the History On command to display in the Debug menu.)

WATCH VARIABLES AND WATCHPOINTS

The Add Watch command in the Debug menu allows you to enter the names of variables or expressions that you want displayed in the watch window. The **watch window** (Figure A-1) displays above the view window whenever watch variables are active. Watching a variable is often combined with the Step mode (F8) or breakpoints to track its value, thus avoiding repeated use of the PRINT statement in the immediate window.

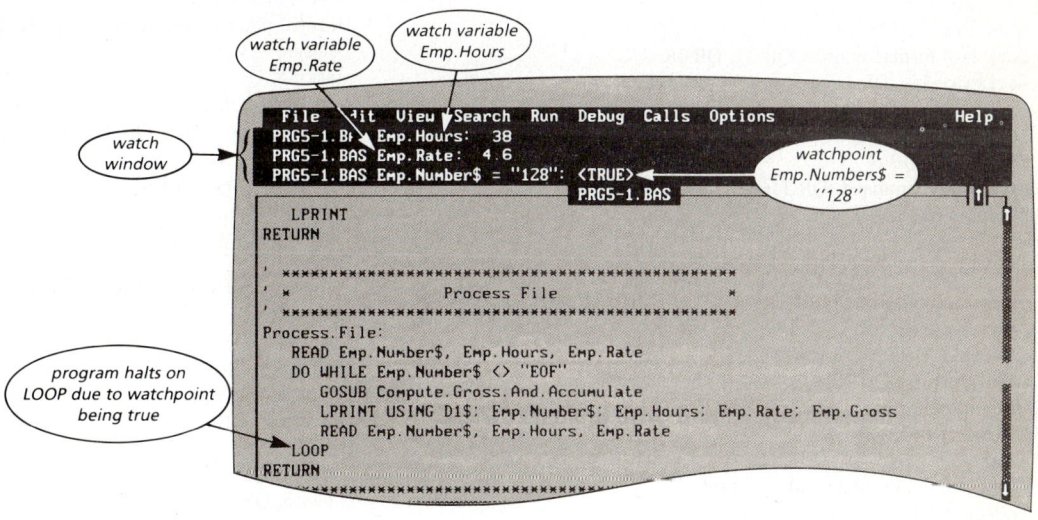

FIGURE A-1
The watch window displays above the view window. Program halts on LOOP statement when Emp.Number$ = "128". Value of Emp.Hours is 38. Value of Emp.Rate is 4.6.

With the commercial version of QuickBASIC, you can add watch variables or conditions to the watch window by pressing Shift + F9 or selecting the Instant Watch command. The main difference between the Instant Watch and Add Watch commands is that with Instant Watch you do not have to type the variable name or condition. You simply select a watch variable by moving the cursor within the variable name in the program. To select a condition, you must use the Shift and arrow keys to highlight it before pressing Shift + F9.

The Watchpoint command in the Debug menu allows you to enter a watchpoint in the watch window. A **watchpoint** (Figure A-1) is a condition that halts program execution when it becomes true.

To delete individual watch variables or watchpoints, select the Delete Watch command in the Debug menu. To delete all watch variables and watch points, select the Delete All Watch command.

QuickBASIC Index

–A–

Accumulator, QB 28
  counter, QB 29
  running total, QB 29
Add Watch command, QB 117
Addition, QB 25
Alt key, QB 17
AND operator, QB 52
Apostrophe. *See* REM statement
APPEND mode for files, QB 83
Appending records, QB 84
Arguments in functions, QB 108
Arithmetic operators, QB 25
Array, QB 99–107
  declaring, QB 100
  lower bound of, QB 100
  name, QB 99, QB 100
  parallel, QB 104
  range of, QB 99
  upper bound of, QB 100

–B–

Backslash format symbol, QB 35, QB 36
Backspace key, QB 16
BASIC. *See* QuickBASIC
BEEP statement, QB 64
Blank, line, QB 6
Breakpoint command, QB 116
Button in dialog box, QB 15

–C–

Calling a subroutine, QB 73
CASE clause, QB 55
CASE ELSE clause, QB 55
Case structure, QB 42, QB 54, QB 55
Circumflex for exponentiation, QB 25
Clause, QB 43, QB 55
Clear
  All Breakpoints command, QB 116
  screen, QB 6, QB 65
Clipboard, QB 17
CLOSE statement, QB 83, QB 84
CLS statement, QB 6
Comma
  format symbol, QB 36
  separator, QB 37
Comparisons
  numeric, QB 9, QB 42, QB 43
  string, QB 9, QB 42, QB 43
Compound condition, QB 51, QB 54
Concatenation operator, QB 110
Condition, QB 43
  compound, QB 51, QB 54
Constant, QB 25
  numeric, QB 25
  string, QB 25

Contents command Help menu, QB 22
Context-senitive help, QB 22
Control structure
  Case, QB 42
  Do-Until, QB 66
  Do-While, QB 66
  If-Then-Else, QB 44
Counter, QB 29
Counter-controlled loop, QB 62, QB 68
Cursor, QB 16
  movement keys, QB 15
Cut and paste, QB 17

–D–

Data, QB 2, QB 25, QB 62–63
  items, QB 2
  validation, QB 65
DATA statement, QB 5, QB 30
DATE$ function, QB 110
Debugging, QB 115
  techniques, QB 115
Decimal point format symbol, QB 35, QB 36
Decision
  making, QB 42
  statement, QB 51, QB 54
  symbol in flowchart, QB 45, QB 66, QB 71
Delete
  All Watch command, QB 117
  key, QB 16
  Watch command, QB 117
Design
  program, QB 1, QB 30–32
  test, QB 1
Detail line, QB 29
Dialog box, QB 15
DIM statement, QB 100
Dimension, QB 100
Dirs/drive box, QB 20
Division, QB 25
Do loop, QB 8, QB 9, QB 31
DO statement, QB 71
DO UNTIL statement, QB 8–10
DO WHILE statement, QB 8–10
Documentation, QB 30
Do-While logic structure, QB 66

–E–

Editing a program, QB 16, QB 33, QB 116
ELSE clause, QB 47
END statement, QB 7
  IF, QB 43, QB 47
  SELECT, QB 55
End-of-file, QB 9, QB 31
  detection, QB 9, QB 91–92
  mark, QB 4, QB 91, QB 96
  routine, QB 9

EOF function, QB 91
Equal sign, QB 31, QB 35
Esc key, QB 13
EXIT FOR statement, QB 105
Expressions, QB 25–26
  match, QB 56
  numeric, QB 25
  string, QB 25

–F–

Field, QB 2
File, QB 2
  appending records to, QB 84
  creating a, QB 84
  extension, QB 20, QB 21, QB 22
  handling statements, QB 83
  name, QB 84
  opening a, QB 83–84
  organization, QB 83
  random, QB 83
  sequential, QB 83
  specification, QB 20, QB 83
Filenumber, QB 83, QB 84
Flowchart, program, QB 2–4
For loop, QB 62, QB 68
  execution of, QB 68
  flowchart representation, QB 68
  nested, QB 27
  range of, QB 68
FOR statement, QB 66, QB 68
Format field, QB 34, QB 36
  symbols, QB 35
Function, QB 108–111
  keys, QB 15
  numeric, QB 25, QB 108
  string, QB 110

–G–

GIGO, QB 65
GOSUB statement, QB 73
Grammatical errors, QB 16, QB 115

–H–

Hard-copy output, QB 18
Header lines, QB 28
Help, QB 13, QB 15, QB 22
  menu, QB 22
  QB Advisor, QB 13, QB 22
Hierarchy
  of arithmetic operations, QB 25
  of logical operators, QB 53
Hyperlinks, QB 22

–I–

IF statement, QB 42–44
  nested, QB 52
If-Then-Else
  logic structure, QB 42–43
  nested forms, QB 46–47
  simple forms, QB 44–46
Immediate window, QB 14, QB 115
Increment value, QB 68

Initialization module, QB 5, QB 30, QB 104
Initialize accumulator, QB 29, QB 30
Input
  prompt, QB 63
  prompt message, QB 63, QB 64
INPUT mode for files, QB 83
INPUT statement, QB 62
INPUT #n statement, QB 85, QB 91
Insert key, QB 16
INT function, QB 108
Interactive programming, QB 62–77

–K–

Keyword, QB 7, QB 25

–L–

Lead read, QB 2
LEFT$ function, QB 110
LEN function, QB 110
LET statement, QB 25, QB 35
Limit value, QB 68, QB 69
LOCATE statement, QB 64, QB 71
LOOP statement, QB 8, QB 62, QB 71
LOOP UNTIL statement, QB 62, QB 71
Lower-bound value, QB 100
LPRINT statement, QB 20, QB 38, QB 50
LPRINT USING statement, QB 38, QB 50

–M–

Main module, QB 73, QB 77, QB 103
Menu bar, QB 14, QB 17
Microsoft QuickBASIC, QB 1
  Advisor, QB 13, QB 22
  editor, QB 16
  functions, R.4–R.5
  help, QB 13, QB 15, QB 22
  quit, QB 16
  reserved words, R.6
  shortcut keys, QB 18
  statements, R.1–R.3
MID$ function, QB 110
Mouse unit, QB 16
  button, QB 15
  pointer, QB 15
Multiple statements per line, QB 45
Multiplication, QB 25

–N–

Nested, QB 27
New command, QB 20, QB 22
NEXT statement, QB 66, QB 68
NOT operator, QB 51
Number sign format symbol, QB 36

–O–

OPEN statement, QB 83
Open command, QB 20, QB 21, QB 22
Operators
  arithmetic, QB 25
  concatenation, QB 53
  logical, QB 50–54
  relational, QB 9, QB 44, QB 51

OR operator, QB 52–53
Order of operations, QB 26
OUTPUT mode for file, QB 83
Output screen, QB 6, QB 18

–P–

Parallel arrays, QB 104
Parentheses, QB 27, QB 54
Precedence, rules of, QB 54
  arithmetic, QB 26
  logical, QB 54
Primary read, QB 2
Print
  command, QB 19
  items, QB 6
  zones, QB 6
PRINT statement, QB 6, QB 28, QB 32, QB 38,
  QB 71, QB 115
PRINT USING statement, QB 28, QB 33–35, QB 71
Problem analysis, QB 1
Process File module, QB 31
Process A Request module, QB 104, QB 105

–Q–

QB Advisor, QB 13, QB 22
QuickBASIC. *See* Microsoft QuickBASIC

–R–

Raising to a power, QB 25
Random file, QB 83
Random numbers, QB 109
RANDOMIZE statement, QB 109
READ statement, QB 7, QB 52
Record, QB 2
Relational operators, QB 9, QB 44, QB 51
REM statement, QB 4, QB 5
Remark line, QB 4, QB 5
Report editing, QB 33
RETURN statement, QB 73
RIGHT$ function, QB 110
RND function, QB 108, QB 109
Run menu, QB 17
Running total, QB 29

–S–

Save As command, QB 20
SELECT CASE statement, QB 42, QB 54–56
Semicolon separator, QB 32, QB 36
Sentinel record, QB 9
Sequential file, QB 83
  creating, QB 83
  organization, QB 83
Set Next statement, QB 116
Shortcut keys, QB 118
SPC function, QB 65
SQR function, QB 108

Status line, QB 14
Step mode, QB 115
String
  comparing, QB 9
  constant, QB 35, QB 37
  expression, QB 34, QB 36, QB 43
  function, QB 25
  sub, QB 110, QB 111
  variable, QB 7, QB 34, QB 36
Subroutine, QB 73
Subscript, QB 100
Subtraction, QB 25

–T–

TAB function, QB 6
Table, QB 99
  hit, QB 105
  lookup, QB 101
  organization, QB 101
  search, QB 99
THEN clause, QB 47
TIME$ function, QB 110
TO attribute, QB 100
Top-down
  approach, QB 72, QB 73
  chart, QB 73, QB 86, QB 102
  programming, QB 62, QB 72
Total line, QB 29, QB 31
Tracing, QB 116
Trailer record, QB 2, QB 9

–U–

Upper-bound value, QB 100

–V–

Validating data, QB 65
Variable, QB 7
  initialize, QB 28, QB 29
  loop, QB 29
  names, QB 7
  numeric, QB 7
  simple, QB 7
  string, QB 7
  subscripted, QB 100
View window, QB 13

–W–

Watch
  variable, QB 117
  window, QB 117
Watchpoint, QB 117
  command, QB 117
Wrap-Up module, QB 12, QB 85, QB 90
WRITE #n statement, QB 83, QB 84–85

MICROSOFT QuickBASIC REFERENCE CARD

Legend: Uppercase letters are required keywords. You must supply items within < >'s. You must select one of the entries within { }'s. Items within [ ]'s are optional. Three ellipsis points (...) indicate that an item may be repeated as many times as you wish. The symbol **b** represents a blank character.

Summary of BASIC Statements

STATEMENT

BEEP
Causes the speaker on the PC to beep for a fraction of a second.

CALL <name> [(argumentlist)]
Transfers control to a subprogram.

CHAIN "<filespec>"
Instructs the PC to stop executing the current program, load another program from auxiliary storage and start executing it.

CHDIR <pathspecification>
Changes the current directory for the specified drive.

CIRCLE <(x, y), radius> [,color [,start,end [,shape]]]
Causes the PC to draw an ellipse, circle, arc, or wedge with center at (x, y).

CLEAR [,,stack]
Reinitializes all program variables, closes files, and sets the stack size.

CLOSE [#] [filenumber] [,[#] [filenumber]]...
Closes specified files.

CLS
Erases the information on the screen and places the cursor in the upper left corner of the screen.

COLOR [background] [,palette]
In medium-resolution graphics mode, sets the color for the background and palette of colors.

COLOR [foreground] [,[background] [,border]
In the text mode, defines the color of the foreground characters, background, and border around the screen.

COM(n) {ON / OFF / STOP}
Enables or disables trapping of communications activity on adaptor n.

COMMON [SHARED] <variable> [,variable]...
Passes specified variables to a chained program.

CONST <constantname> = <expression> [, constantname = expression]...
Declares symbolic constants that can be used in place of numeric or string expressions.

STATEMENT

DATA <data item> [,data item]...
Provides for the creation of a sequence of data items for use by the READ statement.

DATE$ = mm{-/}dd{-/}yy[yy] Sets the system date, where mm = month, dd = day, yy = year, yyyy = 4-digit year.

DECLARE {FUNCTION / SUB} name [(parameterlist)]
Declares references to QuickBASIC procedures and invokes argument-type checking.

DEF FN<name> [(variable, [, variable]...)] = <expression>
Defines and names a function that can be referenced in a program as often as needed. Multiline functions end with an END DEF statement.

DEFtype <letterrange> [,letterrange]...
Sets the data type for variables and functions.

DIM [SHARED] <arrayname(size)> [AS type] [,arrayname(size) [AS type]]...
Reserves storage locations for arrays and declares the array type.

DO
Causes the statements between DO and LOOP to be executed repeatedly. The loop is controlled by a condition in the corresponding LOOP statement.

DO UNTIL <condition>
Causes the statements between DO UNTIL and LOOP to be executed repeatedly until the condition is true.

DO WHILE <condition>
Causes the statements between DO WHILE and LOOP to be executed repeatedly while the condition is true.

DRAW <string expression>
Causes the PC to draw the object that is defined by the value of the string expression.

END {DEF / FUNCTION / IF / SELECT / SUB / TYPE}
Ends a QuickBASIC program, procedure, or block of code.

ERASE <arrayname> [,arrayname]...
Eliminates previously defined arrays.

ERROR <integerexpression>
Simulates the occurrence of a QuickBASIC error or allows the user to define error codes.

EXIT <statement>
Exits statement, where statement is equal to FOR, DO, DEF, FUNCTION, or SUB.

STATEMENT

FIELD <#filenumber, width AS string variable> [,width AS string variable]...
Allocates space for variables in a random file buffer.

FILES [filespecification]
Lists the names of all programs and data files in auxiliary storage on the default drive or the drive specified by file specification.

FOR <loopvariable> = <initial> TO <limit> [STEP increment]
Causes the statements between the FOR and NEXT statements to be executed until the value of loopvariable exceeds the value of the limit.

FUNCTION <name> [(parameterlist)] [STATIC]
Declares the name, the parameters, and initiates a function procedure that ends with an END FUNCTION.

GET <(x₁, y₁) - (x₂, y₂), arrayname>
Reads the colors of the points in the specified area on the screen into an array.

GET <[#]filenumber> [,record number]
Reads the specified record from a random file and transfers it to the buffer that is defined by the corresponding FIELD statement.

GOSUB {linelabel / linenumber} Causes control to transfer to a subroutine beginning at the specified line. Also retains the location of the next statement following the GOSUB statement.

GOTO {linelabel / linenumber} Transfers control to the specified line.

IF <condition> THEN [clause] [ELSE [clause]]
The single line IF statement causes execution of the THEN clause if the condition is true. If the ELSE clause is included, it causes execution of the ELSE clause if the condition is false.

IF <condition> THEN
 [statementblock₁]
[ELSE
 [statementblock₂]]
END IF
The block IF statement allows for multiple lines in the THEN and ELSE clauses. Causes execution of the THEN clause if the condition is true. Causes execution of the ELSE clause if the condition is false. The ELSE IF <condition> THEN clause may be used in place of the ELSE clause.

INPUT [;]["prompt message" {;/,}] <variable> [,variable]...
Provides for the assignment of values to variables from a source external to the program, such as the keyboard.

INPUT <#filenumber, variable> [,variable]...
Provides for the assignment of values to variables from a sequential file in auxiliary storage.

(BASIC Statements continued on page R.2 in left column)

MICROSOFT QuickBASIC REFERENCE CARD

Summary of BASIC Statements (continued)

STATEMENT

KEY {n, string value / ON / OFF / LIST} Assigns a string value to a function key. Also used to display the values and enable or disable the function key display line.

KEY(n) {ON / OFF / STOP} Activates or deactivates trapping of the specified key n.

KILL <filespecification> Deletes a file from disk.

[LET] <variable> = <expression> Causes the evaluation of the expression, followed by the assignment of the resulting value to the variable to the left of the equal sign.

LINE [(x₁, y₁)] −(x₂, y₂) [,[color] [,B[F]]],Style] Draws a line or a box on the screen.

LINE INPUT [;]["prompt message";] <string variable> or
LINE INPUT <#filenumber,> <string variable> Provides for the assignment of a line up to 255 characters from a source external to the program, such as the keyboard or a sequential file.

LOCATE [row] [,column] [,cursor] [,start] [,stop] Positions the cursor on the screen. Can also be used to make the cursor visible or invisible and to control the size of the cursor.

LOCK <[#]filenumber>, {record / [start] TO end} Locks all or some of the records in a file.

LOOP {WHILE / UNTIL} [condition] Identifies the end of a loop.

LPRINT [item] [{, / ; / b}] [item]... Provides for the generation of output to the printer.

LPRINT USING <string expression;> <item> [{, / ; / b} [item]... Provides for the generation of formatted output to the printer.

LSET <string variable> = <string expression> Moves string data left-justified into an area of a random file buffer that is defined by the string variable.

MID$ (<string var, start position [,number]>) = <substring> Replaces a substring within a string.

MKDIR <pathname> Creates a new directory.

NAME <oldfilespecification> AS <newfilespecification> Renames a file on disk.

STATEMENT

NEXT [numeric variable] [,numeric variable]... Identifies the end of the For loop(s).

ON COM(n) GOSUB {linelabel / linenumber} Causes control to transfer to the specified line when data is filling the communications buffer (n).

ON ERROR GOTO {linelabel / linenumber} Enables error trapping and specifies the first line of an error-handling routine that the PC is to branch to in the event of an error. If linenumber is zero, error trapping is disabled.

ON <numeric expression> **GOSUB** {linelabel-list / linenumber-list} Causes control to transfer to the subroutine represented by the selected line. Also retains the location of the next statement following the ON-GOSUB statement.

ON <numeric expression> **GOTO** {linelabel-list / linenumber-list} Causes control to transfer to one of several lines according to the value of the numeric expression.

ON KEY(n) GOSUB {linelabel / linenumber} Causes control to transfer to the specified line when the function key or cursor control key (n) is pressed.

ON PEN GOSUB {linelabel / linenumber} Causes control to transfer to the specified line when the light pen is activated.

ON PLAY(n) GOSUB {linelabel / linenumber} Plays continuous background music. Transfers control to the specified line when a note (n) is sensed.

ON STRIG(n) GOSUB {linelabel / linenumber} Causes control to transfer to the specified line when one of the joystick buttons (n) is pressed.

ON TIMER(n) GOSUB {linelabel / linenumber} Causes control to transfer to the specified line when the specified period of time (n) in seconds has elapsed.

ON UEVENT GOSUB {linelabel / linenumber} Defines the event-handler for a user-defined event.

OPEN <filespec> FOR <mode> AS <[#]filenumber> [LEN = record length] Allows a program to read or write records to a file. If record length is specified, then the file is opened as a random file. If the record length is not specified, then the file is opened as a sequential file.

STATEMENT

OPTION BASE {0 / 1} Assigns a lower bound of 0 or 1 to all arrays declared with only an upper-bound value.

OUT <port>, <data> Sends a byte to a machine I/O port.

PAINT <(x, y)> [[,paint] [,boundary]] Paints an area on the screen with the selected color.

PALETTE [attribute, color] or
PALETTE USING <arrayname> [(arrayindex)] Changes one or more of the colors in the palette.

PCOPY <sourcepage>, <destinationpage> Copies one screen page to another.

PEN(n) {ON / OFF / STOP} Enables or disables the PEN read function used to analyze light pen activity.

PLAY <string expression> Causes the PC to play music according to the value of the string expression.

PLAY {ON / OFF / STOP} Enables, disables, or suspends play event trapping.

POKE <address>, <byte> Writes a byte into a storage location.

PRESET <(x, y)> [,color] Draws a point in the color specified at (x, y). If no color is specified, it erases the point.

PRINT {; / ?} [item] [{, / ; / b} [item]... Provides for the generation of output to the screen.

PRINT {; / ?} <#filenumber,> [item] [{, / ; / b} [item]... Provides for the generation of output to a sequential file.

PRINT USING <string expression;> <item> [{, / ; / b} [item];> Provides for the generation of formatted output to the screen.

PRINT <#filenumber,> USING <string expression;> <item> [{, / ; / b} [item]... Provides for the generation of formatted output to a sequential file.

(BASIC Statements continued on page R.3 in left column)

MICROSOFT QuickBASIC REFERENCE CARD

Summary of BASIC Statements (continued)

STATEMENT

PSET <(x, y)> [,color]
Draws a point in the color specified at (x, y).

PUT <(x₁, y₁), arrayname> [,action]
Writes the colors of the points in the array onto an area of the screen.

PUT <[#]filenumber> [,record number]
Writes a record to a random file from a buffer defined by the corresponding FIELD statement.

RANDOMIZE [numeric expression]
Reseeds the random number generator.

READ <variable> [,variable]...
Provides for the assignment of values to variables from a sequence of data items created from DATA statements.

REDIM [SHARED] <arrayname(size) > [AS type] [arrayname(size) [AS type]]...
Changes the space allocated to an array, declared $DYNAMIC.

{REM} [comment]
{ ' }
Provides for the insertion of comments in a program.

RESET
Closes all disk files.

RESTORE { linelabel }
**   { linenumber }**
Allows the data items in DATA statements to be reread.

RESUME { linelabel }
**   { NEXT   }**
**   { 0   }**
**   { b   }**
Continues program execution at the linelabel, or the line following that which caused the error, after an error-recovery procedure.

RETURN { linelabel   }
**   { linenumber }**
Causes control to transfer from a subroutine back to the statement that follows the corresponding GOSUB or ON-GOSUB statement.

RMDIR <pathname>
Removes a directory from disk after all files and subdirectories have been removed.

RSET <string variable> = <string expression>
Moves string data right-justified into an area of a random file buffer that is defined by string variable.

RUN { linenumber }
**   { linelabel }**
**   { b   }**
Restarts the program in main storage.

SCREEN [mode] [,color switch] [,active page] [,visual page]
Sets the screen attributes for text mode, medium-resolution graphics, or high-resolution graphics.

SEEK <[#]filenumber>, <position>
Sets the position in a file for the next read or write.

STATEMENT

SELECT CASE <testexpression>
  CASE <matchexpression₁>
    [range of statements₁]
  [CASE <matchexpression₂>
    [range of statements₂]
  . . .
  [CASE ELSE
    [range of statementsₙ]
END SELECT
Causes execution of one of several ranges of statements depending on the value of testexpression.

SHARED <variable> [AS type] [,variable [AS type]]...
Gives a SUB or FUNCTION procedure access to variables declared at the module level without passing them as parameters.

SHELL [commandstring]
Places the current QB session in a temporary wait state and returns control to MS-DOS. Can also execute another program or MS-DOS command as specified in commandstring.

SLEEP [seconds]
Suspends execution of the calling program.

SOUND <frequency>, <duration>
Causes the generation of sound through the PC speaker.

STATIC <variablelist>
Causes variables and arrays to be local to either a DEF FN, a FUNCTION, or a SUB, and maintains values between calls.

STOP
Stops execution of a program. Unlike the END statement, files are left open.

STRIG(n) { ON   }
**   { OFF }**
**   { STOP }**
Enables or disables trapping of the joystick buttons.

SUB <globalname> [(parameterlist)] [STATIC]
Establishes the beginning of a subprogram. The end of the subprogram is identified by the END SUB statement.

SWAP <variable₁>, <variable₂>
Exchanges the values of two variables of two elements of an array.

SYSTEM
Closes all open files and returns control to MS-DOS.

TIME$ = hh:mm:ss]
Sets the system time, where hh = hours, mm = minutes, and ss = seconds.

TIMER { ON   }
**   { OFF }**
**   { STOP }**
Enables or disables trapping of timed events.

STATEMENT

TROFF
Disables statement tracing.

TRON
Causes the PC to trace execution of program statements.

TYPE <labelname>
  <fieldname₁> AS <fieldtype>
  . . .
  <fieldnameₙ> AS <fieldtype>
END TYPE
Creates user-defined data types containing one or more elements.

UEVENT { ON   }
**   { OFF }**
**   { STOP }**
Enables, disables, or suspends user-defined event trapping.

UNLOCK <[#]filenumber>, { record   }
**   { [start] TO end }**
Unlocks records in a file.

VIEW [(SCREEN] (x₁, y₁) - (x₂, y₂)] [,color] [,boundary]
Defines a viewport.

VIEW PRINT [topline TO bottomline]
Establishes boundaries for the screen text viewport.

WEND
Identifies the end of a While loop.

WHILE <condition>
Identifies the beginning of a While loop. Causes the statements between WHILE and WEND to be executed repeatedly while the condition is true.

WIDTH { 40 }
**   { 80 }**
Erases the information on the screen, sets the width of the line on the screen to 40 or 80 characters, and places the cursor in the upper left corner of the screen.

WIDTH LPRINT <width>
Sets the printer column width.

WINDOW <[SCREEN] (x₁, y₁) - (x₂, y₂)>
Redefines the coordinates of the viewport. Allows you to draw objects in space and not be bounded by the limits of the screen.

WRITE [expression list]
Writes data to the screen.

WRITE <[#]filenumber,> [item] [{ , } item]...
**   { ; }**
Writes data to a sequential file. Causes the PC to insert commas between the items written to the sequential file.

MICROSOFT QuickBASIC REFERENCE CARD

Summary of BASIC Functions

FUNCTION

ABS(N)
Returns the absolute value of the argument N.

ASC(X$)
Returns a two-digit numeric value that is equivalent in ASCII code to the first character of the string argument X$.

ATN(N)
Returns the angle in radians whose tangent is the value of the argument N.

CDBL(N)
Returns N converted to a double-precision value.

CHR$(N)
Returns a single string character that is equivalent in ASCII code to the numeric argument N.

CINT(N)
Returns N converted to an integer after rounding the fractional part of N.

CLNG(N)
Returns N converted to a long integer after rounding the fractional part of N.

COMMAND$
Returns the command line used to start the program.

COS(N)
Returns the cosine of the argument N where N is in radians.

CSNG(N)
Returns N converted to a single-precision value.

CSRLIN
Returns the vertical (row) coordinate of the cursor.

CVI(X$), CVL(X$), CVS(X$), CVD(X$)
Returns the integer, long integer, single-precision, or double-precision numeric value equivalent to the string X$. Used with random files.

DATE$
Returns the current date (mm-dd-yyyy).

EOF(filenumber)
Returns –1 (true) if the end-of-file has been sensed on the sequential file associated with filenumber. Returns 0 (false) if the end-of-file has not been sensed.

ERDEV
Returns an error code from the last device that caused an error.

FUNCTION

ERDEV$
Returns a string expression containing the name of the device that generated a vital error.

ERL
Returns the line number preceding the line that caused the error. If no line numbers are used, then ERL returns a zero.

ERR
Returns the error code for the last error that occurred.

EXP(N)
Returns e(2.718281...) raised to the argument N.

FILEATTR
Returns the file mode for an open file.

FIX(N)
Returns the value of N truncated to an integer.

FRE(N)
Returns the amount of available stack space (N = –2), string space (N not equal to –1 or –2), or size in bytes of the largest array you can create (N = –1).

FREEFILE
Returns the next free QuickBASIC file number.

HEX$(N)
Returns the hexadecimal equivalent of N.

INKEY$
Returns the last character entered from the keyboard.

INP(N)
Returns the byte read from an I/O port N.

INPUT$(N)
Suspends execution of the program until a string of N characters is received from the keyboard.

INPUT$(N, [#]filenumber)
Returns a string of characters from the specified file.

INSTR(P, X$, S$)
Returns the beginning position of the substring S$ in string X$. P indicates the position at which the search begins in the string X$.

INT(N)
Returns the largest integer that is less than or equal to the argument N.

LBOUND(arrayname[,dimension])
Returns the lower-bound value for the specified dimension of arrayname.

FUNCTION

LCASE$(X$)
Returns X$ in all lowercase letters.

LEFT$(X$, N)
Returns the leftmost N characters of the string argument X$.

LEN(X$)
Returns the length of the string argument X$.

LOC(#filenumber)
With a random file, it returns the number of the last record read or written. With a sequential file, it returns the number of records read from or written to the file.

LOF(#filenumber)
Returns the number of bytes allocated to a file.

LOG(N)
Returns the natural log of the argument N where N is greater than 0.

LPOS(N)
Returns the current position of the line printer's print head within the printer buffer where N is equal to 1 for LPT1, 2 for LPT2, and so on.

LTRIM$(X$)
Returns X$ with leading spaces removed.

MID$(X$, P, N)
Returns N characters of the string argument X$ beginning at position P.

MKI$(N), MKL$(N), MKS$(N), MKD$(N)
Returns the string equivalent of an integer, long integer, single-precision, or double-precision value. Used with random files.

OCT$(N)
Returns the octal equivalent of N.

PEEK(N)
Returns the value of the byte stored at the specified storage location N.

PEN(N)
Returns light pen coordinate information. The information is dependent on the value assigned to N.

PLAY(n)
Returns the number of notes currently in the music background buffer.

PMAP (c, n)
Returns the world coordinate of the physical coordinate c or vice versa. The parameter n varies between 0 and 3, and determines whether c is an x or y coordinate, and whether the coordinate is to be mapped from the physical to the world coordinate or vice versa.

(*BASIC Functions* continued on page R.5 in left column)

MICROSOFT QuickBASIC REFERENCE CARD

Summary of BASIC Functions (continued)

FUNCTION

POINT{(x, y)}{(n)}
With the argument (x, y), the PC returns the foreground color attribute of the point (x, y). With the argument n, the PC returns the physical or world x or y coordinate of the last point referenced. The parameter n varies in the range 0 to 3.

POS(0)
Returns the current position of the cursor on the screen.

RIGHT$(X$, N)
Returns the rightmost N characters of the string argument X$.

RND(N)
Returns a random number between 0 (inclusive) and 1 (exclusive). If N is positive or not included, the next random number is returned. If N is 0 (zero), the previous random number is returned. If N is negative, the random number generator is reseeded before a random number is returned.

RTRIM$(X$)
Returns X$ with trailing spaces removed.

SCREEN(row, column)
Returns the ASCII code for the character at the specified row (line) and column on the screen.

SEEK(filenumber)
Returns the current file position.

SGN(N)
Returns the sign of the argument N: −1 if the argument N is less than 0; 0 if the argument N is equal to 0; or +1 if the argument N is greater than 0.

SIN(N)
Returns the sine of the argument N where N is in radians.

SPACE$(N)
Returns a string of N spaces.

SPC(N)
Displays N spaces. Can be used only in an output statement such as PRINT or LPRINT.

SQR(N)
Returns the square root of the positive argument N.

STICK(N)
Returns the x and y coordinates of joystick N.

STR$(N)
Returns the string equivalent of the numeric argument N.

STRIG(n)
Returns the status of the joystick buttons.

STRING$(N, X$)
Returns N times the first character of X$.

FUNCTION

TAB(N)
Causes the PC to tab over to position N on the output device. Can be used only in an output statement such as PRINT or LPRINT.

TAN(N)
Returns the tangent of the argument N where N is in radians.

TIMER
Returns a value that is equal to the number of seconds elapsed since midnight.

TIME$
Returns the current time (hh:mm:ss).

UBOUND(arrayname[,dimension])
Returns the upper-bound value for the specified dimension of arrayname.

UCASE$(X$)
Returns X$ in all uppercase letters.

VAL(X$)
Returns the numeric equivalent of the string argument X$.

VARPTR(variablename)
Returns the storage address of variablename.

VARPTR$(variablename)
Returns a string representation of the storage address of variablename for use in DRAW and PLAY statements.

Summary of Command Line Options

For the desired effect, append one or more of the following to the QB or QBI command when you enter QuickBASIC:

OPTION	FUNCTION
/ah	Permits arrays to exceed 64 KB.
/b	Designates monochrome display.
/c:size	Sets the size of the communications port buffer.
/cmd str	Passes the string str to the COMMAND$ function.
file	Loads and displays the QuickBASIC program file.
/g	Designates faster video output.
/h	Designates maximum resolution for the video device.
/l[lib]	Loads the specified library or QB.QLB if lib is omitted.
/mbf	Causes conversion functions to treat IEEE-format numbers as Microsoft binary format numbers.
/nohi	Allows monitor that does not support high intensity.
/run file	Loads and executes the QuickBASIC program file before displaying it.

Limits to QuickBASIC

	MAXIMUM	MINIMUM
Variable name	40 characters	1 character
String length	32,767 characters	0 characters
Array dimensions	60	1
Array subscript value	32,767	−32,768
Integers	32,767	−32,768
Long integers	2,147,483,647	−2,147,483,648
Single precision (+)	3.402823E+38	1.401298E−45
Single precision (−)	−1.401298E−45	−3.402823E+38
Double precision (+)	1.797693134862315D+308	4.940656458412465D−324
Double precision (−)	−4.940656458412465D−324	−1.797693134862315D+308

Summary of All Operators

ORDER OF PRECEDENCE	OPERATOR	SYMBOL
Highest	Arithmetic	^
		* or /
		MOD
		+ or − (Unary + or − sign)
		+ or − (Binary + or − sign)
	Concatenation	+
	Relational	=, >, >=, <, <=, or <>
	Logical	NOT
		AND
		OR or XOR
		EQV
Lowest		IMP

Variable Type Definition

APPEND CHARACTER	DECLARATION
%	Integer variable
&	Long integer variable
!	Single-precision variable
#	Double-precision variable
$	String variable

MICROSOFT QuickBASIC REFERENCE CARD

Cursor Movement Keys

KEYS	FUNCTION
←	Character left
→	Character right
↓	Down one line
↑	Up one line
Ctrl + ←	Word left
Ctrl + →	Word right
Ctrl + End	End of program
Ctrl + Enter	Beginning of next line
Ctrl + Home	Beginning of program
Ctrl + Q + E	Top of window
Ctrl + Q + S	Beginning of current line
Ctrl + Q + X	Bottom of window
End	End of line
Home	First indent of current line
Tab	Tab to next tab setting

Scroll Keys

KEYS	FUNCTION
Ctrl + ↓	Line down
Ctrl + ↑	Line up
Page Down	Page down
Page Up	Page up
Ctrl + Page Down	Left one full screen
Ctrl + Page Up	Right one full screen

Execution and Debugging Keys

KEYS	FUNCTION
F5	Continues execution from current statement.
Shift + F5	Starts execution from beginning.
F7	Executes program to cursor.
F8	Executes next program statement.
Shift + F8	Traces execution history backward.
F9	Toggles the Debug menu Breakpoint command.
Shift + F9	Instant watch.
F10	Single step, tracing around a procedure call.
Shift + F10	Traces execution history forward.

Search Keys

KEYS	FUNCTION
F3	Repeats the last find.
Ctrl + \	Searches for selected (highlighted) text.

Help Keys

KEYS	FUNCTION
F1	Displays help on the item in which the cursor is located.
Shift + F1	Displays help on help.
Ctrl + F1	Displays previously requested help topic. (Repeat up to 20 times.)
Shift + Ctrl + F1	Displays next help topic in Help file.
Alt + H	Displays previous help topic in Help file.
Esc	Displays help through Help menu commands.
Letter	Clears help from the screen.
Shift + letter	Moves cursor to help-topic title beginning with letter entered.
Tab	Moves cursor to previous help-topic title beginning with letter entered.
Shift + Tab	Moves cursor to next help-topic title in help screen.
	Moves cursor to previous help-topic title in help screen.

Insert and Copy Keys

KEYS	FUNCTION
Insert	Toggles insert or overtype.
Ctrl + Insert	Copies selection to clipboard and keeps.
Shift + Insert	Inserts contents of clipboard.
Shift + Delete	Copies selection to clipboard and deletes.
Ctrl + Y	Copies current line to clipboard and deletes.
Ctrl + Q + Y	Copies from cursor to end of line to clipboard and deletes.

Delete Keys

KEYS	FUNCTION
Backspace	Deletes character to left.
Ctrl + T	Deletes rest of word.
Delete	Deletes character at cursor or selected text.
Shift + Tab	Deletes leading spaces from selected lines.

Selection (Highlight) Keys

KEYS	FUNCTION
Shift + ←	Character left
Shift + →	Character right
Shift + Ctrl + ←	Word left
Shift + Ctrl + →	Word right
Shift + ↓	Current line
Shift + ↑	Line above
Shift + Page Down	Screen down
Shift + Page Up	Screen up
Shift + Ctrl + Home	To beginning of program
Shift + Ctrl + End	To end of program

View Keys

KEYS	FUNCTION
F4	Toggles between view window and output screen.
F6	Makes next window the active one.

Reserved Words

ABS, ACCESS, ALIAS, AND, ANY, APPEND, AS, ASC, ATN, BASE, BEEP, BINARY, BLOAD, BSAVE, CALL, CALLS, CASE, CDBL, CDECL, CHAIN, CHDIR, CHR$, CINT, CIRCLE, CLEAR, CLOSE, CLS, COLOR, COM, COMMAND$, COMMON, CONST, COS, CSNG, CSRLIN, CVD, CVDMBF, CVI, CVL, CVS, CVSMBF, DATA, DATE$, DECLARE, DEF, DEFDBL, DEFINT, DEFLNG, DEFSNG, DEFSTR, DIM, DO, DOUBLE, DRAW, ELSE, ELSEIF, END, ENDIF, ENVIRON, ENVIRON$, EOF, EQV, ERASE, ERDEV, ERDEV$, ERL, ERR, ERROR, EXIT, EXP, FIELD, FILEATTR, FILES, FIX, FOR, FRE, FREEFILE, FUNCTION, GET, GOSUB, GOTO, HEX$, IF, IMP, INKEY$, INP, INPUT, INPUT$, INSTR, INT, INTEGER, IOCTL, IOCTL$, IS, KEY, KILL, LBOUND, LCASE$, LEFT$, LEN, LET, LINE, LIST, LOC, LOCAL, LOCATE, LOCK, LOF, LOG, LONG, LOOP, LPOS, LPRINT, LSET, LTRIM$, MID$, MKD$, MKDIR, MKDMBF$, MKI$, MKL$, MKS$, MKSMBF$, MOD, NAME, NEXT, NOT, OCT$, OFF, ON, OPEN, OPTION, OR, OUT, OUTPUT, PAINT, PALETTE, PCOPY, PEEK, PEN, PLAY, PMAP, POINT, POKE, POS, PRESET, PRINT, PRINT#, PSET, PUT, RANDOM, RANDOMIZE, READ, REDIM, REM, RESET, RESTORE, RESUME, RETURN, RIGHT$, RMDIR, RND, RSET, RUN, SADD, SCREEN, SEEK, SGN, SELECT, SETMEM, SGN, SHARED, SHELL, SIGNAL, SIN, SINGLE, SLEEP, SOUND, SPACE$, SPC, SQR, STATIC, STEP, STICK, STOP, STR$, STRIG, STRING, STRING$, SUB, SWAP, SYSTEM, TAB, TAN, THEN, TIME$, TIMER, TO, TROFF, TRON, TYPE, UBOUND, UCASE$, UNLOCK, UNTIL, USING, VAL, VARPTR, VARPTR$, VARSEG, VIEW, WAIT, WEND, WHILE, WIDTH, WINDOW, WRITE, WRITE#, XOR